The Wiley Handbook on the Cognitive Neuroscience of Learning

The Wiley Handbook on the Cognitive Neuroscience of Learning

Edited by

Robin A. Murphy and
Robert C. Honey

WILEY Blackwell

This edition first published 2016
© 2016 John Wiley & Sons, Ltd.

Registered Office
John Wiley & Sons, Ltd, The Atrium, Southern Gate, Chichester, West Sussex, PO19 8SQ, UK

Editorial Offices
350 Main Street, Malden, MA 02148-5020, USA
9600 Garsington Road, Oxford, OX4 2DQ, UK
The Atrium, Southern Gate, Chichester, West Sussex, PO19 8SQ, UK

For details of our global editorial offices, for customer services, and for information about how to apply for permission to reuse the copyright material in this book please see our website at www.wiley.com/wiley-blackwell.

The right of Robin A. Murphy and Robert C. Honey to be identified as the authors of the editorial material in this work has been asserted in accordance with the UK Copyright, Designs and Patents Act 1988.

All rights reserved. No part of this publication may be reproduced, stored in a retrieval system, or transmitted, in any form or by any means, electronic, mechanical, photocopying, recording or otherwise, except as permitted by the UK Copyright, Designs and Patents Act 1988, without the prior permission of the publisher.

Wiley also publishes its books in a variety of electronic formats. Some content that appears in print may not be available in electronic books.

Designations used by companies to distinguish their products are often claimed as trademarks. All brand names and product names used in this book are trade names, service marks, trademarks or registered trademarks of their respective owners. The publisher is not associated with any product or vendor mentioned in this book.

Limit of Liability/Disclaimer of Warranty: While the publisher and authors have used their best efforts in preparing this book, they make no representations or warranties with respect to the accuracy or completeness of the contents of this book and specifically disclaim any implied warranties of merchantability or fitness for a particular purpose. It is sold on the understanding that the publisher is not engaged in rendering professional services and neither the publisher nor the author shall be liable for damages arising herefrom. If professional advice or other expert assistance is required, the services of a competent professional should be sought.

Library of Congress Cataloging-in-Publication Data

Names: Murphy, Robin A., editor. | Honey, Robert C., editor.
Title: The Wiley handbook on the cognitive neuroscience of learning / edited by Robin A. Murphy and Robert C. Honey.
Description: Chichester, West Sussex, UK : John Wiley & Sons Inc., [2016] | Includes bibliographical references and index.
Identifiers: LCCN 2015047273 (print) | LCCN 2016003022 (ebook) | ISBN 9781118650943 (cloth) | ISBN 9781118650844 (Adobe PDF) | ISBN 9781118650851 (ePub)
Subjects: LCSH: Learning, Psychology of. | Cognitive learning theory. | Cognitive neuroscience.
Classification: LCC BF318 .W54 2016 (print) | LCC BF318 (ebook) | DDC 153.1/5–dc23
LC record available at http://lccn.loc.gov/2015047273

A catalogue record for this book is available from the British Library.

Cover image: © Olena_T/iStockphoto

Set in 10/12pt Galliard by SPi Global, Pondicherry, India
Printed and bound in Malaysia by Vivar Printing Sdn Bhd

1 2016

Contents

About the Contributors		vii
Preface		x
1	The Cognitive Neuroscience of Learning: Introduction and Intent *Robert C. Honey and Robin A. Murphy*	1

Part I Associative Learning 5

2	The Determining Conditions for Pavlovian Learning: Psychological and Neurobiological Considerations *Helen M. Nasser and Andrew R. Delamater*	7
3	Learning to Be Ready: Dopamine and Associative Computations *Nicola C. Byrom and Robin A. Murphy*	47
4	Learning About Stimuli That Are Present and Those That Are Not: Separable Acquisition Processes for Direct and Mediated Learning *Tzu-Ching E. Lin and Robert C. Honey*	69
5	Neural Substrates of Learning and Attentive Processes *David N. George*	86
6	Associative Learning and Derived Attention in Humans *Mike Le Pelley, Tom Beesley, and Oren Griffiths*	114
7	The Epigenetics of Neural Learning *Zohar Bronfman, Simona Ginsburg, and Eva Jablonka*	136

Part II Associative Representations
Memory, Recognition, and Perception 177

8	Associative and Nonassociative Processes in Rodent Recognition Memory *David J. Sanderson*	179
9	Perceptual Learning: Representations and Their Development *Dominic M. Dwyer and Matthew E. Mundy*	201

10	Human Perceptual Learning and Categorization *Paulo F. Carvalho and Robert L. Goldstone*	223
11	Computational and Functional Specialization of Memory *Rosie Cowell, Tim Bussey, and Lisa Saksida*	249

Space and Time — 283

12	Mechanisms of Contextual Conditioning: Some Thoughts on Excitatory and Inhibitory Context Conditioning *Robert J. McDonald and Nancy S. Hong*	285
13	The Relation Between Spatial and Nonspatial Learning *Anthony McGregor*	313
14	Timing and Conditioning: Theoretical Issues *Charlotte Bonardi, Timothy H. C. Cheung, Esther Mondragón, and Shu K. E. Tam*	348
15	Human Learning About Causation *Irina Baetu and Andy G. Baker*	380

Part III Associative Perspectives on the Human Condition — 409

16	The Psychological and Physiological Mechanisms of Habit Formation *Nura W. Lingawi, Amir Dezfouli, and Bernard W. Balleine*	411
17	An Associative Account of Avoidance *Claire M. Gillan, Gonzalo P. Urcelay, and Trevor W. Robbins*	442
18	Child and Adolescent Anxiety: Does Fear Conditioning Play a Role? *Katharina Pittner, Kathrin Cohen Kadosh, and Jennifer Y. F. Lau*	468
19	Association, Inhibition, and Action *Ian McLaren and Frederick Verbruggen*	489
20	Mirror Neurons from Associative Learning *Caroline Catmur, Clare Press, and Cecilia Heyes*	515
21	Associative Approaches to Lexical Development *Kim Plunkett*	538
22	Neuroscience of Value-Guided Choice *Gerhard Jocham, Erie Boorman, and Tim Behrens*	554

Index — 592

About the Contributors

Robert C. Honey, School of Psychology, Cardiff University, UK

Robin A. Murphy, Department of Experimental Psychology, Oxford University, UK

Helen M. Nasser, Brooklyn College, City University of New York, USA

Andrew R. Delamater, Brooklyn College, City University of New York, USA

Nicola C. Byrom, Department of Experimental Psychology, Oxford University, UK

Tzu-Ching E. Lin, School of Psychology, Cardiff University, UK

David N. George, Department of Psychology, University of Hull, UK

Mike Le Pelley, School of Psychology, University of New South Wales, Australia

Tom Beesley, School of Psychology, University of New South Wales, Australia

Oren Griffiths, School of Psychology, University of New South Wales, Australia

Zohar Bronfman, School of Psychology, Tel-Aviv University, Israel

Simona Ginsburg, Natural Science Department, The Open University of Israel, Israel

Eva Jablonka, The Cohn Institute for the History and Philosophy of Science and Ideas, Tel-Aviv University, Israel

David J. Sanderson, Department of Psychology, Durham University, UK

Dominic M. Dwyer, School of Psychology, Cardiff University, UK

Matthew E. Mundy, School of Psychological Sciences, Monash University, Australia

Paulo F. Carvalho, Department of Psychological and Brain Sciences, Indiana University, USA

Robert L. Goldstone, Department of Psychological and Brain Sciences, Indiana University, USA

Rosie Cowell, Department of Psychological and Brain Sciences, University of Massachusetts Amherst, USA

Tim Bussey, Department of Physiology and Pharmacology, University of Western Ontario, Canada

Lisa Saksida, Department of Physiology and Pharmacology, University of Western Ontario, Canada

Robert J. McDonald, Department of Neuroscience/Canadian Centre for Behavioural Neuroscience, University of Lethbridge, Canada

Nancy S. Hong, Department of Neuroscience/Canadian Centre for Behavioural Neuroscience, University of Lethbridge, Canada

Anthony McGregor, Department of Psychology, Durham University, UK

Charlotte Bonardi, School of Psychology, University of Nottingham, UK

Timothy H. C. Cheung, School of Life Sciences, Arizona State University, USA

Esther Mondragón, Centre for Computational and Animal Learning Research, UK

Shu K. E. Tam, University of Oxford, UK

Irina Baetu, School of Psychology, University of Adelaide, Australia

Andy G. Baker, Department of Psychology, McGill University, Canada

Nura W. Lingawi, Brain & Mind Research Institute, University of Sydney, Australia

Amir Dezfouli, Brain & Mind Research Institute, University of Sydney, Australia

Bernard W. Balleine, Brain & Mind Research Institute, University of Sydney, Australia

Claire M. Gillan, Department of Psychology, University of Cambridge, UK; and Department of Psychology, New York University, USA

Gonzalo P. Urcelay, Department of Neuroscience, Psychology and Behaviour, University of Leicester, UK

Trevor W. Robbins, Department of Psychology, New York University and University of Cambridge, UK

Katharina Pittner, Maastricht University, The Netherlands

Kathrin Cohen Kadosh, Department of Experimental Psychology, University of Oxford, UK

Jennifer Y. F. Lau, Institute of Psychiatry, King's College London, UK

Ian McLaren, School of Psychology, University of Exeter, UK

Frederick Verbruggen, School of Psychology, University of Exeter, UK

Caroline Catmur, Department of Psychology, University of Surrey, UK

Clare Press, Department of Psychological Sciences, Birkbeck, University of London, UK

Cecilia Heyes, All Souls College, University of Oxford, UK

Kim Plunkett, Department of Experimental Psychology, University of Oxford, UK

Gerhard Jocham, Centre for Behavioral Brain Sciences, Otto-von-Guericke-University, Germany

Erie Boorman, Department of Experimental Psychology, University of Oxford, UK; and Wellcome Trust Centre for Neuroimaging, University College London, London, UK

Tim Behrens, Institute of Neurology, University College London, UK; and Nuffield Department of Clinical Neurosciences, University of Oxford, John Radcliffe Hospital, UK.

Preface

This handbook provides a cohesive overview of the study of associative learning as it is approached from the stance of scientists with complementary interests in its theoretical analysis and biological basis. These interests have been pursued by studying humans and animals, and the content of this handbook reflects this fact. Wiley, the publishers of this series of handbooks, gave us free rein in determining the overarching focus of this book, associative learning, and the specific topics that would be included. We have taken full advantage of this latitude and thank them for their support throughout the editorial process. Our choice of topics was determined by a combination of their enduring significance and contemporary relevance. The contributors then chose themselves, as it were, on the basis of their expertise. Inevitably, there has been some bias in our choices, and we have made only a limited attempt to cover all of the domains of research that have resulted in significant scientific progress. However, we hope that you will be as interested to read the contributions that we have selected as we were to receive them. It remains for us to express our thanks to the contributors who have followed, fortunately not slavishly, their individual remits and who have collectively produced a handbook that we hope will be of interest to a broad readership. Finally, we would like to thank Laurence Errington for generating the comprehensive subject index, which provides the reader with an effective tool for negotiating the volume as a whole.

1

The Cognitive Neuroscience of Learning

Introduction and Intent

Robert C. Honey and Robin A. Murphy

If an organism's behavior is to become better tuned to its environment, then there must be plasticity in those systems that interact with that environment. One consequence of such plasticity is that the organism's mental life is no longer bound to the here and now but reflects the interplay between the here and now and the there and then. Scientists from a variety of disciplines have studied the processes of learning that provide the basis for this interplay. While some have inferred the nature of the underlying conceptual or hypothetical processes through the detailed analysis of behavior in a range of experimental preparations, others have examined the neural processes and brain systems involved by making use of these and other preparations. To be sure, the preparations that have been employed often vary considerably in terms of their surface characteristics and the uses to which they are put. But this fact should not distract one from attempting to develop a parsimonious analysis, and it with this principle in mind that this handbook was conceived. Its focus is on the cognitive neuroscience of learning. Our frequent use of the qualifier Associative, as in Associative Learning, reflects either our bias or the acknowledgment of the fact that the formal analysis of all learning requires an associative perspective.

According to an associative analysis of learning, past experiences are embodied in the changes in the efficacy of links among the constituents of that experience. These associative links allow the presence of a subset of the constituents to affect the retrieval of a previous experience in its entirety: they provide a link, both theoretically and metaphorically, between the past and the present. We focus on this process because it has provided the basis for integration and rapprochement across different levels of analysis and different species, and it has long been argued that associative learning provides a potential shared basis for many aspects of behavior and cognition – for many forms of learning that might appear superficially distinct.

> Hence, the temporary nervous connexion is a universal physiological phenomenon both in the animal world and in our own. And at the same time it is likewise a psychic phenomenon, which psychologists call an association, no matter whether it is a combination of various

---

The Wiley Handbook on the Cognitive Neuroscience of Learning, First Edition.
Edited by Robin A. Murphy and Robert C. Honey.
© 2016 John Wiley & Sons, Ltd. Published 2016 by John Wiley & Sons, Ltd.

actions or impressions, or that of letters, words, and thoughts. What reason might there be for drawing any distinction between what is known to a physiologist as a temporary connexion and to a psychologist as an association? Here we have a perfect coalescence, a complete absorption of one by the other, a complete identification. Psychologists seem to have likewise acknowledged this, for they (or at any rate some of them) have made statements that experiments with conditioned reflexes have provided associative psychology ... with a firm basis. (Pavlov, 1941, p. 171)

The breadth of application evident in Pavlov's treatise, and that of some of his contemporaries and successors, has often struck many as overly ambitious, provocative, or even plain misguided. The idea that what seems to be a rather simple process might play a role in such a broad range of phenomena is certainly bold; and some have argued that such an enterprise is flawed for a variety of reasons: where is the direct evidence of the operation of associative processes, how could such a simple process be sensitive to the inherent complexity and ambiguity in the real world, and so on. These and other criticisms have been acknowledged and have played an important role in shaping, for example, investigations of the brain bases of associative learning, and the development and assessment of more complex associative models that explicitly address a broad range of phenomena. This is not to say that the critics have been silenced or have even become any less vocal, and nor is it to imply that they have accepted the changes in the scientific landscape for which they have been partly responsible: they want the changes to be more radical, more enduring. Not to put too finer point on it, they want associationism to be like Monty Python's parrot: an ex-theory. We hope that the contents of this handbook will serve to illustrate that the associative analysis of learning is flourishing, with each chapter highlighting recent advances that have been made by cognitive and behavioral neuroscientists.

The research conducted by cognitive and behavioral neuroscientists uses complementary techniques: ranging from the use of sophisticated behavioral procedures, which isolate key theoretical processes within computational models, to new software tools, that allow vast quantities of imaging data to be rendered in a form that enables changes in neural structures, systems, and their connectivity to be inferred. Some behavioral and neuroscientific techniques are clearly better suited or better developed for some species than others. However, the prospect of understanding the associative process at a variety of levels of analysis and across different species, which was envisaged by previous generations, is now being realized. The chapters in this handbook are intended, both individually and collectively, to provide a synthesis of how cognitive and behavioral neuroscientists have contributed to our understanding of learning that can be said to have an associative origin. To do so, we move from considering relatively simple studies of associative processes in the rat, through to learning involving time and space, to social learning and the development of language. Clearly, the superficial characteristics of the experiences that shape these different forms of learning are quite different, as are the behavioral consequences that these experiences generate. However, there remains the possibility that they are based, at least in part, on the operation of shared associative principles. Where and how these principles are implemented in the brain is an important facet of this handbook. In pursuing answers to these basic questions, of where and of how, we might be forced to reconsider our theoretical analysis of the processes involved in associative learning. This synergy is an exciting prospect that can only be exploited when a common issue is studied from differing vantage points.

Our hope is that this handbook will also help to bridge some gaps between research that has originated from different philosophical orientations and involved different levels of analysis. Briefly, there is a longstanding division between those who use purely behavioral studies to infer the nature of associative processes and those whose principal interests are in the neural bases of learning and memory. Researchers from both traditions make use of a variety of behavioral measures to draw inference about hypothetical processes, on the one hand, and about the role of various systems, structures, or neuronal processes, on the other. At its heart, the dialog does not concern the legitimacy or rigor of the research that is conducted within either tradition, but rather concerns whether or not the research conducted at one level of analysis or in one tradition provides any information that has utility to the other. Of course, it need not; and it is certainly true that historically there has been surprisingly little crosstalk between researchers from the two traditions – a fact that is likely to constrain the opportunity for productive synergy. We believe that this is a pity and hope that the chapters in this handbook will illustrate, in different ways, how such crosstalk can be mutually beneficial.

The study of associative learning is the application of an analytic technique for describing the relation between the here and now and the there and then, and for how the brain deals with this relation and its contents. It is ultimately a description of how the brain works. A theme throughout the chapters in this volume is the conclusion that where we want to understand the brain's workings, we will need to consider how the brain performs the functions described by associative analysis. To this end, we need both the analytic tools for describing the functions and a description of how these functions are implemented at the level of tissue. We are completely aware that the two levels might look very different but also that a complete description will require both.

The counterargument – that we might understand the brain without the associative framework – can be allied to a similar challenge faced by experts in neurophysiology. Here, the question posed is whether brain imaging (which includes any one of a number of techniques for representing the internal workings of the brain in a visual or mathematical manner) goes beyond simple functional mapping of processes and can be used to uncover how the brain codes experience and communicates this experience. Passingham, Rowe, and Sakai (2013) present a convincing defense of the position that at least one technique, fMRI (a technique for using blood flow to track changes in brain activity) has uncovered a new principle of how the brain works. What is perhaps more interesting for this volume is that the principle in question looks very much like the types of associative processes described herein.

As suggested in Passingham *et al.* (2013), it is quite common, and relatively uncontroversial, to use the technique of fMRI to make claims about the localization of cognitive processes. However, it is more difficult to argue that this or similar techniques have informed our understanding of the principles by which the brain processes information. In the case that Passingham *et al.* identify, fMRI was used to show how processing in area A and processing in area B are related to one another with some types of stimuli or context, but activity in area A is related to area C in another context. They then speculate about how this might be achieved through different subpopulations of neurons being active in area A depending on the context. Students of associative learning will recognize the issue of how context-dependent stimulus processing is achieved as one that has dominated the recent associative landscape. It has led to the development of various formal models, some bearing more than a passing resemblance to the implementation described immediately above (e.g., Pearce, 1994; Wagner, 2003), that have been subject to experimental testing through behavioral and neuroscientific analyses. This form of integrated analysis is one to which the associative approach lends itself, as the contents of this volume will, we hope, illustrate.

References

Passingham, R. E., Rowe, J. B., & Sakai, K. (2013). Has brain imaging discovered anything new about how the brain works? *Neuroimage, 66*, 142–150.

Pavlov, I. P. (1941). The conditioned reflex. In *Lectures on conditioned reflexes: conditioned reflexes and psychiatry* (Vol. 2, p. 171). London, UK: Lawrence & Wishart.

Pearce, J. M. (1994). Similarity and discrimination: A selective review and a connectionist model. *Psychological Review, 101*, 587–607.

Wagner, A. R. (2003). Context-sensitive elemental theory. *Quarterly Journal of Experimental Psychology, 56B*, 7–29.

Part I
Associative Learning

2

The Determining Conditions for Pavlovian Learning
Psychological and Neurobiological Considerations

Helen M. Nasser and Andrew R. Delamater

Introduction

From the perspective of classical learning theory, the environment is often described as a complex and often chaotic place with myriad events occurring sometimes at random with respect to one another but also sometimes in predictable ways. Through millions of years of evolution, organisms have evolved the capacities to learn about those predictive relationships among events in the world because such learning provides adaptive advantages. For instance, learning to anticipate that the sudden movement of a branch could indicate the presence of a looming predator lurking behind the bush would enable a foraging animal to act in such a way to avoid its forthcoming attack. Psychologists generally accept that simple associative learning processes are among those that are fundamental in enabling organisms to extract meaning about predictive event relationships in the environment, and in controlling adaptive modes of behavior. However, experimental psychologists have also generally assumed that it is often difficult to analyze complex behavioral adjustments made by animals when studied in real-world naturalistic situations. As a result, two major laboratory paradigms have been developed to investigate different aspects of associative learning. One of these is known as Pavlovian conditioning, or the learning about relationships among different stimulus events, and the other as instrumental conditioning, or the learning about relationships between an organism's own behavior and the stimulus events that follow.

While each of these forms of associative learning has been described in various ways, one of the key assumptions has been that organisms learn about predictive relationships among events by forming associations between them. More formally, in the case of Pavlovian conditioning, theorists usually accept that by learning to associate two events with one another (e.g., the moving branch and the predator), the organism develops new connections between its neural representations of those events (e.g., Dickinson, 1980; Holland, 1990; Pearce & Hall, 1980). In this way, the occurrence of the predictive cue alone can come to activate a representation of the event with which it was associated prior to its actual occurrence. This capacity would surely enable the organism to anticipate future events and, thus, act in adaptive ways.

The study of associative learning has been guided by three fundamental questions (e.g., Delamater & Lattal, 2014; Mackintosh, 1983; Rescorla & Holland, 1976). These are (1) what are the critical conditions necessary for establishing the associative connection between the events in question, (2) what is the content of those associations (or the nature of the representations themselves), and (3) how are such associations translated into observable performance. In the present chapter, we will focus on this first question (establishing the critical conditions for learning), and we will limit our discussion to studies of Pavlovian learning (about which more information is currently available). At the same time, we acknowledge, up front, that answers to these three questions will often be interdependent, and it will be useful to keep this in mind as we proceed with our analysis, particularly at the neural mechanisms level.

For a brief diversion and to illustrate the importance of this issue, let us consider our current conception of Pavlovian learning in somewhat greater detail. We have noted that investigators usually accept that this can be understood in terms of the organism forming a new connection between internal (i.e., neural) representations of conditioned and unconditioned stimuli (CS and US, respectively). However, different authors have characterized the US representation in different ways. For instance, Konorski (1967) speculated that the CS actually developed separate associations with highly specific sensory features of the US, on the one hand, and with more diffuse motivational/affective features of the US, on the other (see also Dickinson & Dearing, 1979). In a more modern context, we acknowledge that any given US might have additional features with which the CS might associate, and these would include their spatial, temporal, hedonic, and response-eliciting properties (Delamater, 2012). If we acknowledge, then, that a CS might come to associate with a host of different aspects of the US, this would suggest that multiple neural systems are actually recruited during simple Pavlovian learning (e.g., Corbit & Balleine, 2005, 2011). Thus, in answer to the question "What are the critical conditions necessary for the establishment of the association?" we should realize that different answers might be forthcoming, depending upon which of these aspects of learning we are studying. This proviso, however, has not been considered in much of the research we shall shortly review, largely because methods used to isolate the different contents of learning have only recently been more intensively explored, and that research is surely just developing.

This qualification notwithstanding, there has been a tremendous amount of behavior-level research over the last 50 years investigating the critical conditions necessary and sufficient for simple forms of Pavlovian learning to take place, and there has additionally been much progress made in recent years translating some of that knowledge to underlying neural mechanisms. The aim of this chapter is to review some of the major findings at each of these levels of analysis.

Major Variables Supporting Pavlovian Learning

Since the time of Pavlov, a number of key variables have been studied for their influence on Pavlovian learning or, in other words, on what we shall refer to as the formation of a CS–US association. Much of this research has been guided by the belief that general laws of learning might be uncovered along the way. Thus, a large number of studies have been performed to identify those variables that affect the course of Pavlovian learning in an effort to uncover both the necessary and sufficient conditions for association formation itself. While finding the truly general laws of learning has proven to be somewhat elusive, we, nevertheless, think that many key discoveries have been made. This section will review some of the major empirical findings and generalizations, and the next section will briefly review some of the major theoretical principles generally assumed to account for many of these findings.

Stimulus intensity and novelty

US intensity The strength of conditioned responding in a Pavlovian learning experiment is generally stronger, the more intense the US. For example, stronger footshocks yield stronger fear conditioning. Using a conditioned suppression task with rats, Annau and Kamin (1961) found that both the rate and level of conditioning was greater with a strong compared with a weak US (see Figure 2.1). Similar findings have been reported in magazine approach conditioning (Morris & Bouton, 2006),

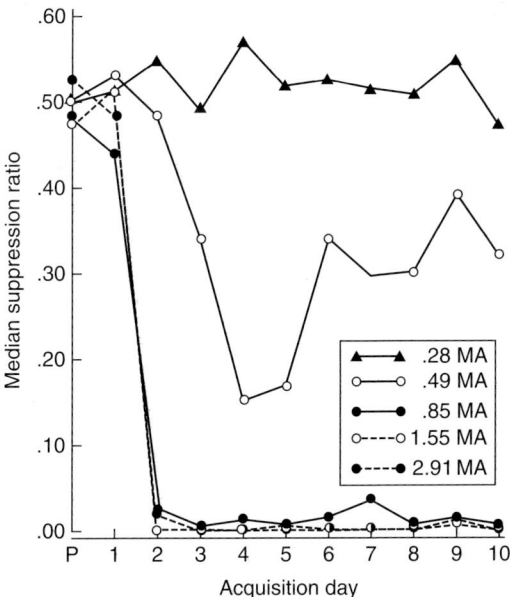

Figure 2.1 Acquisition of various footshock US intensities on a conditioned suppression task. Reproduced from Annau and Kamin (1961).

conditioned flavor preference (Bolles, Hayward, & Crandall, 1981; Smith & Sclafani, 2002), conditioned taste aversion (Barker, 1976), and rabbit eyeblink (Smith, 1968) conditioning paradigms, so these effects appear to be rather general ones.

CS intensity The intensity (or "salience") of the CS has also been shown to be important for learning to occur. Kamin and Schaub (1963) investigated the influence of CS intensity on the acquisition of conditioned suppression. In this experiment, the shock US magnitude remained constant while the intensity of a white-noise CS was varied across groups (49, 62.5, or 81 dB). They observed that the rate of acquisition was directly related to CS intensity but that all groups eventually reached the same asymptotic level of learning. This latter effect has not always been observed (e.g., Kamin, 1965), however, so the generality of this particular finding has not been so clearly established (but see Mackintosh, 1974).

CS and US novelty A number of studies have demonstrated that the CS and US are most effectively learned about when they are novel from the outset of conditioning. Repeatedly presenting a CS without the US during a preexposure phase has been known to slow down learning when the CS and US are subsequently paired. This effect, called "latent inhibition," has been well documented in a wide variety of learning paradigms (e.g., Lubow, 1989) and is likely related to habituation-type (e.g., Wagner, 1978) and memory interference (e.g., Bouton, 1991) processes. Similarly, presenting the US (without the CS) prior to their subsequent pairings also impairs conditioning. This effect, known as the "US preexposure effect," has also been well documented (e.g., Randich & LoLordo, 1979) and is likely related to a class of phenomena known as "stimulus selection" effects (to be discussed later).

Number of CS–US pairings

One of the most basic variables investigated is the number of CS–US pairings. Most studies in the literature have found that conditioned responding generally increases in some fashion with the number of CS–US pairings. This finding has been observed in virtually every Pavlovian learning paradigm explored (e.g., conditioned eyeblink, magazine approach, fear conditioning, taste aversion learning, autoshaping; see Mackintosh, 1974). However, no general consensus has been reached as to the specific form of this function, whether it be logarithmic, exponential, ogival, step-like, linear, etc. (e.g., Gottlieb, 2004). Nevertheless, the most typical result is that conditioned responding monotonically increases with number of CS–US pairings. In some preparations (e.g., fear conditioning, taste aversion), evidence for conditioned responding can be seen after a single pairing (e.g., Albert & Ayres, 1997; Ayres, Haddad, & Albert, 1987; Burkhardt & Ayres, 1978; Mahoney & Ayres, 1976; Shurtleff & Ayres, 1981; Willigen, Emmett, Cote, & Ayres, 1987), but, even in such paradigms, increased levels of conditioned responding often occur with increasing numbers of pairings.

While conditioned responding generally increases with an increasing number of pairings, Gottlieb (2008) noted that studies investigating the number of pairings generally have confounded this variable with the total amount of time subjects spend in the experimental chamber (i.e., with the total intertrial interval time). According to the rate expectancy theory (RET) of Pavlovian learning (Gallistel & Gibbon, 2000), conditioned responding should emerge when the rate of US occurrence attributed to the CS exceeds that attributed to the background by some threshold amount (see Chapter 14). The rate estimate attributed to the CS will not change over trials, since the same US rate applies on each conditioning trial. However, the US rate attributed to the background is inversely related to the total intertrial interval (ITI). Thus, with increasing numbers of conditioning trials, the total ITI time increases as well, and this may very well lead to an increased likelihood of responding over conditioning trials. In Gottlieb's (2008) study, different groups of animals were given either few or many training trials in each experimental session, but the total ITI time was held constant. According to RET, there should be no difference in acquisition of conditioned responding with these parameters, and for the most part, this is what Gottlieb (2008) observed. However, Gottlieb and Rescorla (2010) performed conceptually similar studies using within-subjects experimental designs and, in four separate Pavlovian learning paradigms (magazine approach, taste aversion, taste preference, fear conditioning), observed that greater amounts of conditioned responding occurred to the stimulus given more CS–US pairings. More dramatic differences between cues given relatively few or many conditioning trials were also found by Wagner (1969). Furthermore, in a variant of this general procedure, stimuli given more training trials produced more deepened extinction and more conditioned inhibition to another cue during nonreinforced presentations of the stimulus compound (Rescorla & Wagner, 1972).

These various results are especially convincing when considering the fact that Gottlieb's experimental design confounds the number of pairings with ITI length in an effort to control total ITI time. In other words, when few training trials are compared with many with the overall ITI time held constant, the ITI will be short when there are many training trials, but it will be long with few trials. The well-known trial-spacing effect (Papini & Brewer, 1994; Terrace, Gibbon, Farrell, & Baldock, 1975) shows that the strength of conditioning is weak when conditioning trials are massed (with short ITIs). Thus, this experimental design pits the trial-spacing effect against the effect of number of trials.

Another way of asking the question of whether number of CS–US training trials matters is to ask whether the quality of the learning varies over training. Several lines of studies have, indeed, shown this to be the case. In one investigation, Holland (1998) found that after giving a limited number of pairings of an auditory CS with a distinctive flavored sucrose US, pairing the auditory CS with lithium chloride (LiCl) injections caused the animals to subsequently avoid consuming the sucrose US. In other words, the CS acted as a surrogate for the flavored sucrose US, presumably by activating a detailed representation of the sucrose US at the time of LiCl injections (see Chapter 4). However, this "mediated conditioning" effect only occurred when the number of CS–US pairings was low. In another experiment in this same paper, Holland (1998) demonstrated that the US devaluation effect was not influenced by this amount of training manipulation. In this case, following different numbers of CS–US pairings, the US was itself separately paired with LiCl, and the effect of this on test responding to the CS was later assessed. Independent of how much Pavlovian training was given, animals displayed reduced magazine approach responses to the CS after the US had been devalued compared with when it was not devalued. In both mediated conditioning and US devaluation tasks, a specific representation of the US must be invoked to explain the findings, but unlike US devaluation, the nature of this

US representation that supports mediated conditioning must somehow change over the course of Pavlovian training (see also Holland, Lasseter, & Agarwal, 2008; see also Lin & Honey, this volume).

To reinforce the concept that the amount of training can reveal changes in the nature of the US representation, Delamater, Desouza, Derman, and Rivkin (2014) used a Pavlovian-to-Instrumental task (PIT) to assess learning about temporal and specific sensory qualities of reward. Rats received delayed Pavlovian conditioning whereby the US was delivered either early or late (in different groups) after the onset of the CS, and they were given either minimal or moderate amounts of training (also in different groups). Two distinct CS–US associations were trained in all rats (e.g., tone–pellet, light–sucrose). Independently, the rats were trained with different instrumental response–US relations (e.g., left lever–pellet, right lever–sucrose). Finally, during PIT testing, the rats chose between the two instrumental responses in the presence and absence of each CS. In this test, all rats increased above baseline levels the instrumental response that was reinforced with the same, as opposed to a different, US to that signaled by the CS. However, this effect was most prominently observed around the time when the US was expected (early or late in the CS, depending on group assignment) in animals given more Pavlovian training prior to the PIT test. In animals given limited Pavlovian training, this reward-specific PIT effect was displayed equally throughout the CS period. However, overall responding during the cues increased or decreased across the interval depending on whether the USs occurred during training late or early, respectively, within the CS. These results suggest that during Pavlovian acquisition, the CS forms separate associations with distinct sensory and temporal features of the US, but with more extensive training, the US representation becomes more integrated across these features.

In one final example, the number of Pavlovian conditioning trials has also been shown to change the quality of learning from excitatory to inhibitory or from excitatory to less excitatory. Using a bar-press suppression task with rats, Heth (1976) found that a backward CS functioned as a conditioned excitor of fear after 10 backward (shock–tone) pairings, but this same CS functioned as a conditioned inhibitor of fear after 160 pairings (see also Cole & Miller, 1999). Similarly, in a zero contingency procedure where the CS and US are presented randomly in time during each conditioning session, investigators have reported that a CS can elicit excitatory conditioned responses early in training but then lose this effect after more extensive training (e.g., Benedict & Ayres, 1972; Rescorla, 2000).

All in all, although a certain amount of controversy was raised by Gottlieb (2008) in his tests of RET, the conclusion that increasing numbers of conditioning trials can result in changes in Pavlovian learning seems a secure one. Not only do increasing numbers of conditioning trials result in different levels of conditioned responding (even when total ITI time is controlled), but it can change the quality of learning in interesting ways that will require further investigation.

Order of CS–US pairings

The formation of an excitatory or inhibitory association can be affected by the order in which the CS and US are presented in relation to one another. Tanimoto, Heisenberg, and Gerber (2004; see also Yarali et al., 2008) demonstrated in the fly

(*Drosophila*) that if an olfactory CS was presented before an aversive shock US, the fly learned to avoid the CS. However, if the shock US was presented a comparable amount of time before the olfactory CS, conditioned approach was seen to the CS. Thus, the simple order of presentation of stimuli can significantly affect the quality of the learning. One may conclude that forward conditioning (where the CS *precedes* the US) generally produces excitatory conditioning while backward conditioning (where the CS *follows* the US) produces inhibitory conditioning. This analysis requires that avoidance and approach in this preparation, respectively, reflect excitatory and inhibitory associative learning (see also Hearst & Franklin, 1977). It is noteworthy that inhibitory learning in backward conditioning tasks has also been observed in humans (Andreatta, Mühlberger, Yarali, Gerber, & Pauli, 2010), dogs (Moscovitch & LoLordo, 1968), rabbits (Tait & Saladin, 1986), and rats (Delamater, LoLordo, & Sosa, 2003; Heth, 1976), so it would appear to be a rather general phenomenon. However, under some circumstances (particularly if the US–CS interval is short and, as was noted in the previous section, there are few trials), backward conditioning can also produce excitatory conditioning (e.g., Chang *et al.*, 2003).

CS–US contiguity

Temporal contiguity Another variable that has received much attention in the study of Pavlovian conditioning is temporal contiguity, usually manipulated by varying the time between CS and US onsets. There is a large body of empirical evidence demonstrating that the more closely in time two events occur, the more likely they will become associated (e.g., Mackintosh, 1974). However, given the same CS–US interval, learning is also generally better if there is an overlap between these two events than if a trace interval intervenes between offset of the CS and onset of the US – this is known as the trace conditioning deficit (e.g., Bolles, Collier, Bouton, & Marlin, 1978). This sensitivity to the CS–US interval has been seen in Pavlovian learning paradigms that differ greatly in terms of the absolute times separating CS from US. For instance, in the eyeblink conditioning paradigm, the presentations of stimuli occur within milliseconds of each other. In contrast, in taste aversion learning, the animal usually consumes a distinctively flavored solution, and this can be followed by illness minutes to hours later. Even though the timescales in different learning paradigms differ greatly, the strength of conditioned responding generally deteriorates with long CS–US intervals. This was illustrated elegantly in the aforementioned study with *Drosophila* (Tanimoto *et al.*, 2004). Figure 2.2 shows that over a wide range of forward odor CS–shock US intervals (negative ISI values on the graph), the strength of conditioning (here assessed in terms of an avoidance of a shock-paired odor) initially increases but then decreases with the CS–US interval. As noted above, some backward US–CS intervals (shown in the figure as positive ISI values) result in preference for the CS odor at some but not all backward intervals, indicating that the order of pairings as well as the temporal contiguity is important.

Whereas conditioning within various learning paradigms has generally been observed to occur only when effective CS–US intervals are used, these results have been interpreted to mean that temporal contiguity is a *necessary* condition for Pavlovian learning. Nevertheless, while this generalization holds true, there are several

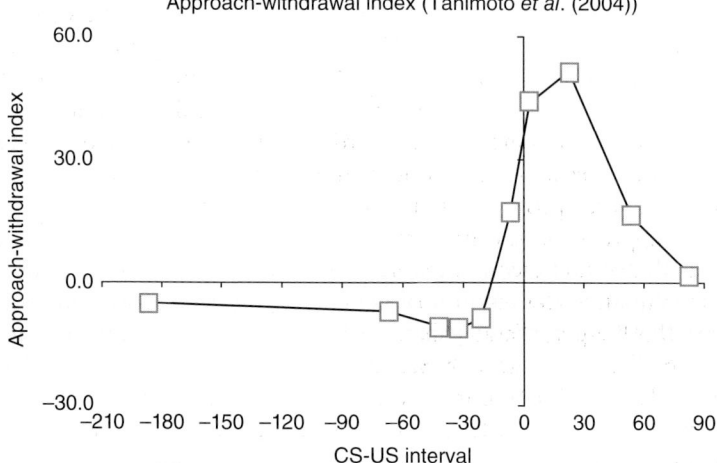

Figure 2.2 Function of *Drosophila* behavior as a function of interstimulus interval (ISI). Redrawn from Tanimoto *et al*, (2004).

important qualifications that must be considered before a complete understanding can be reached concerning the role of temporal contiguity. We will address several of these now.

The idea that temporal contiguity is essential for conditioning suggests that learning would be best achieved in a simultaneous conditioning procedure, where the CS and US are delivered at the same time. Whereas some studies have revealed that simultaneous tone + shock presentations can result in conditioned fear to the tone CS (Burkhardt & Ayres, 1978; Mahoney & Ayres, 1976), the more common result (as depicted in Figure 2.2) is that simultaneous procedures result in less conditioning than in more normal forward delay conditioning procedures where the CS precedes US presentation on each conditioning trial (e.g., Heth, 1976; Heth & Rescorla, 1973). If temporal contiguity were necessary for learning, why would simultaneous conditioning fail to produce the strongest evidence for learning? Several answers can be given to this question.

One possibility is that in simultaneous conditioning, the US occurs at a time before the CS has had a chance to be effectively processed. If CS processing steadily increases over time until some steady state is reached, then US presentations will be most effective at supporting learning when it coincides with optimal CS processing. This would not occur during a simultaneous procedure. A second possibility is that during a simultaneous conditioning procedure, when the CS and US co-occur both must be attended to at the same time, and there might be processing interference of each stimulus as a result. This could have the effect of reducing learning to the CS.

A third possibility is that seemingly poor conditioning in the simultaneous procedure could be a result of stimulus generalization decrement that occurs when the CS is conditioned in the presence of another stimulus (the US) but then tested alone. Rescorla (1980) addressed this concern in a flavor sensory preconditioning task. In this task, two taste cues were mixed together in solution and were immediately followed by a third taste (AB–C). Then, in different subgroups, either taste B or C was separately paired with LiCl to establish an aversion to that taste. Finally, the intake of taste A was assessed. Had simultaneous AB pairings resulted in greater learning than sequential A–C pairings, then an aversion should have transferred more to A when an aversion was established to B than to C. Notice that although testing A by itself would be expected to produce some generalization decrement, this factor would not have applied differentially in the assessment of the simultaneous AB or sequential A–C associations. Rescorla (1980) observed that the AB association was stronger than the A–C association in this task. Thus, at least in this situation, it would appear that simultaneous training produced greater learning than sequential training when equating the amount of generalization decrement. Other data, however, suggest that simultaneous pairings of two taste cues result in a qualitatively different form of learning than sequential pairings of two taste cues (Higgins & Rescorla, 2004), so whether this conclusion would apply more generally is not known (cf. Chapter 4). Nevertheless, the experimental design offers promise for further research.

One final explanation for why simultaneous training generally results in weaker evidence of conditioning than occurs in a normal delay procedure is that the failure is due to a performance mask. Matzel, Held, and Miller (1988) suggested that conditioned fear responses are adaptive and will be evoked by a CS only when it can be used to anticipate the arrival of an aversive event. In a simultaneous fear-conditioning procedure, no fear responses will be observed because the tone CS does not anticipate the future occurrence of the shock US. However, Matzel et al. (1988) further suggested that simultaneous training does result in the formation of a tone–shock association. Such learning could be expressed if another cue (light CS) subsequently was forwardly paired with the tone CS. Under these circumstances, conditioned fear responses were observed to the light CS presumably because it anticipated the tone CS and its associated shock memory.

To summarize this section so far, the notion of temporal contiguity might suggest that simultaneous training should be ideal for establishing good learning. However, this finding has rarely been observed in different learning paradigms. Several reasons for this could involve incomplete stimulus processing, processing interference, generalization decrement, and/or performance masking processes. Determining the ideal interval that supports learning, therefore, requires special experimental design considerations.

A second qualification to the claim that temporal contiguity is critical in establishing learning concerns the role of different response systems. In their classic studies, Vandercar and Schneiderman (1967) were probably the first to demonstrate that different response systems show different sensitivities to interstimulus interval (ISI, i.e., CS–US interval). In particular, the optimal ISI for conditioned eyeblink responses in rabbits was shorter than for conditioned heart rate, and this, in turn, was shorter than for conditioned respiration rate responses. Using very different conditioning preparations, related findings have also been reported by Akins, Domjan, and Gutierrez (1994), Holland (1980), and Timberlake, Wahl, and King (1982). Thus, when discussing the effects of temporal contiguity, it will be important to keep in mind that any rules that emerge are likely to influence different response systems somewhat differently, and this will, ultimately, pose an important challenge to any theoretical understanding of simple Pavlovian learning.

A third qualification to the idea that temporal contiguity is critical for Pavlovian learning to occur comes from studies exploring the effects of absolute versus relative temporal contiguity. In one rather dramatic example of this distinction, Kaplan (1984) studied the effects of different ITIs on trace conditioning in an autoshaping task with pigeons. In different groups of birds, a keylight CS was presented for 12 s, and following its termination, a 12 s trace interval occurred before the food US was presented for 3 s. Different groups of birds were trained on this task with different ITIs that varied in length between 15 and 240 s, on average. If absolute temporal contiguity were fundamental, then the different groups should have all displayed similar learning independent of the ITI. However, excitatory conditioning (conditioned approach to the keylight) resulted when the ITI was long (e.g., 240 s), while conditioned inhibition (conditioned withdrawal from the keylight) was seen when conditioning occurred with a very short ITI (i.e., 15 s). This finding suggests that CS–US temporal contiguity relative to the ITI has a significant impact on conditioned responding.

More generally, it has been proposed that the overall "cycle" to "trial" (C/T) ratio is what governs the acquisition of conditioned responding in Pavlovian tasks (Balsam & Gallistel, 2009; Gallistel & Gibbon, 2000; Gibbon, 1977; Gibbon & and Balsam, 1981), where cycle refers to the time between successive USs, and trial refers to the total time within the CS before the US occurs. In a meta-analysis of early pigeon autoshaping studies, Gibbon and Balsam noted that the number of trials required before an acquisition criterion was reached was inversely related to the C/T ratio, and this occurred over a wide range of conditions differing in absolute CS and ITI durations (see Figure 2.3).

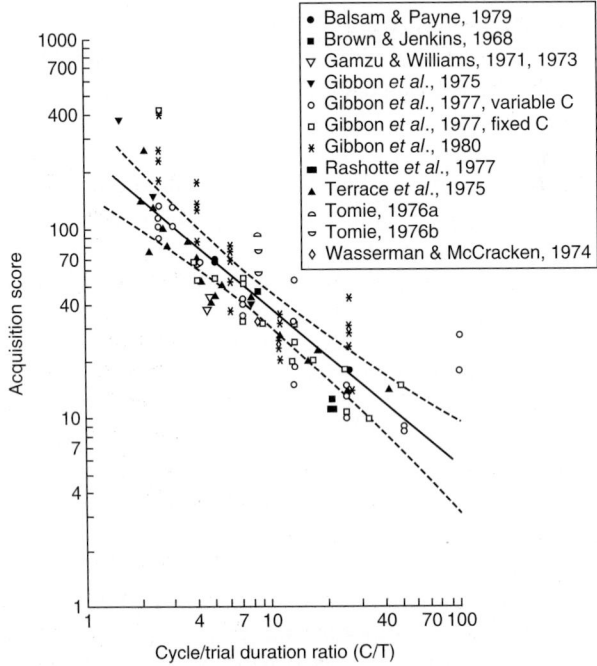

Figure 2.3 Relation between strength of learning (acquisition score) and the ratio of CS period to trial period (C/T). Reproduced from Gibbon and Balsam (1981).

The role of the C/T ratio has been most extensively studied in pigeon autoshaping tasks (e.g., Drew, Zupan, Cooke, Couvillon, & Balsam, 2005; Gibbon, Baldock, Locurto, Gold, & Terrace, 1977; Terrace et al., 1975). However, it has also been studied in other learning paradigms. In one review of the literature, it was concluded that the importance of this ratio is quite general across paradigms (Gallistel & Gibbon, 2000). However, this conclusion may be premature. Studies using the magazine approach paradigm with rats have provided equivocal results (Holland, 2000; Lattal, 1999). Furthermore, it seems doubtful that acquisition of conditioned responding in conditioned taste aversion and rabbit eyeblink conditioning paradigms will show the same sensitivities to C/T as has been found in pigeon autoshaping. For one thing, successful conditioning of the rabbit eyeblink response requires relatively short CS durations (less than approximately 2 s; Christian & Thompson, 2003). Moreover, although some between-experiment comparisons in fear conditioning paradigms reveal C/T sensitivity, results from other experiments provide conflicting evidence. Davis, Schlesinger, and Sorenson (1989), for instance, demonstrated more rapid acquisition of a fear-potentiated startle response to a stimulus trained with a long CS–US interval (52,300 ms) compared with shorter intervals (200 or 3200 ms) when conditioning occurred with ITI and context exposures before the first and after the last training trial held constant. Clearly, some process other than the C/T ratio is at work in this situation.

To summarize, there should be little doubt of the importance of temporal contiguity as a fundamentally important variable in Pavlovian conditioning research, perhaps even as a necessary condition for learning. That being said, a number of ancillary processes are likely involved as well. For instance, CS processing speed, processing interference, generalization decrement, and relative temporal contiguity are all factors that seem to affect the course of Pavlovian conditioning. In addition, the absolute CS duration appears to be a good predictor of conditioned responding, especially at asymptotic levels, although the C/T ratio is predictive of acquisition rate in at least the pigeon autoshaping paradigm. Moreover, the fact that different response systems show different sensitivities to temporal contiguity may imply that more than one associative learning system may be at work in different situations, or that a single associative learning system underlies learned behavior but in different ways across different situations. The basic fact that most learning paradigms, more or less, display the same host of learning phenomena would tend to support the latter position (e.g., Mackintosh, 1983).

Spatial contiguity Although much less extensively studied, the effect of spatial contiguity on Pavlovian learning has also been examined (see Chapter 13). Some findings point to the conclusion that learning can be promoted when the CS and US are contiguous in space. Rescorla and Cunningham (1979) demonstrated that second-order autoshaping of the pigeon's keypeck response was faster when the first- and second-order keylight stimuli were presented in the same spatial location relative to when they were presented in spatially distinct locations. Noticing a potential confound in the amount of temporal contiguity when CS2 is followed by CS1 in the same versus different physical locations, Christie (1996) used a novel apparatus that effectively controlled for this potential temporal confound and observed stronger first-order learning to approach a keylight stimulus that was paired with food when the spatial distance between the two was short compared with long (even though the bird had to travel the same distance to actually retrieve the food in both cases). Further, earlier studies have also relied on the concept of greater spatial or spatio-temporal similarity among certain classes of events to help explain why food-aversion learning appears to be highly "specialized" (e.g., Testa & Ternes, 1977).

Overall, there are fewer studies devoted to investigating the effects of spatial contiguity on learning than studies of temporal contiguity. Nevertheless, the picture that emerges is that the formation of associations between CS and US can be more readily achieved when there is greater temporal and/or spatial contiguity than when contiguity is low.

CS–US similarity

A role for similarity in association formation has long been hypothesized (e.g., Rescorla & Holland, 1976). Although this factor also has not been extensively explored, what evidence does exist is persuasive. Rescorla and Furrow (1977; see also Rescorla & Gillan, 1980) studied this in pigeons using a second-order conditioning procedure. Birds were first trained to associate two keylight stimuli from different stimulus dimensions (color, line orientation) with food (blue–food, horizontal lines–food) and to discriminate these from two other stimuli taken from those dimensions (green–no food, vertical lines–no food). Each of the rewarded stimuli was then used to second-order condition the nonrewarded stimuli taken from these two stimulus dimensions during a subsequent phase. During this phase, the second-order stimuli were presented for 10 s, and then each was followed immediately by one of the first-order stimuli trained in phase 1, but no food was presented on these trials. This procedure is known to result in the development of conditioned keypeck responses to the second-order stimulus. Rescorla and Furrow varied the relation between the two second-order and first-order stimuli during this phase of the experiment. For one group of birds, both stimuli on each second-order conditioning trial were from the same dimension (e.g., green–blue, vertical–horizontal), but for a second group they were from different dimensions (e.g., vertical–blue, green–horizontal). The group of birds exposed to second-order conditioning trials with similar stimuli, that is, both coming from the same stimulus dimension, learned second-order responding more rapidly than the birds trained with dissimilar stimuli. Testa (1975) also demonstrated in a conditioned suppression task with rats that CS–US associations were learned more rapidly when the spatio-temporal characteristics of the two stimuli were similar than when they were dissimilar. Grand, Close, Hale, and Honey (2007) also demonstrated an effect of similarity on paired associates learning in humans. Thus, both first- and second-order Pavlovian conditioning are generally enhanced when the stimuli are more than less similar.

Stimulus selection (contingency, relative cue validity, blocking)

In the late 1960s, a series of experiments performed independently by Rescorla, Wagner, and Kamin resulted in a completely new way in which Pavlovian conditioning was to be conceptualized. Until then, the dominant view was that temporal contiguity was the best general rule describing whether or not excitatory Pavlovian conditioning would occur. However, these three investigators produced results from experiments that questioned the *sufficiency* (though not the *necessity*) of temporal contiguity as a determiner of learning. Collectively, the three types of experiments these investigators performed are often referred to as "stimulus selection" or "cue competition" studies because they illustrate that the conditioning process depends upon important interactions among the various stimuli present on a given conditioning trial (including the general experimental context in which conditioning takes place).

Rescorla (1968) demonstrated this by showing that it was not merely the number of temporally contiguous CS–US pairings that was important for learning, but, rather, it was the overall CS–US contingency that mattered. He assessed the role of contingency in rats by varying the probability of a footshock US occurring during the presence or absence of a tone CS. The most general conclusion from his studies was that excitatory conditioning would develop to the CS whenever the probability of the US was higher in the presence of the CS than in its absence (see Figure 2.4). Moreover, whenever the shock US was equiprobable in the presence and absence of the CS, no conditioning was obtained to the CS in spite of the fact that a number of temporally contiguous CS–US pairings may have occurred. This observation gave rise to the important idea that an ideal control condition in Pavlovian conditioning experiments would be one in which a truly random relationship existed between the CS and US, one that would effectively equate the overall exposures to CS and US across groups but without any predictive relationship in this zero contingency control group (Rescorla, 1967). Finally, the contingency studies advanced our understanding of Pavlovian learning because it gave us a common framework within which to think of excitatory and inhibitory conditioning, two processes that had previously been treated separately. In particular, Rescorla (1969) observed that whenever the US had a higher probability of occurrence in the absence than in the presence of the CS, the CS would

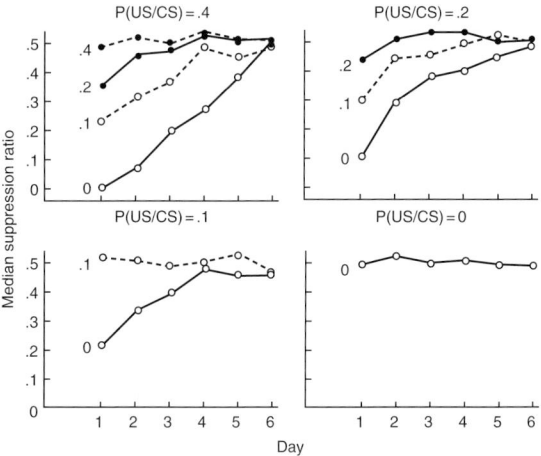

Figure 2.4 Relation between strength of learning (mean lever suppression) as a function of the probability of the US in the presence and absence of the CS. $p(US/US)$ denotes the probability of the shock being delivered during the CS. The lines refer to the probability of the US being delivered during the absence of the US. Reproduced from Rescorla (1968).

function as a conditioned inhibitory stimulus. Remarkably, this would occur even when the CS and US had been paired a number of times, providing that the US was more likely to occur in the absence of the CS.

The important contingency effects found by Rescorla (1968) have been replicated in a number of different learning paradigms and, thus, would appear to be rather general phenomena. These include studies conducted on Hermissenda (Farley, 1987), pigeon autoshaping (e.g., Wasserman, Franklin, & Hearst, 1974), rat magazine approach conditioning (e.g., Boakes, 1977; Murphy & Baker, 2004), rabbit eyeblink conditioning (e.g., Millenson, Kehoe, & Gormezano, 1977), sexual conditioning in birds (e.g., Crawford & Domjan, 1993), and causal judgment tasks with humans (e.g., Shanks & Dickinson, 1990; Vallee-Tourangeau, Murphy, & Drew, 1998).

Wagner, Logan, Haberlandt, and Price (1968) conducted "relative cue validity" studies that also questioned the sufficiency of temporal contiguity. In their studies (conducted in both rabbit eyeblink and rat conditioned suppression paradigms), animals were conditioned with two compound stimuli (AX, BX). In one group of animals, one of these compound stimuli was consistently paired with the US, but the other compound was never paired with the US (AX+, BX−). In a second group of animals, both compound stimuli were paired with the US on 50% of its trials (AX+/−, BX+/−). At issue was whether stimulus X, when tested on its own, would display equal levels of learning in these two groups. In Group 1, X is a relatively poor predictor of the US compared with stimulus A, but in Group 2, X is as valid a predictor of the US as is stimulus A. Wagner et al. (1968) observed that, indeed, X had acquired a greater associative strength in Group 2 than in Group 1. In spite of the fact that X had been paired with the US an equal number of times in these two groups, the amount learned about stimulus X was a function of how well it predicted the US relative to its partner in the stimulus compound. Once again, temporal contiguity alone cannot accommodate this finding.

Kamin (1968, 1969) also observed that temporal contiguity could not alone account for learning in a famous experimental result referred to as the "blocking" effect. In Kamin's study, rats first were trained to fear an auditory CS (A) reinforced with a footshock US (+) in Stage I. During Stage II, A was presented in a compound with a novel visual stimulus (X) and reinforced with footshock (AX+). A control group received Stage II training but not Stage I. In further tests of stimulus X alone, the control group demonstrated robust fear. However, prior presentations of A+ in the experimental group impaired (i.e., "blocked") the development of fear to X. This occurred in spite of the fact that the two groups received the same number of temporally contiguous X–US pairings. Kamin concluded that blocking occurred, in this situation, because the shock US was not surprising in the experimental group following the AX stimulus compound because it was already predicted by A. If only surprising USs can support learning, no learning should occur in this group.

In all three of these "stimulus selection" effects, temporal contiguity alone cannot account for the data. Rather, the learning system appears to select the best predictor of the US at the cost of learning about other cues, be this the experimental context (in the contingency study), the more valid cue (in the relative cue validity study), or the blocking stimulus (in Kamin's study). It is fair to say that these three studies revolutionized our thinking on how learning proceeds in Pavlovian conditioning and, as we will see below, anticipated major developments in the neurobiology of learning.

Stimulus–reinforcer relevance (belonginess)

An additional factor that has been shown to be important in determining learning is known as "stimulus–reinforcer relevance." This refers to the fact that some combinations of CS and US are better learned about than others. The most famous example of this was the experiment by Garcia and Koelling (1966; see also Domjan & Wilson, 1972). In their study, thirsty rats consumed water that was paired with audiovisual and gustatory features (bright-noisy-flavored water), and consumption of this was paired (in different groups) either with a LiCl-induced nausea US or with a footshock US. Several days later, half of the rats were tested with the flavored water in the absence of the audiovisual features. The remaining rats in each of these groups were tested for their intake of bright, noisy water in the absence of the flavor. The rats trained with the illness US drank less of the flavored water but avidly consumed the bright, noisy water, whereas the rats trained with the shock US drank large amounts of the flavored water but not the bright, noisy water (the water paired with the light and sound). Thus, some combinations of CS and US are more readily learned about ("belong" together) than others.

It is important to note that such selective associations have been demonstrated to occur in paradigms other than taste aversion learning, so the phenomenon would not appear to be unique to this situation (e.g., LoLordo, 1979). However, this effect has received different theoretical treatments. On the one hand, Garcia and colleagues argued that such selective associative learning points to important underlying neurobiological constraints that an organism's evolutionary history places upon the learning mechanism (Garcia & Koelling, 1966; Seligman & Hager, 1972). This approach could provide fundamental problems for any effort at finding truly general laws for learning because such laws would be learning-process specific. In contrast, other authors have attempted to explain instances of selective associations by appealing to more general principles. One example of this is the idea that CS–US similarity affects association formation (noted above). If one assumes that the spatio-temporal properties of tastes and illness, for example, are more similar than audiovisual stimuli and illness, then the results from the Garcia and Koelling (1966) study can, in principle, be explained without requiring any major challenges to a more general process approach (e.g., Testa & Ternes, 1977).

Psychological Principles of Pavlovian Learning

Having reviewed the major variables determining Pavlovian excitatory conditioning, we are now in a position to ask what basic psychological principles (i.e., mechanisms) appear to most accurately encompass the major findings we have just discussed. To be sure, there have been a large number of specific learning theories applied to the study of Pavlovian learning (e.g., Pearce & Bouton, 2001), and we will not review these here, but, rather, we will point to what we take to be two rather fundamental principles that are shared, in one way or another, by most of those theoretical treatments, and determine their applicability to the variety of facts we now understand regarding the critical variables for Pavlovian learning to develop. In addition, we will explore the limitations of these basic principles and present, where appropriate, an alternative framework for thinking about the results.

Concurrent activation of CS and US representations

The basic notion that two events will associate with one another to the extent that these events are experienced together in time has played a strong role in theories of Pavlovian learning. For instance, Konorski (1948) suggested that a CS will associate with a US to the extent that its processing co-occurs with a "rise in activation" of the US representation. Conversely, Konorski also speculated that inhibitory associations would develop when the stimulus co-occurs with a "fall in activation" of the US representation. A somewhat more recent version of this approach is Wagner's *sometimes opponent process* (SOP) theory of Pavlovian learning (Wagner, 1981). The idea goes a long way towards helping us achieve some clarity on just why many of the critical variables identified in the previous section are important for Pavlovian learning to occur.

If concurrent activation drives learning, why should the CS–US interval function take the form it most typically does? For instance, why might we expect to see inhibitory or excitatory learning with backward US–CS intervals, relatively weak excitatory learning with simultaneous pairings, somewhat increasingly stronger learning with increases in the CS–US interval, and progressively poorer learning as the CS–US interval increases past its optimal level? The concurrent activation idea, in principle, can explain most of these basic facts. One would need to make the reasonable assumption that when a stimulus is presented, its degree of processing increases with time (e.g., Sutton & Barto, 1981a; Wagner, 1981). With this assumption, very short CS–US intervals could fail to support strong learning because the CS has not had an opportunity to be fully processed by the time the US is presented. Backward US–CS pairings could result in either excitatory or inhibitory learning, depending on whether the CS is primarily coactive with the US or whether its activation coincides more with, in Konorski's (1948) terms, a fall in US activation. Trace conditioning procedures should result in poorer learning compared with normal delay conditioning procedures because the levels of CS activation present at the time of US presentation would favor the delay procedure. Furthermore, the number of CS–US pairings should be important because the strength of the CS–US association should steadily increase with increasing numbers of their coactivations. In addition, it is easy to see why stimulus intensity (CS or US) should also be important (though certain additional assumptions would need to be made to explain why US intensity seems to affect rate and asymptote, while CS intensity seems to primarily affect rate of learning).

The concurrent processing idea may even help us understand the roles of spatial contiguity and similarity in governing learning. For these variables to be understood in such terms, one could assume that the processing of two spatially or physically similar stimuli on a given conditioning trial is different from the processing given to dissimilar stimuli. For instance, Rescorla and Gillan (1980) suggested that the elements of a stimulus that are shared between two similar stimuli effectively become less intense (due to habituation) when two similar stimuli are presented in sequence. This would mean that the distinct features of the stimuli should be more effectively processed and, thus, learned about. This simple mechanism would account for the similarity results noted above, but they would also, under other circumstances, lead to the counterintuitive prediction that sometimes similarity can hinder learning. Rescorla and Gillan (1980) and Grand *et al.* (2007) provided experimental tests in support of these basic ideas. The importance of this analysis is that the fundamental primitive for learning appears not to be similarity per se. Rather, the analysis is consistent with the view that concurrent processing given to two stimuli influences learning, but various factors (e.g., habituation) will need to be considered to determine how these might affect processing of the various features of stimuli to be associated. Ultimately, the appeal of reducing an important variable, similarity, to a more fundamental principle, concurrent processing, can be further appreciated by considering that the explanatory domain of the concurrent processing notion is increased further if stimulus–reinforcer relevance effects can themselves be at least partly understood as a special case of learning by similarity.

In spite of its appeal, a simple notion of concurrent processing also has difficulty in accounting for a number of important variables. First, it is not obvious why, in delay conditioning procedures (where the CS remains on until US delivery), learning should ever be reduced with further increases in the CS–US interval (onset to onset) beyond some optimal level. If the CS processing function increases with time until some maximal processing level is reached, the CS will be maximally coactive with the US at any CS–US interval following the optimal one in the normal delay procedure. Second, it is not obvious from this perspective why different response systems should show different CS–US interval functions. Third, this idea does not fully capture why relative temporal contiguity (and the C/T ratio) should be important. The data from Kaplan's (1984) study, recall, revealed that short ITIs result in inhibitory trace conditioning, whereas long ITIs result in excitatory conditioning. Kaplan (1984) noted that with short ITIs, the US from a previous trial may be processed at the time the CS is presented during the next trial. This could result in inhibitory learning, because the CS would co-occur with a fall in US activation. However, the more general observation that the C/T ratio, at least in pigeon autoshaping, plays an important role over a wide range of CS and ITI durations would not obviously fall out of this perspective. Finally, the three stimulus selection effects considered above (contingency, relative cue validity, blocking) are not well understood with a concurrent processing idea alone. All of these problems require additional considerations.

Prediction Error (US Surprise)

The stimulus selection phenomena noted above reformulated the manner in which theorists view conditioning. Rescorla and Wagner (1972) formalized Kamin's notion that learning will only occur to the extent that the US is surprising (i.e., because of some error in prediction; Chapters 3 and 15). In other words, the predicted US will fail to support new learning because its processing will be greatly diminished (if not totally suppressed). This insight, together with the idea that US predictions depend upon all of the stimuli present on a given conditioning trial (not just the target CS in question; cf. Bush & Mosteller, 1951; Mackintosh, 1975), provides a way to understand the three stimulus selection phenomena noted above, with one simple explanatory mechanism. For example, in Rescorla's contingency studies, the experimental context (i.e., the conditioning chamber) may itself associate with the shock US during the ITI. When a further tone–shock pairing is presented, the occurrence of shock will have already been predicted by the context, and thus no learning should take place. Blocking and relative cue validity effects can be explained in the same way: by making reference to other concurrently presented stimuli that are better at predicting the US than the target CS. Further, the model led to the development of a variety of other tests that depended in different ways on associative changes being brought about by either positive or negative prediction errors. In short, the model became so successful partly because it helped the theorist organize a tremendous amount of phenomena under one framework (Siegel & Allan, 1996).

Notice how this idea is completely compatible with the concurrent processing notion. As Jenkins (1984) noted, one can think of the Rescorla–Wagner model as a temporal contiguity theory. Learning still depends upon concurrent activation of CS and US representations. It is just that the US representation will only be activated and, hence, be able to support new associative learning, when its occurrence (or nonoccurrence) has not been fully predicted. Indeed, in Wagner's SOP theory, this assumption was made explicit by the claim that anticipated USs would be primed and, therefore, less fully activated in a state that would support new excitatory learning. However one imagines the underlying mechanism, the prediction error idea considerably increases the explanatory power of the concurrent processing notion.

Nevertheless, certain problems remain. Even this more embellished idea cannot readily explain why in delay conditioning tasks learning appears to decline with CS–US intervals greater than the optimal one. Here, it would need to be assumed that with very long CS durations, a certain degree of stimulus habituation occurs that may limit its processing (Wagner, 1981). Moreover, the dependence of CS–US interval on response system remains an unsolved problem. The importance of relative contiguity and the C/T ratio could potentially be explained on the basis of differences in background conditioning (Mackintosh, 1983). However, as Balsam and Gallistel (2009) have argued (see also Gibbon & Balsam, 1981), it is not obvious that all quantitative aspects of the C/T ratio experiments will easily fall out of this perspective.

One additional complication with the US prediction error notion comes from a set of studies by Rescorla (2001). Briefly, these studies demonstrated that stimuli conditioned in compound do not show equivalent changes in associative strength on conditioning trials in which there is either a positive or negative US prediction error. The prediction error concept as developed by the Rescorla–Wagner model was based on the idea that all stimuli present on a conditioning trial contribute to the generation of a US prediction. However, Rescorla's studies suggest that those stimuli gaining or losing associative strength on the conditioning trial depend, in part, on their own individual prediction errors. In particular, Rescorla demonstrated that stimuli that predict the US gain less associative strength on a conditioning trial (compared with a nonpredictive cue) in which an unexpected US is presented, while stimuli that predict the absence of the US lose less associative strength when an expected US is omitted. Indeed, Leung and Westbrook (2008) demonstrated that associative changes driven by prediction errors in extinction were regulated by both common and individual prediction error terms (see also Le Pelley, 2004; Rescorla, 2000). It will be important to keep this distinction in mind as the concept is further developed.

Temporal information

A completely different formulation of Pavlovian conditioning arises from a class of approaches known as "comparator" theories (e.g., Gallistel & Gibbon, 2000; Gibbon & Balsam, 1981; Stout & Miller, 2007). According to these approaches, it is assumed that apparent failures of learning reflect failures in performance and not learning per se. In the most recent version of this approach, Balsam and Gallistel (2009; Balsam, Drew, & Gallistel, 2010; Gallistel & Balsam, 2014) emphasize that animals performing in Pavlovian conditioning experiments do not actually learn CS–US associations. Rather, it is assumed that the animal stores the events it experiences within a temporal memory structure, and that decisions to respond or not depend on whether the CS conveys temporal information above that provided by the background. Thus, animals are said to store in memory when CS and US events occur in time, and to calculate the rates of US occurrence both in the presence and in the absence of the CS. To the extent that the US rate estimate within the CS exceeds that to the background, the CS would convey meaningful information and produce a response at the appropriate point in time.

While theories like the Rescorla–Wagner model (Rescorla & Wagner, 1972) have most frequently been applied to so-called "trial-based" situations (but see Buhusi & Schmajuk, 1999; Sutton & Barto, 1981b), such models have not always dealt with issues relating to the specific temporal organization of learned behavior. The Balsam and Gallistel (2009) approach specifically addresses this aspect of learning. However, while this approach readily accommodates the finding that, in autoshaping at least, the C/T ratio governs the acquisition of responding, and while some aspects of timed responding are consistent with the approach (e.g., Drew *et al.*, 2005; but see Delamater & Holland, 2008), there are a number of limitations faced by this approach as well. First, as noted above, while the C/T ratio may describe the rate of acquisition in some preparations, CS duration more accurately describes differences in asymptotic responding. Second, the generality of the importance of the C/T ratio in describing learning has not been established, and conflicting data exist (e.g., Davis *et al.*, 1989; Holland, 2000; Lattal, 1999). Third, because these comparator approaches assume that apparent learning failures (e.g., in blocking, contingency, relative cue validity) are really failures of performance, they face difficulties in accounting for why explicit tests of the learning or performance explanations often favor learning deficits in these tasks (e.g., Delamater *et al.*, 2014; but see Cole, Barnet, & Miller, 1995; Miller, Barnet, & Grahame, 1992; Urushihara & Miller, 2010). In addition, the same problems encountered above concerning response-system differences will also apply to this approach as well.

To summarize so far, we have identified a host of important variables that influence the course of excitatory Pavlovian learning. In this section, we have attempted to explain many of these basic findings by making reference to a limited number of basic psychological principles. In particular, the idea that associative learning develops when there is effective concurrent processing of the representations of the CS and US goes a long way towards helping us understand many of the critical facts of conditioning. This simple idea appears to require an amendment to allow for prediction errors to be critical in defining when USs receive further processing critical for association formation, and the contributions of both "individual" and "common" prediction error terms will need to be adequately addressed. However, some of the behavioral facts may require a more elaborate theoretical treatment of timing processes (see also Delamater et al., 2014). For now, we turn to an analysis of some of the basic neural mechanisms shown to be critical for Pavlovian learning. Our main quest in this highly selective review of the relevant literature will be determining whether there is any neural reality to the suggestions, based on a purely behavioral level of analysis, that concurrent processing and prediction error concepts, for the most part, are responsible for driving Pavlovian learning.

Neural Principles of Conditioning

Major progress towards understanding the neural mechanisms of learning has taken place in recent years, and several different basic Pavlovian learning paradigms have been intensively studied. These include learning of the marine snail *Aplysia*'s gill withdrawal response, the rabbit's eyeblink (or nictitating membrane) response, as well as fear and appetitive conditioning in the rat. The aim of this section is to provide an overview of some of the neural mechanisms that support Pavlovian conditioning. In particular, we will focus on studies that directly relate to the concurrent processing and US surprise ideas identified as being important for association formation by a purely behavior-level analysis. Of course, one should expect that the underlying neural circuits of learning in different paradigms will differ in their details, but the importance of the behavioral work has been to show that similar basic principles may be involved quite ubiquitously throughout the nervous system.

The Hebbian model and temporal contiguity

We have presented behavioral evidence that suggests that concurrent activation of the CS and US is a fundamental principle for learning to occur. Neural evidence at the molecular and cellular level to a large extent supports this concurrent processing idea. The Hebbian hypothesis states that "any two cells or systems of cells that are repeatedly active at the same time will tend to become 'associated,' so that activity in one facilitates activity in the other" (Hebb, 1949, p. 70). This model of neural plasticity directly captures the basic idea from behavioral studies that concurrent activation is critical for associative learning to take place. It also provides us with a neural mechanism for understanding many of the important behavioral aspects of temporal contiguity.

The specific mechanisms involved in this facilitated synaptic communication are complex and are reviewed elsewhere (e.g., Glanzman, 2010). However, in relation to Pavlovian conditioning, the basic concept is that sensory neurons independently process CS and US information, and, in some cases, converge upon a motor output response neuron. The sensory neuron stimulated by the CS itself is not sufficient to drive the motor output neuron but, over the course of conditioning, acquires this ability through presynaptic (e.g., Castellucci & Kandel, 1974, 1976) and postsynaptic mechanisms (i.e., Isaac, Nicoll, & Malenka, 1995; Malenka & Nicoll, 1999).

The strongest evidence to date for this Hebbian hypothesis comes from cellular work in *Aplysia* (for a review, see Kandel, 2001). This work demonstrates that as a result of Pavlovian conditioning, synaptic connectivity between neurons is strengthened via a molecular signaling cascade, and this ultimately causes changes in the ability of the sensory neuron to drive the motor neuron (for a more detailed description of this process, refer to Roberts & Glanzman, 2003). In addition, studies of fear conditioning in mammals also provide support for Hebbian plasticity arising from convergence of CS–US activity in the lateral amygdala (LA). For example, several electrophysiology studies found fear conditioning to occur when weak CS input to LA pyramidal cells coincided with strong US-evoked depolarization of those same cells (see Blair, Schafe, Bauer, Rodrigues, & LeDoux, 2001; Ledoux, 2000; Paré, 2002; Sah, Westbrook, & Lüthi, 2008). This training had the effect of potentiating CS-evoked responses of LA neurons *in vivo* (e.g., Paré & Collins, 2000; Quirk, Repa, & LeDoux, 1995; Rogan, Stäubli, & LeDoux, 1997; Romanski, Clugnet, Bordi, & LeDoux, 1993; Rosenkranz & Grace, 2002). Moreover, pairing a CS with direct depolarization of LA pyramidal neurons (as a surrogate US) also supports fear conditioning (Johansen *et al.*, 2010), and *in vitro* studies have shown that concurrent stimulation of CS and US pathways into LA results in strengthening of CS-to-LA synaptic efficacy (Kwon & Choi, 2009; McKernan & Shinnick-Gallagher, 1997). Morphological evidence also exists for Hebbian-like changes in synaptic plasticity. After multiple pairings of a CS with a fearful US, the postsynaptic density in LA neurons has been observed to increase (Ostroff, Cain, Bedont, Monfils, & Ledoux, 2010). At a molecular level, the mechanisms by which CS–US pairings induce this synaptic plasticity in the LA may be as a result of subsequent intracellular cascades linked to this plasticity (Maren & Quirk, 2004). A review of the intracellular and molecular mechanisms for synaptic plasticity is beyond the scope of this paper, and the reader is referred to Kandel (2001), Orsini and Maren (2012), and Schafe, Nader, Blair, and LeDoux (2001) for such discussions.

One possible mechanism for Hebbian synaptic plasticity is long-term potentiation (LTP). LTP is induced by pairing weak presynaptic stimulation with strong postsynaptic depolarization, and this results in the facilitation of signal transmission (Sigurdsson, Doyère, Cain, & LeDoux, 2007). In the context of Pavlovian conditioning, presynaptic stimulation of sensory afferents is thought to represent activity caused by the CS, whereas postsynaptic depolarization represents the US. The requirement for synchronous neural stimulation suggests that LTP may be a viable mechanism for conditioning. Lin and Glanzman (1997) demonstrated increases in LTP with increases in temporal contiguity between pre- and postsynaptic stimulation (see Figure 2.5). However, it is important to note that this evidence came from cell cultures of *Aplysia*, and it is not known how LTP-induced neurophysiological changes may have mapped onto behavioral output in this study. This is particularly relevant because, in this study, simultaneous stimulation resulted in the optimal amount of LTP, with decreases observed as contiguity was decreased in either the forward or backward directions. At a more behavioral level, as reviewed above, simultaneous and backward procedures tend not to be very effective in supporting conditioned responding.

It is interesting that LTP is sensitive to other variables also shown to be critical for learning to occur. In one study, Scharf *et al.* (2002) demonstrated stronger LTP in

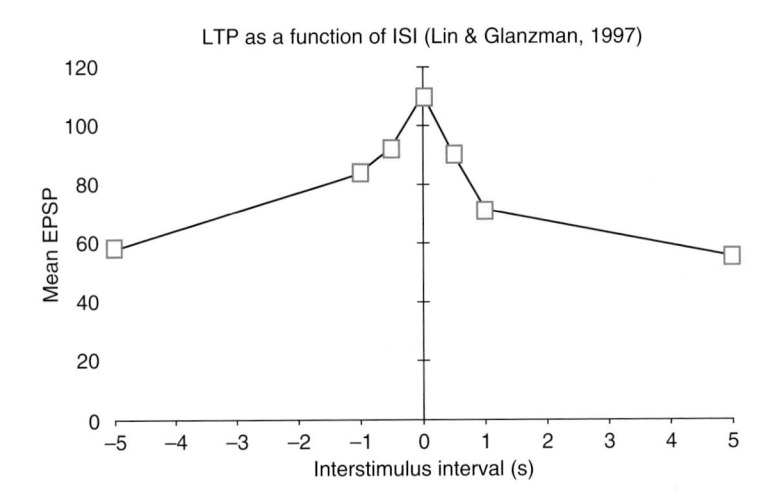

Figure 2.5 Mean EPSPs as a function of interstimulus interval (s). Redrawn from Lin and Glanzman (1997).

hippocampal slices (and stronger behavioral conditioning) when trials were spaced in time (5 min) compared with being massed (20 s). In addition, Bauer, LeDoux, and Nader (2001) observed that LTP, induced by pairing weak presynaptic stimulation with strong postsynaptic depolarization, was itself weakened when the contingency was degraded by adding unpaired postsynaptic depolarizations. Apparently, unpaired postsynaptic depolarizations depotentiated the synapse, effectively reversing LTP. While it is unlikely that this depotentiation effect will explain all types of contingency degradation effects (e.g., Durlach, 1983), it is nevertheless intriguing that organism-level behavioral effects can sometimes be observed at the level of the individual synapse.

Other behavioral characteristics of learning do not so easily map onto LTP at the individual synapse. First, LTP decays fairly rapidly (e.g., Abraham, 2003), but associative learning can last indefinitely. Second, although LTP has been shown to be sensitive to trial spacing, it is unlikely that it will account for all the quantitative aspects of the C/T ratio (Gallistel & Matzel, 2013). Third, although the importance of the order of stimulating pulses in LTP has not been extensively studied (Lin & Glanzman, 1997), the order of CS and US presentations is generally agreed to be important for conditioning at the behavioral level (e.g., Mackintosh, 1974, 1983). Although backward US–CS pairings can sometimes result in excitatory conditioning (e.g., Chang, Blaisdell, & Miller, 2003), the more common result is inhibitory conditioning (e.g., Moscovitch & LoLordo, 1968). It is not clear how this relates to LTP. Forth, Pavlovian conditioning is often highly temporally specific. In other words, conditioned responses often are seen to occur close to the time at which the US is due to arrive (e.g., Drew *et al.*, 2005). How this aspect of learned behavior can be captured by an LTP mechanism remains to be seen. However, it is unfair to expect that all aspects of behavior will be observed at the level of a specific mechanism of plasticity observed at an individual synapse. Associative learning likely entails changes among an entire population of neurons within a larger neural network. LTP is, perhaps, one mechanism that describes changes in connectivity among elements

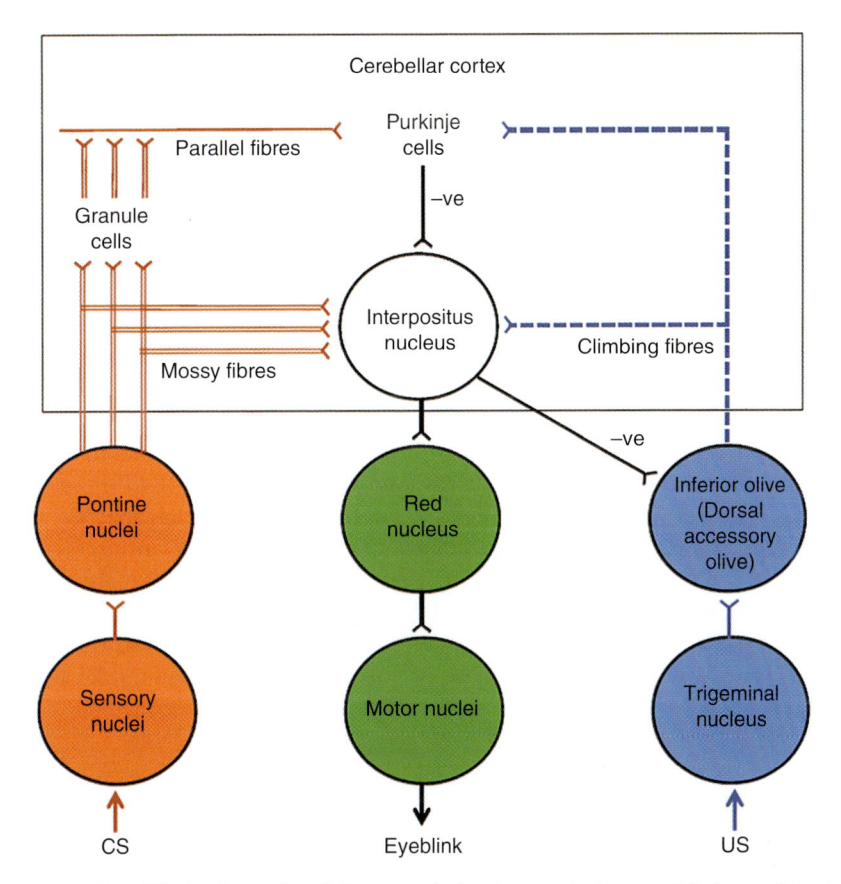

Figure 2.6 Simplified schematic of the neural circuitry underling eyeblink conditioning in the cerebellum. Information about the CS (in orange) and information about US (in blue) converge in the cerebellar cortex in Purkinje cells and the interpositus nucleus via mossy fibers and climbing fibers. CS information is first processed by sensory nuclei, which project to the pontine nuclei, while US information is processed in the trigeminal nucleus, which projects to the inferior olive (where the dorsal accessory olive is located). The output pathway for the conditioned response (in green) includes the interpositus nucleus projection to the red nucleus, which projects to motor nuclei to produce eyeblink. "–ve" indicates inhibitory projections; the remaining projections are excitatory.

within this larger network, but surely the network as a whole would be required to describe many of the key features that characterize learning at the behavioral level.

One interesting example of this is conditioned response timing within the eyeblink conditioning circuit (see Figure 2.6). We mentioned earlier that eyeblink conditioning is very sensitive to the ISI and that the eyeblink CR is extremely well timed (e.g., Schneiderman & Gormezano, 1964). It is now known that CS and US information is conveyed to the cerebellum, respectively, via activation of two major afferents – mossy fibers and climbing fibers – and that output of the cerebellum is responsible for expression of the conditioned eyeblink response (Mauk, Steinmetz, & Thompson, 1986; Steinmetz, Le Coq, & Aymerich, 1989). Plasticity occurs at two points of convergence – within the cerebellar cortex and also in the interpositus nucleus (IPN). It is currently thought that the cerebellar cortex modulates activity within the IPN at the appropriate time to enable a well-timed CR to occur (e.g., Krasne, 2002). How the cerebellar cortex accomplishes this is a matter of some speculation. One idea is that different subsets of cells within the mossy fiber pathway (specifically involving interactions among granule and Golgi cells) are activated with different time delays following a CS input (Buonomano & Mauk, 1994). Those cells that are most active at the time of US delivery would display the most amount of synaptic plasticity, and appropriately timed responses can be the result. In partial support of these ideas is the demonstration that cerebellar cortex lesions disrupt conditioned eyeblink response timing without eliminating learning (Perrett, Ruiz, & Mauk, 1993). Overall, these considerations suggest that populations of the neurons must interact in order to provide a more complete story of the conditioning mechanism.

The evidence presented so far suggests that LTP can be considered as a viable mechanism of synaptic plasticity and learning. However, while LTP is sensitive to some key features of conditioning (temporal contiguity, trial spacing, CS–US contingency), more molar aspects of behavior will likely require an interacting network perspective for their analysis. Another key aspect of learning that also appears to require a network perspective is that the US must be surprising for learning to occur. The stimulus selection studies reviewed above lead to the conclusion that temporal contiguity is not sufficient for learning to occur. Thus, the Hebbian model alone does not entirely explain why conditioning depends upon prediction error.

Neural evidence for the importance of US surprise

Evidence considered above suggests that although temporal contiguity may be necessary for conditioning to occur, it is not sufficient. The other fundamental principle we discussed is that for learning to occur on a given conditioning trial, the US must be surprising, or, in other words, there must be an error in its prediction. There is a wealth of evidence to support this notion at the neural or neural systems levels of analysis, and we now turn to discussing some of that evidence.

Midbrain dopamine neurons

The most recognized neuronal evidence for reward prediction error coding in the brain regards the phasic activation of midbrain dopamine neurons (Matsumoto & Hikosaka, 2009; Schultz, 2006, 2007, 2008; Schultz, Dayan, & Montague, 1997). Correlative evidence from electrophysiological studies in nonhuman primates demonstrates that midbrain dopamine neurons show phasic increases in neural firing as a result of unexpected deliveries of a juice reward US and show phasic inhibition of neural activity as a result of unexpected omission of the reward US (Matsumoto & Hikosaka, 2009; Schultz *et al.*, 1997; see Chapter 3). Furthermore, during conditioning, the response of the dopamine neurons shifts from the delivery of the juice reward to the presentation of the predictive CS, with a fully predicted US losing its ability to phasically activate these neurons. These findings support the US surprise principle that learning occurs as a function of the discrepancy between the actual outcome and the expected outcome (Rescorla & Wagner, 1972; Tobler, Dickinson, & Schultz, 2003; Waelti, Dickinson, & Schultz, 2001).

While the above evidence is largely correlative, recent optogenetic stimulation studies point to a more causal role for prediction error coding by midbrain dopamine neurons. Steinberg *et al.* (2013) optogenetically stimulated dopamine neurons in the rat ventral tegmental area during the compound conditioning phase of a blocking procedure, and observed that such stimulation resulted in increased conditioned responding to the typically blocked cue. Thus, it appears that normal suppression of dopamine activation when a predicted US is presented is responsible for reduced learning to the added cue in a blocking experiment. The specific mechanisms at work in this effect, however, are unclear, but it has been suggested that gamma-aminobutyric acid (GABA)ergic interneurons may play a critical role (Dobi, Margolis, Wang, Harvey, & Morales, 2010; Geisler & Zahm, 2005; Ji & Shepard, 2007; Matsumoto & Hikosaka, 2007). In particular, recent evidence demonstrates that inhibitory input from GABAergic interneurons may counteract the excitatory drive from the reward US when the reward is expected (Cohen, Haesler, Vong, Lowell, & Uchida, 2012).

Eyeblink conditioning in the cerebellum

The most extensively mapped out neural circuit for Pavlovian learning comes from studies of eyeblink conditioning in the rabbit (for a review, see Christian & Thompson, 2003). Here, we shall briefly consider the main processing pathways involved in prediction error coding in this circuitry.

When a US (air puff or electric shock) is delivered to the cornea or paraorbital region of the eye, sensory information is carried to the trigeminal nucleus and relayed both directly and indirectly to various motor nuclei whose output controls different eye muscles that work synergistically to produce an unconditioned blink response to corneal stimulation (for a review, see Christian & Thompson, 2003). The trigeminal nucleus also sends efferent projections to the inferior olive (IO), the most critical region of which is the dorsal accessory olive (Brodal & Brodal, 1981). Climbing fibers from this region send information about the US to the cerebellum (Brodal, Walberg, & Hoddevik, 1975; Thompson & Steinmetz, 2009) and project to both the deep cerebellar nuclei (of the IPN) and Purkinje cells (PCs) in the cerebellar cortex (see Figure 2.6).

Several studies have mapped out CS processing across an array of stimulus modalities (auditory, visual, somatosensory), and while these stimuli project, respectively, to auditory, visual, and somatosensory cortices, all these regions converge upon the pontine nuclei (PN; Glickstein, May, & Mercier, 1985; Schmahmann & Pandya, 1989, 1991, 1993). The PN projects mossy fiber axons that carry CS-related information (Lewis, LoTurco, & Solomon, 1987; Steinmetz *et al.*, 1987; Thompson, 2005) to the cerebellum terminating in both the IPN and at granule cells (GR) of the cerebellar cortex (Steinmetz & Sengelaub, 1992) which, in turn, synapse onto PCs.

Thus, there are two key cerebellar sites of CS–US convergence – the cells of the IPN and PCs of the cortex. In addition to receiving converging CS and US input via the PN and IO, respectively, cells of the IPN receive GABAergic inhibitory input from PCs of the cerebellar cortex. It is currently thought that this inhibitory projection from the cerebellar cortex is involved in the timing of conditioned responding (e.g., Mauk, Medina, Nores, & Ohyama, 2000), whereas whether or not learning will occur depends upon the IPN (Thompson, 2005). Lesions of the lateral IPN and medial dentate nuclei were sufficient to prevent acquisition of CRs in naïve animals (Lincoln, McCormick, & Thompson, 1982) and abolished CRs in well-trained animals (McCormick & Thompson, 1984). Furthermore, temporary inactivation of the IPN (via $GABA_A$ agonist muscimol or the sodium-channel blocker lidocaine) completely prevented learning of CRs in naïve animals (Clark, Zhang, & Lavond, 1992; Krupa & Thompson, 1997; Krupa, Thompson, & Thompson, 1993; Nordholm, Thompson, Dersarkissian, & Thompson, 1993). In contrast, cerebellar cortex lesions have been shown to slow learning, but not prevent it, and also give rise to poorly timed CRs (Thompson, 2005).

A critically important pathway for understanding the nature of prediction error effects in this preparation is the GABAergically mediated inhibitory output projection from the IPN to the IO. Kim, Krupa, and Thompson (1998) recorded PC cells that received climbing fiber input from the IO during eyeblink conditioning. These cells responded more to unpredicted than to predicted US presentations. In addition, infusing a GABA antagonist, picrotoxin, into the olive following conditioning restored the normal response in PC cells to the US, even though it was fully predicted. Most impressively, these authors found that picrotoxin administered in the IO during the compound conditioning phase of a blocking experiment eliminated the blocking effect. Thus, this GABAergic cerebello-olivary projection plays a crucial role in limiting the processing given to a fully predicted US, and appears to provide direct confirmation of the idea from the Rescorla–Wagner model that US processing should be diminished when it is fully predicted.

US prediction errors in conditioned fear

Another learning paradigm whose neural mechanisms have been extensively studied in recent years is fear conditioning in the rat (see also Chapter 18, for the human case). In spite of the explosion of interest in the neural mechanisms of fear learning over the last decade or so, exactly how prediction error mechanisms work in this system is only beginning to be understood. Fanselow (1998) suggested that a well-trained CS evokes an opioid-mediated analgesic reaction whose consequence is to diminish the impact of the shock US when it occurs. More recently, McNally, Johansen, and Blair (2011) have suggested that the critical site for prediction error computations is the ventrolateral periaqueductal gray (vlPAG).

The PAG is an important point of convergence between the processing of aversive sensory inputs (e.g., electric foot shock) and the output of the fear system, particularly the central nucleus of the amygdala (Carrive, 1993). Whereas the amygdala has received most of the focus in fear conditioning research, because this is the region where CS and US information converges and where plasticity takes place (e.g., Romanski *et al.*, 1993), recent studies have revealed that greater responsiveness of cells to unpredicted than predicted shock USs within the LA depends upon such differential activation of cells within the PAG (Johansen, Tarpley, LeDoux, & Blair, 2010). Thus, although plasticity is widely acknowledged to occur within the amygdala in fear conditioning (e.g., Johansen, Cain, Ostroff, & LeDoux, 2011; Maren, 2005; McNally *et al.*, 2011; Orsini & Maren, 2012; Sah *et al.*, 2008; Schafe *et al.*, 2001;

Sigurdsson *et al.*, 2007), the computation of prediction errors appears to depend upon other structures (possibly the vlPAG) that transmit that information to the amygdala.

Focal electrical stimulation of the PAG serves as an effective US during fear conditioning (Di Scala, Mana, Jacobs, & Phillips, 1987). In addition, individual PAG neurons are more responsive to surprising than well-predicted USs. Furthermore, opioid receptors within the vlPAG contribute to predictive fear learning by regulating the effectiveness of the shock US, because it has been shown that unblocking effects can be produced by administering mu opioid receptor antagonists into the vlPAG during the compound conditioning phase of a blocking experiment (e.g., Cole & McNally, 2007). However, the specific mechanisms through which vlPAG opioid receptors determine variations in US effectiveness remain unknown because the PAG does not project directly to the LA.

McNally *et al.* (2011) postulated that the midline thalamus and prefrontal cortex (PFC) may play a key role in relaying the prediction error signal to LA neurons. The PAG projects extensively to the midline and intralaminar thalamus (Krout & Loewy, 2000), and the midline thalamus and PFC show significantly greater cellular activity (Furlong, Cole, Hamlin, & McNally, 2010) and BOLD signals in humans (Dunsmoor, Bandettini, & Knight, 2008) in response to an unexpected than to an expected shock US. This effect is especially seen in individual thalamic neurons that project to the dorsomedial prefrontal cortex (Furlong *et al.*, 2010). Thus, if error signals were computed within the vlPAG, there are known pathways for such a signal to be passed on to other structures. How such signals might find their way to the amygdala, however, has not been well established. Nevertheless, as is true in the eyeblink conditioning circuit, predicted USs lose their effectiveness through some inhibitory feedback process that appears to limit the degree to which a US receives further processing necessary for associative learning.

Conclusions

Thus far, we have reviewed studies showing the importance of some of the major variables in excitatory Pavlovian conditioning. Specifically, such learning is influenced by (1) the number of CS–US pairings, (2) stimulus intensity and novelty, (3) stimulus similarity, (4) the order of CS–US pairings, (5) spatial and temporal contiguity, (6) relative temporal contiguity, (7) CS–US contingency, (8) relative cue validity, and (9) US surprisingness. Further, we have suggested that many of these variables may be important precisely because they reflect the operation of two fundamental underlying psychological principles. The first of these is concurrent activation. This notion has long been recognized as being critical for associative learning and is at the heart of some of the major theoretical approaches to Pavlovian learning (e.g., Wagner, 1981). However, in order to accommodate the various stimulus selection phenomena noted above (contingency, relative cue validity, blocking) one needs to supplement this idea by assuming that the processing given to a US is partly determined by the degree to which it is surprising. In particular, if surprising USs are processed more effectively than expected USs (Rescorla & Wagner, 1972), then the amount of concurrent processing given to a CS and US on a conditioning trial will be strongly influenced by many of the variables noted above.

To be sure, there are more nuanced issues that will need to be addressed more fully. Some of these include determining how best to conceptualize (1) the importance of timing and comparator processes in Pavlovian learning, (2) the nature of response-system differences, (3) CS–US order effects, and (4) the nature of CS–US relevance effects. Nevertheless, the last 50 years of behavioral research has produced a wealth of information concerning the nature of simple Pavlovian conditioning.

In addition, while we have presented a very cursory overview of what is currently known regarding the underlying neurobiology of Pavlovian learning, we hope to have convinced the reader that the two major psychological principles we have discussed seem to have clear neurobiological underpinnings. In particular, the Hebbian synapse, long thought to be critical for synaptic plasticity, seems related to some aspects of learned behavior at a more molar level. Researchers have shown that LTP, for instance, is sensitive to trial spacing, contingency, and interstimulus interval manipulations. While it seems unreasonable to demand that changes at individual synapses should be related in all respects to more molar aspects of behavior, a challenge for neurobiological analyses remains characterizing those more molar aspects. Work on eyeblink conditioning clearly shows how a network perspective can reveal how important molar aspects of behavior can be understood. Changes in US processing, as imagined by the Rescorla–Wagner model, for instance, seem to be clearly indicated within the eyeblink and fear conditioning circuits. Moreover, studies of the midbrain dopamine system reveal clear correlates to this concept in appetitive learning procedures. Thus, the concurrent processing idea seems to be required for synaptic changes, while the US surprise notion has a direct embodiment in the neural network that characterizes learning.

This convergence of evidence between behavior-level and neurobiological-level accounts is surely encouraging and, indeed, exciting. Nevertheless, a number of key issues, some of which have been noted above, remain to be adequately explored. One of these additional issues concerns the characterization of the rules governing inhibitory as well as excitatory conditioning. Another issue concerns determining if the critical conditions required for learning depends upon the nature of learning being assessed. We now turn to a brief consideration of these issues.

Excitatory versus inhibitory conditioning

Most of the literature reviewed here has focused on excitatory Pavlovian conditioning. We have not fully explored the literature examining the critical conditions required for the establishment of inhibitory Pavlovian conditioning. We noted above, for instance, that backward (US–CS) conditioning procedures frequently result in the stimulus acquiring inhibitory behavioral control. However, there are a variety of other conditioning procedures that also result in inhibitory learning (for reviews, see LoLordo & Fairless, 1985; Rescorla, 1969; Williams, Overmier, & LoLordo, 1992). An especially interesting question posed by Rescorla (1968, 1969) is whether the rules governing excitatory and inhibitory conditioning might be symmetrical opposites. Indeed, the Rescorla–Wagner model (Rescorla & Wagner, 1972) suggests this to be the case. While unexpected US presentations (resulting in positive prediction errors) support new excitatory learning, unexpected US omissions (resulting in negative prediction errors) should support new inhibitory learning. Our reading of the literature is that this summary description is the best current account for inhibitory learning (e.g., Mackintosh, 1983). However, while the neurobiology of experimental extinction phenomena (which is merely one method of studying negative prediction errors in behavioral change) has been well developed (e.g., Delamater & Westbrook, 2014; Maren & Quirk, 2004; Quirk & Mueller, 2008), other methods of generating inhibitory Pavlovian learning have not been extensively explored, although interest is currently developing (Christianson et al., 2012; Davis, Falls, & Gewirtz, 2000; Herry et al., 2010; Schiller, Levy, Niv, LeDoux, & Phelps, 2008; Watkins et al., 1998). We expect there to be many exciting discoveries as interest in this topic develops.

Conditions versus contents of learning

While this chapter has largely been concerned with the issue of identifying critical conditions for Pavlovian learning to take place, another key issue (as noted in the introduction section) concerns the basic contents of learning. In other words, following Konorski (1967; also Dickinson & Dearing, 1979), we assume that when CS and US become associated, the CS likely enters into separate associations with distinct properties of the US (e.g., sensory, motivational, temporal, response, etc.). Although this issue has traditionally been addressed separately from identifying the critical conditions for learning, it may very well turn out that learning about different US features obeys different types of learning rules, or that there are interesting interactions among various "learning modules" that would need to be considered (see also Bindra, 1974, 1978; Bolles & Fanselow, 1980; Konorski, 1967; Rescorla & Solomon, 1967). These possibilities have not been extensively examined, but there is some relevant work.

Delamater (1995) demonstrated that CS–US contingency degradation effects are US specific in an appetitive Pavlovian task (see also Ostlund & Balleine, 2008; Rescorla, 2000), a result that was interpreted in terms of US-specific blocking by context. However, Betts, Brandon, and Wagner (1996; see also Rescorla, 1999) found US-specific blocking of consummatory (eyeblink) responses with rabbits, but US-general blocking of preparatory responses (potentiated startle) in the same animals. Collectively, these results imply that the "US prediction errors" that drive learning could be computed by contrasting expected from obtained USs in terms of their specific sensory or general motivational/value features, and that which type of prediction error governs learning is response-system dependent. The more general conclusion is that the basic rule that US surprise governs learning seems to apply to multiple forms of learning that differs in their associative content. Nevertheless, contiguity-based learning mechanisms can also sometimes be observed to occur in parallel with prediction-error-driven learning mechanisms in the same species in different circumstances (e.g., Funayama, Couvillon, & Bitterman, 1995; Ostlund & Balleine, 2008).

One final consideration is whether the different learning "modules" that appear to be involved in learning about multiple features of the US might, themselves, interact with one another. Konorski (1967) suggested that so-called "drive" conditioning occurred more rapidly than consummatory conditioning, but that the former facilitated the latter. There is some evidence in the literature, though surprisingly very little, to suggest that interactions of this sort do occur (see Gewirtz, Brandon, & Wagner, 1998). This will obviously be an area in need of further development at both the behavioral and neurobiological levels of analysis.

Acknowledgments

Preparation for this manuscript was supported by a National Institute on Drug Abuse grant (034995) awarded to ARD. Please direct any email correspondence to either andrewd@brooklyn.cuny.edu or hnasser@brooklyn.cuny.edu.

References

Abraham, W. C. (2003). How long will long-term potentiation last? *Philosophical Transactions of the Royal Society of London. Series B, Biological Sciences, 358*, 735–744.

Akins, C. K., Domjan, M., & Gutierrez, G. (1994). Topography of sexually conditioned behavior in male Japanese quail (*Coturnix japonica*) depends on the CS–US interval. *Journal of Experimental Psychology: Animal Behavior Processes, 20*, 199.

Albert, M., & Ayres, J. J. B. (1997). One-trial simultaneous and backward excitatory fear conditioning in rats: Lick suppression, freezing, and rearing to CS compounds and their elements. *Animal Learning & Behavior, 25*, 210–220.

Andreatta, M., Mühlberger, A., Yarali, A., Gerber, B., & Pauli, P. (2010). A rift between implicit and explicit conditioned valence in human pain relief learning. *Proceedings of the Royal Society B: Biological Sciences*.

Annau, Z., & Kamin, L. J. (1961). The conditioned emotional response as a function of intensity of the US. *Journal of Comparative and Physiological Psychology, 54*, 428–432.

Ayres, J. J. B., Haddad, C., & Albert, M. (1987). One-trial excitatory backward conditioning as assessed by conditioned suppression of licking in rats: Concurrent observations of lick suppression and defensive behaviors. *Animal Learning & Behavior, 15*, 212–217.

Balsam, P. D., & Gallistel, C. R. (2009). Temporal maps and informativeness in associative learning. *Trends in Neurosciences, 32*, 73–78.

Balsam, P., Drew, M., & Gallistel, C. (2010). Time and Associative Learning. *Comparative Cognition & Behavior Reviews, 5*, 1–22.

Barker, L. M. (1976). CS duration, amount, and concentration effects in conditioning taste aversions. *Learning and Motivation, 7*, 265–273.

Bauer, E. P., LeDoux, J. E., & Nader, K. (2001). Fear conditioning and LTP in the lateral amygdala are sensitive to the same stimulus contingencies. *Nature Neuroscience, 4*, 687–688.

Benedict, J. O., & Ayres, J. J. B. (1972). Factors affecting conditioning in the truly random control procedure in the rat. *Journal of Comparative and Physiological Psychology, 78*, 323–330.

Betts, S. L., Brandon, S. E., & Wagner, A. R. (1996). Dissociation of the blocking of conditioned eyeblink and conditioned fear following a shift in US locus. *Animal Learning & Behavior, 24*, 459–470.

Bindra, D. (1974). A motivational view of learning, performance, and behavior modification. *Psychological Review, 81*, 199–213.

Bindra, D. (1978). A behavioristic, cognitive-motivational, neuropsychological approach to explaining behavior. *Behavioral and Brain Sciences, 1*, 83–91.

Blair, H. T., Schafe, G. E., Bauer, E. P., Rodrigues, S. M., & LeDoux, J. E. (2001). Synaptic plasticity in the lateral amygdala: a cellular hypothesis of fear conditioning. *Learning & Memory (Cold Spring Harbor, NY), 8*, 229–242.

Boakes, R. A. (1977). Performance on learning to associate a stimulus with positive reinforcement. *Operant-Pavlovian Interactions, 67*–97.

Bolles, R. C., Collier, A. C., Bouton, M. E., & Marlin, N. A. (1978). Some tricks for ameliorating the trace-conditioning deficit. *Bulletin of the Psychonomic Society, 11*, 403–406.

Bolles, R. C., & Fanselow, M. S. (1980). A perceptual-defensive-recuperative model of fear and pain. *Behavioral and Brain Sciences, 3*, 291–301.

Bolles, R. C., Hayward, L., & Crandall, C. (1981). Conditioned taste preferences based on caloric density. *Journal of Experimental Psychology. Animal Behavior Processes, 7*, 59–69.

Bouton, M. E. (1991). Context and retrieval in extinction and in other examples of interference in simple associative learning. In L. Dachowski & C. F. Flaherty (Eds.), *Current topics in animal learning: Brain, emotion, and cognition* (pp. 25–54). Hillsdale, NJ: Lawrence Erlbaum Associates.

Brodal, A., Walberg, F., & Hoddevik, G. H. (1975). The olivocerebellar projection in the cat studied with the method of retrograde axonal transport of horseradish peroxidase. *The Journal of Comparative Neurology, 164*, 449–469.

Brodal, P., & Brodal, A. (1981). The olivocerebellar projection in the monkey. Experimental studies with the method of retrograde tracing of horseradish peroxidase. *The Journal of Comparative Neurology, 201*, 375–393.

Buhusi, C. V., & Schmajuk, N. A. (1999). Timing in simple conditioning and occasion setting: A neural network approach. *Behavioural Processes, 45*, 33–57.

Buonomano, D. V., & Mauk, M. D. (1994). Neural network model of the cerebellum: temporal discrimination and the timing of motor responses. *Neural Computation, 6*, 38–55.

Burkhardt, P. E., & Ayres, J. J. B. (1978). CS and US duration effects in one-trial simultaneous fear conditioning as assessed by conditioned suppression of licking in rats. *Animal Learning & Behavior, 6*, 225–230.

Bush, R. R., & Mosteller, F. (1951). A mathematical model for simple learning. *Psychological Review, 58*, 313–323.

Carrive, P. (1993). The periaqueductal gray and defensive behavior: functional representation and neuronal organization. *Behavioural Brain Research, 58*, 27–47.

Castellucci, V. F., & Kandel, E. R. (1974). A quantal analysis of the synaptic depression underlying habituation of the gill-withdrawal reflex in aplysia. *Proceedings of the National Academy of Sciences, 71*, 5004–5008.

Castellucci, V., & Kandel, E. R. (1976). Presynaptic facilitation as a mechanism for behavioral sensitization in Aplysia. *Science, 194*, 1176–1178.

Chang, R. C., Blaisdell, A. P., & Miller, R. R. (2003). Backward conditioning: Mediation by the context. *Journal of Experimental Psychology: Animal Behavior Processes, 29*, 171–183.

Christian, K., & Thompson, R. (2003). Neural substrates of eyeblink conditioning: acquisition and retention. *Learning & Memory*, 427–455.

Christianson, J. P., Fernando, A. B. P., Kazama, A. M., Jovanovic, T., Ostroff, L. E., & Sangha, S. (2012). Inhibition of fear by learned safety signals: A mini-symposium review. *The Journal of Neuroscience, 32*, 14118–14124.

Christie, J. (1996). Spatial contiguity facilitates Pavlovian conditioning. *Psychonomic Bulletin & Review, 3*, 357–359.

Clark, R. E., Zhang, A. A., & Lavond, D. G. (1992). Reversible lesions of the cerebellar interpositus nucleus during acquisition and retention of a classically conditioned behavior. *Behavioral Neuroscience, 106*, 879.

Cohen, J. Y., Haesler, S., Vong, L., Lowell, B. B., & Uchida, N. (2012). Neuron-type-specific signals for reward and punishment in the ventral tegmental area. *Nature, 482*, 85–88.

Cole, R. P., Barnet, R. C., & Miller, R. R. (1995). Effect of relative stimulus validity: learning or performance deficit? *Journal of Experimental Psychology. Animal Behavior Processes, 21*, 293–303.

Cole, R. P., & Miller, R. R. (1999). Conditioned excitation and conditioned inhibition acquired through backward conditioning. *Learning and Motivation, 30*, 129–156.

Cole, S., & McNally, G. P. (2007). Opioid receptors mediate direct predictive fear learning: evidence from one-trial blocking. *Learning & Memory (Cold Spring Harbor, NY), 14*, 229–235.

Corbit, L. H., & Balleine, B. W. (2005). Double dissociation of basolateral and central amygdala lesions on the general and outcome-specific forms of Pavlovian-instrumental transfer. *The Journal of Neuroscience, 25*, 962–970.

Corbit, L. H., & Balleine, B. W. (2011). The general and outcome-specific forms of Pavlovian-instrumental transfer are differentially mediated by the nucleus accumbens core and shell. *The Journal of Neuroscience, 31*, 11786–111794.

Crawford, L., & Domjan, M. (1993). Sexual approach conditioning: Omission contingency tests. *Animal Learning & Behavior, 21*, 42–50.

Davis, M., Falls, W., & Gewirtz, J. (2000). Neural systems involved in fear inhibition: Extinction and conditioned inhibition. In M. Myslobodsky & I. Weiner (Eds.), *Contemporary issues in modeling psychopathology SE – 8* (Vol. 1, pp. 113–141). Springer US.

Davis, M., Schlesinger, L. S., & Sorenson, C. A. (1989). Temporal specificity of fear conditioning: effects of different conditioned stimulus-unconditioned stimulus intervals on the fear-potentiated startle effect. *Journal of Experimental Psychology. Animal Behavior Processes, 15*, 295–310.

Delamater, A. R. (1995). Outcome-selective effects of intertrial reinforcement in a Pavlovian appetitive conditioning paradigm with rats. *Animal Learning & Behavior, 23*, 31–39.

Delamater, A. R. (2012). Issues in the extinction of specific stimulus-outcome associations in Pavlovian conditioning. *Behavioural Processes, 90*, 9–19.

Delamater, A. R., Desouza, A., Derman, R., & Rivkin, Y. (2014). Associative and temporal processes: a dual-process approach. *Behavioural Processes, 101*, 38–48.

Delamater, A. R., & Holland, P. C. (2008). The influence of CS–US interval on several different indices of learning in appetitive conditioning. *Journal of Experimental Psychology. Animal Behavior Processes, 34*, 202–222.

Delamater, A. R., LoLordo, V. M., & Sosa, W. (2003). Outcome-specific conditioned inhibition in Pavlovian backward conditioning. *Learning & Behavior, 31*, 393–402.

Delamater, A. R., & Matthew Lattal, K. (2014). The study of associative learning: Mapping from psychological to neural levels of analysis. *Neurobiology of Learning and Memory, 108*, 1–4.

Delamater, A. R., & Westbrook, R. F. (2014). Psychological and neural mechanisms of experimental extinction: A selective review. *Neurobiology of Learning and Memory, 108C*, 38–51.

Di Scala, G., Mana, M. J., Jacobs, W. J., & Phillips, A. G. (1987). Evidence of Pavlovian conditioned fear following electrical stimulation of the periaqueductal grey in the rat. *Physiology & Behavior, 40*, 55–63.

Dickinson, A. (1980). *Contemporary animal learning theory*. Cambridge, UK: Cambridge University Press.

Dickinson, A., & Dearing, M. F. (1979). Appetitive-aversive interactions and inhibitory processes. *Mechanisms of Learning and Motivation*, 203–231.

Dobi, A., Margolis, E. B., Wang, H.-L., Harvey, B. K., & Morales, M. (2010). Glutamatergic and nonglutamatergic neurons of the ventral tegmental area establish local synaptic contacts with dopaminergic and nondopaminergic neurons. *The Journal of Neuroscience, 30*, 218–229.

Domjan, M., & Wilson, N. (1972). Specificity of cue to consequence in aversion learning in the rat. *Psychonomic Science, 26,* 143–145.

Drew, M. R., Zupan, B., Cooke, A., Couvillon, P. A., & Balsam, P. D. (2005). Temporal control of conditioned responding in goldfish. *Journal of Experimental Psychology. Animal Behavior Processes, 31,* 31–39.

Dunsmoor, J. E., Bandettini, P. A., & Knight, D. C. (2008). Neural correlates of unconditioned response diminution during Pavlovian conditioning. *Neuroimage, 40,* 811–817.

Durlach, P. J. (1983). Effect of signaling intertrial unconditioned stimuli in autoshaping. *Journal of Experimental Psychology: Animal Behavior Processes, 9,* 374.

Fanselow, M. S. (1998). Pavlovian conditioning, negative feedback, and blocking: mechanisms that regulate association formation. *Neuron, 20,* 625–627.

Farley, J. (1987). Contingency learning and causal detection in Hermissenda: II. Cellular mechanisms. *Behavioral Neuroscience, 101,* 28–56.

Funayama, E. S., Couvillon, P. A., & Bitterman, M. E. (1995). Compound conditioning in honeybees: Blocking tests of the independence assumption. *Animal Learning & Behavior, 23,* 429–437.

Furlong, T. M., Cole, S., Hamlin, A. S., & McNally, G. P. (2010). The role of prefrontal cortex in predictive fear learning. *Behavioral Neuroscience, 124,* 574–586.

Gallistel, C. R., & Balsam, P. D. (2014). Time to rethink the neural mechanisms of learning and memory. *Neurobiology of Learning and Memory, 108C,* 136–144.

Gallistel, C. R., & Gibbon, J. (2000). Time, rate, and conditioning. *Psychological Review, 107,* 289–344.

Gallistel, C. R., & Matzel, L. D. (2013). The neuroscience of learning: beyond the Hebbian synapse. *Annual Review of Psychology, 64,* 169–200.

Garcia, J., & Koelling, R. A. (1966). Relation of cue to consequence in avoidance learning. *Psychonomic Science, 4,* 123–124.

Geisler, S., & Zahm, D. S. (2005). Afferents of the ventral tegmental area in the rat-anatomical substratum for integrative functions. *The Journal of Comparative Neurology, 490,* 270–294.

Gewirtz, J. C., Brandon, S. E., & Wagner, A. R. (1998). Modulation of the acquisition of the rabbit eyeblink conditioned response by conditioned contextual stimuli. *Journal of Experimental Psychology: Animal Behavior Processes, 24,* 106.

Gibbon, J. (1977). Scalar expectancy theory and Weber's law in animal timing. *Psychological Review, 84,* 279–325.

Gibbon, J., Baldock, M., Locurto, C., Gold, L., & Terrace, H. S. (1977). Trial and intertrial durations in autoshaping. *Journal of Experimental Psychology: Animal Behavior Processes, 3,* 264–284.

Gibbon, J., & Balsam, P. (1981). Spreading association in time. In C. M. Locurto, H. S. Terrace, & J. Gibbon (Eds.), *Autoshaping and conditioning theory* (pp. 219–253). New York, NY: Academic Press.

Glanzman, D. L. (2010). Common mechanisms of synaptic plasticity in vertebrates and invertebrates. *Current Biology, 20,* R31–R36.

Glickstein, M., May, J. G., & Mercier, B. E. (1985). Corticopontine projection in the macaque: The distribution of labelled cortical cells after large injections of horseradish peroxidase in the pontine nuclei. *The Journal of Comparative Neurology, 235,* 343–359.

Gottlieb, D. A. (2004). Acquisition with partial and continuous reinforcement in pigeon autoshaping. *Learning & Behavior, 32,* 321–334.

Gottlieb, D. A. (2008). Is the number of trials a primary determinant of conditioned responding? *Journal of Experimental Psychology. Animal Behavior Processes, 34,* 185–201.

Gottlieb, D. A, & Rescorla, R. A. (2010). Within-subject effects of number of trials in rat conditioning procedures. *Journal of Experimental Psychology. Animal Behavior Processes, 36,* 217–231.

Grand, C., Close, J., Hale, J., & Honey, R. C. (2007). The role of similarity in human associative learning. *Journal of Experimental Psychology: Animal Behavior Processes, 33*, 64–71.

Hearst, E., & Franklin, S. R. (1977). Positive and negative relations between a signal and food: approach-withdrawal behavior. *Journal of Experimental Psychology: Animal Behavior Processes, 3*, 37–52.

Hebb, D. O. (1949). *The organization of behavior: A neuropsychological approach*. New York, NY: John Wiley & Sons.

Herry, C., Ferraguti, F., Singewald, N., Letzkus, J. J., Ehrlich, I., & Lüthi, A. (2010). Neuronal circuits of fear extinction. *The European Journal of Neuroscience, 31*, 599–612.

Heth, C. D. (1976). Simultaneous and backward fear conditioning as a function of number of CS–UCS pairings. *Journal of Experimental Psychology: Animal Behavior Processes, 2*, 117.

Heth, C. D., & Rescorla, R. A. (1973). Simultaneous and backward fear conditioning in the rat. *Journal of Comparative and Physiological Psychology, 82*, 434–443.

Higgins, T., & Rescorla, R. A. (2004). Extinction and retraining of simultaneous and successive flavor conditioning. *Animal Learning & Behavior, 32*, 213–219.

Holland, P. C. (1980). CS–US interval as a determinant of the form of Pavlovian appetitive conditioned responses. *Journal of Experimental Psychology: Animal Behavior Processes, 6*, 155–174.

Holland, P. C. (1990). Event representation in Pavlovian conditioning: Image and action. *Cognition, 37*, 105–131.

Holland, P. C. (1998). Temporal control in Pavlovian occasion setting, *44*, 225–236.

Holland, P. C. (2000). Trial and intertrial durations in appetitive conditioning in rats. *Animal Learning & Behavior, 28*, 121–135.

Holland, P. C., Lasseter, H., & Agarwal, I. (2008). Amount of training and cue-evoked taste-reactivity responding in reinforcer devaluation. *Journal of Experimental Psychology. Animal Behavior Processes, 34*, 119–132.

Isaac, J. T. R., Nicoll, R. A., & Malenka, R. C. (1995). Evidence for silent synapses: implications for the expression of LTP. *Neuron, 15*, 427–434.

Jenkins, H. M. (1984). Time and contingency in classical conditioning. *Annals of the New York Academy of Sciences, 423*, 242–253.

Ji, H., & Shepard, P. D. (2007). Lateral habenula stimulation inhibits rat midbrain dopamine neurons through a GABA(A) receptor-mediated mechanism. *The Journal of Neuroscience, 27*, 6923–6930.

Johansen, J. P., Cain, C. K., Ostroff, L. E., & LeDoux, J. E. (2011). Molecular mechanisms of fear learning and memory. *Cell, 147*, 509–24.

Johansen, J. P., Tarpley, J. W., LeDoux, J. E., & Blair, H. T. (2010). Neural substrates for expectation-modulated fear learning in the amygdala and periaqueductal gray. *Nature Neuroscience, 13*, 979–986.

Kamin, L. J. (1965). Temporal and intensity characteristics of the conditioned stimulus. In W. F. Prokasy (Ed.), *Classical conditioning: A symposium* (pp. 118–147). New York, NY: Appleton-Century-Crofts.

Kamin, L. J. (1968). "Attention-like" processes in classical conditioning. In M. R. Jones (Ed.), *Miami symposium on the prediction of behavior: Aversive stimulation* (pp. 9–33). Miami, FL: University of Miami Press.

Kamin, L. J. (1969). Predictability, surprise, attention, and conditioning. In B. A. Campbell & R. M. Church (Eds.), *Punishment and aversive behavior* (pp. 279–296). New York, NY: Appleton-Century-Crofts.

Kamin, L. J., & Schaub, R. E. (1963). Effects of conditioned stimulus intensity on the conditioned emotional response. *Journal of Comparative and Physiological Psychology, 56*, 502–507.

Kandel, E. R. (2001). The molecular biology of memory storage: a dialogue between genes and synapses. *Science, 294*, 1030–1038.

Kaplan, P. S. (1984). Importance of realtive temporal parameters in trace autoshaping: from extinction to inhibition. *Journal of Experimental Psychology: Animal Behavior Processes, 10,* 113–126.

Kim, J. J., Krupa, D. J., & Thompson, R. F. (1998). Inhibitory cerebello-olivary projections and blocking effect in classical conditioning. *Science, 279,* 570–573.

Konorski, J. (1948). *Conditioned Reflexes and Neuron Organization.* Cambridge, UK: Cambridge University Press.

Konorski, J. (1967). *Integrative activity of the brain: An interdisciplinary approach.* Chicago, IL: University of Chicago Press.

Krasne, F. (2002). Neural analysis of learning in simple systems. In R. Gallistel (Ed.), *Stevens' handbook of experimental psychology third edition vol 3: Learning, motivation, and emotion* (pp. 131–200). New York, NY: John Wiley & Sons.

Krout, K. E., & Loewy, A. D. (2000). Periaqueductal gray matter projections to midline and intralaminar thalamic nuclei of the rat. *The Journal of Comparative Neurology, 424,* 111–141.

Krupa, D. J., Thompson, J. K., & Thompson, R. F. (1993). Localization of a memory trace in the mammalian brain. *Science, 260,* 989–991.

Krupa, D. J., & Thompson, R. F. (1997). Reversible inactivation of the cerebellar interpositus nucleus completely prevents acquisition of the classically conditioned eye-blink response. *Learning & Memory, 3,* 545–556.

Kwon, J.-T., & Choi, J.-S. (2009). Cornering the fear engram: Long-term synaptic changes in the lateral nucleus of the amygdala after fear conditioning. *The Journal of Neuroscience, 29,* 9700–9703.

Lattal, K. M. (1999). Trial and intertrial durations in Pavlovian conditioning: issues of learning and performance. *Journal of Experimental Psychology. Animal Behavior Processes, 25,* 433–450.

Ledoux, J. E. (2000). Emotion circuits in the brain. *Annual Review of Neuroscience, 23,* 155–184.

Le Pelley, M. E. (2004). The role of associative history in models of associative learning: A selective review and a hybrid model. *Quarterly Journal of Experimental Psychology Section B, 57,* 193–243.

Leung, H. T., & Westbrook, R. F. (2008). Spontaneous recovery of extinguished fear responses deepens their extinction: a role for error-correction mechanisms. *Journal of Experimental Psychology: Animal Behavior Processes, 34,* 461–474.

Lewis, J. L., LoTurco, J. J., & Solomon, P. R. (1987). Lesions of the middle cerebellar peduncle disrupt acquisition and retention of the rabbit's classically conditioned nictitating membrane response. *Behavioral Neuroscience, 101,* 151.

Lin, X. Y., & Glanzman, D. L. (1997). Effect of interstimulus interval on pairing-induced LTP of aplysia sensorimotor synapses in cell culture. *Journal of Neurophysiology, 77,* 667–674.

Lincoln, J. S., McCormick, D. A., & Thompson, R. F. (1982). Ipsilateral cerebellar lesions prevent learning of the classically conditioned nictitating membrane/eyelid response. *Brain Research, 242,* 190–193.

LoLordo, V. M. (1979). Selective associations. In A. Dickinson & R. A. Boakes (Eds.), *Mechanisms of learning and motivation: A memorial volume to Jerzy Konorski* (pp. 367–398). Hillsdale, NJ: Lawrence Erlbaum Associates.

LoLordo, V. M., & Fairless, J. L. (1985). Pavlovian conditioned inhibition: The literature since 1969. In R. R. Miller & N. E. Spear (Eds.), *Information processing in animals: Conditioned inhibition* (pp. 1–49). Hillsdale, NJ: Lawrence Erlbaum Associates.

Lubow, R. E. (1989). *Latent inhibition and conditioned attention theory.* Cambridge, UK: Cambridge University Press.

Mackintosh, N. J. (1974). *The psychology of animal learning*. London, UK: Academic Press.

Mackintosh, N. J. (1975). A theory of attention: Variations in the associability of stimuli with reinforcement. *Psychological Review, 82*, 276–298.

Mackintosh, N. J. (1983). *Conditioning and associative learning*. Oxford, UK: Clarendon Press.

Mahoney, W. J., & Ayres, J. J. B. (1976). One-trial simultaneous and backward fear conditioning as reflected in conditioned suppression of licking in rats. *Animal Learning & Behavior, 4*, 357–362.

Malenka, R. C., & Nicoll, R. A. (1999). Long-term potentiation – a decade of progress? *Science, 285*, 1870–1874.

Maren, S. (2005). Synaptic mechanisms of associative memory in the amygdala. *Neuron, 47*, 783–786.

Maren, S., & Quirk, G. J. (2004). Neuronal signalling of fear memory. *Nature Reviews Neuroscience, 5*, 844–852.

Matsumoto, M., & Hikosaka, O. (2007). Lateral habenula as a source of negative reward signals in dopamine neurons. *Nature, 447*, 1111–1115.

Matsumoto, M., & Hikosaka, O. (2009). Two types of dopamine neuron distinctly convey positive and negative motivational signals. *Nature, 459*, 837–841.

Matzel, L. D., Held, F. P., & Miller, R. R. (1988). Information and expression of simultaneous and backward associations: Implications for contiguity theory. *Learning and Motivation, 19*, 317–344.

Mauk, M. D., Medina, J. F., Nores, W. L., & Ohyama, T. (2000). Cerebellar function: Coordination, learning or timing? *Current Biology, 10*, R522–R525.

Mauk, M., Steinmetz, J. E., & Thompson, R. F. (1986). Classical conditioning using stimulation of the inferior olive as the unconditioned stimulus. *Proceedings of the National Academy of Sciences, 83*, 5349–5353.

McCormick, D. A., & Thompson, R. F. (1984). Neuronal responses of the rabbit cerebellum during acquisition and performance of a classically conditioned nictitating membrane-eyelid response. *The Journal of Neuroscience, 4*, 2811–2822.

McKernan, M. G., & Shinnick-Gallagher, P. (1997). Fear conditioning induces a lasting potentiation of synaptic currents in vitro. *Nature, 390*, 607–611.

McNally, G. P., Johansen, J. P., & Blair, H. T. (2011). Placing prediction into the fear circuit. *Trends in Neurosciences, 34*, 283–292.

Millenson, J. R., Kehoe, E. J., & Gormezano, I. (1977). Classical conditioning of the rabbit's nictitating membrane response under fixed and mixed CS–US intervals. *Learning and Motivation, 8*, 351–366.

Miller, R. R., Barnet, R. C., & Grahame, N. J. (1992). Responding to a conditioned stimulus depends on the current associative status of other cues present during training of that specific stimulus. *Journal of Experimental Psychology. Animal Behavior Processes, 18*, 251–64.

Morris, R. W., & Bouton, M. E. (2006). Effect of unconditioned stimulus magnitude on the emergence of conditioned responding. *Journal of Experimental Psychology: Animal Behavior Processes, 32*, 371.

Moscovitch, A., & LoLordo, V. M. (1968). Role of safety in the Pavlovian backward fear conditioning procedure. *Journal of Comparative and Physiological Psychology, 66*, 673–678.

Murphy, R. A., & Baker, A. G. (2004). A role for CS-US contingency in Pavlovian conditioning. *Journal of Experimental Psychology: Animal Behavior Processes, 30*, 229–239.

Nordholm, A. F., Thompson, J. K., Dersarkissian, C., & Thompson, R. F. (1993). Lidocaine infusion in a critical region of cerebellum completely prevents learning of the conditioned eyeblink response. *Behavioral Neuroscience, 107*, 882.

Orsini, C. a, & Maren, S. (2012). Neural and cellular mechanisms of fear and extinction memory formation. *Neuroscience and Biobehavioral Reviews, 36*, 1773–1802.

Ostlund, S. B., & Balleine, B. W. (2008). Differential involvement of the basolateral amygdala and mediodorsal thalamus in instrumental action selection. *The Journal of Neuroscience, 28*, 4398–4405.

Ostroff, L. E., Cain, C. K., Bedont, J., Monfils, M. H., & Ledoux, J. E. (2010). Fear and safety learning differentially affect synapse size and dendritic translation in the lateral amygdala. *Proceedings of the National Academy of Sciences, 107*, 9418–9423.

Papini, M., & Brewer, M. (1994). Response competition and the trial-spacing effect in autoshaping with rats. *Learning and Motivation, 25*, 201–215.

Paré, D. (2002). Mechanisms of Pavlovian fear conditioning: has the engram been located? *Trends in Neurosciences, 25*, 436–7; discussion 437–438.

Paré, D., & Collins, D. R. (2000). Neuronal correlates of fear in the lateral amygdala: multiple extracellular recordings in conscious cats. *The Journal of Neuroscience, 20*, 2701–2710.

Pearce, J. M., & Bouton, M. E. (2001). Theories of associative learning in animals. *Annual Review of Psychology, 52*, 111–139.

Pearce, J. M., & Hall, G. (1980). A model for Pavlovian learning: Variations in the effectiveness of conditioned but not of unconditioned stimuli. *Psychological Review, 87*, 532–552.

Perrett, S. P., Ruiz, B. P., & Mauk, M. D. (1993). Cerebellar cortex lesions disrupt learning-dependent timing of conditioned eyelid responses. *The Journal of Neuroscience, 13*, 1708–1718.

Quirk, G. J., & Mueller, D. (2008). Neural mechanisms of extinction learning and retrieval. *Neuropsychopharmacology, 33*, 56–72.

Quirk, G. J., Repa, J. C., & LeDoux, J. E. (1995). Fear conditioning enhances short-latency auditory responses of lateral amygdala neurons: parallel recordings in the freely behaving rat. *Neuron, 15*, 1029–1039.

Randich, A., & LoLordo, V. M. (1979). Associative and non-associative theories of the UCS preexposure phenomenon: implications for Pavlovian conditioning. *Psychological Bulletin, 86*, 523–548.

Rescorla, R. (1980). Simultaneous and successive associations in sensory preconditioning. *Journal of Experimental Psychology: Animal Behavior Processes, 6*, 207–216.

Rescorla, R. A. (2000). Associative changes with a random CS–US relationship. *The Quarterly Journal of Experimental Psychology. B, Comparative and Physiological Psychology, 53*, 325–340.

Rescorla, R. A. (2001). Are associative changes in acquisition and extinction negatively accelerated? *Journal of Experimental Psychology: Animal Behavior Processes, 27*, 307–315.

Rescorla, R. A. (1967). Pavlovian conditioning and its proper control procedures. *Psychological Review, 74*, 71–80.

Rescorla, R. A. (1968). Probability of shock in the presence and absence of CS in fear conditioning. *Journal of Comparative and Physiological Psychology, 66*, 1–5.

Rescorla, R. A. (1969). Pavlovian conditioned inhibition. *Psychological Bulletin, 72*, 77–94.

Rescorla, R. A. (1999). Learning about qualitatively different outcomes during a blocking procedure. *Animal Learning & Behavior, 27*, 140–151.

Rescorla, R. A., & Cunningham, C. L. (1979). Spatial contiguity facilitates Pavlovian second-order conditioning. *Journal of Experimental Psychology. Animal Behavior Processes, 5*, 152–161.

Rescorla, R. A., & Furrow, D. R. (1977). Stimulus similarity as a determinant of Pavlovian conditioning. *Journal of Experimental Psychology: Animal Behavior Processes, 3*, 203–215.

Rescorla, R. A., & Gillan, D. J. (1980). An analysis of the facilitative effect of similarity on second-order conditioning. *Journal of Experimental Psychology: Animal Behavior Processes, 6*, 339–351.

Rescorla, R. A., & Holland, P. C. (1976). Some behavioral approaches to the study of learning. *Neural Mechanisms of Learning and Memory*, 165–192.

Rescorla, R. A., & Solomon, R. L. (1967). Two-process learning theory: Relationships between Pavlovian conditioning and instrumental learning. *Psychological Review, 74*, 151–182.

Rescorla, R. A., & Wagner, A. R. (1972). A theory of Pavlovian conditioning: Variations in the effectiveness of reinforcement and nonreinforcement. In A. H. Black & W. F. Prokasy (Eds.), *Classical conditioning II: Current research and theory* (pp. 64–99). New York, NY: Appleton-Century-Crofts.

Roberts, A. C., & Glanzman, D. L. (2003). Learning in Aplysia: looking at synaptic plasticity from both sides. *Trends in Neurosciences, 26*, 662–670.

Rogan, M. T., Stäubli, U. V., & LeDoux, J. E. (1997). Fear conditioning induces associative long-term potentiation in the amygdala. *Nature, 390*, 604–607.

Romanski, L. M., Clugnet, M.-C., Bordi, F., & LeDoux, J. E. (1993). Somatosensory and auditory convergence in the lateral nucleus of the amygdala. *Behavioral Neuroscience, 107*, 444.

Rosenkranz, J. A., & Grace, A. A. (2002). Cellular mechanisms of infralimbic and prelimbic prefrontal cortical inhibition and dopaminergic modulation of basolateral amygdala neurons in vivo. *The Journal of Neuroscience, 22*, 324–337.

Sah, P., Westbrook, R. F., & Lüthi, A. (2008). Fear conditioning and long-term potentiation in the amygdala: what really is the connection? *Annals of the New York Academy of Sciences, 1129*, 88–95.

Schafe, G. E., Nader, K., Blair, H. T., & LeDoux, J. E. (2001). Memory consolidation of Pavlovian fear conditioning: a cellular and molecular perspective. *Trends in Neurosciences, 24*, 540–546.

Scharf, M. T., Woo, N. H., Lattal, K. M., Young, J. Z., Nguyen, P. V., Abel, T. E. D., ... Abel, T. (2002). Protein synthesis is required for the enhancement of long-term potentiation and long-term memory by spaced training. *Journal of Neurophysiology, 87*, 2770–2777.

Schiller, D., Levy, I., Niv, Y., LeDoux, J. E., & Phelps, E. A. (2008). From fear to safety and back: Reversal of fear in the human brain. *The Journal of Neuroscience, 28*, 11517–11525.

Schmahmann, J. D., & Pandya, D. N. (1989). Anatomical investigation of projections to the basis pontis from posterior parietal association cortices in rhesus monkey. *The Journal of Comparative Neurology, 289*, 53–73.

Schmahmann, J. D., & Pandya, D. N. (1991). Projections to the basis pontis from the superior temporal sulcus and superior temporal region in the rhesus monkey. *The Journal of Comparative Neurology, 308*, 224–248.

Schmahmann, J. D., & Pandya, D. N. (1993). Prelunate, occipitotemporal, and parahippocampal projections to the basis pontis in rhesus monkey. *The Journal of Comparative Neurology, 337*, 94–112.

Schneiderman, N., & Gormezano, I. (1964). Conditioning of the nictitating membrane of the rabbit as a function of CS–US interval. *Journal of Comparative and Physiological Psychology, 57*, 188–195.

Schultz, W. (2006). Behavioral theories and the neurophysiology of reward. *Annual Review of Psychology, 57*, 87–115.

Schultz, W. (2007). Behavioral dopamine signals. *Trends in Neurosciences, 30*, 203–210.

Schultz, W. (2008). Predictive reward signal of dopamine neurons. *Journal of Neurophysiology, 80*, 1–27.

Schultz, W., Dayan, P., & Montague, P. R. (1997). A neural substrate of prediction and reward. *Science (New York, NY), 275*, 1593–1599.

Seligman, M. E., & Hager, J. L. (1972). *Biological boundaries of learning*. East Norwalk, CT: Appleton-Century-Crofts.

Shanks, D. R., & Dickinson, A. (1990). Contingency awareness in evaluative conditioning: A comment on Baeyens, Eelen, and Van Den Bergh. *Cognition & Emotion, 4*, 19–30.

Shurtleff, D., & Ayres, J. J. B. (1981). One-trial backward excitatory fear conditioning in rats: Acquisition, retention, extinction, and spontaneous recovery. *Animal Learning & Behavior, 9*, 65–74.

Siegel, S., & Allan, L. G. (1996). The widespread influence of the Rescorla–Wagner model. *Psychonomic Bulletin & Review, 3*, 314–321.

Sigurdsson, T., Doyère, V., Cain, C. K., & LeDoux, J. E. (2007). Long-term potentiation in the amygdala: a cellular mechanism of fear learning and memory. *Neuropharmacology, 52*, 215–227.

Smith, J. C., & Sclafani, A. (2002). Saccharin as a sugar surrogate revisited. *Appetite, 38*, 155–160.

Smith, M. C. (1968). CS–US interval and US intensity in classical conditioning of the rabbit's nictitating membrane response. *Journal of Comparative and Physiological Psychology, 66*, 679–687.

Steinberg, E. E., Keiflin, R., Boivin, J. R., Witten, I. B., Deisseroth, K., & Janak, P. H. (2013). A causal link between prediction errors, dopamine neurons and learning. *Nature Neuroscience, 16*, 966–973.

Steinmetz, J. E., Logan, C. G., Rosen, D. J., Thompson, J. K., Lavond, D. G., & Thompson, R. F. (1987). Initial localization of the acoustic conditioned stimulus projection system to the cerebellum essential for classical eyelid conditioning. *Proceedings of the National Academy of Sciences, 84*, 3531–3535.

Steinmetz, J. E., & Sengelaub, D. R. (1992). Possible conditioned stimulus pathway for classical eyelid conditioning in rabbits. I. Anatomical evidence for direct projections from the pontine nuclei to the cerebellar interpositus nucleus. *Behavioral and Neural Biology, 57*, 103–115.

Steinmetz, M., Le Coq, D., & Aymerich, S. (1989). Induction of saccharolytic enzymes by sucrose in *Bacillus subtilis*: evidence for two partially interchangeable regulatory pathways. *Journal of Bacteriology, 171*, 1519–1523.

Stout, S. C., & Miller, R. R. (2007). Sometimes-competing retrieval (SOCR): A formalization of the comparator hypothesis. *Psychological Review, 114*, 759.

Sutton, R., & Barto, A. (1981a). An adaptive network that constructs and uses an internal model of its world. *Cognition and Brain Theory, 4*, 217–246.

Sutton, R. S., & Barto, A. G. (1981b). Toward a modern theory of adaptive networks: expectation and prediction. *Psychological Review, 88*, 135–170.

Tait, R. W., & Saladin, M. E. (1986). Concurrent development of excitatory and inhibitory associations during backward conditioning. *Animal Learning & Behavior, 14*, 133–137.

Tanimoto, H., Heisenberg, M., & Gerber, B. (2004). Event timing turns punishment to reward. *Nature, 430*, 983.

Terrace, H. S., Gibbon, J., Farrell, L., & Baldock, M. D. (1975). Temporal factors influencing the acquisition and maintenance of an autoshaped keypeck. *Animal Learning & Behavior, 3*, 53–62.

Testa, T. J. (1975). Effects of similarity of location and temporal intensity patterns of conditioned and unconditioned stimuli on the acquisition of conditioned suppression in rats. *Journal of Experimental Psychology: Animal Behavior Processes, 104*, 114–121.

Testa, T. J., & Ternes, J. W. (1977). Specificity of conditioning mechanisms in the modification of food preferences. In L. M. Barker, M. R. Best, & M. Domjan (Eds.), *Learning mechanisms in food selection* (pp. 229–253). Waco, TX: Baylor University Press.

Thompson, R. F. (2005). In search of memory traces. *Annual Review of Psychology, 56*, 1–23.

Thompson, R. F., & Steinmetz, J. E. (2009). The role of the cerebellum in classical conditioning of discrete behavioral responses. *Neuroscience, 162*, 732–755.

Timberlake, W., Wahl, G., & King, D. A. (1982). Stimulus and response contingencies in the misbehavior of rats. *Journal of Experimental Psychology: Animal Behavior Processes, 8*, 62.

Tobler, P. N., Dickinson, A., & Schultz, W. (2003). Coding of predicted reward omission by dopamine neurons in a conditioned inhibition paradigm. *The Journal of Neuroscience, 23,* 10402–10410.

Urushihara, K., & Miller, R. R. (2010). Backward blocking in first-order conditioning. *Journal of Experimental Psychology. Animal Behavior Processes, 36,* 281–295.

Vallee-Tourangeau, F., Murphy, R. A., & Drew, S. (1998). Judging the importance of constant and variable candidate causes: A test of the power PC theory. *The Quarterly Journal of Experimental Psychology: Section A, 51,* 65–84.

Vandercar, D. H., & Schneiderman, N. (1967). Interstimulus interval functions in different response systems during classical discrimination conditioning of rabbits. *Psychonomic Science, 9,* 9–10.

Waelti, P., Dickinson, A., & Schultz, W. (2001). Dopamine responses comply with basic assumptions of formal learning theory. *Nature, 412,* 43–48.

Wagner, A. R. (1969). Stimulus validity and stimulus selection in associative learning. *Fundamental Issues in Associative Learning, 90–122.*

Wagner, A. R. (1978). Expectancies and the priming of STM. In S. H. Hulse, H. Fowler, & W. K. Honig (Eds.), *Cognitive processes in animal behavior* (pp. 177–209). Hillsdale, NJ: Lawrence Erlbaum Associates.

Wagner, A. R. (1981). SOP: A model of automatic memory processing in animal behavior. In N. E. Spear & R. R. Miller (Eds.), *Information processing in animals: memory mechanisms* (pp. 5–44). Hillsdale, NJ: Lawrence Erlbaum Associates.

Wagner, A. R., Logan, F. A., Haberlandt, K., & Price, T. (1968). Stimulus selection in animal discrimination learning. *Journal of Experimental Psychology, 76,* 171–180.

Wasserman, E., Franklin, S. R., & Hearst, E. (1974). Pavlovian appetitive contingencies and approach versus withdrawal to conditioned stimuli in pigeons. *Journal of Comparative and Physiological Psychology, 86,* 616–627.

Watkins, L. R., Wiertelak, E. P., McGorry, M., Martinez, J., Schwartz, B., Sisk, D., & Maier, S. F. (1998). Neurocircuitry of conditioned inhibition of analgesia: effects of amygdala, dorsal raphe, ventral medullary, and spinal cord lesions on antianalgesia in the rat. *Behavioral Neuroscience, 112,* 360–378.

Williams, D. A., Overmier, J. B., & LoLordo, V. M. (1992). A reevaluation of Rescorla's early dictums about Pavlovian conditioned inhibition. *Psychological Bulletin, 111,* 275–290.

Willigen, F., Emmett, J., Cote, D., & Ayres, J. J. B. (1987). CS modality effects in one-trial backward and forward excitatory conditioning as assessed by conditioned suppression of licking in rats. *Animal Learning & Behavior, 15,* 201–211.

Yarali, A., Krischke, M., Michels, B., Saumweber, T., Mueller, M. J., & Gerber, B. (2008). Genetic distortion of the balance between punishment and relief learning in *Drosophila*. *Journal of Neurogenetics, 23,* 235–247.

3

Learning to Be Ready
Dopamine and Associative Computations
Nicola C. Byrom and Robin A. Murphy

Summary and Scope

Associative theory treats mental life, very generally, as being dominated by the simplest of mechanisms: the association captures the content of our mental representations (sensations or experiences) with the additional idea that associative links determine how the associates interact. Associative theory is used to describe how we learn from our environment, ultimately allowing scientists to predict behavior. This is arguably one of the fundamental goals of psychology. There are few constraints on which behaviors we may seek to understand, so this could be about understanding the approach behavior of a rat to the visual cues associated with food or that of a human learning to swipe the shiny lit surface of a tablet computer. Associative processes have been used to explain overt behavior in the lab animal and in the human. The development of brain recording and measurement tools has allowed an extension to a similar analysis of the correlated behavior of relevant synapses and neurons. The assumption is that our overt behavior is related to the "behavior" of our neurons. While we are still at the beginning of such an understanding, the discoveries related to the behavior of neurons correlated with learning and memory have already garnered neuroscientists Nobel prizes. Arvid Carllson, Paul Greengard, and Eric Kandel won the Nobel Prize in medicine in 2000 for "discoveries concerning signal transduction in the nervous system." These discoveries for psychology were important not so much for their illumination of the biological process but for the correlation of these processes with overt behavior related to learning and memory. Their recognition comes even though the gap between our understanding of the relation between neural signals and the behaving organism is still in its infancy. In this chapter, we review the development of associative theory and its role in the interpretation of the behavior of neurons related to dopamine. Dopamine is a neurotransmitter that has long been of interest for psychologists, both because of its relation to the psychological and physical symptoms of disorders such as Parkinson's and schizophrenia, and for the disorders related to primary reward systems (e.g., drug addiction) and recently in relation to learning in the form of the prediction error.

The Wiley Handbook on the Cognitive Neuroscience of Learning, First Edition.
Edited by Robin A. Murphy and Robert C. Honey.
© 2016 John Wiley & Sons, Ltd. Published 2016 by John Wiley & Sons, Ltd.

Prediction error is a fundamental concept in learning theory that captures some of the empirical conditions necessary for learning to take place in complex environments where there are multiple possible things to learn about. It is well known that we tend to learn on the basis of how events unfold in time and space, for instance, temporal and spatial contiguity encourage events to be associated (Pavlov, 1927). Some associations reflect the temporal flow of experience; an animal in the lab may learn that a tone precedes the delivery of food, and we learn, for example, that sunrise precedes breakfast (usually) because that is the way that they actual happen. The concept of prediction error captures the idea that initially neither the rat nor the human would be expecting the occurrence of food after the tone or sunrise, and therefore a large *prediction error* occurs when food is delivered. In this chapter, we look at the investigations of overt behavior that shaped the development of our understanding of prediction error and ask whether these investigations can direct future research into the neural correlates of learning.

In many cases, our predictions of what will happen next are determined by lots of different possible associations, and correspondingly associative theory captures how learning is influenced by previous experiences. Associations can reflect both direct and relative experience. For instance, several readers may be familiar with the aftereffects of alcohol and some of the somewhat negative associations that may form following these experiences. We may learn that gin makes us ill, but interestingly subsequent ingestion of gin with the taste of gin masked by the addition of tonic water is not likely to undermine this aversion. In general, associations are less likely to form between a given cue and an outcome, if another cue is present that is already strongly associated with that outcome. This effect is called *blocking* and will be discussed later in the chapter. Associations can reflect direct experience, or, in the case of our experimentation with cocktails, associations are determined by relative experiences. Effects such as *blocking*, *conditioned inhibition*, and *super-learning*, discussed later in the chapter, have been used extensively in investigations of overt behavior, and their precise manipulation of prediction error has shaped the development of associative theory over the last 45 years. In this chapter, we consider how these manipulations of prediction error can be used to generate expectations of when dopamine neurons might be active.

All of the chapters in this handbook make reference to the work of Pavlov (1927) as the founder of the associative perspective on learning. A recipient of the Nobel Prize himself, it was Pavlov's study of learning that provided the empirical foundation that would allow an eventual elaboration of the physiological consequences of associative experience and signal transduction. Pavlovian conditioning characterizes how the laboratory subject (e.g., a rat) learns to respond to a previously neutral stimulus (CS) after pairings with a biologically relevant stimulus (e.g., food; US). Pavlov was interested in the conditions that allowed a previously neutral stimulus to come to have new behavioral controlling properties. As a materialist, Pavlov assumed that there was an underlying physical instantiation of this process in the nervous system.

In this chapter, we present an, admittedly idiosyncratic, perspective on the development of the idea of prediction-error learning, the use of mathematics to describe the computations required to make predictions about future events, and how this has supported the development of an understanding of the behavior of synapses, in particular the role of the neurotransmitter dopamine and D2 dopamine receptors in the midbrain (e.g., Schultz, 1998). We review how investigations of the conditions necessary for associations to develop led to the discovery that the temporal relation between stimuli is an insufficient condition for learning. This realization led to an interest in the conditions necessary for relative predictiveness and the first tests of blocking, which illustrated the role of prediction error in learning. We describe how the idea of prediction error has been incorporated into mathematical models of associative learning and look briefly at the wide range of precise predictions that these models have generated and the studies of overt behavior that have tested these. In the closing sections of the chapter, we consider how this work can support future research in the neural correlates of learning. Associative learning theory provides hypotheses about how learning might proceed, and we can evaluate whether dopamine can be seen as a physical marker of the associative computations for learning. The position to be presented is that our understanding of the activity of neurons as predictors of overt behavior requires a formal analysis of how stimuli come to be learned about, since much of our behavior is on the basis of past experience. Associative theory provides the context for which to understand neural activity.

Conditions for Association

Repeated pairing of two events encourages their association, an idea so simple that it requires little explanation. The experimental work on paired word associate learning confirmed the principle that experience with Western children's nursery rhymes allows the word *sugar* to retrieve a memory of the word *spice* because of their repeated pairing (e.g., Ebbinghaus, 1885/ 1964). This idea was central to early thinkers of psychology such as James (1890/1950). An echo of this thinking is present in connectionist modeling work described in this volume in which both motivationally salient and events and neutral events can be associated (see Chapters 15 and 21).

The associative analysis of animal learning also grapples with the additional contribution that biologically relevant stimuli bring to an experimental task. Unlike the words *sugar* and *spice* for the listening human child, the pairing of the ringing bell and food for a hungry rat involves specific effects that food or other natural rewards and punishers have on the learning process. Some stimuli are satisfying, to use Thorndike's (1933) terms (food when hungry, water when thirsty), and others dissatisfying (e.g., pain) by their specific biological consequences. Thorndike and Pavlov developed a technical language for describing these relations and raised questions about associative learning that have dogged it since its outset. Do reinforcers, as the outcomes (O) of paired associates, enhance the memory of stimuli (S) that happen prior to their occurrence (S → O), or do they modify or reinforce the response that happens in the presence of the stimulus (S → R; see Chapter 16)? Either way, early researchers were aware that reinforcers were able to impart new properties to a stimulus via the associative experience. Since animals came to behave with these stimuli in ways that mimicked the reward or punishment, one obvious conclusion was that the association allows the previously neutral stimuli to substitute for the actual presence of the reinforcer; it may have become a so-called secondary reinforcer or substitute for the reinforcer. In terms of Pavlov's experiments, dogs salivated to the sound of the now-conditioned bell just as they salivated to the presence of food.

Stimulus substitution

Work by researchers such as Pavlov, Thorndike, and Guthrie recognized the simple power of contiguity for learning (for a review, see Hilgard & Bower, 1966). Although contiguity implies simultaneous or overlapping presentation, Pavlov had already shown that delay conditioning was a more powerful conditioning procedure than simultaneous presentations, even though the very notion of contiguity implies the superiority of simultaneous presentations (see Rescorla, 1980). He recognized that the temporal parameters of learning were crucial and assumed that defining the temporal parameters that supported learning would give an insight into the ideal parameters to which neural tissue responded. Any demonstration that a particular temporal constraint on learning was important (e.g., that conditioning with a 10 s CS was most effective if it terminated with US delivery with little or no trace between the two) was seen as probably related to constraints on the neural response. As we shall see, subsequent research has shown that the power of delay or sequential presentation in conditioning reflects the very nature of associative learning; delays allow cues to predict what happens after them.

The physiological psychologist (as neuroscientists were once called), Donald Hebb, captured the notion of temporal contiguity and its relation to neural responses by proposing that the neural basis for such temporal expectations was the co-occurring activity in two centers of the brain. Frequently repeated stimulation causes cells in the brain to come to act as a "closed system" that can excite or inhibit other similar assemblies. Simultaneous activity of particular cells contributes to the facilitation of the pathways between them (Hebb, 1949). In this way, the early theories conceived Pavlovian conditioning as contributing to learning by strengthening pathways of association and thereby allowing a form of stimulus substitution much like that proposed by Pavlov (1927). Stimulus substitution suggests that conditioning is concerned primarily with allowing neutral cues to be imitations of reinforcers and that the neutral events can become proxies or substitutes for the important, biologically relevant, events.

Hebb's (1949) account of the formation of these cell assemblies or engrams is an implied description of how associations between neurons or representations are formed. If the representations of the predictive stimulus or CS (A) and the US (λ) are active at the same time, this will change the association (ΔV) between them.

$$\Delta V_A = k(\lambda * A) \tag{3.1}$$

These associations are formed to the extent that the two events are active and modified by a stimulus-specific parameter or constant (k) that reflects the stimulus-specific properties of the two cues or their unique associability.

If associations reflect learning about important consequences, then an implication is that these newly formed associations might themselves support new learning. That is, you might not need the presence of the physical US if the CS is able to activate the internal representation of the US on its own. The CS itself might be expected to have the power to reinforce other responses or associations. It seems plausible that as food could be used to make an animal make a response to previously neutral stimulus as if it were food, the newly learned stimulus could do the same. Research on learning outlines the sorts of conditions that facilitated the secondary reinforcing properties acquired by a cue during conditioning (e.g., Grice, 1948). Two things may bring each other to mind by association, but by eliciting the same behaviors, the notion of an association achieves its behaviorist or empirical demonstration. Experiments designed to explore the boundaries of temporal contiguity's effectiveness showed the insufficiency of pairings as a condition for effective conditioning.

Researchers at the time of Hebb were fully aware of the idea that neutral stimuli acquire their reinforcing powers if a correlation is prepared between the neutral stimulus and the reinforcer, and that it might need to be "close" and "consistent." The experiments to examine the boundary conditions of secondary reinforcers involved first training rats to press a lever to receive food, which the rats did quite readily (Schoenfeld, Antonitis, & Bersh, 1950). The researchers then simultaneously presented a brief, originally neutral, light (CS) each time the rats received the food reward. By simultaneously activating the light at the exact moment the animal had seized the pellet and began to eat it, the expectation was that the light might come to be associated with food just as in Pavlov's experiments. Both the light and the food were internally activated at the same time and therefore might be expected to form an association. If so, the animal might be expected to press a lever to have the light illuminated. Secondary reinforcement of lever pressing is quite easily produced under certain conditions (see, for example, Dwyer, Starns, & Honey, 2009), but for Shoenfeld *et al.*, there was absolutely no evidence of such transfer of reinforcing powers to the light.

The researchers describe in some detail their tight control over the conditions for learning, how the light stimulus was always present when the animal had started to eat and terminated before eating was finished and that they carefully ensured that the light never preceded the delivery of the pellet. Any presentations of the light either before or after the food might have been considered to be conditions that would undermine the association, since the light would be active in the rat's mind without food. Following a session in which lever pressing for food was extinguished (i.e., a session in which lever pressing was not presented with food), two sessions were presented in which the lever produced now not food but the light. The question was whether during this session rats would increase pressing when the light was presented briefly for each lever press.

The negative results of these studies proved puzzling. Following this type of training, there was little evidence of lever pressing for the light in spite of the positive correlation and pairing between the light and food in the training phase. The experimenters proposed that perhaps the failure reflected an important characteristic of association formation. Importantly, for the development of the idea of prediction error, they recognized that simple pairing was insufficient for secondary reinforcement, even if, on the basis of previous work in their lab, it was sufficient to impart

Pavlovian properties to the light. Learning a Pavlovian relation between a CS and US did not make the CS a substitute for the US (Chapter 2 raises the similar question of why simultaneous presentation is not a better route of learning to pair events if co-occurrence is the driving force behind learning). The answer to why learning is not simply dependent upon pairings lies in the anticipatory nature of many Pavlovian conditioned responses. Associative learning is a more general phenomenon, but if you measure associative learning using a conditioning procedure, then the responses that an animal learns allow it to anticipate or expect (in cognitive terms) or simply perform an action prior to the occurrence of the US. Conditioning is not so much about stimulus substitution, although there is evidence for this, but rather about learning a predictive relation about the occurrence of the US. In the previous experimental situation, the light did not predict the occurrence of the US because by the time the light was presented, the food was already being consumed. The presence of a predictive relation was established as an important condition for learning.

Prediction and priority

This problem regarding priority of occurrence or predictiveness and the rules for conditioning emerged again as researchers explored the now obviously important temporal relations and their controlling influence on conditioned responding. It turned out that the temporal relation itself is also an insufficient condition for learning, as had been implied by experiments like those described by Schoenfeld *et al.* (1950). Even in situations with ideal temporal relations, animals would sometimes not learn about cues. This new style of experiment presented multiple cues to animals, each of which was independently conditionable but now in different temporal positions to each other.

Egger and Miller (1962) tested how different cues might be arranged to have priority in terms of access to the associative system depending on their predictive relation. The experiments involved comparing two cues, each with their own temporal relation to a food reinforcer. The results demonstrated that it was the reliability of a cue as a predictor, that is, its absolute consistency as a predictor and its relative value, that determined conditioned responding. They interpreted their results as suggesting that a cue must be informative if it is to become a conditioned reinforcer, that is, it must be reliable and not redundant.

They studied hungry male rats and examined how well they would learn about a CS that was presented prior to food (US) and tested whether two cues that both appeared prior to the US would be learned about. Pavlov (1927) had studied the case of *overshadowing* in which two cues were presented simultaneously (AB+). Evidence that either one of two simultaneously presented cues might interfere with learning about the other was at the heart of a debate that was relevant for theories of selective attention (see Mackintosh, 1975). But Egger and Miller were not simply testing the case of overshadowing, since, although both cues terminated with the delivery of the US, one of the two cues CS_{early} appeared earlier than CS_{late} (see Figure 3.1A for a schematic). This design asks a simple but important question; CS_{early} might be expected to be a better predictor of the US because it is the earliest signal and therefore has temporal precedence, but CS_{late} might be considered more important, since more of the experience of CS_{late} happens contiguous with the US. According to their hypothesis, CS_{late}

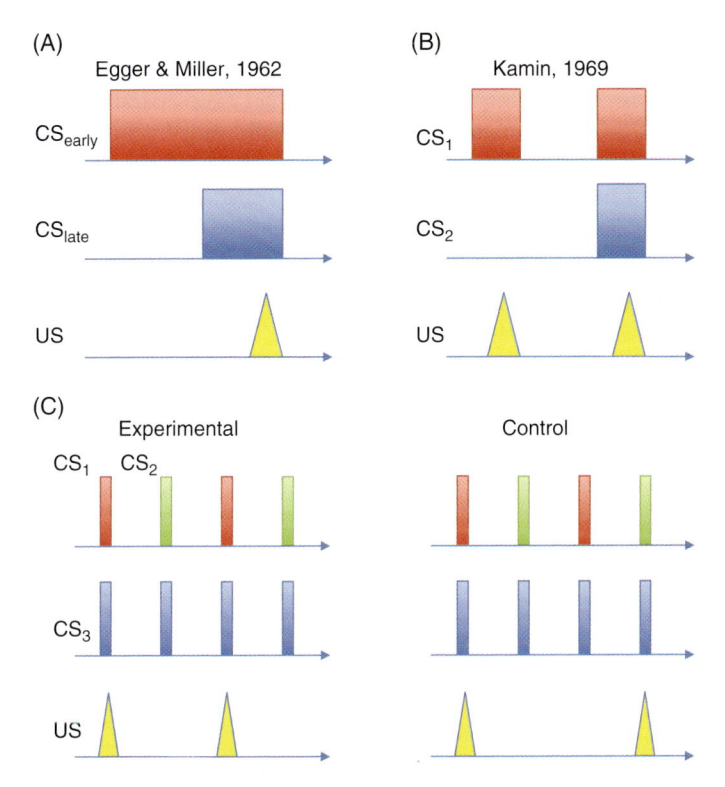

Figure 3.1 Schematic of design for selective learning experiments by (A) Egger and Miller (1962), (B) Kamin (1969), and (C) Wagner et al. (1968).

was expected to be a redundant predictor, and indeed it acquired weak control over responding. They also demonstrated that the strength of the control that CS_{late} had over responding could be increased by presenting CS_{early} on some trials alone in extinction. The control group received the same cues paired with food, but on half of the trials, CS_{early} was presented without CS_{late} or the US. In the control group, CS_{late} now acquired the conditioned response, while in the experimental group, conditioned responding was acquired by CS_{early}. According to their analysis of this design, the priority of relation of CS_{early} was the driving force for making it more informative for the occurrence of food. The question this work raised, then, was: What were the conditions for relative predictiveness?

Tests of relative predictiveness came from experiments designed to contrast the predictiveness of two cues as a signal for an outcome, in this case not rewarding food but aversive electric shock (see Figure 3.1B for a schematic). In Kamin's (1969) *blocking* experiments, prior training with one cue ($CS_1 \rightarrow$ Shock) before pairing a second simultaneously presented cue would be expected to make the second cue redundant (CS_1^+, CS_1, and CS_2^+). These important experiments make an appearance in many of the chapters of this volume because of their general relevance to a number of issues in associative learning. The blocking result was a further failure of contiguity as a condition for associative learning, because, although CS_2 is contiguous with shock, it fails to acquire a strong association. It is important to note that the result is not the consequence of CS_1 overshadowing CS_2 on the compound trials, since, in one of Kamin's control groups for blocking, the first phase involved training cue a separate cue (CS_3). CS_2, in this other control group, is made relatively more valid, not by any change in its own absolute validity as a predictor of shock but by reducing CS_1's relative validity by training with CS_3. One interpretation of this result is that a predictable US has a diminished ability to instigate processing and association (Rescorla & Wagner, 1972). An alternative interpretation is that the predictability of the US renders the new cue redundant, and as the cue is not correlated with any change in reinforcement, it is ignored (see Mackintosh, 1975). Other similar selective learning effects such as CS–US contingency learning (Murphy & Baker, 2004; Rescorla, 1968) and the relative validity effect (Wagner, Logan, Haberlandt, & Price, 1968; see Figure 3.1C) provided further support for relative predictiveness as a constraint on learning. Wagner *et al.*, for instance, demonstrated with compound cues that learning about a partially reinforced (50%) cue was determined by the validity of the cues that were paired with it, such that learning about CS_3 in the experimental group was much lower than in the control group because CS_1 and CS_2 were perfect predictors of US occurrence and absence. The attempts to formalize these relative relations resulted in one of the most cited theories of conditioning and association and of psychology more generally: the Rescorla–Wagner model (see Rescorla & Wagner, 1972; Siegel & Allan, 1996).

Prediction error

The model starts, somewhat innocuously, by proposing that associations are the function of the difference between a value that represents the activity produced by the US and sum of the associative strengths of the stimuli present on that trial. Unlike the Hebb's multiplicative function, the use of differences provides a simple way of representing the gradually decelerating curve observed across studies of learning. Learning involves larger changes early in training and smaller changes as learning proceeds, or as the difference becomes smaller. Earlier theories focused on characterizing the changes in the learned behavior (e.g., Hull, 1950), whereas the Rescorla–Wagner model used this prediction error to describe changes to the internal, cognitive expectancy for the US.

Rescorla and Wagner's theory (1972), more formally, proposes that learning is a process by which a cue comes to be associated with its postcedents or concurrents. Learning is a function of the difference between the level of activation produced by the postcedent (e.g., US), represented by the value for that US (λ), and the value of the sum (Σ) of the activations for that US produced by any associates (ΣV). Initially, potential associates have no associative strength ($V_A = 0$), and so the difference is large ($\lambda > V$). On the first and subsequent experiences, the change in associative strength or the amount of learning that accrues as a function of this difference. Formally, this expectancy discrepancy can be characterized as the difference between the prediction generated by the current cues in a given learning scenario (here represented by the sum of two cues A and B) and the actual US (λ).

$$\Delta V_A = k\left[\left(\lambda - V_A + V_B\right)\right] = k\left(\lambda - \Sigma V\right) \qquad (3.2)$$

Table 3.1 Size of prediction error as a function of stimulus associative strength and outcome presence in a single cue experiment.

		Outcome	
		Occurs (λ = 1)	*Absent (λ = 0)*
Stimulus associative strength	$V = 0$	Simple acquisition / | A+ PE = +1	No learning / | A− PE = 0
	$V = +1$	Presenting a trained stimulus A+ | A+ PE = 0	Simple extinction A+ | A− PE = −1

If the difference is positive ($\lambda > V_{A+}$), then the conditions support acquisition of A's association with the US. The top-left panel of Table 3.1 shows that initially if the US is presented but the association is nonexistent ($V = 0$), then a large prediction (PE = 1) is set up, and learning should occur. Once a strong association is acquired ($V = 1$), if the outcome occurs then no prediction error is anticipated (bottom-left panel of 3.1). The difference can be negative too; a negative prediction error is present if, after acquisition has occurred, the associated outcome is removed ($\lambda = 0$). In this case, the CS is said to be presented in extinction, so $\lambda < V_A$. The omission of the expected US results in gradual extinction or weakening of the positive association and thereby the conditioned response. Of course if a cue A is present without US, but it has never been previously presented with the US, then no prediction error occurs either (top-right panel of Table 3.1). These are the four basic conditions that describe simple learning. However, the Rescorla–Wagner model was proposed to account for the more complex situations that arise when multiple cues are presented. These are outlined in Table 3.2.

Under some conditions, after learning about an expected US, the presentation of a second cue (B) can be taught as a predictor of the absence of the US. Conditioned inhibition is the case when a cue signals the omission of an otherwise expected US (see McLaren, this volume; Rescorla, 1969). If A+ training is accompanied by AB− training, B will become a predictor of US absence. The absence of the US ($\lambda = 0$) normally produces no learning, but in a combination of a US-expectation ($\Sigma V = 1$), the absence of the US generates a negative prediction error, PE = −1, so that B acquires a negative associative strength ($V_B = -1$; see Conditioned Inhibition in Table 3.2). The effect of prediction-error combinations like this, where A and B have different associations, sets up different expectancies for the US, with interesting consequences.

For example, if, after conditioned inhibition training of B, the US is present with the inhibitor (B), an extra-large prediction error is set up, since B will have a negative prediction for the US [PE = $\lambda - (-1) = +2$]. This specific hypothesis was tested by experiments on so-called Super-learning; presenting B with a novel cue (C) followed by the US generates a large prediction error that supports stronger learning about a novel cue (C; Rescorla, 1971; Turner *et al.*, 2004; although see Baker, 1974).

Table 3.2 Size of prediction error as a function of stimulus associative strength and outcome presence in a multi-cue experiment.

		Outcome Occurs ($\lambda = 1$)	Outcome Absent ($\lambda = 0$)
Stimulus associative strength (outcome expectation)	$V = -1$	Super-learning A+ AX– | BX+ PE = +2	Extinction of inhibition A+ AX– | X– PE = +1
	$V = 0$	Release from blocking A+ AX– | ABX+ PE = +1	Protection from extinction A+ AX– B+ | BX – PE = 0
	$V = +1$	Blocking A+ | AB+ PE = 0	Conditioned inhibition A+ | AX– PE = –1
	$V = +2$	Overexpectation A+ B+ | AB+ PE = –1	Extinction of super-learning A+ AX– | BX+ | B– PE = –2

The negative prediction error can also diminish like positive prediction error $\lambda > V$ if the negative expectation of the US is followed by no US.

The model also provides a simple explanation for the selective learning effects. For instance, learning about the first cue (A⁺) in Kamin's blocking procedure results in a strong association between that cue and the outcome. In the second phase, when both cues are trained, B does not acquire associative strength because the prediction error is close to zero [$(\lambda - \Sigma V) = 0$], and therefore the US is ineffective at strengthening B's association.

The model provides an account for interactions between cues and the selective association phenomenon outlined in Table 3.2 (Wagner & Rescorla, 1972). In each of these selective learning effects, it is the prediction error generated by the sum of the cues presented on a trial that determines the conditions for learning. In learning with multiple cues, it is the sum of the US expectancy that determines the prediction error. Overexpectation (Kremer, 1978; Li & McNally, 2014) occurs when two cues that have been trained independently and therefore have strong associations with the US are presented together and with US (see Table 3.2). Since the two cues predict more than the associative strength that λ can support, a negative prediction error is set up: $\lambda < (V_A + V_B)$. Even though both cues might always be paired with the US, during training and during the second phase of training (AB+), the negative prediction error suggests that there will be a weakening of associative strength. In somewhat the same way, super-learning shows how the presence of an inhibitor contributes to increases in the size of the positive prediction error, such that extra strong associations are predicted between the novel cue and paired outcome [$\lambda > (V_{A+} + V_{B-})$]. In these cases, neither the presence of the US nor previous learning about a cue determines whether associations are formed, but rather learning is dependent upon the combination of the cues present.

A similar situation arises with prediction errors generated by the absence of the US. In the presence of an inhibitor (B−), the absence of the US can result in no change in the associative strength of a previously trained cue, A [$0 = (V_{A+} + V_{B-})$], an effect known as protection from extinction (e.g., Murphy, Baker, & Fouquet, 2001), or even an increase in associative strength if the inhibitory strength is stronger than the excitatory strength [$0 < (V_{A+} + V_{B-})$].

What is so striking about this analysis is how simple the components of the theory are and yet how it allows an impressive range of predictions involving multiple cues. It is also the case that it would be quite compelling if the behavioral data were accompanied by a simple neural correlate of this process.

The search for a physiological mechanism of learning that is based on difference calculations can be seen to have a parallel research tradition in one of Pavlov's contemporaries, the mathematician, engineer, and early founder of modern computer science, Charles Babbage (1791–1871). Babbage is recognized as one of the early proponents of the automization of mathematical principles. There is good reason to think that by putting into action and making physical the processes of mathematics, he anticipated and contributed crucially to the development of the physical computer and the software that drives it. The mechanization of memory and logical operations had a transformational effect not simply in terms of its effect on the development of computer hardware and software design but in developing our understanding of psychological and physiological processes. Babbage conceived of his work as developing "thinking machines"; physical structures that had the potential to mimic mental processes by performing mathematical functions over time. Interestingly, these functions were accomplished by using difference calculations (Figure 3.2; see Babbage, 1864).

If the prediction-error hypothesis is correct, brains are, in at least one important way, difference engines. But consider that modern neuroscience has opened up the circuitry of the brain to scrutiny and observation; electrical and chemical reactions mediating cognitive life, which once could only be studied in vitro, can now be monitored online. One of the points where computational principles have been applied to the understanding of neural action has been in the role that dopamine plays in forging associative links (e.g., Wise, 2004). There is evidence that dopamine neurons are active in a manner that suggests that they are related to the type of prediction-error differences described by the Rescorla–Wagner model. Early work with small invertebrates proposed a role for dopamine in increasing the synaptic efficiency between sensory and motor neurons much like that suggested by Hebb's (1949) principle. In mammals, dopamine has been found to have a similar role.

Dopamine Prediction Error

Bertler and Rosengren (1959) measured dopamine concentration in brain tissue in a range of mammals (i.e., cow, sheep, pig, dog, cat, rabbit, guinea-pig and rat) and localized the primary source to the corpus striatum. Initial hypotheses that dopamine was a simple chemical precursor to other important neurochemical reactions were updated when dopamine was manipulated directly. Research on the effects of dopamine receptor agonists for disorders such as Parkinsonism and schizophrenia, and

Figure 3.2 Component of Babbage's difference engine. Reproduced with permission of the Museum of the History of Science Oxford University.

their involvement in mediating the effects of drugs of addiction had indicated an involvement in motor behavior (e.g., Grace, 1991; Wise & Bozarth, 1987). This motor theory of dopamine's action was developed over time to include gradually more sophisticated cognitive functions. For the remainder of this chapter, we will evaluate the evidence for the relation between prediction errors and dopamine responses, specifically the extent of dopamine's involvement in the range of prediction-error subtypes as outlined in Table 3.2.

Dopamine and reward

Dopamine is found in the brains of reptiles, birds, fish, rodents, and primates. In rodents and primates, it is found in the midbrain, in the small midbrain reticular formation and mouse retrorubal fields (A8), in the adjacent densely packed substantia nigra (A9), and in the large ventral tegemental areas (A10; see Figure 3.3). These neurons release dopamine when activated by axonal stimulation from the striatum and frontal cortex, among other regions. Current neuroscience provides a range of techniques for studying the working brain. Correlational inferences can be derived from measuring neural activity and overt responses using full brain scanners (fMRI, DTI) or cellular-level recording technologies (electrophysiology). These are complemented by causal inferences derived from techniques involving lesioning (drug and energy damage), genetic manipulation, and pharmacological, electrical, and magnetic interference. Together, these techniques have resulted in set of experimental tools that have examined the role of dopamine in learning.

Much of the work on dopamine has involved causal experimental techniques. These allow interference in the activity of dopamine neurons and the subsequent measurement of the activity of dopamine neurons when the active animal is engaged in tasks that involve learning to associate.

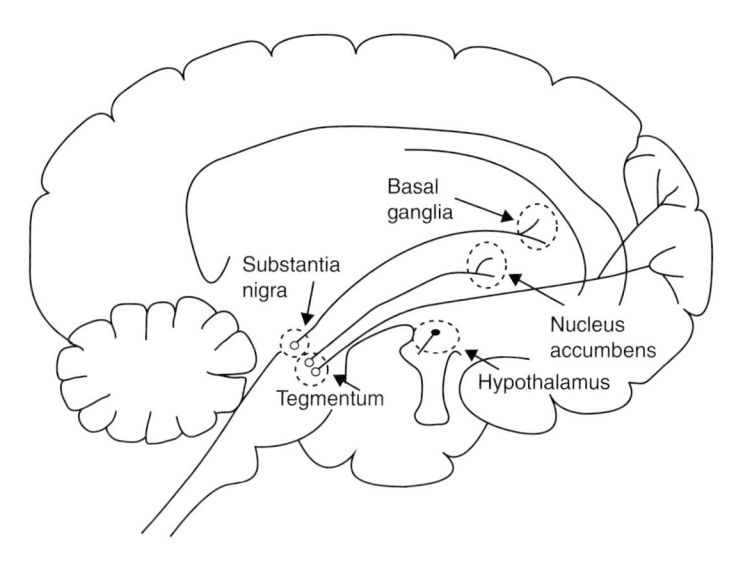

Figure 3.3 Midbrain schematic.

Penfield (1961) pioneered the exploratory investigation of one of the causal mechanisms for studying brain function. Electrical brain stimulation performed during neurosurgery, by his own admission, resulted in fundamental discoveries that were the product of serendipity. He initially conducted this work in conscious patients to map areas ostensibly to minimize unintended permanent damage during brain surgery and facilitate the placement of lesions to reduce epilepsy. He noted that electrical stimulation often had quite local, specific, and unusual effects. At times, stimulation had no discernible effect on the patient, and at other times, the same level of stimulation elicited powerful memories and the positive and negative associates of these memories. The discovery that electrical stimulation of the temporal lobe could retrieve a separate stream of consciousness of previous, experienced events at the same time that the patient was conscious and aware of the surgery was simply groundbreaking. Experiences and their associated interpretations were the subject of temporal lobe excitation. Penfield was aware that the memories themselves were stored elsewhere but observed that the temporal lobe extracted experiences were part of "interpretive signalling" (Penfield, 1961, p. 83). Penfield speculated that perhaps these activated and interpretive percepts in humans were the same as those associative components found in a Pavlovian conditioning procedure.

Subsequent work found that electrical stimulation in free-moving animals compelled them to behave in stereotyped ways, for instance, rats returned to a location at which stimulation took place or would press a lever to receive intracranial stimulation (ICS; Olds & Milner, 1954). In addition to the potential implications that these results might have for motor and spatial components of learning, it was assumed that ICS was interfering, in some way, with learning processes and that stimulation was exciting pathways related to primary rewards (i.e., food, water). These experiments led to the development of the understanding of pathways that might be involved in reward (Olds & Milner, 1954). These pathways were primarily related to the septal pathways including those in the medial forebrain bundle (MFB), ventral tegemental areas (VTA) (Figure 3.3). For instance, electrodes placed into the area of the septum, including the MFB, could be used to electrically stimulate these areas and sustain lever pressing in rats in the absence of any primary reward. Although many sites could generate self-sustaining lever pressing, the role of dopamine in this process was suspected. Studies with animals confirmed that dopamine (and noradrenaline) antagonists could suppress lever pressing for ICS (e.g., Rolls, Kelly, & Shaw, 1974). Whether ICS encouraged stereotyped motor behavior as opposed to activation of reward required further experimental work. Animals might repeatedly press a lever because of the strength of the activation of the lever pressing motor pattern or because of the effects of ICS to mimic those of reward.

Dissociating the motor from and reward effects of dopamine involved an experiment that harnessed the concepts of positive and negative prediction errors, although this terminology is not used in the original paper, to show that a CS associated with ICS or a CS in extinction could contribute to instrumental lever pressing. The experiment involved training rats to lever-press for ICS, and the lever-pressing response was extinguished if either the ICS was removed or a dopamine antagonist (i.e., pimozide) was introduced without removing ICS (e.g., Franklin & McCoy, 1979). The evidence that dopamine antagonists could remove the effect of ICS argued for the role of dopamine in the ICS effect, but one could still argue that the effects of pimozide were on the motor system directly. To counter this idea, Franklin and McCoy showed that extinguished responding could be reinstated while exposed to Pimozide, with the presentation of a CS that had previously been paired with ICS. It is a well-demonstrated effect that the presence of a CS associated with a US can contribute to a transitory reinstatement of extinguished instrumental responding (e.g., Baker, Steinwald, & Bouton, 1991). The CS in this case acted like a substitute for the ICS. The skeptic might still argue that it is still possible that the secondary reinforcing properties of the CS were simply related to motor behavior, but it does seem possible that dopamine acts like ICS to generate the reward signal.

While the evidence for a role for dopamine in rewarding behavior is compelling, it is clear there are still many ways to define its role. Wise (2004) describes a full range of hypotheses that outline dopamine's role in mediating the effects of reward. His dopamine hypothesis for reinforcement, reward, and hedonia is built on the basis of data showing the effects of lesions to dopamine pathways or selective depletion of forebrain dopamine. In addition to specific functional roles in driving drug addiction, the range of hypotheses about dopamine's role in associative learning encompasses all aspects of behavior including reinforcement (the strengthening of behaviors), reward, incentive motivation, conditioned reinforcement, anhedonia, motor, and the more subtle distinctions of wanting versus liking and reward prediction as opposed to simple reward (Wise, 2004). We are primarily interested in the distinction between reward and prediction of reward, since it is this distinction that has been seen to involve some of the principles of the error-prediction models like that provided by the Rescorla–Wagner model. The evidence that dopamine codes prediction error as opposed to some other function is less compelling than the range of effects provided in Tables 3.1 and 3.2; nevertheless, the evidence is growing.

The experiments closely associated with the development of the prediction-error hypothesis are those of Schultz and colleagues. Their importance to neuroscience and the renewed relevance of associative models for neural processes is evidenced by the reference to this work in other chapters in this volume (see Chapters 2, 14–16, and 19). The experiments combine measurements of dopamine release prior to, during, and after learning episodes of varying complexity (see Bayer & Glimcher, 2005).

Miller, Sanghera, and German (1981) reported evidence from studies using both Pavlovian and instrumental conditioning with rodents that dopamine neuron firing rates were correlated with the conditioned response. Similarly, Schultz (1986) reported findings that have provided the basis of the development of the prediction-error hypothesis of dopamine function using primates. Schultz used monkeys and recorded extracellular activity of midbrain dopamine neurons while they were learning. The goal of these studies was to distinguish the behavioral, motoric, and cognitive contributions of these cells and pathways. In the earlier and simpler behavioral tasks, hungry monkeys were trained to retrieve small portions of apple when cued by visual and auditory signals. Levels of dopamine release correlated with different aspects of the temporal stream of learning indicated some strong correlations. It was important for Schultz to identify whether the changes in dopamine activity reflected the behaviors that accompanied reaching and/or eating the food, or were caused by the presence or meaning of the cues that predicted the food. The monkeys were trained to place their finger upon a small button in front of a closed food slot. After a variable period, the food slot opened, a short 100-ms-long sound was played, and the monkey was then free to release the button and take the food. Early movement of the finger off the button stopped the delivery of food. In this manner, animals learned a CS for the availability food and the cue for when they were permitted to emit the quite naturalistic reaching response to retrieve the food.

Measurement of dopamine was conducted using electrophysiology. Electrical activity was recorded from a total of 128 neurons in two monkeys (58 and 70 for monkey A and B) over many trials (up to 50 in some cases). The initial challenge was to discern whether the dopamine activity was initiated by the reaching behavior or the unconditioned perception of the stimuli (sounds and sights of the opening of the food well) as opposed to being related to predictive signaling of the CS. While many of the neural responses related to all of these categories of events, Schultz provides strong statistical evidence that more than half of the recorded dopamine neurons in the monkey midbrain showed a characteristic phasic response to the predictive stimulus, while other slower tonic changes were caused by a range of events related to the task.

At this point, it is worth stating that in these early experiments, the nature of the task determined that all that could be concluded was that dopamine was activated by the predictive cue, and little could be claimed about a generalized, prediction-error-related phasic response other than that the response was related to the pairing of the stimulus with the US. The evidence did not distinguish between a prediction error and a response related to the initiation of the behavioral reaching response that was about to be emitted or even whether the dopamine activity was related to the food that was about to be eaten, since activity was positively correlated with all these features of the tasks. There was good evidence in fact that dopamine was also preparing the animal to move and to eat, but that it was probably not simply being activated by changes in sensory stimulation (i.e., when unusual stimuli were present that were unrelated to the behavior).

These experiments demonstrated a role for dopamine in this reward-learning task but were unable to distinguish between the more general concept of prediction error and one that uses a simpler stimulus substitution-type principle that looks like Hebbian learning. Subsequent experiments by Schultz used Kamin's blocking procedure and a conditioned inhibition paradigm, which are not predicted by Hebbian learning and provide the opportunity to begin to distinguish stimulus substitution from prediction error.

Waelti, Dickinson, and Schultz (2001) conducted experiments using a similar design to that described by Kamin (1969). Monkeys were provided with cues for the availability of fruit juice, and licking responses and eye gaze towards the cues were recorded. Results showed that a visual cue trained in compound with a second pretrained visual cue acquired a conditioned response much more weakly than it did if it had been trained with a cue that was not pretrained. Pretraining interfered with the acquisition (or perhaps expression) of a learned association with the cue. Although the monkeys were able to attend to the different cues as confirmed by the eye gaze data, the conditioned licking showed clear evidence for the blocking effect. In addition, the dopamine responses in midbrain cells in substantia nigra and ventral tegmental areas showed good discrimination between the blocked and unblocked cues. Of the 200 neurons recorded from the two subjects in this experiment, 150 discriminated between the reward predictive and nonpredictive cues, either in an all-or-none fashion or with weaker phasic responding to the nonpredictive cues. Reward presentations that correlated with dopamine activity were related to behavioral learning.

This evidence suggests that dopamine activity seems dependent upon the reinforcement history of the training cues, but Waelti *et al.* (2001) also showed that removing the expected outcome (i.e., extinction) had a particular effect on dopamine. Having learned that a cue was a reliable predictor, the omission of reward generated a depression in dopamine neuron activity, while the presentation of reward following a cue that was not a reliable predictor of reward generated an increase in dopamine neuron activity. On the basis of these findings, the relations between cellular processes, behavioral responses, and the computational principles of error prediction were held to be in place.

While much of this and other evidence related to the role of dopamine in associative tasks has related to correlational techniques (correlating behavior and dopamine activity e.g., Guarraci & Kapp, 1999), direct manipulation of dopamine neurons to simulate their effect on behavior has also supported the case. It is possible to directly alter dopamine cells via lesions (Brozoski, Brown, Rosvold, & Goldman, 1979), electrochemical stimulation (e.g., Rolls, Kelly, & Shaw, 1974) or pharmaceutical manipulation (e.g., Spyraki, Fibiger, & Phillips, 1982) with results that are generally supportive of the previous analysis, but these techniques have limitations in terms of understanding behavior, since they have the potential to interfere with other regions of the brain and therefore other neurons or fibers of passage. While lesions cause permanent damage, dopamine agonists and antagonists are temporary, but they also have the potential to interfere with dopamine neurons that are not part of the targeted brain regions. Genetic manipulation of the DNA related to dopamine neurons has been used to encourage either over- or underexpression of dopamine characteristics, but even this method is limited because of the associated developmental effects. The use of optogenetic manipulations allows much more control over dopamine neuron activity. With this technique, transgenic rats expressing Cre-recombinase are injected with a Cre-dependent virus resulting in photosensitivity of the dopamine neurons. These altered dopamine neurons are receptive to light energy, and the experimenter can use focal laser exposure in the tissue to activate or deactivate dopamine neurons (e.g., Boyden, Zhang, Bamberg, Nagel, & Deisseroth, 2005).

Using the Kamin Blocking experimental design, Steinberg et al. (2013) exposed rats to auditory and visual cues for sucrose and utilized the optogenetic procedure to activate dopamine neurons. When activation of the neurons was caused at a time when reward prediction might have been expected to be low, they found facilitated learning. That is, they were able to induce a positive and negative prediction error not by the relationships between the environmental cues but by the activation of dopamine neurons. The researchers claimed that activation could mimic the effects of experienced learning. For instance, during the presentation of the normally blocked cue and during reward omission trials that normally result in extinction, light activation of the neurons resulted in animals behaving as if they had learned about the outcome.

The hypothesis that dopamine neurons might play a role in the calculations that determine what is learned about is supported by the evidence that conditions designed to manipulate the learnability of cues are accompanied by characteristic dopamine changes. Situations designed to result in either a positive prediction ($\lambda > V_{A+}$; Schultz, 1986) or negative prediction error ($\lambda < V_{A+}$) are accompanied by clear changes to the activity of dopamine neurons. Similarly, important control tests in Schultz's work showed that no dopamine responses were observed when there was no prediction error, when the expectation of reward matched the cue $\lambda = V_{A+}$, and when no reward was presented with a cue that had no predictive history $0 = V_A$.

This latter work involving negative prediction errors and dopamine activity for unexpected absences corresponds with some of the most important predictions of the Rescorla–Wagner model about the nature of inhibition (Wagner & Rescorla, 1972). The absence of expected reward normally extinguishes (reduces) the associative strength of the cue that set up the expectation, but in the presence of a novel cue, the absence of the expected outcome drives inhibitory learning about the novel cue (see Table 3.2). Tobler, Dickinson, and Schultz (2003) tested the phasic dopamine response of neurons with this design, using a similar method to that described by Waelti et al. (2001). The procedure involved *conditioned inhibition* (A+, AB−) designed to train one cue (B−) as an inhibitor of fruit juice reward. Both monkeys in this experiment treated B as an inhibitor for the availability of fruit juice, and B passed the standard behavioral tests of inhibition, the retardation and summation tests (Rescorla, 1969; see also Chapters 12 and 19). These tests involve comparing responding to B with control stimuli that also have never been presented with reward but for which no expectation of reward had been generated. Importantly, many of the dopamine neurons tested showed decreased activity to B. The negative prediction error ($\lambda < V_{A+} + V_{B-}$) was accompanied by a depression in activity from baseline. For these dopamine neurons, the depression was found not only on AB− trials but also on test trials of B alone. B had become a conditioned inhibitor and resulted in depressed dopamine activity when presented alone. Other work, consistent with the error-prediction hypothesis, has examined predictions related to contingency learning [$\lambda - (V_A + V_{Cxt})$, e.g., Nakahara, Itoh, Kawagoe, Takikawa, & Hikosaka, 2004].

This summary of some of the relevant data on the role of dopamine in associative learning suggests a relation between prediction error and its relation to the neurotransmitter dopamine but raises some questions about the theory. First, it is clear that associative theory and prediction error have a much wider range of implications for learning than have been tested in relation to dopamine, particularly in conditions with multiple cues. The literature has focused on the case of blocking, which is only one type of selective association effect. Second, it will be important to demonstrate that prediction errors are consistent with learning in different motivational states, punishment and reward for the generality of prediction error to hold. In fact, the prediction-error notion has been successfully applied in animal and human learning where no reward or punishment is present (e.g., learning the association between any two events might be expected to show effects predicted by associative models; see Chapter 4). Third, there is growing evidence that areas other than the midbrain may be involved in error-prediction learning. Fourth, dopamine neurons may not be the only neurotransmitter system that is involved in error-prediction learning.

Although there is certainly good evidence that dopamine neurons respond in cases of prediction error, we have highlighted the discrepancies between the extent of the general implications of the theory as outlined in Tables 3.1 and 3.2, and the specific evidence for a role of dopamine in prediction error. Dopamine seems to have some involvement in all of the effects described in Table 3.1, but consideration of the effects described in Table 3.2 is less clear. Prediction error, in its general form, in which predictions are generated from the totality of experience and reflect mixtures of competing evidence, is beyond the conclusions that can be drawn from the current evidence. Indeed, the Rescorla–Wagner model is at best an incomplete description of error-prediction learning (see Chapter 14).

Although it is clear that the complete set of predictions generated by the Rescorla–Wagner model or any specific theory of prediction error has not been tested, there is good evidence for the hypothesis that dopamine activity is involved in learning about at least single predictive cues (Chowdury et al., 2013). In the context of deciding how general the prediction error idea is, it is worth pointing out a slightly anomalous feature of the argument as it has been presented so far. While much is made of the correspondence between reward learning and error-prediction theory, as described by the Rescorla–Wagner model, and its relation to Kamin's experimental blocking procedure (e.g., Steinberg et al., 2013; Waelti et al., 2001), none of Kamin's experiments on the study of blocking ever involved reward or reward prediction, as implied by much of the research in this area, but rather involved rats learning about cues for electric shock (i.e., punishment). Even though the two types of stimuli invoke different motivational systems and behavior patterns, the evidence that animals learn to anticipate the occurrence of positive events (food, water, and so forth) and avoid negative events (e.g., electric shock) is clear. This discrepancy has led to a search for prediction error responses in an aversive motivational system. Indeed, Cohen, Haesler, Vong, Lowell, and Uchida (2012) have suggested that dopamine neuron recordings in the VTA indicate that some cells show specific phasic activity coding the error prediction and with other cells showing a temporally graded response. In addition, some of these cells respond to the rewarding, and others the punishing properties of the outcomes. Further evidence supporting this result related to punishment would go some way to supporting the generality of the prediction-error hypothesis, specifically as it applies to the data on blocking.

The generality of the prediction-error hypothesis is supported to the extent that prediction for any type of outcome, not just reward, being coded by dopamine. There is also evidence that the specific localization of prediction-error dopamine neurons in midbrain might be premature. There is evidence that areas other than midbrain neurons have an error-prediction function including prefrontal (Watanabe, 1996) and cingulate (Rushworth & Behrens, 2008), and that other neurotransmitters may code prediction errors perhaps for different motivation systems (e.g., Dayan & Huys, 2008).

Conclusions

Prediction error is embodied in many theories of associative learning (e.g., Le Pelley, 2004; Mackintosh, 1975; Pearce & Hall, 1980). Here, we referred to the principles of error prediction instantiated in the Rescorla–Wagner model and showed how the basic principles can account for a range of learning effects. Prediction error allows for complexity of learning, accounting for effects from simple principles of reinforcement and selective attentional effects. The application of this idea to interpret dopamine activity has provided more questions than answers as to what dopamine is for and how the brain performs prediction-error computations (see also Niv & Schoenbaum, 2008). Some have suggested that dopamine might provide goal-prediction errors as opposed to simple predictors of reward (Flagel et al., 2011), or perhaps that it also relates to reward quantity or timing (Matsumoto & Takada, 2013; Roesch, Calu, Esber, & Schoenbaum, 2010). Others have suggested abandoning a learning style computational theory that captures the acquisition process in favor of an axiomatic propositional-style account relying on a formal logical analysis (Hart, Rutledge, Glimcher, & Philips, 2014). While still others have been unconvinced by the reward-prediction notion and suggested that the timing characteristics of the response make them highly unlikely to be performing the computations just described, they may rather be reflecting action selection (Redgrave, Gurney, & Reynolds, 2008). Developments in our understanding of the neural code for computations have relied on the conceptual advances provided by developments in associative theory without which it would be impossible to make sense of neural action, but there is still considerable work to be done to characterize dopamine's role.

References

Babbage, C. (1864). *Passages from the life of a philosopher*. London, UK: Longman.

Baker, A. G. (1974). Conditioned inhibition is not the symmetrical opposite of conditioned excitation: A test of the Rescorla–Wagner model. *Learning & Motivation, 5*, 369–379.

Baker, A. G., Steinwald, H., & Bouton, M. E. (1991). Contextual conditioning and reinstatement of extinguished instrumental responding. *Quarterly Journal of Experimental Psychology, 43*, 199–218.

Bayer, H. M., & Glimcher, P. W. (2005). Midbrain dopamine neurons encode a quantitative reward prediction error signal. *Neuron, 47*, 129–141.

Bertler, A., & Rosengren, E. (1959). Occurrence and distribution of dopamine in brain and other tissues. *Experientia, 15*, 10–11.

Boyden, E. S., Zhang, F., Bamberg, E., Nagel, G., & Deisseroth, K. (2005). Millisecond-timescale, genetically targeted optical control of neural activity. *Nature Neuroscience, 8*, 1263–1268.

Brozoski, T. J., Brown, R. M., Rosvold, H. E., & Goldman, P. S. (1979). Cognitive deficit caused by regional depletion of dopamine in prefrontal cortex in rhesus monkey. *Science, 205*, 929–932.

Chowdury, R., Guitart-Masip, M., Christian, L., Dayan, P., Huys, Q., Duzel, E., & Dolan, R. J. (2013). Dopamine restores reward prediction errors in old age. *Nature Neuroscience, 16*, 648–653.

Cohen, J. Y., Haesler, S., Vong, L., Lowell, B. B., & Uchida, N. (2012). Neuron-type-specific signals for reward and punishment in the ventral tegmental area. *Nature, 482*, 85–88.

Dayan, P., & Huys, Q. J. M. (2008). Serotonin, inhibition and negative mood. *PLOS Computational Biology, 4*, e4.

Dwyer, D. M., Starns, J., & Honey, R. C. (2009). "Causal reasoning" in rats: A reappraisal. *Journal of Experimental Psychology: Animal Behavior Processes, 35*, 578–586.

Ebbinghaus, H. (1964). *Memory: A contribution to experimental psychology*. Oxford, UK: Dover. (Original work published 1885).

Egger, M. D., & Miller, N. E. (1962). Secondary reinforcement in rats as a function of information value and reliability of the stimulus. *Journal of Experimental Psychology, 64*, 97–104.

Flagel, S. B., Clark, J. J., Robinson, T. E., Mayo, L., Czuj, A., Willun, I., Akers, C. A., Clinton, S. M., Phillips, P. E. M., & Akil, H. (2011). A selective role for dopamine in stimulus–reward learning. *Nature, 469*, 53–59.

Franklin, K. B. J., & McCoy, S. N. (1979). Pimozine-induced extinction in rats: Stimulus control of responding rules out motor deficit. *Pharmacology, Biochemistry & Behavior, 11*, 71–75.

Grace, A. A. (1991). Phasic versus tonic dopamine release and the modulation of dopamine system responsivity: A hypothesis of the etiology of schizophrenia. *Neuroscience, 41*, 1–24.

Grice, G. G. (1948). The relation of secondary reinforcement to delayed reward in visual discrimination learning. *Journal of Experimental Psychology, 38*, 1–16.

Guarraci, F. A., & Kapp, B. S. (1999). An electrophysiological characterization of ventral tegmental area dopaminergic neurons during differential Pavlovian fear conditioning in the awake rabbit. *Behavioral Brain Research, 99*, 169–179.

Hart, A. S., Rutledge, R. B., Glimcher, P. W., & Philips, P. E. M. (2014). Phasic dopamine release in the rat nucleus accumbens symmetrically encodes a reward prediction error term. *The Journal of Neuroscience, 34*, 698–704.

Hebb, D. O. (1949). *The organization of behavior: A neuropsychological theory*. New York, NY: John Wiley & Sons.

Hilgard, E. R., & Bower, G. H. (1966). *Theory of learning*. New York: Appleton-Century-Crofts.

Hull, C. L. (1950). Simple qualitative discrimination learning. *Psychological Review, 57*, 303–313.

James, W. (1950). *The principles of psychology*. New York, NY: Dover (Original work published 1890).

Kamin, L. J. (1969). Selective association and conditioning. In N. J. Mackintosh & W. K. Honig (Eds.), *Fundamental issues in associative learning* (pp. 42–64). Halifax, Canada: Dalhousie University Press.

Kremer, E. F. (1978). Rescorla–Wagner model: losses in associative strength in compound conditioned stimuli. *Journal of Experimental Psychology: Animal Behavior Process, 4*, 22–36.

Le Pelley, M. E. (2004). The role of associative history in models of associative learning: A selective review and a hybrid model. *Quarterly Journal of Experimental Psychology Section B, 57*, 193–243.

Li, S. S.Y & McNally, G. P. (2014). The conditions that promote fear learning: Prediction error and Pavlovian fear conditioning. *Neurobiology of Learning and Memory, 108*, 14–21.

Mackintosh, N. J. (1975). A theory of attention: Variations in the associability of stimuli with reinforcement. *Psychological Review, 82*, 276–298.

Matsumoto, M., & Takada, M. (2013). Distinct representations of cognitive and motivational signals in midbrain dopamine neurons. *Neuron, 79*, 1011–1024.

Miller, J. D., Sanghera, M. K., & German, D. C. (1981). Mesencephalic dopaminergic unit activity in the behaviorally conditioned rat. *Life Sciences, 29*, 1255–1263.

Murphy, R. A., & Baker, A. G. (2004). A role for CS–US contingency in Pavlovian conditioning. *Journal of Experimental Psychology: Animal Behavior Processes, 30*, 229–239.

Murphy, R. A., Baker, A. G., & Fouquet, N. (2001). Relative validity effects with either one or two more valid cues in Pavlovian and instrumental conditioning. *Journal of Experimental Psychology: Animal Behavior Processes, 27*, 59–67.

Nakahara, H., Itoh, H., Kawagoe, R., Takikawa, Y., & Hikosaka, O. (2004). Dopamine neurons can represent context-dependent prediction error. *Neuron, 41*, 269–280.

Niv, Y., & Schoenbaum, G. (2008). Dialogues on prediction errors. *Trends in Cognitive Science, 12*, 265–272.

Olds, J., & Milner, P. (1954). Positive reinforcement produced by electrical stimulation of the septal area and other regions of rat brain. *Journal of Comparative and Physiological Psychology, 47*, 419–427.

Pavlov, I. P. (1927). *Conditioned reflexes. An investigation of the physiological activity of the cerebral cortex.* London, UK: Oxford University Press.

Pearce, J. M., & Hall, G. (1980). A model for Pavlovian learning: variations in the effectiveness of conditioned but not of unconditioned stimuli. *Psychological Review, 87*, 532–552.

Penfield, W. (1961). Activation of the record of human experience. *Annals of the Royal College of Surgeons England, 29*, 77–84.

Redgrave, P, Gurney, K., & Reynolds, J. (2008). What is reinforced by phasic dopamine signals. *Brain Research Review, 58*, 322–339.

Rescorla, R. A. (1968). Probability of shock in the presence and absence of CS in fear conditioning. *Journal of Comparative and Physiological Psychology, 66*, 1–5.

Rescorla, R. A. (1969).Conditioned inhibition of fear resulting from negative CS–US contingencies. *Journal of Comparative and Physiological Psychology, 66*, 1–5.

Rescorla, R. A. (1971). Variation in the effectiveness of reinforcement and nonreinforcement following prior inhibitory conditioning. *Learning & Motivation, 2*, 113–123.

Rescorla, R. A. (1980). Simultaneous and successive associations in sensory preconditioning. *Journal of Experimental Psychology: Animal Behavior Processes, 6*, 207.

Rescorla, R. A., & Wagner, A. R. (1972). A theory of Pavlovian conditioning: Variations in the effectiveness of reinforcement and nonreinforcement. In A. H. Black & W. F. Prokasy (Eds.), *Classical conditioning II: Current research and theory* (pp. 64–99). New York, NY: Appleton-Century-Crofts.

Roesch, M. R., Calu, D. J., Esber, G. R., & Schoenbaum, G. (2010). All that glitters ... dissociating attention and outcome expectancy from prediction errors signals. *Journal of Neurophysiology, 104*, 587–595.

Rolls, E. T., P. H. Kelly, S. G. Shaw. (1974). Noradrenaline, dopamine and brain-stimulation reward. *Pharmacology, Biochemistry Behavior, 2*, 735–740.

Rushworth, M. F. S., & Behrens, T. E. J. (2008). Choice, uncertainty and value in prefrontal and cingulate cortex. *Nature Neuroscience, 11*, 389–397.

Schoenfeld, W. N., Antonitis, J. J., & Bersh, P. J. (1950). A preliminary study of training conditions necessary for secondary reinforcement. *Journal of Experimental Psychology, 40*, 40–45.

Schultz, W. (1986). Responses of midbrain dopamine neurons to behavioral trigger stimuli in the monkey. *Journal of Neurophysiology, 56*, 1439–1461.

Schultz, W. (1998). Predictive reward signal of dopamine neurons. *Journal of Neurophysiology, 80*, 1–27.

Siegel, S., & Allan, L. G. (1996). The widespread influence of the Rescorla–Wagner Model. *Psychonomic Bulletin & Review, 3*, 314–321.

Spyraki, C., Fibiger, H. C., & Phillips, A. G. (1982). Attenuation by haloperidol of place preference conditioning using food reinforcement. *Psychopharmacology, 77*, 379–382.

Steinberg, E. E., Keiflin, R., Boivin, J. R., Witten, I. B., Deisseroth, K., & Janak, P. H. (2013). A causal link between prediction errors, dopamine neurons and learning. *Nature Neuroscience, 16*, 966–973.

Thorndike, E. L. (1933). A proof of the law of effect. *Science, 77*, 173–175.

Tobler, P. N., Dickinson, A., & Schultz, W. (2003). Coding of predicted reward omission by dopamine neurons in a conditioned inhibition paradigm. *The Journal of Neuroscience, 23*, 10402–10410.

Turner, D. C., Aitken, M. R. F., Shanks, D. R., Sahakian, B. J., Robbins, T. W., Schwarzbauer, C., & Fletcher, P. C. (2004). The role of the lateral frontal cortex in causal associative learning: Exploring preventative and super-learning. *Cerebral Cortex, 14*, 872–880.

Waelti, P., Dickinson, A., & Schultz, W. (2001). Dopamine responses comply with basic assumptions of formal learning theory. *Nature, 412*, 43–48.

Wagner, A. R., Logan, F. A., Haberlandt, K., & Price, T. (1968). Stimulus selection in animal discrimination learning. *Journal of Experimental Psychology, 76*, 171–180.

Wagner, A. R., & Rescorla, R. A. (1972). Inhibition in Pavlovian conditioning: Application of a theory. In R. A. Boakes & M. S. Halliday (Eds.), *Inhibition and learning* (pp. 301–336). New York, NY: Academic Press.

Watanabe, M. (1996). Reward expectancy in primate prefrontal neurons. *Nature, 382*, 629–632.

Wise, R. A. (2004). Dopamine, learning and motivation. *Nature Reviews Neuroscience, 5*, 1–12.

Wise, R. A., & Bozarth, M. A. (1987). A psychomotor stimulant theory of addiction. *Psychological Review, 94*, 469–492.

4

Learning About Stimuli That Are Present and Those That Are Not

Separable Acquisition Processes for Direct and Mediated Learning

Tzu-Ching E. Lin and Robert C. Honey

Summary and Scope

Pavlov's analysis of the conditioning process is so well known that it needs no introduction. His procedure provides a powerful way to probe the nature of associative learning in animals. We consider evidence from behavioral and neuroscientific manipulations that informs our understanding of both the conditions that promote the formation of new associative knowledge and the content of this knowledge. Our specific focus here is on the contrast between the acquisition of associative knowledge that reflects real-world relationships, embedded within conditioning procedures, and other forms of mediated learning that do not. By mediated learning, we are referring to cases where an association forms between two memories that is not the product of contiguity between their real-world counterparts. We provide converging evidence, from sensory preconditioning procedures, suggesting that these two forms of learning can be dissociated: by variations in the form of the conditioned response, in their differential reliance on a brain systems and neuronal processes, and by the distinct influences of a simple procedural variable.

Historical Context

In the year before his death, Pavlov summarized the results of his research concerning how stimuli to which animals were initially indifferent (the sound of a bell) came to evoke conditioned reflexes (salivation) as a result of being paired with stimuli that possess unconditioned value (food):

> The essential condition necessary to the formation of a conditioned reflex is in general the coinciding in time (one or several times) of an indifferent stimulation with an unconditioned one. This formation is achieved most rapidly and with least difficulty when the

former stimulations directly precede the latter, as has been shown in the instance of the auditory-acid reflex. (Pavlov, 1941, p. 171)

This summary clearly confirms the importance of (some of) the principles of association (temporal contiguity and frequency) identified with the associationist movement (for a review, see Warren, 1921), and foreshadows many of the empirical and theoretical analyses that would follow (see Mackintosh, 1974, 1983). But Pavlov was not just interested in characterizing the conditions under which behavior changed; he was concerned with the underlying neural bases of what was learned. Pavlov's overarching vision involved his physiologically inspired theoretical analysis of learning finding a rather direct homolog in the brain. This vision, from around one century ago, is captured by the following prophetic image:

If we could look through the skull into the brain of a consciously thinking person, and if the place of optimal excitability were luminous, then we should see playing over the cerebral surface, a bright spot with fantastic, waving borders constantly fluctuating in size and form, surrounded by a darkness more or less deep, covering the rest of the hemispheres. (Pavlov, 1928, p. 222)

The parenthetical use of the term *behavior* in the title of his first collected works reflects Pavlov's vision well; but the behavior*ism* that dominated the ensuing decades did little to encourage such integration. And so we fast-forward a further 40 or 50 years to a period in which the study of Pavlovian learning enjoyed a renaissance, and there was an increased synergy between behavioral and neuroscientific analysis. One impetus for this rapprochement came from the growing conviction that conditioned responding should be, rather than could be, used to infer the nature of the mental lives of animals; a conviction that was supported by the development of sophisticated behavioral tools that provided a rigorous basis for such inferences to be drawn (see Mackintosh & Honig, 1969). In turn, these tools and the theoretical analysis that their use supported provided natural points of contact with a neuroscience community, whose interests were becoming more translational in nature.

Contemporary Animal Learning Theory

The opening chapter of Dickinson's (1980) monograph, the title of which we have borrowed, highlights the fact that convincing demonstrations of sensory preconditioning (e.g., Rizley & Rescorla, 1972; see also Brogden, 1939; Fudim, 1978; Rescorla & Cunningham, 1978; Rescorla & Freberg, 1978) were pivotal in driving the move away from strict behaviorism (see also Mackintosh, 1974, pp. 85–87). In sensory preconditioning procedures, rats might first receive pairings of two neutral stimuli (e.g., a light and a tone) that affect no immediate change in their behavior. However, the fact that they have learned something about the relationship can be revealed by establishing a response to the tone (e.g., fear), by pairing it with an event that has motivational significance and then showing that the light also evokes that response. Dickinson argued that the original light → tone pairings must have resulted in learning that "is best characterized as a modification of some internal cognitive structure."

He immediately follows this analysis with the following statements: "Whether or not we shall be able at some point to identify the neurophysiological substrate of these cognitive structures is an open question. It is clear, however, that we cannot do so at present" (Dickinson, 1980, p. 5). In the following sections, we hope to show how investigations of this phenomenon have begun to inform our understanding of the associative process at a variety of levels of analysis.

Perhaps the most obvious cognitive structure that could underpin sensory preconditioning is an associative chain, the components of which are forged during the first and second stages of training: the memory of the light becoming linked to that of the tone, and the memory of the tone being linked to that of shock. A rat possessing these two associations will show fear to the light to the extent that the activation of the memory of the light passes along the light → tone → shock chain. This account has been widely adopted (e.g., Jones *et al.*, 2012; Wimmer, & Shohamy, 2012) and has the virtue of only appealing to well-established associative processes that allow real-world relationships to be represented. It is not the only explanation, however. For example, it has been argued that sensory preconditioning might be based on a rather different form of learning: retrieval-mediated learning. According to this analysis, to the extent that the second stage of training allows the tone to provoke a memory of the light, this associatively retrieved memory might become associated with the memory of shock. Indeed, Ward-Robinson and Hall (1996) have provided evidence that is consistent with just this type of analysis of sensory preconditioning.

The idea that the associatively retrieved memory of a given stimulus might be learned about in *the same way* as when this memory had being directly activated by its real-world counterpart is entirely consistent with the spirit of an associative analysis of Pavlovian learning (Hall, 1996), even if formal models failed to accommodate it (e.g., Rescorla & Wagner, 1972; Wagner, 1981). The italicized phrase reflects both the simplifying assumption that direct and associative activation converge on the same memory, and a natural corollary of this assumption that (excitatory) associative changes involving this memory are necessarily blind with respect to how it was activated. This general idea is consistent with demonstrations that food aversions, for example, can be established by dint of the associatively activated memory of food (rather than food itself) being coincident with illness (e.g., Holland, 1981; see also Holland, 1983; Holland & Forbes, 1982). It also receives support from studies showing that when the memories of two stimuli are associatively provoked at the same time, an (excitatory) association can be shown to have formed between them (see Dwyer, Mackintosh, & Boakes, 1998).

The studies outlined in the previous paragraph indicate that extant theories of associative learning need to be modified in order to allow the associatively provoked memories to be learned about in the same way as when the memories are being directly activated by their corresponding stimuli. This modification does not appear to undermine the central tenets of an associative analysis of animal learning. The results of more recent studies of sensory preconditioning, however, suggest that mediated learning is dissociable from associative learning involving real-world relationships, and that such dissociations are based upon animals representing the source of mnemonic activity in what they learn (Lin, Dumigan, Dwyer, Good, & Honey, 2013; Lin & Honey, 2011). We shall come to the evidence that bears on these specific claims in due course, but we first establish a prima facie case for the more general claim that mediated learning is based upon changes in cognitive structures that are separable from those that are a product

Mediated Learning During Sensory Preconditioning

The view that mediated learning provides a basis for sensory preconditioning receives indirect support from studies using procedures originally developed by Rescorla and colleagues (e.g., Rescorla & Cunningham, 1978; Rescorla & Freberg, 1978; see also Fudim, 1978). It is worth describing the basic sensory preconditioning effect in some detail, before considering the evidence that suggests it is based on (some form of) mediated learning. Table 4.1 summarizes the procedure, in which thirsty rats are first given access across several days to two flavor compounds (for several minutes each) that are constructed from two dilute flavors (e.g., salt and sour; and sweet and bitter). We will refer to these compounds as AX and BY. Rats then receive access to a flavor from one of the compounds (X; e.g., sour) that is followed by an injection of lithium chloride, which provokes illness several minutes later. The rats also receive access to a flavor from the other compound (Y; e.g., bitter) that is without consequence. This flavor-aversion procedure has a marked effect, reducing consumption of X relative to Y – an effect that has been allied to Pavlovian conditioning, in spite of its relative insensitivity to the long interval between ingestion of the flavor and illness (see left panel of Figure 4.1; results taken from Dwyer, Burgess, & Honey, 2012). Critically, the procedure also results in a reduction in consumption of A relative to B – a sensory preconditioning effect (see left

Table 4.1 Sensory preconditioning: experimental designs.

Stage 1	Stage 2	Test
Flavor-aversion procedures		
AX	X → illness	A
BY	Y → no illness	B
AX	X → illness	AX
BY	Y → no illness	BX
Fear-conditioning procedures		
AX	X → 40 s → shock	AX AY
BY	Y → no shock	BX BY
AX	X → shock	AX AY
BY	Y → no shock	BX BY
AX	X → shock	AX/ax AY/ay
BY	Y → no shock	BX/bx BY/by

Note. For the flavor-aversion procedures: A, B, X, and Y denote flavors. Rats receive preexposure to AX and BY, followed by conditioning trials in which X is paired with illness, and Y was not. During the test, the consumption of A and B, and AX and BX can be assessed. For the fear-conditioning procedures: A and B denote left and right lights; X and Y denote a tone and a clicker. Rats receive preexposure to both AX and BY, followed by a conditioning trials in which X was followed by shock (either after a 40 s trace interval or immediately). During the test, activity is monitored during the compounds (AX, BX, AY, and BY) and the trace periods that immediately follow them (ax, bx, ay, and by).

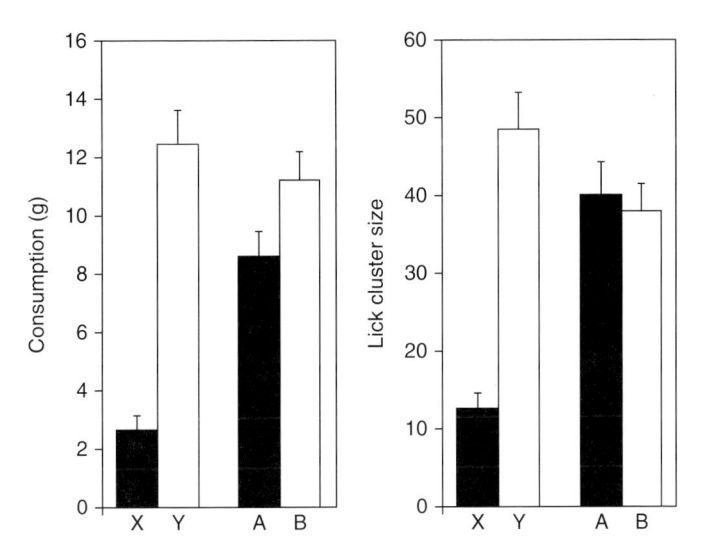

Figure 4.1 Sensory preconditioning in flavor-aversion procedures. Mean consumption (left panel) and mean lick cluster size (right panel; +SEM) of the test flavors X, Y, A, and B. Rats had previously received exposure to flavor compounds AX and BY, and then trials on which X was followed the induction of illness and Y was not. Adapted from: Dwyer, D. M., Burgess, K. V., & Honey, R. C. (2012). Avoidance but not aversion following sensory-preconditioning with flavors: A challenge to stimulus substitution. *Journal of Experimental Psychology: Animal Behavior Processes, 38*, 359–368.

panel in Figure 4.1). In fact, the magnitude and reliability of the sensory preconditioning effect in flavor-aversion learning should give one some cause to reflect: Are there features of this procedure that are especially conducive to observing sensory preconditioning? We shall answer this question later on, when use of a different conditioning procedure allows the relevance of the timing of the stimuli (and their decaying traces) during the conditioning trials and test to be investigated more effectively.

The standard associative chain account of sensory preconditioning assumes that any difference in consumption between the critical test flavors (A and B) is a consequence of their differing capacities to activate the memory of the flavor that was directly paired with illness (i.e., X). This account carries with it the implication that if the propensity of A and B to evoke a conditioned aversion during a test was assessed in the presence of X, then the resulting compounds (i.e., AX and BX) should not produce different levels of consumption: The different capacities of A and B to activate the directly conditioned flavor (X) should now be redundant because X is present and directly activating its memory (and thereby that of illness). However, there is reliable evidence that a sensory preconditioning effect is observed under just such conditions (e.g., Ward-Robinson, Coutureau, Honey, & Killcross, 2005; see also Rescorla & Freberg, 1978). The fact that the presence of the directly conditioned stimulus (X) during the test does not null, as it were, the sensory preconditioning effect can be taken to suggest that A has gained a capacity to evoke the memory of the outcome (e.g., illness) that is independent of what was learned about the directly conditioned stimulus, X. There are two potential bases for this suggestion that rely, in different ways, on the idea of mediating conditioning: Either the memory of A was associatively retrieved by X during conditioning and entered into association with illness; or the presentation of A at test associatively retrieves a memory of X that has properties that are independent of what was learned about the directly activated memory of X. As we will see, both of these process of mediated learning contribute to sensory preconditioning (Lin et al., 2013). However, next we consider additional evidence from flavor-aversion procedures that suggests that mediated learning during sensory preconditioning is not a behavioral homolog of direct conditioning.

The nature or topography of conditioned responding varies as a function of many features of conditioning procedures: For example, in rats, the sensory quality of the conditioned stimulus (e.g., whether it is visual or auditory) affects the nature of the conditioned response (for a reviews, see Holland, 1990). If mediated learning and direct conditioning are based on different cognitive structures – perhaps involving independent memories of the same stimulus – then they might too support different conditioned responses. Clearly, the fact that sensory preconditioning and direct conditioning are routinely assessed using the same response measure neither represents a particularly strong test of this possibility, nor of the prediction, derived from the associative chain account, that sensory preconditioning should obey the principle of stimulus substitution. According to the chaining account, already undermined by the results of Ward-Robinson et al. (2005; see also Rescorla & Freberg, 1978), any change in behavior that direct conditioning brings about to one part of the chain should be reflected in performance to the stimuli from other parts of the chain: Sensory preconditioning should obey the principle of stimulus substitution (Pavlov, 1927). Dwyer et al. (2012) have conducted a test of these predictions, using the flavor-aversion procedure described above, but assessing test performance using two measures: the amount of a flavor that rats consume (as noted above) and the way in which they consume the flavor as revealed by the microstructure of licking activity.

Flavor–illness pairings not only reduce consumption of the conditioned flavor but also affect the way in which rats consume that flavor. Briefly, rats consume liquid in bouts, and the number of licks in a bout of licking decreases when a flavor is paired with illness (see Dwyer, 2012). As we have already seen, Dwyer et al. (2012) replicated the sensory preconditioning effect using consumption as a measure (see left panel of Figure 4.1), but they also simultaneously assessed the microstructure of licking. They observed that the change in lick cluster size, which was apparent in way in which the directly conditioned flavors (X versus Y) were consumed, was not reflected in the test of sensory preconditioning (A versus B; see right panel of Figure 4.1). The fact that sensory preconditioning does not result in strict stimulus substitution is interesting and suggests that sensory preconditioning and direct conditioning have different origins. This suggestion receives converging support from an analysis of the brain mechanisms involved in at least some forms of sensory preconditioning.

Brain Mechanisms of Mediated Learning

The view that learning about stimuli that are currently impinging on an animal and retrieval-mediated learning reflect the operation of different learning processes carries with it the implication that they might be based on different brain mechanisms. There is evidence that is directly relevant to this prediction, not from studies involving sensory preconditioning with flavors (cf. Ward-Robinson et al., 2001) but from the use of a new variant of a sensory preconditioning procedure. In this procedure, rats first received exposure to four patterns of sensory stimulation: A tone was presented in one context (A) but not another (B) in the morning, whereas the tone was presented in context B and not A in the afternoon. The fact that the rats have encoded the four configurations is revealed by pairing the tone with mild shock at midday in a third context, and then showing that the rats are more fearful in the context + time of day configurations in which the tone had originally been presented (i.e., context A in the morning and context B in the afternoon; see Iordanova, Good, & Honey, 2008). This effect is beyond the scope of a simple associative chain analysis: Both of the components of each of the four test configurations were paired with the tone (and click), and so the effect at test must reflect something that the rats had learned about the configurations. One analysis of this effect relies on retrieval-mediated learning: During the first stage, rats encode the four configurations; and when the tone is presented during the conditioning stage it reactivates the configural memories involving the tone (i.e., context A + morning + tone and context B + afternoon + tone). These retrieved memories become linked to the memory of shock and mediate the fear seen to the test configurations (i.e., context A + morning and context B + afternoon).

There are several theoretical grounds for predicting that the hippocampus is likely to be involved in the mnemonic processes that support test performance in the procedure outlined in the previous paragraph: Test performance must be based on configural processes (e.g., Rudy & Sutherland, 1989), and it involves the integration of sensory domains associated with episodic memory (what happened, where, and when; e.g., Aggleton & Brown, 1999; see also Tulving, 2002). To assess the nature of the involvement of the hippocampus in such procedures, we have conducted an extensive series of studies. In one study, for example, prior to behavioral testing a group of rats received excitotoxic lesions of the (dorsal) hippocampus, and another group received sham lesions. The (configural) sensory preconditioning effect described in the previous paragraph was abolished in rats that had received lesions of the hippocampus, but these rats showed normal conditioned responding to the tone (Iordanova, Burnett, Good, & Honey, 2011; Iordanova, Burnett, Aggleton, Good, & Honey, 2009). This pattern of results is at least consistent with the idea that the hippocampus might be involved in mediated learning involving configurations, but not in learning involving stimuli that are present. More compelling evidence that this interpretation has some merit came from a study in which NMDA receptor-dependent synaptic plasticity in the hippocampus was blocked (by local infusions of AP5) during conditioning with the tone (Iordanova, Good, & Honey, 2011).

Figure 4.2 summarizes the results of the test in which the rats were placed in contexts A and B in the morning and afternoon. The scores shown are freezing ratios in which the amount of freezing in context A is expressed as a proportion of freezing in both contexts A and B at a given time of day. Using this measure, scores above 0.50 in the morning and below 0.50 in the afternoon mean that rats are showing sensory preconditioning: They are more fearful in context A than in context B in the morning and the reverse in the afternoon. The rats who had received infusions of artificial cerebrospinal fluid (aCSF) during the fear-conditioning stage (left and center panels of Figure 4.2) showed the pattern of scores that is the signature of sensory preconditioning effect, but those who had received infusions of AP5 into the dorsal hippocampus immediately

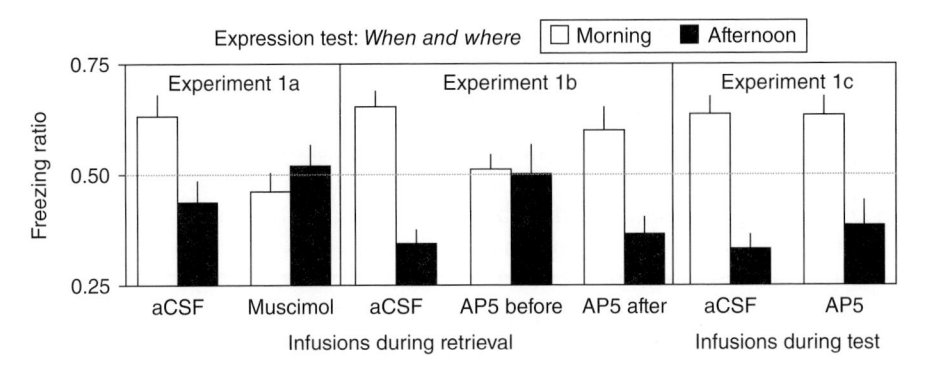

Figure 4.2 Role of the hippocampus in retrieval-mediated learning: mean freezing ratios (+SEM) during the test with the context + time of day configurations. Scores >0.50 in the morning, and scores <0.50 in the afternoon, indicate that retrieval-mediated learning has taken place and is evident at test. The hippocampus was infused with aCSF, muscimol, or AP5 (Experiments 1a and 1b) immediately before (or sometime after) conditioning with the tone and click; or aCSF or AP5 were infused during the test (Experiment 1c). Reproduced from: Iordanova, M. D., Good, M., & Honey, R. C. (2011). Retrieval-mediated learning involving episodes requires synaptic plasticity in the hippocampus. *Journal of Neuroscience, 31*, 7156–7162.

before (but not after) the fear-conditioning stage (or of muscimol, which blocks synaptic transmission) did not. In keeping with the view that AP5 infusions affected retrieval-mediated learning, they had no effect when administered during the test itself (right-hand panel of Figure 4.2). Importantly, AP5 had no effect on differential conditioning to the auditory stimuli that were presented during the fear-conditioning stage (see also Wheeler, Chang, & Holland, 2013).[1]

Our preferred interpretation of the findings outlined in the previous paragraph – that mediated conditioning involving the context + time of day configurations is disrupted, but direct conditioning is not – has received further support from a recent unpublished study. In this study, rats with hippocampal lesions were unimpaired in learning that the context + time of day configurations signaled the presence or absence of a motivationally significant outcome (in this case, food; Dumigan, Lin, Good, & Honey, 2016). That is, rats with dorsal lesions of the hippocampus were capable of directly learning about the same configurations that they fail to learn about through a process of mediated learning in a sensory preconditioning procedure (see also Coutureau *et al.*, 2002).

The evidence outlined in preceding two sections provides a prima facie case for our principal theoretical claim, that learning about stimuli that are present and those that are not rely on separable acquisition processes. Thus, the conditioned response gained through direct conditioning is independent of, and differs in nature from, that established by mediated learning; and disrupting hippocampal function has an effect on mediated learning, but not direct conditioning.[2] The important supplementary theoretical claim, that this separation of learning processes reflects the fact that stimuli in the immediate environment activate one memory and those that are not activate a different memory, requires theoretical elaboration and further empirical analysis. However, next we consider another obvious example where stimuli that are not present enter into excitatory associations: trace conditioning. It transpires that this example is relevant to meeting both of the requirements just identified.

Trace Conditioning As Mediated Learning

The influence of temporal contiguity on conditioning was described by Pavlov (1927), and later captured in the adage *What fires together wires together*. For the mnemonic or neural processes activated by different stimuli to become linked to one another in the brain, it is critical that they occur close together in time (Hebb, 1943; Wagner, 1981, 2003). We have already argued that these processes need not be activated by the stimuli themselves – they can be associatively activated. Trace conditioning represents another example in which learning occurs in spite of the fact that the stimulus itself is not, or no longer, present. While it is usual to focus on the fact that a lack of temporal contiguity disrupts the acquisition of conditioned responding, trace conditioning can still result in appreciable levels of responding. As we will now see, recent research challenges our understanding of the role of temporal contiguity in learning: from behavioral processes, through computational models to brain mechanisms. This research involves the influence of a trace interval during the second stage of a sensory preconditioning procedure.

The design used by Lin *et al.* (Experiment 1, 2013; see also Lin & Honey, 2011) is summarized in the middle panel of Table 4.1. Rats were first preexposed to two 10-s compounds (AX and BY), each constructed from one visual and one auditory stimulus. They then received conditioning trials in which the offset of X alone was followed by shock after a trace of 40 s (and nonreinforced trials with Y; Group Trace) or trials where X was immediately followed by shock (and nonreinforced trials with Y; Group Immediate). During the subsequent test, the level of conditioned responding to AX, BX, AY, and BY was assessed. In Group Trace, there was less activity (i.e., more fear) during compounds containing A (AX and AY) than in those containing B (BX and BY), and there were no marked differences between compounds containing X and Y. This effect replicates those described in a previous section using the flavor-aversion compound test procedure (Ward-Robinson *et al.*, 2005; see also Rescorla & Freberg, 1978). In contrast, Group Immediate showed greater fear to compounds containing X than those containing Y, but there was no evidence of sensory preconditioning (see Figure 4.3).

The pattern of results just described is reliable, having also been observed in a related appetitive conditioning procedure, with food in place of shock (see Lin & Honey, 2011); and it is theoretically challenging: It violates the principle of temporal contiguity that dominates analyses of associative learning, from artificial neural networks, identified with learning theory and connectionism, to synaptic plasticity. However, as already mentioned, it is consistent with the fact that flavor-aversion procedures, which themselves involve a long trace interval, produce a particularly marked sensory preconditioning effect. One plausible interpretation of this pattern of results that is consistent with the general thrust of this chapter relies on the idea that the process of retrieval-mediated learning involving the memory of A is especially effective when there is a trace interval between X and the unconditioned stimulus (e.g., shock): The memory of A, which is associatively retrieved by X, will be more effectively linked to the memory of shock when there is a trace interval between X and shock than when there is no interval. This interpretation was considered in some detail by Ward-Robinson and Hall (1996) in the context of their own results concerning (so-called) backward conditioning. But new evidence suggests that we must look elsewhere for a more coherent interpretation. For example, we have conducted a study of second-order conditioning, which simply involves reversing the order of the first two stages of a sensory

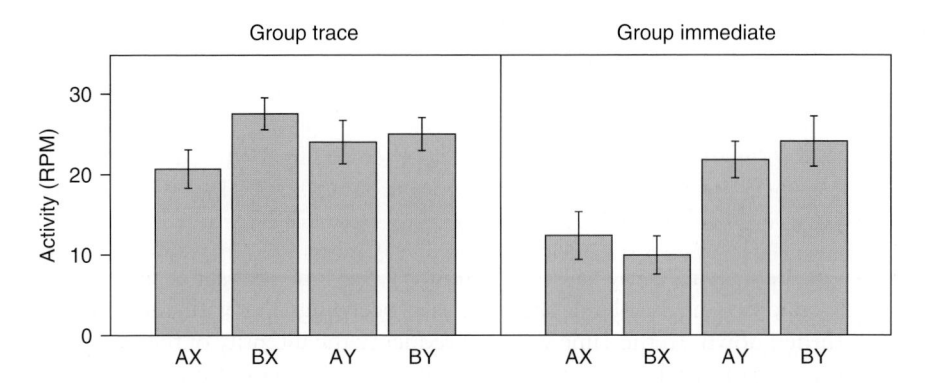

Figure 4.3 Sensory preconditioning in fear-conditioning procedures. Mean activity levels (in responses per minute, RPM; ±SEM) during the test compounds: AX, BX, AY, and BY. Rats had received exposure to AX and BY, prior to either trials where X was followed by shock after a trace interval (and Y was not; left-hand panel) or trials on which X was immediately followed by shock (and Y was not; right-hand panel). Reproduced from: Lin, T. E., Dumigan, N. M., Dwyer, D. M., Good, M. A., & Honey, R. C. (2013). Assessing the encoding specificity of associations with sensory preconditioning procedures. *Journal of Experimental Psychology: Animal Behavior Processes, 39,* 67–75.

preconditioning procedure: After X was paired with food, rats then received A–X pairings and the development of second-order conditioned responding to A was monitored (Lin & Honey, 2011). Over the course of the second stage, stimulus A provoked more second-order responding if conditioned responding to X had been established using a trace conditioning procedure than a standard conditioning procedure (i.e., one without a trace interval). There is no obvious reason to think that either (1) X's ability to activate a memory of A (and A to be linked to a memory of food) or (2) A's ability to activate a memory of X (and then food) should have been enhanced by the trace conditioning procedure. A coherent explanation of the results from sensory preconditioning and second-order conditioning requires one appeal to some other feature of the trace conditioning procedure.

If the influence of a trace interval on sensory preconditioning is not to be explained in terms of enhanced mediated conditioning of the associatively evoked memory of A (cf. Ward-Robinson & Hall, 1996), how should it be explained? Any explanation will need to be consistent both with the evidence presented in the preceding sections and with standard theoretical treatments of conditioning, which have proven explanatory currency. Certainly, the dissociation between the effect of a trace interval on simple Pavlovian conditioning and sensory preconditioning reinforces the idea that these phenomena rely on different mnemonic processes, but how so?

Theoretical Elaboration

We argue that the central problem that standard models of associative learning face with our recent results (i.e., Lin & Honey, 2011; Lin *et al.*, 2013; see also Ward-Robinson & Hall, 1996) stems from their analysis of the "What fires" component of "What fires together wires together." While some of these theoretical treatments suppose that the presentation of a stimulus activates a short-term cascade of mnemonic activity (e.g., Wagner, 1981, 2003), they share the assumption that the stored or encoded form of the memories, which become more or less strongly linked, are the same irrespective of the temporal relationship between them (see Chapter 15). They also assume a simple correspondence between the memory that is activated by the presentation of a stimulus and the memory that is associatively retrieved of the same stimulus.[3] So, to caricature theoretical treatments of this type: Varying the interval between the to-be-connected events (e.g., the tone and food or the tone and shock) is held to allow the memory of the tone to decay, to some extent, by the time that shock is delivered. It is "as if" conditioning involving the tone is proceeding, but with the intensity or volume turned down. In the same way that reducing the intensity of the tone will disrupt learning, so too will the introduction of a trace interval during conditioning. During the sensory preconditioning test, presentations of light will retrieve the memory of the tone; but because the tone is less likely to activate a memory of food after trace conditioning, the light should elicit less responding. This is clearly the opposite pattern to that observed in our studies, hence the need to develop an alternative theoretical analysis. Indeed, even models of animal learning in which temporal information plays an independent role (e.g., Gallistel & Gibbon, 2000; Miller & Barnet, 1993) fail to predict the pattern of results that we observed.

We have proposed an overarching theoretical analysis that attempts to capture the difference between direct learning and mediated learning. Our first assumption is that the memory that is immediately activated by the presentation of a stimulus (we will call M1) is *qualitatively* different from the memory that becomes active during the trace period after the same stimulus (M2; see also Solomon & Corbit, 1974). This assumption has obvious consequences for our appreciation of what is learned during standard conditioning and trace conditioning: While the M1 of X will become linked to the memory of food when there is no trace interval between the X and food, the introduction of a trace interval between the two will mean that the M2 is more likely to be linked to the memory of food during trace conditioning (Lin & Honey, 2011; Lin *et al.*, 2013). The key to explaining the fact that trace conditioning results in more marked sensory preconditioning effect than does standard conditioning is the assumption that the memory of X that is associatively provoked by A (during the test) is its M2 memory rather than its M1 memory (cf. Wagner, 1981). This assumption means that when the presentation of A provokes the M2 memory of X during the sensory preconditioning test, it will result in more conditioned behavior after a trace conditioning procedure than after standard conditioning: After trace conditioning, the light will provoke the M2 memory of the tone, and it was this memory that was linked to food as a consequence of this conditioning procedure. After standard conditioning, the light will again provoke the M2 memory of the tone, but in this case it was the M1 memory of the tone that had been linked to food. Hence, trace conditioning will paradoxically produce a more marked sensory preconditioning effect than will standard conditioning, in spite of the fact that direct conditioning is more effective when there is no trace interval. This analysis also predicts that second-order conditioning will proceed more rapidly after trace conditioning than standard conditioning: Briefly, the trace conditioning procedure, unlike the standard procedure, will result in the M2 memory of the tone becoming linked to food, and the light-tone pairings will result in the light coming to evoke the M2 memory of the tone.

We have interpreted the effects of a trace interval on both sensory preconditioning and second-order conditioning without the need to appeal to a process of (retrieval-) mediated conditioning as it is ordinarily construed (cf. Ward-Robinson & Hall, 1996). And yet our analysis predicts that mediated conditioning involving the associatively evoked (M2) memories should both occur and be dissociable from direct conditioning involving directly activated (M1) memories. In fact, our new analysis makes clear predictions about the test conditions that should be most conducive to revealing such retrieval-mediated learning.

Further Empirical Analysis

The idea that the associatively retrieved memory of a stimulus is equivalent to the trace memory of the same stimulus (here called M2) has its theoretical roots in Wagner's (1981, 2003) influential SOP model of animal memory. This analysis was based, in part, on the fact that conditioned stimuli can provoke responses that resemble those generated by the "aftereffect" of a motivationally significant event: For example, the presentation of a brief footshock to a rat generates a period of hyperactivity followed by hypoactivity, but the conditioned response to a stimulus that has predicted shock is hypoactivity (or freezing) not hyperactivity (cf. Solomon & Corbit, 1974). The new idea that we have developed is that the directly activated M1 memories and the indirectly activated M2 memories of a given stimulus become (part of) what is encoded in the association when the interval between one stimulus and another is changed.[4]

If M2 memories can gain associative strength during trace conditioning, then they should also do so when associatively provoked. It will be remembered that the results from the flavor-aversion procedure, when rats showed a greater reluctance to consume AX than BX, seemed to provide support for this suggestion (e.g., Ward-Robinson *et al.*, 2001). However, we now know that this effect might not have reflected differences in the ability of A and B to directly activate a memory of illness (as a result of retrieval-mediated learning), but rather reflected a difference in the ability of A and B to activate the M2 memory of X. So, how might we reveal learning about the associatively activated (M2) memory of A during a sensory preconditioning procedure? One obvious strategy that we have adopted is to examine test performance during the trace period that immediately follows A. It is during this period that any associatively mediated learning involving the M2 memory of A is predicted to be most evident. Lin *et al.* (Experiment 3, 2013; see also Lin & Honey, 2010) provided direct support for this prediction.

The experimental design that Lin *et al.* used is summarized in the lower panel of Table 4.1. Again, the rats first received exposure to two audio-visual compounds. In fact, these compounds were presented either simultaneously (AX and BX) or successively (A → X and B → Y) – a manipulation that had little effect on the outcome of the final test and is ignored henceforth. After this first stage of training, rats received conditioning trials in which the offset of X was *immediately* followed by shock, and the offset of Y was not. As we have already seen in Figure 4.3, this conditioning procedure results in AX and BX provoking similar levels of fear during the test (Experiment 1, Lin *et al.*, 2013). However, this is unlikely to be the most sensitive test

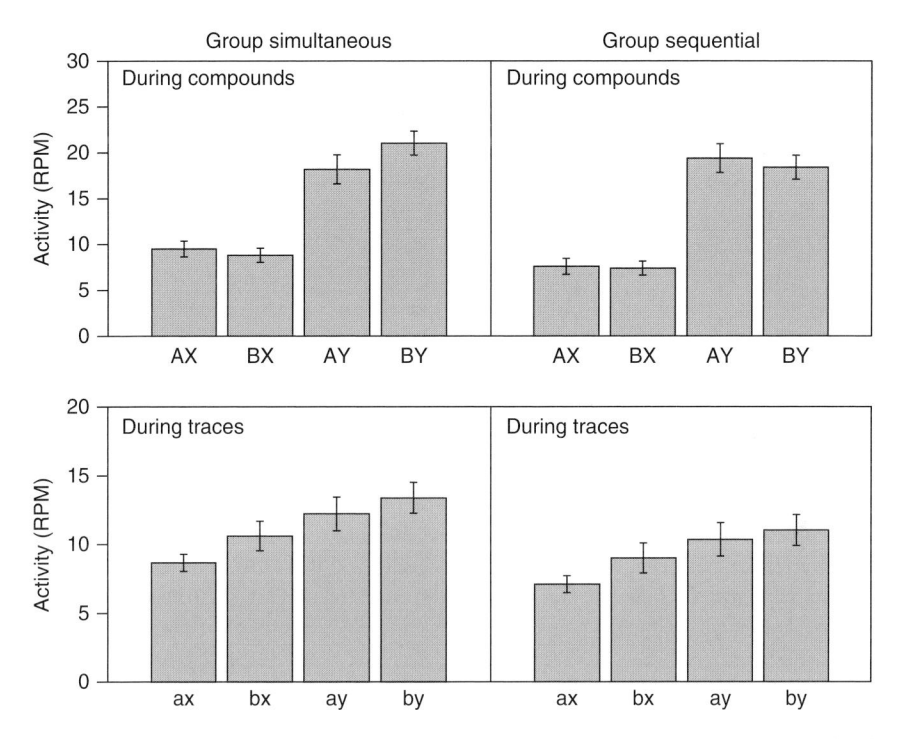

Figure 4.4 Sensory preconditioning in fear-conditioning procedures. Mean activity levels (in responses per minute, RPM; ±SEM) during the test compounds (AX, BX, AY, and BY; upper panel), and during the trace periods that immediately followed these compounds (lower panel). Rats had received exposure to either simultaneous compounds (i.e., AX and BY) or sequential compounds (i.e., A → X and B → Y), prior to trials on which X was immediately followed by shock (and Y was not; ibid.).

of whether X → shock trials allowed the M2 memory of A to become linked to shock, because A will at least initially provoke its M1 memory. Accordingly, we contrasted the rats' behavior during the test compounds (AX, BX, AY, and BY) with their behavior immediately after these compounds, during the traces of the test compounds (i.e., ax, bx, ay, and by). Our prediction was that there should be more fear (i.e., less activity) during AX and BX than AY and BY, because X was paired with shock, and Y was not; and there should be more fear during the traces of the compounds that included A (ax and ay) than during the traces of the compounds that included B (bx and by).

Inspection of Figure 4.4 reveals a striking confirmation of these predictions. The upper panels show that performance during the test compounds was largely determined by the presence of X or Y, with less activity (i.e., more fear) during AX and BX than during AY and BY, and little effect of A and B. In contrast, inspection of the lower panels shows that there was consistently less activity (i.e., more fear) during the traces involving a than the corresponding traces involving b (i.e., ax than bx, and ay than by), with the presence of the x and y traces having a much less marked effect than the presence of X and Y. These results show that an associatively retrieved memory of a stimulus can enter into association with shock, and this fact is most readily observed by examining performance during the trace of that stimulus.

Concluding Comments and Integration

We have considered evidence concerning the nuts and bolts of the process of associative learning: evidence that elucidates the theoretical entities that enter into the associative process and the brain mechanisms that underpin this process. The results originally reported by Lin and colleagues are especially noteworthy with respect to our understanding of the conditions under which learning occurs and the content or nature of such learning: They suggest that the decayed trace of a recently presented stimulus can become associated with an outcome, and this association can be revealed by associatively provoking the memory of that stimulus at test; and similarly, the associatively evoked memory of a stimulus can be linked with an outcome, and this association can be revealed by monitoring performance during the trace of that stimulus (see Lin et al., 2013; see also Lin & Honey, 2010, 2011). This symmetry suggests that the trace of a stimulus and an associatively activated memory of the same stimulus are, at least, related. We have given these memories a common label, M2, to both reflect this relatedness and contrast them with a directly activated memory of the same stimulus, which we have labeled M1. Our results show that M1 and M2 memories of the same stimulus can simultaneously possess different associative properties. The analysis of the neural mechanisms that underpin these associative processes, undertaken by Iordanova and colleagues, suggests that retrieval-mediated or M2 learning involving configurations is based upon NMDA synaptic plasticity in the hippocampus, but that M1 learning is not (Iordanova et al., 2009, 2011). The research upon which we have based our analysis comes from laboratory studies of rodents, and it is appropriate to consider whether there are parallels to be drawn with research undertaken with humans. In fact, there is an intriguing parallel between our evidence from rodents (in particular, Iordanova et al., 2011; Lin et al., 2013) and the results from a recent study that examined the neural correlates of sensory preconditioning using fMRI in humans (Wimmer & Shohamy, 2012). In this study, the sensory preconditioning effect that was observed at test correlated with an index of hippocampal activity during the second stage of training, where we suppose M2 learning is taking place, but not with hippocampal activity during the first stage of training or during the test itself (see also Zeithamova, Dominick, & Preston, 2012). The potential for this type of integration and translation in the study of *higher nervous activity (behavior)* was anticipated a century ago, and it is fitting that the procedures that have enabled it originate in the pioneering analysis of conditioning that was undertaken by Pavlov.

Acknowledgments

We should like to thank Dominic Dwyer for his incisive comments on this chapter. The research reported in this article, involving the authors, was supported by grants from the BBSRC UK and Postgraduate Studentships awarded by the School of Psychology at Cardiff University to T. E. Lin and N. M. Dumigan. Correspondence concerning this article should be addressed to: R. C. Honey, School of Psychology, Cardiff University, Tower Building, Park Place, Cardiff CF10 3AT, UK.

Notes

1. It should be noted that these manipulations had no effect on test performance in procedures that could be operationally defined as elemental. The reader is directed to a recent review for a detailed analysis of this elemental/configural dissociation (Honey, Iordanova, & Good, 2014); but for the present purposes, it is interesting to highlight the fact that the elemental procedure, unlike the configural procedure, allowed sensory preconditioning to be based on a simple associative chain.
2. The fact that a basic sensory preconditioning effect in flavor-aversion learning is not affected by lesions of the dorsal hippocampus (Ward-Robinson et al., 2001) suggests, in combination with the results described above, that test performance can be supported by a simple associative chain in lesioned rats when the procedure allows this possibility.
3. Albeit Wagner (1981) assumed that the transient form of the retrieved memory depends on whether they are directly activated or associatively activated.
4. It is worth noting that this distinction, between M1 and M2 memories, can be implemented within a neural network model with two types of hidden-layer units (corresponding to M1 and M2) with quite different activation profiles (see Grand & Honey, 2008; Honey & Grand, 2011), which result in M1 becoming active upon presentation of a stimulus, and M2 being more likely become active during the trace of that stimulus.

References

Aggleton, J. P., & Brown, M. W. (1999). Episodic memory, amnesia and the hippocampal–anterior thalamic axis. *Behavioral and Brain Sciences, 22*, 425–444.

Brogden, W. J. (1939). Sensory pre-conditioning. *Journal of Experimental Psychology, 25*, 323–332.

Coutureau, E., Killcross, A. S., Good, M., Marshall, V. J., Ward-Robinson, J., & Honey, R. C. (2002). Acquired equivalence and distinctiveness of cues: II. Neural manipulations and their implications. *Journal of Experimental Psychology: Animal Behavior Processes, 28*, 388–396.

Dickinson, A. (1980). *Contemporary animal learning theory*. Cambridge, UK: Cambridge University Press.

Dumigan, N., Lin, T. E., Good, M., & Honey, R. C. (2016). Acquisition of configual *(what-where-when)* discriminations in rats with lesions of the hippocampus. Manuscript in preparation.

Dwyer, D. M. (2012). Licking and liking: The assessment of hedonic responses in rodents. *Quarterly Journal of Experimental Psychology, 65*, 371–394.

Dwyer, D. M., Burgess, K. V., & Honey, R. C. (2012). Avoidance but not aversion following sensory-preconditioning with flavors: A challenge to stimulus substitution. *Journal of Experimental Psychology: Animal Behavior Processes, 38*, 359–368.

Dwyer, D. M., Mackintosh, N. J., & Boakes, R. A. (1998). Simultaneous activation of the representations of absent cues results in the formation of an excitatory association between them. *Journal of Experimental Psychology: Animal Behavior Processes, 24*, 163–171.

Fudim, O. K. (1978). Sensory preconditioning of flavors with a formalin-produced sodium need. *Journal of Experimental Psychology: Animal Behavior Processes, 3*, 276–285.

Gallistel, C. R., & Gibbon, J. (2000). Time, rate and conditioning. *Psychological Review, 107*, 289–344.

Grand, C. S., & Honey, R. C. (2008). Solving XOR. *Journal of Experimental Psychology: Animal Behavior Processes, 34*, 486–493.

Hall, G. (1996). Learning about associatively activated stimulus representations: Implications for acquired equivalence and perceptual learning. *Animal Learning & Behavior, 24*, 233–255.

Hebb, D. O. (1943). *Organization of behavior.* New York, NY: Wiley.

Holland, P. C. (1981). Acquisition of representation-mediated conditioned food aversions, *Learning and Motivation, 12*, 1–18.

Holland, P. C. (1983). Representation-mediated overshadowing and potentiation of conditioned aversions. *Journal of Experimental Psychology: Animal Behavior Processes, 9*, 1–13.

Holland, P. C. (1990). Event representation in Pavlovian conditioning: Image and action. *Cognition, 37*, 105–131.

Holland, P. C., & Forbes, D. T. (1982). Representation-mediated extinction of conditioned flavor aversions. *Learning and Motivation, 13*, 454–471.

Honey, R. C., & Grand, C. S. (2011). Application of connectionist analyses to animal learning: Interactions between perceptual organization and associative processes. In E. Alonso & E. Mondragon (Eds.), *Computational neuroscience for advancing artificial intelligence: models, methods and applications* (pp. 1–14). Hershey, PA: IGI Global.

Honey, R. C., Iordanova, M. D., & Good, M. (2014). Associative structures in animal learning: Dissociating elemental and configural processes. *Neurobiology of Learning and Memory 108*, 96–103.

Iordanova, M. D., Burnett, D, Good, M., & Honey, R. C. (2011). Pattern memory involves both elemental and configural processes: Evidence from the effects of hippocampal lesions. *Behavioral Neuroscience, 125*, 567–577.

Iordanova, M., Burnett, D., Aggleton, J. P., Good, M., & Honey, R. C. (2009). The role of the hippocampus in mnemonic integration and retrieval: Complementary evidence from lesion and inactivation studies. *European Journal of Neuroscience, 30*, 2177–2189.

Iordanova, M. D., Good, M., & Honey, R. C. (2008). Configural learning without reinforcement: Integrated memories for what, where and when. *Quarterly Journal of Experimental Psychology, 61*, 1785–1792.

Iordanova, M. D., Good, M., & Honey, R. C. (2011). Retrieval-mediated learning involving episodes requires synaptic plasticity in the hippocampus. *Journal of Neuroscience, 31*, 7156–7162.

Jones, J. L., Esber, G. R., McDannald, M. A., Gruber, A. J., Hernandez, A., Mirenzi, A., & Schoenbaum, G. (2012). Orbitofrontal cortex supports behavior and learning using inferred but not cached values. *Science, 338*, 953–956.

Lin, T. E., & Honey, R. C. (2010). Analysis of the content of configural representations: The role of associatively evoked and trace memories. *Journal of Experimental Psychology: Animal Behavior Processes, 36*, 501–505.

Lin, T. E., & Honey, R. C. (2011). Encoding specific associative memory: Evidence from behavioral and neural manipulations. *Journal of Experimental Psychology: Animal Behavior Processes, 37*, 317–329.

Lin, T. E., Dumigan, N. M., Dwyer, D. M., Good, M. A., & Honey, R. C. (2013). Assessing the encoding specificity of associations with sensory preconditioning procedures. *Journal of Experimental Psychology: Animal Behavior Processes, 39*, 67–75.

Mackintosh, N. J. (1974). *The psychology of animal learning.* London, UK: Academic Press.

Mackintosh, N. J. (1983). *Conditioning and associative learning.* Cambridge, UK: Cambridge University Press.

Mackintosh, N. J., & Honig, W. K. (1969). *Fundamental issues in associative learning.* Halifax: Dalhousie University Press.

Miller, R. R., & Barnet, R. C. (1993). The role of time in elementary associations. *Current Directions in Psychological Science, 2*, 106–111.

Pavlov, I. P. (1928). *Lectures on conditioned reflexes: twenty-five years of objective study of the higher nervous activity (behaviour) of animals.* New York, NY: International.

Pavlov, I. P. (1941). The conditioned reflex. In *Lectures on conditioned reflexes: conditioned reflexes and psychiatry* (Vol. 2, p. 171). London, UK: Lawrence & Wishart.

Pavlov, I. P. (1927). *Conditioned reflexes.* London, UK: Oxford University Press.

Rescorla, R. A., & Cunningham, C. L. (1978). Within-compound flavor associations. *Journal of Experimental Psychology: Animal Behavior Processes, 4,* 267–275.

Rescorla, R. A., & Freberg, L. (1978). The extinction of within-compound flavor associations. *Learning and Motivation, 9,* 411–424.

Rescorla, R. A., & Wagner, A. R. (1972). A theory of Pavlovian conditioning: Variations in the effectiveness of reinforcement and nonreinforcement. In A. H. Black & W. F. Prokasy (Eds.), *Classical conditioning II: current research and theory* (pp. 64–99). New York, NY: Appleton-Century-Crofts.

Rizley, R. C., & Rescorla, R. A. (1972). Associations in second-order conditioning and sensory preconditioning. *Journal of Comparative and Physiological Psychology, 81,* 1–11.

Rudy, J. W., & Sutherland, R. J. (1989). The hippocampal formation is necessary for rats to learn and remember configural discriminations. *Behavioural Brain Research, 34,* 97–109.

Solomon, R. L., & Corbit, J. D. (1974). An opponent-process theory of motivation: I. Temporal dynamics of affect. *Psychological Review, 81,* 119–145.

Tulving, E. (2002). Episodic memory: From mind to brain. *Annual Review of Psychology, 53,* 1–25.

Wagner, A. R. (1981). SOP: A model of automatic memory processing in animal behavior. In N. E. Spear & R. R. Miller (Eds.), *Information processing in animals: Memory mechanisms* (pp. 5–47). Hillsdale, NJ: Erlbaum.

Wagner, A. R. (2003). Context-sensitive elemental theory. *Quarterly Journal of Experimental Psychology, 23B,* 7–29.

Ward-Robinson, J., & Hall, G. (1996). Backward sensory preconditioning. *Journal of Experimental Psychology: Animal Behavior Processes, 22,* 395–404.

Ward-Robinson, J., Coutureau, E., Good, M., Honey, R. C., Killcross, A. S., & Oswald, C. J. P. (2001). Excitotoxic lesions of the hippocampus leaves sensory preconditioning intact: Implications for models of hippocampal function. *Behavioral Neuroscience, 115,* 1357–1362.

Ward-Robinson, J., Coutureau, E., Honey, R. C., & Killcross, A. S. (2005). Excitotoxic lesions of the entorhinal cortex leave gustatory within-event learning intact. *Behavioral Neuroscience, 119,* 1131–1135.

Warren, H. C. (1921). *A history of the association psychology.* London, UK: Constable and Co.

Wheeler, D. S., Chang, S. E., & Holland, P. C. (2013). Odor-mediated taste learning requires dorsal hippocampus, but not basolateral amygdala activity. *Neurobiology of Learning and Memory, 101,* 1–7.

Wimmer, G. E., & Shohamy, D. (2012). Preference by association: How memory mechanisms in the hippocampus bias decisions. *Science, 338,* 270–273.

Zeithamova, D., Dominick, A. L., & Preston, A. R. (2012). Hippocampal and ventral medial prefrontal activation during retrieval-mediated learning supports novel inference. *Neuron, 75,* 168–179.

5

Neural Substrates of Learning and Attentive Processes

David N. George

Summary

Two prominent theories concerning role of attention in associative learning, advanced by Mackintosh (1975) and Pearce and Hall (1980), have proposed rather different relationships between the reliability with which a cue signals an outcome and the amount of attention that the cue will receive. The former model suggested that cues that are highly predictive of a salient outcome will attract attention, whereas the latter suggested that attention will be directed toward cues that are uncertain predictors. This chapter reviews research on the neural correlates of several behavioral effects predicted by each model and considers what this research can tell us about the psychological processes involved in attention.

Preamble

A wide variety of behavioral phenomena have been attributed to the influence of attention on learning. Despite the diversity of these effects, formal models of attention in associative learning tend to make the same simple assumption that the amount of attention paid to a stimulus affects its ability to enter into associations with other stimuli or events. For four decades, research in this area has been dominated by two attentional theories published by Mackintosh (1975) and by Pearce and Hall (1980; see Chapter 6). These theories differ not so much in what they say about the relation between attention and learning, but rather in the mechanisms that determine how much attention is paid to a stimulus. Mackintosh proposed that animals will attend to stimuli that have been established as good predictors of what follows them. Pearce and Hall, however, suggested that animals will attend a stimulus when it is uncertain what will follow it.

There is evidence in support of both of these theories (see, for example, Pearce & Mackintosh, 2010), and the neural bases of each have been the subject of considerable investigation. Much of this work has been summarized in previous reviews

---

The Wiley Handbook on the Cognitive Neuroscience of Learning, First Edition.
Edited by Robin A. Murphy and Robert C. Honey.
© 2016 John Wiley & Sons, Ltd. Published 2016 by John Wiley & Sons, Ltd.

(e.g., George, Duffaud, & Killcross, 2010; Hampshire & Owen, 2010; Robbins, 2007). In this chapter, I highlight a number of neuroscientific studies that have helped to elucidate the complexity of the psychological mechanisms of attention in associative learning.

Effects of Predictiveness

Attentional set shifting

In an early and now classic demonstration of acquired distinctiveness, Lawrence (1949) showed that learning in one task can facilitate learning in another. He trained rats on a series of discrimination tasks in which one of several stimulus dimensions signaled the location of a food reward. When the same stimulus dimension was relevant in each successive task, learning was more rapid than when the rats had to learn about a previously irrelevant or novel dimension. The full design of Lawrence's experiment was rather complex, but its general findings may be appreciated by considering the treatment received by just two of his 18 groups of animals, shown in Figure 5.1. In the first stage of the experiment, the rats were trained on a simultaneous discrimination in an apparatus consisting of two parallel runways. For the first group of rats, one of the runways was lined with white card, whereas the other runway was lined with black card. The food reward was located at the end of one of the runways, and the rats simply had to learn to choose the correct runway on each trial. For these rats, the location of the food was reliably signaled by the brightness of the runways (for some animals, the food was always in the black runway, whereas for other animals, it was always in the white runway). The second group of animals were trained in the same apparatus, but for them both runways were lined with gray card. Attached to the floor of one runway was a fine wire mesh, and to the floor of the other runway was attached a coarse wire mesh (a mesh of intermediate texture was attached to the floor of each runway for animals in the first group). The texture of the floor signaled the location of the food reward for the second group.

In the second stage of the experiment, the two groups of rats were both trained on the same successive discrimination task. On each trial, they were placed in the start box of a T-maze, which was painted either uniformly white or uniformly black. The texture of the floor was varied from trial to trial by the attachment of either coarse or fine wire mesh. Again, the rats simply had to learn to make an appropriate response to locate a food reward in one or other arm of the maze. For the two groups of animals that we are considering, the brightness of the maze signaled the location of the food. A particular rat may have had to learn to choose the right goal arm when the maze was black but the left goal arm when the maze was white. The texture of the floor was completely unrelated to the location of the food. Lawrence found that the animals that had learned about brightness in the first stage of the experiment learned the successive discrimination more rapidly than the animals that had learned about texture in the first stage. Learning that particular features of the environment reliably predicted reward in one situation facilitated subsequent discrimination learning involving those features in a different situation.

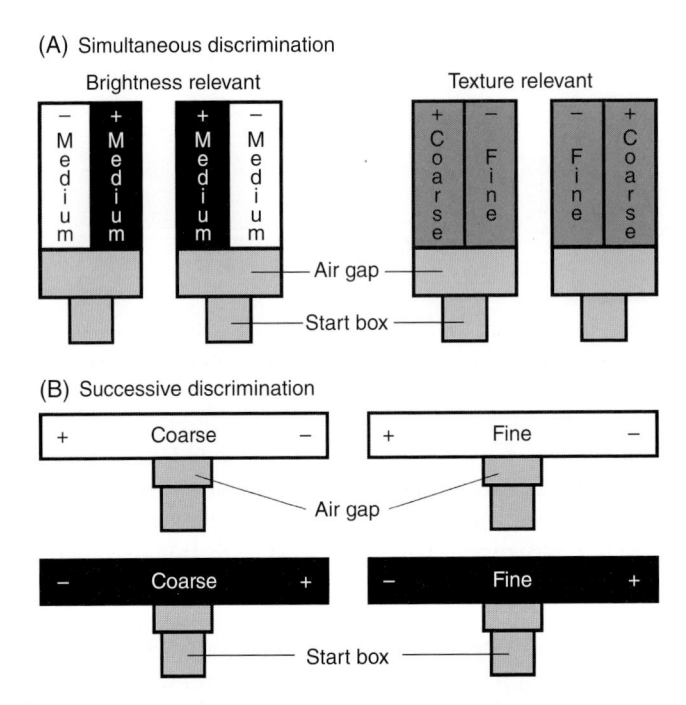

Figure 5.1 Training received by two groups of rats in Lawrence's (1949) acquired distinctiveness experiment. Animals were first trained on a simultaneous discrimination (A) where either runway brightness or floor texture signaled the location of a food reward (+). All animals were then transferred to a successive discrimination task where brightness was relevant (B).

Lawrence's (1950) favored explanation of the acquired distinctiveness effect was that stimuli that an animal had learned were relevant would enter more strongly into associations than those that were not. That is, learning may affect the *associability* of a stimulus. This principle formed the basis of models of attentional learning in the following quarter century. Many of these models (e.g., Lovejoy, 1968; Sutherland & Mackintosh, 1971; Trabasso & Bower, 1968; Zeaman & House, 1963) incorporated some notion of limited capacity and the inverse hypothesis – that increases in attention to some stimuli must be accompanied by a reduction in attention to other stimuli. The model that has proved to be the most enduring of this era was, however, one that made no recourse to the inverse hypothesis. Mackintosh's (1975) model assumes that, following a conditioning event, the associative strength of stimulus A will be updated according to Equation 1, where V_A is the current associative strength of the stimulus, α_A is its associability, θ is a learning rate parameter, and λ is the maximum associative strength supported by the trial outcome:

$$\Delta V_A = \alpha_A \theta (\lambda - V_A) \tag{5.1}$$

Following a conditioning trial, the associability of a stimulus may also be updated using the rules shown in Equations 2a and 2b, where V_X is the sum of the associative strengths of all other stimuli present.

$$\alpha_A \text{ is positive if } |\lambda - V_A| < |\lambda - V_X| \quad (5.2a)$$

$$\alpha_A \text{ is negative if } |\lambda - V_A| \geq |\lambda - V_X| \quad (5.2b)$$

Hence, if a stimulus predicts the outcome better than all other available stimuli combined, then its associability will increase, whereas if it predicts the outcome less well than all other stimuli, its associability will decrease.

It is possible to come up with alternative explanations of Lawrence's (1949) results. Siegel (1967, 1969), for example, suggested that the behavior could be understood in terms of response strategies. Other behavioral effects cited in support of theories of attention in associative learning – transfer along a continuum (also known as the easy-to-hard effect, e.g., Lawrence, 1952; Pavlov, 1927) and the overtraining reversal effect (e.g., Reid, 1953) – provide similarly equivocal evidence (see Mackintosh, 1974, for a discussion). It is much more difficult to dismiss an attentional explanation for the intradimensional–extradimensional (ID–ED) shift effect. The design of an ID–ED shift experiment is shown in Table 5.1. The principle is similar to that of Lawrence's (1949) experiment. Two groups of animals are first trained on a discrimination task where either one or another stimulus dimension is relevant, before both are trained on a task in which just one of those dimensions is relevant. For Group ID, the same dimension is relevant in both stages, whereas for Group ED the dimension that is relevant in Stage 2 was irrelevant in Stage 1 (and vice versa). Faster learning in Stage 2 by Group ID than by Group ED has been observed in numerous species including rats (e.g., Shepp & Eimas, 1964); pigeons (e.g., George & Pearce, 1999; Mackintosh & Little, 1969), monkeys (e.g., Dias, Robbins, & Roberts, 1996a, 1996b; Shepp & Schrier, 1969), honeybees (Klosterhalfen, Fischer, & Bitterman, 1978), and humans (e.g., Eimas, 1966; Wolff, 1967). The ID–ED shift effect is difficult to explain in terms of simple generalization of associative strength between old and new signals for reward because very different stimuli are often employed in the two stages of the experiment. The stimuli, for example, that Mackintosh and Little (1969) used were red or yellow lines that were horizontal or vertical in the first stage of the experiment, and green or blue lines oriented at 45 or 135° to vertical in the second stage. Indeed, Mackintosh (1974, p. 597) wrote that "Perhaps the best evidence that transfer between discrimination problems may be based partly on increases in attention to relevant dimensions and decreases in attention to irrelevant dimensions, is provided by [the ID–ED shift effect]."

Table 5.1 Design of an ID–ED shift experiment.

	Stage 1	*Stage 2 (both groups)*
Group ID	Aw+ BwØ Ax+ BxØ	Cy+ DyØ
Group ED	aW+ aXØ bW+ bXØ	Cz+ DzØ

Note. A–D are stimuli belonging to one stimulus dimension. W–Z are stimuli belonging to a second dimension. + indicates that a stimulus compound signals food; Ø indicates that it does not. Stimuli shown in upper-case letters are relevant to the solution of the discrimination, those shown in lower case are irrelevant.

Neural correlates of attentional set

Prefrontal cortex Around the same time that Lawrence was conducting his experiments on acquired distinctiveness, Berg – inspired by a body of work that suggested that certain patient groups displayed impairments in flexible, or abstract, behavior (e.g., Goldstein & Scheerer, 1941; Weigl, 1941) – developed the Wisconsin Card Sorting Task (WCST; Berg, 1948; Grant & Berg, 1948). In the WCST, participants are required to sort cards according to an undisclosed rule that they must deduce on the basis of corrective feedback provided by the experimenter. Once they have learned the rule, it changes. This aspect of the WCST is, on the surface at least, similar to the extradimensional shift of the ID–ED shift task.

Milner (1963, 1964) was among the first to identify a role for frontal brain regions in the WCST, reporting that patients with lesions to the dorsolateral frontal lobe found it difficult to shift between rules. Typically, these patients made numerous perseverative errors following a rule change, continuing to sort cards by the old rule despite receiving negative feedback. More recently, a number of articles have been published showing that patients with frontal damage (Owen, Roberts, Polkey, Sahakian, & Robbins, 1991), as well as those with schizophrenia (Elliott, McKenna, Robbins, & Sahakian, 1995), obsessive–compulsive disorder (Veale, Sahakian, Owen, & Marks, 1996), Parkinson's disease (Downes *et al.*, 1989), and Huntington's disease (Lawrence *et al.*, 1996), and older adults (Robbins *et al.*, 1998) are all impaired on the ED component of the Cambridge Neuropsychological Test Automated Battery (CANTAB) ID–ED task (Roberts, Robbins, & Everitt, 1988). This task is often described as an analog of the WCST, but it has similarity to a standard ID–ED shift task. The CANTAB ID–ED task employs a sequential, within-subject design. The basic design of the task is shown in Table 5.2. Over numerous stages, participants are presented with a sequence of simultaneous discrimination tasks. In the first stage of the task, participants are given a simple discrimination between two stimuli differing along a single dimension. In the second stage, the compound discrimination (CD) variation on a second dimension is introduced but is irrelevant to the discrimination. In later stages, novel values on each dimension are introduced. One or more intradimensional shift (IDS) discriminations are followed by an eventual extradimensional shift (EDS). Following each of the CD, IDS, and EDS stages, reversals of the discriminations are given where the correct and incorrect responses are swapped.

As would be expected on the basis of the ID–ED shift effect, normal participants tend to solve the EDS discrimination less rapidly than they solve the IDS discrimination. The typical pattern in patients with frontal damage or dysfunction is normal, or near normal, performance on all stages of the task with the exception of the EDS discrimination, where they make many more errors than normal controls; they show an exaggerated ID–ED shift effect. The CANTAB ID–ED task has been adapted for use with nonhuman primates (Dias *et al.*, 1996a) and rodents (Birrell & Brown, 2000). Experiments using these animal versions of the task have found that damage to the lateral prefrontal cortex in marmosets (Dias *et al.*, 1996a, 1996b; Dias, Robbins, & Roberts, 1997) or the medial prefrontal cortex in rats (Birrell & Brown, 2000) results

Table 5.2 Design of the CANTAB IDED shift task.

Stage	Exemplars		Relevant	Irrelevant
Simple discrimination (SD)	S1+	S2Ø	Shape	
Compound discrimination (CD)	S1/L1+	S2/L2Ø	Shape	Line
	S1/L2+	S2/L1Ø		
Reversal (Rev)	S2/L1+	S1/L2Ø	Shape	Line
	S2/L2+	S1/L1Ø		
Intradimensional shift (IDS)	**S3**/L3+	**S4**/L4Ø	Shape	Line
	S3/L4+	**S4**/L3Ø		
Reversal (IDR)	**S4**/L3+	**S3**/L4Ø	Shape	Line
	S4/L4+	**S3**/L3Ø		
Additional IDS and IDR stages	… .	… .	Shape	Line
Extradimensional shift (EDS)	S5/**L5**+	S6/**L6**Ø	Line	Shape
	S6/**L5**+	S5/**L6**Ø		
Reversal (EDR)	S5/**L6**+	S6/**L5**Ø	Line	Shape
	S6/**L6**+	S5/**L5**Ø		

Note. On each trial, participants are required to choose one of two stimuli that differ in the shape (S1–S4) and/or line (L1–L4) of which they consist. In each stage, either shape or line is relevant to the discrimination. + indicates that an exemplar is the correct choice; Ø that it is not. Relevant stimuli are shown in bold.

in impairment on the EDS discrimination, whereas lesions to the orbitofrontal cortex impair reversal learning in both species (Dias et al., 1996a, 1996b, 1997; Tait & Brown, 2008). Over the past 15 or so years, these animal versions of the task have allowed researchers to discover a great deal about the neural systems underlying set shifting behavior (see Bissonette, Powell, & Roesch, 2013; George, Duffaud, & Killcross, 2010; Robbins, 2007 for reviews). The task is also sufficiently flexible, with human participants at least, to allow researchers to differentiate between impairments in the ability to shift attention towards previously irrelevant stimuli or to shift attention away from previously relevant stimuli (e.g., Owen et al., 1993). It has, however, been suggested that the task is not ideal for studying the neural mechanisms of attention, partly because of its serial nature – with multiple ID stages followed by one or two ED shifts, and partly because performance fails to differentiate between the many different patient groups mentioned above who display a wide range of pathologies. Instead, it has been suggested that performance on the CANTAB ID–ED task reflects general problem-solving ability rather than just attentional set shifting ability (Hampshire & Owen, 2010).

Studies using the much simpler strategy-shift task (Figure 5.2) have more recently provided considerable insight into the neural mechanisms of set shifting, as well as revealing the extent to which the psychological processes are fractionated. The strategy shift task involves a single ED shift and nothing else. Rats are trained on two consecutive discriminations in a T-maze, in which they have to learn about different aspects of the environment. In the response-based version, they simply have to learn to always make the same response to find a food reward: For example, exit the start arm of the maze and turn right. In the visual cue-based version, the rats have to learn to always approach (or to always avoid) a stimulus, regardless of where it is located. On day 1 of the experiment, each rat is trained on one of these tasks until it reaches a performance criterion. On the

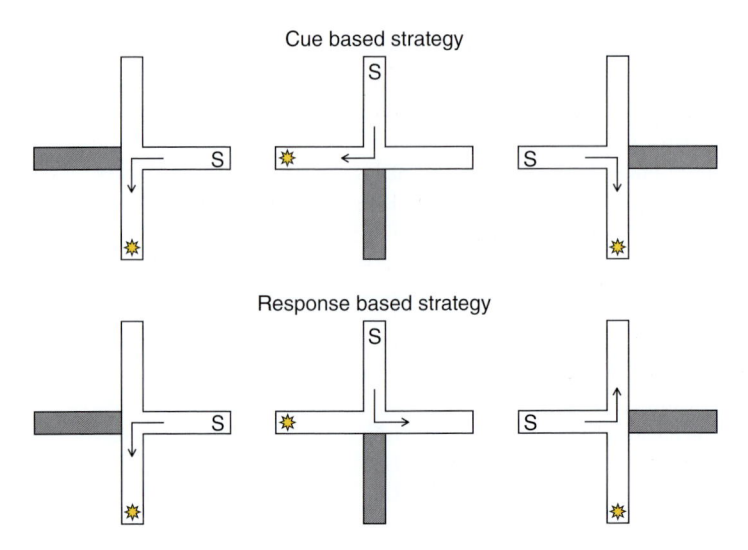

Figure 5.2 Two tasks involved in a typical strategy shifting experiment. On each trial, the rat is placed at the end of the start arm of a T-maze (S); a visual cue is located randomly at the end of one of the other two arms. In the cue-based version of the task, the arm containing the visual cue is baited with a food reward. In the response-based version, the baited arm is always in the same position relative to the start arm (to the left in this example). Here, the path that the rat must follow to earn reward is indicated for each arrangement by the arrow. Rats are trained first on one version of the task and then on the other version.

next day, each rat is trained on the other task. Consistent with the effect of prefrontal lesions on ED shift performance, prefrontal inactivation (e.g., Ragozzino, Ragozzino, Mizumori, & Kesner, 2002) selectively impairs acquisition of the postshift task, whereas inactivation of the orbiofrontal cortex has no effect (Ghods-Sharifi, Haluk, & Floresco, 2008). Although there are some definite advantages to employing completely different stimuli in each stage of a shift experiment (Slamecka, 1968), using the same stimuli can allow a more detailed analysis of different types of errors.

Cortico-striato-thalamic circuitry Block, Dhanji, Thompson-Tardiff, and Floresco (2007) conducted an elegant disconnection study involving disruption of specific elements of the cortico-striato-thalamic network involving the medial prefrontal cortex (mPFC), nucleus accumbens (NAc), and medial nucleus of the thalamus (MD). Three groups of rats received contra-lateral inactivation of two of these structures through infusion of the GABA agonist bupivacaine, whereas various control groups received unilateral inactivation of one structure coupled with infusion of saline into a contra-lateral structure, or two contra-lateral infusions of saline. The pattern of results was understandably complex, but allowed the authors to identify three separate processes involved in set shifting, each served by different parts of the cortico-striato-thalamic network. Careful consideration of the types of errors caused by each of the three disconnections led them to conclude that following a set shift, the network supports a number of coordinated processes. First, the MD passes information about changes in the contingencies between stimuli and/or responses and rewards to the mPFC. Second, in reaction to these changes, the mPFC suppresses the previous, and now incorrect, strategy. Third, the animal then explores new response strategies, and the learning of new reward contingencies is facilitated by suppression of inappropriate strategies by the MD-NAc pathway. Finally, at some point, the correct new strategy will be identified and become established. It is then the role of the mPFC-NAc pathway to help maintain this strategy.

George, Duffaud, and Killcross (2010) suggested that the involvement of the mPFC in set shifting may be fractionated still further. We examined the effects of discrete lesions to subregions of the mPFC on yet another type of shifting design, the optional shift (e.g., Kendler, Kendler, & Silfen, 1964). The design of our experiment is shown in Table 5.3. The key features of this task were that rats were first trained on a discrimination where one dimension was relevant and another was irrelevant, before being trained on a second discrimination task involving novel cues in which both stimulus dimension were equally informative. A test stage was later administered in which the amount that was learned about each dimension in the second stage was assessed. In the second stage, normal control animals tended to learn more about the dimension that was relevant in Stage 1 than they did about the dimension that was irrelevant (Duffaud, Killcross, & George, 2007). Rats with lesions to the prelimbic region of the mPFC behaved in exactly the same way as control animals that had undergone sham surgery. They learned more about the previously relevant dimension. Rats with lesions to the infralimbic mPFC, however, behaved in a most surprising way. They learned significantly more about the previously irrelevant stimuli. In fact, their performance at test was almost the mirror image of the control animals'.

We interpreted these results in the context of other effects of lesions to the infralimbic cortex. These lesions increase the magnitude of spontaneous recovery, reinstatement, and context renewal of conditioned responding following extinction (Rhodes & Killcross, 2004, 2007) and result in an enhanced latent inhibition effect (George, Duffaud, Pothuizen, Haddon, & Killcross, 2010). All of these effects may be attributed to variations in the animals' sensitivity to changes in the environment. Using rather different conditioning procedures, Killcross and Coutureau (2003; Coutureau &

Table 5.3 Design of the optional shift task used by George *et al.* (2010).

Stage	Exemplars		Relevant	Irrelevant
Initial discrimination	**A1/V1**: R1+	**A1**/V2: R2Ø	Auditory	Visual
	A1/V2: R1+	**A1**/V2: R2Ø		
	A2/V1: R2+	**A2**/V1: R1Ø		
	A2/V2: R2+	**A2**/V2: R1Ø		
Shift discrimination	**A3/V3**: R1+	**A3/V3**: R2Ø	Auditory and visual	
	A4/V4: R2+	**A4/V4**: R1Ø		
Optional shift test	A3/V4	A4/V3		

Note. Stimuli A1–A4 were different auditory stimuli; V1–V4 were visual stimuli. R1 and R2 were two response levers. + indicates that responses were reinforced; Ø that they were not. The optional shift test sessions were conducted in extinction. Contingencies are shown for rats for which auditory cues were relevant during the initial discrimination; for other rats, visual cues were relevant, and auditory cues were irrelevant. Relevant stimuli are shown in bold.

Killcross, 2003) found that lesions to, or inactivation of, the infralimbic cortex disrupted the development of behavioral habits. Conversely, lesions to the prelimbic mPFC accelerated the development of habits. On the basis of these findings, we observed (George, Duffaud, & Killcross, 2010) that the infralimbic and prelimbic corticies appear to have complementary and competitive roles in a wide range of situations.

In the case of set shifting, the prelimbic cortex is involved in disengaging from the existing set and triggering the search for a new set when certain changes are detected in the task. These changes may involve negative feedback resulting from different reward contingencies, or changes in the context or stimuli. The infralimbic cortex, however, normally acts to resist the action of the prelimbic cortex and to bias behavior towards established patterns. Through this action, the infralimbic cortex is responsible for the maintenance of the current set when animals are exposed to an intradimensional shift, or when contingencies are reversed. When the infralimbic cortex is damaged, the prelimbic cortex is free to disengage from the current set whenever a change is detected. In the case of our optional shift experiments, this might explain why rats with lesions to the infralimbic cortex appear to perform an EDS and learn more about the previously irrelevant dimension in the second stage of the experiment.

Experiments such as Block *et al.*'s (2007) disconnection study have significantly advanced our understanding of the psychological processes involved in set shifting in the normal brain but may also generate interesting hypotheses about the origin of specific patterns of dysfunction in neurological disorders. Animal studies are often able to reveal information that is not always easily obtainable using functional imaging techniques in humans. This is partly because neuroimaging tends to require averaging over numerous trials, whereas set shifting studies involve a small number of critical shifts. It is also partly because many of the processes identified by Block *et al.* would be expected to operate in concert making them difficult to dissociate in imaging.

Blocking and latent inhibition

Experiments involving animals have allowed researchers to identify several distinct psychological processes involved in attentional set shifting. The results of these experiments suggest that the mechanisms involved in set shifting are somewhat more complex than Mackintosh's (1975) model of attention and associative learning might suggest. Nevertheless, these experiments provide strong support for the notion that animals learn to attend to stimuli that are good predictors. There are a number of other effects such as blocking and latent inhibition that may also be explained by Mackintosh's model. These provide less compelling support for the model, not least because there are several alternative explanations for each effect. Nevertheless, a few words should be devoted to them before we consider Pearce and Hall's (1980) alternative approach to the role of attention in learning.

Kamin (1968) reported the results of an experiment in which the vital comparison was between the levels of conditioned responding to a light in two groups of animals that had received training in which a compound of the light and a noise was paired with an aversive electrical shock. Prior to the compound training, a blocking group received trials on which the noise alone was paired with the shock, whereas a control group did not. At test, the blocking group appeared to have learned less about the relationship between the light and shock than the control group. The pretraining with the noise had "blocked" later learning about the light. While it is possible to explain this blocking effect without recourse to attentional processes (e.g., Rescorla & Wagner, 1972), both Mackintosh (1975) and Pearce and Hall (1980) predict that learning about the light will be retarded for the blocking group due to a reduction in attention to the light. Specifically, the Mackintosh model predicts that at the start of compound training, the noise will be a good predictor of the shock for the blocking group. Since the light is a poorer predictor of the shock than the light, its associability will be reduced, and learning about the relationship between the light and the shock will proceed slowly. For the control group, the light will not experience such a rapid reduction in associability because the noise has not been established as a good predictor of the shock.

It has been shown that blocked cues do suffer from reduced associability in both rats (Mackintosh & Turner, 1971) and humans (Kruschke & Blair, 2000; Le Pelley, Beesley, & Suret, 2007). Compared with attention set shifting, relatively little research has been devoted to the investigation of the neural mechanisms of blocking, but there is evidence that the prefrontal cortex is involved in rats (e.g., Jones & Gonzalez-Lima, 2001) and humans (e.g., Eippert, Gamer, & Büchel, 2012). Furthermore, Iordanova, Westbrook, and Killcross (2006) found that NAc dopamine (DA) activity modulated the blocking effect. Increased DA activation enhanced blocking, reducing the amount learned about the blocked cue. NAc DA blockade had the opposite effect, eliminating the blocking effect. Neither treatment affected learning about the blocking cue. Iordanova *et al.* concluded that NAc DA modulates the ability of good predictors to influence learning about (i.e., attention to) poor predictors of trial outcome. That similar brain regions appear to be involved in both attentional set shifting and blocking is consistent with the suggestion that attention contributes to the blocking effect. We should be cautious when making these assumptions, however. Jones and Haselgrove (2013) tested the associability of both blocked and blocking cues following a standard blocking procedure. They found that attention was greater to the blocked cues, an effect that could be explained simply in terms of the amount of exposure each cue had received during training.

Latent inhibition has also been attributed by some authors to a reduction in attention to a stimulus. In the first published demonstration of the effect, Lubow and Moore (1959) reported that animals learned less rapidly about the relationship between a stimulus and an outcome if the stimulus had previously been presented in the absence of any outcome. The explanation of latent inhibition offered by Mackintosh (1975) is that during preexposure, the stimulus predicts the trial outcome (i.e., nothing) no better than any other cue (e.g., the context), which means that, according to Equation 2b, its associability will decline. A great deal is known about the neural systems involved in latent inhibition. Areas including the hippocampus (HPC), NAc, basolateral nucleus of the amygdala (BLA), and entorhinal cortex have been implicated in the acquisition and expression of latent inhibition (see Weiner, 2003, for a review) as well as both the prelimbic (Nelson, Thur, Marsden, & Cassaday, 2010) and infralimbic prefrontal (George, Duffaud, Pothuizen, *et al.*, 2010) cortices.

There is little agreement, however, that latent inhibition is an effect of learned predictiveness. Bouton (1993) has suggested that latent inhibition is a manifestation of proactive interference. It arises because whatever is learned during preexposure (that the stimulus is insignificant or that it signals no event) interferes with retrieval of the stimulus–outcome association acquired during conditioning. A not dissimilar explanation is offered by the switching model (e.g., Weiner, 2003). Wagner's (1981) SOP model states that how well a stimulus is itself predicted will affect its ability to be learned about. During preexposure, the context will come to predict the CS, reducing its associability. The Pearce–Hall model also explains latent inhibition in terms of a reduction in associability due to there being no uncertainty about what the stimulus predicts during preexposure.

Effects of Uncertainty

A few years after Mackintosh published his model of attentional associability, Pearce and Hall considered a somewhat different attentional process. They observed that rats learned less rapidly about the relationship between a tone and a strong electric shock if they had previously been exposed to pairings of the same tone and a weaker shock than if they had not experienced these pairings (Hall & Pearce, 1979). In seeming opposition to the predictiveness hypothesis proposed by Mackintosh, Pearce and Hall (1980) suggested that the associability of a stimulus is determined by how surprising the events that follow it are. In Hall and Pearce's experiment, the pretrained animals had learned that the tone was a reliable predictor of the weak shock, and hence attention to the tone was reduced. This reduction in attention retarded learning about the tone when it was later paired with the strong shock. Equation 3 shows how the associability of stimulus A on trial n, α_A^n, is determined by how well it predicted events on previous trials according to Pearce, Kaye, and Hall (1982). In this equation, γ is a parameter that may vary between 0 and 1, and determines the extent to which α is influenced by the immediately preceding trial, $n-1$, and how much it is influenced by more distant past trials. V_T^{n-1} is the total associative strength of all stimuli present on the previous trial on which stimulus A was presented, and λ^{n-1} is the intensity of the outcome on that trial.

$$\alpha_A^n = \gamma \left| \lambda^{n-1} - V_T^{n-1} \right| + (1-\gamma)\alpha_A^{n-1} \qquad (5.3)$$

This value of α in turn affects any changes in the associative strength of stimulus A as a consequence of events on trial n, in a manner determined by Equation 4 where S_A^n is the intensity of the stimulus and R^n is the magnitude of the reinforcer.

$$\Delta V_A^n = \alpha_A^n \cdot S_A^n \cdot R^n \qquad (5.4)$$

At first glance, the Pearce–Hall model appears to contradict Mackintosh (1975). Where Mackintosh suggested that the amount of attention paid to a stimulus is determined by how well it predicts the outcome of a trial, Pearce and Hall proposed that it is determined by how surprising the trial outcome is. There is, however, a certain intuitive appeal to each model. It makes sense that an animal should want to attend to stimuli that tell it something important about the world, and to ignore those that provide no new information. At the same time, however, if an important event is well predicted, it makes no sense to expend limited resources processing information about what preceded it. Here, we can see that the two models address rather different properties of a stimulus. Le Pelley (2004) suggested one way to reconcile these two models; the Pearce–Hall model might tell an organism how much it needs to learn about the stimulus situation as a function of how uncertain an outcome was, whereas the Mackintosh model might determine which specific stimuli should be learned about. Reflecting the fact that the perceived conflict between the two models may be resolved in this way, several authors have published hybrid models that incorporate aspects of each (e.g., George & Pearce, 2012; Le Pelley, 2004, 2010; Pearce & Mackintosh, 2010).

Holland, together with several of his colleagues, has devoted significant effort to investigating the neural substrates of Pearce–Hall-type attentive processes in rats (for a review, see Holland & Maddux, 2010). Over the past 20 years or more, he has conducted a program of work that has revealed which brain regions are involved in these processes but also told us a great deal about the relationship between associability and surprise. The foundation of much of this work is the serial conditioning procedure described by Wilson, Boumphrey, and Pearce (1992). The design of Wilson *et al.*'s experiment (henceforth the WBP task) is shown in Table 5.4. In the first stage of the experiment, two groups of rats received the same treatment. On all trials, presentation of a light was followed by a tone. On half of the trials, the tone was followed by the delivery of food, whereas on the other half of the trials, it was not. According to the Pearce–Hall model, the light should lose associability because it is a good predictor of the tone that follows it on every trial. In the second stage of the experiment, Group Consistent received exactly the same training as in Stage 1. For Group Inconsistent, however, the tone was omitted on the trials on which food was not delivered. For this group, the light had become an unreliable predictor of the tone, and, as a consequence, the Pearce–Hall model states that its associability should be reinstated. To test this prediction, both groups were given simple pairings of the light and food in the final, test stage of the experiment. In keeping with the assumptions of the Pearce–Hall model, Group Inconsistent learned more rapidly about the relationship between the light and food than did Group Consistent. Furthermore, at the beginning of Stage 1, rats in both groups exhibited an orienting response (OR) to the light, turning towards and approaching it when it was illuminated. Kaye and Pearce (1984; see also Sokolov, 1963) have suggested that the OR might provide an index of the amount of processing that a stimulus received (or the attention paid to it). Wilson *et al.* observed that the

Table 5.4 Design of the serial conditioning experiment conducted by Wilson *et al.* (1992).

	Stage 1	Stage 2	Test stage
Group Consistent	Light → tone → +	Light → tone → +	Light → +
	Light → tone → Ø	Light → tone → Ø	
Group Inconsistent	Light → tone → +	Light → tone → +	Light → +
	Light → tone → Ø	Light → Ø	

Note. The light and the tone were each presented for 10 s. + indicates that the trial terminated with the delivery of food; Ø that it did not.

OR gradually declined over the course of Stage 1. When the relationship between the light and tone changed for Group Inconsistent at the start of Stage 2, however, the OR returned for those animals. Hence, Wilson *et al.* provided evidence for Pearce–Hall-type attentional changes from two separate behavioral measures.

Holland's work has revealed that different brain systems are involved in expectancy-induced decreases in associability and surprise-induced increases in associability. Furthermore, the neural bases of surprise-induced increases in associability as a consequence of the unexpected delivery of reward and the unexpected omission of reward are distinct. I shall consider each of these systems in turn.

Sensitivity to downshifts in reward

Central amygdala Following observations that lesions to the central nucleus of the amygdala (CeA) disrupt the enhancement of ORs to stimuli during conditioning (Gallagher, Graham, & Holland, 1990), Holland and Gallagher (1993a) examined the effects of these lesions on the WBP task. Unlike normal, control rats, those with CeA lesions did not learn faster at test following inconsistent training than following consistent training. In fact, the lesioned animals showed the opposite pattern. Because the performance of consistently trained animals was entirely unaffected by the lesions, Holland and Gallagher concluded that the CeA was important only for increases in associability following changes in reward predictiveness and not for expectancy-induced decreases in associability. These conclusions are supported by the fact that CeA lesions have no effect on habituation of an OR (Gallagher *et al.*, 1990; Holland & Gallagher, 1993a), blocking (Holland & Gallagher, 1993b), or latent inhibition (Holland & Gallagher, 1993a). On the basis that CeA lesions disrupt surprise-induced increases in associability, but not expectancy-induced decreases in associability, it would be reasonable to expect CeA lesions to abolish any difference in consistent versus inconsistent training histories on test performance on the WBP task. Why, then, did Holland & Gallagher observe slower learning following inconsistent training in the CeA lesioned animals? One explanation is that inconsistently trained animals experienced greater decrements in associability to the light during the second stage of the experiment. For rats receiving inconsistent training, the light is presented alone on some occasions and in compound on other occasions, whereas for rats receiving consistent training, it is always presented in compound. Several authors have reported greater habituation and latent inhibition to stimuli that have been presented alone than to those presented in compound (e.g., Holland & Forbes, 1980; Lubow, Wagner, & Weiner, 1982), and so one might expect animals to attend less to the light following inconsistent training.

The Pearce–Hall model predicts that the associability of a blocked cue will decline very rapidly during compound conditioning because the outcome is reliably predicted by the pretrained cue. Blocking may be reduced, or even abolished, if there is a change in the magnitude of the reinforcing stimulus at the start of the compound conditioning phase (Dickinson, Hall, & Mackintosh, 1976; Holland, 1984). According to Pearce and Hall, this is quite simply because the now novel outcome is not well predicted by the noise. The Pearce–Hall model therefore relies on expectancy-induced reductions in associability to explain blocking, and surprise-induced increases in associability to explain the disruption of blocking following increases or decreases in the magnitude of the reinforcer (upshift- and downshift unblocking, respectively). Hence, it is entirely consistent with Holland's suggestion that the CeA is involved in surprise-induced increases in associability that lesions to the CeA had no effect on blocking but do impair downshift unblocking (Holland & Gallagher, 1993b). Interestingly, upshift-unblocking is unaffected by these lesions, suggesting that the CeA is involved only in increases in associability when an expected reward is omitted (as is the case, of course, in the WBP task), and not when an unexpected reward is delivered.

Substantia nigra pars compacta The CeA is just one part of a circuit that affects stimulus associability. There is substantial evidence that I shall discuss later that the midbrain dopaminergic (DAergic) systems are involved in signaling information about the discrepancy between expected rewards and actual rewards (i.e., prediction error). As we can see from Equation 3, Pearce and Hall (1980) suggest that changes in associability are dependent upon this error. The majority of DA neurons are located within the substantia nigra pars compacta (SNc) and the ventral tegmental area (VTA). The former of these structures is particularly well connected with the CeA. Lee, Youn, O, Gallagher, and Holland (2006) employed a disconnection procedure in which rats received unilateral lesions of the SNc, which selectively damaged DAergic neurons, in combination with unilateral lesions to the CeA in either the ipsi- or contra-lateral hemisphere, before being trained on the WBP task. For rats with ipsilateral lesions, connections between SNc and CeA were preserved in one hemisphere. These animals showed faster learning about the relationship between light and food during the final phase of the experiment following inconsistent training than following consistent training, suggesting that the mechanism of surprise-induced increases in associability was preserved. For rats with contralateral lesions, connections between SNc and CeA were disrupted in both hemispheres, and no difference at test was observed between groups receiving consistent or inconsistent training. The integrity of the CeA–SNc connections is, however, important only at the time of surprise (Lee, Youn, Gallagher, & Holland, 2008), and not during subsequent learning in the test phase. These results suggest that interaction between these structures is important for the processing of prediction-error information, but not for the expression of the influence of associability during learning.

Substantia innominata The CeA and SNc both have connections with the basal forebrain cholinergic system. Pretraining 192IgG-saporin lesions, which specifically target cholinergic neurons, to the substantia innominata (SI) have the same effect as lesions to the CeA on several tasks (Chiba, Bucci, Holland, & Gallagher, 1995). Rats with lesions to the SI show no evidence of surprise-induced increases in associability in the WBP task but do show normal latent inhibition, suggesting that expectancy-induced decreases in associability occur normally. Disconnection of the CeA and SI abolishes the WBP effect (Han, Holland, & Gallagher, 1999) but does not reverse it in the way that lesions to either structure alone do (Chiba *et al.*, 1995; Holland & Gallagher, 1993a). The relationship between SI and CeA in associability modulation turns out not to be quite as straightforward as that between SNc and CeA. Temporary inactivation of these structures at specific points in the WBP task has revealed that whereas involvement of the CeA is important at the time of surprise, the SI has its effect during subsequent learning (Holland & Gallagher, 2006). That is, the CeA is involved in recalculating the prediction error associated with stimuli following the unexpected omission of reward, whereas the SI is involved in applying the new associability value in later learning.

It seems likely that the relatively sparse connections from the CeA to the SI are more important in the processing of prediction error than the much denser reciprocal connections from the SI to CeA. One reason for suggesting this is that the latter neurons are unaffected by the neurotoxin employed by Chiba *et al.* (1995), since they lack the nerve growth factor receptor that it targets. The SI, in turn, projects to several neocortical regions, including the posterior parietal cortex (PPC), which has been implicated in attentional processes in humans (e.g., Behrmann, Geng, & Shomstein, 2004). It should come as no surprise, then, that Bucci, Holland, and Gallagher (1998) found that lesions targeting SI-PPC projections abolished downshift unblocking, and the effects of training history in the WBP task. In the latter task, the lesioned animals showed the same pattern of performance as those with lesions to the SI – equal rates of learning at test in animals that had received consistent or inconsistent training.

Together, this collection of studies suggests that a network of brain regions including, but not limited to, the midbrain DAergic system, CeA, cholinergic basal forebrain, and the neocortex, is involved in the modulation of attention in response to omission of expected rewards.

Sensitivity to upshifts in reward

Basolateral amygdala   Just as decreasing the value of an expected outcome will lead to unblocking, so too will increasing its value. Lesions to the CeA that abolish downshift unblocking do not, however, affect this type of unblocking (Holland, 2006; Holland & Gallagher, 1993b). This suggests that surprise-induced changes in associability due to omission of an expected reward or the delivery of an unexpected reward are mediated by different brain systems.

There are at least two potential mechanisms by which upshift-unblocking may occur. First, new learning could result simply from an increase in the value of the reinforcer – the new outcome is not fully predicted, and so new learning might be driven simply by a Rescorla–Wagner-type process. Second, the upshift might maintain or increase the associability of the blocked cue due to the increase in prediction error. Holland (2006) set out to distinguish between these two mechanisms. Instead of increasing the magnitude of the US, Holland added a second US in the upshift condition. In a compound conditioning phase, a light + noise compound was paired with the delivery of food, which was followed 5 s later by sucrose delivery in a different location to the food. Prior to this training, rats in a blocking group had received training where the light alone was paired with the food → sucrose sequence, whereas for rats in an unblocking group, the light was paired with food alone. In this situation, the Pearce–Hall model predicts that the unblocking animals should show more learning to the noise for both reinforcers. In contrast, the Rescorla–Wagner model predicts unblocking of learning about the sucrose outcome only. The results of Holland's experiment were consistent with the predictions of the Pearce–Hall model. Lesions to the CeA had no effect for either blocking or unblocking groups. Using essentially the same procedure, however, Chang, McDannald, Wheeler, and Holland (2012) found that upshift unblocking that could be attributed to changes in associability was abolished by lesions to the BLA. When unblocking could be due to either Pearce–Hall or Rescorla–Wagner mechanisms (i.e., when the upshift was simply an increase in the number of food pellets delivered), BLA lesions had no effect.

Reductions in attention

Hippocampus The Pearce–Hall model can explain latent inhibition very simply. During preexposure, the cue is established as a good predictor of (the lack of) trial outcome, and as a consequence its associability is reduced. Lesions to areas that are involved in increasing attention to stimuli following unexpected changes in outcome tend not to affect expectancy-induced reductions in attention. Lesions of CeA (Holland & Gallagher, 1993a), BLA (Weiner, Tarrasch, & Feldon, 1995; but see Coutureau, Blundell, & Killcross, 2001), and SI (Chiba et al., 1995), for example, leave latent inhibition intact. Lesions to the HPC, however, have been found to disrupt decreases in attention while having no effect on increases in attention. Han, Gallagher, and Holland (1995) observed that HPC lesions abolished latent inhibition. In the WBP task, rats with these lesions learned faster in the test phase following inconsistent training than following consistent training but also learned faster following either type of training than corresponding groups of animals that had undergone control surgery. These results suggest two things. First, HPC lesions prevent stimuli from losing associability. Second, surprise can increase the associability of stimuli, even when they have not experienced expectancy-induced reductions in associability.[1]

Cholinergic systems Just as the cholinergic neurons in the SI are implicated in increases in associability, other regions of the basal forebrain appear to be involved in reductions in associability. Disruption of cholinergic projections to the HPC from the medial septum and vertical limb of the diagonal band (MS/VDB) abolish latent inhibition (Baxter, Holland, & Gallagher, 1997). The same lesions also disrupt decrements in associability in the WBP task. During the test phase, lesioned animals learned at the same rate as did control animals following inconsistent training, regardless of the training regimen to which they had been exposed. On the basis of Han et al.'s (1995) results following HPC lesions, a selective impairment of decremental associability processing would be expected to preserve the advantage of inconsistent training on test performance. This might suggest that MS/VDB lesions also disrupt incremental associability processing, or that the lesioned animals were at a ceiling of responding that obscured the effect of an increase in associability following inconsistent training. What is clear, however, is that these lesions result in qualitatively different results to lesions of the SI.

In summary, Holland and colleagues have provided clear evidence that increases and decreases in the associability of a stimulus based on the certainty with which it predicts an outcome are mediated by different neural circuits. It is not yet clear exactly what the role of each specific brain area in associability change is, but it is possible that the CeA and HPC act to modulate activity in the cortical targets of the basal forebrain structures to which they project (Holland & Maddux, 2010).

Prediction-Error Signals in the Brain

Both Mackintosh's (1975) and Pearce and Hall's (1980) models propose that the prediction error associated with a cue will influence its associability. This claim might be strengthened by evidence that prediction error is encoded by brain systems. A number of laboratories have sought exactly this type of evidence through the use of procedures such as single unit recording. Of course, showing that the brain codes surprise does not by itself provide any support for a Pearce–Hall- or Mackintosh-type attentional system. After all, most models of learning make the assumption that the amount learned on each trial will be in some way influenced by how surprising the outcome of that trial is (e.g., Rescorla & Wagner, 1972; Sutton, 1988). These models tend, however, to rely on a signed error term (i.e., one that can take either positive or negative values). Consider, for example, the learning rule employed by Rescorla and Wagner (1972) shown in Equation 5. According to this equation, following a conditioning trial the change in the associative strength of stimulus A is dependent upon α_A and β – a couple of learning rate parameters associated with the stimulus and the outcome respectively – and the difference between the actual value of the outcome, λ, and the expected outcome determined by the sum of the associative strengths of all stimuli present, ΣV. It is this last term, $(\lambda - \Sigma V)$, that represents the prediction error. If the actual outcome is larger than expected, the prediction error will be positive, and the associative strength of stimulus A will be incremented. If the outcome is smaller than expected, the prediction error will be negative, and the associative strength of A will be reduced.

$$\Delta V_A = \alpha_A \beta (\lambda - \Sigma V) \qquad (5.5)$$

Signed prediction error

There is strong evidence that signed prediction error is coded by DA neurons. Single unit recording of DA neurons in the VTA and SNc of monkeys has shown increases in firing rates in response to unexpected rewards and decreases in response to the omission of an expected reward (Schultz, Dayan, & Montague, 1997; see Chapter 3). Furthermore, the magnitude of these responses is proportional to the size of the prediction error, with more certain rewards producing smaller responses than less certain rewards (Fiorillo, Tobler, & Schultz, 2003). Changes in the responsiveness of dopamine neurons to conditioned stimuli appear to match the predictions of associative theories of learning (Waelti, Dickinson, & Schultz, 2001). Rather impressively, Steinberg *et al.* (2013) have demonstrated a causal link between DA prediction-error signals and learning. Using a blocking procedure, they found that optogenetic activation of VTA DA neurons was sufficient to support new learning about a blocked cue that did not occur in the absence of this activation.

Unsigned prediction error

The equation used by Pearce *et al.* (1982) to determine the attention paid to a stimulus (Equation 3) relies upon an unsigned error term. It is sensitive simply to how surprising an outcome is and is not affected by whether the outcome is smaller, or larger, than the expected outcome (see Figure 5.3). In Mackintosh's (1975) model, changes in attention similarly rely on an unsigned measure of prediction error (see Equations 2a and 2b). The discovery, therefore, of neurons that respond in a similar fashion to the unexpected delivery of reward and to the omission of an expected reward would strengthen the suggestion that attention is allocated in the manner described by these models.

In addition to cells that provide a signed prediction-error signal, in primates there are also some that code unsigned error in regions including the medial prefrontal cortex (Matsumoto, Matsumoto, Abe, & Tanaka, 2007) and lateral habenula (e.g., Matsumoto & Hikosaka, 2009a). Matsumoto and Hikosaka (2009b) paired three visual stimuli with different probabilities of reward (0%, 50%, 100%), and in a separate training block three other visual stimuli were paired with different probabilities of punishment (0%, 50%, 100%). They identified several populations of DA neurons in SNc and VTA. Some simply responded to the value of the outcome associated with a stimulus. Activity in these cells was excited by reward predicting stimuli and inhibited by punishment predicting stimuli. Other cells responded to the predictive value of a stimulus; their firing rates were proportional to the probability of either reward or punishment. A third population of cells provided a signed prediction error signal. These cells fired most when an unexpected reward was delivered, displayed minimal change in firing when either a fully predicted reward or a fully predicted punishment occurred, and their activity was inhibited by an unexpected punishment. Finally, some cells were excited by an unexpected reward or an unexpected punishment in a graded fashion.

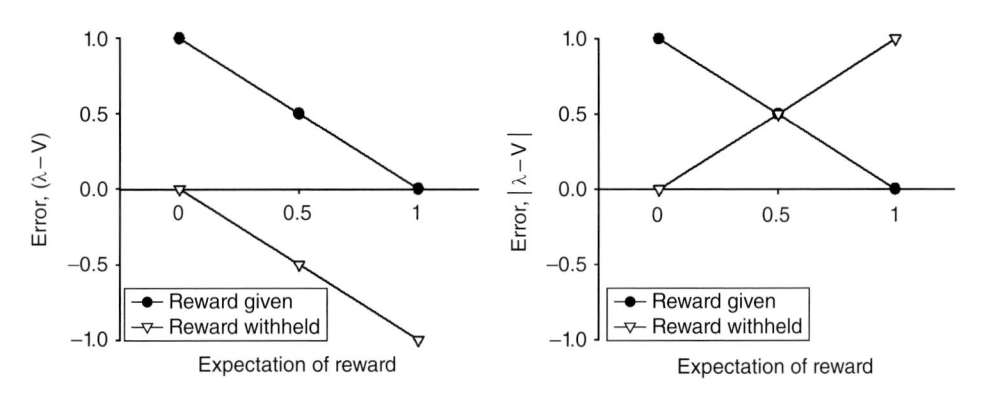

Figure 5.3 Signed (left panel) and unsigned (right panel) prediction error following the delivery or omission of reward as a function of reward expectation.

Unfortunately, it is difficult to be absolutely certain that this last population of cells provide a pure measure of unsigned prediction error because we do not know how they responded to the unexpected omission of reward and punishment.

Much of the clearest evidence for unsigned prediction-error signals comes from the laboratories of Roesch and Schoenbaum. Calu *et al.* (2010) recorded from cells in the CeA while rats were trained on a task in which they learned to expect rewards at specific times. When an expected reward was omitted, activity in some CeA cells increased. Over trials, as new learning occurred and the omission of the reward ceased to be surprising, the firing rate declined again. These neurons did not fire in response to unexpected reward. They were not, however, sensitive to surprise caused by the delivery of an unexpected reward. This is entirely consistent with the effects of lesions to the CeA reported by Holland and Gallagher (1993a, 1993b). Using the same task, however, Roesch, Calu, Esber, and Schoenbaum (2010) found cells in the BLA that were sensitive to both the omission of expected reward and the delivery of unexpected reward. When the rats experienced either a down- or an upshift in the expected reward, the firing rate of BLA cells increased. Over successive trials, as the rats learned about the new outcome, activity in these cells returned to baseline levels. In contrast, activity in DA cells in the VTA provided a signed error signal, increasing after an upshift in reward and decreasing following a downshift before returning to baseline. Projections from VTA to BLA suggest, however, that the signed error signal of the DA system may be the source of the BLA's unsigned error signal. This suggestion is supported by the fact that 6-OHDA lesions to the VTA disrupt the BLA error signal (Esber *et al.*, 2012).

An interesting feature of the BLA's unsigned error signal recorded by Roesch *et al.* (2010) was that surprise induced changes in neuronal activity developed over several trials. That is, there was no change in activity on the first trial on which an up- or downshift in reward was experienced. Instead, there was a more gradual change in activity over the succeeding couple of trials until activity peaked and then a gradual decline over several trials. Activity in these cells is not, then, an index of how surprising the outcome of a trial was. Rather, it appears to reflect the value of α as predicted by Equation 3. Curiously, α is a property of the stimulus and not the outcome, but both Esber *et al.* (2012) and Roesch *et al.* (2010) observed these signals at the time of (expected) reward and not stimulus presentation. It is also worth mentioning that although Roesch *et al.* (2010) found that inactivation of the BLA led to an expected retardation of learning following changes in reward, and disrupted surprise induced changes in orienting behavior, excitotoxic lesions to the BLA have no effect on the WBP task (Holland, Hatfield, & Gallagher, 2001).

Risk and ambiguity

A much larger literature has examined similar phenomena within the framework of risky decision-making. Within this literature, rather little interest is devoted to the effects of predictiveness or uncertainty on learning. Instead, a distinction is made between two types of uncertainty within (relatively) stable systems. If an animal has little or no information about the relationship between a response and any possible reward, the situation is ambiguous. Alternatively, if the response is associated with a known range of outcomes but may be paired by any of these on a given trial, it is considered to be risky. The amount of risk associated with a response is simply the range of possible outcomes. In the same way associative strength and attention may be dissociated in the models of Mackintosh (1975) and Pearce and Hall (1980), in a risky situation the average value of a response may be independent of the risk. For example, if one response always results in the delivery of one food pellet, and a second response earns two pellets 50% of the time but no pellets 50% of the time, then the two responses have the same average value but are associated with different levels of risk. There are obvious parallels between risk in decision-making and uncertainty in associative learning. Neural signals that correlate with risk may, therefore, reflect attention. These signals have been found in a number of brain regions, many of which overlap with those that have already been discussed in this chapter.

In a number of experiments involving primates, the probability and/or size of the outcome associated with a stimulus or a response have been manipulated in a manner consistent with this dissociation between risk and value. If five stimuli, are each associated with a different probability (0%, 25%, 50%, 75%, 100%) that a fixed amount of juice will be delivered, they will differ in both their average value and risk. These two measures are, however, poorly correlated. As the probability of reward increases from 0% to 100%, average value increases monotonically. Risk, however, is at its lowest (i.e., zero) when the outcome is certain at 0% or 100% and has its maximum value when certainty is at its lowest for the 50% stimulus. The effects of value on neural activity in this situation may also be controlled for by including a condition in which several stimuli signal 100% probability of different amounts of juice. In experiments using this type of design, cells in areas including the anterodorsal septal region, midbrain, cingulate cortex, and orbitofrontal cortex have been found to code risk, responding most when the outcome is least certain, whereas other cells in the midbrain, cingulate cortex, and orbitofrontal cortex show activity that is correlated with outcome value (e.g., Fiorillo *et al.*, 2003; McCoy & Platt, 2005; Monosov & Hikosaka, 2013; O'Neill & Schultz, 2010).

In human learning and decision-making experiments conducted in combination with fMRI, activity within the ventral striatum, orbitofrontal cortex, and ventromedial prefrontal cortex has been found to correlate with outcome value, whereas the orbitofrontal, anterior cingulate, and dorsolateral medial prefrontal cortices, and the amygdala appear to signal risk (e.g., Christopoulos, Tobler, Bossaerts, Dolan, & Schultz, 2009; Metereau & Dreher, 2013; Tobler, Christopoulos, O'Doherty, Dolan, & Schultz, 2009; Xue *et al.*, 2009; see Chapter 22).

It is clear that a wide network of brain areas is important in processing information about uncertain rewards, and that there is obvious overlap with those areas that have been shown in lesion studies to be important both in Pearce–Hall attentional processes and in attentional set shifting.

Summary and Conclusions

In this chapter, I have tried to demonstrate how neuroscientific studies, predominantly in animals, have contributed to our understanding of the psychological processes that govern the relationship between learning and attention. There is substantial evidence that both predictability and uncertainty contribute towards changes in attention in ways consistent with the models proposed by Mackintosh (1975) and Pearce and Hall (1980). The psychological processes underlying these changes in attention are, however, much more complex than might be suggested by the simple mathematical nature of those models.

Mackintosh (1975) proposed that attention will increase and decrease to stimuli as a function of how well they predict reward. Studies of attentional set shifting suggest that such changes may, however, be affected by the attentional history of a stimulus. The fact that animals with lesions to the prefrontal cortex are selectively impaired on an ED shift task (e.g., Dias *et al.*, 1996b) suggests that they are able to learn to attend to relevant cues and/or to ignore irrelevant cues, but they have difficulty in reversing these changes in attention. Furthermore, when Dias *et al.* (1997) subjected marmosets to a sequence of multiple ED shifts, these same lesions affected performance only on the first occasion. A second ED discrimination, where the dimension that had been relevant during initial training became relevant once again, was acquired rapidly by lesioned and control animals alike. These results are perhaps more readily explained by the learning of a set of rules, rather than the incremental changes in attention described by Mackintosh. This rule-based view is reinforced by the identification of several distinct processes that contribute to set-shifting behavior by Block *et al.* (2007; see also Floresco, Zhang, & Enomoto, 2009) and the discovery that set shifts are accompanied by abrupt transitions between patterns of neuronal activity in the PFC (Durstewitz, Vittoz, Floresco, & Seamans, 2010). Some recent evidence suggests, however, that both rule-based (top-down) and associative (bottom-up) processes might contribute to attention in people. In a few experiments using a type of optional-shift design not dissimilar to that employed by George, Duffaud, Pothuizen, *et al.* (2010), human participants have been informed at the beginning of the shift discrimination phase that previously predictive cues are unlikely to continue to signal outcome. While the results of these experiments have been mixed, they have in at least some cases revealed an effect of learned predictiveness that is not abolished by the instructions (Shone & Livesey, 2013).

Pearce and Hall's (1980) theory employs an even simpler rule for changing attention than Mackintosh (1975). Rather than specifying separate conditions under which attention to a stimulus might increase or decrease, they simply suggested that the attention paid to a stimulus will be determined by how well the outcome had been predicted on previous occasions on which that stimulus had been encountered. As in the case of set shifting, Holland's systematic approach to investigating the effects of uncertainty on attention has revealed multiple separable processes. One important distinction may be made between a neocortical system that rapidly increases attention in response to surprise and a more gradual process that reduces attention to stimuli that accurately predict other events and is supported by the hippocampus (Holland & Maddux, 2010). This fractionation of processes does not alter the fact that the Pearce–Hall model predicts the effects of uncertainty on learning and attention in a range of behavioral paradigm involving animals. Furthermore, neural signals have been discovered that correspond to the uncertainty-based changes in associability described by the model.

Mackintosh (1975, p. 295) wrote of his theory that "the ideas proposed here are more a program for a theory than a fully elaborated formal model of conditioning and discrimination learning." We should consider, then, that Mackintosh (1975) and Pearce and Hall (1980) described some of the factors that contribute to the attention paid to a stimulus: predictiveness and uncertainty. Although the processes that contribute to attentional changes have been revealed to be considerably more complex than anticipated by these associative models, they may nevertheless rely on calculation of the same prediction error that those models use. Hence, after four decades, there is still plenty of reason to suppose that attentive processes might be sensitive to the associative mechanisms described by Mackintosh (1975) and Pearce and Hall (1980).

Note

1 It should be noted that Honey and Good (1993; see also Coutureau, Galani, Gosselin, Majchrzak, & Di Scala, 1999) found no effect of HPC lesions on latent inhibition. It is not clear why these different experiments had divergent results, but this could be due to differences in stimulus modality, experimental design (within- versus between-subject), or the extent of the lesions. Han *et al.* are not the only authors to report that HPC lesions disrupt latent inhibition (e.g., Kaye & Pearce, 1987; Oswald *et al.*, 2002; Schmajuk, Lam, & Christiansen, 1994).

References

Baxter, M. G., Holland, P. C., & Gallagher, M. (1997). Disruption of decrements in conditioned stimulus processing by selective removal of hippocampal cholinergic input. *Journal of Neuroscience, 17*, 5230–5236.

Behrmann, M., Geng, J. J., & Shomstein, S. (2004) Parietal cortex and attention. *Current Opinion in Neurobiology, 14*, 212–217.

Berg, E. A. (1948). A simple objective technique for measuring flexibility in thinking. *Journal of General Psychology, 39*, 15–22.

Birrell, J. M., & Brown, V. J. (2000). Medial frontal cortex mediates perceptual attentional set shifting in the rat. *Journal of Neuroscience, 20*, 4320–4324.

Bissonette, G. B., Powell, E. M., & Roesch, M. R. (2013). Neural structures underlying set-shifting: Roles of medial prefrontal cortex and anterior cingulated cortex. *Behavioural Brain Research, 250*, 91–101.

Block, A. E., Dhanji, H., Thompson-Tardiff, S. F., & Floresco, S. B. (2007). Thalamic-prefrontal cortical-ventral striatal circuitry mediates dissociable components of strategy set shifting. *Cerebral Cortex, 17*, 1625–1636.

Bouton, M. E. (1993). Context, time, and memory retrieval in the interference paradigms of Pavlovian learning. *Psychological Bulletin, 114*, 80–99.

Bucci, D. J., Holland, P. C., & Gallagher, M. (1998). Removal of cholinergic input to rat posterior parietal cortex disrupts incremental processing of conditioned stimuli. *Journal of Neuroscience, 18*, 8038–8046.

Calu, D. J., Roesch, M. R., Haney, R. Z., Holland, P. C., & Schoenbaum, G. (2010). Neural correlates of variations in event processing during learning in central nucleus of amygdala. *Neuron, 68*, 991–1001.

Chang, S. E., McDannald, M. A., Wheeler, D. S., & Holland, P. C. (2012). The effects of basolateral amygdala lesions on unblocking. *Behavioral Neuroscience, 126*, 279–289.

Chiba, A. A., Bucci, D. J., Holland, P. C., & Gallagher, M. (1995). Basal forebrain cholinergic lesions disrupt increments but not decrements in conditioned stimulus processing. *Journal of Neuroscience, 15*, 7315–7322.

Christopoulos, G. I., Tobler, P. N., Bossaerts, P., Dolan, R. J., & Schultz, W. (2009). Neural correlates of value, risk, and risk aversion contributing to decision making under risk. *Journal of Neuroscience, 29*, 12574–12583.

Coutureau, E., Blundell, P. J., & Killcross, S. (2001). Basolateral amygdala lesions disrupt latent inhibition in rats. *Brain Research Bulletin, 56*, 49–53.

Coutureau, E., Galani, R., Gosselin, O., Majchrzak, M., & Di Scala, G. (1999). Entorhinal but not hippocampal or subicular lesions disrupt latent inhibition in rats. *Neurobiology of Learning and Memory, 72*, 143–157.

Coutureau, E., & Killcross, S. (2003). Inactivation of the infralimbic prefrontal cortex reinstates goal-directed responding in overtrained rats. *Behavioural Brain Research, 146*, 167–174.

Dias, R., Robbins, T. W., & Roberts, A. C. (1996a). Dissociation in prefrontal cortex of affective and attentional shifts. *Nature, 380*, 69–72.

Dias, R., Robbins, T. W., & Roberts, A. C. (1996b) Primate analogue of the Wisconsin Card Sorting Test: effects of excitotoxic lesions of the prefrontal cortex in the marmoset. *Behavioral Neuroscience, 110*, 872–886.

Dias, R., Robbins, T. W., & Roberts, A. C. (1997). Dissociable forms of inhibitory control within prefrontal cortex with an analog of the Wisconsin Card Sorting Test: Restriction to novel situations and independence from "on-line" processing. *Journal of Neuroscience, 17*, 9285–9297.

Dickinson, A., Hall, G., & Mackintosh, N. J. (1976). Surprise and the attenuation of blocking. *Journal of Experimental Psychology: Animal Behavior Processes, 2*, 313–322.

Downes, J. J., Roberts, A. C., Sahakian, B. J., Evenden, J. L., Morris, R. G., & Robbins, T. W. (1989). Impaired extra-dimensional shift performance in medicated and unmedicated Parkinson's disease: Evidence for a specific attentional dysfunction. *Neuropsychologia, 27*, 1329–1343.

Duffaud, A. M., Killcross, S., & George, D. N. (2007). Optional-shift behaviour in rats: A novel procedure for assessing attention processes in discrimination learning. *Quarterly Journal of Experimental Psychology, 60*, 534–542.

Durstewitz, D., Vittoz, N. M., Floresco, S. B., & Seamans, J. K. (2010). Abrupt transitions between prefrontal neural ensemble states accompany behavioural transitions during rule learning. *Neuron, 66*, 438–448.

Eimas, P. D. (1966). Effects of overtraining and age on intradimensional and extradimensional shifts in children. *Journal of Experimental Child Psychology, 3*, 348–355.

Eippert, F., Gamer, M., & Büchel, C. (2012). Neurobiological mechanisms underlying the blocking effect in aversive learning. *Journal of Neuroscience, 32*, 13164–13176.

Elliott, R., McKenna, P. J., Robbins, T. W., & Sahakian, B. J. (1995). Neuropsychological evidence for fronto-striatal dysfunction in schizophrenia. *Psychological Medicine, 25*, 619–630.

Esber, G. R., Roesch, M. R., Bali, S., Trageser, J., Bissonette, G. B., Puche, A. C., Holland, P. C., & Schoenbaum, G. (2012). Attention-related Pearce–Kaye–Hall signals in basolateral amygdala require the midbrain dopaminergic system. *Biological Psychiatry, 72*, 1012–1019.

Fiorillo, C. D., Tobler, P. N., & Schultz, W. (2003). Discrete coding of reward probability and uncertainty by dopamine neurons. *Science, 299*, 1898–1902.

Floresco, S. B., Zhang, Y., & Enomoto, T. (2009). Neural circuits subserving behavioural flexibility and their relevance to schizophrenia. *Behavioural Brain Research, 204*, 396–409.

Gallagher, M., Graham, P. W., & Holland, P. C. (1990). The amygdala central nucleus and appetitive Pavlovian conditioning: Lesions impair one class of conditioned behaviour. *Journal of Neuroscience, 10*, 1906–1911.

George, D. N., Duffaud, A. M., & Killcross, S. (2010). Neural correlates of attentional set. In C. J. Mitchell & M. E. Le Pelley (Eds.), *Attention and associative learning* (pp. 351–383). Oxford, UK: Oxford University Press.

George, D. N., Duffaud, A. M., Pothuizen, H. H. J., Haddon, J. E., & Killcross, S. (2010). Lesions to the ventral, but not the dorsal, medial prefrontal cortex enhance latent inhibition. *European Journal of Neuroscience, 31*, 1474–1482.

George, D. N., & Pearce, J. M. (1999). Acquired distinctiveness is controlled by stimulus relevance not correlation with reward. *Journal of Experimental Psychology: Animal Behavior Processes, 25*, 363–373.

George, D. N., & Pearce, J. M. (2012). A configural theory of attention and associative learning. *Learning & Behavior, 40*, 241–254.

Ghods-Sharifi, S., Haluk, D. M., & Floresco, S. B. (2008). Differential effects of inactivation of the orbitofrontal cortex on strategy set-shifting and reversal learning. *Neurobiology of Learning and Memory, 89*, 567–573.

Goldstein, K., & Scheerer, M. (1941). Abstract and concrete behavior: an experimental study with special tests. *Psychological Monographs, 53* (whole number 239), 1–151.

Grant, D. A., & Berg, E. A. (1948). A behavioural analysis of degree of reinforcement and ease of shifting to new responses in a Weigl-type card-sorting problem. *Journal of Experimental Psychology, 38*, 404–411.

Hall, G., & Pearce, J. M. (1979). Latent inhibition of a CS during CS–US pairings. *Journal of Experimental Psychology: Animal Behavior Processes, 5*, 31–42.

Hampshire, A., & Owen, A. M. (2010). Clinical studies of attention and learning. In C. J. Mitchell & M. E. Le Pelley (Eds.), *Attention and Associative Learning* (pp. 385–405). Oxford, UK: Oxford University Press.

Han, J. S., Gallagher, M., & Holland, P. C. (1995). Hippocampal lesions disrupt decrements but not increments in conditioned stimulus processing. *Journal of Neuroscience, 11*, 7323–7329.

Han, J-S., Holland, P. C., & Gallagher, M. (1999). Disconnection of the amygdala central nucleus and substantia innominata/nucleus basalis disrupts increments in conditioned stimulus processing in rats. *Behavioral Neuroscience, 113*, 143–151.

Holland, P. C. (1984). Unblocking in Pavlovian appetitive conditioning. *Journal of Experimental Psychology: Animal Behavior Processes, 10*, 476–497.

Holland, P. C. (2006). Enhanced conditioning produced by surprising increases in reinforce value are unaffected by lesions of the amygdala central nucleus. *Neurobiology of Learning and Memory, 85*, 30–35.

Holland, P. C., & Forbes, D. T. (1980). Effects of compound or element preexposure on compound flavor aversion conditioning. *Animal Learning & Behavior, 8*, 199–203.

Holland, P. C., & Gallagher, M. (1993a). Amygdala central nucleus lesions disrupt increments, but not decrements, in conditioned stimulus processing. *Behvioral Neuroscience, 107*, 246–253.

Holland, P. C., & Gallagher, M. (1993b). Effects of amygdala central nucleus lesions on blocking and unblocking. *Behavioral Neuroscience, 107*, 235–245.

Holland, P. C., & Gallagher, M. (2006). Different roles for amygdala central nucleus and substantial innominata in the surprise-induced enhancement of learning. *Journal of Neuroscience, 26*, 3791–3797.

Holland, P. C., Hatfield, T., & Gallagher, M. (2001). Rats with lesions of basolateral amygdala show normal increases in conditioned stimulus processing but reduced potentiation of eating. *Behavioral Neuroscience, 115*, 945–950.

Holland, P. C., & Maddux, J-M. (2010) Brain systems of attention in associative learning. In C. J. Mitchell & M. E. Le Pelley (Eds.), *Attention and associative learning* (pp. 305–349). Oxford, UK: Oxford University Press.

Honey, R. C., & Good, M. (1993). Selective hippocampal lesions abolish the contextual specificity of latent inhibition and conditioning. *Behavioral Neuroscience, 107*, 23–33.

Iordanova, M. D., Westbrook, R. F., & Killcross, A. S. (2006). Dopamine activity in the nucleus accumbens modulate blocking in fear conditioning. *European Journal of Neuroscience, 24*, 3265–3270.

Jones, D., & Gonzalez-Lima, F. (2001). Mapping Pavlovian conditioning effects on the brain: Blocking, contiguity, and excitatory effects. *Journal of Neurophysiology, 86*, 809–823.

Jones, P. M., & Haselgrove, M. (2013). Blocking and associability change. *Journal of Experimental Psychology: Animal Behavior Processes, 39*, 249–258.

Kamin, L. J. (1968). "Attention-like" processes in classical conditioning. In M. R. Jones (Ed.), *Miami Symposium on the Prediction of Behavior, 1967: Aversive Stimulation* (pp. 9–31). Coral Gables, FL: University of Miami Press.

Kaye, H., & Pearce, J. M. (1984). The strength of the orienting response during Pavlovian conditioning. *Journal of Experimental Psychology: Animal Behavior Processes, 10*, 90–109.

Kaye, H., & Pearce, J. M. (1987). Hippocampal lesions attenuate latent inhibition and the decline of the orienting response in rats. *Quarterly Journal of Experimental Psychology, 39B*, 107–125.

Kendler, T. S., Kendler, H. H., & Silfen, C. K. (1964). Optional shift behaviour of albino rats. *Psychonomic Science, 1*, 5–6.

Killcross, S., & Coutureau, E. (2003). Coordination of actions and habits in the medial prefrontal cortex of rats. *Cerebral Cortex, 13*, 400–408.

Klosterhalfen, S., Fischer, W., & Bitterman, M. E. (1978). Modification of attention in honey bees. *Science, 201*, 1241–1243.

Kruschke, J. K., & Blair, N. J. (2000). Blocking and backward blocking involve learned inattention. *Psychonomic Bulletin & Review, 7*, 636–645.

Lawrence, A. D., Sahakian, B. J., Hodges, J. R., Rosser, A. E., Lange, K. W., & Robbins, T. W. (1996). Executive and mnemonic functions in early Huntington's disease. *Brain, 119*, 1633–1645.

Lawrence, D. H. (1949). The acquired distinctiveness of cues: I. Transfer between discriminations on the basis of familiarity with the stimulus. *Journal of Experimental Psychology, 39*, 770–784.

Lawrence, D. H. (1950). The acquired distinctiveness of cues: II. Selective associations in a constant stimulus situation. *Journal of Experimental Psychology, 40*, 175–188.

Lawrence, D. H. (1952). The transfer of a discrimination along a continuum. *Journal of Comparative and Physiological Psychology, 45*, 511–516.

Lee, H. J., Youn, J. M., Gallagher, M., & Holland, P. C. (2008). Temporally limited role of substantia nigra-central amygdala connections in surprise-induced enhancement of learning. *European Journal of Neuroscience, 27*, 3043–3049.

Lee, H. J., Youn, J. M., O M. J., Gallagher, M., & Holland, P. C. (2006). Role of substantia nigra-amygdala connections in surprise-induced enhancement of attention. *Journal of Neuroscience, 26*, 6077–6081.

Le Pelley, M. E. (2004). The role of associative history in models of associative learning: A selective review and a hybrid model. *Quarterly Journal of Experimental Psychology, 57B*, 193–243.

Le Pelley, M. E. (2010). The hybrid modeling approach to conditioning. In N. A. Schmajuk (Ed.), *Computational models of conditioning* (pp. 71–107). Cambridge, UK: Cambridge University Press.

Le Pelley, M. E., Beesley, T., & Suret, M. (2007). Blocking of human causal learning involves learned changes in stimulus processing. *Quarterly Journal of Experimental Psychology, 60*, 1468–1476.

Lovejoy, E. (1968). *Attention in discrimination learning.* San Francisco, CA: Holden-Day.

Lubow, R. E., & Moore, A. U. (1959). Latent inhibition: The effect of non-reinforced preexposure to the conditioned stimulus. *Journal of Comparative and Physiological Psychology, 52*, 415–419.

Lubow, R. E., Wagner, M., & Weiner, I. (1982). The effects of compound stimulus preexposure of two elements differing in salience on the acquisition of conditioned suppression. *Animal Learning & Behavior, 10*, 483–489.

Mackintosh, N. J. (1974). *The psychology of animal learning.* London, UK: Academic Press.

Mackintosh, N. J. (1975). A theory of attention: Variations in the associability of stimuli with reinforcement. *Psychological Review, 82*, 276–298.

Mackintosh, N. J., & Little, L. (1969). Intradimensional and extradimensional shift learning by pigeons. *Psychonomic Science, 14*, 5–6.

Mackintosh, N. J., & Turner, C. (1971) Blocking as a function of novelty of CS and predictability of UCS. *The Quarterly Journal of Experimental Psychology, 23*, 359–366.

Matsumoto, M., & Hikosaka, O. (2009a). Representation of negative motivational value in the primate lateral habenula. *Nature Neuroscience, 12*, 77–84.

Matsumoto, M., & Hikosaka, O. (2009b). Two types of dopamine neuron distinctly convey positive and negative motivational signals. *Nature, 459*, 837–841.

Matsumoto, M., Matsumoto, K., Abe, H., & Tanaka, K. (2007). Medial prefrontal cell activity signalling prediction errors of action values. *Nature Neuroscience, 10*, 647–656.

McCoy, A. N., & Platt, M. L. (2005). Risk-sensitive neurons in macaque posterior cingulate cortex. *Nature Neuroscience, 8*, 1220–1227.

Metereau, E., & Dreher, J-C. (2013). Cerebral correlates of salient prediction error for different rewards and punishments. *Cerebral Cortex, 23*, 477–487.

Milner, B. (1963). Effects of different brain lesions on card sorting: The role of the frontal lobes. *Archives of Neurology, 9*, 100–110.

Milner, B. (1964). Some effects of frontal lobectomy in man. In J. M. Warren & K. Akert (Eds.), *The frontal granular cortex and behavior.* New York: McGraw-Hill.

Monosov, I. E., & Hikosaka, O. (2013). Selective and graded coding of reward uncertainty by neurons in the primate anterodorsal septal region. *Nature Neuroscience, 16*, 756–762.

Nelson, A. J. D., Thur, K. E., Marsden, C. A., & Cassaday, H. J. (2010). Catecholaminergic depletion within the prelimbic medial prefrontal cortex enhances latent inhibition. *Neuroscience, 170*, 99–106.

O'Neill, M., & Schultz, W. (2010). Coding of reward risk by orbitofrontal neurons is mostly distinct from coding reward value. *Neuron, 68*, 789–800.

Oswald, C. J. P., Yee, B. K., Bannerman, D. B., Rawlins, J. N. P., Good, M., & Honey, R. C. (2002). The influence of selective lesions to components of the hippocampal system on the orienting response, habituation and latent inhibition. *European Journal of Neuroscience, 15*, 1983–1990.

Owen, A. M., Roberts, A. C., Hodges, J. R., Summers, B. A., Polkey, C. E., & Robbins, T. W. (1993). Contrasting mechanisms of impaired attentional set-shifting in patients with frontal lobe damage or Parkinson's disease. *Brain, 116*, 1159–1175.

Owen, A. M., Roberts, A. C., Polkey, C. E., Sahakian, B. K., & Robbins, T. W. (1991). Extra-dimensional versus intra-dimensional set shifting performance following frontal love excisions, temporal lobe excisions or amygdalo-hippocampectomy in man. *Neuropsychologia, 29*, 993–1006.

Pavlov, I. P. (1927). *Conditioned reflexes.* Oxford, UK: Oxford University Press.

Pearce, J. M., & Hall, G. (1980). A model of Pavlovian learning: Variations in the effectiveness of conditioned but not of unconditioned stimuli. *Psychological Review, 87*, 532–552.

Pearce, J. M., Kaye, H., & Hall, G. (1982). Predictive accuracy and stimulus associability: Development of a model for Pavlovian learning. In M. L. Commons, R. J. Herrnstein, & A. R. Wagner (Eds.), *Quantitative analyses of behavior* (Vol. 3, pp. 241–256). Cambridge, UK: Ballinger.

Pearce, J. M., & Mackintosh, N. J. (2010). Two theories of attention: A review and a possible integration. In C. J. Mitchell & M. E. Le Pelley (Eds.), *Attention and associative learning: From brain to behaviour* (pp. 11–40). Oxford, UK: Oxford University Press.

Ragozzino, M. E., Ragozzino, K. E., Mizumori, S. J. Y., & Kesner, R. P. (2002). Role of the dorsomedial striatum in behavioral flexibility for response and visual cue discrimination learning. *Behavioral Neuroscience, 116*, 105–115.

Rescorla, R. A., & Wagner, A. R. (1972). A theory of Pavlovian conditioning: variations in the effectiveness of reinforcement and nonreinforcement. In A. H. Black & W. F. Prokasy (Eds.), *Classical conditioning II: Current research and theory* (pp. 64–99). New York, NY: Appleton-Century-Crofts.

Reid, L. S. (1953). The development of noncontinuity behaviour through continuity learning. *Journal of Experimental Psychology, 46*, 107–112.

Rhodes, S. E. V., & Killcross, S. (2004) Lesions of rat infralimbic cortex enhance recovery and reinstatement of an appetitive Pavlovian response. *Learning & Memory, 11*, 611–616.

Rhodes, S. E. V., & Killcross, S. (2007) Lesions of rat infralimbic cortex enhance renewal of extinguished appetitive Pavlovian responding. *European Journal of Neuroscience, 25*, 2498–2503.

Roberts, A. C., Robbins, T. W., & Everitt, B. J. (1988). The effects of intradimensional and extradimensional shifts on visual discrimination learning in humans and non-human primates. *Quarterly Journal of Experimental Psychology, 40B*, 321–341.

Robbins, T. W. (2007) Shifting and stopping: fronto-striatal substrates, neurochemical modulation and clinical implications. *Philosophical Transactions of the Royal Society of London. Series B, Biological Sciences, 362*, 917–932.

Robbins, T. W., James, M., Owen, A. M., Sahakian, B. J., Lawrence, A. D., McInnes, L., & Rabbit, P. M. A. (1998). A study of performance on tests from the CANTAB battery sensitive to frontal lobe dysfunction in a large sample of normal volunteers: Implications for theories of executive functioning and cognitive ageing. *Journal of the International Neuropsychological Society, 4*, 474–490.

Roesch, M. R., Calu, D. J., Esber, G. R., & Schoenbaum, G. (2010). Neural correlates of variations in event processing during learning in basolateral amygdala. *Journal of Neuroscience, 30*, 2464–2471.

Schmajuk, N. A., Lam, Y-W., Christiansen, B. A. (1994). Latent inhibition of the rat eyeblink response: Effect of hippocampal aspiration lesions. *Physiology & Behavior, 55*, 597–601.

Schultz, W., Dayan, P., & Montague, P. R. (1997). A neural substrate of prediction and reward. *Science, 275*, 1593–1599.

Shepp, B. E., & Eimas, P. D. (1964). Intradimensional and extradimensional shifts in the rat. *Journal of Comparative and Physiological Psychology, 57*, 357–364.

Shepp, B. E., & Schrier, A. M. (1969). Consecutive intradimensional and extradimensional shifts in monkeys. *Journal of Comparative and Physiological Psychology, 67*, 199–203.

Shone, L., & Livesey, E. (2013). Automatic and instructed attention in learned predictiveness. In *35th Annual Meeting of the Cognitive Science Society (COGSCI 2013)*. Austin, TX: Cognitive Science Society.

Siegel, S. (1967). Overtraining and transfer processes. *Journal of Comparative and Physiological Psychology, 64*, 471–477.

Siegel, S. (1969). Discrimination overtraining and shift behaviour. In R. M. Gilbert & N. S. Sutherland (Eds.), *Animal discrimination learning*. New York, NY: Academic Press.

Slamecka, N. J. (1968). A methodological analysis of shift paradigms in human discrimination learning. *Psychological Bulletin*, 69, 423–438.

Sokolov, E. N. (1963). *Perception and the conditioned reflex*. Oxford, UK: Pergamon Press.

Steinberg, E. E., Keiflin, R., Boivin, J. R., Witten, I. B., Deisseroth, K., & Janak, P. H. (2013). A causal link between prediction errors, dopamine neurons and learning. *Nature Neuroscience*, 16, 966–973.

Sutherland, N. S., & Mackintosh, N. J. (1971). *Mechanisms of animal discrimination learning*. New York, NY: Academic Press.

Sutton, R. S. (1988) Learning to predict by the method of temporal difference. *Machine Learning*, 3, 9–44.

Tait, D., S., & Brown, V. J. (2008). Lesions of the basal forebrain impair reversal learning but not shifting of attentional set in rats. *Behavioural Brain Research*, 187, 100–108.

Tobler, P. N., Christopoulos, G. I., O'Doherty, J. P., Dolan, R. J., & Schultz, W. (2009). Risk-dependent reward value signal in human prefrontal cortex. *Proceedings of the National Academy of Sciences of the USA*, 106, 7185–7190.

Trabasso, T., & Bower, G. H. (1968). *Attention in learning: Theory and research*. New York, NY: John Wiley & Sons.

Veale, D. M., Sahakian, B. J., Owen, A. M., & Marks, I. M. (1996). Specific cognitive deficits in tests sensitive to frontal lobe dysfunction in obsessive–compulsive disorder. *Psychological Medicine*, 26, 1261–1269.

Waelti, P., Dickinson, A., & Schultz, W. (2001). Dopamine responses comply with basic assumptions of formal learning theory. *Nature*, 412, 43–48.

Wagner, A. R. (1981). SOP: A model of automatic memory processing in animal behavior. In N. E. Spear & R. R. Miller (Eds.), *Information processing in animals: Memory mechanisms* (pp. 5–47). Hillsdale, NJ: Erlbaum.

Weiner, I. (2003). The "two-headed" latent inhibition model of schizophrenia: modelling positive and negative symptoms and their treatment. *Psychopharmacology*, 169, 257–297.

Weiner, I., Tarrasch, R., & Feldon, J. (1995). Basolateral amygdala lesions do not disrupt latent inhibition. *Behavioural Brain Research*, 72, 73–81.

Weigl, E. (1941). On the psychology of the go-called processes of abstraction. *Journal of Abnormal and Social Psychology*, 36, 3–33.

Wilson, P. N., Boumphrey, P., & Pearce, J. M. (1992). Restoration of the orienting response to a light by a change in its predictive accuracy. *Quarterly Journal of Experimental Psychology*, 44B, 17–36.

Wolff, J. L. (1967). Concept-shift and discrimination-reversal learning in humans. *Psychological Bulletin*, 68, 369–408.

Xue, G., Lu, Z., Levin, I. P., Weller, J. A., Li, X., & Bechara, A. (2009). Functional dissociations of risk and reward processing in the medial prefrontal cortex. *Cerebral Cortex*, 19, 1019–1027.

Zeaman, D., & House, B. J. (1963). The role of attention in retardate learning. In N. R. Ellis (Ed.), *Handbook of mental deficiency: Psychological theory and research* (pp. 159–223). New York, NY: McGraw-Hill.

6

Associative Learning and Derived Attention in Humans

Mike Le Pelley, Tom Beesley, and Oren Griffiths

Derived Attention

Attention describes the collection of cognitive mechanisms that act to preferentially allocate mental resources to the processing of certain aspects of sensory input. As such, attention plays a central role in determining our interactions with the sensory world. Research into attentional processes in the cognitive psychology and neuroscience literature has traditionally focused on two fundamental issues (for reviews, see Jonides, 1981; Yantis, 2000). First, how much control do we have over our deployment of attention? For example, if we are instructed to monitor location X, we will typically be faster to detect events occurring at location X than at an unattended location Y (Posner, 1980). This suggests that people can deploy attention in a controlled fashion in order to enhance certain aspects of stimulus processing. Second, to what extent is attention influenced by the properties of stimuli that we encounter? For example, if we are instructed to monitor location X, a sudden flash at location Y will nevertheless automatically summon attention to this location and (transiently) speed detection of other events occurring there (Posner & Cohen, 1984). This suggests that stimulus properties (such as color, intensity, or abruptness of onset) can influence deployment of attention in a relatively automatic fashion.

In contrast, researchers working within the conditioning and associative learning literature have tended to focus on how attention to stimuli is influenced by learning about the significance of those stimuli. That is, this research investigates how attention is malleable, as a function of organisms' experience of the relationships between events in the world. The idea that learning might influence the amount of attention paid to a stimulus – that stimuli with meaningful consequences might "stand out" – is certainly not new. William James (1890/1983) introduced the concept of *derived attention*; a form of attention to a stimulus that "owes its interest to association with some other immediately interesting thing" (p. 393). While the idea has been with us for some time, this chapter describes important advances that have been made in recent years in elucidating the nature and operation of derived attention in studies of human learning.

Part 1: Learned Predictiveness

Formal theories of derived attention – often referred to as attentional theories of associative learning – have existed for over 50 years (e.g., Lovejoy, 1968; Mackintosh, 1975; Sutherland & Mackintosh, 1971; Trabasso & Bower, 1968; Zeaman & House, 1963). These theories have in common the idea that attention to a stimulus is not a fixed consequence of its physical characteristics, but rather that it can vary with an organism's experience of the correlation between that stimulus and other events. One of the most influential of these attentional theories of associative learning has been Mackintosh's (1975) model, which states that attention is a function of the *learned predictiveness* of a stimulus. Suppose that a doctor examines a series of ill patients and finds that the type of rash on each person's skin reveals the type of virus they have contracted, while other symptoms (swollen glands, clammy hands, etc.) do not reliably signal which type of virus the patient has. Hence, the type of rash is a better predictor of type of virus than are these other symptoms. According to Mackintosh's theory, the doctor will therefore learn to pay more attention to rashes than to other symptoms when making diagnoses in the future.

There is now a wealth of empirical evidence, from both humans and animals, that experience of learned predictiveness produces some kind of change in the processing of stimuli. Traditionally, these studies have examined the extent to which previous learning about the predictiveness of stimuli influences the rate of future learning about those stimuli. These studies are predicated on the reasonable assumption that organisms will learn more rapidly about stimuli for which they are attending than those they are ignoring. Suppose that our doctor has learned to pay attention to rashes and to ignore other symptoms. A new strain of bacterium now evolves that reliably causes a particular type of rash *and* clammy hands. As a consequence of his previously learned difference in attention to the different symptoms, the doctor might be more likely to learn about the relationship between the rash and this new bacterium than between clammy hands and the same bacterium, even though both symptoms actually have the same diagnostic value.

This idea that previous experience of predictiveness will influence the rate of new learning about stimuli has now been confirmed countless times in animals and humans, in experiments that are conceptually similar to the doctor example given above (see Mitchell & Le Pelley, 2010). In humans at least, the results of these experiments have typically been in line with the spirit of Mackintosh's (1975) model, with faster learning about stimuli previously experienced as predictive than those experienced as nonpredictive (Beesley & Le Pelley, 2010; Bonardi, Graham, Hall, & Mitchell, 2005; Kruschke, 1996; Le Pelley & McLaren, 2003; Le Pelley, Turnbull, Reimers, & Knipe, 2010; but see also Griffiths, Johnson, & Mitchell, 2011).

These findings are consistent with the idea that learning about predictiveness influences the perceived salience of stimuli. The logic runs thus: (1) Studies have shown that the rate of learning is influenced by the perceptual salience of stimuli in animals and humans (e.g., Denton & Kruschke, 2006; Kamin & Schaub, 1963); (2) the studies mentioned in the previous paragraph show that the rate of learning is influenced by previous learning about predictiveness; so maybe (3) previous learning about predictiveness modulates the perceptual salience of stimuli. On this view, the data from human studies suggest that predictive stimuli become more salient and hence more likely to capture attention in the future.

The weakness of this logic is clear: There are many reasons why people might learn faster about a stimulus that are unrelated to its salience. Perhaps stimuli experienced as predictive develop stronger and/or more distinct representations in memory than those experienced as nonpredictive, and this allows subsequent information to be more accurately addressed to (associated with) the stronger stimulus representation of predictive stimuli (see Honey, Close, & Lin, 2010; Le Pelley, Reimers, et al., 2010). Or perhaps people draw a conscious inference that stimuli that were previously useful in making predictions will continue to be useful in making predictions in future. Hence, people would place more weight on these previously predictive stimuli when judging relationships of contingency in future (Mitchell, Griffiths, Seetoo, & Lovibond, 2012).

The problem with these previous tests of attentional theories of learning is that measuring the rate of learning about a stimulus provides only a very indirect measure of attention to that stimulus, and learning rate can be influenced by many other, non-attentional factors. This has led researchers to develop other, more direct and more diagnostic ways to assess the relationship between associative learning and attention.

Perhaps foremost among these has been the use of eye tracking. One of the most obvious features of visual attention is that it tends to coincide with where our eyes are looking, referred to as *overt* attention. While it is possible to make *covert* shifts of attention that are not accompanied by eye movements (Posner, 1980), eye movements and attentional shifts are generally tightly coupled (Deubel & Schneider, 1996), especially when dealing with the sorts of relatively complex stimuli (words and complex pictures) typically used in studies of human contingency learning.

Many studies have now used eye tracking to demonstrate that associative learning does indeed exert an influence on overt attention (Beesley & Le Pelley, 2011; Hogarth et al., 2008; Kruschke, Kappenman, & Hetrick, 2005; Le Pelley, Beesley, & Griffiths, 2011; Rehder & Hoffman, 2005; Wills, Lavric, Croft, & Hodgson, 2007). To the extent that these studies provide support for a particular view of this relationship, they once again tend to concord with Mackintosh's (1975) suggestion that predictive stimuli will capture more attention than nonpredictive stimuli (Le Pelley et al., 2011; Le Pelley, Mitchell, et al., 2013; Rehder & Hoffman, 2005; but see Hogarth et al., 2008).

What do these findings really tell us? In all of these studies, overt attention was measured while people were performing a contingency learning task. On each trial, stimuli were presented, and participants were required to make a response to those stimuli. They would then be told whether this prediction was correct or not, and could use this feedback to learn the various stimulus–outcome relationships present in the experiment. As an example, consider the commonly used "food allergist" cover-story, in which participants must predict the type of allergic reaction (headache or nausea) that a patient will suffer as a result of eating particular foods. Suppose that, over previous trials, apple had consistently been paired with headache (and hence was predictive), while carrot had been equally followed by headache and nausea (and hence was nonpredictive). Now, apples and carrot are presented together, and the participant is asked to make an allergy prediction. If the participant happens to look first at "apple," they can confidently respond "headache" without needing to gather further information. In contrast, if the participant looks first at "carrot," they cannot respond confidently; they would need to keep gathering information until they established that "apple" was also present, at which point they could respond. Consequently, if the overt attention that is measured using eye tracking correlates with this process of information gathering, it is not surprising that it should show the advantage for predictive cues that is observed experimentally: Predictive stimuli are the only cues that *need* to be identified in order to perform accurately.

In order to establish that associative learning about predictiveness exerts a more fundamental influence on the processing of a stimulus, we instead need to examine whether learning can produce a bias in the attentional processing of a stimulus that operates even when it is not required. That is, a bias that is orthogonal to the demands of the task being performed, or which may even hinder performance on that task. We know of just two studies in humans that may fulfill this criterion (Le Pelley, Vadillo, & Luque, 2013; Livesey, Harris, & Harris, 2009).

Livesey et al. (2009) used a complicated procedure, but essentially people were trained with a task in which the appearance of certain target letters in a rapid stream of stimuli predicted which of two responses they would subsequently be required to make, while other target letters did not predict the correct response. In a separate test phase that followed, participants showed an advantage in detecting previously predictive target letters in rapidly presented letter streams, relative to previously nonpredictive targets; specifically, these previously predictive letters were less susceptible to the so-called *attentional blink* effect (Raymond, Shapiro, & Arnell, 1992).

This finding is certainly consistent with the idea that associative learning effectively increases the salience of (and extent of attentional capture by) predictive stimuli, thereby increasing their detectability. And importantly, this advantage for predictive stimuli was observed in a test that was independent of the learning task used to establish that predictiveness, unlike in the previously cited eye-tracking studies. However, an alternative interpretation is possible. Suppose that, during the initial training phase, predictive letters come to be represented more strongly in memory by virtue of their consistent pairings with particular responses (cf. Honey et al., 2010). As a consequence, in the test phase participants may simply have been more likely to *report* these previously predictive letters even if they had not *detected* them. So, the advantage for predictive letters in the test phase might reflect participants being more likely to guess these letters (in terms of signal detection theory, a difference in criterion β) rather than reflecting a difference in detectability (d'). Unfortunately, Livesey et al. (2009) do not report the false alarm rates that could rule out this account.

Le Pelley et al. (2013) also used a procedure in which the test phase was separate from the training phase in which predictiveness was established (Figure 6.1). During the training phase, certain stimuli predicted the correct response to be made on a trial (pressing the up or down arrow key), while other stimuli provided no information regarding the correct response and hence were nonpredictive. After many trials of training on this task, during which time participants learned the stimulus–outcome relationships, they moved on to a test phase that involved a variant of the *dot probe* procedure (MacLeod, Mathews, & Tata, 1986). On each trial of this test phase two stimuli were presented, one on either side of the screen. One of these stimuli had been predictive in the training phase, and the other had been nonpredictive. After a stimulus-onset asynchrony (SOA) of 350 ms, a dot probe (a small white triangle)

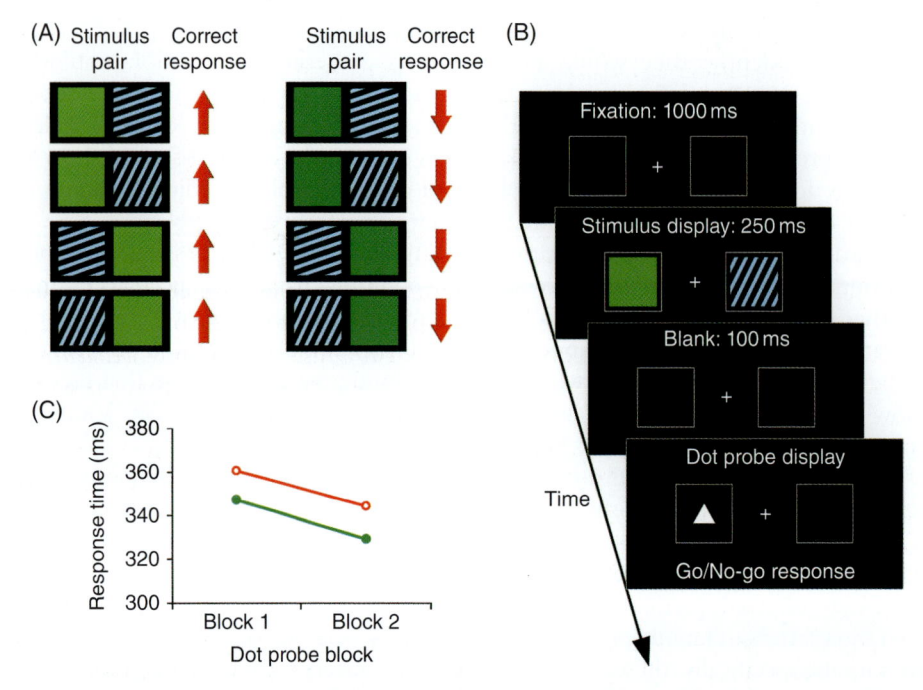

Figure 6.1 Experiment 1 reported by Le Pelley *et al.* (2013) involved two phases. (A) On each trial of the training phase, a pair of stimuli appeared – a green square and some oblique lines – and participants were required to make either an "up" or "down" response, with corrective feedback. For half of the participants, the shade of the green square predicted the correct response, while the orientation of the oblique lines provided no information regarding the correct response and hence was nonpredictive. This is the situation shown in (A). For the other half of participants, this stimulus assignment was reversed, so that the orientation was predictive, and the shade of green was nonpredictive. (B) On trials of the subsequent test phase, a pair of stimuli (one green square and one set of lines) appeared briefly and were sometimes followed by a dot probe (the white triangle). The participants' task was to press the spacebar as quickly as possible if and when this probe appeared, and to withhold this response otherwise. Importantly, the probe was equally likely to appear in the location of the stimulus that had been predictive of the correct response in the training phase as in the location of the stimulus that had been nonpredictive. (C) Nevertheless, responses to the dot probe were faster when it appeared in the same location as the stimulus that had been predictive (green line) than the location of the nonpredictive stimulus (red line).

sometimes appeared in the location of one of these stimuli, and participants were required to press the spacebar as rapidly as possible if and when the probe appeared. Importantly, across trials of the test phase, the dot probe was equally likely to appear in the location of the stimulus that had been predictive during the training phase as it was to appear in the location of the nonpredictive stimulus. Hence, there was no advantage to be gained in directing attention to either location prior to dot probe presentation. Indeed, participants were explicitly informed that in order to respond to the dot probe as quickly as possible, their best strategy was to ignore the initially presented stimuli. Despite this instruction, dot probe responses were significantly faster when the probe appeared in the location of the predictive stimulus than when it appeared in the location of the nonpredictive stimulus.

The implication is that the predictive stimulus captured participants' spatial attention and hence sped responses to events occurring in that location, in this case, the onset of the dot probe (see Posner, 1980, for more on the relationship between spatial attention and response speed). This attentional capture occurred, even though (1) it was not required by the task, (2) it was not adaptive with regard to that task, and (3) the short SOA meant that there was little time for participants to consciously process and respond to the stimuli on each test trial. Le Pelley, Vadillo, *et al.* (2013) demonstrated that providing more time for participants to consciously process the stimuli – by increasing the SOA on test trials to 1000 ms – significantly *weakened* the influence of predictiveness on dot probe responding. This suggests that the pattern observed at short SOA is not a result of conscious, controlled processing but instead reflects a rapid and relatively automatic effect of predictiveness on attentional capture. A long SOA then provides sufficient time for participants to use controlled processes to correct for the automatic attentional orienting caused by presentation of the stimuli, returning attention to the center of the display (cf. Klauer, Roßnagel, & Musch, 1997).

Thus, Le Pelley *et al.*'s (2013) dot probe data support the suggestion that associative learning about predictiveness can influence the effective salience of stimuli, with predictive stimuli becoming more likely to capture attention in future. We also note that this pattern of greater attention to predictive than nonpredictive stimuli is consistent with Mackintosh's (1975) attentional theory of associative learning.

Learned Value

In all of the studies described in the previous section, the events used to establish the differential predictiveness of cues (types of allergic reaction suffered by fictitious patients; up or down arrows, etc.) did not have strong motivational value. This leaves open the question of whether attention to stimuli might be influenced not only by how associated or predictive they are but also by the value of their associates, their *learned value*.

This question has recently come under empirical scrutiny (Anderson, Laurent, & Yantis, 2011a, 2011b; Anderson & Yantis, 2012; Della Libera & Chelazzi, 2009; Kiss, Driver, & Eimer, 2009; Le Pelley, Mitchell, & Johnson, 2013; Theeuwes & Belopolsky, 2012). These studies have used reward-learning tasks to examine changes in attention to discriminative stimuli as a function of outcome value.

Le Pelley, Mitchell, and Johnson (2013) trained people on a task in which certain stimuli consistently signaled a response that produced a large reward (150 Space Credits; participants exchanged Space Credits for real money at the end of the experiment), while others signaled a response that produced a small reward (1 Space Credit). Note that both types of stimulus were equally (and perfectly) predictive of reward; they differed only in the value of the reward that they predicted. During this training, people showed a bias in overt attention – measured using an eye tracker – toward stimuli that signaled large reward ("high-value" stimuli) over those that signaled small reward ("low-value" stimuli). Moreover, after this training, participants were faster to learn new associations involving high-value stimuli than low-value stimuli.

These findings are consistent with the idea that learning about the value of an outcome predicted by a stimulus produces a change in the effective salience of (and attentional capture by) that stimulus. However, as in the case of studies of learned predictiveness, which use learning rate and eye gaze as dependent variables (discussed earlier), other interpretations are possible. The influence of learned value on learning rate may not be mediated by attention; for example, it may instead reflect a difference in the extent to which stimuli are represented in memory. And the influence of learned value on overt attention was demonstrated only during the learning task itself; as such, the effect may be specific to the way in which people learn to attribute predictive power in this task. That is, participants may look more at high-value stimulus X than at low-value stimulus Y not because stimulus X has become generally more salient, and hence more likely to grab attention automatically, but instead because they have learned that stimulus X has greater meaning within the learning task, and hence it is more important to ensure it has been identified correctly so as to be confident of making the correct response.

As in the case of learned predictiveness, clearer evidence of a more automatic and general influence of learned value on attentional processing would come from a procedure in which attentional bias is measured separately from the learning task, and when it will (if anything) hinder performance during the test phase. Anderson *et al.* (2011a; see also Anderson *et al.*, 2011b) describe just such a procedure, using a visual search task. Each trial of an initial training phase presented six differently colored circles (Figure 6.2A). Each display contained a target circle, which could be red or green. Participants responded as rapidly as possible to the orientation of a line segment inside the target circle (vertical or horizontal). Correct responses made within 600 ms were rewarded, with the amount of reward related to the color of the target (red or green) on that trial. One of the target colors (the high-value color) was paired with high reward (5¢) on 80% of trials and low reward (1¢) on 20% of trials. The other, low-value target color was paired with high reward on 20% of trials and low reward on 80%. Participants were not explicitly informed of this reward contingency, but learned it over the course of 1,008 training trials.

In a subsequent test phase, on each trial participants were again presented with six shapes: either five circles and one diamond (Figure 6.2B) or one circle and five diamonds. The target on each trial was now defined by the unique shape; e.g., on a trial with five circles and one diamond, the target was the diamond. As before, participants responded to the orientation of a line segment within this target (no monetary rewards were provided during the test phase). Importantly, on some trials one of the nontarget shapes in this test display was colored either red or green (all other shapes were black). Participants were explicitly informed that color was irrelevant to this task and should be ignored, and that the target would never be red or green. Nevertheless, Anderson *et al.* (2011a) found that test phase response times were influenced by the color of the nontarget shape. Responses were slower if the test display contained a nontarget in the high-value color than if it contained a nontarget in the low-value color.

Theeuwes and Belopolsky (2012; see also Anderson & Yantis, 2012) describe a similar experiment. Each of 240 training trials presented six red shapes: four circles,

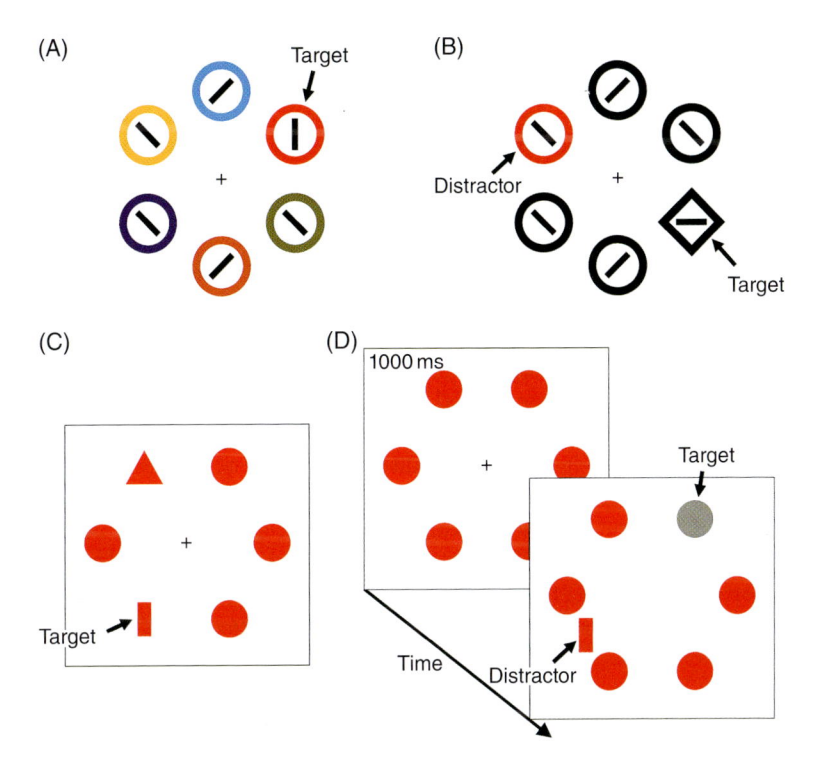

Figure 6.2 Example training phase (A) and test phase (B) displays from the study by Anderson et al. (2011a). In the training phase, the target was defined as a red or green circle, and participants were required to respond according to the orientation of the line segment (horizontal or vertical) inside this target circle. The color of the target circle determined the size of the reward for a correct response. In the test phase, the target was defined as a shape oddball: either a diamond among circles (as shown here) or a circle among diamonds. In the test phase, one of the nontarget circles (the distractor) could appear rendered in either red or green. Example training phase (C) and test phase (D) displays from the study by Theeuwes and Belopolsky (2012). In the training phase, the target was defined as a vertical or horizontal bar, and participants were required to make a saccade to this target as quickly as possible. The orientation of the target circle determined the size of the reward for a correct response. In the test phase, the target was as a gray circle. A distractor bar could appear, oriented either vertically or horizontally.

one triangle, and one rectangular bar, which could be oriented vertically or horizontally (Figure 6.2C). Participants were instructed to make a single saccade to the bar as quickly and accurately as possible. Correct saccades (measured using an eye tracker) were rewarded, with the amount of reward depending on whether the bar was vertical or horizontal. Correct responses to one of the orientations (high-value stimulus) were followed by high reward (10¢) on 80% of trials and low reward (1¢) on 20%; correct responses to the other orientation (low-value stimulus) were followed by high reward on 20% of trials and low reward on 80%. The assignment of vertical and horizontal orientations to high- and low-value stimuli was counterbalanced across participants.

In a subsequent, unrewarded test phase, each trial began with presentation of six red circles. After 1000 ms, one of these circles changed color to gray, and participants were required to make a saccade to this target stimulus as quickly and accurately as possible. On some test trials, at the same time as the target appeared a vertical or horizontal bar also appeared (Figure 6.2D) but was irrelevant to the task. However, participants sometimes made their first eye movement toward this distractor, rather than toward the target. And crucially, the likelihood of this oculomotor capture by the distractor was significantly greater when the distractor was the high-value stimulus than when it was the low-value stimulus.

Thus, in the studies by Anderson et al. (2011a) and Theeuwes and Belopolsky (2012), a task-irrelevant distractor previously associated with high reward interfered more strongly with performance (by slowing visual search or capturing eye gaze) than a distractor previously associated with smaller reward, even though the physical salience of these distractors was matched across participants by counterbalancing. The implication is that the high-value stimulus is more likely than the low-value stimulus to capture attention when it appears as a distractor in the test phase, and hence slow processing of the target. Thus, these findings demonstrate that learned value influences attentional capture. Notably, this attentional capture must surely be involuntary, since the high- and low-value stimuli are irrelevant to the participants' task in the test phase, and attending to them will, if anything, hinder performance.

In support of the suggestion that this *value-driven capture* reflects the influence of selective attention, Kiss et al. (2009) used a training procedure similar to that of Anderson et al. (2011a), combined with electroencephalography, to demonstrate that the learned value of target stimuli modulates event-related potential (ERP) signatures of attentional selection. Specifically, the N2pc ERP component occurred earlier, and had greater magnitude, for targets rendered in a high-value color than targets in a low-value color. The N2pc is an early, lateralized component emerging around 180–220 ms after display onset, and extensive study of singleton visual search has identified it as an important correlate of visual target selection (see Eimer, 1996; Woodman & Luck, 1999).

The nature of the learning that underlies this value-driven attentional capture remains open to debate, however. Notably, in all of the studies described above, during the initial training stage the stimuli that predicted reward were *task-relevant* for participants. In the training phase of the studies by Anderson et al. (2011a, b), participants were required to attend to the colored circles, since they constituted the targets to which responses were made during the initial training stage. That is, the stimuli that predicted reward were also the stimuli that participants responded to in order to obtain that reward. This raises the possibility that capture of attention by similar-colored circles in the subsequent test phase was simply a "hangover' of an overlearned attentional orienting response to these stimuli that was previously established in the training phase. Similarly, by the end of the training phase of Theeuwes and Belopolsky's (2012) eye-tracking study, participants had received a large reward 96 times for making an eye movement toward (say) a vertical bar. Having been strongly conditioned to make this oculomotor response, it is perhaps unsurprising that participants should continue (at least for a while) to make oculomotor responses toward similar vertical bars in the test phase.

These prior experiments demonstrate that the task relevance of stimuli during training is sufficient for value-driven attentional capture to occur. But is it *necessary*? This is an important question, because in the real world, stimuli that signal reward are not always direct causes of those rewards. For example, an addict may typically take drugs in a particular room. This room signals the drug's rewarding effect but has no instrumental relationship with achieving that reward: Entering the room does not itself elicit a drug reward, and the drug would have a similar rewarding effect if ingested elsewhere. In this sense, the room is task-irrelevant with respect to the goal of achieving drug reward.

We have investigated whether task relevance is necessary for value-driven attentional capture in a recent series of experiments, which used training in which the critical stimuli were *never* task relevant for participants (Le Pelley, Pearson, Griffiths, & Beesley, 2015). The final experiment of this series used a gaze-contingent procedure, in which eye movements not only provided our measure of attention but also were the means by which participants made responses during the experiment. Specifically, on each trial, participants were required to move their eyes to the location of a diamond-shaped target among circles (Figure 6.3A), as quickly as possible. A distractor circle could be rendered in either a high-value color or a low-value color (red or blue, counterbalanced across participants). A response was registered when 100 ms of eye gaze had accumulated in a small region of interest (ROI) surrounding the diamond target. On trials with a distractor in the high-value color, rapid responses earned a large reward (10¢). On trials with a distractor in the low-value color, rapid responses earned a small reward (1¢). Importantly, however, if at any point participants' gaze was registered in a relatively large ROI surrounding the distractor, the reward on that trial was cancelled; these were termed *omission trials*.

Thus, while the distractor predicted reward magnitude, it was not the stimulus to which participants were required to respond (or direct their attention) in order to

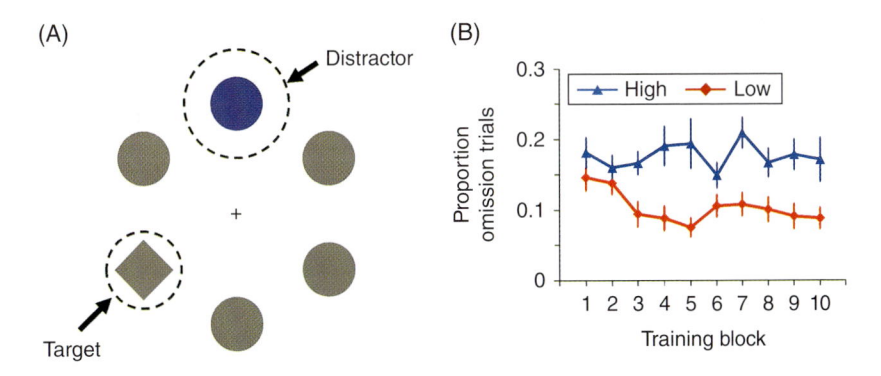

Figure 6.3 (A) Example stimulus display from the study by Le Pelley *et al.* (2015). Participants responded by moving their eyes to the diamond target. One of the nontarget circles (the distractor) could be red or blue. Dotted lines (not visible to participants) indicate the ROI around the target and distractor within which eye gaze was defined as falling on the corresponding stimulus. Fast, correct responses received a monetary reward, depending on the distractor color. A high-value distractor color reliably predicted a large reward; a low-value color reliably predicted a small reward. If gaze fell within the distractor ROI at any point, the trial was deemed an omission trial, and no reward was delivered. (B) Mean proportion of omission trials across the 10 training blocks, for trials with high-value and low-value distractors. High-value distractors produced significantly more omission trials than did low-value distractors. Error bars show within-subjects SEM.

obtain that reward. Hence, throughout the entire experiment, the distractor was irrelevant with respect to participants' goal of obtaining reward. Indeed, our design went further than this, in that participants were never rewarded if they looked at or near the distractor. As such, there was no reinforcement for participants to develop an attentional orienting response toward the distractor. Nevertheless, even under these conditions, participants still developed an attentional bias toward high-value distractors. Figure 6.3B shows the proportion of omission trials in each of the 10 training blocks of this study. The key finding is that high-value distractors produced significantly more omission trials than did low-value distractors ($p = .004$). That is, participants were more likely to make eye movements toward high-value distractors than low-value distractors, even though doing so was directly counterproductive because if these eye movements occurred, the reward was omitted. This experiment therefore provides an intriguing example of reward learning promoting a response (shifting overt attention to the distractor) that has never been rewarded. In another experiment, Le Pelley et al. (2015) demonstrated that this maladaptive capture by high-value distractors persisted over extended training (1,728 trials over 3 days), suggesting that this is a stable pattern. Even with extensive experience, participants did not come to show an adaptive pattern wherein they suppressed attention to the high-value distractor, which would have increased their payoff.

These findings demonstrate clearly that value-driven attentional capture can develop for stimuli that have never been task relevant; i.e., stimuli that participants have never been rewarded for attending to. The implication is that the crucial determinant of capture is not learning about the reward value produced by orienting attention to a stimulus (which we might term *response-value*). Instead, capture seems to depend on learning about the reward value signaled by the presence of a stimulus (*signal-value*). In our experiments, the high-value color is clearly a signal of large reward, since a large reward can be obtained only when a high-value distractor is present in the stimulus array. Similarly, the low-value color is a reliable signal of small reward. Thus, our findings suggest that signals of large reward become more likely to capture attention than signals of small reward. In the more traditional terminology of conditioning research, our data suggest that value-driven capture is a process of Pavlovian, rather than instrumental, conditioning.[1]

To the best of our knowledge, only one other study, by Della Libera and Chelazzi (2009), has examined the influence of reward learning on attention to distractors in humans. In a complicated training procedure, when critical stimuli appeared as distractors, they signaled (with 80% validity) whether the trial would have large or small reward. Evidence from Della Libera and Chelazzi's Experiment 1 suggested that this training led to reduced capture by distractors that signaled large reward (compared with those signaling small reward). This is the opposite of the current findings, and suggests that response-value was the critical variable in their case. The reason for this discrepancy remains unclear; however, we note the following. First, the effect for distractors in Experiment 1 of Della Libera and Chelazzi was observed on only one of two response measures (at $p = .04$), and did not replicate in Experiment 2. In contrast, the effect that we observed was replicated across three experiments with medium to large effect sizes, and in two dependent variables (proportion of omission trials and response times). Second, attentional capture by distractors did not have any influence on rewards obtained in Della Libera and Chelazzi; in our experiments, capture by distractors resulted in reduced reward, rendering it counterproductive. Third, Della Libera and Chelazzi's procedure had no consistent distinction between targets and distractors; a given stimulus acted as a target on some trials and as a distractor on others, but signaled reward magnitude only when it appeared in one of these roles. Thus, participants had extensive experience of receiving reward for responding to "distractor" stimuli when these same stimuli appeared as targets. In our experiments, colored stimuli only ever appeared as distractors, so participants were never required to respond to these stimuli. Fourth, the relationship between stimuli and reward magnitude in Della Libera and Chelazzi was relatively weak. Eight different predictive distractors signaled reward magnitude with 80% validity when they appeared as distractors; when they appeared as targets (which happened equally often), they provided no information. Our experiments had only two or three colored stimuli, and the high- and low-value distractors signaled reward magnitude with 100% validity. Fifth, Della Libera and Chelazzi's training involved spatially coincident, overlaid stimuli; our experiments used spatially distinct stimuli in a visual search task.

The findings of Le Pelley et al. (2015) are more similar to those of a study by Peck et al. (2009) using monkeys. On each trial of that study, a peripheral visual reward cue (RC) predicted whether the trial outcome would be a juice reward (RC+) or no reward (RC−). However, to achieve this outcome, monkeys were required to make an eye movement toward a target cue whose location was independent of the RC. Even though RCs had no operant role in achieving reward (and hence were task irrelevant), over the course of training the RC+ became more likely to attract overt attention and the RC− to repel attention (measured using eye tracking). This suggests that, as in our experiments with humans, attention was under the control of learning about the signal-value of the RC rather than its response-value. These findings thus provide an interesting parallel between value-driven attention in humans and nonhuman animals.

Using single-unit recording, Peck et al. (2009) showed that attentional modulation in their task was encoded in posterior parietal cortex, specifically in the lateral intraparietal area. This is notable because, as noted earlier, Kiss et al. (2009) demonstrated a difference in the N2pc ERP component as a function of reward value in human participants (in a study in which the critical reward-predictive stimuli were task-relevant throughout). Importantly, neural source analyses based on magnetoencephalography implicate both posterior parietal cortex and extrastriate visual cortex as brain regions contributing to the N2pc induced by task-relevant items in visual search (e.g., Hopf et al., 2000). Thus, we have two studies implicating the posterior parietal cortex in value-driven attentional capture. Kiss et al.'s study (in humans) used task-relevant stimuli, and hence the capture in this study could reflect either instrumental learning about response-value or Pavlovian learning about signal-value. Peck et al.'s study (in monkeys) used task-irrelevant stimuli, and hence the capture in this study must reflect Pavlovian learning about signal-value. The most parsimonious explanation of both sets of findings, then, would be that posterior parietal cortex encodes the Pavlovian signal-value of stimuli, and that it is this signal-value (rather than response-value) that is the primary determinant of attentional capture. However, given the current scarcity of empirical evidence, this interpretation must remain tentative for the time being.

Derived Attention and Stimulus Processing: A Summary

In the previous sections, we have seen that recent studies provide strong evidence that attentional processing of stimuli is influenced by learning about the predictiveness of those stimuli, and the value of the outcome that they predict. It is as though this associative learning produces a change in the effective salience of these stimuli so that, for example, a stimulus that signals a high-value reward becomes more salient to participants (and hence more likely to capture attention) than a stimulus that signals a low-value reward.

In support of this interpretation in terms of changes in the effective salience of stimuli as a result of learning, neuroscientific evidence supports the general thesis that learning can influence fundamental aspects of stimulus perception. Specifically, learning about rewards predicted by visual stimuli has been shown to modulate the neural activity elicited by those stimuli at very early stages of the visual system, including primary visual cortex (area V1), in rats (Shuler & Bear, 2006), monkeys (Stănişor, van der Togt, Pennartz, & Roelfsema, 2013), and humans (Serences, 2008; Serences & Saproo, 2010). So, associative learning influences activity in sensory cortices that represent low-level stimulus features. The implication is that learning about stimuli (in particular their predictiveness, and the value of events that they predict) might change the fundamental way in which those stimuli are perceived, and/or the resources dedicated to processing of those stimuli, at a very early stage of perception. In particular, such processes might produce a change in the effective salience of stimuli that underlies the attentional effects of learning observed behaviorally.

Turning to theoretical accounts, as noted earlier the suggestion of a relationship between learning and attention is not novel; William James described the possibility in 1890, and formal attentional models of associative learning have existed for over 50 years (Mackintosh, 1975, provides an early review). Most of the previous research on attentional learning in the associative tradition has tended to focus on learned predictiveness, rather than learned value. As a consequence, the theories developed to account for the findings of this research tend to be better suited to accounting for effects of predictiveness (e.g., Kruschke, 2001; Le Pelley, 2004; Mackintosh, 1975; Pearce & Hall, 1980). But that is not to say that such theories cannot account for effects of learned value on attention. Consider, for example Mackintosh's (1975) model, which has been successful in accounting for predictiveness effects in humans (see Le Pelley, 2010). This model states that following each learning trial, the associative strength of each presented stimulus A (V_A) is updated according to the following equation:

$$\Delta V_A = S\alpha_A (\lambda - V_A) \quad (6.1)$$

where S is a fixed learning-rate parameter. The *prediction error* ($\lambda - V_A$) represents the discrepancy between the actual magnitude of the outcome occurring on that trial (λ); (see Chapter 3) and the extent to which stimulus A predicts that outcome (the associative strength of A, V_A). Critically, α_A is a variable representing the attention paid to stimulus A. According to Mackintosh's model as it was originally formulated, attention α is determined by comparing how well the outcome is predicted by A (given by the absolute value of the prediction error for A, $|\lambda - V_A|$) with how well the outcome is predicted by all other presented stimuli X ($|\lambda - V_X|$). If A is a better predictor of the outcome than is X, then attention to A (α_A) should increase; if A is a poorer predictor, then α_A should decrease. Following Le Pelley (2004), this principle can be implemented by updating α_A according to:

$$\Delta \alpha_A = \theta \left(|\lambda - V_X| - |\lambda - V_A| \right) \quad (6.2)$$

where θ is a fixed rate parameter, and α_A is constrained to lie between a lower limit (here we use 0.1) and an upper limit (here we use 1).

In this version of the model, attention to predictive stimuli will tend to increase toward the upper limit, regardless of exactly what outcome they predict. However, the *rate* of this increase depends on the value of the outcome, λ. This is because early in training when V_A is small, a large value of λ will produce a large prediction error in Equation 1 and hence rapid learning. This will in turn mean that the predictiveness of the stimulus is established rapidly, so attention to the stimulus will increase quickly according to Equation 2. Consequently, at least early in training, this model correctly anticipates that attention will be greater to stimuli that predict a high-value outcome than those that predict a low-value outcome (Figure 6.4A). However, at asymptote, the model anticipates that attention will depend on learned predictiveness (i.e., attention will be greater to predictive cues than nonpredictive cues) but not learned value (i.e., attention will not depend on the value of the outcome that a predictive cue predicts).

It is straightforward to modify this approach so that it is better equipped to account for effects of both learned predictiveness and learned value, even after extended training. Rather than basing attention on a comparison of the predictiveness of different stimuli (as in Equation 2), an alternative approach has attention to a stimulus determined by the absolute associative strength of that stimulus:

$$\alpha_A = |V_A| \quad (6.3)$$

with a lower limit of 0.1. The resulting model still accounts for most, if not all, previous demonstrations of an attentional advantage for predictive over nonpredictive stimuli, because the predictive stimuli in these studies typically have greater associative strengths. Notably, in this alternative model, attention is also a direct function of learned value, because asymptotic associative strengths for stimuli paired with high-value outcomes will be greater than for stimuli paired with low-value outcomes (Figure 6.4B). (Formally: According to Equation 1, learning reaches asymptote when $V_A = \lambda$; since asymptotic V_A depends on outcome magnitude λ, then according to Equation [3], asymptotic α_A will also depend on λ.) A more complex, and probably more representative, model implementing attentional learning along these lines has recently been developed by Esber and Haselgrove (2011).

Finally, it is worth considering how the derived attention described in the preceding sections fits within the language of attention research alluded to in the introduction to this chapter. An influential framework in the cognitive psychology literature distinguishes between *goal-directed* (also referred to as endogenous) and *stimulus-driven* (exogenous) processes in attention (e.g., Yantis, 2000). Goal-directed processes refer to controlled, subject-driven attention that encompasses a person's intentions. Hence,

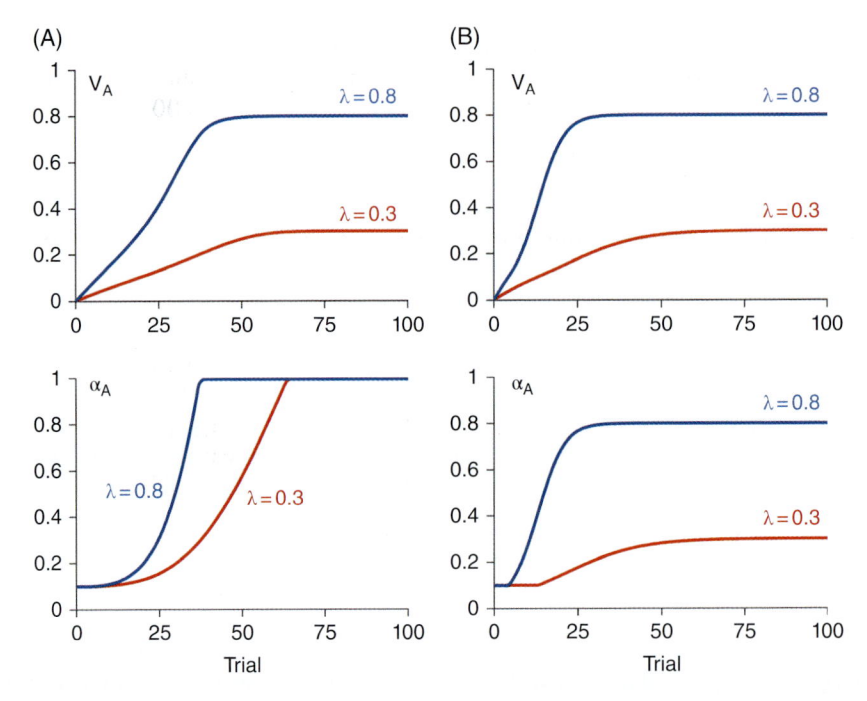

Figure 6.4 Simulation results using variants of Mackintosh's (1975) attentional theory of associative learning. Simulations comprised 100 trials on which cues A and X were together paired with an outcome (AX+), alternated with 100 trials on which X alone was presented without the outcome (X−). Thus, A represents a reliable predictor of the outcome, while X represents a nonpredictive stimulus. Upper panels show the associative strength of A (V_A) across training, and lower panels show attention to A (α_A). Blue lines show simulation results for a high-value outcome ($\lambda = 0.8$), and red lines show results for a low-value outcome ($\lambda = 0.3$). (A) Attention calculated based on a comparison of relative predictiveness (Equation 2). Since A is the most predictive stimulus regardless of outcome magnitude, α_A increases to the upper limit of 1 in both cases. However, it approaches this limit more rapidly when outcome magnitude is large ($\lambda = 0.8$) than when it is small ($\lambda = 0.3$). Therefore, this model anticipates an influence of learned value on attention early in training, but not at asymptote (other parameters: $S = \theta = 0.2$). (B) Attention determined by absolute associative strength (Equation 3). As A develops associative strength, α_A increases for both $\lambda = 0.8$ and $\lambda = 0.3$. However, since attention is determined by associative strength, which is in turn limited by λ, asymptotic attention is greater when the outcome magnitude is larger than when it is small. Therefore, this model anticipates a persistent influence of learned value on attention (other parameter: $S = 0.3$).

while looking at the pages of a book, we can choose to attend to the written words, and to ignore a conversation that is going on nearby. In contrast, stimulus-driven attentional processes relate to attention-grabbing characteristics that are intrinsic to the stimulus: its brightness, onset, color, and so forth. Thus, even while our goal is to concentrate on reading our book, a loud bang from behind us will nevertheless capture our attention in an automatic, stimulus-driven fashion. Where does the influence of learning on attention fit into this framework? It is not goal directed – at least, not always – since several of the studies of learning described in this chapter demonstrate attentional biases that conflict with people's intentions and with the demands of the tasks they are carrying out. But neither is it stimulus-driven. The sensory properties of a red circle do not change merely because it is consistently followed by reward; it remains equally red, bright, circular, and so forth The attentional bias toward the circle is a consequence of an event occurring within the participant (associative learning) rather than being a property of the world. Hence, it would seem that at least some demonstrations of the influence of learning on attention fall outside the standard framework of attentional effects. Consequently, it would seem that derived attention merits its own category within an updated language of attention research.

Derived Attention, Drug Addiction, and Psychosis

The concept of derived attention is important because it demonstrates that our automatic processing of sensory input is not a fixed function of physical salience, but is instead malleable and based on our experiences. This enhanced automatic processing may bring adaptive advantages by improving and speeding detection of meaningful stimuli in our environment. But it may also create problems. For example, many drugs of abuse produce potent neural reward signals (Dayan, 2009; Hyman, 2005; Robinson & Berridge, 2001). Consequently, the derived attention processes described in this chapter would promote involuntary attentional capture by stimuli that are experienced as being associated with these drug rewards (such as drug paraphernalia, or people and locations associated with drug supply). However, clinical research has established that such involuntary capture by drug-associated stimuli predicts relapse in recovering addicts (Cox, Hogan, Kristian, & Race, 2002; Marissen *et al.*, 2006; Waters *et al.*, 2003).

A dysfunction of the relationship between learning and attention has also been implicated in the development of psychotic symptoms that are a characteristic feature of schizophrenia. In an influential article, Kapur (2003; see also Frank, 2008) argued that psychosis reflects a state of *aberrant salience*, wherein patients attribute undue salience to mundane or irrelevant events. This fits well with patients' reports of their own experiences; "Everything seems to grip my attention … Often the silliest little things that are going on seem to interest me … I find myself attending to them and wasting a lot of time" (McGhie & Chapman, 1961). This aberrant salience might in turn generate exaggerated, amplified, and unusually vibrant internal percepts of events, which manifest as hallucinations. It would also drive patients to form internal explanations of those aberrant experiences, which manifest as delusions.

Kapur suggested that aberrant salience results from a dysfunction in the dopaminergic system that normally regulates the salience of stimuli as a function of their motivational value. Notably, this encompasses the case of derived attention wherein the effective salience of stimuli is modulated by learning about their motivational consequences (in terms of learned value and predictiveness). This possibility is rendered plausible by neuroimaging studies demonstrating that the effects of reward value reach down to the earliest sensory processing levels of the cerebral cortex (Serences, 2008; Serences & Saproo, 2010; Shuler & Bear, 2006; Stănișor *et al.*, 2013), such that any dysfunction of reward learning could feasibly have a profound effect on fundamental aspects of perception. So, is there empirical evidence for a general dysfunction of derived attention in psychosis?

Unfortunately, the best answer that can currently be provided is "maybe." Studies have demonstrated abnormalities in the phenomena of latent inhibition (e.g., Baruch, Hemsley, & Gray, 1988; but see also Schmidt-Hansen & Le Pelley, 2012), blocking (e.g., Jones, Gray, & Hemsley, 1992), and learned irrelevance (Morris, Griffiths, Le Pelley & Weickert, 2013; Roiser *et al.*, 2009) in psychotic patients with schizophrenia. Without going into great detail, in each case patients learned more than healthy controls about stimuli that had previously been experienced as irrelevant to the occurrence of outcomes; that is, stimuli with low learned predictiveness and/or learned value. These findings *could* be interpreted in terms of a dysfunction of derived attention: Patients fail to downregulate the effective salience of inconsequential stimuli, such that these stimuli continue to capture attention and hence engage in learning. However, as noted earlier, measuring the rate/amount of learning about a stimulus provides only an indirect measure of attention to that stimulus, and learning can be influenced by many other, nonattentional factors. For example, these data could equally be explained in terms of a schizophrenia-related deficit in memory representation or inferential reasoning (cf. Honey *et al.*, 2010; Mitchell *et al.*, 2012).

The new techniques for assessing derived attention described in this chapter are important in this regard, because they could potentially provide a more selective demonstration of an abnormal relationship between learning and the effective salience of stimuli (i.e., their ability to capture attention) in psychotic patients. If patients are less able to downregulate attention to stimuli that have low learned predictiveness, they should not show a reduction in the extent to which those stimuli capture attention (relative to highly predictive stimuli) in the dot probe task used by Le Pelley, Vadillo, and Luque (2013). Similarly, if patients do not downregulate salience of stimuli with low learned value, they would show a decreased effect of value on attentional orienting in Anderson *et al.*'s (2011a) visual search task.

Such findings would demonstrate convincingly that psychosis is associated with a deficit in the ability to modulate the salience of stimuli as a function of learning about their motivational value, and so would provide strong support for Kapur's (2003) theory of aberrant salience.[2] These important studies remain a task for the future.

Conclusions

Attention and learning are two of the most fundamental processes in human cognition. Attention determines which stimuli in the environment we select for processing and action; learning allows us to adapt how we respond to those stimuli in order to maximize rewards. The concept of derived attention, first introduced by William James over a century ago, describes how associative learning can produce changes in the effective salience of stimuli – the extent to which they grab our attention, regardless of whether we want them to. Indeed, over the course of this chapter, we have seen that attention and learning interact at an automatic level. It is through such influences that the impact of learning seeps into many areas of psychology, and this is why an understanding of the mechanisms underlying associative learning is so important for researchers from a wide array of fields.

Finally, in this chapter we have restricted ourselves to discussing the influence of learning on the attentional processing of stimuli that predict outcomes. We have not discussed how learning might also influence the processing of the *outcome* events, but of course this is also an interesting question. Just as learning seems to influence our perception of the stimulus that affords a prediction, it also influences our perception of the event that is the target of that prediction. We end with a powerful demonstration of this by Pariyadath and Eagleman (2007), who examined the influence of learning on the perceived duration of stimuli. Participants were presented either with the sequence 1, 2, 3, 4, 5 or with a scrambled series that began with 1 but was otherwise unsequenced (e.g., 1, 5, 4, 3, 2). In each series, all stimuli apart from the first were presented for 500 ms. The duration of the initial "1" varied from 300 to 700 ms, and after the series was complete, participants reported whether this "1" appeared longer or shorter than the stimuli that followed. For scrambled series, people were fairly accurate at this task. However, for the sequential series, they systematically overestimated the duration of the initial item. In this sequential condition, each item allowed participants to predict the identity of the following item. This suggests that the predictable nature of later items in the sequence caused them to contract in perceived duration, such that the initial item (which could not be predicted, since it was not preceded by anything) was judged to have lasted for longer. The implication is that perceived duration is influenced by associative learning, with unpredictable stimuli seeming to last for longer than predictable stimuli of the same objective duration. When combined with the studies of visuospatial attention cited earlier, it is tempting to conclude that associative learning influences our perception of both space and time. How could learning be more fundamental?

Notes

1 Recall that, in our gaze-contingent eye-tracking study (Le Pelley et al., 2015), if participants looked at the distractor, the reward was omitted. This means that participants must have learned the signal-value of the distractor colors (e.g., red signals high-value reward, and blue signals low-value reward) *on trials on which they did not look at the distractor*. That is, participants must have encoded the presence of a particular distractor color in the array using peripheral vision, and this supported learning about the relationship between the presence of that color and the reward value obtained on that trial.

2 Interestingly, studies of patients with anxiety disorders have used tasks such as the dot probe to reveal enhanced salience of threat-related stimuli in these patients (e.g., the word *murder*, angry faces, or pictures of spiders for spider-phobics; see Cisler & Koster, 2010, for a review). This could be a consequence of derived attention, wherein an aversive experience involving (say) a spider has led to a disproportionate increase in the attention-capturing capacity of spiders. Hence, it would also be interesting to test for a general dysfunction of derived attention in anxiety patients, to see if these people typically show an abnormally large increase in attention to stimuli that are paired with aversive consequences.

References

Anderson, B. A., Laurent, P. A., & Yantis, S. (2011a). Learned value magnifies salience-based attentional capture. *PLoS ONE, 6*.

Anderson, B. A., Laurent, P. A., & Yantis, S. (2011b). Value-driven attentional capture. *Proceedings of the National Academy of Sciences of the United States of America, 108*, 10367–10371.

Anderson, B. A., & Yantis, S. (2012). Value-driven attentional and oculomotor capture during goal-directed, unconstrained viewing. *Attention Perception & Psychophysics, 74*, 1644–1653.

Baruch, I., Hemsley, D. R., & Gray, J. A. (1988). Differential performance of acute and chronic-schizophrenics in a latent inhibition task. *Journal of Nervous and Mental Disease, 176*, 598–606.

Beesley, T., & Le Pelley, M. E. (2010). The effect of predictive history on the learning of subsequence contingencies. *Quarterly Journal of Experimental Psychology, 63*, 108–135.

Beesley, T., & Le Pelley, M. E. (2011). The influence of blocking on overt attention and associability in human learning. *Journal of Experimental Psychology: Animal Behavior Processes, 37*, 114–120.

Bonardi, C., Graham, S., Hall, G., & Mitchell, C. J. (2005). Acquired distinctiveness and equivalence in human discrimination learning: Evidence for an attentional process. *Psychonomic Bulletin & Review, 12*, 88–92.

Cisler, J. M., & Koster, E. H. W. (2010). Mechanisms of attentional biases towards threat in anxiety disorders: An integrative review. *Clinical Psychology Review, 30*, 203–216.

Cox, W. M., Hogan, L. M., Kristian, M. R., & Race, J. H. (2002). Alcohol attentional bias as a predictor of alcohol abusers' treatment outcome. *Drug and Alcohol Dependence, 68*, 237–243.

Dayan, P. (2009). Dopamine, reinforcement learning, and addiction. *Pharmacopsychiatry, 42*, S56–S65.

Della Libera, C., & Chelazzi, L. (2009). Learning to attend and to ignore is a matter of gains and losses. *Psychological Science, 20*, 778–784.

Denton, S. E., & Kruschke, J. K. (2006). Attention and salience in associative blocking. *Learning & Behavior, 34*, 285–304.

Deubel, H., & Schneider, W. X. (1996). Saccade target selection and object recognition: Evidence for a common attentional mechanism. *Vision Research, 36*, 1827–1837.

Eimer, M. (1996). The N2pc component as an indicator of attentional selectivity. *Electroencephalography and Clinical Neurophysiology, 99*, 225–234.

Esber, G. R., & Haselgrove, M. (2011). Reconciling the influence of predictiveness and uncertainty on stimulus salience: a model of attention in associative learning. *Proceedings of the Royal Society B: Biological Sciences, 278*, 2553–2561.

Frank, M. J. (2008). Schizophrenia: A computational reinforcement learning perspective. *Schizophrenia Bulletin, 34*, 1008–1011.

Griffiths, O., Johnson, A. M., & Mitchell, C. J. (2011). Negative transfer in human associative learning. *Psychological Science, 22*, 1198–1204.

Hogarth, L., Dickinson, A., Austin, A., Brown, C., & Duka, T. (2008). Attention and expectation in human predictive learning: The role of uncertainty. *Quarterly Journal of Experimental Psychology, 61*, 1658–1668.

Honey, R. C., Close, J., & Lin, E. (2010). Acquired distinctiveness and equivalence: A synthesis. In C. J. Mitchell & M. E. Le Pelley (Eds.), *Attention and associative learning: from brain to behaviour* (pp. 159–186). Oxford, UK: Oxford University Press.

Hopf, J. M., Luck, S. J., Girelli, M., Hagner, T., Mangun, G. R., Scheich, H., & Heinze H. J. (2000). Neural sources of focused attention in visual search. *Cerebral Cortex, 10*, 1233–1241.

Hyman, S. E. (2005). Addiction: A disease of learning and memory. *American Journal of Psychiatry, 162,* 1414–1422.

James, W. (1983). *The principles of psychology.* Cambridge, MA: Harvard University Press (Original work published 1890).

Jones, S. H., Gray, J. A., & Hemsley, D. R. (1992). Loss of the Kamin blocking effect in acute but not chronic schizophrenics. *Biological Psychiatry, 32,* 739–755.

Jonides, J. (1981). Voluntary versus automatic control over the mind's eye's movement. In J. B. Long & A. D. Baddeley (Eds.), *Attention and performance IX* (pp. 187–203). Hillsdale, NJ: Erlbaum.

Kamin, L. J., & Schaub, R. E. (1963). Effects of conditioned stimulus intensity on the conditioned emotional response. *Journal of Comparative and Physiological Psychology, 56,* 502–507.

Kapur, S. (2003). Psychosis as a state of aberrant salience: A framework linking biology, phenomenology, and pharmacology in schizophrenia. *American Journal of Psychiatry, 160,* 13–23.

Kiss, M., Driver, J., & Eimer, M. (2009). Reward priority of visual target singletons modulates event-related potential signatures of attentional selection. *Psychological Science, 20,* 245–251.

Klauer, K. C., Roßnagel, C., & Musch, J. (1997). List-context effects in evaluative priming. *Journal of Experimental Psychology: Learning, Memory, and Cognition, 23,* 246–255.

Kruschke, J. K. (1996). Dimensional relevance shifts in category learning. *Connection Science, 8,* 225–247.

Kruschke, J. K. (2001). Towards a unified model of attention in associative learning. *Journal of Mathematical Psychology, 45,* 812–863.

Kruschke, J. K., Kappenman, E. S., & Hetrick, W. P. (2005). Eye gaze and individual differences consistent with learned attention in associative blocking and highlighting. *Journal of Experimental Psychology: Learning, Memory, and Cognition, 31,* 830–845.

Le Pelley, M. E. (2004). The role of associative history in models of associative learning: A selective review and a hybrid model. *Quarterly Journal of Experimental Psychology, 57B,* 193–243.

Le Pelley, M. E. (2010). Attention and human associative learning. In C. J. Mitchell & M. E. Le Pelley (Eds.), *Attention and associative learning: from brain to behaviour* (pp. 187–215). Oxford, UK: Oxford University Press.

Le Pelley, M. E., Beesley, T., & Griffiths, O. (2011). Overt attention and predictiveness in human associative learning. *Journal of Experimental Psychology: Animal Behavior Processes, 37,* 220–229.

Le Pelley, M. E., & McLaren, I. P. L. (2003). Learned associability and associative change in human causal learning. *Quarterly Journal of Experimental Psychology, 56B,* 68–79.

Le Pelley, M. E., Mitchell, C. J., & Johnson, A. M. (2013). Outcome value influences attentional biases in human associative learning: Dissociable effects of training and of instruction. *Journal of Experimental Psychology: Animal Behavior Processes, 39,* 39–55.

Le Pelley, M. E., Pearson, D., Griffiths, O., & Beesley, T. (2015). When goals conflict with values: Counterproductive attentional and oculomotor capture by reward-related stimuli. *Journal of Experimental Psychology: General, 144,* 158.

Le Pelley, M. E., Reimers, S. J., Calvini, G., Spears, R., Beesley, T., & Murphy, R. A. (2010). Stereotype formation: Biased by association. *Journal of Experimental Psychology: General, 139,* 138–161.

Le Pelley, M. E., Turnbull, M. N., Reimers, S. J., & Knipe, R. L. (2010). Learned predictiveness effects following single-cue training in humans. *Learning & Behavior, 38,* 126–144.

Le Pelley, M. E., Vadillo, M. A., & Luque, D. (2013). Learned predictiveness influences rapid attentional capture: Evidence from the dot probe task. *Journal of Experimental Psychology: Learning, Memory, and Cognition, 39,* 1888–1900.

Livesey, E. J., Harris, I. M., & Harris, J. A. (2009). Attentional changes during implicit learning: Signal validity protects a target stimulus from the attentional blink. *Journal of Experimental Psychology: Learning, Memory, and Cognition, 35*, 408–422.

Lovejoy, E. (1968). *Attention in discrimination learning.* San Francisco, CA: Holden-Day.

Mackintosh, N. J. (1975). A theory of attention: Variations in the associability of stimuli with reinforcement. *Psychological Review, 82*, 276–298.

MacLeod, C., Mathews, A., & Tata, P. (1986). Attentional bias in emotional disorders. *Journal of Abnormal Psychology, 95*, 15–20.

Marissen, M. A. E., Franken, I. H. A., Waters, A. J., Blanken, P., van den Brink, W., & Hendriks, V. M. (2006). Attentional bias predicts heroin relapse following treatment. *Addiction, 101*, 1306–1312.

McGhie, A., & Chapman, J. (1961). Disorders of attention and perception in early schizophrenia. *British Journal of Medical Psychology, 34*, 103–116.

Mitchell, C. J., Griffiths, O., Seetoo, J., & Lovibond, P. F. (2012). Attentional mechanisms in learned predictiveness. *Journal of Experimental Psychology: Animal Behavior Processes, 38*, 191–202.

Mitchell, C. J., & Le Pelley, M. E. (Eds.). (2010). *Attention and associative learning: From brain to behaviour.* Oxford, UK: Oxford University Press.

Morris, R. W., Griffiths, O., Le Pelley, M. E., & Weickert, T. W. (2013). Attention to irrelevant cues is related to positive symptoms in schizophrenia. *Schizophrenia Bulletin, 39*, 575–582.

Pariyadath, V., & Eagleman, D. (2007). The effect of predictability on subjective duration. *PLoS ONE, 2*, 1–6.

Pearce, J. M., & Hall, G. (1980). A model for Pavlovian conditioning: Variations in the effectiveness of conditioned but not of unconditioned stimuli. *Psychological Review, 87*, 532–552.

Peck, C. J., Jangraw, D. C., Suzuki, M., Efem, R., & Gottlieb, J. (2009). Reward modulates attention independently of action value in posterior parietal cortex. *Journal of Neuroscience, 29*, 11182–11191.

Posner, M. I. (1980). Orienting of attention. *Quarterly Journal of Experimental Psychology, 32*, 3–25.

Posner, M. I., & Cohen, Y. (1984). Components of visual orienting. In H. Bouma & D. Bouwhuis (Eds.), *Attention and performance X* (pp. 531–556). Hillsdale, NJ: Erlbaum.

Raymond, J. E., Shapiro, K. L., & Arnell, K. M. (1992). Temporary suppression of visual processing in an RSVP task: An attentional blink? *Journal of Experimental Psychology: Human Perception and Performance, 18*, 849–860.

Rehder, B., & Hoffman, A. B. (2005). Eyetracking and selective attention in category learning. *Cognitive Psychology, 51*, 1–41.

Robinson, T. E., & Berridge, K. C. (2001). Incentive-sensitization and addiction. *Addiction, 96*, 103–114.

Roiser, J. P., Stephan, K. E., den Ouden, H. E. M., Barnes, T. R. E., Friston, K. J., & Joyce, E. M. (2009). Do patients with schizophrenia exhibit aberrant salience? *Psychological Medicine, 39*, 199–209.

Schmidt-Hansen, M., & Le Pelley, M. E. (2012). The positive symptoms of schizophrenia and latent inhibition in humans and animals: Underpinned by the same process(es)? *Cognitive Neuropsychiatry, 17*, 473–505.

Serences, J. T. (2008). Value-based modulations in human visual cortex. *Neuron, 60*, 1169–1181.

Serences, J. T., & Saproo, S. (2010). Population response profiles in early visual cortex are biased in favor of more valuable stimuli. *Journal of Neurophysiology, 104*, 76–87.

Shuler, M. G., & Bear, M. F. (2006). Reward timing in the primary visual cortex. *Science, 311*, 1606–1609.

Stănişor, L., van der Togt, C., Pennartz, C. M. A., & Roelfsema, P. R. (2013). A unified selection signal for attention and reward in primary visual cortex. *Proceedings of the National Academy of Sciences of the United States of America, 110,* 9136–9141.

Sutherland, N. S., & Mackintosh, N. J. (1971). *Mechanisms of animal discrimination learning.* New York, NY: Academic Press.

Theeuwes, J., & Belopolsky, A. V. (2012). Reward grabs the eye: Oculomotor capture by rewarding stimuli. *Vision Research, 74,* 80–85.

Trabasso, T. R., & Bower, G. H. (1968). *Attention in learning: Theory and research.* New York, NY: Wiley.

Waters, A. J., Shiffman, S., Sayette, M. A., Paty, J. A., Gwaltney, C. J., & Balabanis, M. H. (2003). Attentional bias predicts outcome in smoking cessation. *Health Psychology, 22,* 378–387.

Wills, A. J., Lavric, A., Croft, G. S., & Hodgson, T. L. (2007). Predictive learning, prediction errors, and attention: Evidence from event-related potentials and eye tracking. *Journal of Cognitive Neuroscience, 19,* 843–854.

Woodman, G. F., & Luck, S. J. (1999). Electrophysiological measurement of rapid shifts of attention during visual search. *Nature, 400,* 867–869.

Yantis, S. (2000). Goal-directed and stimulus-driven determinants of attentional control. In S. Monsell & J. Driver (Eds.), *Attention and performance XVIII* (pp. 73–103). Cambridge, MA: MIT Press.

Zeaman, D., & House, B. J. (1963). The role of attention in retardate discrimination learning. In N. R. Ellis (Ed.), *Handbook of mental deficiency: Psychological theory and research* (pp. 378–418). New York, NY: McGraw-Hill.

7
The Epigenetics of Neural Learning

Zohar Bronfman, Simona Ginsburg, and Eva Jablonka

Introduction

Learning, which involves neural plasticity and memory, is manifest at many levels of biological organization: at the single-cell level, at the level of local cell assemblies or networks, and at the system level of dedicated structures such as the hippocampus in mammals. We review recent data that focus on the intracellular level and the intercellular synapse-mediated level in the nervous system, showing that several interacting epigenetic mechanisms underlie learning and plasticity. On the basis of the survey of the literature, we show that there are consistent correlations between global changes in epigenetic regulation and the capacity for learning. We suggest that learning dynamics may be reflected by cumulative epigenetic changes at the neuron level, and discuss the implications of epigenetic mechanisms for the study of the inheritance and evolution of learning.

The search for cellular correlates of memory started toward the end of the 19th century, when cytology became an established discipline, and the mechanisms for the transmission of information were sought within the structures and dynamics of the cell. Initially, some of this searching was associated with the idea that memory and heredity form a continuum: that repetition of activities leads to memorization and to the formation of automatic habits during the life-time of the individual, and that these habits are inherited. Eventually, they produce instincts and an orderly innate succession of embryonic stages that recapitulate the sequence in which the behaviors were learned. Heredity was therefore seen as "unconscious memory" (Butler, 1920, discussed in Schacter, 2001).

An original and comprehensive notion of biological memory was developed by the German zoologist Richard Semon in the early 20th century (Semon, 1909/1921). Like other mnemonic-evolutionary theorists, Semon suggested that the processes that lead to the development of new behaviors and other characteristics acquired by an individual through learning or through direct environmental effects leave traces in the individual's biological organization, and some of these traces are transmitted to its descendants. Semon called these traces "engrams" and suggested that they are reactivated and retrieved when similar or associated conditions occur during subsequent phases of the development of the individual. Semon did not think that a single mechanism underlies memorization and recall at all levels of biological organization, but he did think that a *common principle*, which he called the Mneme, is manifest at the cellular level (cell memory), the level of the nervous system (neural memory), and the phylogenetic level (heredity). His Mneme was a tripartite conceptualization of memory: Semon suggested that in all memory systems, at all levels, there are processes of *encoding and storage* (which he called engraphy), and *retrieval* (which he called ecphory), a conceptualization that has become fundamental to memory research. As Schacter (2001) has documented, Semon's focus on the distinct and constructive nature of retrieval had to wait nearly 70 years to be appreciated, and although his major book, *The Mneme*, did generate some critical interest when published, his views were criticized and eventually discarded and forgotten. However, the idea of cell memory persisted and was already being explored empirically by developmental biologists and microbiologists in the 1950s, and investigations gathered momentum with the discovery of epigenetic mechanisms such as DNA methylation, which were shown to underlie both the regulation of gene expression and cell memory (Holliday & Pugh, 1975; Riggs, 1975; Vanyushin, Nemirovsky, Klimenko, Vasiliev, & Belozersky, 1973; this history is reviewed in Jablonka & Lamb, 2011). At the same time, molecular investigations of neural memory and learning became of increasing interest as neurobiology and molecular biology provided insights into synaptic plasticity – the ability to modify the properties of preexisting synapses and to generate new ones. It was found that short-term memory in animals entails only covalent changes in existing proteins, and this plasticity expresses itself as changes in the strength of preexisting synaptic connections. In contrast, long-term types of memory needed for learning – our main focus in this chapter – require, in addition, alterations in gene expression: the transcription of new mRNAs and their translation into new proteins (reviewed in Bailey & Kandel, 2008; Kandel, 2012). In view of the turnover of proteins, a major question for memory research was how the transcriptional and translational states persist once the original triggering stimulus disappears. Which molecular mechanisms and factors underlie this enduring neural memory?

The two strands of research, into cell memory and into neural encoding through synaptic plasticity, soon came together. An early suggestion was that metabolic self-sustaining autocatalytic loops, triggered by neural firing, encode mental memories (Griffith, 1967). A different, more explicit, molecular link between cell memory and enduring memory at the organismal level was suggested by Griffith and Mahler (1969), who proposed that changes in DNA methylation follow neural firing and encode the firing patterns, an idea also suggested by Crick (1984) and developed by Holliday (1999). Today, these speculative suggestions have been fleshed out and modified by epigenetic research. Moreover, a connection between cell memory and transgenerational heredity that is mediated by many different epigenetic mechanisms has been corroborated (reviewed in Jablonka & Raz, 2009).

Before presenting an overview of the extensive new data on the epigenetic basis of learning, we will describe the essential features of learning and its relation to memory in a way that is applicable to different levels of biological organization, including the cellular level, which is our main focus in this chapter.

A General Characterization of Learning and Memory

Like many other definitions in the literature (see Roediger III, Dudai, & Frizpatrick, 2007 for examples and analyses), our characterization focuses on the three processes identified by Semon: encoding, storage, and retrieval. How each of these processes occurs and how exactly they relate to one another may differ for different levels and types of learning and memory. Taking a very broad view that is not specific to neural learning, we say that learning occurs when:

1 A pattern of external or self-generated inputs starts an internal reaction or a series of reactions that alter patterns of internal interactions and culminate in a functional response. The interactions are selected through the operations of value systems, and can be said to *encode* the relation between the input and the response.
2 The encoded input–response relation is maintained or *stored*. By stored, we mean that some physical traces of the relation persist, even when the original input is no longer present and the response is no longer manifest; a latent memory trace, an engram, is formed. The engram may be realized in many ways at multiple levels of biological organization – as an epigenetic chromosomal mark, as a self-sustaining intracellular network, as a persistent change in cellular architecture (in the synapse, for example), as a local change in the connectivity of a neural network, or as an altered multinetwork pattern of activity within a distinct anatomical structure (e.g., the hippocampus). Engrams may be unique or multiple, and can be laid down both in parallel and sequentially.
3 The memory trace, the engram, can be activated, and the relation can be recalled or *retrieved* upon later exposure to a similar, partial, and/or associated type of input conditions resulting in a modified functional response. Retrieval can occur at all the levels mentioned previously and may involve complex processes of reconstruction rather than simple triggering; it leads to new processes of encoding that alter existing engrams.

This characterization can be applied to different types of learning, from the sensitization and habituation found in single-celled *Paramecia* (Ginsburg & Jablonka, 2009) to episodic learning and memory in humans. It can also be applied to processes such as repeated ectopic head-regeneration in planarians (Oviedo *et al.*, 2010; Tseng & Levin, 2013) and to learning in nonneural, multicell systems like the immune system. Although the immune system and the nervous system may have coevolved (Bayne, 2003), and the same epigenetic mechanisms operate in *all* eukaryotic cells, in this chapter we focus on the cellular epigenetic mechanisms underlying neural learning and memory, a topic that has been intensely studied since the beginning of the 21st century. Because the term epigenetics is sometimes used inconsistently, and there are several different types of epigenetic mechanisms, we first define the terms as they are employed in this chapter (based on Jablonka & Lamb, 2014).

Epigenetic Mechanisms

Epigenetics, a term coined by Waddington in the late 1930s, is used today to describe the study of developmental processes that lead to persistent changes in the states of organisms, their components, and their lineages (Jablonka & Lamb, 2011, 2014). Persistent developmental changes are mediated by *epigenetic mechanisms*, which underlie developmental plasticity and canalization. Developmental plasticity is the ability of a single genotype to generate variable phenotypes in response to different environmental circumstances; its mirror image is canalization, the adjustment of developmental pathways so as to bring about a uniform phenotypic outcome in spite of genetic and environmental variations. At the cellular level, epigenetic mechanisms establish and maintain, through auto- and hetero-catalytic processes, the changes that occur during ontogeny in both nondividing cells, such as neurons, and dividing cells, such as stem cells (Jablonka & Lamb, 2014). *Cell memory*, the dynamic maintenance of developmentally induced cellular states in the absence of the triggering stimulus, and *cell heredity*, which leads to the persistence of cell memory-patterns in daughter cells following cell division, are mediated by epigenetic mechanisms. When information is transmitted to cells during cell division and reproduction, and variations in the transmitted information are not determined by variations in DNA sequence (i.e., the same DNA sequence has more than one cell-heritable epigenetic state), *epigenetic inheritance* is said to occur. Some epigenetic mechanisms are found in prokaryotes (cells that have no distinct nucleus, such as bacteria), but the focus of most epigenetic research is on the epigenetic systems discovered in nucleated eukaryotic cells, where four types have been recognized (see Figure 7.1 for a schematic depiction). All four are found in neurons and play a role in learning and memory; furthermore, their interactions and complementarity are what render learning so robust and flexible.

Chromatin marking

Chromatin is the complex of DNA, proteins, and RNAs that constitute the chromosome. It can assume different local and global conformations as it changes in response to signals (Figure 7.1A and B depict closed and open conformations respectively). Chromatin marks, the variable non-DNA parts of a chromosomal locus, are generated and maintained by dedicated molecular machinery. Chromatin marks partake in the regulation of transcription and all other known chromosomal behaviors, such as transposition, recombination, and repair. They can be divided into four major categories.

DNA methylation marks (see Yu, Baek, & Kaang, 2011, for a neurobiology-oriented review) are the small chemical groups (such as the methyl group $-CH_3$ or the hydroxymethyl group $-CH_2OH$) that are covalently bound to cytosines. Cytosines are often methylated in the cytosine–guanine dinucleotides (CpG) of DNA, although the methylation of cytosines in a non-CpG context (CH methylation, where H can be any nucleotide) is prevalent in neurons. DNA methylation patterns (both CpG and CH methylation) present in CG-rich promoter regions repress transcription, whereas hydroxymethylation and an absence of methylation in such regions is generally associated with increased transcriptional activity (Figure 7.1C). Preexisting methylation patterns in CpG doublets are maintained by specific methyltransferase enzymes

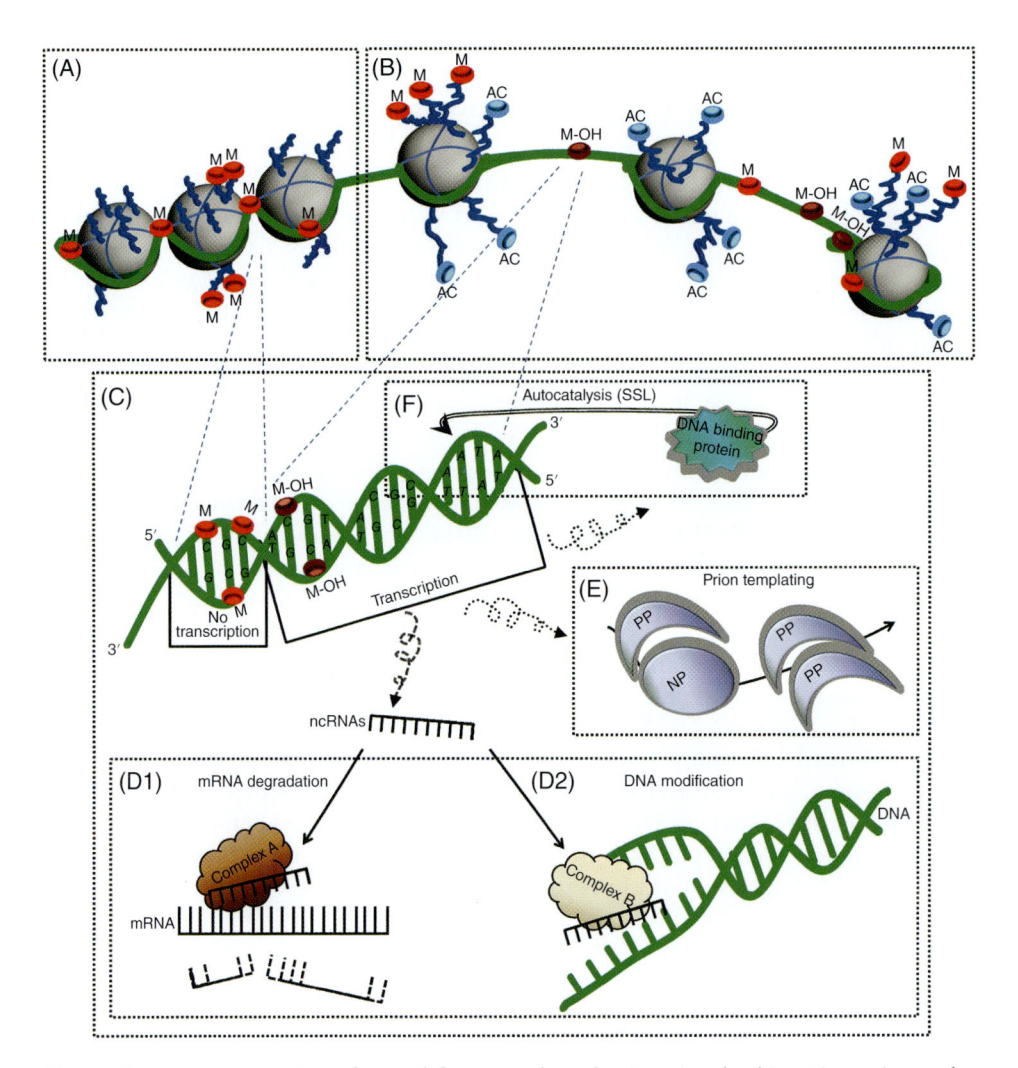

Figure 7.1 Schematic view of several factors and mechanisms involved in epigenetic regulation. DNA (green ribbon) is wound around a nucleosome (gray ball), which is made up of four different histone dimers. Histone tails can be acetylated (blue buttons on blue tails, AC) methylated (red buttons, M, on blue tails). DNA can have an added methyl group (red buttons, M) or a hydroxyl-methyl group (brown button M-OH). (A) Compacted, "closed" chromatin, with crowded nucleosomes. Three nucleosomes have nonacetylated tails (no blue buttons), and one has methyl groups added to some of its histone tails (red buttons, M). The DNA is heavily methylated in CG-rich promoter regions. (B) An open chromatin conformation. The histone tails are acetylated (blue buttons, AC) and some tails are methylated (red buttons, M) or are modified in other ways (not shown). The DNA (green ribbon) has few methyl groups (red button, M) in CG-rich promoter regions and is also marked with some hydroxymethyl groups (M-OH). (C) Close-up of DNA regions shown in (A) and (B): DNA with many methyl groups in CpG promoter regions is not transcribed, while more sparsely methylated DNA and DNA marked with M-OH are transcribed. Transcribed small regulatory RNAs can lead to the degradation of mRNAs with homolog sequences (D1) or to the modification of DNA (D2). Other transcribed regions are translated into proteins (NP), some of which (E) assume a self-templating prion conformation (PP) or act as positive regulators of their own transcription (F) forming a self-sustaining loop (SSL). The mechanisms leading to the maintenance of DNA methylation and histone modifications are not shown, and DNA-binding epigenetic factors, including the H1 histone are not depicted. Note that histone tails can be methylated in both closed and open conformations, although the pattern is different.

[DNA methyltransferase (DNMT)1 in animals]; new methyl groups are added to unmethylated cytosines by other DNMT enzymes (DNMT3a and DNMT3b), and methyl groups can be actively removed by excision-repair enzymes and DNMTs in response to developmental and environmental signals.

Histone modifications are chemical groups, such as acetyl and methyl groups, that are enzymatically added to and removed from particular amino acids of the histones H2a, H2b, H3 and H4 that make up the octamer around which the DNA duplex is wound (see Gräff & Tsai, 2013; Peixoto & Abel, 2013 for general reviews that focus on neural memory). For example, the acetylation of histones (the addition of acetyl group to the N-terminus of lysine in histones), which makes them more accessible to transcription factors, is catalyzed by HATs, and the deacetylation of histones, which has the opposite effect, is catalyzed by HDACs. With histone methylation, up to three methyl groups can be added to lysines, leading to mono- di-, or trimethylation patterns that have been shown to affect transcriptional regulation of the locally wound DNA (Figure 7.1A,B). Histone H1, a histone protein that is bound to nucleosomes in regions of condensed chromatin, is involved in the compaction of chromatin and in core-histone tail modifications that lead to silencing.

Histone variants are specific histone proteins that take the place of the usual histones and alter the conformation of chromatin and its accessibility to modifying enzymes.

Nonhistone proteins that are bound to DNA, some of which (e.g., HAT) are enzymes involved in chromatin marking; they regulate chromatin condensation, affect its three-dimensional topology, and control or stabilize other chromosomal functions.

Chromatin marks can be dynamically maintained over a long time. In dividing cells, some hitchhike on DNA replication and segregate (through complex and not fully understood interactions with trans-acting factors), with parental marks nucleating the reconstruction of similar marks on daughter DNA molecules. The different chromatin marks are functionally and mechanistically related and often work synergistically.

RNA-mediated epigenetic regulation

Regulatory RNA molecules are important epigenetic factors that control transcription and translation. Silent states of gene activity are initiated and actively maintained through repressive interactions between noncoding, small RNA molecules and the RNA to which they are complementary (Bernstein & Allis, 2005; see Spadaro & Bredy, 2012 for a neuro-focused review). Silencing through small noncoding RNA (ncRNA) mediation, which has become known as *RNA interference* (RNAi), can occur through (1) posttranscriptional silencing, when mRNAs that have sequences complementary to small RNAs are degraded, or their translation is suppressed (Figure 7.1D1); (2) transcriptional silencing, when small RNAs interact with DNA in ways that cause long-term and cell-heritable silencing modifications of marks such as DNA methylation (Figure 7.1D2); and (3) RNA-mediated targeted gene deletions and amplifications (not shown). Complex systems of enzymes, which are highly conserved in eukaryotes, are responsible for these silencing processes, and small RNAs have multiple functions. For example, small interfering RNAs are important for defense against genomic parasites, microRNAs play a central role in developmental regulation in all cell types including neurons, and Piwi-interacting RNAs (piRNAs) are involved in the regulation of transcription in neurons, as well as in gametic surveillance and transgenerational transmission. The long-term developmental maintenance of silenced states can occur through several different mechanisms (Jablonka & Lamb, 2014). Small ncRNAs can migrate from cell to cell, so silencing can spread horizontally within an organism (Hoy & Buck, 2012), and their number is modulated by different mechanisms, including circular RNAs with complementary sequences, which can attach to and act as "sinks" for complementary small RNAs (Ledford, 2013). In addition to small ncRNAs, long ncRNAs are also important regulators of genomic activity (LaSalle, Powell, & Yasui, 2013; Ulitsky, Shkumatava, Jan, Sive, & Bartel, 2011).

Structural templating

Another type of epigenetic mechanism involves the active maintenance and regeneration of alternative conformations of proteins, protein complexes, and membrane components (Jablonka & Lamb, 2014). With this mechanism, preexisting three-dimensional cellular structures that are altered during development can act as templates for the production of similar structures within the same cell or in daughter cells. Structural templating includes a wide spectrum of processes, the best understood being that which leads to the maintenance, propagation, and sometimes the cellular inheritance of prions (Shorter & Lindquist, 2005; Figure 7.1E).

Self-sustaining autocatalytic loops

A specific pattern of intracellular activity can be maintained when genes and their products form autocatalytic loops (Figure 7.1F). Such loops can occur at all levels of information processing, and can involve many different types of feedback interactions (Shoval & Alon, 2010). An example is the auto-activation of calcium/calmodulin dependent protein kinase II by Ca^{2+}/calmodulin. The enzyme becomes phosphorylated upon very strong synaptic stimulation, and this phosphorylation prevents an inhibitory subunit from binding to the catalytic domain. This in turn enables the site to be continually phosphorylated by neighboring subunits within the holoenzyme in the absence of the initiating Ca^{2+}/calmodulin triggers (Lisman, Schulman, & Cline, 2002).

The different epigenetic mechanisms depicted in Figure 7.1 often interact. They affect the topology of the chromosome and lead to the formation of robust yet flexible and responsive patterns of activity. They underlie developmental plasticity: For example, they mark the determined state of different stem cell types that breed true (e.g., Bibikova *et al.*, 2006); they are involved in caste determination in honey bees (queen and workers have different inducible epigenetic patterns; Kucharski, Maleszka, Foret, & Maleszka, 2008; Lyko *et al.*, 2010); and as we describe in the following sections of this chapter, they are integral to the neural plasticity underlying learning and memory, including the affective and cognitive dispositions that drive behavior.

Epigenetic Memory Systems in Neurons: Memory All the Way Down

All forms of neural learning and memory in animals are based on the cell-memory systems found in all eukaryotic cells, from protists through plants and fungi to animals. Highly complex learning and memory-dedicated structures such as the mushroom bodies in insects, and hippocampal and cortical structures in mammals, depend on intercellular synaptic mechanisms and on epigenetic mechanisms in the nucleus: Memory goes all the way down! The memory mechanisms depend on each other and form a nested hierarchical system.

Although epigenetic mechanisms are universal, and all or most of them are present in all eukaryotic cells, at the level of the single cell they can endow it with only limited learning potential (a constraint resulting from the multifunctionality of the components that constitute cellular networks). Toy models and experiments with single-celled organisms such as *Paramecium* have shown that cellular epigenetic memory systems can underlie habituation, sensitization, and even limited associative learning (where only a very small, highly constrained number of associations can be formed) at the single-cell level (Ginsburg & Jablonka, 2009). More flexible types of associative learning require intercellular interactions mediated through synaptic connections. Even more complex types of learning, such as contextual fear conditioning and spatial learning, require intricate neural computations, mapping relations, and dedicated neural structures (Zovkic, Guzman-Karlsson, & Sweatt, 2013; see Chapters 12 and 13).

The molecular epigenetics of persistent neural plasticity, which, in addition to learning and memory, includes neural changes resulting from behavioral maturation, ageing, obesity, traumas, and other experiences, is a vast topic and reviewing all its aspects is beyond the scope of this chapter. However, studies of all aspects of neural plasticity in all animal taxa show that both the basic molecular mechanisms and the specific factors participating in them, such as the second messenger cyclic AMP, the protein kinase A, the DNA-binding proteins cAMP response element-binding (CREB) 1 and CREB2, and the RNA-binding protein cytoplasmic polyadenylation element-binding protein, are highly conserved and are key players in its regulation – including the epigenetic facets of this regulation (Kandel, 2012). The same is true for the basic epigenetic mechanisms discussed in the previous section, especially DNA methylation (when present), histone modifications, and the RNA control systems that regulate and are regulated by learning-associated proteins. Moreover, it seems that several different epigenetic factors and mechanisms join together in memory formation in neurons. First, different epigenetic mechanisms interact: For example, various small RNAs, DNA methylation, and histone modifications are all intimately interrelated through feedback loops (Cheng, Wang, Cai, Rao, & Mattson, 2003). Second, a single neuron can have thousands of connections with different synaptic strengths that may need to be maintained locally; epigenetic mechanisms operating solely at the transcriptional levels may not be sufficient for the generation of these synaptic memories (Yu *et al.*, 2011), but interactions between these mechanisms and synapse-sensitive epigenetic mechanisms can enable such local plasticity. Hence, we expect (and find) a great complexity of factors, mechanisms, and interactions in the nervous system, and there are excellent recent reviews on the role of different epigenetic mechanisms such as histone modifications, especially acetylation and deacetylation (Gräff & Tsai, 2013), noncoding RNAs (Spadaro & Bredy, 2012), and DNA methylation and demethylation (Li, Wei, Ratnu, & Bredy, 2013; Yu et al., 2011) in learning and memory.

Table 7.1 summarizes the main results and conclusions from research on the epigenetics of learning. The table brings together studies exploring the epigenetic basis of learning in rodents (e.g., fear learning, taste learning, object recognition), and in other species, among them marmoset monkeys, *Aplysia*, *Drosophila*, *Caenorhabditis elegans*, snails, crabs, and bees. It does not cover *all* the studies reported in the literature, but it illustrates the scope and range of research in the area today, and points to some interesting generalizations. As the table clearly shows, investigations of the epigenetics of fear conditioning and extinction in rats and mice are most numerous (Blaze & Roth, 2013; Zovkic et al., 2013).

Epigenetics of Fear Conditioning and Fear Extinction in Rodents

Epigenetic mechanisms not only are important for any persistent biological function, but also have the capacity to dynamically store encoded information and thus contribute to the long-term storage that is the hallmark of neural memory. As we have noted earlier, the importance of epigenetic mechanisms for storing information led to the expectation that persistent patterns of activity in brain-expressed genes that are known to affect learning will be found to alter their epigenetic state following conditioning or other behavioral manipulations.

Studies investigating the epigenetic basis of fear conditioning in rats were pioneered by David Sweatt and his group members. Their experiments showed that rats that received shocks in a training chamber and exhibited freezing behavior upon subsequent exposures to the chamber (i.e., learned that the chamber is associated with shock) had increased acetylation of histone H3 in the CA1 area of the hippocampus, an area where transcription is known to increase following contextual learning. Other histone modifications were also found to change following contextual fear conditioning: Di- and tri-methylation of histones was increased in the hippocampus following conditioning, whereas no change was observed in the entorhinal cortex, but inhibition of histone di-methylation in the entorhinal cortex (but not in the hippocampus) enhanced memory formation (Gupta-Agarwal et al., 2012). It was also found that although the acetylation of histone H4 was unaffected by fear conditioning, this histone became acetylated following latent inhibition – interference in the development of a conditioned response, in this case freezing in the training room, when the conditioned stimulus was presented alone before the conditioning session (Levenson et al., 2004). Since latent inhibition may involve the learning of associations between the CS and the context (e.g., Honey, Iordanova, & Good, 2010) this result suggests that H4 acetylation is dependent on the specific nature of the association of the CS with the context. Another type of fear conditioning, cued fear conditioning, in which a cue such as a sound is associated with foot shock, showed that conditioning resulted in changes in patterns of histone modifications at the *Homer1a* promoter (*Homer1a* is a gene required for memory formation) in hippocampal and amygdala neurons (Mahan et al., 2012). Another study demonstrated that administration of an HDAC inhibitor before fear conditioning rescued learning in mice with genetically knocked out neuronal nitric oxide synthase (which is a key factor in the nitric oxide pathway that plays a role in synaptic plasticity and long-term memory) and facilitated the extinction of fear memory of wild-type mice for several weeks (Itzhak, Anderson, Kelley, & Petkov, 2012).

Additional studies of contextual fear conditioning by Sweatt's group uncovered temporally and spatially orchestrated changes in various brain regions in both DNA methylation and histone modifications of specific learning-associated genes. The investigators demonstrated that global DNA methylation is required for the maintenance of memory: DNMT expression was significantly enhanced within the hippocampus after contextual fear conditioning, and blocking the activity of DNMT abolished fear memory. When looking at specific genes, the studies showed that DNA methylation at the *reelin* gene, which is associated with memory formation, decreased following conditioning, while DNA methylation at the *PP1* gene, which is considered to be a memory repressor, increased (Miller & Sweatt, 2007). Another gene involved in the persistence of fear memories, the brain-derived neurotrophic factor gene (*BDNF*), underwent changes in its pattern of methylation at several different sites along the gene, and these changes were associated with concomitant changes in histone acetylation and methylation (Gupta *et al.*, 2010; Lubin, Roth, & Sweatt, 2008). These epigenetic changes were relatively short-lived, but subsequent studies showed that remote, long-term memory that consolidates within 30 days was accompanied by increased DNA methylation in *calcineurin* (a suppressor of memory) (Miller *et al.*, 2010; for reviews of these studies, see Day & Sweatt, 2010, 2011; Zovkic *et al.*, 2013).

DNA methylation is also important for the consolidation and reconsolidation of cued fear conditioning: Using DNMT inhibitors to block DNA methylation in the lateral nucleus of the amygdala, it was found that this inhibition impaired both retrieval-related H3 acetylation and fear memory reconsolidation. Manipulation of histone acetylation by inhibiting HDAC reversed the effects of DNMT inhibition, showing that both DNA methylation and histone acetylation are important for memory reconsolidation in this region of the brain (Maddox & Schafe, 2011).

The explosion of studies on the role of small ncRNAs in neural development and functioning includes a growing number that show that changes in the activities of microRNAs affect learning and memory. The expression level of half of the 187 measured microRNAs in rats changed in response to contextual fear conditioning (Kye *et al.*, 2011). In mice, knocking out of *Dicer1*, a gene coding for one of the key enzymes in the biogenesis of the microRNA pathway, led to improvements in both fear memory and spatial memory (Konopka *et al.*, 2010) suggesting that microRNAs (miRs) may have a role in the inhibition of learning. Other studies demonstrate the associations between particular microRNAs and fear conditioning and extinction. For example, extinction of fear in mice was associated with an increase in the expression of miR-128b, which disrupted the stability of plasticity-related target genes in the infralimbic PFC (Lin *et al.*, 2011).

The formation and elimination of dendritic spines reflect the changes in neural networks that form during associative learning such as Pavlovian conditioning. A study of fear conditioning in mice showed that pairing an auditory cue with a foot-shock increased the rate of elimination of dendritic spines in the association cortex nine days after exposure to the paired stimuli, whereas the repeated presentation of the auditory cue without a foot-shock (i.e., extinction) led to an increase in the rate of spine formation at the same dendritic branches, and reconditioning induced the elimination of the dendritic spines that were formed after extinction (Lai, Franke, & Gan, 2012). Although not investigated in the same study, dendritic spine remodeling is known to be associated with the activity of microRNAs and is crucial for synaptic plasticity and learning. The neural microRNAs miR-132, miR-134, and miR-138 regulate the actin cytoskeleton in mammalian hippocampal neurons (Fortin, Srivastava, & Soderling, 2012); moderate increases in miR132, a particularly versatile microRNA that seems to be involved in multiple learning-related functions, was shown to increase cognitive capacity in transgenic mice. When highly expressed, on the other hand, it led to a significant impairment of spatial memory capacity and an enrichment of dendritic spines (Hansen, Sakamoto, Wayman, Impey, & Obrietan, 2010; Hansen et al., 2012).

The studies presented in Table 7.1, which, in addition to fear conditioning, include other forms of learning and species other than rodents, lead to several general conclusions and suggest possible directions for future research. First, multiple and interacting epigenetic mechanisms affect all types, modes, and durations of learning and memory. The table reflects the current predominance of studies on the involvement of histone acetylation and DNA methylation in learning, although there are also some studies of the effects of histone methylation (e.g., Castellano et al., 2012; Gupta-Agarwal et al., 2012). Studying other chromatin marks and other epigenetic factors will complete, and no doubt complicate, the current picture. Second, the local and specific epigenetic changes observed depend on the particular learning task, the time elapsed after learning, the brain region investigated, the particular genes that are suppressed or activated, and the signaling cascade that regulates and is regulated by the epigenetic changes. Additional factors, such as the effects of age, the general state of health, and specifically the integrity of the immune system (Ziv et al., 2006), are also likely to have a significant influence on learning and memory. Third, in some cases, epigenetic-mediated transfer of information from one brain region (hippocampus) to another (prefrontal cortex) accompanies long-term (remote) memory, and the study of such transfer is becoming one of the major challenges of neural epigenetics.

The data presented in Table 7.1 reveal interesting and surprisingly consistent correlations between epigenetic processes and learning:

1 In 32/36 studies (rows 1–11, 14–24, 26–28, 30–34, 47, 49) in which general changes in HAT or HDAC were investigated, improved learning was positively correlated with global increase in acetylation, whatever the learning task and the species investigated.
2 In 9/9 studies (rows 37, 39, 41–42, 46–49, 52) that investigated the relation between global methylation and learning, a decrease in DNA methylation (through the inhibition of one of the DNMTs) was associated with decreased learning; improved learning was associated with increased expression of methylating enzymes (DNMTs). In line with this global effect, a gain-of-function mutation in the *Mecp2* gene (a gene that produces a protein that binds to methylated DNA and contributes to the inhibition of transcription) enhances both its binding to methylated DNA and learning (row 37). The observation (row 61) that knocking out Piwi genes, which contribute to DNA methylation, results in reduced long-term facilitation (LTF), whereas Piwi overexpression enhances it, is also compatible with a general effect of increased methylation on learning.

3   Small RNAs, both microRNAs, and piRNAs can have general effects on learning: *Dicer* deletion leads to increased learning, whereas overexpression of Piwi genes in *Aplysia* (row 61) results in enhanced LTF through its effect on DNA methylation in the promoter of the gene coding for CREB2, a major memory inhibitor. However, as yet, there are only a few reports of these global effects, so this conclusion is far more tentative than that based on the global effects of DNA methylation and histone acetylation.

4   At the level of the *specific* DNA sequence, DNA methylation at particular sites may increase or decrease during learning (rows 38, 40, 43–46, 49–51). The effects of the enzyme GADD45B, which is needed for the demethylation of specific promoters, is variable (rows 46, 49). Similarly, the specificity and pattern of histone-tail acetylation depend on local interacting factors, brain area, learning paradigm, and other contingent factors (for details, see Peixoto & Abel, 2013).

5   The amount of *specific* microRNAs and piRNAs needs to be finely balanced to promote learning (rows 53, 55–63).

6   Prion-like proteins, whose conformation is altered as a result of signal transduction and that dynamically maintain and propagate the altered architecture of the synapse through 3D-templating, may be part of the local memory system of the synapse (rows 64, 65).

Locus-specific changes in acetylation, DNA methylation, or the level of specific ncRNAs are always the result of multiple local effects, none of which, in isolation, is likely to be necessary or sufficient. We therefore did not expect to find regularities in epigenetic regulation at the single locus or synapse level. Nevertheless, structural 3D-templating is a memory mechanism, which, if shown to be ubiquitous, might account for the persistence of memory at the synapse level and provide a high level of specificity. Unfortunately, at present, we have only a few examples of prion-like synaptic proteins (Table 7.1, rows 64 and 65), so generalizations are premature, although because of their potential to template cellular structures at the synapse, we believe that 3D-templating of prion-like proteins or complexes of proteins will be found to be an important and general feature of synaptic memory.

But how can one explain the robust relationship between *general* epigenetic changes – such as a global increase in histone acetylation and increased DNA methylation – and enhanced learning (Figure 7.2)? Since, in all experiments, different neural cell types with (presumably) cell-specific levels of gene expression and chromatin regulation have been used, the fact that these global changes have a consistent effect on learning requires a special explanation. HATs seem to recruit transcription factors, and increased histone acetylation seems to loosen chromatin and make the "open" chromosome region more accessible to regulatory factors, among them the positive and negative regulators of learning-associated genes. It is therefore not surprising that enhanced learning ability is associated with global histone acetylation. Relaxation of chromatin and recruitment of transcription factors may be a necessary condition for long-term memory, just like the mechanistically related need for RNA and protein synthesis. Two exceptions to the robust correlation between histone acetylation and enhanced learning (rows 12 and 13) involve fear extinction, which, as suggested by Bahari-Javan *et al.* (2012), may entail interactions with repressive regulatory factors that are specific to this type of active learning to unlearn. Another exception (row 25)

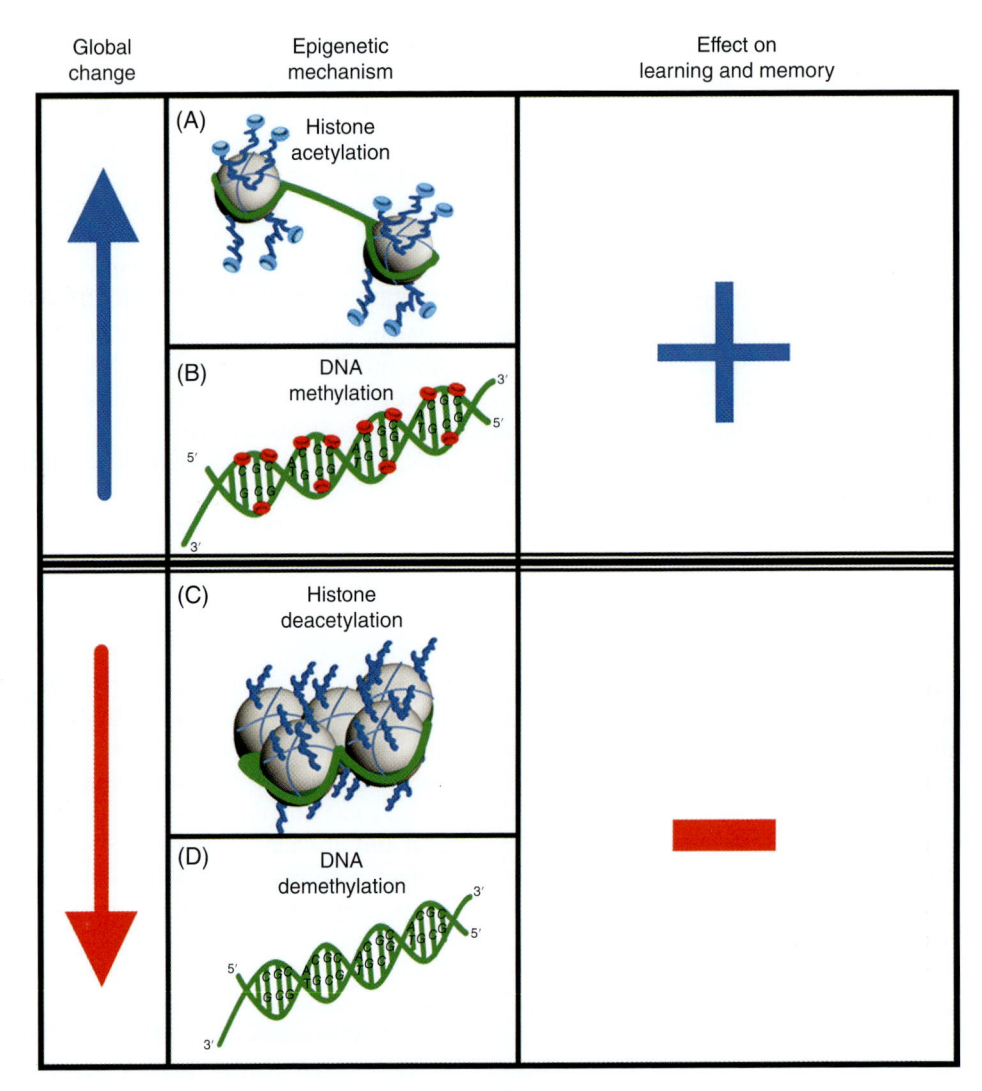

Figure 7.2 Global epigenetic effects on learning. Global increase (blue arrow) in histone acetylation (A) and in DNA methylation (B) is correlated with increased learning; global decrease (red arrow) in acetylation (C) and in DNA methylation (D) is correlated with decreased learning.

is the finding that chronic HDAC inhibition prevents the BDNF-induced increase in dendritic spine density and changes in dendritic spine morphology *in vitro*, but this observation is contradicted by several other experiments, so it may be the result of the experimental procedure used. The remaining exception (row 29), which neither contradicts nor supports the general observation, is that both over- and underexpression of HDAC impair courtship learning in *Drosophila*; it shows the need for a balance in the amount of epigenetic enzymes. Although it is clear that the present picture is extremely partial, and there are many open questions, such as whether histone acetylation must precede activation or need only follow and stabilize it (or, as seems most likely, both), the global effect of increased histone acetylation on improved learning seems to be a robust general principle.

Unlike the relationship between HAT activity and enhanced learning, the correlation between a general *increase* in DNA methylation and enhanced learning seems paradoxical, since DNA methylation is usually associated with a more "closed" chromatin conformation and gene silencing, especially in gene promoter regions (Yu et al., 2011). The explanations offered in the literature are that (1) methylation leads to the repression of the synthesis of specific memory-repressors, and hence to improved learning (e.g., Yu et al., 2011; Sui, Wang, Ju, & Chen, 2012); (2) increased methylation in the body of the gene is associated with increased transcriptional activity; or (iii) DNMTs are involved in both DNA methylation and demethylation (Chen, Wang, & Shen, 2012). However, although such suggestions may explain specific effects, they do not account very well for the correlation between *global* increase in DNA methylation and improved learning in mammals. We propose that in addition to the effects mentioned above, increased DNA methylation leads to the silencing of clusters of microRNA genes, which globally suppress learning. Hence, our suggestion is that the more downstream cause for the observed decrease in learning associated with DNMT inhibition is the effect of this inhibition on small microRNA transcription (a process that may be guided by piRNAs in the nucleus that positively interact with the DNA methylation system; see Rajasethupathy et al., 2012). This hypothesis is easy to test, since it predicts that DNMT inhibition would be followed by increased expression of microRNAs (but not piRNAs). The hypothesis is compatible with the observed increase in learning following knocking out *Dicer*, which leads to a decreased level of small microRNAs and to the suppression of the inhibition that they impose. The effects of increased methylation and impaired biogenesis of microRNAs seem to reflect the importance of active inhibition in associative learning: Learning always involves selection and the concomitant inhibition of the myriad of irrelevant (nonselected) associations. But whatever their mechanistic explanations turn out to be, the robust correlations between the activities of the enzymes that regulate epigenetic mechanisms at the neuron level and learning, which occurs at the whole animal level, are striking and predictive.

The global effects of increased acetylation, increased methylation, and decreased biogenesis of microRNAs on enhanced learning and memory raise the question of the costs of these global effects. It is clear that inhibition is a fundamental facet of learning and that an increase in transcriptional activity is not necessarily related to increased learning ability. As a study charting DNA methylation dynamics in the brains of mice and humans has recently shown, there are developmental changes in patterns of DNA methylation in cortical neurons, with CH methylation, which is associated with transcriptional silencing, increasing throughout early childhood and adolescence, and becoming dominant in mature neurons (Lister et al., 2013). Moreover, although it may seem that improved memory is always advantageous, the effects of global epigenetic factors are not confined to neurons, and may have costs because global changes in gene activity may impair biological functions in other cell types (e.g., in interacting immune system cells). Even when considering just the nervous system and neural learning, we must remember that forgetting is very important: Persistent memory of already irrelevant relations may be maladaptive, and both passive and active forgetting have evolved (Hardt, Nader, & Nadel, 2013). Furthermore, enhanced memory of a recently learned task may come at the expense of memories of past tasks, or of the learning of (different) future tasks. Experimental investigation of learning dynamics can lead to a better understanding of the constraints on the epigenetic mechanisms of learning and memory at different stages of development.

Some General Implications and Future Directions

Our review of the epigenetics of learning is inevitably incomplete. We have been unable to cover many important research areas and speculative suggestions. For example, we have not presented the intriguing data about epigenetically controlled transposition in mouse neurons, which is increased during exposure to stress conditions (Singer, McConnell, Marchetto, Coufal, & Gage, 2010) and during engagement in voluntary motor activity (Muotri, Marchetto, Zhao, & Gage, 2009). These findings suggest that learning in traumatic situations or during intense physical activity (which is often linked to stress) may increase transposition and lead to enhanced neuronal variability (Singer *et al.*, 2010), and possibly also to some targeted genetic changes in neurons. Another possibility, which is at present unexplored, is that the postsynaptic density complex, which in mammals includes over a thousand different proteins and RNAs, has prion-like architectural properties; these may enable three-dimensional guided assembly during the formation of new synapses during learning, comparable with the 3D templating that reproduces structures in ciliates (see Grimes & Aufderheide, 1991, for a review). Yet another topic that has not been addressed here is the role of spatial bioelectric organization, which involves not only neuronal systems but also somatic systems in the encoding and storage of memory (Tseng & Levin, 2013). We cannot do justice to these and to many other fascinating areas of work, so we conclude with a short discussion of some issues that seem to us particularly pertinent for understanding the epigenetics of associative learning discussed in this chapter.

Epigenetic Mechanisms and the Formation of Cellular Associations

In addition to their role in mediating learning-related gene expression, epigenetic mechanisms are themselves learning mechanisms that have an inherent ability to store information about the specific developmental history of individual neurons (Rajasethupathy *et al.*, 2012). For example, both sensitization and priming can be described at the single-cell level in terms of quantitative change in chromatin marks that alter the threshold of sensitivity to transcription (Ginsburg & Jablonka, 2009). This implies that the epigenetic profile of a neuron may determine its future capacity for learning and memory, and thus provide the nervous system with an additional, "history-sensitive," computational affordance. The interacting epigenetic mechanisms within each cell can therefore shape the cell's learning curve.

Learning curves describe the relation between learning and experience, or more directly the change in responding over time. Qualitatively speaking, a learning curve can be linear, diminishing, or accelerating. For example, a diminishing learning curve relating a synaptic stimulation with changes in synaptic potentiation shows that subsequent stimulations will result in a diminishing increase in potentiation so that the "strongest" learning occurs during early stimulations, while later stimulations have a relatively small impact. At the cellular-epigenetic level, a neuron in which past learning has resulted in an altered pattern of epigenetic marks such as addition of transcription-enhancing marks that assist future learning will have an accelerating learning curve, while a neuron in which learning led to removal of enhancing marks or to the addition of suppressing marks will exhibit a diminishing learning curve. Hence, a neuron's epigenetic pattern may determine the neuron's learning curve. We suggest that the learning curve at the neuron level, which is determined by the pattern of the epigenetic marks that affect its synaptic plasticity, influences, and may partially reflect, the learning curve at the behavioral level.

If neurons have the ability to communicate their epigenetic profile to their neighbors, epigenetic learning at the cell level can exhibit prediction-error-like properties. Learning is modulated by the predictability measure of the reinforcing stimulus (e.g., Rescorla & Wagner, 1972). This means that the increase in the strength of the association between a CS and a US is not based solely on the contiguity of the CS and the US but rather is based on the extent to which all cues present on a trial predict or are sufficiently associated with the US. The bigger the difference between the actual outcome and the outcome predicted by the CS (the "prediction error"), the stronger the increment (e.g., Schultz & Dickinson, 2000; see Chapter 1). Since epigenetic mechanisms "keep track" of neurons' learning history, the prediction error can be calculated from the relevant cells' epigenetic profile. Furthermore, if we assume that epigenetic patterns, including those leading to inhibition of synapse formation, can be communicated to neighboring neurons, even more complex learning effects involving stimulus selection, such as blocking (Kamin, 1969), may be inferred from altered patterns of modulations at the cellular level.

Memory Through the Formation of Intercellular Associations

The intracellular epigenetic factors and mechanisms on which we have focused are directly related to the *inter*cellular neural communication that takes place across the synapses that connect neurons. The classical and established processes underlying memory formation are the LTP and long-term depression (LTD) that occur in synapses. As our discussion of fear conditioning shows, epigenetic factors, notably chromatin marks and microRNAs, are involved in these processes. Furthermore, as noted earlier, the morphological growth and retraction of dendritic spines that occur during learning are under epigenetic control through the actions of specific microRNA (Fortin *et al.*, 2012; Lai *et al.*, 2012).

Prions may turn out to be additional vehicles of intercellular neural communication. Prions have been shown to influence synaptic transmission, exerting their effects both presynaptically and postsynaptically. For example, Caiati *et al.* (2013) showed that the prion protein, PrP^C, can control synaptic plasticity toward LTP or LTD. But prions may also have more far-reaching effects by being transported from neuron to neuron through exosome shuttling. Exosomes are vesicles measuring

50–90 nm contained in larger intracellular multivesicular bodies (MVBs). Exosomes are released from certain cells into the extracellular environment by MVBs fusing with the plasma membrane. Porto-Carreiro, Février, Paquet, Vilette, and Raposo (2005) showed that exosomes are involved in mobilizing prions in many neurodegenerative disorders, and different conformations of prion protein have been found in them (Chivet *et al.*, 2013). Neurons are known to secrete exosomes (Lachenal *et al.*, 2010; Lai & Breakefield, 2012) that contain – among other epigenetic factors – microRNAs (Valadi *et al.*, 2007) and prions. A vast array of new possibilities have therefore been opened up, with exosomes as mediators of intercellular neural communication. Prions and microRNAs, released from exosomes that cross the boundaries between neurons, may (1) enable synapse-specific inhibition and (2) allow alliances and stabilizations among communicating neurons that can lead to coordination and long-term stability within the network, and between the CNS and the peripheral nervous system.

The storage of memories as chromatin marks in stem cells and as small RNA molecules that migrate among neurons may underlie puzzling observations such as the memory of adult moths that remember the associations they learned as caterpillars (Blackiston, Silva Casey, & Weiss, 2008). Such epigenetic mechanisms may also be part of the explanation of the ability of planarians that have regenerated a new head and brain following decapitation to remember what they had learned with the old head (Shomrat & Levin, 2013). Because it is possible to experimentally manipulate epigenetic mechanisms using mutations and chemical inhibitors, it should be possible to elucidate some of the mechanistic basis for encoding such developmental memory.

Beyond Long-Term Memory

Long-term memory is an amazing feat, and memory retention following head-brain metamorphosis is even more astounding, but even this is not the most remarkable type of memory persistence. In recent years, it has been found that conditions such as environmental enrichment, social defeat, and the quality of maternal care can have *transgenerational* cognitive and affective effects affecting learning and memory. The transgenerational effects of ancestral behavior can occur in two mutually nonexclusive ways. The first, referred to as soma-soma or experiential transmission, is through developmental reconstruction that bypasses the gametes (Jablonka & Lamb, 2014). For example, a low amount of licking-grooming (LG) of her offspring by a mother rat leads to an increased stress response and neophobia in these offspring; her daughters, when they become mothers, also exhibit low LG and then pass it on to their own daughters, and so on (Weaver *et al.*, 2004). These developmental changes are underlain by epigenetic changes in DNA methylation and histone modification in the rat brain. The second type of transgenerational transfer, germline transmission, is *direct transmission of epigenetic information through the gametes*. For example, deficient maternal behavior is transmitted through the gametes in mice; in rats, gametic transmission of mate preference and an altered response to stress involved DNA methylation and histone modifications are found after treating their great-grandmother with the fungicide vinclozolin. Table 7.2 lists details of many other examples of both types of transgenerational transmission. We can safely predict that in all cases in which the molecular mechanisms have not yet been identified, epigenetic processes will be found to play a key role. It seems that, after 110 years, some of Semon's derided suggestions are being vindicated!

It is important to stress that there is a fundamental difference between the ontogenetic learning that we described earlier and inherited learning-affecting effects. The example of fear-related learning showed that epigenetic changes underlie memorization of the specific learned associations acquired during ontogeny. It is difficult to imagine how such specific complex associations can be transmitted between generations because such memory requires the formation of multiple specific engrams at the synaptic level, and these cannot be inherited. Nonetheless, psychological changes in ancestors (resulting from environment enrichment, various types of stress, addiction, and so on) can lead to either a decrease or increase in *general* cognitive and learning abilities, or to altered *specific dispositions* (e.g., disposition to be attracted or startled by particular odorants) through the gametic transmission of memory factors such as neural ncRNAs. Table 7.2 lists examples of both general and specific types of transgenerational effects. In nematodes, for example, inherited changes in specific dispositions were observed after the worms have been exposed for five (F0–F4) generations to a particular odorant, which led to very stable inheritance (40 generations) of a preference for that odorant (Remy, 2010). An example of a general effect on learning is seen in mice when environmental enrichment in the parents' generation (which has effects on both cognition and emotions) leads to beneficial effects in the offspring's general learning abilities. A specific effect was demonstrated in mice following olfactory fear conditioning. Mice that have been trained to fear a particular smell (acetophenone or propanol) transmitted an enhanced sensitivity and a greater startle response to that smell to their offspring and grand-offspring (F1 and F2) through both sperm and egg, and the CG methylation of locus responsive to one of the odorant was heritably altered in sperm (Dias & Ressler, 2014). Another interesting example of a specific change in disposition was found in rats, where cocaine addiction in the paternal generation led to a compensatory effect of increased tolerance to the drug in the offspring, demonstrating that transgenerational effects need not lead to similarity between parents and offspring. Clearly, the nature (similar or compensatory) and intergenerational persistence of an acquired/learned trait depend on the exposure conditions and their duration.

The realization that epigenetic mechanisms play a key role in the expression of persistent cognitive traits that impact learning has huge medical implications, because detrimental epigenetic effects may be alleviated by administering inhibitors or enhancers of epigenetic factors. Although existing epigenetic interventions are still crude, more specific interventions are being developed and hold great promise for the mitigation of mental diseases, age-related cognitive deterioration, and cognitive and affective retardation. Moreover, the realization that chronic stress leads to transgenerational effects has alarming social and political implications: For example, long-lasting ethnic conflicts or persistent starvation can lead to detrimental cognitive and affective effects in whole populations, thus aggravating and reinforcing social problems for generations to come.

Implications for the Evolution of Associative Learning

What are the implications of the new epigenetic findings for evolutionary questions pertaining to learning and memory? First, the possibility of transgenerational epigenetic inheritance has population-wide implications: Population dynamics are different from those expected if genetic variation alone is considered. For example, rates of evolution can be very high (Day & Bonduriansky, 2011; Geoghegan & Spencer, 2012) and can be further accelerated through social learning and cultural transmission. Second, the realization that epigenetic mechanisms and factors are important for learning and memory makes it necessary to investigate the evolution of the epigenetic pathways that affect neural learning. The work of the Jensen group shows that stressing domesticated females chickens impairs learning in their offspring (see Table 7.2), whereas stressing jungle fowl parents, the species from which the chicken evolved, has no detrimental effects on offspring. This suggests that the development of learning pathways in domesticated chicken has been destabilized. Since the domestication of the chicken involved massive changes in DNA methylation (Nätt et al., 2012), identifying the epigenetically altered genes may help us to understand the processes of both domestication and learning, and to unravel the pathways involved. On a broader scale, the evolution of flexible associative learning from simpler types of learning during the early evolution of animals must have involved changes in epigenetic factors, for example the introduction of new microRNAs. The identification of these epigenetic factors through comparative studies between taxa that learn predominately through sensitization and/or limited associative learning (e.g., cnidarians) and species that manifest flexible, open-ended associative learning should shed light on this fundamental question (Ginsburg & Jablonka, 2010).

There is no doubt that the study of the epigenetics of memory enriches and expands our understanding of learning and provides a bridge between different types of memory. Cellular life cannot exist without basic forms of memory, and neural learning and memory are the hallmarks of animal life, the foundations of its amazing richness, and the drivers of its evolution. Epigenetics is fundamental to all aspects of the biology of learning.

Table 7.1 Epigenetic correlates of learning and memory.

No.	Species	Type of plasticity/ learning task	Brain area/s involved	Reported results	Experimental timescale	Reference
Histone acetylation and deacetylation						
1	Mice	Contextual fear conditioning	Hippocampus	Inhibitors of class I HDACs restore performance to normal levels for a 6-month-old mouse model of Alzheimer's disease; these inhibitors cause repeated cycles of histone acetylation/deacetylation throughout the genome	1 and 14 days	Kilgore et al. (2010)
2	Mice	Contextual fear conditioning	Hippocampus and amygdala	Administration of an HDAC inhibitor before conditioning rescues learning in mice with genetically knocked-out nitric oxide synthase (a key factor in the nitric oxide pathway which plays a role in synaptic plasticity and long-term memory) and facilitates extinction memory in WT mice	Weeks	Itzhak et al. (2012)
3	Mice	Contextual fear conditioning	Hippocampus and cortex	Environmental enrichment correlates with increased histone-tail acetylation; increased histone acetylation by inhibitors of HDAC induces sprouting of dendrites, increased number of synapses and reinstated learning behavior along with access to long-term memories	Weeks	Fischer, Sananbenesi, Wang, Dobbin, and Tsai (2007)
4	Mice	Contextual and cued fear conditioning	Lateral amygdala	Inhibition of PP1 (a suppressor of LTM) leads to increase in acetylation and decrease in HDAC activity, increases LTP, and enhances contextual and tone fear memory	24 hr	Koshibu, Gräff, and Mansuy (2011)

(*Continued*)

Table 7.1 (Continued)

No.	Species	Type of plasticity/learning task	Brain area/s involved	Reported results	Experimental timescale	Reference
5	Mice	Contextual and cued fear conditioning	Hippocampal and amygdala	Inhibition of HDAC enhances contextual but not cued fear conditioning and enhances *Homer1* H3 acetylation in the hippocampus	24 hr	Mahan *et al.* (2012)
6	Mice	Contextual fear conditioning and spatial memory	Hippocampus	Overexpression of HDAC2 decreases dendritic spine density, synapse number, synaptic plasticity and memory formation; HDAC2 deficiency results in increased synapse number and memory facilitation.	24 hr	Guan *et al.* (2009)
7	Mice	Contextual fear conditioning and spatial memory	Hippocampus	Aged (16 months) mice treated with HDAC inhibitor show improved memory and elevated H4K12 acetylation	30 and 60 min; 24 and 48 hr	Peleg *et al.* (2010)
8	Mice	Contextual fear conditioning and novel object recognition	CA1 area of the hippocampus and cortical areas	p300 knock-out mice exhibited memory impairments: both lower preference for a novel object and lower freezing upon reexposure to the fear-learned context	24 hr	Oliveira *et al.* (2011)
9	Mice	Contextual fear conditioning and novel object recognition; LTP	CA1 area of the hippocampus	Neurons lacking CBP demonstrate impairments to LTP and long-term memory (contextual fear and novel object location), but not short-term memory	24 hr	Barrett *et al.* (2011)
10	Mice	Contextual fear conditioning; spatial memory; object recognition	Hippocampus and cortex	CBP knock-out mice exhibit robust impairment in long- and short-term memory formation	30 and 60 min (short term); 24 hr and 4 weeks (long term)	Chen, Zou, Watanabe, van Deursen, and Shen (2010)

11	Mice	Contextual fear conditioning and extinction	Hippocampus and infralimbic cortex	Administration of HDAC inhibitor facilitates extinction	1 and 14 days	Stafford, Raybuck, Ryabinin, and Lattal (2012)
12	Mice	Contextual fear extinction	Hippocampus	Overexpression of HDAC1 enhances fear extinction learning; inhibition of HDAC1 impairs fear extinction; during fear extinction HDAC1 deacetylates H3K9 at the *c-Fos* promoter, which allows for H3K9 trimethylation, leading to repression of the *c-Fos* gene (an early gene that is upregulated after contextual fear conditioning and whose protein levels are reduced after extinction)	Days	Bahari-Javan *et al.* (2012)
13	Mice	Fear conditioning and extinction	Infralimbic prefrontal cortex	p300 inhibition facilitates extinction memory and LTP	24 hr	Marek *et al.* (2011)
14	Mice	Fear conditioning and extinction	Prefrontal cortex	extinction is accompanied by increase in histone H4 acetylation around the *BDNFP4* gene promoter	2 hr	Bredy *et al.* (2007)
15	Mice	Novel object recognition	Dorsal hippocampus	HAT inhibition immediately after training impairs memory consolidation	24 hr	Zhao, Fan, Fortress, Boulware, and Frick (2012)
16	Mice	Novel object recognition	Dorsal hippocampus	Deletion of HDAC3 leads to an increased *Nr4a2* (a CREB-dependent gene that has been implicated in long-term memory) expression and enhanced long-term memory for object location	24 hr and 7 days	McQuown *et al.* (2011)

(*Continued*)

Table 7.1 (Continued)

No.	Species	Type of plasticity/ learning task	Brain area/s involved	Reported results	Experimental timescale	Reference
17	Mice	Novel object recognition	Forebrain	Mice lacking CBP have reduced neuronal histone acetylation and impaired object memory	24 hr	Valor et al. (2011)
18	Mice	Novel object recognition	Hippocampus and prefrontal cortex	PTMs (including histone acetylation and methylaton) increase accompanies memory consolidation; when their increase is pharmacologically blocked, memory consolidation is prevented	24 hr and 7 days	Gräff, Woldemichael, Berchtold, Dewarrat, and Mansuy (2012)
19	Mice	Novel object recognition	Hippocampus	HDAC inhibition enhances memory for familiar objects	24 hr and 7 days	Stefanko, Barrett, Ly, Reolon, and Wood (2009)
20	Mice	Novel taste learning	Insular cortex	Learning results in an increase in HAT activity	Many hours after the initial stimulus	Swank and Sweatt (2001)
21	Mice	Object-location memory	Dorsal hippocampus	HDAC inhibition enhances memory	24 hr	Hawk, Florian, and Abel (2011)
22	Mice	Object-location memory	Hippocampus	HDAC inhibition enhances memory in a CBP dependent manner	24 hr	Haettig et al. (2011)
23	Mice	Spatial memory	Hippocampus	HAT (CBP/p300) activation (by CSP-TTK21) enhances the persistence of memory (extending the time during which memory can be retrieved)	2 days	Chatterjee et al. (2013)
24	Rats	Contextual fear conditioning and extinction	CA1 area of the hippocampus	Conditioning is accompanied by increased H3 acetylation; extinction leads to an increase in the acetylation of H4; injection of HDAC inhibitor prior to conditioning enhances the formation of long-term memory	24 hr	Levenson et al. (2004)

25	Rats	*In vitro*	CA1 area of the hippocampus	Chronic HDAC inhibition prevents the BDNF-induced increase in dendritic spine density and changes of dendritic spine morphology	24 hr	Calfa *et al.* (2012)
26	Rats	Spatial memory	Hippocampus	Acetylation levels of the H2B and H4 histones are increased during memory formation; learning results in enhanced CBP transcription	3 days	Bousiges *et al.* (2010)
27	Rats	Spatial memory	Hippocampus	Following learning, histone H3 acetylation becomes induced across all regions of the hippocampus, while acetylation of lysine 9 on H3 is downregulated selectively in CA1. H4 acetylation is influenced in opposite directions in CA1 and DG, and is insensitive in CA3	2 hr	Castellano *et al.* (2012)
28	*Helix lucorum* (snail)	Food aversion	Right parietal ganglion	Conditioning is accompanied by increased H3 acetylation	15 min	Danilova, Kharchenko, Shevchenko, and Grinkevich (2010)
29	*Drosophila* (fruit fly)	Courtship memory	Mushroom body	Both knockdown and overexpression of HDAC (*Rpd3*) impairs LTM	24 hr	Fitzsimons and Scott (2011)
30	*Chasmagnathus granulatus* (crab)	Context-signal memory	Central brain	Strong training induces a significant increase in H3 acetylation; HDAC inhibition enhances memory	1 hr after training	Federman, Fustiñana, and Romano (2009)
31	*Chasmagnathus granulatus* (crab)	Context-signal memory reconsolidation	Central brain	Increased H3 acetylation during reconsolidation; p300 HAT inhibitor impaired reconsolidation of strong memory; HDAC inhibitor enhances reconsolidation of a weak memory and an increase in histone H3 acetylation	1 hr after reconsolidation	Federman, Fustiñana, and Romano (2012)

(*Continued*)

Table 7.1 (Continued)

No.	Species	Type of plasticity/ learning task	Brain area/s involved	Reported results	Experimental timescale	Reference
32	*C. elegans* (nematode worm)	Thermotaxic task	Nervous system	Deletion of the *hda4*, a homolog of the mammalian *HDAC4* leads to enhanced memory, while the overexpression of this gene diminishes it	18–48 hr	Wang *et al.* (2011)
33	*Aplysia* (mollusk)	*In vitro* sensitization and depression	Sensory neurons	Long-term sensitization leads to enhanced histone acetylation, while long-term depression (LTD) is associated with histone deacetylation	Days	Guan *et al.* (2002)
Histone methylation
34	Mice and rats	Contextual fear conditioning	Hippocampus	Conditioning induces both trimethylation of H3K4 and dimethylation of H3K9; HDAC inhibitor elevates trimethylation of H3K4 and decreases dimethylation of H3K9; deletion of Mll, a known regulator of histone methylation, leads to significant deficits in memory consolidation; fear conditioning increases trimethylation of H3K4 at the *Zif268* gene	24 hr	Gupta *et al.* (2010)
35	Rats	Contextual fear conditioning	CA1 area of the hippocampus and the entorhinal cortex	Di- and tri-methylation of histones increased in the hippocampus following conditioning, while no change is observed in the entorhinal cortex, yet inhibition of histone di-methylation in the entorhinal (but not in the hippocampus) enhances memory formation	24 hr and longer	Gupta-Agarwal *et al.* (2012)
36	*Drosophila*	Habituation and courtship-related memory	Mushroom body	Deletion of euchromatin histone methyl transferase, one of the histone modifying enzymes, impairs learning and memory	30 min and 24 hr	Kramer *et al.* (2011)

DNA methylation					
37	Mice	*In vitro*	Hippocampus	Exposure of slices to DNMT inhibitor results in an immediate diminution of LTP; inhibition of DNMT activity can block PKC-mediated changes in histone acetylation	3 hr	Levenson *et al.* (2006)
38	Mice	Contextual fear conditioning	Hippocampus	Specific CpG sites in Bdnf CpG island 2 are hypomethylated 0.5 hr after conditioning with levels maintained up to 24 hr	24 hr	Mizuno, Dempster, Mill, and Giese (2012)
39	Mice	Contextual fear conditioning	Hippocampus	Mutation in *MeCP2* (a molecular linker between DNA methylation, chromatin remodeling and transcription regulation) that increases binding to methylated DNA leads to enhanced LTP and to an increase in excitatory synaptogenesis	24 hr	Li *et al.* (2011)
40	Mice	Contextual fear conditioning	Hippocampus	*gadd45b* (a gene associated with active DNA demethylation) KO mice exhibit memory impairment	24 hr	Leach *et al.* (2012)
41	Mice	Spatial memory and fear conditioning	CA1 area of the hippocampus	Mice that lack both *Dnmt1* and *Dnmt3a* show significantly smaller neurons, abnormal LTP and deficits in learning and memory	8–12 days for spatial memory and 24 hr for fear conditioning	Feng *et al.* (2010)
42	Mice	Conditioned place preference	Hippocampus	DNMT inhibition impairs memory acquisition (but not retrieval)	24 hr	Han, Li, Wang, Wei, Yang, and Suian (2010)

(*Continued*)

Table 7.1 (Continued)

No.	Species	Type of plasticity/learning task	Brain area/s involved	Reported results	Experimental timescale	Reference
43	Mice	LTP; contextual fear conditioning and spatial memory	Hippocampus	*gadd45b* knock-out mice exhibit enhanced memory in various tasks	24 hr to 28 days	Sultan, Wang, Tront, Liebermann, and Sweatt (2012)
44	Rats	Contextual fear conditioning	Dorsomedial prefrontal cortex; hippocampus	Following conditioning, *calcineurin*, a suppressor of memory, undergoes robust methylation in its CpG-rich promoter region	1–30 days	Miller *et al.* (2010)
45	Rats	Contextual fear conditioning	Hippocampus	The pattern of methylation on *BDNF* is altered in several different sites along the gene; NMDA receptor blockade prevents memory-associated alterations in bdnf DNA methylation and a deficit in memory formation	Less than 24 hr	Lubin *et al.* (2008)
46	Rats	Contextual fear conditioning	Hippocampus	Enhanced DNMT expression after conditioning; blocking DNMT's activity abolishes memory; methylation at the *reelin* gene is decreased; enhanced methylation at the PP1 gene	Less than 24 hr	Miller and Sweatt (2007)
47	Rats	Cued fear conditioning	Lateral amygdala	Conditioning is associated with an increase in histone H3 acetylation and DNMT3A expression. Infusion of HDAC inhibitor increases H3 acetylation and enhances long-term memory. Conversely, infusion of DNMT inhibitor impairs memory consolidation	90 min	Monsey, Ota, Akingbade, Hong, and Schafe (2011)
48	Rats	Cued fear conditioning and reconsolidation	Lateral amygdala	Inhibition of DNMT impairs both retrieval-related H3 acetylation and memory reconsolidation	3 hr and 24 hr	Maddox and Schafe (2011)

49	Rats	*In vitro*	Medial prefrontal cortex	LTP induction elevates total DNMTs, total HATs and global acethylation of H3 and H4. Demethylation of *reelin* and *bdnf* genes is upregulated in the process of LTP induction	2 hr or 24 hr	Sui *et al.* (2012)
50	Rats	Novel object recognition	Hippocampus	Positive correlation between recognition-performance and DNA methylation of BDNF-1	3 hr	Muñoz, Aspe, Contreras, and Palacios (2010)
51	Marmoset monkeys	Repeated cocaine injections in a conditioned place preference	Not described	"Acquisition of a conditioned place preference decreases methylation at the NK3 receptor coding gene (*TACR3*)"	Days	Barros *et al.* (2011)
52	Honey bee	Pavlovian olfactory discrimination and extinction	Mushroom body	Learning involves DNMT3 upregulation, and, depending on treatment time, DNMT inhibition reduces the acquisition and retention of memory and alters its extinction	5 hr	Lockett *et al.* (2010)
ncRNAs						
53	Mice	Cued fear conditioning and extinction	Infralimbic PFC	An increase in the expression of miR-128b (mediates dopamine transmission) disrupts stability of plasticity-related target genes	24 hr	Lin *et al.* (2011)
54	Mice	Cued fear conditioning and spatial memory	CA1 and CA3 areas of the hippocampus	Knock-out of *Dicer1*, one of the key enzymes in the biogenesis of the microRNA pathway, leads to improved memory	48 hr and 5 days	Konopka *et al.* (2010)

(*Continued*)

Table 7.1 (Continued)

No.	Species	Type of plasticity/learning task	Brain area/s involved	Reported results	Experimental timescale	Reference
55	Mice	Spatial memory	Medial temporal lobe	miR132 regulates neural spinogensis: when its amount is moderately increased, memory is enhanced, while when highly expressed, it leads to significant impairment	24 hr	Hansen et al. (2010, 2012)
56	Mice and rats	Contextual fear conditioning	CA1 area of the hippocampus	Expression level of half of the 187 measured miRNAs is changed in an NMDA (glutamate) receptor-dependent manner	24 hr	Kye et al. (2011)
57	Rats	Cued fear conditioning	Lateral amygdala	Overexpression of miR-182 represses actin-regulating protein (but not mRNA degradation) and disrupts memory formation	24 hr	Griggs, Young, Rumbaugh, and Miller (2013)
58	Rats	Novel object recognition	Hippocampus	Overexpression of miR-132 interferes with muscarinic acetylcholine receptors-dependent plasticity and impairs memory	20 min	Scott et al. (2012)
59	Drosophila	Olfactory conditioning	Mushroom body	When miR-276a function is reduced, DopR (defective proboscis extension response) gene levels increase, and memory is impaired	24 hr	Li, Cressy, et al. (2013)
60	C. elegans	Synapse remodeling	Ventral and dorsal body muscles	miR-84 is involved in genetically programmed synaptic remodeling	12–19 hr	Thompson-Peer, Bai, Hu, and Kaplan (2012)
61	Aplysia	In situ (in vitro preparation, but with the whole circuitry examined)	CNS	Knockdown of Piwi genes (which methylate DNA) results in reduced LTF; Piwi overexpression enhances it	Days	Rajasethupathy et al. (2012)

62	*Aplysia*	*In situ* (*in vitro* preparation, but with the whole circuitry examined)	Pleural ganglia neurons	LTF between sensory and motor neurons results in reduced levels of miR-124 – the effect is mediated by transcriptional regulation of CREB	Hours	Rajasethupathy *et al.* (2009)
63	*C. elegans*	Odor adaptation	Olfactory sensory neurons (AWC)	Endogenous RNAi promotes odor adaptation by repressing the *odr-1* gene: learning results with increased levels of NRDE-3-bound odr-1 siRNA and nuclear RNAi Ago NRDE-3 is required in the AWC neuron to promote adaptation	1–3 hr	Juang *et al.* (2013)
Prion-like proteins						
64	*Drosophila*	Courtship suppression	Mushroom body	The neuronal protein, *Orb2*, is required for the persistence of long-term memory possibly on the basis of its prion-like properties	Beyond 48 hr	Majumdar *et al.* (2012); Mastushita-Sakai, White-Grindley, Samuelson, Seidel, and Si (2010)
65	*Aplysia*	*In situ* (*in vitro* preparation, but with the whole circuitry examined)	Sensory neurons	A neuron-specific isoform of CPEB (an RNA-binding protein) with prion-like properties plays a role in activating molecules that take part in synaptic growth that occurs during LTF	Days	Si, Choi, White-Grindley, Majumdar, and Kandel (2010); Si, Lindquist, and Kandel (2003)

Table 7.2 Examples of epigenetically mediated inheritance of learning-related behaviors.

Species	Psychological trait in parents (F0)	Psychological and behavioral change in descendants' traits	Epigenetic mechanism/s	Mode of transgenerational transmission	Reference
Rattus rattus (rat)	Low quality of maternal care (low licking-grooming, LG) during a critical period (6 days postnatally)	Neophobia, stress susceptibility, reduced quality of maternal care in female offspring	Decreased histone acetylation, increased DNA methylation of *glucocorticoid receptor*; increased methylation of *estrogen receptor alpha* DNA in female offspring of neglecting mothers	Soma-soma (through behavioral reconstruction); several generations	Champagne (2011); Weaver *et al.* (2004)
	Abusive maternal behavior	Stress susceptibility; quality of maternal care in female offspring	DNA methylation (hypermethyaltion of *BDNF* in the prefrontal cortex)	Soma-soma and some germline, transmitted to F1 (not entirely reversed by fostering)	Roth, Lubin, Funk, and Sweatt (2009)
	Prenatal stress of pregnant dams	Feminization of males	DNA methylation, microRNAs	Germline (transmission through stressed F1 males)	Morgan and Bale (2011)
	Treating with vinclozolin during pregnancy	Mate preference; response to stress	DNA methylation	Germline transmission for at least three generations	Crews *et al.* (2012)
	Addiction of fathers (self-administration of cocaine)	Cocaine tolerance	Histone acetylation of *Bdnf* promoter	Presumably germline; transmitted to F1 males	Vassoler, White, Schmidt, Sadri-Vakili, and Pierce (2013)
Mus musculus (mouse)	Defective early maternal care	Altered social behavior, stress response, spatial learning	DNA methylation, small ncRNAs	Germline transmission to F3	Franklin *et al.* (2010); Franklin, Linder, Russig, Thöny, and Mansuy (2011); Weiss, Franklin, Vizi, and Mansuy (2011)

Relief of poor quality of maternal care in previous generations by enriched social environment (communal nesting)	Anxiety behavior	DNA methylation	Soma-soma, transmitted to F2	Curley, Davidson, Bateson, and Champagne (2009)
Environmental enrichment	Improved memory	Involves changes in histone acetylation and DNA methylation	Soma-soma transmitted to F1	Arai and Feig (2011); Arai, Li, S., Hartley, and Feig (2009)
Chronic social defeat in fathers	Depressive behavior	Not described	Soma-soma and possibly small germline contribution; transmitted to F1	Dietz and Nestler (2012)
Parental care style: bi-parental care or mono parental care	Learning in males; motor coordination and social investigation in females	Not described	Soma-soma?	Mak, Antle, Dyck, and Weiss (2013)
Conditioned fear response to odorants (acetophenone and propanol)	Increased sensitivity to odorants and display of startled response	Involves change in the methylation of the *Olfr151* gene (responsive to acetophenone)	Germline; transmitted to F2 through both males and females	Dias and Ressler (2013)

(*Continued*)

Table 7.2 (Continued)

Species	Psychological trait in parents (F0)	Psychological and behavioral change in descendants' traits	Epigenetic mechanism/s	Mode of transgenerational transmission	Reference
Gallus gallus domesticus (domesticated longhorn chicken)	Stress in parents	Learning ability	Changes in the expression pattern of genes in hypothalamus and pituitary; multiple DNA methylation changes	Soma-soma? transmitted to F1	Lindqvist *et al.* (2007); Nätt *et al.* (2012)
Drosophila melanogaster (fruit fly)	Pentylenetetrazole administered to adult males induced long-term brain plasticity	Brain plasticity	Not described; changes in RNA expression profile	Germline; transmitted to F2 males	Sharma and Singh (2009)
Gryllus pennsylvanicus (field cricket)	Exposure to high density of predators by gravid females	Enhanced antipredatory behavior	Not described	Soma to soma?	Storm and Lima (2010)
Caenorhabditis elegans (nematode)	Exposure to certain odors for five consecutive generations (F0–F4)	Odor preference	Not described; probably small ncRNA	Germline transmitted for at least 40 generations	Remy (2010)

Acknowledgments

We are very grateful to Marion Lamb, Oded Rechavi, and the editors of this volume for their constructive comments.

References

Arai, J. A., & Feig, L. A. (2011). Long-lasting and transgenerational effects of an environmental enrichment on memory formation. *Brain Research Bulletin, 85*, 30–35.

Arai, J. A., Li, S., Hartley, D. M., & Feig, L. A. (2009). Transgenerational rescue of genetic defect in long-term potentiation and memory formation by juvenile enrichment. *Journal of Neuroscience, 29*, 1496–1502.

Bahari-Javan, S., Maddalena, A., Kerimoglu, C., Wittnam, J., Held, T., Bähr, M., ... Sananbenesi, F. (2012). HDAC1 regulates fear extinction in mice. *Journal of Neuroscience 32*, 5062–5073.

Bailey, C. H., & Kandel, E. R. (2008). Synaptic remodeling, synaptic growth and the storage of long-term memory in *Aplysia*. *Progress in Brain Research, 169*, 179–98.

Barrett, R. M., Malvaez, M., Kramar, E., Matheos, D. P., Arrizon, A., Cabrera, S. M., ... Wood, M. A. (2011). Hippocampal focal knockout of CBP affects specific histone modifications, long-term potentiation, and long-term memory. *Neuropsychopharmacology, 36*, 1545–1556.

Bayne, C. J. (2003). Origins and evolutionary relationships between the innate and adaptive arms of immune systems. *Integrative Comparative Biology, 43*, 293–299.

Bernstein, E., & Allis, C. D. (2005). RNA meets chromatin. *Genes and Development, 19*, 1635–1655.

Bibikova, M., Chudin, E., Wu, B., Zhou, L., Garcia, E. W., Liu, Y., ... Fan, J. B. (2006). Human embryonic stem cells have a unique epigenetic signature. *Genome Research, 16*, 1075–1083.

Blackiston, D. J., Silva Casey, E., & Weiss, M. R. (2008). Retention of memory through metamorphosis: can a moth remember what it learned as a caterpillar? *PLoS ONE, 3*, e1736.

Blaze, J., & Roth, T. L. (2013). Epigenetic mechanisms in learning and memory. *WIREs Cognitive Science, 4*, 105–115.

Bousiges, O., Vasconcelos, A. P., Neidl, R., Cosquer, B., Herbeaux, K., Panteleeva, I., ... Boutillier, A. L. (2010). Spatial memory consolidation is associated with induction of several lysine-acetyltransferase (histone acetyltransferase) expression levels and H2B/H4 acetylation-dependent transcriptional events in the rat hippocampus. *Neuropsychopharmacology, 35*, 2521–2537.

Bredy, T. W., Wu, H., Crego, C., Zellhoefer, J., Sun, Y. E., & Barad, M. (2007). Histone modifications around individual bdnf gene promoters in prefrontal cortex are associated with extinction of conditioned fear. *Learning and Memory, 14*, 268–276.

Butler, S. (1920). *Unconscious memory*. London, UK: A. C. Fifield.

Caiati, M. D., Safiulina, V. F., Fattorini, G., Sivakumaran, S., Legname, G., & Cherubini, E. (2013). PrP^C controls via protein kinase A the direction of synaptic plasticity in the immature hippocampus. *Journal of Neuroscience, 33*, 2973–2983.

Calfa, G., Chapleau, C. A., Campbell, S., Inoue, T., Morse, S. J., Lubin, F. D., & Pozzo-Miller, L. (2012). HDAC activity is required for BDNF to increase quantal neurotransmitter release and dendritic spine density in CA1 pyramidal neurons. *Hippocampus, 22*, 1493–1500.

Castellano, J. F., Fletcher, B. R., Kelley-Bell, B., Kim, D. H., Gallagher, M., & Rapp, P. R. (2012). Age-related memory impairment is associated with disrupted multivariate epigenetic coordination in the hippocampus. *PLoS ONE, 7*, e33249.

Champagne, F. A. (2011). Maternal imprints and the origins of variation. *Hormones and Behavior*, 60, 4–11.

Chatterjee, S., Mizar, P., Cassel, R., Neidl, R., Selvi, B. R., Mohankrishna, D. V., ... Boutillier, A. L. (2013). A novel activator of CBP/p300 acetyltransferases promotes neurogenesis and extends memory duration in adult mice. *Journal of Neuroscience*, 33, 10698–10712.

Chen, C.-C., Wang, K.-Y., & Shen, C.-K. J. (2012). The mammalian *de novo* DNA methyltransferases DNMT3A and DNMT3B are also DNA 5-hydroxymethylcytosine dehydroxymethylases. *Journal of Biological Chemistry*, 287, 33116–33121.

Chen, G., Zou, X., Watanabe, H., van Deursen, J. M., & Shen, J. (2010). CREB binding protein is required for both short-term and long-term memory formation. *Journal of Neuroscience*, 30, 13066–13077.

Cheng, A., Wang, S., Cai, J., Rao, M. S., & Mattson, M. P. (2003). Nitric oxide acts in a positive feedback loop with BDNF to regulate neural progenitor cell proliferation and differentiation in the mammalian brain. *Developmental Biology*, 258, 319–333.

Chivet, M., Javalet, C., Hemming, F., Pernet-Gallay, K., Laulagnier, K., Fraboulet, S., & Sadoul, R. (2013). Exosomes as a novel way of interneuronal communication. *Biochemical Society Transactions*, 41, 241–244.

Crews, D., Gillette, R., Scarpino, S. V., Manikkam, M., Savenkova, M. I., & Skinner, M. K. (2012). Epigenetic transgenerational inheritance of altered stress responses. *Proceedings of the National Academy of Sciences USA*, 109, 9143–9148.

Crick, F. (1984). Memory and molecular turnover. *Nature*, 312, 101.

Curley, J. P., Davidson, S., Bateson, P., & Champagne, F. A. (2009). Social enrichment during postnatal development induces transgenerational effects on emotional and reproductive behavior in mice. *Frontiers in Behavioral Neuroscience*, 3, 25.

Danilova, A. B., Kharchenko, O. A., Shevchenko, K. G., & Grinkevich, L. N. (2010). Histone H3 acetylation is asymmetrically induced upon learning in identified neurons of the food aversion network in the mollusk helix lucorum. *Frontiers in Behavioral Neuroscience*, 4, 180.

Day, J., & Sweatt, J. D. (2010). DNA methylation and memory formation. *Nature Neuroscience*, 13, 1319–1323.

Day, J., & Sweatt, J. D. (2011). Cognitive neuroepigenetics: A role for epigenetic mechanisms in learning and memory. *Neurobiology of Learning and Memory*, 96, 2–12.

Day, T., & Bonduriansky, R. (2011). A unified approach to the evolutionary consequences of genetic and nongenetic inheritance. *American Naturalist*, 178, E18–E36.

Dias, B. G., & Ressler, K. J. (2014). Parental olfactory experience influences behavior and neural structure in subsequent generations. *Nature Neuroscience*, 17, 89–96.

Dietz, D. M., & Nestler, E. J. (2012). From father to offspring: paternal transmission of depressive-like behaviors. *Neuropsychopharmacology*, 37, 311–312.

Federman, N., Fustiñana, M. S., & Romano, A. (2009). Histone acetylation is recruited in consolidation as a molecular feature of stronger memories. *Learning and Memory*, 16, 600–606.

Federman, N., Fustiñana, M. S., & Romano, A. (2012). Reconsolidation involves histone acetylation depending on the strength of the memory. *Neuroscience*, 219, 145–156.

Feng, J., Zhou, Y., Campbell, S. L., Le, T., Li, E., Sweatt, J. D., Silva, A. J., & Fan, G. (2010). Dnmt1 and Dnmt3a maintain DNA methylation and regulate synaptic function in adult forebrain neurons. *Nature Neuroscience*, 13, 423–430.

Fischer, A., Sananbenesi, F., Wang, X., Dobbin, M., & Tsai, L. H. (2007). Recovery of learning and memory is associated with chromatin remodelling. *Nature*, 447, 178–182.

Fitzsimons, H. L., & Scott, M. J. (2011). Genetic modulation of Rpd3 expression impairs long-term courtship memory in *Drosophila*. *PLoS ONE* 6, e29171.

Fortin, D. A., Srivastava, T., & Soderling, T. R. (2012). Structural modulation of dendritic spines during synaptic plasticity. *The Neuroscientist*, 18, 326–341.

Franklin, T. B., Linder, N., Russig, H., Thöny, B., & Mansuy, I. M. (2011). Influence of early stress on social abilities and serotonergic functions across generations in mice. *PLoS ONE, 6*, e21842.

Franklin, T. B., Russig, H., Weiss, I. C., Gräff, J., Linder, N., Michalon, A., ... Mansuy, I. M. (2010). Epigenetic transmission of the impact of early stress across generations. *Biological Psychiatry, 68*, 408–415.

Geoghegan, J. L., & Spencer, H. G. (2012). Population-epigenetic models of selection. *Theoretical Population Biology, 81*, 232–242.

Ginsburg, S., & Jablonka, E. (2009). Epigenetic learning in non-neural organisms. *Journal of Bioscience, 34*, 633–646.

Ginsburg, S., & Jablonka, E. (2010). Associative learning: a factor in the Cambrian explosion. *Journal of Theoretical Biology, 266*, 11–20.

Gräff, J., & Tsai, L-H. (2013). Histone acetylation: molecular mnemonics on the chromatin. *Nature Reviews Neuroscience, 14*, 97–111.

Gräff, J., Woldemichael, B. T., Berchtold, D., Dewarrat, G., & Mansuy, I. M. (2012). Dynamic histone marks in the hippocampus and cortex facilitate memory consolidation. *Nature Communications, 3*, 991.

Griffith, J. S. (1967). *A view of the brain.* Oxford, UK: Oxford University Press.

Griffith, J. S., & Mahler, H. R. (1969). DNA ticketing theory of memory. *Nature, 223*, 580–582.

Griggs, E. M., Young, E.J., Rumbaugh, G., & Miller, C. A. (2013). MicroRNA-182 regulates amygdala-dependent memory formation. *Journal of Neuroscience, 33*, 1734–1740.

Grimes, G. W., & Aufderheide, K. J. (1991). *Cellular aspects of pattern formation: the problem of assembly. Monographs in developmental biology, Vol. 22.* Basel: Karger.

Guan, J. S., Haggarty, S. J., Giacometti, E., Dannenberg, J. H., Joseph, N., Gao, J., ... Tsai, L. H. (2009). HDAC2 negatively regulates memory formation and synaptic plasticity. *Nature, 459*: 55–60.

Guan, Z., Giustetto, M., Lomvardas, S., Kim, J. H., Miniaci, M. C., Schwartz, J. H., ... & Kandel, E. R. (2002). Integration of long-term-memory-related synaptic plasticity involves bidirectional regulation of gene expression and chromatin structure. *Cell, 111*, 483–493.

Gupta, S., Kim, S. Y., Artis, S., Molfese, D. L., Schumacher, A., Sweatt, J. D., ... Lubin, F. D. (2010). Histone methylation regulates memory formation. *Journal of Neuroscience, 30*, 3589–3599.

Gupta-Agarwal, S., Franklin, A. V., Deramus, T., Wheelock, M., Davis, R. L., McMahon, L. L., & Lubin, F. D. (2012). G9a/GLP histone lysine dimethyltransferase complex activity in the hippocampus and the entorhinal cortex is required for gene activation and silencing during memory consolidation. *Journal of Neuroscience, 32*, 5440–5453.

Haettig, J., Stefanko, D. P., Multani, M. L., Figueroa, D. X., McQuown, S. C., & Wood, M. A. (2011). HDAC inhibition modulates hippocampus-dependent long-term memory for object location in a CBP-dependent manner. *Learning and Memory, 18*, 71–79.

Han, J., Li, Y., Wang, D., Wei, C., Yang, X., & Suian, N. (2010). Effect of 5-aza-2-deoxycytidine microinjecting into hippocampus and prelimbic cortex on acquisition and retrieval of cocaine-induced place preference in C57BL/6 mice *European Journal of Pharmacology, 642*, 93–98.

Hansen, K. F., Karelina, K., Sakamoto, K., Waymanm G., Impey, S., & Obrietan, K. (2012). miRNA-132: a dynamic regulator of cognitive capacity. *Brain Structure and Function, 218*, 817–831.

Hansen, K. F., Sakamoto, K., Wayman, G.A., Impey, S., & Obrietan, K. (2010). Transgenic miR132 alters neuronal spine density and impairs novel object recognition memory. *PLoS ONE, 5*, e15497.

Hardt, O., Nader, K., & Nadel, L. (2013). Decay happens: the role of active forgetting in memory. *Trends in Cognitive Sciences, 17*, 111–20.

Hawk, J. D., Florian, C., & Abel, T. (2011). Post-training intrahippocampal inhibition of class I histone deacetylases enhances long-term object-location memory. *Learning and Memory, 18*, 367–370.

Holliday, R. (1999). Is there an epigenetic component in long-term memory? *Journal of Theoretical Biology, 200*, 339–341.

Holliday, R., & Pugh, J. E. (1975). DNA modification mechanisms and gene activity during development. *Science, 187*, 226–232.

Honey, R. C., Iordanova, M.D & Good, M. A. (2010). Latent inhibition and habituation: evaluation of an associative analysis. In R. E. Lubow & I. Weiner (Eds.), *Latent inhibition: data, theories, and applications to schizophrenia* (pp. 163–182). New York, NY: Cambridge University Press.

Hoy, A. M., & Buck, A. H. (2012). Extracellular small RNAs: what, where, why? *Biochemical Society Transactions, 40*, 886–890.

Itzhak, Y., Anderson, K. L., Kelley, J. B., & Petkov, M. (2012). Histone acetylation rescues contextual fear conditioning in nNOS KO mice and accelerates extinction of cued fear conditioning in wild type mice. *Neurobiology of Learning and Memory, 97*, 409–417.

Jablonka, E., & Lamb, M. J. (2011). Changing thought styles: the concept of soft inheritance in the 20th century. In R. Egloff & J. Fehr (Eds.), *Vérité, Widerstand, development: at work with / Arbeiten mit / Travailler avec Ludwik Fleck* (pp. 119–157). Zürich: Collegium Helveticum Heft 12.

Jablonka, E., & Lamb, M. J. (2014). *Evolution in four dimensions: genetic, epigenetic, behavioral, and symbolic variation in the history of life* (2nd ed.). Cambridge, MA: MIT Press.

Jablonka, E., & Raz, G. (2009). Transgenerational epigenetic inheritance: prevalence, mechanisms, and implications for the study of heredity and evolution. *Quarterly Review of Biology 84*, 131–176.

Juang, B. T., Gu, C., Starnes, L., Palladino, F., Goga, A., Kennedy, S., & L'Etoile, N. D. (2013). Endogenous nuclear RNAi mediates behavioral adaptation to odor. *Cell 154*, 1010–1022.

Kamin, L. J. (1969). Predictability, surprise, attention, and conditioning. In B. A. Campbell & R. M. Church (Eds.), *Punishment and aversive behavior*, pp. 279–296. New York, NY: Appleton-Century-Crofts.

Kandel, E. R. (2012). The molecular biology of memory: cAMP, PKA, CRE, CREB-1, CREB-2, and CPEB. *Molecular Brain 5*, 14.

Kilgore, M., Miller, C. A., Fass, D. M., Hennig, K,M., Haggarty, S. J., Sweatt, J. D., & Rumbaugh, G. (2010). Inhibitors of class 1 histone deacetylases reverse contextual memory deficits in a mouse model of Alzheimer's disease. *Neuropsychopharmacology, 35*, 870–880.

Konopka, W., Kiryk, A., Novak, M., Herwerth, M., Parkitna, J. R., Wawrzyniak, M., … Schütz, G. (2010). MicroRNA loss enhances learning and memory in mice. *Journal of Neuroscience, 30*, 14835–14842.

Koshibu, K., Gräff, J., & Mansuy, I. M. (2011). Nuclear protein phosphatase-1: An epigenetic regulator of fear memory and amygdala long-term potentiation. *Neuroscience, 173*, 30–36.

Kramer, J. M., Kochinke, K., Oortveld, M., Marks, H., Kramer, D., de Jong, E. K., … Schenck, A. (2011). Epigenetic regulation of learning and memory by *Drosophila* EHMT/G9a. *PLoS Biology, 9*, e1000569.

Kucharski, R., Maleszka, J., Foret, S., & Maleszka, R. (2008). Nutritional control of reproductive status in honey bees via DNA methylation. *Science, 319*, 1827–1830.

Kye, M. J., Neveu, P., Lee, Y.-S., Zhou, M., Steen, J. A., Sahin, M., … Silva, A. J. (2011). NMDA mediated contextual conditioning changes miRNA expression. *PLoS ONE, 6*, e24682.

Lachenal, G., Pernet-Gallay, K., Chivet, M., Hemming, F. J., Belly, A., Bodon, G., ... Sadoul, R. (2010). Release of exosomes from differentiated neurons and its regulation by synaptic glutamatergic activity. *Molecular and Cellular Neuroscience, 46*, 409–418.

Lai, C. P.-K., & Breakefield, X. O. (2012). Role of exosomes/microvesicles in the nervous system and use in emerging therapies. *Frontiers in Physiology, 3*, 228.

Lai, C. S. W., Franke, T. F., & Gan, W-B. (2012). Opposite effects of fear conditioning and extinction on dendritic spine remodelling. *Nature 483*, 87–91.

LaSalle, J. M., Powell, W. T., & Yasui, D. H. (2013). Epigenetic layers and players underlying neurodevelopment. *Trends in Neuroscience 36*, 460–470.

Leach, P. T., Poplawski, S. G., Kenney, J. W., Hoffman, B., Liebermann, D. A., Abel, T., & Gould, T. J. (2012). Gadd45b knockout mice exhibit selective deficits in hippocampus dependent long-term memory. *Learning and Memory, 19*, 319–324.

Ledford, H. (2013). Circular RNAs throw genetics for a loop. *Nature, 494*, 415.

Levenson, J. M., O'Riordan, K. J., Brown, K. D., Trinh, M. A., Molfese, D. L., & Sweatt, J. D. (2004). Regulation of histone acetylation during memory formation in the hippocampus. *Journal of Biological Chemistry, 279*, 40545–40559.

Levenson, J. M., Roth, T. L., Lubin, F. D., Miller, C. A., Huang, I. C., Desai, P., ... Sweatt, J. D. (2006). Evidence that DNA (cytosine-5) methyltransferase regulates synaptic plasticity in the hippocampus. *Journal of Biological Chemistry, 281*, 15763–15773.

Li, H., Zhong, X., Chau, K. F., Williams, E. C., & Chang, Q. (2011). Loss of activity-induced phosphorylation of MeCP2 enhances synaptogenesis, LTP and spatial memory. *Nature Neuroscience, 14*, 1001–1008.

Li, W., Cressy, M., Qin, H., Fulga, T., Van Vactor, D., & Dubnau, J. (2013). MicroRNA-276a functions in ellipsoid body and mushroom body neurons for naive and conditioned olfactory avoidance in *Drosophila*. *Journal of Neuroscience, 33*, 5821–5833.

Li, X., Wei, W., Ratnu, V. S., & Bredy, T. W. (2013). On the potential role of active DNA demethylation in establishing epigenetic states associated with neural plasticity and memory. *Neurobiology of Learning and Memory, 105*, 125–132.

Lin, Q., Wei, W., Coelho, C. M., Li, X., Baker-Andresen, D., Dudley, K., ... Bredy, T. W. (2011). The brain-specific microRNA miR-128b regulates the formation of fear-extinction memory. *Nature Neuroscience, 14*, 1115–1117.

Lindqvist, C., Janczak, A. M., Nätt, D., Baranowska, I., Lindqvist, N., Wichman, A., ... & Jensen, P. (2007). Transmission of stress-induced learning impairment and associated brain gene expression from parents to offspring in chickens. *PLoS ONE, 2*, e364.

Lisman, J., Schulman, H., & Cline, H. (2002). The molecular basis of CaMKII function in synaptic and behavioural memory. *Nature Reviews Neuroscience, 3*, 175–190.

Lister, R., Mukamel, E. A., Nery, J. R., Urich, M., Puddifoot, C. A., Johnson, N. D., ... Ecker, J. R. (2013). Global epigenomic reconfiguration during mammalian brain development. *Science, 341*.

Lockett, G. A., Helliwell, P., & Maleszka, R. (2010). Involvement of DNA methylation in memory processing in the honey bee. *Neuroreport, 12*, 812–816.

Lubin, F. D., Roth, T.L., & Sweatt, J. D. (2008). Epigenetic regulation of bdnf gene transcription in the consolidation of fear memory. *Journal of Neuroscience, 28*, 10576–10586.

Lyko, F., Foret, S., Kucharski, R., Wolf, S., Falckenhayn, C., & Maleszka, R. (2010).The honey bee epigenomes: differential methylation of brain DNA in queens and workers. *PLoS Biology, 8*, e1000506. [Correction in: *PLoS Biology, 9*, January 2011. 10.1371/annotation/2db9ee19-faa4-43f2-af7a-c8aeacca8037.]

Maddox, S. A., & Schafe, G. E. . (2011). Epigenetic alterations in the lateral amygdala are required for reconsolidation of a Pavlovian fear memory. *Learning and Memory, 18*, 579–593.

Mahan, A. L., Mou, L., Shah, N., Hu, J. H., Worley, P. F., & Ressler, K. J. (2012). Epigenetic modulation of *Homer1a* transcription regulation in amygdala and hippocampus with Pavlovian fear conditioning. *Journal of Neuroscience, 32*, 4651–4659.

Majumdar, A., Cesario, W. C., White-Grindley, E., Jiang, H., Ren, F., Khan, M. R., ... Si, K. (2012). Critical role of amyloid-like oligomers of *Drosophila* Orb2 in the persistence of memory. *Cell, 148,* 515–529.

Mak, G. K., Antle, M. C., Dyck, R. H., & Weiss, S. (2013) Bi-parental care contributes to sexually dimorphic neural cell genesis in the adult mammalian brain. *PLoS ONE 8,* e62701.

Marek, R., Coelho, C. M., Sullivan, R. K., Baker-Andresen, D., Li, X., Ratnu, V., ... Bredy, T. W. (2011). Paradoxical enhancement of fear extinction memory and synaptic plasticity by inhibition of the histone acetyltransferase p300. *Journal of Neuroscience, 31,* 7486–7491.

Mastushita-Sakai, T., White-Grindley, E., Samuelson, J., Seidel, C., & Si, K. (2010). *Drosophila* Orb2 targets genes involved in neuronal growth, synapse formation, and protein turnover. *Proceedings of the National Academy of Sciences USA, 107,* 11987–11992.

McQuown, S. C., Barrett, R. M., Matheos, D. P., Post, R. J., Rogge, G. A., Alenghat, T., ... Wood, M. A. (2011). HDAC3 is a critical negative regulator of long-term memory formation. *Journal of Neuroscience, 31,* 764–774.

Miller, C. A., Gavin, C. F., White, J. A., Parrish, R. R., Honasoge, A., Yancey, C. R., ... Sweatt, J. D. (2010). Cortical DNA methylation maintains remote memory. *Nature Neuroscience, 13,* 664–666.

Miller, C. A., & Sweatt, J. D. (2007). Covalent modification of DNA regulates memory formation. *Neuron, 53,* 857–869.

Mizuno, K., Dempster, E., Mill, J., & Giese, K. P. (2012). Long-lasting regulation of hippocampal bdnf gene transcription after contextual fear conditioning. *Genes Brain and Behavior, 11,* 651–659.

Monsey, M. S., Ota, K. T., Akingbade, I. F., Hong, E. S., & Schafe, G. E. (2011). Epigenetic alterations are critical for fear memory consolidation and synaptic plasticity in the lateral amygdala. *PLoS ONE, 6,* e19958.

Morgan, C. P., & Bale, T. L. (2011). Early prenatal stress epigenetically programs dysmasculinization in second-generation offspring via the paternal lineage. *Journal of Neuroscience, 31,* 11748–11755.

Muñoz, P. C., Aspe, M. A., Contreras, L. S., & Palacios, A. G. (2010). Correlations of recognition memory performance with expression and methylation of brain-derived neurotrophic factor in rats. *Biological Research, 43,* 251–258.

Muotri, A. R., Marchetto, M. C. N., Zhao, C., & Gage, F. H. (2009). Environmental influence on L1 retrotransposons in the adult hippocampus. *Hippocampus, 19,* 1002–1007.

Nätt, D., Rubin, C-J., Wright, D., Johnsson, M., Beltéky, J. Andersson, L., & Jensen, P. (2012). Heritable genome-wide variation of gene expression and promoter methylation between wild and domesticated chickens. *BMC Genomics, 13,* 59.

Oliveira, A. M., Estevez, M. A., Hawk, J. D., Grimes, S., Brindle, P. K., & Abel, T. (2011). Subregion-specific p300 conditional knock-out mice exhibit long-term memory impairments. *Learning and Memory, 18,* 161–169.

Oviedo, N. J., Morokuma, J., Walentek, P., Kema, I. P., Gu, M. B., Ahn, J. M., ... Levin, M. (2010). Long-range neural and gap junction protein-mediated cues control polarity during planarian regeneration. *Developmental Biology, 339,* 188–199.

Peixoto, L., & Abel, T. (2013). The role of histone acetylation in memory formation and cognitive impairments. *Neuropsychopharmacology, 38,* 62–76.

Peleg, S., Sananbenesi, F., Zovoilis, A., Burkhardt, S., Bahari-Javan, S., Agis-Balboa, R. C., ... Fischer, A. (2010). Altered histone acetylation is associated with age-dependent memory impairment in mice. *Science, 328,* 753–756.

Porto-Carreiro, I., Février, B., Paquet, S., Vilette, D., & Raposo, G. (2005). Prions and exosomes: From PrP^c trafficking to PrP^{sc} propagation. *Blood Cells, Molecules, and Diseases, 35,* 143–148.

Rajasethupathy, P., Antonov, I., Sheridan, R., Frey, S., Sander, C., Tuschl, T., & Kandel, E. R. (2012). A role for neuronal piRNAs in the epigenetic control of memory-related synaptic plasticity. *Cell, 149,* 693–707.

Rajasethupathy, P., Fiumara, F., Sheridan, R., Betel, D., Puthanveettil, S. V., Russo, J. J., ... Kandel, E. (2009). Characterization of small RNAs in *Aplysia* reveals a role for miR-124 in constraining synaptic plasticity through CREB. *Neuron, 63,* 803–817.

Remy, J-J. (2010). Stable inheritance of an acquired behavior in *Caenorhabditis elegans*. *Current Biology, 20,* R877–R878.

Rescorla, R. A., & Wagner, A. R. (1972). A theory of Pavlovian conditioning: Variations in the effectiveness of reinforcement and nonreinforcement. In A. H. Black & W. F. Prokasy (Eds.), *Classical conditioning II: current research and theory* (pp. 64–99). New York, NY: Appleton-Century-Crofts.

Riggs, A. D. (1975). X inactivation, differentiation, and DNA methylation. *Cytogenetics and Cell Genetics, 14,* 9–25.

Roediger III, H. L., Dudai, Y., & Frizpatrick, S. M. (2007). *Science of memory: concepts.* New York, NY: Oxford University Press.

Roth, T. L., Lubin, F. D., Funk, A. J., & Sweatt, J. D. (2009). Lasting epigenetic influence of early-life adversity on the BDNF gene. *Biological Psychiatry, 65,* 760–769.

Schacter, D. L. (2001) *Forgotten ideas, neglected pioneers. Richard Semon and the story of memory.* Philadelphia, PA: Psychology Press.

Schultz, W., & Dickinson, A. (2000). Neuronal coding of prediction errors. *Annual Review of Neuroscience, 23,* 473–500.

Scott, H. L., Tamagnini, F., Narduzzo, K. E., Howarth, J. L., Lee, Y.-B., Wong, L.-F., ... Uney, J. B. (2012). MicroRNA-132 regulates recognition memory and synaptic plasticity in the perirhinal cortex. *European Journal of Neuroscience, 36,* 2941–2948.

Semon, R. (1921). *The mneme* (3rd ed.). London, UK: Allen & Unwin (Original work published 1909)

Sharma, A., & Singh, P. (2009). Detection of transgenerational spermatogenic inheritance of adult male acquired CNS gene expression characteristics using a *Drosophila* systems model. *PLoS ONE 4,* e5763.

Shomrat, T., & Levin, M. (2013). An automated training paradigm reveals long-term memory in planaria and its persistence through head regeneration. *Journal of Experimental Biology, 216,* 3799–3810.

Shorter, J., & Lindquist, S. (2005). Prions as adaptive conduits of memory and inheritance. *Nature Reviews Genetics, 6,* 435–450.

Shoval, O., & Alon, U. (2010). SnapShot: network motifs. *Cell, 143,* 326–326.

Si, K., Choi, Y. B., White-Grindley, E., Majumdar, A., & Kandel, E. R. (2010). *Aplysia* CPEB can form prion-like multimers in sensory neurons that contribute to long-term facilitation. *Cell, 140,* 421–435.

Si, K., Lindquist, S., & Kandel, E. R. (2003). A neuronal isoform of the aplysia CPEB has prion-like properties. *Cell, 115,* 879–891.

Singer, T., McConnell, M. J., Marchetto, M. C. N., Coufal, N. G., & Gage, F. H. (2010). LINE-1 retrotransposons: Mediators of somatic variation in neuronal genomes? *Trends in Neurosciences, 33,* 345–54.

Spadaro, P. A., & Bredy, T. W. (2012). Emerging role of non-coding RNA in neural plasticity, cognitive function, and neuropsychiatric disorders. *Frontiers in Genetics 3,* 132.

Stafford, J. M., Raybuck, J. D., Ryabinin, A. E., & Lattal, K. M. (2012). Increasing histone acetylation in the hippocampus infralimbic network enhances fear extinction. *Biological Psychiatry, 72,* 25–33.

Stefanko, D. P., Barrett, R. M., Ly, A. R., Reolon, G. K., & Wood, M. A. (2009). Modulation of long-term memory for object recognition via HDAC inhibition. *Proceedings of the National Academy of Sciences USA, 106,* 9447–9452.

Storm, J. J., & Lima, S. L. (2010) Mothers forewarn offspring about predators: a transgenerational maternal effect on behavior. *The American Naturalist, 175,* 382–390.

Sui, L., Wang, Y., Ju, L., & Chen, M. (2012). Epigenetic regulation of reelin and brain-derived neurotrophic factor genes in long-term potentiation in rat medial prefrontal cortex. *Neurobiology of Learning and Memory, 97,* 425–440.

Sultan, F. A., Wang, J., Tront, J., Liebermann, D. A., & Sweatt, J. D. (2012). Genetic deletion of gadd45b, a regulator of active DNA demethylation, enhances long-term memory and synaptic plasticity. *Journal of Neuroscience, 32*, 17059–17066.

Swank, M. W., & Sweatt, J. D. (2001). Increased histone acetyltransferase and lysine acetyltransferase activity and biphasic activation of the ERK/RSK cascade in insular cortex during novel taste learning. *Journal of Neuroscience, 21*, 3383–3391.

Thompson-Peer, K. L., Bai, J., Hu, Z., & Kaplan, J. M. (2012). HBL-1 patterns synaptic remodeling in *C. elegans*. *Neuron, 73*, 453–465.

Tseng, A., & Levin, M. (2013). Cracking the bioelectric code: probing endogenous ionic controls of pattern formation. *Communicative & Integrative Biology, 6*, 1–8.

Ulitsky, I., Shkumatava, A., Jan, C. H., Sive, H., & Bartel, D. P. (2011). Conserved function of lincRNAs in vertebrate embryonic development despite rapid sequence evolution. *Cell, 147*, 1537–1550.

Valadi, H., Ekström, K., Bossios, A., Sjöstrand, M., Lee, J. J., & Lötvall, J. O. (2007). Exosome-mediated transfer of mRNAs and microRNAs is a novel mechanism of genetic exchange between cells. *Nature Cell Biology, 9*, 654–659.

Valor, L. M., Pulopulos, M. M., Jimenez-Minchan, M., Olivares, R., Lutz, B., & Barco, A. (2011). Ablation of CBP in forebrain principal neurons causes modest memory and transcriptional defects and a dramatic reduction of histone acetylation but does not affect cell viability. *Journal of Neuroscience, 31*, 1652–1663.

Vanyushin, B. F., Nemirovsky, L. E., Klimenko, V. V., Vasiliev, V. K., & Belozersky, A. N. (1973). The 5-methylcytosine in DNA of rats. Tissue and age specificity and the changes induced by hydrocortisone and other agents. *Gerontologia, 19*, 138–152.

Vassoler, F. M., White, S. L., Schmidt, H. D., Sadri-Vakili, G., & Pierce, R. C. (2013). Epigenetic inheritance of a cocaine-resistance phenotype. *Nature Neuroscience, 16*, 42–47.

Wang, W.H., Cheng, L.C., Pan, F.Y., Xue, B., Wang, D.Y., Chen, Z., & Li, C.J. (2011). Intracellular trafficking of histone deacetylase 4 regulates long-term memory formation. *Anatomical Record, 294*, 1025–1034.

Weaver, I. C. G., Cervoni, N., Champagne, F. A., D'Alessio, A. C., Sharma, S., Seckl, J. R., ... Meaney, M. J. (2004). Epigenetic programming by maternal behavior. *Nature Neuroscience, 7*, 847–854.

Weiss, I. C., Franklin, T. B., Vizi, S., & Mansuy, I. M. (2011). Inheritable effect of unpredictable maternal separation on behavioral responses in mice. *Frontiers in Behavioral Neuroscience, 5*, 3.

Yu, N-K., Baek, S. H., & Kaang, B-K. (2011). DNA methylation-mediated control of learning and memory. *Molecular Brain, 4*, 5.

Zhao, Z., Fan, L., Fortress, A. M., Boulware, M. I., & Frick, K. M. (2012). Hippocampal histone acetylation regulates object recognition and the estradiol-induced enhancement of object recognition. *Journal of Neuroscience, 32*, 2344–2351.

Ziv, Y., Ron, N., Butovsky, O., Landa, G., Sudai, E., Greenberg, N., Cohen, H., ... Schwartz, M. (2006). Immune cells contribute to the maintenance of neurogenesis and spatial learning abilities in adulthood. *Nature Neuroscience, 9*, 268–275.

Zovkic, I. B., Guzman-Karlsson, M. C., & Sweatt, J. D. (2013). Epigenetic regulation of memory formation and maintenance. *Learning and Memory, 20*, 61–74.

Part II
Associative Representations
Memory, Recognition, and Perception

8
Associative and Nonassociative Processes in Rodent Recognition Memory

David J. Sanderson

In the study of human recognition memory, there is disagreement over the number of processes that determine the strength of recognition memory (e.g., Brown & Aggleton, 2001; Cowel, Bussey, & Saksida, 2010; Squire, Wixted, & Clark, 2007; Yonelinas, 1999). The dual-process theory (e.g., Brown & Aggleton, 2001) proposes that two different forms of memory, familiarity and recollection, combine to determine the degree to which a previously encountered stimulus is recognized. Whereas recollection requires recalling specific details to do with the instance or the context in which the stimulus was encountered, familiarity relies on the sense of knowing that a stimulus was previously encountered without necessarily remembering the encounter (Brown & Aggleton, 2001; Mandler, 1980). Neuroanatomical dissociations between familiarity and recollection judgments have provided strong support for the dual-process account. For example, it has been argued that the hippocampus is necessary for recollection but not familiarity, whereas the perirhinal cortex is important for familiarity (Aggleton & Brown, 1999, 2006; Brown & Aggleton, 2001; see also Chapter 11). In contrast to the dual-process theory, it has been argued that the dissociations between recollection and familiarity reflect differences only in memory strength (Squire *et al.*, 2007) or differences in the memory representation (Cowel *et al.*, 2010), rather than qualitative differences in the memory processes. According to such analyses the observed dissociations could reflect the operation of a single psychological process.

The neuroanatomical dissociations that are seen in human studies are also found with other animals. Recognition memory in animals has been studied using procedures in which animals respond selectively to stimuli on the basis of whether they have been experienced previously or not. In rodents, recognition memory can be studied by measuring the spontaneous preference for exploring novel objects over previously explored, familiar objects. Studies examining the psychological basis of spontaneous novelty preference behavior in rodents have demonstrated that more than one process determines performance (e.g., Ennaceur & Delacour, 1988; Good, Barnes, Staal, McGregor, & Honey, 2007; Sanderson & Bannerman, 2011). Furthermore, under

---

The Wiley Handbook on the Cognitive Neuroscience of Learning, First Edition.
Edited by Robin A. Murphy and Robert C. Honey.
© 2016 John Wiley & Sons, Ltd. Published 2016 by John Wiley & Sons, Ltd.

certain conditions, the processes that determine spontaneous novelty preference behavior are competitive, with manipulations that increase the influence of one factor decreasing the influence of another factor.

In this chapter, I will discuss the evidence for multiple processes in the rodent recognition memory as measured by the spontaneous novelty preference procedure. In line with the analysis described by Honey and Good (2000a), I propose that an associative model, developed by Allan Wagner (Wagner, 1976, 1978, 1979, 1981), may provide a new theoretical framework for formulating hypotheses the role of particular brain regions in rodent recognition memory, which may inform accounts of human recognition memory.

Spontaneous Novelty Preference Task

Berlyne (1950) developed a version of the novelty preference procedure to study recognition memory. Rats were initially allowed to explore a set of identical objects (e.g., wooden cubes). Then, in a test phase, one of the objects was replaced with a new object that had not previously been explored (e.g., a cardboard cylinder). Rats showed greater exploration of the "novel" object than the familiar objects. This result demonstrates that the rats were able to discriminate between the objects, and did so on the basis of their prior exposure. The procedure was popularized by Ennaceur and Delacour (1988) and has become a widely used tool for studying cognition in animal models of disease (Ennaceur, 2010; Lyon, Saksida, & Bussey, 2012).

One low-level explanation for such a novelty preference is that it represents an instance of stimulus-specific habituation based on the decline in the efficacy of a stimulus–response pathway (Groves & Thompson, 1970; Horn, 1967; Horn & Hill, 1964). According to this simple analysis, during exposure the link between the sensory processes activated by the training object and the unconditioned response (exploration) will decline. Provided it is the case that the novel test object does not activate the same sensory processes as the familiar object, the rat will preferentially explore the novel object.

Competitive Short-Term and Long-Term Processes in Habituation

If spontaneous novelty preferences reflect stimulus-specific habituation, then factors that affect habituation must also affect spontaneous novelty preference behavior. The causes and characteristics of habituation have been extensively studied (Groves & Thompson, 1970; Rankin et al., 2009). An important finding is that habituation can sometimes be short-term; if the interval between exposures to a stimulus is short, there is a reduction in unconditioned responding (i.e., habituation), but if the interval is long, there is little or no reduction in responding. Habituation can also be long-term; exposure to a stimulus leads to a long-term, durable reduction in the unconditioned response. A study by Davis (1970) demonstrated that short-term and long-term habituation reflect qualitatively, rather than merely quantitatively, dissociable processes. Davis examined the effect of the interval between presentations of a loud tone on habituation of the startle response in rats. One group of rats received exposure to the tone in which each presentation was separated by a short, 2 s interval (Group 2 s). Another group of rats received exposure in which each presentation of the tone was separated by a longer, 16 s interval (Group 16 s). One minute after the exposure phase, both groups were assessed for their long-term habituation to the tone. It is important to note that because both groups were tested after a common 1-min interval, any difference between the two groups during the test phase must be due to the effect of the interval used in the exposure phase on long-term habituation. During the exposure phase, Group 2 s showed greater habituation of the startle response than Group 16 s. This result demonstrates that habituation was short-term: The effect of a stimulus exposure on habituation was reduced over time. Surprisingly, however, in the test phase, Group 2 s showed weaker habituation than Group 16 s. Although a 2 s interval between exposures resulted in strong habituation during the exposure phase, it resulted in weak habituation in the test phase.

The results described above demonstrate that habituation must be the consequence of more than one process. The interval between exposures had opposite effects on short-term and long-term habituation. Therefore, the difference between short-term and long-term habituation cannot be due to weak and strong effects of stimulus exposure. Instead, short-term and long-term habituation must be caused by separate, qualitatively different processes that, at some level, interact with one another.

Competitive Short-Term and Long-Term Processes in Spontaneous Novelty Preference Behavior

The same interaction between short-term and long-term processes is also observed using the novelty preference procedure (Sanderson & Bannerman, 2011). Spatial novelty preference behavior was assessed using a Y-shaped maze, with walls made out of clear Perspex that permitted the sampling of extramaze, room cues (Sanderson *et al.*, 2007). Mice received ten 2-min exposure trials in which they were allowed to explore two arms of the Y-maze (the start arm and the sample arm). During the exposure phase, access to the third arm was blocked. After the last exposure, trial mice were returned to the Y-maze and were allowed to explore all three arms: the start arm, the sample, familiar arm, and the novel, previously unexplored arm. During the test, the time spent in the novel arm and the familiar arm was used to provide a measure of novelty preference. For one group of mice, the interval between exposure trials was 1 min. For a second group, the interval was 24 hr. Within each of these groups, half the mice received the test trial 1 min after the last exposure trial, and for the other half the test trial was conducted after 24 hr. The design permitted the effect of the interstimulus interval on short-term and long-term habituation to be examined within a single test. Thus, any short-term effect would be demonstrated by an effect of the test interval on the strength of the novelty preference, and any long-term effect would be demonstrated by an effect of the interstimulus interval used in the exposure phase.

The results of the test trial are shown in Figure 8.1. Mice that were tested after a short, 1-min interval showed a significantly greater novelty preference than mice tested after a long, 24-hr interval. However, mice that received exposure trials that were spaced by a short, 1-min interval showed a smaller novelty preference than mice that received exposure trials that were spaced by a long, 24-hr interval. The results of this test of spatial novelty preference mirror those of Davis's (1970) test of habituation of the startle response. A short interval resulted in a marked short-term, novelty preference, as indicated by the effect of the test interval. However, during the exposure phase, the short interval led to a weaker novelty preference than the long interval, suggesting the short interval interfered with a long-term process that allows the novelty preference to be a durable effect.

The opposite effects of short and long intervals on short-term and long-term novelty preference behavior are also found with procedures using object stimuli. The short-term nature of recognition memory is demonstrated by the finding that an increase in the interval between object exposure and test decreases the strength of preference for the novel object (e.g., Ennaceur & Delacour, 1988). In contrast, when rodents receive repeated exposures to objects before a novelty preference test, a short interval between exposure trials produces weaker long-term novelty preference than long intervals (Anderson, Jablonski, & Klimas, 2008; Whitt & Robinson, 2013).

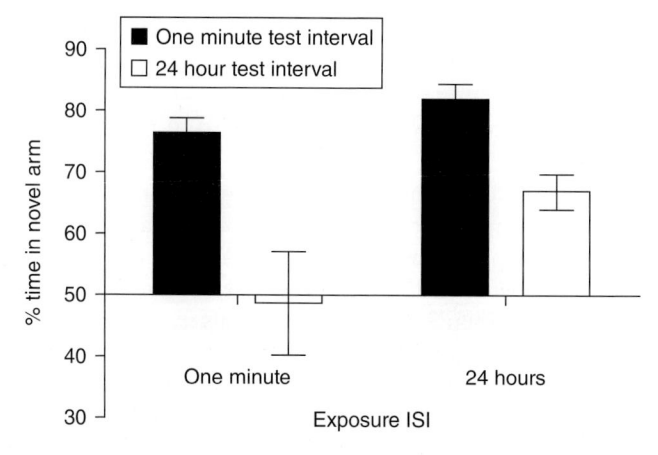

Figure 8.1 Opposite effects of the interstimulus interval on short- and long-term spontaneous spatial novelty preference behavior. Mice received repeated exposure to an arm of a Y-maze before a novelty preference test in which they were allowed to explore the previously explored arm and a novel arm. Preference for the novel is demonstrated by spending more than 50% of the exploration time in the novel arm. When exposure trials were separated by a 1-min interstimulus interval (ISI) mice showed a weaker preference for the novel arm than when the ISI was 24 hr. In contrast, when the interval between the last exposure trial and the novelty preference test was 1 min, mice showed a stronger preference for the novel arm than when the test interval was 24 hr. Data reproduced from Sanderson and Bannerman (2011).

Wagner's Standard Operating Procedures Model

The parallel between the results of Davis's (1970) experiment and those of Sanderson and Bannerman (2011) suggest that habituation and spontaneous novelty preference behavior share a common cause. Importantly, the results of the experiments demonstrate that the consequence of exposure to a stimulus has separate short-term and long-term effects. Furthermore, the short-term and long-term effects are the result of qualitatively dissociable causes.

Wagner's (1981) Standard Operating Procedures (SOP) theory provides an explanation of the opposing effects of short and long intervals on short-term and long-term habituation and spatial novelty preference behavior (see also Wagner, 1976, 1978, 1979). The SOP model was developed as a real-time extension of the Rescorla–Wagner trial-based analysis of Pavlovian conditioning (Rescorla & Wagner, 1972; Wagner & Rescorla, 1972). The model proposes that stimuli are represented in memory as a set of elements. Elements of stimulus representations can be in one of three possible states at any one time. The different states and the transitions between them are shown in Figure 8.2. A stimulus has no influence over behavior when its elements are in an inactivate state (I). When a stimulus is presented, its elements transfer from the inactive state to the A1 state, the primary activity state. From the A1 state, the elements rapidly decay to the A2 state, the secondary activity state. From the A2 state, the elements eventually decay back into the inactive state. When elements are in the A1 state, they are able to elicit strong levels of responding. However, when they are in the A2 state, they are able to elicit only weak levels of responding (see Chapter 4).

The rules for response generation and transitions between activity states provide an explanation of short-term habituation. When a stimulus is first presented, it will be able to activate its elements into the A1 state, and responding will be strong. The

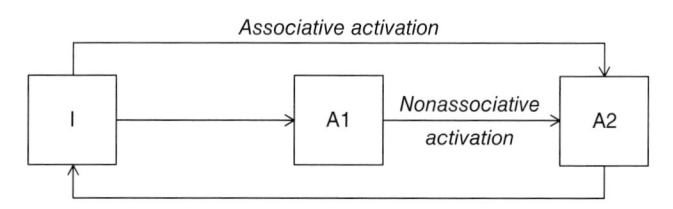

Figure 8.2 Wagner's (1981) SOP model. When a stimulus is presented, the elements of its mnemonic representation transfer from the inactive state (I) to the primary activity state (A1), then rapidly decay into a secondary activity state (A2) before eventually returning to the inactivate state. Elements in the A1 state can elicit strong levels of responding, but only weak levels in the A2 state. Elements in the A2 state cannot transfer back to the A1 state when a stimulus is re-presented, thus resulting in habituation. Elements of a stimulus representation can be in the A2 state because the stimulus has been presented recently (nonassociative activation) or because the presentation of another stimulus has led to the retrieval of the representation directly into the A2 state (associative activation). Associations form between the elements of stimulus representations that are concurrently in the A1 state. Nonassociative activation of elements in the A2 state reduces the ability of stimuli to form associations. Thus, nonassociative activation of elements in the A2 state undermines the process that allows associative activation to occur.

elements then decay into the A2 state where they remain before eventually returning to the inactivate state. Importantly, elements in the A2 state cannot return to the A1 state if the stimulus is re-presented. Consequently, if the stimulus is presented while its elements are in the A2 state, there will be a reduction in the number of elements in the A1 state, resulting in reduced responding. If sufficient time has elapsed since a stimulus presentation, then its elements will have returned to the inactive state, and the presentation of the stimulus will again be capable of provoking its elements into the A1 state. The model predicts that a recent stimulus presentation results in a short-term, time-dependent, form of habituation.

Wagner's (1981) SOP model uses an associative mechanism to account for long-term habituation. The model states that elements of stimulus representations that are in the A1 state at the same time are able to form excitatory associations with one another. The consequence of an association is that presentation of a stimulus results in the retrieval of the memories of other stimuli with which it is associated into the A2 state. That is, when a stimulus is presented, the elements of stimuli with which it is associated move from the inactive state directly into the A2 state. If a stimulus is presented when its elements have been associatively activated into the A2 state, it will not be able to activate its elements into the A1 state, and habituation will occur, but in this case, it is the product of long-term, associative processes.

The SOP model predicts that long-term habituation is context dependent. When a stimulus is presented, it enters into an association with the context in which it is presented, because of their concurrent A1 state activation. Consequently, the context will retrieve the representation of the stimulus into the A2 state, and habituation will occur. The associative activation of elements into the A2 state results in a long-term form of habituation. Thus, the extent of habituation is not dependent on how recently the stimulus has been presented but is dependent on the strength of the association between the context and the habituated stimulus. Long-term habituation is long-term, not because it is simply strong, but because it is the result of a time-independent, associative process.

Short-term and long-term habituation are, therefore, consequences of different routes of activation into the A2 state: a nonassociative route (A1 to A2) and an associative route (I to A2). Given the qualitative differences between these routes of activation, the model correctly predicts that short-term and long-term habituation can be independent, dissociable processes. Therefore, short- and long-term memory do not simply reflect the strength of the memory.

Competition between short-term and long-term memory occurs because A2 activation caused by a recent stimulus presentation interferes with the associative process that underlies long-term habituation. Long-term habituation is dependent on associations formed between stimulus representations that are in the A1 state at the same time. If a stimulus has been presented recently, its representation will be in the A2 state for a period of time before returning to the inactive state. If the stimulus is presented while its representation is in the A2 state, its elements will not be able to return to the A1 state. This will result in short-term habituation, but it will also limit the ability of the stimulus to form associations with other stimuli whose representations are in the A1 state. Therefore, a short interval between stimulus exposures results in short-term habituation, but also undermines the associative mechanism that results in long-term habituation; nonassociative A2 activation reduces associative learning that causes associative activation.

Context-Dependent Spontaneous Novelty Preference Behavior

One way to test the associative mechanism for recognition memory is to manipulate the retrieval cues. If long-term habituation is due to the effect of an association between a stimulus and the context in which it is presented, then long-term habituation will be context dependent. That is, if after exposure to a stimulus in one context that stimulus is presented in either the same or a different context, then it is predicted that habituation will be greatest in the original context. This prediction has received support. For example, a change of context reduces habituation of lick suppression (Jordan, Strasser, & McHale, 2000). Furthermore, long-term habituation has been demonstrated in conditioning paradigms in which, instead of the context, a punctate conditioned stimulus is used to associatively retrieve the representation of the unconditioned stimulus into the A2 state (Donegan, 1981; Kimmel, 1966; Kimble & Ost, 1961). If the unconditioned stimulus is preceded by a conditioned stimulus with which it has not previously been paired, then unconditioned responding is more vigorous than when it is preceded by conditioned stimulus with which it has been paired. More relevant to the case of object recognition is the fact that a similar effect has been shown for the orienting response to visual stimuli in rats (Honey & Good, 2000a, 2000b; Honey, Good, & Manser, 1998; Honey, Watt, & Good, 1998). In a study by Honey et al. (1998), rats received trials in which different auditory stimuli (A1 and A2) preceded different visual stimuli (V1 and V2) on separate trials (A1 → V1, A2 → V2). In a test phase, rats were presented with either the same audiovisual pairings (match trials: A1 → V1, A2 → V2) or rearrangements of the audiovisual pairings (mismatch trials: A1 → V2, A2 → V1). Rats showed weaker levels of orienting on match trials than on mismatch trials, demonstrating that an association, formed between the auditory stimuli and the specific visual stimuli, resulted in long-term, time-independent habituation.

Consistent with Wagner's (1981) associative analysis of long-term habituation, spontaneous novelty preference for objects is context dependent. In a study by Dix and Aggleton (1999), two copies of an object (A) were presented in one context (X), and two copies of another object (B) were presented in a different context (Y). In the test phase, one copy of each object was presented in one of the contexts (e.g., A and B were presented in context X). Rats showed a preference for exploring the object that was previously not paired with the test context (i.e., B).

Although the results of the object-in-context study by Dix and Aggleton (1999) are consistent with the hypothesis that long-term spontaneous novelty preference behavior is caused by an associative process, the effect may be explained in a different manner. An alternative account is that the perception of an object is altered in different contexts. Consequently, dishabituation will appear to have occurred when an object is presented in a different context, not because of habituation process rather because is not perceived as the same stimulus as it was when it was originally presented in the training context. For example, if an object was originally presented in a dark context and then presented in a light context, then it may not be recognized given its new "light" qualities. In this example, long-term habituation is context dependent, but it does not depend on associative retrieval.

An experiment by Whitt, Haselgrove, and Robinson (2012) tested whether associative retrieval is sufficient for long-term spontaneous novel object preference by eliminating the potential for any perceptual confound. The design of the task is shown in Figure 8.3. Similar to the design of the study by Dix and Aggleton (1999), rats

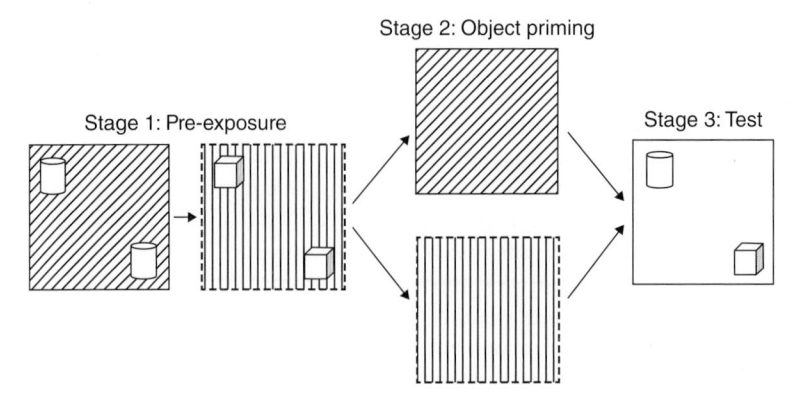

Figure 8.3 Design of the experiment by Whitt *et al.* (2012). In stage 1, rats were exposed to two copies of an object in one context before being exposed to two copies of another object in a different context. In stage 2, rats were placed in one of the two previously explored contexts (either the first or the second context), but in the absence of any objects. Shortly afterwards, in stage 3, rats were placed in a novel context and were allowed to explore a single copy of the two different, previously exposed objects. Rats showed a preference for exploring the object that was not previously paired with the context that was explored in stage 2.

were initially allowed to explore two copies one object (A) in one context (X), and two copies of another object (B) in a different context (Y). In the second stage, rats were placed in one of the two contexts (X or Y) in the absence of any objects. According to SOP, the context will prime the representation of the associated object into the A2 state. To test if this was the case, rats were then placed into a new context (Z) and were allowed to explore objects A and B. It was found that rats showed a greater preference for exploring the object that had not been primed by the prior context exposure. For example, if rats had previously been exposed to context X, they showed a preference for object B. These results cannot be explained by dishabituation caused by a perceptual change: In the test trial, both objects were placed in a novel context. Therefore, any perceptual change would be equal for both objects. The selective preference for one object over another in the test trial was caused by the prior exposure of one of the contexts. Thus, prior exposure to either context resulted in the retrieval of the representation of the object with which it had been previously paired. These results demonstrate that spontaneous novelty preference behavior is caused by associative retrieval of the mnemonic representation of the familiar stimulus.

In the study by Whitt *et al.* (2012), the context was used to retrieve the memory of an object. However, it has also been demonstrated that an object can retrieve the memory of the spatial context in which it was presented (Eacott, Easton, & Zinkivskay, 2005). Therefore, the association formed between objects and the context in which they are presented is bidirectional. The design of an experiment by Eacott *et al.* (2005) is shown in Figure 8.4. Rats were placed in one context (X) and were allowed to explore objects A and B, which were in different locations (A on the left, B on the right). In a second exposure trial, the rats were placed in a different context (Y), and now the location of each object was switched (A on the right, B on the left). In the second stage, rats were placed in a new context (Z) and were allowed to explore either object A or B. According to SOP, the object will prime a memory of the spatial

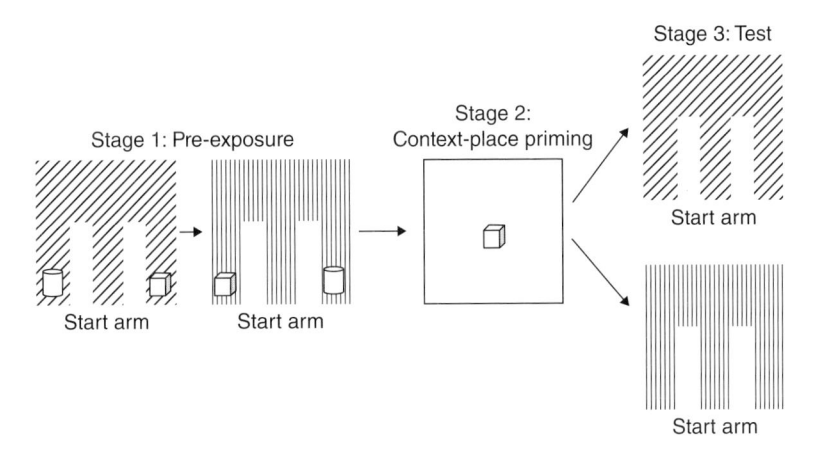

Figure 8.4 Design of the experiment by Eacott *et al.* (2005). In stage 1, rats were exposed to two different objects in an E-shaped maze with distinctive contextual cues. One object was placed in the outer left arm of the maze, and the other was placed in the outer right arm. The middle arm was used as the start arm from which rats were always released. In a second exposure trial, rats were exposed to the objects in the E-maze, but now the locations of the objects were swapped, and the E-maze contained different contextual cues. In stage 2, rats were placed into an open field and were exposed to one of the previously explored objects. Shortly afterwards, in stage 3, rats were returned to the E-maze in the presence of the contextual cues from either the first or the second exposure trial. Rats showed a preference for exploring the arm of the maze that had not been paired with the object that was previously exposed in stage 2.

context in which it has been previously paired. However, because an object had previously been presented in two different locations in different contexts, a number of memories will be retrieved. For example, if rats were exposed to object A in the second stage, a memory of the left location in context X will be retrieved, and a memory of the right location in context Y will also be retrieved. In the test trial, rats were returned to either context X or context Y in the absence of any objects. Rats showed a preference for exploring the spatial location of the context that was not associated with the object that was exposed in the second stage. For example, if rats were exposed to object A in the second stage and then tested in context X, they showed a preference for exploring the location on the right, but if they were tested in context Y, they showed a preference for exploring the location on the left. Therefore, the object that was previously exposed in the second stage primed memories of the spatial contexts with which it had previously been paired. Similar to the results in Whitt *et al.*'s (2012) study, Eacott *et al.*'s (2005) findings cannot be explained by renewed exploration caused by changes in perception, but can be explained by an associative retrieval process.

Importance of Competitive Processes for the Study of Recognition Memory in Animals

In humans, evidence that multiple processes contribute to recognition memory has been sought from measures of the confidence of recognition memory judgments, using an established but quite different analytic framework, the analysis of receiver operating characteristic (ROC) curves (e.g., Yonelinas, 1999; Yonelinas & Parks, 2007). The logic of this analysis is that familiarity is a continuum, and recognition that reflects familiarity will be accompanied by variable levels of confidence. Accordingly, it is suggested that familiarity reflects a signal-detection process. Recollection, however, is an all-or-nothing process, whereby memories either meet the threshold for recollection or do not. Therefore, recognition caused by recollection will by accompanied by a high level of confidence. These signal-detection and threshold processes have different effects on the ROC curves in which the false alarm rate is plotted against the hit rate at different confidence levels. The signal-detection process results in curvilinearity, whereas the threshold process results in asymmetry. The assumptions about the shape of ROC curves for supporting a dual-process model of recognition memory are controversial (Mickes, Wais, & Wixted, 2009; Squire et al., 2007; Wixted, 2007; Wixted & Mickes, 2010) and it has been argued that single-process, signal-detection models may, instead, be sufficient for explaining the properties of ROC curves (Wixted, 2007).

Recently, the same analysis has been applied to recognition memory in animals (Eichenbaum, Fortin, Sauvage, Robitsek, & Farovik, 2010; Farovik, Dupont, Arce, & Eichenbaum, 2008; Farovik, Place, Miller, & Eichenbaum, 2011; Fortin, Wright, & Eichenbaum, 2004; Sauvage, Beer, & Eichenbaum, 2010; Sauvage, Fortin, Owens, Yonelinas, & Eichenbaum, 2008). Lesions of brain regions proposed to be involved in recognition have been found to change the shape of the ROC curve. For example, lesions of the hippocampus increase the curvilinearity of the curve, suggesting that lesioned animals rely on familiarity (Sauvage et al., 2008). Similar to the debate in the human literature, analysis of ROC curves in animals has proved controversial (Wixted & Squire, 2008). The main issue is that the analysis of ROC curves in animals relies on a number of assumptions. First, there is the assumption that levels of confidence relate to distinct memory processes, which in turn have a direct effect on performance. Second, there is the assumption that particular behavioral manipulations affect levels of confidence or bias in making responses in a manner that is useful for interpreting hit and false alarm rates.

The problem with the analysis of ROC curves in animals is that if the assumptions are not valid, there may be no reason to accept a dual-process account of recognition memory. However, the results of the experiment by Sanderson and Bannerman (2011) demonstrate that there are multiple processes that determine recognition memory without making assumptions about confidence judgments. Thus, the competitive nature of short-term and long-term processes provides evidence against a single-process account of recognition memory in animals without recourse to assumptions about behavioral, confidence biases and how they affect the expression of memory.

A further criticism of evidence for a dual-process account of recognition from analysis of ROC curves is that recollection and familiarity are confounded with memory strength (Squire et al., 2007). This criticism does not hold for the evidence of competitive processes in rodent recognition memory. The competitive nature of short-term, nonassociative and long-term, associative processes in rodent recognition memory is predicted by Wagner's (1981) SOP model, which, importantly, assumes that both of these processes may vary equally in the strength of memory that is produced. Thus, nonassociative A2 state activation that occurs as a result of a recent stimulus presentation is dependent on the interval between stimulus exposures. If the stimulus has been presented recently, then A2 state activation will be strong, and spontaneous novelty preference behavior will be marked. If the stimulus has been presented less recently, then A2 state activation will be weak, and spontaneous novelty preference behavior will be less marked. If the stimulus has not been presented recently, then there will be no A2 state activation, and animals will not show novelty preference behavior. Associative A2 state activation is dependent on the strength of associations. If there is a high level of associative strength, then A2 state activation will be strong, and spontaneous novelty preference will be marked. If there is a low level of associative strength, then A2 state activation will be weak, and spontaneous novelty preference behavior will be less marked. If there is no associative strength between cues, then there will be no A2 state activation, and animals will not show spontaneous novelty preference behavior. The benefit of this analysis is that it requires no assumptions about the nature of the cause of memory based on the strength of memory that is produced as is required by the analysis of ROC curves (Squire et al., 2007).

Role of the GluA1 AMPAR Subunit in Short-Term, Recency-Dependent Memory

The strength of Wagner's (1981) SOP model is that it makes clear predictions for the conditions that affect the separate nonassociative and associative processes, and the conditions that will place the two processes in competition with each other. It turns out that this is particularly helpful when considering the neural substrates that underlie recognition memory in rodents.

We have conducted a series of studies examining the role of the GluA1 AMPA glutamate receptor subunit in short-term, recency-dependent and long-term, context-dependent recognition memory (Sanderson et al., 2007, 2009; Sanderson, Hindley, et al., 2011; Sanderson, Sprengel, Seeburg, & Bannerman, 2011). The GluA1 AMPA receptor subunit is a key mediator of hippocampal plasticity (Erickson, Maramara, & Lisman, 2009; Hoffman, Sprengel, & Sakmann, 2002; Romberg et al., 2009; Zamanillo et al., 1999) and has previously been found to be necessary for nonassociative memory, but not for associative memory (Reisel et al., 2002; Schmitt, Deacon, Seeburg, Rawlins, & Bannerman, 2003). Moreover, GluA1 deletion has been found to enhance associative learning under particular circumstances (Schmitt et al., 2003; Taylor et al., 2011). Consistent with these findings, we demonstrated that GluA1 deletion impairs short-term recognition memory, but can enhance long-term recognition memory (Sanderson et al., 2009). These results, which are discussed below, thereby provide further evidence that rodent recognition memory is determined by competitive processes.

Short-term and long-term recognition memory were assessed in genetically altered mice that lack the GluA1 subunit (GluA1$^{-/-}$ mice) using a spatial novelty preference task (Sanderson et al., 2009). Mice received five 2-min exposure trials to two arms of Y-shaped maze (start arm and sample arm) before receiving a novelty preference test in which they were allowed to explore all three arms of the Y-maze (i.e., the start arm, familiar, previously sampled arm, and novel, previously unexplored arm). Mice were tested in two conditions. In one condition, the interval between each exposure trial and between the last exposure trial and the novelty preference test was 1 min. In the other condition, the interval was 24 hr. Performance in the test trial was predicted to be differentially affected by short-term and long-term processes in the two conditions. In the 1-min condition, performance was predicted to be affected by nonassociative A2 state activation, whereas in the 24 hr condition, it was expected that nonassociative A2 state activation will have decayed and, therefore, performance was more likely to reflect associative A2 state activation.

The results of the experiment are shown in Figure 8.5. As predicted, GluA1$^{-/-}$ mice showed less exploration of the novel arm in the 1-min condition, suggesting that GluA1 deletion impaired short-term, recency-dependent recognition memory. However, GluA1$^{-/-}$ mice showed significantly enhanced novel arm exploration in the 24-hr condition. The opposite effects of GluA1 deletion on short-term and long-term novelty preference behavior would appear paradoxical if short-term and long-term memory were expression of a single process. Therefore, these results are consistent with the notion that short-term and long-term memory reflect dissociable processes (Alvarez, Zola-Morgan, & Squire, 1994). Moreover, the results suggest that short-term memory and long-term memory are interacting processes. This interaction may be explained in terms of Wagner's (1981) SOP model in which the nonassociative process that results in short-term memory can reduce the associative process that results in long-term memory.

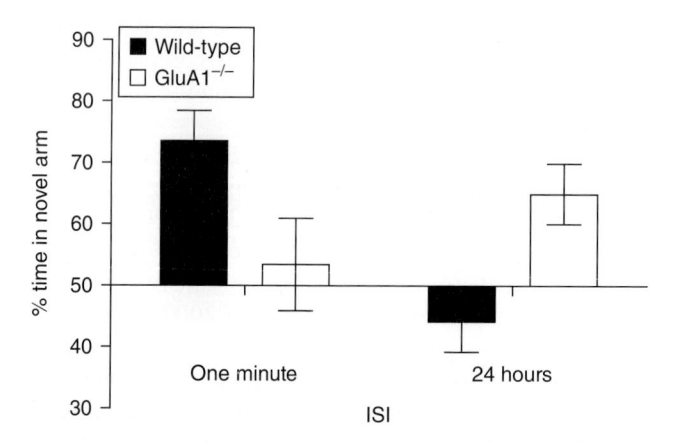

Figure 8.5 GluA1 deletion impairs short-term spatial novelty preference behavior, but enhances long-term spatial novelty preference behavior. Mice received repeated exposures to an arm of Y-maze before receiving a novelty preference test in which they were allowed to explore the previously explored arm and a novel arm. In one condition, the exposure trials were separated by a 1-min ISI, and the novelty preference was also conducted 1 min after the last exposure trial. In another condition, the ISI was 24 hr, and the novelty preference test was also conducted after 24 hr. Preference for the novel arm is demonstrated by spending more than 50% of the exploration time in the novel arm. When the ISI was 1 min, wild-type control mice showed a strong preference for the novel arm. GluA1$^{-/-}$ mice were impaired and failed to show a significant novelty preference. When the ISI was 24 hr, GluA1$^{-/-}$ mice showed a significant preference for the novel arm that was significantly greater than the preference of the wild-type mice. Data reproduced from Sanderson et al. (2009).

If GluA1 deletion reduce the competition between short-term and long-term processes in habituation, what is the precise role of GluA1? Before this question can be answered, it is necessary to consider first the performance of the wild-type mice in the experiment by Sanderson *et al.* (2009). In the 24-hr condition, wild-type, control mice failed to show a significant preference suggesting that five exposure trials were not sufficient for long-term memory. This is in contrast to the similar study by Sanderson and Bannerman (2011) in which 10 exposure trials were used, and successful long-term memory was found (Figure 8.1). This suggests that the cumulative exposure to stimuli aids long-term memory. This is consistent with the account that long-term habituation reflects an association between cues that can be incrementally strengthened with repeated exposures (Wagner, 1979). GluA1 deletion resulted in facilitating this incremental, long-term process (Sanderson *et al.*, 2009). One way in which GluA1 deletion may have increased long-term learning is by increasing the time that elements of stimuli stay in the A1 state. This would result in greater increments in excitatory associative strength per exposure, such that five exposures were sufficient for long-term habituation in GluA1$^{-/-}$ mice, but this was not the case in the wild-type mice.

A reduction in the rate of decay from the A1 state to the A2 state would result in impaired short-term habituation because elements would remain in the A1 state for longer such that there was no difference between the extent of A1 state activation for the novel stimulus and for the recently, exposed, familiar stimulus. Given this analysis of the short-term habituation deficit in GluA1$^{-/-}$ mice, it might be predicted that under certain conditions, a recent stimulus presentation that normally is expected to show an effect of habituation might not show this effect because of the number of elements in the A1 state. In contrast, the recent present presentation might be expected to result in short-term sensitization, in which a recent stimulus exposure potentiates the unconditioned response to the stimulus. Thus, an initial stimulus exposure will activate a portion of its elements into the A1 state. If those elements have not decayed to the A1 state when the stimulus is presented for a second time, then the second presentation will lead to further activation of elements that exceeds the extent of activation that was achieved on the first exposure trial.

This prediction has also been supported by a study that examined the short-term effects of a stimulus exposure on orienting to a light (Sanderson, Sprengel, *et al.*, 2011). Mice received trials in which a visual stimulus was presented (V1 or V2), followed 30 s later by either the same visual stimulus (V1 → V1 or V2 → V2) or a different visual stimulus (V1 → V2 or V2 → V1). Mice were trained to collect sucrose pellets from a magazine in an operant box, and suppression of magazine activity was used as an indirect measure of unconditioned, orienting behavior to the visual stimuli. On trials in which the two visual stimuli differed, wild-type mice showed a level of suppression that was consistent across the first visual stimulus and the second. This was also true for GluA1$^{-/-}$ mice. However, the groups differed on trials in which the first and second visual stimuli were the same. Whereas wild-type mice showed a reduction in suppression to the second stimulus, GluA1$^{-/-}$ mice showed an increase in suppression. Thus, wild-type mice showed short-term habituation of unconditioned responding to the visual stimuli, but GluA1$^{-/-}$ mice showed short-term sensitization. A recent stimulus exposure had opposite effects in the two groups.

This result is consistent with the hypothesis that GluA1 regulates the rate at which elements decay from the A1 state to the A2 state, and that deletion of GluA1 reduces the rate of transfer.

The rate of decay between the A1 state to the A2 state limits the number of elements that accrue in the A1 state during a stimulus presentation. Thus, if a stimulus activates a proportion of its elements into the A1 state moment by moment, then the number of elements in the A1 state may initially increase, but as time progresses, the number of elements will reach a maximum level before being reduced as a consequence of elements entering the A2 state. This theory explains why stimuli of an intermediate duration condition more readily than stimuli that are either of a short or long duration (Smith, 1968). The result of the Sanderson, Sprengel, et al. (2011) study suggests that in GluA1$^{-/-}$ mice, a recent stimulus exposure increased the number of elements in the A1 state such that the unconditioned response was potentiated. Therefore, GluA1 deletion may have reduced the rate at which elements decayed from the A1 state to the A2 state, increasing the overall level of elements that could be activated into the A1 state.

The results of the studies with GluA1$^{-/-}$ mice show dissociations between different forms of recognition memory. However, performance was affected not because of impaired memory but because of changes in the expression of memory under different conditions. Therefore, the temporal dynamics of the rates of decay between the different activation states determined the expression of short-term recognition memory and also determined the extent of associative learning. Wagner's (1981) SOP model provides a framework in which the seemingly paradoxical effects of GluA1 deletion may be interpreted, and from which novel predictions can be derived. Similarly, this model can be used to understand the multiple memory process account via different brain areas.

Role of the Hippocampus in Associative and Nonassociative Recognition Memory Processes

One of the main controversies in the debate over single-process versus dual-process models of recognition is the role of the hippocampus. In the human literature, it is not clear whether the hippocampus contributes to both recollection and familiarity or just to recollection (Aggleton & Brown, 2006; Brown & Aggleton, 2001; Squire et al., 2007). In rodents, hippocampal lesions often spare performance on the standard spontaneous object-recognition procedure in which the preference for a novel object over a familiar object is assessed (e.g., Good et al., 2007; Winters, Forwood, Cowell, Saksida, & Bussey, 2004). In contrast, hippocampal lesions in rodents impair context-dependent spontaneous object recognition (Good et al., 2007; Mumby, Gaskin, Glenn, Schramek, & Lehmann, 2002). The dissociation between the standard object-recognition procedure and the context-dependent procedure has been taken as evidence for a selective role of the hippocampus in recollection (Aggleton & Brown, 2006; Brown & Aggleton, 2001). Thus, whereas the context-dependent procedure requires retrieval of associated memories for correct performance, the standard object-recognition procedure may be solved on the basis of familiarity alone. However, a number of studies have found that hippocampal lesions can impair performance on the standard object-recognition procedure (Broadbent, Gaskin, Squire, & Clark, 2010; Broadbent, Squire, & Clark, 2004), suggesting that the hippocampus may have a general role in recognition memory and, furthermore, potentially arguing against a dual-process account (Squire *et al.*, 2007).

Despite the ambiguity of the role of the hippocampus in the standard object-recognition memory procedure, there is a clearer role of the hippocampus in object recognition that is determined by the temporal order of the presentation of objects (Barker & Warburton, 2011; Good *et al.*, 2007). In these procedures, an object (A) is first presented, and then a different object (B) is subsequently presented. In the test trial, both objects A and B are presented. Normal rats show a preference for exploring the object that was presented first, but hippocampal lesioned rats fail to show the preference. While the temporal order procedure may be perfomed on the basis of relative recency (see Murphy, Mondragon, Murphy, & Fouquet, 2004, for a discussion on temporal order learning), it has been argued that, similar to the context-dependent procedure, the temporal order procedure requires an associative-retrieval, recollection-like process and cannot be solved on the basis of familiarity alone (Devito & Eichenbaum, 2011).

At first glance, the effects of lesions of the hippocampus on the variations of the object-recognition procedure pose a problem for the analysis of recognition memory in terms of the mechanisms of Wagner's (1981) SOP model. The dissociation between the standard object-recognition procedure and the context-dependent object-recognition procedure suggests that the standard object-recognition procedure may reflect performance on the basis of nonassociative A2 activation alone and that the hippocampus is necessary for processes that lead to associative A2 activation, but not for nonassociative A2 activation. However, this conclusion is at odds with the effect of hippocampal lesions on the temporal order object-recognition procedure. In this procedure, both objects have equal opportunity for forming an association with the context; therefore, the context will associatively retrieve a memory of the objects equally on the test trial. Consequently, it is unlikely that associative retrieval caused by the context contributes to the preference for the less recently presented object. However, it is likely that the nonassociative A2 activation of the second presented object will be stronger than that of the first object, because the second object is the more recently presented object at the test trial.

Given the analysis of the temporal order version of the object-recognition procedure, if hippocampal lesions spare nonassociative A2 activation why do they impair the temporal order procedure? One answer to this question is that performance on the temporal order recognition procedure may not rely purely on nonassociative A2 activation. There is the potential during exposure trials for associations to form, other than object-context associations, which may affect performance during the test trial. According to Wagner's (1981) SOP model, while excitatory associations form between elements of representations that are concurrently in the A1 state, inhibitory associations form between stimulus representations that are in the A1 state and representations that are in the A2 state. In the temporal order object-recognition procedure, if the representation of the first object is in the A2 state when the second object is presented, then the second object will form an inhibitory association with the first object (see Moscovitch & LoLordo, 1968). During the test trial, the context will have the potential to associatively retrieve the representations of both the first and second presented objects into the A2 state. However, the ability of the representation of the first object to enter the A2 state will be reduced by the presentation of the second object. Thus, the inhibitory association will hinder retrieval of memory. The consequence of this is that the first object will be able to activate more of its elements into the A1 state than the second object, and exploration of the first object will be higher than the second object. This associative analysis of performance on the temporal order object-recognition procedure provides an explanation of how animals are able to show a preference for the first presented object after long test intervals in which it is unlikely that short-term, nonassociative A2 activation supports performance (Mitchell & Laiacona, 1998).

The explanation of temporal order object-recognition memory in terms of the effects of inhibitory associations on associative A2 activation rather than nonassociative, recency-dependent A2 activation may provide a way of reconciling the effects hippocampal lesions on the different variations of the object-recognition procedure. Thus, hippocampal lesions may impair performance on the temporal order object-recognition procedure, but not the standard object-recognition procedure because the former depends on the associative A2 activation, whereas the latter may rely on only nonassociative A2 activation. However, the associative A2 activation account holds only when the exploration of the first and second presented objects is measured in a simultaneous, preference test. Thus, the second object has to be present to affect exploration of the first object. The inhibitory effect of the second object would be avoided if unconditioned exploration of the two objects was assessed in separate, independent tests. This could be achieved by testing exploration of the first and second presented objects in a between-subjects design. Such a between-subjects design would allow a pure test of the effects of temporal order on nonassociative A2 activation. If it were found that hippocampal lesions impaired performance on the temporal order object-recognition procedure when preference for the first object could be caused only by nonassociative activation, then this would provide evidence against a selective role of the hippocampus in associative memory. While this test has not, to my knowledge, been conducted using objects, it has been conducted using exploration of distinctive contexts (Honey, Marshall, McGregor, Futter, & Good, 2007). Rats received trials in which they were allowed to explore two contexts in a specific temporal order, and then, 1 min after the last context exposure, they were returned to either the first context or the second context. It was found that rats with hippocampal lesions differed from sham lesioned rats and on the test trial showed greater exploration of the more recently explored context. This result is consistent with the idea that hippocampus is involved in nonassociative A2 activation and is not simply involved in associative-retrieval. Importantly, the results of Honey *et al.*'s (2007) study demonstrate that hippocampal lesions did not eliminate performance but instead altered the expression of memory. Thus, hippocampal lesions resulted in recency-dependent sensitization of exploration. This suggests that the memory of the context is not stored in the hippocampus and that the hippocampus modulates the influence of memory on behavior.

The finding that hippocampal lesions affect nonassociative A2 activation in the temporal order recognition procedure (Honey *et al.*, 2007) fails to provide support for the hypothesis that the hippocampus plays a selective role in associative-retrieval, recollection-like processes in recognition memory. Consequently, we return to the question of why hippocampal lesions sometimes spare performance on the standard object-recognition memory procedure, but impair performance on the temporal order objection recognition procedure. One simple explanation that cannot yet be ruled out is that hippocampal lesions impair A2 activation caused by nonassociative priming as well as associative priming, and that the temporal order procedure provides a more sensitive measure of memory than the standard object-recognition procedure.

Although hippocampal lesions can spare performance on the standard object-recognition procedure, there are a number of examples of a hippocampal lesion impairment on the procedure (e.g., Broadbent et al., 2004, 2010). Thus, while the hippocampus may not always be necessary for performance, there is evidence that suggests that damage to the hippocampus is sufficient to impair performance. This observation is consistent with the procedure sensitivity account. Furthermore, delay-dependent effects of manipulations of the hippocampus (Hammond, Tull, & Stackman, 2004) may reflect an increase in procedure difficulty due to reduced A2 activation over time. However, it is also possible that performance after longer test intervals reflects associative A2 state activation, whereas at shorter intervals, performance may rely on both nonassociative and associative A2 activation. Nonetheless, the collective results suggest that any dissociation between the effects of hippocampal lesions on the variants of the object-recognition procedure may be due to quantitative effects related to the sensitivity of the procedure, and need not reflect a qualitative dissociation of the role of the hippocampus in the respective procedures. Thus, a potential compromise between the opposing single-process (Squire et al., 2007) and dual-process (Brown & Aggleton, 2001) accounts is that recognition memory reflects two processes and that the hippocampus plays a part in both processes. While, the data do not, at present, allow us to decide between the different accounts of hippocampal function, by unpicking the psychological processes underlying recognition memory we may then form testable predictions for evaluating the opposing theories.

The analysis of rodent recognition memory in terms of Wagner's (1981) SOP model provides a new insight into the role of the hippocampus in memory processes. In line with other dual-process accounts of recognition memory, Wagner's (1981) SOP model claims that there are two separate processes that determine recognition memory. However, whereas other dual-process models assume that the processes have an additive effect on recognition performance, Wagner's (1981) SOP model claims that the processes involved can be competitive, and thus successfully provides an account of the opposite effects of short and long interstimulus intervals on short-term and long-term recognition memory (Sanderson & Bannerman, 2011). In contrast, and in disagreement with dual-process accounts, when the results of hippocampal lesions on recognition memory are viewed in terms of terms of Wagner's (1981) SOP model, the dissociable effects are likely to reflect quantitative, rather than qualitative, differences. Therefore, the hippocampus likely plays a role in both nonassociative and associative recognition memory. While, single-process accounts have claimed that the hippocampus is necessary for both recollection and familiarity, because they both reflect the same, single memory process, there is no need to make this assumption. Instead, it has been claimed that the hippocampus is necessary not for storing or retrieving memories but for how memory is expressed (Marshall, McGregor, Good,

& Honey, 2004). This theory can explain results demonstrating that hippocampal lesions fail to abolish memory, but qualitatively change the nature of how memory is expressed behaviorally (Honey & Good, 2000b; Honey et al., 2007; Marshall et al., 2004), which current single-process accounts (e.g., Squire et al., 2007), dual-process accounts (e.g., Aggleton & Brown, 2006), and representational accounts (Cowel et al., 2010) of recognition memory fail to explain.

Conclusion

Research with rodents has been used to examine the neurobiological basis of recognition memory. Interpretation of the results has been hindered by disagreement over the potential psychological mechanisms required for recognition memory (Aggleton & Brown, 2006; Squire et al., 2007). However, recent behavioral analyses of recognition memory in rodents have demonstrated that recognition memory is determined by separate, yet competitive, interacting mechanisms (Sanderson & Bannerman, 2011; Whitt et al., 2012; Whitt & Robinson, 2013). These results are predicted by an associative theory of learning (Wagner, 1981) that is able to explain a wide range of experimental findings (see Brandon, Vogel, & Wagner, 2003; Vogel, Brandon, & Wagner, 2003). Wagner's (1981) SOP model provides a new theoretical framework for deriving predictions and assessing the effects of neural manipulations. While it is possible that the psychological mechanisms of recognition memory in animals may ultimately differ from those in humans, it is necessary to have an adequate, accurate understanding of the psychological basis of behavior in animals so that the usefulness of animal models for studying the neurobiology of recognition memory can be assessed.

References

Aggleton, J. P., & Brown, M. W. (1999). Episodic memory, amnesia, and the hippocampal–anterior thalamic axis. *Behavioral and Brain Sciences, 22,* 425–444; discussion 444–489.

Aggleton, J. P., & Brown, M. W. (2006). Interleaving brain systems for episodic and recognition memory. *Trends in Cognitive Sciences, 10,* 455–463.

Alvarez, P., Zola-Morgan, S., & Squire, L. R. (1994). The animal model of human amnesia: long-term memory impaired and short-term memory intact. *Proceedings of the National Academy of Sciences of the United States of America, 91,* 5637–5641.

Anderson, M. J., Jablonski, S. A., & Klimas, D. B. (2008). Spaced initial stimulus familiarization enhances novelty preference in Long-Evans rats. *Behav Processes, 78,* 481–486.

Barker, G. R., & Warburton, E. C. (2011). When is the hippocampus involved in recognition memory? *Journal of Neuroscience, 31,* 10721–10731.

Berlyne, D. E. (1950). Novelty and curiosity as determinants of exploratory behavior. *British Journal of Psychology – General Section, 41,* 68–80.

Brandon, S. E., Vogel, E. H., & Wagner, A. R. (2003). Stimulus representation in SOP: I. Theoretical rationalization and some implications. *Behavioral Processes, 62,* 5–25.

Broadbent, N. J., Gaskin, S., Squire, L. R., & Clark, R. E. (2010). Object recognition memory and the rodent hippocampus. *Learning and Memory, 17,* 5–11.

Broadbent, N. J., Squire, L. R., & Clark, R. E. (2004). Spatial memory, recognition memory, and the hippocampus. *Proceedings of the National Academy of Sciences of the United States of America, 101*, 14515–14520.

Brown, M. W., & Aggleton, J. P. (2001). Recognition memory: What are the roles of the perirhinal cortex and hippocampus? *Nature Reviews Neuroscience, 2*, 51–61.

Cowel, R. A., Bussey, T. J., & Saksida, L. M. (2010). Components of recognition memory: dissociable cognitive processes or just differences in representational complexity? *Hippocampus, 20*, 1245–1262.

Davis, M. (1970). Effects of interstimulus interval length and variability on startle-response habituation in the rat. *Journal of Comparative and Physiological Psychology, 72*, 177–192.

Devito, L. M., & Eichenbaum, H. (2011). Memory for the order of events in specific sequences: contributions of the hippocampus and medial prefrontal cortex. *Journal of Neuroscience, 31*, 3169–3175.

Dix, S. L., & Aggleton, J. P. (1999). Extending the spontaneous preference test of recognition: evidence of object-location and object-context recognition. *Behavioral Brain Research, 99*, 191–200.

Donegan, N. H. (1981). Priming-produced facilitation or diminution of responding to a Pavlovian unconditioned stimulus. *Journal of Experimental Psychology Animal Behavior Processes, 7*, 295–312.

Eacott, M. J., Easton, A., & Zinkivskay, A. (2005). Recollection in an episodic-like memory task in the rat. *Learning and Memory, 12*, 221–223.

Eichenbaum, H., Fortin, N., Sauvage, M., Robitsek, R. J., & Farovik, A. (2010). An animal model of amnesia that uses Receiver Operating Characteristics (ROC) analysis to distinguish recollection from familiarity deficits in recognition memory. *Neuropsychologia, 48*, 2281–2289.

Ennaceur, A. (2010). One-trial object recognition in rats and mice: Methodological and theoretical issues. *Behavioral Brain Research, 215*, 244–254.

Ennaceur, A., & Delacour, J. (1988). A new one-trial test for neurobiological studies of memory in rats .1. Behavioral-data. *Behavioral Brain Research, 31*, 47–59.

Erickson, M. A., Maramara, L. A., & Lisman, J. (2009). A single 2-spike burst induces GluR1-dependent associative short-term potentiation: a potential mechanism for short-term memory. *Journal of Cognitive Neuroscience*.

Farovik, A., Dupont, L. M., Arce, M., & Eichenbaum, H. (2008). Medial prefrontal cortex supports recollection, but not familiarity, in the rat. *Journal of Neuroscience, 28*, 13428–13434.

Farovik, A., Place, R. J., Miller, D. R., & Eichenbaum, H. (2011). Amygdala lesions selectively impair familiarity in recognition memory. *Nature Neuroscience, 14*, 1416–1417.

Fortin, N. J., Wright, S. P., & Eichenbaum, H. (2004). Recollection-like memory retrieval in rats is dependent on the hippocampus. *Nature, 431*, 188–191.

Good, M. A., Barnes, P., Staal, V., McGregor, A., & Honey, R. C. (2007). Context- but not familiarity-dependent forms of object recognition are impaired following excitotoxic hippocampal lesions in rats. *Behavioral Neuroscience, 121*, 218–223.

Groves, P. M., & Thompson, R. F. (1970). Habituation: a dual-process theory. *Psychological Review, 77*, 419–450.

Hammond, R. S., Tull, L. E., & Stackman, R. W. (2004). On the delay-dependent involvement of the hippocampus in object recognition memory. *Neurobiology of Learning and Memory, 82*, 26–34.

Hoffman, D. A., Sprengel, R., & Sakmann, B. (2002). Molecular dissection of hippocampal theta-burst pairing potentiation. *Proceedings of the National Academy of Sciences of the United States of America, 99*, 7740–7745.

Honey, R. C., & Good, M. (2000a). Associative components of recognition memory. *Current Opinion in Neurobiology, 10,* 200–204.

Honey, R. C., & Good, M. (2000b). Associative modulation of the orienting response: distinct effects revealed by hippocampal lesions. *Journal of Experimental Psychology: Animal Behavior Processes, 26,* 3–14.

Honey, R. C., Good, M., & Manser, K. L. (1998). Negative priming in associative learning: Evidence from a serial-habituation procedure. *Journal of Experimental Psychology: Animal Behavior Processes, 24,* 229–237.

Honey, R. C., Marshall, V. J., McGregor, A., Futter, J., & Good, M. (2007). Revisiting places passed: sensitization of exploratory activity in rats with hippocampal lesions. *Quarterly Journal of Experimental Psychology (Hove), 60,* 625–634.

Honey, R. C., Watt, A., & Good, M. (1998). Hippocampal lesions disrupt an associative mismatch process. *Journal of Neuroscience, 18,* 2226–2230.

Horn, G. (1967). Neuronal mechanisms of habituation. *Nature, 215,* 707–711.

Horn, G., & Hill, R. M. (1964). Habituation of the response to sensory stimuli of neurones in the brain stem of rabbits. *Nature, 202,* 296–298.

Jordan, W. P., Strasser, H. C., & McHale, L. (2000). Contextual control of long-term habituation in rats. *Journal of Experimental Psychology Animal Behavior Processes, 26,* 323–339.

Kimble, G. A., & Ost, J. W. (1961). A conditioned inhibitory process in eyelid conditioning. *Journal of Experimental Psychology, 61,* 150–156.

Kimmel, H. D. (1966). Inhibition of the unconditioned response in classical conditioning. *Psychological Review, 73,* 232–240.

Lyon, L., Saksida, L. M., & Bussey, T. J. (2012). Spontaneous object recognition and its relevance to schizophrenia: a review of findings from pharmacological, genetic, lesion and developmental rodent models. *Psychopharmacology, 220,* 647–672.

Mandler, G. (1980). Recognizing – the judgment of previous occurrence. *Psychological Review, 87,* 252–271.

Marshall, V. J., McGregor, A., Good, M., & Honey, R. C. (2004). Hippocampal lesions modulate both associative and nonassociative priming. *Behavioral Neuroscience, 118,* 377–382.

Mickes, L., Wais, P. E., & Wixted, J. T. (2009). Recollection is a continuous process: implications for dual-process theories of recognition memory. *Psychological Science, 20,* 509–515.

Mitchell, J. B., & Laiacona, J. (1998). The medial frontal cortex and temporal memory: tests using spontaneous exploratory behavior in the rat. *Behavioral Brain Research, 97,* 107–113.

Moscovitch, A., & LoLordo, V. M. (1968). Role of safety in the Pavlovian backward fear conditioning procedure. *Journal of Comparative and Physiological Psychology, 66,* 673–678.

Mumby, D. G., Gaskin, S., Glenn, M. J., Schramek, T. E., & Lehmann, H. (2002). Hippocampal damage and exploratory preferences in rats: memory for objects, places, and contexts. *Learning and Memory, 9,* 49–57.

Murphy, R. A., Mondragon, E., Murphy, V. A., & Fouquet, N. (2004). Serial order of conditional stimuli as a discriminative cue for Pavlovian conditioning. *Behavioural Processes, 67,* 303–311.

Rankin, C. H., Abrams, T., Barry, R. J., Bhatnagar, S., Clayton, D. F., Colombo, J., Coppola, G., ... Thompson, R. F. (2009). Habituation revisited: an updated and revised description of the behavioral characteristics of habituation. *Neurobiology of Learning and Memory, 92,* 135–138.

Reisel, D., Bannerman, D. M., Schmitt, W. B., Deacon, R. M., Flint, J., Borchardt, T., Seeburg, P. H., ... Rawlins, J. N. P. (2002). Spatial memory dissociations in mice lacking GluR1. *Nature Neuroscience, 5,* 868–873.

Rescorla, R. A., & Wagner, A. R. (1972). A theory of Pavlovian conditioning: variations in the effectiveness of reinforcement and nonreinforcement. In A. H. Black & W. F. Prokasy

(Eds.), *Classical conditioning, II: Current research and theory* (pp. 64–99). New York, NY: Appleton-Century-Crofts.

Romberg, C., Raffel, J., Martin, L., Sprengel, R., Seeburg, P. H., Rawlins, J. N., Bannerman, D. M., ... Paulsen, O. (2009). Induction and expression of GluA1 (GluR-A)-independent LTP in the hippocampus. *European Journal of Neuroscience, 29*, 1141–1152.

Sanderson, D. J., & Bannerman, D. M. (2011). Competitive short-term and long-term memory processes in spatial habituation. *Journal of Experimental Psychology Animal Behavior Processes, 37*, 189–199.

Sanderson, D. J., Good, M. A., Skelton, K., Sprengel, R., Seeburg, P. H., Rawlins, J. N., & Bannerman, D. M. (2009). Enhanced long-term and impaired short-term spatial memory in GluA1 AMPA receptor subunit knockout mice: evidence for a dual-process memory model. *Learning and Memory, 16*, 379–386.

Sanderson, D. J., Gray, A., Simon, A., Taylor, A. M., Deacon, R. M., Seeburg, P. H., Sprengel, R., ... Bannerman, D. M. (2007). Deletion of glutamate receptor-A (GluR-A) AMPA receptor subunits impairs one-trial spatial memory. *Behavioral Neuroscience, 121*, 559–569.

Sanderson, D. J., Hindley, E., Smeaton, E., Denny, N., Taylor, A., Barkus, C., Sprengel, R., ... Bannerman, D. M. (2011). Deletion of the GluA1 AMPA receptor subunit impairs recency-dependent object recognition memory. *Learning and Memory, 18*, 181–190.

Sanderson, D. J., Sprengel, R., Seeburg, P. H., & Bannerman, D. M. (2011). Deletion of the GluA1 AMPA receptor subunit alters the expression of short-term memory. *Learning and Memory, 18*, 128–131.

Sauvage, M. M., Beer, Z., & Eichenbaum, H. (2010). Recognition memory: adding a response deadline eliminates recollection but spares familiarity. *Learning and Memory, 17*, 104–108.

Sauvage, M. M., Fortin, N. J., Owens, C. B., Yonelinas, A. P., & Eichenbaum, H. (2008). Recognition memory: opposite effects of hippocampal damage on recollection and familiarity. *Nature Neuroscience, 11*, 16–18.

Schmitt, W. B., Deacon, R. M., Seeburg, P. H., Rawlins, J. N., & Bannerman, D. M. (2003). A within-subjects, within-task demonstration of intact spatial reference memory and impaired spatial working memory in glutamate receptor-A-deficient mice. *Journal of Neuroscience, 23*, 3953–3959.

Smith, M. C. (1968). CS–US interval and US intensity in classical conditioning of the rabbit's nictitating membrane response. *Journal of Comparative and Physiological Psychology, 66*, 679–687.

Squire, L. R., Wixted, J. T., & Clark, R. E. (2007). Recognition memory and the medial temporal lobe: A new perspective. *Nature Reviews Neuroscience, 8*, 872–883.

Taylor, A. M., Niewoehner, B., Seeburg, P. H., Sprengel, R., Rawlins, J. N., Bannerman, D. M., & Sanderson, D. J. (2011). Dissociations within short-term memory in GluA1 AMPA receptor subunit knockout mice. *Behavioral Brain Research, 224*, 8–14.

Vogel, E. H., Brandon, S. E., & Wagner, A. R. (2003). Stimulus representation in SOP: II. An application to inhibition of delay. *Behav Processes, 62*, 27–48.

Wagner, A. R. (1976). Priming in STM: An information processing mechanism for self-generated or retrieval-generated depression in performance. In T. J. Tighe & R. N. Leaton (Eds.), *Habituation: Perspectives from child development, animal behavior, and neurophysiology* (pp. 95–128). Hillsdale, NJ: Lawrence Erlbaum Associates.

Wagner, A. R. (1978). Expectancies and the priming of STM. In S. H. Hulse, H. Fowler, & W. K. Honig (Eds.), *Cognitive Processes in Animal Behavior* (pp. 177–209). Hillsdale, NJ: Lawrence Erlbaum Associates.

Wagner, A. R. (1979). Habituation and memory. In A. Dickinson & R. A. Boakes (Eds.), *Mechanisms of learning and motivation: A memorial volume for Jerry Konorski* (pp. 53–82). Hillsdale, NJ: Erlbaum.

Wagner, A. R. (1981). SOP: A model of automatice memory processing in animal behavior. In N. E. Spear & R. R. Miller (Eds.), *Information processing in animals: Memory mechanisms* (pp. 5–47). Hillsdale, NJ: Lawrence Erlbaum Associates Inc.

Wagner, A. R., & Rescorla, R. A. (1972). Inhibition in Pavlovian conditioning: Application of a theory. In R. A. Boakes & M. S. Halliday (Eds.), *Inhibition and learning*. London, UK: Academic Press.

Whitt, E., Haselgrove, M., & Robinson, J. (2012). Indirect object recognition: evidence for associative processes in recognition memory. *Journal of Experimental Psychology Animal Behavior Processes, 38*, 74–83.

Whitt, E., & Robinson, J. (2013). Improved spontaneous object recognition following spaced preexposure trials: evidence for an associative account of recognition memory. *Journal of Experimental Psychology Animal Behavior Processes, 39*, 174–179.

Winters, B. D., Forwood, S. E., Cowell, R. A., Saksida, L. M., & Bussey, T. J. (2004). Double dissociation between the effects of peri-postrhinal cortex and hippocampal lesions on tests of object recognition and spatial memory: heterogeneity of function within the temporal lobe. *Journal of Neuroscience, 24*, 5901–5908.

Wixted, J. T. (2007). Dual-process theory and signal-detection theory of recognition memory. *Psychological Review, 114*, 152–176.

Wixted, J. T., & Mickes, L. (2010). A continuous dual-process model of remember/know judgments. *Psychological Review, 117*, 1025–1054.

Wixted, J. T., & Squire, L. R. (2008). Constructing receiver operating characteristics (ROCs) with experimental animals: cautionary notes. *Learning and Memory, 15*, 687–690.

Yonelinas, A. P. (1999). The contribution of recollection and familiarity to recognition and source-memory judgments: A formal dual-process model and an analysis of receiver operating characteristics. *Journal of Experimental Psychology: Learning Memory and Cognition, 25*, 1415–1434.

Yonelinas, A. P., & Parks, C. M. (2007). Receiver operating characteristics (ROCs) in recognition memory: a review. *Psychological Bulletin, 133*, 800–832.

Zamanillo, D., Sprengel, R., Hvalby, O., Jensen, V., Burnashev, N., Rozov, A., Kaiser, K. M., … Sakmann, B. (1999). Importance of AMPA receptors for hippocampal synaptic plasticity but not for spatial learning. *Science, 284*, 1805–1811.

9

Perceptual Learning
Representations and Their Development
Dominic M. Dwyer and Matthew E. Mundy

It is somewhat of a cliché to begin a discussion of perceptual learning by quoting Gibson's definition of it from *Annual Review of Psychology* in 1963 as "any relatively permanent and consistent change in the perception of a stimulus array, following practice or experience with this array" (Gibson, 1963, p. 29). We have not departed from this tradition because the definition focuses on the *effects* of experience and is thus instructive in its agnosticism regarding the underlying mechanisms by which these effects take place. In contrast, Goldstone's superficially similar statement in the same journal that "Perceptual learning involves relatively long-lasting changes to an organism's perceptual system that improve its ability to respond to its environment" (Goldstone, 1998, p. 585) carries with it the implication that there is a distinction between "true" perceptual learning and higher-level cognitive processes (an implication that Goldstone made explicit later in his paper). A similar tendency can be seen in Fahle's (2002) introduction to a more recent volume on perceptual learning that sought to distinguish perceptual learning from other processes and, in particular, from associative learning. The idea that associative processes have no role to play in perceptual learning is anathema to the motivating spirit of this volume but also flies in the face of a long tradition of theorists who have offered associative accounts of how experience impacts on the development of representations and the discrimination between them (e.g., Hall, 1991; James, 1890; McLaren & Mackintosh, 2000; Postman, 1955). Taken very generally, studies of perceptual learning can be divided into two broad streams: an "associative" one noted already, and one conducted in the broad context of psychophysics and perception. While we will be focusing mainly on the associative stream of perceptual learning research, it will become clear that the two traditions may not be as divergent as might be supposed given some of the definitional tendencies noted above (cf. Mitchell & Hall, 2014).

The *psychophysical* stream of research is generally characterized by the use of relatively simple stimuli such as vernier acuity (e.g., McKee & Westheimer, 1978), motion direction (e.g., Ball & Sekuler, 1982), line orientation (e.g., Vogels & Orban, 1985), and texture discrimination (e.g., Karni & Sagi, 1991) – but there are exceptions such as the examination of object recognition (e.g., Furmanski & Engel, 2000) or faces (e.g., Gold, Bennett & Sekuler, 1999). Studies in this stream also tend to compare performance after learning (based on either simple exposure or discrimination practice with feedback) with performance either before training or on untrained stimuli. In contrast, the associative stream is typically characterized by the use of relatively complex stimuli such as morphed faces (e.g., Mundy, Honey, & Dwyer, 2007), complex checkerboards (e.g., McLaren, 1997), collections of visual icons (e.g., de Zilva & Mitchell, 2012), or flavor compounds (e.g., Dwyer, Hodder & Honey, 2004). Moreover, this associative stream has focused on learning without explicit feedback, and the contrast between how different forms of exposure affect later discrimination. The study of how the structure of stimulus exposure contributes to perceptual learning is perhaps the most unique contribution of the associative stream, as it has not been addressed elsewhere. Before describing this contribution in detail, however, it is worth considering the rationale and generalizability of a common assumption that is central to the associative stream – namely that the representations of stimuli can be considered as collections of elements.

A Note on Terminology, Elements, and Representations

Associative theorists are fond of describing their stimuli and experimental designs in rather abstract terms (e.g., As, Bs, Xs, and Ys) that make no direct reference to the physical nature of the stimuli themselves.[1] It is common to consider difficult-to-discriminate stimuli (which are the mainstay of perceptual learning) as overlapping collections of elements, where the difficulty of discrimination is presumed to lie in the fact that the stimuli share a number of common elements alongside some that are unique. So, two similar stimuli might be described as AX and BX (where A and B refer to their unique elements and X to the elements they have in common). In many cases, this distinction between common and unique elements reflects the fact that the stimuli are explicitly constructed as compounds of simpler features: such as salt–lemon and sucrose–lemon flavor compounds (e.g., Dwyer et al., 2004) or checkerboards constructed by placing one of a number of distinct features on a common background image (e.g., Lavis & Mitchell, 2006; but see Jones & Dwyer, 2013). In others, the elements are not explicit in the construction of the stimuli but can reasonably be thought to exist as a product of the way they are produced: such as with the morphing between two faces to produce intermediate and confusable face images (e.g., Mundy et al., 2007). Without preempting the detailed discussion that follows, the crux of associative analyses of perceptual learning lies in the effects that exposure has on the representation of these unique and common elements, and the relationships between them. Most generally, exposure could produce a perceptual learning effect if it reduced the sensitivity or response to the common elements in favor of selectively responding to the unique elements (Gibson, 1969).

However, the general tendency within the associative stream, to use complex compound stimuli, raises the question of whether associative analyses only make sense in the context of stimuli that comprise separable elements. If far simpler stimuli such as line orientation or motion direction simply do not admit decomposition then an associative (or any other) analysis of them in terms of unique and common features is untenable.

In this light, it is instructive to consider the analysis of motion direction discrimination in terms of the action of a hypothetical population of neurons, each differing in their peak sensitivities to specific orientations, but also responding to a broad and overlapping range of motion orientations (e.g., McGovern, Roach, & Webb, 2012). Here, the most informative neurons for detecting small deviations around vertical motion will actually be those that have their peak response somewhat away from the to-be-discriminated orientations because it is in these more distant neurons that the largest differences in firing rate occur (as opposed to neurons centered on vertical motion, as these would have common changes to small deviations left and right of vertical; see Figure 9.1). Thus, even a simple stimulus such as motion direction can be decomposed into the effects of that motion on a variety of channels with different peak sensitivities. Indeed, classic descriptions of many perceptual adaptation effects are based on the presumption that seemingly simple stimuli are decomposed into overlapping detection channels (e.g., Mollon, 1974).

When considered in light of a broadly Gibsonian perspective on perceptual learning, the idea that simple stimuli can be decomposed into a number of overlapping channels implies that it should be possible to improve discrimination performance by reducing the activity of channels that respond to both of the to-be-discriminated stimuli, or to impair discrimination by reducing the activity of the channels that respond predominantly to one stimulus or other. A demonstration of this manipulation has been performed using an adaptation procedure. When subjects were discriminating between motion directions displaced slightly to the left or right of vertical, adaptation to upward motion (which should reduce the sensitivity of channels responding in common to both of the to-be-discriminated orientations) enhances discrimination accuracy. In addition, adapting to motion ±20° from vertical (which corresponds to the channels that respond most differently to stimuli that are to the left vs. right of vertical) reduces accuracy (McGovern, Roach, *et al.*, 2012). Thus, although research on perceptual learning conducted in the psychophysical tradition may not typically use stimuli that explicitly comprise compounds of separate elements, the idea that perceptual learning can be analyzed in terms of the effects on representations that are decomposed into overlapping collections of elements is still entirely applicable.

Impact of Exposure Schedule

One of the simplest possible explanations for perceptual learning is that the discriminability of stimuli is a direct function of the frequency with which the to-be-discriminated stimuli have been encountered (i.e., perceptual learning is a simple product of familiarity, e.g., Gaffan, 1996; Hall, 1991). Perhaps the first concrete suggestion that this idea might not be correct came from the demonstration (in rats) that the discrimination between two compound stimuli, saline–lemon and sucrose–lemon, was improved by exposure to the common lemon element alone (Mackintosh, Kaye, & Bennett, 1991). Here, exposure to the common element alone (i.e., X) does not affect the familiarity of the unique features (i.e., A and B) upon which the ability to discriminate AX and BX must be based, and so familiarity per se cannot explain the exposure-dependent

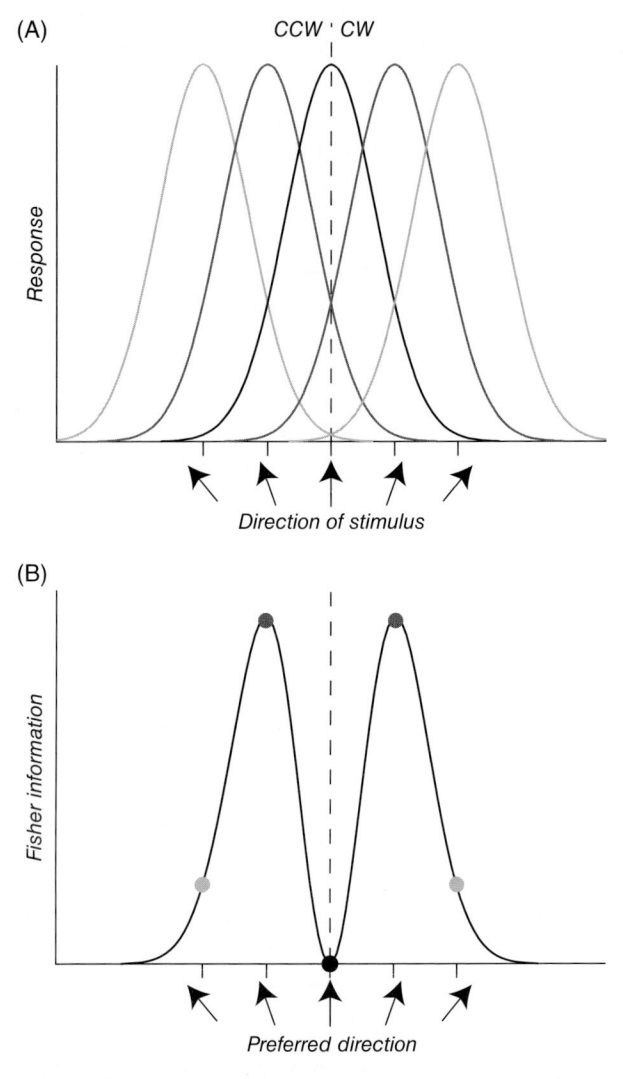

Figure 9.1 Fisher information carried by a homogeneous population of neurons performing a fine discrimination task. (A) Tuning functions of direction-selective neurons responding to upward motion (black) and directions offset symmetrically ±20° (dark gray) and ±40° (light gray) from upward. (B) Fisher information for performing this task is highest for neurons tuned to directions ±20° from upward (dark gray circles) because small deviations from upward produce the largest differential firing rate. Neurons tuned to upward (black circle) and directions ±40° from upward (light gray circles) convey no or very little information because their differential firing rates to small deviations from upward are zero or negligible, respectively. The vertical dashed line indicates the boundary around which neurons discriminate whether a stimulus was moving in a direction clockwise (CW) or counterclockwise (CCW) from upward. Fisher information is calculated as follows: $FI = f'_i(\theta)^2 / n_i(\theta)$, where $f'_i(\theta)$ is the differential firing rate to small deviations from upward, and $n_i(\theta)$ is the variance of the Poisson-distributed response. Figure and legend adapted with permission from McGovern, Roach, et al. (2012).

improvement in discrimination. Nor is this result restricted to taste stimuli in rodent experiments: Mundy *et al.* (2007) demonstrated that exposure to the midpoint on the morph between two similar faces (which presumably reflects the features that the two faces share) improved subsequent discrimination between them, while Wang and Mitchell (2011) found that discrimination between two checkerboards consisting of a unique feature placed on a common background was facilitated by exposure to the common background alone.

While the effects of common element exposure do question a simple familiarity account of perceptual learning to some extent, the most direct evidence against this idea comes from the analysis of studies in which the schedule of exposure was manipulated while the total amount of exposure to the relevant stimuli (and hence their overall familiarity) was held constant. This issue was first considered in chicks with the demonstration that intermixed exposure to two stimuli that differed only on one dimension resulted in better subsequent discrimination between them than did the equivalent amount of exposure given in separate blocks (Honey, Bateson, & Horn, 1994). This advantage for intermixed over blocked exposure schedules has proved to be highly reliable in both animals (e.g., Symonds & Hall, 1995) and humans (e.g., Dwyer *et al.*, 2004; Lavis & Mitchell, 2006), and cannot be reduced simply to differences in the frequency of exposure (e.g., Mitchell, Nash, & Hall, 2008). The generality of this intermixed/blocked effect across species and stimuli suggests that the manner in which stimuli are exposed is critically important for perceptual learning over and above the simple amount of exposure.

Gibson (1963, 1969) herself provided one of the earliest theoretical accounts of perceptual learning that anticipated the advantage of intermixed over blocked exposure. She suggested that the opportunity for comparison between stimuli would be particularly effective in producing perceptual learning because it would best support a process of stimulus differentiation whereby the effectiveness of the features that were unique to each of the exposed stimuli was enhanced relative to those features that were shared or common to both. While the mechanism behind this stimulus differentiation was not made explicit, the prediction that comparison would enhance perceptual learning was entirely clear. But in this respect, the results from human and animal based studies diverge. Mitchell and Hall (2014) provide an extended discussion of this issue, but in short, animal studies examining alternation often involve trials separated by periods of several hours or more, which does not afford direct comparison in any meaningful sense (e.g., Dwyer & Mackintosh, 2002; Symonds & Hall, 1995), and reducing the interval between stimuli, which should facilitate direct comparison, can actually impair perceptual learning (e.g., Bennett & Mackintosh, 1999; Honey & Bateson, 1996). In contrast, human studies have shown that simultaneous exposure, which should best facilitate comparison, produces larger perceptual learning effects than does alternating exposure (Mundy *et al.*, 2007; Mundy, Honey, & Dwyer, 2009), and inserting a distractor between alternating stimuli in the exposure phase, thus presumably reducing the opportunity for direct comparison between them, attenuates the beneficial effects of alternating exposure (Dwyer, Mundy, & Honey, 2011). Thus, while the structure of exposure clearly influences perceptual learning in both humans and other animals, the particular beneficial effects of comparison between stimuli have only been demonstrated in human studies.

Before turning to the analysis of mechanisms by which comparison influences perceptual learning, it is worth noting that the effects of intermixed exposure in the absence of the opportunity for comparison do admit explanation in terms of associative principles. For example, McLaren and Mackintosh (2000) note that alternating exposure to AX and BX will mean that on BX trials, the representation of A will be retrieved in its absence (by its connection with X), and the converse will happen for B on AX trials. Thus, the absence of one unique element is explicitly paired with the presence of the other unique element; something whereby standard accounts of associative learning predict should lead to the formation of mutual inhibitory associations between the two unique elements. In turn, these inhibitory associations should reduce generalization between the stimuli. There is evidence that intermixed exposure does indeed produce such inhibitory links in rodents (e.g., Dwyer, Bennett, Mackintosh, 2001; Dwyer & Mackintosh, 2002; Espinet, Iraola, Bennett, & Mackintosh, 1995) and humans (e.g., Artigas, Chamizo, & Peris, 2001; Mundy, Dwyer, & Honey, 2006). Alternatively, Hall (2003) suggested that the mere associative activation of a stimulus in its absence might increase its salience. As noted above, intermixed exposure will ensure that both of the unique elements A and B will be retrieved in their absence and thus receive a salience boost, but the common elements X will not. Again, there is evidence consistent with a salience boost in rodents (e.g., Hall, Blair, & Artigas, 2006; but see Dwyer & Honey, 2007; Mondragon & Murphy, 2010). However, it must be remembered that both of these mechanisms require the activation of a stimulus in its absence, which should not be possible with the simultaneous presentation of stimuli, and neither of these accounts offers an explanation of why perceptual learning is attenuated when a distractor is used to disrupt comparison (Dwyer et al., 2011). Because it is abundantly clear that the opportunity for comparing the to-be-discriminated stimuli is a critical determinant of perceptual learning in humans, accounts of perceptual learning that explicitly or implicitly neglect comparison do not offer a complete account of the phenomenon in humans.[2]

Adaptation and Unpacking "Comparison"

If accounts of perceptual learning based on standard associative principles do not provide a full explanation of how exposure schedules promoting comparison, then what can? What needs to be unpacked is the mechanism by which exposure influences the effectiveness of the unique features of a stimulus. Perhaps the most central feature of exposure schedules that afford comparison between two stimuli is that they produce a situation where the to-be-discriminated stimuli are encountered repeatedly in close succession. Such repeated exposure is likely to produce adaptation of the stimuli involved, thus reducing the degree to which they are processed on each presentation. However, this adaptation will not be equivalent for all features of the stimulus. When exposure to BX follows experience of AX, the common element X will already be adapted to some extent, and thus the unique elements of BX (B) will be relatively better processed than the common elements (X). Similarly, when AX is subsequently encountered, the common elements X will remain more adapted than the unique elements, thus biasing the processing to the unique features A. Obviously, focusing on the unique as opposed to common elements would facilitate discrimination, but for this adaptation-produced bias in processing to have enduring effects, it must influence the aspects of the stimuli that are stored or represented because the direct effects of adaptation are short-lived, while perceptual learning effects can endure for some time. This idea that short-term processes of adaptation will have enduring effects on the subsequent representation of stimuli has been entertained several times (e.g., Dwyer *et al.*, 2011; Honey & Bateson, 1996; Honey, Close, & Lin, 2010; Mundy *et al.*, 2007) and can be simply illustrated by considering the formation of representations as the actions of a multilayer network. Here, the mapping between input layer units and hidden layer configural nodes could be affected by adaptation in a bottom-up fashion as it would reduce the activity of the input units for the common elements – which would reduce the weight of any connections between the common element and any hidden layer representation, and (perhaps most importantly) reduce the possibility that two overlapping patterns (e.g., AX and BX) would be drawn into a single hidden layer representation (see Figure 9.2).[3]

The interaction between the degree of processing and the subsequent representation of stimuli can also been considered in a rather different fashion. Mitchell *et al.* (2008) also argue that the degree to which a feature is encoded as part of the representation of a stimulus as a whole will be related to the amount of processing it receives. But, instead of relying on stimulus-driven bottom-up processes, they note that recently presented (and thus well-remembered) features would be less processed than more novel features (see Jacoby, 1978). Similarly, short-term adaptation of the nondiagnostic common elements should leave the critical unique elements more salient. In turn, this might allow them to attract attention more successfully than the common elements, and this greater attentional weighting of the unique features would support better discrimination (Mundy *et al.*, 2007).

Thus, the idea that short-term processes of adaptation will have enduring effects on the subsequent representation of stimuli can be understood in terms of either top-down (memory/attention) or bottom-up (stimulus-driven) mechanisms. Evidence from representational updating studies is consistent with the idea that the degree of overlap between successively presented stimuli affects the degree to which they are drawn into a single configural representation (Honey, Mundy, & Dwyer, 2012). However, while the updating data show that the idea of bottom-up processes determining representation formation is plausible, these studies explicitly controlled for the schedule by which the critical stimuli were presented, and thus do not speak directly to the effects of comparison. Although one might make an argument for a bottom-up account of the interplay between adaptation and representation development on a priori grounds of parsimony, there is no direct evidence to select between a top-down memory/attentional understanding and a bottom-up stimulus-driven one.

Quality Versus Quantity in Perceptual Learning and the Potential Role for Brain Imaging

This chapter began with the definition of perceptual learning as a change in perception as a product of experience, and has reviewed evidence demonstrating that discrimination between otherwise confusable stimuli is improved by exposure,

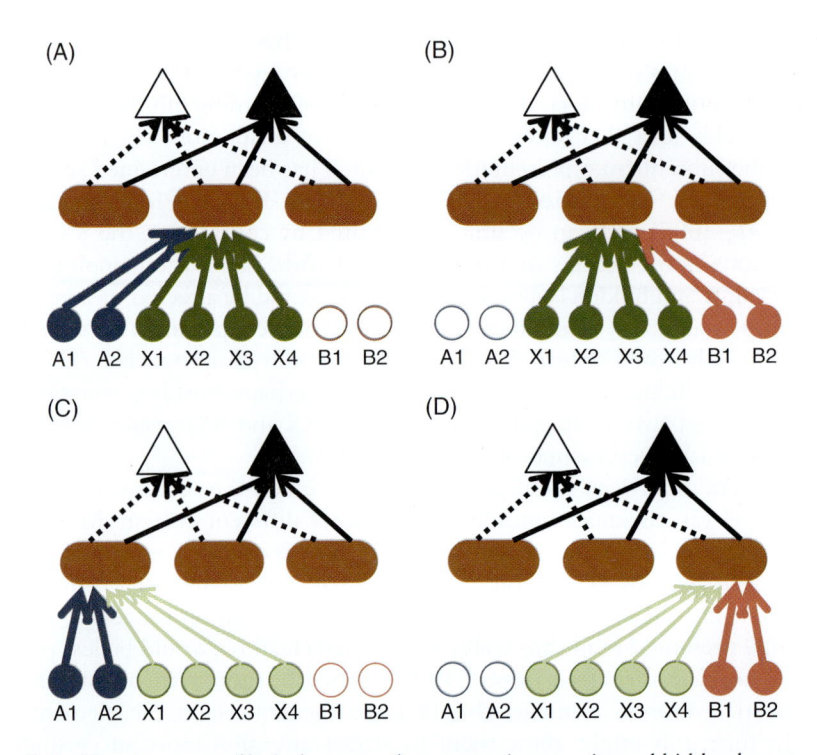

Figure 9.2 Development of links between the sensory input units and hidden layer representations. The intensity of the coloring in the sensory units represents the level of activation, and the weighting of the connections is represented by the breadth of the arrows. Panels (A) and (B) illustrate the development of links between the sensory input units and hidden layer representations in the absence of selective adaptation. The sensory units corresponding to AX and BX are drawn into the same hidden layer representation due to the predominance of input coming from the common elements X1–X4. In addition, the strength of connections across input units is approximately equal, as the level of initial activations is similar. Panels (C) and (D) illustrate the situation where exposure has reduced the response to the common elements by adaptation. Now, the sensory units corresponding to AX and BX are linked to different hidden layer units because the adaptation of X1–X4 means that AX and BX are dominated by the unique elements A1/A2 and B1/B2 respectively. In addition, the strength of connections from the common elements X1–X4 is less than from the unique elements A1/A2 and B1/B2 because the common elements were activated to a lesser degree during exposure.

especially when that exposure affords comparison between the to-be-discriminated stimuli. Thus far, the evidence for such improvements in discrimination has been dealt with in a relatively undifferentiated fashion – in particular, it has yet to be asked whether exposure influences the type of mechanism underpinning the discrimination (i.e., the nature of the discrimination) or merely the accuracy with which these discriminations occur (i.e., the degree or amount of discrimination). To illustrate this issue, remember that during intermixed exposure, the interval between presentations of the unique features of two similar stimuli is greater than between those of the common features. This difference in the patterning of exposure to the unique and common elements is a particularly effective means of adapting or habituating the common features of the two stimuli, leaving the unique elements to become better represented and available to be learned about subsequently. When the stimuli are presented the same number of times in a blocked fashion, the time between separate presentations is the same for both unique and common features, so the relative timing cannot contribute to the degree of adaptation. But it remains the case that the features that are common to all stimuli will be encountered more often than features that are unique to one or other stimulus – and so the common features will be adapted more than the unique features. Thus, there are still grounds for the unique features to gain relatively greater weighting in the representation of the stimulus as a whole. Of course, novel stimuli afford neither the opportunity for adaptation to differentially weight attention between common and unique features nor the chance to form an integrated representation of the stimulus at all. Thus, the general idea that short-term processes of adaptation will have enduring effects on the subsequent representation of stimuli can be applied to both perceptual learning as a product of exposure per se and the products of the structure of exposure.

That said, the fact that a single mechanism could be responsible for effects due to both the amount and structure of exposure does not mean that it is the only mechanism in operation or even that the output of a single mechanism can only have quantitatively different effects. For example, if the degree of overlap between two stimuli is particularly large, then it is possible that no amount of blocked exposure might prevent both becoming linked to the same hidden layer unit, while intermixed exposure could retain the possibility of separating them. Unfortunately, the behavioral tasks described thus far are unsuited to determining whether perceptual learning (based on either the amount or structure of exposure) has qualitative or quantitative effects on discrimination performance. This is because they tend to simply ask whether two stimuli can be discriminated or not, but are silent with respect to how that discrimination might take place. This is one issue where the study of brain activity, or correlates thereof, might be of particular value. If perceptual learning simply influences the accuracy of discrimination performance, then the effects of exposure on the brain activity associated with discrimination performance should vary by degree but perhaps not by brain region. However, if the mechanisms underlying discrimination performance are differentially affected by the structure of exposure, then it is at least possible that this might be reflected in differences in the brain regions that are recruited. Moreover, the question of whether the interaction between adaptation and stimulus representation reflects bottom-up or top-down mechanisms has also been unresolved by purely behavioral analyses, but might well be amenable to an imaging analysis. For example, if the brain structures associated with attentional mechanisms and those linked to basic sensory processing are separable, examining the relationships between activity in these regions as a function of exposure could help to adjudicate between the top-down and bottom-up conceptions described previously. Therefore, the remainder of this chapter will be concerned with reviewing the results of imaging studies of perceptual learning in light of these two general issues. Although the study of the brain mechanisms involved in perceptual learning has received some recent attention from studies undertaken in the associative tradition, this is very much in its infancy in comparison with comparable work undertaken the psychophysical tradition. Thus it is to this line of research that we will turn first.

Brain Imaging in the Psychophysical Tradition of Perceptual Learning Research

Even before studies of brain imaging were performed, the question of what the brain substrates of perceptual learning might be had emerged as a key issue for consideration. It was well known that many examples of perceptual learning are highly specific to the training situation (e.g., Ball & Sekuler, 1982; Fiorentini & Berardi, 1980; Karni & Sagi, 1991; Poggio, Fahle, & Edelman, 1992). For example, the enhanced discriminability produced by experience was typically restricted to the stimulus orientation and retinal position used in training and did not transfer to situations in which these were changed. Given that neurons with the requisite location and orientation specificity are found in primary visual cortex and not further along the visual processing stream, such results appeared to be consistent with primary sensory cortex playing a critical role in perceptual learning. However, this reasoning has been challenged by the demonstration that the response properties of even primary sensory cortex neurons are subject to contextual control (e.g., Gilbert, Ito, Kapadia & Westheimer, 2000; Li, Piech & Gilbert, 2004) and even more recently by the fact that, under appropriate training methods, perceptual learning can transfer across changes in location, stimulus orientation, and task (e.g., McGovern, Webb, & Peirce, 2012; Xiao et al., 2008; J. Y. Zhang et al., 2010; T. Zhang, Xiao, Klein, Levi, & Yu, 2010). The complete transfer of training-dependent improvement in discrimination, despite changes in the characteristics of stimulus and task directly challenges the idea that location and stimulus specificity is a key feature of perceptual learning. In turn, this questions the idea that retinotopically organized visual cortex is the neural site for perceptual learning and requires that at least some more central mechanisms are involved. That said, it does not rule out any involvement of primary sensory cortex (Dwyer, 2008), especially as the hyperacuity displayed following some perceptual learning experiments appears to require levels of spatial resolution only found in the visual cortex (Poggio et al., 1992). In short, the behavioral study of perceptual learning implicates both sensory cortex and more central mechanisms, and so the direct characterization of the brain mechanisms involved could help separate these possibilities.

When functional imaging methods have been used to examine the effects of perceptual learning on brain activity, the involvement of primary visual cortex has been repeatedly identified across a variety of visual stimuli and tasks. For example, Schiltz et al. (1999), using positron emission tomography, reported a reduction in activation in visual cortex following extended training with contrast discrimination, and Mukai et al. (2007), in an fMRI study, found a decrease in activity in the visual cortex after training with sinusoidal gratings (for related effects in face processing, see Dubois et al., 1999). Moreover, Mukai et al. observed that it was not simply the case that activity in visual cortex changed as a result of learning, but the decrease in activity was only seen in participants who displayed improvements in behavioral performance. Those who did not show perceptual learning effects at a behavioral level also showed no change in brain activity. It should also be noted that while decreases in the activation of visual brain regions were indeed associated with an improvement in perceptual performance, this decrease came from higher baseline levels of activation than seen in subjects who did not show perceptual improvements with experience. As a result, the enhancement in neural response that was seen at the start of training for people who subsequently showed strong perceptual learning was observed when levels of behavioral performance did not differ between learners and nonlearners. Yet, when the levels of behavioral performance had diverged between the learner and nonlearner groups toward the end of testing, levels of brain activity did not differ between groups. Thus, while a decrease in brain activity with experience is linked to an increase in performance in this study, there was no simple relationship between absolute levels of visual cortex activation and behavioral performance.

The involvement of visual cortex in perceptual learning has been confirmed in many other studies; however, the fact that its involvement reflects a reduction in activity has not. For example, Schwartz, Maquet, and Frith (2002) report an increase in primary visual cortex activity following training with a texture discrimination that was specific to the trained eye and retinotopic location (as was the improvement in behavioral performance). Furmanski, Schluppeck, and Engel (2004) observed increases in visual cortex activity following extended training with a contrast-detection task. It has also been demonstrated that the increases in activity following texture discrimination training gradually attenuate over time, even as the exposure-dependent improvement in behavioral performance is maintained (Yotsumoto, Watanabe, & Sasaki, 2008). Thus, while the reason that some studies show increases and others show decreases in activation of the primary visual cortex after stimulus exposure is unclear, it may relate in part to the amount of training involved (for some other suggestions, see Schwarzkopf, Zhang, & Kourtzi, 2009).

The involvement of visual cortex in perceptual learning is also reinforced by the use of electroencephalography methods. Casco, Campana, Grieco, and Fuggetta (2004) observed improvements in texture-orientation discrimination, across a single training session, which were related to visually evoked potentials. In addition, comparing the pattern of evoked responses on trials with consistent and inconsistent textural information suggested that, relative to the responses elicited at the beginning of training, neural responses increased for features relevant to the discrimination and decreased for features irrelevant to the discrimination – something that suggests a further complication for aggregated measures of brain activity as increases in the response to relevant stimuli might be offset by decreases to irrelevant ones if both are processed in the same general regions. Pourtois, Rauss, Vuilleumier, and Schwartz (2008) examined the effects of training on a texture-discrimination task on visually evoked potentials localized as consistent with neural generators within primary visual cortex and observed a reduction in amplitude of components starting 40 ms after stimulus onset. As well as confirming the visual cortex involvement per se, this is informative because top-down influences on visual cortex activity are typically seen only after 100 ms (Li *et al.*, 2004), and therefore this result supports a bottom-up influence or a reinterpretation of previous limits to the top-down mechanisms.

While the involvement of visual cortex in perceptual learning is not in doubt, it is most certainly not the only region involved. For example, in addition to the visual cortex effects noted above, Mukai *et al.* (2007) also report decreases in the activity of frontal and supplementary eye-fields and dorsolateral prefrontal cortex as a function of exposure learning. In light of the theoretical suggestion of attentional mechanisms contributing to perceptual learning, it is interesting to note that these regions have been identified as part of a dorso-frontal attentional network (Corbetta & Shulman, 2002). Moreover, the decrease in activity in these attentional regions was only seen in participants who displayed improvements in behavioral performance, and initial levels of activation were also higher in those who subsequently showed a learning effect. That is, in Mukai *et al.* (2007), the same relationships were seen between the improvement in behavioral performance (or not) and activation in both visual and attentional brain regions.

The involvement of brain regions associated with attention is not only seen in studies where perceptual learning produces decreases in visual cortex activation. For example, Lewis, Baldassarre, Committeri, Romani, and Corbetta (2009) report increases in visual cortex activity after training with a shape-discrimination task at the same time as decreases in the activity of the same dorso-frontal attentional network regions described by Mukai *et al.* (2007). Importantly, the changes in activity in both the visual cortex and the attentional areas were correlated with the improvements in behavioral performance (positively for visual cortex, negatively for the attentional areas). Thus, as well as confirming the involvement of brain regions linked to basic sensory processing, functional imaging also reliably confirms the involvement of regions linked to attentional mechanisms.

In summary, functional imaging studies of perceptual learning dovetail with purely behavioral analyses. There is evidence that visual cortex activity is modulated by perceptual learning (with both increases and decreases being observed). Brain regions linked to attention are also modulated by perceptual learning (but here the observation of learning-dependent decreases is more consistent). Moreover, the links between behavioral performance and visual and attentional brain activity suggest that both are directly linked to the changes in perception produced by experience, especially when the time-course of visual cortex activity is considered. The involvement of both attentional and stimulus-driven mechanisms in perceptual learning is consistent with the two broad interpretations of the interaction between adaptation and representation development outlined above. In addition, the suggestion from electroencephalography studies that perceptual learning is linked to an increase in the response to relevant over irrelevant features is also consistent with the associative analysis of perceptual learning. That said, it should be remembered that all of these experiments compared trained and untrained responses, and thus only speak to the effects of the simple brute fact of experience. In order to directly address the questions raised above in light of the associative analysis of perceptual learning, it is necessary to examine functional imaging in the context of manipulations of exposure schedule as well as the amount of exposure. It is to this that we turn next.

Brain Imaging and Exposure Schedule

To our knowledge, there only two functional imaging studies have directly addressed the effects of exposure schedule on perceptual learning. The first of these (Mundy, Honey, Downing *et al.*, 2009) is a rather brief report, while the latter has been described across two separate publications (Mundy, Downing, Dwyer, Honey, &

Graham, 2013; Mundy et al., 2014). Moreover, both studies were reported with a focus on stimulus-specific mechanisms (In particular, for faces as compared with other stimulus types). Thus, we will give both studies a detailed consideration in order to place the emphasis on the effects that are common across visual stimuli.

The basic experimental design used by Mundy, Honey, Downing, et al. (2009) was taken from our previous studies of schedule effects in perceptual learning in which participants were exposed (without any explicit feedback) to one pair of stimuli in alternation while another pair of stimuli received the same amount of exposure in blocks (see Table 9.1). Each presented image was shown five times for 2 s each with a 1 s interval between them.[4] There was then a test phase where participants made the same/different judgments on the intermixed stimuli, blocked stimuli, and an additional novel pair of stimuli. The protocol was repeated six times for each participant: three times with morphed faces as stimuli (e.g., Mundy et al., 2007) and three times with complex checkerboards (e.g., Mundy et al., 2009). The published report focused on the contrast between intermixed and blocked stimuli during the test phase – that is, on the effects of exposure schedule on neural activity controlling for the amount of exposure (see the upper panel of Figure 9.3). The most salient product of this contrast when taking faces and checkerboards together (i.e., examining stimulus-general effects of exposure) was that intermixed stimuli elicited greater activity in visual cortex than did blocked stimuli. It was also observed that activity was greater for blocked than for intermixed stimuli in the superior frontal gyrus (including the frontal eye field), mid frontal gyrus, and cingulate gyrus (including the supplementary eye field). These areas were substantially similar to the attentional regions that Mukai et al. (2007) reported as decreasing in activation as a product of perceptual learning. While the bulk of the differences between intermixed and blocked exposure were common across face and checkerboard stimuli, there were some notable differences, in particular in the face fusiform area – but also in the medial temporal lobe, although signal dropout for medial temporal regions meant that this could not be assessed with any certainty.

The published report focused on the discussion of the contrast between intermixed and blocked stimuli – reflecting perceptual learning based on the schedule of exposure. It is also possible to interrogate the data from this experiment to investigate the effects

Table 9.1 Experimental design for Mundy, Honey, Downing, et al. (2009).

Condition	Exposure	Discrimination
Intermixed	AX, BX, AX, BX, AX, BX, AX, BX, AX, BX	AX versus BX
Blocked	CY, DY, CY, DY, CY, DY, CY, DY, CY, DY	CY versus DY
Control	No exposure	EZ versus FZ

Note. AX/BX to EZ/FZ represent pairs of difficult to discriminate stimuli. A within-subjects factorial design was used that manipulated exposure type (intermixed, blocked, and control) and stimulus type (morphed faces and random checkerboards). Each presented image was shown five times for 2 s each with a 1-s ISI. After an exposure stage (AX/BX intermixed, CY/DY blocked), participants received a same/different test phase in which the exposed stimuli and a novel pair of stimuli (EZ/FZ) were presented. This design was repeated six times (three times each with faces and checkerboards) with different stimuli as AX–FZ. The scanning data (see Figure 9.3) were taken from the test phase and averaged across the two types of stimuli.

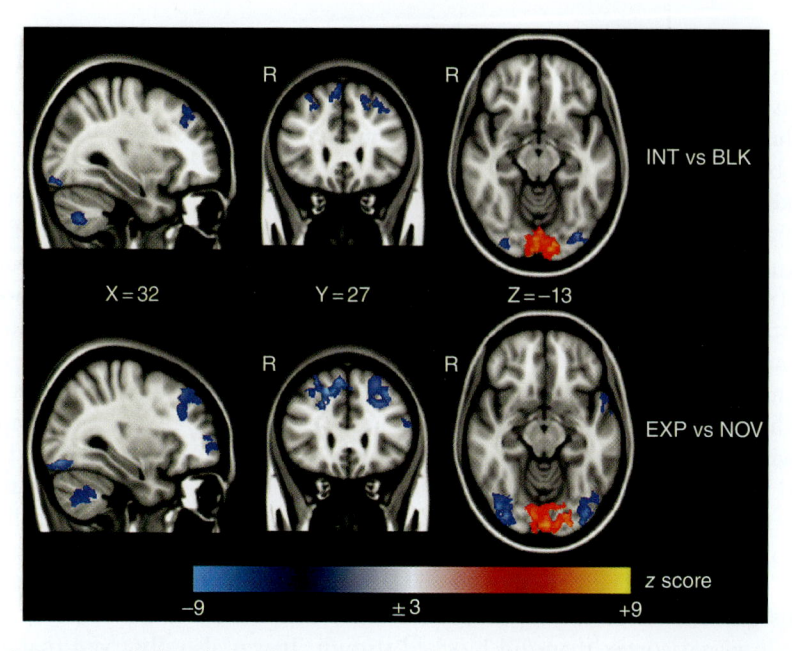

Figure 9.3 Expanded analysis of the results from Mundy, Honey, Downing, et al. (2009). The upper row of images shows the main effect of intermixed (INT) versus blocked stimuli (BLK). The lower row shows the main effect of exposed (i.e. intermixed and blocked combined – EXP) versus novel stimuli (NOV). Contrasts in a group analysis ($n = 12$) were overlaid on an MNI-152 standard template brain. Co-ordinates are in MNI space: saggital slices are shown at $x = 32$; coronal slices $y = 27$; axial slices $z = -13$. R = right. Effects were color-coded such that intermixed > blocked (or exposed > novel) are in red–yellow, and blocked > intermixed (or novel > exposed) are in blue–lightblue. Statistics were thresholded using clusters determined by a z value greater than 3 and a (corrected) cluster significance threshold of $p = 0.05$.

of perceptual learning based on the amount of exposure by examining the contrast between exposed (intermixed and blocked combined) and novel stimuli. These data are shown in the lower panel of Figure 9.3. Comparing the upper and lower panels of Figure 9.3, the same general patterns of activation were seen following perceptual learning based on either the schedule or the amount of exposure (with the latter tending to produce larger effects). Moreover, although there was insufficient power to detect a correlation between behavioral performance and activation changes in any region, a post-hoc analysis was performed using a median split to divide subjects on the basis of the difference between intermixed and blocked performance (that is, separating the best and worst perceptual learners). This revealed that the difference in activation in visual cortex between intermixed and blocked stimuli was smaller for the better learners than for those that learned less (even though the activation was greater for intermixed than blocked stimuli for all subjects). This pattern of results is at least consistent with the report by Mukai et al. (2007) that successful perceptual learning was associated with a reduction in visual cortex activity (from a high initial baseline), although this should be considered with some caution due to the lack of power and the post-hoc nature of the analysis. In summary, Mundy, Honey, Downing, et al. (2009) demonstrated that perceptual learning using brief, nonreinforced, exposure to complex stimuli involved both visual cortical regions and some higher attentional regions – a pattern of effects similar to that seen with extended reinforced exposure to more simple stimuli. In addition, the study provided preliminary evidence that the effects of both exposure schedule and amount of exposure were similar. However, because the study lacked the power to examine the links between behavioral performance and the pattern of brain activation in any detail, it was more suggestive than definitive.

In order to address these issues (and others – especially relating to stimulus specificity), we reexamined the same basic behavioral design (i.e., comparing intermixed, blocked, and novel stimuli) while adding to the range and power of the analysis by increasing the number of runs in each exposure condition, broadening the analysis to three stimulus types (faces, scenes, and random-dot patterns), performing a formal retinotopic mapping procedure, and using a larger subject group (Mundy et al., 2013, 2014). The primary focus of the Mundy et al. (2013) report was on the stimulus-specific role of subregions of the medial temporal lobe for face and scene stimuli, in particular the fact that a face-selective region in the perirhinal cortex was modulated by discrimination accuracy with faces while a scene-selective region in the posterior hippocampus was modulated by discrimination accuracy with scenes. The stimulus-specific importance of these regions in discrimination performance was confirmed by the examination of patients with medial temporal lobe damage. While these stimulus-specific effects are clearly important in understanding the function of the medial temporal lobe, for the current concerns it is important that the only stimulus-general relationships between activity and discrimination accuracy were found in the visual cortex.

The analysis of stimulus-general (i.e., combining faces, scenes and dot stimuli) is the main focus of Mundy et al. (2014). A whole-brain analysis across all subjects revealed that activity was higher for intermixed than for novel stimuli in the occipital pole (including V1 and V2) and that activity was higher for novel than for intermixed stimuli for the lateral occipital and lingual gyri (including V3 and V4); intraparietal sulcus; superior frontal gyrus (at the junction of the precentral sulcus, encompassing the frontal eye field); mid frontal gyrus, extending to dorsolateral prefrontal cortex; precuneus; and cingulate gyrus (extending to the upper part of the paracentral sulcus, containing the supplementary eye field). The contrast between intermixed and blocked stimuli revealed the same general pattern. These regions broadly correspond to those identified by Mukai et al. (2007) and confirm the suggestion from Mundy, Honey, Downing, et al. (2009) that similar brain regions are involved in perceptual learning based on differences in exposure schedule and those based on exposure per se. Moreover, they also confirm the idea that similar regions are involved when perceptual learning involves brief exposure to complex stimuli and long exposure to simple stimuli.

In addition to these group-based analyses, the additional power of this experiment afforded a correlational analysis of the relationship between behavioral performance and activity changes. This revealed that in both visual cortex (V1–V4) and attentional regions (intraparietal sulcus, frontal eye field, supplementary eye field, and dorsolateral prefrontal cortex), there was a negative correlation between the size of the behavioral effect of perceptual learning (performance on intermixed stimuli – performance on novel stimuli) and the difference in activity (intermixed stimuli – novel stimuli). That is, in all of these regions, the difference in activity elicited by intermixed stimuli relative to novel stimuli was greatest in subjects for whom the improvement in behavioral performance produced by perceptual learning was small and lowest in subjects who showed large behavioral effects of perceptual learning. The only difference in this relationship across regions was the overall level of activity – for example, in V1 and V2, activity was greater for intermixed than for novel in participants who showed the smallest effects of perceptual learning on behavioral performance, and this difference decreased as the behavioral effects of exposure increased, while in V3 and V4 there was little or no difference in activity elicited by intermixed and novel stimuli for weak perceptual learners, but the novel stimuli elicited progressively greater activity as the behavioral effects increased. Perhaps most critically, the same relationships were seen for the contrast between intermixed and blocked stimuli, with the exception of V1 and V2, where there was no correlation between performance and activity. A significant interaction between the activity/behavior relationships intermixed versus blocked (exposure schedule) and intermixed versus novel (amount of exposure) in V1 and V2 confirmed that this was a genuine difference in these regions. The similarity of the activity/behavior relationships for the remainder of the regions analyzed was attested to by the absence of any such interactions outside V1 and V2.

Putting the differences in V1 and V2 aside for one moment, these behavior/activity correlations are particularly interesting with respect to the brain mechanisms underpinning visual perceptual learning. First, they are broadly consistent with the idea that the development of discrimination ability with experience might reflect a reduction in brain activity (perhaps as a result of refining the representations to focus on the critical features of the stimuli). Second, the fact that different regions – most obviously V1 and V2 compared with V3 and V4 in this experiment – showed different baseline levels of activation might help explain the apparent discrepancies across previous studies if it is assumed that the weighting across visual cortex for different stimuli/situations might vary.

These correlations are also interesting with respect to the general questions regarding the nature of perceptual learning outlined above. First, the fact that similar behavior/activity relationships are seen in both visual cortex and attentional regions is consistent with the contribution of both top-down and bottom-up processes to the development of stimulus representations. Of course, because these are correlations, it is not possible to make a definitive causal interpretation with respect to either set of regions (e.g., the activity in attentional regions might be the product of stimulus-driven processes making some features more salient than others). But even with this caveat, it is important that neither the top-down nor stimulus-driven bottom-up account has been invalidated. Second, the fact that the bulk of the behavior/activity correlations were common to both the effects of exposure schedule and amount of exposure suggests that they share, at least in part, a common neural basis. Of course, the existence of a common brain substrate need not indicate that a single cognitive mechanism underlies perceptual learning, and the lack of V1 or V2 differential activity following intermixed versus blocked exposure (and the presence of this differential activity when contrasting intermixed with novel stimuli) points to some level of divergence in brain processing. That said, the fact that the bulk of the behavior/activity correlations were common to both sources of perceptual learning is certainly consistent with largely common cognitive and brain mechanisms. Indeed, if there are external reasons why V1 and V2 might not be differentially activated after intermixed and blocked exposure, then entirely common mechanisms might well be responsible. For example, V1 and V2 might initially be involved in local, feature discriminations, but they might be superseded once more complex configural information becomes available (cf. the reverse hierarchy theory of perceptual learning, Ahissar and Hochstein, 2004), and if the same local features are present in all stimuli, they might not amenable to the effects of comparison over and above simple exposure. It is also important to recognize here that the relationship between blood-oxygen-level-dependent response (BOLD) in these regions and implied neural function is neither simple nor entirely understood (e.g., Logothetis & Wandell, 2004). It remains a matter for further investigation to relate our understanding of neural mechanisms with more complex modeling of the BOLD response in visual areas (e.g., Kay, Winawer, Rokem, Mezer, & Wandell, 2013).

In summary, functional imaging studies of perceptual learning suggest that the brain mechanisms recruited by visual perceptual learning are remarkably similar despite great disparities in terms of the stimuli and general training procedures. This commonality supports the suggestion made above that perceptual learning within psychophysical and associative traditions might not be as divergent as they have been supposed. In particular, the possibility that both top-down attentional and bottom-up stimulus-driven mechanisms contribute to perceptual learning has been reinforced. Moreover, taken alongside the fact that the behavioral products of comparing exposed with novel, and intermixed with blocked exposure are similar (they both produce an improvement in the ability to discriminate between stimuli), the commonality of the brain processes recruited suggests that the nature of exposure primarily influences the degree or speed of perceptual learning rather than the quality or kind of that learning – at least when considering brief exposure to relatively complex stimuli. This is not to say that only the amount of exposure is important for perceptual learning (cf. Gaffan, 1996), but rather there is a difference in the degree to which different schedules of exposure afford the involvement of the cognitive and brain mechanisms supporting perceptual learning.

Concluding Comments

The chapter began by outlining the somewhat separate associative and psychophysical traditions of perceptual learning research. Notwithstanding the general differences in the types of stimuli and exposure methods used, it is encouraging that there appears to be a substantial commonality in the underlying cognitive and brain mechanisms being considered within both traditions. In particular, some combination of top-down and bottom-up mechanisms appears to be required to explain the range of behavioral and functional imaging results observed. Moreover, the most general insight from the associative tradition regarding the importance of exposure schedule (and its ability to facilitate comparison between stimuli) has been reinforced by the demonstration of exposure schedule effects on the brain mechanisms recruited by perceptual learning, and refined by the discovery that these brain mechanisms substantially overlap with those recruited by the amount of exposure alone. However, it should be remembered that these suggestions are derived from the analysis of largely correlational techniques. To truly demonstrate that attentional and stimulus-driven mechanisms are required for perceptual learning from stimuli ranging from the complex to the very simple, for exposure ranging from seconds to weeks, and for the schedule and amount of exposure, this will require confirmation from studies that directly investigate the functionality of the relevant brain regions and putative cognitive processes. One means to this end is exemplified by the examination of patients' focal brain damage to confirm the causal role of subregions of the medial temporal lobe in stimulus-specific aspects of perceptual learning and discrimination (Mundy *et al.*, 2013), while another might be to use techniques such as transcranial direct current stimulation or transcranial magnetic stimulation to temporarily manipulate the function of specific brain regions. The themes emerging from the functional imaging of perceptual learning and the cross-fertilization between associative and psychophysical research traditions are exciting but remain to be fully explored.

Notes

1 Perhaps associative theorists are too fond of such mock-algebraic descriptions, for many nonspecialists have complained about the impenetrable lists of As and Bs. However, this abstract terminology can be very convenient, and so we shall not entirely avoid it here in the hope of exemplifying its utility while attempting to avoid further contributions to "the barbarous terminology" that comprises "one of the most repellent features of the study of conditioning" (Mackintosh, 1983, p. 19).
2 See Dwyer *et al.* (2011) and Mundy *et al.* (2007) for a more detailed explanation of why the accounts of perceptual learning presented by Hall (2003) and McLaren and Mackintosh (2000) cannot provide a complete explanation of how comparison influences perceptual learning in humans.
3 The idea that perceptual learning might depend on reweighting the connections between basic visual detection channels and a decision unit (rather than changes in the basic detection mechanisms, or in the action of the decision unit) has also been considered within the psychophysical tradition (e.g., Dosher & Lu, 1999; Petrov, Dosher, & Lu, 2005).
4 While this is much shorter exposure than is typical for experiments conducted within the psychophysical tradition, it has been shown to produce reliable differences between exposed and novel stimuli as well as between stimuli exposed according to different schedules (Dwyer *et al.*, 2004, 2011; Mundy *et al.*, 2006, 2007; Mundy, Honey, & Dwyer, 2009).

References

Ahissar, M., & Hochstein, S. (2004). The reverse hierarchy theory of visual perceptual learning. *Trends in Cognitive Sciences*, 8, 457–464.

Artigas, A. A., Chamizo, V. D., & Peris, J. M. (2001). Inhibitory associations between neutral stimuli: A comparative approach. *Animal Learning and Behavior*, 29, 46–65.

Ball, K., & Sekuler, R. (1982). A specific and enduring improvement in visual–motion discrimination. *Science, 218,* 697–698.
Bennett, C. H., & Mackintosh, N. J. (1999). Comparison and contrast as a mechanism of perceptual learning? *Quarterly Journal of Experimental Psychology, 52B,* 253–272.
Casco, C., Campana, G., Grieco, A., & Fuggetta, G. (2004). Perceptual learning modulates electrophysiological and psychophysical response to visual texture segmentation in humans. *Neuroscience Letters, 371,* 18–23.
Corbetta, M., & Shulman, G. L. (2002). Control of goal-directed and stimulus-driven attention in the brain. *Nature Reviews Neuroscience, 3,* 201–215.
de Zilva, D., & Mitchell, C. J. (2012). Effects of exposure on discrimination of similar stimuli and on memory for their unique and common features. *Quarterly Journal of Experimental Psychology, 65,* 1123–1138.
Dosher, B. A., & Lu, Z. L. (1999). Mechanisms of perceptual learning. *Vision Research, 39,* 3197–3221.
Dubois, S., Rossion, B., Schiltz, C., Bodart, J. M., Michel, C., Bruyer, R., & Crommelinck, M. (1999). Effect of familiarity on the processing of human faces. *Neuroimage, 9,* 278–289.
Dwyer, D. M. (2008). Perceptual learning: Complete transfer across retinal locations. *Current Biology, 18,* R1134–R1136.
Dwyer, D. M., Bennett, C. H., Mackintosh, N. J. (2001). Evidence for inhibitory associations between the unique elements of two compound flavours. *Quarterly Journal of Experimental Psychology, 54B,* 97–109.
Dwyer, D. M., Hodder, K. I., & Honey, R. C. (2004). Perceptual learning in humans: Roles of preexposure schedule, feedback, and discrimination assay. *Quarterly Journal of Experimental Psychology, 57B,* 245–259.
Dwyer, D. M., & Honey, R. C. (2007). The effects of habituation training on compound conditioning are not reversed by an associative activation treatment. *Journal of Experimental Psychology: Animal Behavior Processes, 33,* 185–190.
Dwyer, D. M., & Mackintosh, N. J. (2002). Perceptual learning: Alternating exposure to two compound flavours creates inhibitory associations between their unique features. *Animal Learning & Behavior, 30,* 201–207.
Dwyer, D. M., Mundy, M. E., & Honey, R. C. (2011). The role of stimulus comparison in human perceptual learning: Effects of distractor placement. *Journal of Experimental Psychology: Animal Behavior Processes, 37,* 300–307.
Espinet, A., Iraola, J. A., Bennett, C. H., & Mackintosh, N. J. (1995). Inhibitory associations between neutral stimuli in flavor-aversion conditioning. *Animal Learning and Behavior, 23,* 361–368.
Fahle, M. (2002). Introduction. In M. Fahle & T. Poggio (Eds.), *Perceptual learning* (pp. ix–xx). Cambridge, MA: MIT Press.
Fiorentini, A., & Berardi, N. (1980). Perceptual-learning specific for orientation and spatial-frequency. *Nature, 287,* 43–44.
Furmanski, C. S., & Engel, S. A. (2000). Perceptual learning in object recognition: object specificity and size Invariance. *Vision Research, 40,* 473–484.
Furmanski, C. S., Schluppeck, D., & Engel, S. A. (2004). Learning strengthens the response of primary visual cortex to simple patterns. *Current Biology, 14,* 573–578.
Gaffan, D. (1996). Associative and perceptual learning and the concept of memory systems. *Cognitive Brain Research, 5,* 69–80.
Gibson, E. J. (1963). Perceptual learning. *Annual Review of Psychology, 14,* 29–56.
Gibson, E. J. (1969). *Principles of perceptual learning and development.* New York, NY: Appelton-Century-Crofts.

Gilbert, C., Ito, M., Kapadia, M., & Westheimer, G. (2000). Interactions between attention, context and learning in primary visual cortex. *Vision Research, 40,* 1217–1226.

Gold, J., Bennett, P. J., & Sekuler, A. B. (1999). Signal but not noise changes with perceptual learning. *Nature, 402,* 176–178.

Goldstone, R. L. (1998). Perceptual learning. *Annual Review of Psychology, 49,* 585–612.

Hall, G. (1991). *Perceptual and associative learning.* Oxford, UK: Clarendon Press/Oxford University Press.

Hall, G. (2003). Learned changes in the sensitivity of stimulus representations: Associative and nonassociative mechanisms. *Quarterly Journal of Experimental Psychology, 56B,* 43–55.

Hall, G., Blair, C. A. J., & Artigas, A. A. (2006). Associative activation of stimulus representations restores lost salience: Implications for perceptual learning. *Journal of Experimental Psychology: Animal Behavior Processes, 32,* 145–155.

Honey, R. C., & Bateson, P. (1996). Stimulus comparison and perceptual learning: Further evidence and evaluation from an imprinting procedure. *Quarterly Journal of Experimental Psychology, 49B,* 259–269.

Honey, R. C., Bateson, P., & Horn, G. (1994). The role of stimulus comparison in perceptual learning: An investigation with the domestic chick. *Quarterly Journal of Experimental Psychology, 47B,* 83–103.

Honey, R. C., Close, J., & Lin, T. E. (2010). Acquired distinctiveness and equivalence: A synthesis. In C. J. Mitchell & M. E. Le Pelley (Eds.), *Attention and associative learning: From brain to behaviour* (pp. 159–186). Oxford, UK: Oxford University Press.

Honey, R. C., Mundy, M. E., & Dwyer, D. M. (2012). Remembering kith and kin is underpinned by rapid memory updating: Implications for exemplar theory. *Journal of Experimental Psychology: Animal Behavior Processes, 38,* 433–439.

Jacoby, L. L. (1978). Interpreting the effects of repetition: Solving a problem versus remembering a solution. *Journal of Verbal Learning and Verbal Behavior, 17,* 649–667.

James, W. (1890). *The principles of psychology.* Oxford, UK: Holt.

Jones, S. P., & Dwyer, D. M. (2013). Perceptual learning with complex visual stimuli is based on location, rather than content, of discriminating features. *Journal of Experimental Psychology: Animal Behavior Processes, 39,* 152–165.

Karni, A., & Sagi, D. (1991). Where practice makes perfect in texture-discrimination – Evidence for primary visual-cortex plasticity. *Proceedings of the National Academy of Sciences of the United States of America, 88,* 4966–4970.

Kay, K. N., Winawer, J., Rokem, A., Mezer, A., & Wandell, B. A. (2013). A two-stage cascade model of BOLD responses in human visual cortex. *PLoS Computational Biology, 9.*

Lavis, Y., & Mitchell, C. (2006). Effects of preexposure on stimulus discrimination: An investigation of the mechanisms responsible for human perceptual learning. *Quarterly Journal of Experimental Psychology, 59,* 2083–2101.

Lewis, C. M., Baldassarre, A., Committeri, G., Romani, G. L., & Corbetta, M. (2009). Learning sculpts the spontaneous activity of the resting human brain. *Proceedings of the National Academy of Sciences of the United States of America, 106,* 17558–17563.

Li, W., Piech, V., & Gilbert, C. D. (2004). Perceptual learning and top-down influences in primary visual cortex. *Nature Neuroscience, 7,* 651–657.

Logothetis, N. K., & Wandell, B. A. (2004). Interpreting the BOLD signal. *Annual Review of Physiology, 66,* 735–769.

Mackintosh, N. J. (1983). *Conditioning and associative learning.* Oxford, UK: Carendon Press.

Mackintosh, N. J., Kaye, H., & Bennett, C. H. (1991). Perceptual learning in flavour aversion conditioning. *Quarterly Journal of Experimental Psychology, 43B,* 297–322.

McGovern, D. P., Roach, N. W., & Webb, B. S. (2012). Perceptual learning reconfigures the effects of visual adaptation. *Journal of Neuroscience, 32,* 13621–13629.

McGovern, D. P., Webb, B. S., & Peirce, J. W. (2012). Transfer of perceptual learning between different visual tasks. *Journal of Vision, 12*, 4.

McKee, S. P., & Westheimer, G. (1978). Improvement in vernier acuity with practice. *Perception and Psychophysics, 24*, 258–262.

McLaren, I. P. L. (1997). Categorization and perceptual learning: An analogue of the face inversion effect. *Quarterly Journal of Experimental Psychology, 50A*, 257–273.

McLaren, I. P. L., & Mackintosh, N. J. (2000). An elemental model of associative learning: I. Latent inhibition and perceptual learning. *Animal Learning and Behavior, 28*, 211–246.

Mitchell, C., & Hall, G. (2014). Can theories of animal discrimination explain perceptual learning in humans? *Psychological Bulletin. 140*, 283–307.

Mitchell, C., Nash, S., & Hall, G. (2008). The intermixed-blocked effect in human perceptual learning is not the consequence of trial spacing. *Journal of Experimental Psychology: Learning Memory and Cognition, 34*, 237–242.

Mollon, J. (1974). Aftereffects and the brain. *New Scientist, 61*, 479–482.

Mondragon, E., & Murphy, R. A. (2010). Perceptual learning in an appetitive conditioning procedure: Analysis of the effectiveness of the common element. *Behavioural Processes, 83*, 247–256.

Mukai, I., Kim, D., Fukunaga, M., Japee, S., Marrett, S., & Ungerleider, L. G. (2007). Activations in visual and attention-related areas predict and correlate with the degree of perceptual learning. *Journal of Neuroscience, 27*, 11401–11411.

Mundy, M. E., Downing, P. E., Dwyer, D. M., Honey, R. C., & Graham, K. S. (2013). A critical role for the hippocampus and perirhinal cortex in perceptual learning of scenes and faces: complementary findings from amnesia and FMRI. *The Journal of Neuroscience, 33*, 10490–10502.

Mundy, M. E., Downing, P. E., Honey, R. C., Singh, K. D., Graham, K. S., & Dwyer, D. M. (2014). Brain correlates of perceptual learning based on the amount and schedule of exposure. *PLoS ONE, 9*, e101011.

Mundy, M. E., Dwyer, D. M., & Honey, R. C. (2006). Inhibitory associations contribute to perceptual learning in humans. *Journal of Experimental Psychology: Animal Behavior Processes, 32*, 178–184.

Mundy, M. E., Honey, R. C., Downing, P. E., Wise, R. G., Graham, K. S., & Dwyer, D. M. (2009). Material-independent and material-specific activation in functional MRI after perceptual learning. *Neuroreport, 20*, 1397–1401.

Mundy, M. E., Honey, R. C., & Dwyer, D. M. (2007). Simultaneous presentation of similar stimuli produces perceptual learning in human picture processing. *Journal of Experimental Psychology: Animal Behavior Processes, 33*, 124–138.

Mundy, M. E., Honey, R. C., & Dwyer, D. M. (2009). Superior discrimination between similar stimuli after simultaneous exposure. *Quarterly Journal of Experimental Psychology, 62*, 18–25.

Petrov, A. A., Dosher, B. A., & Lu, Z. L. (2005). The dynamics of perceptual learning: An incremental reweighting model. *Psychological Review, 112*, 715–743.

Poggio, T., Fahle, M., & Edelman, S. (1992). Fast perceptual-learning in visual hyperacuity. *Science, 256*, 1018–1021.

Postman, L. (1955). Association theory and perceptual learning. *Psychological-Review, 62*, 438–446.

Pourtois, G., Rauss, K. S., Vuilleumier, P., & Schwartz, S. (2008). Effects of perceptual learning on primary visual cortex activity in humans. *Vision Research, 48*, 55–62.

Schiltz, C., Bodart, J. M., Dubois, S., Dejardin, S., Michel, C., Roucoux, A., et al.... Orban, G. A. (1999). Neuronal mechanisms of perceptual learning: Changes in human brain activity with training in orientation discrimination. *Neuroimage, 9*, 46–62.

Schwartz, S., Maquet, P., & Frith, C. (2002). Neural correlates of perceptual learning: A functional MIR study of visual texture discrimination. *Proceedings of the National Academy of Sciences of the United States of America, 99*, 17137–17142.

Schwarzkopf, D. S., Zhang, J., & Kourtzi, Z. (2009). Flexible learning of natural statistics in the human brain. *Journal of Neurophysiology, 102*, 1854–1867.

Symonds, M., & Hall, G. (1995). Perceptual learning in flavour aversion conditioning: Roles of stimulus comparison and latent inhibition of common elements. *Learning and Motivation, 26*, 203–219.

Vogels, R., & Orban, G. A. (1985). The effect of practice on the oblique effect in line orientation judgments. *Vision Research, 25*, 1679–1687.

Wang, T., & Mitchell, C. J. (2011). Attention and relative novelty in human perceptual learning. *Journal of Experimental Psychology: Animal Behavior Processes, 37*, 436–445.

Xiao, L.-Q., Zhang, J.-Y., Wang, R., Klein, S. A., Levi, D. M., & Yu, C. (2008). Complete transfer of perceptual learning across retinal locations enabled by double training. *Current Biology, 18*, 1922–1926.

Yotsumoto, Y., Watanabe, T., & Sasaki, Y. (2008). Different dynamics of performance and brain activation in the time course of perceptual learning. *Neuron, 57*, 827–833.

Zhang, J. Y., Zhang, G. L., Xiao, L. Q., Klein, S. A., Levi, D. M., & Yu, C. (2010). Rule-based learning explains visual perceptual learning and its specificity and transfer. *Journal of Neuroscience, 30*, 12323–12328.

Zhang, T., Xiao, L. Q., Klein, S. A., Levi, D. M., & Yu, C. (2010). Decoupling location specificity from perceptual learning of orientation discrimination. *Vision Research, 50*, 368–374.

10
Human Perceptual Learning and Categorization

Paulo F. Carvalho and Robert L. Goldstone

A rainbow is a continuous range of wavelengths of light. If we perceived the physical world directly, we would see a continuous set of shades (akin to shades of gray). However, when we look at a rainbow, what we see is a distinct number of bands of color (usually seven). This is a striking example of how our perception is warped by our categories – in this case, color. Why does this happen? The world is a highly complex environment. If we were to perceive every single pressure oscillation, light wavelength, and so forth, the world would be a "blooming, buzzing, confusion" (James, 1981, p. 462) of sounds, and sights. However, as with the rainbow, our perception of the world is highly organized into objects, places, groups. This organization is both perceptual and conceptual in nature and is governed not only by the physical properties of the world but also by our experiences.

Perceptual learning has been defined as "any relatively permanent and consistent change in the perception of a stimulus array, following practice or experience with this array" (Gibson, 1963, p. 29). More broadly, it is common to conceptualize the behavioral rather than perceptual effects in terms of, for instance an improvement in performance in perceptual tasks following experience (Garrigan & Kellman, 2008). These improvements on how information is "picked up" can take place at different levels. For example, improvement as a result of experience has been seen for low-level perceptual tasks such as orientation discrimination (Furmanski & Engel, 2000; Petrov, Dosher, & Lu, 2006) or motion perception (Liu & Vaina, 1998; Matthews, Liu, Geesaman, & Qian, 1999), among others. Improvements at this level are usually highly specific to the parameters of the stimuli and task, from the color of the stimuli (Matthews *et al.*, 1999), stimulus orientation (Furmanski & Engel, 2000; Petrov *et al.*, 2006), retinal position (Dill & Fahle, 1999), and retinal size (Ahissar & Hochstein, 1993), down to the eye used during training (Karni & Sagi, 1991). This specificity has been taken to demonstrate the plasticity of the early stages of visual processing, and in fact, single-cell recording studies have shown shifts in receptive field position (neural reorganization) following training (Pons *et al.*, 1991). Perceptual improvements can also be seen for higher-level perceptual tasks such as object recognition (Furmanski & Engel, 2000) or face discrimination (Dwyer, Mundy, Vladeanu, & Honey, 2009), for example. Neuroimaging correlates of changes in early visual

---

The Wiley Handbook on the Cognitive Neuroscience of Learning, First Edition.
Edited by Robin A. Murphy and Robert C. Honey.
© 2016 John Wiley & Sons, Ltd. Published 2016 by John Wiley & Sons, Ltd.

processing resulting from this kind of experience have also been demonstrated (Dolan et al., 1997; for a more complete analysis of the neural basis of perceptual learning, see Chapter 9). Perhaps not surprisingly, many of these perceptual improvements have been demonstrated to take place within the first seven years of life (Aslin & Smith, 1988), but evidence shows that they may also occur throughout life when a perceptual reorganization is beneficial. For instance, adult human chicken sorters show improvements in sexing young chickens with perceptual experience (Biederman & Shiffrar, 1987).

All things considered, the evidence from perceptual learning research indicates that our perception (from higher levels in the visual stream hierarchy down to low-level perceptual areas, such as V1) is tuned to the perceptual input available in our environment. Another source of perceptual structuring of our environment can be categorization. When we look around, we usually do not see series of linear segments and wavelengths, but rather we blue mugs and white books. Categorization is a highly pervasive human activity (Murphy, 2002). Identifying an animal as a cat or the person across the street as Mary are examples of categorization in everyday life. Moreover, the concepts we form are directly linked to our experience of the world, reducing the amount of information provided by the world to meaningful units (Goldstone, Kersten, & Carvalho, 2012). In much the same way that the rainbow is not perceived as a continuous set of shades, the world is internally organized in discrete categories.

Categories constitute equivalence classes. Every time we categorize something as "X" for a purpose, it is treated like every other object in the same category and is treated as more similar to all the other Xs than it would have been if it were not so categorized (Goldstone, 1995; Sloman, 1996). This cognitive equivalence has been shown to have impacts at a perceptual level. Sometimes, these new categorical structures can be learned by using previously existent perceptual features (Nosofsky, Palmeri, & McKinley, 1994). In fact, in many traditional models of categorization, categories are defined as having a fixed set of features or dimension values (e.g., Kruschke, 1992; Nosofsky, 1986).

However, categorization can also "shape" perception by creating new perceptual units that did not exist before the categorization experience (Schyns, Goldstone, & Thibaut, 1998; Schyns & Murphy, 1994). Similarly, categorization experience can change the way perceptual information is segmented or parsed (Hock, Webb, & Cavedo, 1987; Wills & McLaren, 1998). Categorization, in this sense, not only provides organization to an otherwise hopelessly complex world but works to adapt the perceptual features used to perceive this world. Categorization is thus the result of perceptual experience and simultaneously a pervasive influence on that same perceptual experience (Goldstone, 2000; Goldstone, Steyvers, Spencer-Smith & Kersten, 2000; Lin & Murphy, 1997; Schyns et al., 1998; Schyns & Murphy, 1994; Schyns & Rodet, 1997).

Although category learning and perceptual learning constitute two substantially different processes of information structuring (for instance, in their specificity and level of abstraction), they are intrinsically related in their contribution to perceptual flexibility and adaptation of our perceptual systems to the environment. In fact, both are the result of perceptual experience with the world and both act to shape that same perceptual experience for future use. This intricate relation makes it likely that they partake of some of the same mechanisms of change (Spratling & Johnson, 2006). In fact, to some extent, shared brain loci have been identified in neuroimaging (Xu et al., 2010).

The goal of the present review is to highlight empirical and theoretical developments from both perceptual learning and category learning that suggest a shared set of mechanisms between the two learning processes. A unified treatment of perceptual and category learning has precedence in the literature (Austerweil & Griffiths, 2013; Goldstone, 2003; Mundy, Honey, & Dwyer, 2007; Wills, Suret, & McLaren, 2004) but is still fairly novel in the context of separately developing literature. The majority of models of category learning assume a fixed, preestablished perceptual representation to describe the objects to be categorized (Aha & Goldstone, 1992; Kruschke, 1992; Nosofsky, 1986), and conversely, the majority of models of perceptual learning do not describe how the adapted perceptual representations are included in conceptual representations (Dosher & Lu, 1998; Lu & Dosher, 2004). This review will include research at different levels of analysis (including psychophysics and developmental approaches using low-level and higher-order perceptual tasks) and both human and nonhuman animal studies.

Mechanisms of Perceptual Change

There are several different ways in which perception can change through experience (either perceptual or conceptual). In the following sections, we review evidence of changes in attentional weighting to different dimensions, differentiation of dimensions and unitization of dimensions of stimuli, following simple exposure (perceptual learning) and category learning exposure (see also Goldstone, 1998).

Attentional weighting

One of the important ways in which experience with categorizing objects can shape perception is by changing what is attended, highlighting perceptual aspects that are important for a purpose. In general, categorization acts to emphasize task-relevant dimensions (e.g., color) while deemphasizing previously salient features that are not relevant for a task (Livingston & Andrews, 1995). Simultaneously, this experience leads to decreased discriminability between dimensions that are not relevant for categorization (Honey & Hall, 1989).

The role of attention in perceptual learning has been emphasized before. Attention to relevant features has been shown to be necessary for perceptual learning (Ahissar & Hochstein, 1993; Ahissar, Laiwand, Kozminsky, & Hochstein, 1998; Schoups, Vogels, Qian, & Orban, 2001; Tsushima & Watanabe, 2009; but see Watanabe, Nanez, & Sasaki, 2001). Moreover, passively attending to relevant features can improve performance in an unrelated task (Gutnisky, Hansen, Iliescu, & Dragoi, 2009). Attention has also been shown to modulate activity in early cortical areas of visual processing (Posner & Gilbert, 1999; Sengpiel & Hübener, 1999; Watanabe, Harner, et al., 1998; Watanabe, Sasaki, et al., 1998), usually by enhancing the signal for task-relevant stimuli (Moran & Desimone, 1985) and inhibiting task-irrelevant signals (for reviews, see Desimone & Duncan, 1995; Friedman-Hill, Robertson, Desimone, & Ungerleider, 2003). In the auditory modality, Weinberger (1993) describes evidence that cells in the primary auditory cortex become tuned to the frequency of often-repeated tones, and training in a selective attention task produces differential responses as early as the cochlea (Puel, Bonfils, & Pujol, 1988). This amazing degree of top-down modulation of a peripheral neural system is mediated by descending pathways of neurons that project from the auditory cortex all the way back to olivocochlear neurons, which directly project to outer hair cells within the cochlea – an impressively peripheral locus of modulation.

Attentional weighting can also happen at later levels in the perceptual system. For example, English-speaking children have a strong bias toward attending to shape when categorizing new objects (the "shape bias"; Landau, Smith, & Jones, 1988). One main hypothesis is that, through repeated experience with objects, English-speaking children learn that shape is a strongly reliable cue for category membership, thus reinforcing attention toward shape compared with any other dimension of the object (Landau et al., 1988). The role of previous experience can be demonstrated by the absence of a shape bias in children with less categorization experience (Jones & Smith, 1999) and the extension of novel nouns to novel shape matching objects following extensive experience with novel shape-based categories (Smith, Jones, Landau, Gershkoff-Stowe, & Samuelson, 2002).

In the same fashion, experience with categories can lead adults to attend to dimensions that were previously relevant for categorization (acquired distinctiveness) or ignore dimensions that are category-irrelevant (acquired equivalence). For example, Goldstone and Steyvers (2001 Experiment 1) had adults learn to categorize morphed images of four faces into two categories using one of two arbitrary dimensions (see Figure 10.1 for stimuli examples and main results). Participants then completed a transfer categorization task in which the relevance of the dimensions from the initial categorization was manipulated. Interestingly, best transfer performance from a learned categorization to a novel one was achieved when both categorizations shared either relevant or irrelevant dimensions, even when the exemplars of the transfer categorization had nothing in common with the original ones (thus, the values along those dimensions were different; see also Op de Beeck, Wagemans, & Vogels, 2003).

The nature of the categorization experience can also change how stimuli are perceived and encoded. Archambault, O'Donnell, and Schyns (1999) presented learners with images of scenes containing different objects and had participants learn the objects either at a general level of categorization (e.g., "it is a computer") or at a specific level of categorization (e.g., "it is Mary's computer"). Participants then completed a change-detection task in which they had to indicate what changed between two familiar scenes. The results show that participants had to see a pair of images more times to be able to identify a change in objects they had learned at the general level than objects they had learned at the specific level. No difference was seen for objects not categorized during the initial categorization task. Similar results were obtained by Tanaka, Curran, and Sheinberg (2005) in a training experiment that controlled for the amount of exposure at different levels of categorization. In this experiment, after completing a pretest bird-discrimination task, participants completed a discrimination training session where they were trained to discriminate between different bird images at either the species (basic) level or at the family

(A)

Dimension A

1   2

3

Dimension B

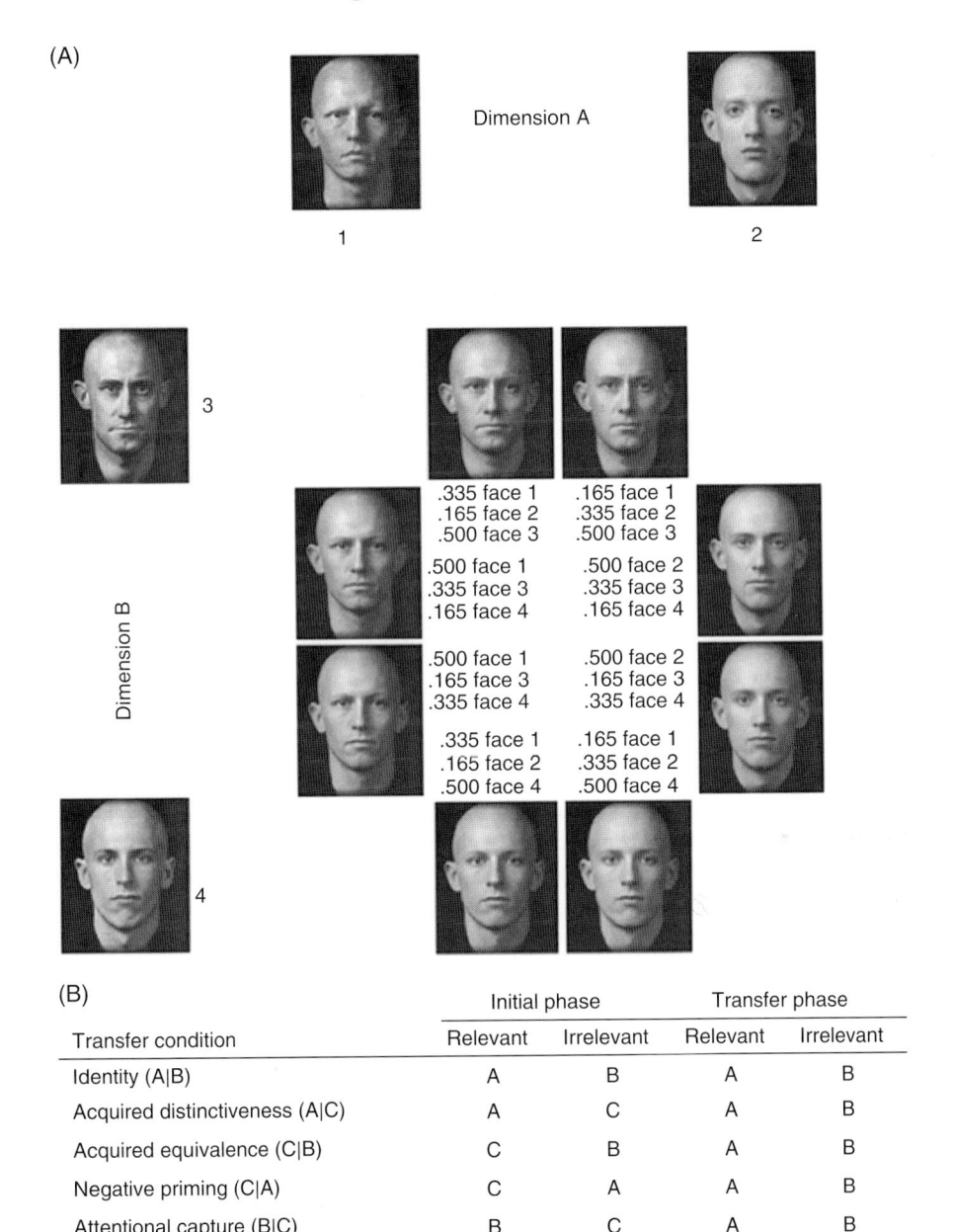

.335 face 1   .165 face 1
.165 face 2   .335 face 2
.500 face 3   .500 face 3

.500 face 1   .500 face 2
.335 face 3   .335 face 3
.165 face 4   .165 face 4

.500 face 1   .500 face 2
.165 face 3   .165 face 3
.335 face 4   .335 face 4

.335 face 1   .165 face 1
.165 face 2   .335 face 2
.500 face 4   .500 face 4

4

(B)

	Initial phase		Transfer phase	
Transfer condition	Relevant	Irrelevant	Relevant	Irrelevant
Identity (A|B)	A	B	A	B
Acquired distinctiveness (A|C)	A	C	A	B
Acquired equivalence (C|B)	C	B	A	B
Negative priming (C|A)	C	A	A	B
Attentional capture (B|C)	B	C	A	B
90 degree rotation (B|A)	B	A	A	B
Neutral control (C|D)	C	D	A	B

Figure 10.1 (A) Stimuli used in Goldstone and Steyvers (2001, Experiment 1). (B) Complete set of conditions, schematically depicted. Participants studied categories with two dimensions, one relevant for categorization and the other irrelevant, and then completed a transfer test. (C) Main results. As can be seen, the best performance was achieved when the transfer and study tasks shared one of the dimensions, regardless of relevance for categorization. Adapted from Goldstone and Steyvers (2001).

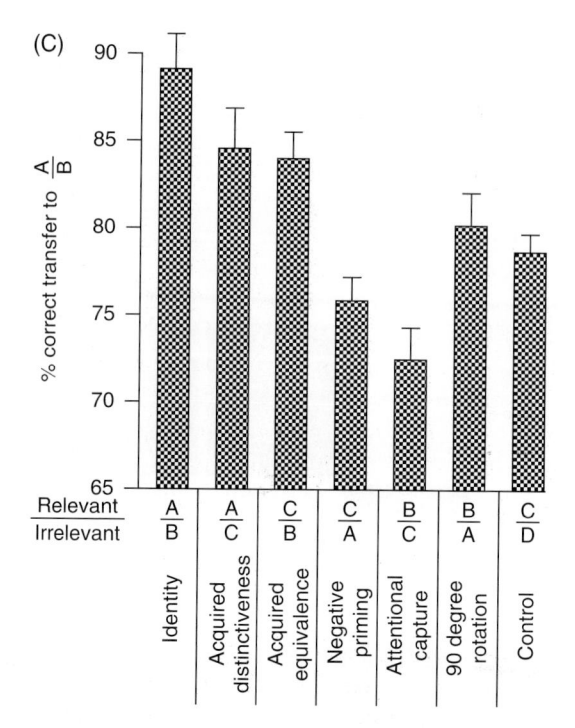

Figure 10.1 (Continued)

(subordinate) level. The results showed improved performance for birds from both groups but also better discrimination between birds of new species following training at the subordinate level. Taken together, these results indicate that the category level at which the images were studied changed what dimensions were attended to and thus how the images were perceived and later recalled.

Are these changes perceptual in nature or decisional ones? Most evidence suggests a perceptual shift and not a strategic one. For example, children attend to shape even when shape is not a reliable categorization cue in laboratory experiments. Given that attending to shape is not relevant for the task or strategic, this might be indicative of perceptual biases and not just decisional process to attend to the relevant properties (Graham, Namy, Gentner, & Meagher, 2010). Similarly, adults completing a visual search task continue to preferentially look for the item that had consistently been presented as the target, even when they know the item is no longer the target (Shiffrin & Schneider, 1977). The reverse is also true: People are slower finding a target that had previously been a distractor (i.e., negative priming, Tipper, 1992). Additionally, practice with one perceptual task does not improve performance in a different perceptual task when the two tasks depend on different attributes of the same stimuli (Ahissar & Hochstein, 1993). While some researchers argue that changes of attention to stimulus elements should be considered pre- or postperceptual (Pylyshyn, 1999), habitual attention to task-relevant features leads to their perceptual sensitization and affects how the objects are subjectively perceived (see Macpherson, 2011, for a theoretical analysis of some of the evidence for this) as well as perceptual discriminations that one can make (Goldstone, 1994).

All in all, attentional weighting and attention more broadly have been identified as an important mechanism of attentional change in both perceptual and category learning, with effects at different levels of the visual processing stream. Through attentional weighting, the way information is picked up is substantially altered, changing subsequent encounters with the same materials. These changes seem to take place at higher levels of the perceptual system as well as at lower levels. However, directing one's attention to certain dimensions requires the ability to perceive each of the stimuli's dimensions separately. This is not always possible. For instance, dimensions separable for adults, such as brightness and the size of a square, are not perceived as separable by children (Kemler & Smith, 1978; Smith & Kemler, 1978) and thus cannot be individually attended. Children also have difficulty making discriminations based on one single feature of objects but succeed at discriminations involving an integration of all the features (Smith, 1989). When two dimensions are perceived as fused, but only one dimension is deemed relevant from previous experience, differentiation takes place.

Differentiation

Differentiation involves an increase in the ability to discriminate between dimensions or stimuli that were psychologically fused together. Dimensions become separable when, as in the previous examples, one has the ability to attend to one of the dimensions while ignoring the other, even though this ability was originally absent. An important distinction between differentiation and attentional weighting lies in their different temporal profiles. Differentiation precedes the ability to differently attend to different dimensions in the sense that dimensions or stimuli that are psychologically fused together cannot be separately attended to. Thus, attentional weighting is a relatively rapid process that makes use of existing perceptual organizations, while differentiation requires more time and considerably more practice, *creating* novel perceptual organization.

Differentiation has been extensively studied in the animal learning literature as an example of experience-based perceptual change. A classic example is the finding that rats raised in cages where images of geometrical shapes are available are better at discriminating other geometrical shapes in subsequent tests (Gibson & Walk, 1956). Interestingly, this effect does not seem to be related to the greater plasticity of perceptual systems early in development (Hall, 1979) and has been replicated with shorter preexposure durations (Channell & Hall, 1981). Differentiation between geometrical shapes was achieved in these studies by repeated training with discriminations along the relevant dimension.

Similarly, improved perceptual taste discriminations are found in rats given exposure to two compound flavors, AX and BX, both quinine based (X), one with added sucrose (A), and another with added lemon (B). Later, only one of these compounds is paired with an injection of lithium chloride (LiCl), which induces illness and aversion to that taste. The measure of interest is usually how much of the other solution rats drink: If rats generalize the aversive conditioning from the paired solution to the other one, they will drink less of it. What is found is that preexposure to both compound solutions leads to less generalization of the aversion condition – thus suggesting increased discrimination between the two solutions (Honey & Hall, 1989; Mackintosh, Kaye, & Bennett, 1991; Symonds & Hall, 1995, 1997).

Although perceptual in nature, these results have been parsimoniously explained by associative theories. For example, Hall (1991, 2003) proposes that repeating a common feature (X) will result in continuous activation of that feature and habituation to it. The discriminating features (A and B), on the other hand, will only be activated associatively, which will reverse the process of habituation (for similar proposals involving increased attention to discrimination features, see Mitchell, Kadib, Nash, Lavis, & Hall, 2008; Mundy, Honey, & Dwyer, 2007, 2008). A similar explanation has been proposed, based on the establishment of inhibitory links between A and B (because each one predicts the absence of the other; McLaren & Mackintosh, 2000). Interestingly, contrary to cases of differentiation usually described as perceptual learning, such as orientation discrimination (e.g., Petrov, Dosher, & Lu, 2006) or motion perception (e.g., Liu & Vaina, 1998; Matthews, Liu, Geesaman, & Qian, 1999), the cases of differentiation often reported in animal learning are dependent less on the exact characteristics of the objects used during training. Evidence supporting this comes from work showing that the differentiation often transfers between objects or tasks. For example, Pick (1965) trained people to make a discrimination between two shapes, A and B, based on a dimension such as curvature of one of the lines or orientation of the base. People showed better transfer to a new discrimination when the same dimension was relevant for discriminating new objects, C and D, compared with a discrimination that involved one of the old shapes but a new dimension. This might indicate that different perceptual mechanisms are at work in different situations that require different levels of perceptual change. It is possible that perceptual changes resulting from novel associations between existing perceptual experiences require a different process than perceptual changes that result from reorganization of perceptual receptors, which speaks to the malleability of our perceptual system at multiple points in the information processing stream.

Another good example of differentiation comes from work with auditory stimuli. The Japanese language presents no distinction between the English sounds for /r/ and /l/. Thus, native Japanese speakers often have difficulty discriminating between these two sounds in English (Miyawaki et al., 1975; Werker & Logan, 1985). However, when given extensive experience with English words that include these two sounds, produced by several speakers and with immediate feedback, Japanese speakers can succeed at this discrimination (Lively, Logan, & Pisoni, 1993; Logan, Lively, & Pisoni, 1991). Moreover, this training improves Japanese speakers' utterances of words that include these sounds (Bradlow, Pisoni, Akahane-Yamada, & Tohkura, 1997).

Parallel results have also been found with human subjects using complex visual stimuli. For example, Wills, Suret, and McLaren (2004; see also Wills & McLaren, 1998) gave half of the participants repeated exposure to checkerboards similar to those presented in Figure 10.2. Each new checkerboard was created by randomly replacing squares of one of two base patterns. The other half of the participants completed an unrelated task. Critically, participants given preexposure with the checkerboards were better able to discriminate between the checkerboards than non-preexposed participants – preexposure enhanced learning to categorize the checkerboards into two groups. This basic result has been replicated and expanded in recent years, indicating not only improved discrimination between the stimuli but also improved attention and memory for the relevant dimensions of the stimuli or specific spatial

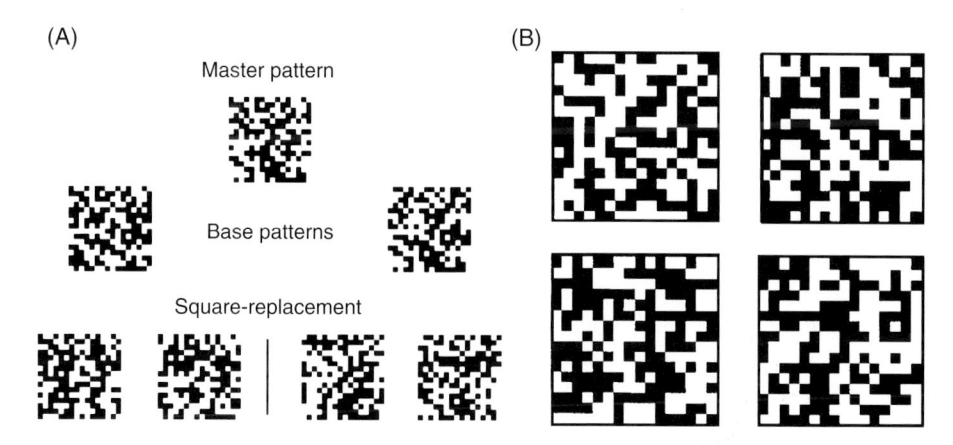

Figure 10.2 Examples of four checkerboard stimuli used by Wills *et al.* (2004) and Wills and McLaren (1998). (A) Example of the process by which the stimuli were created. (B) Examples of the type of checkerboard used. Adapted from Wills and McLaren (1998) and Wills *et al.* (2004).

locations (Carvalho & Albuquerque, 2012; de Zilva & Mitchell, 2012; Lavis & Mitchell, 2006; Wang, Lavis, Hall, & Mitchell, 2012; Wang & Mitchell, 2011). Studies that test both familiar and unfamiliar features in spatial positions that have been learned to be relevant show better discrimination for the former, suggesting that learning features does not always involve only learning to attend to specific locations (Hendrickson & Goldstone, 2009).

There is evidence that practice on these hard discriminations has cascading effects at multiple stages of the perceptual system as early as V1. One good example is the finding that practice in discriminating small motions in different directions significantly alters electrical brain potentials that occur within 100 ms of the stimulus onset (Fahle, 1994). These electrical changes associated with practice are centered over the part of visual cortex primarily responsible for motion perception (the medial temporal visual area MT) and relatively permanent, suggesting plasticity in early visual processing. Furmanski *et al.* (2004) used functional magnetic resonance imaging to measure brain activity before and after one month of practice detecting hard-to-see oriented line gratings. Training increased V1 response for the practiced orientation relative to the other orientations, and the magnitude of V1 changes was correlated with detection performance. Similarly, Bao *et al.* (2010) trained human subjects for one month to detect a diagonal grating, and found EEG differences in V1 for trained versus untrained orientations within 50–70 ms after the onset of the stimulus. The rapidity of the EEG difference combined with the demanding nature of the primary behavioral task during testing make it unlikely that the earliest EEG differences were mediated by top-down feedback from higher cortical levels. In the somewhat later visual area V4, single-cell recording studies in monkeys have also shown activity changes of cells in early visual cortex (Yang & Maunsell, 2004). Individual neurons with receptive fields overlapping the trained location of a line orientation discrimination developed stronger responses, and more narrow tuning, to the particular trained orientation, compared with neurons with receptive fields that did not fall on the trained location.

Changes in perceptual discrimination ability can also be found when participants are trained with categorizing the checkerboards, instead of simply being exposed to them. McLaren, Wills, and Graham (2010) report an experiment in which participants learned to differentiate between two categories of stimuli. In their experiment, participants were trained to categorize distortions of two prototypes (see Figure 10.2). Following this task, participants completed a discrimination task that included the prototype exemplars (never presented before), new exemplar distortions (similar to those presented before, but never presented), and new stimuli never presented (prototypes and exemplars from another participant). Participants were better at discriminating prototype and exemplar stimuli belonging to the categories previously presented, demonstrating learned differentiation between the categories studied, but not overall familiarization with the type of stimuli, which would have been demonstrated by better or equivalent performance for new, similar stimuli that were never presented.

Categorization can also improve discrimination between initially unseparable dimensions. For instance, saturation and brightness are usually perceived as fused together in adults (Burns & Shepp, 1988; Melara, Marks, & Potts, 1993). Goldstone (1994) demonstrated that it is possible to differentiate these two initially nondiscriminable dimensions via categorization training. Specifically, practice in a categorization task in which only one of these dimensions was relevant increased participants' discrimination in a same–different task involving that dimension (but not category-irrelevant dimensions). When both dimensions were relevant, discrimination was not selectively improved for just one of the dimensions, suggesting that categorization affects the separability of dimensions over and above simple exposure to the stimuli. Similar results were also found for dimensions initially perceived as separate, such as size and brightness (Goldstone, 1994).

Pevtzow and Goldstone (1994) extended these results to more complex dimensional spaces. Participants were initially given categorization practice with stick figures composed of six lines, in which a spatially contiguous subset was relevant for categorization. In a later phase, participants completed a whole–part task in which they had to judge whether a part was present or absent from the whole presented. Participants were significantly faster making this decision when it involved parts that were relevant for the previous categorization task, or complement parts that were left over in the whole object once the category-relevant parts were removed. Thus, segmentation of complex stimuli seems also to be influenced by previous categorization experience. Similar results were found for differentiation of initially integral dimensions following appropriate category training of shapes (Hockema, Blair, & Goldstone, 2005; but see Op de Beeck *et al.*, 2003).

Some of the neural substrata for these perceptual changes have also been identified. Following category training in which some dimensions were relevant and others were not, neurons in inferior temporal cortex of monkeys generate larger responses for discriminations along the relevant than the irrelevant dimension (Sigala & Logothetis, 2002). These changes indicate that category-level feedback shaped the sensitivity of inferior temporal neurons to the diagnostic dimensions (Hasegawa & Miyashita, 2002; Spratling & Johnson, 2006). Similarly, monkeys given discrimination training at a specific pitch frequency show improvements in discriminations for that frequency only, along with associated changes in primary auditory cortex (Recanzone, Schreiner, & Merzenich, 1993).

Another classic example of differentiation resulting from perceptual experience is face perception. People are generally better at identifying faces with which they are familiar (Shapiro & Penrod, 1986). O'Toole and Edelman (1996) tested both Japanese and American participants on discriminations between male and female faces, and found that these discriminations were quicker if the faces belonged to people from the same ethnicity as the participant. This discrimination is most likely connected with extensive experience discriminating faces and is accordingly likely to involve perceptual learning.

An interesting phenomenon in face perception is the face-inversion effect (Valentine & Bruce, 1986). In general terms, people are better at discriminating faces presented upright than upside down. This difference in performance is greater than that seen for other kinds of materials (Diamond & Carey, 1986). One possibility is that this is an expertise effect; continued experience discriminating faces makes adult humans experts at discriminating upright faces, but this performance deteriorates when faces are presented upside down, possibly due to the holistic processing of faces, related to unitization (see the next section) and the specificity associated with perceptual learning. Evidence for this claim comes from work showing no evidence of a face inversion effect in children younger than 10 years of age (Carey & Diamond, 1977; Flin, 1985), and studies with experts that show inversion effects with pictures of objects in their area of expertise (Carey & Diamond, 1977).

A similar effect can be found using abstract categories created with a prototype (hence sharing a common category structure, much like faces do). McLaren (1997) had participants categorize checkerboards created by adding random noise to each of two prototypes. Participants engaged in this categorization training until they reached a categorization criterion, that is, they were able to successfully categorize the exemplars at a criterion accuracy rate. In a subsequent discrimination task with novel stimuli drawn from the same categories, participants were more accurate in discriminating checkerboards presented upright than inverted (thus demonstrating an inversion effect). This inversion effect was not seen for untrained controls. Interestingly, when categories were created by shuffling rows in the checkerboard rather than adding noise to a prototype, no inversion effect was seen. This experiment demonstrates well how learning categories organized around a common perceptual organization helps tune the system to that common perceptual structure without involving an overall sensitization to stimuli sharing the same components but organized in different structures.

The evidence reviewed in this section makes it clear that perceptual differentiation of initially undifferentiated dimensions can be achieved by extensive experience. Finally, these changes seem to have an impact not only in how information is used but also at different steps of the perceptual system. Although the different loci of perceptual change between perceptual learning changes (early cortical areas) and conceptual-driven perceptual change (higher cortical areas) might at first sight seem indicative of differences between perceptual and conceptual learning, we would like to argue that they are better understood as part of a broader perceptual system (see Conclusions).

Unitization

In much the same way that initially fused dimensions become psychologically separable by differentiation, unitization is the process of fusing together features that were initially separately perceived. For example, work by Wheeler (1970) indicates that people are quicker at identifying the presence of a letter when words are presented compared with when letters are presented alone (see also Reicher, 1969). This might be indicative that when presented together in a coherent whole, letters in a word are perceived as a "unit."

Moreover, a familiar region of an ambiguous image is more likely to be perceived as the figure (i.e., the whole; Peterson & Gibson, 1993, 1994; Peterson & Lampignano, 2003; Vecera, Flevaris, & Filapek, 2004; Vecera & O'Reilly, 1998), and exposure to novel object configurations can bias subsequent object groupings (Zemel, Behrmann, Mozer, & Bavelier, 2002). Developmentally, it has been demonstrated that 3-year old children segment objects into smaller units than do 5-year-olds or adults (Tada & Stiles, 1996), and over the course of development children will increasingly rely more on the whole configuration of spatial patterns when making similarity judgments (Harrison & Stiles, 2009). Taken together, these results suggest that the units of perceptual processing change with experience and development toward more complex unitized components.

Shiffrin and Lightfoot (1997) showed that extensive experience with stimuli during a visual search task can result in unitization of the object's parts. In a search task, the number of distractors influences the speed of response to find a target if more than one feature is needed to identify the target from among the distractors. Shiffrin and Lightfoot's (1997) search task included target and distractors objects that were composed of several line segments. Critically, the target shared a line segment with each of the distractors, so that at any given time, at least two line segments were necessary to identify the target. Initially, search time was a function of number of distractors; however, after approximately 20 days of performing this task, participants experienced "pop-out." Pop-out is seen in search tasks when the time to find a target is not affected by the number of distractors and usually takes place when target and distractors differ in a single feature (Treisman & Gelade, 1980). Thus, after prolonged experience, participants perceived the entire object as a feature, and the target could be distinguished from the distractors by the single, whole-object feature. These data demonstrate that, with prolonged experience, people can come to represent as a single unit dimensions that were initially separate (for similar results, see Austerweil & Griffiths, 2009, 2013).

Face processing is also a good example of unitization. It has been argued that faces are processed more holistically (i.e., configural processing), and people are better at identifying whole faces than their individual parts separately (Tanaka & Farah, 1993). Several studies have demonstrated that this configural processing, which combines all of the parts into a single, viewpoint-specific, unit, is the result of prolonged experience with faces (Carey, 1992; Le Grand, Mondloch, Maurer, & Brent, 2001). These findings have been extended to familiar objects (Diamond & Carey, 1986) and novel objects as well (Gauthier & Tarr, 1997; Gauthier, Williams, Tarr, & Tanaka, 1998).

Unitization can also be achieved through extensive categorization practice. In a series of experiments using stimuli composed of several complex segments, Goldstone (2000) demonstrated that categorizations requiring five segments to be taken into account simultaneously resulted in the organization of these segments into a single unit (see Figure 10.3). Participants completed a speeded categorization task in which evidence from five components had to be processed to make a reliably correct categorization. Across the task, large improvements were seen in reaction times, and eventual response times were faster than predicted by a model that independently combined

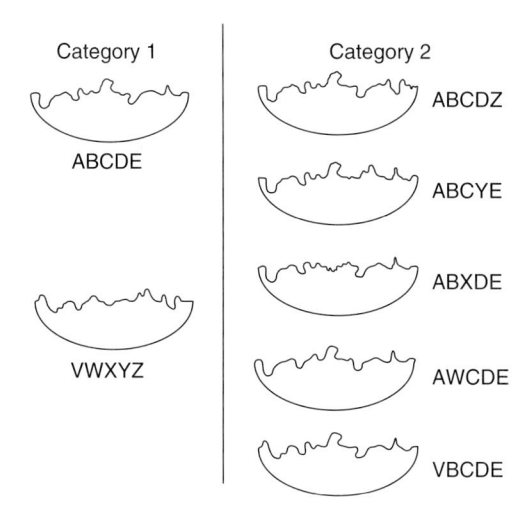

```
            Category 1              Category 2

                                     ABCDZ

              ABCDE
                                     ABCYE

                                     ABXDE

              VWXYZ
                                     AWCDE

                                     VBCDE
```

Figure 10.3 Examples of four stimuli used by Goldstone (2000). Each letter identifies one part of the object. The stimuli in Category 1 were created so that processing of all of its parts was necessary for successful categorization. Adapted from Goldstone (2000).

evidence from five segments, indicating improved processing efficiency achieved by unitization. Comparable benefits were not seen when only one part was needed for category assignment or when more than one part was needed, but these were randomly ordered, thereby preventing unit formation.

Taken as whole, this research suggests that repeated exposure and categorization experience can similarly shape our perceptual system toward a more unitized view of object's features that were initially perceived separated. Differentiation and unitization might, on first appearance, be interpreted as antagonist processes. However, they are likely to work simultaneously in shaping how the world is organized by creating the perceptual units that are needed for a particular environment and task set. For instance, category learning leads learners to divide objects into different parts based on their relevance for category learning (Schyns & Murphy, 1994; Schyns & Rodet, 1997). This process is likely to involve both differentiation and unitization of the objects' segments into units useful for supporting the categorization. Parts that co-occur frequently tend to be unitized together, particularly if their co-occurrence is diagnostic of an important category. Likewise, parts that tend to occur independently of one another tend to be differentiated, particularly if these parts differ in their relevance (Goldstone, 2003). During a typical category-learning task involving complex objects, some of the objects' parts will be joined together into units at the same time that these units are psychologically isolated from each other based on their functional relevancy (Schyns & Murphy, 1994). For example, perceiving a novel shape requires unitization of several line segments together while also requiring differentiation between these unitized wholes and other similar segments. Another example of unitization and differentiation possibly reflecting a single process is when rats are exposed to two similar stimuli, AX and BX. It has been argued (e.g., McLaren & Mackintosh, 2000) that the elements A and X will become linked, as will B and X. The linking of both A and B to X leads to their inhibiting one another, supporting their differentiation.

Categorical Perception

In the previous sections, we discussed different ways in which changes in how perceptual information is used can take place, through both simple exposure and categorization. A related phenomenon is categorical perception (Harnad, 1987), which is likely to involve attentional weighting, differentiation, and unitization (Goldstone, 1998). Categorical perception occurs for learned, not only built-in, categories and refers to the phenomenon of increased perceptual sensitivity for discriminating objects that straddle a category boundary relative to objects that fall on the same side of a category boundary. Thus, smaller physical differences will be detected following category training. This increased sensitivity for discriminating objects that span a category boundary is often accompanied by decreased discriminability for stimuli belonging to the same category. That is, following category learning, larger perceptual differences are not as easily detected for stimuli that fall into a common category – an effect similar to perceptual assimilation (Goldstone, 1995).

Interesting examples of categorical perception come from cross-cultural studies. Language use constitutes a widely pervasive categorization tool (Lupyan, Thompson-Schill, & Swingley, 2010; see Chapter 21). Languages often differ in how objects are categorized. One such example is the existence of two blue categories in Russian (roughly equivalent to "light blue" and "dark blue" in English) that do not exist as separate, common, lexicalized words in English. Winawer et al. (2007) showed that Russian speakers were quicker at differentiating between light blue and dark blue squares than between squares with the same type of blue (see also Roberson, Davidoff, Davies, & Shapiro, 2005). English speakers, on the other hand, did not show this effect. Moreover, when a verbal interference task is performed simultaneously, which disrupts access to linguistic information and thus the categorical distinction between light and dark blue for Russian speakers, the advantage for Russians for distinguishing between blues that straddle the lexicalized category boundary is lost, which is not seen when a spatial interference task (which does not interfere with access to linguistic information) is used instead (see also Roberson & Davidoff, 2000). These results have been replicated by teaching English speakers different categories that separate two hue values that are usually referred to using the same label in English (Ozgen & Davies, 2002). Additionally, this effect seems to be linked to lower perceptual thresholds for performing discriminations at the category boundary (Ozgen, 2004).

Similar effects have been found for other types of visual stimuli in training experiments. For instance, improved sensitivity for discriminations that span a category boundary has been shown following category training using face-morph continua between two anchor faces with an arbitrarily placed boundary. This has been shown for novel faces (Gureckis & Goldstone, 2008; Kikutani, Roberson, & Hanley, 2010; Levin & Beale, 2000), other-race faces, and inverted faces (Levin & Beale, 2000). Interestingly, categorical perception for faces seems to benefit from using familiar faces as the end-points and labeling the end-points in case of novel faces (Kikutani, Roberson, & Hanley, 2008).

Categorical perception effects have also been demonstrated using complex visual stimuli, showing that the increased sensitivity across a category boundary is highly specific to the characteristics of the trained stimuli (Notman, Sowden, & Ozgen, 2005), consistent with high levels of selectivity found in primary areas of the visual stream

(Posner & Gilbert, 1999; Sengpiel & Hübener, 1999). In addition, some of the findings with novel visual stimuli already discussed as attentional weighting and differentiation examples following category learning are easily interpreted as categorical perception (Goldstone, 1994; Goldstone & Steyvers, 2001). Participants trained on a categorization between morphed images of two known objects also show more accurate discriminations for stimuli that cross the category boundary (Newell & Bülthoff, 2002). In addition, decreased sensitivity for differences between novel objects within the same category without increased sensitivity across the category boundary has also been demonstrated (Livingston, Andrews, & Harnad, 1998). This phenomenon is not unique to the visual domain. Similar effects have been demonstrated in auditory (Miyawaki *et al.*, 1975) and haptic modalities (Gaißert, Waterkamp, Fleming, & Bülthoff, 2012).

One prominent question in the perceptual learning literature is: How is categorical perception taking place? One possibility is that categorization is acting not to change perception but rather to change temporary and online verbal associations or attentional strategies. This would mean that categorical perception could only act on initially separable dimensions, and perceptual sensitization to the category boundary would not take place for dimensions that were initially perceived as fused. Evidence showing the impact of labels (Kikutani *et al.*, 2008) and clear end-points in face-morphing space (Kikutani *et al.*, 2010), as well as an absence of categorical perception in some situations (Op de Beeck *et al.*, 2003), seem to favor this position. Further support for this view comes from neuroimaging studies showing no evidence of category-specific neural tuning in relevant brain areas following category learning (Jiang *et al.*, 2007). In light of this evidence, it would seem that categorical perception takes place not by changing perceptual sensitivity but rather through the use of novel attentional strategies acquired during category learning, such as the use of labels or specific salient stimuli in the morphing space.

However, there is also evidence showing that the representation of objects can be fundamentally altered due to categorization experience. Goldstone, Lippa, and Shiffrin (2001) found that objects belonging to the same category are rated as more similar to each other following category training, but also become more similar in how they are judged relative to novel, uncategorized objects. This is contrary to the idea that category learning is just changing similarity judgments by a simple heuristic such as "if the objects received the same category label, then increase their judged similarity by some amount." Moreover, there is evidence that, when categorical perception effects are seen in behavioral tasks, they are accompanied by increased sensitivity to category-relevant changes in regions of the anterior fusiform gyrus (Folstein, Palmeri, & Gauthier, 2013). Additionally, Folstein, Gauthier, and Palmeri (2012) demonstrated that whether increased sensitivity along the category-relevant dimension and the creation of novel functional dimensions were found or not is a function of the type of morphing space used. The authors propose that category learning can indeed change perceptual representations in a complex space, and the findings showing that those effects could only be found for separable dimensions might have been a result of the type of space used. More specifically, evidence for the creation of functional dimensions is mostly seen with factorial morphing techniques (two morph lines forming the sides of the space) but not with blended morph spaces (in which the original, or parents, of the space form the angles; see Figure 10.4). This is an interesting proposal, perhaps speaking to the limits of perceptual flexibility.

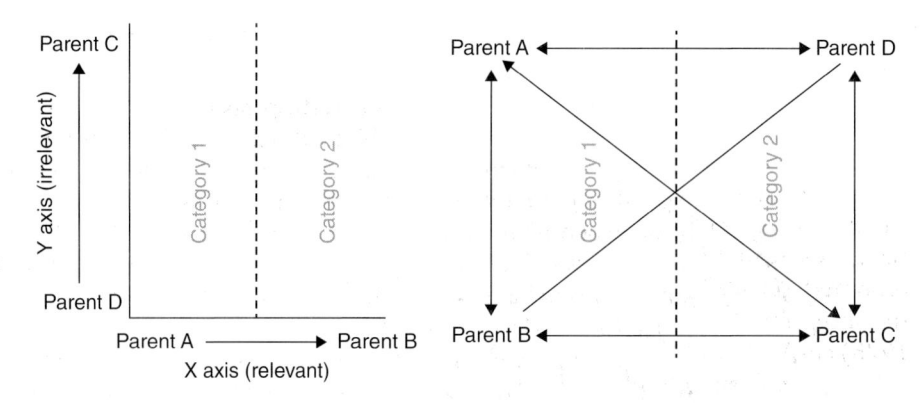

Figure 10.4 Schematic representation of two different types of morph spaces: a factorial morphing space (left panel) and a blended morphed space (right panel). Adapted from Folstein et al. (2012).

Conclusions

Throughout this paper, evidence has been reviewed showing that perceptual changes occur during perceptual and category learning. These effects are sometimes very similar, and, under some circumstances, it might be hard to say what sets apart categorization from perceptual discrimination. Strong relations between category learning and perceptual learning do not imply that both share a common set of mechanisms. However, if we consider that (1) perceptual learning is the tuning of perceptual systems to relevant environmental patterns as the result of experience and (2) that category learning is a prevalent structuring pressure in human experience capable of inducing such perceptual tuning, it is easy to imagine that category and perceptual learning might result from overlapping mechanisms.

One argument against this view is that the early perceptual system is changed by perceptual learning in a bottom-up way but not in a top-down way by category learning. Bottom-up perceptual changes could be achieved by, for example, changing how perceptual units coming from perceptual receptors are organized later on in the perceptual system – but not fundamentally changing those receptors for the task at hand. A related possibility is that most of the influence of high-level cognition on perception is the result of decisional or strategic changes on how a perceptual task is "tackled" (Pylyshyn, 2003). In general, this view would propose that although category learning receives inputs from perception, it does not share mechanisms with perceptual learning. Category learning, by this view, only applies attentional or decisional constraints on the outputs of fixed perceptual areas.

This perspective is very much related to the classic view of the perceptual system as a unidirectional flow of information from primary sensory areas to higher cognitive levels in which low-level perceptual information is processed before high-level information (Hubel & Wiesel, 1977). However, current theories propose a feedforward set (from low-level to high-level information), but also in the opposite direction (a feedback system Hochstein & Ahissar, 2002; Lamme & Roelfsema, 2000; Lamme, Super, & Spekreijse, 1998). Current evidence makes it clear that prior learning affects sensory processing even before sensory processing begins. In particular, learning influences how objects will impinge upon our sensory organs. In many cases, perceptual learning involves acquiring new procedures for actively probing one's environment (Gibson, 1969), such as learning procedures for efficiently scanning the edges of an object (Salapatek & Kessen, 1973). The result is that adults look at objects differently than children, and experts look at objects differently than novices; and since each fixates objects differently, the visual patterns that fall on an observer's retina vary with experience. Perceptual changes are found at many different neural loci, and a general rule seems to be that earlier brain regions are implicated in finer, more detailed perceptual training tasks (Ahissar & Hochstein, 1997). Thus, although it is clear that perceptual learning and category learning have different neuronal loci of change, it should not be taken to mean that they result from different mechanisms. The evidence of bidirectional connections between brain regions indicates that these different loci of change for different types of change are better understood as a single system, resulting from the same set of mechanisms of perceptual change. One such prominent view is the Reverse Hierarchy Theory (RHT; Ahissar & Hochstein, 2004; Hochstein & Ahissar, 2002), which proposes that learning starts at higher levels of the perceptual system and descends toward lower levels when finer-grained information is needed.

The claim for widespread neural plasticity in brain regions related to perception should not be interpreted as an argument for the equipotentiality of brain regions for implementing modifications to perception. Evidence for plasticity at the earliest visual processing area of the cortex, V1, remains controversial (Crist, Li, & Gilbert, 2001; Kourtzi & DiCarlo, 2006). Some of the observed activity pattern differences in V1 may be attributable to top-down influences after a first forward sweep of activity has passed. However, the very presence of large recurrent connections from more central to more peripheral brain regions attests to the evolutionary importance of tailoring input representations to one's tasks. Properties of V1 cells depend on the perceptual task being performed and experience, in the sense that neurons respond differently to identical visual patterns under different discrimination tasks and with different experiences. Moreover, these top-down influences are seen from the onset of neural response to a stimulus (Li, Piëch, & Gilbert 2004). The perceptual change, thus, is early both in the information-processing stream of the brain and chronometrically. The use of this framework can parsimoniously account, for example, for how participants in Shiffrin and Lightfoot's (1997) experiment perceive the properties of objects after prolonged experience as unitized. In this situation, perception is organized by previous knowledge, and finer-grained information is not accessed because it is not needed (instead, the larger units are perceived; for a review of how learning can have long-term effects in simple perceptual tasks, see Ahissar et al., 1998). In much the same way, finer-grained information will start being accessed following category learning that requires such specialized perceptual units, as seen in differentiation cases (Goldstone, 1994; Goldstone & Steyvers, 2001) or in cases of categorical perception.

This influence of conceptual knowledge on low-level perception has also been clearly demonstrated in the context of shape perception (I. Bülthoff, Bülthoff, & Sinha, 1998; Kourtzi & Connor, 2011; Sinha & Poggio, 1996). For example, Sinha and Poggio (1996) demonstrated that extensive training in which the mean angle projection of a 2D object and its 3D structure were associated resulted in participants imposing the learned 3D structure onto novel objects with the same mean angle projection but not onto objects with different angle projection. This resulted in perceiving rigid rotating objects as nonrigid and misperception of stereoscopic depth. Thus, conceptual learning had long-term specific consequences on how objects were perceived.

Models implementing processes similar to those described by RHT have been proposed. For instance, Spratling and Johnson (2006) proposed a neural network model that includes feedforward as well as feedback connections between low-level perceptual and conceptual processing. This model demonstrates that feedback connections allow previous learning to influence later perceptual processing, resulting in tuned perceptual and conceptual processing.

Through experience, our perceptual system becomes "tuned" to the environment. This adaptation is achieved by bottom-up influences on perception as well as by top-down influences from previous conceptual knowledge. This flexibility and interchange between conceptual and perceptual learning is particularly clear in cases of categorical perception. The evidence presented here makes it clear that perceptual learning and category learning can both be considered as the result of similar mechanisms within a single perceptual system.

Acknowledgments

Preparation of this chapter was supported by National Science Foundation REESE grant DRL-0910218, and Department of Education IES grant R305A1100060 to RLG and Graduate Training Fellowship SFRH/BD/78083/2011 from the Portuguese Foundation for Science and Technology, cosponsored by the European Social Found to PFC. The authors would like to thank Linda Smith and Rich Shiffrin for feedback in early versions of this work. Correspondence concerning this chapter should be addressed to rgoldsto@indiana.edu or Robert Goldstone, Psychology Department, Indiana University, Bloomington, IN 47405, USA. Further information about the laboratory can be found at http://www.indiana.edu/~pcl.

References

Aha, D. W., & Goldstone, R. L. (1992). Concept learning and flexible weighting. In *Proceedings of the Fourteenth Annual Conference of the Cognitive Science Society* (pp. 534–539).
Ahissar, M., & Hochstein, S. (1993, June). Early perceptual learning. *Proceedings of the National Academy of Sciences, 90*, 5718–5722.
Ahissar, M., & Hochstein, S. (1997). Task difficulty and the specificity of perceptual learning. *Nature, 387*, 401–406.
Ahissar, M., & Hochstein, S. (2004). The reverse hierarchy theory of visual perceptual learning. *Trends in Cognitive Sciences, 8*, 457–464.
Ahissar, M., Laiwand, R., Kozminsky, G., & Hochstein, S. (1998). Learning pop-out detection: building representations for conflicting target–distractor relationships. *Vision Research, 38*, 3095–3107.
Archambault, A., O'Donnell, C., & Schyns, P. G. (1999). Blind to object changes: When learning the same object at different levels of categorization modifies its perception. *Psychological Science, 10*, 249.

Aslin, R. N., & Smith, L. B. (1988). Perceptual development. *Annual Review of Psychology, 39,* 435–473.

Austerweil, J. L., & Griffiths, T. L. (2009). The effect of distributional information on feature learning. In N. A. Taatgen & H. van Rijn (Eds.), *31st Annual Conference of the Cognitive Science Society.* Austin, TX: Cognitive Science Society.

Austerweil, J. L., & Griffiths, T. L. (2013). A nonparametric Bayesian framework for constructing flexible feature representations. *Psychological Review, 120*, 817–851.

Bao, M., Yang, L., Rios, C., & Engel, S. A. (2010). Perceptual learning increases the strength of the earliest signals in visual cortex. *Journal of Neuroscience, 30,* 15080–15084.

Biederman, I., & Shiffrar, M. M. (1987). Sexing day-old chicks: A case study and expert systems analysis of a difficult perceptual-learning task. *Journal of Experimental Psychology: Learning, Memory, and Cognition, 13,* 640–645.

Bradlow, A. R., Pisoni, D. B., Akahane-Yamada, R., & Tohkura, Y. (1997). Training Japanese listeners to identify English /r/ and /l/: IV. Some effects of perceptual learning and speech production. *Journal of the Acoustical Society of America, 101,* 2299–2310.

Burns, B., & Shepp, B. E. (1988). Dimensional interactions and the structure of psychological space – the representation of hue, saturation, and brightness. *Perception & Psychophysics, 43,* 494–507.

Bülthoff, I., Bülthoff, H., & Sinha, P. (1998). Top-down influences on stereoscopic depth-perception. *Nature Neuroscience, 1,* 254–257.

Carey, S. (1992). Becoming a face expert. *Philosophical Transactions of the Royal Society of London, 335,* 95–102.

Carey, S., & Diamond, R. (1977). From piecemeal to configurational representation of faces. *Science, New Series, 195,* 312 314.

Carvalho, P. F., & Albuquerque, P. B. (2012). Memory encoding of stimulus features in human perceptual learning. *Journal of Cognitive Psychology, 24,* 654–664.

Channell, S., & Hall, G. (1981). Facilitation and retardation of discrimination learning after exposure to the stimuli. *Journal of Experimental Psychology: Animal Behavior Processes, 7,* 437–446.

Crist, R. E., Li, W., & Gilbert, C. D. (2001). Learning to see: experience and attention in primary visual cortex. *Nature Neuroscience, 4,* 519–525.

de Zilva, D., & Mitchell, C. J. (2012). Effects of exposure on discrimination of similar stimuli and on memory for their unique and common features. *Quarterly Journal of Experimental Psychology, 65,* 1123–1138.

Desimone, R., & Duncan, J. (1995). Neural mechanisms of selective visual attention. *Annual Review of Neuroscience, 18,* 193–222.

Diamond, R., & Carey, S. (1986). Why faces are and are not special: An effect of expertise. *Journal of Experimental Psychology: General, 115,* 107–117.

Dill, M., & Fahle, M. (1999). Display symmetry affects positional specificity in same–different judgment of pairs of novel visual patterns. *Vision Research, 39,* 3752–3760.

Dolan, R. J., Fink, G. R., Rolls, E., Booth, M., Holmes, A., Frackowiak, R. S. J., & Friston, K. J. (1997). How the brain learns to see objects and faces in an impoverished context. *Nature, 389,* 596–599.

Dosher, B. A., & Lu, Z. L. (1998). Perceptual learning reflects external noise filtering and internal noise reduction through channel reweighting. *Proceedings of the National Academy of Sciences, 95,* 13988–13993.

Dwyer, D. M., Mundy, M. E., Vladeanu, M., & Honey, R. C. (2009). Perceptual learning and acquired face familiarity: Evidence from inversion, use of internal features, and generalization between viewpoints. *Visual Cognition, 17,* 334–355.

Fahle, M. (1994). Human pattern recognition: Parallel processing and perceptual learning. *Perception, 23,* 411–427.

Flin, R. H. (1985). Development of face recognition: An encoding switch? *British Journal of Psychology, 76*, 123–134.

Folstein, J. R., Gauthier, I., & Palmeri, T. J. (2012). How category learning affects object representations: Not all morphspaces stretch alike. *Journal of Experimental Psychology: Learning, Memory, and Cognition, 38*, 807–820.

Folstein, J. R., Palmeri, T. J., & Gauthier, I. (2013). Category learning increases discriminability of relevant object dimensions in visual cortex. *Cerebral Cortex, 23*, 814–823.

Friedman-Hill, S. R., Robertson, L. C., Desimone, R., & Ungerleider, L. G. (2003). Posterior parietal cortex and the filtering of distractors. *Proceedings of the National Academy of Sciences of the United States of America, 100*, 4263–4268.

Furmanski, C. S., & Engel, S. A. (2000). Perceptual learning in object recognition: object specificity and size invariance. *Vision Research, 40*, 473–484.

Furmanski, C. S. Schluppeck, D., & Engel, S. A. (2004) Learning strengthens the response of primary visual cortex to simple patterns. *Current Biology, 14*, 573–578

Gaißert, N., Waterkamp, S., Fleming, R. W., & Bülthoff, I. (2012). Haptic categorical perception of shape. *PloS One, 7*, e43062.

Garrigan, P., & Kellman, P. J. (2008). Perceptual learning depends on perceptual constancy. *Proceedings of the National Academy of Sciences, 105*, 2248–2253.

Gauthier, I., & Tarr, M. J. (1997). Becoming a "greeble" expert: exploring mechanisms for face recognition. *Vision Research, 37*, 1673–1682.

Gauthier, I., Williams, P., Tarr, M. J., & Tanaka, J. W. (1998). Training "greeble" experts: a framework for studying expert object recognition processes. *Vision Research, 38*, 2401–2428.

Gibson, E. J. (1963). Perceptual learning. *Annual Review of Psychology, 14*, 29–56.

Gibson, E. J. (1969). *Principles of perceptual learning and development.* New York, NY: Appleton-Century-Crofts.

Gibson, E. J., & Walk, R. D. (1956). The effect of prolonged exposure to visually presented patterns on learning to discriminate them. *Journal of Comparative and Physiological, 49*, 239–242.

Goldstone, R. L. (1994). Influences of categorization on perceptual discrimination. *Journal of Experimental Psychology: General, 123*, 178–200.

Goldstone, R. L. (1995). Effects of categorization on color perception. *Psychological Science, 6*, 298–304.

Goldstone, R. L. (1998). Perceptual learning. *Annual Review of Psychology, 49*, 585–612.

Goldstone, R. L. (2000). Unitization during category learning. *Journal of Experimental Psychology: Human Perception and Performance, 26*, 86–112.

Goldstone, R. L. (2003). *Learning to perceive while perceiving to learn.* Perceptual Organization in Vision: Behavioral and Neural Perspectives, 233–278.

Goldstone, R. L., & Steyvers, M. (2001). The sensitization and differentiation of dimensions during category learning. *Journal of Experimental Psychology: General, 130*, 116–139.

Goldstone, R. L., Kersten, A., & Carvalho, P. F. (2012). Concepts and Categorization. In A. F. Healy & R. W. Proctor (Eds.), *Handbook of psychology, volume 4 – experimental psychology* (2nd ed., pp. 607–630). New York, NY: Wiley.

Goldstone, R. L., Lippa, Y., & Shiffrin, R. M. (2001). Altering object representations through category learning. *Cognition, 78*, 27–43.

Goldstone, R. L., Steyvers, M., Spencer-Smith, J., & Kersten, A. (2000). Interactions between perceptual and conceptual learning. In E. Diettrich & A. B. Markman (Eds.), *Cognitive dynamics: conceptual change in humans and machines* (pp. 191–228). Hillsdale, NJ: Lawrence Erlbaum Associates.

Graham, S. A., Namy, L. L., Gentner, D., & Meagher, K. (2010). The role of comparison in preschoolers' novel object categorization. *Journal of Experimental Child Psychology, 107*, 280–290.

Gureckis, T. M., & Goldstone, R. L. (2008). The effect of the internal structure of categories on perception. In *Proceedings of the 30th Annual Conference of the Cognitive Science Society* (pp. 1876–1881). Austin, TX: Cognitive Science Society.

Gutnisky, D. A., Hansen, B. J., Iliescu, B. F., & Dragoi, V. (2009). Attention alters visual plasticity during exposure-based learning. *Current Biology, 19*, 555–560.

Hall, G. (1979). Exposure learning in young and adult laboratory rats. *Animal Behaviour, 27*, 586–591.

Hall, G. (1991). *Perceptual and associative learning.* Oxford, UK: Clarendon Press/Oxford University Press.

Hall, G. (2003). Learned changes in the sensitivity of stimulus representations: associative and nonassociative mechanisms. *The Quarterly Journal of Experimental Psychology. B, Comparative and Physiological Psychology, 56*, 43–55.

Harnad, S. (1987). Psychophysical and cognitive aspects of categorical perception: A critical overview. In S. Harnad (Ed.), *Categorical perception: the groundwork of cognition* (pp. 1–52). New York, NY: Cambridge University Press.

Harrison, T. B., & Stiles, J. (2009). Hierarchical forms processing in adults and children. *Journal of Experimental Child Psychology, 103*, 222–240.

Hasegawa, I., & Miyashita, Y. (2002). Categorizing the world: expert neurons look into key features. *Nature Neuroscience, 5*, 90–91.

Hendrickson, A. T., & Goldstone, R. L. (2009). *Perceptual unitization in part–whole judgments.* In *Proceedings of the Thirty-First Annual Conference of the Cognitive Science Society* (pp. 1084–1089). Amsterdam, Netherlands: Cognitive Science Society.

Hochstein, S., & Ahissar, M. (2002). View from the top: hierarchies and reverse hierarchies review. *Neuron, 36*, 791–804.

Hock, H. S., Webb, E., & Cavedo, L. C. (1987). Perceptual learning in visual category acquisition. *Memory & cognition, 15*, 544–556.

Hockema, S. A., Blair, M. R., & Goldstone, R. L. (2005). *Differentiation for novel dimensions* (pp. 953–958). Presented at the Proceedings of the 27th Annual Conference of the Cognitive Science Society.

Honey, R. C., & Hall, G. (1989). Acquired equivalence and distinctiveness of cues. *Journal of Experimental Psychology: Animal Behavior Processes, 15*, 338–346.

Hubel, D. H., & Wiesel, T. N. (1977). Ferrier lecture: Functional architecture of macaque monkey visual cortex. *Proceedings of the Royal Society of London. Series B, Biological Sciences, 198*, 1–59.

James, W. (1981). *The principles of psychology.* Cambridge, MA: Harvard University Press.

Jiang, X., Bradley, E., Rini, R. A., Zeffiro, T., VanMeter, J., & Riesenhuber, M. (2007). Categorization training results in shape- and category-selective human neural plasticity. *Neuron, 53*, 891.

Jones, S. S., & Smith, L. B. (1999). Object name learning and object perception: a deficit in late talkers. *Journal of Child Language, 32*, 223–240.

Karni, A., & Sagi, D. (1991). Where practice makes perfect in texture discrimination: evidence for primary visual cortex plasticity. *Proceedings of the National Academy of Sciences of the United States of America, 88*, 4966–4970.

Kemler, D. G., & Smith, L. B. (1978). Is there a developmental trend from integrality to separability in perception? *Journal of Experimental Child Psychology, 26*, 498–507.

Kikutani, M., Roberson, D., & Hanley, J. R. (2008). What's in the name? Categorical perception for unfamiliar faces can occur through labeling. *Psychonomic Bulletin & Review, 15*, 787–794.

Kikutani, M., Roberson, D., & Hanley, J. R. (2010). Categorical perception for unfamiliar faces. The effect of covert and overt face learning. *Psychological Science, 21*, 865–872.

Kourtzi, Z., & Connor, C. E. (2011). Neural representations for object perception: structure, category, and adaptive coding. *Annual Review of Neuroscience, 34*, 45–67.

Kourtzi Z., & DiCarlo J. J. (2006). Learning and neural plasticity in visual object recognition. *Current Opinion in Neurobiology*, 16, 152–158.

Kruschke, J. K. (1992). ALCOVE: An exemplar-based connectionist model of category learning. *Psychological Review*, 99, 22–44

Lamme, V. A., & Roelfsema, P. R. (2000). The distinct modes of vision offered by feedforward and recurrent processing. *Trends in Neurosciences*, 23, 571–579.

Lamme, V. A., Super, H., & Spekreijse, H. (1998). Feedforward, horizontal, and feedback processing in the visual cortex. *Current Opinion in Neurobiology*, 8, 529–535.

Landau, B., Smith, L. B., & Jones, S. S. (1988). The importance of shape in early lexical learning. *Cognitive Development*, 3, 299–321.

Lavis, Y., & Mitchell, C. J. (2006). Effects of preexposure on stimulus discrimination: an investigation of the mechanisms responsible for human perceptual learning. *Quarterly Journal of Experimental Psychology*, 59, 2083–2101.

Le Grand, R., Mondloch, C. J., Maurer, D., & Brent, H. P. (2001). Neuroperception: Early visual experience and face processing. *Nature*, 410, 890–890.

Levin, D. T., & Beale, J. M. (2000). Categorical perception occurs in newly learned faces, other-race faces, and inverted faces. *Perception & Psychophysics*, 62, 386–401.

Li, W., Piëch, V., & Gilbert, C. D. (2004). Perceptual learning and top-down influences in primary visual cortex. *Nature Neuroscience*, 7, 651–657.

Lin, E. L., & Murphy, G. L. (1997). Effects of background knowledge on object categorization and part detection. *Journal of Experimental Psychology: Human Perception and Performance*, 23, 1153–1169.

Liu, Z., & Vaina, L. M. (1998). Simultaneous learning of motion discrimination in two directions. *Cognitive Brain Research*, 6, 347–349.

Lively, S. E., Logan, J. S., & Pisoni, D. B. (1993). Training Japanese listeners to identify English /r/ and /l/. II: The role of phonetic environment and talker variability in learning new perceptual categories. *The Journal of the Acoustical Society of America*, 94, 1242–1255.

Livingston, K. R., & Andrews, J. K. (1995). On the interaction of prior knowledge and stimulus structure in category learning. *The Quarterly Journal of Experimental Psychology Section A*, 48, 208–236.

Livingston, K. R., Andrews, J. K., & Harnad, S. (1998). Categorical perception effects induced by category learning. *Journal of Experimental Psychology: Learning, Memory, and Cognition*, 24, 732–753.

Logan, J. S., Lively, S. E., & Pisoni, D. B. (1991). Training Japanese listeners to identify English/r/and/l: A first report. *The Journal of the Acoustical Society of America*, 89, 874–886.

Lu, Z. L., & Dosher, B. A. (2004). Perceptual learning retunes the perceptual template in foveal orientation identification. *Journal of Vision*, 4, 44–56.

Lupyan, G., Thompson-Schill, S. L., & Swingley, D. (2010). Conceptual penetration of visual processing. *Psychological Science*, 21, 682–691.

Mackintosh, N. J., Kaye, H., & Bennett, C. H. (1991). Perceptual learning in flavour aversion conditioning. *The Quarterly Journal of Experimental Psychology Section B*, 43, 297–322.

Macpherson, F. (2011). Cognitive penetration of colour experience: Rethinking the issue in light of an indirect mechanism. *Philosophy and Phenomenological Research*, 84, 24–62.

Matthews, N., Liu, Z., Geesaman, B. J., & Qian, N. (1999). Perceptual learning on orientation and direction discrimination. *Vision Research*, 39, 3692–3701.

McLaren, I. P. L. (1997). Categorization and perceptual learning: an analogue of the face inversion effect. *The Quarterly Journal of Experimental Psychology A*, 50, 257–273.

McLaren, I. P. L., & Mackintosh, N. J. (2000). An elemental model of associative learning: I. Latent inhibition and perceptual learning. *Animal Learning & Behavior*, 28, 211–246.

McLaren, I. P. L., Wills, A. J., & Graham, S. (2010). Attention and perceptual learning. In C. J. Mitchell (Ed.), *Attention and associative learning* (pp. 131–158). New York, NY: Oxford University Press.

Melara, R. D., Marks, L. E., & Potts, B. C. (1993). Primacy of dimensions in color-perception. *Journal of Experimental Psychology: Human Perception and Performance, 19*, 1082–1104.

Mitchell, C. J., Kadib, R., Nash, S., Lavis, Y., & Hall, G. (2008). Analysis of the role of associative inhibition in perceptual learning by means of the same–different task. *Journal of Experimental Psychology: Animal Behavior Processes, 34*, 475–485.

Miyawaki, K., Jenkins, J. J., Strange, W., Liberman, A. M., Verbrugge, R., & Fujimura, O. (1975). An effect of linguistic experience: The discrimination of [r] and [l] by native speakers of Japanese and English. *Perception & Psychophysics, 18*, 331–340.

Moran, J., & Desimone, R. (1985). Selective attention gates visual processing in the extrastriate cortex. *Science, 229*, 782–784.

Mundy, M. E., Honey, R. C., & Dwyer, D. M. (2007). Simultaneous presentation of similar stimuli produces perceptual learning in human picture processing. *Journal of Experimental Psychology: Animal Behavior Processes, 33*, 124–138.

Mundy, M. E., Honey, R. C., & Dwyer, D. M. (2008). Superior discrimination between similar stimuli after simultaneous exposure. *The Quarterly Journal of Experimental Psychology, 62*, 18–25.

Murphy, G. L. (2002). *The big book of concepts.* Cambridge, MA: MIT Press.

Newell, F. N., & Bülthoff, H. H. (2002). Categorical perception of familiar objects. *Cognition, 85*, 113–143.

Nosofsky, R. M. (1986). Attention, similarity, and the identification–categorization relationship. *Journal of Experimental Psychology: General, 115*, 39.

Nosofsky, R. M., Palmeri, T. J., & McKinley, S. C. (1994). Rule-plus-exception model of classification learning. *Psychological Review, 101*, 53–79.

Notman, L. A., Sowden, P. T., & Ozgen, E. (2005). The nature of learned categorical perception effects: a psychophysical approach. *Cognition, 95*, B1–B14.

O'Toole, A. J., & Edelman, S. (1996). *Face distinctiveness in recognition across viewpoint: An analysis of the statistical structure of face spaces* (pp. 10–15). Presented at the Proceedings of the Second International Conference on Automatic Face and Gesture Recognition, IEEE.

Op de Beeck, H., Wagemans, J., & Vogels, R. (2003). The effect of category learning on the representation of shape: dimensions can be biased but not differentiated. *Journal of Experimental Psychology: General, 132*, 491–511.

Ozgen, E. (2004). Language, learning, and color perception. *Current Directions in Psychological Science, 13*, 95–98.

Ozgen, E., & Davies, I. R. L. (2002). Acquisition of categorical color perception: A perceptual learning approach to the linguistic relativity hypothesis. *Journal of Experimental Psychology. General, 131*, 477–493.

Peterson, M. A., & Gibson, B. S. (1993). Shape recognition inputs to figure-ground organization in three-dimensional displays. *Cognitive Psychology, 25*, 383–429.

Peterson, M. A., & Gibson, B. S. (1994). Object recognition contributions to figure-ground organization: Operations on outlines and subjective contours. *Perception & Psychophysics, 56*, 551–564.

Peterson, M. A., & Lampignano, D. W. (2003). Implicit memory for novel figure-ground displays includes a history of cross-border competition. *Journal of Experimental Psychology: Human Perception and Performance, 29*, 808–822.

Petrov, A. A., Dosher, B. A., & Lu, Z.-L. (2006). Perceptual learning without feedback in non-stationary contexts: Data and model. *Vision Research, 46*, 3177–3197.

Pevtzow, R., & Goldstone, R. L. (1994). *Categorization and the parsing of objects* (pp. 717–722). Presented at the Proceedings of the Sixteenth Annual Conference of the Cognitive Science Society, Hillsdale, NJ.

Pick, A. D. (1965). Improvement of visual and tactual form discrimination. *Journal of Experimental Psychology, 69*, 331–339.

Pons, T. P., Garraghty, P. E., Ommaya, A. K., Kaas, J. H., Taub, E., & Mishkin, M. (1991). Massive cortical reorganization after sensory deafferentation in adult macaques. *Science, New Series, 252*, 1857–1860.

Posner, M. I., & Gilbert, C. D. (1999). Attention and primary visual cortex. *Proceedings of the National Academy of Sciences of the United States of America, 96*, 2585–2587.

Puel, J. L., Bonfils, P., & Pujol, R. (1988). Selective attention modifies the active micromechanical properties of the cochlea. *Brain Research, 447*, 380–383.

Pylyshyn, Z. W. (1999). Is vision continuous with cognition? The case for cognitive impenetrability of visual perception. *Behavioral and Brain Sciences, 22*, 341–423.

Pylyshyn, Z. W. (2003). *Seeing and visualizing: it's not what you think*. Cambridge, MA: MIT Press.

Recanzone, G. H., Schreiner, C. E., & Merzenich, M. M. (1993). Plasticity in the frequency representation of primary auditory cortex following discrimination training in adult owl monkeys. *The Journal of Neuroscience, 13*, 87–103.

Reicher, G. M. (1969). Perceptual recognition as a function of meaningfulness of stimulus material. *Journal of Experimental Psychology, 81*, 275–280.

Roberson, D., & Davidoff, J. (2000). The categorical perception of colors and facial expressions: the effect of verbal interference. *Memory & cognition, 28*, 977–986.

Roberson, D., Davidoff, J., Davies, I. R. L., & Shapiro, L. R. (2005). Color categories: Evidence for the cultural relativity hypothesis. *Cognitive Psychology, 50*, 378–411.

Salapatek, P., & Kessen, W. (1973). Prolonged investigation of a plane geometric triangle by the human newborn. *Journal of Experimental Child Psychology, 15*, 22–29.

Schoups, A., Vogels, R., Qian, N., & Orban, G. (2001). Practising orientation identification improves orientation coding in V1 neurons. *Nature, 412*, 549–553.

Schyns, P. G., & Murphy, G. L. (1994). The ontogeny of part representation in object concepts. *Psychology of Learning and Motivation: Advances in Research and Theory, 31*, 305–349.

Schyns, P. G., & Rodet, L. (1997). Categorization creates functional features. *Journal of Experimental Psychology: Learning, Memory, and Cognition, 23*, 681–696.

Schyns, P. G., Goldstone, R. L., & Thibaut, J.-P. (1998). The development of features in object concepts. *The Behavioral and Brain Sciences, 21*, 1–17; discussion 17–54.

Sengpiel, F., & Hübener, M. (1999). Visual attention: spotlight on the primary visual cortex. *Current Biology, 9*, R318–R321.

Shapiro, P. N., & Penrod, S. (1986). Meta-analysis of facial identification studies. *Psychological Bulletin, 100*, 139–156.

Shiffrin, R. M., & Lightfoot, N. (1997). Perceptual learning of alphanumeric-like characters. *The Psychology of Learning and Memory, 36*, 45–81.

Shiffrin, R. M., & Schneider, W. (1977). Controlled and automatic human information processing: II. Perceptual learning, automatic attending and a general theory. *Psychological Review, 84*, 127.

Sigala, N., & Logothetis, N. K. (2002). Visual categorization shapes feature selectivity in the primate temporal cortex. *Nature, 415*, 318–320.

Sinha, P., & Poggio, T. (1996). Role of learning in three-dimensional form perception. *Nature*.

Sloman, S. A. (1996). The empirical case for two systems of reasoning. *Psychological Bulletin, 119*, 3–22.

Smith, L. B. (1989). A model of perceptual classification in children and adults. *Psychological Review, 96*, 125–144.

Smith, L. B., Jones, S. S., Landau, B., Gershkoff-Stowe, L., & Samuelson, L. (2002). Object name learning provides on-the-job training for attention. *Psychological Science, 13*, 13–19.

Smith, L. B., & Kemler, D. G. (1978). Levels of experienced dimensionality in children and adults. *Cognitive Psychology, 10,* 502–532.

Spratling, M. W., & Johnson, M. H. (2006). A feedback model of perceptual learning and categorization. *Visual Cognition, 13,* 129–165.

Symonds, M., & Hall, G. (1995). Perceptual learning in flavor aversion conditioning: Roles of stimulus comparison and latent inhibition of common stimulus elements. *Learning and Motivation, 26,* 203–219.

Symonds, M., & Hall, G. (1997). Contextual conditioning with lithium-induced nausea as the US: Evidence from a blocking procedure. *Learning and Motivation, 28,* 200–215.

Tada, W. L., & Stiles, J. (1996). Developmental change in children's analysis of spatial patterns. *Developmental Psychology, 32,* 951–970.

Tanaka, J. W., & Farah, M. J. (1993). Parts and wholes in face recognition. *Quarterly Journal of Experimental Psychology Section A: Human Experimental Psychology, 46,* 225–245.

Tanaka, J. W., Curran, T., & Sheinberg, D. L. (2005). The training and transfer of real-world perceptual expertise. *Psychological Science, 16,* 145–151.

Tipper, S. P. (1992). Selection for action: The role of inhibitory mechanisms. *Current Directions in Psychological Science, 1,* 105–109.

Treisman, A. M., & Gelade, G. (1980). A feature-integration theory of attention. *Cognitive Psychology, 12,* 97–136.

Tsushima, Y., & Watanabe, T. (2009). Roles of attention in perceptual learning from perspectives of psychophysics and animal learning. *Learning & Behavior, 37,* 126–132.

Valentine, T., & Bruce, V. (1986). The effect of race, inversion and encoding activity upon face recognition. *Acta Psychologica, 61,* 259–273.

Vecera, S. P., & O'Reilly, R. C. (1998). Figure-ground organization and object recognition processes: an interactive account. *Journal of Experimental Psychology: Human Perception and Performance, 24,* 441–462.

Vecera, S. P., Flevaris, A. V., & Filapek, J. C. (2004). Exogenous spatial attention influences figure-ground assignment. *Psychological Science, 15,* 20–26.

Wang, T., & Mitchell, C. J. (2011). Attention and relative novelty in human perceptual learning. Journal of Experimental Psychology: *Animal Behavior Processes.*

Wang, T., Lavis, Y., Hall, G., & Mitchell, C. J. (2012). Preexposed stimuli are more discriminable than novel stimuli: implications for salience-modulation theories of perceptual learning. *Journal of Experimental Psychology: Animal Behavior Processes,* 1–40.

Watanabe, T., Harner, A. M., Miyauchi, S., Sasaki, Y., Nielsen, M., Palomo, D., & Mukai, I. (1998). Task-dependent influences of attention on the activation of human primary visual cortex. *Proceedings of the National Academy of Sciences of the United States of America, 95,* 11489–11492.

Watanabe, T., Nanez, J. E., & Sasaki, Y. (2001). Perceptual learning without perception. *Nature, 413,* 844–848.

Watanabe, T., Sasaki, Y., Miyauchi, S., Putz, B., Fujimaki, N., Nielsen, M., et al. (1998). Attention-regulated activity in human primary visual cortex. *Journal of Neurophysiology, 79,* 2218–2221.

Weinberger, N. M. (1993). Learning-induced changes of auditory receptive fields. *Current Opinion in Neurobiology, 3,* 570–577.

Werker, J. F., & Logan, J. S. (1985). Cross-language evidence for three factors in speech perception. *Perception & Psychophysics, 37,* 35–44.

Wheeler, D. D. (1970). Processes in word recognition. *Cognitive Psychology, 1,* 59–85.

Wills, A. J., & McLaren, I. P. L. (1998). Perceptual learning and free classification. *Quarterly Journal of Experimental Psychology Section B, 51,* 235–270.

Wills, A. J., Suret, M., & McLaren, I. P. L. (2004). Brief communication: The role of category structure in determining the effects of stimulus preexposure on categorization accuracy. *The Quarterly Journal of Experimental Psychology Section B, 57,* 79–88.

Winawer, J., Witthoft, N., Frank, M. C., Wu, L., Wade, A. R., & Boroditsky, L. (2007). Russian blues reveal effects of language on color discrimination. *Proceedings of the National Academy of Sciences, 104*, 7780–7785.

Xu, P., Lu, Z.-L., Wang, X., Dosher, B. A., Zhou, J., Zhang, D., & Zhou, Y. (2010). Category and perceptual learning in subjects with treated Wilson's disease. *PloS One, 5*, 1–9.

Yang, T., & Maunsell, J. H. (2004) The effect of perceptual learning on neuronal responses in monkey visual area V4. *Journal of Neuroscience, 24*, 1617–1626.

Zemel, R. S., Behrmann, M., Mozer, M. C., & Bavelier, D. (2002). Experience-dependent perceptual grouping and object-based attention. *Journal of Experimental Psychology: Human Perception and Performance, 28*, 202–217.

11
Computational and Functional Specialization of Memory

Rosie Cowell, Tim Bussey, and Lisa Saksida

Introduction

In this chapter, we describe how our work on the neural and cognitive mechanisms of perception and memory provides an example of an interdisciplinary research approach that allows the rapprochement between theory, observation of behavior, and neural mechanism. We have developed a theory of visual and mnemonic processing in the ventral visual stream (VVS) and medial temporal lobe (MTL) that is situated at a relatively coarse-grained neurobiological level, explaining cognition primarily in terms of the organization of object representations in the brain. It draws on observations of perceptual and mnemonic behavior, on knowledge of systems-level anatomical organization, on data regarding the neural mechanisms of information processing in cortex, and on simple, well-understood principles of associative learning. The theory ties these strands together using explicit, computationally instantiated neural network models. This general approach has provided a framework for interpreting existing empirical results and has generated a large number of predictions for further experiments. The results of such experiments, in tandem with further development of the models, are now enabling the development of a broader and more unified theory of visual and mnemonic cognition in the mammalian brain.

Modular Organization of Visual Memory and Visual Perception in the Brain

Early work in experimental psychology attempted to render the field of human cognition more amenable to study by dividing it up into separable, self-contained portions and assuming that each could be studied in isolation. This was an era in which we knew little about the processes underlying thought and behavior, and less still about the neural mechanisms upon which these processes depended. And so divisions within the broad subject matter of cognition fell naturally along the lines suggested by introspection: Labels such as memory, perception, attention and emotion were used to designate separate branches of the human cognition that could be assumed to operate largely independently. Although some research approaches such as animal learning theory and connectionism have not assumed independence of these processes, many areas of psychology and cognitive neuroscience still do make tacit assumptions of functional modularity that respect the same boundaries (Cowell, Bussey, & Saksida, 2010).

The assumption of a modular distinction between memory and perception was solidified, at least in the visual domain, on the basis of evidence from animal neuropsychology. Specifically, it stemmed from an extensive experimental literature examining the effects of damage to the ventral visual pathway on a number of visual discrimination learning tasks (Blake, Jarvis, & Mishkin, 1977; Butter, 1972; Cowell et al., 2010; Wilson & Kaufman, 1969; Cowey & Gross, 1970; Dean, 1974; Gross, Cowey, & Manning, 1971; Iversen & Humphrey, 1971; Iwai & Mishkin, 1968; Kikuchi & Iwai, 1980; Manning, 1971a, 1971b; Wilson & Kaufman, 1969; Wilson, Zieler, Lieb, & Kaufman, 1972). Broadly speaking, the authors of these studies used a visual discrimination learning paradigm with two different variants, one of which was presumed to tax basic visual perception and the other of which was supposed to involve greater mnemonic demands. These tasks were presented to animals with two classes of brain damage: posterior VVS and anterior VVS.

The basic task is as follows. Visual stimuli are assigned to fixed pairs, of which one is designated as "rewarded" and the other "nonrewarded." Animals are presented with each pair of visual stimuli in the set and are required to learn which of the pair must be selected in order to obtain a food reward. All stimulus pairs are presented many times, with training proceeding until the animal reaches some predetermined criterion specifying the number of errors allowed within a certain number of trials. In the "perceptual" variant of this paradigm, tasks tended to use few pairs of discriminanda – perhaps as few as one pair – and to use simple visual stimuli such as basic geometric shapes rendered in black and white on a two-dimensional plaque. By contrast, in the "mnemonic" variant of the task, a larger number of stimulus pairs were typically used, and animals were required to learn all pairs concurrently; that is, each training epoch involved cycling through the entire set without repeating any one pair successively. In addition, the mnemonic tasks typically employed more visually complex stimuli, such as three-dimensional, color junk objects. It was assumed that the concurrent retention of many pairs, in combination with the detailed nature of the stimulus material, placed a greater load on memory in this variant of the paradigm.

A double dissociation in this paradigm was repeatedly found, with anterior lesions in the ventral visual pathway causing impairments on the "mnemonic" variant of the task, and posterior lesions causing problems in performance on the "perceptual" variant (e.g., Iwai & Mishkin, 1968; see Cowell et al., 2010 for a review); hence the conclusion that posterior ventral visual regions are critical for visual perception, whereas more anterior regions, toward MTL, are instead important for associative memory.

At the same time as this modular view was developing and gaining widespread influence, a parallel literature examining the nature and neural organization specifically of declarative memory – memory for facts and events – was emerging. The striking memory impairment observed in the amnesic patient H.M., in the apparent absence of perceptual impairment, reinforced the strong assumption at the core of theories of perception and memory in the mammalian brain: that these two psychologically defined functions – declarative memory and visual perception – are performed relatively independently, by distinct neural systems. Furthermore, the dominant new view of memory emphasized further modularity within memory, including a delineation between MTL-based declarative memory (i.e., abstract, semantic knowledge and long-term episodic memory), perceptually grounded learning assumed to rely upon neocortical areas outside of the MTL (such as repetition priming or perceptual learning), and subcortically based types of procedural learning (also known as "habit learning" or motor learning). The class of theories assuming the separability of memory from perception and, additionally, the existence of functionally and neuroanatomically separate systems within memory itself, became known as the "Multiple Memory Systems" (MMS) view (e.g., Cohen & Squire, 1980; Packard, Hirsh, & White, 1989; Sherry & Schacter, 1987).

A related question was whether distinct structures in MTL could also be differentiated along functional lines and, if yes, what the specific contributions of each structure to declarative memory were. For example, evidence from animal models has pointed to a role for the hippocampus in the recognition of places and for object-in-place memory (Bachevalier & Nemanic, 2008; Barker & Warburton, 2015; Jackson-Smith, Kesner, & Chiba, 1993; Komorowski, Manns, & Eichenbaum, 2009; Sanderson et al., 2007). This can be contrasted with the observed role of the perirhinal cortex (PRC) in recognition memory for objects per se, that is, judging the familiarity of single items (e.g., Eacott, Gaffan, & Murray, 1994; Meunier, Bachevalier, Mishkin, & Murray, 1993; Zola-Morgan, Squire, Amaral, & Suzuki, 1989).

In differentiating between the contributions of MTL structures to memory for objects versus memory for more complex stimuli (such as events, episodes, and spatial relations), this literature touched upon some of the same ideas as the foregoing body of work on visual discrimination learning. That prior literature had laid the foundations for the idea that object memory was mediated by regions in or near to anterior temporal lobe, and the newer research into the nature of object-recognition memory (ORM) in MTL began to flesh out more specifically the mechanisms and neural underpinnings of ORM. The classic "memory" manipulation that was used is the length of the delay between studying an object and testing the memory of it: the longer the delay, the greater the memory load, and the worse any memory impairment should be in individuals with damage to brain regions critical for memory. In line with this, the performance of subjects with PRC lesions gets worse with longer study–test delays. But what is the mechanism by which PRC damage causes this extra forgetting over a delay? The standard explanation was that there are two systems: short-term memory (STM) and long-term memory (LTM). STM is intact in animals with PRC damage, so their performance at very short delays is spared, and memory impairments are revealed only when the time frame of STM is exceeded (e.g., Buffalo, Reber, & Squire, 1998; Jeneson & Squire, 2012; Liu & Bilkey, 1998).

Puzzling Findings and Problems with the Modular View

The above section reveals two key assumptions of prevailing theories of object processing. The first is that visual perception and visual memory are served by distinct cognitive and neural mechanisms. The second is that any residual memory performance at short delays in individuals with MTL damage must be underpinned by an STM system that is distinct from an MTL-dependent memory operating at longer delays. However, both of these assumptions face certain challenges, which we outline below.

Assumption 1: Visual perception and visual memory are served by distinct cognitive and neural mechanisms

According to the MMS view, PRC is part of the MTL memory system critical for declarative memory and declarative memory only (Squire, Stark, & Clark, 2004; Squire & Wixted, 2011; Squire & Zola-Morgan, 1991). However, in the late 1990s, a number of studies began to show that this brain structure was important for visual discrimination tasks – in the absence of an overt declarative mnemonic component – in certain cases.

Buckley and Gaffan carried out a number of influential studies examining the role of PRC in object perception. In most of these experiments, a concurrent visual discrimination learning paradigm, similar to the visual discrimination learning tasks described above, was used. As in those earlier studies, a series of pairs of visual stimuli are presented to the animal, with one stimulus in each pair being consistently rewarded on each presentation, and the other unrewarded (e.g., A+ vs. B–, C+ vs. D–, E+ vs. F–, etc., where each letter represents an individual stimulus). Animals typically see all pairs in the series many times, and training continues until some performance criterion is reached. In a previous study of rhinal cortex using this task (Gaffan & Murray, 1992), animals with rhinal cortex lesions were unimpaired when stimuli were presented in pairs and with small set sizes (10 pairs of stimuli, i.e., 10 discrimination problems). However, when Buckley and Gaffan (1997) modified the paradigm by increasing the number of distracter stimuli, so that the target had to be selected from an array of seven or 14 stimuli, rather than a pair of stimuli, they found that animals with PRC lesions were impaired. In the same study, increasing the number of problems that had to be learned concurrently (to a set size of 40, 80, or 160 problems) also revealed impairments in PRC-lesioned animals. Interestingly, the same authors found that discrimination impairments following PRC lesions could be observed with problem set sizes as small as 10, if the task was manipulated in other ways, such as constructing the stimuli according to the biconditional problem, such that no individual feature of an object can predict reward (e.g., a set containing the two problems: AB+ vs. BC– and CD+ vs. AD–, where a pair of letters represents a whole stimulus; Buckley & Gaffan, 1998a).

These findings concerning the role of PRC in visual discrimination learning, when taken together, were puzzling. If the PRC was unimportant for perception per se, then perceptual manipulations such as constructing the stimuli configurally, or changing the viewing angle of a stimulus, should not influence whether PRC lesions cause impairments. On the other hand, if PRC was important for perception, why did it only seem to be critical under certain perceptual demands? Buckley and Gaffan (1997, 1998b) suggested a role for PRC in object identification because it seemed that PRC was necessary not for the perception of basic visual attributes (e.g., color), but specifically for the perception of objects, particularly in situations where the ability to discriminate one object from another might be taxed. In particular, Buckley and Gaffan suggested that PRC was important for forming "coherent concepts" of objects (Buckley & Gaffan, 1998b). But there remained an important, unanswered question: Exactly *why* was a role for PRC in forming coherent object concepts important for object identification, and why was it important only under the specific conditions outlined above? Nonetheless, these results were a critical step forward in our understanding of the mechanisms of object memory and perception in the brain, because they began to question the notion that PRC was important only for declarative memory (Gaffan, 2002; Murray & Bussey, 1999).

Assumption 2: Residual memory performance at short delays following MTL damage is underpinned by an STM system that is distinct from the MTL system for declarative memory

The use of a dual-system (STM vs. LTM) account to explain animals' performance on these tasks suggests that if animals with lesions in MTL structures have intact STM, their performance on object recognition tasks ought to be well preserved whenever there is a very short delay (e.g., less than 5 s). However, under some conditions, this is true, but under certain other conditions, it is not.

Eacott *et al.* (1994) used a test of ORM (delayed matching to sample, DMS) in monkeys and showed that, with a large stimulus set size, animals with rhinal cortex lesions (which included PRC) were impaired relative to controls in two conditions designed to minimize mnemonic demands: the "zero delay" and "simultaneous matching" conditions. That is, even when the task should have been easily soluble on the basis of intact STM, animals with damage to the putative long-term declarative memory system were impaired. In a similar vein, Bartko, Winters, Cowell, Saksida, and Bussey (2007b) found that rats with PRC damage were impaired relative to controls on a test of object recognition when zero delay was interposed between study and test. The impairment was revealed only when the task was made challenging by requiring the discrimination of the familiar object from a novel object that was a previously unseen combination of previously seen parts. Similarly, Bartko, Winters, Cowell, Saksida, and Bussey (2007a) reported an impairment in ORM in rats with PRC lesions on a task that used a zero study–test delay, but only when the perceptual similarity of the novel and familiar objects in the recognition test phase was increased. The foregoing findings are problematic for the dual-system (STM/LTM) account of ORM. This account predicts that animals with damage to PRC should show impaired object memory after delays longer than a few seconds, but that these animals' memory for a studied object should always be intact in the period immediately following study. Moreover, the STM–LTM account offers no explanation for why an impairment should be revealed at zero delay in some conditions (when the novel and familiar test stimuli are perceptually similar, or when the novel foil is composed of familiar parts), but not revealed in others (when the test objects are more perceptually distinct, or when the novel object is composed of novel parts).

Representational–Hierarchical Framework

Motivated by the puzzles outlined above, we sought an entirely new account of object perception and ORM in PRC (Bussey & Saksida, 2002; Bussey, Saksida, & Murray, 2002; Cowell, Bussey, & Saksida, 2006; Cowell et al., 2010; Saksida, 1999). In this account, we moved away from the traditional, modular approach to understanding the functions of object perception and recognition memory in the brain. In particular, we rejected the assumption of two separate systems – STM and LTM – to explain ORM behavior. Moreover, with a single-system theory, we aimed to incorporate not only an explanation of the delay-dependent memory deficits induced by PRC lesions, but also an account of the apparently perception-related impairments that follow PRC damage. Below, we describe the specific computational instantiations of the theory that provided an account of existing empirical findings, and generated novel predictions, across the domains of both memory and perception.

Computational modeling was a vital conduit for the development of the general theoretical framework, because it allowed us to bring together simple assumptions about the organization of object representations in the brain with candidate information-processing mechanisms and, through simulation, test the consequences of those assumptions and mechanisms for cognitive outcomes. What emerged from the computational studies was a novel account of object processing. This account eschews the notion of separable processes for functions such as *recognition memory* and *visual discrimination* in distinct brain regions. Instead – more in keeping with animal learning theory approaches – it emphasizes the representations that each brain region contains and explains the contribution of each brain region to any given cognitive function (recognition memory, perceptual discrimination, and so on) according to whether the representations that the region contains are necessary for that task.

A model of visual discrimination learning in PRC

It was undisputed that PRC has a critical role in ORM. Many researchers argued, in addition, that it had no role in perception. Other researchers had found PRC lesions to influence visual discrimination behavior – clearly a "perceptual" function – but only under specific circumstances, which seemed to depend on the use of particular stimulus material or the imposition of certain task demands. If the PRC was involved in memory and some, but not all, perceptual tasks, how could its role in cognition best be explained? It seemed likely that an account of PRC function that could explain all of these related findings might best avoid psychological labels such as *memory* and *perception* altogether, instead asking how the object representations that the PRC contains might determine its contribution to a given cognitive task. In short, the puzzles in the literature demanded a "representational" account of cognition.

As mentioned above, Buckley and Gaffan suggested a role for PRC in object identification, but this account did not specify the mechanism by which PRC was critical for object-level perception. That is, what precise aspect of object perception – what mechanism, process, or representational property – was compromised by PRC lesions, and why did it cause the specific pattern of impairments observed? For example, why was object identification possible in PRC-lesioned individuals if the distracter stimuli were viewed from the same angle, but not from different angles? Why did increasing the number of distracters increase the discrimination problems seen following PRC lesions? One possibility was that whenever the task could be solved on the basis of simple visual features alone, PRC was not necessary. But whenever the stimulus material and task demands conspired to require the discrimination of object-level stimuli such that there were overlapping visual features between the choices to be made, animals with PRC lesions were impaired.

We refined this notion by considering that PRC may have been resolving a property of certain tasks that we came to refer to as "feature-level ambiguity": a situation that occurs when a given feature is rewarded when it is part of one object but not rewarded when part of another. In other words, the feature is ambiguous with respect to reward. To consider this hypothesis in terms of the neural representations of objects within the brain, we began with the well-established idea that visual representations build up in complexity across the VVS, with simple features represented in early regions and representations of the conjunctions of those features emerging downstream (Desimone, Albright, Gross, & Bruce, 1984; Desimone & Schein, 1987; Hubel & Wiesel, 1962). Given its anatomical placement at the end of the ventral visual pathway, we suggested that the PRC might also be considered part of the ventral visual pathway, important for representing objects in their full complexity (Bussey & Saksida, 2002; Murray & Bussey, 1999). Following from this, a mechanism that could potentially explain the pattern of results in the visual discrimination literature was based on the possibility that the object-level representations extant in PRC were complex conjunctions of the basic visual features, combined in such a way that the "whole is greater than the sum of the parts." That is, two stimuli sharing three out of four features would each elicit a level of activation much less than 75% of the maximum in each other's representation (e.g., Pearce, 1994). If there is significant feature ambiguity in a task, then exactly this type of complex, conjunctive representation would be necessary to resolve the ambiguity. PRC representations of this nature would provide unique representations of *combinations* of features that are not activated by a partial match; this ensures that the representation of an object that has been associated with reward will not be activated by a different stimulus that shares some, but not all, features with the rewarded object. Thus, reward will not be predicted by a different stimulus that was never associated with reward during training, even if it shares some features, and feature-level ambiguity can be resolved.

We built a very simple connectionist network (Bussey & Saksida, 2002), which instantiated a hierarchical scheme of object representations, and used it to simulate performance on visual discrimination learning tasks (see also Chapters 15 and 21). The model assumes that simple visual features of objects are represented in posterior regions of the VVS, whereas complex conjunctions of those simple features are represented in anterior regions, with representational complexity reaching the level of a whole object in PRC (Figure 11.1, top panel). The connectionist model possessed a simple feature layer corresponding to posterior visual cortex and a feature-conjunction layer corresponding to PRC (Figure 11.1, bottom panel). Critically, in this network, representations in the PRC layer were activated according to a formula that ensured that "the whole is greater than the sum of the parts," in line with evidence that representations in the brain possess this property (Baker, Behrmann, & Olson, 2002;

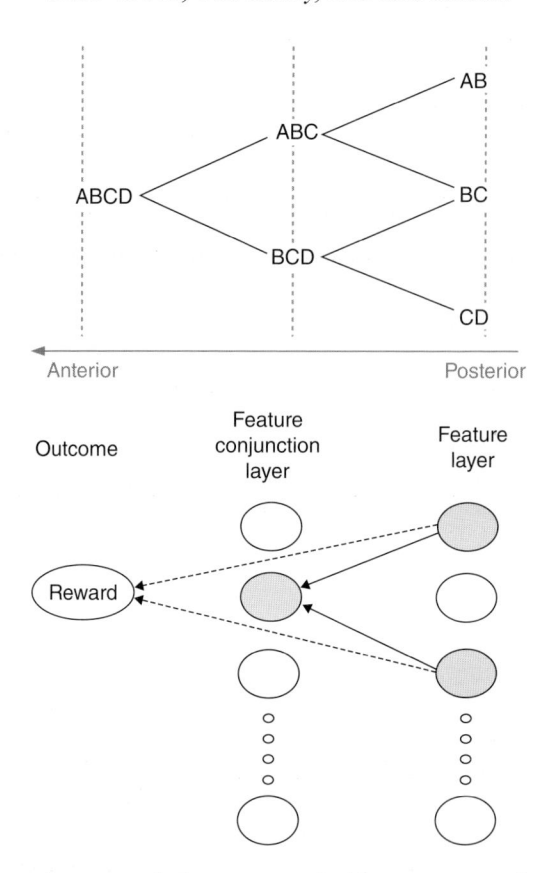

Figure 11.1 Top: schematic of the system of object representations assumed by the Representational–Hierarchical view to exist in the ventral visual stream. A single letter represents a simple, individual visual feature such as the orientation of a line. With progression from posterior to anterior regions, simple features are combined into increasingly complex conjunctions. In the PRC, the complexity of a representation corresponds to a unique, whole object. Bottom: architecture of the earliest connectionist network instantiating the Representational–Hierarchical view (Bussey and Saksida, 2002). In the first layer, corresponding to a posterior region in ventral visual stream, a unit represents a simple visual feature; in the second layer, corresponding to the PRC, a unit represents the complex conjunction of visual features that specifies a whole object. Adapted from Bussey and Saksida (2002).

Eysel, Worgotter, & Pape, 1987; Sillito, 1979; Sillito, Kemp, Milson, & Berardi, 1980). Stimulus representations in both layers were hard-wired (i.e., assumed to be developed and fixed, having been acquired by an animal during its life experience), and any active unit forming part of a stimulus representation could be associated with reward, during training, through a simple associative learning mechanism – a variant of the Rescorla–Wagner or delta rule (Rescorla & Wagner, 1972). Both layers of the model were subject to exactly the same learning rules; thus, we avoided assumptions of functional modularity in which different cognitive processes are presumed to occur in the posterior versus anterior ends of the pathway, and instead assumed that the only important way in which PRC differs from posterior visual cortex is the level of complexity of the representations it houses. The model enabled us to simulate visual discrimination learning by training networks – which amounted to updating the associative weights between stimulus representations and reward outcomes – on a series of visual discrimination problems. Moreover, the effects of PRC lesions on visual discrimination learning performance could be simulated by lesioning (i.e., removing) the layer corresponding to PRC. Training and testing such lesioned networks provided an explicit demonstration of the mechanism by which the simple assumptions instantiated in the model could explain the puzzling behavioral findings. In addition, the simulations produced explicit, novel predictions for further experimental work.

The model was able to account for the puzzling findings described in the foregoing review of the visual discrimination learning literature. That is, the model successfully simulated the deleterious effect of PRC lesions on large, but not small, set sizes, and on small set sizes for stimuli constructed according to the biconditional problem. In addition, the networks were able to successfully simulate the previously puzzling finding that the retention, postoperatively, of previously learned discriminations is consistently impaired after PRC lesions, but that the acquisition of new discrimination problems is only sometimes impaired. The model also generated novel predictions for further empirical work, which are described in the section on experimental work driven by the model below (Bussey et al., 2002; Bussey, Saksida, & Murray, 2003).

A key component of the model's mechanistic account of PRC function was relating the notion of feature ambiguity (and its resolution by PRC) to all of the various tasks on which PRC lesions had revealed impairments. That is, explaining how each case involved feature ambiguity, and thus how the feature-conjunction model was able to simulate the behavioral findings. The case of the biconditional problem is plainly explained by a "conjunctive representation" solution: Each individual feature in the stimulus set is fully ambiguous with respect to reward. Thus, only by creating configural representations, in which a representation of the object whole is not activated by partially matching stimuli, can each stimulus be correctly associated with reward or nonreward. However, the explanations for other tasks were less obvious. In the case of set size, feature ambiguity arises whenever the same visual features occur in different objects within the set, by chance. Among a small number of objects, the features comprising those objects might be relatively unique; however, once the pool of objects increases, so does the probability that two or more objects in the pool will share features in common. Thus, at large set sizes, individual visual features appear as part of both rewarded and nonrewarded objects, giving rise to feature ambiguity. Finally, the finding that postoperative retention of previously learned discriminations is consistently impaired after PRC lesions can be explained by the model because the surgery (in networks, the removal of the PRC layer) destroyed the object representations in PRC that were associated with reward during preoperative training, necessitating the relearning of the object–reward associations after training, with whatever residual object representations remained. According to the model, in the case of postoperatively learned discriminations, whether PRC lesions affected the acquisition or not depended on whether the discrimination task contained feature ambiguity; hence these tasks were sometimes impaired and sometimes not.

A single-system account of dissociations between perception and memory

As discussed above, arguably the most fundamental and widespread assumption made by theories of visual cognition in the 20th century was that the mechanisms of memory and visual perception are functionally and neuroanatomically distinct. From a cognitive neuroscience perspective, this assumption has profound implications for the functional organization of the brain: Visually responsive regions must contribute to no more than one of the two domains, perception and memory; no region can contribute to both. However, the results indicating that PRC – a structure that, according to the modular view, is part of the MTL memory system and so should contribute to declarative memory and declarative memory only – is critical for visual discrimination learning under certain conditions suggested that this view needed to be reconsidered. However, an important challenge in building a new representational account of the neural and cognitive mechanisms in PRC was to demonstrate that the earliest evidence for neuroanatomical modularity of perception and memory could be explained by our alternative account that allowed a given brain region to contribute to both functions, depending on the task.

To this end, we revisited the neuropsychological literature on visual discrimination learning from the 1960s and 1970s, exemplified by the study of Iwai and Mishkin (1968; see Figure 11.2). We asked: Can a single-system model – in which all processing stations along the ventral visual pathway perform the same computational operations – account for the observed double dissociation in discrimination learning performance, following anterior versus posterior lesions (Cowell et al., 2010)? To build such a model, we assumed the same principles of representational organization as in the original model of PRC function. In addition, we used very similar rules governing the construction of representations and the learning of associations. For this model, however, we extended the network, including three layers of stimulus representation, so that several different points along the VVS could be simulated. Furthermore, we employed an input layer that could send stimulus activation independently to all layers of representations, so that early layers could be lesioned without a total blockade of information reaching later layers; this is in line with evidence for parallel, or "jumping," connections that exist alongside the serial connections in the ventral visual pathway of the brain (Lennie, 1998; Nakamura, Gattass, Desimone, & Ungerleider, 1993).

We used this extended network to simulate performance on the visual discrimination learning tasks used by Iwai and Mishkin, and in other studies like theirs, both with and without the kinds of brain lesions employed by those authors. The model assumed that the organization of object representations in the brain is the critical factor determining the behavioral effects of lesions at different points along the ventral pathway. Simple, feature-based visual representations are located in posterior regions, and complex conjunctions of those features are housed in more anterior regions, as in the previous instantiation of the model, shown in Figure 11.1. When a given brain region is damaged, performance will be impaired on any task that is best solved using the representations at the level of complexity usually found in the damaged region. The extended connectionist model included three layers of units, corresponding to three different levels of complexity of the stimulus representations, spanning posterior regions such as V1 through to anterior parts of the temporal lobe (Figure 11.3).

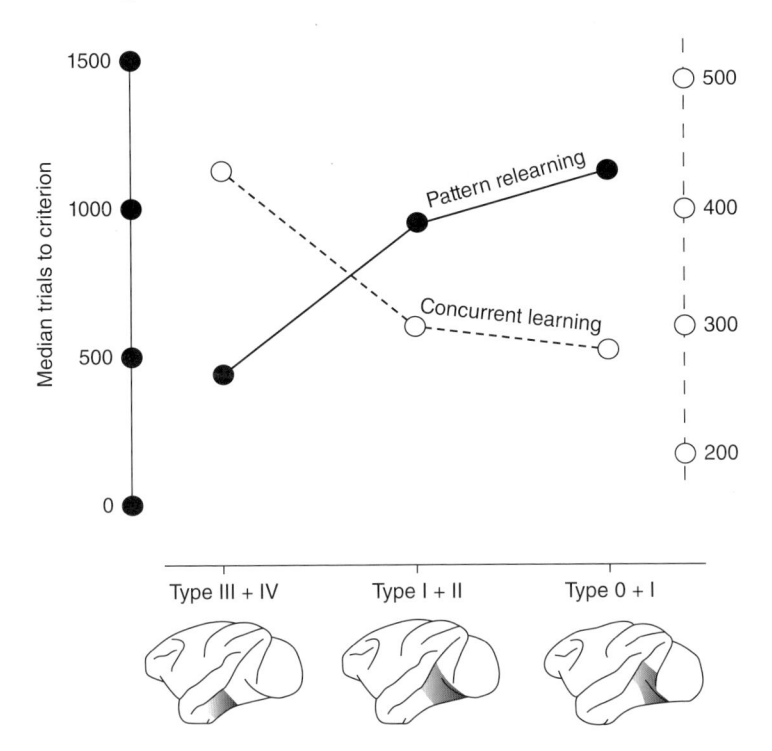

Computational and Functional Specialization of Memory 259

Figure 11.2 Data from Iwai and Mishkin (1968). The "Pattern Relearning" Task was a putative test of perception, in which monkeys were required to learn to discriminate a single pair of very simple visual stimuli. The "Concurrent Learning" task was a putative test of memory, in which monkeys had to learn concurrently to discriminate several pairs of complex visual objects. See the section entitled "The modular organization of visual memory and visual perception in the brain" for further details on the tasks and their interpretation. Lesions at different points in the ventral visual stream produced strikingly different impairments on the two tasks; this double dissociation was taken as evidence for the functional and anatomical independence of visual perception and visual memory. Adapted from Cowell et al. (2010).

Like the two-layer model of visual discrimination learning that was used to understand PRC function (Bussey & Saksida, 2002), this extended model used three very simple assumptions. First, we assumed that the organization of object representations in the VVS is hierarchical, with simple conjunctions of features being represented in early regions, and complex conjunctions of those simpler conjunctions being represented in later regions. Second, in all layers, we used lateral inhibition to ensure that "the whole is greater than the sum of the parts," such that any given representation corresponding to a particular object would be activated to a level much less than half of its maximum activation by a stimulus containing half of the features belonging to the corresponding object. Third, we assumed that object representations at all points could become associated with outcomes such as reward, through a simple associative learning mechanism. Importantly, we removed the problematic assumption of most other accounts of visual cognition that there are differential contributions of different regions along the VVS to perception and memory. Instead, in this model, the object-processing mechanisms underlying learning and discrimination behavior were identical at all points in the pathway.

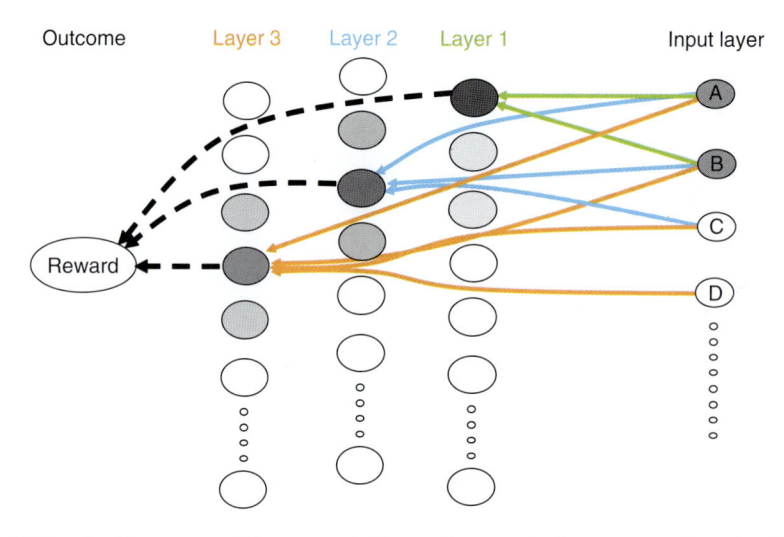

Figure 11.3 Archictecture of the extended neural network that was used to simulate data from Iwai and Mishkin (1968). The network contains an input layer and three layers of representations, ranging in complexity from simple conjunctions of two visual features (in Layer 1) to complex conjunctions of four visual features (in Layer 3). Darker gray indicates a higher degree of activation. The stimulus pattern displayed across the network corresponds to a "simple" two-featured visual stimulus. Solid lines depict fixed (nonadjustable weights), whereas dotted lines indicate weights that are learned through an associative mechanism. Adapted from Cowell et al. (2010).

To simulate the visual discrimination learning tasks of Iwai and Mishkin (1968) and the associated literature, we proposed that the complex objects used in the "mnemonic" version of those tasks contained more visual features than the simple two-dimensional stimuli used in the "perceptual" versions. Because the layers of the network were independent and corresponded to different points along the VVS, we could lesion the network in both anterior and posterior layers in order to simulate the neuropsychology experiments of the 1970s. In doing so, two important assumptions of the model came together to allow an account of the behavioral findings. The fact that simple conjunctions were represented on Layer 1, and complex conjunctions were represented on Layer 3 (see Figure 11.3), meant that the simple stimuli were a good match to representational units on Layer 1, whereas the complex (mnemonic) stimuli were a good match to Layer 3 units. In addition, the "whole is greater than the sum of the parts" assumption meant that simple stimuli were well discriminated by units in Layer 1 but poorly discriminated by units in Layers 2 and 3. Conversely, complex stimuli were well discriminated by units in Layer 3 but poorly discriminated by units in Layers 2 and 1 (see Figure 11.4). This scheme led to exactly the pattern of results observed in the monkey literature. When networks were lesioned in Layer 3 (the anterior end of VVS), only discrimination tasks employing complex stimuli were severely impaired, whereas when networks had Layer 1 removed (the posterior end of VVS), tasks using simple stimuli were selectively severely impaired, as shown in Figure 11.5.

As with the foregoing account of PRC function, a computational approach to reinterpreting the literature allowed us to bring together knowledge from neuroscience

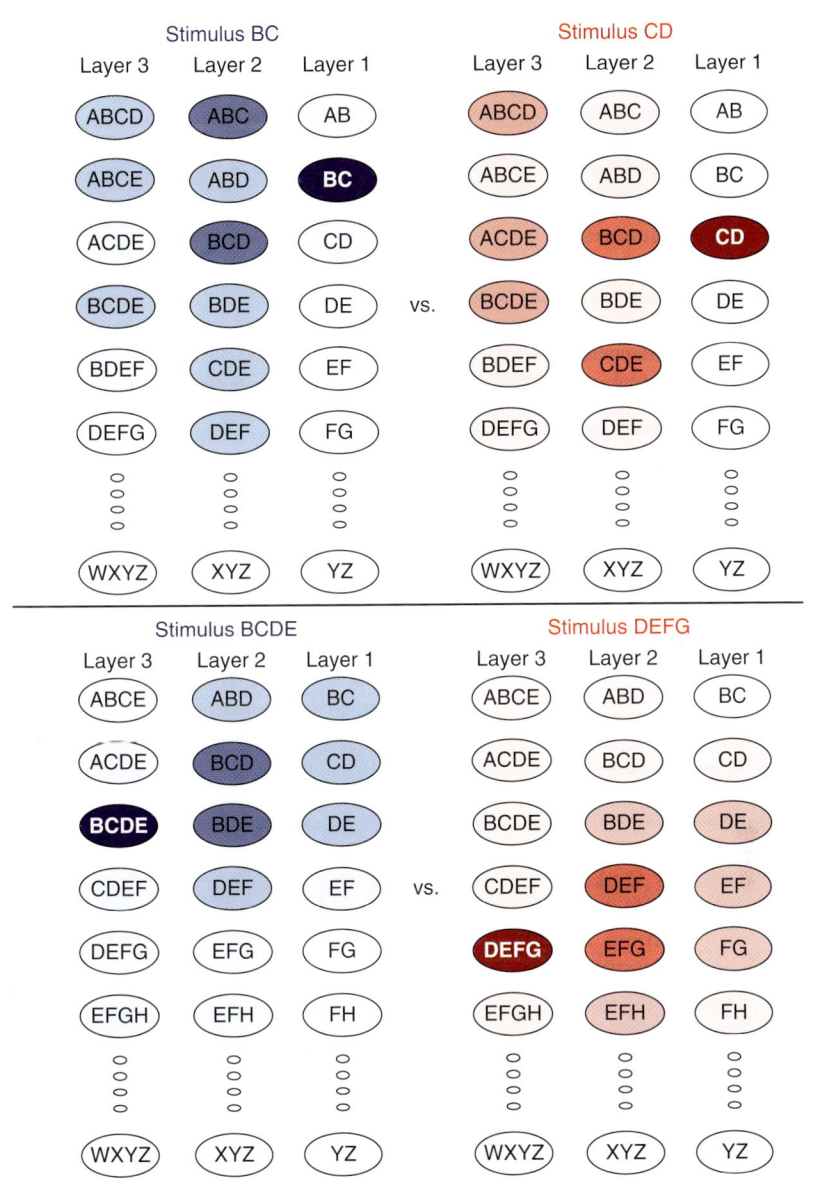

Figure 11.4 Schematic depicting the activation patterns corresponding to a simple (top panel) and a complex (bottom panel) stimulus, across the network. Simple stimuli are well discriminated by units in Layer 1, because each stimulus provides an exact match to one, and only one, unit in the layer, which leads to a "sharp" representation in which only one unit is highly active for each stimulus, and the two stimuli have highly distinct activation patterns. In contrast, a simple stimulus is poorly discriminated by units in Layers 2 and 3, since they never provide an exact match to units in those layers and thus elicit weak activation across many units, rendering the patterns corresponding to two different simple stimuli highly similar. Conversely, complex stimuli are well discriminated by units in Layer 3 because each stimulus provides an exact match to one Layer 3 unit, but poorly discriminated by units in Layers 2 and 1, because in those layers, the multifeatured objects activate multiple (simple) units and the lateral inhibition fails to produce one clear winner for each stimulus that would allow efficient discrimination.

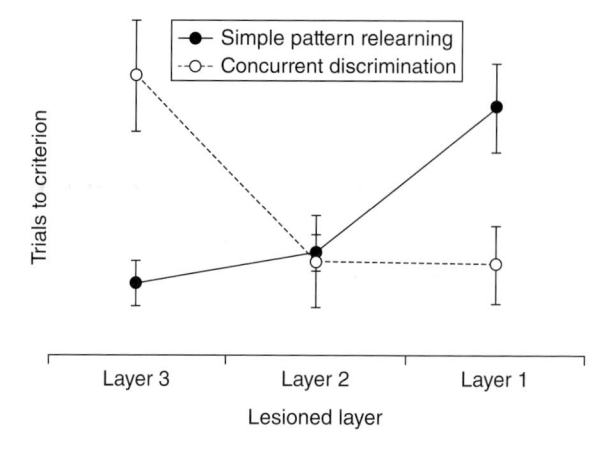

Figure 11.5 Simulation data from Cowell *et al.* (2010), reproducing the results of Iwai and Mishkin (1968). For the "Pattern Relearning" task, networks were repeatedly presented with a single pair of two-featured stimuli; for the "Concurrent Learning" task, networks were required to learn, through multiple presentations, to discriminate multiple pairs of complex, four-featured stimuli. A lesion was simulated by removing the layer of interest, thus forcing networks to learn the discrimination problem using only the remaining layers. Adapted from Cowell *et al.* (2010).

(concerning the organization of the visual pathway, and the properties of neural representations) with principles and mechanisms from associative learning theory (the Rescorla–Wagner or delta rule; and concepts of elemental and configural processing) and test their consequences for behavior. By lesioning networks, we could test the behavioral consequences of the removal of representations in those regions, to demonstrate that a "representational account" of cognition in VVS could explain the observed double dissociation. The chief novel contribution of this representational account was the claim that the contribution of each brain region to cognition is determined by the representations it contains, and not by a psychological label that ascribes to it a particular cognitive function.

A model of ORM in PRC

A central building block of the nonmodular account of visual cognition was put in place by providing the foregoing single-system account of observed double dissociations in visual discrimination learning. But to show that performance on a *visual learning task* can be explained in terms of compromised stimulus representations is one thing; to demonstrate that this same representational account can explain the effects of brain lesions on a *classic memory task* would be quite another. ORM is thought to rely wholly upon the MTLs, according to the traditional "MMS" view, and ORM tasks are widely used in animal models of amnesia. Therefore, another key building block of the nonmodular account would be to use this same general, theoretical framework to account for ORM. Moreover, since PRC is the MTL structure known to be critical for ORM performance, any theoretical account that attempts to explain object processing in PRC must ultimately incorporate an explanation of this important cognitive function.

The logical extension of our representational account is that – like regions of the ventral visual pathway, whose contributions to visual discrimination learning we explained in terms of the stimulus representations they contain, rather than in terms of an exclusive role in perception or memory – the contribution of PRC to both visual perception and visual memory can be explained in terms of its representations. The idea seemed unconventional, but the approach held instant appeal: expanding the Representational–Hierarchical view to account for object memory in PRC would provide a unifying theoretical framework that brought a common set of assumptions and mechanisms to bear upon a range of cognitive tasks and an extended set of brain regions.

We thus set out to test the idea that the deleterious effect of PRC lesions on ORM could be explained under the Representational–Hierarchical account (Cowell et al., 2006). We assumed the same scheme of representations as in the model of visual discrimination learning (Figure 11.1, top panel), but it was necessary to adapt the computational instantiation for this application because, in the previous model, stimulus representations were hard-wired. To simulate ORM, a mechanism for the *development* of stimulus representations is necessary, so that networks can provide a familiarity signal for objects that have been viewed (i.e., to which they have been exposed) in order to differentiate familiar objects from novel objects (to which networks have not been exposed). We therefore replaced the hard-wired stimulus representation layers in the previous model with self-organizing feature maps, or Kohonen networks (Kohonen, 1982), in which stimulus representations develop without supervision when networks are exposed to perceptual stimuli. Self-organizing feature maps are typically laid out in two dimensions, such that each unit has a fixed position in the network layer, rather like each neuron in the cortical sheet. This property, along with the biological plausibility of the learning rules they employ, makes them well suited to modeling the learning processes occurring in cortex. Furthermore, the dimensionality of the representations in a Kohonen network can be set to any desired level, simply by choosing the number of inputs: A Kohonen network with eight input units will contain eight-dimensional representations, because all inputs are connected to each "stimulus representation" unit in the Kohonen network. To model the increasing complexity of representations advancing along the VVS, we built two stimulus representation layers using Kohonen networks: a "posterior VVS" layer, in which we employed four separate networks with low-dimensional representations, and a layer corresponding to PRC, containing a single representational network with high dimensionality (Figure 11.6). This produced representations of objects that manifested as four distinct, two-dimensional feature "chunks" in the posterior layer (in four low-dimensional representational spaces) and one unified high-dimensional object representation (in one high-dimensional representational space) in the PRC layer. We made a strong but simple assumption about the composition of visual objects in the world: that all objects are composed from a limited pool of simple visual features. That is, while there are an almost infinite number of possible unique objects in the world, there are a finite, relatively small number of elemental building blocks – simple visual features – of which all objects are composed, with each object's uniqueness being defined by the exact combination or conjunction of features that it comprises.

We pretrained networks by presenting a large number of stimuli, thus allowing networks to learn about the whole stimulus space through a self-organizing learning algorithm. We then simulated encoding in a memory task by presenting a single stimulus for several successive cycles of learning, so that its representation became

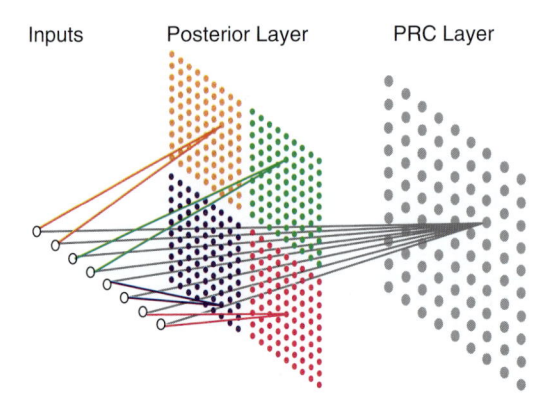

Figure 11.6 Architecture of neural network model used to simulate object recognition memory. The input layer, on the far right, consists of eight inputs or "dimensions." The "Posterior Layer" contains four separate self-organizing maps (shown in distinct colors), each of which receives inputs from two input units and thus represents a simple, two-dimensional chunk of an object that we term a "visual feature." The "Perirhinal Layer" contains a single self-organizing map in which each unit receives inputs from all eight input units, thus creating complex eight-dimensional representations in this layer that correspond to a whole visual object. After Cowell *et al.* (2006).

"sharpened" (i.e., familiar) on the stimulus representation layers of the model (see Figure 11.7). This process was identical on both layers; it resulted in four sharp feature representations on the posterior layer and one sharp object representation on the PRC layer. We used the sharpness of a stimulus representation as an index of familiarity.

We made a further assumption about the mechanism of forgetting over a delay: interference in the form of a stream of objects played out in the activity of visual cortex. This interference could arise from real or imagined visual stimuli. Because objects are drawn from an extremely high-dimensional space (i.e., a very large pool) the chances of seeing a particular object during a delay period are very low; the chances of seeing it twice are vanishingly small. By contrast, the features that constitute the objects occur repeatedly but as part of different objects. As the length of the delay increases, so the number of viewed objects increases, and each feature in the limited pool appears again and again; eventually, its representation on the posterior layer of the network begins to sharpen and appear familiar. After a sufficiently long delay, all features in the pool appear familiar on the posterior layer of the model. In contrast, on the PRC layer, all stimuli are represented as unique, high-dimensional whole objects. Since no object appears more than once during the delay, no representations become familiar-looking as a result of interference. The only objects that appear familiar on the PRC layer at the end of the delay are those that have been repeatedly presented to networks in an explicit study phase.

Presumably, individuals with PRC lesions must rely solely upon posterior representations in order to judge familiarity. After a delay, all feature-level representations are sharpened, giving the impression, at least at the level of neural networks, that all objects are familiar. Without the PRC, an individual can no longer discriminate novel from previously seen objects on the basis of familiarity (Figure 11.8).

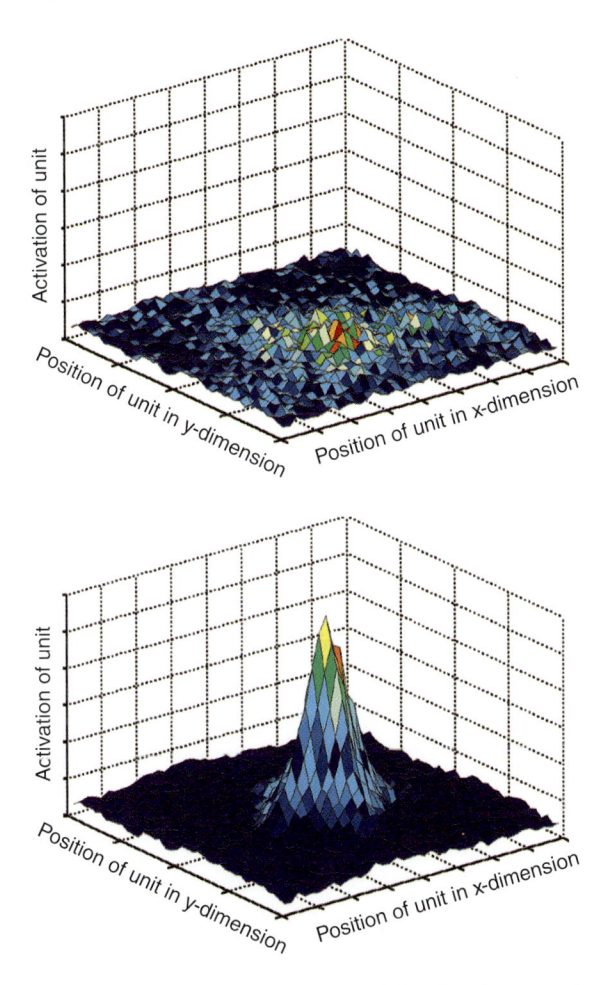

Figure 11.7 Representation of a stimulus in the model before (top panel) and after (bottom panel) encoding has taken place. Each point on the grid corresponds to a unit in the layer; the height and color of the point indicate the activation level of the unit. Before encoding, all units are activated to a similar level; after encoding, there is a peak of activation around the "winning" unit. The encoding process operates in the same manner for both posterior and perirhinal self-organizing maps. After Cowell et al. (2006).

Having developed an account of delay-dependent forgetting, we also simulated the effect of PRC lesions on the list length effect and found that the model replicated empirical data well: Effectively, the effect of increasing the length of the list of to-be-remembered items was identical to the effect of presenting interfering items during a delay. Thus, PRC-lesioned networks were impaired at increasing list lengths. Moreover, in line with the empirical evidence, removing the PRC layer of the model had no effect on repeated-items object recognition. This is because, in the model, neither the posterior feature layer nor the PRC layer can usefully contribute to such a task: Two items that are highly familiar through repeated recent presentation cannot be discriminated on the basis of familiarity.

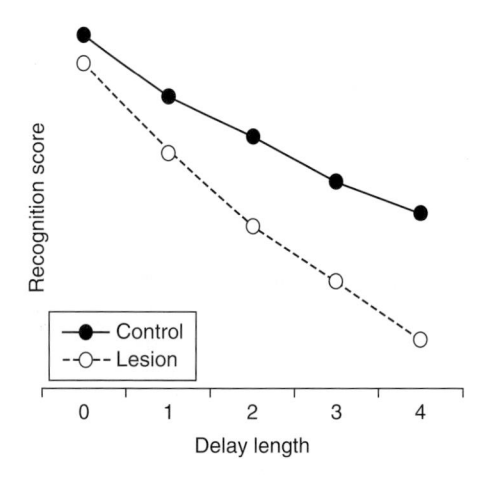

Figure 11.8 Simulation data from the model of object recognition memory. Following a delay, networks with PRC lesions (i.e., in which the PRC layer has been removed and performance relies upon the Posterior Layer alone) show a deficit in object recognition memory. Adapted from Cowell et al. (2006).

A particular strength of this model is that it provides a single-system account of delay-dependent forgetting. This account contrasts with the dual-system STM/LTM account (e.g., Buffalo et al., 1998; Jeneson & Squire, 2012; Liu & Bilkey, 1998), and it does not suffer the problem of being unable to explain the deleterious effects of PRC lesions on ORM at zero delay. Rather, this model provides a natural account of this result. The contribution of PRC to ORM rests upon its provision of complex, conjunctive stimulus representations that specify a whole object uniquely. In ORM, these representations shield an individual from feature-level interference that builds up during a delay between study and test. However, the interposition of a delay is not the only means by which a task may demand the resolution of feature-level interference or ambiguity. If the novel and familiar object stimuli in the choice phase share a sufficient number of features, then feature-based representations in posterior regions may be insufficient to distinguish the objects on the basis of familiarity. Indeed, this hypothesis is supported by data from Bartko et al. (2007a) and Eacott et al. (1994). For example, a novel object sharing three out of four features with the familiar object will elicit a familiarity signal in posterior regions that is approximately 75% as strong as that for the familiar object itself, greatly diminishing the discriminability of the two stimuli on the basis of familiarity. Discriminating these objects, even at zero delay, instead requires whole-object representations in PRC for which "the whole is greater than the sum of the parts," such that even similar objects with several shared features do not strongly excite each other's representation (Bartko et al., 2007a). This application of the account demonstrates a key tenet of the Representational–Hierarchical Framework: that any given brain region will contribute to any cognitive task for which the stimulus representations contained in the region are necessary. The object-level representations in PRC are necessary for most novel–familiar discriminations after a study–test delay – a "memory" contribution – and for certain novel–familiar discriminations (e.g., between similar stimuli) at zero delay – a "perceptual" contribution.

Summary of the Representational–Hierarchical computational framework

The Representational–Hierarchical computational framework takes empirically determined details of neural representations and the mechanisms that operate upon them (e.g., the hierarchical organization of object representations, lateral inhibition mechanisms that render individual object representations highly selective) and integrates it with information-processing ideas from associative learning theory (e.g., the delta rule), to explain observed behavior. Under the Representational–Hierarchical account, the explanatory legwork is carried out through combination of three basic ingredients: (1) a simple idea about the organization of object representations in the brain; (2) some simple assumptions about how those representations might be used by the brain to produce behavior, based on standard ideas in the literature (e.g., sharpening of representations signaling familiarity, or associative learning between a representation and a rewarding outcome producing discrimination learning); and (3) a simple assumption that the many unique visual objects in the world are composed from a limited set of commonly occurring, simple, visual features – a state of affairs that creates feature ambiguity in many object-processing tasks. These three basic ingredients produce an account in which complex, conjunctive representations in later regions of the ventral visual pathway are important for object processing across an array of tasks – both perceptual and mnemonic – in which feature-level interference, or feature ambiguity, arises, while early regions of the same pathway are important for the processing of very simple visual stimuli. This framework has been used to provide a unifying, single-system account of behavioral data from a range of cognitive tasks and, through this account, explain some puzzling and contradictory findings. However, the most powerful means by which any formal model can advance and refine theoretical understanding is via the generation of novel predictions and the testing of those predictions with experimental work. This process is the subject of the next section.

Experimental Work Driven by the Representational–Hierarchical Framework

Visual discrimination learning

The first set of experimental findings driven by the Representational–Hierarchical view followed directly from its first computational instantiation, and tested predictions of the model for visual discrimination behavior after PRC lesions. The simple connectionist model of PRC function made three novel predictions (Bussey & Saksida, 2002; Saksida, 1999). First, the degree of impairment in visual discrimination learning following PRC lesions should be related to the degree of feature ambiguity between the to-be-discriminated stimuli. Second, PRC damage should impair the acquisition of perceptually ambiguous discriminations (in which the stimuli share many features) more than perceptually nonambiguous discriminations, and that the degree of impairment should be unrelated to the speed of acquisition of the problem by control animals (i.e., not due to difficulty per se). Third, PRC lesions should impair perceptually ambiguous discriminations, even in the absence of any learning. For example, if a lesioned animal learns a low feature ambiguity discrimination problem to some criterion without impairment, a subsequent increase in the feature ambiguity of the problem (by rendering the stimuli more similar to one another) should reveal impairments in the lesioned animal's discrimination performance that cannot be attributed to a deficit in learning.

We tested the first prediction with a study in rhesus monkeys (Bussey et al., 2002). Animals learned a visual discrimination task, in which stimuli were constructed from grayscale photographs and grouped into pairs, designating one stimulus in each pair to be consistently rewarded during training. Three levels of difficulty were created by explicitly manipulating the degree to which the visual features of the stimuli were ambiguous in their predictions of reward: In the "Maximum Feature Ambiguity" condition, all visual features appeared equally often as part of a rewarded and an unrewarded stimulus (AB+, CD+, BC−, AD−, as in the biconditional problem); in the "Minimum Feature Ambiguity" condition, all visual features only ever appeared in either a rewarded or an unrewarded stimulus (AB+, CD+, EF−, GH−); in an "Intermediate" condition, half of all visual features were ambiguous, and half provided unambiguous predictions of reward (AB+, CD+, CE±, AF±), as shown in Figure 11.9. Thus, as the degree of feature ambiguity increased, the task demanded greater and greater reliance upon configural stimulus representations, because only the specific conjunctions of features comprising unique stimuli provided unambiguous information as to which stimulus would lead to reward. We found, as predicted, that monkeys with PRC lesions were unimpaired at Minimum Feature Ambiguity, mildly impaired in the

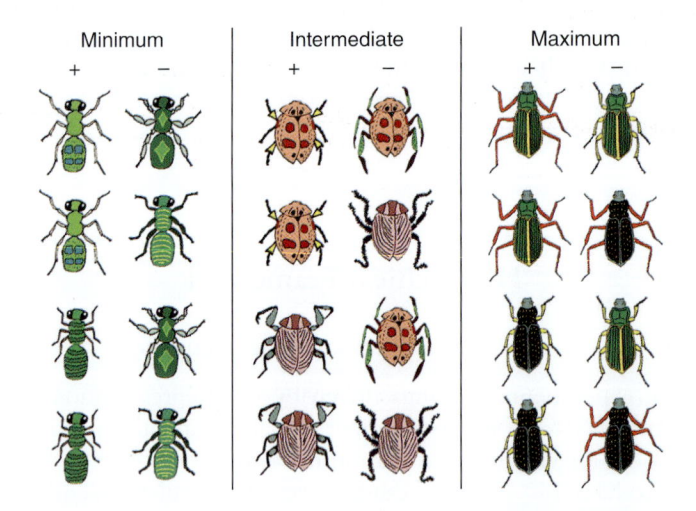

Figure 11.9 Stimuli from the "Feature Ambiguity" experiment of Barense et al. (2005). These followed the same structural design as the photographic stimuli of Bussey et al. (2002). The columns show the sets of "bug" stimuli used to create Minimum, Intermediate and Maximum levels of Feature Ambiguity. In the Minimum condition, all features are unambiguous, being consistently rewarded or unrewarded. In the Intermediate condition, half of all features are ambiguous, appearing equally often as part of rewarded and unrewarded stimuli, while the other half of the features are unambiguous, only ever being rewarded or unrewarded. In the Maximum condition, all features are ambiguous, appearing equally often as part of rewarded and unrewarded stimuli; thus only the specific conjunction of features gives an unambiguous prediction of reward.

Intermediate condition, and severely impaired in the Maximum condition. In subsequent work we found that alternative manipulations of feature ambiguity, such as morphing the discriminanda together, led to a similar pattern of results (Bussey et al., 2003; Saksida, Bussey, Buckmaster, & Murray, 2007). It is important to note that the same monkeys with PRC lesions were not impaired when required to discriminate objects with low feature ambiguity ; nor were they impaired when required to acquire difficult color or size discriminations.

We followed this up in a collaboration to test this same prediction in humans with MTL damage. In Barense et al. (2005), we adapted the visual discrimination learning paradigm used in monkeys for human participants, creating three different sets of stimuli – barcodes, fictitious insects (as shown in Figure 11.8) and abstract blobs – that each contained stimulus pairs constructed, just as for monkeys, with three levels of feature ambiguity: Minimum, Intermediate, and Maximum. In addition, one further stimulus set, comprising mythical beasts (say, the head of a horse with the body of a leopard) contained only two levels of feature ambiguity: Minimum and Maximum. Four groups of participants were tested: patients with extensive MTL damage (including PRC), patients with focal hippocampal damage (excluding PRC), and two sets of matched control subjects, one for each patient group. For all four stimulus sets, an analysis of the discrimination learning measure (number of trials to reach a fixed performance criterion) revealed a greater deviation from control performance in the MTL group than in the HC group, as feature ambiguity increased. Closer inspection of each group's performance on the different conditions showed that MTL patients performed normally in all but one of the minimum ambiguity conditions, but poorly in all conditions involving feature ambiguity, whereas HC patients performed indistinguishably from controls in all conditions, regardless of feature ambiguity. In line with the model of PRC function, these results imply that PRC – in humans – is indeed critical for object perception, but only in situations where conjunctive object-level representations are needed to resolve ambiguity at the level of individual visual features.

Simultaneous visual discrimination

The findings of Barense et al. (2005) were critical to demonstrating that the Representational–Hierarchical account applied not only to animals but also to humans with MTL damage. However, the study incorporated an element of learning, in that each stimulus had to be associated with reward or nonreward. To make an unequivocal demonstration that the cognitive deficit caused by PRC damage could not be due to impairments in learning, it was necessary to test such a group of patients on a task that eliminated all learning. To that end, Barense, Gaffan, and Graham (2007) devised a series of "oddity" tasks, in which participants were presented with all stimuli, targets and distracters, simultaneously. Any deficit in performance under such conditions must necessarily be attributable to perceptual problems. These tasks were modeled after work in the monkey literature (e.g., Buckley, Booth, Rolls, & Gaffan, 2001), which had shown that PRC-lesioned animals were impaired on oddity discrimination tasks, but only under certain conditions such as when a variety of viewing angles of the objects were used, and when complex object-level stimuli had to be discriminated.

Three different tests of simultaneous object discrimination were assessed, in addition to two tests of basic visual perception that were matched for difficulty to the object tasks. In one object task, novel three-dimensional objects (*Fribble* stimuli, originally constructed by Williams & Simons, 2000) were presented in arrays of seven items, in which three items were identical pairs, and one item was the "odd one out." Arrays were constructed with three levels of feature ambiguity – Minimum, Intermediate, and Maximum – analogous to the visual discrimination learning tasks described above. That is, in the Minimum condition, no unique objects (i.e., no objects except those in identical pairs) shared any features; in the Intermediate condition, all unique objects consisted half of unique features and half of features appearing in other unique objects; and in the Maximum condition, all unique objects were composed entirely of features that appeared in more than one unique object. In the other two object tasks, participants were presented with arrays containing four stimuli, each pictured from a different angle; one image depicted a unique object, whereas the other three images were three different views of the same object. One of these tasks used Greebles (Gauthier & Tarr, 1997); the other used photographs of everyday objects. In all three object tasks, participants were required to choose the unique object. Selection of the correct target item required the ability to discriminate between objects that shared many features and could not be performed by analyzing a simple image feature (i.e., a simple feature always pictured from the same angle). By contrast, in the two basic visual perception tasks, participants were required to make very difficult size or color discriminations, which necessitated highly accurate representations of basic visual features. Patients with lesions in hippocampus that excluded PRC performed similarly to controls on all conditions. In contrast, patients with damage that included PRC were significantly impaired whenever the task required discrimination of objects that shared a large number of visual features in common, but not when the discriminations could easily be solved on the basis of simple visual features possessed by the objects. These results are consistent with earlier work showing that monkeys with selective hippocampal lesions are unimpaired on PRC-dependent feature-ambiguous visual discriminations (Saksida, Bussey, Buckmaster, & Murray, 2006).

Having translated these important findings from the animal to the human domain, we and others were motivated to test further implications of the theoretical framework, extending it to consider the possibility that the hippocampus, too, is involved in visual perception, whenever a task taxes the particular kind of conjunctive representations that are housed within it. Whereas, under the Representational–Hierarchical view, PRC is the critical locus for conjunctive object-level representations, the hippocampus would be situated at a higher level in the hierarchy, providing representations of higher-order conjunctions (Bussey & Saksida, 2005; Cowell et al., 2006). Such conjunctions may contain multiple individual objects, the spatial relations between objects, the spatial, temporal, or interoceptive context of an item or event, and other associative information present during a given experience (Chapters 4 and 12). As such, one class of stimulus that should depend strongly upon hippocampal representations is spatial scenes. According to the Representational–Hierarchical view, the hippocampus should be important for the perceptual discrimination of scenes, even in the absence of any memory demands, when those scenes contain many shared items or features, such that the task cannot be solved on the basis of object-level or feature-level representations alone (Chapter 13).

Lee and colleagues have tested this hypothesis for hippocampal function. Using oddity tasks similar to those of Barense *et al.* (2007), Lee *et al.* (2005a) tested discrimination of virtual scenes and discrimination of faces, in patients with focal hippocampal damage, in patients with more widespread MTL damage including both HC and PRC, and in matched control subjects. In one version of the task, for each stimulus type all distracter stimuli in the simultaneously presented array were pictured from different views (as in Barense *et al.*, 2007; Buckley *et al.*, 2001). In another version, all distracter stimuli were presented from the same view, presumably enabling the use of a single image feature to group together all distracter items and distinguish them from the target. Lee *et al.* found that the discrimination of scenes in the different views condition was impaired by HC damage (i.e., it was impaired in both patient groups), but scene discrimination in the same views condition was not. There was no effect of additional PRC damage (i.e., no difference between focal HC and patients with HC and PRC damage) on either version of the scene discrimination task. For face stimuli, focal HC damage did not impair discrimination, regardless of the viewing angle of the distracter stimuli. In contrast, patients whose damage included PRC were impaired on the different views condition for faces, but not for the same views condition. The authors concluded, in line with the Representational–Hierarchical account, that HC is important for scene discrimination, but only when the scenes cannot be discriminated on the basis of simple visual features, and it is not critical for face discrimination. Moreover, PRC is not critical for scene discrimination, but is important for face discrimination, and – analogous to the role of HC for scenes – the PRC contributes to face perception only when the faces cannot be distinguished on the basis of simple features.

The same team of researchers used the same oddity tests of face and object discrimination to assess patients with either Alzheimer's disease (AD) or semantic dementia (SD; Lee *et al.*, 2006). Given that AD patients have predominantly hippocampal atrophy within the MTL, whereas SD patients have more perirhinal damage, these two patient groups provide a second test of the contributions of these two MTL structures to perceptual function. The authors found essentially the same pattern of results: AD patients were impaired at scene oddity discriminations, whereas SD patients were not; SD patients were impaired at face oddity discriminations, whereas AD patients were not.

In two further studies, Lee and coworkers tested the ability of patients with MTL damage to perform visual discriminations, this time making the tasks difficult by blending, or morphing, pairs of visual stimuli, such that, in the hardest conditions, discriminations could not be performed on the basis of isolating and utilizing a salient visual feature. They found, both in patients with MTL damage (Lee *et al.*, 2005b; cf. Kim *et al.*, 2011) and in patients with AD versus SD (Lee *et al.*, 2007), evidence for a role for hippocampus in the visual perception of scenes and a role for MTL neocortical structures (such as PRC) in the visual perception of single, complex items such as objects and faces.

A final, important piece of evidence for the application of the Representational–Hierarchical account to hippocampal function comes from an imaging study in healthy human participants. Using the aforementioned oddity judgment paradigm, Lee, Scahill, and Graham (2008) found that oddity judgments for scene stimuli were associated with increased posterior hippocampus and parahippocampal cortex activity, when contrasted with the activation elicited by performing face oddity judgments or difficult size oddity discriminations. In contrast, PRC and anterior hippocampus were more strongly activated during the face oddity task than by performance of the scene or size oddity task. In this study, the size oddity task involved detecting which square in an array of squares was slightly larger or smaller than the rest; it served as a control condition, matched for difficulty to the other tasks, in which the visual discrimination could be made on the basis of a simple perceptual feature. The findings corroborate the evidence from patients described above, supporting the idea that PRC is involved in object discriminations and the hippocampus in scene discriminations, in particular during tasks in which the discriminations cannot be solved by attending to simple perceptual features.

ORM

The Representational–Hierarchical framework provided a parsimonious, single-system account of the delay-dependent deficits observed in MTL amnesia (Chapter 8). It also accounted for other extant findings from subjects with PRC damage, such as the effects on recognition memory performance of increasing the length of the list of to-be-remembered items, and using repeated-items rather than trial-unique stimuli. More importantly, the modeling work also generated a number of novel predictions, which have subsequently been tested empirically both in our own laboratory and by others.

The first novel prediction is that, following PRC damage, recognition memory will be impaired if the novel and familiar stimuli presented at test are made perceptually similar by increasing the number of shared features they possess. This prediction arises because, in the model, any features of a novel object that appeared as part of a studied object will appear familiar; in PRC-lesioned networks that must rely on individual feature representations in the posterior layer, this renders the novel object more familiar-looking. This prediction holds, even with no delay between the study and test phases of the task; indeed, a true test of this prediction requires a zero-delay paradigm to avoid potential confound with the effect of delay. We tested this prediction in a study with rats (Bartko *et al.*, 2007a). Using a spontaneous recognition paradigm, we introduced an instantaneous transition between the study and test phases (Figure 11.10), thus eliminating any delay. The novel and familiar stimuli presented in the test phase were made of Lego™ and explicitly manipulated to share many perceptual features (e.g., by possessing a similar global shape and blocks of the same color in similar locations on the two stimuli). As predicted by the model, rats with lesions in PRC were impaired in the "perceptually difficult" condition, in which novel and familiar stimuli shared many visual features, but not in the "perceptually easy" condition, in which stimuli shared fewer visual features.

The second novel prediction is that individuals with PRC damage will show deficits in the recognition of novel combinations of familiar parts. This is because the model says that, in the absence of PRC, an individual must rely upon feature-based representations to judge familiarity; in any scenario in which the individual features of a novel object are familiar, ORM will be impaired. Put another way, the feature-based representations in posterior visual cortex cannot be used to detect novelty at the object- or feature-conjunction level. In our test of this prediction, we used an object recognition

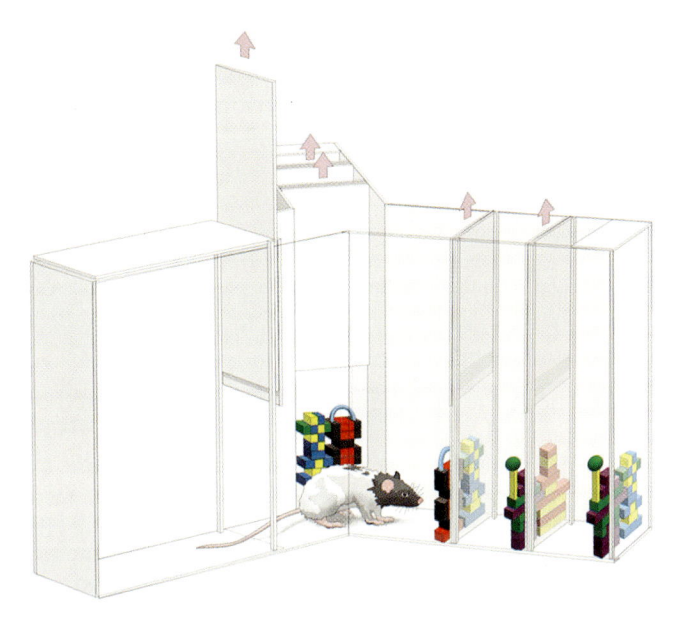

Figure 11.10 Modified Y-maze apparatus showing two sets of interior walls, with objects attached to the base of each wall. The interior walls can be removed quickly, which simultaneously removes the objects, allowing immediate progression of the rat from sample (study) phase to choice (test) phase, thus eliminating any study–test delay. In this illustration, three sets of objects are shown, comprising two sample phases and a final test phase (as in Bartko et al., 2010). In Bartko et al. (2007a), only two phases were used: study and test.

task in which stimuli were constructed "configurally" (Bartko et al., 2007b). All stimuli were composed of two parts. In the configural object condition, the novel stimulus was novel only in that it comprised a novel recombination of parts that were individually familiar. Those parts had been made familiar by presenting them as part of a different composite object during an earlier study phase. In the control object condition, stimuli were again constructed of two parts, but the novel object comprised two unfamiliar parts, such that both the component features and the combination defining the object whole were novel (see Table 11.1). As predicted by the model of ORM, rats with lesions in PRC were impaired in the configural object condition, in which all features of the novel object were familiar, and unimpaired in control object condition in which the novel object contained novel features.

The third novel prediction of the ORM model is that recognition memory in individuals with PRC damage should be impaired by the interposing interfering visual stimulus material between the study and test phases of a recognition task. Critically, the impairment will be greater when interfering stimuli share a larger number of features with the stimulus items presented in the test phase. We tested this prediction with a study in rats (Bartko, Cowell, Winters, Bussey, & Saksida, 2010) in which we interposed visual material between the study and the test phases of a Stimulus–Organism–Response (SOR) task. Stimuli in the study and test phases were always composed of colored Lego blocks. In one condition (Low Interference), the interfering material comprised black and white photographs of everyday objects; in the

Table 11.1 Stimulus construction in the 'Control' and 'Configural' conditions of Bartko et al. (2007b).

	Control condition		Configural condition	
Sample Phase 1	EF	EF	BC	BC
Sample Phase 2	GH	GH	AD	AD
Choice Phase	EF	AB	BC	AB

Each compound stimulus was composed of two halves. Each stimulus half is depicted by a single upper-case letter; a whole stimulus is depicted by a pair of letters.

other (High Interference), the interfering material was constructed of colored Lego blocks in the same manner that the study and test objects were constructed. Clearly, the latter condition introduced a much greater degree of feature overlap between interfering items and, critically, the novel object presented in the test phase. As predicted, animals with PRC lesions were more seriously impaired in the High Interference condition than in the Low Interference condition. This was in line with the model's prediction that the features of the novel object would appear familiar after experiencing a high degree of feature-level visual interference, and that animals lacking a conjunctive object representation in PRC would be unable to discriminate the novel and familiar objects on the basis of familiarity.

The fourth novel prediction that arose from the model of ORM is arguably the most counterintuitive, radical, and unexpected. The model of ORM was originally developed to account for three existing findings from animals with PRC lesions, as outlined above. In developing the model, we tried many potential mechanisms to simulate these phenomena, before finally hitting upon one that worked. Only then did we realize that this mechanism entailed the strong and highly novel prediction that, in MTL amnesia, subjects fail at ORM because novel objects look familiar (McTighe, Cowell, Winters, Bussey, & Saksida, 2010). As discussed earlier, an assumption of the model is that that during the delay between study and test, the subject will view other, nonexperimental visual stimuli in the surrounding area. These stimuli are very likely to share some features, such as color or aspects of shape, in common with the novel object. This can lead to interference, because as a result of this experience, features in the novel object will now be familiar. That is, they will be perceived as having been seen before (in the computational model, this corresponds to possessing a more sharply tuned representation). However, because it is very unlikely that the exact whole object presented during the test phase will have been seen by chance during the delay, the unique, object-level representations in PRC will not be familiar and therefore can protect the individual from this interference. However, if the subject has to rely on the simpler, feature-based memory that is highly susceptible to interference, they will be impaired on the task because the studied object looks familiar. This prediction contrasts with the account provided by nearly all theories of amnesia, which assume that such individuals suffer impairments because familiar objects appear novel.

We set out to test this prediction in rats, again using the SOR paradigm (McTighe et al., 2010). However, the standard form of the SOR paradigm offers the rat two objects for exploration in the test phase, one novel and one familiar. This imposes a two-alternative forced choice on the animal, measuring the *relative* preference for the novel object, which precludes the assessment of the absolute value of each object's novelty. Rats that fail to discriminate could be either unduly excited by the familiar object or unduly bored by the novel object, leaving us unable to distinguish between the prediction of our model of amnesia and the prediction of all others. To gauge absolute novelty, we redesigned the SOR task, decoupling the presentation of the novel and familiar (Figure 11.11, left panel). This allowed determination of whether rats that failed to discriminate (i.e., treated the familiar and the novel objects the same) did so because they explored the familiar object more, or the novel object less (Figure 11.11, right panel). The results of this study are shown in the left panel of Figure 11.12. As predicted, rats with PRC lesions failed to discriminate the novel and familiar objects, and this was expressed via a reduction in exploration of the novel object, relative to control animals' behavior. Interestingly, we have also found that the TgCRND8 mouse model of AD, which displays aberrant synaptic plasticity in PRC, is impaired on SOR in the same way (Romberg *et al.*, 2012).

Further to this, we tested the model's assumption that forgetting in the lesioned group was due to visual interference in the delay between study and test. If, as the model suggests, the problem for these animals was the interposition of visual stimulation, such that feature-level interference made the novel objects look familiar, then reducing the amount of visual information experienced during the delay should "rescue" the performance of the lesioned group. We tested this by placing animals in

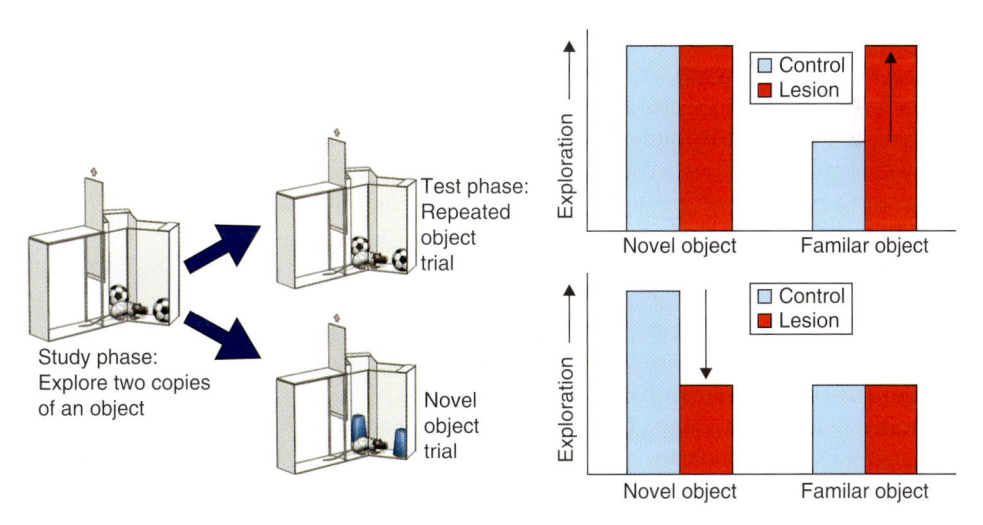

Figure 11.11 Left: modified SOR paradigm, in which the choice phase is decoupled into two separate types of trials: Novel Object and Repeated Object. The decoupling ensures independent exploration of each object type, so that each type of trial gives an estimate of the absolute perceived novelty of each type of stimulus. Right: predictions of traditional theories of amnesia (top) and the Representational–Hierarchical view (bottom). Traditional theories would predict that old objects look new in amnesic subjects, producing increased exploration of repeated (familiar) items relative to control subjects. The Representational-hierarchical view predicts that new objects look old, producing reduced exploration of novel items relative to control subjects. After McTighe *et al.* (2010).

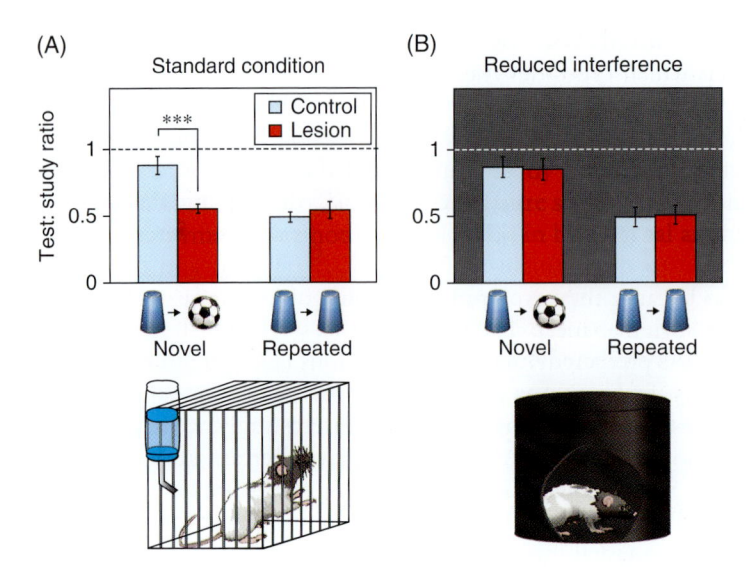

Figure 11.12 (A) Rats with PRC lesions explored the repeated (familiar) object to the same level as controls, but showed reduced exploration of the novel objects, in line with the model's prediction of a reduction in perceived novelty of novel objects. (B) Reduction in visual interference between study and test, by placing animals in the dark, rescued the performance of the lesioned group. Adapted from McTighe *et al.* (2010).

the dark between the study and test phases (Figure 11.12, right panel). As predicted, in this condition, animals with PRC lesions explored the novel objects to the level of controls, in the choice phase, discriminating them effectively from familiar items. A final test of their recognition memory under the standard condition, in which animals were allowed to observe the testing room during the delay, reinstated the memory impairment originally seen, which confirmed that animals had not performed well in the "black bin" condition by recovering from surgery or learning to employ a new strategy. The deficit in the TgCRND8 model can also be rescued in the same way (Romberg *et al.*, 2012).

We have recently begun to develop analogs of these animal studies for use with human participants, to test the validity of the Representational–Hierarchical account of amnesia in humans (cf. Dewar, Garcia, Cowan, & Della Sala, 2009; Dewar, Pesallaccia, Cowan, Provinciali, & Della Sala, 2012). We have developed a spontaneous or implicit measure of object recognition in order to test the "novel appears familiar" hypothesis in patients with Mild Cognitive Impairment, a cognitive disorder that is a precursor to AD (Petersen *et al.*, 1999) in which sufferers are at risk for incipient MTL damage. In this study (Yeung, Ryan, Cowell, & Barense, 2013), we presented streams of photographs of everyday objects. This was a passive viewing task, with subjects beingmonitored for the appearance of a target stimulus (a black square) between photographic stimuli, and recognition memory was measured implicitly through the analysis of eye-movement data. During the latter part of each block, photographic items were presented that were novel, high interference (shared a large number of features with a previously viewed item), or low interference (did not explicitly share features with a previously viewed item). In healthy control subjects, previously viewed objects elicited generally fewer fixations than novel items did, in line with the assumption that fewer fixations to an object indicate greater perceived familiarity (Hannula, Baym, Warren, & Cohen, 2012). Older adults at risk for developing Mild Cognitive Impairment showed false recognition to high-interference novel items, relative to controls, but normal novelty responses to low-interference novel items. Analogous to the rodent studies of McTighe *et al.* (2010) and Romberg *et al.* (2012), humans with probable incipient MTL damage were thus susceptible to feature-level interference in an implicit recognition memory paradigm. In rats, we were able to rescue the memory performance of animals with brain damage by reducing the amount of visual interference via sensory deprivation; analogously, in humans, abnormal performance in the experimental group was ameliorated in a reduced interference condition, i.e., a subset of trials in which novel items possessed fewer visual features in common with previously viewed items.

Summary of the experimental work driven by the Representational–Hierarchical account

Thus, the experimental work driven by the Representational–Hierarchical account has confirmed a wide range of predictions for perceptual and mnemonic function in rats, but those animal paradigms are now also being translated for use in humans. Moving forward, we intend to examine the ability of the Representational–Hierarchical account to explain aspects of human cognition and, ultimately, the devastating effects of brain damage that may be caused by accident, injury, or one of several increasingly common diseases that can ravage the MTL in older people.

In developing the Representational–Hierarchical view, the strong theoretical framework underlying the approach and the explicit computational implementation of its ideas were both critical to building a persuasive account. By providing a concrete and well-specified model to demonstrate the consequences of the framework's simple assumptions for behavior, and by generating novel predictions (sometimes unexpected, even by us) for experimental work, we were able to explain more clearly the proposed mechanisms and demonstrate more convincingly the power of the theory than would have been possible with a verbal theory, alone. By driving experimental work that translates from animals to humans, and by promoting a shift in thinking in the field of human neuropsychology, such a framework has significant potential benefits to the search for rehabilitative treatments and better diagnostic tools for disorders of the MTL, in humans.

Conclusions

In the field of cognitive neuroscience, simple assumptions can be easily married, and their consequences for behavior effectively tested, with computational modeling. The behavioral predictions that emerge from such models lead to thoughtfully guided experimental work and, we argue, a faster route to deepening our understanding of cognitive mechanisms. Thus, computational modeling is an approach that has allowed the rapprochement between theory and observation of behavior. Moreover, a critical contribution to this endeavor has come from associative learning theory, which has taught us that representations are critical, and that we can achieve much by simply considering the nature of psychological representations and some simple rules for acquiring information about them.

References

Bachevalier, J., & Nemanic, S. (2008). Memory for spatial location and object-place associations are differently processed by the hippocampal formation, parahippocampal areas TH/TF and perirhinal cortex. *Hippocampus, 18*, 64–80.

Baker, C. I., Behrmann, M., & Olson, C. R. (2002). Impact of learning on representation of parts and wholes in monkey inferotemporal cortex. *Nature Neuroscience, 5*, 1210–1216.

Barense, M. D., Bussey, T. J., Lee, A. C. H., Rogers, T. T., Davies, R. R., Saksida, L. M., ... Graham, K. S. (2005). Functional specialization in the human medial temporal lobe. *Journal of Neuroscience, 25*, 10239–10246.

Barense, M. D., Gaffan, D., & Graham, K. S. (2007). The human medial temporal lobe processes online representations of complex objects. *Neuropsychologia, 45*, 2963–2974.

Barker, G. R., & Warburton, E. C. (2015). Object-in-place associative recognition memory depends on glutamate receptor neurotransmission within two defined hippocampal-cortical circuits: a critical role for AMPA and NMDA receptors in the hippocampus, perirhinal, and prefrontal cortices. *Cerebral Cortex, 25*, 472–481.

Bartko, S. J., Cowell, R. A., Winters, B. D., Bussey, T. J., & Saksida, L. M. (2010). Heightened susceptibility to interference in an animal model of amnesia: Impairment in encoding, storage, retrieval – or all three? *Neuropsychologia, 48*, 2987–2997.

Bartko, S. J., Winters, B. D., Cowell, R. A., Saksida, L. M., & Bussey, T. J. (2007a). Perceptual functions of perirhinal cortex in rats: Zero-delay object recognition and simultaneous oddity discriminations. *Journal of Neuroscience, 27*, 2548–2559.

Bartko, S. J., Winters, B. D., Cowell, R. A., Saksida, L. M., & Bussey, T. J. (2007b). Perirhinal cortex resolves feature ambiguity in configural object recognition and perceptual oddity tasks. *Learning & Memory, 14*, 821–832.

Blake, L., Jarvis, C. D., & Mishkin, M. (1977). Pattern-discrimination thresholds after partial inferior temporal or lateral striate lesions in monkeys. *Brain Research, 120*, 209–220.

Buckley, M. J., Booth, M. C., Rolls, E. T., & Gaffan, D. (2001). Selective perceptual impairments after perirhinal cortex ablation. *Journal of Neuroscience, 21*, 9824–9836.

Buckley, M. J., & Gaffan, D. (1997). Impairment of visual object-discrimination learning after perirhinal cortex ablation. *Behavioral Neuroscience, 111*, 467–475.

Buckley, M. J., & Gaffan, D. (1998a). Perirhinal cortex ablation impairs configural learning and paired-associate learning equally. *Neuropsychologia, 36*, 535–546.

Buckley, M. J., & Gaffan, D. (1998b). Perirhinal cortex ablation impairs visual object identification. *Journal of Neuroscience, 18*, 2268–2275.

Buffalo, E. A., Reber, P. J., & Squire, L. R. (1998). The human perirhinal cortex and recognition memory. *Hippocampus, 8*, 330–339.

Bussey, T. J., & Saksida, L. M. (2002). The organization of visual object representations: a connectionist model of effects of lesions in perirhinal cortex. *European Journal of Neuroscience, 15*, 355–364.

Bussey, T. J., & Saksida, L. M. (2005). Object memory and perception in the medial temporal lobe: an alternative approach. *Current Opinion in Neurobiology, 15*, 730–737.

Bussey, T. J., Saksida, L. M., & Murray, E. A. (2002). Perirhinal cortex resolves feature ambiguity in complex visual discriminations. *European Journal of Neuroscience, 15*, 365–374.

Bussey, T. J., Saksida, L. M., & Murray, E. A. (2003). Impairments in visual discrimination after perirhinal cortex lesions: testing "declarative" vs. "perceptual-mnemonic" views of perirhinal cortex function. *European Journal of Neuroscience, 17*, 649–660.

Butter, C. M. (1972). Detection of masked patterns in monkeys with inferotemporal, striate or dorsolateral frontal lesions. *Neuropsychologia, 10*, 241.

Cohen, N. J., & Squire, L. R. (1980). Preserved learning and retention of pattern-analyzing skill in amnesia – dissociation of knowing how and knowing that. *Science, 210*, 207–210.

Cowell, R. A., Bussey, T. J., & Saksida, L. M. (2006). Why does brain damage impair memory? A connectionist model of object recognition memory in perirhinal cortex. *Journal of Neuroscience, 26*, 12186–12197.

Cowell, R. A., Bussey, T. J., & Saksida, L. M. (2010). Functional dissociations within the ventral object processing pathway: cognitive modules or a hierarchical continuum? *Journal of Cognitive Neuroscience, 22*, 2460–2479.

Cowey, A., & Gross, C. G. (1970). Effects of foveal prestriate and inferotemporal lesions on visual discrimination by rhesus monkeys. *Experimental Brain Research, 11*, 128.

Dean, P. (1974). Choice reaction-times for pattern discriminations in monkeys with inferotemporal lesions. *Neuropsychologia, 12*, 465–476.

Desimone, R., Albright, T. D., Gross, C. G., & Bruce, C. (1984). Stimulus-selective properties of inferior temporal neurons in the macaque. *Journal of Neuroscience, 4*, 2051–2062.

Desimone, R., & Schein, S. J. (1987). Visual properties of neurons in area V4 of the macaque – sensitivity to stimulus form. *Journal of Neurophysiology, 57*, 835–868.

Dewar, M., Garcia, Y. F., Cowan, N., & Della Sala, S. (2009). Delaying interference enhances memory consolidation in amnesic patients. *Neuropsychology, 23*, 627–634.

Dewar, M., Pesallaccia, M., Cowan, N., Provinciali, L., & Della Sala, S. (2012). Insights into spared memory capacity in amnestic MCI and Alzheimer's disease via minimal interference. *Brain and Cognition, 78*, 189–199.

Eacott, M. J., Gaffan, D., & Murray, E. A. (1994). Preserved recognition memory for small sets, and impaired stimulus identification for large sets, following rhinal cortex ablations in monkeys. *European Journal of Neuroscience, 6*, 1466–1478.

Eysel, U. T., Worgotter, F., & Pape, H. C. (1987). Local cortical lesions abolish lateral inhibition at direction selective cells in cat visual cortex. *Experimental Brain Research, 68*, 606–612.

Gaffan, D. (2002). Against memory systems. *Philosophical Transactions of the Royal Society B: Biological Sciences, 357*, 1111–1121.

Gaffan, D., & Murray, E. A. (1992). Monkeys (*Macaca fascicularis*) with rhinal cortex ablations succeed in object discrimination-learning despite 24-hr intertrial intervals and fail at matching to sample despite double sample presentations. *Behavioral Neuroscience, 106*, 30–38.

Gauthier, I., & Tarr, M. J. (1997). Becoming a "greeble" expert: Exploring mechanisms for face recognition. *Vision Research, 37*, 1673–1682.

Gross, C. G., Cowey, A., & Manning, F. J. (1971). Further analysis of visual discrimination deficits following foveal prestriate and inferotemporal lesions in rhesus monkeys. *Journal of Comparative and Physiological Psychology, 76*, 1.

Hannula, D. E., Baym, C. L., Warren, D. E., & Cohen, N. J. (2012). The eyes know: eye movements as a veridical index of memory. *Psychological Science, 23*, 278–287.

Hubel, D. H., & Wiesel, T. N. (1962). Receptive fields, binocular interaction and functional architecture in the cat's visual cortex. *The Journal of Physiology, 160*, 106–154.

Iversen, S. D., & Humphrey, N. K. (1971). Ventral temporal lobe lesions and visual oddity performance. *Brain Research, 30,* 253.

Iwai, E., & Mishkin, M. (1968). Two visual foci in the temporal lobe of monkeys. In N. Yoshii, & N. Buchwald (Eds.), *Neurophysiological basis of learning and behavior* (pp. 1–11). Osaka, Japan: Osaka University Press.

Jackson-Smith, P., Kesner, R. P., & Chiba, A. A. (1993). Continuous recognition of spatial and nonspatial stimuli in hippocampal-lesioned rats. *Behavioral and Neural Biology, 59,* 107–119.

Jeneson, A., & Squire, L. R. (2012). Working memory, long-term memory, and medial temporal lobe function. *Learning & Memory, 19,* 15–25.

Kikuchi, R., & Iwai, E. (1980). The locus of the posterior subdivision of the inferotemporal visual learning area in the monkey. *Brain Research, 198,* 347–360.

Kim, S., Jeneson, A., van der Horst, A. S., Frascino, J. C., Hopkins, R. O., & Squire, L. R. (2011). Memory, visual discrimination performance, and the human hippocampus. *Journal of Neuroscience, 31,* 2624–2629.

Kohonen, T. (1982). Self-organized formation of topologically correct feature maps. *Biological Cybernetics, 43,* 59–69.

Komorowski, R. W., Manns, J. R., & Eichenbaum, H. (2009). Robust conjunctive item-place coding by hippocampal neurons parallels learning what happens where. *Journal of Neuroscience, 29,* 9918–9929.

Lee, A. C., Buckley, M. J., Gaffan, D., Emery, T., Hodges, J. R., & Graham, K. S. (2006). Differentiating the roles of the hippocampus and perirhinal cortex in processes beyond long-term declarative memory: a double dissociation in dementia. *Journal of Neuroscience, 26,* 5198–5203.

Lee, A. C., Levi, N., Davies, R. R., Hodges, J. R., & Graham, K. S. (2007). Differing profiles of face and scene discrimination deficits in semantic dementia and Alzheimer's disease. *Neuropsychologia, 45,* 2135–2146.

Lee, A. C. H., Buckley, M. J., Pegman, S. J., Spiers, H., Scahill, V. L., Gaffan, D., ... Graham, K. S. (2005a). Specialization in the medial temporal lobe for processing of objects and scenes. *Hippocampus, 15,* 782–797.

Lee, A. C. H., Bussey, T. J., Murray, E. A., Saksida, L. M., Epstein, R. A., Kapur, N., ... Graham, K. S. (2005b). Perceptual deficits in amnesia: challenging the medial temporal lobe "mnemonic" view. *Neuropsychologia, 43,* 1–11.

Lee, A. C. H., Scahill, V. L., & Graham, K. S. (2008). Activating the medial temporal lobe during oddity judgment for faces and scenes. *Cerebral Cortex, 18,* 683–696.

Lennie, P. (1998). Single units and visual cortical organization. *Perception, 27,* 889–935.

Liu, P., & Bilkey, D. K. (1998). Excitotoxic lesions centered on perirhinal cortex produce delay-dependent deficits in a test of spatial memory. *Behavioral Neuroscience, 112,* 512–524.

Manning, F. J. (1971a). Punishment for errors and visual-discrimination learning by monkeys with inferotemporal cortex lesions. *Journal of Comparative and Physiological Psychology, 75,* 146.

Manning, F. J. (1971b). Selective attention deficit of monkeys with ablations of foveal prestriate cortex. *Psychonomic Science, 25,* 291–292.

McTighe, S. M., Cowell, R. A., Winters, B. D., Bussey, T. J., & Saksida, L. M. (2010). Paradoxical false memory for objects after brain damage. *Science, 330,* 1408–1410.

Meunier, M., Bachevalier, J., Mishkin, M., & Murray, E. A. (1993). Effects on visual recognition of combined and separate ablations of the entorhinal and perirhinal cortex in rhesus-monkeys. *Journal of Neuroscience, 13,* 5418–5432.

Murray, E. A., & Bussey, T. J. (1999). Perceptual-mnemonic functions of the perirhinal cortex. *Trends in Cognitive Sciences, 3,* 142–151.

Nakamura, H., Gattass, R., Desimone, R., & Ungerleider, L. G. (1993). The modular organization of projections from Area-V1 and Area-V2 to Area-V4 and Teo in macaques. *Journal of Neuroscience, 13,* 3681–3691.

Packard, M. G., Hirsh, R., & White, N. M. (1989). Differential-effects of fornix and caudate-nucleus lesions on 2 radial maze tasks – evidence for multiple memory-systems. *Journal of Neuroscience, 9,* 1465–1472.

Pearce, J. M. (1994). Similarity and discrimination – a selective review and a connectionist model. *Psychological Review, 101,* 587–607.

Petersen, R. C., Smith, G. E., Waring, S. C., Ivnik, R. J., Tangalos, E. G., & Kokmen, E. (1999). Mild cognitive impairment – clinical characterization and outcome. *Archives of Neurology, 56,* 303–308.

Rescorla, R. A., & Wagner, A. R. (Eds.) (1972). *A theory of Pavlovian conditioning: Variations in the effectiveness of reinforcement and nonreinforcement.* New York, NY: Appleton Century Crofts.

Romberg, C., McTighe, S. M., Heath, C. J., Whitcomb, D. J., Cho, K., Bussey, T. J., & Saksida, L. M. (2012). False recognition in a mouse model of Alzheimer's disease: rescue with sensory restriction and memantine. *Brain, 135,* 2103–2114.

Saksida, L. (1999). *A competitive connectionist model of the effect of experience on perceptual representations.* Unpublished doctoral dissertation. Carnegie Mellon University, Pittsburgh, PA.

Saksida, L. M., Bussey, T. J., Buckmaster, C. A., & Murray, E. A. (2006). No effect of hippocampal lesions on perirhinal cortex-dependent feature-ambiguous visual discriminations. *Hippocampus, 16,* 421–430.

Saksida, L. M., Bussey, T. J., Buckmaster, C. A., & Murray, E. A. (2007). Impairment and facilitation of transverse patterning after lesions of the perirhinal cortex and hippocampus, respectively. *Cerebral Cortex, 17,* 108–115.

Sanderson, D. J., Gray, A., Simon, A., Taylor, A. M., Deacon, R. M. J., Seeburg, P. H., ... Bannerman, D. M. (2007). Deletion of glutamate receptor-A (GluR-A) AMPA receptor subunits impairs one-trial spatial memory. *Behavioral Neuroscience, 121,* 559–569.

Sherry, D. F., & Schacter, D. L. (1987). The evolution of multiple memory-systems. *Psychological Review, 94,* 439–454.

Sillito, A. M. (1979). Inhibitory mechanisms influencing complex cell orientation selectivity and their modification at high resting discharge levels. *The Journal of Physiology, 289,* 33–53.

Sillito, A. M., Kemp, J. A., Milson, J. A., & Berardi, N. (1980). A re-evaluation of the mechanisms underlying simple cell orientation selectivity. *Brain Research, 194,* 517–520.

Squire, L. R., Stark, C. E., & Clark, R. E. (2004). The medial temporal lobe. *Annual Review of Neuroscience, 27,* 279–306.

Squire, L. R., & Wixted, J. T. (2011). The cognitive neuroscience of human memory since H. M. *Annual Review of Neuroscience, 34,* 259–288.

Squire, L. R., & Zola-Morgan, S. (1991). The medial temporal-lobe memory system. *Science, 253,* 1380–1386.

Williams, P., & Simons, D. J. (2000). Detecting changes in novel, complex three-dimensional objects. *Visual Cognition, 7,* 297–322.

Wilson, M., & Kaufman, H. M. (1969). Effect of inferotemporal lesions upon processing of visual information in monkeys. *Journal of Comparative and Physiological Psychology, 69,* 44.

Wilson, M., Zieler, R. E., Lieb, J. P., & Kaufman, H. M. (1972). Visual identification and memory in monkeys with circumscribed inferotemporal lesions. *Journal of Comparative and Physiological Psychology, 78,* 173.

Yeung, L. K., Ryan, J. D., Cowell, R. A., & Barense, M. D. (2013). Recognition memory impairments caused by false recognition of novel objects. *Journal of Experimental Psychology: General, 142,* 1384–1397.

Zola-Morgan, S., Squire, L. R., Amaral, D. G., & Suzuki, W. A. (1989). Lesions of perirhinal and parahippocampal cortex that spare the amygdala and hippocampal formation produce severe memory impairment. *Journal of Neuroscience, 9,* 4355–4370.

Space and Time

12

Mechanisms of Contextual Conditioning

Some Thoughts on Excitatory and Inhibitory Context Conditioning

Robert J. McDonald and Nancy S. Hong

Introduction

The abilities to learn and remember constitute two of the most important functions mediated by the mammalian brain. These cognitive functions are important because they allow the organism to negotiate complex environments and situations, increasing the possibility of success, happiness, and well-being, as well as survival and reproductive advantage. In short, the ability to learn and remember is highly adaptive.

There has been an impressive scholarly effort and tradition of trying to account for how behavior is shaped by exposure to specific events and environmental conditions (Bouton, 1993; Holland, 1983; Hull, 1943; Mackintosh, 1975; Pavlov, 1927; Pearce & Hall, 1980; Rescorla & Wagner, 1972; Thorndike, 1932) and the neural systems responsible (Balleine & Dickinson, 1992; Everitt, Cador, & Robbins, 1989; Good & Honey, 1991; Holland, Lamoureux, Han, & Gallagher, 1999; Kapp, Frysinger, Gallagher, & Haselton, 1979; Quirk & Gehlert, 2003; Sanderson et al., 2010; Sutherland & Rudy, 1989; White & McDonald, 2002). This undertaking has made many impressive advances in our understanding of the conditions and mechanisms of learning in human and nonhuman animals and has had a huge impact on modern society. For example, this work is revolutionizing our understanding of the nature and causes of psychiatric disorders including addictive behaviors (Crombag, Bossert, Koya, & Shaham, 2008; Everitt, Dickinson, & Robbins, 2001; White, 1996), anxiety (Grillon, 2002; Zelinski, Hong, Halsall, & McDonald, 2010), posttraumatic stress disorder (Lolordo & Overmier, 2011), and obesity (Holland & Petrovich, 2005; Polivy, Herman, & Coelho, 2008). The contribution of animal learning to our understanding of these human maladies, in our

---

The Wiley Handbook on the Cognitive Neuroscience of Learning, First Edition.
Edited by Robin A. Murphy and Robert C. Honey.
© 2016 John Wiley & Sons, Ltd. Published 2016 by John Wiley & Sons, Ltd.

view, has overshadowed even the much-vaunted modern genetics approach (Chapter 7). It could also be argued that this work has been harnessed by corporations to drive consumer behavior (Allen & Shimp, 1990) and influence fundamental decision processes including crucial governmental decisions. Despite this range of impacts, many important issues concerning conditioning processes remain unknown.

One obvious feature of learning is that it always occurs in some type of context. Context has been defined in different ways. Balsam (1985) argued that there are at least two main types of context. The first is a cognitive or associative context of what has been learned before. The second type of context is the environmental context that is defined by the location, specific features, and time of the task at hand. It is the latter type of context that will be the focus of the present chapter. We acknowledge that recent formulations argue that there are many forms of contextual representations that can influence a wide range of functions and abilities. For example, Maren *et al.* (2013) have suggested at least five major forms of context representations including spatial, temporal, interoceptive, cognitive, and social and cultural.

Understanding the effects of physically defined contextual cues on learning and performance is fundamental to our understanding of normal and abnormal manifestations of mammalian behavior. Historically, the influence of context emerged to explain the complexity of associative structures acquired in simple situations. Early theories and empirical work suggested that learning involved simple binary associations between central representations of CS and US or CS and responses (Guthrie, 1935; Hull, 1943; Pavlov, 1927; Skinner, 1938; Thorndike, 1932). It is clearly much more complicated than that. Simple associative learning theories failed to account for all learned phenomena, and the idea of context was crucial in boosting our understanding of the conditions and rules of learning. The integration of the role(s) of context into general learning theories improved the breadth and depth of predictions and increased explanatory power.

An example of how context can influence learning processes and conditioned behavior is the now classic demonstration of how a static training context competes for associative strength or attentional processes with other punctate stimuli (Mackintosh, 1975; Rescorla & Wagner, 1972; Chapter 2). In one important demonstration, a group of rats were presented CS and US randomly over a specified training period. In this training situation, the CS and US occur together sometimes and not at other times. Another group of rats experience the same CS and US except that they always occur together. In both cases, the CS and US occur together the same amount of times, but in the former, the CS and US are uncorrelated. Only the latter group show good conditioning to the CS while the former produce little or no conditioning. Other work has shown that significant conditioning is accrued to the context in the former but not as much in the latter (Rescorla, 1967, 1968).

This chapter will describe two distinct roles of contextual cues. The first type involves the formation of direct context–US associations, and the second involves the contextual control of extinction. We describe these different forms of learning, various key experiments, and the key roles played by the hippocampus and other brain systems in supporting these functions.

Context–US Associations

One of the most obvious, directly observable, and easily tested functions of context during learning is via their direct associations with the US. In its simplest form, this kind of learning utilizes a context chamber, similar to those used for operant conditioning, in which a rat is exposed to a distinct context that is associated with an appetitive or aversive unconditioned stimulus. For example, early experiments by Balsam (1985) gave doves 25 training sessions of unsignaled food presentations in a distinct context. After training, five extinction sessions occurred; half of the subjects received extinction in the same context and the other half in a different context (defined by visual, auditory, and tactile changes), and activity levels were recorded during these trials as a measure of appetitive conditioning. The subjects extinguished in the same context as original training showed elevated activity levels compared with the subjects in the nontraining context. This is evidence that a context–US association was formed during the original food presentations. The subjects learned that food availability was associated with the context as defined by their specific features. One of the goals of understanding the role of context has been to define more precisely which features an animal might learn about. We have argued that different variations of the task can provide evidence on this question.

More sophisticated versions of appetitive context conditioning procedures have emerged since this time. One version, sometimes referred to as a conditioned place preference task (CPP), has many design features that make it a convincing demonstration of context–US associations. Interestingly, this task was developed to assess the rewarding properties of stimuli and was used extensively by behavioral pharmacologists as a tool to understand drugs of abuse and mechanisms of drug addiction (Mucha, van der Kooy, O'Shaughnessy, & Bucenieks, 1982). The procedure has three phases: preexposure, training, and preference test. The task utilizes an apparatus made up of two chambers with a connecting tunnel. Although variations exist, the two chambers normally differ in many ways including visual, olfactory, and tactile features. The preexposure phase is that in which rats are given free access to the two contexts via the connecting tunnel. Time spent in the two chambers is recorded as a measure of initial preference before conditioning. When initiating these kinds of experiments, a series of pilot experiments should be run to manipulate the strength and type of these cues to ensure that a group of normal animals do not show an initial preference to either of the chambers during the preexposure phase. If this initial result is achieved, this is considered an unbiased CPP method, which allows the experimenter to infer that any preference towards the reinforced chamber is based upon the contingencies that have been arranged. Following preexposure, training ensues in a counterbalanced manner. The training conditions include assignment to one of the contexts in which they will receive the reinforcer and whether they receive reinforcement on the first or second day of a training block. On the final preference day, the tunnel connecting the two context chambers is open, and the rat is allowed to move freely throughout the apparatus for 10 min in the absence of the reinforcer. Time spent in the different contexts is recorded and used as a measure of context preference.

We have argued (McDonald, Hong, & Devan, 2004) that this is an excellent paradigm for demonstrating Pavlovian context conditioning because the animal sits in the paired chamber and eats the food for most of the training interval. There is no clear instrumental response that the animal has to make or does make to obtain the food. The unbiased method and proper counterbalancing for reinforced context and order of reinforcement also make this a powerful tool for assessing Pavlovian-mediated context–US associations.

Another method differs from the CPP in several important ways. First, it utilizes foot-shock as the US. Second, in many cases, a discrete CS is associated with the US (Kim & Fanselow, 1992; Phillips & Ledoux, 1992) in the training context. Third, the paradigm utilizes only one context, making it, from a context conditioning perspective, nondiscriminative. After multiple CS-US pairings, the rats are placed back in the training context 24 hr after the final day of training, and freezing is assessed in the absence of the CS and US. Freezing is a species-typical fear response. Unconditioned and conditioned fear response is found in rodents in which the subject becomes almost completely motionless except for movements associated with breathing (Blanchard & Blanchard, 1969). On a final test, the rats are placed in a novel context, and CS presentations occur. Using this paradigm, the results show that the rats acquire fear to both the context and the predictive cue (Fanselow, 1990; Kim & Fanselow, 1992).

In another variant that also does not compare responding between contexts or use a discrete CS (Phillips & Ledoux, 1992), rats are exposed to a novel context for several minutes and then receive several mild unsignaled foot-shocks. The rats are then removed from the apparatus and returned to their home cage. On the next day, the rats are placed back into the training context and freezing recorded. During this test, normal rats show a substantial increase in freezing when exposed to the training context, even in the absence of the US. The fear exhibited by the subject during this phase is considered the expression of an associative memory formed between the experimental context and the aversive event.

We have been critical of nondiscriminative fear conditioning to context paradigms because they have significant flaws as an unequivocal measure of context–US associations (McDonald *et al.*, 2004). One issue with the nondiscriminative procedure is that it is difficult to know which aspects of the testing procedure and apparatus are actually being associated with fear. That is, the fearful experience in these experiments could be associated with removal from the colony, the trip to the testing room, the testing room, the general apparatus, the experimenter, the time of day, etc.

Another potential issue with nondiscriminative procedures is that fear responses can be activated via nonassociative processes and are not differentiated from conditioned fear responses. One type of nonassociative processes is a general enhancement of arousal or fear that could potentially last for several days following an aversive event. This general sensitization effect would result in the appearance of conditioned fear 24 hr following training but would not reflect an expression of an association between the fear context and fear responses. In an attempt to circumvent this issue, researchers have instituted a transfer test at the end of testing in which the subjects are placed in a novel context to ensure that conditioning is specific to the original testing chamber (Kim & Fanselow, 1992; Martin, 1966). However, we have argued that this procedure is not a clear demonstration of context-specific conditioning because a lack of freezing in the novel context could be an instance of novelty-induced exploration that could compete with freezing behavior. Other forms of discriminative procedures have been developed to assess fear conditioning but have since been abandoned (Fanselow & Baackes, 1982; Garcia, Kimeldorf, & Hunt, 1957; Martin, 1966; Martin & Ellinwood, 1974; Overall, Brown, & Logie, 1959).

Discriminative fear conditioning to context

In response, we developed a discriminative version of the fear conditioning to context paradigm (McDonald, Koerner, & Sutherland, 1995) that was inspired by the design of the unbiased conditioned place preference paradigm (Carr, Fibiger, & Phillips, 1989; Hiroi & White, 1991) and as such is essentially an aversively motivated version of the CPP task.

The apparatus for this task consists of two chambers and one connecting arena. One chamber is black and triangle-shaped with a fruity odor (iso-amyl acetate). The other chamber is a white square, and a menthol odor (eucalyptus) serves as the olfactory cue. During training, a rat is placed in one of these chambers with the connecting tunnel closed for 5 min and receives several mild foot-shocks. On the next day, the rat is placed in the other chamber for 5 min, and nothing happens. This cycle is repeated four times. On the following day, the rat is placed in one chamber for a specified time (5, 10, or 20 min), and freezing behavior (a well-established measure of fear in the rodent) is assessed. The day after, the rat is placed in the other chamber for the same amount of time, and freezing behavior recorded. Normal rats show high levels of freezing in the context previously paired with the aversive stimulus and low levels of freezing in the other context. On the final day, each rat is given access to the two chambers via the connecting tunnel, and a preference score is obtained.

Context chamber and context testing room conditioning

While completing pilot experiments for this paradigm, we made an interesting discovery. Using what we thought was a sufficient number of training trials (8 days of training) and the appropriate US intensity (1 mA), control animals did not show differential or discriminative fear conditioning, but they did show elevated fear to both chambers (Figure 12.1, top panel). One idea was that this was a demonstration of generalized fear. That is, the rats learned that shock was associated with this episode-removal from the vivarium, presence of the experimenter, the testing room, time of day, etc.-but were unable to associate the shock specifically with the appropriate context. To test this idea, we slightly modified the paradigm. The new version was identical to the original except that two training rooms with identical set-ups consisting of the equipment described above were used. One of the training rooms was designated the "shock room" in which all of the subjects experienced the context-shock pairings regardless of the context assigned to the reinforcer. The other training room was designated the "safe room" in which all subjects experienced the context-no-shock pairings. Importantly, the safe room was the location in which conditioned fear was assessed. Using this slight variation of the original paradigm, the results showed that a group of normal rats showed discriminative fear conditioning to the context with the same amount of training trials and US intensity as in the original pilot experiment

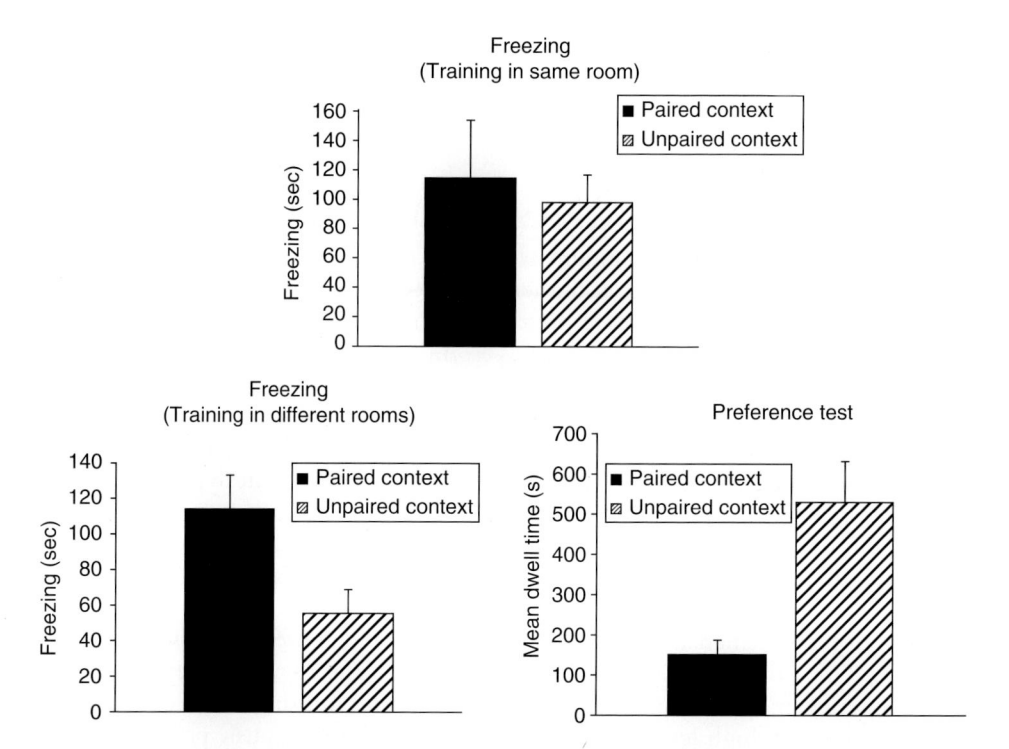

Figure 12.1 Previously unpublished data showing discriminative fear conditioning to context, as measured by freezing behavior in the same testing room in which shock and no-shock training occurred (top panel) versus in a room in which only no-shock training occurred (bottom left panel). When tested in the same room that training occurred, rats did not show discriminative fear conditioning. When tested in a different training room, the group of rats showed discriminative conditioned freezing behavior and showed an aversion for the shock context during a preference test (bottom right panel).

(Figure 12.1, bottom left panel). Our interpretation of this effect was that a significant amount of fear accrues to the testing room that interferes or competes with specific fear to the context chambers. The rats also showed a preference for the context in which no foot-shock was presented using this modified paradigm (Figure 12.1, bottom right panel).

The implications of this finding are significant in our view. First, when using non-discriminative fear conditioning procedures, it is unclear what the subject is associating with the fear, and it is possible that it is not the context chamber. Second, by using the discriminative version of this task and employing different rooms for shock and no-shock trials, one can be confident that elevated fear levels in the paired versus unpaired chamber during testing are a demonstration of context-specific fear conditioning to context. Third, the results indicate that there are multiple levels of context, each of which can be associated with the negative or positive experience. Finally, this paradigm opens up the possibility of manipulating the level of discriminative ambiguity by increasing cue overlap in the paired and unpaired contexts. This is of interest because the hippocampus has been implicated in similar pattern separation functions (Sutherland & McDonald, 1990; Sutherland, McDonald, Hill, & Rudy, 1989).

Multiple measures of fear

Another weakness of the standard, nondiscriminative fear conditioning to context procedure is that in most cases they only assess a single fear response. It is well documented that a state of fear is based on a wide array of physiological and behavioral responses mediated by a heterogeneous collection of brain areas from the spinal cord up to the neocortex (Kapp, Wilson, Pascoe, Supple, & Whalen, 1990). It follows that if we are to get a full understanding of the complexities of fear-induced emotional responses and related learning processes that occur during these experiences, it is important to assess a full range of fear responses. Accordingly, our version of the discriminative fear conditioning to context paradigm assessed multiple measures of unconditioned and conditioned fear. These responses included: avoidance, freezing, heart rate, ultrasonic vocalizations, defecation, body temperature, urination, and locomotion. We showed that these different measures of fear can become associated with specific contexts and that they are learned at different rates (Antoniadis & McDonald, 1999). The demonstration of different learning rate parameters for fear responses reinforced our belief that expanded testing-windows are also an important feature of a valid fear conditioning to context paradigm.

Forebrain learning and memory systems

Evidence from various laboratories using the nondiscriminative paradigm is supportive of a popular view of the neural circuits underlying fear conditioning to context. The data suggest that both the functions of the hippocampus and amygdala are required for normal fear conditioning to a static context (Kim & Fanselow, 1992; Maren, 2008; Phillips & Ledoux, 1992; Sanders, Wiltgen, & Fanselow, 2003). The hippocampus is thought to form a polymodal representation of the context features, and this information is sent to the amygdala to access unconditioned fear circuits in the hypothalamus and brainstem.

We have used our discriminative fear conditioning to context paradigm to reassess the contributions of various forebrain structures implicated in these learning and memory processes. Specifically, we have assessed the effects of neurotoxic lesions of the amygdala or hippocampus on discriminative fear conditioning to context as measured by multiple fear responses. The results showed that both the amygdala and hippocampus are key players in the neural circuitry supporting fear conditioning to context (Antoniadis & McDonald, 1999, 2000, 2001). The amygdala contributes exclusively to the emergence of conditioned heart rate while the hippocampus contributes exclusively to conditioning of defecation and body temperature. The amygdala and hippocampus appear to synergistically interact to mediate conditioned freezing, ultrasonic vocalizations, locomotion, and preference. These results suggest a different view of the organization of forebrain learning and memory systems underlying discriminative fear conditioning to context.

Our new model posits that there are three parallel neural circuits that acquire, store, and express fear conditioning to context. The first circuit, based on synergistic interactions with the hippocampus and amygdala, mediates the association of certain fear responses (freezing, locomotion, ultrasonic vocalizations) with the context, which can be expressed in that same context in the future. During conditioning, hippocampal processing is believed to form a complex representation of the context in which the aversive event occurs (Fanselow, 1990; Sutherland & McDonald, 1990). This context information is then sent to the amygdala and associated with fear responses mediated via subcortical structures. The second circuit is centered on the amygdala, which acts as a parallel circuit. The amygdala probably associates elements of the context with heart-rate changes elicited by fear, which can be subsequently expressed in the same context. The final circuit is centered on the hippocampus, which links complex context information with two fear responses (body temperature changes and increased levels of defecation), which can be expressed in the same context in the future.

Amount of cue overlap as a determinant of the necessity of hippocampal processing during context conditioning

Clearly, from this analysis, the response the experimenter measures determines which neural circuits will be necessary for contextual fear conditioning. On the basis of the preceding analysis, it is clear that the experimenter's choice of response measures is important: different response measures are sensitive to different neural circuits that contribute to contextual fear conditioning. Another factor that might be critical is the level of cue overlap. Cue overlap increases cue ambiguity and is a further factor that determines hippocampal involvement (Antoniadis & McDonald, 1999; McDonald & White, 1995; McDonald et al., 1997). In the case of context conditioning, hippocampal function is thought to be necessary for discriminative abilities between two similar contexts (high cue ambiguity). Nondiscriminative fear conditioning to context, according to our analysis, has low levels of cue ambiguity and as such does not require the hippocampus for conditioning to occur (Frankland, Cestari, Filipkowski, McDonald, & Silva, 1998; Maren, Aharonov, & Fanselow, 1997; Wiltgen, Sanders, Anagnostaras, Sage, & Fanselow, 2006). This pattern of involvement, in which there is an effect or lack of effect following hippocampal lesions, is thought to occur because, as outlined above, there are at least two parallel learning and memory systems at play during context fear conditioning: the hippocampus and amygdala. The hippocampus is thought to form a relational representation of the context during first exposure to the new environment (Fanselow, 1990), and this representation can be associated with fear responses (Kapp et al., 1979). The amygdala tracks cues that predict the presence of positive and negative events. However, when a context has some cue overlap, it requires more training sessions for the amygdala to generate sufficient associative strength to the unique cues differentiating the two contexts. The more cue overlap, the harder it is for amygdala processing to differentiate between the paired and unpaired context.

There is some evidence for these claims. First, although rats with hippocampal lesions induced before training on the single context fear conditioning paradigm are not impaired, there is growing evidence that rats with hippocampal lesions induced after training on the same paradigm are severely impaired (McDonald and Hong, 2013). One explanation of this effect is that when the hippocampus is intact during learning, it interferes with other systems from acquiring a fear conditioning memory. When the hippocampus is absent during conditioning, the nonhippocampal systems are free to acquire an independent context-fear memory. If there is a high level of cue overlap, as in our discriminative version of the task, and the hippocampus is dysfunctional, it seems likely that the amygdala would require many more training trials to acquire enough associative strength to distinguish between the two chambers and associate one with an aversive outcome. Consistent with this idea, a study assessed the effects of repeated training sessions before induction of hippocampal damage would allow the nonhippocampal learning and memory system sufficient trials to support fear conditioning in the retrograde direction. The results showed that if sufficient context–US pairings occur before the hippocampus is damaged, rats with hippocampal lesions are not impaired at fear conditioning to context, although they are with less training (Lehmann et al., 2010). The results suggest that a nonhippocampal learning and memory system can support learning under certain conditions but that high cue ambiguity makes it more difficult for the amygdala to accomplish (see Rudy, 2009, for an alternative explanation).

Our discriminative version of context conditioning has a medium level of cue ambiguity and is sensitive to hippocampal dysfunction (Antoniadis & McDonald, 1999; Frankland et al., 1998). Consistent with the idea that the hippocampus is required for discriminations with high cue overlap, we have shown that rats with hippocampal dysfunction are also impaired on both spatial and configural tasks that have a high cue overlap and yet show normal performance on similar tasks with a low cue overlap (Antoniadis & McDonald, 1999; McDonald & White, 1995; McDonald et al., 1997). For example, the spatial navigation cue overlap experiments used an eight-arm radial maze in which groups of rats with or without hippocampal damage were required to make arm discriminations based on arms that were adjacent to or far apart from one another (McDonald & White, 1995). The configural cue overlap experiments (McDonald et al., 1997) used variants of cued instrumental tasks developed for operant chambers in which cue overlap was high or low and within or across testing sessions. The low-ambiguity task was a conditional context discrimination whereby, in one context, one cue (tone) was reinforced, and another was not (light), and the reverse was true in the other context. Subjects were trained in one context on one day and the other context the next day. The medium-ambiguity task was similar to the first discrimination except that the discriminations in the two contexts were completed each day. Finally, the high-ambiguity task was a negative patterning task in which lever pressing was reinforced when a tone or light was presented but not reinforced when the tone and light were presented together. In all of these experiments, the rats with hippocampal damage were impaired on the tasks with high but not low cue ambiguity.

Summary

In this section, we have tried to provide some insight into the learning processes that are involved in forming and expressing simple associations that result from pairing a context with an event of motivational significance. One issue that was raised is that there are different versions of tasks used to assess this kind of conditioning, and we feel that certain variants have advantages over others for providing unequivocal evidence for context–US associations. The discriminative fear conditioning paradigm using multiple measures of fear was singled out as a strong candidate for these purposes. Using this paradigm, several potentially important findings were obtained. First, a view of how different neural systems implicated in learning and memory contribute to this form of conditioning emerged. Second, it was shown that rats learn a significant amount about the testing room associated with fear that might override or compete with conditioning to the context chamber. Third, manipulating the level of cue overlap between the paired and unpaired chamber makes the task more difficult to resolve (more training required) and increases the sensitivity of the task to hippocampal dysfunction.

Context-Specific Conditioned Inhibition

In the previous section, we discussed a role for contexts in excitatory fear conditioning, but contexts can also play inhibitory roles. One fundamental learning and memory function that most organisms possess is the ability to discriminate between different cues and situations. This is an important process because cues and situations predict the presence or absence of reinforcers and allow the animal to elicit appropriate behaviors towards these signals. The issue of stimulus control has a long tradition in the classic animal learning field, and much is known about discrimination learning (Pearce, 1997; Roberts, 1998), generalization gradients (Honig et al., 1963), and the contributions of excitatory and inhibitory conditioning (Konorski, 1948; Rilling, 1977; Sutherland & Mackintosh, 1971) to discriminative behavior (Chapter 19). The latter demonstration that, during discrimination learning, the reinforced cue acquires excitatory potential, and the nonreinforced cue acquires inhibitory potential is the focus of the latter portion of this chapter.

Our interest in discrimination learning emerged from trying to understand the organization of learning and memory in the mammalian brain. This work has been guided by the theory that there are multiple learning and memory systems in the mammalian brain (White & McDonald, 2002). These systems are located in different parts of the brain and acquire and store different types of information. In normal circumstances, these systems interact either cooperatively or competitively to produce coherent behavior. These systems include, but are not limited to, the hippocampus, dorso-lateral striatum (DLS), and amygdala.

The hippocampus is thought to be an associative learning and memory system important for pulling together the disparate elements of an experience into a coherent representation of the event or episode. The cortical brain regions representing the original experience are "reactivated" by the hippocampus through synaptic processes sometimes via a single retrieval cue. A good example of a task dependent on the hippocampus in the rodent is a discriminative fear conditioning to context task (Antoniadis & McDonald, 1999) described in depth in the previous section. It is thought that normal rats use their hippocampus to form a coherent representation of each context that allows them to identify and remember which context was associated with the foot-shock and which context was safe. Consistent with this idea, rats with hippocampal damage show similar levels of fear in both chambers.

The DLS is thought to be involved in the acquisition and expression of stimulus–response associations (Devan, Hong, & McDonald, 2011; Packard & Knowlton, 2002). Specifically, this system is tracking the co-occurrence of stimuli and motor responses that result in reinforcement or punishment. With many repetitions, the stimulus triggers the specific motor response in a reflexive or habitual manner (i.e., insensitive to the changing instrumental or goal contingencies). A good example of a learning task dependent on the DLS is the conditional discrimination task developed for operant chambers. For this task, rats are reinforced with a palatable food reward for pressing a lever when a light is on and pulling a chain when a tone is present. After a significant training period, the rats respond at high rates to the lever only when the light is on and chain pulling when the tone is present. It is thought that the DLS forms an association, during the many training trials that the animal experiences, between each cue and response, and the appropriate response is triggered when the cue is presented. Consistent with this idea, rats with neurotoxic damage to the DLS are impaired at the acquisition and retention of this instrumental task (Featherstone & McDonald, 2004, 2005).

A large body of evidence supports the idea that the amygdala is critical for forms of emotional learning and memory (White & McDonald, 2002). Specifically, the amygdala seems to track the co-occurrence of neutral stimuli and positive or negative events, and forms a representation of these associations so that the previously neutral cues can retrieve the emotional experience associated with that cue (Cador, Robbins, & Everitt, 1989; Everitt *et al.*, 1989; Hiroi & White, 1991; Hitchcock & Davis, 1986). A good example of a learning task dependent on the neural circuitry of the amygdala is cued fear conditioning. In this paradigm, rabbits are exposed to two types of training trials. One trial consists of the presentation of a neutral cue (light) and an aversive stimulus (paraorbital shock), and the other type of trial consists of the presentation of another neutral cue (tone) with no consequence. After sufficient training, the rabbit shows decreased heart rates (bradycardia) during presentations of the light alone, but not during presentations of the tone alone. The idea is that the amygdala forms an association between the light and the aversive event, forming the basis of an emotional memory that can be used by the rat later to avoid potentially dangerous situations. Rats with damage to the amygdala do not form this association under these training conditions (Kapp *et al.*, 1979).

One interesting experiment using variants of the eight-arm radial maze task showed that these different learning and memory systems can act independently of one another. Rats with damage to the hippocampus, DLS, or amygdala were trained on three different versions of the radial maze task including: spatial, stimulus–response, and classical conditioning versions. The results showed that rats with hippocampal damage were impaired on the spatial but not the other learning tasks. The rats with DLS damage were impaired on the stimulus–response version but not the other tasks. The rats with amygdala damage were impaired on the classical conditioning task but not the others. These results were interpreted to indicate that these systems act in parallel and can function in the absence of the others (McDonald & White, 1993).

Following this work, we wanted to delve further into the visual discrimination task developed for the radial maze (the S–R task) to understand how this discrimination was learned and what the nature of the representation was that supported this behavior. This task was of particular interest because it was discriminative, and we wanted to determine if both excitatory and inhibitory learning were occurring during training. If this was the case, how did each of these associative representations contribute to asymptotic performance, and what was the neural basis of these different forms of learning?

The final parts of this chapter will review research that provides evidence that during training on this visual discrimination task, rats acquire both excitatory and inhibitory associations. The inhibitory association appears to be context specific, and the excitatory association is not. We provide new evidence that the inhibitory association is broken down more slowly during reversal learning while new excitatory conditioning is quicker, suggesting that these are mediated by different neural systems. Further evidence is presented showing that the purported inhibitory association acquired during visual discrimination learning passes the summation test of conditioned inhibition (Rescorla, 1971). The neural circuits mediating this form of conditioned inhibition are also presented, including work showing different roles for the ventral hippocampus, medial prefrontal cortex, and medial striatum. Finally, the implications of this work for understanding the organization of learning and memory in the mammalian brain are discussed.

Visual discrimination task

We have completed a large set of experiments using a visual discrimination task developed for the eight-arm radial maze (Packard, Hirsh, & White, 1989). This is a task in which rats are reinforced for entering lit arms and not reinforced for entering the dark arms. During training, four arms are selected as the reinforced arms each day; food is placed in a food dish, and a light found on that arm is illuminated (McDonald & Hong, 2004). A rat is placed in the center of the radial maze and allowed to forage freely for food for 10 min or until all of the available reinforcers are obtained. The learning curve had a gradual slope indicating slow and incremental improvement over the training experience. This kind of acquisition pattern is consistent with the kind of learning theorized by Hull and colleagues (Hull, 1943).

This visual discrimination task can best be described as an instrumental task in which a particular stimulus (light) was associated with a particular response (body turn), and this stimulus–response association was always reinforced with a palatable food. It was thought that the rats with DLS lesions were impaired on this task because the dorsal striatum was a central module of a learning and memory system mediating stimulus–response habit learning (Packard, Hirsh, & White, 1989).

Consistent with the idea that this instrumental visual discrimination task taps into stimulus–response habit learning and memory functions, Knowlton and colleagues (Sage & Knowlton, 2000) showed that performance on the visual discrimination task is affected by devaluation of the reinforcer in the early, but not the later phases of training. This pattern of effects is traditionally interpreted as evidence that a goal-directed learning and memory system controls behavior early in training and that after many reinforced trials, a stimulus–response habit system takes over (Yin, Ostlund, Knowlton, & Balleine, 2005). The former is thought to be mediated by the dorso-medial striatum and the latter by the DLS (Chapter 16; Yin, Knowlton, & Balleine, 2004).

Triple dissociation within a triple dissociation: Necessary versus incidental associations

Although it appears from previous work that the hippocampus and amygdala are not necessary for solving the visual discrimination task developed for the eight-arm radial maze, it is possible that these systems acquire and/or store information that could influence future behavior. We conducted a series of experiments using the visual discrimination task to explore this prediction. Initial experiments were completed using normal rats and several task manipulations, including context shifts and reversal learning to assess the context specificity of the potential excitatory and inhibitory associations acquired during learning.

Context specificity of visual discrimination learning

For the experiments using normal subjects, rats were trained on the visual discrimination task in a distinct testing room (context A); after reaching asymptotic performance, half of the group continued training in the original context, and the other half were switched to a different context with a virtually identical radial maze and resumed visual discrimination training. The results, presented in Figure 12.2, showed that the group of rats switched to context B after reaching asymptotic levels of performance showed no alteration in their performance of the discrimination despite the fact that they did detect the change in training context (McDonald, King, & Hong, 2001). These experiments showed that the expression of visual discrimination learning was not context specific.

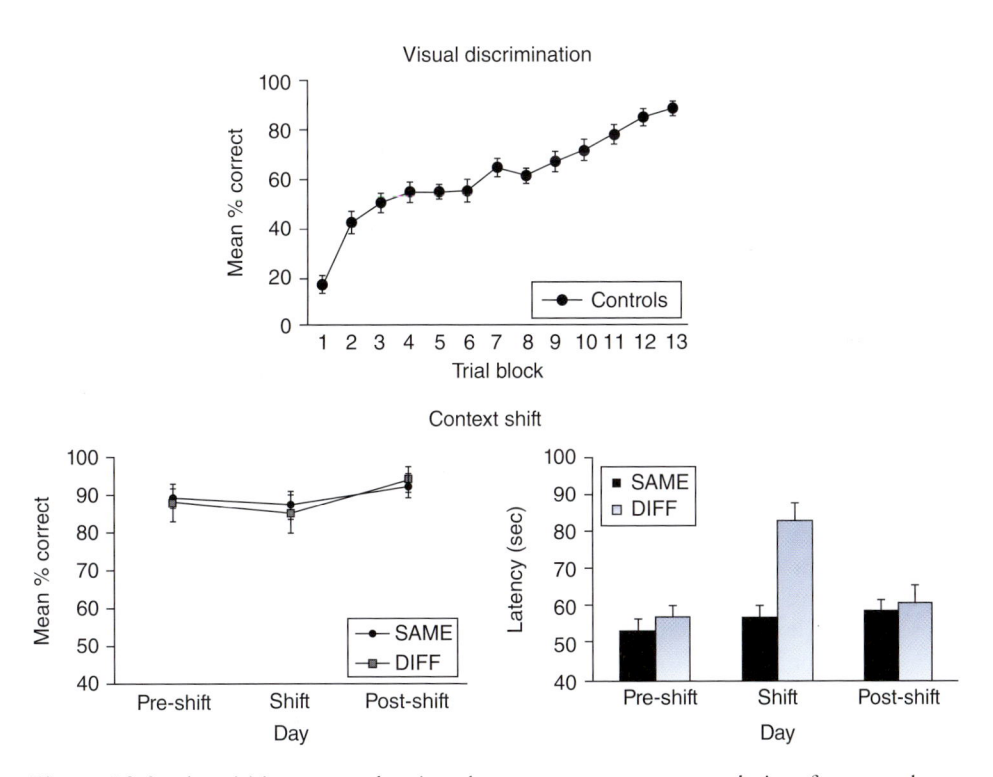

Figure 12.2 Acquisition curve showing the mean percent correct choices for control rats during visual discrimination training on the eight-arm radial maze. As can be seen, learning was slow and incremental (top panel). Bottom left panel: effects of shifting the training context on visual discrimination performance as measured by choice accuracy. Transfer to a different context had no effect on discrimination performance. The rats in the context shift experiment did notice the context change as measured by latency to complete the task before and after the context shift (bottom right panel).

Despite the demonstration that this form of visual discrimination learning was not dependent on the context in which training occurred, it was possible that contextual information was acquired incidentally. One idea was that an excitatory association was acquired during training to the light cue, and this conditioning was sufficient to drive high levels of performance in the different context. This is based on claims that excitatory conditioning is not context specific (Holland & Bouton, 1999). One hypothesis that we were interested in testing was that inhibitory conditioning was accrued to the nonreinforced cue and that this association was the context specific.

Evidence for encoding of a context-specific inhibitory association: reversal learning and renewal tests

For these experiments, a large group of normal rats were trained to asymptotic levels on the visual discrimination task in context A; then half of the rats were given reversal training in the original training context, while the other half were shifted to a different training room (context B) and given reversal training. Reversal training consisted of a switching of the reinforcement contingencies from the lit arms being reinforced to a dark arms being reinforced. Interestingly, rats that received the reversal in a different context from original training showed a rapid acquisition of the reversal learning compared with the rats given the reversal in the original training context (Figure 12.3, top panel; McDonald et al., 2001). This pattern of results was interpreted as indicating that a context-specific inhibitory association was acquired to the nonreinforced dark arm. This hypothesized inhibitory association was acquired during the original discrimination, was context specific, and reduced the probability that the rat would enter dark arms. During reversal learning in the original context, the rat has to undo both the original excitatory association to the reinforced light cue and the inhibitory association accrued to the dark cue; whereas the rats undergoing reversal training in the different context would have to break down the original excitatory association, since it transfers to other contexts, but would not have to undo the inhibitory association, since it was context specific. Evidence for the idea that rats acquire a context-specific inhibitory association to the nonreinforced dark cue during original acquisition was obtained from a transfer test. The transfer test involved returning the group of rats trained in the original context A and reversed in context B, back to context A. The idea behind this transfer test was that the most recently acquired excitatory association would transfer back to the original training context and increase the probability that the rats would enter dark arms. This tendency to enter dark arms would compete with the context-specific inhibitory association accrued to the dark cue in the original context, thereby decreasing entries into dark arms, and result in chance performance. This was the pattern of results obtained for the transfer test (Figure 12.3, bottom panel) providing what we think is compelling evidence for a context-specific inhibitory association.

Further evidence that the nonreinforced dark arm is a conditioned inhibitor

Some have argued that a suspected conditioned inhibitor should pass two empirical tests to be considered a bona fide inhibitory association (Rescorla, 1971). These tests are called the retardation and summation tests, respectively. We have little doubt that

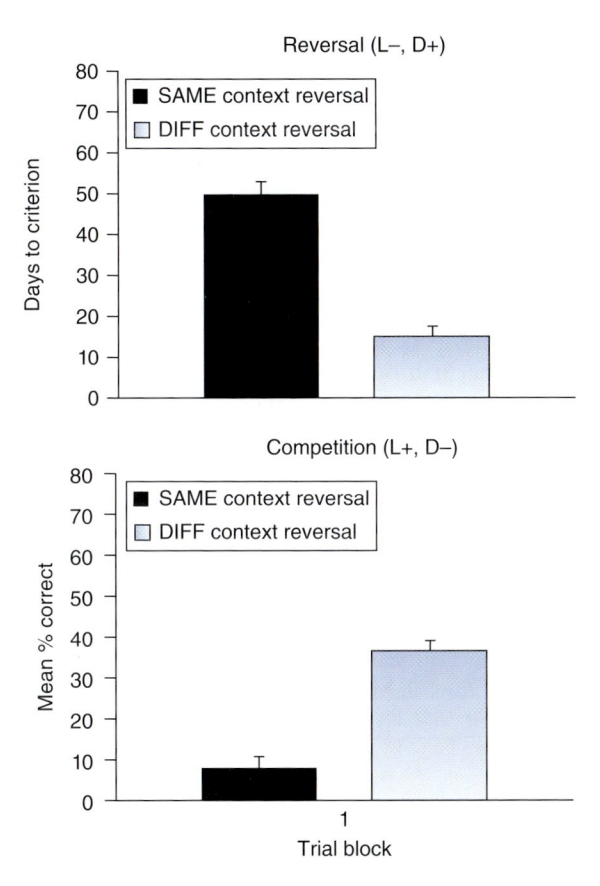

Figure 12.3 Trials to criterion for reversal learning in the same context as original training versus a different context (top panel). A group of rats given reversal training in the same context took much longer to solve the discrimination than a group reversed in a different context. The effects of a competition test in which a group of control rats reversed in a different context from original discrimination training were returned to the latter context, and choice accuracy was assessed (bottom panel). The results showed that the rats performed at approximately 50% choice accuracy. This was interpreted as a competition between the recently acquired excitatory conditioning to the dark arm (trained in the other context) and an inhibitory association with the dark arm linked exclusively to the original context.

the dark arm, following training to asymptotic levels of performance, would retard acquisition of a new discrimination using the dark arms as the newly reinforced cue based on the pattern of our reversal data. However, further experiments to provide direct confirmation of this assumption need to be completed. A more intriguing experiment, in our view, was the summation test using our initial training procedure. An experiment was completed in which we simultaneously pretrained a group of rats to asymptotic performance levels on a visual and tactile discrimination on the radial maze in different rooms and then ran a summation test.

To ascertain whether conditioned inhibition accrued to the nonreinforced arms, a series of summation tests were performed whereby a novel reinforced cue (from the other training context) was simultaneously presented with the nonreinforced cue in four of the maze arms, and the remaining arms had the normally reinforced cue. Since we know that the excitatory conditioning transfers to other contexts, whereas the presumed inhibitory conditioning does not (e.g., McDonald et al., 2001), it was surmised that if the nonreinforced cue was conditioned, the rats would enter the arms containing the reinforced cue of that context more frequently than arms that contained the inhibitory cue in combination with the novel excitatory cue. Entry into an inhibitory arm with the novel excitatory cue was interpreted as the nonreinforced cue not being a classical conditioned inhibitor. For each of the two test days, the context in which the rat was tested in first (A or B) was counterbalanced so that half of the rats were tested in A first on the first day and B first on the second day, and vice versa for the other half of the rats. In context A, the novel reinforced cue from context B (rough flooring panel) was paired with the nonreinforced cue (dark arm) in half the arms, and the reinforced cue (lit arms) was presented with the smooth flooring panel in the other arms. In context B, the novel reinforced cue from context A (light) was turned on with the nonreinforced cue (smooth flooring panel) in four of the eight arms, and the normally reinforced cue (rough flooring) was presented with a dark arm in the remaining arms. The first four arm choices and trial latency were recorded during this test. The results showed that, in both contexts, the rats entered the excitatory arms more than the arms containing the inhibitory cue and the novel excitatory cue, although this result was more prominent in Context B. This pattern of results is consistent with the idea that during visual discrimination learning, the nonreinforced cue acquires inhibitory processes that are context specific (McDonald & Hong, 2013).

What is the status of excitatory and inhibitory conditioning during the midpoint of reversal learning in the same context as original training?

Another feature of the association accrued to the nonreinforced cue during visual discrimination training was how fast this inhibitory association was broken down during reversal learning. Our hypothesis was that the acquisition of the new excitatory association to the dark arm (D+) and the breakdown or extinction of the old context-specific inhibitory association to the dark arm (D−) would occur at a similar pace during reversal learning in the original training context. To test this idea, we designed an experiment in which three groups of rats were trained to asymptotic performance on the visual discrimination task (L+, D−) in Context A. The "same" and "same–diff" groups were then given reversal training in the same context, and the "diff" group was reversed in Context B, the different context. When the group in Context B started learning the reversal (70%), the same–diff group (that was not discriminating owing to context-specific inhibitory association linked to the original context) was switched to Context B, and all the groups continued reversal training. We were interested to see what happens to discriminative performance once the group of rats were removed from the original context. The pattern of results would give some clue as to the associative status of the new excitatory and old inhibitory conditioning to the dark arm. The results showed that the different context reversal group continued to perform with increasing accuracy, the same context reversal group displayed slow incremental improvement, and the same–diff reversal group improved readily once they were transferred to the different context. For the *competition test*, the rats either remained in or were transferred back to context A, and their first four choices were recorded. Entries into lit arms were considered to be correct for this test. The results showed that the group that had reversal training in the same context entered more dark arms than the different and same–diff context reversal groups that entered lit and dark arms almost equally.

Taken together, the results from this experiment showed that the same–diff group had lower choice accuracy scores on the reversed contingencies while they were still in the same context compared with the different context reversal group. Interestingly, once the same–diff group were transferred to another context, their performance improved rapidly and became quite similar to the different context reversal group. These data suggest that the new excitatory conditioning to the dark arm was learned earlier on in reversal training than what was reflected in their performance. The learning was likely masked by the still influential inhibitory association accrued to the dark arm, linked to the original training context, suggesting that this association takes longer to diminish its influence on behavior. Therefore, animals undergoing reversal training in the different context, and the rats that were transferred out of the same to the different context, do not have this inhibitory association competing with the reversal learning for performance outcome. During the competition test, the same reversal group continued to enter dark arms, whereas the same–diff and different context reversal groups entered lit and dark arms almost equally. This strongly suggests that the context inhibitory association with the dark arm was never broken down or extinguished in the latter groups and thus was inhibiting them from approaching the now reinforced dark arm.

Evidence for encoding of a context-specific inhibitory association in the hippocampus during visual discrimination learning

The demonstration of excitatory conditioning to the light cue that appears to be context independent, and thought to be mediated by the DLS, provided a unique opportunity to assess a potential role of the hippocampus in visual discrimination learning. The idea was that during discrimination learning, an excitatory stimulus–response association to the reinforced light cue was acquired by the DLS, and simultaneously an inhibitory association to the nonreinforced dark cue was acquired by the hippocampus. The latter was hypothesized to be unnecessary for acquisition of the visual discrimination but could affect future behavior if task demands were altered. The hippocampus has long been thought to be involved in context conditioning processes (Good & Honey, 1991; Kim & Fanselow, 1992; Sutherland & McDonald, 1990) and, in our mind, was an obvious candidate learning and memory system for this inhibitory association.

To test this idea, we replicated the series of experiments described above in rats with neurotoxic lesions to the hippocampus. The results showed that rats with hippocampal damage showed normal acquisition of the visual discrimination task but, during reversal learning, did not show an inhibition of learning in the original training context. Furthermore, rats with hippocampal damage reversed in a different context from original training (context B) and then returned to the original training room (context A) did not show a competition between the most recent excitatory association (dark cue) and the presumed context-specific inhibitory association (dark cue in context A), as their behavior was controlled by the most recent excitatory association. Taken together, this pattern of results was interpreted as evidence that the hippocampus acquired the context-specific inhibitory association during original training. Although this association was not necessary for normal levels of performance on the task, it could affect behavioral patterns when task requirements or parameters are altered (McDonald, Ko, & Hong, 2002).

Evidence suggests that different subregions of the hippocampus have different functions (Moser & Moser, 1998; Nadel, 1968). We wanted to test the possibility that this unique context-specific inhibitory association might be mediated by one of the subregions of the hippocampus. Specifically, we assessed the effects of neurotoxic lesions of the dorsal versus ventral hippocampus (Figure 12.4). The results clearly showed that the ventral hippocampus, and not the dorsal region, was essential for acquiring the context-specific inhibitory association (McDonald, Jones, Richards, & Hong, 2006). This result, combined with our other work showing that the dorsal hippocampus was important for spatial learning and memory functions, is to our knowledge the first demonstration of unique learning and memory functions dependent on the neural circuitry of these different regions.

We also tested the hypothesis that the medial prefrontal cortex (MPFC), via interactions with the ventral hippocampus, inhibits responding to the nonreinforced cue during visual discrimination learning. The MPFC has been implicated in a variety of complex functions, including recall of hippocampal memories, control of motor sequences, behavioral inhibition processes, and extinction (McDonald, Foong, Rizos, & Hong, 2008). Identical experiments to those described above were undertaken in rats with neurotoxic lesions of the MPFC including the infralimbic, prelimbic, and anterior cingulate cortices. Rats with MPFC lesions showed normal acquisition of the visual discrimination task and reversal learning in the different context from original training. Interestingly, reversal learning in the same context was accelerated in the MPFC-damaged animals (Figure 12.5, top panel), an effect reminiscent of the ventral hippocampal lesion-induced impairment. However, the behavioral effects of the two lesions appear to be different in one important way. When rats with ventral hippocampal lesions that were reversed in the different context are brought back into the original context, they show no evidence of acquiring the conditioned inhibition to the nonreinforced cue, but the rats with MPFC damage do (Figure 12.5, bottom panel).

In summary, the MPFC is a neural system that also contributes to context-specific inhibitory processes during discrimination learning and reversals. This cortical system maintains hippocampal control of behavior for as long as possible during times of changing contingencies.

Other evidence for a role of hippocampus in inhibitory processes

The idea that the hippocampus might be involved in inhibitory processes is not a new idea. One early and popular theory of hippocampal function (Gray, 1982) hypothesized that the hippocampus was not a substrate for learning and memory, but was needed for a more general process in detection and resolution of conflicts between incompatible responses or goals. Essentially, the idea was that the hippocampus was a general inhibitory system. When conflict is detected, the hippocampus is thought to

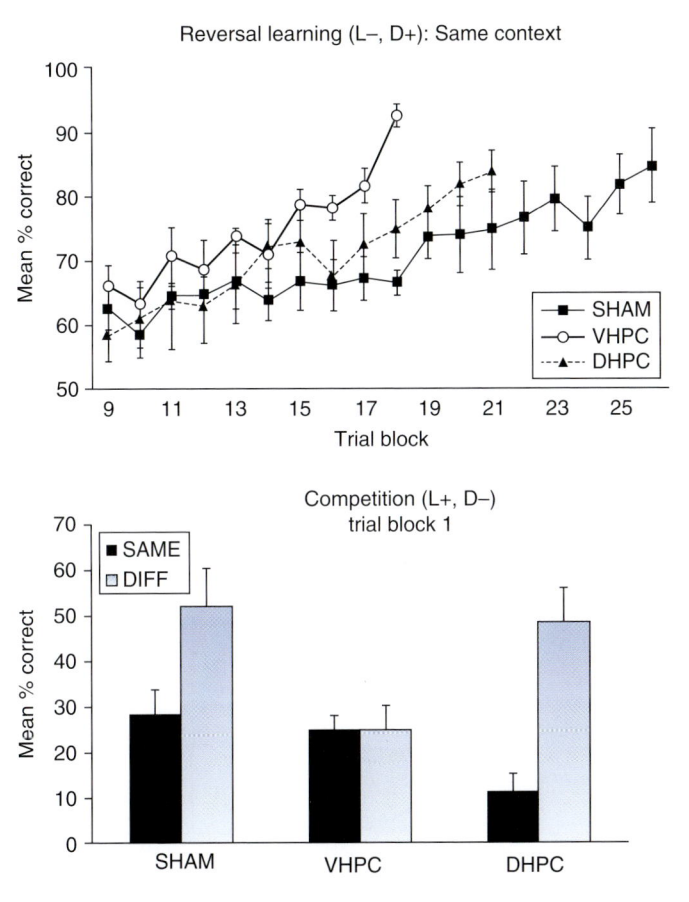

Figure 12.4 Visual discrimination reversal learning in the same context as original training in rats with dorsal or ventral hippocampal lesions compared with controls (top panel). As can be seen, rats with a dysfunctional ventral hippocampus showed accelerated reversal learning compared with the other two groups. When the control group and the group of rats with dorsal hippocampal lesions were reversed in the different context and returned to the original training context, they showed a normal competition between the new excitatory association to the dark arm and the inhibitory association to the dark arm acquired in the original context. In contrast, the rats with ventral hippocampal lesions chose to enter dark arms, the most recent excitatory association accrued to the dark arm in the other context (bottom panel). This pattern of effects suggests that the ventral hippocampus is a critical part of the neural circuitry involved in the acquisition and/or expression of the context-specific inhibitory association acquired during visual discrimination training (adapted from McDonald *et al.*, 2006).

send a signal that increases the influence or associative strength of information with a negative valence. The result of this output signal is that there will be an inhibition of approach or responding to the goal. The basic idea is that rats and humans without a hippocampus are unable to inhibit responding during these conflicting information situations, and this causes impairments on behavioral tasks, not problems with spatial/relational learning and memory problems as some have hypothesized (Moser & Moser, 1998; O'Keefe & Nadel, 1978).

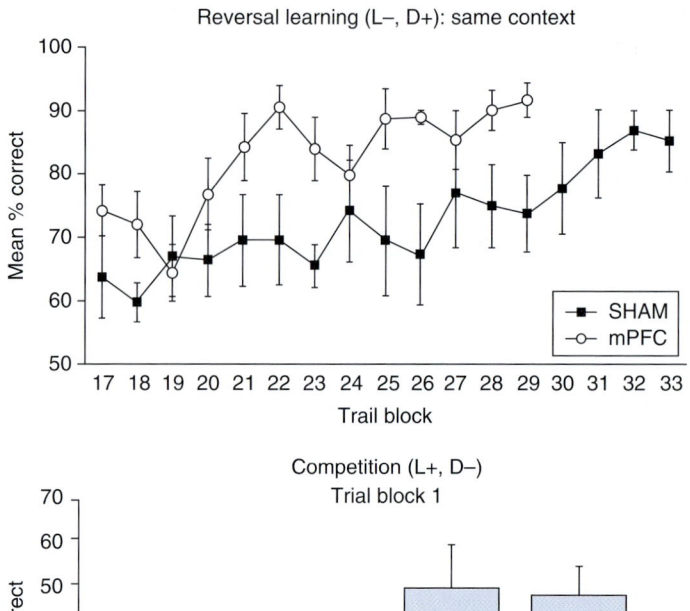

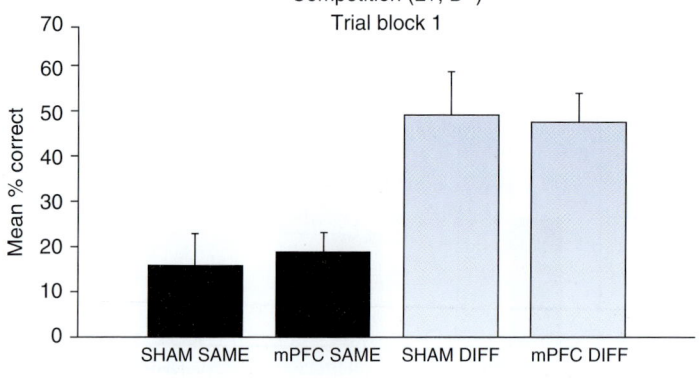

Figure 12.5 Effects of neurotoxic lesions to the MPFC on visual discrimination reversal learning in the same context as original training. Results showed that damage to the MPFC resulted in accelerated reversal learning in the same context (top panel). Although this effect was similar to that reported following ventral hippocampal lesions, there was one difference. When rats with MPFC lesions were reversed in the different context and returned to the original training context, they showed a normal competition between the new excitatory association with the dark arm and the inhibitory association with the dark arm acquired in the original context. This pattern of data suggests that the MPFC actively maintains the control of the context-specific inhibitory association during reversal learning (adapted from McDonald, Foong, Ray, Rios, & Hong, 2007).

Although there are some interesting features of this theory, the patterns of data that have followed since this theory was proffered are not consistent with even the most basic of the predictions of the main idea (but see Davidson & Jarrard, 2004). For example, one key finding used to support this view is the demonstration that rats with hippocampal damage show impairments in extinction (Schmaltz & Theios, 1972). According to Gray (1982), during extinction the nonreward causes the hippocampus to send an output signal that increases inhibition to approach the goal site, and the animal starts showing extinction. Without a hippocampus, the animal continues to approach the previously rewarded goal site. Modern views of extinction suggest otherwise (Bouton & Bolles, 1979). They argue that during extinction trials, a new representation is formed in which the CS is associated with nonreinforcement and becomes inhibitory and context dependent. This function appears to depend on the amygdala, hippocampus, and portions of prefrontal cortex (Orsini, Kim, Knapska, & Maren, 2011) with convergent inputs from both the ventral hippocampus and prelimbic portions of the prefrontal cortex to the basolateral amygdala to mediate the contextual control of fear after extinction.

The role of the hippocampus in one form of inhibition, latent inhibition, has received a significant amount of attention in the past. Latent inhibition occurs when a subject is preexposed to a CS in the absence of a reinforcer prior to training. When that CS is then subsequently paired with a US, conditioning is slowed or inhibited (Lubow, 1973). One interesting aspect of this learning phenomenon is that it is normally context specific so that if the preexposure and conditioning phases of the experiment occur in different contexts, the latent inhibition effect is significantly reduced (Channell & Hall, 1983). Honey and Good (1993) assessed the effects of neurotoxic lesions of the hippocampus on latent inhibition using a Pavlovian conditioning procedure. They found that rats with large neurotoxic lesions of the hippocampus did not show a context-specific latent inhibition effect, although they did show latent inhibition. They and others (Bouton) have interpreted these effects as impairments in contextual retrieval processes originally proposed by Hirsh (1974). The idea is that the hippocampus is required to disambiguate the meaning of the CS in these types of learning paradigms. The meaning of the CS changes across the different training phases and contexts so that in the preexposure phase, the CS predicts nonreinforcement, while during the conditioning phase, in a different context, the CS predicts reinforcement. The hippocampus is thought to use orthogonal representations of the two contexts to aid in retrieval of the appropriate association.

Maren and colleagues expanded on these empirical findings and interpretations by assessing context-specific latent inhibition during the retrieval process as the other studies used pretraining neurotoxic lesions that confound the role of the hippocampus in learning from retrieval processes. The results showed that expression of context-specific latent inhibition was impaired in rats that received temporary inactivations of the dorsal hippocampus (Maren & Holt, 2000), but latent inhibition processes in general were not altered.

Another line of work has assessed the role of inhibitory processes during extinction (Bouton, 1993). Evidence suggests that the original CS–US association is not reduced during extinction, but the CS acquires a new association, CS–no reinforcer (Bouton & King, 1983). According to this view, whether the subject exhibits extinction depends on the context in which conditioning and extinction occur. If the subject is trained in one context, and this conditioning is extinguished in another context, conditioning will renew if the subject is placed back into the original context. Ji and Maren (2005) showed that rats with dorsal hippocampal lesions did not show this renewal effect in extinction (but see Wilson, Brooks, & Bouton, 1995). Some have argued that it is not the inhibitory conditioning that makes the processes described above context and dorsal hippocampal dependent; instead, it is what is learned second about the CS that becomes highly context- and hippocampal dependent (Holland & Bouton, 1999).

In contrast, our work using the visual discrimination task showing a ventral hippocampal mediated context-specific inhibitory association is not consistent with the above reviewed research. Our research showed that during acquisition of a visual discrimination, excitatory and inhibitory conditioning simultaneously occurred, with the latter being highly context dependent. Further, the context-specific inhibitory association was dependent on the ventral and not the dorsal hippocampus.

There are several differences in the work reviewed above and the work reported from our laboratory. First, most of the experiments carried out by the other groups investigated extinction or latent inhibition, and there may be fundamental differences between the types of inhibitory processes at work during these tasks versus discrimination tasks. Second, almost all of the work carried out on inhibitory processes and the hippocampus has focused on classical conditioning except for our radial maze experiments. It is entirely possible that classical and instrumental conditioning paradigms result in different forms of inhibitory conditioning, and the neural substrates might be different. Consistent with this idea, there is evidence that the nature of the representations formed during operant versus classical conditioning extinction is different (Colwill, 1991; Rescorla, 1993). Lastly, our contexts are actually laboratory testing rooms, not the traditional operant chamber or box that is most often used. It is possible that these different types of contexts are utilized differently by the organism. One possible difference is the amount of movement and movement-related hippocampal processing that might occur in the two different sizes of contexts. Movement through space activates certain types of waveform activity in the hippocampus, called theta rhythms. Theta oscillatory activity is thought to be involved in hippocampal learning and memory processes (Hasselmo, 2005), and it is possible that these learning processes might be different than when a subject is confined in a small box. Further research is required to test some of these ideas.

Summary

In this section, we have reviewed a body of work directed at describing and understanding the influence of inhibitory associations. A specific focus was on a class of these associations called conditioned inhibition, and a demonstration of these associations during acquisition of a visual discrimination task developed for the eight-arm radial maze. The results showed several interesting features of this conditioned inhibition including: (1) it was context specific; (2) it passed a summation test; (3) it was dependent on ventral hippocampal circuitry; (4) extinction processes associated with reversal learning in the same context as original training are dependent on the MPFC. Other demonstrations of inhibitory associations including latent inhibition and extinction were also reviewed, with an emphasis on the role of hippocampus in some of these conditioning phenomena.

General Conclusions

This chapter has described two different types of context conditioning and discussed various empirical and theoretical issues around these demonstrations. The first type of context learning considered is mediated by direct context–US associations, which are considered the most direct measure of context conditioning, and there are a variety of paradigms that have been designed to assess this type of conditioning. We provided evidence that a discriminative fear conditioning version is an excellent tool for assessing context–US associations with the potential to ask important empirical and theoretical questions that are not afforded by nondiscriminative versions. The second type of context learning we assessed is linked to tasks that have an inhibitory conditioning component to them like discrimination, latent inhibition, and extinction tasks, in which it has been shown that this type of conditioning is context specific. We focused on our work investigating a form of context-specific conditioned inhibition acquired during acquisition of a visual discrimination task in normal rats. We also presented evidence that the ventral hippocampus is essential for this form of learning, and the role of the MPFC was also described. Finally, other paradigms involving inhibitory conditioning were discussed with an emphasis on whether they were context specific and what role, if any, the hippocampus played. From this and other work, a pattern emerged, indicating that there are different forms of excitatory and inhibitory context conditioning, having a wide range of influences on behavior, with different neural subcircuits mediating them.

References

Allen, C. T., & Shimp, T. A. (1990). On using classical conditioning methods for researching the impact of ad-evoked feelings. In S. J. Agras, J. A. Edell, & T. M. Dubitsky (Eds.), *Emotion in advertising: Theoretical and practical explorations.* Westport, CT: Quorum Books.

Antoniadis, E. A., & McDonald, R. J. (1999). Discriminative fear conditioning to context expressed by multiple measures of fear in the rat. *Behavioural Brain Research, 101,* 1–13.

Antoniadis, E. A., & McDonald, R. J. (2000). Amygdala, hippocampus, and discriminative fear conditioning to context. *Behavioural Brain Research, 108,* 1–19.

Antoniadis, E. A., & McDonald, R. J. (2001). Amygdala, hippocampus, and unconditioned fear. *Experimental Brain Research, 138,* 200–209.

Balleine, B., & Dickinson, A. (1992). Signalling and incentive processes in instrumental reinforce devaluation. *Quarterly Journal of Experimental Psychology B, 45,* 285–301.

Balsam, P. D. (1985). The functions of context in learning and performance. In: P. D. Balsam & A. Tomie (Eds.), *Context and learning* (pp. 1–22). Hillsdale, NJ: Lawrence Erlbaum Associates.

Blanchard, R. J., & Blanchard, D. C. (1969). Crouching as an index of fear. *Journal of Comparative Physiological Psychology, 67,* 370–375.

Bouton, M. E. (1993). Context, time, and memory retrieval in the interference paradigms of Pavlovian learning. *Psychological Bulletin, 114,* 80–99.

Bouton, M. E., & Bolles, R. C. (1979). Role of conditioned contextual stimuli in reinstatement of extinguished fear. *Journal of Experimental Psychology and Animal Behavior Processes, 5,* 368–378.

Bouton, M. E., & King, D. A. (1983). Contextual control of the extinction of conditioned fear: tests for the associative value of the context. *Journal of Experimental Psychology: Animal Behavioral Processes, 9,* 248–265.

Cador, M., Robbins, T. W., & Everitt, B. J. (1989). Involvement of the amygdala in stimulus–reward associations: interaction with the ventral striatum. *Neuroscience, 30,* 77–86.

Carr, G. D., Fibiger, H. C., & Phillips, A. G. (1989). Conditioned place preference as a measure of drug reward. In J. M. Leibman & S. J. Cooper (Eds.), *The neuropharmacological basis of reward* (pp. 264–319). Oxford, UK: Oxford University Press.

Channell, S., & Hall, G. (1983). Contextual effects in latent inhibition with an appetitive conditioning procedure. *Animal Learning & Behavior, 11,* 67–74.

Colwill, R. W. (1991). Negative discriminative stimuli provide information about the identity of omitted response-contingent outcomes. *Animal Learning & Behavior, 19,* 326–336.

Crombag, H. S., Bossert, J. M., Koya, E., & Shaham, Y. (2008). Context-induced relapse to drug seeking: a review. *Philosophical Transactions of the Royal Society B, 363,* 3233–3243.

Davidson, T. L., & Jarrard, L. E. (2004). The hippocampus and inhibitory learning: a "Gray" area? *Neuroscience & Biobehavioural Reviews, 28,* 261–271.

Devan, B. D., Hong, N. S., & McDonald, R. J. (2011). Parallel associative processing in the dorsal striatum: segregation of stimulus–response and cognitive control subregions. *Neurobiology of Learning and Memory, 96,* 95–120.

Everitt, B. J., Cador, M., & Robbins, T. W. (1989). Interactions between the amygdala and ventral striatum in stimulus–reward associations: Studies using a second-order schedule of reinforcement. *Neuroscience, 30,* 63–75.

Everitt, B. J., Dickinson, A., & Robbins, T. W. (2001). The neuropsychological basis of addictive behavior. *Brain Research Reviews, 36,* 129–138.

Fanselow, M. S. (1990). Factors governing one-trial contextual conditioning. *Animal Learning & Behavior, 18,* 264–270.

Fanselow, M. S., & Baackes, M. P. (1982). Conditioned fear-induced opiate analgesia on the formalin test: Evidence for two aversive motivational systems. *Learning and Motivation, 13,* 200–221.

Featherstone, R. E., & McDonald, R. J. (2004). Dorsal striatum and stimulus–response learning: lesions of the dorsolateral, but not dorsomedial, striatum impair acquisition of a stimulus–response-based instrumental discrimination task, while sparing conditioned place preference learning. *Neuroscience, 124,* 23–31.

Featherstone, R. E., & McDonald, R. J. (2005). Lesions of the dorsolateral or dorsomedial striatum impair performance of a previously acquired simple discrimination task. *Neurobiology of Learning and Memory, 84,* 159–167.

Frankland, P. W., Cestari, V., Filipkowski, R. K., McDonald, R. J., & Silva, A. J. (1998). The dorsal hippocampus is essential for context discriminations, but not for context recognition. *Behavioral Neuroscience, 112,* 863–874.

Garcia, J., Kimeldorf, D. J., Hunt, E. L. (1957). Spatial avoidance in the rats as a result of exposure to ionizing radiation. *British Journal of Radiology, 30,* 318–321.

Good, M., & Honey, R. C. (1991). Conditioning and contextual retrieval in hippocampal rats. *Behavioral Neuroscience, 105,* 499–509.

Gray, J. A. (1982). *The neuropsychology of anxiety: an enquiry into the function of the septo-hippocampal system.* Oxford, UK: Oxford University Press.

Grillon, C. (2002). Startle reactivity and anxiety disorders: aversive conditioning, context, and neurobiology. *Biological Psychiatry, 52,* 958–975.

Guthrie, E. R. (1935). *The psychology of learning.* New York, NY: Harper & Row.

Hasselmo, M. E. (2005). What is the function of hippocampal theta rhythm? Linking behavioral data to phasic properties of field potential and unit recording data. *Hippocampus, 15,* 936–949.

Hiroi, N., & White, N. M. (1991). The lateral nucleus of the amygdala mediates expression of the amphetamine conditioned place preference. *Journal of Neuroscience, 11,* 2107–2116.

Hirsh, R. (1974). The hippocampus and contextual retrieval of information from memory: A theory. *Behavioral Biology, 12,* 421–444.

Hitchcock, J., & Davis, M. (1986). Lesions of the amygdala, but not of the cerebellum or red nucleus, block conditioned fear as measured with the potentiated startle paradigm. *Behavioral Neuroscience, 100,* 11–22.

Holland, P. C. (1983). "Occasion-setting" in conditional discriminations. In M. Commons, R. Hernstein, & A. R. Wagner (Eds.), *Quantitative analyses of behavior: Vol. 4: Discrimination processes*. New York, NY: Ballinger.

Holland, P. C., & Bouton, M. E. (1999). Hippocampus and context in classical conditioning. *Current Opinion in Neurobiology, 9*, 195–202.

Holland, P. C., Lamoureux, J. A., Han, J. S., & Gallagher, M. (1999). Hippocampal lesions interfere with pavlovian negative occasion setting. *Hippocampus, 9*, 143–157.

Holland, P. C., & Petrovich, G. D. (2005). A neural system analysis of the potentiation of feeding by conditional stimuli. *Physiology and Behavior, 86*, 747–761.

Honey, R. C., & Good, M. (1993). Selective hippocampal lesions abolish the contextual specificity of latent inhibition and conditioning. *Behavioral Neuroscience, 107*, 23–33.

Honig, W. K., Boneau, C. A., Burstein, K. R., & Pennypacker, H. S. (1963). Positive and negative generalization gradients obtained under equivalent training conditions. *Journal of Comparative and Physiological Psychology, 56*, 111–116.

Hull, C. L. (1943). *Principles of behavior*. New York, NY: Appleton-Century-Crofts.

Ji, J., & Maren, S. (2005). Electrolytic lesions of the dorsal hippocampus disrupt renewal of conditional fear after extinction. *Learning and Memory, 12*, 270–276.

Kapp, B. S., Frysinger, R. C., Gallagher, M., & Haselton, J. B. (1979). Amygdala central nucleus lesions: Effect on heart rate conditioning in the rabbit. *Physiology and Behavior, 23*, 1109–1117.

Kapp, B. S., Wilson, A., Pascoe, J. P., Supple, W. F., & Whalen, P. J. (1990). A neuroanatomical systems analysis of conditioned bradycardia in the rabbit. In M. Gabriel, & J. Moore (Eds.), *Neurocomputation and learning: foundations of adaptive networks* (pp. 55–90). New York, NY: Bradford Books.

Kim, J. J., & Fanselow, M. S. (1992). Modality-specific retrograde amnesia of fear. *Science, 256*, 675–677.

Konorski, J. (1948). The physiological bases of memory. *Mysl Wspolczenosc, 5*, 214–232.

Lehmann, H., Sparks, F. T., Spanswick, F. T., Hadikin, C., McDonald, R. J., & Sutherland, R.J (2010). Making context memories independent of the hippocampus. *Learning and Memory, 16*, 417–420.

Lolordo, V. M., & Overmier, J. B. (2011). Trauma, learned helplessness, its neuroscience, and implications for posttraumatic stress disorder. In T. R. Schachtman & S. Reilly (Eds.), *Associative learning and conditioning theory: Human and non-human applications*. New York, NY: Oxford University Press.

Lubow, R. E. (1973). Latent inhibition. *Psychological Bulletin, 79*, 398–407.

Mackintosh, N. J. (1975). Theory of attention. *Psychological Review, 72*, 276–298.

Maren, S. (2008). Pavlovian fear conditioning as a behavioural assay for hippocampus and amygdala function: cautions and caveats. *Behavioral Neuroscience, 28*, 1661–1666.

Maren, S., Aharonov, G., & Fanselow, M. S. (1997). Neurotoxic lesions of the dorsal hippocampus and Pavlovian fear conditioning in rats. *Behavioural Brain Research, 88*, 261–274.

Maren, S., & Holt, W. (2000). The hippocampus and contextual memory retrieval in Pavlovian conditioning. *Behavioural Brain Research, 110*, 97–108.

Maren, S., Phan, K. L., & Liberzon, I. (2013). The contextual brain: implications for fear conditioning, extinction, and psychopathology. *Nature Reviews Neuroscience, 14*, 417–428.

Martin, J. C. (1966). Spatial avoidance in a paradigm in which ionizing radiation precedes spatial confinement. *Radiation Research, 27*, 284–289.

Martin, J. C., & Ellinwood Jr., E. H. (1974). Conditioned aversion in spatial paradigms following methamphetamine injection. *Psychopharmacologia, 36*, 323–335.

McDonald, R. J., Koerner, A., & Sutherland, R. J. (1995). Contextual fear conditioning and the hippocampus. *Society for Neuroscience Abstracts, 21*, 1218.

McDonald, R. J., Murphy, R. A., Guarraci, F. A., Gortler, J. R., White, N. M., & Baker, A. G. (1997). A systematic comparison of the effects of hippocampal and fornix-fimbria lesions on acquisition of three configural discrimination tasks. *Hippocampus, 7*, 371–388.

McDonald, R. J., Foong, N., Ray, C., Rios, Z., & Hong, N. S. (2007). The role of medial prefrontal cortex in context-specific inhibition processes. *Experimental Brain Research, 177*, 509–519.

McDonald, R. J., Foong, N., Rizos, Z., & Hong, N. S. (2008). Neurotoxic lesions of the medial prefrontal cortex or medial striatum impair multiple-location place learning in the water task: evidence for neural structures with complementary roles in behavioural flexibility. *Experimental Brain Research, 187*, 419–427.

McDonald, R. J., & Hong, N. S. (2004). A dissociation of dorso-lateral striatum and amygdala function on the same stimulus-response habit task. *Neuroscience, 124*, 507–513.

McDonald, R. J., & Hong, N. S. (2013). How does a learning and memory system gain control over behavior? *Hippocampus, 23*, 1084–1102.

McDonald, R. J., Hong, N. S., & Devan, B. D. (2004). The challenges of understanding mammalian cognition and memory-based behaviours: an interacting learning and memory systems approach. *Neuroscience and Biobehavioural Reviews, 28*, 719–746.

McDonald, R. J., Jones, J., Richards, B., & Hong, N. S. (2006). A double dissociation of dorsal and ventral hippocampal function on a learning and memory task mediated by the dorso-lateral striatum. *European Journal of Neuroscience, 24*, 1789–1801.

McDonald, R. J., King, A. L., & Hong, N. S. (2001). Context-specific interference on reversal learning of a stimulus–response habit. *Behavioural Brain Research, 121*, 149–165.

McDonald, R. J., Ko, C., & Hong, N. S. (2002). Attenuation of context-specific inhibition on reversal learning of a stimulus–response habit in rats with hippocampal damage. *Behavioural Brain Research, 136*, 113–126.

McDonald, R. J., & White, N. M. (1993). A triple dissociation of memory systems: hippocampus, amygdala, and dorsal striatum. *Behavioral Neuroscience, 107*, 3–22.

McDonald, R. J., & White, N. M. (1995). Hippocampal and non-hippocampal contributions to place learning. *Behavioral Neuroscience, 109*, 579–593.

Moser, E. I., & Moser, M. B. (1998). Functional differentiation in the hippocampus. *Hippocampus, 8*, 608–619.

Mucha, R. F., van der Kooy, D., O'Shaughnessy, M., & Bucenieks, P. (1982). Drug reinforcement studied by the use of place conditioning in rat. *Brain Research, 243*, 91–105.

Nadel, L. (1968). Dorsal and ventral hippocampal lesions and behavior. *Physiology and Behavior, 3*, 891–900.

O'Keefe, J., & Nadel, L. (1978). *The hippocampus as a cognitive map*. Oxford, UK: Oxford University Press.

Orsini, C. A., Kim, J. H., Knapska, E., & Maren, S. (2011). Hippocampal and prefrontal projections to the basal amygdala mediate contextual regulation of fear after extinction. *Journal of Neuroscience, 31*, 17269–17277.

Overall, J. E., & Brown, W. L., & Logie, L. C. (1959). Instrumental behaviour of albino rats in response to incident X-irradiation. *British Journal of Radiology, 32*, 411–414.

Packard, M. G., Hirsh, R., & White, N. M. (1989). Differential effects of fornix and caudate nucleus lesions on two radial maze tasks: evidence for multiple memory systems. *Journal of Neuroscience, 9*, 1465–1472.

Packard, M. G., & Knowlton, B. J. (2002). Learning and memory functions of the basal ganglia. *Annual Review of Neuroscience, 25*, 563–593.

Pavlov, I. P. (1927). *Conditioned reflexes*. Oxford, UK: Oxford University Press.

Pearce, J. M. (1997). *Animal learning and cognition* (2nd ed.). Hove, UK: Psychology Press.

Pearce, J. M., & Hall, G. (1980). A model for Pavlovian learning: variations in the effectiveness of conditioned but not unconditioned stimuli. *Psychological Review, 87*, 532–552.

Phillips, R. G., & Ledoux, J. E. (1992). Differential contribution of amygdala and hippocampus to cued and contextual fear conditioning. *Behavioral Neuroscience, 106,* 274–285.

Polivy, J., Herman, C. P., & Coelho, J. (2008). Caloric restriction in the presence of attractive food cues: external cue, eating, and weight. *Physiology and Behavior, 94,* 729–733.

Quirk, G. J., & Gehlert, D. R. (2003). Inhibition of the amygdala: key to pathological states? *Annals of the New York Academy of Sciences, 985,* 263–272.

Rescorla, R. A. (1967). Pavlovian conditioning and its proper control procedures. *Psychological Review, 74,* 71–80.

Rescorla, R. A. (1968). Probability of shock in the presence and absence of CS in fear conditioning. *Journal of Comparative Physiology and Psychology, 66,* 1–5.

Rescorla, R. A. (1971). Summation and retardation tests of latent inhibition. *Journal of Comparative Physiological Psychology, 75,* 77–81.

Rescorla, R. A. (1993). Inhibitory associations between S and R in extinction. *Animal Learning & Behavior, 21,* 327–336.

Rescorla, R. A., & Wagner, A. R. (1972). A theory of Pavlovian conditioning: variations in the effectiveness of reinforcement and nonreinforcement. In A. H. Black & W. F. Prokasy (Eds.), *Classical conditioning II: Current theory and research*. New York, NY: Appleton-Century-Crofts.

Rilling, M. (1977). Stimulus control and inhibitory processes. In W. K. Honig & J. E. R. Staddon (Eds.), *Handbook of operant behavior* (pp. 432–480). Englewood Cliffs, NJ: Prentice-Hall.

Roberts, W. A. (1998). *Principles of animal cognition*. Boston: McGraw-Hill.

Rudy, J. W. (2009). Context representations, context functions, and the parahippocampal–hippocampal system. *Learning and Memory, 16,* 573–585.

Sage, J. R., & Knowlton, B. J. (2000). Effects of US devaluation on win–stay and win–shift radial maze performance in rats. *Behavioral Neuroscience, 114,* 295–306.

Sanders, M. J., Wiltgen, B. J., & Fanselow, M. S. (2003). The place of the hippocampus in fear conditioning. *European Journal of Pharmacology, 463,* 217–223.

Sanderson, D. J., McHugh, S. B., Good, M. A., Sprengel, R., Rawlins, J. N., & Bannerman, D. M. (2010). Spatial working memory deficits in GluA1 AMPA receptor subunit knockout mice reflect impaired short-term habituation: evidence for Wagner's dual-process memory model. *Neuropsychologia, 48,* 2303–2315.

Schmaltz, L. W., & Theios, J. (1972). Acquisition and extinction of a classically conditioned response in hippocampectomized rabbits (*Oryctolagus cuniculus*). *Journal of Comparative Physiological Psychology, 79,* 328–333.

Skinner, B. F. (1938). *The behavior of organisms: An experimental analysis*. Englewood Cliffs, NJ: Prentice-Hall.

Sutherland, N. S., & Mackintosh, N. J. (1971). *Mechanisms of animal discrimination learning*. New York, NY: Academic Press.

Sutherland, R. J., & McDonald, R. J. (1990). Hippocampus, amygdala and memory deficits. *Behavioural Brain Research, 37,* 57–79.

Sutherland, R. J., McDonald, R. J., Hill, C. R., & Rudy, J. W. (1989). Damage to the hippocampal formation in rats selectively impairs the ability to learn cue relationships. *Behavioral and Neural Biology, 52,* 331–356.

Sutherland, R. J., & Rudy, J. W. (1989). Configural association theory: the role of the hippocampal formation in learning, memory, and amnesia. *Psychobiology, 17,* 129–144.

Thorndike, E. L. (1932). *The fundamentals of learning*. New York, NY: Teachers College Press.

White, N. M. (1996). Addictive drugs as reinforcers: Multiple partial actions on memory systems. *Addiction, 91,* 921–949.

White, N. M., & McDonald, R. J. (2002). Multiple memory systems in the rat brain: A review. *Neurobiology of Learning and Memory, 77,* 125–184.

Wilson, A., Brooks, D. C., Bouton, M. E. (1995). The role of the rat hippocampal system in several effects of context in extinction. *Behavioral Neuroscience, 109,* 828–836.

Wiltgen, B. J., Sanders, M. J., Anagnostaras, S. G., Sage, J. R., & Fanselow, M. S. (2006). Context fear learning in the absence of the hippocampus. *Journal of Neuroscience, 26,* 5484–5491.

Yin, H. H., Knowlton, B. J., & Balleine, B. W. (2004). Lesions of dorsolateral striatum preserve outcome expectancy but disrupt habit formation in instrumental learning. *European Journal of Neuroscience, 19,* 181–189.

Yin, H. H., Ostlund, S. B., Knowlton, B. J., & Balleine, B. W. (2005). The role of the dorsomedial striatum in instrumental conditioning. *European Journal of Neuroscience, 22,* 513–523.

Zelinski, E., Hong, N. S., Halsall, B., & McDonald, R. J. (2010). Prefrontal cortical contributions during discriminative fear conditioning, extinction, and spontaneous recovery in rats. *Experimental Brain Research, 203,* 285–297.

13

The Relation Between Spatial and Nonspatial Learning

Anthony McGregor

Faced with the problem of returning to an important location, such as a nest or a source of food, an animal could use any number of strategies. Some may be unrelated to learning based on cues provided naturally by the environment that could indicate the spatial goal location. For example, an animal could follow a pheromone trail laid down by conspecifics (e.g., trail-laying in ants; Leuthold, 1968). Another is for an animal to keep track of its own body movements and the distance it has traveled to calculate a vector from its current position back to where it began. This strategy, known as path integration or dead reckoning, is used by a range of species, from insects (e.g., Wehner & Srinivasan, 1981) to humans (e.g., Loomis *et al.*, 1993), and may be used without any reference to the environment in which the animal finds itself. However, most often, animals navigate to a location in an environment made familiar through experience, and in this case learning is involved. The purpose of this chapter is to examine how spatial learning involves the same associative processes thought to underlie nonspatial learning, the conditions under which spatial learning progresses, and how learning is translated into performance.

What is Learned?

S–R associations

Spatial behavior has been used to examine the fundamental nature of associative learning in animals since the birth of experimental psychology. Early psychologists documented the gradual manner in which rats seemed to learn to navigate through mazes. Small (1901) noted, after observing rats run through a complex maze with a series of left and right turns, and many alleys leading to dead ends, the "gradually increasing certainty of knowledge" and "the almost automatic character of the movements" in his later experiments (p. 218). Such observations led behaviorists such as Watson to analyze spatial learning in terms of the habits, which they argued were the basis of all learning. Watson (1907) reported that manipulations the special senses, such as vision and olfaction, had no effect on the ability of rats to learn to run through a maze, and came to the conclusion that they learned a series of responses controlled by internal kinesthetic feedback to the brain from joints and muscles. Though criticized at the time and subsequently for ignoring compensation from other senses, Watson argued that spatial behavior involved the initiation of a chain of automatic responses, learned through the development of complex S–R motor habits and unaffected by the presence of external stimuli. Such a view seemed to gain some support in subsequent studies. In Carr and Watson's (1908) famous "kerplunk" experiment, rats were trained to run down an alley-like maze for food. When the alley was shortened, rats ran past the now-closer food and straight into the wall at the end of the alley, making the "kerplunk" noise that gave the study its name. Other reports by Dennis (1932) and Gingerelli (1929) provided similar evidence of reflexive running through a maze, and Stoltz and Lott (1964) showed that rats trained to locate food at the end of a maze would run straight past food placed in unexpected locations.

S–S associations

In contrast to the prevailing views of S–R theorists such as Hull (1943), Tolman (1932, 1948, 1949) claimed that many studies of spatial behavior demonstrated that associative learning involved the acquisition of information about the relationships among stimuli and outcomes, in what may be termed S–S learning. For Tolman, such S–S associations enabled animals to learn the interrelations among stimuli in their environments, and the location of reinforcers such as food, allowing the formation of a spatial map (see section below). Tolman's argument that animals did not learn simply as the result of strengthened response tendencies gained support from two sources of evidence. First, animals seemed to learn about their spatial environments in the absence of explicit reinforcement (e.g., Tolman & Honzik, 1930), a finding that conflicted with the S–R theorists' concept of how learning occurred. Second, studies showed that animals were capable of using external stimuli in their environments to guide their navigation. For example, Tolman, Ritchie, and Kalish (1947) trained rats to run from a fixed start arm in a T-maze to where food was located at one of the two goal arms. At the end of training, rats received a probe in which the entire maze was rotated 180° so the rats now started from the diametrically opposite location from the start position during training. The rats could either follow the response made during training (e.g., turn left at the choice point) or go to the location in the room where the food was placed during training (e.g., the east side of the room). These "response" and "place" strategies would lead the rats to opposite locations in the T-maze. Tolman *et al.* (1947; see also Tolman, Ritchie, & Kalish, 1946b) showed that rats were capable of learning both strategies, and subsequent studies showed that the preference for one over the other depended on the nature and availability of environmental cues and the amount of training given (see Restle, 1957, for a review). More recently, neurobiological studies using the same T-maze paradigm have shown that the hippocampus supports place learning, while the dorsal striatum seems to be involved in response learning (e.g., Packard & McGaugh, 1996). In conjunction with human neuropsychological evidence supporting the distinction between procedural and declarative memory (Cohen & Squire, 1980), and animal studies on the role of the hippocampus in memory (Hirsch, 1974), such dissociations have popularized the view that place learning involves S–S associations.

However, at a behavioral level, it is possible that both place and response learning reflect the association of different stimuli with responses – place learning reflecting S–R associations with respect to stimuli in the environment and response learning to internal stimuli, such as the kinesthetic feedback. What evidence is there that spatial learning involves the representation of the outcome; that is, is it goal directed? That animals should learn to navigate in a goal-directed fashion seems evident from spontaneous alternation behavior, in which rats will learn quickly to run to the alternative arm in a Y-maze after depleting the food from the other (Dember & Fowler, 1958), and from more complex win-shift tasks such as successfully solving a radial arm maze (Olton & Samuelson, 1976). At least, an account of spatial learning based on the reinforcement of previously made responses (e.g., left and right turns in a maze) seems unable to account for such results. One proposed explanation for win-shift behavior is that it reflects simple short-term memory processes. Rather than goal-directed navigation, avoiding a recently visited location and selecting one more novel may be the result of habituation to the previously experienced stimulus (Sanderson & Bannerman, 2012) if an animal favors selection of novel stimuli in its environment (Cowan, 1976). More convincing evidence that place learning is goal-directed comes from studies that have made use of outcome devaluation procedures. For example, Yin and Knowlton (2002) trained rats to find distinctively flavored food in one arm of a radial arm maze, while another (nonadjacent) arm never contained food. Other arms in the maze were blocked. Following training, rats were fed the distinctive food in their home cages before being injected with either LiCl, which induces an aversive response, or saline, which is neutral. The taste aversion treatment was effective, with those animals injected with LiCl rejecting the food when given the opportunity to eat it again. Critically, when they were placed back into the radial maze with the food removed, they spent less time in the arm associated with food than those animals that had been injected with saline, which continued to spend more time in the food arm than the nonfood arm. Similar results in conditioning procedures have been interpreted as evidence that animals represent the outcome of events (in Pavlovian tasks; e.g., Holland & Straub, 1979) or their actions (in instrumental tasks; e.g., Adams & Dickinson, 1981) in a goal-directed fashion. In contrast, Sage and Knowlton (2000) also trained rats to run arms in a radial arm maze before devaluation of the food reward but used a specific visual cue to signal food (a light). The location of cued arms varied between trials, so rats had to follow the cue rather than the spatial location. Lesions of the dorsolateral striatum impaired acquisition of a similar win-stay foraging task (Packard, Hirsh & White, 1989), suggesting that Sage and Knowlton's task was dependent upon S–R associations. The taste-aversion treatment being effective, animals in Sage and Knowlton's study continued to visit the lit arms that were associated with food, and which the animals rejected when given the opportunity to eat it. The results indicated that such win-stay tasks involve response learning that is not goal-directed. Despite such results, the brain regions mediating goal-directed and habit-based learning are not always so clear. Although lesions to the fornix (Packard, Hirsh & White, 1989) and hippocampus (Olton, Walker, & Gage, 1978) impair performance in the win-shift variant of the radial arm maze, which has been argued to reflect goal-directed learning (White, 2008), other experiments by Sage and Knowlton (2000) failed to show that outcome devaluation had any effect on arm choice in such tasks.

Experiments conducted by Pearce and colleagues have provided evidence that spatial learning in the water maze also involves a representation of the goal rather than simply learning the route that leads to escape from the pool. Early studies presumed such a representation. For example, Morris (1981) argued that the ability of rats to swim to a submerged platform in a water maze reflects the formation of a representation of the location of the platform and the rat's position within the pool with reference to the landmarks outside it. After being trained to swim to the platform from one position at the side of the pool, one group in Morris's study was released from a novel location. The rats in this group appeared to be unaffected by the change in release points, apparently indicating that the animals had learned the location of the platform regardless of the path they had taken during training, which Morris argued should be the case if animals learned to navigate in the swimming pool by S–R associations. However, Horne, Gilroy, Cuell, and Pearce (2012) pointed out that nearly every rat in Morris's study started out swimming in a different direction to that expected if the animal had learned in a goal-directed manner. It was impossible for Morris to ensure rats had not experienced a particular route to the platform during training, meaning it was still possible for an S–R account to explain the observed behavior (see also Sutherland, Chew, Baker, & Linggard, 1987). In Morris's study it is possible that rats initially swam randomly until they recognized a familiar stimulus, which would evoke the response they had previously made when they had previously reached the platform. To overcome this criticism, Horne et al. prevented rats from forming such S–R associations by placing them directly onto the platform in a rectangular pool that was surrounded by curtains that obscured the extramaze cues (see also Jacobs, Zaborowski, & Whishaw, 1989a, 1989b; Keith & McVety, 1988; Sutherland & Linggard, 1982, for similar direct placement studies that required the use of extramaze cues). In addition, between trials, the rectangular pool was rotated inside the curtains to ensure that no other cues emanating from the room could be used by the rats. In a test trial, at the end of training, the rats were finally given the opportunity to swim in the rectangle, but in the absence of the platform. They spent more time in the corner associated with the platform and the diametrically opposite one (the correct corners) than in the corners that had never contained the platform during training, which Horne et al. argued must have been as a result of the formation of a representation of the platform location during training. In another experiment, they sought to determine how such a representation influenced behavior during the test trial. One possibility is that the rats swam at random around the pool until they found themselves in one of the correct corners, at which point they would recognize it as a corner in which they were placed onto the platform and spend time searching there. Alternatively, when introduced to the pool, the rats may have identified the correct corner after examining the available cues and headed to one of the correct corners to search. On the test trial, significantly more rats headed directly to one of the correct corners than to the incorrect corners, indicating that the latter explanation was more likely.

In addition to learning the locations of goals or reinforcers in relation to cues in the environment, recent studies have examined the extent to which associations form

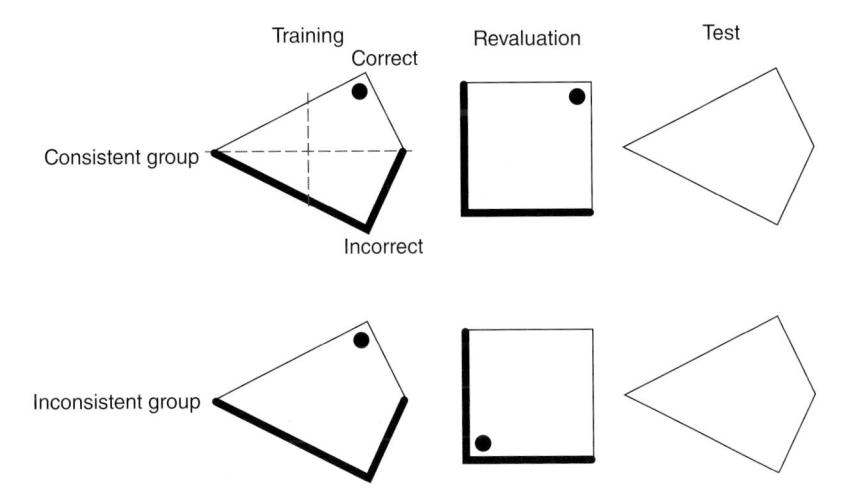

Figure 13.1 Plan view of the apparatus used in the study by Horne and Pearce (2009a). Both the consistent and inconsistent groups were trained to locate the platform in one corner of the kite-shaped pool, with the colors of the walls also indicative of the platform's location. In the revaluation stage in a square, the consistent group was trained to find the platform in the corner with the same colors as during training, while the inconsistent group learned a reversal, with the opposite colors now associated with the platform. During the test in the kite-shaped pool, group inconsistent spent less time searching in the previously correct corner than group consistent.

between stimuli that could indicate a goal's location. Pearce, Graham, Good, Jones, and McGregor (2006; see also Graham, Good, McGregor, & Pearce, 2006) proposed that associations formed between stimuli provided by environmental geometry and nongeometric features such as the colors of the walls creating the shape. Horne and Pearce (2009a) demonstrated the existence of such associations by training rats to swim to a platform in one of the right-angled corners of a kite-shaped pool with two adjacent long walls and two adjacent short walls, such that the two right-angled corners were mirror opposites of one another (see Figure 13.1). In addition to the shape of the pool, the rats were also able to learn the location of the platform with reference to the colors of the walls. The walls creating the right-angled corner containing the platform were white, while those creating the incorrect corner were black. Following training in this manner, the rats were split into two groups for a second stage of training, in which they were transferred to a square arena. The walls of the square were also black or white. For half of the animals, the platform was still located in the all-white corner of the square, while for the remainder, the platform was now located in the all-black corner. The effect of this training on the animals' performance was dramatic when they were placed back into the kite-shaped arena, which was now made up from four white walls. The platform was removed from the pool for this test trial, and the time spent in the correct and incorrect right-angled corners was recorded. Those animals with consistent training in stages 1 and 2 continued to discriminate the correct from incorrect corners in the kite. However, despite the same right-angled corner indicating the platform's location for both groups throughout training, the animals that underwent reversal training in stage 2 training in the black and white square lost their preference for the correct right-angled corner in the kite. Such a result is difficult to explain if we were to suppose that associations had formed only between a particular stimulus and the platform, or between a stimulus and an action (S–R association). Instead, the observed behavior must have been the result of an association forming between some cue or cues provided by the shape of the arena and cues provided by the colors of the walls. In the test trial in the kite, the sight of the shape cues would evoke a memory of the colored walls with which they were associated during training, and the rats' inclination to approach the corner would be driven by whether or not the colored walls were still associated with the platform.

Similar experiments have revealed that such associations form between colored walls and geometry in an appetitive rather than an aversive version of the task (Rhodes, Creighton, Killcross, Good, & Honey, 2009; see also Rescorla & Durlach, 1987, for a nonspatial example of this effect), and also between geometry and discrete landmarks, rather than colored walls, in the water maze (Austen, Kosaki, & McGregor, 2013). Austen *et al.* have argued that such associations account for unexpected cue effects in spatial learning, which are discussed in more detail in the section on conditions of learning later in the chapter.

Cognitive maps

Tolman's argument was that learning involved the acquisition of information or "knowledge" in the form of S–S associations that represent the interrelations among stimuli and events. In spatial learning, these S–S associations supported a map-like representation that Tolman termed a "cognitive map." However, despite more than 80 years of research into spatial learning, psychologists still disagree about what is meant by the term, and how animals represent space. What interrelations are learned? Are they integrated into a cognitive map? The notion of a cognitive map has perhaps shifted away from that conceived by Tolman. Many modern theories of spatial learning suppose that a cognitive map functions separately from other forms of learning and obeys different rules to those that account for conditioning (e.g., Gallistel, 1990; O'Keefe & Nadel, 1978). Such accounts have gained popularity, but are at odds with domain-general accounts of learning such as those provided by theories of associative learning. This popularity is due to a large extent to the discovery of cells in the hippocampus that respond selectively to the animal's location in space, regardless of its orientation and current view (O'Keefe & Dostrovsky, 1971). The firing properties of these "place" cells have led to influential theories about their function as the basis of a cognitive map (e.g., Burgess & O'Keefe, 1996; O'Keefe & Nadel, 1978). Place cell firing is invariant to the orientation of the animal, or the manner in which the animal finds itself in a location, which has been argued to be the result of a special representation that is independent of the animal's own body movements (O'Keefe & Dostrovsky, 1971). Place cells do respond to particular environmental cues, however. For example, place fields (locations in the environment that are associated with maximal firing of place cells) are particularly influenced by the distal geometric properties of the environment (Burgess & O'Keefe, 1996; Lever, Wills, Cacucci, Burgess, & O'Keefe, 2002; O'Keefe & Burgess, 1996), but seem not to detect changes to the locations of proximal landmarks (Cressant, Muller, & Poucet, 1997). The foregoing evidence suggests, then, that the firing properties of place cells reflect the representation of "place" in the place/response distinction drawn above. The discovery has led to further insights in cellular activity in relation to spatial representation. Other cells respond when the animal is facing a particular direction but are invariant to the animal's actual position (e.g., Taube, Muller, & Ranck, 1990). These "head direction" cells, together with the more recently discovered "grid" cells in the entorhinal cortex (e.g., Hafting, Fyhn, Molden, Moser, & Moser, 2005), have been proposed to provide a metric input of distance and direction information to the place cells in the hippocampus (McNaughton, Battaglia, Jensen, Moser, & Moser, 2006). More recently still, some cells in the entorhinal cortex and the subiculum seem to respond selectively to barriers or boundaries (Lever, Burton, Jeewajee, O'Keefe, & Burgess, 2009; Solstad, Boccara, Kropff, Moser, & Moser, 2008). Jeffery (2010) has argued that these specialized cell functions in hippocampus-based spatial learning should be considered the basis of a quasi-modular representation that concerns itself exclusively with the formation of a cognitive map. Certainly, lesions of the hippocampus seem to impair spatial learning based on place strategies, but not on response learning (see discussion above; Eichenbaum, Stewart, & Morris, 1990; Morris, Garrud, Rawlins, & O'Keefe, 1982). However, it must be pointed out that lesions to the hippocampus impair a number of other memory functions, including decision-making, temporal order, sequences of events, episodic memory, priming, and contextual learning (Fortin, Agster, & Eichenbaum, 2002; Good, Barnes, Staal, McGregor, & Honey, 2007; Honey & Good, 2000; Kesner, Gilbert, & Barua, 2002; Mariano *et al.*, 2009; Marshall, McGregor, Good, & Honey, 2004). In addition, the dorsal and ventral portions of the hippocampus have been dissociated in terms of memory and emotional processing (reviews in Bannerman *et al.*, 2014; Gray & McNaughton, 2000). Although the hippocampus undoubtedly has a spatial function and is associated with specialized cells tuned to particular aspects of spatial processing, an understanding of the psychological representation of space cannot be determined from their activity alone. Instead, we must turn to behavioral evidence of a map-like representation of space, and only in the light of this evidence can we hope to understand the function of place cells.

Definitions of cognitive maps vary (e.g., Gallistel, 1990; Leonard & McNaughton, 1990; O'Keefe & Nadel, 1978), and some have argued that the concept of a cognitive map is flawed specifically for this reason (e.g., Bennett, 1996). However, it is generally recognized that they should allow the animal to represent the interrelations of objects and surfaces in its environment and that this representation should be in some sense independent of the animal's own position, such that it can place itself into this map-like representation for navigation. If an animal possesses a cognitive map, it should be able to make a novel shortcut if it has the opportunity, and to navigate a detour if a familiar route becomes blocked. The evidence for such abilities is mixed. The evidence that animals are capable of navigating a direct path to a goal from a novel start position (Morris, 1981) has been discussed above and challenged (Horne *et al.*, 2012). However, Tolman was the first to examine detour behavior in experiments conducted in a "sunburst" maze (Tolman, Ritchie, & Kalish, 1946a). Rats were trained to run along an alley that began from an elevated circular table. The alley consisted of a series of left and right turns that led to a goal box containing food. Following training, the original path was blocked, and new paths radiating from the circular table were added, hence the name of the maze. If the animal had formed a cognitive map during training, then on the test trial it should have chosen the path that would lead directly to the goal box. Although most rats did run down the correct arm, a number of authors have pointed out the flaw in the experiment: The goal box was signaled by a light shining directly above it. If the animal associated the light with the food, then it could be used simply as a beacon that the animal then would approach. As Mackintosh (2002) pointed out, such behavior may be regarded as an example of simple Pavlovian conditioning. Similar experiments from Tolman's laboratory (Ritchie, 1948) and others (e.g., Chapuis, Durup, & Thinus-Blanc, 1987; Gould, 1986) suffered from the same flaw. If objects in the environment (beacons if they are at the goal location, or landmarks if they are further away) can be seen from both the start position and the goal, then any apparent shortcut or detour behavior may be explained without appealing to the concept of a cognitive map. Indeed, Muir and Taube's (2004) attempt to replicate Tolman *et al.*'s findings in the sunburst maze without the light above the goal box failed. Chapuis and Scardigli (1993) were able to control the cues visible to the hamsters in their experiments by training them in a hexagonal maze that had boxes at the ends of six radial alleys that met in the middle of the maze. In addition, six alleys connected the boxes around the circumference of the maze (Figure 13.2). The hamsters were trained to run along the circumference alleys from one box to reach food in another. The maze was rotated between trials, ruling out the use of visual cues outside the maze for efficient performance. In addition, although the start and goal box locations were maintained relative to each other, they were varied between trials, so the hamsters could not use cues within the maze to navigate. Following training, the radial alleys were opened to determine if the animals

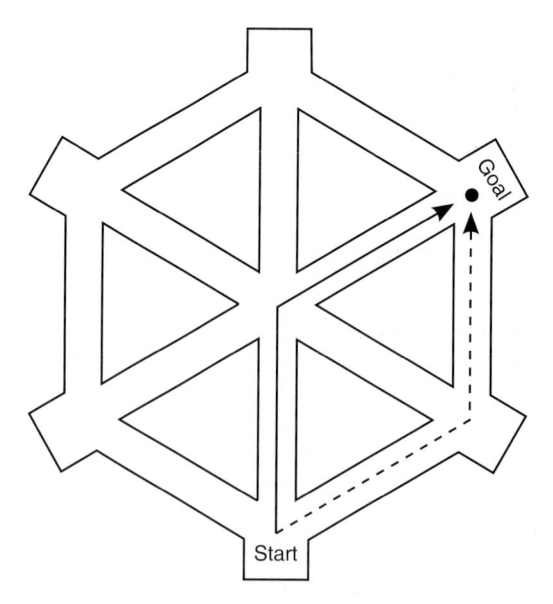

Figure 13.2 Hexagonal maze used by Chapuis and Scardigli (1993) showing the circumference alleys used during training (dashed line) and the radial alleys used during the shortcut tests. The position of the goal box varied for different groups of hamsters.

could make the correct detour to the location of the correct box. When the circumference path (dashed line in Figure 13.2) taken in training was short, involving only two of the six circumference alleys, then shortcut behavior through the radial paths, shown in the solid line, was quite efficient. However, as the task became more difficult with three or four circumference alleys in training, the shortcut choice through the radial arms fell to chance. The results can be explained readily by the hamsters' use of dead reckoning during training. During repeated trials, the animal may have learned from vestibular and proprioceptive feedback that the goal was a constant distance and direction from the start box. When the usual path was blocked, it was thus able to select the correct detour on the basis of these internal cues. As Collett (1996) pointed out, errors in the calculation of distance and direction traveled accumulate as the path length increases, thus explaining Chapuis and Scardigli's pattern of results. The evidence for shortcut and detour behavior is similarly explicable through nonmapping processes elsewhere in the literature.

A second property of a cognitive map is that it should be a representation of the interrelations of the stimuli in an animal's familiar environment. Gallistel (1990) has defined a cognitive map in terms of a representation of the geometric relations among surfaces in the environment, and Leonard and McNaughton (1990) discussed a cognitive map as a global representation of objects within a kind of coordinate system so that spatial relations among the objects can be determined. If an animal possesses such a global representation, it should be able to make use of the geometry of the environment to aid navigation. Cheng (1986) demonstrated just such an effect with rats trained to locate food in one corner of a rectangular box. After finding and eating some of the food, the animals were removed from the box before being replaced and given the opportunity to eat the remainder. Despite visual and/or odor cues that could be used to distinguish between the different corners, the rats appeared to ignore these and use only the geometric properties of the box to relocate the food. This led to them searching in the correct corner, and also in the diametrically opposite but geometrically equivalent corner. Similar results in other animals and in humans (reviewed in Cheng & Newcombe, 2005) have led to the popular view that many animals possess a geometric module that serves to represent the global geometric shape of the environment. Cheng and Spetch (1998) specifically defined animals' use of geometry as a configural representation of the broad shape of the environment, which did not involve the use of the elemental stimuli that made up the shape. However, Pearce, Good, Jones, and McGregor (2004) questioned such an interpretation. They argued that an animal in Cheng's (1986) study that was trained to locate food in a corner constructed of a long wall to the left of a short wall could have learned to move to the left end of the short wall, or the right end of the long wall, rather than learn about the overall shape of the arena. Alternatively, it may have searched for a corner with a long wall to the left and a short wall to the right: That is, it may have learned about the geometric structure of the correct corner but without reference to the global shape. Such alternatives would have led to the same behavior as that observed by Cheng.

To determine whether rats did make use of the entire shape of the arena, Pearce et al. (2004) trained them to swim to a submerged platform in a rectangular water maze, shown in Figure 13.3A. The platform was always placed in the same corner, and the rats were released from the center of each of the four walls once within a

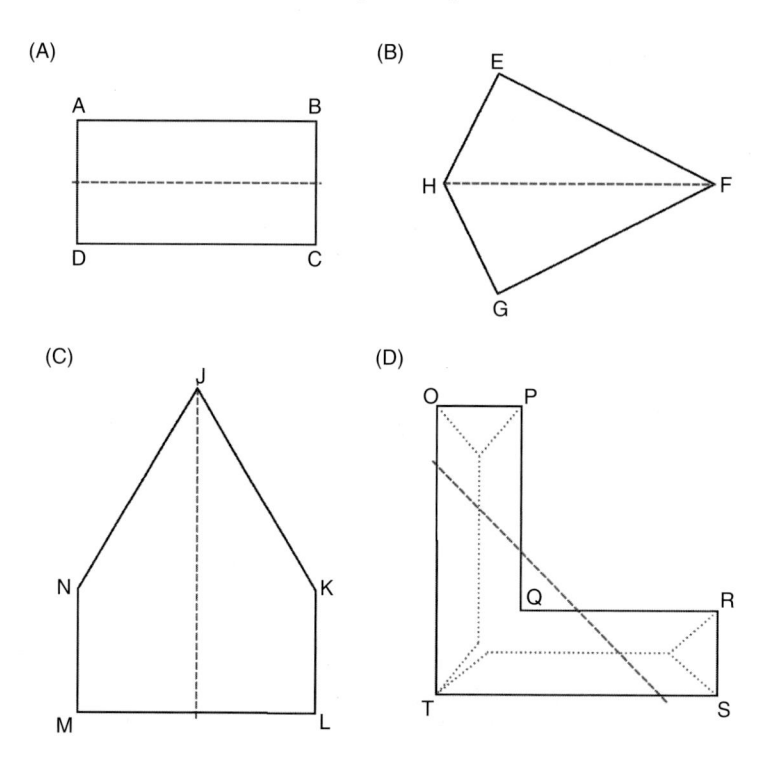

Figure 13.3 Plan views of the arenas used in various experiments to test the nature of the spatial representation of geometry. (A) Rectangle used by Pearce *et al.* (2004) and others. (B) Kite used by Pearce *et al.* (2004). (C) "House" used by McGregor *et al.* (2006). (D) "L" used by Kelly *et al.* (2011).

training session to prevent them from developing a habit of swimming in a fixed direction from the release point. In addition, the pool was surrounded by curtains, and the arena was rotated randomly between trials to prevent the animals from making use of the cues outside the curtains for learning the position of the platform. Performance during training was recorded by the rats' tendency to swim directly to the corner containing the platform (e.g., corner A) or the diametrically opposite one (corner C), which was geometrically identical. Each of these corners was termed "correct." In test trials at the end of training, by which time the rats were swimming directly to one of the correct corners on the majority of trials, the arrangement of walls was altered so that the arena was now kite shaped, with the two long walls adjacent to each other (Figure 13.3B). The corners where the long and short walls met were still right-angled (corners E and G), and the elements (long and short walls) of the arena from training were all present in the kite, but the overall shape had changed. A representation based on the overall rectangular shape of the arena during training would be of little use in the test in the kite. However, rats may be expected to discriminate between the corners if they had learned about the geometric structure (the spatial arrangement of long and short walls) of the correct corner during training. The rats did swim to the correct corner in the kite more often than to the incorrect right-angled corner, presenting a problem for the notion that they formed a global representation of the rectangle during training. However, they also swam to the apex corner (corner F), formed from the conjunction of the two long walls. Pearce *et al.* (2004) argued it was possible that this tendency reflected the animals learning to swim to a particular end of a long wall during training in the rectangle. In the kite, if they selected one of the walls (e.g., wall EF), this would lead to the correct corner, but selecting the other (wall FG) would lead to the apex. Cheng and Spetch's (1998) interpretation of Cheng's (1986) findings in terms of a global representation of space cannot explain this pattern of results.

As might be expected, Cheng and Gallistel (2005) offered an alternative interpretation for the results reported by Pearce *et al.* Rather than forming a map-like representation of the overall shape, rats may have abstracted from the shape information based on the axes of symmetry. Orienting with reference to the principal axis in the rectangle (the dashed line in Figure 13.3A) would allow the animals to swim to the correct corners and avoid the incorrect corners. Following the same rule in the kite (dashed line in Figure 13.3B) would lead them to the correct corner and to the apex. McGregor, Jones, Good, and Pearce (2006) assessed this possibility by training rats to swim to a platform in a water maze in the shape of an irregular pentagon, shown in Figure 13.3C. The platform was always located in one of two right-angled corners that were mirror images of one another (corners L and M). The principal axis in this shape is shown as the dashed line in Figure 13.3C. Following training, the rats were tested in a rectangle. If the rats learned to orient with reference to the principal axis in the pentagon, then transferring that strategy to the rectangle (as Cheng & Gallistel, 2005 had proposed) would lead them to the incorrect corners with respect to the geometric arrangement of walls. In fact, the animals headed to the incorrect corners on only about 20% of trials, and to the correct corners on the remainder. For example, if the correct corner in the pentagon was L, then in the rectangle we would expect the rats to search for the platform in corners A and C if they had learned with reference to the local geometric cues, but B and D if they transferred from using the principal axis during their initial training in the pentagon.

The theoretical analysis favored by McGregor *et al.* (2006) receives support from a study involving spontaneous object recognition by Poulter, Kosaki, Easton, and McGregor (2013), who removed the component of extensive training from the Pearce *et al.* (2004) design. Rats were exposed to two different objects (e.g., ceramic ornaments) in each of two different corners of a rectangular arena (e.g., corners A and B in the rectangle shown in Figure 13.3) and allowed to explore them for 2 min. They were then removed to a different testing room and placed into a kite in which copies of one of the two objects were located in each of the right-angled corners (E and G in Figure 13.3b). Rats have a tendency to explore objects they have not encountered before (e.g., Ennaceur & Delacour, 1988) or a familiar object in a novel location (e.g., Dix & Aggleton, 1999). On the one hand, if the animals had formed a representation of the overall shape of the rectangle in the first exploration phase, then the objects in the kite would both seem to be in novel locations, because of the lack of correspondence between the shapes. In that case, we would have expected the rats to explore both objects equally. On the other hand, if the rat detected an incongruence between the corner in which the object was located in the kite and the corner in which it was previously encountered in the rectangle, then it would be expected to explore the copy of the object in that corner more than the alternative. Over a series of days with different objects in different locations, the rats spent more time exploring the object in the corner of the kite that had incongruent local geometric properties to the corner in which it was located in the rectangle, consistent with the idea that learning based on shape did not involve a global representation.

Another compelling example of the use of local geometric information comes from the final experiment of the aforementioned paper by Horne et al. (2012). By placing the rats directly onto the platform in one corner of a rectangle, they prevented them from forming S–R associations. When they were given the opportunity to swim in a kite in the absence of the platform, they spent more time swimming in the corner with the same local geometric properties as the one in which the platform was located in the rectangle than in the incorrect right-angled corner. Intriguingly, the rats did not spend any more time searching in the apex than in the other incorrect corners, which is inconsistent with Pearce et al.'s (2004) findings. Such a result could indicate that at least some of the search behavior of rats in Pearce et al.'s (2004) study was the result of S–R associations. It also implies that Cheng and Gallistel's (2005) suggestion of orientation based on the principal axis was incorrect because the rats failed to explore the apex. It could be claimed that Horne et al.'s results are the result of a limited representation of space based on only the closest cues to the platform during training. If the rats were to learn only about the properties of the closest corner in the rectangle and swim to that location during the test trial in the kite, then we would expect them to search only at the correct right-angled corner and not at the apex. However, Gilroy and Pearce (2014) have recently shown that when rats are placed directly onto a platform in a featureless corner of a square arena, they are able to learn about the features of a distant corner to guide their subsequent search behavior. Such a result extends our understanding of what might be termed a local feature in that it need not be immediately adjacent to the goal location to be used.

It remains possible that animals form both global and local representations of the shape of the environment, and by altering the overall shape, the animal is able to rely only on local information to guide its behavior. Kelly, Chiandetti, and Vallortigara (2011) trained pigeons and chicks to find food in one corner of a rectangle similar to that shown in Figure 13.3A before transferring them to the L-shaped arena shown in Figure 13.3D for a test trial in the absence of the food. The principal axis of this shape is shown as a dashed line. Although it is not obvious which corner the animals should search during the test if they transferred their behavior based on the principal axis of the rectangle, it seems rather more clear what to expect if they matched the local geometric information provided by corners. We might expect an animal trained to find food in corner A of the rectangle to search in corners P and S of the L-shaped arena, because in each case a long wall is located to the right of a short wall. This is where both pigeons and chicks searched, but they also searched in corner T some of the time, with pigeons searching there more than chicks. The authors argued that the chicks relied primarily on the local geometry of the correct corner during training, but secondarily on the medial axes of the L-shape, shown in dotted lines in Figure 13.3D. Pigeons relied on medial axes. The use of medial axes may imply that the animals were able to abstract some spatial information from the original shape other than the simple arrangement of the walls in the correct corner, which Cheng and Gallistel (2005) argued would require less computational power than learning many different local geometries. An alternative to this view is that searching at corner T reflected some unconditioned preference, or generalization from what was previously learned about the local geometry in the rectangle. Interest in the exact nature of the geometric information learned in an environment with a distinctive shape remains high and has more recently extended to studies with humans, with results suggesting that both local and global solutions may be available to them (e.g., Ambosta, Reichert, & Kelly, 2013; Bodily, Eastman, & Sturz, 2011; Lew *et al.*, 2014), though none have yet adopted the spontaneous or placement training approaches taken by Poulter *et al.* (2013) and Horne *et al.* (2012).

Spatial relations

If animals do not represent the overall shape of their environments, what spatial relationships are learned? One simple relation is between a beacon and a goal, with searching behavior being based on Pavlovian conditioning, such that an animal learns to approach or avoid cues in the environment that are associated with the presence of absence of reinforcement. There is plenty of evidence that animals are capable of using such information. In the water maze, a visible platform (Morris, 1981) or a stick attached to the platform (Redhead, Roberts, Good, & Pearce, 1997) may be considered as examples of beacon use. An object not far from the goal could also be used as a beacon if the animal engages in a process of random search once in the approximate location, which Tinbergen's (1951) classic experiments on digger wasps showed could serve an animal well. Alternatively, if an object is not placed directly at the goal location, it may be considered a landmark in that a spatial relationship between the object, and the goal location must be derived for efficient navigation. To do so may require the animal to learn that the location it is searching for is a certain distance and direction from the landmark. Cartwright and Collett (1983) showed that honeybees learned such information by matching their current view of a landmark to a memory or "retinal snapshot" of the view of the landmark from the goal location. Reducing or enlarging the size of the landmark caused the honeybees to alter where they searched for a reward of sucrose. Gerbils tested in a similar manner did not show such a change in their behavior when the landmark size was altered (Collett, Cartwright, & Smith, 1986), which seemed to indicate that they had calculated a vector containing information about both the distance and direction of the landmark to the goal. The nature of such vector learning in terms of the associations involved is not well understood, but some elegant experiments characterizing how vectors are used (Cheng, 1989, 1995; Gould-Beierle & Kamil, 1996) have led to ideas about how they can be averaged to produce efficient spatial search (Biegler, McGregor, & Healy, 1999; Kamil & Cheng, 2001).

If a landmark appears to be different from different viewpoints, then it may itself be able to provide multiple distinct direction-specific cues from the landmark to the goal. However, in the examples in the previous paragraph, the landmark was symmetrical, so at best it gave unreliable directional information. Therefore, some other source of information is required to denote direction. Presumably, this information is provided by cues reasonably far from the landmark that change little as the animal moves around its environment. These could be distal extramaze cues, smells or sounds emanating from a particular source, or even magnetic cues (Muheim, Edgar, Sloan, & Phillips, 2006). Often, the source of such information is unknown to the experimenter, though it may be much clearer when more than one landmark is present.

Collett et al. (1986) tested gerbils in such a task in which the directional information could be more clearly established. They were trained to find a sunflower seed hidden among stone chippings in a fixed position with respect to an array of two identical landmarks. The food was hidden such that the landmarks and food together formed the vertices of a notional triangle. The array and the sunflower seed were moved between trials, so there was no fixed route to the goal from the start position, though their orientation within the room was always the same. Once the animals were running directly to the sunflower seed, a series of test trials were conducted. In one, when one of the landmarks was removed, the gerbils searched in two discrete locations that corresponded with the distance and direction of the food with respect to each of the landmarks during training. This result suggests that the animals had learned different vectors from each of the two landmarks, but were unable to determine which of the landmarks was present. It also suggests that during training, the presence of both landmarks disambiguated which landmark was which, meaning that one landmark provided directional information for the vector calculated from the other.

McGregor, Good, and Pearce (2004) showed that directional information for vector learning could be derived simultaneously from local cues, within the water maze in which their rats were trained, and distal cues, from outside the pool. They trained rats with symmetrical but distinctive landmarks in a manner similar to Collett et al. (1986), with the array of landmarks and the platform again forming the vertices of a notional triangle. The landmarks and platform were moved between trials, but they always maintained the same spatial relations to one another, and the landmarks were always in the same orientation with respect to the distal cues outside the pool. As such, the directional information for each vector could be derived from the position of the other landmark or from the distal cues. When either of the landmarks was removed, the rats found the platform significantly more quickly when it was placed in a position consistent with training compared with when it was placed on the opposite side of the landmark, suggesting that the distal cues provided the directional information for each vector. However, when the distal cues were obscured by a curtain, and the landmark array was rotated by 90°, the rats were equally able to locate the platform on the correct side of the array, meaning that they were able to use the other landmark for direction. Result suggests that animals may be able to use multiple sources of directional information and multiple landmarks for navigation. As such, experiments that have previously been argued to support the existence of a cognitive map (e.g., Morris, 1981; Rodriguez, Duran, Vargas, Torres, & Salas, 1994; Suzuki, Augerinos, & Black, 1980) may instead reflect animals' use of complex spatial relations between landmarks and extramaze cues to locate a goal. Certainly, the use of such relations can be impressive, as with the case of pigeons' use of a configuration of landmarks to control their search (Spetch, Cheng, & MacDonald, 1996) or Clark's nutcrackers' use of a geometric rule to determine where a nut is buried (Jones & Kamil, 2001; Kamil & Jones, 2000). However, the difficulty of determining whether complex spatial behavior is the result of the formation of a cognitive map or a combination of simpler processes such as vector learning, generalization, and perceptual matching has led a number of authors to question whether the notion of a cognitive map is useful for understanding what is learned in spatial learning (e.g., Benhamou, 1996; Bennett, 1996; Healy, Hodgson, & Braithwaite, 2003; Leonard & McNaughton, 1990; Mackintosh, 2002).

This section has highlighted that animals may learn quite complex spatial relations among cues in the environment and important target locations. Such spatial relations seem to go beyond the simple approach and avoid responses we might expect to observe if spatial learning were based on the same principles as Pavlovian conditioning. Therefore, the argument that spatial learning involves the same associations as those found in conditioning procedures is at best incomplete. Gallistel (1990, 1994) discussed the kinds of unique computations that must be required for such learning, which he argued allows the animal to construct a map in the absence of a direct role for associative processes. The idea that spatial learning involves two processes, one based on associative learning and another special form of learning, has become influential since O'Keefe and Nadel's (1978) book (e.g., Doeller & Burgess, 2008; Gallistel, 1990; Jacobs & Schenk, 2003). As such, studying the conditions under which spatial learning progresses may inform us further about the nature of an animal's spatial representation.

Conditions of Learning

O'Keefe and Nadel's (1978) account of spatial learning was based largely on neurobiological evidence for the representation of space in the hippocampus, described briefly above with more recent discoveries of cells outside of the hippocampus that seem to represent metric information about the environment and the animal's movement through it. From this evidence they identified two forms of learning, which they termed taxon and locale learning. Taxon learning can be described broadly in terms of response strategies and beacon homing. However, true spatial learning, they argued, involved more complex representations of the interrelations among stimuli that are independent of cues provided by the animal's own body movements that may be termed "egocentric." Instead, locale learning underlies allocentric spatial learning such that the animal learns the positions of cues in the environment with reference to one another rather than with reference to the animal itself. Such allocentric representations undoubtedly exist, but I have argued that they do not necessarily confirm the existence of a cognitive map. The previously discussed properties of hippocampal place cells add weight to the notion that hippocampal-dependent spatial learning is incidental. Addition or removal of landmarks from a familiar environment seems to have little effect on the firing of place cells (Barry & Muller, 2011; O'Keefe & Conway, 1978), though their rotation does result in a corresponding rotation of the place fields (O'Keefe & Speakman, 1987). The nature of the cues thought to control place cell activity has changed more recently from individual landmarks or landmark arrays to environmental boundaries (Burgess & O'Keefe, 1996; Doeller, King, & Burgess, 2008), which are also argued to be learned about incidentally (Doeller & Burgess, 2008).

Functionally, incidental spatial learning makes sense. Shettleworth (2010) argued that a representation of space that includes all available cues could be important because different cues could act as backups if navigation on one set of cues fails. The finding that food-storing birds rely primarily on the spatial arrangement of cues in the environment before using the visual features of those cues to guide their behavior may be seen as evidence of the utility of learning about all aspects of the environment (Brodbeck, 1994). Similarly, pigeons' use of various environmental cues for homing could be viewed as evidence for incorporating redundancy into a spatial map (Healy & Braithwaite, 2010). The question of interest is whether the conditions under which spatial learning occurs are different to those that apply to associative learning. If this proved to be the case, then spatial learning would be quite different from associative learning, in which many procedures have shown that redundant information is not well learned about.

Exploration and latent learning

Studies showing that spatial learning could occur in the absence of any obvious reinforcement while the animal explores its environment have been argued to support the notion that true spatial learning is incidental (e.g., Blodgett, 1929; Tolman & Honzik, 1930). Although it was written contemporaneously with many developments in the study of associative learning, O'Keefe and Nadel's two-process learning model did not reflect a modern view of associative learning that included the formation of S–S associations in the absence of a reinforcer (e.g., Rescorla & Cunningham, 1978; Rizley & Rescorla, 1972; Dickinson, 1980). Subsequent developments have supported the involvement of response–outcome (R–O) and conditional S–(R–O) associations in instrumental conditioning (e.g., Adams & Dickinson, 1981; Rescorla, 1991); results that demonstrate the complexity of associative learning and that reveal S–R theory to be an incomplete account of learning. In addition, it was argued at the time (Hull, 1952; Spence, 1951) and subsequently (Mackintosh, 1974) that S–R theory, albeit with some modifications, was still capable of explaining apparent latent learning. The uncertainty of the mechanism underlying latent learning means it does not necessarily provide evidence that spatial learning is special. Instead of focusing on latent learning, it may be more fruitful to examine the conditions known to be necessary for spatial learning.

Exploration, though often conflated with the notion of latent learning, does seem to be important for effective spatial learning. One way of demonstrating its importance is to consider experiments in which exposure to sections of the environment is restricted. Ellen, Soteres, and Wages (1984) trained rats to find food on one of three tables connected by a Y-shaped alley with a central platform, in a manner similar to Maier's (1932) three-table task. In the absence of any food in the arena, the rats were able to explore one table and arm, two connected tables along two arms, or the whole maze for a number of days before a test trial. In the test, food was presented on one of the tables, and the number of occasions on which the rats ran to the correct table was recorded. Those animals with limited exposures to the arms and tables took longer to learn the location of the food than those that were able to explore the whole maze. A flaw in the study was that the different groups did not receive equal experience of running along the alleys, with the group exposed to the whole maze gaining more experience. However, the results are consistent with the idea that experience is necessary for the formation of a representation of where food might be from any given start point. Another example is presented in a study by Sutherland *et al.* (1987). Morris (1981) claimed that rats reaching a submerged platform from a novel location provided evidence of a cognitive map. Their view of the pool from the novel release point was quite different from that experienced during training, so transfer of performance must have been due to the formation of a cognitive map of the environment during training. However, Sutherland *et al.* (1987) pointed out that the rats' view of the pool was unrestricted during the early stages of training, so they were likely to have viewed the cues outside the pool from many different locations. Sutherland *et al.* tested whether restricting a rat's experience of different parts of a swimming pool during training impaired its ability to locate the platform from a novel location. While some rats were able to swim through the maze without any restriction, others had their movement restricted by a transparent barrier across the center of the pool. These animals were only ever released within the part of the pool in which the platform was located and could not swim to the other half of the pool, though they could view all of the extramaze cues. When the barrier was removed, and these animals were released from the previously restricted part of the pool, they were considerably slower in locating the platform than those that had never had their movement restricted. Another group of animals also experienced the transparent barrier but were able to swim beneath it to each side of the pool during training trials. These animals were unimpaired when released from a novel position in the pool, suggesting that the performance of the restricted group was not simply a matter of failing to generalize between training and testing conditions. Similar results were demonstrated in humans using a computer-generated navigation task (Hamilton, Driscoll, & Sutherland, 2002), and other experiments that restrict the views of animals and humans as they explore the environment seem to show limited evidence of their ability to stitch together spatial representations into a single map, providing evidence against Morris's (1981) claim of cognitive map formation (e.g., Benhamou, 1996; Gibson and Kamil, 2001; Wang & Brockmole, 2003).

Opposing these results are some examples of integration of spatial information following an opportunity to explore the environment. Chamizo, Rodrigo, and Mackintosh (2006) trained rats to find a platform in a swimming pool that was always in a fixed location with respect to landmarks placed at the edge of the pool. In alternate trials, different landmarks were present, with the exception that one landmark was always present and was common to both arrays. At test, some landmarks selected from each of the arrays were present, but the common landmark was not. Rats found the platform readily at test compared with a group that was trained with the same array with which they were tested. Chamizo *et al.*'s results fit well with those of a similar experiment by Blaisdell and Cook (2005). In their experiment (see also Sawa, Leising, & Blaisdell, 2005), pigeons found food that had a fixed relationship to two different landmarks. During a second phase of training, only one of these landmarks was present, and its spatial relationship to the food was different from initial training. In a test trial, the landmark not presented during the second phase was reintroduced, in the absence of any other landmark. Blaisdell and Cook found that the pigeons behaved as though they had inferred the location of the food from their memory of the second landmark's position with respect to the first. Such a result was interpreted as evidence that animals integrated their memories through a process of sensory preconditioning. Similarly, Chamizo *et al.*'s (2006) results could be thought of as occurring as the result of some S–S association, in a manner similar to the earlier description of Horne and Pearce's (2009a) results. Quite why humans in a computer-based analog of

Blaisdell and Cook's pigeon experiment did not integrate spatial information is something of a mystery (Sturz, Bodily, & Katz, 2006), though mirror those of Hamilton et al. (2002).

Changes in associability and discriminability

How may an understanding of the conditions under which associative learning is known to occur help us explain the foregoing effects of exploration on spatial learning? Although it is commonly found that repeated exposure to a stimulus retards later learning involving that stimulus, the latent learning examples above appear not to support such a prediction. However, latent inhibition (Lubow, 1973; Lubow & Weiner, 2010) is not the only effect that we might predict on the basis of studies of associative learning. For example, preexposure to more than one stimulus is sometimes found to enhance subsequent discrimination between them (Hall, 1991; McLaren & Mackintosh, 2000). According to McLaren and Mackintosh (2000), preexposure can lead either to latent inhibition or to facilitation of learning through a perceptual learning effect, owing to the reduction in the associability of the elements that different stimuli in the environment share. In fact, there is evidence for both increases (perceptual learning) and decreases (latent inhibition) in spatial learning following preexposure. Chamizo and Mackintosh (1989; see also Trobalon, Chamizo, & Mackintosh, 1992) showed that preexposure to the arms of a Y-maze led to slower learning when one of the arms was subsequently baited with food, but only when the arms were readily discriminable, like a latent inhibition effect. However, when the arms were made more similar, learning was facilitated compared with animals in a control condition. The effects are consistent with the latent inhibition and perceptual learning effects predicted by McLaren and Mackintosh (2000). They would not be predicted by cognitive mapping theory, however, which supposes a map to form through incidental learning as a result of exploration regardless of the discriminability of the stimuli. It could be argued that discriminating textures and visual features in a Y-maze is very different from true spatial learning, but similar effects have been obtained when the arms were discriminable only by their spatial location (Trobalon, Sansa, Chamizo, & Mackintosh, 1991) and when extramaze landmarks indicated the location of a platform in a water maze (Prados, Chamizo, & Mackintosh, 1999).

Changes in attention

Some of the experiments outlined above involve what can be regarded as passive, or at least nonreinforced, exposure to spatial information. A second way in which exposure to cues in the environment could enhance spatial learning is by the modulation of attention to the cues. The process is rather different to the one described above that supposes the associability of the cues changes through preexposure. Instead, several authors have proposed the attention paid to a stimulus to change if it predicts a significant outcome (e.g., George & Pearce, 1999; Mackintosh, 1975; Sutherland & Mackintosh, 1971). Prados, Redhead, and Pearce (1999) were able to determine if attention was a factor in spatial learning by training rats to swim to a platform in a water maze that had a beacon attached to it. In addition, landmarks were suspended from the ceiling at the edge of the pool just inside a curtain that obscured the rest of the room. Three groups of rats were trained before a test phase with the beacon removed from the platform but with the landmarks present. For group Stable-Same, the arrangement of the landmarks remained the same throughout training and testing. Another group, Stable-Diff, was trained identically, but in the test phase a new arrangement of the landmarks was used. For this group, the formation of a cognitive map from the configuration of the landmarks during training would be of little use in the test phase, when the configuration was different. So, it was expected that at test, group Stable-Diff would be slower than group Stable-Same in finding the platform if rats had formed a cognitive map. However, for both groups, the landmarks provided reliable information about the position of the platform throughout training, so attention to the landmarks should be high at the beginning of the test phase, and performance should be similar, if attention is an important factor. The inclusion of a third group, group Mixed, enabled Prados *et al.* to distinguish between the attentional prediction and one based on an associability account that also predicts similar performance in groups Stable-Same and Stable-Diff because they each experienced similar preexposure to the landmarks (McLaren & Mackintosh, 2000; see also McLaren, Kaye, & Mackintosh, 1989). For group Mixed, the landmarks were moved with respect to each other between trials, but in the test phase the configuration was fixed, as it was for the other two groups. The total amount of preexposure for all three groups was equivalent, so according to the associability account, the escape latencies should be similar at test for all rats. According to the attentional account, however, the attention to the landmarks should be low for group Mixed because they did not provide reliable information about the position of the platform during training. The attentional account therefore predicts group Mixed be significantly slower than the other two groups. The results followed the predictions of the attentional account: groups Stable-Same and Stable-Diff found the platform quickly, with little difference between the groups; however, group Mixed was considerably slower. The results are not consistent with the associability or cognitive mapping accounts. Further evidence for the role of attention in spatial learning comes from demonstrations of intradimensional extradimensional (ID–ED) shift both in radial mazes (Trobalon, Miguelez, McLaren, & Mackintosh, 2003) and in the water maze (Cuell, Good, Dopson, Pearce, & Horne, 2012).

Cue competition

Certain behavioral phenomena, such as overshadowing and blocking, are regarded by many as a hallmark of associative learning. When more than one cue signals an outcome, then standard theories of associative learning (e.g., Rescorla & Wagner, 1972) predict them to compete for control over behavior, such that learning based on one necessarily restricts learning based on another. In learning to navigate a familiar environment, an animal may encounter many cues that could indicate a goal location. A question that has concerned many psychologists is what happens when such redundancy is experienced in spatial learning. A number of excellent reviews have documented the evidence for cue competition effects in spatial learning (e.g., Chamizo, 2003; Pearce, 2009; Shettleworth, 2010). For the purposes of this chapter, I shall discuss cue competition in relation to theories of spatial learning that suppose there are special circumstances that preclude the development of such effects.

As discussed at the beginning of this section on the conditions of learning, O'Keefe and Nadel (1978) set out a number of phenomena that characterized locale learning within their cognitive map hypothesis. One of these was that true spatial learning should progress independently as a result of the animal's exploration of its environment. As an animal encounters cues in its environment, they should be incorporated into its cognitive map. As such, we should expect the absence of cue competition in tasks that are said to engage an animal's cognitive map. However, in both the radial-arm and water mazes, several experiments have demonstrated the presence of both overshadowing and blocking of spatial learning (e.g., Diez-Chamizo, Sterio, & Mackintosh, 1985; March, Chamizo, & Mackintosh, 1992; Roberts & Pearce, 1998). In each of these examples, proximal cues restricted concurrent (in the case of overshadowing) or subsequent (in the case of blocking) place learning based on distal cues. For example, Roberts and Pearce trained rats to swim to a platform, the location of which was indicated by a beacon attached directly to it. Curtains were drawn around the water maze to prevent the animals from using distal extramaze cues, which Morris (1981) and others have argued rats use to form a cognitive map for locating the platform. In a second stage of training, the curtains were opened to reveal the extramaze cues. If O'Keefe and Nadel's (1978) account of spatial learning was correct, it would be expected that these cues would be incorporated into the animal's cognitive map. However, the test results, in which the platform and beacon were removed from the pool, revealed that the rats spent less time searching in the correct portion of the pool than the control group. This group received no training in stage 1 with the curtains drawn and instead were trained only to locate the platform with reference to a combination of the beacon and extramaze cues in stage 2 of the experiment. Similar results have been obtained in bees (Cheng, Collett, Pickhard, & Wehner, 1987) and pigeons (Spetch, 1995), and the same beacon overshadows learning based on extramaze cues (Redhead *et al.*, 1997).

The studies already mentioned provide strong evidence that learning based on one spatial strategy, such as navigating to a beacon, restricts learning based on another, such as navigating with reference to the spatial relations among cues. Other experiments show that cue competition also occurs when learning relies on only one strategy, such as learning a goal location with reference to the positions of landmarks. Rodrigo, Chamizo, McLaren, and Mackintosh (1997) showed that training rats to learn the location of a platform in a water maze with reference to a configuration of landmarks subsequently blocked learning based on new landmark configurations. Similar blocking and overshadowing results have been obtained with rats in a water maze (Sanchez-Moreno, Rodrigo, Chamizo, & Mackintosh, 1999) and in an open field arena (Biegler & Morris, 1999), and in humans navigating in a computer-generated environment (e.g., Hamilton & Sutherland, 1999).

Geometric module

Although the nonassociative nature of what might be termed cognitive mapping is questioned by the foregoing discussion, there have been circumstances under which it has been difficult to establish cue competition effects in spatial learning. The most notable of these is when an animal has to learn a location with reference to the shape of the environment. Cheng's (1986) demonstration of the control that environmental geometry can take of an animal's spatial behavior has been discussed previously in relation to the nature of the geometric representation. However, he also argued that his results demonstrated that learning based on the geometry of the environment was unaffected by the presence of nongeometric features, such as landmarks. This was apparent when the rats seemingly ignored features that could disambiguate otherwise geometrically identical corners, unless they were trained repeatedly to relocate food in one particular corner. Under these circumstances, he argued, rats could "paste on" the features to their representation of the shape, but this process would still leave the representation of shape unimpaired, such that removal of the features would reveal unrestricted learning based on geometry. A number of studies intended to examine such a prediction seemed to agree with the geometric module hypothesis in both rats (e.g., Hayward, Good, & Pearce, 2004; Hayward, McGregor, Good, & Pearce, 2003; McGregor, Horne, Esber, & Pearce, 2009; Pearce, Ward-Robinson, Good, Fussell, & Aydin, 2001; Wall, Botly, Black, & Shettleworth, 2004) and humans (e.g., Redhead & Hamilton, 2007, 2009). Visible nongeometric features, such as visible platforms or discrete landmarks placed near the platform, appeared to have no effect on learning based on concurrent or subsequent learning based on geometry.

However, more recently, it has been shown that integrating colors into the walls of a distinctively shaped could restrict geometry learning. Gray, Bloomfield, Ferrey, Spetch, and Sturdy (2005) were the first to show overshadowing of geometry learning using mountain chickadees as subjects. They trained the birds to find food, the position of which could be learned with reference both to the geometry of the arena and to the color of the walls making up the arena. When tested in a uniformly colored arena, they chose the correct corner less often than birds that had been trained to rely on geometry only. Subsequent experiments with rats showed similar overshadowing effects and also demonstrated blocking (Graham *et al.*, 2006; Pearce *et al.*, 2006). Furthermore, whereas earlier studies had failed to that discrete landmarks had any effect on geometry learning, recent experiments have demonstrated both overshadowing and blocking under these conditions as well (e.g., Horne & Pearce, 2009b; Kosaki, Austen, & McGregor, 2013; see Wilson & Alexander, 2008, for a similar demonstration in humans). Rodriguez, Chamizo, and Mackintosh (2011) proposed that the reason for the previous failures of landmarks to restrict geometry learning was differences in the relative salience of landmarks and geometry. Rodriguez, Torres, Mackintosh, and Chamizo (2010) had previously shown that the shape of the environment gained most control over male rats' spatial behavior, when trained with both geometric cues and a landmark to indicate a platform's location. In contrast, female rats showed the opposite pattern of results, with the landmark gaining more control over their behavior than geometry. Consistent with Mackintosh's (1975) theory, Rodriguez *et al.* (2011) showed that the landmark was capable of blocking and overshadowing learning based on geometry for females, but not for males. For males, the geometry both blocked and overshadowed learning based on the landmark. Rather different evidence for the importance of the relative salience of landmarks and geometry comes from a study by Kosaki *et al.* (2013). They aimed to manipulate the salience of geometric cues by training rats to find a platform in either the acute or obtuse corners of a rhombus-shaped arena. When the platform was moved between acute and obtuse corners during training, the rats learned more rapidly about the acute corner, though a control group showed no unconditioned preference for one corner over the other. In two subsequent experiments, discrete landmarks were unable to overshadow geometry learning if the platform was consistently in the acute corner, but overshadowed learning based on the obtuse corner. They also showed that overshadowing was more likely if the landmark was a relatively more valid cue than the geometry.

In apparent contrast to the cue competition effects described above, some experiments have instead shown the opposite effect, with an enhancement of geometry learning compared with the appropriate control condition, an effect known as potentiation. The designs of the experiments that have shown potentiation follow a familiar overshadowing design, with a landmark or other nongeometric feature being presented in compound with geometry to indicate a goal location. Subsequent tests with the nongeometric cue removed show stronger behavioral control by geometry than for animals trained with geometry only (e.g., Cole, Gibson, Pollack, & Yates, 2011; Horne & Pearce, 2011; Pearce et al., 2001, 2006). This enhancement of learning about one cue when trained in the presence of another seems to contradict theories of associative learning that incorporate a global error term to explain cue competition (e.g., Rescorla & Wagner, 1972), though it has been demonstrated in conditioning procedures (e.g., Durlach & Rescorla, 1980). Relatively few experiments have examined potentiation of geometry learning directly, though Horne and Pearce (2011) showed that the relative salience of the nongeometric and geometric cues was important. In their experiment, they found that panels attached to the corners of a rectangle overshadowed geometry learning if they were of relatively high salience, but potentiated learning if they were of relatively low salience. Horne and Pearce's (2011) analysis was that not only did associations form between the geometric cues and the platform and the panels and the platform, but also associations formed between the cues after they had been presented in compound. The relative expression of the different associations determined the overshadowing or potentiation effect observed. Their view was that the panel-geometry within-compound association caused a representation of the absent cue (the panel) to be evoked if the other cue from the compound (geometry) was presented alone, driving responding to the cue that was present. At the same time, if the panel–platform association was strong, then it strongly overshadowed learning based on geometry, counteracting the compensatory effect of the within-compound association. However, if the panel-platform association was weak, because the relative salience of the panel was low, then the compensation from the within-compound association outweighed the overshadowing of geometry learning, and potentiation was observed. This analysis support from a study by Austen et al. (2013) that showed that both high and low salience landmarks entered within-compound associations with geometry, but that only the low salience landmark potentiated geometry learning (see Figure 13.4).

The results from studies of geometry learning have failed to support the hypothesis that learning based on the geometry of the environment progresses independently of learning based on nongeometric information, at least when an animal has to repeatedly return to a location (see Gallistel & Matzel, 2013). Even failure to demonstrate cue competition can be explained by differences in the relative salience of cues (Kosaki *et al.*, 2013; Rodriguez *et al.*, 2011), relative validity of the cues

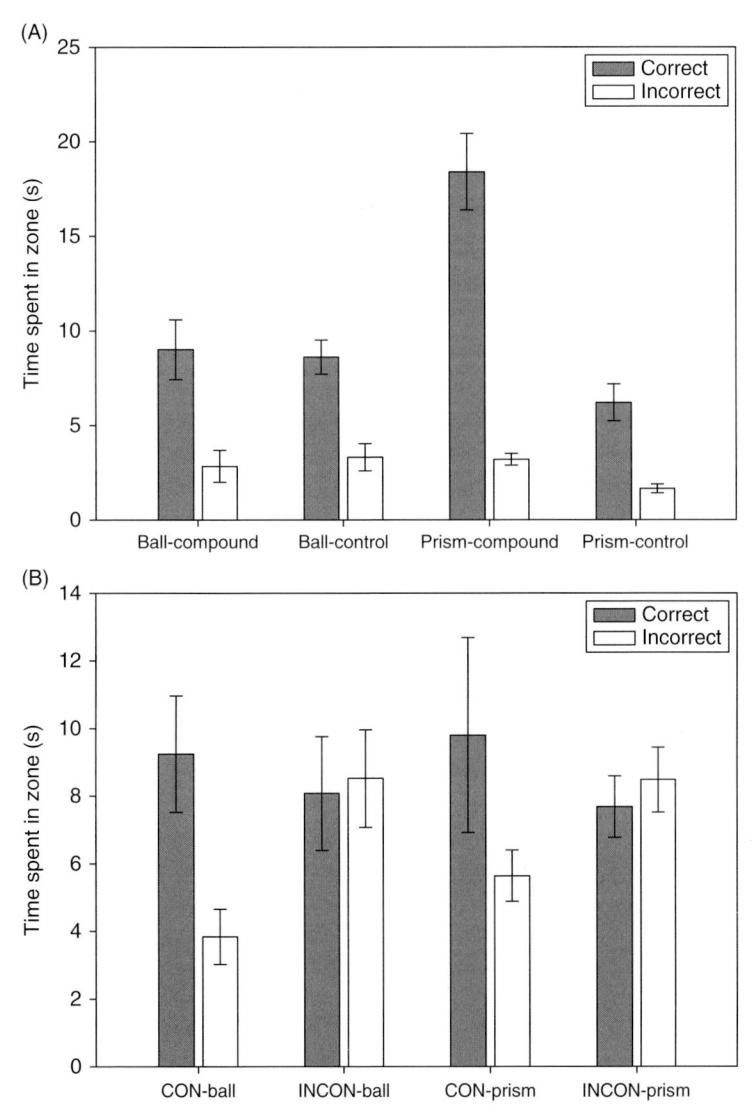

Figure 13.4 (A) Results from experiment 2 of Austen *et al.* (2013). Rats trained to locate a platform with reference to both a landmark and geometry in compound (Ball–Compound and Prism–Compound) were compared with rats trained with only geometry relevant (Ball–Control and Prism–Control) in a test trial with only geometric cues present. The lower salience prism cue significantly potentiated learning based on geometry, while the higher salience ball cue appeared to have no effect on learning. (B) Results from experiment 3 of Austen *et al.* (2013). For both Ball- and Prism-trained rats, the revaluation of the landmark–platform association (Incon-groups) reduced the discrimination of geometric cues in a geometry test trial, compared with Con-groups that underwent no revaluation.

(Kosaki *et al.*, 2013), or the compensatory effects of within-compound associations (Austen *et al.*, 2013; Horne & Pearce, 2011), effects all explained by principles of associative learning.

Performance

The least well-understood aspect of spatial learning is how learning is translated into performance. I have considered the nature of the associative structures involved in spatial learning, and some of these may provide more or less direct paths to performance. For example, to the extent that a given behavior is driven by S–R associations or a chain of S–R associations provides an obvious mechanism: Provided it is the case that the appropriate S becomes active, then the R will occur to the extent that the two are connected. Brown and Sharp (1995) proposed a neurophysiological model that translated such S–R learning into performance. It depended on hypothetical roles for place cells and head direction cells that had excitatory and inhibitory connections to motor units that would be associated through reinforcement with specific actions. While the model would allow an animal to navigate effectively from one place to another, it would have the unfortunate consequence of fixing an animal to a fixed path; and it would provide no explanation for latent learning. It would also mean that short-cut and detour behavior were not possible, since the animal would have no representation of the distances between locations or their direction other than in terms of the next movement required in the response chain.

Cognitive map models have also been tied to the cellular correlates of spatial behavior that O'Keefe and colleagues have observed. One example is from Burgess, Recce, and O'Keefe (1994), in which the activity of place cells in the hippocampus is coupled to hippocampal theta rhythm. As the animal explores its environment, the firing of place cells in the animal's path is linked to the activity of goal cells. The output of these goal cells enables the animal to estimate distance and direction to the goal from anywhere along the path. Other goal cell populations would be linked to obstacles in the environment that enable the animal to use these vectors to make detours around them. Such a map would allow the animal to navigate in a more flexible fashion than in Brown and Sharp's (1995) model, but Burgess *et al.*'s model suffers from the problem that it relies on hypothetical neural units that have not yet been detected. Even if they were, as Biegler (2003) points out, how learning based on the outputs of place cells and goal cells is actually translated to performance is not specified in the model. Other neural models of spatial learning suffer from similar problems.

At the other extreme, a simple mechanism for performance of spatial behavior is to act to minimize the discrepancy between the animal's current view and that held in memory, a "retinal snapshot" (Cartwright & Collett, 1983). Although this kind of model may be thought to be inadequate to describe vertebrate navigation (Collett *et al.*, 1986), it has been used with some success to explain a number of behavioral results with rats in geometrically distinct environments (Cheung, Stürzl, Zeil, & Cheng, 2008; Stürzl, Cheung, Cheng, & Zeil, 2008). In these models, the environment is divided into a large number of panoramic views. An animal that finds itself in one part of the arena can compare its current view with the adjacent views and then move toward the view that best matches the view from the goal location, which is held in memory. A performance rule means that if the animal finds itself in a location that is a better match for the goal location than all of the adjacent views but is still incorrect, it can still move away from the incorrect location and continue its search. Although the model seems able to explain the transfer of search behavior observed by Pearce *et al.* (2004), it is unable to explain all of the reports of blocking and overshadowing of geometry discussed above.

A similar though less view-dependent mechanism for translating learning to performance was proposed by Reid and Staddon (1998). Their model incorporated generalization gradients around expectation values that are assigned to each location in the animal's environment. At the beginning of exploration, only goal locations have expectation values above zero, though these values generalize to nearby locations. Similarly to Cheung *et al.* (2008), the animal's current expectation value is compared with the adjacent values, and the animal moves to the location with highest value. The current location expectation value is then set to zero to prevent the animal from becoming stuck in one place. Like Burgess *et al.* (1994), Reid and Staddon's model is linked to place cells and hypothetical goal cells. An advantage of this model is that the path chosen can be flexible, as it is not linked to a previously reinforced set of motor repsonses. However, like other cognitive map models, it seems not to take into account the associative effects that behavioral studies have revealed.

Like Cheung *et al.* (2008), Miller and Shettleworth (2007) also proposed a model of performance to explain geometry learning, but with the view that it could be applied to any spatial learning. Theirs is an associative model in which the strength of an association between a cue and an outcome, progressing according to the Rescorla and Wagner (1972) model, was directly related to the tendency to approach the cue. Again, a performance rule was applied in which the probability of approaching a location was proportionate to the total associative strengths of all of the cues in that location. The model supposed no special role for geometric information but was still able to account for blocking, overshadowing, potentiation, and absence of cue competition. However, the predictions of the circumstances under which these effects should occur have not been supported by experimental evidence (Austen *et al.*, 2013; Horne & Pearce 2011; McGregor *et al.*, 2009). Despite these apparent flaws, Miller and Shettleworth's model is the only one to incorporate associative strengths in trying to understand spatial performance. Given the strong evidence discussed earlier that spatial learning largely conforms to the principles of associative learning, the development of other associative models that can account for more aspects of observed behavior is an important pursuit.

Summary

In this chapter, I have reviewed the contents of spatial learning and the conditions under which spatial learning occurs. There is evidence for both S–R and S–S associations, with S–S associations enabling learning based on the relations among stimuli and a representation of the outcome of an animal's behavior. Whether the contents of these associations are identical to those underlying nonspatial learning is difficult to say, since it can be argued that some uniquely spatial representation is necessary for true spatial learning. However, I have argued that complex spatial behavior does not necessarily require a cognitive map that obeys unique nonassociative rules in its formation. In fact, an examination of the conditions under which spatial learning progresses reveals associative processes wherever they have been sought. The least well-understood aspect of spatial behavior is how the contents of spatial learning translate into performance. The reviewed models seem unable to capture all of the processes revealed by behavioral studies, and an important future endeavor is to provide accounts of performance that can match the knowledge that research into the nature of spatial learning has provided.

Acknowledgment

I would like to thank Joe Austen for help in creating the figures and for helpful discussions regarding this chapter.

References

Adams, C. D., & Dickinson, A. (1981). Instrumental responding following reinforcer devaluation. *Quarterly Journal of Experimental Psychology Section B: Comparative and Physiological Psychology, 33,* 109–121.

Ambosta A. H., Reichert J. F., & Kelly D. M. (2013). Reorienting in virtual 3D environments: Do adult humans use principal axes, medial axes or local geometry? *PLoS ONE, 8,* e78985.

Austen, J. M., Kosaki, Y., & McGregor, A. (2013). Within-compound associations explain potentiation and failure to overshadow learning based on geometry by discrete landmarks. *Journal of Experimental Psychology: Animal Behavior Processes, 39,* 259–272.

Bannerman, D. M., Sprengel, R., Sanderson, D. J., McHugh, S. B., Rawlins, J. N. P., Monyer, H., & Seeburg, P. H. (2014). Hippocampal synaptic plasticity, spatial memory and anxiety. *Nature Reviews Neuroscience, 15,* 181–192.

Barry, J., & Muller, R. (2011). Updating the hippocampal representation of space: place cell firing fields are controlled by a novel spatial stimulus. *Hippocampus, 21,* 481–494.

Benhamou, S. (1996). No evidence for cognitive mapping in rats. *Animal Behaviour, 52,* 201–212.

Bennett, A. T. D. (1996). Do animals have cognitive maps? *Journal of Experimental Biology, 199,* 219–224.

Biegler, R. (2003). Reading cognitive and other maps: how to avoid getting buried in thought. In K. J. Jeffery (Ed.), *The neurobiology of spatial behaviour* (pp. 259–273). Oxford, UK: Oxford University Press.

Biegler, R., McGregor, A., & Healy, S. D. (1999). How to animals "do" geometry? *Animal Behaviour, 57,* F4–F8.

Biegler, R., & Morris, R. G. M. (1999). Blocking in the spatial domain with arrays of discrete landmarks. *Journal of Experimental Psychology: Animal Behavior Processes, 25,* 334–351.

Blaisdell, A. P., & Cook, R. G. (2005). Integration of spatial maps in pigeons. *Animal Cognition, 8,* 7–16.

Blodgett, H. C. (1929). The effect of the introduction of reward upon the maze performance of rats. *University of California Publications in Psychology, 4,* 113–134.

Bodily, K. D., Eastman, C. K., & Sturz, B. R. (2011). Neither by global nor local cues alone: evidence for a unified orientation process. *Animal Cognition, 14,* 665–674.

Brodbeck, D. R. (1994). Memory for spatial and local cues – a comparison of a storing and a nonstoring species. *Animal Learning & Behavior, 22,* 119–133.

Brown, M. A., & Sharp, P. E. (1995). Simulation of spatial-learning in the Morris water maze by a neural-network model of the hippocampal-formation and nucleus-accumbens. *Hippocampus, 5,* 171–188.

Burgess, N., & O'Keefe, J. (1996). Neuronal computations underlying the firing of place cells and their role in navigation. *Hippocampus, 6,* 749–762.

Burgess, N., Recce, M., & J. O'Keefe (1994). A model of hippocampal function. *Neural Networks, 7,* 1065–1081.

Carr, H., & Watson, J. B. (1908). Orientation in the white rat. *Journal of Comparative Neurology and Psychology, 18,* 27–44.

Cartwright, B. A., & Collett, T. S. (1983). Landmark learning in bees – experiments and models. *Journal of Comparative Physiology, 151,* 521–543.

Chamizo, V. D. (2003). Acquisition of knowledge about spatial location: assessing the generality of the mechanism of learning. *Quarterly Journal of Experimental Psychology Section B: Comparative and Physiological Psychology, 56,* 102–13.

Chamizo, V. D., & Mackintosh, N. J. (1989). Latent learning and latent inhibition in maze discriminations. *Quarterly Journal of Experimental Psychology Section B: Comparative and Physiological Psychology, 41,* 21–31.

Chamizo, V. D., Rodrigo, T., & Mackintosh, N. J. (2006). Spatial integration with rats. *Learning & Behavior, 34,* 348–354.

Chapuis, N., Durup, M., & Thinus-Blanc, C. (1987). The role of exploratory experience in a shortcut task by golden-hamsters (*Mesocricetus auratus*). *Animal Learning & Behavior, 15,* 174–178.

Chapuis, N., & Scardigli, P. (1993). Shortcut ability in hamsters (*Mesocricetus auratus*) – the role of environmental and kinesthetic information. *Animal Learning & Behavior, 21,* 255–265.

Cheng, K. (1986). A purely geometric module in the rats spatial representation. *Cognition, 23,* 149–178.

Cheng, K. (1989). The vector sum model of pigeon landmark use. *Journal of Experimental Psychology: Animal Behavior Processes, 15,* 366–375.

Cheng, K. (1995). Landmark-based spatial memory in the pigeon. *Psychology of Learning and Motivation, 33,* 1–21.

Cheng, K., Collett, T. S., Pickhard, A., & Wehner, R. (1987). The use of visual landmarks by honeybees – bees weight landmarks according to their distance from the goal. *Journal of Comparative Physiology A: Sensory Neural and Behavioral Physiology, 161,* 469–475.

Cheng, K., & Gallistel, C. R. (2005). Shape parameters explain data from spatial transformations: Comment on Pearce *et al.* (2004) and Tommasi & Polli (2004). *Journal of Experimental Psychology: Animal Behavior Processes, 31,* 254–259.

Cheng, K., & Newcombe, N. S. (2005). Is there a geometric module for spatial orientation? Squaring theory and evidence. *Psychonomic Bulletin & Review, 12,* 1–23.

Cheng, K., & Spetch, M. L. (1998). Mechanisms of landmark use in mammals and birds. In S. D. Healy (Ed.), *Spatial representation in animals* (pp. 1–17). Oxford, UK: Oxford University Press.

Cheung, A., Stürzl, W., Zeil, J., & Cheng, K. (2008). The information content of panoramic images II: view-based navigation in nonrectangular experimental arenas. *Journal of Experimental Psychology: Animal Behavior Processes, 34,* 15–30.

Cohen, N. J., & Squire, L. R. (1980). Preserved learning and retention of pattern-analyzing skill in amnesia – dissociation of knowing how and knowing that. *Science, 210,* 207–210.

Cole, M. R., Gibson, L., Pollack, A., & Yates, L. (2011). Potentiation and overshadowing of shape by wall color in a kite-shaped maze using rats in a foraging task. *Learning and Motivation, 42,* 99–112.

Collett, T. S. (1996). Insect navigation *en route* to the goal: multiple strategies or the use of landmarks. *Journal of Experimental Biology, 199,* 227–235.

Collett, T. S., Cartwright, B. A., & Smith, B. A. (1986). Landmark learning and visuospatial memories in gerbils. *Journal of Comparative Physiology A: Sensory Neural and Behavioral Physiology, 158,* 835–851.

Cowan, P. E. (1976). The new object reaction of *Rattus rattus* L.: the relative importance of various cues. *Behavioral Biology, 16,* 31–44.

Cressant, A., Muller, R. U., & Poucet, B. (1997). Failure of centrally placed objects to control the firing fields of hippocampal place cells. *Journal of Neuroscience, 17,* 2531–2542.

Cuell, S. F., Good, M. A., Dopson, J. C., Pearce, J. M., & Horne, M. R. (2012). Changes in attention to relevant and irrelevant stimuli during spatial learning. *Journal of Experimental Psychology: Animal Behavior Processes, 38,* 244–254.

Dember, W. N., & Fowler, H. (1958). Spontaneous-alternation behavior. *Psychological Bulletin, 55,* 412–428.

Dennis, W. (1932). Multiple visual discrimination in the block elevated maze. *Journal of Comparative Psychology, 13,* 391–396.

Dickinson, A. (1980). *Contemporary animal learning theory.* Cambridge, UK: Cambridge University Press.

Diez-Chamizo, V., Sterio, D., & Mackintosh, N. J. (1985). Blocking and overshadowing between intra-maze and extra-maze cues – a test of the independence of locale and guidance learning. *Quarterly Journal of Experimental Psychology Section B: Comparative and Physiological Psychology, 37,* 235–253.

Dix, S. L., & Aggleton, J. P. (1999). Extending the spontaneous preference test of recognition: evidence of object-location and object-context recognition. *Behavioural Brain Research, 99,* 191–200.

Doeller, C. F., & Burgess, N. (2008). Distinct error-correcting and incidental learning of location relative to landmarks and boundaries. *Proceedings of the National Academy of Sciences of the United States of America, 105,* 5909–5914.

Doeller, C. F., King, J. A., & Burgess, N. (2008). Parallel striatal and hippocampal systems for landmarks and boundaries in spatial memory. *Proceedings of the National Academy of Sciences of the United States of America, 105,* 5915–5920.

Durlach, P. L., & Rescorla, R. A. (1980). Potentiation rather than overshadowing in flavor-aversion learning: an analysis in terms of within-compound associations. *Journal of Experimental Psychology: Animal Behavior Processes, 6,* 175–187.

Eichenbaum, H., Stewart, C., & Morris, R. G. M. (1990). Hippocampal representation in place learning. *Journal of Neuroscience, 10,* 3531–3542.

Ellen, P., Soteres, B. J., & Wages, C. (1984). Problem-solving in the rat – piecemeal acquisition of cognitive maps. *Animal Learning & Behavior, 12,* 232–237.

Ennaceur, A., & Delacour, J. (1988). A new one-trial test for neurobiological studies of memory in rats .1. Behavioral-data. *Behavioural Brain Research, 31,* 47–59.

Fortin, N. J., Agster, K. L., & Eichenbaum, H. B. (2002). Critical role of the hippocampus in memory for sequences of events. *Nature Neuroscience, 5,* 458–462.

Gallistel, C. R. (1990). Representations in animal cognition – an introduction. *Cognition, 37,* 1–22.

Gallistel, C. R. (1994). Space and time. In N. J. Mackintosh (Ed.), *Animal learning and cognition* (pp. 221–253). San Diego, CA: Academic Press.

Gallistel, C. R., & Matzel, L. D. (2013). The neuroscience of learning: beyond the Hebbian synapse. *Annual Review of Psychology, 64,* 169–200.

George, D. N., & Pearce, J. M. (1999). Acquired distinctiveness is controlled by stimulus relevance not correlation with reward. *Journal of Experimental Psychology: Animal Behavior Processes, 25*, 363–373.

Gibson, B. M., & Kamil, A. C. (2001). Tests for cognitive mapping in Clark's nutcrackers (*Nucifraga columbiana*). *Journal of Comparative Psychology, 115*, 403–417.

Gilroy, K. E., & Pearce, J. M. (2014). The role of local, distal, and global information in latent spatial learning. *Journal of Experimental Psychology: Animal Learning and Cognition, 40*, 212–24.

Gingerelli, J. A. (1929). Preliminary experiments on the causal factors in animal learning. II *Journal of Comparative Psychology, 9*, 245–274.

Good, M. A., Barnes, P., Staal, V., McGregor, A., & Honey, R. C. (2007). Context- but not familiarity-dependent forms of object recognition are impaired following excitotoxic hippocampal lesions in rats. *Behavioral Neuroscience, 121*, 218–23.

Gould, J. L. (1986). The locale map of honey-bees – do insects have cognitive maps? *Science, 232*, 861–863.

Gould-Beierle, K. L., & Kamil, A. C. (1996). The use of local and global cues by Clark's nutcrackers, *Nucifraga columbiana*. *Animal Behaviour, 52*, 519–528.

Graham, M., Good, M. A., McGregor, A., & Pearce, J. M. (2006). Spatial learning based on the shape of the environment is influenced by properties of the objects forming the shape. *Journal of Experimental Psychology: Animal Behavior Processes, 32*, 44–59.

Gray, E. R., Bloomfield, L. L., Ferrey, A., Spetch, M. L., & Sturdy, C. B. (2005). Spatial encoding in mountain chickadees: features overshadow geometry. *Biology Letters, 1*, 314–317.

Gray, J. A., & McNaughton, N. (2000). Neural anxiety systems: Relevant fault-lines to trace and treat disorders. *European Journal of Neuroscience, 12*, 311–311.

Hafting, T., Fyhn, M., Molden, S., Moser, M. B., & Moser, E. I. (2005). Microstructure of a spatial map in the entorhinal cortex. *Nature, 436*, 801–806.

Hall, G. (1991). *Perceptual and associative learning*. Oxford, UK: Clarendon Press.

Hamilton, D. A., Driscoll, I., & Sutherland, R. J. (2002). Human place learning in a virtual Morris water task: some important constraints on the flexibility of place navigation. *Behavioural Brain Research, 129*, 159–170.

Hamilton, D. A., & Sutherland, R. J. (1999). Blocking in human place learning: Evidence from virtual navigation. *Psychobiology, 27*, 453–461.

Hayward, A., Good, M. A., & Pearce, J. M. (2004). Failure of a landmark to restrict spatial learning based on the shape of the environment. *Quarterly Journal of Experimental Psychology Section B: Comparative and Physiological Psychology, 57*, 289–314.

Hayward, A., McGregor, A., Good, M. A., & Pearce, J. M. (2003). Absence of overshadowing and blocking between landmarks and the geometric cues provided by the shape of a test arena. *Quarterly Journal of Experimental Psychology Section B: Comparative and Physiological Psychology, 56*, 114–126.

Healy, S. D., & Braithwaite, V. A. (2010). The role of landmarks in small and large scale navigation. In F. Dollins & R. Mitchell (Eds.), *Spatial cognition and spatial perception: mapping the self and space* (pp. 52–179). Cambridge, UK: Cambridge University Press.

Healy, S. D., Hodgson, Z., & Braithwaite, V. A. (2003). Do animals use maps? In K. J. Jeffery (Ed.), *The neurobiology of spatial behaviour* (pp. 104–118). Oxford, UK: Oxford University Press.

Hirsch, R. (1974). The hippocampus and contextual retrieval of information from memory: A theory. *Behavioral Biology, 12*, 421–444.

Holland, P. C., & Straub, J. J. (1979). Differential effects of 2 ways of devaluing the unconditioned stimulus after Pavlovian appetitive conditioning. *Journal of Experimental Psychology: Animal Behavior Processes, 5*, 65–78.

Honey, R. C., & Good, M. (2000). Associative modulation of the orienting response: Distinct effects revealed by hippocampal lesions. *Journal of Experimental Psychology: Animal Behavior Processes, 26,* 3–14.

Horne, M. R., Gilroy, K. E., Cuell, S. F., & Pearce, J. M. (2012). Latent spatial learning in an environment with a distinctive shape. *Journal of Experimental Psychology: Animal Behavior Processes, 38,* 139–147.

Horne, M. R., & Pearce, J. M. (2009a). Between-cue associations influence searching for a hidden goal in an environment with a distinctive shape. *Journal of Experimental Psychology: Animal Behavior Processes, 35,* 99–107.

Horne, M. R., & Pearce, J. M. (2009b). A landmark blocks searching for a hidden platform in an environment with a distinctive shape after extended pretraining. *Learning & Behavior, 37,* 167–178.

Horne, M. R., & Pearce, J. M. (2011). Potentiation and overshadowing between landmarks and environmental geometric cues. *Learning & Behavior, 39,* 371–382.

Hull, C. L. (1943). *Principles of behavior.* New York, NY: Appleton-Century-Crofts.

Hull, C. L. (1952). *A behavior system.* New Haven, CT.: Yale University Press.

Jacobs, L. F., & Schenk, F. (2003). Unpacking the cognitive map: The parallel map theory of hippocampal function. *Psychological Review, 110,* 285–315.

Jacobs, W. J., Zaborowski, J. A., & Whishaw, I. Q. (1989a). Rats repeatedly placed on a hidden platform learn but quickly forget its location. *Journal of Experimental Psychology: Animal Behavior Processes, 15,* 36–42.

Jacobs, W. J., Zaborowski, J. A., & Whishaw, I. Q. (1989b). Failure to find latent spatial-learning in the morris water task – retraction. *Journal of Experimental Psychology: Animal Behavior Processes, 15,* 286–286.

Jeffery, K. J. (2010). Theoretical accounts of spatial learning: A neurobiological view (commentary on Pearce, 2009). *Quarterly Journal of Experimental Psychology, 63,* 1683–1699.

Jones, J. E., & Kamil, A. C. (2001). The use of relative and absolute bearings by Clark's nutcrackers, *Nucifraga columbiana*. *Animal Learning & Behavior, 29,* 120–132.

Kamil, A. C. & Cheng, K. (2001). Way-finding and landmarks: The multiple-bearings hypothesis. *Journal of Experimental Biology, 204,* 103–113.

Kamil, A. C., & Jones, J. E. (2000). Geometric rule learning by Clark's nutcrackers (Nucifraga columbiana). *Journal of Experimental Psychology: Animal Behavior Processes, 26,* 439–453.

Keith, J. R., & McVety, K. M. (1988). Latent place learning in a novel environment and the influences of prior training in rats. *Psychobiology, 16,* 146–151.

Kelly, D. M., Chiandetti, C., & Vallortigara, G. (2011). Re-orienting in space: do animals use global or local geometry strategies? *Biology Letters, 7,* 372–375.

Kesner, R. P., Gilbert, P. E., & Barua, L. A. (2002). The role of the hippocampus in memory for the temporal order of a sequence of odors. *Behavioral Neuroscience, 116,* 286–290.

Kosaki, Y., Austen, J. M., & McGregor, A. (2013). Overshadowing of geometry learning by discrete landmarks in the water maze: effects of relative salience and relative validity of competing cues. *Journal of Experimental Psychology: Animal Behavior Processes, 39,* 126–139.

Leonard, B., & McNaughton, B. (1990). Spatial representation in the rat: Conceptual, behavioral, and neurophysiological perspectives. In R. P. Kesner & D. S. Olton (Eds.), *Neurobiology of comparative cognition,* 363–422. Hillsdale, NJ: Erlbaum.

Leuthold, R. H. (1968). A tibial gland scent-trail and trail-laying behavior in the ant *Crematogaster ashmaedi*. *Psyche, 75,* 233–248.

Lever, C., Burton, S., Jeewajee, A., O'Keefe, J., & Burgess, N. (2009). Boundary vector cells in the subiculum of the hippocampal formation. *Journal of Neuroscience, 29,* 9771–9777.

Lever, C., Wills, T., Cacucci, F., Burgess, N., & O'Keefe, J. (2002). Long-term plasticity in hippocampal place-cell representation of environmental geometry. *Nature, 416,* 90–94.

Lew, A. R., Usherwood, B., Fragkioudaki, F., Koukoumi, V., Smith, S. P., Austen, J. M., & McGregor, A. (2014). Transfer of spatial search between environments in human adults and young children (*Homo sapiens*): Implications for representation of local geometry by spatial systems. *Developmental Psychobiology, 56,* 421–434.

Loomis, J. M., Klatzky, R. L., Golledge, R. G., Cicinelli, J. G., Pellegrino, J. W., & Fry, P. A. (1993). Nonvisual navigation by blind and sighted – assessment of path integration ability. *Journal of Experimental Psychology: General, 122,* 73–91.

Lubow, R. E. (1973). Latent inhibition. *Psychological Bulletin, 79,* 398–407.

Lubow, R. E., & Weiner, I. (2010). *Latent inhibition: cognition, neuroscience and applications to schizophrenia.* Cambridge, UK: Cambridge University Press.

Mackintosh, N. J. (1974). *The psychology of animal learning.* London, UK: Academic Press.

Mackintosh, N. J. (1975). Theory of attention – variations in associability of stimuli with reinforcement. *Psychological Review, 82,* 276–298.

Mackintosh, N. J. (2002). Do not ask whether they have a cogntiive map, but how they find their way about. *Psicologica, 23,* 165–185.

Maier, N. R. F. (1932). A study of orientation in the rat. *Journal of Comparative Psychology, 14,* 387–399.

March, J., Chamizo, V. D., & Mackintosh, N. J. (1992). Reciprocal overshadowing between intra-maze and extra-maze cues. *Quarterly Journal of Experimental Psychology Section B: Comparative and Physiological Psychology 45B:* 49–63.

Mariano, T. Y., Bannerman, D. M., McHugh, S. B., Preston, T. J., Rudebeck, P. H., Rudebeck, S. R., Rawlins, J. N. P., Walton, M. E., Rushworth, M. F. S., Baxter, M. G., & Campbell, T. G. (2009). Impulsive choice in hippocampal but not orbitofrontal cortex-lesioned rats on a nonspatial decision-making maze task. *European Journal of Neuroscience, 30,* 472–484.

Marshall, V. J., McGregor, A., Good, M., & Honey, R. C. (2004). Hippocampal lesions modulate both associative and nonassociative priming. *Behavavioral Neuroscience, 118,* 377–82.

McGregor, A., Good, M. A., & Pearce, J. M. (2004). Absence of an interaction between navigational strategies based on local and distal landmarks. *Journal of Experimental Psychology: Animal Behavior Processes, 30,* 34–44.

McGregor, A., Horne, M. R., Esber, G. R., & Pearce, J. M. (2009). Absence of overshadowing between a landmark and geometric cues in a distinctively shaped environment: a test of Miller and Shettleworth (2007). *Journal of Experimental Psychology: Animal Behavior Processes, 35,* 357–370.

McGregor, A., Jones, P. M., Good, M. A., & Pearce, J. M. (2006). Further evidence that rats rely on local rather than global spatial information to locate a hidden goal: Reply to Cheng and Gallistel (2005). *Journal of Experimental Psychology: Animal Behavior Processes, 32,* 314–321.

McLaren, I. P. L., Kaye, H., & Mackintosh, N. J. (1989). An associative theory of the representation of stimuli: Applications to perceptual learning and latent inhibition. In R. G. M. Morris (Ed.), *Parallel distributed processing: Implications for psychology and neurobiology* (pp. 102–130). Oxford, UK: Clarendon Press.

McLaren, I. P. L., & Mackintosh, N. J. (2000). An elemental model of associative learning: I. Latent inhibition and perceptual learning. *Animal Learning & Behavior, 28,* 211–246.

McNaughton, B. L., Battaglia, F. P., Jensen, O., Moser, E. I., & Moser, M. B. (2006). Path integration and the neural basis of the "cognitive map." *Nature Reviews Neuroscience, 7,* 663–678.

Miller, N. Y., & Shettleworth, S. J. (2007). Learning about environmental geometry: An associative model. *Journal of Experimental Psychology: Animal Behavior Processes, 33*, 191–212.

Morris, R. G. M. (1981). Spatial localization does not require the presence of local cues. *Learning and Motivation, 12*, 239–260.

Morris, R. G. M., Garrud, P., Rawlins, J. N. P., & O'Keefe, J. (1982). Place navigation impaired in rats with hippocampal-lesions. *Nature, 297*, 681–683.

Muheim, R., Edgar, N. M., Sloan, K. A., & Phillips, J. B. (2006). Magnetic compass orientation in C57BL/6J mice. *Learning & Behavior, 34*, 366–373.

Muir, G. M., & Taube, J. S. (2004). Head direction cell activity and behavior in a navigation task requiring a cognitive mapping strategy. *Behavioural Brain Research, 153*, 249–253.

O'Keefe, J., & Burgess, N. (1996). Geometric determinants of the place fields of hippocampal neurons. *Nature, 381*, 425–428.

O'Keefe, J., & Conway, D. H. (1978). Hippocampal place units in freely moving rat – why they fire where they fire. *Experimental Brain Research, 31*, 573–590.

O'Keefe, J., & Dostrovsky.J (1971). Hippocampus as a spatial map – preliminary evidence from unit activity in freely-moving rat. *Brain Research, 34*, 171–175.

O'Keefe, J., & Nadel, L. (1978). *The hippocampus as a cognitive map*. Oxford, UK: Clarendon Press.

O'Keefe, J., & Speakman, A. (1987). Single unit activity in the rat hippocampus during a spatial memory task. *Experimental Brain Research, 68*, 1–27.

Olton, D. S., & Samuelson, R. J. (1976). Remembrance of places passed – spatial memory in rats. *Journal of Experimental Psychology: Animal Behavior Processes, 2*, 97–116.

Olton, D. S., Walker, J. A., & Gage, F. H. (1978). Hippocampal connections and spatial discrimination. *Brain Research, 139*, 295–308.

Packard, M. G., Hirsh, R., & White, N. M. (1989). Differential-effects of fornix and caudate-nucleus lesions on 2 radial maze tasks – evidence for multiple memory-systems. *Journal of Neuroscience, 9*, 1465–1472.

Packard, M. G., & McGaugh, J. L. (1996). Inactivation of hippocampus or caudate nucleus with lidocaine differentially affects expression of place and response learning. *Neurobiology of Learning and Memory, 65*, 65–72.

Pearce, J. M. (2009). The 36th Sir Frederick Bartlett lecture: an associative analysis of spatial learning. *Quarterly Journal of Experimental Psychology, 62*, 1665–84.

Pearce, J. M., Good, M. A., Jones, P. M., & McGregor, A. (2004). Transfer of spatial behavior between different environments: Implications for theories of spatial learning and for the role of the hippocampus in spatial learning. *Journal of Experimental Psychology: Animal Behavior Processes, 30*, 135–147.

Pearce, J. M., Graham, M., Good, M. A., Jones, P. M., & McGregor, A. (2006). Potentiation, overshadowing, and blocking of spatial learning based on-the shape of the environment. *Journal of Experimental Psychology: Animal Behavior Processes, 32*, 201–214.

Pearce, J. M., J. Ward-Robinson, Good, M., Fussell, C., & Aydin, A. (2001). Influence of a beacon on spatial learning based on the shape of the test environment. *Journal of Experimental Psychology: Animal Behavior Processes, 27*, 329–344.

Poulter, S. L., Kosaki, Y., Easton, A., & McGregor, A. (2013). Spontaneous object recognition memory is maintained following transformation of global geometric properties. *Journal of Experimental Psychology: Animal Behavior Processes, 39*, 93–98.

Prados, J., Chamizo, V. D., & Mackintosh, N. J. (1999). Latent inhibition and perceptual learning in a swimming-pool navigation task. *Journal of Experimental Psychology: Animal Behavior Processes, 25*, 37–44.

Prados, J., Redhead, E. S., & Pearce, J. M. (1999). Active preexposure enhances attention to the landmarks surrounding a Morris swimming pool. *Journal of Experimental Psychology: Animal Behavior Processes, 25*, 451–460.

Redhead, E. S., & Hamilton, D. A. (2007). Interaction between locale and taxon strategies in human spatial learning. *Learning and Motivation, 38*, 262–283.

Redhead, E. S., & Hamilton, D. A. (2009). Evidence of blocking with geometric cues in a virtual watermaze. *Learning and Motivation, 40*, 15–34.

Redhead, E. S., Roberts, A., Good, M., & Pearce, J. M. (1997). Interaction between piloting and beacon homing by rats in a swimming pool. *Journal of Experimental Psychology: Animal Behavior Processes, 23*, 340–350.

Reid, A. K., & Staddon, J. E. R. (1998). A dynamic route finder for the cognitive map. *Psychological Review, 105*, 585–601.

Rescorla, R. A. (1991). Associative relations in instrumental learning – the 18th Bartlett Memorial Lecture. *Quarterly Journal of Experimental Psychology Section B: Comparative and Physiological Psychology, 43*, 1–23.

Rescorla, R. A., & Cunningham, C. L. (1978). Within-compound flavor associations. *Journal of Experimental Psychology: Animal Behavior Processes, 4*, 267–275.

Rescorla, R. A., & Durlach, P. J. (1987). The role of context in intertrial interval effects in autoshaping. *Quarterly Journal of Experimental Psychology Section B: Comparative and Physiological Psychology, 39*, 35–48.

Rescorla, R. A., & Wagner, A. (1972). A theory of Pavlovian conditioning: Variations in the effectiveness of reinforcement and non-reinforcement. In A. H. Black & W. F. Prokasy (Eds.), *Classical conditioning II: Current research and theory* (pp. 64–99). New York, NY: Appleton-Century-Crofts.

Restle, F. (1957). Discrimination of cues in mazes – a resolution of the place-vs-response question. *Psychological Review, 64*, 217–228.

Rhodes, S. E. V., Creighton, G., Killcross, A. S., Good, M., & Honey, R. C. (2009). Integration of geometric with luminance information in the rat: evidence from within-compound associations. *Journal of Experimental Psychology: Animal Behavior Processes, 35*, 92–98.

Ritchie, B. F. (1948). Studies in spatial learning. 6. Place orientation and direction orientation. *Journal of Experimental Psychology, 38*, 659–669.

Rizley, R. C., & Rescorla, R. A. (1972). Associations in second-order conditioning and sensory preconditioning. *Journal of Comparative and Physiological Psychology, 81*, 1–11.

Roberts, A. D. L., & Pearce, J. M. (1998). Control of spatial behavior by an unstable landmark. *Journal of Experimental Psychology: Animal Behavior Processes, 24*, 172–184.

Rodrigo, T., Chamizo, V. D., McLaren, I. P. L., & Mackintosh, N. J. (1997). Blocking in the spatial domain. *Journal of Experimental Psychology: Animal Behavior Processes, 23*, 110–118.

Rodriguez, C. A., Chamizo, V. D., & Mackintosh, N. J. (2011). Overshadowing and blocking between landmark learning and shape learning: the importance of sex differences. *Learning & Behavior, 39*, 324–335.

Rodriguez, C. A., Torres, A., Mackintosh, N. J., & Chamizo, V. D. (2010). Sex differences in the strategies used by rats to solve a navigation task. *Journal of Experimental Psychology: Animal Behavior Processes, 36*, 395–401.

Rodriguez, F., Duran, E., Vargas, J. P., Torres, B., & Salas, C. (1994). Performance of goldfish trained in allocentric and egocentric maze procedures suggests the presence of a cognitive mapping system in fishes. *Animal Learning & Behavior, 22*, 409–420.

Sage, J. R., & Knowlton, B. J. (2000). Effects of US devaluation on win-stay and win-shift radial maze performance in rats. *Behavioral Neuroscience, 114*, 295–306.

Sanchez-Moreno, J., Rodrigo, T., Chamizo, V. D., & Mackintosh, N. J. (1999). Overshadowing in the spatial domain. *Animal Learning & Behavior, 27*, 391–398.

Sanderson, D. J., & Bannerman, D. M. (2012). The role of habituation in hippocampus-dependent spatial working memory tasks: Evidence from GluA1 AMPA receptor subunit knockout mice. *Hippocampus, 22*, 981–994.

Sawa, K., Leising, K. J., & Blaisdell, A. P. (2005). Sensory preconditioning in spatial learning using a touch screen task in pigeons. *Journal of Experimental Psychology: Animal Behavior Processes, 31*, 368–375.

Shettleworth, S. J. (2010). *Cognition, evolution, and behavior* (2nd ed.). Oxford, UK: Oxford University Press.

Small, W. S. (1901). Experimental study of the mental processes in the rat II. *American Journal of Psychology, 12*, 206–239.

Solstad, T., Boccara, C. N., Kropff, E., Moser, M. B., & Moser, E. I. (2008). Representation of geometric borders in the entorhinal cortex. *Science, 322*, 1865–1868.

Spence, K. W. (1951). Theoretical interpretations of learning. In S. S. Stevens (Ed.), *Handbook of experimental psychology* (pp. 690–729). New York, NY: Wiley.

Spetch, M. L. (1995). Overshadowing in landmark learning – touch-screen studies with pigeons and humans. *Journal of Experimental Psychology: Animal Behavior Processes, 21*, 166–181.

Spetch, M. L., Cheng, K., & MacDonald, S. E. (1996). Learning the configuration of a landmark array. 1. Touch-screen studies with pigeons and humans. *Journal of Comparative Psychology, 110*, 55–68.

Stoltz, S. B., & Lott, D. F. (1964). Establishment in rats of a persistent response producing a net loss of reinforcement. *Journal of Comparative and Physiological Psychology, 57*, 147–149.

Sturz, B. R., Bodily, K. D., & Katz, J. S. (2006). Evidence against integration of spatial maps in humans. *Animal Cognition, 9*, 207–217.

Stürzl, W., Cheung, A., Cheng, K., & Zeil, J. (2008). The information content of panoramic images I: The rotational errors and the similarity of views in rectangular experimental arenas. *Journal of Experimental Psychology: Animal Behavior Processes, 34*, 1–14.

Sutherland, N. S., & Mackintosh, N. J. (1971). *Mechanisms of animal discrimination learning*. New York, NY: Academic Press.

Sutherland, R. J., Chew, G. L., Baker, J. C., & Linggard, R. C. (1987). Some limitations on the use of distal cues in place navigation by rats. *Psychobiology, 15*, 48–57.

Sutherland, R. J., & Linggard, R. (1982). Being there – a novel demonstration of latent spatial-learning in the rat. *Behavioral and Neural Biology, 36*, 103–107.

Suzuki, S., Augerinos, G., & Black, A. H. (1980). Stimulus-control of spatial-behavior on the 8-arm maze in rats. *Learning and Motivation, 11*, 1–18.

Taube, J. S., Muller, R. U., & Ranck, J. B. (1990). Head-direction cells recorded from the postsubiculum in freely moving rats. 1. Description and quantitative-analysis. *Journal of Neuroscience, 10*, 420–435.

Tinbergen, N. (1951). *The study of instinct*. Oxford, UK: Oxford University Press.

Tolman, E. C. (1932). *Purposive behavior in animals and men* New York, NY: Century.

Tolman, E. C. (1948). Cognitive maps in rats and men. *Psychological Review, 55*, 189–208.

Tolman, E. C. (1949). There is more than one kind of learning. *Psychological Review, 56*, 144–155.

Tolman, E. C., & Honzik, C. H. (1930). Introduction and removal of reward and maze performance in rats. *University of California Publications in Psychology, 4*, 257–275.

Tolman, E. C., Ritchie, B. F., & Kalish, D. (1946a). Studies in spatial learning. 1. Orientation and the short-cut. *Journal of Experimental Psychology, 36*, 13–24.

Tolman, E. C., Ritchie, B. F., & Kalish, D. (1946b). Studies in spatial learning. 2. Place learning versus response learning. *Journal of Experimental Psychology*, 221–229.

Tolman, E. C., Ritchie, B. F., & Kalish, D. (1947). Studies in spatial learning. 4. The transfer of place learning to other starting paths. *Journal of Experimental Psychology, 37*, 39–47.

Trobalon, J. B., Chamizo, V. D., & Mackintosh, N. J. (1992). Role of context in perceptual-learning in maze discriminations. *Quarterly Journal of Experimental Psychology Section B: Comparative and Physiological Psychology 44B*: 57–73.

Trobalon, J. B., Miguelez, D., McLaren, I. P. L., & Mackintosh, N. J. (2003). Intradimensional and extradimensional shifts in spatial learning. *Journal of Experimental Psychology: Animal Behavior Processes, 29*, 143–152.

Trobalon, J. B., Sansa, J., Chamizo, V. D., & Mackintosh, N. J. (1991). Perceptual-learning in maze discriminations. *Quarterly Journal of Experimental Psychology Section B: Comparative and Physiological Psychology, 43*, 389–402.

Wall, P. L., Botly, L. C. P., Black, C. K., & Shettleworth, S. J. (2004). The geometric module in the rat: Independence of shape and feature learning in a food finding task. *Learning & Behavior, 32*, 289–298.

Wang, R. X. F., & Brockmole, J. R. (2003). Human navigation in nested environments. *Journal of Experimental Psychology: Learning Memory and Cognition, 29*, 398–404.

Watson, J. B. (1907). Kinaesthetic and organic sensations: their role in the reactions of the white rat to the maze. *Psychological Monographs, 8*, 1–100.

Wehner, R., & Srinivasan, M. V. (1981). Searching behavior of desert ants, genus Cataglyphis (Formicidae, Hymenoptera). *Journal of Comparative Physiology, 142*, 315–338.

White, N. M. (2008). Multiple memory systems in the brain: cooperation and competition. In H. B. Eichenbaum (Ed.), *Memory systems* (pp. 9–46). Oxford, UK: Elsevier.

Wilson, P. N., & Alexander, T. (2008). Blocking of spatial learning between enclosure geometry and a local landmark. *Journal of Experimental Psychology: Learning Memory and Cognition, 34*, 1369–1376.

Yin, H. H., & Knowlton, B. J. (2002). Reinforcer devaluation abolishes conditioned cue preference: Evidence for stimulus–stimulus associations. *Behavioral Neuroscience, 116*, 174–177.

14
Timing and Conditioning
Theoretical Issues
Charlotte Bonardi, Timothy H. C. Cheung, Esther Mondragón, and Shu K. E. Tam

Introduction

In a typical conditioning task, a CS is reliably followed by an outcome of motivational value (US). As a result, a conditioned response (CR) develops during the CS, indicating anticipation of the US. This chapter will consider the temporal characteristics of this process, and examine the extent to which they may be explained by *trial-based associative theories*,[1] comparing them with the alternative, *information-theoretic time-accumulation accounts* of conditioning and timed behavior. Then, we will review what is known about the neural substrates underlying these different temporal characteristics of conditioning, and theoretical issues that arise. We will focus on conditioning in the seconds-to-minutes range and thus not consider procedures such as eyeblink conditioning, in which timed responses occur over much shorter intervals (e.g., White, Kehoe, Choi, & Moore, 2000), or flavor aversion learning (e.g., Garcia & Koelling, 1966), in which CS and US can become associated even when separated by several hours. We will also neglect the well-known role of the cerebellum in the temporal aspects of subsecond conditioning (e.g., McCormick & Thompson, 1984). We conclude that recent developments of trial-based associative theories are able to provide a plausible account of conditioning and timing, but that further developments are still required before they can provide a comprehensive account of the effects of neural manipulations on timed behavior.

Temporal Factors and Associative Learning

Temporal contiguity

According to *trial-based associative theories*, conditioning results from the formation of an association between the mental representations of CS and US, so presenting the CS can activate the US representation and thus elicit the CR. But although such

---

The Wiley Handbook on the Cognitive Neuroscience of Learning, First Edition.
Edited by Robin A. Murphy and Robert C. Honey.
© 2016 John Wiley & Sons, Ltd. Published 2016 by John Wiley & Sons, Ltd.

theories implicitly assume that CS and US must occur close together in time on a conditioning trial for an association to form, many incorporate no mechanism for detecting temporal contiguity (e.g., Mackintosh, 1975; Pearce & Hall, 1980; Rescorla & Wagner, 1972; see Gallistel, Craig, & Shahan, 2014, for a recent discussion). This limits their ability to specify whether or not learning occurs, and to account for phenomena with explicit temporal features such as *trace* conditioning, in which a trace interval separates CS offset and food delivery. Such CSs elicit less conditioned responding than when CS offset coincides with US delivery, and the CR becomes progressively weaker as the trace interval increases in duration.

Nonetheless, there are trial-based theories that can explain such observations. For example, Hebb (1949) postulated that learning occurs when neural activity produced by the CS and US overlaps in time. This ensures that contiguity is sufficient for learning, and also – provided the neural activity associated with the CS decays gradually after its offset – that learning decreases as CS-US contiguity is reduced. Wagner (1981) proposed a more detailed version of such a theory, suggesting that a stimulus may be conceptualized as a set of constituent elements that can exist in different memory states. When a stimulus is first presented, some of its constituent elements go from an inactive state (I) to a primary state of activation (A1), whence they decay rapidly to a secondary state of activation (A2), and then slowly to their initial inactive state. For two events to be associated, their elements must both be in A1 at the same time, and the greater the overlap in their A1 activity, the more learning will occur. Once associated, the CS develops the ability to send the US elements directly into A2, producing anticipation of the US during CS presentation and elicitation of the CR. In addition, when the CS is in A1 but the US is in A2, an inhibitory association forms; the resultant inhibitor opposes the tendency of an excitatory CS to put the US elements directly into A2.

Hebb's theory, unlike Wagner's, refers to underlying neural processes; but both assume that the closer two events are in time, the more strongly they will become associated – so the consequences of contiguity emerge directly from the models' structure. But Wagner's adaptation, unlike Hebb's, instantiates a second important principle of associative learning – that temporal contiguity of CS and US, although necessary, is not sufficient for an association to form: The US must also be *surprising* – not associatively predicted by any other cue (Rescorla & Wagner, 1972). For example, in blocking a CS, A, is paired with a US in the presence of a second stimulus, B, that has been pretrained as a signal for the same US (i.e., $B \rightarrow US$; $AB \rightarrow US$). The pairings of A and the US do not result in an association because the US is not surprising. The mechanism for this requirement is incorporated in Wagner's (1981) model. On the first trial on which CS and US are paired, the elements of both are in A1, allowing an association to form; but this association will allow the CS to put some of the US elements into A2 on the trial that follows. The distinction between a surprising and predicted US is thus captured by the elements of a *surprising* US being primarily in A1, but that the more that US comes to be *predicted*, the more of its elements will be in A2. As a consequence predicted USs support less learning because more of their elements are in A2, meaning fewer will be available for recruitment into A1 and thus able to support learning (see Mackintosh, 1975; Pearce & Hall, 1980, for alternative ways of accommodating this general principle). The blocked CS, A, is thus paired with a US whose elements have already been put into A2 by the pretrained B – and this is why learning about A is curtailed.

In summary, although some of the earlier versions of trial-based associative theories did not provide a mechanism for contiguity detection or explain why trace conditioning is less effective than delay conditioning, a theory like Wagner's (1981) can accommodate effects of this type quite easily and is also able to explain cue competition effects.

Effect of intertrial interval and CS duration on conditioning: the I/T ratio

There are other ways in which conditioning is sensitive to temporal factors, but that trial-based associative theories seem unable to accommodate. For example, the speed with which the CR develops (Gibbon, Baldock, Locurto, Gold, & Terrace, 1977) and its final asymptotic rate (Lattal, 1999; Perkins *et al.*, 1975; Terrace, Gibbon, Farrell, & Baldock, 1975) are directly related to the ratio of the intertrial interval (I) to the duration of the CS (T) – the I/T *ratio*. Higher I/T ratios, achieved by increasing the intertrial interval and/or decreasing CS duration, foster faster conditioning. This relationship is reportedly both orderly and quantitatively reliable: As long as the I/T ratio is held constant, measures of learning are roughly invariant over a range of CS and ITI durations (Gallistel & Gibbon, 2000).

Trial-based associative theories can provide a *qualitative* explanation of this effect. They anticipate that increasing ITI duration will enhance conditioning (cf. Sunsay & Bouton, 2008), because of the requirement that for associative learning to occur the US must be surprising. During conditioning, the context will also acquire associative strength, and thus, when CS and US are paired, the extent to which the context predicts the US will attenuate learning about the CS (*overshadowing*). Longer ITIs entail greater exposure to the context in the absence of the US, weakening the context → US association and promoting learning about the CS. However, this common sense view hides an implicit assumption – that a longer ITI is somehow equivalent to more nonreinforced presentations of the context than a shorter one. Trial-based associative models typically conceptualize stimuli as being punctate, and cannot accommodate this notion without making extra assumptions. Nonetheless, if such assumptions are made, then the effect can be accounted for – and evidence has been generated in favor of this interpretation (e.g., Sunsay & Bouton, 2008). Moreover, applying the same logic to the CS implies that a long CS is effectively a series of nonreinforced *extinction* trials followed by a final, reinforced trial. Thus, shorter CSs produce better conditioning than longer ones simply because shorter CSs comprise fewer of these extinction trials than longer ones.

Sunsay, Stetson, and Bouton (2004) noted that an additional reason for the detrimental effect of short ITIs on conditioning may emerge from Wagner's theory. Because of the slow rate of decay from A2 to the inactive state, and the lack of a direct route from A2 to A1, this theory predicts that when a CS is presented twice in quick succession, as when the ITI is short, on the second presentation some of its elements will still be in the A2 state. This means they will be unavailable for recruitment into A1, which limits the degree to which the CS can associate with the US. The same logic applies to US presentations: If A2 activity in the US representation persisting from the previous trial overlaps with A1 activity of the CS, this results in inhibitory conditioning, which will reduce the degree to which the CS can elicit the CR. Sunsay *et al.* (2004) provided evidence for this mechanism.

Trial-based associative theories can, therefore, explain *qualitative* aspects of the effect of I/T ratio on conditioning. However, the claim is that there is a precise *quantitative* relation between I/T ratio and speed of conditioning (e.g., Gallistel & Gibbon, 2000) – and it has been argued that no extant trial-based associative accounts could generate such predictions (Gallistel & Gibbon, 2000). However, some have questioned whether the control of I/T ratio over conditioning is as invariant as was previously thought. For example, Holland (2000) demonstrated that differences in conditioned responding were obtained in animals trained with identical I/T ratios (see also Bouton & Sunsay, 2003). The failure of trial-based associative theories to explain I/T ratio effects may, therefore, be of less theoretical significance than was originally thought.

The relevance of these studies also depends on the measures of conditioning employed. Theories to which I/T ratio are fundamental, such as Rate Expectancy Theory (RET; Gallistel & Gibbon, 2000 discussed below) make predictions only about the rate of CR *acquisition* (e.g., trials to criterion) – *not* the final asymptotic rate (Gallistel & Gibbon, 2000). In contrast, trial-based associative theories typically make predictions about the rate of CR, rather than the speed with which it is acquired.[2] In fact, very few studies have attempted to evaluate the predictions of trial-based associative theories using measures that would be regarded as relevant to theories like RET (although see, for example, Harris, 2011; Jennings, Alonso, Mondragón, Franssen, & Bonardi, 2013; Killeen, Sanabria, & Dolgov, 2009).

CR timing

Temporal factors also control the distribution of the CR across the course of the CS with astonishing precision. Pavlov (1927) himself first described *inhibition of delay*, in which maximum CR occurs at the end of temporally extended CSs. It is now well established that, after training with a fixed duration CS, conditioned responding gradually increases to a maximum at the point of US delivery. On test trials in which the CS is extended and reinforcement omitted (the *peak* procedure), a clear peak of responding is seen roughly at the time at which food was delivered during training. As this point is not explicitly signaled by any environmental cues, this suggests the use of some internal timing mechanism (Holland, 2000; Kirkpatrick & Church, 2000; Ohyama, Horvitz, Kitsos, & Balsam, 2001). Moreover, the spread of responding round the peak, indicating precision of timing, increases roughly linearly with the timed duration, so that the *relative* variability of timed responding is roughly invariant (Gibbon, 1991; Holland, 2000; Kirkpatrick & Church, 2000) – the *scalar invariance property*. Trial-based associative theories, as we have seen, do not typically assume differentiation within a CS and, even with the assumptions suggested earlier, cannot easily account for this orderly pattern of behavior.

Information-Theoretic Approach

An alternative to associative analysis is provided by the class of theories which adopts *an information-processing decision-based* perspective; these theories reject associations, and instead assume that emergence of the CR stems from a decision made on the basis of information extracted from the conditioning episode – giving the trial no special status. One example of such an account is RET (Gallistel & Gibbon, 2000; see also Balsam, 1984; Balsam, Drew, & Gallistel, 2010; Balsam & Gallistel, 2009). RET assumes that information about the temporal properties of the environment during learning is *accumulat*ed over a series of conditioning trials – hence models of this type are termed *time-accumulation* models. The rate of US delivery during the CS, and in the CS's absence, is then computed, and a comparison between these values indicates the degree to which the CS increases the probability of US occurrence. Once this comparison reaches a certain threshold, a decision is made to respond. This framework explains the orderly relationship between conditioning and the I/T ratio, as the durations of CS and ITI are inversely related to reinforcement rates in their presence.

These principles are then integrated with those of Scalar Expectancy Theory (SET; Gibbon, 1977), a model previously developed to model timing of the CR. SET comprises a pacemaker, from which pulses may be transferred via a switch to an accumulator. At CS onset, the switch diverts pulses into the accumulator until US delivery, and then the number of pulses in the accumulator is transferred into long-term memory (LTM), multiplied by a scaling parameter, K, that approximates to 1. When the CS is next presented, the number of pulses accumulating in the accumulator is compared with one of the values in LTM; when the difference between them is sufficiently small relative to the duration of the target interval, responding occurs. Although, on any trial, there is an abrupt transition from low to high responding, there is trial-to-trial instability in the point at which this transition occurs, because of variability in the pacemaker and in memory encoding – for example, a range of reinforced values is stored in LTM, any of which may be selected on a particular trial. Thus, when averaged over a number of trials, this model can explain how, for a fixed duration CS, the average rate of conditioned responding increases gradually until the point at which the US is delivered – effectively *timing* US occurrence. This account can also explain the scalar property of timing: For example, the transfer of pulses from the accumulator to LTM is multiplicative and noisy, ensuring that the error in the stored value is always proportional to the mean; in addition, the decision to respond is based on the difference between the experienced and stored duration values expressed as a proportion of the stored duration.

A Challenge to Trial-Based Associative Theory?

Because time-accumulation models can provide an integrated explanation of conditioning and timing, and explain the quantitative effect of I/T ratio on conditioning and the distribution of timed responding, some have argued that they should supersede trial-based theories (e.g., Church & Broadbent, 1990; Kirkpatrick & Church, 1998). Nonetheless, there are a number of arguments against this position, which will now be considered.

Theoretical evaluation

RET, in common with other time-accumulation models, relies on the detection of CS/US contiguity to compute reinforcement rate during the CS – yet no *mechanism* for this is specified. Moreover, according to RET, conditioning should not occur to a trace-conditioned CS, as the reinforcement rate *during* the CS is zero. The model explains the responding that occurs to trace-conditioned CSs because the *timing* mechanism computes that CS onset is a better signal for US delivery than the previous US (Gallistel & Gibbon, 2000, p. 305; see also Balsam, 1984, for a different solution to this problem).

A second issue is that for time-accumulation theories to explain effects such as blocking (for a detailed discussion of trial-based accounts of blocking, see Chapter 3), they require an additional decision rule. For example, if a CS *A* is trained in compound with a previously conditioned CS B (i.e., B+, AB+), because the rate of reinforcement in B does not change with the addition of A, the decision rule dictates that it may be attributed entirely to B – so that no CR will be elicited by A. Yet, typically, a blocked CS does command some CR – which the model explains as an averaging artifact (e.g., Balsam & Gallistel, 2009; Gallistel & Gibbon, 2000), through some animals showing perfect blocking and some none; but this view contradicts empirical evidence suggesting that blocking is a graded effect, even in individual subjects (Balsam & Gallistel, 2009).

Third, although time-accumulation models provide detailed temporal information about *when* the US will occur, they say nothing about what its sensory or motivational properties might be, or the extent to which information about one US generalizes to another. Associative trial-based theories thus provide a richer description of the information encoded during conditioning, as well as being able to explain a wider variety of conditioning effects.

Empirical considerations

Recent work has attempted to discriminate these two approaches experimentally (e.g., Bouton & Sunsay, 2003; Bouton, Woods, & Todd, 2014; Sunsay et al., 2004 described above; see also Harris, 2011). This includes some of our own work, which concentrated on the theories' differing assumptions about whether learning occurs on a trial-by-trial basis, or is based on accumulation of information over a number of trials. We compared conditioning to fixed duration cues with that to cues that *varied in duration from trial to trial*, but with the same mean duration (Jennings et al., 2013). According to time-accumulation accounts, as the mean duration of these two CS types is equated, their conditioning should be identical. In contrast, trial-based associative accounts, while not all making specific predictions, are conceptually equipped to accommodate differences in learning to these two types of cue. Rates of CR were reliably higher to the fixed CS, consistent with it having more associative strength than the variable stimulus; moreover, this was not a performance effect, as the difference was maintained when animals were tested under identical conditions. RET also predicts that the *rate* of CR acquisition should be the same for fixed and variable CSs. The definition of rate of acquisition is beyond the scope of this article, but Jennings *et al.* (2013) also found reliable differences in the rate of CR acquisition to fixed and variable CSs – inconsistent with the predictions of RET. Fixed duration CSs also produced better overshadowing and better blocking than their variable counterparts (Bonardi & Jennings, 2014; Bonardi, Mondragón, Brilot, & Jennings, 2015), further supporting this interpretation.

A Different Associative Approach

Wagner's model

Given these limitations of the time-accumulation approach, the question arises as to whether trial-based associative theory could be modified to better explain the temporal features of conditioning. Some have attempted to do so; for example, Wagner and colleagues (Vogel, Brandon, & Wagner, 2003) proposed a modification of Wagner's original model, according to which a proportion of a CS's elements are always activated in the same order on each trial. Thus, when a fixed duration stimulus is reinforced, certain specific elements will always be active near the time of food delivery and acquire the most associative strength. Such assumptions could yield a timing function, with animals responding at an increasing rate as US delivery approaches. Similar ideas are incorporated in formal timing models such as the Behavioral Theory of Timing model (Killeen & Fetterman, 1988) and the Learning-to-Time model (Machado, 1997; Machado, Malheiro, & Erlhagen, 2009). As we have already seen that Wagner's model can account for the effects of CS/US contiguity, and the qualitative effect of I/T ratio on conditioning, the fact that it can be adapted to explain timing effects means that it can accommodate many of the effects of temporal factors on conditioning; moreover simulations suggest that it could predict the scalar invariance of timed intervals (Vogel *et al.*, 2003). In a related vein, Lin and Honey (2011) have suggested a modification of Wagner's approach, arguing that differential conditioning to A1 and A2 activity could support some patterns of time-based responding (see Chapter 4).

Temporal difference model

A different example of such a theory is the Temporal Difference (TD) model (Sutton & Barto, 1987, 1990) – effectively a real-time extension of the Rescorla–Wagner model (Rescorla & Wagner, 1972). According to Rescorla–Wagner, the amount of learning on each trial depends on the degree to which the US is surprising – the difference between the predicted and actual outcome, or *prediction error* – which decreases as training progresses. The TD model differs from the Rescorla–Wagner model in estimating prediction error not at the end of each trial, but at *each time unit of the CS*. This is achieved by comparing the difference between successive CS unit *predictions*, rather than between the CS and the actual US at the end of a trial. At each time unit, the TD error is calculated by subtracting from the US value the difference between the previous unit $(t-1)$ prediction and the current unit (t) prediction, modulated by a discount factor. This error is then used to update the prediction at time $t + 1$ to bring it more in line with what was experienced. The update is tuned by an eligibility trace (Figure 14.1), a sort of memory trace that modulates the extent to which each CS unit is susceptible to learning. The conjoint action of the discount factor and the eligibility trace results in an exponentially decaying prediction function, reflecting the fact that predictors closer to the reinforcer are based on more recent, accurate information, thus conveying a stronger association. In short, TD inherits cue competition and error correction from the Rescorla–Wagner model, and frames it in real time.

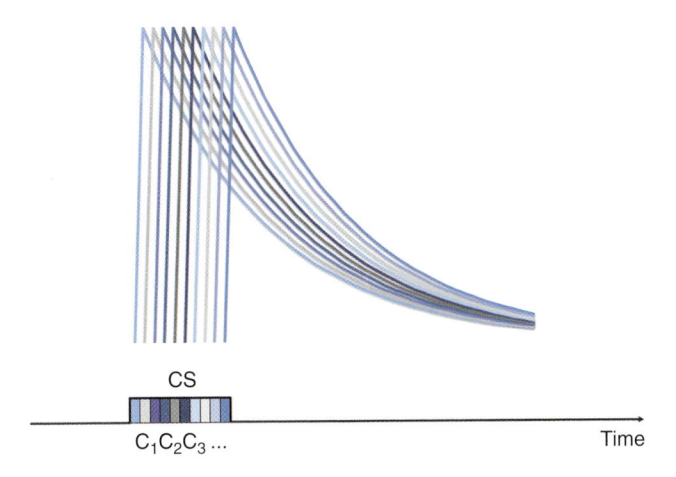

Figure 14.1 Eligibility traces of a CS across time in the CSC temporal difference representation.

The standard interpretation of TD, the Complete Serial Compound (CSC) representation (Moore, Choi, & Brunzell, 1998; see Gray, Alonso, Mondragón, & Fernández, 2012 for an online simulator), conceptualizes a stimulus as a temporally distributed set of components. Each component is effectively treated as a distinct cue and is active only during one time unit and has an *eligibility trace* (a kind of memory trace) attached that modulates the extent to which the component's associative strength is susceptible to change. A component's eligibility trace is maximal while the component is present and decays with time afterwards. In delay conditioning, the CS is contiguous with the US, and therefore the eligibility trace of the component closest to the time of reinforcement is high. In contrast, in a trace-conditioning procedure, the trace of the last stimulus component decays during the trace interval and is at a much lower level by the time the US occurs, allowing for less learning. The total amount of associative strength accruing to successive components is then adjusted by a parameter, gamma (γ), so that the asymptotic predictions exponentially decrease (γ^2, γ^3, γ^4) with distance from the US. Thus, the associative strength acquired by each component is exponentially constrained, such that later portions of the CS condition more effectively than earlier ones. CSC TD is thus able to predict temporal discrimination accurately. When the stimulus's associative strength is estimated as the mean of all its CSC values, CSC TD is also able to correctly predict that short CSs condition more than long ones (see also Chapter 15).

More recently, alternative representations based on so-called *microstimuli* have been proposed to accommodate temporal generalization (Ludvig, Sutton, & Kehoe, 2012). Mondragón, Gray, Alonso, Bonardi, and Jennings (2014; see also Mondragón, Gray, & Alonso, 2013) have further extended CSC TD to process simultaneous and serial compound stimuli, thus allowing them to model stimulus generalization and many complex discriminations (e.g., patterning and serial structural learning).

The TD model allows trial-based associative theory to address most of the various effects of timing on conditioning outlined above. We have seen how it can explain trace conditioning and timing; moreover, by assuming context conditioning, TD can

Table 14.1 Summary of whether the SOP, TD, and RET models can explain various learning phenomena.

Phenomena	SOP	TD	RET
Contiguity detection	Yes	Yes	No
Cue competition	Yes	Yes	(Yes[a])
Trace conditioning	Yes	Yes	(Yes[b])
Timing	(No[c])	Yes[d]	Yes
Scalar invariance of timing	(No[c])	No	Yes
Effect of I on conditioning (qualitative)	Yes	Yes	Yes
Effect of T on conditioning (qualitative)	Yes	Yes	Yes
Effect of I/T ratio on conditioning (quantitative)	No	No	Yes

[a] Additional assumptions about response decision rules are required to explain cue competition effects.
[b] Can explain responding in a trace conditioning procedure, but without additional assumptions these are due to timing rather than conditioning.
[c] Vogel's adaptation is able to explain both timing and its scalar invariance.
[d] Preasymptotically.

provide a qualitative (although not quantitative) account of I/T ratio effects in a similar way to the more orthodox associative models. For example, during longer ITIs, the context will undergo more extinction than during short ITIs; moreover, it can also predict that shorter CSs condition more effectively than longer ones. It cannot, however, explain the scalar variance of timing effects (Table 14.1).[3]

Neural Substrates of Timing Mechanisms

So far, we have outlined various temporal aspects of the conditioning process: (1) the requirement to detect CS/US contiguity, specifically when the US is surprising; (2) the attenuation of conditioning when CS and US are separated by a trace interval; (3) the dependence of the degree of conditioning on temporal factors such as the I/T ratio; and (4) the ability of animals to time US delivery, and the scalar invariance of this process. We have also considered how two theoretical approaches, trial-based associative and time-accumulation models, explain these features of learning. There follows a selective review of potential neural substrates of these effects. First, we discuss the role of the hippocampus: Much evidence suggests that this structure shows properties relevant to trace conditioning (2), and also to the timing of US delivery (4) and the scalar property of timing (4).

We will then consider the dopamine system – increasingly implicated in temporal cognitive processes. First, we will briefly review evidence that dopaminergic neurons originating in the midbrain show a phasic response that seemingly tracks the occurrence of surprising appetitive events, or their omission, accurately in time – see (1) and (4). Second, we will discuss the involvement of dopaminergic and cholinergic neurotransmitter systems in timing behavior, and the evidence suggesting that this dopaminergic mediation of timing may, at least in part, be localized in the dorsal striatum, and also be relevant to timing appetitive USs (4).

Involvement of the Hippocampus in Temporal Cognition

There is longstanding literature relating the hippocampus to timed behavior. Older studies tended to use lesion techniques, revealing a role for the hippocampus in both trace conditioning and timing, while later studies suggest its involvement in the discrimination of stimulus order. Finally, work using electrophysiological techniques has provided fascinating insights into the role of the hippocampus in timing.

Lesion studies

Trace conditioning It has long been suggested that the hippocampus is crucial for maintaining stimulus traces within the seconds-to-minutes range (Rawlins, 1985). Consistent with this idea, hippocampal damage often impairs formation of associations between CSs and *aversive* USs that are separated in time. For example, in fear trace conditioning in which a CS terminates before footshock delivery, the CS evokes conditioned freezing or enhances startle responses in rats with an intact hippocampus. Animals with hippocampal lesions show little conditioned freezing (Bangasser, Waxler, Santollo, & Shors, 2006; McEchron, Bouwmeester, Tseng, Weiss, & Disterhoft, 1998; Yoon & Otto, 2007) or fear-potentiated startle during CS presentation (Burman, Starr, & Gewirtz, 2006; Fendt, Fanselow, & Koch, 2005; Trivedi & Coover, 2006). No deficit is observed in these studies when the CS and US are presented closely in time, suggesting that lesioned animals do not suffer from a general deficit in fear conditioning (although this is sometimes found: Maren, Aharonov, & Fanselow, 1997; Richmond et al., 1999).

Hippocampal lesion effects on fear trace conditioning, however, are highly dependent on the form of CR measured, only being found in freezing and fear-potentiated startle paradigms. Rawlins and Tanner (1998) measured the extent to which a CS paired with an aversive US after a trace interval would suppress lever-pressing, and no hippocampal lesion deficit was found (see also Tam, 2011). In addition, the effect of hippocampal lesion on trace conditioning appears to be dependent on the use of aversive USs, as hippocampal damage does not impair formation of associations between CSs and *appetitive* USs that are separated in time, irrespective of the form of CR measured: rearing (Ross, Orr, Holland, & Berger, 1984), licking (Thibaudeau, Doré, & Goulet, 2009; Thibaudeau, Potvin, Allen, Doré, & Goulet, 2007), or approach responses (Lin & Honey, 2011; Tam & Bonardi, 2012a; although see Chan, Shipman, & Kister, 2014). Thus, the hippocampus seems to mediate trace conditioning only in certain paradigms – and this selectivity suggests it is not crucial for maintaining stimulus traces across time as originally suggested by Rawlins (1985).

Timing Although hippocampal damage does not impair formation of associations between CS and appetitive USs, it does affect how CRs are distributed within trials. A series of studies on the peak procedure conducted by Meck and colleagues (Meck, 1988; Meck, Church, & Olton, 1984) looked at the effect of lesions of the fimbria-fornix, fibers connecting the hippocampus with other subcortical structures, on an operant peak task reinforcement is provided for the first response after a fixed interval has elapsed since cue onset, and then accuracy of response timing is examined on test trials without US delivery. In control animals, responding gradually increased across the trial, reached a maximum at approximately the time of US delivery, and declined gradually afterwards. Animals with hippocampal damage showed similar Gaussian-shaped response distributions, but showed maximal responding at *earlier* time points than the control animals, suggesting an underestimation of target times.

Early studies also examined differential reinforcement of low rates (DRL), in which a lever press is followed by food delivery only if the response is separated from the previous response by a minimum target period. Control animals normally show little premature responding (interresponse time < target time) but relatively high responding around the time when food became available. Damage to the hippocampus led to a shortening of interresponse times (Bannerman, Yee, Good, Heupel, Iversen, & Rawlins, 1999; Braggio & Ellen, 1976; Clark & Isaacson, 1965; Costa, Bueno, & Xavier, 2005; Jaldow & Oakley, 1990; Jarrard & Becker, 1977; Johnson, Olton, Gage, & Jenko, 1977; Rawlins, Winocur, & Gray, 1983; Rickert, Bennett, Anderson, Corbett, & Smith, 1973; Sinden, Rawlins, Gray, & Jarrard, 1986).

We have found effects similar to those reported by Meck and colleagues when damage is confined to the dorsal hippocampus (Tam & Bonardi, 2012a, 2012b; Tam, Jennings, & Bonardi, 2013; see also Balci *et al.*, 2009; Yin & Meck, 2014). Tam and Bonardi (2012a) employed a Pavlovian version of the peak task used by Meck *et al.* in which different CS–food intervals were used on the conditioning trials (15 s and 30 s), and the accuracy and precision of response timing were examined on test trials without US delivery. Animals given lesions of the dorsal hippocampus before training on this task showed maximal responding at earlier time points than the control animals, and the time of peak responding was significantly shorter than the actual CS–food interval in lesioned but not in control subjects. A similar timing deficit was also observed in rats with damage to the dorsal CA3 and CA1 subregions but intact dentate gyrus; in addition, the width of the response distributions in the lesioned group was also broader than that in the control group, suggesting less precise timing (Tam, Jennings, & Bonardi, 2013).

Thus, hippocampal damage systematically reduces the observed peak time, and shortens the interresponse times on DRL tasks, suggesting a deficit in temporal learning. However, these effects could also result from more impulsive responding (Cheung & Cardinal, 2005) or a more general deficit in response inhibition (Davidson & Jarrard, 2004). It is not possible to distinguish between these alternatives in the DRL task, but it is in appetitive conditioning tasks. For example, in Tam *et al.* (2013), animals were given test trials on which gaps of different duration, 0.5 s, 2.5 s, and 7.5 s, interrupted the early part of the CS. On these gap trials, the dorsal-hippocampal-lesioned animals showed maximal responding *later*, instead of earlier, relative to the control animals. Meck *et al.* (1984; Olton, Meck, & Church, 1987; Olton, Wenk, Church, & Meck, 1988) found similar effects in animals with fimbria-fornix lesions. These findings do not provide support for the idea that lesioned animals responded impulsively or were unable to inhibit appetitive responses, because if this were the case, they would have shown maximal responding at earlier time points, on trials both with and without intervening gaps.

In summary, damage to the hippocampus frequently affects timing in the peak procedure, both reducing the observed peak time on peak trials and producing a *later* peak after insertion of a gap. In terms of SET, the former effect is typically interpreted as a reduction in the scaling parameter, K, by which the number of pulses stored in the accumulator is multiplied before transfer into LTM. The remembered time of reinforcement will thus be systematically shorter than that registered in the accumulator, resulting in animals responding too early (see Meck, Church, & Matell, 2013, for a recent review); it is less clear, however, how such an account can explain the effects observed in the gap procedure.[4]

In contrast to SET, the trial-based associative theories outlined above cannot explain effects such as the reduction in peak time without additional assumptions, because they do not make this distinction between time values stored in the accumulator and in LTM; although they regard the processes of perceiving and encoding a stimulus as different, the default assumption is that the perceived stimulus corresponds exactly to the stimulus that is encoded. These theories assert that times of significant events are coded by conditioning a specific group of time-locked CS elements (cf. Vogel *et al.*, 2003), a specific pattern of memory state activity (cf. Lin & Honey, 2011), or specific CS components (the TD model). Any effect on timing produced by a lesion presumably stems from an alteration in the speed with which these time-locked patterns of activity develop. But if lesions are given before training (e.g., Tam & Bonardi, 2012a; Tam *et al.*, 2013), any alteration produced by the lesion will be the *same* for both current and stored values, with the result that timing will remain accurate – even if the pattern of activation present during reinforcement differs from that in control subjects. Further development of these models is therefore needed for them to accommodate effects of this type.

Discriminating stimulus order The hippocampus also seems to mediate temporal order discrimination of serially presented stimuli. When animals with an intact hippocampus are presented with different stimuli, usually objects, in a serial manner (e.g., A → B → C), and subsequently given a choice between two of the stimuli in the series (e.g., A vs. C), they spontaneously orient to the stimulus that has been experienced *earlier* in time (i.e., A; Mitchell & Laiacona, 1998). This kind of discrimination is abolished after hippocampal damage (Good, Barnes, Staal, McGregor, & Honey, 2007), suggesting the involvement of the hippocampus in differentiating stimulus order. The lesion effect becomes more subtle when it is confined to the dorsal CA1 subregion. Kesner *et al.* (Hoge & Kesner, 2007; Hunsaker, Fieldsted, Rosenberg, & Kesner, 2008; Hunsaker & Kesner, 2008) found that CA1-lesioned animals still distinguished between stimuli presented serially, but they oriented to the stimulus that had been experienced *later*, instead of earlier, in time.

Single-unit recording studies

Timing an aversive US Findings from single-unit recording studies in rats (Delacour & Houcine, 1987) and rabbits (McEchron, Tseng, & Disterhoft, 2003) suggest that a small proportion of hippocampal cells expresses information about when an unpleasant US will be delivered with respect to a stable temporal landmark.

Delacour and Houcine (1987) trained rats with a fixed-time procedure, in which the US (whisker stimulation) was delivered once every 24 s in the absence of any explicit CS. After extended training, their subjects showed little conditioned whisker movement during the early portion of the ITI, but the level of CR increased across the ITI period and reached a maximum a few seconds before delivery of the US. Delacour and Houcine (1987) found that a small group of cells in the dentate gyrus of the hippocampus fired in a way that was similar to CR timing. Their firing rates were low at the beginning of the ITI, but increased gradually to a maximum a few seconds before US delivery. Another small group of cells showed the opposite pattern, their firing being initially high but decreasing across the ITI period. Collectively, these two groups of cells provided information on how much time had elapsed since the last US delivery. As the animals were partially restrained and remained in the same place during the recording sessions, the firing patterns observed could not be attributed to spatial location, running direction, or running speed——variables that influence firing of hippocampal pyramidal cells in foraging and spatial navigation tasks (e.g., Wiener, Paul, & Eichenbaum, 1989).

Timing signals in the hippocampus are also observed in a task with an explicit CS. McEchron *et al.* (2003) gave rabbits a trace-conditioning task, in which a 3-s tone was followed by an empty interval of 10 or 20 s, the termination of which was followed by delivery of a paraorbital shock. Another group of rabbits received a pseudoconditioning procedure with the same number of explicitly unpaired CSs and USs. On nonreinforced test trials, the trace group showed a greater change in heart rate during the CS period and during the 10- or 20-s period that followed CS termination than the pseudoconditioning controls, suggesting acquisition of conditioned fear in the former subjects. Among these subjects, a small group of their pyramidal cells in the CA1 subregion showed timing signals similar to those observed by Delacour and Houcine (1987). Firing was relatively low during most of the nonreinforced test trial period, but the cells fired maximally around the time of US delivery on the conditioning trials; no timing signal was observed in the pseudoconditioning controls. During extinction trials when no USs were delivered, conditioned heart-rate responses in the conditioning group declined across blocks of test trials. McEchron *et al.* (2003) observed that the reduction in CRs across extinction was mirrored by a reduction in the number of cells showing a timing signal, resulting in a significant correlation between the two variables. As in the study by Delacour and Houcine (1987), the animals were completely restrained during the recording sessions, so the firing patterns observed could not be attributed to other behavioral variables such as head direction or running speed. However, Gilmartin and McEchron (2005) failed to observe any significant timing signal in the dentate gyrus and pyramidal cells in the conditioning group relative to the pseudoconditioning group; but the absence of timing signal could be due to differences in the training protocol used in the two studies (e.g., number of conditioning trials per day), which would have resulted in a different degree of associative strength relative to the pseudoconditioning controls.

Timing an appetitive US Findings from a single-unit recording study in rats (Young & McNaughton, 2000) suggest that a small proportion of hippocampal cells also reflect the timing of the occurrence of a pleasant US.

In this study, rats were trained on a DRL task in which a lever press was rewarded with a food pellet only if the response was separated by at least 15 s from the previous one. After sufficient training, the subjects tended to show few premature responses (i.e., interresponse interval <15 s), but relatively high responding around the criterion time. Presenting a 0.5-s auditory cue halfway through the criterion time did not facilitate timing performance, suggesting that the subjects treated it as irrelevant, and relied on the response cue, instead of the auditory cue, to time the occurrence of food delivery.

Young and McNaughton (2000) observed that a small group of CA3 and CA1 cells showed signals that are similar to those observed by Delacour and Houcine (1987) during the interresponse period. Firing was relatively high at the beginning of the period, but decayed at a constant rate as time elapsed, reaching a minimum just before the subjects pressed the lever; firing then resumed at a relatively high level after the lever press, suggestive of resetting of interval timing. A second group of cells showed a different pattern with relatively constant rates of firing during most of the interresponse period (except a few seconds prior to lever pressing), suggesting that the former, but not the latter, group of cells provided information on how much time had elapsed since the last response or US delivery. These two distinct patterns of firing were not observed in cells in the entorhinal cortex, which provides a major source of input to the dentate gyrus via the perforant pathway (e.g., Amaral & Witter, 1989). Thus, it is unlikely that the timing signal was computed in the entorhinal cortex and sent from there to the hippocampus (see also Naya & Suzuki, 2011). Both the hippocampal and entorhinal cells treated the auditory cue halfway through the criterion time as irrelevant, as their firing was not influenced by its presence. Young and McNaughton (2000) also noted that the hippocampal cells that showed a timing signal comprised only a very small proportion of all recorded cells (20 out of 317 cells), the majority of which showed event-firing patterns that were distinct from one another, and hence they could not be categorized.

Temporal information from combined activation of different hippocampal cell populations More recent evidence suggests that, during tasks in which animals are required to maintain stimulus representation across an empty interval, different subsets of CA3 and CA1 cells are activated at specific moments that combine to provide an index of the flow of time. MacDonald, Lepage, Eden, and Eichenbaum (2011) trained their rats in a conditional learning task, in which one object signaled that one odor cue would be rewarded, and a different object signaled that another odor cue would be rewarded (A → x+, B → y+), but the reverse pairings were not rewarded (A → y–, B → x–). There was an empty interval of 10 s between presentation of the object and odor cues, so that the subjects had to maintain object representations across the gap period.

MacDonald et al. (2011) observed that during the gap period, different CA3 and CA1 cells fired maximally at different moments. Cells that fired maximally during the early portion of the gap tended to have a relatively narrow firing distribution, whereas those that fired maximally later in time had a broader firing distribution, conforming to the timescale invariance property of interval timing at the behavioral level (e.g., Gallistel & Gibbon, 2000). The cumulative activation of these cells led to a gradual, incremental change in population activity across the gap period, giving rise to an internal flow of time. On trials in which the duration of the gap was extended to 20 s, some cells showed an entirely different firing pattern, becoming active at a different moment in time. A small group of cells, however, continued to fire maximally at the same moments relative to the gap onset, suggesting that they signaled the flow of absolute time. In contrast, another small group of cells expanded their firing distributions such that the rescaled firing patterns superimposed with the original ones when plotted on a relative scale, suggesting that they signaled the flow of relative, instead of absolute, time.

Similar patterns have been observed in the hippocampus of macaques during a temporal order learning task (Naya & Suzuki, 2011). The subjects in this study were presented on a touch screen with two different visual stimuli that were separated in time by 0.92 s; the termination of the second stimulus was shortly followed by delivery of one drop of water. After a short variable delay, the subjects were given a choice of three cues, two of which had been encountered before the delay period and one that had not, the latter acting as a distractor. Drops of water were delivered if the subjects selected the two cues in the same order as they were encountered before the variable delay period. Naya and Suzuki (2011) observed that, after sufficient training, hippocampal cells fired preferentially at different moments in time during serial presentation of the two cues. Some cells showed little firing during the first cue but started to increase firing gradually during the 0.92-s gap period, and firing reached a maximum shortly after the termination of the second cue. Other cells showed the opposite pattern of firing, which was relatively high during the first cue but declined to a minimum during the second cue. The cumulative activation of these cells resulted in a gradual, incremental change in population activity across trial time, similar to that observed by MacDonald *et al.* (2011) in rats. Similar patterns have also been observed in the hippocampus of macaques (Naya & Suzuki, 2011).

Summary and Implications for Theory

Hippocampal damage can disrupt formation of associations between CSs and aversive USs that are separated in time. The effect, however, is dependent on the form of CR measured, and as yet no parallel impairment has been observed in appetitive trace conditioning. Damage to the structure also disrupts timing of appetitive USs in different classical and instrumental conditioning paradigms. Thus, it is at least possible that the reported effects of hippocampal damage on aversive trace conditioning may stem from a more general effect of such damage on the timing of the CR. However, we are not aware of any study explicitly examining the effect of lesion on timing of aversive USs, so on the basis of lesion data, it is currently unclear whether the hippocampus has a general involvement in timing the occurrence of biologically significant stimuli regardless of their hedonic value. Nonetheless, findings from single-unit recording studies (see below) suggest this is likely to be the case. Finally, hippocampal damage affects stimulus discrimination on the basis of the order in which stimuli are experienced.

Studies reviewed in the sections "Lesion studies" and "Single-unit recording studies" also found an involvement of the hippocampus in timing the occurrence of biologically significant events regardless of their hedonic values. Cells in the dentate gyrus and CA3–1 subregions express information about when an appetitive or aversive US will be delivered with respect to a temporal landmark (Delacour & Houcine, 1987; McEchron *et al.*, 2003; Young & McNaughton, 2000), and activity in populations of hippocampal cells combines to yield quite subtle temporal information.

These findings provide support for the notion that the hippocampus is important for temporal learning and memory (Kesner, 1998; Olton, 1986; Sakata, 2006). Moreover, the strength of some of this time-related cell activation was correlated with performance of the CR, which is at least consistent with the proposal that the strength of a putative timing signal is intimately related to the degree of associative strength (e.g., McEchron *et al.*, 2003). This observation sits more easily with theories like the TD model, according to which timing is an emergent property of the conditioning process, than those time-accumulation accounts (such as RET) that assume that timing and conditioning are mediated by independent mechanisms.

Theories such as SET assume the existence of a pacemaker to explain response timing (although it has been argued that no plausible neural system has been found that could play such a role; e.g., Staddon, 2005). In contrast, associative theories often assume that the onset of a CS triggers sequential activation of some hypothetical elements, each being activated at a specific moment in time (Fraisse, 1963; Kehoe, Ludvig, & Sutton, 2009; Machado *et al.*, 2009; Vogel *et al.*, 2003). Studies reviewed have identified a neural correlate for this mechanism. Stimuli that are valid predictors of USs trigger sequential activation of a population of hippocampal cells, which fire preferentially at different, but overlapping, moments across trial time (MacDonald *et al.*, 2011; Naya & Suzuki, 2011). Moreover, the firing properties of these cells render them capable of encoding both absolute and relative time, which corresponds with the scalar invariance of timing outlined above. This internally generated sequence of hippocampal activity could also provide animals with a directionality of time or a gradual change in temporal context (Bouton, 1993), thereby allowing formation and retrieval of associations at different moments. Yet, as we saw above, the reduction in peak time produced by hippocampal damage cannot be easily explained by current associatively based timing theories without additional assumptions. Future work is required to develop these theories to the point that they are able to explain such effects. But whichever theoretical approach proves to be more effective, the behavioral findings we have described strongly suggest that the hippocampus mediates various aspects of temporal cognition.

Phasic Firing of Dopaminergic Neurons

A response to temporally unexpected reward

Another neurophysiological system that appears to be intimately related to timing is the dopaminergic system. Dopaminergic neurons originating from substantial nigra and ventral tegmental area show increased phasic (burst) firing to unexpected appetitive reward (reviewed by Schultz, 2002, 2006; see Chapter 3). This dopamine response changes during learning: If the reward is consistently preceded by a CS, then as training progresses, the phasic dopamine response evoked by the reward gradually diminishes – but the CS progressively *gains* the ability to evoke this same response. Parallel changes in dopamine efflux are observed in the nucleus accumbens core (AcbC; Clark, Collins, Sanford, & Phillips, 2013; Day, Roitman, Wightman, & Carelli, 2007; Sunsay & Rebec, 2008). No dopamine response is evoked by a CS that has been blocked (Waelti, Dickinson, & Schultz, 2001), and the (surprising) presentation of a reward after a blocked CS evokes a dopamine response, as does the presentation of an unexpected reward (Waelti et al., 2001).

The orderly way in which this phasic dopamine response changes during learning suggests that dopamine is involved in the process of conditioning, and its precise role is currently a subject of intense research. One theory suggests that it serves as a *reward prediction error signal* (Montague, Dayan, & Sejnowski, 1996; Schultz, 2002), similar to the error signal in the Rescorla–Wagner and TD models, and is therefore critical to learning (although see Berridge & Robinson, 1998). A detailed discussion of the prediction error hypothesis is beyond the scope of this chapter (see Chapter 3); however, the phasic dopamine response has two interesting temporal properties that we will highlight below.

First, the phasic dopamine response is sensitive to the *timing* of the appetitive US. In well-trained animals, the dopamine response elicited by the reward is greater if the reward is presented at a *different* time from when it was delivered during conditioning, and omission of reward causes the firing of dopaminergic neurons to decrease around the time when the reward is usually delivered (Fiorillo, Song, & Yun, 2013; Fiorillo, Yun, & Song, 2013; Hollerman & Schultz, 1998; Ljungberg, Apicella, & Schultz, 1991). These findings suggest that dopaminergic neuron activity is closely related to the expected timing of the US.

Second, the longer the CS–US duration, the smaller the CS-evoked dopamine response. Dopaminergic neurons fire only to the onset of CSs and not to their offset, even when the offset is a better predictor of reward (Schultz & Romo, 1990). As the CS duration is increased, the transfer of the evoked dopamine response from the US to the CS is reduced (Fiorillo, Song, & Yun, 2013; Fiorillo, Yun, & Song, 2013). This observation has been interpreted in terms of phasic dopamine serving as a prediction error signal (Fiorillo, Song, & Yun, 2013; Fiorillo, Yun, & Song, 2013): As CS duration is increased, the time of US occurrence is more difficult to predict because timing imprecision scales with CS duration (Gibbon, 1991). Therefore, US occurrence retains some of its surprise value and evokes a smaller dopamine response.

The prediction-error-signal account of the phasic dopamine response assumes that the CS must be unpredicted, or it should not elicit a dopamine response. Normally this is likely, because in standard conditioning procedures, CSs are often preceded by an ITI that is variable or so long that it would be difficult to predict the occurrence of each CS from the CS or US that precedes it. This account predicts that when the ITI-CS duration is fixed and short, the CS will show only a limited ability to evoke a dopamine response, because it can be fully predicted by the occurrence of the previous reward. To our knowledge, this prediction has not yet been empirically tested.

Summary and implications for theory

The dopamine phasic response appears to track, with some temporal precision, the occurrence or omission of unexpected rewards, and of CSs that predict reward. This corresponds with the assertion of the TD model, that there is a different error signal for different components of the CS, such that later components of the CS predict US occurrence effectively, but earlier components less so, due to eligibility trace decay. Moreover, the observation that the dopamine response can migrate to the onset of the CS mirrors the prediction of TD, that components of the CS closest to the US begin to acquire associative strength first, but that, as learning progresses, the error-prediction signal gradually propagates backwards across earlier CS components, until the start of the predictive cue also becomes an unexpected signal for reward (Sunsay & Rebec, 2008; although see Pan, Schmidt, Wickens, & Hyland, 2005).

Whether phasic firing of dopaminergic neurons is sufficient and/or necessary for reward learning is currently under debate (Adamantidis *et al.*, 2011; Parker *et al.*, 2010; Rossi, Sukharnikova, Hayrapetyan, Yang, & Yin, 2013). Moreover, if the phasic dopamine response were to underlie a general learning mechanism, then it should not be restricted to rewarding events – and yet there is controversy over whether activity in these neurons is elevated or suppressed by unexpected *aversive* reinforcers (Fiorillo, Yun, & Song, 2013; Winton-Brown, Fusar-Poli, Ungless, & Howes, 2014). Some have argued that this inconsistency stems from the existence of different subclasses of neuron, some of which are activated by aversive events, and some inhibited (e.g., Matsumoto & Hikosaka, 2009).

A general learning mechanism should also be able to accommodate the fact that associations can form between two motivationally neutral stimuli – ostensibly at odds with the reward-prediction error hypothesis (e.g., Hollerman & Schultz, 1998; Romo & Schultz, 1990; Schultz, 2010). Yet it has long been known that the phasic dopamine response can also be elicited by salient neutral stimuli (which, it has been argued, were effectively rewarding by virtue of their novelty, or via generalization from truly rewarding stimuli; e.g., Ungless, 2004). Moreover, some authors have convincingly argued on the basis of electrophysiological observations that the phasic dopamine response is simply too fast to be able to detect whether an event is rewarding or not (e.g., Redgrave, Gurney, & Reynolds, 2008). Others have questioned the assertion that different subclasses of neuron respond to appetitive and aversive stimuli, and reported that many of these neurons respond to *both* appetitive and aversive events, but also that at short latencies, their activation is related to their *physical intensity* rather than their motivational value (Fiorillo, Song, & Yun, 2013; Fiorillo, Yun, & Song, 2013). This has led to the suggestion that the phasic dopamine response might be more accurately regarded as a system for detecting salient stimuli, rather than having any intrinsic requirement for these stimuli to have motivational value (e.g., Winton-Brown *et al.*, 2014). We argued above that our current theoretical models of conditioning and timing require a system for detecting contiguity of to-be-associated events, and this must be able to monitor the occurrence of any surprising event in time with temporal precision. Observations of the type described in this section suggest that the phasic dopamine response might be able to achieve this. Nonetheless, at present, the extent to which this neural mechanism underlies conditioning and timing of events other than appetitive USs remains to be seen.

Involvement of Neurotransmitters in Timing Behavior

The previous section described how the phasic dopamine response is tied closely to *when* unexpected rewarding events occur. Given these observations, it is perhaps not surprising that manipulating the dopamine system also alters timing of the response.

This has been shown in operant versions of the peak procedure [described in 4a(ii) above] and also in the Free-Operant Psychophysical Procedure (FOPP). In this latter task, subjects are trained to switch their responding from one lever to another halfway through the trial in order to keep earning reinforcers on a variable interval schedule. Test trials without reinforcers are occasionally inserted, during which the index of timing, the Point of Subjective Equality (PSE), is recorded. The PSE is the time at which response rates on the two levers are equal. Because the appropriate switch time is not explicitly signaled, subjects need to use internal mechanisms to time. Subjects tend to switch from the "early" to the "late" lever halfway through the trial, and the variability of timing is roughly scalar invariant (Bizo & White, 1997; Stubbs, 1980). The similarity in timing performance across different timing tasks – the ability to track the criterion time and the scalar invariance of timing variability – has led researchers to assume that a single timing mechanism governs timing performance across all tasks. As we will see below, results from several neurobiological studies suggest that such an assumption may be too simple.

Dopaminergic and serotonergic compounds

Timing on the peak procedure is altered by dopaminergic compounds (reviewed by Coull, Cheng, & Meck, 2011). Acute treatment with dopamine receptor agonists produces an *immediate* leftward shift in the peak function, reducing peak time, while dopamine receptor antagonists have the opposite effect (Drew, Fairhurst, Malapani, Horvitz, & Balsam, 2003; MacDonald & Meck, 2005; Meck, 1996; Saulsgiver, McClure, & Wynne, 2006; although see Buhusi & Meck, 2002a). With continued treatment, these shifts in peak time progressively decline until eventually the baseline peak value is restored (Maricq, Roberts, & Church, 1981; Meck, 1996; Saulsgiver et al., 2006; although see Frederick and Allen, 1996; Matell, King, & Meck, 2004).

Information-processing theories such as SET account for these results by proposing that pacemaker speed is respectively increased and decreased by activation and blockade of dopamine receptors. Acute treatment leads to immediate peak shifts because the stored peak time (computed with an "accurate" pacemaker) is achieved earlier or later (Meck, 1996), while continued exposure allows subjects to store new peak values generated at the time of reward delivery with the altered pacemaker speed; this "recalibration" allows the subject to perform correctly (Meck, 1996). Associative theories account for these findings in a similar manner: For example, if activating dopamine receptors *speeds up* the sequential activation of components that encode time, the reinforced component will occur earlier, shifting peak time. But this previously reinforced component will no longer coincide with US delivery and so will slowly extinguish, while the component that *is* now coincident with the US will acquire associative strength, producing the recalibration effect.

Acute treatment with the serotonin 2A (5-HT$_{2A}$) receptor agonist 1-(2,5-dimethoxy-4-iodophenyl)-2-aminopropane (DOI) also immediately reduces peak time in the peak procedure (Asgari et al., 2006); DOI also transiently reduces the PSE in the FOPP task (Body et al., 2003, 2006; Cheung et al., 2007a, 2007b); moreover, after extended DOI treatment, when the PSE has returned to its original value, the ability of amphetamine, a nonselective dopamine receptor agonist, to reduce PSE is blocked – but that of quinpirole, a dopamine D_2 receptor agonist, is not (Cheung *et al.*, 2007a, 2007b). The blocking of amphetamine's effect is consistent with the assumption that once a subject has recalibrated to faster subjective timing after DOI treatment, it would have adapted to faster subjective timing in general; the lack of effect with quinpirole suggests that quinpirole reduces PSE via a separate mechanism. This latter effect is not readily explicable in theoretical terms, either by SET or by associative theories.

In terms of SET, quinpirole might reduce the response criterion – the threshold of how similar the current pulse count has to be to the reinforced values stored in reference memory before the subject decides to respond (that is, switch to the "late" lever). This would predict that quinpirole should not show a recalibration effect – a prediction that has not, to our knowledge, been tested.

Cholinergic compounds

Chronic systemic treatment with cholinergic compounds that increase (or decrease) synaptic levels of acetylcholine (ACh) have a slightly different effect, *gradually* reducing (or increasing) the peak time over several sessions (Meck, 1996). SET explains these gradual shifts by assuming a memory encoding deficit: Increased levels of ACh reduce the number of counts transferred to the LTM, while blocking ACh receptors has the opposite effect. These changes in memory encoding have no immediate effects on timing behavior, but with continued exposure the criterion values in memory are increasingly "contaminated" by the incorrect number of pulses translated from the accumulator, resulting in gradual shifts in peak time. This suggestion is consistent with the involvement of the cholinergic system in memory processes (see reviews by Gold, 2003; Power, Vazdarjanova, & McGaugh, 2003). In contrast, it is more difficult to see how associative theories can accommodate *gradual* effects on peak time without making extra assumptions.

Summary and implications for theory Both SET and trial-based associative theories can explain immediate effects of neuropharmacological manipulations on timing performance by assuming they alter the rate of "subjective flow of time" – pacemaker speed for SET, rate of sequential activation of associative elements for associative theories. However, associative theories are less able to explain gradual effects of cholinergic manipulations, for the same reason they cannot account for the shifts in peak time produced by hippocampal damage. In contrast, SET is able to explain these findings because its multistage informational processing structure gives it greater flexibility – although one could argue that this makes SET not as well constrained and testable as associative theories.

Dorsal Striatum and Timing Behavior

Role of dorsal striatum in timing

The dorsal striatum has been shown to be involved in operant peak timing. Matell, Meck, and Nicolelis (2003) reported that a subset of dorsolateral striatal neurons increased their firing rate roughly around the peak times, while a human fMRI study found that the activity of the right putamen, part of the dorsal striatum, peaked around criterion times in a modified peak procedure (Meck & Malapani, 2004).

The involvement of dorsal striatal neurons in the peak procedure may be intimately related to the nigrostriatal dopaminergic system. Meck (2006) reported that radiofrequency lesion or dopamine depletion of the dorsal striatum completely abolished peak timing – lesioned rats responded at a constant rate throughout the trial, and responding failed to peak around the criterion time. Treatment with the dopamine precursor L-DOPA restored peak timing in rats with nigral dopamine depletion, but was ineffective in rats with radiofrequency lesion of the dorsal striatum. These results suggest that timing on the peak procedure requires both intact dorsal striatum and functional dopaminergic input to this area.

Striatal beat frequency model: a synthesis?

Evidence of this type has led to the development of the striatal beat frequency model (SBF; Buhusi & Oprisan, 2013; Matell & Meck, 2000, 2004). SBF is one of the first attempts to translate a theoretical approach to timing to neurobiologically plausible mechanisms. It is based on the multiple oscillator model (Church & Broadbent, 1990), an approach that rejects the idea of a single pacemaker with one period, and instead assumes multiple oscillators with different periods, which in combination can time durations much longer than the oscillator with the longest period. A brief description of SBF is given below (for a complete description, see Buhusi & Oprisan, 2013; Oprisan & Buhusi, 2011).

The medium spiny neurons (MSNs) in the dorsal striatum, which project out of the striatum, each receive input from a large number of cortical neurons (Wilson, 1995). SBF proposes that these cortical neurons oscillate at different intrinsic frequencies, and their convergent projections to MSNs allow the latter to detect the pattern of their coincident activity and to use this pattern as a timer (see Figure 14.2). At the onset of the timed signal, the oscillatory cortical neurons reset their phases and begin to fire according to their different intrinsic frequencies, such that different subsets of these neurons will be active at different points during the timed interval. The release of dopamine in the dorsal striatum evoked by subsequent reinforcement increases the synaptic strength between the set of input cortical neurons that are active at that particular time and their targeted dendritic spines on the MSNs, via long-term potentiation. After training, the set of cortical neurons that is usually active close to the criterion time is proposed to trigger MSN firing, via spatial summation, at around the criterion time. Thus, in SBF, passage of time is represented by the particular set of cortical neurons that are firing, and reference memory of criterion time is stored spatially in MSNs as synaptic strength on particular dendritic spines. Computer simulation has shown that SBF can replicate the pattern of responding seen in the peak procedure, as well as the scalar invariance property (Oprisan & Buhusi, 2011). Also consistent with this model is the fact that prefrontal cortex has been found to be active during several timing tasks, including the peak procedure and the FOPP (Jin, Fujii, & Graybiel, 2009; Matell et al., 2003; Valencia-Torres et al., 2011, 2012a, 2012b), and its inactivation impairs temporal discrimination (Kim, Jung, Byun, Jo, & Jung, 2009).

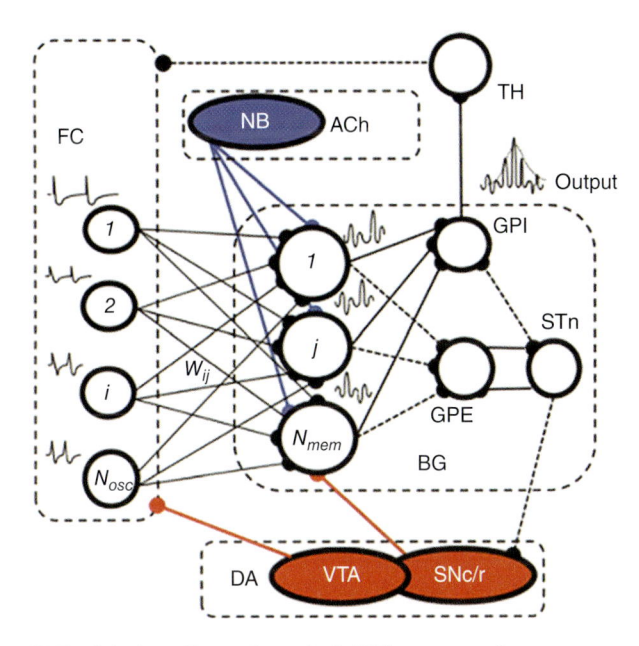

Figure 14.2 SBF of timing. Frontal cortical (FC) neurons form convergent projections to MSNs in the striatum in the basal ganglia (BG). At CS onset, phasic dopamine (DA) release in the FC causes FC neurons to reset their phases and to start oscillating at different intrinsic frequencies. Their coincident-activation signal is detected by striatal MSNs, and the linear combination of these signals acts as a timer whose period is much longer than those of individual FC neurons. Reward delivery of reward causes phasic dopamine release in the striatum, which allows long-term potentiation between the subset of FC neurons that are active at the time of the reward and their corresponding MSN dendrites, analogous to increasing their associative strength. With training, coincidental firing of this subset of FC neurons alone triggers a timing response via the MSNs close to the criterion time. Note that although the memorized time is proposed to be scaled by ACh levels, it is difficult for SBF to account for it mechanistically (Buhusi & Oprisan, 2013, p. 68). GPE = globus pallidus external; GPI = globus pallidus internal; NB = nucleus basalis; STn = subthalamic nucleus; SNc/r = substantia nigra pars compacta/reticulata; TH = thalamus. Adapted with permission from Buhusi and Oprisan (2013).

SBF is related to trial-based associative models, insofar as it proposes an association between the temporal elements active at the time of reward (input cortical neurons) and the reward (phasic dopamine release) whose strength, stored on MSN dendritic spines, is updated on a trial-to-trial basis. Dopaminergic compounds are assumed to alter the firing frequency of the cortical oscillatory neurons to cause the clock speed effects described above (Oprisan & Buhusi, 2011). However, because SBF stores criterion time spatially instead of using a pulse count, it has difficulties accounting for the quantitatively orderly "memory effects" of cholinergic compounds (Buhusi & Oprisan, 2013).

Summary The finding that the striatal MSNs receive convergent cortical inputs and that dopamine is implicated in reward timing has led to the development of the SBF model, which provides a neurobiological account of how a subject learns about when a rewarding event will occur. This model has many advantages. It proposes a timer that is distributed among a large population of cortical neurons, which sidesteps a problem faced by SET – that neurobiological studies so far have failed to find evidence of a single pacemaker capable of timing behaviorally relevant durations (e.g., Staddon, 2005). Another notable strength is that computer simulation has shown that SBF can predict scalar invariance of timing variability. Nonetheless, SBF is more designed to explain timing than conditioning, and it is currently unclear whether it can explain learning phenomena such as cue competition effects, although it is possible that a hybrid model integrating SBF's multiple-oscillator timing and Rescorla–Wagner-like update rules could do so. Finally, because of SBF's spatial representation of time, it cannot easily accommodate findings such as the proposed memory effects of cholinergic treatments. Perhaps, in this respect, neuroanatomical and electrophysiological findings that suggest how time might be represented neurally may constrain the types of model that are developed to explain timing effects. Alternatively, one could argue that if a theoretical model of timing is sufficiently powerful, it may not matter whether its neurobiological implementation is viable or not.

The model also has some general problems. We saw in section 4 that a large body of evidence implicates the hippocampus as playing an integral part in timing – yet SBF gives no role to this structure. The connection between the hippocampus and striatum is likely to play an important role in learning (Pennartz, Ito, Verschure, Battaglia, & Robbins, 2011; Yin & Meck, 2014), and future neurobiological theories of learning and timing will need to address the role played by both structures. Moreover, SBF places huge importance on the detection of reward by phasic dopamine – and yet the ability to time is not confined to appetitive events (Shionoya et al., 2013; Vogel et al., 2003) – although as we saw in section 5, the phasic dopamine response might be more general than was previously thought. Finally, the findings that the same neurobiological manipulation can have different timing effects on different tasks pose a problem for both trial-based associative theories and information-processing theories. Nonetheless, whether or not it turns out to be correct, the development of SBF has led to some interesting insights into the interaction between neuroscientific findings and our existing theoretical models.

Conclusions

We have reviewed the effects on associative learning of temporal factors in the second-to-minutes range. We have seen that associative learning entails the ability to encode in time the occurrence of surprising outcomes, and that learning is modulated by the interval between CS offset and the occurrence of such outcomes. Moreover, the level and speed of conditioning are very sensitive to the temporal relationship between the duration of the CS and the intertrial interval. Animals also modulate their rate of responding over the course of a CS, reflecting their ability to time US occurrence. We have discussed the ability of trial-based associative theories to explain such effects and compared them with the class of time-accumulation information-theoretic models. Our suggestion is that, on both theoretical and empirical grounds, the more recent generation of associative theories might have the edge in being able to provide a comprehensive account of conditioning and timing effects – although significant challenges remain.

We have also reviewed the evidence for neural mediators of these effects. We have seen that the hippocampus is strongly implicated in an animal's ability to time the occurrence of both appetitive and aversive outcomes, and that cell assemblies in this structure have shown firing patterns that seem capable of encoding both relative and absolute time. We have also suggested that the role of the hippocampus in trace conditioning – a deficit that is often viewed as diagnostic of damage to this structure – may be less ubiquitous than is widely believed, and may even be interpretable as secondary to a timing impairment. We have also described how the phasic dopamine response is a very plausible candidate for a mediator of temporal encoding of surprising outcomes, at least in the appetitive case, and so might be an example of how, more generally, conditioning is sensitive to this factor. We have discussed the effects of various pharmacological manipulations on timing behavior, and seen how these findings give us some insight into how a theoretical pacemaker might function. Finally, we have considered the role of the dorsal striatum in timing, and considered the strengths and weaknesses of the SBF model – one of the first attempts to develop a theory of timing in terms of neurobiological mechanisms. We hope that the material reviewed in this chapter gives a taste of the exciting research currently being undertaken on this topic, work that promises to give a greater insight into the important cognitive processes of associative learning and timing, and the neural mechanisms that underlie them.

Notes

1 By trial-based associative theory, we refer to a subset of theories employing the concept of association, but whose primary aim is to specify the mechanisms underlying *formation* of associations as a result of presentations of a CS that may or may not be followed by a US – such presentations being termed *trials*.
2 Even predictions about phenomena such as latent inhibition, in which the rate of acquisition of the CR is supposedly reduced following nonreinforced exposure to a CS, are typically evaluated by comparing levels of CR at different points of acquisition training.
3 In fact, the model never attempted to do so, although see Shapiro and Wearden (2001) for a proposal to introduce a scalar neural clock system within the TD model.
4 It would also predict that the spread of responding round the peak should be reduced in proportion to the timed interval, so that the scalar property of timing is maintained; but although a reduction in spread has been observed after damage to the whole hippocampus (Buhusi & Meck, 2002b), or lesions of the fimbria fornix (Meck, 1984), we found either no effect (Tam & Bonardi, 2012a, 2012b; although see Yin & Meck, 2014) or an increase in spread after dorsal hippocampal damage (Tam et al., 2013). This might suggest an additional, nonscalar source of timing error after these more specific lesions (see Tam et al., 2013).

References

Adamantidis, A. R., Tsai, H.-C., Boutrel, B., Zhang, F., Stuber, G. D., Budygin, E. A., Touriño, C., Bonci, A., Deisseroth, K., & de Lecea, L. (2011). Optogenetic interrogation of dopaminergic modulation of the multiple phases of reward-seeking behavior. *The Journal of Neuroscience*, *31*, 10829–10835.

Amaral, D. G., & Witter, M. P. (1989). The three-dimensional organization of the hippocampal formation: A review of anatomical data. *Neuroscience, 31,* 571–591.

Asgari, K., Body, S., Zhang, Z., Fone, K. C. F., Bradshaw, C. M., & Szabadi, E. (2006). Effects of 5-HT1A and 5-HT2A receptor stimulation on temporal differentiation performance in the fixed-interval peak procedure. *Behavioural Processes, 71,* 250–257.

Balci, F., Meck, W. H., Moore, H., & Brunner, D. (2009). Timing deficits in aging and neuropathology. In J. L. Bizon & A. Woods (Eds.), *Animal models of human cognitive aging* (pp. 1–41). Totowa, NJ: Humana Press.

Balsam, P. D. (1984). Relative time in trace conditioning. *Annals of the New York Academy of Sciences, 423,* 211–225.

Balsam, P. D., Drew, M. R., & Gallistel, C. R. (2010). Time and associative learning. *Comparative Cognition and Behavior Reviews, 5,* 1–22.

Balsam, P. D., & Gallistel, C. R. (2009). Temporal maps and informativeness in associative learning. *Trends in Neurosciences, 32,* 73–78.

Bangasser, D. A., Waxler, D. E., Santollo, J., & Shors, T. J. (2006). Trace conditioning and the hippocampus: The importance of contiguity. *Journal of Neuroscience, 26,* 8702–8706.

Bannerman, D. M., Yee, B. K., Good, M. A., Heupel, M. J., Iversen, S. D., & Rawlins, J. N. P. (1999). Double dissociation of function within the hippocampus: A comparison of dorsal, ventral, and complete hippocampal cytotoxic lesions. *Behavioral Neuroscience, 113,* 1170–1188.

Berridge, K. C., & Robinson, T. E. (1998). What is the role of dopamine in reward: hedonic impact, reward learning, or incentive salience? *Brain Research Reviews, 28,* 309–369.

Bizo, L. A., & White, K. G. (1997). Timing with controlled reinforcer density: Implications for models of timing. *Journal of Experimental Psychology: Animal Behavior Processes, 23,* 44–55.

Body, S., Cheung, T. H. C., Bezzina, G., Asgari, K., Fone, K. C. F., & Glennon, J. C., Bradshaw, C. M., & Szabadi, E. (2006). Effects of D-amphetamine and DOI (2,5-dimethoxy-4-iodoamphetamine) on timing behavior: interaction between D-1 and 5-HT2A receptors. *Psychopharmacology, 189,* 331–343.

Body, S., Kheramin, S., Ho, M-Y., Miranda, F., Bradshaw, C. M., & Szabadi, E. (2003). Effects of a 5-HT2 receptor agonist, DOI (2,5-dimethoxy-4-iodoamphetamine), and antagonist, ketanserin, on the performance of rats on a free-operant timing schedule. *Behavioral Pharmacology, 14,* 599–607.

Bonardi, C., & Jennings, D. J. (2014). *Blocking by fixed and variable duration stimuli.* Manuscript in preparation.

Bonardi, C., Mondragón, E., Brilot, B., & Jennings, D. J. (2015). Overshadowing by fixed- and variable-duration stimuli. *The Quarterly Journal of Experimental Psychology, 68,* 523–542.

Bouton, M. E. (1993). Context, time, and memory retrieval in the interference paradigms of Pavlovian learning. *Psychological Bulletin, 114,* 80–99.

Bouton, M. E., & Sunsay, C. (2003). Importance of trials versus accumulating time across trials in partially reinforced appetitive conditioning. *Journal of Experimental Psychology: Animal Behavior Processes, 29,* 62–77.

Bouton, M. E., Woods, A. M., & Todd, P. T. (2014). Separation of time-based and trial-based accounts of the partial reinforcement extinction effect. *Behavioural Processes, 101,* 23–31.

Braggio, J. T., & Ellen, P. (1976). Cued DRL training – effects on permanence of lesion-induced overresponding. *Journal of Comparative and Physiological Psychology, 90,* 694–703.

Buhusi, C. V., & Meck, W. H. (2002a). Differential effects of methamphetamine and haloperidol on the control of an internal clock. *Behavioral Neuroscience, 116,* 291–297.

Buhusi, C. V., & Meck, W. H. (2002b). Ibotenic acid lesions of the hippocampus disrupt attentional control of interval timing. *Society for Neuroscience Abstracts,* Abstract No. *183.*10.

Buhusi, C. V., & Oprisan, S. (2013). Time-scale invariance as an emergent property in a perceptron with realistic, noisy neurons. *Behavioural Processes, 95*, 60–70.

Burman, M. A., Starr, M. J., & Gewirtz, J. C. (2006). Dissociable effects of hippocampus lesions on expression of fear and trace fear conditioning memories in rats. *Hippocampus, 16*, 103–113.

Chan, K., Shipman, M. L., & Kister, E. (2014). Selective hippocampal lesions impair acquisition of appetitive trace conditioning with long intertrial interval and long trace intervals. *Behavioral Neuroscience, 128*, 92–102.

Cheung, T. H. C., Bezzina, G. Body, S., Fone, K. C. F., Bradshaw, C. M., & Szabadi, E. (2007a). Tolerance to the effect of 2,5-dimethoxy-4-iodoamphetamine (DOI) on free-operant timing behaviour: interaction between behavioural and pharmacological mechanisms. *Psychopharmacology, 192*, 521–535.

Cheung, T. H. C., Bezzina,G., Hampson, C. L., Body, S., Fone, K. C. F., Bradshaw, C. M., & Szabadi, E. (2007b). Effect of quinpirole on timing behaviour in the free-operant psychophysical procedure: evidence for the involvement of D-2 dopamine receptors. *Psychopharmacology, 193*, 423–436.

Cheung, T. H. C., & Cardinal, R. N. (2005). Hippocampal lesions facilitate instrumental learning with delayed reinforcement but induce impulsive choice in rats. *BMC Neuroscience, 6*, 36.

Church, R. M., & Broadbent, H. A. (1990). Alternative representations of time, number and rate. *Cognition, 37*, 55–81.

Clark, C. V. H., & Isaacson, R. L. (1965). Effect of bilateral hippocampal ablation on DRL performance. *Journal of Comparative and Physiological Psychology, 59*, 137–140.

Clark, J. J., Collins, A. L., Sanford, C. A., & Phillips, P. E. M. (2013). Dopamine encoding of Pavlovian incentive stimuli diminishes with extended training. *Journal of Neuroscience, 33*, 3526–3532.

Costa, V. C. I., Bueno, J. L. O., & Xavier, G. F. (2005). Dentate gyrus-selective colchicine lesion and performance in temporal and spatial tasks. *Behavioural Brain Research, 160*, 286–303.

Coull, J. T., Cheng, R. K., & Meck, W. H. (2011). Neuroanatomical and Neurochemical substrates of timing. *Neuropsychopharmacology, 36*, 3–25.

Davidson, T. L., & Jarrard, L. E. (2004). The hippocampus and inhibitory learning: A "Gray" area? *Neuroscience and Biobehavioral Reviews, 28*, 261–271.

Day, J. J., Roitman, M. F., Wightman, R. M., & Carelli, R. M. (2007). Associative learning mediates dynamic shifts in dopamine signaling in the nucleus accumbens. *Nature Neuroscience, 10*, 1020–1028.

Delacour, J., & Houcine, O. (1987). Conditioning to time: evidence for a role of hippocampus from unit recording. *Neuroscience, 23*, 87–94.

Drew, M. R., Fairhurst, S., Malapani, C., Horvitz, J. C., & Balsam, P. D. (2003). Effects of dopamine antagonists on the timing of two intervals. *Pharmacology Biochemistry and Behavior, 75*, 9–15.

Fendt, M., Fanselow, M. S., & Koch, M. (2005). Lesions of the dorsal hippocampus block trace fear conditioned potentiation of startle. *Behavioral Neuroscience, 119*, 834–838.

Fiorillo, C. D., Song, M. R., & Yun, S. R. (2013). Multiphasic temporal dynamics in responses of midbrain dopamine neurons to appetitive and aversive stimuli. *Journal of Neuroscience, 33*, 4710–4725.

Fiorillo, C. D., Yun, S. R., & Song, M. R. (2013). Diversity and homogeneity in responses of midbrain dopamine neurons. *Journal of Neuroscience, 33*, 4693–4709.

Fraisse, P. (1963). *The psychology of time.* Translated by J. Leith. New York, NY: Harper & Row.

Frederick, D. L., & Allen, J. D. (1996). Effects of selective dopamine D1- and D2-agonists and antagonists on timing performance in rats. *Pharmacology Biochemistry and Behavior, 53*, 759–764.

Gallistel, C. R., Craig, A. R., & Shahan, T. A. (2014). Temporal contingency. *Behavioural Processes, 101*, 89–96.

Gallistel, C. R., & Gibbon, J. (2000). Time, rate and conditioning. *Psychological Review, 107*, 289–344.

Garcia, J., & Koelling, R. A. (1966). Relation of cue to consequence in avoidance learning. *Psychonomic Science, 5*, 121–122.

Gibbon, J. (1977). Scalar expectancy theory and Weber's law in animal timing. *Psychological Review, 84*, 279–325.

Gibbon, J. (1991). Origins of scalar timing. *Learning and Motivation, 22*, 3–38.

Gibbon, J., Baldock, M. D., Locurto, C., Gold, L., & Terrace, H. S. (1977). Trial and intertrial intervals in autoshaping. *Journal of Experimental Psychology: Animal Behavior Processes, 3*, 264–284.

Gilmartin, M. R., & McEchron, M. D. (2005). Single neurons in the dentate gyrus and CA1 of the hippocampus exhibit inverse patterns of encoding during trace fear conditioning. *Behavioral Neuroscience, 119*, 164–179.

Gold, P. E. (2003). Acetylcholine modulation of neural systems involved in learning and memory. *Neurobiology of Learning and Memory, 80*, 194–210.

Good, M. A., Barnes, P., Staal, V., McGregor, A., & Honey, R. C. (2007). Context- but not familiarity-dependent forms of object recognition are impaired following excitotoxic hippocampal lesions in rats. *Behavioral Neuroscience, 121*, 218–223.

Gray, J., Alonso, E., Mondragón, E., & Fernández, A (2012). *Temporal difference simulator © V.1 [Computer software]*. London, UK: CAL-R. Retrieved from http://www.cal-r.org/index.php?id=software)

Harris, J. A. (2011). The acquisition of conditioned responding. *Journal of Experimental Psychology: Animal Behavior Processes, 37*, 151–164.

Hebb, D. O. (1949). *The organization of behavior*. Wiley: New York.

Hoge, J., & Kesner, R. P. (2007). Role of CA3 and CA1 subregions of the dorsal hippocampus on temporal processing of objects. *Neurobiology of Learning and Memory, 88*, 225–231.

Holland, P. C. (2000). Trial and intertrial interval durations in appetitive conditioning in rats. *Animal Learning and Behavior, 28*, 121–135.

Hollerman, J. R., & Schultz, W. (1998). Dopamine neurons report an error in the temporal prediction of reward during learning. *Nature Neuroscience, 1*, 304–309.

Hunsaker, M. R., Fieldsted, P. M., Rosenberg, J. S., & Kesner, R. P. (2008). Evaluating the differential roles of the dorsal dentate gyrus, dorsal CA3, and dorsal CA1 during a temporal ordering for spatial locations task. *Hippocampus, 18*, 955–964.

Hunsaker, M. R., & Kesner, R. P. (2008). Dissociating the roles of dorsal and ventral CA1 for the temporal processing of spatial locations, visual objects, and odors. *Behavioral Neuroscience, 122*, 643–650.

Jaldow, E. J., & Oakley, D. A. (1990). Performance on a differential reinforcement of low-rate schedule in neodecorticated rats and rats with hippocampal esions. *Psychobiology, 18*, 394–403.

Jarrard, L. E., & Becker, J. T. (1977). The effects of selective hippocampal lesions on DRL behavior in rats. *Behavioral Biology, 21*, 393–404.

Jennings, D. J., Alonso, E., Mondragón, E., Franssen, M., & Bonardi, C. (2013). The effect of stimulus duration distribution form on the acquisition and rate of conditioned responding. *Journal of Experimental Psychology: Animal Behavior Processes, 39*, 233–248.

Jin, D. Z. Z., Fujii, N., & Graybiel, A. M. (2009). Neural representation of time in cortico-basal ganglia circuits. *Proceedings of the National Academy of Sciences of the United States of America, 106*, 19156–19161.

Johnson, C. T., Olton, D. S., Gage, F. H., & Jenko, P. G. (1977). Damage to hippocampus and hippocampal connections: Effects on DRL and spontaneous alternation. *Journal of Comparative and Physiological Psychology, 91*, 508–522.

Kehoe, E. J., Ludvig, E. A., & Sutton, R. S. (2009). Magnitude and timing of conditioned responses in delay and trace classical conditioning of the nictitating membrane response of the rabbit (*Oryctolagus cuniculus*). *Behavioral Neuroscience, 123,* 1095–1101.

Kesner, R. P. (1998). Neural mediation of memory for time: Role of the hippocampus and medial prefrontal cortex. *Psychonomic Bulletin and Review, 5,* 585–596.

Killeen, P. R., & Fetterman, J. G. (1988). A behavioral theory of timing. *Psychological Review, 95,* 274–295.

Killeen, P. R., Sanabria, F., & Dolgov, I. (2009). The dynamics of conditioning and extinction. *Journal of Experimental Psychology: Animal Behavior Processes, 35,* 447–472.

Kim, J., Jung, A. H., Byun, J., Jo, S., & Jung, M. W. (2009). Inactivation of medial prefrontal cortex impairs time interval discrimination in rats. *Frontiers in Behavioral Neuroscience, 3,* 9.

Kirkpatrick, K., & Church, R. M. (1998). Are separate theories of conditioning and timing necessary *Behavioral Processes, 44,* 163–182.

Kirkpatrick, K., & Church, R. M. (2000). Independent effects of stimulus and cycle duration in conditioning: The role of timing processes. *Animal Learning and Behavior, 28,* 373–388.

Lattal, K. M. (1999). Trial and intertrial durations in Pavlovian conditioning: Issues of learning and performance. *Journal of Experimental Psychology: Animal Behavior Processes, 25,* 433–450.

Lin, T.-C. E., & Honey, R. C. (2011). Encoding specific associative memory: Evidence from behavioral and neural manipulations. *Journal of Experimental Psychology: Animal Behavior Processes, 37,* 317–329.

Ljungberg, T., Apicella, P., & Schultz, W. (1991). Responses of monkey midbrain dopamine neurons during delayed alternation performance. *Brain Research, 567,* 337–341.

Ludvig, E. A., Sutton, R. S., & Kehoe, E. J. (2012). Evaluating the TD model of classical conditioning. *Learning and Behavior, 40,* 305–319.

MacDonald, C. J., Lepage, K. Q., Eden, U. T., & Eichenbaum, H. (2011). Hippocampal "time cells" bridge the gap in memory for discontiguous events. *Neuron, 25,* 737–749.

MacDonald, C. J., & Meck, W. H. (2005). Differential effects of clozapine and haloperidol on interval timing in the supraseconds range. *Psychopharmacology, 182,* 232–244.

Machado, A. (1997). Learning the temporal dynamics of behavior. *Psychological Review, 104,* 241–265.

Machado, A., Malheiro, M. T., & Erlhagen, W. (2009). Learning to Time: A Perspective. *Journal of the Experimental Analysis of Behavior, 92,* 423–458.

Mackintosh, N. J. (1975). A theory of attention: variation in the associability of stimuli with reinforcement. *Psychological Review, 82,* 276–298.

Maren, S., Aharonov, G., & Fanselow, M. S. (1997). Neurotoxic lesions of the dorsal hippocampus and Pavlovian fear conditioning in rats. *Behavioural Brain Research, 88,* 261–274.

Maricq, A. V., Roberts, S., & Church, R. M. (1981). Methamphetamine and time estimation. *Journal of Experimental Psychology: Animal Behavior Processes, 7,* 18–30.

Matell, M. S., King, G. R., & Meck, W. H. (2004). Differential modulation of clock speed by the administration of intermittent versus continuous cocaine. *Behavioral Neuroscience, 118,* 150–156.

Matell, M. S., & Meck, W. H. (2000). Neuropsychological mechanisms of interval timing behavior. *Bioessays, 22,* 94–103.

Matell, M. S., & Meck, W. H. (2004). Cortico-striatal circuits and interval timing: coincidence detection of oscillatory processes. *Cognitive Brain Research, 21,* 139–170.

Matell, M. S., Meck, W. H., & Nicolelis, M. A. L. (2003). Interval timing and the encoding of signal duration by ensembles of cortical and striatal neurons. *Behavioral Neuroscience, 117,* 760–773.

Matsumoto, M., & Hikosaka, O. (2009). Two types of dopamine neuron distinctly convey positive and negative motivational signals. *Nature*, *459*, 837–841.

McCormick, D. A., & Thompson, D. A. (1984). Cerebellum – Essential involvement in the classically conditioned eyelid response. *Science*, *223*, 296–299.

McEchron, M. D., Bouwmeester, H., Tseng, W., Weiss, C., & Disterhoft, J. F. (1998). Hippocampectomy disrupts auditory trace fear conditioning and contextual fear conditioning in rat. *Hippocampus*, *8*, 638–646.

McEchron, M. D., Tseng, W., & Disterhoft, J. F. (2003). Single neurons in CA1 hippocampus encode trace interval duration during trace heart rate (fear) conditioning in rabbit. *Journal of Neuroscience*, *23*, 1535–1547.

Meck, W. H. (1984). Attentional bias between modalities: Effect on the internal clock, memory, and decision stages used in animal time discrimination. *Annals of the New York Academy of Sciences*, *423*, 528–541.

Meck, W. H. (1988). Hippocampal function is required for feedback control of an internal clock's criterion. *Behavioral Neuroscience*, *102*, 54–60.

Meck, W. H. (1996). Neuropharmacology of timing and time perception. *Cognition and Brain Research*, *3*, 227–242.

Meck, W. H. (2006). Neuroanatomical localization of an internal clock: A functional link between mesolimbic, nigrostriatal, and mesocortical dopaminergic systems. *Brain Research*, *1109*, 93–107.

Meck, W. H., Church, R. M., & Matell, M. S. (2013). Hippocampus, time, and memory – A retrospective analysis. *Behavioral Neuroscience*, *127*, 642–654.

Meck, W. H., Church, R. M., & Olton, D. S. (1984). Hippocampus, time, and memory. *Behavioral Neuroscience*, *98*, 3–22.

Meck, W. H., & Malapani, C. (2004). Neuroimaging of interval timing. *Cognitive Brain Research*, *21*, 133–137.

Mitchell, J. B., & Laiacona, J. (1998). The medial frontal cortex and temporal memory: Tests using spontaneous exploratory behaviour in the rat. *Behavioural Brain Research*, *97*, 107–113.

Mondragón, E., Gray, J., & Alonso, E. (2013). A complete serial compound temporal difference simulator for compound stimuli, configural cues and context representation. *Neuroinformatics*, *11*, 259–261.

Mondragón, E., Gray, J., Alonso, E., Bonardi, C., & Jennings, D. J. (2014). SSCC TD: a serial and simultaneous configural-cue compound stimuli representation for temporal difference learning. *PLOS One*, *23*, e102469.

Montague, P. R., Dayan, P., & Sejnowski, T. J. (1996). A framework for mesencephalic dopamine systems based on predictive Hebbian learning. *Journal of Neuroscience*, *16*, 1936–1947.

Moore, J. W., Choi, J., & Brunzell, D. H. (1998). Predictive timing under temporal uncertainty: the TD model of the conditioned response. In D. Rosenbaum, & A. C. E. Collyer (Eds.), *Timing of behavior: neural, computational, and psychological perspectives* (pp. 3–34). Cambridge, MA: MIT Press.

Naya, Y., & Suzuki, W. A. (2011). Integrating what and when across the primate medial temporal lobe. *Science*, *333*, 773–776.

Ohyama, T., Horvitz, J. C., Kitsos, E., & Balsam, P. D. (2001). The role of dopamine in the timing of Pavlovian conditioned keypecking in ring doves. *Pharmacology Biochemistry and Behavior*, *69*, 617–627.

Olton, D. S. (1986). Hippocampal function and memory for temporal context. In R. L. Isaacson & K. H. Pribram (Eds.), *The hippocampus* (Vol. 4). New York, NY: Plenum Press.

Olton, D. S., Meck, W. H., & Church, R. M. (1987). Separation of hippocampal and amygdaloid involvement in temporal memory dysfunctions. *Brain Research*, *404*, 180–188.

Olton, D. S., Wenk, G. L., Church, R. M., & Meck, W. H. (1988). Attention and the frontal cortex as examined by simultaneous temporal processing. *Neuropsychologia, 26,* 307–318.

Oprisan, S., & Buhusi, C. V. (2011). Modelling pharmacological clock and memory patterns of interval timing in a striatal beat-frequency model with realistic noisy neurons. *Frontiers in Integrative Neuroscience, 5,* 60–70.

Pan, W. X., Schmidt, R., Wickens, J. R., & Hyland, B. I. (2005). Dopamine cells respond to predicted events during classical conditioning: Evidence for eligibility traces in the reward-learning network. *Journal of Neuroscience, 25,* 52.

Parker, J. G., Zweifel, L. S., Clark, J. J., Evans, S. B., Phillips, P. E. M., & Palmiter, R. D. (2010). Absence of NMDA receptors in dopamine neurons attenuates dopamine release but not conditioned approach in Pavlovian conditioning. *Proceedings of the National Academy of Sciences, 107,* 13492–13496.

Pavlov, I. (1927). *Conditioned reflexes.* Oxford University Press.

Pearce, J. M., & Hall, G. (1980). A model for Pavlovian learning: Variations in the effectiveness of conditioned but not of unconditioned stimuli. *Psychological Review, 87,* 532–552.

Pennartz, C. M. A., Ito, R., Verschure, P. F. M. J., Battaglia, F. P., & Robbins, T. W. (2011). The hippocampal–striatal axis in learning, prediction and goal-directed behavior. *Trends in Neurosciences, 34,* 548–559.

Perkins, C. C., Beavers, W. O., Hancock, R. A., Hemmendinger, P. C., Hemmendinger, D., & Ricci, J. A. (1975). Some variables affecting rate of key pecking during response-independent procedures (autoshaping). *Journal of the Experimental Analysis of Behavior, 24,* 59–72.

Power, A. E., Vazdarjanova, A., & McGaugh, J. L. (2003). Muscarinic cholinergic influences in memory consolidation. *Neurobiology of Learning and Memory, 80,* 178–193.

Rawlins, J. N. P. (1985). Associations across time: The hippocampus as a emporary memory store. *Behavioral and Brain Sciences, 8,* 479–497.

Rawlins, J. N. P., & Tanner, J. (1998). The effects of hippocampal aspiration lesions on conditioning to the CS and to a background stimulus in trace conditioned suppression. *Behavioural Brain Research, 91,* 61–72.

Rawlins, J. N. P., Winocur, G., & Gray, J. A. (1983). The hippocampus, collateral behavior, and timing. *Behavioral Neuroscience, 97,* 857–872.

Redgrave, P., Gurney, K., & Reynolds, J. (2008). What is reinforced by phasic dopamine signals? *Brain Research Reviews, 58,* 322–339.

Rescorla, R. A., & Wagner, A. R. (1972). A theory of Pavlovian conditioning: Variations in the effectiveness of reinforcement. In A. H. Black & W. F. Prokasy (Eds.), *Classical conditioning: II. Theory and research* (pp. 64–99). New York, NY: Appleton-Century-Crofts.

Rickert, E. J., Bennett, T. L., Anderson, G. J., Corbett, J., & Smith, L. (1973). Differential performance of hippocampally ablated rats on nondiscriminated and discriminated DRL schedules. *Behavioral Biology, 8,* 597–609.

Richmond, M. A., Yee, B. K., Pouzet, B., Veenman, L., Rawlins, J. N. P., Feldon, J., & Bannerman, D. M. (1999). Dissociating context and space within the hippocampus: Effects of complete, dorsal, and ventral excitotoxic hippocampal lesions on conditioned freezing and spatial learning. *Behavioral Neuroscience, 113,* 1189–1203.

Romo, R., & Schultz, W. (1990). Dopamine neurons of the monkey midbrain: contingencies of responses to active touch during self-initiated arm movements. *Journal of Neurophysiology, 63,* 592–606.

Ross, R. T., Orr, W. B., Holland, P. C., & Berger, T. W. (1984). Hippocampectomy disrupts acquisition and retention of learned conditional responding. *Behavioral Neuroscience, 98,* 211–225.

Rossi, M. A., Sukharnikova, T., Hayrapetyan, V. Y., Yang, L., & Yin, H. H. (2013). Operant self-stimulation of dopamine neurons in the substantia nigra. *Plos One, 8,* e65799.

Sakata, S. (2006). Timing and hippocampal theta in animals. *Reviews in Neurosciences*, *17*, 157–162.
Saulsgiver, K. A., McClure, E. A., & Wynne, C. D. L. (2006). Effects of D-amphetamine on the behavior of pigeons exposed to the peak procedure. *Behavioural Processes*, *71*, 268–285.
Schultz, W. (2002). Getting formal with dopamine and reward. *Neuron*, *36*, 241–263.
Schultz, W. (2006). Behavioral theories and the neurophysiology of reward. *Annual Review of Psychology*, *57*, 87–115
Schultz, W. (2010). Dopamine signals for reward value and risk: basic and recent data. *Behavioral Brain Function*, *6*, 9.
Schultz, W., & Romo, R. (1990). Dopamine neurons of the monkey midbrain: contingencies of responses to stimuli eliciting immediate behavioral reactions. *Journal of Neurophysiology*, *63*, 607–624.
Shapiro, J. L., & Wearden, J. (2001). Reinforcement learning and time perception – a model of animal experiments. Paper presented at 25th Annual Conference on Neural Information Processing Systems (NIPS) (pp. 115–122). Cambridge, MA: MIT Press. Granada, Spain, December 12–17. eScholarID:2h1115.
Shionoya, K., Hegoburu, C., Brown, B. L., Sullivan, R. M., Doyère, V., & Mouly, A. M. (2013). It's time to fear! Interval timing in odor fear conditioning in rats. *Frontiers in Behavioral Neuroscience*, *7*. 10.3389/fnbeh.2013.00128.
Sinden, J. D., Rawlins, J. N. P., Gray, J. A., & Jarrard, L. E. (1986). Selective cytotoxic lesions of the hippocampal formation and DRL performance in rats. *Behavioral Neuroscience*, *100*, 320–329.
Staddon, J. R. (2005). Interval timing: memory, not a clock. *Trends in Cognitive Neuroscience*, *9*, 312–314.
Stubbs, D. A. (1980). Temporal discrimination and a free-operant psychophysical procedure. *Journal of the Experimental Analysis of Behavior*, *33*, 167–185.
Sutton, R. S., & Barto, A. G. (1987). *A temporal difference model of classical conditioning* (Technical Report No. TR 87-509.2). Waltham, MA: GTE Lab.
Sutton, R. S., & Barto, A. G. (1990). Time derivative models of Pavlovian reinforcement. In M. R. Gabriel & J. W. Moore (Eds.), *Learning and computational neuroscience: Foundations of adaptive networks* (pp. 497–537). Cambridge, MA: MIT Press.
Sunsay, C., & Bouton, M. E. (2008). Analysis of a trial-spacing effect with relatively long intertrial intervals. *Learning and Behavior*, *36*, 104–115.
Sunsay, C., & Rebec, G. V. (2008). Real-time dopamine efflux in the nucleus accumbens core during Pavlovian conditioning. *Behavioral Neuroscience*, *122*, 358–367.
Sunsay, C., Stetson, L., & Bouton, M. E. (2004). Memory priming and trial-spacing effects in Pavlovian learning. *Learning and Behavior*, *32*, 220–229.
Tam, S. K. E. (2011). *The role of the dorsal hippocampus in learning*. Unpublished doctoral thesis, University of Nottingham.
Tam, S. K. E., & Bonardi, C. (2012a). Dorsal hippocampal involvement in appetitive trace conditioning and interval timing. *Behavioral Neuroscience*, *126*, 258–269.
Tam, S. K. E., & Bonardi, C. (2012b). Dorsal hippocampal lesions disrupt Pavlovian delay conditioning and conditioned-response timing. *Behavioural Brain Research*, *230*, 259–267.
Tam, S. K. E., Jennings, D. J., & Bonardi, C. (2013). Dorsal hippocampal involvement in conditioned-response timing and maintenance of temporal information in the absence of the CS. *Experimental Brain Research*, *227*, 547–559.
Terrace, H.S, Gibbon, J., Farrell, L., & Baldock, M. D. (1975). Temporal factors influencing the acquisition and maintenance of an autoshaped keypeck. *Animal Learning and Behavior Processes*, *3*, 53–62.
Thibaudeau, G., Doré, F. Y., & Goulet, S. (2009). Additional evidence for intact appetitive trace conditioning in hippocampal-lesioned rats. *Behavioral Neuroscience*, *123*, 707–712.

Thibaudeau, G., Potvin, O., Allen, K., Doré, F. Y., & Goulet, S. (2007). Dorsal, ventral, and complete excitotoxic lesions of the hippocampus in rats failed to impair appetitive trace conditioning. *Behavioural Brain Research, 185*, 9–20.

Trivedi, M. A., & Coover, G. D. (2006). Neurotoxic lesions of the dorsal and ventral hippocampus impair acquisition and expression of trace-conditioned fear-potentiated startle in rats. *Behavioural Brain Research, 168*, 289–298.

Ungless, M. A. (2004). Dopamine: the salient issue. *Trends in Neurosciences, 27*, 702–706.

Valencia-Torres, L., Olarte-Sanchez, C. M., Body, S., Cheung, T. H. C., Fone, K. C. F., Bradshaw, C. M., & Szabadi, E. (2012a). Fos expression in the prefrontal cortex and ventral striatum after exposure to a free-operant timing schedule. *Behavioural Brain Research, 235*, 273–279.

Valencia-Torres, L., Olarte-Sanchez, C. M., Body, S., Fone, K. C. F., Bradshaw, C. M., & Szabadi, E. (2011). Fos expression in the prefrontal cortex and nucleus accumbens following exposure to retrospective timing tasks. *Behavioral Neuroscience, 125*, 202–214.

Valencia-Torres, L., Olarte-Sanchez, C. M., Body, S., Fone, K. C. F., Bradshaw, C. M., & Szabadi, E. (2012b). Fos expression in the orbital prefrontal cortex after exposure to the fixed-interval peak procedure. *Behavioural Brain Research, 229*, 372–377.

Vogel, E. H., Brandon, S. E., & Wagner, A. R. (2003). Stimulus representation in SOP: II. An application to inhibition of delay. *Behavioural Processes, 62*, 27–48.

Waelti, P., Dickinson, A., & Schultz, W. (2001). Dopamine responses comply with basic assumptions of formal learning theory. *Nature, 412*, 43–48.

Wagner, A. R. (1981). SOP: A model of automatic memory processing in animals. In N. E. Miller & R.R. Spear (Eds.), *Information processes in animals: Memory mechanisms* (pp. 95–128). Hillsdale, NJ: Erlbaum.

White, N. E., Kehoe, E. J., Choi, J. S., & Moore, J. W. (2000). Coefficients of variation in timing of the classically conditioned eyeblink in rabbits. *Psychobiology, 28*, 520–524.

Wiener, S. I., Paul, C. A., & Eichenbaum, H. (1989). Spatial and behavioral-correlates of hippocampal neuronal-activity. *Journal of Neuroscience, 9*, 2737–2763.

Wilson, C. J. (1995). The contribution of cortical neurons to the firing pattern of striatal spiny neurons. In J. C. Houk, J. L. Davis, & D. G. Beiser (Eds.), *Models of information processing in the basal ganglia* (pp. 29–50). Cambridge, MA: MIT Press.

Winton-Brown, T. T., Fusar-Poli, P., Ungless, M. A., & Howes, O. D. (2014). Dopaminergic basis of salience dysregulation in psychosis. *Trends in Neurosciences, 27*, 85–94.

Yin, B., & Meck, W. H. (2014). Comparison of interval timing behaviour in mice following dorsal or ventral hippocampal lesions with mice having d-opiod receptor gene deletion. *Philosophical Transactions of the Royal Society, 369*.

Yoon, T., & Otto, T. (2007). Differential contributions of dorsal vs ventral hippocampus to auditory trace fear conditioning. *Neurobiology of Learning and Memory, 87*, 464–475.

Young, B., & McNaughton, N. (2000). Common firing patterns of hippocampal cells in a differential reinforcement of low rates of response schedule. *Journal of Neuroscience, 20*, 7043–7051.

15
Human Learning About Causation
Irina Baetu and Andy G. Baker

Humans and animals can detect contingencies between events in the world, and initiate a course of action based on this information. Moreover, this behavior often meets the criterion of rational generative transmission, but the constituents of our neurobiology are probably not individually rational. One of the challenges for neuroscience is to bridge the gap between neurons that individually are not rational and actions of the whole organism that, at least, appear to be rational. This is also the main challenge of associationism. We discuss possible mechanisms, which are not themselves made up of rational elements, that would allow people to process empirical causal evidence and behave rationally. The parallels between human causal learning and animal learning suggest common mechanisms, which might be associative in nature (e.g., Baker *et al.*, 1996; Dickinson, Shanks, & Evenden, 1984). Here, we show how associative models that were developed to describe animal conditioning phenomena, and which on the surface at least are analogous to neural structure, can be used to explain how people infer causal relationships between observed events.

Learning About Generative Causes

In the simplest case, both cause and outcome are binary events (i.e., they either occur or do not occur). If a generative cause truly generates an outcome, then when the cause occurs, the outcome should be more likely to follow than when the cause does not occur. Here we discuss the associative mechanisms that might give rise to the perception that a cause generates an outcome from experience with the two events.

Associative models posit that experiencing various events occurring together, or separately, changes the connections between the internal representations of these events. A potential cause, or cue, that is frequently followed by the occurrence of an outcome is assumed to become associated with it. Subsequently, presentation of the cue alone will retrieve the memory of the outcome via this shared connection. This mechanism simulates how one is able to anticipate a future event (the outcome) based on past experience with the cue–outcome relationship. According to the associative approach, the contingency between the cue and the outcome and their temporal contiguity are not consciously used to evaluate a causal relationship; rather,

---

The Wiley Handbook on the Cognitive Neuroscience of Learning, First Edition.
Edited by Robin A. Murphy and Robert C. Honey.
© 2016 John Wiley & Sons, Ltd. Published 2016 by John Wiley & Sons, Ltd.

they dictate whether the conditions are favorable for the cue–outcome association to be learned, and it is this association, once formed, that generates our perception of causality. In their simplest form, purely associative models assume that we react to causal structures rather than understand them. This often results in adaptive behavior and sensitivity to causal relationships. Importantly, postulating a simple associative mechanism does not preclude some higher process using the output of the associator to deduce the causal structure. Such a reasoning mechanism, however, is often not necessary to behave adaptively and may be less parsimonious.

Role of redundancy in the perception of causality

One of the most important findings in the associative learning literature is that repeated cue–outcome pairings are not always sufficient to produce learning of a cue–outcome relationship. There is evidence suggesting that learning the relationship proceeds more readily if the cue conveys unique information about the occurrence of the outcome. This is well demonstrated by the *blocking effect* (Kamin, 1969), which has been shown in a variety of species and preparations, including human causal learning (e.g., Shanks, 1985). In a blocking design, participants first learn that a cue (A) predicts an outcome (A–Outcome), and then observe the same outcome follow a combination of that cue and a novel, target, cue (AX–Outcome; see Table 15.1). The participants' causal ratings of the target cue X are typically lower than ratings of a control cue (Y) that is presented with a cue that has never been paired with the outcome in Phase 1. Thus, learning that the first cue (A) signals, or causes, the outcome seems to reduce, or "block," learning that the target cue (X) is also a predictor of the outcome.

There are several possible explanations for the blocking effect. The initial training with A might block the expression of a learned X–Outcome relationship during the test (Miller & Matzel, 1988), or might change the extent to which X is processed (Mackintosh, 1975). Alternatively, one could argue that the blocking effect suggests that we learn only the information that is necessary to predict the near future and ignore redundant information. In the blocking design, cue A is sufficient to predict every outcome, making X redundant. This latter interpretation has led to the development of models that attempt to capture this redundancy. It seems that a cue–outcome association is changed only if the organism fails to anticipate the occurrence or nonoccurrence of the outcome. This idea was formalized in Rescorla and Wagner's (1972) model and is at the heart of many other associative models (e.g., Baetu & Baker, 2009, Delamater, 2012; Graham, 1999; Ludvig, Sutton, & Kehoe, 2012; McLaren & Mackintosh, 2000; Schmajuk, Lam, & Gray, 1996; Thorwart, Livesey, & Harris, 2012). The finding that little seems to be learned about redundant cues using

Table 15.1 Typical design and results of a blocking experiment.

Condition	Training Phase 1	Training Phase 2	Test	Typical Blocking Effect
Blocking	A–Outcome	AX–Outcome	X	X is considered to be a weaker predictor of the Outcome than Y
Control (Overshadowing)		BY–Outcome	Y	

the blocking and other experimental designs (Baker, Mercier, Vallée-Tourangeau, Frank, & Pan, 1993; Wagner et al., 1968) also implies that learning requires an outcome that is poorly anticipated or, in other words, surprising (Kamin, 1969).

Redundancy implemented in an error-correction rule

One way in which redundancy might affect associative learning is through associative change being a function of prediction error. Prediction error can be thought of as a formalization of surprise. A connection between a cue and an outcome is altered only if the occurrence or nonoccurrence of the outcome is surprising. On every trial, the change in the strength of a cue–outcome connection is directly related to the difference between the experienced outcome and the expectation of the outcome retrieved from memory.

$$\text{Prediction Error} = \text{Experienced Outcome} - \text{Expected Outcome} \quad (15.1)$$

The first time an outcome follows a cue, the outcome should generate a strong positive prediction error because it was not anticipated. This is assumed to strengthen the cue–outcome association. Following repeated cue–outcome pairings, the cue–outcome association allows the cue to retrieve the memory of the outcome, which, in turn, reduces the prediction error. Thus, this rule updates associations in order to better approximate the outcome's occurrence and reduce prediction error in the future (see Chapter 3).

Most error-correction models assume that the expectation of the outcome on every trial is generated by all cues present on that trial (e.g., Graham, 1999; McLaren & Mackintosh, 2000; Pearce, 1994; Rescorla & Wagner, 1972). If one of the presented cues reduces the prediction error, then all cue–outcome associations will remain largely unchanged. This mechanism ensures that redundant cues (i.e., cues that do not uniquely signal the outcome) are learned about less. This mechanism can explain the blocking effect (Table 15.1) and other related phenomena (see Miller, Barnet, & Grahame, 1995, for a review). When the target cue X is introduced on AX–Outcome trials, the outcome is already predicted by A (because of the earlier A–Outcome pairings), and there is no opportunity for the X → Outcome connection to strengthen because there is little prediction error. Thus, despite the fact that X and the outcome are repeatedly paired, an association between the two does not form.

Role of temporal information in the perception of causality

The associative analysis presented so far assumes that whenever an outcome follows a cue, these stimuli occur close enough in time to be perceived as a pairing, as both occurring together. The analysis as described so far has been silent with respect to temporal properties of the stimuli, such as their duration, the interval of time that separates them, and the order in which they are experienced. The timing of the stimuli, however, has a strong influence on both the ability of animals to exhibit anticipatory conditioned responses and humans' ability to detect a causal relationship. A cue, or cause, might be consistently followed by an outcome, but if the temporal gap between the two is extended (sometimes by even as little as 2 s), learning of a cue–outcome or action–outcome relationship is generally poor. This occurs in animals (Dickinson, Watt, & Griffiths, 1992) and in humans (e.g., Shanks, Pearson, & Dickinson, 1989). Furthermore, performance is poor if the cue and outcome are presented in reverse order, that is, when the outcome precedes the putative generative cause. This has also been demonstrated in both animals (using a backward conditioning preparation; Hall, 1984) and in humans (e.g., Lagnado & Sloman, 2006).

This temporal precedence in causation can, of course, be explained, at least in humans, by arguing that they think rationally (Lagnado & Sloman, 2006). If there is a causal relationship between a cue and an outcome, then the cue should occur before rather than after the outcome, and, generally, most causes have immediate effects. This rational analysis, however, provides no mechanism through which rationality can be achieved. From an associative point of view, the challenge is to design a model that generates judgments that mirror this rational structure despite the fact that each component of the model is not rational.

Several researchers have taken on this challenge and developed associative models that can learn from temporal information (e.g., Aitken & Dickinson, 2005; Baetu & Baker, 2009; Harris, 2006; McClelland & Rumelhart, 1988; McLaren & Mackintosh, 2000; Schmajuk et al., 1996; Sutton & Barto, 1981; Wagner, 1981). These models generally adopt a realistic stimulus representation in order to account for timing effects. In real life, events unfold over time; consequently, these models adopt a "real-time" stimulus representation.

Temporal information implemented in real-time models

In this section, we describe the model we use to simulate causal learning, the auto-associator (full details of the model are described in Baetu & Baker, 2009; McClelland & Rumelhart, 1988; note that we use McClelland & Rumelhart's terminology in which an "auto-associative" structure refers to a fully interconnected set of units as opposed to other more restricted structures in which only some connections exist). Because the auto-associator's assumptions about stimulus representation are similar to those of other real-time models, the simulations of the auto-associator are shared with some of these other models. We have chosen the auto-associator to illustrate how real-time models learn from temporal information because it is simpler than many of the other real-time models. For instance, unlike other models (Harris, 2006; McLaren & Mackintosh, 2000; Schmajuk et al., 1996), it does not learn to modulate attention to stimuli as a result of experience, and hence cannot account for effects that seem to rely on additional processes involving attention (see Chapter 6; note, however, that a model similar to the auto-associator has been modified to account for attention effects; see McLaren & Mackintosh, 2000). Because a secondary process like attention is not necessary to explain the effects we are about to describe, this simpler version of the model will suffice to demonstrate the advantage of real-time representations.

An auto-associator is a network of units in which each unit represents a stimulus or a stimulus feature. Figure 15.1 illustrates the way stimulus occurrences are represented in the model. When a stimulus (A) is presented for a brief period of time, the activation level of the unit or units that represent it gradually increases from a resting value of zero into the positive range. This is the result of updating the activation

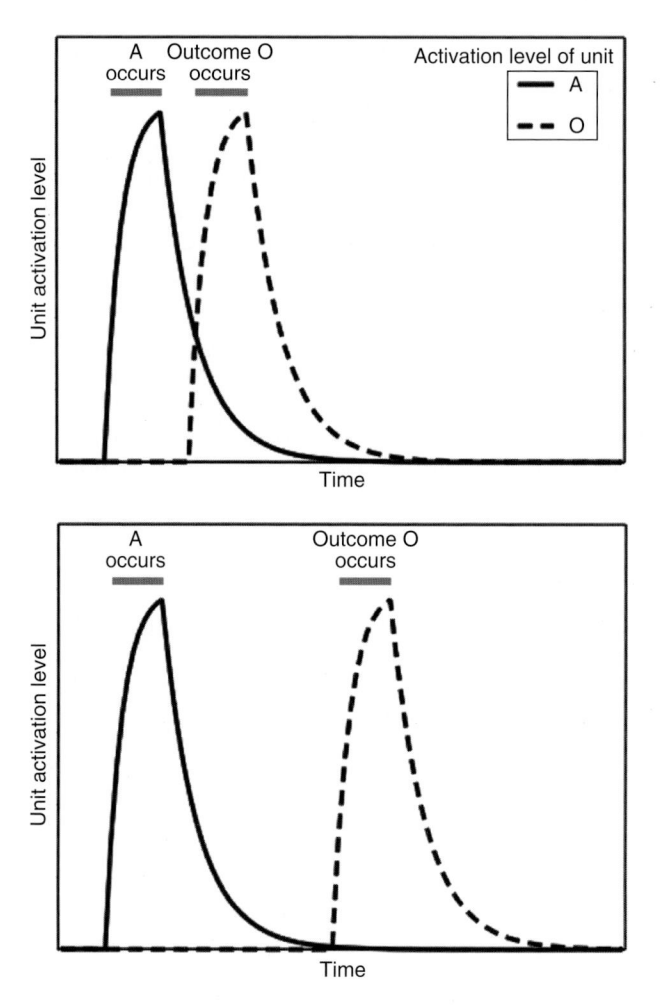

Figure 15.1 Simulated activity in units representing a cue (A) and an outcome (O) when they are first presented together but are separated by a short (upper panel) or a long (lower panel) delay.

level of that unit over a series of discrete time steps. When that stimulus ceases to be present, its activation level gradually decays back to zero. Thus, although stimulus A might be a binary event (it either occurs or does not occur), the activity of its mental representation is graded: It can gradually rise or decrease over time, thus taking on the properties of a continuous variable.

If a second stimulus, such as an outcome, is presented before the activation level of A has decayed to zero (upper panel), then there is an opportunity for an association to form between unit A and the outcome unit. If the outcome is presented after a longer period of time when the activation level of unit A has decayed to a low level (lower panel), then the opportunity for an association to form is lost. Thus, the model explains the effect of delays between a potential cause and an effect simply by allowing a stimulus representation to decay from memory once the stimulus is no longer present.

In this model, there are unidirectional connections between each possible pair of units in the network (e.g., there is a connection from unit A to unit B, and one from B to A). These connections are initially set to zero, but their strength can change as a result of experience with the stimuli represented by these units. Because there are connections between any two units in the network, the network can learn to associate cues to outcomes, but it can also learn to associate pairs of cues or even make backward outcome → cue associations (although the latter are usually much weaker). All associations are updated using an error-correction rule similar to that described in Equation 1. For example, the change in the association between cue A and an outcome ($\Delta w_{A-Outcome}$) is a function of how surprising the outcome is (i.e., the amount of prediction error, Equation 1) and the activity level of unit A:

$$\Delta w_{A-Outcome} = f(\text{Outcome Prediction Error} \times \text{Activity in unit A})$$
$$= f\left[(\text{Experienced Outcome} - \text{Expected Outcome}) \times \text{Activity in unit A}\right]$$
(15.2)

The activity level of unit A depends both upon whether the unit receives sensory input (when A is physically present) and whether other active units in the network share an association with it and activate it (Figure 15.2). The outcome's prediction error is computed as the difference between the sensory input that is received by the outcome unit (the experienced outcome) and the expectation of the outcome generated

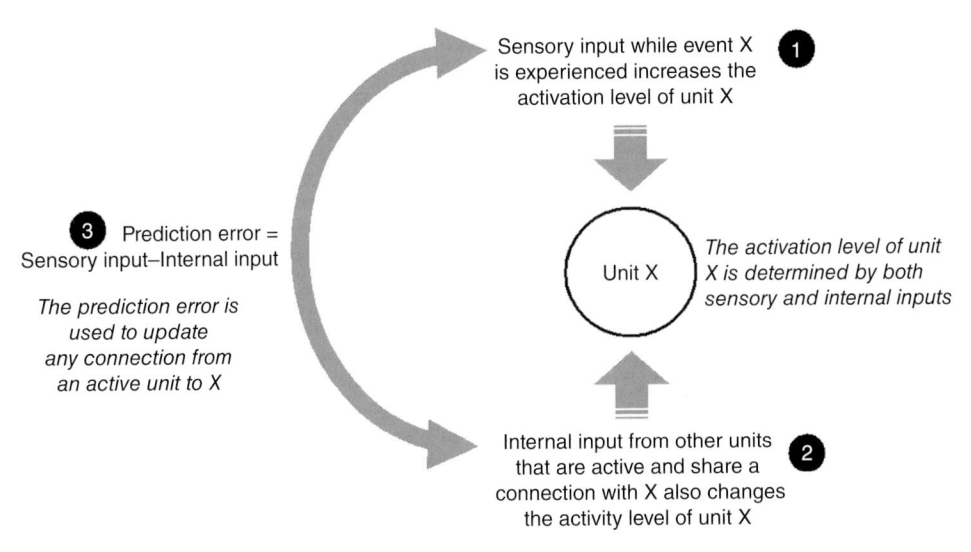

Figure 15.2 Activation level of any unit, X, is determined by (1) sensory input that takes on a positive value when event X is experienced and a value of zero when X is not experienced, and (2) internally generated input from other active units in the network that share an association with X. The sensory input represents the experienced event X, whereas the internal input represents the extent to which X was retrieved from memory by other active units, in other words, the extent to which X was anticipated. Prediction error for unit X is computed as the difference between the sensory and internal inputs that feed into unit X (3). This prediction error is used to update any connection that links a unit that has a non-zero activity level to unit X.

on that trial (the expected outcome). A large prediction error for the outcome might increase the strength of the connection between A and the outcome units, but only if the activation of unit A is not zero, as is the case in the upper panel of Figure 15.1. This is because the change in the association from A to the outcome depends not only on how surprising the outcome is (the prediction error term) but also on the activation level of A.

A large prediction error for the outcome might increase the strength of the connection between A and the outcome units, but only if the activation of unit A is not zero, as is the case in the upper panel of Figure 15.2. This is because the change in the association from A to the outcome depends not only on how surprising the outcome is (the prediction error term) but also on the activation level of A.

The model can represent the order in which events usually occur. For example, if A precedes the outcome (e.g., Figure 15.1, upper panel), the model is sensitive to this temporal order. It shows this sensitivity because it forms an association from A to the outcome (A → Outcome) that is stronger than the association from the outcome to A (Outcome → A). Whereas the model updates the A → Outcome association using Equation 2, it updates the Outcome → A association using the following formula:

$$\Delta w_{\text{Outcome A}} = f\left[(\text{Experienced A} - \text{Expected A}) \times \text{Activity in the Outcome unit}\right]$$
(15.3)

This analysis anticipates that the forward A → Outcome association will be stronger than the backward Outcome → A association on the following basis. At the outset of training, when the forward association is updated, A's activation level has a positive (decayed) value and the outcome's prediction error will also be positive. This results in strengthening of the A → Outcome association (Equation 2). In contrast, when the backward association is updated, the outcome's activation level will be positive, but A's prediction error value will no longer be positive because "Experienced A" equates to sensory input (and A is absent when the outcome occurs; see Figure 15.2). Thus, the Outcome → A association cannot become strong if A precedes the outcome in time because this association requires both a high prediction error for A and a high outcome unit activation level (Equation 3), but they do not happen simultaneously.

Thus, after training, A might be able to activate a strong representation of the outcome through the A → Outcome association, but the outcome will only activate a very weak representation of A since the Outcome → A association is weak. Thus, if presented with the cue, the network is able to retrieve from memory the pattern it had been trained with (i.e., it expects the outcome to follow A), but it does not retrieve the reversed temporal pattern that it never experienced (in which the outcome is followed by cue A). This mechanism can represent causal precedence whereby people typically interpret the first event as the cause of the second, and not vice versa (Lagnado & Sloman, 2006). It also explains why animals often fail to acquire a conditioned response in a backward conditioning preparation in which the outcome, or unconditioned stimulus, is presented before the cue. It is worth noting that this explanation accounts for discriminations between A → B and B → A, but that even this account fails to learn more complex temporal order patterns (e.g., Murphy, Mondragón, Murphy, & Fouquet, 2004).

Learning About Preventive Causes

So far, we have discussed learning about generative causes and have argued that from an associative perspective, it can be understood to rely on the formation of a cue → outcome association. In associative terms, this association is *excitatory*, allowing the cue to retrieve the memory of the outcome. But some causes have the opposite effect. A preventive cause signals the absence of the outcome and suppresses the expectation that the outcome will occur. Many associative models, including the auto-associator, assume that learning about preventive causes involves the acquisition of an *inhibitory* association between the cause and the outcome (see Chapter 19), although there are notable exceptions (Konorski, 1967; Miller & Matzel, 1988; Pearce & Hall, 1980). Inhibitory associations (that we denote by the symbol ⊸) have opposite properties to excitatory associations: An inhibitory association suppresses activity in the outcome representation and makes it more difficult for excitatory associations to activate it.

Pavlov (1927) was the first to study inhibitory learning using a conditioned inhibition design. In this design, cue A is paired with the outcome (A–Outcome), but when it is presented in combination with cue X, the outcome does not occur (AX–No Outcome). Humans and other animals are typically sensitive to the negative correlation between X and the outcome (e.g., Baetu & Baker, 2010; Baker, 1977; Pavlov, 1927; Rescorla, 1969). In associative terms, X becomes an inhibitor. Models that use prediction error to change associations can anticipate this inhibition. The A–Outcome trials should generate an excitatory association. When the two cues are presented together (AX–No Outcome), A generates the expectation of the outcome, which is then omitted. Thus, the prediction error (Experienced − Expected Outcome) is negative. This causes a negative change in associative strength, which both weakens the A → Outcome association and forces the initially neutral X to form a negative or inhibitory association with the outcome.

Role of redundancy in preventive learning

We and others have shown that, just like generative learning, preventive learning is sensitive to redundancy and may be blocked (Baetu & Baker, 2010, 2012; Baker et al., 1993; Darredeau et al., 2009; Lotz, Vervliet, & Lachnit, 2009; Vallée-Tourangeau, Murphy, & Baker, 1998). Similar to generative blocking, the extent to which an inhibitory cue uniquely signals the absence of the outcome influences the strength of inhibitory associations. A simplified version of a design that we (Baetu & Baker, 2010) used to test this idea is presented in Table 15.2. Here, the target inhibitory cue X is blocked by a more informative inhibitory cue B. That is, cue B signals the omission of the outcome that normally follows A regardless of whether X is also present. Cue X adds nothing new to this prediction, because, although it is always followed by the absence of the outcome, it predicts only a subset of these absences. Thus, X is a redundant and less informative predictor of the outcome's absence. Consequently, learning that B predicts the outcome's absence should "block" learning that X is also inhibitory. Moreover, less should be learned about X compared with a control cue (Y) that also signals the absence of the outcome, but does so in competition with an equivalent predictor (C) that does not signal the outcome's omission in

Table 15.2 Simplified version of the design used by Baetu and Baker (2010, 2012) to test for blocking of conditioned inhibition.

Training	Test the target cues
A–Outcome	
AB–No Outcome	
ABX–No Outcome	X (blocked)
ACY–No Outcome	Y (overshadowed control)

Note. The training trials were randomly intermixed.

the absence of Y. Similar to the generative blocking effect reported earlier, conditioned inhibition was blocked. In our experiments, learning that X prevents the outcome was weak compared with learning that Y prevents the outcome. A similar finding in animals has been reported by Suiter and LoLordo (1971), but failures to find the effect have also been reported (see Moore & Stickney, 1985; Schachtman, Matzel, & Miller, 1988).

Models that use prediction error to modify associations readily explain blocking of conditioned inhibition. They generate negative prediction errors on no-outcome trials because A should cause the outcome to be expected, but the outcome does not happen. Because B signals the absence of the outcome on AB–No Outcome trials, it should acquire a strong inhibitory association with the outcome. This strong inhibitory B⟶Outcome association should prevent strengthening of the inhibitory X⟶Outcome association because whenever X is present (on ABX–No Outcome trials), B cancels the outcome expectation caused by A, so there is no negative prediction error. This absence of prediction error should leave X with a weak or zero association with the outcome. Thus, redundancy seems to play an important role in the acquisition of inhibitory associations, and this can be captured by an error-correction rule.

Asymmetries Between Preventive and Generative Learning

The fact that both generative and preventive learning are influenced by redundancy suggests that there are certain parallels between the mechanisms for the acquisition of excitatory and inhibitory associations. Nonetheless, there seem to be differences between generative and preventive learning. For example, preventive learning seems more robust, than excitatory learning, to extinction treatments in which the target cue is presented by itself in the absence of the outcome (e.g., Yarlas, Cheng, & Holyoak, 1995; Lysle & Fowler, 1985). Consequently, some researchers have developed models in which the principles that govern excitatory associations are different from those that govern inhibitory associations (e.g., Zimmer-Hart & Rescorla, 1974; see also Baker, 1974).

One of the difficulties in evaluating whether excitatory and inhibitory mechanisms are similar is the fact that excitatory and inhibitory cues are typically trained and tested in different ways (e.g., an inhibitory cue is always presented in compound with an excitor, whereas an excitatory cue is usually presented in the absence of other cues except for a neutral or slightly excitatory context). We recently investigated this issue in human learning by keeping the training and testing conditions similar for generative and preventive cues (Baetu & Baker, 2012). Even under such conditions, we did find some asymmetries between generative and preventive learning. For instance, preventive learning was weaker than generative learning. Although this might suggest that excitatory and inhibitory learning are different, at least quantitatively, it is possible that excitatory and inhibitory associations might not have symmetrical influences on external behavior, even though the same kind of processes might generate excitatory and inhibitory associations. Potential reasons for this asymmetry seen in performance are explained below.

According to the present associative analysis, generative learning depends on positive prediction errors, and preventive learning depends on negative prediction errors. But although positive and negative prediction errors are computed in the same way, negative prediction errors depend on previous excitatory learning, whereas positive prediction errors do not. This is a direct consequence of the fact that, in order for the prediction error to be negative, the expected outcome should be larger than the experienced outcome. Because the expected outcome relies on existing excitatory associations, these associations must be in place before a negative prediction error can be generated. For example, in order for X to become inhibitory in a conditioned inhibition experiment (A–Outcome, AX–No Outcome), an excitatory A → Outcome association must be formed before A can generate an outcome expectation that will be violated on AX–No Outcome trials. In contrast, positive prediction errors do not require existing associations. Large prediction errors can be generated when learning has not yet taken place, making the outcome very surprising.

Furthermore, an inhibitory association might not be independent of excitatory associations because X is always presented in compound with the excitatory cue A, so there is an opportunity for AX to become associated. Thus, even though X might develop a direct inhibitory association with the outcome, its ability to suppress the activity of the outcome node might be limited if it indirectly excites the outcome representation via an X → A → Outcome associative chain (see the left panel of Figure 15.3). This might explain why we, and others, have found that preventive learning is often weaker than excitatory learning. This idea has received some empirical support from animal studies that show that extinguishing the excitor A after inhibitory training increases the inhibitory potential of X (Tobler, Dickinson, & Schultz, 2003; Williams, Travis, & Overmier, 1986; but see Lysle & Fowler, 1985). This might happen because the excitatory X → A → Outcome chain is weakened, reducing its ability to interfere with the direct inhibitory X⊣Outcome association.

Because negative prediction errors require previous excitatory learning, inhibitory associations should develop relatively slowly. So during conditioned inhibition training, if the A–Outcome and AX–No Outcome trials are intermixed, an error-correction model like the auto-associator will represent the associative structure in Figure 15.3 by first forming excitatory X → A and A → Outcome associations and then forming inhibitory X⊣Outcome associations. This means that X will initially develop excitatory properties because it will be able to retrieve the memory of the outcome via the X → A and A → Outcome excitatory associations (a phenomenon usually referred to as second-order, or higher-order, conditioning; Pavlov, 1927). Because the outcome is omitted on every AX trial, the negative prediction error

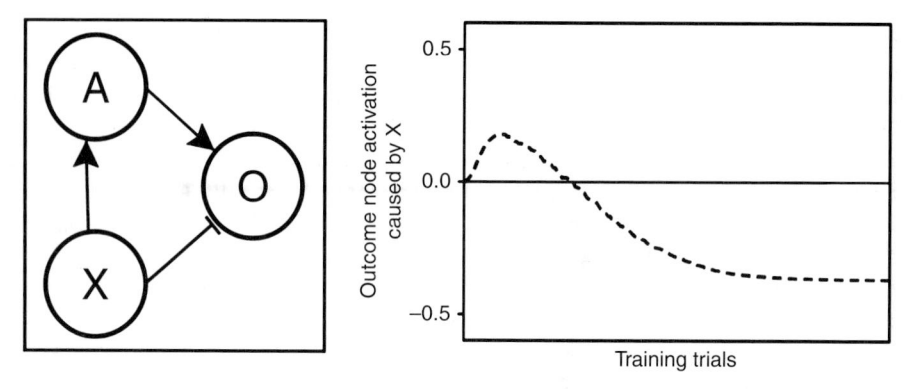

Figure 15.3 Left: Associative structure formed by the auto-associator after training with intermixed A-Outcome and AX-No Outcome trials. The letter O in the left panel represents the outcome. Arrows represent excitatory associations, and the flat-ended line represents an inhibitory association. Note that an excitatory association from A to X is also formed (not shown), but it is weaker than the association from X to A because it is extinguished on trials on which A occurs without X. Right: simulated effect of X on the outcome node during training. Early on, X increases the activity of the outcome node, whereas with extended training, X suppresses the activity of the outcome node.

generated on these trials will strengthen a direct inhibitory X—⊣Outcome association that will gradually counteract the excitatory effect of the X → A → Outcome chain of associations, and finally endow X with net inhibitory properties. This is illustrated in the right panel of Figure 15.3, which shows simulations from the auto-associator (similar simulations have been reported with other models, e.g., Kutlu & Schmajuk, 2012). Early during training, X activates the outcome node (it is effectively an excitatory cue) via the X → A → Outcome chain. Only with more training trials will the inhibitory X—⊣Outcome association overcome the excitatory X → A → Outcome chain and suppress the activity of the outcome node. This prediction has received empirical support from animal studies (Stout, Escobar, & Miller, 2004; Yin, Barnet, & Miller, 1994).

Inferring Larger Causal Structures from Individual Causal Links

In the simulations shown in Figure 15.3, X's ability to increase the activity of the outcome node early in training critically depends on the X → A → Outcome chain of associations. This depends on the ability to integrate the X → A and A → Outcome associations into a chain, despite the fact that these associations were learned on separate trials (on AX–No Outcome and A–Outcome trials, respectively). The ability to integrate associations that were learned separately into a larger structure is interesting from a causal learning point of view, because it might explain how people integrate several pieces of information into a larger causal model or schema without ever experiencing the whole causal structure. We often seem to be able to integrate multiple pieces of information effortlessly, allowing us to draw inferences about relationships that were not observed directly.

Recently, we investigated how people integrate two associations, which had been acquired independently on separate trials, into a larger causal model (Baetu & Baker, 2009). In particular, we were interested in the way generative and preventive links, or associations, are integrated into a chain. We were interested in examining how people infer the relationship between the distal events of a chain, even though they never observed the complete chain. We also investigated whether an associative model could capture such apparently rational inferences without appealing to the notion of rationality. This might provide a possible mechanism through which a simple system made up of nonrational units (such as neurons) could generate an output that is considered rational. Our participants learned about two links involving three stimuli (A → B and B → C) and were later asked to evaluate the relationship between A and C, despite the fact that they had no opportunity to form a direct A → C association (but see Chapter 4). So one obvious way in which they could evaluate the A–C relationship was by integrating the separate A → C and B → C links into an A → B → C chain. One problem with separately learning the two links of an A → B → C chain is that it is analogous to the conditioned inhibition experiment (where A, B and C are equivalent to X, A, and the Outcome from the previous section). Thus, seeing only A → B implies that C is not present, or seeing only B → C implies that A is not present. This could lead to unintended inhibitory A⊣C associations complicating the picture when the participants are later asked to construct the A → B → C chain. This possible inhibitory learning might mask learning or reporting the A → B → C chain. One way to avoid this is to prevent learning of a direct A⊣C association by not allowing participants to observe whether or not C occurred following the A → B presentations and preventing them from seeing A on the B → C presentations. Thus, they cannot form direct sensory associations between A and C because only information from the A → B and B → C contingencies is available for inferring the workings of the A → B → C chain. In our scenario, participants were asked to discover whether three colored lights (displayed on a computer screen) were connected, such that the lights in a chain might turn the subsequent light on or off. On any trial, participants observed only two of the lights; the third was covered so they could not see whether it was on or off (Figure 15.4). For the sake of simplicity, we will label the three lights A, B, and C. On every trial, participants could observe either lights A and B (C was covered) or lights B and C (A was covered). Thus, they could directly observe the A → B and B → C links, but they never observed the relationship between A and C, since one of these two lights was always covered. Nevertheless, participants were asked to evaluate whether A would have an influence on C, that is, whether light A might turn light C on or off. This allowed us to investigate whether participants could infer an A → B → C chain from their observation of the A → B and B → C links without the opportunity to observe a direct link between A and C (this direct A–C link is analogous to the direct X⊣Outcome association shown in Figure 15.3).

Our participants did infer that light A would turn light C on if they observed positive contingencies between lights A and B, and between lights B and C. But more interesting is the way they integrated negative links into a chain. In some of the conditions, the lights were negatively correlated, that is, whenever one of the lights was on, the other was likely to be off, and vice versa. Table 15.3 summarizes our results. When one of the two observed contingencies was positive and the other negative, participants judged a negative relationship between A and C, meaning that they

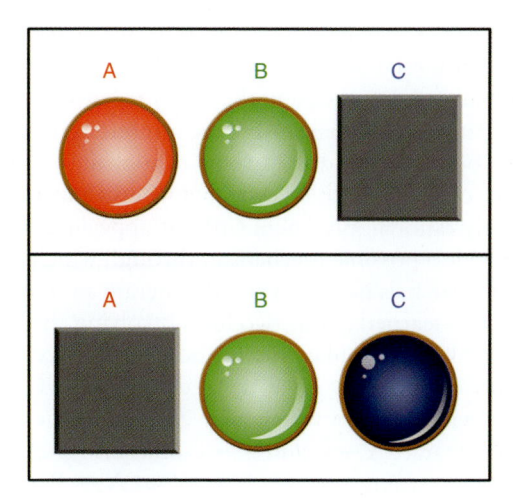

Figure 15.4 Schematic diagram of two types of trial used in the experiments by Baetu and Baker (2009). Upper panel: example of trial on which lights A and B are on, and light C is covered. Lower panel: example of trial on which light B is on, light C is off, and light A is covered. Note that the lights were labeled by color rather than by letters in the experiments.

Table 15.3 Summary of design and results of the experiments reported by Baetu and Baker (2009).

Observed contingencies		
A–B	B–C	*Inferred A–C relationship*
Positive	Positive	Positive
Positive	Negative	Negative
Negative	Positive	Negative
Negative	Negative	Positive
Positive	Zero	Zero
Negative	Zero	Zero
Zero	Zero	Zero

expected light A to switch light C off. Moreover, if both observed contingencies were negative, they inferred that light A would switch light C on. Finally, when one or both observed contingencies were zero, i.e., two of the lights were uncorrelated (last three rows of Table 15.3), participants concluded that there was no relationship between lights A and C. These results mirror the normative algebraic rule of signs for combining positive and negative contingencies into chains. They also follow simple logical rules. For example, if A makes B more likely (a positive A → B link), but B makes C less likely (a preventive or negative B—|C link), then presenting A should make C less likely to occur (the A → B—|C chain has a negative influence on C). And, of course, making any link zero breaks the chain. In short, the participants behaved normatively or rationally. This is merely a description of their behavior, but we further investigated possible associative mechanisms that might generate such apparently rational behavior and help us understand how these inferences were achieved.

Our participants' behavior is exactly what the auto-associator model, which has no explicit representation of the rational rules but allows activation to spread through a chain of excitatory or inhibitory associations, would predict. In our simulations, the network learned excitatory or inhibitory A–B and B–C associations whenever the contingencies were positive or negative, respectively. After this training, we activated unit A to test whether the network could infer an A–C relationship. That is, we tested whether the network could "anticipate" unit C to be on, or off, when it experienced A. The network's behavior in each of the conditions summarized in Table 15.3 was very much like our participants' estimates of the A–C relationship. For example, when the two observed contingencies were positive, activating unit A resulted in a gradual activation of unit B, which was followed by activity in unit C. Thus, the network anticipated A to be followed by B, and then by C. Hence, this simple network could make rational inferences about the unobserved A–C causal relationship despite the fact that none of the individual components was capable of rational thinking. This might give us some indirect insight into how some of our rational thinking is achieved by a neural system whose components lack any rationality.

So far, our examples show how human causal learning and also some apparently rational rule-inference can be explained within an associative framework. We argue that this framework is more biologically plausible than other frameworks (e.g., Cheng, 1997; Griffiths & Tenenbaum, 2005), and is thus useful for discovering how causal reasoning is achieved by a network of neurons, thus helping us bridge the gap between brain and mind (Baker *et al.*, 2005; Barberia, Baetu, Murphy, & Baker, 2011). But if this associative framework is (at least somewhat) biologically plausible, then we should be able to observe some congruency between some neurobiological features and some of the basic tenets of these associative models. In the next section, we explore this issue and discuss some evidence from studies of the relationship between learning and brain activity.

Brain Activity Consistent with Outcome Expectations and Prediction Errors

There is now a strong body of research showing that brain activity during learning tasks is consistent with basic associative principles, although some of these findings are also consistent with other accounts. Most of these tasks have involved learning whether certain cues signal a particular outcome through trial and error, so these tasks resemble causal discovery. A wealth of imaging and electrophysiological studies have found brain responses that occur at the time of cue presentation that correlate with behavioral and model-predicted outcome expectancy (e.g., Flor *et al.*, 1996; Knutson, Taylor, Kaufman, Peterson, & Glover, 2005; O'Doherty, Deichmann, Critchley, & Dolan, 2002; Rothemund *et al.*, 2012; Simons, Ohman, & Lang, 1979). According to associative models, outcome expectancy is based on the strength of the learned cue–outcome association; however, other alternative explanations are possible. For example, outcome expectancy might be based on some statistical computation of the cue–outcome relationship (e.g., Cheng, 1997; Griffiths & Tenenbaum, 2005), and such computations can yield similar predictions to those made by associative models (Baker *et al.*, 1996; Chapman & Robbins, 1990; Wasserman, Elek, Chatlosh, & Baker, 1993). So, evidence that brain activity is consistent with outcome expectations does not uniquely support associative models, especially given that these simple tasks usually do not provide the opportunity to contrast the two classes of theory.

More compelling evidence favoring associative models comes from studies showing that brain activity is consistent with the trial-by-trial variations in prediction error anticipated by many associative models (e.g., Rescorla & Wagner, 1972), but not by alternative statistical models (e.g., Cheng, 1997). Consistent with error-correction associative models, electrophysiological studies found event-related potentials, at the time when the outcome is delivered or omitted, that are correlated with prediction error (e.g., Bellebaum & Daum, 2008; Philiastides, Biele, Vavatzanidis, Kazzer, & Heekeren, 2010; Walsh & Anderson, 2011; Yeung & Sanfey, 2004), and imaging studies have measured these prediction-error-like signals, locating them mainly in the striatum and the prefrontal cortex (e.g., McClure, Berns, & Montague, 2003; Morris *et al.*, 2011; O'Doherty, Dayan, Friston, Critchley, & Dolan, 2003; Pagnoni, Zink, Montague, & Berns, 2002; Ploghaus *et al.*, 2000). For example, Ploghaus *et al.* (2000) reported frontal responses consistent with prediction error when participants learned to associate cues with a painful outcome, and Morris *et al.* (2011) showed that the activity of the ventral striatum is consistent with both positive and negative prediction errors when learning to associate visual cues with monetary rewards.

Many of the studies above investigated learning to predict outcomes that are emotionally or motivationally salient, but similar effects have been observed in more neutral causal learning tasks; for example, tasks in which participants discover whether a hypothetical patient is allergic to various foods (Corlett *et al.*, 2004; Fletcher *et al.*, 2001; Turner *et al.*, 2004). These studies have mostly found prefrontal activation consistent with prediction error, but also, despite the fact that these neutral tasks involve outcomes that are probably not motivationally significant, they found some striatal activation. Even though it has been argued that striatal activity is modulated by motivation or saliency (e.g., McClure *et al.*, 2003), it might play a role in forming associations between neutral events as well. It is worth noting that some of these results provide particularly compelling evidence in favor of error-correction models because the experimental designs controlled for potential factors that had been correlated with prediction error in previous studies, such as the novelty of the stimuli on surprising versus unsurprising trials (Corlett *et al.*, 2004; Turner *et al.*, 2004). These studies found prefrontal activity consistent with prediction error, and, furthermore, Turner and colleagues found that this activity also correlated with behavioral adjustments when making outcome predictions on subsequent trials. This suggests that this error-dependent activity generated changes in cue–outcome associations and, hence, in subsequent cue-triggered outcome expectations.

These findings are also consistent with many animal studies. For example, the seminal work of Schultz and colleagues showed that, in monkeys, the phasic firing of striatal dopamine neurons is consistent with both outcome expectancy and prediction error (see Chapter 3). This was demonstrated not only in a conditioning paradigm in which the animals learned simple associations between a single cue and reward (Schultz, Dayan, & Montague, 1997), but also in more complex designs such as blocking (Waelti, Dickinson, & Schultz, 2001) and conditioned inhibition (Tobler, Dickinson, & Schultz, 2003). This suggests that learning processes recruit the dopamine system, and many argue that learning in humans similarly depends on dopamine (e.g., Corlett, Honey, & Fletcher, 2007; Holroyd & Coles, 2002). If this is so, then it is possible that variations in dopaminergic genes might account for individual differences in learning. This topic is briefly reviewed in the next section.

Genetic Markers that Correlate with Learning

Although causal links between specific genotypes and phenotypes are difficult to establish because of possible interactions among genes, the study of individual differences that are linked to genetic factors is useful from at least two points of view. First, although these studies are correlational in nature in humans (see Steinberg *et al.*, 2013, for a more causal manipulation in nonhuman animals), they provide us with some insight into the neurobiology of learning because they allow us to investigate whether genetic correlates of specific neural substrates are linked to variations in learning (see also Chapter 7). This knowledge is a useful step in investigating learning processes, and can be complemented by pharmacological manipulations. Second, even though a causal relationship between a specific genotype and learning might be difficult to establish, genetic markers can nevertheless be used to predict an individual's propensity to learn from experience with rewards or punishments. This has clinical implications for diagnosis and treatment of disorders that seem to involve some form of abnormal learning, such as addiction (Noble, 2003), obesity (Epstein *et al.*, 2007), or anxiety disorders (Soliman *et al.*, 2010).

The studies reviewed in this section investigated polymorphisms in genes that directly regulate the function of the dopamine system. Polymorphic genes exhibit more than one allele at that gene's locus within a population. Figure 15.5 summarizes some of the findings reviewed in more detail below. Although we focus our discussion on dopaminergic genes, it is worth noting that other genotypes have also been found to correlate with individual differences in learning, including polymorphisms in the brain-derived neurotrophic factor gene (Soliman *et al.*, 2010), the mu-opioid receptor (OPRM1) gene (Lee *et al.*, 2011), and the serotonin transporter gene linked polymorphic region (5-HTTLPR; Hermann *et al.*, 2012).

Protein phosphatase 1 regulatory subunit 1B and the dopamine D2 receptor genes

Several studies have examined polymorphisms in genes that affect dopamine D1 and D2 receptors. In general, they suggest that these receptors may play different roles in learning through their sensitivity to either positive or negative prediction errors, respectively. Frank, Moustafa, Haughey, Curran, and Hutchinson (2007) investigated learning from positive and negative prediction errors using a forced-choice task in which two visual stimuli (cues) were shown on every trial, and participants were asked to choose one of them. They were then shown the consequence of their choice (the outcome), which was a statement about whether their choice was correct or incorrect. Although no stimulus signaled the outcome perfectly, some of the stimuli had a higher probability of being correct than others. Thus, participants could learn

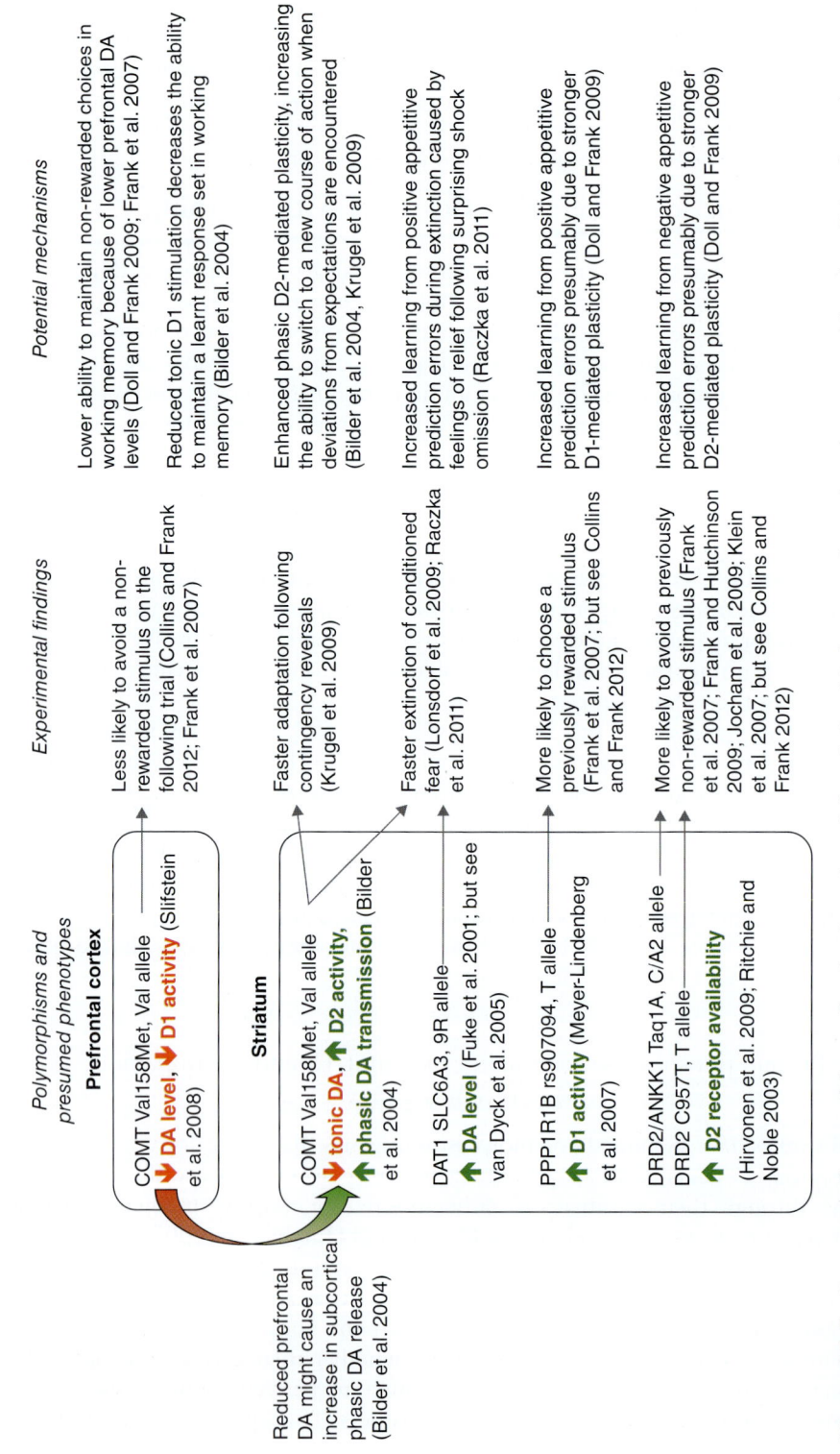

Polymorphisms and presumed phenotypes	Experimental findings	Potential mechanisms
Prefrontal cortex		
COMT Val158Met, Val allele ↓ DA level, ↓ D1 activity (Slifstein et al. 2008)	Less likely to avoid a non-rewarded stimulus on the following trial (Collins and Frank 2012; Frank et al. 2007)	Lower ability to maintain non-rewarded choices in working memory because of lower prefrontal DA levels (Doll and Frank 2009; Frank et al. 2007)
		Reduced tonic D1 stimulation decreases the ability to maintain a learnt response set in working memory (Bilder et al. 2004)
Striatum		
COMT Val158Met, Val allele ↓ tonic DA, ↑ D2 activity, ↑ phasic DA transmission (Bilder et al. 2004)	Faster adaptation following contingency reversals (Krugel et al. 2009)	Enhanced phasic D2-mediated plasticity, increasing the ability to switch to a new course of action when deviations from expectations are encountered (Bilder et al. 2004, Krugel et al. 2009)
DAT1 SLC6A3, 9R allele ↑ DA level (Fuke et al. 2001; but see van Dyck et al. 2005)	Faster extinction of conditioned fear (Lonsdorf et al. 2009; Raczka et al. 2011)	Increased learning from positive appetitive prediction errors during extinction caused by feelings of relief following surprising shock omission (Raczka et al. 2011)
PPP1R1B rs907094, T allele ↑ D1 activity (Meyer-Lindenberg et al. 2007)	More likely to choose a previously rewarded stimulus (Frank et al. 2007; but see Collins and Frank 2012)	Increased learning from positive appetitive prediction errors presumably due to stronger D1-mediated plasticity (Doll and Frank 2009)
DRD2/ANKK1 Taq1A, C/A2 allele DRD2 C957T, T allele ↑ D2 receptor availability (Hirvonen et al. 2009; Ritchie and Noble 2003)	More likely to avoid a previously non-rewarded stimulus (Frank et al. 2007; Frank and Hutchinson 2009; Jocham et al. 2009; Klein et al. 2007; but see Collins and Frank 2012)	Increased learning from negative appetitive prediction errors presumably due to stronger D2-mediated plasticity (Doll and Frank 2009)

Reduced prefrontal DA might cause an increase in subcortical phasic DA release (Bilder et al. 2004)

Figure 15.5 Summary of some of the studies that investigated the relationship between dopaminergic genes and learning. DA = dopamine; green up-arrows = increase; red down-arrows = decrease.

by trial and error to choose stimuli that were more likely to result in positive (correct) feedback and avoid stimuli that were more likely to be followed by negative (incorrect) feedback. In a subsequent test phase, participants were confronted with novel choice pairs that tested their ability to choose a previously correct stimulus versus their ability to avoid a previously incorrect stimulus. This type of task resembles causal learning tasks in which participants are asked to discover the underlying relationships between potential causes (or cues) and outcomes, although it has an additional choice component whereby participants may not only learn the cue–outcome relationships, but also choose the cues that they think are more likely to be classified as correct.

Frank and colleagues tested the hypothesis that dopamine D1 receptors are involved in learning from positive prediction errors, whereas D2 receptors are involved in learning from negative prediction errors (Doll & Frank, 2009; Frank et al., 2007; Frank & Hutchinson, 2009). According to this hypothesis, the participants' choices are influenced by two learning pathways: A "go" pathway that enables them to learn to choose stimuli that lead to rewards, and a "no-go" pathway that enables them to learn to avoid stimuli that are not rewarded. According to Frank and colleagues, striatal dopamine regulates both pathways. They argue that positive prediction errors in response to unanticipated rewards cause bursts of phasic dopamine release, which in turn cause long-term potentiation at D1 receptors. This D1-mediated plasticity along the "go" pathway is assumed to underlie the ability to choose rewarded stimuli when they are encountered again. In contrast, negative prediction errors in response to unanticipated reward omissions cause dips in phasic dopamine release, which in turn should cause long-term potentiation at D2 receptors. This D2-mediated plasticity of the "no-go" pathway is assumed to underlie the ability to avoid nonrewarded stimuli. Consequently, genotypes that affect D1 and D2 receptors should be correlated with individual differences in the ability to learn from positive and negative prediction errors. Frank and colleagues tested this hypothesis by investigating learning differences associated with polymorphisms in the protein phosphatase 1 regulatory subunit 1B (PPP1R1B) and dopamine D2 receptor (DRD2) genes, which affect D1 and D2 receptors, respectively (Frank et al., 2007; Frank & Hutchinson, 2009).

The PPP1R1B gene codes for the dopamine- and cAMP-regulated neuronal phosphoprotein (DARPP-32), a protein that influences dopaminergic transmission, including D1 receptor stimulation in the striatum. Frank and colleagues studied one of the polymorphisms in the PPP1R1B gene (rs907094), which has been associated with differential protein mRNA expression, whereby carriers of the T allele show greater expression compared with carriers of the C allele (Meyer-Lindenberg et al., 2007). Consistent with their hypothesis, that increased D1 signaling should facilitate learning from positive prediction errors, they found that during the final test phase of their task, the T allele was associated with a stronger preference for stimuli that had been followed by correct feedback during training (Frank et al., 2007; also see correction reported in Frank et al., 2009, supplemental materials). Contrary to this, however, there was no effect of this polymorphism in a more recent study that used a different learning task (Collins & Frank, 2012).

Furthermore, these researchers found that polymorphisms in the DRD2 gene were associated with learning from negative-prediction errors. The DRD2 gene affects D2 receptor density in the striatum. Commonly studied polymorphisms in the DRD2 gene are the TAQ-IA polymorphism (rs1800497; note that this polymorphism was more recently classified as belonging to the adjacent ANKK1 gene) and the C957T polymorphism (rs6277), but other polymorphisms have been studied as well (e.g., Frank & Hutchinson, 2009). The absence of the A1 allele of the TAQ-IA polymorphism and the presence of the T allele of the C957T polymorphism are both associated with increased D2 receptor density (Hirvonen et al., 2005; Ritchie & Noble, 2003). Once again, consistent with their hypothesis, Frank and colleagues found that these genotypes were generally associated with a stronger tendency to avoid incorrect stimuli during the final test phase, thereby strengthening the claim for an association between D2 receptors and learning from negative prediction errors (Frank et al., 2007; Frank & Hutchinson, 2009; but see Collins & Frank, 2012).

Using the same task as Frank et al. (2007), Klein et al. (2007) also found that a genotype associated with increased D2 receptor density (the absence of the A1 allele of the TAQ-IA polymorphism in the DRD2/ANKK1 gene, that is, the A2/A2 genotype) is positively associated with the ability to avoid incorrect stimuli during the test phase. This is consistent with the results of Frank et al. (2007) and Frank and Hutchinson (2009). Furthermore, Klein et al. (2007) recorded brain activity in response to positive and negative feedback during the training phase. This, in principle, would allow them to determine sensitivity to positive and negative prediction errors that followed correct and incorrect choices, respectively. They found stronger activation of the posterior medial frontal cortex in response to negative feedback in the A2/A2 genotype group associated with a higher D2 receptor density (see also Jocham et al., 2009).

Dopamine transporter gene

The dopamine transporter (DAT1) gene recaptures extracellular dopamine after release, thus limiting dopamine availability. The 9-repeat (9R) allele of the SLC6A3 (rs28363170) polymorphism of the DAT1 gene is associated with reduced expression of DAT1 and reduced DAT binding, hence higher dopamine availability, relative to the 10-repeat (10R) allele (Fuke et al., 2001; VanNess, Owens, & Kilts, 2005; but see van Dyck et al., 2005). Hence, the 9R allele is presumably associated with increased levels of synaptic dopamine in the striatum, given that this is one of the areas in which DAT1 expression is high (Schott et al., 2006).

Consistent with the finding that the activity of the striatum is sensitive to reward expectancy, some studies found that the DAT1 9R allele, with its presumably higher level of dopamine, correlates with stronger striatal activation in anticipation of reward (see Hoogman et al., 2012, for a review). Moreover, the 9R allele also correlates with stronger striatal activity in response to prediction errors. This evidence comes from a study of fear extinction in which participants first learned that a cue was followed by an electric shock, followed by an extinction phase in which the cue was no longer followed by shock. The study found that carriers of the 9R allele (with presumably higher striatal dopamine availability) showed higher prediction-error signals in the ventral striatum in response to surprising shock omissions, and faster extinction of fear responses (Raczka et al., 2011). Interestingly, these authors suggest that aversive negative prediction errors (generated by the surprising omission of an aversive event) can be interpreted as positive appetitive prediction errors (generated by feelings of relief). This might explain the involvement of the dopamine system in fear extinction, as dopamine has generally been associated with learning about rewards rather than punishments (Pessiglione, Seymour, Flandin, Dolan, & Frith, 2006; Schultz et al., 1997). This idea is consistent with previous proposals of two antagonistic motivational systems suggesting that stimuli that signal the absence of a significant (aversive or appetitive) event effectively signal the presence of an event of opposite affective value (e.g., Dickinson & Pearce, 1977). Although this is an interesting idea, it raises an important issue: It is sometimes difficult to interpret the valence of a given hypothesized prediction error, as an aversive prediction error might be interpreted as an appetitive prediction error of opposite sign, and vice versa. This could in principle pose problems when one tries to infer the role of the various components of the dopamine system in other studies as well, including those mentioned previously. For example, a choice that is classified as "incorrect" in the task described by Frank *et al.* (2007) could generate an appetitive negative prediction error (an unexpected omission of reward), but also an aversive positive prediction error (an unexpected punishment). Interpreting this event as an appetitive negative prediction error requires one to make strong assumptions about the way the "incorrect" feedback is encoded. These assumptions might be supported by previous research (e.g., Schultz *et al.*, 1997) if one assumes that the stimuli used in these different studies are similar. Nevertheless, even though one might question the sign of the hypothesized prediction error signals, the results of Frank and colleagues suggest that the roles of dopamine D1 and D2 receptors may be dissociable.

Catechol-*O*-methyltransferase enzyme gene

Catechol-*O*-methyltransferase (COMT) is an enzyme that catabolizes released dopamine mostly in the prefrontal cortex. It is encoded by the COMT gene, which contains a polymorphism (Val158Met, rs4680) that has been associated with differential enzyme activity. Individuals who carry the Met allele have been shown to have reduced COMT activity presumably leading to increased prefrontal dopamine levels (Chen *et al.*, 2004).

Although Frank and colleagues hypothesize that striatal D1 and D2 receptors mediate learning from positive and negative prediction errors, respectively, they do not attribute a similar role to COMT. They assume that COMT affects prefrontal, but not subcortical, dopamine levels (Egan *et al.*, 2001; but see Bilder *et al.*, 2004). Hence, they do not anticipate a relationship between COMT and striatal-mediated habit learning from prediction errors. Instead, they argue that the COMT genotype influences working memory via its influence on dopamine levels in the prefrontal cortex. According to their hypothesis, higher prefrontal dopamine levels conferred by the Met allele are associated with a higher working memory capacity, which facilitates the adjustment of cue–outcome associations (Collins & Frank, 2012; Frank *et al.*, 2007). Thus, Met carriers would have an increased ability to remember a previously nonreinforced choice when it appears again despite the fact that the two presentations were separated by a number of intervening trials.

Consistent with this idea, Met carriers showed better behavioral adaptation after negative feedback (Frank et al., 2007). Furthermore, Collins and Frank (2012) showed that the advantage of Met carriers was even more pronounced when the number of stimuli participants had to learn about was increased. This presumably should have increased working memory demands by increasing the delay between trials of the same type.

Other studies, however, found an advantage for the Val allele. Krugel, Biele, Mohr, Li, and Heekaeren (2009) found the Val allele to be associated with faster learning, including faster adaptation following contingency reversals. Val carriers also exhibited greater changes in striatal activity in response to positive and negative prediction errors. Furthermore, Lonsdorf et al. (2009) found that individuals with the Met/Met genotype failed to extinguish a conditioned fear response, whereas Val carriers extinguished their conditioned responses rapidly. A common feature of these studies that found better performance in carriers of the COMT Val allele is the fact these tasks included contingency reversals, whereby participants experienced unannounced switches in cue–outcome contingencies (e.g., cues that were previously paired with an outcome were suddenly no longer followed by the outcome). These results are better understood in the context of the tonic-phasic dopamine hypothesis proposed by Bilder and colleagues to account for the seemingly complex effects of COMT on behavior and cognition (Bilder et al., 2004). In contrast to the assumption put forward by Frank and colleagues, Bilder proposes that COMT not only regulates prefrontal dopamine levels but also has an opposite effect on dopamine release in the striatum. The Met allele might thus be associated with higher dopamine levels in the prefrontal cortex, but lower phasic dopamine release in the striatum, whereas the opposite might be true of the Val allele (Bilder et al., 2004; Meyer-Lindenberg & Weinberger, 2006). Like Frank and colleagues, Bilder and colleagues also relate COMT to working memory; however, they distinguish between two working memory abilities: the ability to maintain information active in one's mind that might depend upon tonic prefrontal dopamine, and the ability to reset or update the contents of working memory that might depend upon phasic dopamine release in the striatum. The hypothesized enhanced ability to maintain information in working memory in Met carriers is consistent with Frank et al.'s (2007) interpretation of the effect of the Val158Met COMT polymorphism and their results. Bilder's additional assumption that Met carriers also have lower striatal phasic dopamine release and might thus be less able to flexibly adapt to changes in the environment is consistent with the studies that found that the Val allele, rather than the Met allele, is associated with better learning following contingency reversals (Krugel et al., 2009; Lonsdorf et al., 2009).

We have discussed some of the genotypes that influence behavioral and neural correlates of associative learning in healthy individuals. Many of these studies have taken a computational approach investigating the relationship between genetic markers and specific hypothesized learning processes, such as learning from positive versus negative prediction errors. This is an interesting area of research that has potential to shed light on the neurochemical factors underlying learning processes. Such knowledge might not only explain some of the variance in performance within the population at large, but also contribute to a fuller understanding of how certain pathologies develop (e.g., Epstein et al., 2007; Soliman et al., 2010).

Conclusion

Associative models predict trial-by-trial fluctuations in expectations and prediction errors. Furthermore, real-time models make predictions about specific times when outcome expectations and prediction errors are expressed and can model the temporal dynamics of these signals within every trial (e.g., Sutton & Barto, 1981). We have shown that real-time models are useful for understanding the influence of temporal parameters on learning. Furthermore, it is possible to fit model parameters that best match the behavioral performance or brain activity of each individual participant (e.g., Frank et al., 2007; Krugel et al., 2009; O'Doherty et al., 2003). This technique is particularly useful for investigating the relative contribution of different model parameters in capturing individual differences that might be linked, for example, to genetic factors or specific clinical symptoms. Such computational approaches provide a powerful tool that can be used to model and understand learning processes in general including those that support causal reasoning, and to predict learning performance at the group and individual levels.

We have provided just a few examples of how causal learning, and other forms of learning, can be modeled by an associative framework. This approach has spurred interest in discovering the neural substrates that might perform the computations assumed by associative models (e.g., Fanselow, 1998; Holroyd & Coles, 2002; Kim, Krupa, & Thompson, 1998; McNally, Johansen, & Blair, 2011). Such findings, in turn, have led to the development of more sophisticated computational models of learning that assign different roles or learning rules to various brain structures (e.g., Doll & Frank, 2009; Holroyd & Coles, 2002; McClelland McNaughton, & O'Reilly, 1995). This iterative process of searching for neural correlates of hypothesized associative processes and using these possible neural mechanisms to improve associative models has a great potential to lead to computational models of learning that have a higher degree of biological plausibility. This, we hope, will lead to a better understanding of how our neurobiology supports our ability to learn from experience, which is often required for complex forms of cognition such as causal reasoning and decision-making.

References

Aitken, M. R., & Dickinson, A. (2005). Simulations of a modified SOP model applied to retrospective revaluation of human causal learning. *Learning & Behavior, 33*, 147–159.

Baetu, I., & Baker, A. G. (2009). Human judgments of positive and negative causal chains. *Journal of Experimental Psychology: Animal Behavior Processes, 35*, 153–168.

Baetu, I., & Baker, A. G. (2010). Extinction and blocking of conditioned inhibition in human causal learning. *Learning & Behavior, 38*, 394–407.

Baetu, I., & Baker, A. G. (2012). Are preventive and generative causal reasoning symmetrical? Extinction and competition. *Quarterly Journal of Experimental Psychology, 65*, 1675–1698.

Baker, A. G. (1974). Conditioned inhibition is not the symmetrical opposite of conditioned excitation: A test of the Rescorla–Wagner model. *Learning and Motivation, 5*, 369–379.

Baker, A. G. (1977). Conditioned inhibition arising from a between-sessions negative correlation. *Journal of Experimental Psychology: Animal Behaviour Processes, 3*, 144–155.

Baker, A. G., Mercier, P., Vallée-Tourangeau, F., Frank, R., & Pan, M. (1993). Selective associations and causality judgments: Presence of a strong causal factor may reduce judgments of a weaker one. *Journal of Experimental Psychology: Learning, Memory, and Cognition, 19*, 414–432.

Baker, A. G., Murphy, R. A., Mehta, R., & Baetu, I. (2005). Mental models of causation: A comparative view. In A. J. Wills (Ed.), *New directions in human associative learning* (pp. 11–40). Mahwah, NJ: Lawrence Erlbaum.

Baker, A. G., Murphy, R. A., & Vallée-Tourangeau, F. (1996). Associative and normative models of causal induction: Reacting to versus understanding cause. In D. R. Shanks, K. J. Holyoak & D. L. Medin (Eds.), *The psychology of learning and motivation* (Vol. 34, pp. 1–45). San Diego, CA: Academic Press.

Barberia, I., Baetu, I., Murphy, R. A., & Baker, A. G. (2011). Do associations explain mental models of cause? *International Journal of Comparative Psychology, 24*, 365–388.

Bellebaum, C., & Daum, I. (2008). Learning-related changes in reward expectancy are reflected in the feedback-related negativity. *European Journal of Neuroscience, 27*, 1823–1835.

Bilder, R. M., Volavka, J., Lachman, H. M., & Grace, A. A. (2004). The catechol-O- methyltransferase polymorphism: relations to the tonic-phasic dopamine hypothesis and neuropsychiatric phenotypes. *Neuropsychopharmacology, 29*, 1943–1961.

Chapman, G. B., & Robbins, S. J. (1990). Cue interaction in human contingency judgment. *Memory & Cognition, 18*, 537–545.

Chen, J., Lipska, B. K., Halim, N., Ma, Q. D., Matsumoto, M., Melhem, S., ... Weinberger, D. R. (2004). Functional analysis of genetic variation in catechol-O-methyltransferase COMT: Effects on mRNA, protein, and enzyme activity in postmortem human brain. *American Journal of Human Genetics, 75*, 807–821.

Cheng, P. W. (1997). From covariation to causation: A causal power theory. *Psychological Review, 104*, 367–405.

Collins, A. G. E., & Frank, M. J. (2012). How much of reinforcement learning is working memory, not reinforcement learning? A behavioral, computational and neurogenetic analysis. *European Journal of Neuroscience, 35*, 1024–1035.

Corlett, P. R., Aitken, M. R., Dickinson, A., Shanks, D. R., Honey, G. D., Honey, R. A., ... Fletcher, P. C. (2004). Prediction error during retrospective revaluation of causal associations in humans: fMRI evidence in favor of an associative model of learning. *Neuron, 44*, 877–88.

Corlett, P. R., Honey, G. D., & Fletcher, P. C. (2007). From prediction error to psychosis: ketamine as a pharmacological model of delusions. *Journal of Psychopharmacology, 21*, 238–252.

Darredeau, C., Baetu, I., Baker, A. G., & Murphy, R. A. (2009). Competition between multiple causes of a single outcome in causal reasoning. *Journal of Experimental Psychology: Animal Behavior Processes, 35*, 1–14.

Delamater, A. R. (2012). On the nature of the CS and US representations in Pavlovian learning. *Learning & Behavior, 40*, 1–23.

Dickinson, A., & Pearce, J. M. (1977). Inhibitory interactions between appetitive and aversive stimuli. *Psychological Bulletin, 844*, 690–711.

Dickinson, A., Shanks, D., & Evenden, J. (1984). Judgement of act-outcome contingency: The role of selective attribution. *Quarterly Journal of Experimental Psychology A: Human Experimental Psychology, 36*, 29–50.

Dickinson, A., Watt, A., & Griffiths, W. J. H. (1992). Free-operant acquisition with delayed reinforcement. *Quarterly Journal of Experimental Psychology, 45B*: 241–258.

Doll, B. B., & Frank, M. J. (2009). The basal ganglia in reward and decision making: Computational models and empirical studies. In J. Dreher & L. Tremblay Eds., *Handbook of Reward and Decision Making* (pp. 399–425). Oxford, UK: Academic Press.

Egan, M. F., Goldberg, T. E., Kolachana, B. S., Callicott, J. H., Mazzanti, C. M., Straub, R. E., ... Weinberger, D. R. (2001). Effect of COMT Val108/158 Met genotype on frontal lobe function and risk for schizophrenia. *Proceedings of the National Academy of Sciences of the United States of America, 98,* 6917–6922.

Epstein, L. H., Temple, J. L., Neaderhiser, B. J., Salis, R. J., Erbe, R. W., & Leddy, J. J. (2007). Food reinforcement, the dopamine D2 receptor genotype, and energy intake in obese and nonobese humans. *Behavioral Neuroscience, 121,* 877–886.

Fanselow, M. S. (1998). Pavlovian conditioning, negative feedback, and blocking: Mechanisms that regulate association formation. *Neuron, 20,* 625–627.

Fletcher, P. C., Anderson, J. M., Shanks, D. R., Honey, R., Carpenter, T. A., Donovan, T., ... Bulmore, E. T. (2001). Responses of human frontal cortex to surprising events are predicted by formal associative learning theory. *Nature Neuroscience, 4,* 1043–1048.

Flor, H., Birbaumer, N., Roberts, L. E., Feige, B., Lutzenberger, W., Hermann, C., & Kopp, B. (1996). Slow potentials, event-related potentials, "gamma-band" activity, and motor responses during aversive conditioning in humans. *Experimental Brain Research, 112,* 298–312.

Frank, M. J., Doll, B. B., Oas-Terpstra, J., & Moreno, F. (2009). Prefrontal and striatal dopaminergic genes predict individual differences in exploration and exploitation. *Nature Neuroscience, 12,* 1062–1068.

Frank, M. J., & Hutchinson, K. (2009). Genetic contributions to avoidance-based decisions: Striatal D2 receptor polymorphisms. *Neuroscience, 164,* 131–140.

Frank, M. J., Moustafa, A. A., Haughey, H. M., Curran, T., & Hutchinson, K. E. (2007). Genetic triple dissociation reveals multiple roles for dopamine in reinforcement learning. *Proceedings of the National Academy of Sciences of the United States of America, 104,* 16311–16316.

Fuke, S., Suo, S., Takahashi, N., Koike, H., Sasagawa, N., & Ishiura, S. (2001). The VNTR polymorphism of the human dopamine transporter DAT1 gene affects gene expression. *Pharmacogenomics Journal, 1,* 152–156.

Graham, S. (1999). Retrospective revaluation and inhibitory associations: Does perceptual learning modulate our perception of the contingencies between events? *Quarterly Journal of Experimental Psychology: Comparative and Physiological Psychology, 52:* 159–185.

Griffiths, T. L., & Tenenbaum, J. B. (2005). Structure and strength in causal induction. *Cognitive Psychology, 51,* 334–384.

Hall, J. F. (1984). Backward conditioning in Pavlovian type studies: Revaluation and present status. *Pavlovian Journal of Biological Science, 19,* 163–168.

Harris, J. A. (2006). Elemental representations of stimuli in associative learning. *Psychological Review, 113,* 584–605.

Hermann, A., Küpper, Y., Schmitz, A., Walter, B., Vaitl, D., Hennig, J., ... Tabbert, K. (2012). Functional gene polymorphisms in the serotonin system and traumatic life events modulate the neural basis of fear acquisition and extinction. *PLoS One, 7,* e44352.

Hirvonen, M., Laakso, A., Nagren, K., Rinne, J., Pohjalainen, T., & Hietala, J. (2005). C957t polymorphism of the dopamine d2 receptor drd2 gene affects striatal drd2 availability in vivo. *Molecular Psychiatry, 10,* 889.

Hirvonen, M. H., Lumme, V., Hirvonen, J., Pesonen, U., Någren, K., Vahlberg, T., ... Hietala, J. (2009). C957T polymorphism of the human dopamine D2 receptor gene predicts extrastriatal dopamine receptor availability in vivo. *Progress in Neuro-Psychopharmacology & Biological Psychiatry, 33,* 630–636.

Holroyd, C. B., & Coles, M. G. (2002). The neural basis of human error processing: Reinforcement learning, dopamine, and the error-related negativity. *Psychological Review, 109,* 679–709.

Hoogman, M., Onnink, M., Cools, R., Aarts, E., Kan, C., Arias Vasquez, A., ... & Franke, B. (2012). The dopamine transporter haplotype and reward-related striatal responses in adult ADHD. *European Psychopharmacology, 236,* 469–478.

Jocham, G., Klein, T. A., Neumann, J., von Cramon, D. Y., Reuter, M., & Ullsperger, M. (2009). Dopamine DRD2 polymorphism alters reversal learning and associated neural activity. *Journal of Neuroscience, 29,* 3695–3704.

Kamin, L. J. (1969). Selective associations and conditioning. In W. K. Honig & N. J. Mackintosh (Eds.), *Fundamental issues in associative learning* (pp. 42–64). Halifax, NS: Dalhousie University Press.

Kim, J. J., Krupa, D. J., & Thompson, R. F. (1998). Inhibitory cerebello-olivary projections and blocking effect in classical conditioning. *Science, 279,* 570–573.

Klein, T. A., Neumann, J., Reuter, M., Hennig, J., von Cramon, D. Y., & Ullsperger, M. (2007). Genetically determined differences in learning from errors. *Science, 318,* 1642–1645.

Knutson, B., Taylor, J., Kaufman, M., Peterson, R., & Glover, G. (2005). Distributed neural representation of expected value. *Journal of Neuroscience, 25,* 4806–4812.

Konorski, J. (1967). *Integrative activity of the brain: An interdisciplinary approach.* Chicago, IL: Chicago University Press.

Krugel, L. K., Biele, G., Mohr, P. N. C., Li, S. C., & Heekaeren, H. R. (2009). Genetic variation in dopaminergic neuromodulation influences the ability to rapidly and flexibly adapt decisions. *Proceeding of the National Academy of Sciences of the United States of America, 106,* 17951–17956.

Kutlu, M. G., & Schmajuk, N. A. (2012). Solving Pavlov's puzzle: Attentional, associative, and flexible configural mechanisms in classical conditioning. *Learning & Behavior, 40,* 269–291.

Lagnado, D. A., & Sloman, S. A. (2006). Time as guide to cause. *Journal of Experimental Psychology: Learning, Memory, and Cognition, 32,* 451–460.

Lee, M. R., Gallen, C. L., Zhang, X., Hodgkinson, C. A., Goldman, D., Stein, E. A., & Barr, C. S. (2011). Functional polymorphism of the mu-opioid receptor gene OPRM1 influences reinforcement learning in humans. *PLoS One, 6,* e24203.

Lonsdorf, T. B., Weike, A. I., Nikamo, P., Schalling, M., Hamm, A. O., & Ohman, A. (2009). Genetic gating of human fear learning and extinction: possible implications for gene–environment interaction in anxiety disorder. *Psychological Science, 20,* 198–206.

Lotz, A., Vervliet, B., & Lachnit, H. (2009). Blocking of conditioned inhibition in human causal learning: No learning about the absence of outcomes. *Experimental Psychology, 56,* 381–385.

Ludvig, E. A., Sutton, R. S., & Kehoe, E. J. (2012). Evaluating the TD model of classical conditioning. *Learning & Behavior, 40,* 305–319.

Lysle, D. T., & Fowler, H. (1985). Inhibition as a "slave" process: Deactivation of conditioned inhibition through extinction of conditioned excitation. *Journal of Experimental Psychology: Animal Behavior Processes, 11,* 71–94.

Mackintosh, N. J. (1975). A theory of attention: Variations in the associability of stimuli with reinforcement. *Psychological Review, 82,* 276–298.

McClelland, J. L., McNaughton, B. L., & O'Reilly, R. C. (1995). Why there are complementary learning systems in the hippocampus and neocortex: Insights from the successes and failures of connectionist models of learning and memory. *Psychological Review, 102,* 419-57.

McClelland, J L., & Rumelhart, D. E. (1988). *Explorations in parallel distributed processing: A handbook of models, programs, and exercises.* Boston, MA: MIT Press.

McClure, S. M., Berns, G. S., & Montague, P. R. (2003). Temporal prediction errors in a passive learning task activate human striatum. *Neuron, 38,* 339–346.

McLaren, I. P. L., & Mackintosh, N. J. (2000). Associative learning and elemental representations. I: A theory and its application to latent inhibition and perceptual learning. *Animal Learning & Behavior*, 26, 211–246.

McNally, G. P., Johansen, J. P., & Blair, H. T. (2011). Placing prediction into the fear circuit. *Trends in Neurosciences*, 34, 283–292.

Meyer-Lindenberg, A., Straub, R. E., Lipska, B. K., Verchinski, B. A., Goldberg, T., Callicott, J. H., ... Weinberger, D. R. (2007). Genetic evidence implicating DARPP-32 in human frontostriatal structure, function, and cognition. *Journal of Clinical Investigation*, 117, 672–682.

Meyer-Lindenberg, A., & Weinberger, D. R., 2006. Intermediate phenotypes and genetic mechanisms of psychiatric disorders. *Nature Reviews Neuroscience*, 7, 818–827.

Miller, R. R., Barnet, R. C., & Grahame, N. J. (1995). Assessment of the Rescorla–Wagner model. *Psychological Bulletin*, 117, 363–386.

Miller, R. R., & Matzel, L. D. (1988). The comparator hypothesis: A response rule for the expression of associations. In G. H. Bower (Ed.), *The psychology of learning and motivation* (Vol. 22, pp. 51–92). San Diego, CA: Academic Press.

Moore, J. W., & Stickney, K. J. (1985). Antiassociations: Conditioned inhibition in attentional-associative networks. In R. R. Miller & N.E Spear (Eds.), *Information processing in animals: Conditioned inhibition* (pp. 209–232). Hillsdale, NJ: Erlbaum.

Morris, R. W., Vercammen, A., Lenroot, R., Moore, L., Short, B., Langton, J. M., ... Weickert, T. W. (2011). Disambiguating ventral striatum fMRI-related bold signal during reward prediction in schizophrenia. *Molecular Psychiatry*, 17, 280–289.

Murphy, R. A., Mondragón, E., Murphy, V. A., & Fouquet, N. (2004). Serial order of conditioned stimuli as a discriminative cue for Pavlovian conditioneding. *Behavioural Processes*, 67, 303–311.

Noble, E. P. (2003). D2 dopamine receptor gene in psychiatric and neurologic disorders and its phenotypes. *American Journal of Medical Genetics Part B*, 116, 103–125.

O'Doherty, J., Dayan, P., Friston, K. J., Critchley, H. D., & Dolan, R. J. (2003). Temporal difference models and reward-related learning in the human brain. *Neuron*, 382, 329–337.

O'Doherty, J. P., Deichmann, R., Critchley, H. D., & Dolan, R. J. (2002). Neural responses during anticipation of a primary taste reward. *Neuron*, 33, 815–826.

Pagnoni, G., Zink, C. F., Montague, P. R., & Berns, G. S. (2002). Activity in human ventral striatum locked to errors of reward prediction. *Nature Neuroscience*, 5, 97–98.

Pavlov, I. P. (1927). *Conditioned reflexes*. London, UK: Oxford University Press.

Pearce, J. M. (1994). Similarity and discrimination: A selective review and a connectionist model. *Psychological Review*, 101, 587–607.

Pearce, J. M., & Hall, G. (1980). A model of Pavlovian learning: Variations in the effectiveness of conditioned but not unconditioned stimuli. *Psychological Review*, 87, 532–552.

Pessiglione, M., Seymour, B., Flandin, G., Dolan, R. J., & Frith, C. D. (2006). Dopamine-dependent prediction errors underpin reward-seeking behaviour in humans. *Nature*, 442, 1042–1045.

Philiastides, M. G., Biele, G., Vavatzanidis, N., Kazzer, P., & Heekeren, H. R. (2010). Temporal dynamics of prediction error processing during reward-based decision making. *NeuroImage*, 53, 221–232.

Ploghaus, A., Tracey, I., Clare, S., Gati, J. S., Rawlins, J. N., & Matthews, P. M. (2000). Learning about pain: the neural substrate of the prediction error for aversive events. *Proceeding of the National Academy of Sciences of the United States of America*, 97, 9281–9286.

Raczka, K. A., Mechias, M. L., Gartmann, N., Reif, A., Deckert, J., Pessiglione, M., & Kalisch, R. (2011). Empirical support for an involvement of the mesostriatal dopamine system in human fear extinction. *Translational Psychiatry*, 1, e12.

Rescorla, R. A. (1969). Pavlovian conditioned inhibition. *Psychological Bulletin, 72,* 77–81.

Rescorla, R. A., & Wagner, A. R. (1972). A theory of Pavlovian conditioning: Variations in the effectiveness of reinforcement and non-reinforcement. In A. H. Black & W. F. Prokasy (Eds.), *Classical conditioning II: Current theory and research* (pp. 64–99). New York, NY: Appleton-Century-Crofts.

Ritchie, T., & Noble, E. P. (2003). Association of seven polymorphisms of the D2 dopamine receptor gene with brain receptor-binding characteristics. *Neurochemical Research, 28,* 73–82.

Rothemund, Y., Ziegler, S., Hermann, C., Gruesser, S. M., Foell, J., Patrick, C. J., & Flor, H. (2012). Fear conditioning in psychopaths: event-related potentials and peripheral measures. *Biological Psychology, 90,* 50–9.

Schachtman, T. R., Matzel, L. D., & Miller, R. R. (1988). Retardation of conditioned excitation following operational inhibitory blocking. *Animal Learning & Behavior, 16,* 100–104.

Schmajuk, N. A., Lam, Y. W., & Gray, J. A. (1996). Latent inhibition: A neural network approach. *Journal of Experimental Psychology: Animal Behavior Processes, 22,* 321–349.

Schultz, W., Dayan, P., & Montague, R. (1997). A neural substrate of prediction and reward. *Science, 275,* 1593–1599.

Shanks, D. R. (1985). Forward and backward blocking in human contingency judgment. *Quarterly Journal of Experimental Psychology B: Comparative and Physiological Psychology, 37,* 1–21.

Shanks, D., Pearson, S. M., & Dickinson, A. (1989). Temporal contiguity and the judgment of causality by human subjects. *Quarterly Journal of Experimental Psychology: Comparative and Physiological Psychology, 41,* 139–159.

Schott, B. H., Seidenbecher, C. I., Fenker, D. B., Lauer, C. J., Bunzeck, N., Bernstein, H. G., … Duzel, E. (2006). The dopaminergic midbrain participates in human episodic memory formation: evidence from genetic imaging. *Journal of Neuroscience, 26,* 1407–1417.

Simons, R. F., Ohman, A., & Lang, P. J. (1979). Anticipation and response set: Cortical, cardiac and electrodermal correlates. *Psychophysiology, 16,* 222–233.

Slifstein, M., Kolachana, B., Simpson, E.H., Tabares, P., Cheng, B., Duvall, M., … Abi-Dargham, A. (2008). COMT genotype predicts cortical-limbic D1 receptor availability measured with [11C]NNC112 and PET. *Molecular Psychiatry, 13,* 821–827.

Soliman, F., Glatt, C. E., Bath, K. G., Levita, L., Jones, R. M., Pattwell, S. S., … Casey, B. J. (2010). A genetic variant BDNF polymorphism alters extinction learning in both mouse and human. *Science, 327,* 863–866.

Stout, S., Escobar, M., & Miller, R. R. (2004). Trial number and compound stimuli temporal relationship as joint determinants of second-order conditioning and conditioned inhibition. *Learning & Behavior, 32,* 230–239.

Suiter, R. D., & LoLordo, V. M. (1971). Blocking of inhibitory Pavlovian conditioning in the conditioned emotional response procedure. *Journal of Comparative & Physiological Psychology, 76,* 137–141.

Sutton, R. S., & Barto, A. G. (1981). Toward a modern theory of adaptive networks: expectation and prediction. *Psychological Review, 88,* 135–70.

Steinberg, E. E., Keiflin, R., Boivin, J. R., Witten, I. B., Deisseroth, K., & Janak, P. H. (2013). A causal link between prediction errors, dopamine neurons and learning. *Nature Neuroscience, 16,* 966–973.

Thorwart, A., Livesey, E. J., & Harris, J. A. (2012). Normalization between stimulus elements in a model of Pavlovian conditioning: Showjumping on an elemental horse. *Learning & Behavior, 40,* 334–346.

Tobler, P. N., Dickinson, A., & Schultz, W. (2003). Coding of predicted reward omission by dopamine neurons in a conditioned inhibition paradigm. *Journal of Neuroscience, 23,* 10402–10410.

Turner, D. C., Aitken, M. R., Shanks, D. R., Sahakian, B. J., Robbins, T. W., Schwarzbauer, C., & Fletcher, P. C. (2004). The role of the lateral frontal cortex in causal associative learning: exploring preventative and super-learning. *Cerebral Cortex, 14,* 872–80.

Vallée-Tourangeau, F., Murphy, R. A., & Baker, A. G. (1998). Causal induction in the presence of a perfect negative cue: Contrasting predictions from associative and statistical models. *Quarterly Journal of Experimental Psychology: Comparative and Physiological Psychology, 51:* 173–191.

van Dyck, C. H., Malison, R. T., Jacobsen, L. K., Seibyl, J. P., Staley, J. K., Laruelle, M., ... & Gelernter, J. (2005). Increased dopamine transporter availability associated with the 9-repeat allele of the SLC6A3 gene. *Journal of Nuclear Medicine, 46,* 745–751.

VanNess, S. H., Owens, M. J., & Kilts, C. D. (2005). The variable number of tandem repeats element in DAT1 regulates in vitro dopamine transporter density. *BMC Genetics, 6,* 55.

Waelti, P., Dickinson, A., & Schultz, W. (2001). Dopamine responses comply with basic assumptions of formal learning theory. *Nature, 412,* 43–48.

Wagner, A. R. (1981). SOP: A model of automatic memory processing in animal behavior. In N. E. Spear & R. R. Miller (Eds.), *Information processing in animals: Memory mechanisms* (pp. 5–47). Hillsdale, NJ: Erlbaum.

Wagner, A. R., Logan, F. A., Haberlandt, K., & Price, T. (1968). Stimulus selection in animal discrimination learning. *Journal of Experimental Psychology, 76,* 171–180.

Walsh, M. M., & Anderson, J. R. (2011). Modulation of the feedback-related negativity by instruction and experience. *Proceedings of the National Academy of Sciences of the United States of America, 108,* 19048–19053.

Wasserman, E. A., Elek, S. M., Chatlosh, D. L., & Baker, A. G. (1993). Rating causal relations: Role of probability in judgments of response-outcome contingency. *Journal of Experimental Psychology: Learning, Memory, and Cognition, 19,* 174–188.

Williams, D. A., Travis, G. M., & Overmier, J. B. (1986). Within-compound associations modulate the relative effectiveness of differential and Pavlovian conditioned inhibition procedures. *Journal of Experimental Psychology: Animal Behavior Processes, 12,* 351–362.

Yarlas, A. S., Cheng, P. W., & Holyoak, K. J. (1995). Alternative approaches to causal induction: The probabilistic contrast versus the Rescorla–Wagner model. In J. F. Lehman & J. D. Moore (Eds.), *Proceedings of the Seventeenth Annual Conference of the Cognitive Science Society* (pp. 431–436). Hillsdale, NJ: Erlbaum.

Yeung, N., & Sanfey, A. G. (2004). Independent coding of reward magnitude and valence in the human brain. *Journal of Neuroscience, 24,* 6258–6264.

Yin, H., Barnet, R. C., & Miller, R. R. (1994). Second-order conditioning and Pavlovian conditioned inhibition: Operational similarities and differences. *Journal of Experimental Psychology: Animal Behavior Processes, 20,* 419–428.

Zimmer-Hart, C. L., & Rescorla, R. A. (1974). Extinction of Pavlovian conditioned inhibition. *Journal of Comparative and Physiological Psychology, 86,* 837–845.

Part III

Associative Perspectives on the Human Condition

16

The Psychological and Physiological Mechanisms of Habit Formation

Nura W. Lingawi, Amir Dezfouli, and Bernard W. Balleine

Habits are ubiquitous phenomena; so ubiquitous in fact that they may seem to warrant little elaboration. The word itself often conjures up negative associations; the term "bad habit" is frequently used to describe various undesirable behaviors. However, habitual behaviors are critical for efficient and effective functioning in everyday life. Actions that have become habitual and reflexive relieve cognitive and attentional load; rather than having to evaluate all available actions at every choice point, habits allow for actions to be executed fluidly and rapidly. Consider, for example, getting ready for work every morning without the seamless succession of actions attained through years of repetition. Tying our shoes and making a cup of coffee would require such abundant attention that we would be mentally drained before even stepping out the door. Indeed, in his classic 1890 text, *Principles of Psychology*, William James refers to habits as "the enormous flywheel of society, its most precious conservative agent" (James, 1918, p. 121), and certainly they simplify our movements and alleviate our conscious attention.

In recent years, there has been a growing body of research aimed at elucidating the psychological factors and neural substrates of habitual behavior. Attaining a better understanding of these factors not only provides us with greater knowledge of our own overt actions, but provides an insight into the way we adapt to a changing environment. As a result, in this chapter, we will discuss how we study habitual behavior empirically as well as the psychological and neural mechanisms of habit development. Finally, we will discuss how habits interact with nonhabitual actions and the structure in which actions are selected.

Defining Habits from an Instrumental Learning Perspective

Various definitions of the term "habit" have emerged from a range of fields, but, particularly within contemporary research in psychology and neuroscience, the most common definition is an empirical one developed from studies of instrumental learning. This field has a particular interest in investigating what learning occurs as animals perform specific action and experience the consequences of those actions. Early descriptions of instrumental behavior, particularly those advocated by Hull (1943), proposed that it be viewed, like other reflexes, as the consequence of specific eliciting stimuli coming to provoke responding through the selective application of a biologically potent reinforcer, a view rooted in Thorndike's (1911) law of effect. From the Hullian perspective, reinforcers serve to strengthen the formation of an association between any prevailing sensory stimuli and specific motor responses, resulting in an S–R association. As an example, consider the case of a hungry rat that has been trained to press a lever in an operant chamber to earn access to a food pellet. From the S–R standpoint, the stimuli (in this case, the situational stimuli of the context, the presentation of the lever, etc.) will elicit a response (a lever press) because the reinforcing properties of the food pellet have previously served to strengthen the association between these stimuli and the response. Thus, the rat in this situation will press the lever, not because of knowledge of the outcome or its value but because the antecedent stimuli elicit the action. Other theorists, most notably Dickinson and colleagues (Adams & Dickinson, 1981; Dickinson, 1985, 1989, 1994), have argued that, although sufficient, such S–R processes are not necessary to acquire instrumental actions; that other associative processes can support instrumental conditioning. Chief among the viable alternatives has been the suggestion that, in addition to S–R associations, animals can also form direct associations between actions and their consequences or outcomes. That is, they can form action–outcome (A–O) associations. Whereas habitual responses do not rely on a representation of the reinforcer and are driven by contextual or situational stimuli, recent research suggests that the performance of actions mediated by the A–O association are controlled both by knowledge of the instrumental contingency between the action and its specific outcome, and by the current value of that outcome (Adams, 1980; Balleine & Dickinson, 1998; Corbit, Muir, & Balleine, 2001, 2003; Dickinson & Nicholas, 1983; Dickinson, Nicholas, & Adams, 1983; Yin, Knowlton, & Balleine, 2006). As a consequence, actions mediated by A–O learning are commonly referred to as goal-directed actions. Thus, in contemporary research, it has become customary to view instrumental learning as governed by two associative learning processes involving A–O learning for goal-directed actions and S–R learning for habits.[1] As a consequence of this development, defining an action as goal-directed or habitual requires first establishing the associative structure supporting its performance.

Differentiating Habitual and Goal-Directed Behaviors

Manipulating the A–O contingency

One way of differentiating goal-directed from habitual actions is to determine whether the contingency between performance of the action and outcome delivery is controlling performance. In the case of a rat pressing a lever for a particular outcome, for example, the contingency between action and outcome will be degraded if the outcome is made freely available. Animals using the encoded A–O contingency to control performance should decrease their performance of the degraded action, whereas other nondegraded actions should be maintained. Hammond (1980) demonstrated that the instrumental performance of rats can be sensitive to these types of changes in contingency and that they reduce lever pressing when the probability of the outcome given the action had decreased. Dickinson and Charnock (1985), among others (Holland, 1979; Kosaki & Dickinson, 2010), attained similar results when contingencies were manipulated. There are, however, situations in which animals are insensitive to these types of changes in A–O contingency (see, for example, Balleine & Dickinson, 1998; Corbit *et al.*, 2001, 2003; Yin *et al.*, 2006), and these will be discussed further below.

Manipulating outcome value

Although contingency manipulations are a reliable method for differentiating goal-directed from habitual actions, the more frequently used method involves changes to outcome value. As such, the majority of the discussion regarding these two distinct learning processes will use outcome devaluation as the experimental procedure. Modifications in behavior due to changes in outcome value are viewed as evidence that the representation of the outcome contributes to the associative structure that elicits the response (Adams, 1980); that is, that the A–O association mediates appropriate increases or decreases in performance of an action due to the change in outcome value. Importantly, changes in instrumental responding due to shifts in motivation rely on incentive learning, or updating the current value of the outcome while in the now new motivational state (for a discussion of incentive learning, see Dickinson, 1994; Dickinson & Balleine, 1993).

Two of the most common means of manipulating outcome value involve changing value after the animal has learned about the A–O associations. Take, for example, our hungry rat that has learned to lever press for a food pellet. One way to devalue the outcome is to prefeed the rat with pellets before testing its lever press performance during a test where no outcomes are delivered. Since the animal has become sated on the outcome, its value has decreased and is now devalued. Consequently, if the rat's behavior is generated by an A–O association, responding should be attenuated during the test when compared with another rat that did not receive pellets, but that received some other outcome (such as their maintenance diet, to control for the effects of general satiety) during the prefeeding phase, or when compared with an action that delivers a different outcome entirely. However, if the behavior is habitual, responding is predicted to be similar in both of the devalued and nondevalued conditions. This specific-satiety procedure has been used in a number of experiments, in both single-action (Killcross & Coutureau, 2003) and in binary choice tasks (see, for example, Colwill & Rescorla, 1986; Dickinson & Balleine, 2002 for review). It is important to emphasize that tests that assess knowledge of outcome value are generally conducted in extinction, where no outcomes are presented. This ensures that any reduction in performance seen during the test phase reflects the animals' knowledge of the outcome values encoded during the training sessions, and precludes the animal from using any feedback to adjust their actions during the test.

An alternative form of devaluation consists in conditioning a taste aversion to the outcome. Animals readily associate gastric malaise with specific foods and tastes (Garcia, Kimeldorf, & Koelling, 1955). Lithium chloride (LiCl) induces a gastric malaise in rats when injected intraperitoneally, and by pairing the consumption of the outcome with injections of LiCl, animals attribute the illness to the outcome it had just consumed. Like specific satiety, if the animal's behavior is goal directed and guided by A–O associations, then pairing an outcome with LiCl should decrease the performance of actions that were associated with that outcome during training compared with animals that did not receive the pairing. However, if the behavior is habitual, then the performance of animals that had the LiCl–food pairings is generally found to be similar to those that did not receive the pairings. Indeed, like contingency degradation, there are certain circumstances and conditions that have been found to render instrumental performance impervious to these outcome devaluation procedures. Based on the argument that two learning processes can control instrumental performance together with the other considerations above, it is generally assumed that the absence of a devaluation effect is due to the control of performance by the S–R habit system. The conditions under which S–R associations strengthen and cause animals to behave in an inflexible and habitual manner are discussed in the next section.

Perspectives on Habit Formation

Correlation theory

Early experiments using the conditioned taste aversion procedure to examine instrumental learning (see, for example, Adams, 1980; Holman, 1975) found results in conflict with subsequent experiments (Adams, 1982; Adams & Dickinson, 1981; Balleine & Dickinson, 1991; Colwill & Rescorla, 1985; Dickinson et al., 1983). Whereas the latter found evidence of sensitivity to outcome devaluation, the former did not. This discrepancy led to a reconsideration of the nature of habit learning. One view of habits held that they only emerge after extended training (Kimble & Perlmuter, 1970). Evidence for this view came from Adams's 1982 experiments that varied the amount of instrumental training rats received before devaluation. In one experiment, the performance of rats that had received extended instrumental training (500 pairings of the lever press with sucrose pellets) was found to be impervious to devaluation induced by LiCl injections (see group Overtrained in Figure 16.1). In contrast, devaluation was effective in reducing lever-press responding in animals that had received relatively limited instrumental training (see group Undertrained in Figure 16.1).

This effect of overtraining on sensitivity to outcome devaluation has subsequently been demonstrated in numerous experiments comparing habitual and goal-directed control of instrumental actions (Coutureau & Killcross, 2003; Dickinson, Balleine, Watt, Gonzalez, & Boakes, 1995; Lingawi & Balleine, 2012; Quinn, Pittenger, Lee, Pierson, & Taylor, 2013; Wassum, Cely, Maidment, & Balleine, 2009; Yin, Knowlton, & Balleine, 2004, 2005). However, as Dickinson (1985) pointed out, this insensitivity to outcome devaluation cannot be due solely to the amount of training the rats received. Indeed, the results of the early studies suggested that the number of reinforced actions and the schedule on which the reinforcer was delivered were both important determinants. For example, Holman used variable interval schedules of reinforcement and found no evidence of sensitivity to outcome devaluation, whereas Adams and Dickinson (1981) gave rats training comparable to

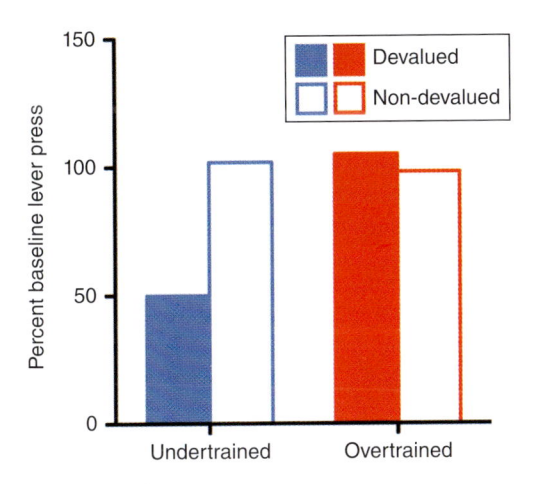

Figure 16.1 Results (adapted from Adams, 1982) demonstrating that the amount of training affects the influence of outcome devaluation on instrumental conditioning. With limited training (Undertrained), a devaluation effect can be seen: Animals reduce their responding for a devalued outcome (in this instance, a food that had previously been paired with illness), but continue to respond if the outcome is still valuable (i.e., has not been paired with illness; Nondevalued). However, after extended instrumental training, they are insensitive to outcome value and continue to respond for a devalued outcome. Adapted from Adams (1982).

that described in Holman (1975) but using ratio schedules of reinforcement and found that the rats were sensitive to outcome devaluation during an extinction test (Adams & Dickinson, 1981).

Dickinson (1985, 1994) proposed, therefore, that the critical element causing variations in the sensitivity to outcome devaluation was not the amount of training the animals received, per se, but knowledge of the relationship between the rate of performance and the rate of outcome delivery. This idea is rooted in a theory advanced by Baum (1973), suggesting that the interaction of rewarding feedback with the performance of an action increased with the strength of the *correlation* between response rate and reward rate. Drawing on this correlational theory, Dickinson (1985) asserted that this correlation determined the strength of the A–O association. Specifically, a high correlation between response rate and reward rate will strengthen the A–O association, which will be manifest in the performance of goal-directed actions, whereas a reduction in this correlation will result in a weaker A–O association and habitual behavior.

Correlation theory can account for the effects of overtraining in terms of the feedback the animal experiences as a result from varying response rates at different stages of training. As Figure 16.2 illustrates, during the initial training sessions, animals experience feedback from a wide range of response rates. This results in a strong behavior–outcome correlation, and sensitivity to outcome value. In contrast, when animals are overtrained, response rates toward the later stages of training reach an asymptote. As a consequence, the variation in the response rate, and hence the reward rate, tends to be low, and the experienced correlation across these latter training

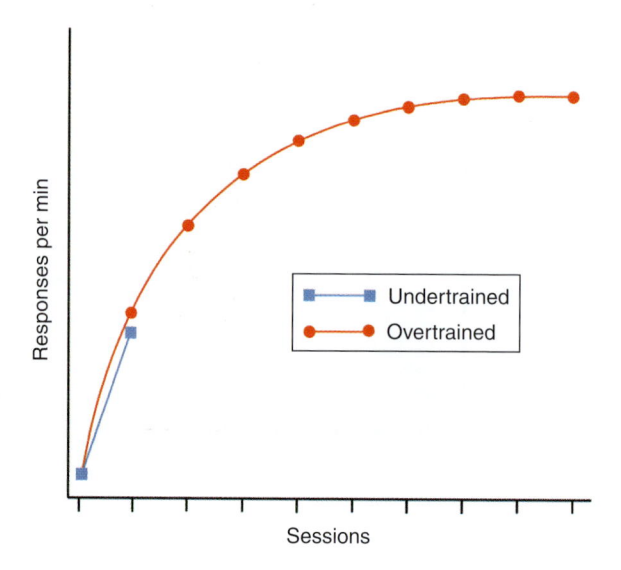

Figure 16.2 Schematic function depicting variations in rates of responding for undertrained and overtrained conditions. Initially, response rates vary markedly, whereas, with extended training, variations in response rates decrease. Decreases in response rate variability cause a decrease in response–reward correlation, causing S–R associations to strengthen and habits to form. Adapted from Dickinson (1985).

sessions between action and outcome is correspondingly low, resulting in a reduction in the A–O association. As a result, they are likely to show insensitivity to outcome devaluation. This shift from goal-directed to habitual control of actions after extended training can be best conceptualized using Dickinson *et al.*'s (1995) two-process view of the influence of A–O and S–R associations on behavior depicted in Figure 16.3. In this view, net performance is determined by the sum of A–O and S–R associations. As shown in Figure 16.3, A–O associations are strong when an animal initially learns about its actions and their consequences, but their influence declines with training. However, S–R associations start out weak, but gain strength as training progresses. This results in the performance of habitual responses that are relatively insensitive to outcome devaluation after extended training.

Interval versus ratio schedules

If it is true that the critical element that leads to the predominance of S–R associations, reflected behaviorally as insensitivity to outcome devaluation, is the correlation between response and reward rates, then schedules of reinforcement that vary this correlation should similarly affect performance after outcome devaluation. This is indeed the case. Ratio schedules establish a strong positive relationship between response rate and outcome delivery. This is akin, in practical terms, to the contingencies facing predatory animals, such as a lion hunting for food: The more she hunts, the more likely she will gain access to food. Interval schedules, on the other hand, deliver an outcome after a response but only after a specified period of time has lapsed; animals that gather fruit, grass, nectar, and so on are faced with

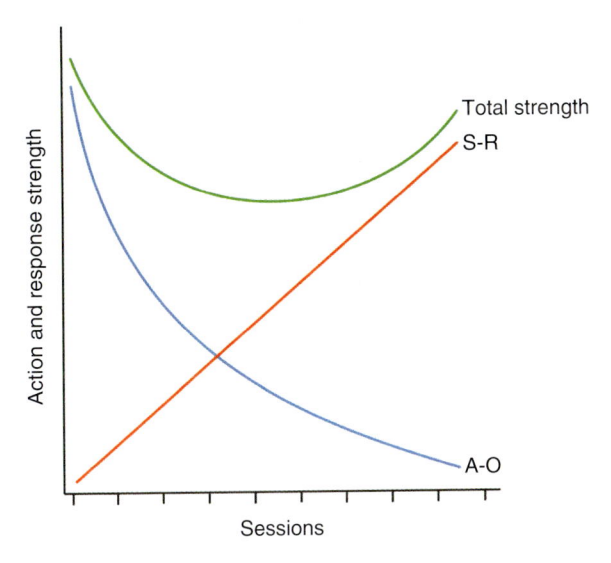

Figure 16.3 Shift from goal-directed to habitual action control as a result of overtraining. As training progresses, S–R associations increase in strength, guiding behavior, resulting in insensitivity to outcome devaluation. Adapted from Dickinson et al. (1995).

this kind of contingency; once a resource is depleted, it takes time to replenish; no amount of gathering will procure more food until time has lapsed. Thus, under interval schedules, the rate of responding does not necessarily correlate with the rate of outcome delivery, particularly if the specified interval is long, and the rate of responding is high. To test the predictions made by the correlational account advocated by Dickinson, he and colleagues (Dickinson et al., 1983) assessed sensitivity to outcome devaluation induced by conditioned taste aversion after training on ratio or on interval schedules. As predicted by the correlational account, animals trained on ratio schedules were sensitive to outcome devaluation, whereas animals trained on interval schedules were not. This was true even when the devalued outcome was delivered during the test, either contingent or noncontingent on the lever press response.

Dickinson (1985) pointed out that the critical difference between ratio and interval schedules is the feedback functions these distinct schedules provide. These feedback functions are presented in Figure 16.4; under ratio schedules, a positive correlation exists between performance of the action and outcome delivery, where the more an animal performs an action, the more outcomes it will procure. In contrast, this relationship does not exist with interval schedules; increasing response rates under interval schedules does not necessarily lead to the delivery of more outcomes.

Choice between actions

Rats typically remain sensitive to outcome devaluation despite being overtrained if they are given a choice between two actions that lead to different outcomes during training (Colwill & Rescorla, 1985, 1986). For example, Kosaki and Dickinson (2010) overtrained

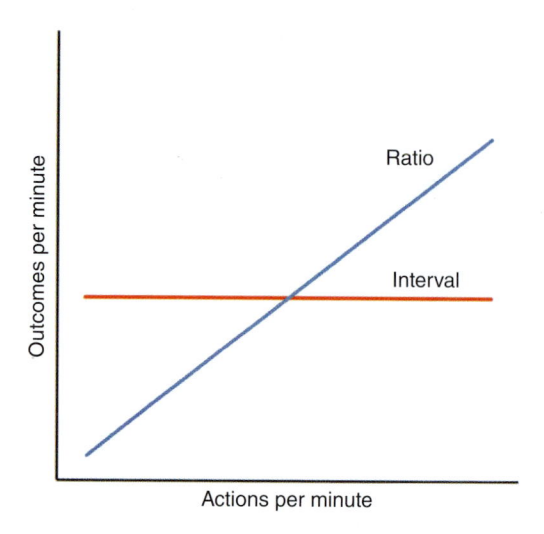

Figure 16.4 Rates of outcome delivery as a function of response rate under ratio and interval schedules of reinforcement. Under ratio schedules, there is a positive correlation between response rate and outcome delivery rate (i.e., the more actions performed, the more outcomes delivered). However, under interval schedules, an increase in performance rate does not necessarily produce increases in outcome rate. Adapted from Dickinson (1994).

rats to press two different levers to earn two rewards. Despite overtraining, instrumental responding in these rats remained sensitive to outcome devaluation caused by LiCl injections (see also Colwill & Rescorla, 1988). In contrast, rats that were overtrained on only one lever while receiving the second outcome noncontingently showed insensitivity to outcome devaluation. As the authors explain, A–O associations will weaken when the correlation between response rate and outcome rate is low, resulting in animals using S–R associations to drive behavior. However, training an animal to perform two different actions ensures that there are times when the animal is not performing one action because it is performing the other. This ensures the correlation between the rate of responding and the rate of outcome delivery remains high, causing the animal to be sensitive to outcome devaluation.

Experience of noncontingent outcomes

Rats show sensitivity to contingency degradation; responding for an earned reinforcer declines if that outcome becomes freely available (Balleine & Dickinson, 1998; Colwill & Rescorla, 1986; Dickinson & Mulatero, 1989; Hammond, 1980). However, the influence of a noncontingent outcome on a specific A–O association depends on its identity with respect to the earned outcome; whereas noncontingent delivery of the earned outcome weakens A–O associations, delivery of a different outcome tends to leave these associations unaffected.

Carefully considered, using this factor to alter the strength of A–O associations may also influence the rate of habit acquisition; that is, factors that discourage A–O learning could encourage S–R learning. We tested this hypothesis in our laboratory and found that it was indeed the case that manipulations of the strength of the A–O association

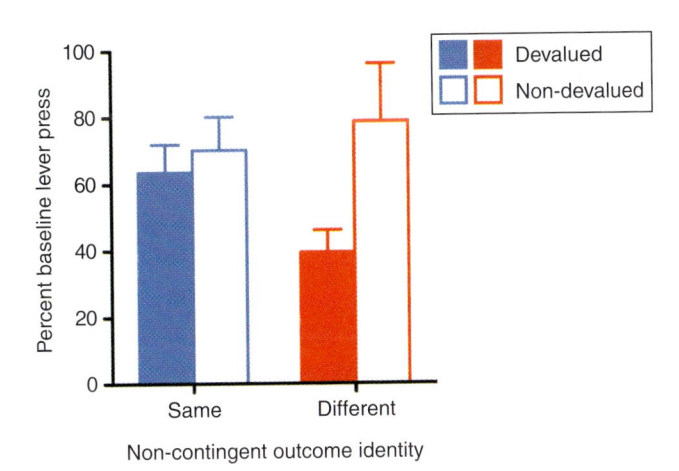

Figure 16.5 Results showing that the type of outcome noncontingently delivered determines the rate of habit acquisition. Delivery of noncontingent outcomes that were the same as the earned outcome (Group Same) caused rats to be impervious to outcome devaluation. These rats displayed habitual behavior during a 5-min extinction test conducted after outcome devaluation by conditioned taste aversion. In contrast, the delivery of noncontingent outcomes that were different from the earned outcome preserved A–O association, and rats remained goal directed at test, as determined by their relative lever press responding from baseline (±SEM).

affected the rate of habit acquisition. Specifically, rats that were trained to press a lever for an outcome (O1) and received noncontingent deliveries of that same outcome (O1; Group Same) were subsequently insensitive to outcome devaluation, induced by conditioned taste aversion, in a later extinction test (Figure 16.5). In contrast, rats that received a different noncontingent outcome (O2; Group Different) remained sensitive to outcome value. One interpretation of these results is that noncontingent O1 presentations resulted in a more rapid strengthening of the S–R association in Group Same, causing their actions to become habitual faster than those in Group Different. This finding is also consistent with the correlational account; the free delivery of the earned outcome should have decreased the correlation between response rate and outcome rate. This low correlation between the action and outcome could also have been augmented by the fact that the outcome was fully predicted by the context (i.e., the operant chamber), causing the correlation between the lever press and O1 to weaken further. In any case, these data suggest that manipulations that reduce the strength of the A–O contingency might facilitate the rate of habit formation.

Habits as model-free reinforcement learning

An alternative, currently popular, account of habits has been derived from reinforcement learning theories of adaptive behavior (Sutton & Barto, 1998). Reinforcement learning (RL) addresses the computational problem of choosing an action among other available actions in order to maximize future rewards. The main elements of an RL model are states, actions, rewards, and values. States refer to the situations of the environment that an agent can perceive through its sensory inputs. Within each state, there are one or several actions an agent can choose to execute. After executing an action, the agent is transferred to a new state and receives a reward (which can be positive or negative). The goal of an RL agent is to choose the course of action that leads to the highest future reward. This is achieved by predicting the value of the different actions in any particular state in order to guide action selection. The value of an action is the amount of reward that the agent expects to gain by taking that action.

RL models can be divided into two broad categories based on what aspects of the environment are being learned: *model-free* and *model-based*.[2] In model-free RL, an agent learns a value for each action using a reward-prediction error. Reward-prediction error (denoted by δ) refers to the difference between predicted value of an action (denoted by V_A) and the actual reward earned after executing that action (denoted by r):

$$\delta = r - V_A$$

This prediction error is a teaching signal used by the agent to update the value of the executed action:

$$\Delta V_A = \alpha \delta$$

where α is a learning rate. Take, for example, a rat that is placed for the first time in the conditioning chamber and allowed to press a lever to earn food pellets. While exploring the environment, it presses the lever for the first time and receives a food pellet. If this is rewarding, a positive reward-prediction error will be generated, since the reward was unexpected. This positive prediction error will cause an increase in the value of the lever press, increasing the chance of pressing the lever in the future. In this manner, actions leading to reward will be assigned higher values and so will be chosen more frequently. This form of learning is roughly similar to the learning of S–R associations, where the strength of a connection between a stimulus (or state in RL terms) and a response is modulated by the change in the reward prediction generated by the outcome of the response (Daw, Niv, & Dayan, 2005; Doya, 1999; Keramati, Dezfouli, & Piray, 2011).

The action values in model-free RL are driven by the prediction error signal, which does not convey any information about the specific source of reward. As a result, the representations of action values are not linked to a specific outcome or state that results as a consequence of the action, and so any offline change in the value of an outcome will leave the value of the actions unaffected. This predicts that an agent guided by model-free RL will not show sensitivity to outcome devaluation, a characteristic of habitual action control (Daw et al., 2005; Keramati et al., 2011).

In contrast to model-free RL, a model-based agent encodes the outcomes of actions and the reward associated with each outcome, which in sum constitutes a model of the environment. Having learned a model of the environment, the agent calculates the value of actions at each choice point based on their resultant outcomes, and reward associated with those outcomes. This is denoted by the following equation:

$$V_A = \sum_i P(O_i | A) R_{O_i}$$

where $P(O_i | A)$ is the probability of earning outcome O_i by executing action A – which can be interpreted as A–O contingency in psychological terms – and R_{O_i} is the reward of outcome O_i. Here, a change in the value of an outcome will instantly affect the computed value of an action; thus, action control will be sensitive to changes in the value of the outcome, a characteristic feature of goal-directed action control. Thus, model-free RL generates a form of action control similar to habits, whereas model-based RL is similar to goal-directed action control (Daw et al., 2005; Keramati et al., 2011).

Within this framework, both model-free and model-based RL have been argued to coexist with an arbitrator coordinating their contribution to actions. Based on the principle of reward maximization, this arbitration component selects the system at each choice point that is predicted to yield the greatest future reward. To achieve this, various arbitration rules have been suggested, and these too can be divided into two classes (Figure 16.6). In the first class (Figure 16.6A), an arbitrator receives inputs from both model-based and model-free RL systems in order or to determine the degree of contribution of each system to actions (Daw et al., 2005; Lee, Shimojo, & O'Doherty, 2014). The inputs that the arbitrator receives convey information about the quality of the predictions made by each system, which can be quantified as the uncertainty of each system about its predictions. The arbitrator then uses the uncertainty of each system to determine its relative contribution to actions (less uncertainty, higher contribution). This kind of arbitration rule implies that at each choice point, both of the systems are engaged in action control. Even when the behavior is completely habitual or goal directed, the other system remains operating in the background to provide input for making choices.

The first class of models assumes that there are situations in which predictions of the model-based RL, which has access to the model of the environment, will be worse than the model-free RL. This has been argued to be due to working memory limitations, or a sort of noise during neural computation of model-based values (Daw et al.,

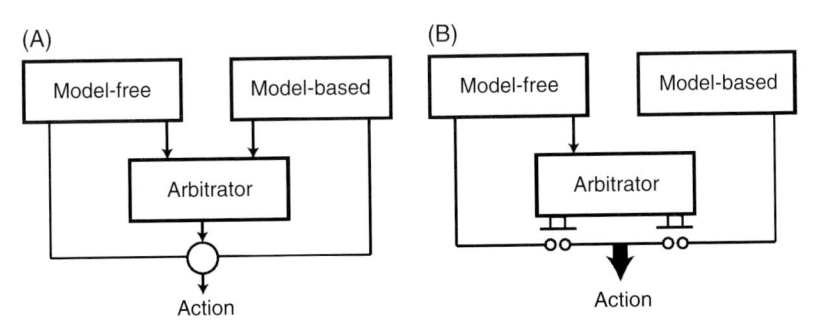

Figure 16.6 Model showing how two classes of arbitrators coordinate the contribution of model-free and model-based RL systems. (A) First class of arbitration models. The arbitrator receives inputs from both model-free and model-based systems to determine the degree of contribution of each system (W). Within this class, both systems are engaged at each choice point. (B) Second class of arbitration models, in which the arbitrator only receives inputs from the model-free system. If the quality of the prediction made by the model-free system is satisfactory, then the model-based system will not engage (the left switch will be closed, and the right switch will be open). Otherwise, the arbitrator calls on the model-based system to make a choice (the right switch will be closed, and the left switch will be open).

2005). In contrast to this assumption, the second class of models assume that the model-based RL always has perfect information about value of actions; however, engaging in the model-based action control has a cost (due to its slowness in calculating actions values or cognitive loads), and the value of perfect information provided by model-based RL should outweigh this cost in order to justify engaging in model-based action control (Keramati et al., 2011). Within this arbitration rule, the arbitrator requires inputs only from the model-free RL, and model-based RL will be activated only if the arbitrator decided not to use habits (Figure 16.6B), in contrast to the first class in which both models are always engaged.

Habits as action sequences

Although powerful, the alignment of habits with model-free RL has a number of problems. The first of these is the suggestion that the feedback that strengthens or reinforces state-action (i.e., specific S–R) associations is a function of the reward-prediction error. As we have argued previously (Dezfouli & Balleine, 2012), this anticipates that treatments that increase error should lead to rapid acquisition of new habits; for example, if, after a period of overtraining, rats are shifted from a contingent reinforcement schedule to an omission schedule, the large positive and negative prediction errors produced by this shift should result in rapidly learning responses incompatible with responding. This is not true, however. Overtrained rats are insensitive both to devaluation and to shifts in the instrumental contingency (cf. Dezfouli & Balleine, 2012; Dickinson, Campos, Varga, & Balleine, 1996). Similarly, this account predicts that the rate of acquisition of habits should reflect the strength of the error signal and so should be relatively less likely to control behavior if the error signal is weak. One way of reducing the error signal induced by the delivery of an outcome after the performance of an action (and hence the reinforcement signal) is to increase the predictability of that reinforcing event, that is, to reinforce a habit in the presence of a cue that also predicts the outcome. We have already described such an experiment in which the specific outcome used to reinforce an action was also delivered noncontingently in the absence of the action from the start of training. In this situation, the action should be a weak predictor of the outcome, and the context a relatively much stronger predictor; as such, the prediction error produced by outcome delivery after the action should also be relatively diminished. As shown above in Figure 16.5, however, training rats in the presence of noncontingent delivery of the instrumental outcome in this way still resulted in habits. Despite the fact that the experimental context should have become a relatively strong predictor of the outcome weakening the prediction error produced by outcome delivery in the context, habits emerged with the usual degree of overtraining.

Most tellingly, perhaps, equating habits with model-free RL provides no explanation for another common feature of habits, Namely, that they are not performed as independent actions but, during repetition, are chunked together with other actions to form part of a longer sequence of actions (Graybiel, 2008). In essence this means that action control transitions from being closed-loop, sensitive to environmental feedback from individual actions, to being open-loop, and hence performed in absence of such feedback. In this latter situation, feedback is reserved for the sequence in which an action is chunked rather than individual actions. Importantly, the model-free

RL explanation of habits applies only to closed-loop behavior in which the action selection is guided by the current state of the agent, and such states are, by definition, determined by sensory inputs from the environment. Hence, each action is determined by such feedback, and sequences, should they form, can only be explained in closed-loop terms. Hence, chunked habit sequences that emerge through repetition and that run off in an open looped fashion lie outside the model-free RL of habits; they cannot be explained or even described in model-free RL terms.

Recently, we have advanced an alternative perspective on the interaction of goal-directed and habitual actions based on the idea that simple goal-directed actions and habit sequences interact hierarchically for action control (Dezfouli & Balleine, 2012, 2013; Dezfouli, Lingawi, & Balleine, 2014). According to this view, habit sequences are represented independently of the individual actions and outcomes embedded in them such that the decision-maker treats the whole sequence of actions as a single response unit. As a consequence, action sequences are evaluated independently of any offline environmental changes in individual A–O contingencies or the value of outcomes inside the sequence boundaries and are executed irrespective of the outcome of each individual action, i.e., without requiring immediate feedback. On this hierarchical view, these action sequences are utilized by a goal-directed system (model-based RL) in order to efficiently achieve specific goals. This is achieved by learning the contingencies between action sequences and goals, and assessing whether an agent can achieve that goal. In essence, the goal-directed system functions at a higher level and selects which habit should be executed, whereas the role of habits is limited to the efficient implementation of the decisions made by the goal-directed process.

Although this is not the place to consider this account in detail, there is now considerable evidence for this perspective (cf. Dezfouli & Balleine, 2012, 2013; Dezfouli *et al.*, 2014). Generally, the hierarchical perspective predicts (1) if the first action in a habit sequence is selected, then the next action in that sequence is more likely to be selected; and (2) because sequences of actions are executed more rapidly than individual actions, when selecting the first element of a sequence, the second element should be executed with a reduced reaction time. Using a two-stage discrimination task, we have recently found evidence for both predictions. Furthermore, when, using Bayesian model comparison, we pitted a flat architecture (i.e., model-free models of habits explained in the previous section) against the hierarchical architecture (action sequence model of habits), a family of hierarchical RL models provided a better fit of behavior on the task than a family of flat models. Although these findings do not rule out all possible model-free accounts of instrumental conditioning, they do show that such accounts are not necessary to explain habitual actions and support a hierarchical theory of the way goal-directed and habitual actions interact.

Neural Correlates of Habitual Behavior

We now turn to examining the neural substrates involved in the formation of habitual behavior, a field within behavioral neuroscience, which has been of particular interest due to the implications it has for maladaptive behavior and aberrant decision-making. Habits were originally considered to be a form of a procedural, hippocampal-independent memory system (Squire & Zola-Morgan, 1988). It was not until the

1980s that the basal ganglia were implicated in habit learning, a suggestion first proposed by Mishkin (Mishkin, Malamut, & Bachevalier, 1984). Since then, extensive evidence elucidated the neural structures involved in learning and performing habits, and, most notably, the dorsolateral striatum (DLS) and its dopaminergic afferents from the substantia nigra pars compacta (SNc) have emerged as the major foci of interest in this regard. Additionally, the infralimbic region of the medial prefrontal cortex (IL) and the amygdala central nucleus (CeN) have both been implicated in habit formation. The anatomy and connectivity of these regions as well as evidence of their involvement in habits are discussed below; a summary of the connectivity among these regions is provided in Figure 16.7 together with the structures and connectivity shown to be involved in goal-directed behaviors.

Dorsolateral striatum

The striatum, the rodent homolog to the caudate/putamen, is commonly subdivided into the dorsal and ventral aspects, and within the dorsal region, the medial and lateral areas are functionally distinct. Inhibitory GABAergic Medium Spiny Neurons (MSN) comprise ~95% of the neurons of the striatum (Bolam, Hanley, Booth, & Bevan, 2000). These MSNs express D1 or D2 dopamine (DA) receptors, which make up the direct and indirect pathways, respectively. The traditional model of striatal function holds that these two types of MSNs have distinct efferents, and the different pathways they comprise have opposing influences on motor function (see Bagetta et al., 2011; Bolam et al., 2000 for discussion). An advantage of this model is that these D1 and D2 expressing MSNs can use dopamine signals to learn which actions are appropriate in future situations (Maia & Frank, 2011).

Recently, inactivation and lesion studies have provided clear evidence for the role of the DLS in habits. Yin et al. (2004) demonstrated that pretraining lesions of the DLS cause rats to be sensitive to outcome devaluation despite overtraining. Additionally, temporary inactivation of the DLS before testing disrupted the performance of habitual behavior, as evidenced by increased sensitivity to an omission schedule after overtraining (Yin et al., 2006). These results provide clear evidence for the role of the DLS in habit acquisition and performance. Furthermore, Featherstone and McDonald (2004) demonstrated similar deficits in S–R learning in discrimination tasks following DLS lesions. In humans, similar deficits have been shown in patients with striatal dysfunction (Knowlton, Mangels, & Squire, 1996; Poldrack et al., 2001), and neuroimaging studies have confirmed the role of the DLS in habitual control of actions; Tricomi, Balleine, and O'Doherty (2009) reported an increase in the fMRI BOLD signal in the right posterior putamen during overtraining on an instrumental task (see also De Wit et al., 2012; Haruno & Kawato, 2006).

The dopamine input to the DLS from the SNc is critical to habit formation, particularly the influence of dopamine release D2 receptor expressing neurons in the DLS. These inputs contribute to dopamine-dependent Long Term Depression (LTD) in the DLS, which is thought to underpin the acquisition of habits. It has been demonstrated that unexpected primary rewards activate phasic dopamine bursts (Schultz, 1997; see Chapter 3), and when an action is followed by a dopamine burst into the striatum, corticostriatal synapses onto D1 expressing neurons are strengthened by Long Term Potentiation (LTP). Concurrently, corticostriatal neurons projecting onto

Mechanisms of Habit Formation 425

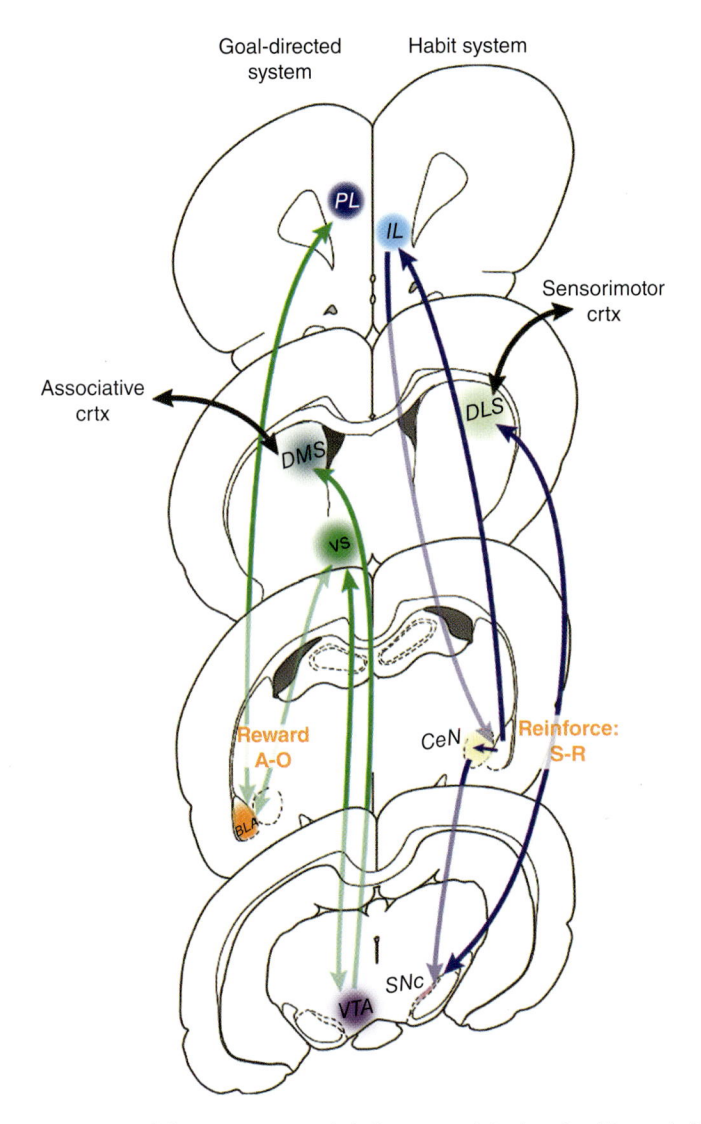

Figure 16.7 Summary of the structures and their connectivity involved in goal-directed (left) and habitual behaviors (right). The habit system involves communication between the infralimbic cortex (IL), amygdala central nucleus (CeN), substantia nigra pars compacta (SNc), and dorsolateral striatum (DLS). The goal-directed system recruits the prelimbic cortex (PL), basolateral amygdala (BLA), ventral striatum (VS), ventral tegmental area (VTA), and dorsomedial striatum (DMS), as well as the medial dorsal thalamus (not shown). Atlas sections taken from Paxinos and Watson (1998) 6th edition.

D2 expressing MSN are weakened by LTD (Maia & Frank, 2011). This LTD in the DLS involves presynaptic binding of endocannabinoids (the endogenous ligand of cannabinoid receptors) to CB1 receptors, which causes a decrease in the probability of glutamate release at the corticostriatal synapse, specifically on neurons expressing

D2 receptors (Gerdeman, Partridge, & Lupica, 2003). This release of endocannabinoids onto the presynaptic cell at the corticostriatal synapse is critical for habit formation, as transgenic animals without CB1 receptors are incapable of acquiring habits (Hilário, Clouse, Yin, & Costa, 2007). Furthermore, neuronal firing patterns within the DLS undergo changes during habit formation (Jog, Kubota, Connolly, Hillegaart, & Graybiel, 1999; Yin et al., 2004).

Nigrostriatal dopaminergic projection

The dopaminergic afferents on the DLS are critical for the development of habits. 6-Hydroxydopamine (6-OHDA) injected into the DLS, which causes deafferentation of the ascending nigrostriatal DA neurons, has been found to disrupt the formation of habits (Faure, Haberland, Conde, & El Massioui, 2005); rats with lesions of this type were shown to be sensitive to outcome devaluation despite being overtrained. Furthermore, this loss of habitual control after DA deafferentation seems to be irreversible; introduction of DA agonists failed to restore habit performance in overtrained animals (Faure, Leblanc-Veyrac, & El Massioui, 2010). Interestingly, the involvement of SNc in habits seems to transcend outcome modality, as animals that habitually self-administered nicotine show an increase in cellular activity in the SNc as compared with nonhabitual animals (Clemens, Castino, Cornish, Goodchild, & Holmes, 2014). In people, Parkinsons disease leads to the degeneration of nigrostriatal dopamine system. Parkinson's patients show similar disruptions in S–R associations, as evidenced by impairments in a probabilistic classification task designed to study nonmotor habits (Knowlton et al., 1996). In line with this, amphetamine sensitization, which critically alters dopamine function (Vanderschuren & Kalivas, 2000), was found to accelerate the transition from goal-directed to habitual behavior in rats (Nelson & Killcross, 2006) as does cocaine sensitization (Corbit, Chieng, & Balleine, 2014). This DA input likely plays a role in modulating LTP and plasticity within the corticostriatal circuit, as stimulation of the nigrostriatal DA pathway results in potentiation of these synapses (Reynolds, Hyland, & Wickens, 2001).

It is also worth noting another critical feature of dopamine in habit learning. Dopamine activity has been shown to be sensitive to the expectation of reward delivery (Montague, Dayan, & Sejnowski, 1996; Schultz, 1997) and has been described as the signal encoding reward-prediction error (Murray et al., 2007; Schultz, 1997; Suri & Schultz, 1999). Firing of these neurons during the presentation of rewarding and unpredicted events may serve as a reinforcement signal causing the animal to perform the action again in the future, thus strengthening the S–R association (Seger & Spiering, 2011), although, as discussed above, this is unlikely to be due to information regarding the prediction error per se. The results obtained from Faure et al.'s (2005) study, in particular, provide support for this. By this account, disruptions to nigrostriatal DA signaling that strengthens S–R associations should attenuate the performance of habits, which was demonstrated. This nigrostriatal pathway, at least in part, seems to be modulated by inputs from the amygdala central nucleus (CeN; Gerfen, Staines, Arbuthnott, & Fibiger, 1982; Gonzales & Chesselet, 1990; Kelley et al., 1982; Shinonaga, Takada, & Mizuno, 1992), a region we will discuss in more detail below.

Infralimbic cortex

The infralimbic cortex is a region within the medial prefrontal cortex that, like the dorsolateral striatum, has been implicated in learning and expressing habitual behaviors. Lesions and inactivation of the IL have been shown to disrupt the performance of habits by causing rats to be sensitive to outcome value (Coutureau & Killcross, 2003; Killcross & Coutureau, 2003). For example, inactivation of the IL disrupts the performance of an overtrained action after outcome devaluation, while leaving goal-directed actions unaffected. More recently, it was shown that optogenetic perturbation of the IL during the execution of a T-maze task similarly disrupted S–R guided behavior in rats overtrained on this task (Smith & Graybiel, 2013). The critical distinction between the IL and the DLS, however, is that the DLS seems necessary for both the acquisition and the performance of habits, whereas the IL has only been shown to be required for performance.

Amygdala central nucleus

It is interesting to note that two regions we have discussed, the IL and DLS, though both involved in habits, are not directly connected anatomically. Thus, there likely exists another structure functioning as an interface between these two regions. One possibility is that the amygdala central nucleus (CeN) serves this role. Glutamatergic projections from the IL to the amygdala, particularly to the inhibitory intercalated cells that lie between the basolateral and central regions, have been of particular interest to those studying the extinction of conditioned fear. Within this literature, it has been demonstrated that stimulation of the IL results in decreased responsiveness of projection neurons within the CeN (Quirk, Likhtik, Pelletier, & Paré, 2003). Thus, it has been proposed that IL activation of ITCs during fear extinction modulates the excitatory input from the basolateral to the central amygdala, causing a reduction in fear responses (Busti et al., 2011; Paré, Quirk, & LeDoux, 2004). In line with this view, the IL may function in a similar manner in appetitive instrumental conditioning, influencing output of the CeN that then affects the acquisition and/or performance of habits.

Indeed, recent evidence from our laboratory has demonstrated the involvement of the CeN in habit learning. Pretraining lesions to the anterior region of the amygdala central nucleus (aCeN) disrupts the formation of habitual behaviors (Lingawi & Balleine, 2012). Specifically, it was found that lesions to the aCeN caused rats trained to respond for a food outcome to remain sensitive to outcome devaluation by conditioned taste aversion despite overtraining. Importantly, this region of the central amygdala appears to interact with the DLS during habit learning. This was tested by functionally disconnecting their communication with asymmetrical lesions. Contralateral lesions of the aCeN and DLS disrupt their communication bilaterally while preserving their function in the nonlesioned hemisphere. Ipsilateral lesions of these regions, however, preserve the communication between the aCeN and DLS in one hemisphere (likely via the substantia nigra pars compacta). In our experiment, it was found that unilateral lesions of the aCeN and DLS in contralateral hemispheres disrupted habit formation, whereas habitual behavior was preserved in rats that received ipsilateral control lesions. These data suggest that the aCeN is a critical structure for habit formation and that it communicates with the DLS, likely altering striatal plasticity via its influence on the ascending nigrostriatal DA pathway (see Lingawi & Balleine, 2012, for discussion).

Another important element of these experiments was the effects on habit learning seen after lesions to distinct areas of the CeN. Specifically, lesions of the anterior, but not of the posterior, CeN disrupted subsequent habitual behavior. It seems likely that this dissociation is due to the target projection locations of these two regions. The anterior region of the CeN sends dense projections to the lateral SNc, the region of the substantia nigra that heavily innervates the region of the DLS implicated in habits (Gonzales & Chesselet, 1990). This has been further illustrated in tracing studies conducted in our laboratory. For example, when the retrograde tracer, Fluoro-Gold, was injected into the region of the DLS implicated in habit learning, imaging of the SNc shows dense labeling throughout the lateral and dorsal regions (Figure 16.8B). Additionally, when Fluoro-Gold was injected into the SNc, there was abundant labeling in the anterior CeN (Figure 16.9). Whereas more posterior regions of the CeN also project to the SNc, these projections are sparser. To further examine this circuitry, we injected retrograde and anterograde tracers into the DLS and aCeN, respectively, to visualize the convergence of their connections in the SNc. As can be viewed in Figure 16.10, there was a high level of convergence between the projections from the aCeN and the dopamine neurons (stained for tyrosine hydroxylase; TH) extending to the DLS (Figure 16.10D). Thus, we suggest there exists a circuitry involving the IL and CeN along with the DLS, which causes the development of habits; with excitatory inputs from the IL to the CeN alter phasic DA activity in the nigrostriatal pathway via the amygdalonigral projections to the dopamine projection neurons in the SNc. This altered phasic dopamine signal leads to the strengthening of S–R associations via plasticity in the striatum, resulting in habit formation.

On the Interaction Between Habitual and Goal-Directed Systems: Evidence for Hierarchical Neural Control

When considered from the perspective of Dickinson *et al.*'s (1995) two-process account, the relationship of actions and habits would appear to be an antagonistic one, that is, one in which there is a mutual inhibition between these two processes. There has certainly been no shortage of evidence from studies assessing the neural bases of actions and habits to support this conclusion. Anatomical studies suggest that there are separate basal-ganglia-cortical circuits that lead to the development of goal-directed and habitual behaviors (Alexander, DeLong, & Strick, 1986; Reep, Cheatwood, & Corwin, 2003) with striatonigrostriatal loops described as extending medially to laterally to allow for one region of the striatum to exert inhibitory control over activity in another (Haber, Fudge, & McFarland, 2000; Joel & Weiner, 2000). Furthermore, separate yet adjacent regions of the amygdala, striatum and prefrontal cortex have been implicated in these two types of learning processes, suggesting that there may be a degree of mutual inhibition between them (see Figure 16.7). The prelimbic region of

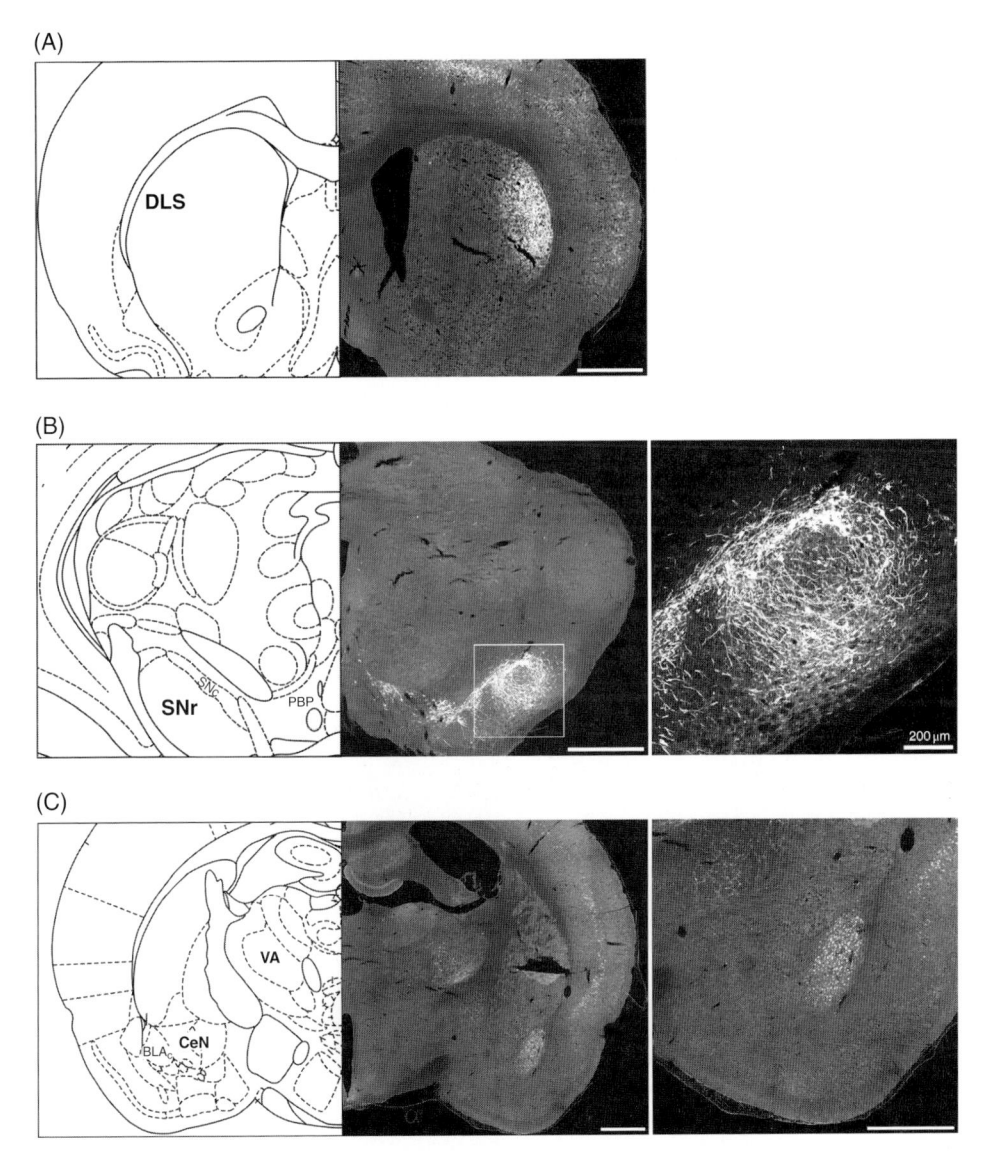

Figure 16.8 Projections to the dorsolateral striatum (DLS) visualized by retrograde tracer Fluoro-Gold. (A) Fluoro-Gold injection site into the DLS (right), as well as the corresponding stereotaxic location (left). Retrograde labeling seen in the substantia nigra (B) and amygdala (C) as well as their relative stereotaxic locations (left). Atlas sections taken from Paxinos and Watson (1998) at +0.7, −5.3, and −1.8 mm relative to bregma, respectively. Abbreviations: BLAC = basolateral complex of the amygdala; CeN = amygdala central nucleus; DLS = dorsolateral striatum; PBP = parabrachial pigmented nucleus; SNc = substantia nigra pars compacta; SNr = substantia nigra pars reticulata; VA = ventral anterior thalamic nucleus. Scale bars: 1 mm, except where indicated.

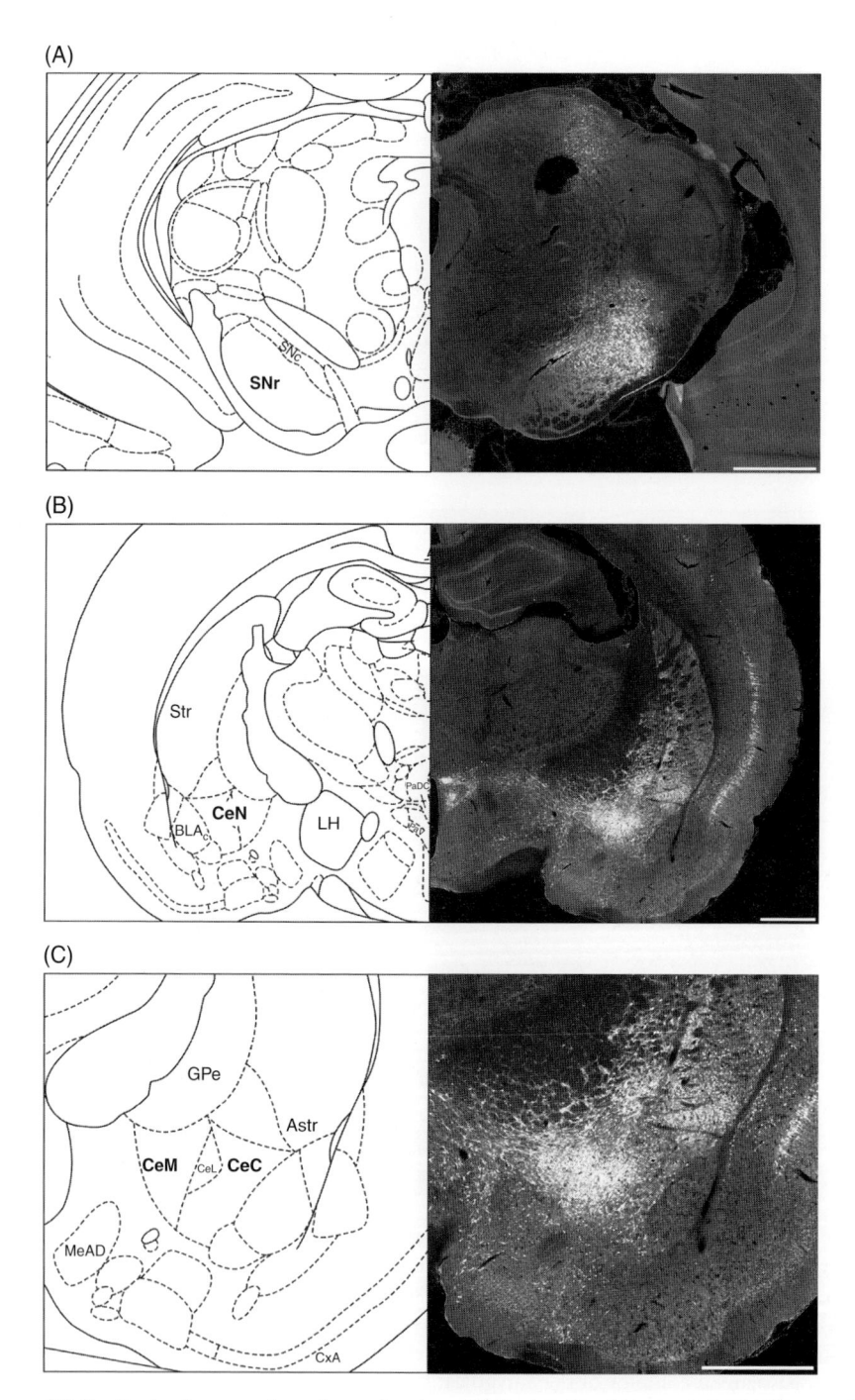

Figure 16.9 Projections to the substantia nigra (SN) visualized by retrograde Fluoro-Gold staining. (A) Fluoro-Gold injection site into the SN (right) as well as its stereotaxic location (left). (B, C) Retrograde labeling seen in the anterior amygdala (right), as well as its stereotaxic location (left). Atlas sections taken from −5.3 and −1.8 mm relative to bregma, respectively. Abbreviations: Astr = amygdalostriatal transition area; BLAC = basal and lateral amygdala complex; CeC = amygdala central nucleus, capsular division; CeL = amygdala central nucleus, lateral division; CeM = amygdala central nucleus, medial division; CeN = amygdala central nucleus; DLS = dorsolateral striatum; CxA = cortex–amygdala transistion zone; GPe = external globus pallidus; MeAD = anterodorsal part of the medial amygdalaloid nucleus; SNc = substantia nigra pars compacta; SNr = substantia nigra pars reticulata; Stri = striatum. Scale bars, 1 mm.

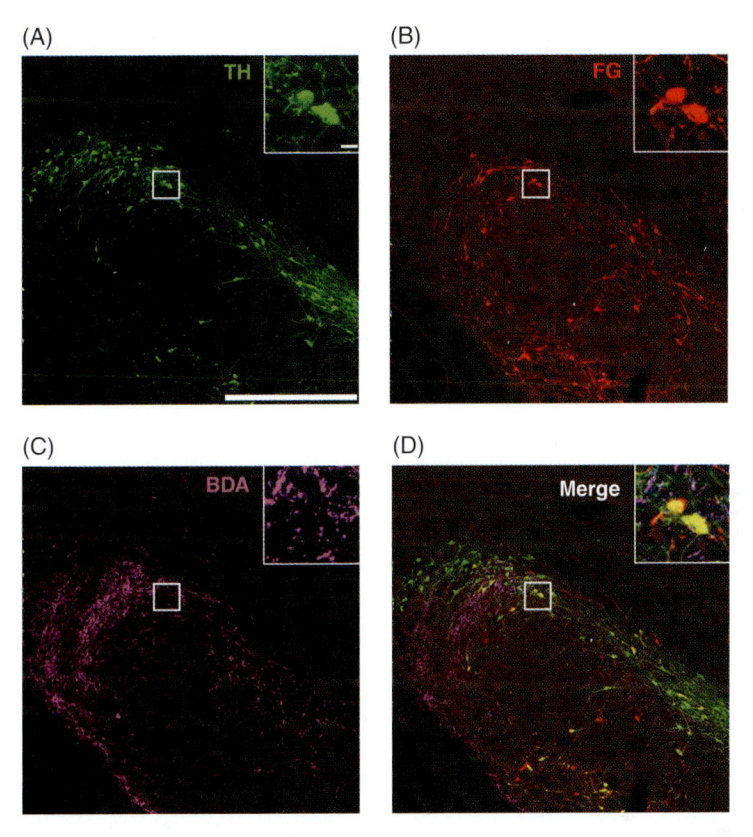

Figure 16.10 Brain images showing that anterograde tracing from the CeN and retrograde tracing from the DLS converge in the SN pars compacta. (A) TH staining (green) labels dopaminergic cells in the SNc, distinguishing it from the neighboring SNr. (B) Cells retrogradely labeled with Fluoro-Gold (red) after injection of Fluoro-Gold into the DLS. (C) Presynaptic boutons and axons extending from the CeN after an injection of neuronal tracer biotinylated dextran amine (BDA) shown in magenta. These three images are merged in (D). A high level of convergence of the anterograde and retrograde tracers can be seen within the SNc, suggesting that the CeN is synapsing onto nigrostriatal dopaminergic projection neurons. Scale bar: 500 μm; inset: 10 μm.

the medial prefrontal cortex (PL) has been shown to be critical for acquiring goal-directed actions (Balleine & Dickinson, 1998) and lies immediately dorsal to the infralimbic cortex, which is involved in habits. In addition, the dorsomedial striatum (DMS) has consistently been demonstrated to be involved in goal-directed action, whereas the adjacent dorsolateral striatum has been implicated in habits. Similarly, the basolateral amygdala (BLA) has been found to assign incentive value to an outcome by establishing a relationship between motivationally important events and their sensory-specific properties, and thus is critical for the performance goal-directed behaviors, whereas it appears that the central nucleus of the amygdala is involved in the propagation of the reinforcement signal for habits. Indeed, a most striking relationship exists between these parts of the amygdala: The basolateral and central nuclei appear to parse the instrumental outcome into rewarding and reinforcing feedback for goal-directed and habit learning respectively.

Accordingly, lesions of the PL, the DMS or the BLA all disrupt goal-directed learning. Nevertheless, animals learn to perform instrumental actions, but they do so by relying entirely on habit-learning processes; their actions are insensitive to changes in outcome value and instrumental contingency (Balleine & Dickinson, 1998; Balleine et al., 2003; Blundell, Hall, & Killcross, 2001; Cardinal, Parkinson, Hall, & Everitt, 2002; Parkes & Balleine, 2013; Schoenbaum, Chiba, & Gallagher, 1998; Wang, Ostlund, Nader, & Balleine, 2005; Wassum, Cely, Balleine, & Maidment, 2011; Yin, Knowlton, & Balleine, 2005; Yin, Ostlund, Knowlton, & Balleine, 2005). Conversely, lesions to the IL, DLS, and CeN all abolish habits and force animals to acquire actions and to maintain them under goal-directed control. Hence, it appears that goal-directed processes inhibit habits, and habits can inhibit goal-directed actions.

Other data fail to support this idea of mutual inhibition, however, and appear instead to suggest that animals can shift flexibly between habits and goal-directed actions in certain circumstances. For example, in a recent study (cf. Dezfouli et al., 2014), when overtrained rats were tested in a 5-min extinction test after outcome devaluation, their initial responding was characteristic of a habitual animal, that is, no devaluation effect was seen. However, with continued extinction, rats that had the food–LiCl pairings began to show goal-directed behavior by decreasing their responding on the devalued action relative to the nondevalued group. These data suggest that over time, when the habits had failed them, the rats were able to shift back to goal-directed control, indicating that the goal-directed system was not irretrievable once habits had emerged. Keramati and colleagues (2011) made this point using a computational modeling system, proposing that the habitual system is utilized once a degree of certainty of attaining a rewarding outcome has been attained. Thus, a serial model of instrumental behavior seems parsimonious with respect to what the animal knows about its environment and appropriate actions to take.

This notion of serial development followed by the opportunity for concurrent selection is, of course, also consistent with the general hypothesis that the interaction between goal-directed actions and habits is hierarchical. Within the hierarchical theory of instrumental conditioning, once acquired both goal-directed and habitual actions exist at the same level and are both available for selection by the hierarchical controller. Likewise, on this view, such a controller could inhibit the selection of either form of action and select an alternative strategy. This kind of control will sound prodigious, but in fact it relies on the evaluation of the relative value of the consequences of adopting any behavioral strategy: At the choice point, if a goal-directed action has a greater value, it will be selected; if a habit has greater value, it will be selected instead. It appears that at a neural level, too, there is evidence supporting this hierarchical approach.

It has long been known that the distinction between goal-directed actions and habit sequences is not encoded within the motor system; at that level, all actions appear to activate the motor cortex similarly whether performed singly or as part of a sequence (Tanji & Shima, 1994, 2000). In contrast, considerable research has found that, taken together, the premotor complex, involving premotor, cingulate motor, supplementary motor (SMA), and presupplementary motor (preSMA) areas, is heavily involved in movement preparation, maintains extensive connections with primary motor cortex and spinal motor pools, and is activated during both the acquisition and performance of sequential actions (Gentilucci et al., 2000; Parsons, Sergent, Hodges, & Fox, 2005; see Nachev, Kennard, & Husain, 2008, for a review). Generally, although premotor and motor cortices are activated by externally triggered motor movement, the SMA and preSMA appear more heavily involved in self-generated movements than those controlled by internal feedback (Cunnington, Windischberger, Deecke, & Moser, 2002). Perhaps as a consequence, these areas are activated during the acquisition and performance of action sequences; damage to them removes previously acquired sequences and attenuates the acquisition of new sequences.

Generally, this premotor complex maintains strong connections with the dorsal striatum, and both the dorsomedial and dorsolateral striatum in particular. In addition, this complex also projects to a central part of dorsal striatum lying between the medial and lateral subregions called the dorsocentral striatum (Reep & Corwin, 1999). From both a behavioral and anatomical perspective, therefore, the premotor complex satisfies many of the conditions one might expect from a hierarchical controller mediating the selection of goal-directed actions and of action sequences.

Although speculative, we have recently reported evidence from an experiment using rats as subjects that appears directly to support this hypothesis (see Ostlund, Winterbauer, & Balleine, 2009). In this experiment, rats were given either bilateral NMDA-induced lesions of the premotor complex, centered on the medial agranular area, or sham surgery. After recovery and a period of pretraining, all of the rats were food deprived and trained to perform a sequence of two lever press actions for a food outcome (Figure 16.11), R1 and R2, such that R1 → R2 → O1 and R2 → R1 → Ø. In a second phase, the order of actions required for reward was reversed, and correct performance of the sequence produced a different outcome, R2 → R1 → O2 and R1 → R2 → Ø, where O1 and O2 were sucrose pellets and a 20% polycose solution. Finally, in a third phase, the rats were allowed to make both sequences concurrently such that R1 → R2 → O1 and R2 → R1 → O2. We analyzed performance in terms of how likely the rats were to perform the specific sequences trained in the different phases as a percentage of all possible sequences, and, as shown in Figure 16.11 A, we found that the sham and lesioned rats were able to perform the appropriate sequences and did so to a similar degree across each of the phases.

The question we were mainly concerned with, however, was whether animals with lesions of the premotor complex were able to exert a similar degree of hierarchical control over their decision-making to the sham rats. To examine this question, we altered the value of the outcome of one of the two sequences trained in Phase 3 using a specific satiety outcome devaluation procedure. We then gave the rats a test in which they were free to press both levers but in extinction, that is, in the absence of any feedback from outcome delivery. The results of this test are presented in Figure 16.11B,C. Although the lesion did not appear to affect performance of the sequences during training, when forced to choose in the absence of feedback it was clear that the lesions of the premotor complex significantly attenuated the rats hierarchical control over their actions. In the sham rats, outcome devaluation attenuated

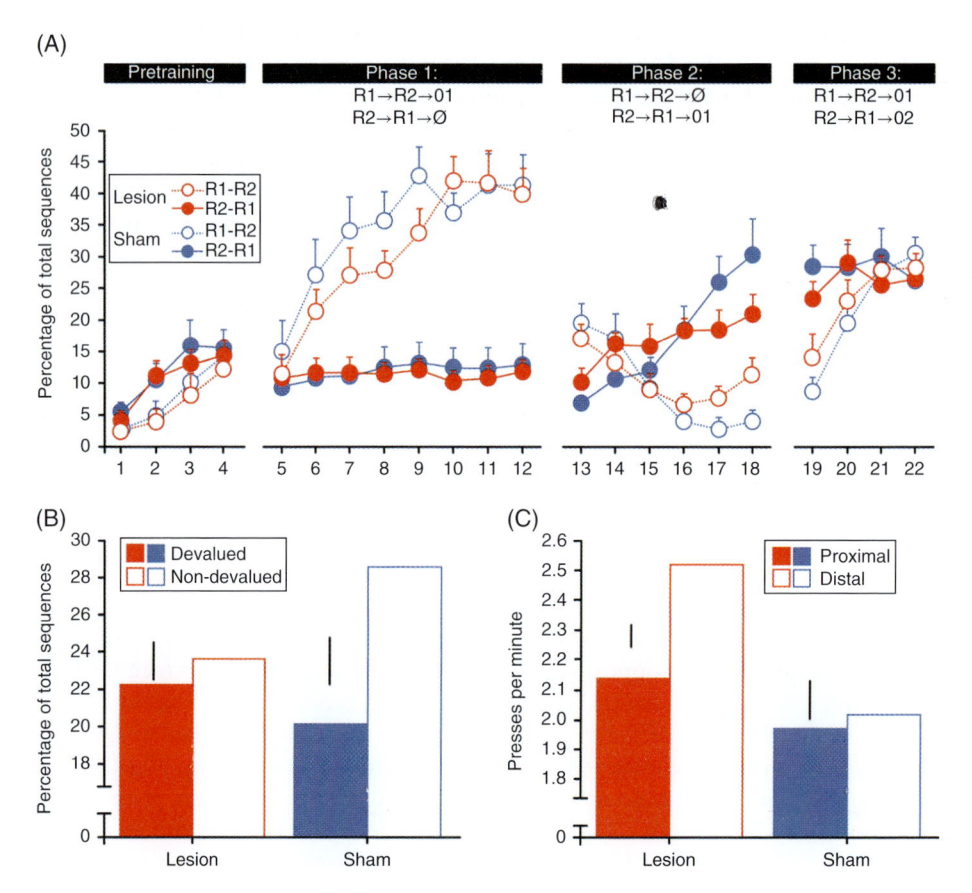

Figure 16.11 Results of an experiment showing that lesions of the premotor complex in rats do not affect the performance of actions sequences but abolish hierarchical decision-making. In (A), both sham and lesions rats appear similarly to acquire the performance of a sequence of lever press actions (Phase 1), to reverse that sequence (Phase 2), and to perform two concurrent sequences for different outcomes (Phase 3). In sham-lesioned rats, the devaluation of O1 by specific satiety resulted in a reduction in the selection of its associated sequence (B, right bars) but did not affect the performance of the action proximal to O1 delivery (i.e., R2) any more than the action proximal to O2 (i.e., R1; C, left bars); evidence that the single actions had become habitual within the sequence. In contrast, lesions to the premotor complex rendered rats unable to choose appropriately between the devalued and nondevalued sequences (B, left bars). In the absence of this hierarchical control, they reverted to choosing on the basis of the individual actions and so showed a significant outcome devaluation effect on the action proximal to O1 relative to the action proximal to O2 (C, left bars). See Ostlund et al. (2009) for details.

their performance of the specific sequence that produced that sequence in training relative to the other sequence. Furthermore, in further evidence of hierarchical control, devaluation did not differentially affect the actions proximal to outcome delivery; in essence these proximal actions appeared habit-like performed at the same rate regardless of the value of their proximal outcome.

This was not true of the rats with lesions of the premotor complex. In this group, devaluation did not affect sequence selection; the rats appeared unable to use hierarchical control to select the appropriate sequence (Figure 16.11B). In contrast, the rats in the lesioned group reverted to control by single actions: As is clear from Figure 16.11C, in contrast to the sham group the lesioned rats showed a significant devaluation effect on the lever proximal to the devalued outcome. As a consequence of losing their capacity to select the goal-directed sequence (and the habitual actions that form a part of that sequence), they reverted to goal-directed control over individual actions. This is exactly the pattern of results that one should predict in the absence of hierarchical action control.

We believe, therefore, that the current evidence favors an analysis of the interaction between actions and habits in terms of a hierarchical structure. As has been amply demonstrated above, actions and habits are mediated by distinct associative structures, distinct forms of feedback, distinct learning rules, and distinct anatomical structures. Nevertheless, rather than being independent, and so subject to some form of arbitration, we believe they constitute two alternative modes of acting that can be selected by a single hierarchical controller as the exigencies of the situation and the consequent values of those distinct courses of action demand.

Acknowledgments

The preparation of this chapter and any unpublished research described were supported by a Laureate Fellowship #FL0992409 from the Australian Research Council and by grant #APP1051280 from the National Health and Medical Research Council of Australia to BWB.

Notes

1. The use of the different terms "actions" and "responses" here is intentional. Although the terms often refer to the same motor topography (such as a lever press), "response" implies that this physical process is reflexive and elicited by some external event or stimulus. "Action," on the other hand, implies a degree of purpose. Indeed, Dickinson (1985) made these distinctions, and many have adopted this nomenclature. Still others use the term "response" to refer to both goal-directed and habitual movements.
2. Here, for simplicity, we assume that values of actions represent their immediate outcomes. For an extension of the learning rules to the condition that values of actions represent all the subsequent outcome, see, for example, Sutton and Barto (1998).

References

Adams, C. D. (1980). Post-conditioning devaluation of an instrumental reinforcer has no effect on extinction performance. *The Quarterly Journal of Experimental Psychology, 32,* 447–458.

Adams, C. D. (1982). Variations in the sensitivity of instrumental responding to reinforcer devaluation. *The Quarterly Journal of Experimental Psychology, 34,* 77–98.

Adams, C. D., & Dickinson, A. (1981). Instrumental responding following reinforcer devaluation. *The Quarterly Journal of Experimental Psychology, 33,* 109–121.

Alexander, G. E., DeLong, M. R., & Strick, P. L. (1986). Parallel organization of functionally segregated circuits linking basal ganglia and cortex. *Annual Review in Neuroscience, 9,* 357–381.

Bagetta, V., Picconi, B., Marinucci, S., Sgobio, C., Pendolino, V., Ghiglieri, V., ... Calabresi, P. (2011). Dopamine-dependent long-term depression is expressed in striatal spiny neurons of both direct and indirect pathways: implications for Parkinson's disease. *The Journal of Neuroscience, 31,* 12513–12522.

Balleine, B., & Dickinson, A. (1991). Instrumental performance following reinforcer devaluation depends upon incentive learning. *Quarterly Journal of Experimental Psychology, 4311,* 279–296.

Balleine, B. W., & Dickinson, A. (1998). Goal-directed instrumental action: contingency and incentive learning and their cortical substrates. *Neuropharmacology, 37,* 407–419.

Balleine, B. W., Killcross, A. S., & Dickinson, A. (2003). The effect of lesions of the basolateral amygdala on instrumental conditioning. *The Journal of Neuroscience, 23,* 666–675.

Baum, W. M. (1973). The correlation-based law of effect. *Journal of Experimental Analysis of Behavior, 20,* 137–153.

Blundell, P., Hall, G., & Killcross, S. (2001). Lesions of the basolateral amygdala disrupt selective aspects of reinforcer representation in rats. *Journal of Neuroscience, 21,* 9018–9025.

Bolam, J. P., Hanley, J. J., Booth, P., & Bevan, M. D. (2000). Synaptic organisation of the basal ganglia. *Journal of Anatomy, 196,* 527–542.

Busti, D., Geracitano, R., Whittle, N., Dalezios, Y., Manko, M., Kaufmann, W... . Ferraguti, F. (2011). Different fear states engage distinct networks within the intercalated cell clusters of the amygdala. *Journal of Neuroscience, 31,* 5131–5144.

Cardinal, R., Parkinson, J., Hall, J., & Everitt, B. (2002). Emotion and motivation: the role of the amygdala, ventral striatum, and prefrontal cortex. *Neuroscience & Biobehavioral Reviews, 26,* 321–352.

Clemens, K. J., Castino, M. R., Cornish, J. L., Goodchild, A. K., & Holmes, N. M. (2014). Behavioral and neural substrates of habit formation in rats intravenously self-administering nicotine. *Neuropsychopharmacology, 39,* 2584–2593.

Colwill, R., & Rescorla, R. (1985). Postconditioning devaluation of a reinforcer affects instrumental responding. *Journal of Experimental Psychology: Animal Behavior Processes, 11,* 120–132.

Colwill, R. M., & Rescorla, R. A. (1986). Associative structures in instrumental learning. In G. H. Bower (Ed.), *The psychology of learning and motivation* (Vol. 20, pp. 55–104). New York, NY: Academic Press.

Colwill, R. M., & Rescorla, R. A. (1988). Associations between the discriminative stimulus and the reinforcer in instrumental learning. *Journal of Experimental Psychology: Animal Behavior Processes, 14,* 155–164.

Corbit, L. H., Chieng, B. C., & Balleine, B. W. (2014). Effects of repeated cocaine exposure on habit learning and reversal by N-acetylcysteine. *Neuropsychopharmacology, 39,* 1893–901.

Corbit, L. H., Muir, J. L., & Balleine, B. W. (2001). The role of the nucleus accumbens in instrumental conditioning: evidence of a functional dissociation between accumbens core and shell. *The Journal of Neuroscience, 21,* 3251–3260.

Corbit, L. H., Muir, J. L., & Balleine, B. W. (2003). Lesions of mediodorsal thalamus and anterior thalamic nuclei produce dissociable effects on instrumental conditioning in rats. *European Journal of Neuroscience, 18,* 1286–1294.

Coutureau, E., & Killcross, S. (2003). Inactivation of the infralimbic prefrontal cortex reinstates goal-directed responding in overtrained rats. *Behavioural Brain Research*, 146, 167–174.

Cunnington, R., Windischberger, C., Deecke, L., & Moser, E. (2002). The preparation and execution of self-initiated and externally-triggered movement: a study of event-related fMRI. *Neuroimage*, 15, 373–385.

Daw, N. D., Niv, Y., & Dayan, P. (2005). Uncertainty-based competition between prefrontal and dorsolateral striatal systems for behavioral control. *Nature Neuroscience*, 8, 1704–1711.

De Wit, S., Watson, P., Harsay, H. A., Cohen, M. X., van de Vijver, I., & Ridderinkhof, K. R. (2012). Corticostriatal connectivity underlies individual differences in the balance between habitual and goal-directed action control. *The Journal of Neuroscience*, 32: 12066–12075.

Dezfouli, A., & Balleine, B. W. (2012). Habits, action sequences and reinforcement learning. *European Journal of Neuroscience*, 35, 1036–51.

Dezfouli, A., & Balleine, B. W. (2013). Actions, action sequences and habits: evidence that goal-directed and habitual action control are hierarchically organized. *PLoS Computational Biology*, 9, e1003364.

Dezfouli, A., Lingawi, N. W., & Balleine, B. W. (2014). Habits as action sequences: Hierarchical action control and changes in outcome value. *Philosophical Transactions of the Royal Society B*, 369.

Dickinson, A. (1985). Actions and habits: the development of behavioural autonomy. *Philosophical Transactions of the Royal Society of London*, 308, 67–78.

Dickinson, A. (1989). Expectancy theory in animal conditioning. In S. Klein (Ed.), *Contemporary learning theories: Pavlovian conditioning and the status of traditional learning theory* (pp. 297–308). New York, NY: Lea.

Dickinson, A. (1994). Instrumental conditioning. In J. N. Mackintosh (Ed.), *Animal learning and cognition* (pp. 45–78). San Diego, CA: Academic Press.

Dickinson, A., & Balleine, B. (1993). Actions and responses: The dual psychology of behaviour. In N. Eilan, R. A. McCarthy, & B. Brewer (Eds.), *Spatial representation: problems in philosophy and psychology* (pp. 277–293). Malden, MA: Blackwell.

Dickinson, A., & Balleine, B. W. (2002). The role of learning in the operation of motivational systems. In C. R. Gallistel (Ed.), *Steven's handbook of experimental psychology: Learning, motivation and emotion* (Vol. 3, 3rd ed., pp. 497–534). New York: John Wiley & Sons.

Dickinson, A., & Charnock, D. J. (1985). Contingency effects with maintained instrumental reinforcement. *The Quarterly Journal of Experimental Psychology (B)*, 37, 397–416.

Dickinson, A., & Mulatero, C. W. (1989). Reinforcer specificity of the suppression of instrumental performance on a non-contingent schedule. *Behavioural Processes*, 19, 167–180.

Dickinson, A., & Nicholas, D. J. (1983). Irrelevant incentive learning during instrumental conditioning: the role of the drive-reinforcer and response-reinforcer relationships. *Quarterly Journal of Experimental Psychology (B)*, 35, 249–263.

Dickinson, A., Balleine, B. W., Watt, A., Gonzalez, F., & Boakes, R. (1995). Motivational control after extended instrumental training. *Animal Learning and Behavior*, 23, 197–206.

Dickinson, A., Campos, J., Varga, Z. L., & Balleine, B. W. (1996). Bidirectional instrumental conditioning. *Quarterly Journal of Experimental Psychology (B)*, 49, 289–306.

Dickinson, A., Nicholas, D. J., & Adams, C. D. (1983). The effect of the instrumental training contingency on susceptibility to reinforcer devaluation. *Quarterly Journal of Experimental Psychology (B)*, 35, 35–51.

Doya, K. (1999). What are the computations of the cerebellum, the basal ganglia and the cerebral cortex? *Neural Networks*, 12, 961–974.

Faure, A., Haberland, U., Conde, F., & El Massioui, N. (2005). Lesion to the nigrostriatal dopamine system disrupts stimulus–response habit formation. *The Journal of Neuroscience*, 25, 2771–2780.

Faure, A., Leblanc-Veyrac, P., & El Massioui, N. (2010). Dopamine agonists increase perseverative instrumental responses but do not restore habit formation in a rat model of Parkinsonism. *Neuroscience*, 168, 744–486.

Featherstone, R. E., & McDonald, R. J. (2004). Dorsal striatum and stimulus-response learning: lesions of the dorsolateral, but not dorsomedial, striatum impair acquisition of a stimulus-response-based instrumental discrimination task, while sparing conditioned place preference learning. *Neuroscience*, 124, 23–31.

Garcia, J., Kimeldorf, D. J., & Koelling, R. A. (1955). Conditioned aversion to saccharin resulting from exposure to gamma radiation. *Science* 122, 157–158.

Graybiel, A. M. (2008). Habits, rituals, and the evaluative brain. *Annual Review Neuroscience*, 31, 359–387.

Gentilucci, M., Bertolani, L., Benuzzi, F., Negrotti, A., Pavesi, G., & Gangitano, M. (2000). Impaired control of an action after supplementary motor area lesion: a case study. *Neuropsychologia*, 38, 1398–404.

Gerdeman, G. L., Partridge, J. G., & Lupica, C. R. (2003). It could be habit forming: drugs of abuse and striatal synaptic plasticity. *Trends in Neuroscience*, 26, 184–192.

Gerfen, C. R., Staines, W. A., Arbuthnott, G. W., & Fibiger, H. C. (1982). Crossed connections of the substantia nigra in the rat. *The Journal of Comparative Neurology*, 207, 283–303.

Gonzales, C., & Chesselet, M. F. (1990). Amygdalonigral pathway: An anterograde study in the rat with *Phaseolus vulgaris* leucoagglutinin (PHAL). *The Journal of Comparative Neurology*, 297, 182–200.

Haber, S. N., Fudge, J. L., & McFarland, N. R. (2000). Striatonigrostriatal pathways in primates form an ascending spiral from the shell to the dorsolateral striatum. *The Journal of Neuroscience*, 20, 2369–2382.

Hammond, L. (1980). The effect of contingency upon the appetitive conditioning of free-operant behavior. *Journal of the Experimental Analysis of Behavior*, 34, 297.

Haruno, M., & Kawato, M. (2006). Different neural correlates of reward expectation and reward expectation error in the putamen and caudate nucleus during stimulus-action–reward association learning. *Journal of Neurophysiology*, 95, 948–959.

Hilário, M. R. F., Clouse, E., Yin, H. H., & Costa, R. M. (2007). Endocannabinoid signaling is critical for habit formation. *Frontiers in Integrative Neuroscience*, 1, 1–12.

Holland, P. C. (1979). Differential effects of omission contingencies on various components of Pavlovian appetitive conditioned responding in rats. *Journal of Experimental Psychology: Animal Behavior Processes*, 5, 178–193.

Holman, E. (1975). Some conditions for the dissociation of consummatory and instrumental behavior in rats. *Learning and Motivation*, 6, 385–366.

Hull, C. (1943). *Principles of behavior*. New York, NY: Appleton-Century-Crofts.

James, W. (1918). *Principles of psychology, volume one*. New York, NY: Dover Publications

Joel, D., & Weiner, I. (2000). The connections of the dopaminergic system with the striatum in rats and primates: an analysis with respect to the functional and compartmental organization of the striatum. *Neuroscience*, 96, 451–474.

Jog, M. S., Kubota, Y., Connolly, C. I., Hillegaart, V., & Graybiel, A. M. (1999). Building neural representations of habits. *Science*, 286, 1745–1749.

Kelley, A. E., Domesick, V. B., & Nauta, W. J. H. (1982). The amygdalostriatal projection in the rat-an anatomical study by anterograde and retrograde tracing methods. *Neuroscience*, 7, 615–630.

Keramati, M. M., Dezfouli, A., & Piray, P. (2011). Speed/accuracy trade-off between the habitual and the goal-directed processes. *PLOS Computational Biology*, 7, e1002055.

Kimble, G. A., & Perlmuter, L. C. (1970). The problem of volition. *Psychological Review, 77,* 361–384.

Knowlton, B. J., Mangels, J. A., & Squire, L. R. (1996). A neostriatal habit learning system in humans. *Science, 273,* 1399–1402.

Kosaki, Y., & Dickinson, A. (2010). Choice and contingency in the development of behavioral autonomy during instrumental conditioning. *Journal of Experimental Psychology: Animal Behavior Processes, 36,* 334–342.

Killcross, S., & Coutureau, E. (2003). Coordination of actions and habits in the medial prefrontal cortex of rats. *Cerebral Cortex, 13,* 1–9.

Lee, S. W., Shimojo, S., & O'Doherty, J. P. (2014). Neural computations underlying arbitration between model-based and model-free learning. *Neuron, 81,* 687–99.

Lingawi, N. W., & Balleine, B. W. (2012). Amygdala central nucleus interacts with dorsolateral striatum to regulate the acquisition of habits. *Journal of Neuroscience, 32,* 1073–1081.

Maia, T. V., & Frank, M. J. (2011). From reinforcement learning models to psychiatric and neurological disorders. *Nature Neuroscience, 14,* 154–162.

Mishkin, M., Malamut, B., & Bachevalier, J. (1984). Memories and habits: Two neural systems. In G. Lynch, J. L. McGaugh, & N. M. Weinberger (Eds.), *The neurobiology of learning and memory* (pp. 65–88). New York, NY: The Guilford Press.

Montague, P., Dayan, P., & Sejnowski, T. (1996). A framework for mesencephalic dopamine systems based on predictive Hebbian learning. *The Journal of Neuroscience, 16,* 1936–1947.

Murray, G. K., Corlett, P. R., Clark, L., Pessiglione, M., Blackwell, A. D., Honey, G.,... Fletcher, P. C. (2007). Substantia nigra/ventral tegmental reward prediction error disruption in psychosis. *Molecular Psychiatry, 13,* 267–276.

Nachev, P., Kennard, C., & Husain, M. (2008). Functional role of the supplementary and pre-supplementary motor areas. *Nature Reviews Neuroscience, 9,* 856–869.

Nelson, A., & Killcross, S. (2006). Amphetamine exposure enhances habit formation. *The Journal of Neuroscience, 26,* 3805–3812.

Ostlund, S. B., Winterbauer, N. E., & Balleine, B. W. (2009). Evidence of action sequence chunking in goal-directed instrumental conditioning and its dependence on the dorsomedial prefrontal cortex. *Journal of Neuroscience, 29,* 8280–8287.

Paré, D., Quirk, G. J., & LeDoux, J. E. (2004). New vistas on amygdala networks in conditioned fear. *Journal of Neurophysiology, 92,* 1–9.

Parkes, S. L., & Balleine, B. W. (2013). Incentive memory: evidence the basolateral amygdala encodes and the insular cortex retrieves outcome values to guide choice between goal-directed actions. *Journal of Neuroscience, 33,* 8753–63.

Parsons, L. M., Sergent, J., Hodges, D.A., & Fox, P. T. (2005). The brain basis of piano performance. *Neuropsychologia, 43,* 199–215.

Paxinos, G., & Watson, C. (1998). *The rat brain in stereotaxic coordinates.* New York: Academic Press.

Poldrack, R. A., Clark, J., Pare-Belagoev, E. J., Shohamy, D., Moyano, J. C., Myers, C., & Gluck, M. A. (2001). Interactive memory systems in the human brain. *Nature, 414,* 546–550.

Quinn, J. J., Pittenger, C., Lee, A. S., Pierson, J. L., & Taylor, J. R. (2013). Striatum-dependent habits are insensitive to both increases and decreases in reinforcer value in mice. *European Journal of Neuroscience, 37,* 1012–1021.

Quirk, G. J., Likhtik, E., Pelletier, J. G., & Paré, D. (2003). Stimulation of medial prefrontal cortex decreases the responsiveness of central amygdala output neurons. *The Journal of Neuroscience, 23,* 8800–8807.

Reep, R. L., Cheatwood, J. L., & Corwin, J. V. (2003). The associative striatum: Organization of cortical projections to the dorsocentral striatum in rats. *The Journal of Comparative Neurology, 467*, 271–292.

Reep, R. L., & Corwin, J. V. (1999). Topographic organization of the striatal and thalamic connections of the rat medial agranular cortex. *Brain Research, 841*, 43–51.

Reynolds, J. N., Hyland, B. I., & Wickens, J. R. (2001). A cellular mechanism of reward-related learning. *Nature, 413*, 67–70.

Schoenbaum, G., Chiba, A. A., & Gallagher, M. (1998). Orbitofrontal cortex and basolateral amygdala encode expected outcomes during learning. *Nature Neuroscience, 1*, 155–159.

Schultz, W. (1997). A neural substrate of prediction and reward. *Science, 275*, 1593–1599.

Seger, C. A., & Spiering, B. J. (2011). A critical review of habit learning and the basal ganglia. *Frontiers in Systems Neuroscience, 5*, 1–9.

Shinonaga, Y., Takada, M., & Mizuno, N. (1992). Direct projections from the central amygdaloid nucleus to the globus pallidus and substantia nigra in the cat. *Neuroscience, 51*, 691–703.

Smith, K. S., & Graybiel, A. M. (2013). Using optogenetics to study habits. *Brain Research, 1511*, 102–114.

Squire, L. R., & Zola-Morgan, S. (1988). Memory: brain systems and behavior. *Trends in Neurosciences, 11*, 170–175.

Suri, R. E., & Schultz, W. (1999). A neural network model with dopamine-like reinforcement signal that learns a spatial delayed response task. *Neuroscience, 91*, 871–890.

Sutton, R. S., & Barto, A. G. (1998). *Reinforcement learning: an introduction*. Cambridge, MA: MIT Press.

Tanji, T., & Shima, K. (1994). Role for supplementary motor area cells in planning several movements ahead. *Nature, 371*, 413–416.

Tanji, T., & Shima K. (2000). Neuronal activity in the supplementary and presupplementary motor areas for temporal organization of multiple movements. *Journal of Neurophysiology, 84*, 2148–2160.

Thorndike, E. L. (1911). *Animal intelligence: experimental studies*. New York, NY: Macmillan.

Tricomi, E., Balleine, B. W., & O'Doherty, J. P. (2009). A specific role for posterior dorsolateral striatum in human habit learning. *European Journal of Neuroscience, 29*, 2225–2232.

Vanderschuren, L. J. M. J., & Kalivas, P. W. (2000). Alterations in dopaminergic and glutamatergic transmission in the induction and expression of behavioural sensitization: a critical review of preclinical studies. *Psychopharmacology, 151*, 99–120.

Wang, S.H., Ostlund, S. B., Nader, K., & Balleine, B. W. (2005). Consolidation and reconsolidation of incentive learning in the amygdala. *The Journal of Neuroscience, 25*, 830–835.

Wassum, K. M., Cely, I. C., Balleine, B. W., & Maidment, N. T. (2011). Mu-opioid receptor activation in the basolateral amygdala mediates the learning of increases but not decreases in the incentive value of a food reward. *The Journal of Neuroscience, 31*, 1591–1599.

Wassum, K. M., Cely, I. C., Maidment, N. T., & Balleine, B. W. (2009). Disruption of endogenous opioid activity during instrumental learning enhances habit acquisition. *Neuroscience, 163*, 770–780.

Yin, H. H., Knowlton, B. J., & Balleine, B. W. (2004). Lesions of dorsolateral striatum preserve outcome expectancy but disrupt habit formation in instrumental learning. *European Journal of Neuroscience, 19*, 181–189.

Yin, H. H., Knowlton, B. J., & Balleine, B. W. (2005). Blockade of NMDA receptors in the dorsomedial striatum prevents action–outcome learning in instrumental conditioning. *European Journal of Neuroscience, 22*, 505–512.

Yin, H. H., Knowlton, B. J., & Balleine, B. W. (2006). Inactivation of dorsolateral striatum enhances sensitivity to changes in the action–outcome contingency in instrumental conditioning. *Behavioural Brain Research, 166*, 189–196.

Yin, H. H., Ostlund, S. B., Knowlton, B. J., & Balleine, B. W. (2005). The role of the dorsomedial striatum in instrumental conditioning. *European Journal of Neuroscience, 22*, 513–523.

17

An Associative Account of Avoidance

Claire M. Gillan, Gonzalo P. Urcelay, and Trevor W. Robbins

Introduction

Humans can readily learn that certain foods cause indigestion, that traveling at 5 pm on a weekday invariably puts one at risk of getting stuck in traffic, or that overindulging in the free bar at the office Christmas party is likely to lead to future embarrassment. Importantly, we are also equipped with the ability to learn to avoid these undesired consequences. We can categorize avoidance behaviors as passive, active, and whether active avoidance starts before or during the aversive experience. So, we can *passively* refrain from eating certain foods, *actively* choose to take an alternate route during rush-hour, or even *escape* the perils of the office party by slipping out when we start to get a bit tipsy (Figure 17.1).

Although avoidance is as ubiquitous in everyday life as reward-seeking, or appetitive behavior, there exists a stark asymmetry in our understanding of the associative mechanisms involved in these two processes. While the learning rules that govern the acquisition of appetitive instrumental behavior are reasonably well understood (Dickinson, 1985), far fewer strides have been made in capturing the associative mechanisms that support avoidance learning. In appetitive instrumental learning, a broad consensus has been reached that behavior is governed by a continuum of representation that produces action ranging from reflexive responses to stimuli that are stamped in by reinforcement learning (Thorndike, 1911) to more considered actions that are more purposeful or goal-directed, and sensitive to dynamic changes in the value of possible outcomes and in environmental action–outcome contingencies (Tolman, 1948). One might assume that these constructs could be readily applied to avoidance, perhaps with the insertion of a well-placed minus sign to capture the aversive nature of the reinforcement. Unfortunately, theoretical black holes, such as the *avoidance problem*, have stagnated development in this area. Baum (1973, p. 142) captures the essence of the experimental problem.

The Wiley Handbook on the Cognitive Neuroscience of Learning, First Edition.
Edited by Robin A. Murphy and Robert C. Honey.
© 2016 John Wiley & Sons, Ltd. Published 2016 by John Wiley & Sons, Ltd.

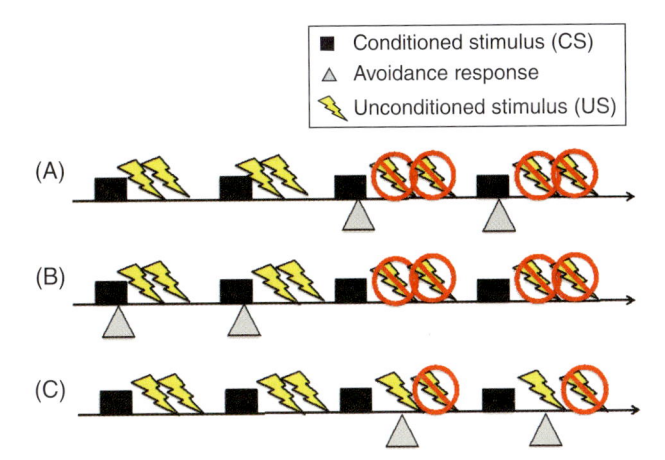

Figure 17.1 Categories of avoidance. Active avoidance (A) describes situations where a subject makes a response within an allotted time frame, and therefore cancels an otherwise imminent aversive US. Passive avoidance (B) is a case where, if a subject refrains from performing a response, they will avoid exposure to an aversive US. Escape (C), much like active avoidance, involves making a response in order to avoid shock. It differs from active avoidance in that the response is performed after the aversive US has been, in part, delivered.

> A man will not only flee a fire in his house; he will take precautions against fire. A rat will not only jump out of a chamber in which it is being shocked; it will jump out of a chamber in which it has been shocked in the past, if by doing so it avoids the shock. In both examples, no obvious reinforcement follows the behavior to maintain it. How then is the law of effect to account for avoidance? (Baum, 1973, p. 142)

Here, we will bridge the historic theoretical literature with new research facilitated by recent advances in the neurosciences. We will first recount the nature of the avoidance debate, and outline a consensus view of the conditions necessary for the acquisition and maintenance of avoidance, derived from these theories. We will then move forward and analyze the content of the associations involved in avoidance, providing evidence for a dual-process account in which goal-directed (action–outcome) and habit-based (stimulus–response), associations can coexist. We then discuss how these factors lead to the performance of avoidance, by evoking recent developments in computational and neuroimaging research on avoidance learning. This analytic framework is borrowed from Dickinson (1980) in his associative review of contemporary learning theory, which focused primarily on the appetitive domain. By adopting this structure for our treatise, we aim to formalize the study of avoidance behavior and bridge the gap with existing associative accounts of appetitive instrumental learning. We will focus our discussion primarily on *active avoidance*, which are cases where an animal must make a response in order to avoid an aversive US such as shock, because this area has been extensively researched in rodents and humans. This is distinct from *passive avoidance*, which describes situations where, in order to avoid an aversive US, a response must be withheld or, in other words, a punishment contingency. To begin, we will outline the theories of avoidance that have predominated the literature up until this point, recounting and reappraising the vibrant avoidance debate.

Associative Theories of Avoidance

Avoidance as a Pavlovian response

Ivan Pavlov coined the term "signalization" (what we now call conditioning) to describe his series of now famous observations wherein the sound of a metronome, a CS, could elicit a consummatory response in a dog, if the sound of the metronome had been previously paired with food delivery (Pavlov, 1927). If, rather than food, an acid solution was delivered to the dog's mouth, then the metronome would elicit a range of defensive responses; wherein, for example, the dog would shake its head. In the above example, the head-shaking response could be characterized in two ways: as a conditioned Pavlovian response equivalent to that emitted when the US is presented, or as an instrumental avoidance response if the experimental conditions are such that shaking of the head prevents the acid from entering their mouth.

The popular account of avoidance at the time was, and still is, based on the assumption that avoidance in animals is an adaptive function, acquired and executed in order to prevent the animal from coming to harm. Robert Bolles (1970) sought to turn this view on its head. He highlighted the fact that in nature, predators rarely give notice to their prey prior to an attack; nor do they typically provide enough trials to its prey for learning to occur. He contended that rather than an instrumental and adaptive response, the kind of avoidance described in nature is an innate defensive reaction that occurs to surprising or sudden events. Though not explicitly appealing to the notion of a Pavlovian model of avoidance, Bolles's account advances the convergent notion that conditioned responses to a CS, such as flight, are not learned but rather biologically prepared reactions to stimuli that are unexpectedly presented. Bolles termed these "species-specific defence reactions" (SSDRs). He suggested that many so-called learned avoidance response experiments utilized procedures in which animals learned very quickly with little exposure to the US. For instance, a common shuttle-box apparatus involves an animal moving from one side to the other side of the box to avoid an aversive US (i.e., shock). In other studies, where the desired avoidance response is not in the animal's repertoire of SSDRs (e.g., a rat pressing a lever), avoidance is acquired much more slowly (Riess, 1971), and in cases where the required avoidance response conflicts with an SSDR, avoidance conditioning is extremely difficult to obtain (Hineline & Rachlin, 1969). Further support for the Pavlovian view of avoidance came from studying the behavior of high and low avoiding strains of rat (Bond, 1984). In his experiments, Bond observed that these strains were selected for fleeing and freezing, respectively, and that a cross of these breeds displayed moderate performance of both of these behaviors. He concludes that, in line with a Pavlovian account of avoidance, defensive reactions in animals are under hereditary control, rather than being controlled primarily by the instrumental avoidance contingency.

Although Bolles's theory was extremely valuable in highlighting the importance of Pavlovian SSDRs in the acquisition of avoidance, the conclusion that avoidance behaviors can be reduced to classical conditioning is widely refuted. Mackintosh (1983) makes an astute rebuttal of this notion, reasoning that in order for a Pavlovian account to be upheld, animals trained with a Pavlovian relation might be expected to acquire avoidance relations at rates of responding that were superior to instrumentally trained ones. Mackintosh cites a series of studies showing that this is not the case. Instead, instrumental avoidance contingencies greatly enhance response rates relative to equivalent classical conditioning procedures (Bolles, Stokes, & Younger, 1966; Brogden, Lipman, & Culler, 1938; Kamin, 1956; Scobie & Fallon, 1974). Further, rather than being a purely stimulus-driven phenomenon, as might be expected on the basis of the Pavlovian analysis, avoidance can be acquired and maintained in the absence of any predictive stimulus (Herrnstein & Hineline, 1966; Hineline, 1970; Sidman, 1953). Moreover, Sidman (1955) discovered that if a warning CS was introduced to his free-operant procedure, rather than potentiating avoidance responding, as a Pavlovian account of avoidance might predict, the CS actually depressed it. This is because rats began to wait for the CS to be presented before responding, suggesting that it served a discriminative function, allowing them to perform only necessary responses. Together, these data point to the existence of a more purposeful mechanism of controlling avoidance behavior.

Two-factor theory

By far the most widely held and influential account of avoidance is Mowrer's (1947) two-factor theory, which was inspired by Konorski and Miller (1937). Although Mowrer was satisfied that a simple Pavlovian account of avoidance was insufficient to explain what he saw as the clearly beneficial effect of introducing an instrumental contingency, he reasoned that if avoidance behavior follows Thorndike's (1911) Law of Effect, wherein behavior is excited or inhibited on the basis of reinforcement, there remained a considerable explanatory gap to be bridged:

> How can a shock which is not experienced, i.e. which is avoided, be said to provide either a source of motivation or of satisfaction? Obviously the factor of fear has to be brought into such an analysis. (Mowrer, 1947, p. 108)

Mowrer (1940) provided the evidence, from rats and later guinea pigs, that began to provide a solution to this puzzle (Figure 17.2). The experiments involved three experimental groups. The first group were placed in a circular grill and, at 1-min intervals, were presented with a tone CS that predicted a shock (Figure 17.1A). If the animals moved to another section of the grill upon hearing the tone, the shock was omitted. He found that the animals readily learned this behavior. In the second group, rather than being presented at regular 1-min intervals, the CS was presented at variable time points (15, 60, or 120 s), averaging 1 min (Figure 17.2B). A final group received the same procedure as the first group, except that during the 1-min ITI, unavoidable (i.e., unsignaled) shocks were delivered every 15 s, forcing the animals to move to another section of the grill to escape the shock (Figure 17.2C). Mowrer observed retarded conditioning of the avoidance response in the second and third groups relative to the first group. He hypothesized that the superiority of conditioning observed in the first group, who had received a schedule with regular ITIs, was a result of the amount of fear reduction or relief that was experienced when the animal produced the conditioned avoidance response. In the other groups, he postulated that relief was attenuated due to the irregular ITIs employed in one group and the addition of unavoidable shocks in the final group, producing a relatively more "annoying state of affairs" (Mowrer, 1947). In essence, this analysis proposed that

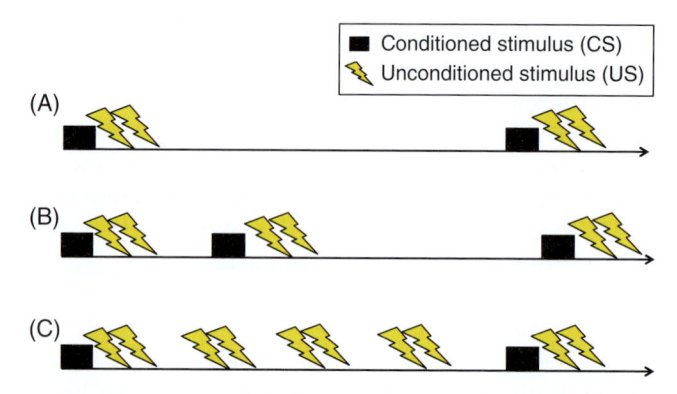

Figure 17.2 Task design (Mowrer, 1940). Group A were presented with avoidable shocks at 1-min intervals. Group B were presented with avoidable shocks at variable intervals, 15, 60, or 120 s, which averaged to 1 min. Group C received avoidable shocks on the same schedule as group A, but during the 1-min intertrial interval, they were presented with unsignaled shocks, which they could escape but not avoid.

avoidance behavior was acquired through negative reinforcement, wherein the reduction of fear was the reinforcer of behavior. In order for this negative reinforcement to take place, the animal first needs to acquire this fear, constituting the two factors necessary for avoidance learning.

> This is accomplished by assuming (i) that anxiety, i.e., mere anticipation of actual organic need or injury, may effectively motivate human beings and (ii) that reduction of anxiety may serve powerfully to reinforce behavior that brings about such a state of "relief" or "security." (Mowrer, 1939, p. 564)

Although popularized by Mowrer, an earlier experiment by Konorski and Miller (1937) foreshadows the notion of a two-factor process of avoidance (recounted by Konorski, 1967). In this experiment, the authors exposed a dog to trials in which a noise (CS) predicted the delivery of intraoral acid (US). They subsequently gave the dog CS presentations, wherein they would passively flex the rear leg of the dog, and withhold the aversive US. They found that the dog began to actively flex their leg following exposure to the CS and that the aversive Pavlovian salivary response diminished as a result of (or was coincident with) the instrumental avoidance response. The avoidance response, according to Konorski and Miller, had become a conditioned inhibitor of the salivation, that is, the conditioned response to the acid.

Mowrer and Lamoreaux (1942) found further support for fear reduction as a construct with the demonstration that, if the avoidance response caused the CS to terminate, their animals conditioned even more readily. As the CS served as the fear-elicitor in their experiment, the finding that terminating this fearful CS enhanced avoidance was strikingly in line with the notion that fear reduction motivates avoidance. However, the theory that escape from fear is what reinforces avoidance was undermined by a series of experiments reported by Sidman. These experiments illustrated that avoidance behavior could be acquired during procedures where there was no external warning CS. Sidman's (1953) free-operant avoidance schedule is one in which animals can learn to avoid shocks that are delivered using an interval timer, which is reset after each avoidance or escape response. Sidman reported successful conditioning in 50 animals using this procedure, and these results were later used to deliver a considerable challenge to (CS based) or "fear-reduction" theories of avoidance. In response to this criticism, the definition of the CS in avoidance was expanded to include internally generated temporal stimuli (Anger, 1963). Anger hypothesized that in a free-operant chamber, where no physical CS signals shock, the duration since the last response becomes a salient CS. If the avoidance response results in omission or delay of a scheduled shock, as time passes, aversiveness increases until another avoidance response is emitted as a conditioned response to this temporal CS. He also argued that in other experimental conditions, there is likely reinforcement from the termination of the avoidance response itself, wherein the termination of the response has been paired with no shock, and the omission of the response is paired with shock. Therefore, the termination of the response becomes fear reducing or, in other words, a fear inhibitor (Konorski, 1967). Herrnstein, one of the most vocal critics of two-factor theory, argued that these extensions to the specification of the CS in the two-factor theory had to "find or invent, a stimulus change" making them so tautological that it was no longer amenable to experimental test (Herrnstein, 1969). Notwithstanding these claims, Herrnstein proceeded to provide just such empirical tests, which will be described later.

Mowrer (1960) responded to the observation that rats acquire instrumental avoidance under free-operant procedures. His new formulation of two-factor theory postulated that the *degree of stimulus change* after an avoidance response was a tractable variable that could have reinforcing properties. Indeed, this idea was supported by experiments in which a discrete stimulus was presented contingently upon avoidance responses, so-called safety signals. Safety signals undoubtedly increase the rate of acquisition of avoidance behavior (Dinsmoor, 2001), and there is strong evidence that safety signals can acquire reinforcing properties (Dinsmoor & Sears, 1973; Morris, 1974, 1975), thus supporting and maintaining avoidance behavior. For example, in recent experiments, Fernando, Urcelay, Mar, Dickinson, and Robbins (2014) showed that performance of an avoidance response is enhanced with presentation of a safety signal. They trained rats in a free-operant procedure where, on each day of training, one of two levers was randomly presented, and a 5-s signal was turned on after each avoidance or escape response. Thus, the signal was associated with both levers. They then set up a situation in which both levers were present and functional (i.e., both levers avoided), but only one of them was followed by the safety signal. Rats readily chose to selectively press the lever that resulted in the presentation of the safety signal, despite the fact that both levers would avoid shock presentation, a result that was also found in a test session where shocks were not present (i.e., in extinction). The mechanism by which safety signals become reinforcing is easily handled by standard associative theories (Rescorla & Wagner, 1972): They predict that such signals become fear inhibitors, and as such, others hypothesize that they may even elicit a positive emotional reaction (i.e., relief: Dickinson & Dearing, 1979; Konorski, 1967). These findings lent further support to the argument that the learned value of a safety signal could enter into the avoidance question.

Another challenge to two-factor theory was the observation that fear responses to the CS, typically indexed using appetitive bar-press suppression, reliably diminish over time as animals master the avoidance response (Kamin, Brimer, & Black, 1963; Linden, 1969; Neuenschwander, Fabrigoule, & Mackintosh, 1987; Solomon, Kamin, & Wynne, 1953; Starr & Mineka, 1977). If, according to Mowrer, fear drives avoidance behavior, then logic follows that avoidance behavior should extinguish as the conditioned fear response diminishes. In other words, conditioned fear should be tightly correlated with the vigor of the avoidance response. A number of studies have convincingly shown that avoidance responding and Pavlovian conditioned fear response measures are dissociable, regardless of whether fear is measured using conditioned suppression as in the aforementioned studies, or using autonomic measures in both nonhuman animals (Brady & Harris, 1977; Coover, Ursin, & Levine, 1973) and humans (Solomon, Holmes, & McCaul, 1980). Furthermore, avoidance responding is known to persist sometimes for extremely long periods in spite of the introduction of a Pavlovian extinction procedure, which is one where the CS no longer predicts an aversive US, when subjects respond on all trials (Levis, 1966; Seligman & Campbell, 1965; Solomon et al., 1953). The persistence of avoidance when fear responses are greatly reduced is considered to be the most serious problem for two-factor theory, as Mineka (1979) concedes in her critique of two-factor theory. However, no experiment had yet demonstrated avoidance behavior in the *complete* absence of fear. Since 1979, researchers have come no closer to making this observation.

Cognitive expectancy theories

Seligman and Johnston (1973) were the original proponents of an elaborated so-called "cognitive theory" of avoidance, proposing that avoidance behavior is not controlled by stimulus–response associations, which are stamped in through reinforcement, but by two expectancies. The first is an expectancy that if the animal does *not* respond, they will receive an aversive CS, and the second is an expectancy that if they do respond, they will *not* receive an aversive CS. The key difference between this and prior models is that cognitive theory supposes that avoidance behavior is not negatively reinforced by the aversive US, but rather relies upon propositional knowledge of action–outcome expectations. While these expectations could of course be supported by associative processes (links), the cognitive component is captured by the way such expectations interact with preferences (for no shock over shock) and bring about avoidance behavior. In a more general sense, of course, these ideas had been around for much longer, dating back to when Tolman first posited a goal-directed account of instrumental action (Tolman, 1948).

> We feel, however, that the intervening brain processes are more complicated, more patterned and often, pragmatically speaking, more autonomous than do the stimulus–response psychologists. (Tolman, 1948, p. 192)

As said, expectancies, in this formulation, can be considered graded variables, which like stimulus–response links, can be captured by an association. Expectancies can be modified not only by direct experience (reinforcement, nonreinforcement), but also by verbal instructions, that is, "symbolically" (in humans). The propositional nature of the resulting representation is considered to reflect a higher-order cognitive process, rather than the *automatic* linking of events. One advantage of cognitive theory is that it can account for the striking persistence of avoidance behavior during CS–US extinction. It predicts that when animals reach an asymptote of avoidance behavior in which they are responding on every trial, they experience only response – no shock contingencies and never experiencing the disconfirming case of *no* response – no shock and therefore continue indefinitely. Seligman and Johnston's cognitive explanation for avoidance learning was, however, still a two-factor approach, as Pavlovian conditioning was considered necessary to motivate avoidance, a factor they termed emotional and reflexive, in line with two-factor theory. They are, however, explicit in their assertion that fear reduction plays no role in reinforcing avoidance behavior. Subsequent attempts have expanded this framework to also account more generally for Pavlovian fear learning (Reiss, 1991). Based largely on self-report and interview data from human anxiety patients (e.g., McNally & Steketee, 1985), Reiss's expectancy theory surmised that pathological fear is at least partially motivated by expectations of future negative events (e.g., "I expect the plane will crash"). Lovibond (2006) subsequently united the instrumental component of Seligman and Johnston's (1973) cognitive account with Reiss's and his own earlier theory positing that expectancy mediated appetitive Pavlovian conditioned responding (Lovibond & Shanks, 2002; Reiss, 1991), to form an integrated cognitive expectancy account. This account posits that if an aversive US is *expected*, anxiety will increase, and stimuli that are signals of the occurrence or absence of aversive outcomes will potentiate and depress expectancy, respectively. A similar account, which suggests that avoidance behavior functions as a negative occasion setter, that is, modifying the known relationship between stimuli and aversive outcomes, makes a similar case regarding the role of expectancy in avoidance (De Houwer, Crombez, & Baeyens, 2005).

In opposition to these accounts, Maia (2010) argued that if avoidance is supported purely by expectations and beliefs, then there is no reason why response latencies should decrease to the point where they are much shorter than what is necessary to avoid shock. Furthermore, these latencies have been shown to continue to decrease into extinction (Beninger, Mason, Phillips, & Fibiger, 1980; Solomon *et al.*, 1953). Cognitive accounts are silent about this effect, and indeed it is difficult to imagine how this could be reconciled within the expectancy framework. Another observation that does not sit well with expectancy/belief perspectives is the observation that in cases of extreme resistance to extinction, dogs will continue to make a well-trained avoidance response, even if it means they will effectively jump into an electrified shock chamber. Solomon *et al.* (1953) first reported this phenomenon when they attempted to discourage a highly extinction-resistant dog from responding when presented with the previously trained aversive CS on an extinction procedure. He introduced an intense shock that would be delivered on the new side of the shuttle box on each trial, that is, a punishment contingency. That the dog persisted to jump *into* shock is a very challenging result for cognitive theories, given the evident lack of instrumentality of the response.

Besides these challenges, opposition to the cognitive theory of avoidance has been relatively limited. One explanation is that due to its relative recency, direct tests of its major tenets have not yet been conducted. However, it has been suggested that the theory is silent about mechanisms and therefore lacks the specificity necessary to be amenable to experimental test. One promising avenue for formalizing the role of expectancy in avoidance came from recent computational accounts of Maia (2010) and Moutoussis, Bentall, Williams, and Dayan (2008). These authors forward an actor-critic (Sutton & Barto, 1998) model of avoidance, in which the expectancies invoked by Lovibond can be formalized associatively in terms of temporal difference learning, wherein expectancies of reward are accrued over the course of experience, and deviations from expectations produce prediction errors (Rescorla & Wagner, 1972; Schultz, Dayan, & Montague, 1997), which can be used to correct expectations for the future. Within this framework, instances where aversive USs are predicted but not delivered following the performance of an avoidance response are hypothesized to produce a positive prediction error (i.e., one that is better than expected), which reinforce the action, and in turn act as an appetitive reinforcer. This account has the advantage of incorporating the notion of expectancy into a two-factor account, which posits that "relief" acts as the reinforcer of avoidance. Although these models can account for much of the preexisting literature on avoidance, including the persistence of avoidance long into extinction, without an experimental test, the question of whether these models possess any predictive validity remains open.

The most influential associative theories of avoidance have now been outlined. Although these theories differ in their interpretation of the particular association that drives behavior, and how that association enters into the learning process, they share a common feature. Each of these theories relies on the idea that associations between environmental events shape the acquisition and retention of avoidance behavior. In the following section, we will formalize our understanding of the conditions, specifically the associations, necessary for avoidance, in part, by juxtaposing these theoretical frameworks.

Conditions Necessary for Avoidance

Pavlovian contingency (CS–US): avoidance acquisition

The acquisition of avoidance responses is sensitive to many of the same conditions governing other forms of associative learning. Contiguity refers to the notion that stimuli that are presented together in time or space are more easily associated. By varying the interval between CS and US, Kamin (1954) demonstrated that the number of trials needed to acquire an avoidance criterion was modulated by temporal contiguity. Specifically, he showed that the weaker the contiguity, the slower the acquisition of avoidance. Despite this clear result, the subsequent discovery of the Blocking effect (Kamin, 1969), together with the observation that contingency strongly determines behavioral control (Rescorla, 1968), eliminated the need of characterizing contiguity as a sufficient condition for learning, and hence for avoidance. Contingency, as opposed to contiguity, refers to the relative probability of an outcome in the presence and absence of a stimulus, $p(US/CS)$ and, $p(US/noCS)$ respectively. The importance of contingency for the acquisition of instrumental avoidance was tested by Rescorla (1966), when he trained three groups of dogs using a Sidman avoidance procedure. One group received training in which a CS predicted a shock US, another received training where the CS predicted the absence of shock, and a third received random presentations of CS and US. He found that avoidance behavior was increased and decreased in the conditions where the CS predicted the presence and absence of the US, respectively. In the noncontingent condition, he found that the CS had no effect on avoidance responding, in spite of the chance pairings of the two events.

As noted earlier, problems for stimulus-based theories of avoidance (i.e., Pavlovian accounts and two-factor theory) came about when critics highlighted that during Sidman's early experiments, free-operant avoidance could be acquired in the absence of a warning CS (Sidman, 1953). In an effort to explain this result within the framework of two-factor theory, some theorists sought to expand the definition of the CS. According to Schoenfeld (1950), stimuli that become conditioned during the avoidance-learning procedure are not limited to that which the experimenter deems relevant to the procedure. Anger (1963), like Schoenfeld, proposed that the temporal conditions inherent in an experiment and also the proprioception associated with aspects of the response could act as CSs, motivating the animal to escape the fear they elicit. Although Herrnstein (1969) made a valid point regarding the difficulty associated with measuring these somewhat elusive CSs, a simple way of characterizing the various stimuli involved in conditioning is to consider them components of the broader experimental context. The role of the context in associative learning only emerged in the latter half of the 20th century, but is now a rich area of study (Urcelay & Miller, 2014). Assuming that environmental cues can enter into association with the shock, we can think of the exteroceptive context as a global warning signal that predicts the occurrence of shock, thus eliciting avoidance behavior owing to its correlation with shock, at least early on in training (Rescorla & Wagner, 1972).

Pavlovian contingency (CS–US): avoidance maintenance

Although likely critical for acquisition, the role of CS–US contingency in the maintenance of avoidance is much less clear. Borne out of the observation that the avoidance behavior evident in anxiety disorders persists despite unreinforced presentations of the CS (e.g., in posttraumatic stress disorder: PTSD), researchers began to speculate that if conditioning is a good model of human anxiety, then avoidance in the laboratory should be particularly resistant to extinction of the CS–US contingency (Eysenck, 1979). The first reported case of extreme resistance to extinction in animal avoidance was described in research by Solomon and colleagues (1953). Two dogs were trained to jump from one side of a shuttle box to the other at the sound of a buzzer and the raising of the central gate separating the compartments of the box, to avoid receiving a highly intense shock. After training to criterion, the dogs were no longer shocked, regardless of their behavior, thus attempting to extinguish responding. Much to the experimenter's surprise, the dogs continued to make the avoidance response for days following the introduction of extinction. They stopped running one animal after 190 extinction trials and the other at 490, neither showing signs of extinction, in fact their response latencies gradually decreased over extinction (i.e., became faster). Strikingly, they reported that the animal that was finally stopped at 490 trials had only received 11 shocks during training. As mentioned earlier, subsequent attempts to discourage avoidance by introducing a punishment contingency were unsuccessful, demonstrating the quite remarkable inflexibility of the avoidance response.

Although Solomon's early observations provided compelling evidence in support of the then popular conditioning model of anxiety, the first analyses of this postulate surmised that persistent resistance to CS–US extinction was not always a feature of avoidance, based on a host of studies demonstrating that in general, avoidance extinguishes quite readily in animals in a number of different paradigms once the CS ceases to predict an aversive outcome (Mackintosh, 1974). This stance was generally accepted but soon reversed when it was observed that paradigms using multiple CSs, presented in series (e.g., a tone, followed by a light, followed by a noise), could reliably induce avoidance behavior that was resistant to CS–US extinction in animals (Levis, 1966; Levis, Bouska, Eron, & McIlhon, 1970; Levis & Boyd, 1979; McAllister, McAllister, Scoles, & Hampton, 1986) and humans (Malloy & Levis, 1988; Williams & Levis, 1991). The serial CS procedure, which was also employed by Solomon in his original work, is thought to reflect more closely the reality of human conditioning, where cues are typically multidimensional, rather than the type of unidimensional cues used in most conditioning procedures. Indeed, direct comparisons between serial and nonserial paradigms clearly demonstrate the disparity in the resulting sensitivity to extinction, wherein serial cues tend to induce greater resistance to extinction than discrete cues (Malloy & Levis, 1988). One explanation for resistance to extinction in avoidance is that unlike appetitive instrumental behavior, the successful outcome of action is a nonevent, or the absence of an expected aversive US (Lovibond, 2006). It follows that when avoidance behavior reaches a high rate prior to extinction, subsequent exposure to the new contingency (CS–noUS) is disrupted by the intervening response, such that the animal is never exposed to the new contingency. From a different theoretical standpoint, the Rescorla–Wagner theory (Rescorla & Wagner, 1972) also predicts that the response should protect the CS from extinguishing, because the avoidance response becomes a conditioned inhibitor of fear, a point originally made by Konorski (1967; see also Soltysik, 1960). In general, it seems that CS–US contingency, although widely considered to be necessary for the development of avoidance, may not be critical for the maintenance of this behavior. It should be noted, however, that the broad individual differences in sensitivity to extinction are typically reported (Sheffield & Temmer, 1950; Williams & Levis, 1991).

Instrumental contingency (R–no US; no R–US)

Perhaps the most widely accepted condition necessary for avoidance behavior to emerge is for an instrumental contingency to exist between performance of the response and the delivery of an aversive event. In other words, avoidance is acquired on the basis that it is effective in preventing undesirable outcomes. This condition for avoidance was first taken out of the realm of tacit assumption and into the laboratory by Herrnstein and colleagues (Boren, Sidman, & Herrnstein, 1959; Herrnstein & Hineline, 1966), who tested the relationship between avoidance and shock intensity, and avoidance and shock-frequency reduction, respectively. This effort was made to resolve an issue arising from Pavlov's (1927) earlier experiments:

> How effective would Pavlov's procedure be if the salivary response did not moisten the food, dilute the acid or irrigate the mouth? (Herrnstein, 1969, p. 50)

What Herrnstein references here is the inability for Pavlov's experiments to distinguish between the instrumental and Pavlovian nature of the responses observed in his classical conditioning studies. In an effort to demonstrate the instrumentality inherent in avoidance responses, Herrnstein and Hineline (1966) designed a free-operant paradigm wherein presentations of a foot shock were delivered at random intervals, with no spatial or temporal CS signal. This design sought to deal with the attempt by Anger (1963), described before, to characterize their earlier results as a consequence of the inherent temporal contingency in the Sidman avoidance procedure. Using this procedure they demonstrated that response rates were directly related to the level of shock reduction. The strong conclusion made by Herrnstein, that avoidance is solely dependent on the reduction in shock rate, is perhaps overstated, given the evidence cited above for the role of context in associative learning. Nonetheless, the tight coupling between response rate and shock frequency reduction observed in this study makes a strong case for the role of R–noUS contingency in avoidance behavior.

Further support was provided by some elegant studies in rodents and humans using flooding (i.e., response prevention). In one such study, after an avoidance criterion was reached using a shuttle-box shock avoidance apparatus, Mineka and Gino (1979) tested the effect of flooding on the conditioned emotional response (CER), an assay for conditioned fear, during extinction training in rats. The experimental flooding group received nonreinforced CS exposure (extinction) in their training cage. Critically, a metal barrier was positioned in place of the hurdle barrier that the rats had previously used to avoid shock, thereby preventing the rats from performing the avoidance response. Two control groups received an equivalent period in their home cage, and CS–US extinction training with no flooding, respectively. In line with an expectancy account of avoidance, they found that the animals receiving flooding showed an initial increase in the CER (i.e., greater fear response) during their extinction training in the presence of flooding compared with the control groups. This effect was also observed by Solomon *et al.* (1953) in his initial experiments with dogs, described earlier in the chapter. What these data suggest is that the avoidance response is associated with avoided shock, and therefore when the opportunity to avoid is removed, the animal predicts shock. Lovibond, Saunders, Weidemann, and Mitchell (2008) demonstrated a similar effect in humans, wherein response prevention increased participants' level of shock expectancy during extinction training compared with a group who were permitted to continue to avoid. There was a similar effect on skin conductance level (SCL), a tonic measure of arousal related to anxiety, in that subjects receiving response prevention had greater SCL than comparison groups. That the prevention of the avoidance response causes an increase in anxiety and shock expectancy suggests that, as in the Mineka and Gino (1979) study, the absence of shock is contingent on the subject performing the avoidance response. In a subsequent experiment, Lovibond, Mitchell, Minard, Brady, and Menzies (2009) found that the availability (and utilization) of the avoidance response during extinction training causes an increase in levels of shock expectancy ratings and SCL when subsequently tested in the absence of the avoidance response, illustrating that continued avoidance can prevent safety learning about CS–noUS contingency, which is a basic tenet of exposure and response prevention therapy for obsessive–compulsive disorder (OCD).

Content of the Associations

Having discussed what we assume are the two conditions necessary for the acquisition and maintenance of avoidance, contingency between stimuli and reinforcers, and between actions and their outcomes, we turn now to the difficult question of delineating what form these associations take in terms of the content of the representation that modulates avoidance behavior. Here, we describe and evaluate a dual-process account of avoidance analogous to that described by Dickinson (1980) for appetitive conditioning. Not to be confused with two-factor theory, which assumes that Pavlovian and instrumental associations are necessary for avoidance, dual-process theories refers to whether the representations that control behavior are stimulus–response, automatic, or habit-based, or if they are driven instead by the value of outcomes, and the relationship between actions and outcomes, and are therefore goal-directed. By virtue of their ubiquity, the representations comprising a dual-system account have appeared in different guises throughout the history of psychology. What Dickinson (1985) termed goal-directed and habitual, others have described as related processes such as declarative and procedural (Cohen & Squire, 1980), model-based and model-free (Daw, Niv, & Dayan, 2005), explicit and implicit (Reber, 1967), or controlled and automatic (Schneider & Shiffrin, 1977). Although the terminology and indeed phenomenology differ, these are all characterizations of a dual-process system of learning and are thought to interrelate. Seger and Spiering (2011) concluded that there are five common definitional features of what we will henceforth call habit learning and goal-directed behavior. Specifically, habits are inflexible, slow or incremental, unconscious, automatic, and insensitive to reinforcer devaluation. As these definitions are partially overlapping, we will use just two of Seger and Spiering's characteristics of habit learning to explore the assertion that the representations that govern avoidance, much like appetitive instrumental behavior, can be understood from a dual-process perspective.

Flexibility

Evidence for goal-directed associations in avoidance comes from many avenues, the first of which is the evident flexibility of avoidance to changes in the environment. Declercq, De Houwer, and Baeyens (2008) investigated if avoidance behavior was capable of this kind of flexibility by testing the ability of subjects to adapt their behavior solely on the basis of new information provided to them. This is in contrast to learning by direct reinforcement. To test this, they arranged a scenario in which a Pavlovian contingency existed between three CSs and unavoidable aversive USs: shock, white noise, and both (i.e., noise + shock), respectively. Subsequently, subjects were given the opportunity to perform one of two avoidance responses (R1 or R2) following the presentation of the third stimulus, which predicted simultaneous presentation of both of the aversive USs (noise + shock). Here, subjects could learn that pressing R1 in the presence of this CS caused the omission of shock, but not noise, whereas pressing R2 caused the omission of the noise, and not the shock. To test for inferential reasoning in avoidance, the authors then presented participants with the other two discriminative stimuli from stage 1, the CS that predicted shock only, and the CS that predicted noise only. They tested if subjects could use R1 when presented with the CS that predicted shock and R2 when presented with the CS that predicted noise. This behavior could rely only on inferential reasoning based on learning during the intervening stage. Declercq and colleagues found that students could indeed make this inferential step, bolstering the claim that avoidance can indeed be goal-directed in nature. However, it is notable that in order to reveal this effect, the authors had to exclude participants from experiment 1 on the basis of the degree to which they acquired propositional (self-report) knowledge of the training stages of the task. These results were even then not altogether convincing, and so the authors repeated the experiment with the introduction of a "learning to criteria" component, designed to improve subjects' propositional knowledge of the initial task contingencies. Indeed, propositional knowledge was improved in this experiment, and the subjects performed the inference task above chance level. This kind of analysis, however, could be considered circular, as participants are selected on the basis of a criterion known to relate to the dependent measure.

Although these data suggest that avoidance behavior has the capacity to be flexible, it highlights how verbal instructions can play a critical role in mediating a shift between flexible and inflexible representations, possibly by promoting propositional knowledge and decreasing sensitivity to direct reinforcement (Li, Delgado, & Phelps, 2011). That when the instructions are sparse, even healthy humans have difficulty making basic inferences in avoidance, suggests that other mechanisms besides expectancy may be supporting avoidance learning. In addition, these experiments employ symbolic outcomes, leaving open the question of whether this kind of instrumentality can be demonstrated using a more traditional avoidance learning paradigm. In addition to the necessity for paradigms to include abundant instructions in order to produce flexible avoidance, further support for the notion that avoidance can also be represented by stimulus–response associations in the habit system can be derived from an observation by Solomon and colleagues (1953), described earlier, in which dogs persist in avoidance despite the introduction of a punishment schedule. In a more structured experiment, Boren and colleagues (1959) found that indeed the intensity of stimulation is a reliable predictor of subsequent resistance to extinction. This suggests that one way in which control of avoidance shifts from being goal-directed to habit-based is through the intensity of the US, which may serve to "stamp in" stimulus–response associations more readily.

Reinforcer devaluation

Reinforcer devaluation was described by Adams and Dickinson (1981) as a method for testing whether appetitive instrumental behavior in the rodent is goal-directed or habit-based. In this procedure, rats were trained to lever-press for a certain food outcome and exposed to noncontingent presentations of another food. In a subsequent stage, the researchers paired consumption of one of the foods with injections of lithium chloride to instill a taste aversion in these subjects (i.e., outcome devaluation). They then tested two groups of rats, one group that had received the taste aversion to the noncontingently presented food and the other to the instrumentally acquired food in stage 1. They found that the rats that had acquired a conditioned taste aversion to the noncontingently presented food persisted to respond on the lever for the other food, while rats that had acquired an aversion to the instrumentally acquired food decreased their rate of responding. Although this provided strong evidence for the goal-directed nature of appetitive behavior in the rodent, Adams (1982) subsequently demonstrated that following extended training, behavior lost its sensitivity to outcome devaluation and became a stimulus–response habit. While reinforcer devaluation has been much studied in appetitive conditions, there are just three examples in avoidance learning (Declercq & De Houwer, 2008; Gillan et al., 2013; Hendersen & Graham, 1979).

In the first such study, Hendersen and Graham (1979) manipulated the value of a heat outcome by altering the ambient temperature in which it was presented. The heat-lamp outcome was aversive in a warm context and less aversive, or "devalued" in a cold context. Animals were trained to avoid the heat US in a warm context and then subsequently placed in a cold environment where half of the rats were given exposure to the heat US, while the other half were not. The rats were then placed into the avoidance apparatus and extinguished in either the warm or cold context, creating four groups in total. When Hendersen and Graham compared rats that were tested in the cold environment, they found that extinction of the avoidance response was facilitated by the intervening heat devaluation procedure (i.e., exposure to the heat US in the cold environment). There was no difference in extinction rate between the groups extinguished in the warm environment. Together, these data suggest that rodents must have learned that the heat US is not aversive in the cold environment, in order to show sensitivity to whether the CS is presented in a warm or cold setting. It therefore appears that, in rodents, avoidance behavior can display characteristics of goal-directed behavior that is sensitive to outcome value. It should be noted, however, that there was no significant difference in behavior between the groups on the first trial of extinction in this study, suggesting that the effects of outcome devaluation were not immediately translated into behavior, as would be predicted by a goal-directed account.

Declercq and De Houwer (2008) attempted to rectify this problem. They trained healthy humans on an avoidance procedure, wherein they could press an available response button to avoid two USs associated with monetary loss that were predicted by two discrete CSs. They then conducted a symbolic *revaluation* procedure, where subjects were shown that one of the USs was now associated with monetary gain, instead of loss. In a subsequent test phase, they observed that subjects refrained from performing the avoidance response to the CS associated with the revalued US, and maintained avoidance to the CS that predicted the still-aversive US. Furthermore, this dramatic behavior change was evident from the first trial of the test phase, suggesting that humans used knowledge of the value of the US to guide their decision whether or not to respond to a given CS, without any new reinforcement experience with the response and the revalued outcome.

The final example of reinforcer devaluation in avoidance comes from our own work studying habit formation in patients with OCD. OCD is an anxiety disorder in which patients feel compelled to perform avoidance responses that they, rather counterintuitively, readily report are senseless or, at a minimum, disproportionate to the situation. Despite this awareness, patients have difficulty overcoming the compulsion to act, in spite of mounting negative consequences associated with performing these avoidance responses. Examples of compulsive behavior range from excessive repetition of common behaviors, such as hand-washing or checking, to superstitious acts such as ritualistic counting or flicking light switches. A recent model of compulsivity in OCD characterizes this behavior as a manifestation of excessive habit formation (Robbins et al., 2012), based on data demonstrating that OCD patients have a deficit in goal-directed behavioral control following appetitive instrumental learning using outcome devaluation of symbolic reinforcers (Gillan et al., 2011). Although these data looked promising, given that compulsions in OCD are avoidant, rather than appetitive, we reasoned that excessive avoidance habit learning is a more ecologically valid model of the disorder and determined that if excessive habit formation was a good model of OCD, then habits must be experimentally demonstrable in avoidance, as well as following appetitive instrumental training.

To test if stimulus–response associations can support avoidance learning, we set up a shock-avoidance procedure with brief and extended training components. We trained OCD patients and a group of matched healthy control subjects on a novel avoidance paradigm, wherein one stimulus predicted a shock to the subjects' left wrist, and another predicted one to the right (Gillan et al., 2013). Participants could avoid receiving a shock if they pressed the correct foot-pedal while a warning CS was on the screen. A third stimulus was always safe and served as a control measure for general response disinhibition. Reinforcer devaluation was implemented by disconnecting the shock electrodes from one of the subjects' wrists while leaving the other connected. We informed subjects explicitly that the stimulus that previously predicted this outcome was now safe and would not lead to further shocks. Following extended training, OCD patients made considerably more habit responses to the devalued stimulus compared with controls, indicative of a relative lack of goal-directed control over action. Notably, both groups demonstrated quite prominent devaluation, indicating that avoidance behavior unequivocally displays goal-directed characteristics.

In this experiment, we also took a posttest measure of shock expectancy during the devaluation test. We found that OCD patients had an equally low expectancy that shock would follow the CS that was associated with the now devalued outcome. This suggests that when habits are formed, avoidance behavior persists in a manner that is insensitive to explicit knowledge of outcome value and task contingency. As noted above, healthy participants in this study did not exhibit habits following extended training. We hypothesized that the failure of our procedure to instill habits in the healthy cohort was because exposure to the devaluation test following brief training may have increased their sensitivity to outcome value at the second test, following overtraining. Therefore, in a subsequent experiment, which is unpublished, we attempted to instill habits in two groups of healthy undergraduates who received different training durations (long vs. short). We found that subjects who received a longer duration of training showed a poorer sensitivity to devaluation. Although significant using a one-tailed test ($p = 0.03$), the weakness of the effect led us to conclude that it is exceedingly difficult to demonstrate robust avoidance habits in a healthy student cohort (Gillan et al., unpublished data). The likely explanation for this difficulty is that the level of instruction, which must (for ethical reasons) be provided in human avoidance experiments, tends to favor propositional, goal-directed control.

In this section, we have reviewed the experimental evidence relevant to a dual-process account, such that the content of the associations supporting avoidance might fall into two categories, goal-directed or habitual. The data presented suggest that much like appetitive instrumental learning, avoidance can and is often supported by goal-directed, flexible representations, but in some situations, avoidance appears to be solely controlled by stimulus–response links based on prior reinforcement of action and that are insensitive to goals.

Mechanisms of Avoidance

Having already discussed various theoretical positions regarding the mechanisms supporting the acquisition of instrumental avoidance, in this section we aim to synthesize these accounts with findings from modern neuroscience. Currently available evidence suggests that prediction error is the most tenable psychological mechanism that can account for the acquisition and maintenance of avoidance. This is an opinion forwarded in recent temporal difference accounts by Maia (2010) and Moutoussis and colleagues (2008), which manage rather seamlessly to integrate two-factor theory with the notion of cognitive expectancy. In this section, we advocate that avoidance learning involves an interaction between (1) learning to predict an imminent threat and (2) learning which instrumental actions can successfully cancel the impending threat, wherein each process relies on prediction error. Prediction errors, discrepancies between what is expected and what is received, are used by the organism to learn how to mitigate potentially aversive events in the environment, just as they are widely believed to aid the organism in the promotion of rewarding events (see Chapter 3). It is important to clarify here that this stance is orthogonal to the issue of the putative "dual-process" content of avoidance associations (habit vs. goal-directed) reviewed in the previous section.

The last three decades have seen a large amount of research investigating the neural basis of avoidance learning, leading to the identification of a network that comprises the amygdala, a temporal lobe structure involved in processing emotional information, cortical regions involved in decision-making, and, unsurprisingly, the striatal complex, that is, the striatum and in particular the NAc, which is a cognitive–emotional interface critical for action, and a putative hub for prediction error. In agreement with the involvement of the neurotransmitter dopamine (DA) in prediction error (Schultz & Dickinson, 2000), DA has a key role in avoidance, and this has led to the use of avoidance tasks as a behavioral assay for antipsychotics, which mainly target dopaminergic function (Kapur, 2004). Correlational studies have found higher levels of tonic DA in the NAc (a region of the rat's ventral striatum) after rats performed an active avoidance session (McCullough, Sokolowski, & Salamone, 1993).

Furthermore, both general (Cooper, Breese, Grant, & Howard, 1973) and NAc-selective (McCullough *et al.*, 1993), DA depletions, achieved by intracerebroventricular infusion of a neurotoxic agent that selectively targets and destroys dopaminergic neurons (6-OHDA), impair active lever-press avoidance performance, providing causal evidence for the involvement of DA in the performance of active avoidance. This is consistent with an experiment using microdialysis to measure DA concentrations that found a selective role for DA in avoidance learning. In this study, rats learned a two-way active avoidance task over five blocks of training. Tonic DA release in the NAc increased consistently during early blocks of training, when prediction error should have been highest, and diminished as subjects mastered the task. Both avoidance learning and DA release were abolished in rats that, prior to training, received lesions of dopaminergic neurons in the substantia nigra, containing a portion of the midbrain dopaminergic neurons projecting to the striatum (Dombrowski et al., 2013). However, above, we have identified several components in avoidance learning, and the specific role of DA may not be captured by studies, given that is has poor temporal resolution (Salamone & Correa, 2012). To address this limitation, Oleson, Gentry, Chioma, and Cheer (2012) used fast-scan voltammetry to investigate the role of phasic DA release in avoidance at the subsecond level in rodents. Of note, they used parameters in their task so that animals could only avoid in 50% of trials, a situation that closely resembles learning (i.e., prediction error) rather than performance. Using these parameters, they measured subsecond DA release in the NAc to the warning signal, safety period, and avoidance responses. A trial-by-trial analysis revealed that DA responses to the warning signal were increased in trials in which animals successfully avoided, and thus predicted whether animals were to avoid or not, but were dampened on trials in which animals did not avoid and thus escaped after receiving shocks. Regardless of whether animals avoided or escaped, a safety signal that followed the instrumental response always was correlated with DA release. This is consistent with recent experiments using a free-operant avoidance paradigm in which a safety signal also followed avoidance responses (Fernando, Urcelay, Mar, Dickinson, & Robbins, 2013).

Fernando and colleagues observed that D-amphetamine infusions in the shell subdivision of the NAc (but not the core) increased responding during presentations of the safety signal, reflecting a disruption of the fear-inhibiting properties of the safety signal. All together, these studies provide a causal role for DA in the acquisition and performance of avoidance behavior, a role that is consistent with the involvement of DA release in prediction error (Schultz & Dickinson, 2000). The amygdala consists of separate nuclei, of which the lateral, basal, and anterior subnuclei (sometimes referred to as the basolateral complex) receive inputs from different sensory modalities and project to the central amygdala (CeA), a nucleus that sends output projections to different response networks. The amygdala, especially the CeA, is widely believed to be the most important region involved in Pavlovian fear conditioning (Killcross, Robbins, & Everitt, 1997; Kim & Jung, 2006; LeDoux, Iwata, Cicchetti, & Reis, 1988; Phelps & LeDoux, 2005). It was noted in the 1990s that human patients with amygdala lesions exhibited deficits in fear conditioning (Bechara et al., 1995; LaBar, Ledoux, Spencer, & Phelps, 1995) and in recognizing fearful emotional faces (Adolphs, Tranel, Damasio, & Damasio, 1994). Human functional magnetic resonance imaging (fMRI) has since been used to investigate the specific role of the amygdala in Pavlovian conditioning (see Sehlmeyer et al., 2009, for meta-analysis), with studies consistently finding that activation in the amygdala is increased following presentation of a neutral CS that is predictive of an aversive US (LaBar, Gatenby, Gore, LeDoux, & Phelps, 1998), and this activation correlates with the intensity of the conditioned fear response, for example, skin conductance responses (LaBar et al., 1998; Phelps, Delgado, Nearing, & LeDoux, 2004). From the perspective of a two-process view of avoidance, given that the amygdala has been heavily implicated in Pavlovian fear learning, it is not surprising that it has also been implicated in avoidance.

In humans, one study used high-resolution fMRI to probe amygdala activation during avoidance and found evidence to suggest that laterality exists in the contribution of amygdala subregions to avoidance and appetitive instrumental learning (Prévost, McCabe, Jessup, Bossaerts, & O'Doherty, 2011). The authors found that activity in the CeA was correlated with the magnitude of an expected reward following an action choice, whereas the same action value signals in avoidance were found in the basolateral amygdala. This finding is in line with a study in rodents, where Lazaro-Munoz, LeDoux, and Cain (2010) found that lesions of the lateral or basal amygdala both lead to severely retarded acquisition of active avoidance, whereas lesions of the CeA had a smaller effect that, if any, went in the opposite direction. Indeed, in a subset of rats that did not acquire active avoidance, posttraining lesions of the central amygdala revealed almost intact learning that had been hindered by competition from freezing responses. This finding again ties in with the human neuroimaging results from Prévost and colleagues, where they also observed that when cues were presented, expected outcome signals were apparent in the CeA for avoidance. Therefore, it could be argued that the CeA mediates passive components of avoidance (e.g., the freezing response), and the basolateral amygdala has a strong role in active avoidance, as it does in punishment (Killcross et al., 1997). Overall, this is consistent with the basic tenets of a two-factor view of avoidance by which cued fear responses such as freezing can compete with the acquisition of instrumental avoidance. In line with this account, Lazaro-Munoz and colleagues observed that none of these lesions had an effect when carried out after animals had acquired the avoidance response, suggesting that the involvement of the amygdala is most critical during acquisition. Using fMRI, Delgado and colleagues (2009) found that activation in the striatum and amygdala were closely coupled as participants acquired an instrumental shock-avoidance response. This finding, though only correlational, suggests that the striatum, although informed by the amygdala during acquisition, may ultimately control the instrumental component of avoidance.

Finally, a few studies have investigated the role of the medial prefrontal cortex (mPFC) in active avoidance. The rat mPFC projects to multiple regions including the basolateral amygdala and the ventral striatum (Voorn, Vanderschuren, Groenewegen, Robbins, & Pennartz, 2004), thus closing a "loop" between these three regions critical for avoidance. In one study, depletion of DA in the rat mPFC did not have a strong effect on avoidance, but did significantly depress escape responding (Sokolowski, McCullough, & Salamone, 1994). The authors suggest that this perhaps reflects a specific role for mPFC DA in responding to direct presentations of aversive events, as opposed to cues that predict them. Recently, a study dissociated prelimbic and infralimbic subregions of the mPFC. Whereas electrolytic lesions of the prelimbic cortex had no effect on active avoidance, infralimbic lesions impaired active avoidance (Moscarello & LeDoux, 2013). What is striking about these findings is that the deficit in active avoidance acquisition was related to freezing to the CS; infralimbic lesioned rats took longer to acquire the task and also froze more to the CS. In addition to this, the opposite pattern was observed after CeA lesions, with these rats freezing less to the CS (at least early in training) and learning active avoidance *faster* than sham controls. The infralimbic cortex projects to a population of inhibitory neurons (intercalated cell masses; Paré, Quirk, & Ledoux, 2004) located in between the basolateral amygdala and the central amygdala, so overall these results suggest that a network involving the prefrontal cortex, the amygdala, and the striatum is implicated in responding to fear and overcoming fear with active behaviors.

Kim, Shimojo, and O'Doherty, (2006) investigated the possibility that avoiding an aversive outcome is in fact equivalent to receiving a reward as alluded to earlier (Dickinson & Dearing, 1979) and would therefore be reflected by a similar pattern of activation. Healthy humans were trained to use two response keys to avoid, or experience monetary loss, respectively. On reward trials, they could select between two visual cues, associated with either a high or low probability of monetary gain. Similarly, on avoidance trials, subjects could select cues that had a high or low probability of monetary loss. At the time of outcome delivery, they found that activation in the orbitofrontal cortex was similar for trials where reward was delivered, and punishment omitted. Computationally derived prediction errors were found to correlate with activation in the insula, thalamus, mPFC, and midbrain on avoidance trials.

To summarize, evidence from the neurosciences points to a key role for the striatum, prefrontal cortex, and amygdala in the acquisition of avoidance behavior. A two-factor account can easily capture these data, which suggest that prediction errors are the learning mechanism through which Pavlovian fear ("expectancy") is first acquired, and instrumental (active or passive) avoidance later manifests.

Summary

In this chapter, we have provided a contemporary review of the existing literature on the associative basis of avoidance, synthesizing historic debate with empirical study in rodents and humans from the fields of behavioral, cognitive, and neuroscience research. We have two main conclusions that we would like to summarize briefly. The first is that a dual-process account of avoidance can reconcile with issues that previously precluded the synthesis of cognitive and reinforcement learning based accounts. The basic tenet of this argument is that although there is ample evidence for goal sensitivity in avoidance, this has typically only been achieved when the experimental conditions are such that propositional knowledge is artificially enhanced, or specifically selected. Frequently, human and nonhuman animal avoidance displays the inflexibility characteristic of stimulus–response, habits. Conversely, stimulus-based accounts of avoidance learning have difficulty accounting for the capacity for some animals to make rapid changes in their avoidance responses based on inference, that is, without any new experience. Habit and goal-directed accounts of the content of associations in avoidance need not be divided into one of two opposing theoretical camps, but as in the appetitive literature, there is it seems ample evidence to consider them orthogonal to a basic understanding of the mechanism of avoidance. Once we dispense with debate on this outdated issue and assume that control of avoidance can oscillate between these controllers, there is good convergence for a two-factor account of avoidance, in which Pavlovian and instrumental prediction errors provide the mechanism of associative avoidance learning. This model has the advantage of possessing generality; that is, it can be applied across avoidance and appetitive preparations, and it can capture many of the observations that initially posed problems for two-factory theory (Maia, 2010). This view is largely based on historical observation and computational simulation; therefore, new, direct tests of this postulate are wanting. However, the neuroimaging evidence reviewed in this chapter converges with this account, identifying a clear role for prediction error in avoidance. This account is currently restricted to the habit domain, but there is no reason to suggest that it would not be possible also to formalize the role of prediction error in the goal-directed acquisition of avoidance, a process that has already begun in the appetitive learning (Daw et al., 2005). This distinction will be of particular importance to researchers hoping to use our theories of pathological avoidance to understand psychiatric disorders like OCD, where stimulus–response avoidance habits, and their interaction with conditioned fear, are thought to play a central role.

References

Adams, C. D. (1982). Variations in the sensitivity of instrumental responding to reinforcer devaluation. *Quarterly Journal of Experimental Psychology Section B: Comparative and Physiological Psychology, 34,* 77–98.

Adams, C. D., & Dickinson, A. (1981). Instrumental responding following reinforcer devaluation. *Quarterly Journal of Experimental Psychology Section B: Comparative and Physiological Psychology, 33,* 109–121.

Adolphs, R., Tranel, D., Damasio, H., & Damasio, A. (1994). Impaired recognition of emotion in facial expressions following bilateral damage to the human amygdala. *Nature, 372,* 669–672.

Anger, D. (1963). The role of temporal discriminations in the reinforcement of Sidman avoidance behavior [Supplement]. *Journal of the Experimental Analysis of Behavior, 6,* 477–506.

Baum, W. M. (1973). Correlation-based law of effect. *Journal of the Experimental Analysis of Behavior, 20,* 137–153.

Bechara, A., Tranel, D., Damasio, H., Adolphs, R., Rockland, C., & Damasio, A. R. (1995). Double dissociation of conditioning and declarative knowledge relative to the amygdala and hippocampus in humans. *Science, 269,* 1115–1118.

Beninger, R. J., Mason, S. T., Phillips, A. G., & Fibiger, H. C. (1980). The use of conditioned suppression to evaluate the nature of neuroleptic-induced avoidance deficits. *Journal of Pharmacology and Experimental Therapeutics, 213,* 623–627.

Bolles, R. (1970). Species-specific defense reactions and avoidance learning. *Psychological Review, 77,* 32–48.

Bolles, R. C., Stokes, L. W., & Younger, M. S. (1966). Does CS termination reinforce avoidance behavior. *Journal of Comparative and Physiological Psychology, 62,* 201.

Bond, N. W. (1984). Avoidance, classical, and pseudoconditioning as a function of species-specific defense reactions in high-avoider and low-avoider rat strains. *Animal Learning & Behavior, 12,* 323–331.

Boren, J. J., Sidman, M., & Herrnstein, R. J. (1959). Avoidance, escape, and extinction as functions of shock intensity. *Journal of Comparative and Physiological Psychology, 52,* 420–425.

Brady, J. V., & Harris, A. (1977). The experimental production of altered physiological states. In W. K. Honig & J. E. R. Staddon (Eds.), *Handbook of operant behavior.* Englewood Cliffs, NJ: Prentice-Hall.

Brogden, W. J., Lipman, E. A., & Culler, E. (1938). The role of incentive in conditioning and extinction. *American Journal of Psychology, 51,* 109–117.

Cohen, N. J., & Squire, L. R. (1980). Preserved learning and retention of pattern-analyzing skill in amnesia – dissociation of knowing how and knowing that. *Science, 210,* 207–210.

Cooper, B. R., Breese, G. R., Grant, L. D., & Howard, J. L. (1973). Effects of 6-hydroxydopamine treatments on active avoidance responding – evidence for involvement of brain dopamine. *Journal of Pharmacology and Experimental Therapeutics, 185*, 358–370.

Coover, G. D., Ursin, H., & Levine, S. (1973). Plasma corticosterone levels during active-avoidance learning in rats. *Journal of Comparative and Physiological Psychology, 82*, 170–174.

Daw, N. D., Niv, Y., & Dayan, P. (2005). Uncertainty-based competition between prefrontal and dorsolateral striatal systems for behavioral control. *Nature Neuroscience, 8*, 1704–1711.

De Houwer, J., Crombez, G., & Baeyens, F. (2005). Avoidance behavior can function as a negative occasion setter. *Journal of Experimental Psychology: Animal Behavior Processes, 31*, 101–106.

Declercq, M., & De Houwer, J. (2008). On the role of US expectancies in avoidance behavior. *Psychonomic Bulletin & Review, 15*, 99–102.

Declercq, M., De Houwer, J., & Baeyens, F. (2008). Evidence for an expectancy-based theory of avoidance behaviour. *Quarterly Journal of Experimental Psychology (Colchester), 61*, 1803–1812.

Delgado, M. R., Jou, R. L., LeDoux, J. E., & Phelps, E. A. (2009). Avoiding negative outcomes: tracking the mechanisms of avoidance learning in humans during fear conditioning. *Frontiers in Behavioral Neuroscience, 3.* 10.3389/neuro.08.033.2009

Dickinson, A. (1980). *Contemporary animal learning theory*. Cambridge, UK: Cambridge University Press.

Dickinson, A. (1985). Actions and habits: the development of behavioural autonomy. *Philosophical Transactions of the Royal Society of London. Series B, Biological Sciences, 308*, 67–78.

Dickinson, A., & Dearing, M. F. (1979). Appetitive–aversive interactions and inhibitory processes. In A. Dickinson & R. A. Boakes (Eds.), *Mechanisms of learning and motivation* (pp. 203–231). Hillsdale, NJ: Erlbaum.

Dinsmoor, J. A. (2001). Stimuli inevitably generated by behavior that avoids electric shock are inherently reinforcing. *Journal of the Experimental Analysis of Behavior, 75*, 311–333.

Dinsmoor, J. A., & Sears, G. W. (1973). Control of avoidance by a response produced stimulus. *Learning and Motivation, 4*, 284–293.

Dombrowski, P. A., Maia, T. V., Boschen, S. L., Bortolanza, M., Wendler, E., Schwarting, R. K. W., ... Da Cunha, C. (2013). Evidence that conditioned avoidance responses are reinforced by positive prediction errors signaled by tonic striatal dopamine. *Behavioural Brain Research, 241*, 112–119.

Eysenck, H. J. (1979). The conditioning model of neurosis. *Behavioral and Brain Sciences, 2*, 155–166.

Fernando, A. B., Urcelay, G. P., Mar, A. C., Dickinson, T. A., & Robbins, T. W. (2013). The role of the nucleus accumbens shell in the mediation of the reinforcing properties of a safety signal in free-operant avoidance: dopamine-dependent inhibitory effects of D-amphetamine. *Neuropsychopharmacology*.

Fernando, A. B. P., Urcelay, G. P., Mar, A. C., Dickinson, A., & Robbins, T. W. (2014). Safety signals as instrumental reinforcers during free-operant avoidance. *Learning & Memory, 21*, 488–497.

Gillan, C. M., Morein-Zamir, S., Urcelay, G. P., Sule, A., Voon, V., Apergis-Schoute, A. M., ... Robbins, T. W. (2013). Enhanced avoidance habits in obsessive–compulsive disorder. *Biological Psychiatry, 75*, 631–638.

Gillan, C. M., Papmeyer, M., Morein-Zamir, S., Sahakian, B. J., Fineberg, N. A., Robbins, T. W., & de Wit, S. (2011). Disruption in the balance between goal-directed behavior and habit learning in obsessive–compulsive disorder. *American Journal of Psychiatry, 168*, 718–726.

Hendersen, R. W., & Graham, J. (1979). Avoidance of heat by rats – effects of thermal context on rapidity of extinction. *Learning and Motivation*, 10, 351–363.

Herrnstein, R. J. (1969). Method and theory in study of avoidance. *Psychological Review*, 76, 49.

Herrnstein, R. J., & Hineline, P. N. (1966). Negative reinforcement as shock-frequency reduction. *Journal of the Experimental Analysis of Behavior*, 9, 421–430.

Hineline, P. N. (1970). Negative reinforcement without shock reduction. *Journal of the Experimental Analysis of Behavior*, 14, 259.

Hineline, P. N., & Rachlin, H. (1969). Escape and avoidance of shock by pigeons pecking a key. *Journal of the Experimental Analysis of Behavior*, 12, 533.

Kamin, L. J. (1954). Traumatic avoidance learning – the effects of CS–US interval with a trace-conditioning procedure. *Journal of Comparative and Physiological Psychology*, 47, 65–72.

Kamin, L. J. (1956). The effects of termination of the CS and avoidance of the US on avoidance learning. *Journal of Comparative and Physiological Psychology*, 49, 420–424.

Kamin, L. J. (1969). Predictability, surprise, attention and conditioning. In B. A. Campbell & R. M. Church (Eds.), *Punishment and aversive behavior* (pp. 279–296). New York, NY: Appleton-Century Crofts.

Kamin, L. J., Brimer, C. J., & Black, A. H. (1963). Conditioned suppression as a monitor of fear of CS in course of avoidance training. *Journal of Comparative and Physiological Psychology*, 56, 497.

Kapur, S. (2004). How antipsychotics become anti-"psychotic" – from dopamine to salience to psychosis. *Trends in Pharmacological Sciences*, 25, 402–406.

Killcross, S., Robbins, T. W., & Everitt, B. J. (1997). Different types of fear-conditioned behaviour mediated by separate nuclei within amygdala. *Nature*, 388, 377–380.

Kim, H., Shimojo, S., & O'Doherty, J. P. (2006). Is avoiding an aversive outcome rewarding? Neural substrates of avoidance learning in the human brain. *PLoS Biology*, 4, e233.

Kim, J. J., & Jung, M. W. (2006). Neural circuits and mechanisms involved in Pavlovian fear conditioning: A critical review. *Neuroscience and Biobehavioral Reviews*, 30, 188–202.

Konorski, J. (1967). *Integrative activity of the brain: An interdisciplinary approach*. Chicago, IL: University of Chicago Press.

Konorski, J., & Miller, S. (1937). On two types of conditioned reflex. *The Journal of General Psychology*, 16, 264–272.

LaBar, K. S., Gatenby, J. C., Gore, J. C., LeDoux, J. E., & Phelps, E. A. (1998). Human amygdala activation during conditioned fear acquisition and extinction: a mixed-trial fMRI study. *Neuron*, 20, 937–945.

LaBar, K. S., Ledoux, J. E., Spencer, D. D., & Phelps, E. A. (1995). Impaired fear conditioning following unilateral temporal lobectomy in humans. *Journal of Neuroscience*, 15, 6846–6855.

Lazaro-Munoz, G., LeDoux, J. E., & Cain, C. K. (2010). Sidman instrumental avoidance initially depends on lateral and basal amygdala and is constrained by central amygdala-mediated Pavlovian processes. *Biological Psychiatry*, 67, 1120–1127.

LeDoux, J. E., Iwata, J., Cicchetti, P., & Reis, D. J. (1988). Different projections of the central amygdaloid nucleus mediate autonomic and behavioral correlates of conditioned fear. *Journal of Neuroscience*, 8, 2517–29.

Levis, D. J. (1966). Effects of serial CS presentation and other characteristics of CS on conditioned avoidance response. *Psychological Reports*, 18, 755.

Levis, D. J., Bouska, S. A., Eron, J. B., & McIlhon, M. D. (1970). Serial CS presentation and one-way avoidance conditioning – noticeable lack of delay in responding. *Psychonomic Science*, 20, 147–149.

Levis, D. J., & Boyd, T. L. (1979). Symptom maintenance – infrahuman analysis and extension of the conservation of anxiety principle. *Journal of Abnormal Psychology*, 88, 107–120.

Li, J., Delgado, M., & Phelps, E. (2011). How instructed knowledge modulates the neural systems of reward learning. *Proceedings of the National Academy of Sciences of the United States of America, 108*, 55–60.

Linden, D. R. (1969). Attenuation and reestablishment of cer by discriminated avoidance conditioning in rats. *Journal of Comparative and Physiological Psychology, 69*, 573.

Lovibond, P. F. (2006). Fear and avoidance: An integrated expectancy model. In M. G. Craske, D. Hermans & D. Vansteenwegen (Eds.), *Fear and learning: From basic processes to clinical implications* (pp. 117–132). Washington, DC: American Psychological Association.

Lovibond, P. F., Mitchell, C. J., Minard, E., Brady, A., & Menzies, R. G. (2009). Safety behaviours preserve threat beliefs: Protection from extinction of human fear conditioning by an avoidance response. *Behaviour Research and Therapy, 47*, 716–720.

Lovibond, P. F., Saunders, J. C., Weidemann, G., & Mitchell, C. J. (2008). Evidence for expectancy as a mediator of avoidance and anxiety in a laboratory model of human avoidance learning. *Quarterly Journal of Experimental Psychology (Colchester), 61*, 1199–1216.

Lovibond, P. F., & Shanks, D. R. (2002). The role of awareness in Pavlovian conditioning: empirical evidence and theoretical implications. *Journal of Experimental Psychology Animal Behavior Processes, 28*, 3–26.

Mackintosh, A. H. (1983). *Conditioning and associative learning*. Oxford University Press: Oxford, UK.

Mackintosh, N. (1974). *The psychology of animal learning*. New York, NY: Academic Press.

Maia, T. V. (2010). Two-factor theory, the actor-critic model, and conditioned avoidance. *Learning & Behavior, 38*, 50–67.

Malloy, P., & Levis, D. J. (1988). A laboratory demonstration of persistent human avoidance. *Behavior Therapy, 19*, 229–241.

McAllister, W. R., McAllister, D. E., Scoles, M. T., & Hampton, S. R. (1986). Persistence of fear-reducing behavior – relevance for the conditioning theory of neurosis. *Journal of Abnormal Psychology, 95*, 365–372.

McCullough, L. D., Sokolowski, J. D., & Salamone, J. D. (1993). A neurochemical and behavioral investigation of the involvement of nucleus-accumbens dopamine in instrumental avoidance. *Neuroscience, 52*, 919–925.

McNally, R. J., & Steketee, G. S. (1985). The etiology and maintenance of severe animal phobias. *Behaviour Research and Therapy, 23*, 431–435.

Mineka, S. (1979). The role of fear in theories of avoidance-learning, flooding, and extinction. *Psychological Bulletin, 86*, 985–1010.

Mineka, S., & Gino, A. (1979). Dissociative effects of different types and amounts of nonreinforced CS-exposure on avoidance extinction and the cer. *Learning and Motivation, 10*, 141–160.

Morris, R. G. M. (1974). Pavlovian conditioned inhibition of fear during shuttlebox avoidance behavior. *Learning and Motivation, 5*, 424–447.

Morris, R. G. M. (1975). Preconditioning of reinforcing properties to an exteroceptive feedback stimulus. *Learning and Motivation, 6*, 289–298.

Moscarello, J. M., & LeDoux, J. E. (2013). Active avoidance learning requires prefrontal suppression of amygdala-mediated defensive reactions. *Journal of Neuroscience, 33*, 3815–3823.

Moutoussis, M., Bentall, R. P., Williams, J., & Dayan, P. (2008). A temporal difference account of avoidance learning. *Network-Computation in Neural Systems, 19*, 137–160.

Mowrer, O. (1947). On the dual nature of learning: A reinterpretation of conditioning and problem solving. *Harvard Educational Review, 17*, 102–148.

Mowrer, O. H. (1939). A stimulus-response analysis of anxiety and its role as a reinforcing agent. *Psychological Review, 46*, 553.

Mowrer, O. H. (1940). Anxiety-reduction and learning. *Journal of Experimental Psychology, 27*, 497–516.

Mowrer, O. H. (1960). *Learning theory and behavior.* New York, NY: Wiley.

Mowrer, O. H., & Lamoreaux, R. R. (1942). Avoidance conditioning and signal duration – a study of secondary motivation and reward. *Psychological Monographs, 54,* 1–34.

Neuenschwander, N., Fabrigoule, C., & Mackintosh, N. J. (1987). Fear of the warning signal during overtraining of avoidance. *Quarterly Journal of Experimental Psychology Section B: Comparative and Physiological Psychology, 39,* 23–33.

Oleson, E. B., Gentry, R. N., Chioma, V. C., & Cheer, J. F. (2012). Subsecond dopamine release in the nucleus accumbens predicts conditioned punishment and its successful avoidance. *Journal of Neuroscience, 32,* 14804–14808.

Paré, D., Quirk, G. J., & Ledoux, J. E. (2004). New vistas on amygdala networks in conditioned fear. *Journal of Neurophysiology, 92,* 1–9.

Pavlov, I. (1927). *Conditioned reflexes: an investigation of the physiological activity of the cerebral cortex.* London: Oxford University Press.

Phelps, E. A., Delgado, M. R., Nearing, K. I., & LeDoux, J. E. (2004). Extinction learning in humans: Role of the amygdala and vmPFC. *Neuron, 43,* 897–905.

Phelps, E. A., & LeDoux, J. E. (2005). Contributions of the amygdala to emotion processing: From animal models to human behavior. *Neuron, 48,* 175–187.

Prévost, C., McCabe, J. A., Jessup, R. K., Bossaerts, P., & O'Doherty, J. P. (2011). Differentiable contributions of human amygdalar subregions in the computations underlying reward and avoidance learning. *European Journal of Neuroscience, 34,* 134–145.

Reber, A. S. (1967). Implicit learning of artificial grammars. *Journal of Verbal Learning and Verbal Behavior, 6,* 855.

Reiss, S. (1991). Expectancy model of fear, anxiety, and panic. *Clinical Psychology Review, 11,* 141–153.

Rescorla, R. (1966). Predictability and number of pairings in Pavlovian fear conditioning. *Psychonomic Science, 4,* 383–384.

Rescorla, R., & Wagner, A. (1972). A theory of Pavlovian conditioning: Variations in the effectiveness of reinforcement and non-reinforcement. In A. Black (Ed.), *Classical conditioning II* (pp. 64–99). New York, NY: Appleton-Century-Crofts.

Rescorla, R. A. (1968). Probability of shock in presence and absence of CS in fear conditioning. *Journal of Comparative and Physiological Psychology, 66,* 1.

Riess, D. (1971). Shuttleboxes, skinner boxes, and sidman avoidance in rats – acquisition and terminal performance as a function of response topography. *Psychonomic Science, 25,* 283–286.

Robbins, T. W., Gillan, C. M., Smith, D. G., de Wit, S., & Ersche, K. D. (2012). Neurocognitive endophenotypes of impulsivity and compulsivity: towards dimensional psychiatry. *Trends in Cognitive Sciences, 16,* 81–91.

Salamone, J., & Correa, M. (2012). The mysterious motivational functions of mesolimbic dopamine. *Neuron, 76,* 470–485.

Schneider, W., & Shiffrin, R. M. (1977). Controlled and automatic human information-processing. 1. Detection, search, and attention. *Psychological Review, 84,* 1–66.

Schoenfeld, W. N. (1950). An experimental approach to anxiety, escape and avoidance behaviour. In P. H. Hoch & J. Zubin (Eds.), *Anxiety* (pp. 70–99). New York, NY: Grune & Stratton.

Schultz, W., Dayan, P., & Montague, P. R. (1997). A neural substrate of prediction and reward. *Science, 275,* 1593–1599.

Schultz, W., & Dickinson, A. (2000). Neuronal coding of prediction errors. *Annual Review of Neuroscience, 23,* 473–500.

Scobie, S. R., & Fallon, D. (1974). Operant and Pavlovian control of a defensive shuttle response in goldfish (*Carassius auratus*). *Journal of Comparative and Physiological Psychology, 86,* 858–866.

Seger, C. A., & Spiering, B. J. (2011). A critical review of habit learning and the basal ganglia. *Frontiers in Systems Neuroscience, 5*, 66.

Sehlmeyer, C., Schoening, S., Zwitserlood, P., Pfleiderer, B., Kircher, T., Arolt, V., & Konrad, C. (2009). Human fear conditioning and extinction in neuroimaging: a systematic review. *Plos One, 4*, e5865.

Seligman, M., & Johnston, J. (1973). A cognitive theory of avoidance learning. In F. McGuigan & D. Lumsden (Eds.), *Contemporary approaches to condition and learning*. Washington, DC: Winston-Wiley.

Seligman, M. E., & Campbell, B. A. (1965). Effect of intensity and duration of punishment on extinction of an avoidance response. *Journal of Comparative and Physiological Psychology, 59*, 295.

Sheffield, F. D., & Temmer, H. W. (1950). Relative resistance to extinction of escape training and avoidance training. *Journal of Experimental Psychology, 40*, 287–298.

Sidman, M. (1953). Avoidance conditioning with brief shock and no exteroceptive warning signal. *Science, 118*, 157–158.

Sidman, M. (1955). Some properties of the warning stimulus in avoidance behavior. *Journal of Comparative and Physiological Psychology, 48*, 444–450.

Sokolowski, J. D., McCullough, L. D., & Salamone, J. D. (1994). Effects of dopamine depletions in the medial prefrontal cortex on active-avoidance and escape in the rat. *Brain Research, 651*, 293–299.

Solomon, R. L., Kamin, L. J., & Wynne, L. C. (1953). Traumatic avoidance learning – the outcomes of several extinction procedures with dogs. *Journal of Abnormal and Social Psychology, 48*, 291–302.

Solomon, S., Holmes, D. S., & McCaul, K. D. (1980). Behavioral-control over aversive events – does control that requires effort reduce anxiety and physiological arousal? *Journal of Personality and Social Psychology, 39*, 729–736.

Soltysik, S. (1960). Studies on avoidance conditioning III: Alimentary conditioned reflex model of the avoidance reflex. *Acta Biologiae Experimentalis, Warsaw, 20*, 183–191.

Starr, M. D., & Mineka, S. (1977). Determinants of fear over course of avoidance-learning. *Learning and Motivation, 8*, 332–350.

Sutton, R. S., & Barto, A. G. (1998). Time-derivative models of Pavlovian reinforcement. In M. R. Gabriel & J. Moore (Eds.), *Foundations of adaptive networks* (pp. 497–537). Cambridge, MA: MIT Press.

Thorndike, A. (1911). *Animal intelligence: Experimental studies*. New York, NY: Macmillan.

Tolman, E. C. (1948). Cognitive maps in rats and men. *Psychological Review* 55.

Urcelay, G. P., & Miller, R. R. (2014). The functions of contexts in associative learning. *Behavioural Processes, 104*, 2–12.

Voorn, P., Vanderschuren, L., Groenewegen, H. J., Robbins, T. W., & Pennartz, C. M. A. (2004). Putting a spin on the dorsal–ventral divide of the striatum. *Trends in Neurosciences, 27*, 468–474.

Williams, R. W., & Levis, D. J. (1991). A demonstration of persistent human avoidance in extinction. *Bulletin of the Psychonomic Society, 29*, 125–127.

18

Child and Adolescent Anxiety
Does Fear Conditioning Play a Role?

Katharina Pittner, Kathrin Cohen Kadosh, and Jennifer Y. F. Lau

Anxiety disorders are commonly reported in childhood and adolescence with prevalence rates between 5.3% and 17% (Cartwright-Hatton, McNicol, & Doubleday, 2006). For a significant number of these children and adolescents, these anxiety problems can persist into adulthood (Pine, Cohen, Gurley, Brook, & Ma, 1998). The principles of association described by learning theory have long been used to explain how anxiety problems develop (e.g., Watson & Rayner, 1920). However, most studies investigating the nature of fear learning difficulties in anxious and nonanxious individuals have focused on adults when presumably much of the learning related to the anxiety response has already taken place.

Fear learning in experimental settings is commonly assessed using Pavlovian conditioning procedures, the process in which a neutral stimulus (CS+) is repeatedly paired with a frightening stimulus (US), such that the neutral stimulus acquires a fear-provoking value. Conditioning is often found to be more effective with repeated pairings of the neutral stimulus (or situation) with the aversive event (or outcome). However, one-trial learning in rats and humans (e.g., Garcia, McGowan, & Green, 1972; Öhman, Eriksson, & Olofsson, 1975) shows that an association between a neutral stimulus can also be easily acquired with a single traumatic event. As not everyone exposed to such an experience develops an anxiety disorder, contemporary learning theories of anxiety assume a diathesis stress model in which conditioned experiences only result in anxiety responses in individuals who are particularly vulnerable (Mineka & Zinbarg, 2006), possibly because of an inherited predisposition (Hettema, Annas, Neale, Kendler, & Fredrikson, 2003) or acquired through social learning from anxious parents (Field & Lester, 2010). This inherited/acquired vulnerability may manifest through impairments in learning: Research in human adults has shown that anxious individuals (1) respond with higher fear levels to a newly acquired CS+ compared with nonanxious adults (Lissek *et al.*, 2005), (2) exhibit heightened fear reactions in response to stimuli not paired with the US (CS−) seeming to overgeneralize fear from CS+ to CS− (Lissek *et al.*, 2005), and (3) more tentatively,

---

The Wiley Handbook on the Cognitive Neuroscience of Learning, First Edition.
Edited by Robin A. Murphy and Robert C. Honey.
© 2016 John Wiley & Sons, Ltd. Published 2016 by John Wiley & Sons, Ltd.

respond with greater fear to the context in which fear associations are formed (Baas, 2012; Grillon, 2002).

Differences in acquisition of fear are accompanied by differences in the loss or extinction of fear. Here, the neutral stimulus is presented without the frightening stimulus over several trials to allow for either a reduction in excitatory association or a new association with safety to be formed; in either case, the CS+ loses its fear-provoking value, and anxiety is usually reduced. Thus, fear learning can also be applied to understand anxiety reduction, and exposure therapy that relies on extinction principles is an integral part of most anxiety treatments (Anderson & Insel, 2006; Delgado, Olsson, & Phelps, 2006). However, again, not all individuals who have experienced the same traumatic events show a reduction in fear across time – and indeed, it may be that those with clinical anxiety seek help because extinction has not occurred naturally. This is consistent with empirical data showing that anxious patients have greater difficulties extinguishing fear (e.g., Michael, Blechert, Vriends, Margraf, & Wilhelm, 2007).

Considerably less is known about how disruptions in fear learning and extinction can explain persistent fears and worries in childhood and adolescence. In this chapter, we focus on two key questions looking at evidence from human and animal models: (1) Individual differences, that is, are some children and adolescents more prone to anxiety than others because of difficulties in fear learning and extinction, and what might the neural basis be using studies of functional magnetic resonance imaging (fMRI)? (2) Qualitative developmental change, that is, does the nature of fear learning change across age through experience-dependent maturation of the PFC and amygdala using lesion studies in animals and fMRI studies in humans – and can this explain why anxiety typically onsets in adolescence?

Individual Differences in Human Fear Learning

Fear-conditioning and extinction paradigms can be divided into two types: (1) simple fear-conditioning paradigms, where a neutral stimulus is paired with an unconditioned stimulus (UCS), thereby becoming a conditioned threat stimulus (CS+); and (2) simple differential fear-conditioning paradigms, where two neutral stimuli are presented. One stimulus is paired with the UCS (CS+), and a second stimulus is never paired with the UCS (CS−). Thereby, the CS− acquires a conditioned safety value. In the first of these paradigms, CRs to the CS+ alone are measured during (or after) conditioning and during (or after) extinction. In the second paradigm, CRs to both the CS+ and CS− can be measured across phases in addition to their difference.

Studies of fear conditioning in anxious and nonanxious youth

Clinically anxious *adults* have been found to show greater CRs to the CS+ compared with nonanxious adults in simple conditioning. However, results from studies using differential conditioning paradigms have been less consistent. Often, greater CRs to the CS+ *and* CS− in anxious than nonanxious individuals have been found with no significant group differences in the differential CR to the CS+ relative to the

CS− responses (Lissek et al., 2005). Only five studies (Table 18.1) have explored the relationship between anxiety and fear learning in youth, with the majority reporting group differences – however these have varied over where the group differences lie. Perhaps the most consistent finding is that indices of conditioned fear responses, for example, skin conductance responses (SCR) and verbal fear ratings, are higher in clinically anxious children and adolescents to the CS+ (Craske et al., 2008; Waters, Henry, & Neumann, 2009), similar to findings from the adult literature (Lissek et al., 2005).

Also, similar to adult findings, anxious children and adolescents appear more afraid of the CS− too (Craske et al., 2008; Lau et al., 2008; Waters et al., 2009; but see Liberman, Lipp, Spence, & March, 2006). This means that in general, there are no group differences found in differential conditioning (the difference between responses to the CS+ and CS−). Thus, these studies suggest that anxious, like nonanxious, youth can differentiate fear to the CS+ and the CS− (though see Liberman et al., 2006) but that anxious youth manifest enhanced fear to the CS+ that generalizes to the CS−. This could imply sensitization (enhanced fear to all experimental stimuli and the wider context) but could also occur because of an inability to discriminate between stimuli that are perceptually similar. These questions have been investigated in anxious adults (Haddad, Pritchett, Lissek, & Lau, 2012; Lissek et al., 2005) but not yet in anxious children and adolescents. Of note, studies of children and adolescents do not typically employ electric shock as the UCS – instead relying on more mildly aversive stimuli, such as loud noises. A possible reason for the more mixed findings in the child and adolescent literature is that these UCSs are not sufficient in producing conditioned fear – this possibility is explored in more detail below.

Studies of fear extinction in anxious and nonanxious youth

In adults, meta-analyses have found that overall, compared with nonanxious controls, anxious individuals show stronger fear responses to the CS+ during extinction in simple conditioning paradigms. However, no differences between anxious and nonanxious participants emerge when comparing the magnitude of the difference in fear to the CS+ versus CS− in differential conditioning paradigms (similar to at the end of acquisition; Lissek et al., 2005). Studies investigating extinction in highly anxious children and adolescents have again yielded mixed findings. One study found a higher fear response in anxious children and adolescents to the CS+ (Waters et al., 2009), whereas another study found the opposite with a higher fear response in nonanxious children and adolescents (Craske et al., 2008).

Findings on differential conditioning are similarly inconclusive. While there is evidence that during extinction, there are within-group differences to the stimuli in all participants, that is, *both* anxious and nonanxious children and adolescents are more afraid of the CS+ than the CS− (Lau et al., 2008), there is also evidence that only anxious children and adolescents display differential fear responses (Liberman et al., 2006; Waters et al., 2009). Still other studies have reported an absence of differential SCR during extinction in both anxious and nonanxious children and adolescents – but that anxious individuals were generally more afraid of both the CS+ and CS− compared with nonanxious children and adolescents (Craske et al., 2008; Liberman et al., 2006; Waters et al., 2009).

Section summary

Clearly, the evidence of differences in either fear learning or extinction between anxious and nonanxious youth is mixed. One reason for the inconsistencies is that there is a paucity of fear-conditioning studies in children and adolescents – and therefore the inconsistent results in this small number of studies could be attributed to methodological differences between the studies. Studies use quite different fear indices, and there is a lack in standardization of the conditioning protocol. Additionally, studying fear processes in youth requires balancing practical and ethical considerations. Electrical shocks, the most powerful UCS in adults, are not appropriate for adolescents. Less noxious UCSs however, such as loud auditory stimuli or shocking or unpleasant photographs, while useful in working with children, provoke minimal fear in the adolescent age range (Lau et al., 2008). To tackle this problem, a novel paradigm has recently been introduced that uses a piercing female scream as the aversive UCS. The "screaming lady paradigm" has been successfully used in both healthy and clinical populations (Lau et al., 2008, 2011).

A further drawback is that research on fear learning during development to date has used discrete cue conditioning, a paradigm that is best suited for explaining transient fear states in both anxious and nonanxious individuals. Context conditioning or conditioning to diffuse nonspecific "background" cues has been used to explain situations of more generalized and sustained fear responses, in other words, anxiety. Contextual fear may be related to the background context during which an aversive stimulus was experienced or acts as a moderator of the effects of the exogenous threat cue itself. Previous work with adults suggests that this contextual fear is greater under conditions when the CS/UCS association is less predictable, that is, when the UCS does not necessarily follow the CS (Grillon, Baas, Cornwell, & Johnson, 2006). This draws on earlier animal work that demonstrated that the CS is unlikely to elicit a CR during the testing stage if, during training, the UCS had a higher probability in the absence than in the presence of the CS (Rescorla, 1968) – probably because the context attained a higher predictive value than the CS (Goddard & Jenkins, 1987). Recent work with anxious adults has shown that this contextual fear response under unpredictable circumstances is even more enhanced in high-anxious individuals (Baas, 2012). In a recent study, Kadosh and colleagues (2015) investigated developmental differences in threat learning in different context conditions in a sample of high- and low-anxious adolescents (aged 13–18). They showed that high-anxious adolescents failed to establish a discriminate response between threat and safety cues, by overgeneralizing fear responses from the CS+ to the contexts in which they appeared. This finding led the authors to suggest that high trait anxiety early in development may be associated with an inability to discriminate cues and contexts, and a misunderstanding of safety or ambiguous signals.

Finally, specific fear learning deficits may explain anxiety during some stages of development but not during others. More particularly, if fear conditioning and extinction rely on certain brain regions that are undergoing structural and functional maturation from late childhood and across adolescence to early adulthood, perhaps the ease with which conditioned fear arises and abates, and the extent to which it explains individual differences in anxiety changes across these developmental phases.

The next section will consider age-associated changes in the sensitivity to different fear-learning indices including during acquisition and extinction – and retention of these learned associations. As most of the work has been conducted in rodents, these will be reviewed first.

Developmental Changes in Fear Learning

Nonhuman animal work

There has been a longstanding tendency to use animal subjects for the study of fear learning, starting with Pavlov (1927). Animal subjects offer unique options in methodology, and not surprisingly, rodents have become the most commonly used subjects in recent years. Rodent studies have several advantages. For example, novel drugs can be administered systematically (Milad & Quirk, 2012), brain areas can be lesioned, and brains can be dissected postmortem to gain a better understanding of the underlying neuronal circuitry. The neural circuits involved in adult fear acquisition and extinction have been found to be comparable in rodents and humans (Graham & Milad, 2011). Even though prefrontal areas in humans are more developed than in rats (Milad, Rauch, Pitman, & Quirk, 2006), the prelimbic (PL) and infralimbic (IL) regions in rodents have been established as homologs to the human medial PFC (Milad & Quirk, 2012). This cross-species validity allows one to translate findings from rodent studies to understand human processes. Crucially, studies of how fear learning develops with age can also benefit from this translational work, given that rats and humans undergo similar developmental stages. Postnatal day (P) 16 in rats is comparable with human infancy. At P24, a rat is a juvenile (or preadolescent), while P28 and P35 correspond approximately to early and late adolescence respectively, and P70 corresponds to adulthood.

Studies of fear conditioning

Previous research suggests that the capacity to learn fear-relevant associations develops gradually across infancy, first appearing at the age of P10 (Figure 18.1). In two studies, rats at various stages in infancy were exposed to an odor that was paired with a shock (Sullivan Landers, Yeaman, & Wilson, 2000; Thompson, Sullivan, & Wilson, 2008) and subsequently tested on a two-odor choice test. In this test, rats were placed in a Y-maze and had to choose to walk toward either the conditioned or another familiar odor. At P8, rats displayed a preference for the conditioned odor, indicating that acquisition was probably unsuccessful and that rats of this age had not learned to fear the odor despite being paired with a UCS. In contrast, from P10, rats were able to learn to avoid an aversive stimulus; and moreover, by P12, the two-odor choice test revealed that this conditioned avoidant response lasted at least 4 hr and even 24 hr after acquisition.

At P16, as few as two pairings were sufficient for a rat to learn to fear (indexed by freezing behavior) a CS when tested immediately after acquisition (Kim, Li, Hamlin, McNally, & Richardson, 2012); and at the beginning of extinction, 7 or 8 days after acquisition (Kim & Richardson, 2010; Yap, Stapinski, & Richardson, 2005). However, even though fear learning appears to be present at P16, crucial differences between P16 and older rats have been observed. For instance, several studies administered more pairings to P16 rats than the older rats to obtain comparable levels of fear (e.g., Kim, Hamlin, & Richardson, 2009) – and P16 rats also show greater spontaneous loss of responding (perhaps related to forgetting; see next section).

By P28 (early adolescence), fear learning can be reliably generated, although more subtle changes have been documented. Hefner and Holmes (2007) found enhanced fear acquisition in P28 mice compared with adult mice, but by P35 these age-associated differences disappeared (Kim *et al.*, 2011; McCallum, Kim, & Richardson, 2010). To investigate this effect further, Den and Richardson (2013) compared delayed and trace conditioning in P23, P28, and P35 rats. During delayed fear conditioning, the CS+ and UCS overlap in time, while in trace fear conditioning, CS+ offset and UCS onset are separated by several seconds, a procedure that makes it more difficult to learn the association between CS+ and US. While neither P23 nor adult rats were able to acquire fear learning when the CS+ and UCS were separated by 20 or 40 s, P35 rats showed successful acquisition under both conditions, with freezing rates comparable with delay fear conditioning. Taken together, these data suggest that between P28 and P35, rats may be more sensitive in detecting the relationships between the neutral and the aversive stimuli.

An important caveat to note when interpreting these results is that appropriate measures of conditioned fear may also depend on age. For example, fear-potentiated startle (FPS) develops later than freezing and avoidance (Richardson, Fan, & Parnas, 2003; Richardson, Paxinos, & Lee, 2000; Richardson, Tronson, Bailey, & Parnas, 2002): By P16 and P20, rats show successful fear learning by avoiding a CS paired with shock but equal levels of FPS to the unpaired CS as to the paired CS. At P23 and P75, learned fear is evident when indicated by either avoidance or FPS (Richardson *et al.*, 2000). These data underscore the need for developmentally appropriate measurement tools to investigate age-associated changes in fear learning.

The behavioral changes in fear learning across infancy, adolescence, and adulthood are accompanied by changes in neural activity of relevant brain regions. The amygdala has been consistently implicated in fear conditioning (Milad & Quirk, 2012). In early development, when rats do not yet show fear learning, they also do not display neural activity in the amygdala during fear acquisition – coinciding with decreased levels of synaptic plasticity in the basolateral amygdala (BLA) at P8 (Thompson *et al.*, 2008). However, from P10 onwards, increased neural activity in the amygdala emerges in response to acquisition, and synaptic plasticity is also observed in the BLA. Interestingly, if synaptic plasticity in the amygdala is disrupted by blocking gamma-aminobutyric acid (GABA) receptors in P12 rats, fear conditioning is also disrupted (Sullivan *et al.*, 2000; Thompson *et al.*, 2008). The development of synaptic plasticity may be related to N-methyl-D-aspartate (NMDA) receptors, which play an important role in controlling synaptic plasticity in adulthood. Injecting P16 and P23 rats with MK-801, an NMDA antagonist, during acquisition similarly impairs fear acquisition (Langton, Kim, Nicholas, & Richardson, 2007).

The medial PFC (mPFC), particularly the infralimbic cortex (IL) and the prelimbic cortex (PL), also play important roles in the modulation of amygdala activity during rodent fear learning (Quirk & Beer, 2006). The PL in particular has been found to be important for fear expression, whereas the IL is more involved in fear inhibition (Sotres-Bayon & Quirk, 2010). At P23, fear acquisition involves an enhancement of synaptic transmission at the PL glutamatergic synapses, but by P29 this synaptic transmission did not change in response to acquisition (Pattwell et al., 2012).

Studies of spontaneous forgetting and reactivation

As mentioned above, although there is evidence that P16 rats show fear learning, there may be memory differences compared with P24 rats, such that P16 rats display spontaneous loss of responding or forgetting after acquisition. P16 rats show substantially lower levels of freezing in response to the CS if tested 48 h after acquisition compared with an immediate test (Kim et al., 2012). This spontaneous decrease in the CR does not characterize P24 rats. These findings have been supported by another study that also found that P23, but not P16, rats displayed heightened fear levels to the CS+ 2 days after acquisition. Thus, even though rats can acquire a CS+–US relationship at P16, they seem less efficient in retaining learned fear (Kim & Richardson, 2007a; Kim et al., 2012) unless they receive more pairings of the CS+ and UCS (e.g., six acquisition trials rather than just two). There is evidence, however, that even when P16–P17 rats show signs of spontaneous forgetting, the memory does not seem to be completely lost over time. That is, using a process called reactivation or reinstatement (Bouton, 2002), where reminder shock is administered 1 day before testing, learned fear can be successfully elicited 3–7 days after acquisition (Kim & Richardson, 2007a; Li, Kim, & Richardson, 2012b).

These age differences in the expression of the fear memory appear to be independent of amygdala functioning. For example, Kim et al. (2012) found that although only the older (P23) rats showed higher levels of freezing toward the CS+ postacquisition, there was elevated phosphorylated mitogen-activated protein kinase (pMAPK)-immunoreactive neuronal activation in the amygdala in both P16 and P23 rats. In P16 rats who showed improved acquisition memory after six CS–US pairings, the pMAPK count was equally high in the group that received six, two, and no pairings. In contrast, differences in the expression of acquired fear may be reliant on the prelimbic (PL) region of the vmPFC. Following PL inactivation (which was achieved by injecting muscimol, a GABAergic agonist), P23 rats behaved like P16 rats with lower levels of freezing (Li et al., 2012a). Together, these findings lend support to the notion that the PL is not crucial for the expression of learned fear at P16 but becomes critical at P23.

Extinction and extinction retention

In contrast to the acquisition of fear, extinction (i.e., when the CS is no longer paired with the UCS) appears to vary less with age, with similar declines in fear-expression rates (as measured by freezing) being reported in P16 rats as P24 rats (e.g., Langton et al., 2007; McCallum et al., 2010). We note that this does depend on the number of extinction trials presented, with most studies reporting successful extinction across 30 trials but not five (Pattwell et al., 2012).

However, when it comes to maintaining acquired knowledge, there are age-associated changes. Successful extinction retention 24 hr after extinction has been found in rats at P70 (adulthood; McCallum *et al.*, 2010) but also earlier on in development, at P16/17 and P23/24 (e.g., Langton *et al.*, 2007). These effects are strikingly persistent with low levels of freezing, hence successful extinction retention, continuing to characterize P16 rats even after 6–7 days postextinction learning (Kim & Richardson, 2010; Yap & Richardson, 2007). Interestingly, the retention of extinction was impaired in adolescent rats (Kim, Li, & Richardson, 2011; McCallum *et al.*, 2010) and mice (Pattwell *et al.*, 2012) compared with preadolescent and adult animals – and only emerged under two conditions: (1) when the extinction experience was doubled (Kim *et al.*, 2011; McCallum *et al.*, 2010) or (2) when D-cycloserine (DCS), an NMDA partial agonist, was administered immediately after extinction (McCallum *et al.*, 2010). DCS has been found to facilitate extinction in adult rats (Ledgerwood, Richardson, & Cranney, 2003).

Thus, while adolescent rats and mice show normal within-session extinction (Hefner & Holmes, 2007; Kim *et al.*, 2011), extinction retention appears to be attenuated in this age range (Kim *et al.*, 2011; McCallum *et al.*, 2010). As with fear conditioning, these behavioral changes related to extinction retention during development occur in tandem with changes in the engagement of neural circuits, possibly because certain brain regions reach maturity at different stages. Most studies have noted similar engagement of the amygdala during extinction learning (Kim *et al.*, 2009). However, age-associated changes during extinction learning have been reported in the vmPFC, particularly in the infralimbic (IL) region (Kim *et al.*, 2009), which, in adult rats, has been found to be involved in mediating extinction acquisition and retention by inhibiting central amygdala responses to suppress fear expression (Sotres-Bayon & Quirk, 2010). In a series of studies conducted by Kim *et al.* (2009), the pMAPK count in the IL, and to some extent in the PL, was found to be elevated in P24 rats in response to extinction learning but not in P17 rats. pMAPK is an enzyme that is part of the intracellular signaling pathway and is important for activity-dependent modulation of synaptic strength. Furthermore, inactivating the mPFC before extinction severely impaired extinction retention in P24 rats but had no effect in P17 rats. Together, these data imply that only at P24 do rats rely on mPFC for extinction retention.

Other changes also occur in the role of the IL and the PL during the retention of extinction during the adolescent years. For example, Pattwell *et al.* (2012) found that, in line with Kim *et al.* (2009), IL activity increased, and PL activity decreased in P23 and adult mice but not in P29 1 day after extinction (compared with control groups who did not receive extinction training). In P23 and adult mice, these changes in activity were also accompanied by an enhancement of glutamatergic synaptic transmission in the IL L5 pyramidal neurons. As with behavioral findings, when the adolescent rats received 60 trials of extinction instead of 30, not only was extinction retention improved but pMAPK counts in the IL and PL were higher than in rats that received no extinction or 30 extinction trials only. Thus, adolescent rodents are able to engage the IL and PL during extinction retention if extinction is increased. Together, these data imply less efficient neural networks in adolescent rodents (Kim *et al.*, 2011).

Return of fear

Originally, it was assumed that successful extinction leads to the erasure (or unlearning) of the fear memory (Rescorla & Wagner, 1972). However, since then, a vast number of studies have shown that under the appropriate circumstances fear returns (e.g., spontaneous recovery; Quirk, 2002). The most common paradigms to study the return of fear are renewal, reinstatement, and spontaneous recovery (Bouton, 2002). Renewal refers to the process in which fear returns in a context different from extinction. This effect is particularly strong when the subject is returned to the context in which acquisition took place. Reinstatement is when a return of the fear response appears after extinction when subjects are presented with the US alone (reinstatement). Spontaneous recovery refers to the finding that the mere passage of time after extinction leads to reemergence of conditioned fear. Fear also commonly returns after extinction when the CS+ is presented in a context other than the extinction context – classically the acquisition context. Collectively, these phenomena of the return of fear suggest that extinction leads to new learning as opposed to memory erasure.

Several studies now show that renewal does not occur in P16 rats. For instance, one study systematically controlled the context in which fear learning took place. As a result, one group of rats received acquisition, extinction, and testing in the same environment (AAA). Others received acquisition in one context, and extinction and testing in another (ABB). In both cases, extinction and testing context were identical. Rats in the renewal condition either were placed into context A during acquisition, then placed into context B during extinction and returned to context A for testing (ABA), or received acquisition and extinction in the same context but placed in another context for testing (AAB). These last two conditions are considered examples of renewal, as the extinction and testing context were different. While P16 and P23 rats show extinction retention to a similar extent in the AAA and ABB condition, only P23 rats show renewal in the ABA condition. This lack of return of fear in P16 rats could indicate that at this age, extinction may look more like the erasure of the acquisition memory.

Similar to the findings on renewal, reinstatement does not appear to be present in rats younger than P23 (Callaghan & Richardson, 2011; Kim & Richardson, 2007b). P23 rats showed reinstatement in response to a US reminder in the form of a postextinction shock. Their freezing levels were elevated compared with rats that did not receive a reminder. P16 rats, on the other hand, showed equally low levels of freezing in the reminder and no-reminder group, and hence displayed no reinstatement. Of note is the fact that P23 rats did not show return of fear when the reminder was presented in a context different from the context in which extinction and testing took place. Thus, reinstatement was modulated by the context in preadolescent rats.

Results for spontaneous recovery are more mixed. One study observed increased freezing levels in response to the CS+ 7 days after extinction in P23 mice, while P16 mice displayed substantially lower levels of freezing. This indicates successful extinction but simultaneously can be interpreted as the absence of spontaneous recovery (Gogolla, Caroni, Lüthi, & Herry, 2009). In contrast, Pattwell *et al.* (2012) observed only slight increases in freezing 24 h after extinction in P29 and adult mice but not at P23. However, the experimental procedures involved in these studies were very different, especially over the delay between extinction and testing.

Taken together these findings show that P16 rats fail to exhibit renewal, reinstatement, and spontaneous recovery suggesting that at this developmental juncture, extinction may well erase fear memories more permanently. It appears that, whereas new learning takes place in P23 and adult rats, unlearning takes place in P16 rats. The fear memory is permanently erased. Alternatively, contextual manipulations in these experiments could be less effective for younger rats.

With regards to the underlying brain networks, it has been shown that the amygdala is a crucial brain structure in both acquisition and extinction from P10. Interestingly, there is an increase in perineuronal nets in the BLA between P16 and P21, which has been interpreted as evidence that perineuronal nets protect the fear memory from being overwritten by extinction. Also, consistent with this interpretation: When perineuronal nets were destroyed in adult mice, these mice resembled P16 mice with a failure to exhibit renewal or spontaneous recovery (Gogolla et al., 2009).

Humans

Studies of fear conditioning

Table 18.1 also displays studies comparing fear learning across development. As with rodents, differential conditioning has been found in young children as early as 3 years (Gao et al., 2010). Unlike rodent studies, the evidence for age-associated differences in the learning of fear associations is less convincing. Only one study has reported such differences: Comparing 8- to 10-year olds and 11- with 13-year olds, this study reported greater differences between CS+ and CS– in the older age group using FPS (Glenn, Klein, et al., 2012). In other studies, one study with an age range of 5–28 found that age had no effect on the SCR in response to either CS+ or CS– (Pattwell et al., 2012), and in another, differential SCR to the CS+ and CS– did not vary in adolescence (10 to –17 years) relative to adults (18–50 years), although overall greater fear responses emerged in the adolescent group.

Studies of fear extinction

In terms of extinction, again mirroring rodent studies, preadolescent children appear capable of reducing their fear to a previously fearfult stimulus (Neumann, Waters, Westbury, & Henry, 2008). Moreover, this acquired fear reduction appeared no different to that found in adults (Pattwell et al., 2012): Thus, both groups displayed a strong decrease in SCR from the first to the last extinction trial. Interestingly, this study, which also included an adolescent group, showed that within-session extinction was clearly attenuated in adolescence. If replicated, these findings show a good parallel to rodent studies: notably that extinction in humans (and retention of extinction in rodents) is more problematic in the adolescent years compared with childhood or adulthood – a finding that carries implications for the understanding of why there may be an onset of persistent anxiety in adolescence.

Section summary

The nature of fear learning changes dramatically throughout life (see Table 18.2 and Figure 18.1), possibly driven by a combination of maturational and experience-dependent processes. Infant rats show associative learning during both the acquisition and extinction of fear, but it is clear from retention studies, notably studies of spontaneous forgetting and the return of fear after extinction, that as juveniles, these fear memories are not stable. The poorer capacity to retain learned fear associations may arise from developmental differences in amygdala functioning, which have been attributed to developmental immaturity of this region. Another shift in fear learning occurs in the transition across adolescence. During this period, fear is reliably acquired, but there appears to be a greater sensitivity for acquiring fear-relevant associations. In addition, while there are no age-associated differences in extinction learning, preliminary data are suggestive of adolescent-specific declines in the retention of extinguished fears. Thus, in contrast to juvenile and adult rodents, adolescent rodents require more extinction trials (or pharmacological agents) – a finding that may be mediated by immature medial PFC engagement.

How do these rodent findings map onto age-associated differences in human fear learning? The paucity of studies comparing different age groups in fear acquisition and extinction makes drawing parallels difficult – but there is tentative evidence that adolescents may show greater acquired fear to threat cues (relative to safety cues), while extinction learning is more difficult to acquire. If these findings are replicated, this may provide a plausible reason why adolescence is a period associated with the onset of more persistent forms of anxiety. It is also interesting to note that as structures such as the medial PFC are involved in processes such as extinction learning (Phelps, Delgado, Nearing, LeDoux, 2004) – and that such structures are still maturing in adolescence (relative to subcortical structures such as the amygdala; Casey et al., 2008), this may explain the observed differences in fear learning particu-

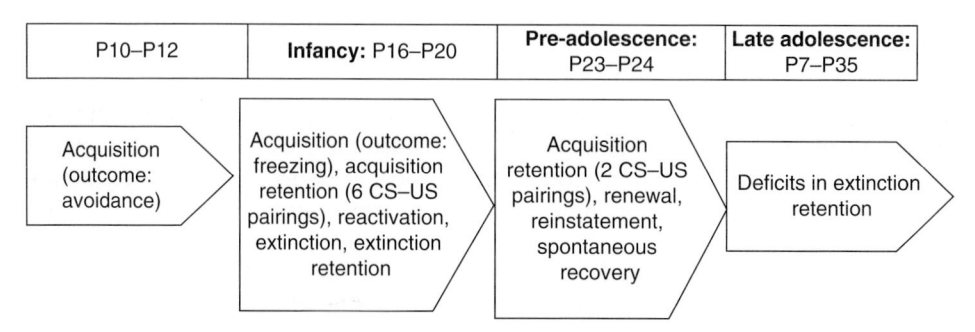

Figure 18.1 Illustration of how fear learning develops across age in rodent studies.

larly extinction. Clearly, these suggestions are based on a limited number of behavioral studies in humans, but as many rodent studies find more convincing developmental differences in general and adolescent-associated differences in particular in studies that examine the retention of these fear memories, this should be an avenue for future studies to explore.

Conclusions

This chapter has reviewed the nature of fear learning in children and adolescents, examining both how fear learning difficulties may characterize anxious and nonanxious youth, and the emergence of the associative processes related to fear-learning capacity and the underlying neural substrates across age. Although the limited number of studies makes drawing strong conclusions premature, it is clear that fear learning may play some role in explaining why some children and young people develop anxiety problems. However, fear learning may also explain why many persistent anxiety disorders first emerge in adolescence. The vital clue involves examining the nature of fear learning in childhood, adolescence, and adulthood – and there is now an emerging corpus of data (mostly from rodent studies) that suggest enhanced sensitivity to acquiring fear associations in adolescence and difficulties acquiring/retaining these associations after extinction.

These findings have clear implications for understanding the developmental time course not only of anxiety, but also of its treatment. In humans, extinction is assumed to be the underlying mechanism of exposure therapy (Rothbaum & Davis, 2003), and successful extinction is a potential predictor of treatment success. Adults that show better retention of extinction also improve more in social anxiety symptoms following exposure therapy (Berry, Rosenfield, & Smits, 2009). The presented research suggests that exposure therapy might be effective for childhood anxiety but less successful for adolescent anxiety. These findings point toward ways to enhance exposure therapy, for example by extending the number of sessions or introducing pharmacological interventions, which might facilitate exposure treatment in adolescents, such as the NMDA agonists DCS (McCallum et al., 2010). In human adults, DCS has been found to be a promising way to enhance exposure therapy (Byrne, Farrell, & Rapee, 2011). Alternatively, anxious adolescents may benefit more from other forms of psychological treatments such as cognitive therapy or more recently developed cognitive bias modification training programs (Lau, 2013).

Table 18.1 Fear learning in humans.

				Acquisition					Results	
Authors	Age	Anxiety measure	Outcome	CS+	CS−	US	%	No.	Verbal	SCR	FPS

Individual differences in anxiety

| Craske et al. (2008) | 7–12.9 | Clinical severity rating of 4 or higher for separation anxiety disorder, panic disorder, generalized anxiety disorder, social anxiety disorder or specific phobia with a CSR of 4 or greater if accompanied by another anxiety disorder diagnosis with a CSR of 3 | SCR, verbal (arousal ratings) | Trapezoid | Triangle | Aversive tone | N/A | 16 | CS+ was rated as significantly less pleasant by the anxiety than control group; no difference in their ratings of the CS− | FIR: differential conditioning in all groups, no group effect SIR and TIR: no differential conditioning in either group; overall, larger magnitude in anxiety group | |
| Liberman et al. (2006) | 7–14 | Meeting clinical diagnostic criteria for one or more anxiety disorders | Verbal, SCR, FPS | Picture | picture | Loud tone | N/A | 12 | Differential conditioning only in nonanxious group (fear) | Anxiety group did not differ from nonanxiety group; | No differential conditioning |

Study	Age	Inclusion criteria	Measures	CS+	CS−	US	ITI (s)	Trials per CS	Main results
Waters et al. (2009)	8–12	Clinical severity rating of 4 or higher social phobia, generalized anxiety disorder, or specific phobia	Verbal, SCR	Trapezoid/ triangle	Trapezoid/ triangle	Loud tone	N/A	16	100% of anxious children correctly reported the CS–US relationship, whereas only 55% of control children did; higher arousal ratings of CS+ in anxiety group FIR: differential conditioning (except two blocks in anxiety group); overall, larger magnitude in anxiety group SIR: differential conditioning in both groups; no group effect TIR: differential conditioning, overall, larger magnitude in anxiety group
Lau et al. (2009)	13.64 (2.37)	Meeting clinical diagnostic criteria of the DSM-IV for an anxiety disorder	Verbal	Face1	Face2	Face1 (scared) + scream	75	32	Differential conditioning in both groups; overall, higher fear ratings in anxiety group

(*Continued*)

Table 18.1 (Continued)

Authors	Age	Anxiety measure	Outcome	Acquisition CS+	CS−	US	%	No.	Results Verbal	SCR	FPS
Developmental studies											
Gao et al. (2010)	3–8		SCR	Tone1	Tone2	Loud tone	66	12 (9/3)	All components: SCR magnitude increases across ages FIR and TIR: differential conditioning SIR: CS+ elicited a sign larger response at age 8 but not at other ages		
Pattwell et al. (2012)	5–11 12–17 18–28		SCR	Square1	Square2	Loud tone	50	48		Differential conditioning in all age groups – no main effect of age group to either stimulus type-trait anxiety was unrelated to fear acquisition	

Study	Ages	Methods	CS	US	N	Findings
Glenn, Lieberman, and Hajcak (2012)	8–10, 11–13	Verbal, FPS	Face1	Face2	Scream + Face 1 (scared)	16 75	Age was not associated with differential conditioning	Differential conditioning across age groups, greater differential FPS in older age group; in contrast to younger children, older children displayed a linear generalization pattern (increase from CS− to GS to CS+), which is similar to adults
Lau et al. (2011)	10–17, 18–50	Verbal (E1&2), SCR E1), BOLD(E2)	Face1	Face2	Scream + Face1 (scared)	20/60 80/50	*Experiment 1:* GSR: differential conditioning in both groups; overall, higher responses in adolescents Verbal: differential conditioning, no age differences *Experiment 2:* Verbal: differential conditioning in both group, stronger differential conditioning in adults BOLD: differential BOLD response in right hippocampus in adolescents and adults, differential BOLD response in right amygdala and left hippocampus only in adolescents, greater activity in DLPFC correlated with higher fear ratings to the CS− in adults, but lower activity predicted more fear to the CS− in adolescents

Table 18.2 Fear learning in childhood and adolescence, a cross-species comparison.

	P8–P9	P10–P12	Infancy: P16–P20	Preadolescence: P23–P24	Early adolescence: P28–P29	Late adolescence: P35	Adulthood: P70–75
Acquisition	No	Yes[a]	Mixed Yes No Freezing and FPS, freezing avoidance	Yes	Yes	Yes	Yes
Acquisition retention	No evidence	No evidence	Mixed Yes No 6 CS–US 2 CS–US pairings pairings	Yes	No evidence	No evidence	Yes
Reactivation	No evidence	No evidence	Yes	No evidence	No evidence	No evidence	No evidence
Extinction	No evidence	No evidence	Yes	Yes	Yes	Yes	Yes
Extinction retention	No evidence	No evidence	Yes	Yes	No evidence	No	Yes
Renewal	No evidence	No evidence	No	Yes	No evidence	No evidence	Yes
Reinstatement	No evidence	No evidence	No	Yes	No evidence	No evidence	Yes
Spontaneous recovery	No evidence	No evidence	No	Yes	Yes	No evidence	Yes

[a] Only tested for avoidance as outcome.

References

Anderson, K. C., & Insel, T. R. (2006). The promise of extinction research for the prevention and treatment of anxiety disorders. *Biological Psychiatry, 60*, 319–321.

Baas, J. M. (2012). Individual differences in predicting aversive events and modulating contextual anxiety in a context and cue conditioning paradigm. *Biological Psychology, 92*, 17–25.

Berry, A. C., Rosenfield, D., & Smits, J. A. J. (2009). Extinction retention predicts improvement in social anxiety symptoms following exposure therapy. *Depression and Anxiety, 26*, 22–27.

Bouton, M. E. (2002). Context, ambiguity, and unlearning: Sources of relapse after behavioral extinction. *Biological Psychiatry, 52*, 976–986.

Byrne, S. P., Farrell, L. J., & Rapee, R. M. (2011). Using cognitive enhancers to improve the treatment of anxiety disorders in young people: Examining the potential for D-cycloserine to augment exposure for child anxiety. *Clinical Psychologist, 15*, 1–9.

Callaghan, B. L., & Richardson, R. (2011). Maternal separation results in early emergence of adult-like fear and extinction learning in infant rats. *Behavioral Neuroscience 125*, 20–28.

Cartwright-Hatton, S., McNicol, K., & Doubleday, E. (2006). Anxiety in a neglected population: Prevalence of anxiety disorders in pre-adolescent children. *Clinical Psychology Review, 26*, 817–833.

Casey, B. J., Jones, R. M., & Hare, T. A. (2008). The adolescent brain. *Annals of the New York Academy of Sciences, 1124*, 111–126.

Craske, M. G., Waters, A. M., Bergman, R. L., Naliboff, B., Lipp, O. V., Negoro, H., & Ornitz, E. M. (2008). Is aversive learning a marker of risk for anxiety disorders in children? *Behaviour Research and Therapy, 46*, 954–967.

Delgado, M. R., Olsson, A., & Phelps, E. A. (2006). Extending animal models of fear conditioning to humans. *Biological Psychology, 73*, 39–48.

Den, M. L., & Richardson, R. (2013). Enhanced sensitivity to learning fearful associations during adolescence. *Neurobiology of Learning and Memory, 104*, 92–102.

Field, A. P., & Lester, K. J. (2010). Learning of information processing biases in anxious children and adolescents. In J. Hadwin & A. P. Field (Eds.), *Information processing biases and anxiety: a developmental perspective*. Chichester, UK: Wiley.

Gao, Y., Raine, A., Venables, P. H., Dawson, M. E., & Mednick. S. A. (2010). The development of skin conductance fear conditioning in children from ages 3 to 8 years. *Developmental Science 13*, 201–212.

Garcia, J., McGowan, B. K., & Green, K. F. (1972). Biological constraints on conditioning. *Classical Conditioning, 2*, 3–27.

Glenn, C. R., Klein, D. N., Lissek, S., Britton, J. C., Pine, D. S., & Hajcak, G. (2012). The development of fear learning and generalization in 8–13 year olds. *Developmental Psychobiology, 54*, 675–684.

Glenn, C. R., Lieberman, L., & Hajcak, G. (2012). Comparing electric shock and a fearful screaming face as unconditioned stimuli for fear learning. *International Journal of Psychophysiology, 86*, 214–219.

Goddard, M. J., & Jenkins, H. M. (1987). Effect of signaling extra unconditioned stimuli on autoshaping. *Animal Learning & Behavior, 15*, 40–46.

Gogolla, N., Caroni, P., Lüthi, A., & Herry, C. (2009). Perineuronal nets protect fear memories from erasure. *Science, 325*, 1258–1261.

Graham, B. M., & Milad, M. R. (2011). The study of fear extinction: Implications for anxiety disorders. *American Journal of Psychiatry, 168*, 1255–1265.

Grillon, C. (2002). Startle reactivity and anxiety disorders: aversive conditioning, context, and neurobiology. *Biological Psychiatry, 52*, 958–975.

Grillon, C., Baas, J. M., Cornwell, B., & Johnson, L. (2006). Context conditioning and behavioral avoidance in a virtual reality environment: effect of predictability. *Biological Psychiatry, 60*, 752–759.

Haddad, A. D. M., Pritchett D., Lissek S., & Lau, J. Y. F. (2012). Trait anxiety and fear responses to safety cues: Stimulus generalization or sensitization? *Journal of Psychopathology and Behavioral Assessment, 34*, 323–331.

Hefner, K., & Holmes, A. (2007). Ontogeny of fear-, anxiety- and depression-related behavior across adolescence in C57BL/6J mice. *Behavioural Brain Research, 176*, 210–215.

Hettema, J. M., Annas, P., Neale, M. C., Kendler, K. S., & Fredrikson, M. (2003). A twin study of the genetics of fear conditioning. *Archives of General Psychiatry, 60*, 702–707.

Kadosh, K. C., Haddad, A. D., Heathcote, L. C., Murphy, R. A., Pine, D. S., & Lau, J. Y. (2015). High trait anxiety during adolescence interferes with discriminatory context learning. *Neurobiology of Learning and Memory, 123*, 50–57.

Kim, J. H., Hamlin, A. S., & Richardson, R. (2009). Fear extinction across development: The involvement of the medial prefrontal cortex as assessed by temporary inactivation and immunohistochemistry. *The Journal of Neuroscience, 29*, 10802–10808.

Kim, J. H., Li, S., Hamlin, A. S., McNally, G. P., & Richardson, R. (2012). Phosphorylation of mitogen-activated protein kinase in the medial prefrontal cortex and the amygdala following memory retrieval or forgetting in developing rats. *Neurobiology of Learning and Memory, 97*, 59–68.

Kim, J. H., Li, S., & Richardson, R. (2011). Immunohistochemical analyses of long-term extinction of conditioned fear in adolescent rats. *Cerebral Cortex, 21*, 530–538.

Kim, J. H., & Richardson, R. (2007a). Immediate post-reminder injection of gamma-amino butyric acid (GABA) agonist midazolam attenuates reactivation of forgotten fear in the infant rat. *Behavioral Neuroscience, 121*, 1328–1332.

Kim, J. H., & Richardson, R. (2007b). A developmental dissociation in reinstatement of an extinguished fear response in rats. *Neurobiology of Learning and Memory, 88*, 48–57.

Kim, J. H., & Richardson, R. (2010). New findings on extinction of conditioned fear early in development: Theoretical and clinical implications. *Biological Psychiatry, 67*, 297–303.

Langton, J. M., Kim, J. H., Nicholas, J., & Richardson, R. (2007). The effect of the NMDA receptor antagonist MK-801 on the acquisition and extinction of learned fear in the developing rat. *Learning & Memory, 14*, 665–668.

Lau, J. Y. (2013). Cognitive bias modification of interpretations: a viable treatment for child and adolescent anxiety? *Behaviour Research and Therapy, 51*, 614–22.

Lau, J. Y., Britton, J. C., Nelson, E. E., Angold, A., Ernst, M., Goldwin, M., ... Pine D. S. (2011). Distinct neural signatures of threat learning in adolescents and adults. *Proceedings of the National Academy of Sciences, 108*, 4500–4505.

Lau, J. Y. F., Lissek, S., Nelson, E. E., Lee, Y., Robertson-Nay, R., Poeth, K.... Pine, D. (2008). Fear conditioning in adolescents with anxiety disorders: Results from a novel experimental paradigm. *Journal of the American Academy of Child and Adolescent Psychiatry, 47*, 94–102.

Ledgerwood, L., Richardson, R., & Cranney, J. (2003). Effects of D-cycloserine on extinction of conditioned freezing. *Behavioral Neuroscience, 117*, 341–349.

Li, S., Kim, J. H., & Richardson, R. (2012a). Differential involvement of the medial prefrontal cortex in the expression of learned fear across development. *Behavioral Neuroscience, 126*, 217–225.

Li, S., Kim, J. H., & Richardson, R. (2012b). Updating memories – Changing the involvement of the prelimbic cortex in the expression of an infant fear memory. *Neuroscience, 222*, 316–325.

Liberman, L. C., Lipp, O. V., Spence, S. H., & March, S. (2006). Evidence for retarded extinction of aversive learining in anxious children. *Behaviour Research and Therapy, 44*, 1491–1502.

Lissek, S. Powers, A. S., McClurea, E. B., Phelps, E. A., Woldehawariata, G., Grillon, C., & Pine, D. S. (2005). Classical fear conditioningin the anxiety disorders: A meta-analysis. *Behaviour Research and Therapy, 43*, 1391–1424.

McCallum, J., Kim, J. H., & Richardson, R. (2010). Impaired extinction retention in adolescent rats: Effects of D-cycloserine. *Neuropsychopharmacology, 35*, 2134–2142.

Michael, T., Blechert, J., Vriends, N., Margraf, J., &Wilhelm, F. H. (2007). Fear conditioning in panic disorder: enhanced resistance to extinction. *Journal of Abnormal Psychology, 116*, 612–617.

Milad, M. R., & Quirk, G. J. (2012). Fear extinction as a model for translational neuroscience: ten years of progress. *Annual Reviews of Psychology, 63*, 129–151.

Milad, M. R., Rauch, S. L., Pitman, R. K., & Quirk, G. J. (2006). Fear extinction in rats: Implications for human brain imaging and anxiety disorders. *Biological Psychology, 73*, 61–71.

Mineka, S., & Zinbarg, R. (2006). A contemporary learning theory perspective on the etiology of anxiety disorders: It's not what you thought it was. *American Psychologist, 61*, 10–26.

Neumann, D. L., Waters, A. M., Westbury, H. R., & Henry, J. (2008). The use of an unpleasant sound unconditional stimulus in an aversive conditioning procedure with 8- to 11-year-old children. *Biological Psychology, 79*, 337–342.

Öhman, A., Eriksson, A., & Olofsson, C. (1975). One-trial learning and superior resistance to extinction of autonomic responses conditioned to potentially phobic stimuli. *Journal of Comparative and Physiological Psychology, 88*, 619–627.

Pattwell, S. S., Duhoux, S., Hartley, C. A., Johnson, D. C., Jing, D., Elliott, M. D., ... Leea, F. S. (2012). Altered fear learning across development in both mouse and human. *Proceedings of the National Academy of Sciences of the United States of America, 109*, 16318–16323.

Pavlov I. (1927). *Conditioned reflexes*. London, UK: Oxford University Press.

Phelps, E. A., Delgado, M. R., Nearing, K. I., & LeDoux, J. E. (2004). Extinction learning in humans: Role of the amygdala and vmPFC. *Neuron, 43*, 897–905.

Pine, D. S., Cohen, P., Gurley, D., Brook, J., & Ma, Y. (1998). The risk for early-adult anxiety and depressive disorders in adolescents with anxiety and depressive disorders. *Archives of General Psychiatry, 55*, 56–64.

Quirk, G. J. (2002). Memory for extinction of conditioned fear is long-lasting and persists following spontaneous recovery. *Learning & Memory, 9*, 402–407.

Quirk, G. J., & Beer, J. S. (2006). Prefrontal involvement in the regulation of emotion: Convergence of rat and human studies. *Current Opinion in Neurobiology, 16*, 723–727.

Rescorla, R. A. (1968). Probability of shock in the presence and absence of CS in fear conditioning. *Journal of Comparative and Physiological Psychology, 66*, 1–5.

Rescorla, R. A., & Wagner, A. R. (1972). A theory of Pavlovian conditioning: Variations in the effectiveness of reinforcement and nonreinforcement. In A. H. Black & W. F. Prokasy (Eds.), *Classical conditioning II: Current research and theory* (pp. 64–99). New York, NY: Appleton-Century-Crofts.

Richardson, R., Fan, M., & Parnas, A. S. (2003). Latent inhibition of conditioned odor potentiation of startle: A developmental analysis. *Developmental Psychobiology, 42*, 261–268.

Richardson, R., Paxinos, G., & Lee, J. (2000). The ontogeny of conditioned odor potentiation of startle. *Behavioral Neuroscience, 114*, 1167–1173.

Richardson, R., Tronson, N., Bailey, G. K., & Parnas, A. S. (2002). Extinction of conditioned odor potentiation of startle. *Neurobiology of Learning and Memory, 78*, 426–440.

Rothbaum, B. O., & Davis, M. (2003). Applying learning principles to the treatment of post-trauma reactions. *Annals of the New York Academy of Sciences, 1008*, 112–121.

Sotres-Bayon, F., & Quirk, G. J. (2010). Prefrontal control of fear: More than just extinction. *Current Opinion in Neurobiology, 20*, 231–235.

Sullivan, R. M., Landers, M., Yeaman, B., & Wilson, D. A. (2000). Good memories of bad events in infancy. *Nature, 407*, 38–39.

Thompson, J. V., Sullivan, R. M., & Wilson, D. A. (2008). Developmental emergence of fear learning corresponds with changes in amygdala synaptic plasticity. *Brain Research, 1200*, 58–65.

Waters, A. M., Henry, J., & Neumann, D. L. (2009). Aversive Pavlovian conditioning in childhood anxiety disorders – impaired response inhibition and resistance to extinction. *Journal of Abnormal Psychology, 118*, 311–321.

Watson, J. B., & Rayner, R. (1920). Conditioned emotional reactions. *Journal of Experimental Psychology, 3*, 1–14.

Yap, C. S. L., & Richardson, R. (2007). Extinction in the developing rat – An examination of renewal effects. *Developmental Psychobiology, 49*, 565–575.

Yap, C. S., Stapinski, L., & Richardson, R. (2005). Behavioral expression of learned fear – updating of early memories. *Behavioral Neuroscience, 119*, 1467–1476.

19

Association, Inhibition, and Action
Ian McLaren and Frederick Verbruggen

Introduction and Manifesto

What is inhibition? The "problem of inhibition" is one that has puzzled learning theorists for many decades. Once it had been demonstrated that pairing a CS (such as a tone or a light) with a US (such as food or shock) produced excitatory conditioning (Pavlov, 1927, and see chapter 2 of Mackintosh, 1974), it was natural to consider if a signal could "undo" the effect of an excitatory CS. We now call such a signal a *conditioned inhibitor*. A viable recipe for producing conditioned inhibition is to use a design such as A+ AB−, which simply denotes trials where A and the US are paired, interspersed with trials where A and B occur in compound but without the US. The result is that B acquires the properties of being hard to condition to that US (i.e., it passes the retardation test for a conditioned inhibitor), and of suppressing excitatory responding when presented in compound with A or with another excitatory CS that has been conditioned with the same US (i.e., it passes the summation test for conditioned inhibition). In this chapter, we will ask what it is about B that enables it to pass these tests, and what it is about the A+ AB− design that confers these properties. But first we must consider another use of the term "inhibition," one that is just as prevalent among cognitive psychologists, but gives a somewhat different meaning to the concept.

Inhibitory control is often invoked in the domain of cognition and action. If one is trying to suppress a thought or withhold an inappropriate or irrelevant action, then we speak of inhibiting that thought or action as part of the solution to the problem. This type of inhibition is considered to be one of the "executive processes" available to us, a deliberate top-down act of control enabling us to cope with ever-changing circumstances (e.g., Baddeley, 1996; Logan, 1985; Miyake *et al.*, 2000). As such, the parallel with the research alluded to in the first paragraph, which has often been with rats, rabbits, or pigeons as subjects, is not particularly obvious. But more recent research has found that this act of cognitive control can, in fact, become associatively mediated (e.g., Verbruggen & Logan, 2008b). In other words, cues that are reliably paired with stopping a response can prime and potentiate that act of control, and may even be able to instigate it in their own right. We shall argue that this is another form of conditioned inhibition, and one of the questions we wish to explore in this chapter is to what extent it shares similarities with the older construct used by learning theorists that goes by the same name.

The Wiley Handbook on the Cognitive Neuroscience of Learning, First Edition.
Edited by Robin A. Murphy and Robert C. Honey.
© 2016 John Wiley & Sons, Ltd. Published 2016 by John Wiley & Sons, Ltd.

We begin by reviewing some of the basic properties of conditioned inhibition as studied in animals, and consider the extent to which these phenomena also apply to humans. Our focus then switches to top-down cognitive and motor inhibition and an evaluation of the extent to which it can be associatively mediated. We review the evidence for this phenomenon and again seek to establish some of its basic characteristics. We end by taking an overtly computational perspective on both sets of phenomena as we look for similarities and differences between them.

Basic Phenomena I: Conditioned Inhibition

Conditioning

If we pair an initially neutral stimulus such as a tone or a light (the CS), with a motivationally significant stimulus such as food or shock (the US), then we expect an animal exposed to these contingencies to learn that the CS predicts the US (given that the stimuli are sufficiently salient, the timing between presentation of the CS and US is appropriate, etc.). This is demonstrated by means of a change in behavior of the animal (and various neural signatures; Chapter 3). For example, when the light comes on, it may run to the magazine where the food is delivered, or when the tone sounds, it freezes, interrupting its current behavior in preparation for an anticipated shock. These are examples of Pavlovian conditioning and are conventionally explained by positing that an association from some representation of the CS to some representation of the US has been set up in the animal's mind, such that activation of the CS representation now leads to associatively mediated activation of the US representation, which is sufficient to generate the observed change in behavior. This explanation of learning, as being due to the formation of an excitatory link between CS and US representations, is not without its problems, but it does capture many of the basic phenomena of Pavlovian conditioning, including the observation that responses elicited by a trained CS are often similar to that elicited by the US with which it has been paired (cf. Pavlov's principle of stimulus substitution; cf. Chapter 4). This principle states that the CS becomes a substitute for the US, and hence elicits a reaction that is similar in its topography to that elicited by presentation of the US itself.

Conditioned inhibition

Once a CS (denoted as A) has been established as an excitor for a US by means of A+ training (where the + denotes the US), we can use a basic feature-negative design to create a conditioned inhibitor. We simply present the animal with trials in which a compound of A and another CS, namely B, are presented in the absence of the US (AB− trials), while still interspersing A+ trials to maintain A as an excitor. B is the "negative feature" in this design, because the otherwise expected reinforcement (predicted by the presence of A) is not delivered when B occurs. One way of expressing this is to say that B has a negative correlation with the US in this design (Chapter 15). The consequence of this procedure is that responding to the compound of A and B diminishes over trials and can completely disappear. As a result, we infer that B becomes a conditioned inhibitor, able to function as a kind of "safety signal" when the US is aversive (e.g., shock). But initially there was considerable debate about the status of B, because when presented on its own, it is quite possible for it to have no detectable effect on behavior. Indeed, as we shall see, presenting B on its own after this type of training procedure can have little effect on the status of B as well.

Tests for inhibition

In order to reveal the effects of feature-negative training on B, we conventionally use retardation and summation tests (Rescorla, 1969). Taking the latter test first, this involves presenting the conditioned inhibitor, B in a compound with a quite different CS, C, which is also an excitor for the US. When C is presented on its own, it causes the conditioned response associated with that combination of CS and US (e.g., freezing if we are dealing with tone and shock). But if it is presented in compound with B, then this response is diminished, and to a greater extent than if we had simply presented C with D, another CS that is equally familiar but has not been trained as a conditioned inhibitor (or excitor). Thus, we can see that B is able to have an influence over behavior, even in the absence of A, and warrants its status as a conditioned inhibitor in its own right. The retardation test takes a somewhat different approach by pairing B with the US for which it is a conditioned inhibitor. The result is that B+ training proceeds more slowly than D+ training, indicating that some "inhibition" has to be overcome to turn B into an excitor. Thus, both the summation and retardation tests demonstrate that A+ AB− training has changed the status of B from a neutral CS to something that now has an effect that is, in some sense, the opposite to that of an excitor.

Acquisition

One characteristic of conditioned inhibition is that it typically develops more slowly than excitation. Obviously if one has to first establish A as an excitor by means of A+ training before we can use AB− to confer inhibitory properties on B, then this necessarily follows for trivial reasons. A more interesting demonstration of this point can be found by comparing acquisition of this feature-negative design with its feature-positive counterpart. Thus, if we contrast the A+ AB− design with C− CD+, in the former B acquires inhibitory control over the discrimination, whereas in the latter D develops excitatory control in the feature-positive equivalent. The standard result here is that the feature-positive discrimination is acquired more rapidly than the feature-negative, suggesting that it takes longer to develop B as a conditioned inhibitor than it does D as a conditioned excitor (see Lotz, Uengoer, Koenig, Pearce, & Lachnit, 2012).

Another point to note is that it is not necessary to use a full A+ AB− design to make B a conditioned inhibitor; a design of the form A+ AB+ will also work, where A is followed by a greater magnitude of reinforcement (+) than AB (+). The reduction in the reinforcement (or in the probability of reinforcement) is itself enough to confer inhibitory properties on B (Cotton, Goodall, & Mackintosh, 1982; Harris, Kwok, & Andrew, 2014). These studies, and others like them, suggest that what is crucial in developing conditioned inhibition is that an expectation of one level or rate of reinforcement is contradicted by experience, and that this leads to the development of something quite different to simple excitatory learning. For example, if we were to contrast B in Cotton et al.'s experiment to another stimulus D that had received CD+ training in the absence of any prior training to C, then we would not expect D to have acquired any inhibitory properties (quite the reverse!).

Extinction

Perhaps one of the most eye-catching characteristics of conditioned inhibition is that, according to Zimmer-Hart and Rescorla (1974), inhibitors cannot themselves be extinguished. After establishing a CS (B) as a conditioned inhibitor, B can be presented on its own for a number of extinction trials, B–, without diminishing its capacity to inhibit (i.e., it will still pass summation and retardation tests). Even if we extend the extinction procedure to a point well beyond that needed to reduce responding to an excitor to floor, the inhibitory properties of B persist, suggesting once again that there is something rather different about an inhibitory association when contrasted with an excitatory one (which extinguish very readily).

Mediated inhibition: the Espinet effect

Inhibition can manifest in conventional CS–US designs as well as in what are in effect simple sensory preconditioning designs. If we preexpose two sets of compound stimuli (e.g., a solution of sucrose+lemon and another of saline+lemon; AX and BX), then a straightforward analysis of the stimulus contingencies leads to the conclusion that the saline and the sucrose features of these stimuli should come to inhibit one another because of the negative correlation between their presentation: Whenever the sucrose (A) occurs, the saline (B) does not, and vice versa (see McLaren, Kaye, & Mackintosh, 1989; McLaren & Mackintosh, 2000, 2002; McLaren, Forrest, & McLaren, 2012, for a more detailed analysis). More specifically, as a result of pairing A and X, X becomes associated with A, and when we now present BX, we have a recipe for establishing an inhibitory association from B to A (because B signals the absence of A). A similar process will establish inhibitory associations from A to B. We can reveal the existence of these mediated inhibitory associations by conditioning A (Espinet, Iraola, Bennett, & Mackintosh, 1995). After a few A+ trials (pairing sucrose with lithium chloride to make the animal feel ill) the animal will become averse to drinking A. But when solution B is subsequently tested, we find no aversion relative to controls. Furthermore, B passes the summation and retardation tests: It *reduces* aversion to another CS, C, which has also been paired with LiCl, when tested in compound with it (summation test), and is itself harder to condition an aversion to than another flavor, D (retardation test). This is the Espinet effect, and the most plausible interpretation of these results is that B has the ability to depress the activity of A via an inhibitory association with A, and that this then in turn expresses itself via the association between A and the US but with the opposite sign to normal excitatory activation. Thus, what we have in effect here is an example of mediated conditioning (cf. Chapter 4), but with the mediation via an inhibitory rather than an excitatory association. Later on, we will argue that this result and others like it require a particular implementation of an inhibitory association that differs from that more commonly involved in conditioned inhibition.

The reason we are able to assert this last conclusion is that Bennett, Scahill, Griffiths, and Mackintosh (1999) have shown that the effect is asymmetric with respect to which of A or B is conditioned after alternating exposure to AX and BX. If the exposure is such that, on each day, experience of AX is always followed by BX, but then there is no further trial until the next day, our analysis implies that the inhibitory B → A association should be strong, but that from A → B should be relatively weak. This is because the AX trial leads to a strong X → A association, which allows the development of an inhibitory B → A association, but the B → X association will have decayed considerably before AX is experienced on the next day reducing learning of the inhibitory A → B association. If we now condition A after this preexposure to AX and BX, we find good evidence that B has acquired inhibitory properties. Our explanation of this is that the inhibitory link from B → A can activate a representation of A in such a way as to depress the US representation now associated with A. But if instead we were to condition B, we would find little evidence of A acquiring inhibitory properties, suggesting that the lack of an inhibitory link from A to B prevents the Espinet effect from occurring in this case.

Backward conditioned inhibition

One version of the basic conditioned inhibition procedure can be summarized as A+ | AB–. If conditioning A is followed by compound presentations of A with B in the absence of the US, B becomes inhibitory. This design can be more fully characterized as *forward conditioned inhibition*. *Backward conditioned inhibition* simply involves reversing the ordering of presentation of A+ and AB–, thus AB– | A+. Remarkably, the effect is very similar to that obtained with a forward design, namely that B becomes inhibitory. This effect was discovered in humans by Chapman (1991) and subsequently replicated and further investigated by Le Pelley, Cutler, and McLaren (2000). It is not susceptible to the same explanation as that offered for the Espinet effect as the association between A and B in this case must be excitatory. Thus, an explanation in terms of associatively retrieved representations entering into learning with the opposite sign to perceptually activated representations (e.g., modified SOP, Dickinson & Burke, 1996; negative alpha, Van Hamme & Wasserman, 1994), postacquisition comparison (Miller & Schachtman, 1985) or memory-based effects as a consequence of retrieval (Le Pelley & McLaren, 2001), must be deployed. We do not have the space here to discuss these alternative explanations of the phenomenon, but simply note that it exists and that the backward procedure is another effective method for producing inhibitory effects.

Inhibition in humans

It is worth stating that most of the effects we have considered so far can be demonstrated in humans. For demonstations of backward conditioned inhibition, see Graham, Jie, Minn, McLaren, and Wills (2011), Le Pelley and McLaren (2001), and also Le Pelley *et al.* (2000). Graham (1999) obtained the Espinet effect in humans using a medical diagnosis paradigm and demonstrated the asymmetry found by Bennett *et al.* (1999). Similarly, Mundy, Dwyer, and Honey (2006) were able to establish the existence of this asymmetry using procedures that closely paralleled those used by Bennett *et al.* (1999) with rats. Thus, these effects seem to be general and characteristic of associative learning across species.

What is Learned During Inhibitory Conditioning?

There are two main accounts of what is learned during inhibitory conditioning. The first account states that subjects learn an inhibitory association between the CS and the US, which suppresses the US representation (Konorski, 1948; see Chapters 2 and 15). The basic idea here is that an inhibitory association is simply a negative excitatory one. This type of associative structure (shown in the left panel of Figure 19.1) emerges naturally from the Rescorla–Wagner view of conditioning (Rescorla & Wagner, 1972), and from the idea that inhibition is the consequence of a disconfirmed expectation of an outcome. In essence, the contingencies involved in the A+ AB– training lead to the development of the excitatory connection from the representation of A to the US representation, and the inhibitory connection from the representation of B to that same US representation. Thus, excitation is simply the converse of inhibition and vice versa. The fact that there is little evidence for relatively long-distance inhibitory connections at the neural level is not an immediate argument invalidating this architecture, as we can imagine the inhibitory connection being made up of a long-distance excitatory connection directly to an inhibitory neurone that operates at a local level. By "long-distance" connection, we simply mean a connection between different (distant) brain regions, whereas a short-distance connection refers to a connection between neurons within the same brain region.

The idea of there being a long-distance excitatory connection to some other neurone that then expresses this connection via a local inhibitory interneuron leads fairly straightforwardly to another possible instantiation of inhibition that depends on the existence of mutual antagonism between different centers. This second account posits that, instead of implementing some (relatively) direct negative link from the

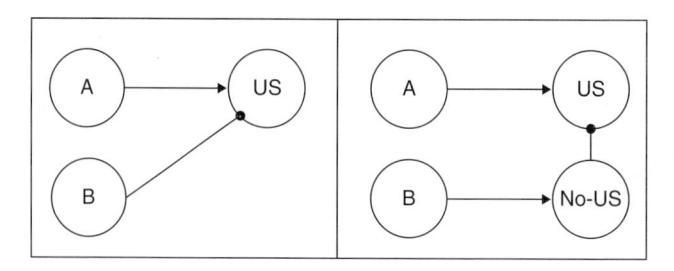

Figure 19.1 Two different associative structures for the implementation of inhibition. The panel on the left shows a direct inhibitory connection from the representation of the CS to the US representation. The panel on the right shows an indirect inhibitory mechanism whereby the CS representation excites a "No-US" representation that then inhibits the US representation via an inhibitory interneurone.

representation of the inhibitory CS to the US representation, an excitatory link forms from the representation of the inhibitory CS to a "No-US" center or representation that then inhibits the US representation (e.g., Konorski, 1967; Le Pelley, 2004; Pearce & Hall, 1980). The key difference between this structure and the earlier one is the use of this "No-US" representation making the inhibition in some sense indirect (see the right panel of Figure 19.1), and the No-US representation is susceptible to at least two different interpretations. In one (favored by Konorski), the representation is US specific, and so, in the case where A is trained with food pellets, the No-US representation would be "No food pellets," but in the case where A is trained with sucrose, the No-US representation would be "No sucrose." Another approach to implementing the "No-US" account is to first posit that all conditioning is either appetitive or aversive and that there are "centers" corresponding to this that mutually inhibit one another (e.g., Dickinson & Dearing, 1979; see also Konorski, 1967). These centers can function as the US and No-US centers, with the aversive acting as the No-US center for appetitive learning and vice versa. This approach depends more on the interaction of two systems that differ in their motivational significance, and as such has more general implications for behavior, as we shall see. It does not require an ability to target a No-US representation in a US-specific fashion, or that there be a distinct No-US representation for each US representation. For this reason, the appetitive/aversive centers approach seems to us to be a better complement to the more direct implementation of conditioned inhibition shown in the left panel of Figure 19.1.

We are now in a position to debate these two alternatives, and start by asserting that any account of conditioned inhibition that appeals solely to some interference mechanism is not viable in the light of the evidence available from the animal studies reviewed in this chapter. We can justify this claim by returning to the demonstration by Cotton *et al.* (1982) showing that conditioned inhibition can be obtained by simply reducing the magnitude of the reinforcer delivered when A and B were presented together (A+ AB+). A tone (playing the role of A) was accompanied by a 1-mA shock, and a tone/light compound (AB) was followed by a 0.4-mA shock. The control group had either the tone conditioned alone (followed by a 1-mA shock) or the light conditioned alone (followed by a 0.4-mA shock). This control group is effectively A+ B+. If the apparent inhibition in the experimental group is due to interference caused by the light (B) predicting a 0.4-mA shock rather than a 1-mA shock, then B should produce a similar effect in the B-alone control group. It did not. Clearly, there is something special about B in the conditioned inhibition group that stems from the fact that it occurs when a larger shock is expected than that delivered. It is worth noting that the light alone group (A+ B+) in Cotton *et al.* (1982) would quite probably pass the retardation test for inhibition, because we know from Hall and Pearce (1979) that if a tone is first paired with a weak shock, this retards subsequent acquisition of a tone → strong shock relationship. Thus, Cotton *et al.* have clearly demonstrated that true conditioned inhibition is more than interference. We note that Pearce and Hall (1980) favor an alternative explanation of this result couched in terms of changes in the associability of a stimulus in any case (see also McLaren & Dickinson, 1990).

Additional evidence on this point can be found in the work of Kremer (1978). He showed that compounding a stimulus (B) with stimuli X and Y, which had been separately trained to a given US so that the US was still presented to the compound BXY, conferred inhibitory properties on B. This result relies on the phenomenon of "overexpectation" first demonstrated by Rescorla (1970). If X and Y are both trained individually (X+ Y+) and then trained in compound with the same reinforcer (XY+), the result is that at test, X and Y will both elicit less responding in the animal than after the initial training involving the individual stimuli. Thus, a reduction in associative strength is deemed to have taken place as a result of the two stimuli "overpredicting" the US when offered in compound. Kremer predicted that if BXY+ was trained after the X+ Y+ pretraining, the overexpectation effect should confer inhibitory status on the initially neutral B. Kremer observed exactly this. Our point is that at no stage in this procedure does the outcome (delivery of the same US) change, making any interference account of this phenomenon hard to sustain. This is not to say that interference may not play a role in some demonstrations of what is termed "inhibition," but we do not believe that it can be the full story. This point will take on added significance when we review some of the human data in a later section.

Which brings us back to the question: Which of the associative architectures shown in Figure 19.1 is to be preferred? The evidence that tends to favor the direct link shown in the left-hand panel of Figure 19.1 is that involving CS–CS associations, such as the Espinet effect. To understand this, it is necessary to realize that the role of A in the figure is being played by the common element X (lemon in this case), the role of B by saline, and the role of the US by sucrose. Thus, a preexposure trial involving sucrose + lemon leads to an association between their representations forming as shown between A and the US in the figure. Now, a trial following this in which saline + lemon is presented will allow the representation of lemon (A) to activate the representation of sucrose (US), so that the representation of saline (B) forms an inhibitory link to that representation of sucrose (which is not physically present). We have already explained why the effect is thought to be mediated via the ability of saline, say, to inhibit the representation of sucrose after experience of sucrose + lemon/saline + lemon exposure. Clearly, it makes little sense to talk of saline exciting an aversive center when both the sucrose and saline solutions are essentially neutral prior to conditioning (the rats have a mild liking for both at the concentrations used).

We are forced to the conclusion that either the No-US representation has to be very specific (i.e., in this case "No-Sucrose"), or an inhibitory link to the sucrose representation itself is required. Both structures amount to much the same thing once we realize that the "No-Sucrose" structure is effectively an implementation of the direct inhibitory link that gets around the need for relatively long-distance pathways for inhibition (see above). Hence, we are proposing an excitatory link to some local interneuron that then inhibits (locally) the representation of sucrose. Clearly, we would also need to postulate some resting activation of this sucrose representation in order for this inhibition mediated via activation of some representation of saline to be effective and to give us the Espinet effect.

The type of evidence that tends to favor the mutually inhibitory appetitive/aversive centers structure draws on studies of trans-reinforcer blocking. Dickinson and Dearing (1979) were able to show that training B to be an inhibitor for a food US enabled it to successfully block learning involving a shock US. That is, once the A+ AB– training was completed using the food US, the next phase was CB+ where the + now denotes shock. Compared with controls, this group learned less about the association between C and shock, suggesting that the prior training of B was, to some extent, blocking acquisition for C. A result of this type fits in well with the idea that the "No-US" center could indeed be some general appetitive or aversive motivational representation, such that a stimulus that came to predict the absence of food that was otherwise expected could itself acquire aversive properties. It is difficult to see how a result of this type could be generated with the architecture shown in the left-hand panel of Figure 19.1. For a review of motivational conditioning and interactions between the appetitive and aversive system, see Dickinson and Balleine (2002).

Our final position, then, is that there is evidence for (1) a general form of inhibition mediated via excitatory connections to appetitive/aversive centers that mutually inhibit one another and (2) a more specific form of inhibition that is equivalent to a direct inhibitory link to the stimulus representation (be it CS or US) in question. The first mechanism relates more strongly to the motivationally significant stimuli (USs) used in conditioning, the second to structures in what might be termed associative memory.

Basic Phenomena II: Conditioned Inhibitory Control

All our examples of inhibition so far relate to what is called Pavlovian or classical conditioning where associations are formed between representations of events that occur in the environment. But this is simply one form of what Dickinson calls event–event learning (Dickinson, 1980). Now we turn to the issue of inhibition in an instrumental context, where the task is to withhold or cancel a thought or action rather than detect the unexpected absence of an event. To do this, we will focus on human experiments that investigate the role of inhibition in executive control. Our review of this area will conclude that in many cases, it is unnecessary to appeal to inhibition to explain performance, But there are some circumstances where the case for inhibition seems to be strong, and we will focus on these once we have identified them.

In the last few decades, "inhibition" has become a central concept in many theories of attentional and executive control. The general tenet is that humans need inhibitory mechanisms to suppress irrelevant stimuli, thoughts, actions, and emotions to deal effectively with the constant inflow of information and multitude of response options. Within the executive control domain, inhibition is not regarded as a unitary construct, and several taxonomies have been proposed. Nigg (2000) distinguished between (1) *cognitive inhibition*, which refers to the suppression of irrelevant thoughts and information in working memory; (2) *interference control*, which refers to suppression of irrelevant stimuli; (3) *behavioral* or *motor inhibition*, which refers to the suppression of automatic, prepared, or cued responses; and (4) *oculomotor inhibition*, which refers to the effortful suppression of reflexive saccades. Similar taxonomies and distinctions between cognitive and behavioral (or motor) inhibition have been proposed by Friedman and Miyake (2004) and Harnishfeger (1995), among others. The case for cognitive inhibition is weak (see, e.g., Raaijmakers & Jakab, 2013; MacLeod *et al.*, 2003). Therefore, we will focus on the inhibition of responses.

Top-down response inhibition in interference tasks

The role of inhibition in interference control or congruency tasks, such as the Eriksen flanker task or the Stroop task, is still disputed. Popular dual-route models (e.g., Kornblum, Hasbroucq, & Osman, 1990) assume that responses in congruency tasks are activated via a direct activation route and an indirect activation route.

Activation via the direct route is unconditional and automatic, independent of the task instructions. By contrast, activation of the response via the indirect route is deliberate and controlled. Inhibitory accounts state that conflict or interference is resolved by strengthening the processing of relevant information via the indirect route and by selectively inhibiting irrelevant information and responses that were activated via the direct route (e.g., Ridderinkhof, 2002). Some have argued that inhibition is required to suppress all motor responses globally when conflict between alternative actions is detected (Frank, 2006; Wiecki & Frank, 2013). This would effectively allow the system to prevent premature responses and to select the appropriate response.

In recent years, evidence both in favor and against inhibitory accounts of interference control has been forthcoming. First, several studies have demonstrated that top-down inhibition may not be required to resolve interference, as this can be achieved by top-down enhancement of relevant information alone. Several computational models of interference control assume that task demand units or representations of the relevant categories will bias processing in the subordinate pathways, enhancing the processing of task-relevant information (e.g., Cohen, Dunbar, & McClelland, 1990; Herd, Banich & O'Reilly, 2006). It may be that activation of task-relevant information leads to inhibition of competing task-irrelevant processing via lateral inhibitory connections. But it is important to stress that this inhibition is achieved locally and not via top-down inhibitory connections. Thus, inhibition of task-irrelevant information would be a local "side-effect" of top-down excitation of task-relevant information. Again, this would help to get around the need for relatively long-distance pathways for inhibition.

But the top-down response-inhibition account has also received support, primarily from neuroscience studies (but see also Ridderinkhof, 2002). For example, a recent study tested the response inhibition account using motor-evoked potentials (MEPs) elicited by transcranial magnetic stimulation of the right motor cortex (Klein, Petitjean, Olivier, & Duque, 2014). The authors found reduced MEPs for trials on which the distractors were mapped onto a left response. This suggests that suppression of motor excitability is a component of interference control (see also van den Wildenberg et al., 2010). It is possible that interference and competition caused by irrelevant stimuli is resolved by activating relevant features and stimulus processing, whereas response competition is resolved by activating the relevant response and selectively suppressing the irrelevant response via separate Go and NoGo pathways between prefrontal cortex and the basal ganglia (e.g., Frank, 2005). More specifically, the relevant response can be activated via activation of "Go" cells in the striatum that inhibit the *internal* segment of the globus pallidus (GPi); this reduces inhibition of the thalamus, leading to the execution of a motor response (the direct cortical–subcortical pathway; Nambu, Tokuno, & Takada, 2002).[1] Irrelevant responses can be suppressed via activation of "Nogo" striatal cells, which inhibit the *external* segment of the globus pallidus (GPe); this reduces tonic inhibition between GPe and the GPi, resulting in increased activity in GPi and, consequently, increased inhibition of the thalamus (the indirect cortical–subcortical pathway; Nambu et al., 2002). Note that global suppression of all motor output, as postulated by Frank and colleagues, could be achieved via a third pathway, namely the hyperdirect pathway. This involves activation of the subthalamic nucleus, which has in turn a broad effect on GPi, leading to global suppression of the thalamus. Prefrontal areas, such as the presupplementary motor area and the right inferior frontal gyrus, are thought to activate the Nogo cells in the striatum or the subthalamic nucleus.

Aftereffects of top-down inhibition: negative priming

After a stimulus has appeared as a distractor in congruency tasks such as a picture-naming task or an Eriksen flanker task, responding to it on the next trial is usually impaired. This finding is referred to as "negative priming." The dominant inhibition account of negative priming assumes that when an item is a distractor, its representation or the process linking the representation with the response becomes suppressed, and that residual inhibition impairs responding to the item on the following trial (e.g., Tipper, 2001). However, this impairment could be caused by the retrieval of stimulus- and response information from the previous trial (e.g., Neill, Valdes, Terry, & Gorfein, 1992; Rothermund, Wentura, & De Houwer, 2005). For example, Neill and colleagues proposed that a distractor becomes associated with a do-not-respond representation; when it is repeated on the next trial as a target, the do-not-respond association is activated via associative retrieval, and this will interfere with responding. By contrast, Rothermund et al. (2005) suggested that the distractor becomes associated with the response to the target on the prime trial; retrieval of this response association will interfere with responding on the current probe trial because the retrieved information is usually inconsistent with the currently relevant response (see Jones, Wills, & McLaren, 1998, for an example of how this type of response interference might be implemented). Mayr and Buchner (2007) reviewed the negative priming literature, and argued that the available data generally favor the memory account over the distractor-inhibition account.

There is a parallel to draw between the memory retrieval accounts of negative priming and the conditioned inhibition accounts discussed in the section "Basic Phenomena I: Conditioned Inhibition". The response-interference account of negative priming is akin to the interference account of conditioned inhibition that assumes US–US interference. As discussed above, interference between CS or US representations may contribute to conditioned inhibition, but it seems unlikely that it is the only mechanism responsible for the effects we have covered. Similarly, Rothermund et al. (2005, p. 493) noted that "stimulus–response retrieval is not the only mechanism that produces negative priming, it is one of the underlying mechanisms." One of the other mechanisms could be the establishment of a link between the stimulus and a "do not respond" or "no response" representation, similar to a "no-US" representation in conditioned inhibition paradigms. This "no-response" representation could be specific (e.g., "no left response," akin to a "no-A" representation) or more general. Consistent with the latter option, Frings, Moeller, and Rothermund (2013) have argued that both stimuli and responses may be represented by abstract conceptual codes; for example, responses would be coded in terms of approach or avoidance. In the context of negative priming, this would imply that distractors are linked to a general "avoid/aversive" representation. Indeed, several recent studies suggest that conflict is aversive (e.g., Fritz & Dreisbach, 2013; van Steenbergen, Band, & Hommel, 2009; see also Botvinick, 2007). Furthermore, work by Raymond and colleagues suggests that ignoring a distractor could lead to its devaluation (e.g., Raymond, Fenske, &

Tavassoli, 2003). Again, this is consistent with the idea that stimuli can be linked with general appetitive/approach and aversive/avoidance centers, which mutually inhibit each other. Later on, we will argue that there is good reason to suppose the existence of both mutually inhibitory appetitive/aversive centers *and separate* approach/avoidance centers, which we will refer to as "go" and "stop" centers.

Top-down inhibition of behavior

The idea that responses or motor actions can be inhibited in a top-down fashion receives the strongest support from paradigms such as the go/no-go paradigm and the stop-signal paradigm. Therefore, we will focus on these two paradigms in the remainder of this chapter. In the go/no-go paradigm, subjects are presented with a series of stimuli and are told to respond when a go stimulus is presented and to withhold their response when a no-go stimulus is presented (e.g., press the response key for a square, but do not press the response key for a diamond; Figure 19.2, left panel). One could argue that the go/no-go task corresponds to an AX+ | BX– design, with A and B as the go stimulus and the no-go stimulus, respectively, and X as the task context. In the stop-signal paradigm, subjects usually perform a choice reaction task on no-signal trials (e.g., press the left response key for a square and press the right response key for a diamond; Figure 19.2, right panel). On a random selection of the trials (stop-signal trials), a stop signal (e.g., an auditory tone or a visual cue, such as the outline of the go stimulus turning bold) is presented after a variable delay (stop-signal delay; SSD), which instructs subjects to withhold the response to the go stimulus on those trials. This corresponds to an A+ | AB– design, with A corresponding to the go stimuli, and B the stop signal.

Behaviorally, performance in both paradigms can be modeled as an independent race between a go process, which is triggered by the presentation of a go stimulus, and a stop process, which is triggered by the presentation of the no-go stimulus or the stop signal (Logan & Cowan, 1984; Logan, Van Zandt, Verbruggen, & Wagenmakers,

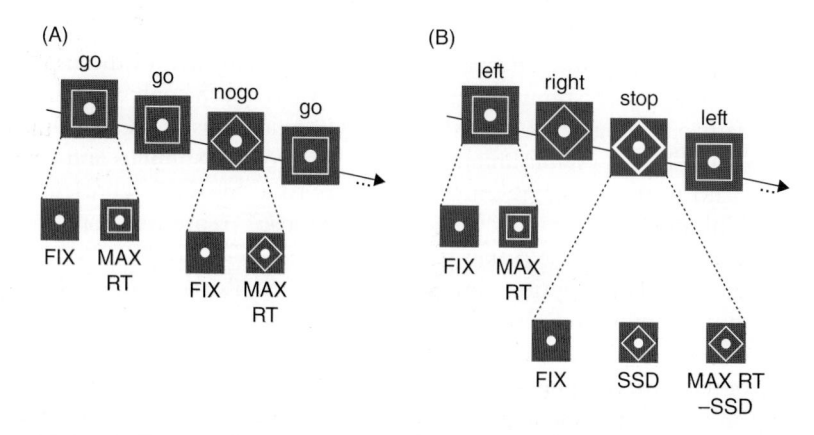

Figure 19.2 Schematic illustration of the go/no-go and stop-signal paradigms. FIX = duration of the fixation interval; MAX RT = maximum response latency; SSD = variable stop-signal delay in the stop-signal paradigm.

2014; Verbruggen & Logan, 2009). When the stop process finishes before the go process, response inhibition is successful, and no response is emitted (signal-inhibit); when the go process finishes before the stop process, response inhibition is unsuccessful, and the response is incorrectly emitted (signal-respond). In the stop-signal task, the covert latency of the stop process (stop-signal reaction time or SSRT) can be estimated from the independent race model (Logan & Cowan, 1984). SSRT has proven to be an important measure of the cognitive control processes that are involved in stopping. For recent reviews of studies of response inhibition in cognitive psychology, cognitive neuroscience, developmental science, and psychopathology, see, for example, Bari and Robbins (2013), Chambers, Garavan, and Bellgrove (2009), and Verbruggen and Logan (2008c).

Neurally, response inhibition processes primarily engage a fronto-basal-ganglia inhibition network, which includes the right (and possibly left) inferior frontal gyrus, the presupplementary motor area, the anterior cingulate cortex, the dorsolateral prefrontal cortex, parietal regions, and basal ganglia (Aron, Robbins, & Poldrack, 2014; Bari & Robbins, 2013; Chambers *et al.*, 2009; Swick, Ashley, & Turken, 2011).[2] On go trials, activation in frontal and parietal areas could lead to activation of a go response via the direct fronto-basal ganglia pathway (see above). In the case of response inhibition, activation in prefrontal areas could lead to a suppression of motor output via the hyperdirect fronto-basal ganglia pathway (see above), resulting in fast and global suppression of motor output. This might affect all response tendencies including activation in muscles that are irrelevant to the task (Badry *et al.*, 2009; Greenhouse, Oldenkamp, & Aron, 2011; Majid, Cai, George, Verbruggen, & Aron, 2012). More selective inhibition of a specific response could potentially be achieved via activation of the indirect fronto-basal pathway (Majid *et al.*, 2012; Smittenaar, Guitart-Masip, Lutti, & Dolan, 2013). The exact cognitive role of the frontal regions is debatable, partly because a detailed processing framework is lacking in many neuroscience studies (McLaren, Verbruggen, & Chambers, 2014). Moreover, the prefrontal areas that are involved in top-down response inhibition are generally recruited by tasks that require selection of competing actions (Bunge, 2004; Duncan & Owen, 2000) and reprogramming or updating actions (Buch, Mars, Boorman, & Rushworth, 2010; Verbruggen, Aron, Stevens, & Chambers, 2010). Thus, response selection and response inhibition may be two sides of the same coin (see also Mostofsky & Simmonds, 2008), relying on overlapping prefrontal brain areas that bias processing in subordinate systems in a context-dependent fashion.

The independent race model of Logan and Cowan (1984) assumes stochastic independence between the go and stop processes. However, the cognitive neuroscience of stopping indicates that go and stop processes interact to produce controlled movements (see also the discussion of the basal ganglia pathways above). To address this "paradox," Boucher, Palmeri, Logan, and Schall (2007) proposed an interactive model. In their model, the go process is initiated by the go stimulus, and a go representation is activated after an afferent delay. The stop process is initiated by the stop signal, and a stop representation is also activated after an afferent delay. Once the stop representation is activated, it inhibits go processing strongly and quickly. In this interactive model, SSRT primarily reflects the period before the stop unit is activated, during which stop and go processing are independent, so its predictions correspond to those of the independent model (Logan & Cowan, 1984).

Conditioned inhibitory control?

Performance in response-inhibition paradigms is usually attributed to a top-down act of control (Verbruggen & Logan, 2008b; McLaren, Verbruggen, & Chambers, 2014). However, in recent years, several studies have examined both the short-term and long-term aftereffects of stopping a response. This work suggests that stop representations may be activated via the retrieval of stimulus–stop associations. Eventually, this could lead to automaticity of stopping (Logan, 1988; Verbruggen & Logan, 2008b). In other words, inhibitory control may become conditioned.

Several stop-signal studies have observed that response latencies on no-signal trials increase after both successful and unsuccessful stopping. This response slowing has been attributed to strategic control adjustments: Subjects must try to find a balance between responding quickly on no-signal trials (speed) and stopping on stop-signal trials (caution); this balance would be adjusted in favor of caution after a stop-signal trial (Bissett & Logan, 2011). However, the slowing is more pronounced when the stimulus or stimulus category of the previous trial is repeated (Bissett & Logan, 2011; Enticott, Bradshaw, Bellgrove, Upton, & Ogloff, 2009; Oldenburg, Roger, Assecondi, Verbruggen, & Fias, 2012; Rieger & Gauggel, 1999; Verbruggen & Logan, 2008a; Verbruggen, Logan, Liefooghe, & Vandierendonck, 2008). This analysis suggests some contribution of memory retrieval. Logan (1988) argued that every time people respond to a stimulus, processing episodes are stored as instances in memory. These episodes consist of the stimulus (e.g., a shape), the interpretation given to a stimulus (e.g., "square"), the task goal ("shape judgment"), and the response ("left"). When the stimulus is repeated, previous processing episodes are retrieved, facilitating performance if the retrieved information is consistent with the currently relevant information but impairing performance if the retrieved information is inconsistent. On a stop-signal trial, the go stimulus or stimulus category becomes associated with stopping; when the stimulus (or category) is repeated, the stimulus–stop association is retrieved, and this interferes with responding on no-signal trials. The idea here, then, is that the go response/goal and the stop response/goal are mutually inhibitory (cf. Boucher et al., 2007) in much the way that Dickinson and Dearing (1979) postulate appetitive and aversive stimuli are. This stimulus–stop association account is related to the "do-not-respond tag" account of the negative priming effect, mentioned earlier (Neill & Valdes, 1992; Neill et al., 1992); of course this is no coincidence because both accounts are based on the Instance Theory of Logan (1988). The stimulus–stop effects are observed up to 20 trials after the presentation of the stop signal (Verbruggen & Logan, 2008a). Similar long-term effects have been observed in task-switching studies, suggesting that stimuli can become associated with tasks or task goals (Waszak, Hommel, & Allport, 2003, 2004, 2005).

Theoretically, repetition priming effects can be viewed as the first step toward automatization (Logan, 1990). According to Logan, automatization involves a transition from performance based on cognitive algorithms or rules to performance based on memory retrieval. Therefore, the observation that a stimulus could prime stopping after a signal trial raises the question whether inhibitory control may become a bottom-up act of control, driven by retrieval of stimulus–stop associations from memory, instead of a top-down act of control. In a series of experiments, we examined the bottom-up idea (Verbruggen & Logan, 2008b). Initially, we used go/no-go tasks in which the stimulus category defined whether subjects had to respond (e.g., natural objects = go) or not (e.g., man-made objects = no-go). We trained subjects to stop their response to a specific stimulus, and then reversed the go/no-go mappings in a test phase. In this test phase, subjects were slower to respond to that stimulus compared with stimuli that they had not seen before (Verbruggen & Logan, 2008b, Experiment 1). Furthermore, learning the new go association was slowed, so one could argue that it passes a retardation test for inhibition. The response slowing was still observed when the tasks changed from training to test: Subjects made natural/man-made judgments in training but large/small judgments in test (or vice versa; Experiment 2), and RTs were longer for inconsistent items (i.e., no-go in one task but go in the other task) than for consistent items (i.e., go in both tasks). This last is a result akin to that obtained in summation tests for inhibition if training for a given stimulus in one category was natural + stimulus = no-go, then on test small + stimulus = go; the inhibition derived from training has transferred to the novel test situation in a manner analogous to combining an inhibitor with a novel excitor. We also demonstrated (Experiment 3) that the effect was not entirely category driven, as stimulus-specific slowing was observed when the category-stop mappings were inconsistent in training: Here, the go/no-go mappings changed every block (e.g., natural = go and man-made = no-go, vs. natural = no-go, man-made = go), but we used different words for each go/no-go rule (resulting in consistent stimulus–stop mappings). Based on these findings, we proposed the automatic inhibition hypothesis: "automatic inhibition" occurs when old no-go stimuli retrieve the stop goal when they are repeated, and this interferes with go processing (Verbruggen & Logan, 2008b). The stimulus–stop mapping is typically consistent in the go/no-go paradigm, so automatic inhibition is likely to occur. However, automatic inhibition can also occur in the stop-signal task when the mapping is manipulated (Verbruggen & Logan, 2008b; experiment 5).

The experiments of Verbruggen and Logan demonstrated behaviorally that response inhibition is not always an effortful or deliberate act of control. A follow-up neuroimaging study showed that the right inferior frontal gyrus, which is part of the fronto-basal-ganglia network that supports deliberate response inhibition (see above), was also activated when stimuli previously associated with stopping were presented in a stop-signal task (Lenartowicz, Verbruggen, Logan, & Poldrack, 2011). Thus, at least part of the top-down inhibition network was activated in the absence of external stop signals. However, the rIFG has been associated with a multitude of roles (e.g., attentional reorientation, context monitoring, response selection, reversal learning), and so this finding does not necessarily allow strong inferences about the underlying cognitive mechanisms.

What is learned during conditioning of inhibitory control?

What is learned during go/no-go and stop-signal tasks is still unclear. Based on Logan's (1988) Instance Theory of Automatization, we hypothesized that stimuli became associated with a stop goal or stop representation in training, which impaired responding to them at test (Verbruggen et al., 2008; Verbruggen & Logan, 2008b).

Like "No-US" representations (section "Basic Phenomena I: Conditioned Inhibition"), stop representations can be interpreted in different ways. First, the stop representation could be response specific. When a cue or stimulus is trained with stopping a left manual response, the stop representation would be "stop left response" (or, to be even more specific, "stop left-hand response"); but when the stimulus is trained with stopping a right response, the stop representation would be "stop right response." Second, the stop representation could be more general. Previously, we have argued that in stop-signal tasks, a stimulus becomes associated with an abstract and general representation of going or stopping; in other words, it does not specify which specific response or motor program has to be executed or stopped (Verbruggen & Logan, 2008b). The study of Giesen and Rothermund (2014) provides direct support for this general representation idea. These authors demonstrated that responding to a stimulus that was previously associated with stopping was delayed even when the expected go response had changed. More specifically, the color of a letter indicated whether subjects had to execute a left or right response; the identity of the letter ("D" or "L") was irrelevant. They found that responding to a letter was slowed down if a stop signal was presented on the previous trial, regardless of the "to-be-executed" or "to-be-stopped" response (e.g., a green D on the prime, followed by a red D). This suggests that the stimulus–stop associations are general. Note that the "general stop representation" idea is also indirectly supported by the observation that stopping often has general effects on the motor system (see above).

Recent work on stopping to motivationally salient stimuli suggests a third interpretation. Several studies have found that consistent pairing of food-related pictures to stopping in a go/no-go or stop-signal-paradigm reduced subsequent food consumption (e.g., Houben, 2011; Houben & Jansen, 2011; Lawrence, Verbruggen, Adams, & Chambers, 2013; Veling, Aarts, & Papies, 2011; Veling, Aarts, & Stroebe, 2012). Furthermore, a similar procedure with alcohol-related stimuli reduced alcohol intake in the laboratory (Jones & Field, 2013) and even self-reported weekly alcohol intake of heavy drinking students (Houben, Havermans, Nederkoorn, & Jansen, 2012; but see Jones & Field, 2013). These effects could be mediated by devaluation of the stimuli that were associated with stopping (e.g., Houben *et al.*, 2012; Kiss, Raymond, Westoby, Nobre, & Eimer, 2008; Veling, Holland, and van Knippenberg, 2008). Ferrey, Frischen, and Fenske (2012) showed that stop associations impact not only on the hedonic value of the stimuli associated with stopping but also on their behavioral incentive. They paired sexually attractive images with either going or stopping in a training phase, and then asked subjects to rate the attractiveness of the images. They found that the no-go (stop) images were rated less positively than the go images. This is similar to the findings of Raymond *et al.*, who showed that ignoring a distractor leads to its devaluation. In a second study, Ferrey *et al.* showed that subjects were less willing to work to see the erotic images that were paired with stopping. Thus, conditioned inhibitory control may impact on the motivational value of stimuli, perhaps via creating links between the stimuli and the appetitive/aversive centers postulated by Dickinson and Dearing (1979).

Central to the "conditioned inhibitory control" idea is the notion that the retrieval of stop representations will impair responding. However, such impairments could arise in at least two different processing stages: action selection and action execution.[3] First, in go/no-go and stop-signal tasks, subjects must select an action on each trial (Gomez, Ratcliff, & Perea, 2007; Logan *et al.*, 2014). The retrieval of stop information could interfere with selecting the appropriate "go" action. This would be akin to "central" interference between two competing go responses when selecting a response. This also implies that conditioned inhibitory control could be achieved via lateral local inhibitory connections between competing action options. This interference or conflict account receives some support from short-term aftereffect studies, which demonstrated that stopping on the previous trial affected the stimulus-locked parietal P300, but only when the stimulus was repeated (Oldenburg *et al.*, 2012). Response-locked motor components were not influenced, arguing against a motor locus for the effect (see also Enticott *et al.*, 2009). Second, the retrieval of the stimulus–stop association could serve as a conditioned stop "signal," activating the indirect or hyperdirect pathways that suppress motor output. This would be more similar to the direct, unconditional, automatic activation of an incorrect go response in interference tasks. Consistent with the motor suppression idea, Chiu, Aron, and Verbruggen (2012) showed that motor excitability was suppressed a mere 100 ms after the presentation of stimuli that were previously associated with stopping, but now required going. Of course, the two options are not exclusive. They may even rely on overlapping neural structures. The detection of conflict (defined as the competition between response options) could trigger a braking mechanism via the No-go cells of the indirect pathway or the hyperdirect pathway (see above; Frank, 2006; Ratcliff & Frank, 2012). If conflict between go and stop representations is detected early enough, this braking mechanism could account for the reduced motor excitability observed in Chiu *et al.* (2012). Thus, the main difference between the "automatic suppression" account and the "conflict" account is the trigger of the braking or stopping mechanism: the stimulus itself or the conflict caused by the retrieved information, respectively. Future work is required to determine how exactly stop representations influence responding in various situations.

In combination, the work above suggests that inhibitory control can be conditioned or become "automatized." Dickinson and Dearing (1979) made a strong case for motivational influences and an appetitive–aversive interaction in Pavlovian conditioning. The work on conditioned inhibitory control suggests that very similar mechanisms might operate in instrumental inhibitory conditioning, despite the fact that Pavlovian and instrumental conditioning differ in many other ways (cf. Dickinson & Balleine, 2002). In the next section, we will focus on integrating these findings and develop a theory of how "conditioned" or "automatic" inhibition might operate.

Integration: Inhibition and Association

Here, we ask if it is possible to bring these two very different areas (animal conditioning and human cognitive psychology) together and arrive at a unified treatment of "inhibition" that would make sense in both domains. Our (somewhat tentative) answer is that it may be possible to develop an integrated approach that captures an emerging consensus in the two separate areas. This consensus revolves more around the associative structures that need to be posited to capture the notion of inhibition than the particular learning algorithms needed to operate within those structures, and so our treatment will mostly focus on the general architecture of inhibition at this point rather than exactly how it develops within this architecture (though the two issues are clearly not independent of one another).

To recap, the work reviewed in the section "Basic Phenomena I: Conditioned Inhibition" suggests that there is a general form of inhibition mediated via excitatory connections to appetitive/aversive centers that mutually inhibit one another, and a more specific form of inhibition that is equivalent to a direct inhibitory link to the stimulus representation (be it CS or US) in question. Both will contribute to learning, and task contexts might determine the relative contribution of the two. The work reviewed in the section "Basic Phenomena II: Conditioned Inhibitory Control" suggests that inhibition of responses is an integral part of executive control, but in many situations, this top-down response inhibition can become "automatized." Recent work suggests that subjects learn a general form of response inhibition, which transfers between tasks. This could be mediated by the same excitatory connections to the appetitive and aversive centers that are a key component of Pavlovian conditioning. Indeed, learning to stop or not to respond to a certain stimulus not only slows responding to it (e.g., Lenartowicz et al., 2011; Neill et al., 1992; Verbruggen & Logan, 2008b) but also reduces its hedonic value and motivational incentive (e.g., Ferrey et al., 2012; Houben et al., 2012; Kiss et al., 2008; Raymond et al., 2003; Veling et al., 2008). Our interpretation of this is that when a distractor or no-go/stop stimulus becomes associated with an avoidance/aversive center, presentation of it will directly activate the avoidance/aversive center, which in turn will suppress activation of the approach/appetitive center (cf. Dickinson & Balleine, 2002). This could explain both the slower responding in an RT task and the lower hedonic values in a stimulus evaluation task using ratings.

In a sense, then, we are arguing that "Go" and "Stop" are the instrumental equivalents of the Pavlovian "Good" and "Bad," and a scheme that implements this idea is shown in outline in Figure 19.3. Of course, Pavlovian and instrumental conditioning should not be equated entirely, as they appear to be influenced in different ways by

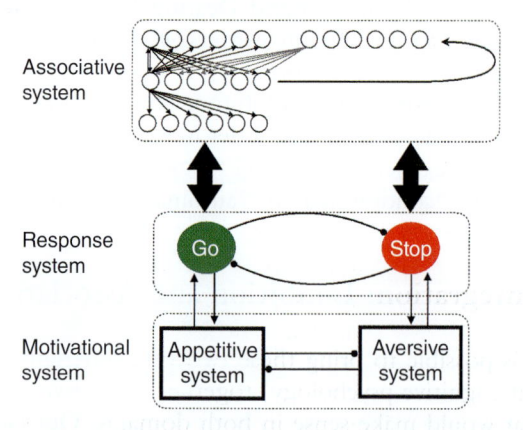

Figure 19.3 Model integrating associative and motivational subsystems that would enable implementation of our proposals for conditioned inhibition. The associative system contains both an auto-associative network and recurrence, giving it the ability to capture statistical regularities in the environment and between actions and outcomes. The motivational and response systems are a synthesis of Dickinson and Balleine's (2002) implementation of Konorski's proposal with an instrumental Stop/Go system along the lines proposed by Boucher et al. (2007). "Direct" conditioned inhibition takes place within the associative system, and is outcome specific. "General" conditioned inhibition takes place via links from the associative system to the other systems either at the Stop/Go instrumental level or at the Appetitive/Aversive Pavlovian level.

manipulations of contexts and omission schedules (Dickinson & Balleine, 2002), and they are supported by different corticostriatal loops (for a short review, see Guitart-Masip, Duzel, Dolan, & Dayan, 2014). Nevertheless, recent work suggests that Pavlovian and instrumental conditioning interact in a go/no-go task (Guitart-Masip et al., 2014). For example, in a study by Guitart-Masip et al. (2012), subjects had to learn stimulus-go/no-go contingencies. They learned them faster when correct go responses were rewarded and incorrect no-go responses were punished, than the other way around. This was attributed to a hard-wired Pavlovian equivalence between reward/punishment and approach/avoidance, respectively. The Konorskian model, as discussed in Dickinson and Balleine (2002), also links the aversive system with avoidance (withdrawal, suppression) and the appetitive system with approach (go). Therefore, it seems plausible to suggest that when subjects always have to stop their response to a specific stimulus, a link between this stimulus and the aversive/avoidance system will be created.

Despite the seemingly overwhelming evidence for a strong link between go and appetite/reward and between no-go and aversion/punishment, a few findings appear inconsistent with the no-go/aversion account. For example, some studies have shown that response inhibition might be impaired rather than enhanced when negative emotional or threatening stimuli are presented (e.g., De Houwer & Tibboel, 2010; Pessoa, Padmala, Kenzer, & Bauer, 2012; Verbruggen & De Houwer, 2007). Because these studies showed similar impairments when positive stimuli were presented, the effect of emotional and threatening stimuli has been attributed to arousal (rather than valence): Arousing stimuli tend to attract attention (and are processed centrally when they high in threat), causing "dual-task" interference. In other words, effects of arousal (attention) may have counteracted or dominated the effects of valence (positive/negative). Perhaps this is not very surprising given recent work that suggests that most of the stopping latency is occupied by afferent or sensory processes (Boucher et al., 2007; Salinas & Stanford, 2013); in other words, activation of the avoidance/aversive center may only have a small influence on the overall SSRT, compared with the effect of arousal, because of the different time courses for the processes involved. In the study by Pessoa et al. (2012; Experiment 2) in particular, the latency for activation of any aversive center due to associations between the stimulus and some motivationally significant outcome may have been too long for it to have much effect on stopping in the stop-signal task, making any effect entirely dependent on a more cognitive appraisal of the stimulus.

So far, we have focused mostly on the link between conditioned inhibitory control and appetitive/aversive valence. But our discussion of the conditioned inhibition literature suggests that performance cannot be explained using a single inhibitory mechanism. Apart from the direct link between the CS and the appetitive/aversive centers, there is the more specific link between the CS and US (or another CS). In the case of conditioned inhibition, this link will be inhibitory. Of course, in many other situations, this link will be excitatory (as in the original work of Pavlov). It seems likely that in the context of conditioned inhibitory control, subjects can also learn associations between the representation of the go stimulus and the representation of the stop signal (Verbruggen et al., 2014). Factors such as the number and kind of stop or no-go signals could determine the relative contribution of stimulus–stimulus associations versus stimulus–approach/avoidance associations.

Conclusion: Inhibition in Cognitive Control and Associative Learning

We have tried to provide a modern approach to the problem of inhibition that draws on many of the classic studies in the animal learning tradition that exemplify the contribution that experimental psychology can make to current issues in cognitive neuroscience. We hope that this integration of the old and the new will prove fruitful in providing a framework for future research on behavioral inhibition.

Notes

1 Note that the cortico-basal-ganglia pathways do not directly map on to the direct and indirect routes discussed in dual-route frameworks.
2 Inhibition of eye movements may recruit a different network. Single-cell studies indicate that it relies primarily on the activation of movement- and fixation-related neurons in frontal eye fields in dorsolateral prefrontal cortex and superior colliculus in midbrain (for a review, see Schall & Godlove, 2012).
3 In Verbruggen, Best, Bowditch, Stevens, and McLaren (2014), we discuss a third possibility, namely that attention and signal detection become conditioned.

References

Aron, A. R., Robbins, T. W., & Poldrack, R. A. (2014). Inhibition and the right inferior frontal cortex: One decade on. *Trends in Cognitive Sciences, 18*, 177–185.

Baddeley, A. (1996). Exploring the central executive. *Quarterly Journal of Experimental Psychology, 49A*, 5–28

Badry, R., Mima, T., Aso, T., Nakatsuka, M., Abe, M., Fathi, D., . . . Fukuyama, H. (2009). Suppression of human cortico-motoneuronal excitability during the stop-signal task. *Clinical Neurophysiology, 120*, 1717–1723.

Bari, A., & Robbins, T. W. (2013). Inhibition and impulsivity: Behavioral and neural basis of response control. *Progress in Neurobiology, 108*, 44–79.

Bennett, C. H., Scahill, V. L., Griffiths, D. P., & Mackintosh, N. J. (1999). The role of inhibitory associations in perceptual learning. *Learning & Behavior, 27*, 333–345.

Bissett, P. G., & Logan, G. D. (2011). Balancing cognitive demands: Control adjustments in the stop-signal paradigm. *Journal of Experimental Psychology: Learning, Memory, and Cognition, 37*, 392–404.

Botvinick, M. M. (2007). Conflict monitoring and decision making: reconciling two perspectives on anterior cingulate function. *Cognitive, Affective, & Behavioral Neuroscience, 7*, 356–366.

Boucher, L., Palmeri, T. J., Logan, G. D., & Schall, J. D. (2007). Inhibitory control in mind and brain: an interactive race model of countermanding saccades. *Psychological Review, 114*, 376–397.

Buch, E. R., Mars, R. B., Boorman, E. D., & Rushworth, M. F. (2010). A network centered on ventral premotor cortex exerts both facilitatory and inhibitory control over primary motor cortex during action reprogramming. *The Journal of Neuroscience, 30*, 1395–1401.

Bunge, S. A. (2004). How we use rules to select actions: A review of evidence from cognitive neuroscience. *Cognitive, Affective & Behavioral Neuroscience, 4*, 564–579.

Chambers, C. D., Garavan, H., & Bellgrove, M. A. (2009). Insights into the neural basis of response inhibition from cognitive and clinical neuroscience. *Neuroscience and Biobehavioral Reviews, 33*, 631–646.

Chapman, G. B. (1991). Trial-order affect s cue interaction in contingency judgement. *Journal of Experimental Psychology: Learning, Memory and Cognition, 17*, 837–854.

Chiu, Y. C., Aron, A. R., & Verbruggen, F. (2012). Response suppression by automatic retrieval of stimulus–stop association: Evidence from transcranial magnetic stimulation. *Journal of Cognitive Neuroscience, 24*, 1908–1918.

Cohen, J. D., Dunbar, K., & McClelland, J. L. (1990). On the control of automatic processes: A parallel distributed processing account of the Stroop effect. *Psychological Review, 97*, 332–361.

Cotton, M. M., Goodall, G., & Mackintosh, N. J. (1982). Inhibitory conditioning resulting from a reduction in the magnitude of reinforcement. *Quarterly Journal of Experimental Psychology, 34B*, 163–180.

De Houwer, J., & Tibboel, H. (2010). Stop what you are not doing! Emotional pictures interfere with the task not to respond. *Psychonomic Bulletin & Review, 17*, 699–703.

Dickinson, A. (1980). *Contemporary animal learning theory*. Cambridge, UK: CUP.

Dickinson, A., & Balleine, B. (2002). The role of learning in the operation of motivational systems. In R. Gallistel (Ed.), *Stevens' handbook of experimental psychology* (3rd ed., Vol. 3, pp. 497–534). New York, NY: John Wiley & Sons.

Dickinson, A., & Burke, J. (1996). Within-compound associations mediate the retrospective revaluation of causality judgements. *Quarterly Journal of Experimental Psychology, 49B*, 60–80.

Dickinson, A., & Dearing, M. F. (1979). Appetitive–aversive interactions and inhibitory processes. In A. Dickinson & R. A. Boakes (Eds.), *Mechanisms of learning and motivation* (pp. 203–232). Englewood Cliffs, NJ: Erlbaum.

Duncan, J., & Owen, A. M. (2000). Common regions of the human frontal lobe recruited by diverse cognitive demands. *Trends in Neurosciences, 23*, 475–483.

Enticott, P. G., Bradshaw, J. L., Bellgrove, M. A., Upton, D. J., & Ogloff, J. R. (2009). Stop task after-effects: The extent of slowing during the preparation and execution of movement. *Experimental Psychology, 56*, 247–251.

Espinet, A., Iraola, J. A., Bennett, C. H., & Mackintosh, N. J. (1995). Inhibitory associations between neutral stimuli in flavor-aversion conditioning. *Animal Learning & Behavior, 23*, 361–368.

Ferrey, A. E., Frischen, A., & Fenske, M. J. (2012). Hot or not: response inhibition reduces the hedonic value and motivational incentive of sexual stimuli. *Frontiers in Psychology, 3*.

Frank, M. J. (2005). Dynamic dopamine modulation in the basal ganglia: a neurocomputational account of cognitive deficits in medicated and nonmedicated Parkinsonism. *Journal of Cognitive Neuroscience, 17*, 51–72.

Frank, M. J. (2006). Hold your horses: A dynamic computational role for the subthalamic nucleus in decision making. *Neural Networks, 19*, 1120–1136.

Friedman, N. P., & Miyake, A. (2004). The relations among inhibition and interference control functions: A latent-variable analysis. *Journal of Experimental Psychology. General, 133*, 101–135.

Frings, C., Moeller, B., & Rothermund, K. (2013). Retrieval of event files can be conceptually mediated. *Attention, Perception, & Psychophysics, 75*, 700–709.

Fritz, J., & Dreisbach, G. (2013). Conflicts as aversive signals: Conflict priming increases negative judgments for neutral stimuli. *Cognitive, Affective & Behavioral Neuroscience, 13*, 311–317.

Giesen, C., & Rothermund, K. (2014). You better stop! Binding "stop" tags to irrelevant stimulus features. *The Quarterly Journal of Experimental Psychology, 67*, 809–832.

Gomez, P., Ratcliff, R., & Perea, M. (2007). A model of the go/no-go task. *Journal of Experimental Psychology. General*, *136*, 389–413.

Graham, S. (1999). Retrospective revaluation and inhibitory associations: does perceptual learning modulate our perception of the contingencies between events? *Quarterly Journal of Experimental Psychology*, 52B, 159–185.

Graham, S., Jie, H. L., Minn, C. H., McLaren, I. P. L., & Wills, A. J. (2011). Simultaneous backward conditioned inhibition and mediated conditioning. *Journal of Experimental Psychology: Animal Behavior Processes*, *37*, 241–245.

Greenhouse, I., Oldenkamp, C. L., & Aron, A. R. (2011). Stopping a response has global or non-global effects on the motor system depending on preparation. *Journal of Neurophysiology*, *107*, 384–392.

Guitart-Masip, M., Duzel, E., Dolan, R., & Dayan, P. (2014). Action versus valence in decision making. *Trends in Cognitive Sciences*, *18*, 194–202

Guitart-Masip, M., Huys, Q. J., Fuentemilla, L., Dayan, P., Duzel, E., & Dolan, R. J. (2012). Go and no-go learning in reward and punishment: interactions between affect and effect. *Neuroimage*, *62*, 154–166.

Hall, G., & Pearce, J. M. (1979). Latent inhibition of a CS during CS–US parings. *Journal of Experimental Psychology: Animal Behaviour Processes*, *5*, 31–43.

Harris, J. A., Kwok, D. W. S., & Andrew, B. J. (2014). Conditioned inhibition and reinforcement rate. *Journal of Experimental Psychology: Animal Learning & Cognition*, *40*, 335–354.

Harnishfeger, K. K. (1995). The development of cognitive inhibition: Theories, definitions, and research evidence. In F. N. Dempster & C. J. Brainerd (Eds.), *Interference and inhibition in cognition* (pp. 175–204). San Diego, CA: Academic Press.

Herd, S. A., Banich, M. T., & O'Reilly, R. C. (2006). Neural mechanisms of cognitive control: An integrative model of stroop task performance and FMRI data. *Journal of Cognitive Neuroscience*, *18*, 22–32.

Houben, K. (2011). Overcoming the urge to splurge: Influencing eating behavior by manipulating inhibitory control. *Journal of Behavior Therapy and Experimental Psychiatry*, *42*, 384–388.

Houben, K., Havermans, R. C., Nederkoorn, C., & Jansen, A. (2012). Beer à no-go: Learning to stop responding to alcohol cues reduces alcohol intake via reduced affective associations rather than increased response inhibition. *Addiction*, *107*, 1280–1287.

Houben, K., & Jansen, A. (2011). Training inhibitory control. A recipe for resisting sweet temptations. *Appetite*, *56*, 345–349.

Jones, A., & Field, M. (2013). The effects of cue-specific inhibition training on alcohol consumption in heavy social drinkers. *Experimental and Clinical Psychopharmacology*, *21*, 8–16.

Jones, F., Wills, A. J., & McLaren, I. P. L. (1998). Perceptual categorisation: connectionist modelling and decision rules. *Quarterly Journal of Experimental Psychology*, 51B, 33–58.

Kiss, M., Raymond, J. E., Westoby, N., Nobre, A. C., & Eimer, M. (2008). Response inhibition is linked to emotional devaluation: Behavioural and electrophysiological evidence. *Frontiers in Human Neuroscience*, *2*, 13.

Klein, P. A., Petitjean, C., Olivier, E., & Duque, J. (2014). Top-down suppression of incompatible motor activations during response selection under conflict. *NeuroImage*, *86*, 138–149.

Konorski, J. (1948). *Conditioned reflexes and neuron organisation*. Cambridge, UK: Cambridge University Press.

Konorski, J. (1967). *Integrative activity of the brain: An interdisciplinary approach*. Chicago, IL: University of Chicago Press.

Kornblum, S., Hasbroucq, T., & Osman, A. (1990). Dimensional overlap: Cognitive basis for stimulus–response compatibility – a model and taxonomy. *Psychological Review*, *97*, 253–270.

Kremer, E. F. (1978). The Rescorla–Wagner model: Losses of associative strength in compound conditioned stimuli. *Journal of Experimental Psychology: Animal Behavior Processes*, *4*, 22–36.

Lawrence, N. S., Verbruggen, F., Adams, R. C., & Chambers, C. D. (2013). *Stopping to food cues reduces snack food intake: Effects of cue specificity, control conditions and individual differences.* Manuscript in preparation.

Lenartowicz, A., Verbruggen, F., Logan, G. D., & Poldrack, R. A. (2011). Inhibition-related activation in the right inferior frontal gyrus in the absence of inhibitory cues. *Journal of Cognitive Neuroscience*, *23*, 3388–3399.

Le Pelley, M. E. (2004). The role of associative history in models of associative learning: A selective review and a hybrid model. *Quarterly Journal of Experimental Psychology*, *57B*, 193–243.

Le Pelley, M. E., Cutler, D. L., & McLaren, I. P. L. (2000). Retrospective effects in human causality judgment. In *Proceedings of the Twenty-Second Annual Conference of the Cognitive Science Society*. Englewood Cliffs, NJ: Erlbaum.

Le Pelley, M. E., & McLaren, I. P. L. (2001). Retrospective revaluation in humans: Learning or memory? *Quarterly Journal of Experimental Psychology*, *54B*, 311–352.

Logan, G. D. (1985). Executive control of thought and action. *Acta Psychologica*, *60*, 193–210.

Logan, G. D. (1988). Toward an instance theory of automatization. *Psychological Review*, *95*, 492–527.

Logan, G. D. (1990). Repetition priming and automaticity: Common underlying mechanisms? *Cognitive Psychology*, *22*, 1–35.

Logan, G. D., & Cowan, W. B. (1984). On the ability to inhibit thought and action: A theory of an act of control. *Psychological Review*, *91*, 295–327.

Logan, G. D., Van Zandt, T., Verbruggen, F., & Wagenmakers, E. J. (2014). On the ability to inhibit thought and action: General and special theories of an act of control. *Psychological Review*, *121*, 66–95.

Lotz, A., Uengoer, M., Koenig, S., Pearce, J. M., & Lachnit, H. (2012). An exploration of the feature-positive effect in adult humans. *Learning & Behavior*, *40*, 222–230.

Mackintosh, N. J. (1974). *The psychology of animal learning*. London, UK: Academic Press.

MacLeod, C. M., Dodd, M. D., Sheard, E. D., Wilson, D. E., & Bibi, U. (2003). In opposition to inhibition. In *Psychology of learning and motivation: Advances in research and theory* (Vol. 43, pp. 163–214). London, UK: Academic Press.

Majid, D. S., Cai, W., George, J. S., Verbruggen, F., & Aron, A. R. (2012). Transcranial magnetic stimulation reveals dissociable mechanisms for global versus selective corticomotor suppression underlying the stopping of action. *Cerebral Cortex*, *22*, 363–371.

Mayr, S., & Buchner, A. (2007). Negative priming as a memory phenomenon. *Zeitschrift Für Psychologie/Journal of Psychology*, *215*, 35–51.

McLaren, I. P. L., & Dickinson, A. (1990). The conditioning connection. *Philosophical Transactions of the Royal Society B: Biological Sciences*, *329*, 179–186.

McLaren, I. P. L., Forrest, C. L., & McLaren, R. P. (2012). Elemental representation and configural mappings: Combining elemental and configural theories of associative learning. *Learning and Behavior*, *40*, 320–333.

McLaren, I. P. L., Kaye, H., & Mackintosh, N. J. (1989). An associative theory of the representation of stimuli: applications to perceptual learning and latent inhibition. In R. G. M. Morris (Ed.), *Parallel distributed processing – implications for psychology and neurobiology*. Oxford, UK: Oxford University Press.

McLaren, I. P. L., & Mackintosh, N. J. (2000). An elemental model of associative learning: I. Latent inhibition and perceptual learning. *Animal Learning and Behavior*, 38, 211–246.

McLaren, I. P. L., & Mackintosh, N. J. (2002). Associative learning and elemental representation: II. Generalization and discrimination. *Animal Learning & Behavior*, 30, 3, 177–200.

Miller, R. R., & Schachtman, T. R. (1985). Conditioning context as an associative baseline: Implications for response generation and the nature of conditioned inhibition. In R. R. Miller & N. E. Spear (Eds.), *Information processing in animals: Conditioned inhibition* (pp. 51–88). Englewood Cliffs, NJ: Erlbaum.

Miyake, A., Friedman, N. P., Emerson, M. J., Witzki, A. H., Howerter, A., & Wager, T. D. (2000). The unity and diversity of executive functions and their contributions to complex "frontal lobe" tasks: A latent variable analysis. *Cognitive Psychology*, 41, 49–100.

Mostofsky, S. H., & Simmonds, D. J. (2008). Response inhibition and response selection: Two sides of the same coin. *Journal of Cognitive Neuroscience*, 20, 751–761.

Mundy, M. E., Dwyer, D. M., & Honey, R. C. (2006). Inhibitory associations contribute to perceptual learning in humans. *Journal of Experimental Psychology: Animal Behavior Processes*, 32, 178–184.

Nambu, A., Tokuno, H., & Takada, M. (2002). Functional significance of the cortico–subthalamo–pallidal 'hyperdirect' pathway. *Neuroscience Research*, 43, 111–117.

Neill, W. T., & Valdes, L. A. (1992). Persistence of negative priming – steady-state or decay. *Journal of Experimental Psychology: Learning Memory and Cognition*, 18, 565–576.

Neill, W. T., Valdes, L. A., Terry, K. M., & Gorfein, D. S. (1992). Persistence of negative priming: II. Evidence for episodic trace retrieval. *Journal of Experimental Psychology: Learning Memory and Cognition*, 18, 993–1000.

Nigg, J. T. (2000). On inhibition/disinhibition in developmental psychopathology: Views from cognitive and personality psychology and a working inhibition taxonomy. *Psychological Bulletin*, 126, 220–246.

Oldenburg, J. F., Roger, C., Assecondi, S., Verbruggen, F., & Fias, W. (2012). Repetition priming in the stop signal task: The electrophysiology of sequential effects of stopping. *Neuropsychologia*, 50, 2860–2868.

Pavlov, I. P. (1927). *Conditioned reflexes*. Oxford, UK: Oxford University Press.

Pearce, J. M., & Hall, G. (1980). A model for Pavlovian conditioning: Variations in the effectiveness of conditioned but not of unconditioned stimuli. *Psychological Review*, 87, 532–552.

Pessoa, L., Padmala, S., Kenzer, A., & Bauer, A. (2012). Interactions between cognition and emotion during response inhibition. *Emotion*, 12, 192–197.

Raaijmakers, J. G., & Jakab, E. (2013). Is forgetting caused by inhibition? *Current Directions in Psychological Science*, 22, 205–209.

Ratcliff, R., & Frank, M. J. (2012). Reinforcement-based decision making in corticostriatal circuits: mutual constraints by neurocomputational and diffusion models. *Neural Computation*, 24, 1186–1229.

Raymond, J. E., Fenske, M. J., & Tavassoli, N. T. (2003). Selective attention determines emotional responses to novel visual stimuli. *Psychological Science*, 14, 537–542.

Rescorla, R. A. (1969). Conditioned inhibition of fear resulting from negative CS–US contingencies. *Journal of Comparative and Physiological Psychology*, 67, 504–509.

Rescorla, R. A. (1970). Reduction in the effectiveness of reinforcement after prior excitatory conditioning. *Learning and Motivation*, 1, 372–381.

Rescorla, R. A., & Wagner, A. R. (1972). A theory of Pavlovian conditioning: Variations in the effectiveness of reinforcement and non-reinforcement. In A. H. Black & W. F. Prokasy (Eds.), *Classical conditioning II: Current research and theory* (pp. 64–99). New York, NY: Appleton-Century-Crofts.

Ridderinkhof, K. R. (2002). Activation and suppression in conflict tasks: Empirical clarification through distributional analyses. In *Attention and performance XIX: Common mechanisms in perception and action* (pp. 494–519). Oxford: Oxford University Press.

Rieger, M., & Gauggel, S. (1999). Inhibitory after-effects in the stop signal paradigm. *British Journal of Psychology, 90*, 509–518.

Rothermund, K., Wentura, D., & De Houwer, J. (2005). Retrieval of incidental stimulus–response associations as a source of negative priming. *Journal of Experimental Psychology: Learning, Memory, and Cognition, 31*, 482–495.

Salinas, E., & Stanford, T. R. (2013). The countermanding task revisited: fast stimulus detection is a key determinant of psychophysical performance. *The Journal of Neuroscience, 33*, 5668–5685.

Schall, J. D., & Godlove, D. C. (2012). Current advances and pressing problems in studies of stopping. *Current Opinion in Neurobiology, 22*, 1012–1021.

Smittenaar, P., Guitart-Masip, M., Lutti, A., & Dolan, R. J. (2013). Preparing for selective inhibition within frontostriatal loops. *The Journal of Neuroscience, 33*, 18087–18097.

Swick, D., Ashley, V., & Turken, A. U. (2011). Are the neural correlates of stopping and not going identical? Quantitative meta-analysis of two response inhibition tasks. *NeuroImage, 56*, 1655–1665.

Tipper, S. P. (2001). Does negative priming reflect inhibitory mechanisms? A review and integration of conflicting views. *The Quarterly Journal of Experimental Psychology: Section A, 54*, 321–343.

van den Wildenberg, W. P. M., Wylie, S. A., Forstmann, B. U., Burle, B., Hasbroucq, T., & Ridderinkhof, K. R. (2010). To head or to heed? Beyond the surface of selective action inhibition: A review. *Frontiers in Human Neuroscience, 4*, 222.

Van Hamme, L. J., & Wasserman, E. A. (1994). Cue competition in causality judgements: The role of nonpresentation of compound stimulus elements. *Learning and Motivation, 25*, 127–151.

van Steenbergen, H., Band, G. P., & Hommel, B. (2009). Reward counteracts conflict adaptation. Evidence for a role of affect in executive control. *Psychological Science, 20*, 1473–1477.

Veling, H., Aarts, H., & Papies, E. K. (2011). Using stop signals to inhibit chronic dieters' responses toward palatable foods. *Behaviour Research and Therapy, 49*, 771–780.

Veling, H., Aarts, H., & Stroebe, W. (2012). Using stop signals to reduce impulsive choices for palatable unhealthy foods. *British Journal of Health Psychology, 18*, 354–368.

Veling, H., Holland, R. W., & van Knippenberg, A. (2008). When approach motivation and behavioral inhibition collide: Behavior regulation through stimulus devaluation. *Journal of Experimental Social Psychology, 44*, 1013–1019.

Verbruggen, F., Aron, A. R., Stevens, M. A., & Chambers, C. D. (2010). Theta burst stimulation dissociates attention and action updating in human inferior frontal cortex. *Proceedings of the National Academy of Sciences of the United States of America, 107*, 13966–13971.

Verbruggen, F., Best, M., Bowditch, W., Stevens, T., McLaren, I. P. L. (2014). The inhibitory control reflex. *Neuropsychologia, 65*, 263–278.

Verbruggen, F., & De Houwer, J. (2007). Do emotional stimuli interfere with response inhibition? Evidence from the stop signal paradigm. *Cognition & Emotion, 21*, 391–403.

Verbruggen, F., & Logan, G. D. (2008a). Long-term aftereffects of response inhibition: Memory retrieval, task goals, and cognitive control. *Journal of Experimental Psychology: Human Perception and Performance, 34*, 1229–1235.

Verbruggen, F., & Logan, G. D. (2008b). Automatic and controlled response inhibition: Associative learning in the go/no-go and stop-signal paradigms. *Journal of Experimental Psychology: General, 137*, 649–672.

Verbruggen, F., & Logan, G. D. (2008c). Response inhibition in the stop-signal paradigm. *Trends in Cognitive Sciences*, *12*, 418–424.

Verbruggen, F., & Logan, G. D. (2009). Models of response inhibition in the stop-signal and stop-change paradigms. *Neuroscience and Biobehavioral Reviews*, *33*, 647–661.

Verbruggen, F., Logan, G. D., Liefooghe, B., & Vandierendonck, A. (2008). Short-term after-effects of response inhibition: Repetition priming or between-trial control adjustments? *Journal of Experimental Psychology: Human Perception and Performance*, *34*, 413–426.

Verbruggen, F., McLaren, I. P. L., & Chambers, C. D. (2014). Banishing the control homunculi in studies of action control and behaviour change. *Perspectives on Psychological Science*, *9*, 497–524.

Waszak, F., Hommel, B., & Allport, A. (2003). Task-switching and long-term priming: Role of episodic stimulus-task bindings in task-shift costs. *Cognitive Psychology*, *46*, 361–413.

Waszak, F., Hommel, B., & Allport, A. (2004). Semantic generalization of stimulus-task bindings. *Psychonomic Bulletin & Review*, *11*, 1027–1033.

Waszak, F., Hommel, B., & Allport, A. (2005). Interaction of task readiness and automatic retrieval in task switching: Negative priming and competitor priming. *Memory & Cognition*, *33*, 595–610.

Wiecki, T. V., & Frank, M. J. (2013). A computational model of inhibitory control in frontal cortex and basal ganglia. *Psychological Review*, *120*, 329–355.

Zimmer-Hart, C. L., & Rescorla, R. A. (1974). Extinction of Pavlovian conditioned inhibition. *Journal of Comparative and Physiological Psychology*, *86*, 837–845.

20

Mirror Neurons from Associative Learning

Caroline Catmur, Clare Press, and Cecilia Heyes

Associative learning theory has typically been used to explain the behavior of whole animals; to understand why organisms make particular kinds of responses to focal stimuli and contextual cues. In this chapter, we use research on associative learning in a slightly different way, in an attempt to explain the behavior – the firing patterns – of individual neurons, rather than whole animals. The neurons in question are known as "mirror neurons" (MNs), and the behavior that has made MNs famous is their tendency to fire not only when a macaque performs an action, but also when the macaque passively observes a similar action performed by another. Neurons with this capacity to match observed and executed actions were originally found in area F5 of the ventral premotor cortex (PMC; di Pellegrino, Fadiga, Fogassi, Gallese, & Rizzolatti, 1992) and subsequently in the inferior parietal lobule (IPL; Fogassi *et al.*, 2005) of the macaque brain. A substantial body of evidence now suggests that MNs are also present in the human brain (Molenberghs, Cunnington, & Mattingley, 2012).

A variety of functions have been ascribed to MNs. Popular suggestions relate to action understanding (Gallese & Sinigaglia, 2011; Rizzolatti, Fadiga, Gallese, & Fogassi, 1996), imitation (Iacoboni *et al.*, 1999), and language processing (Rizzolatti & Arbib, 1998). A great deal of interest has also been generated in the wider scientific and public media: MNs have been hailed as "cells that read minds" (Blakesee, 2006), "the neurons that shaped civilization" (Ramachandran, 2009), and a "revolution" in understanding social behavior (Iacoboni, 2008).

Whereas much research has focused on theorizing and speculation about MN functions, this chapter's primary focus is the origin of MNs. We ask not "What are MNs for?," but "What is the process that gives MNs their 'mirrorness'; their fascinating capacity to match observed with executed actions?" The standard answer to this question (e.g., Rizzolatti & Craighero, 2004) is evolution. The "adaptation account" assumes that the mirrorness of MNs was produced by natural selection acting on genetic variation. In contrast, we will argue that the balance of evidence supports the "associative account" (Catmur, Press, Cook, Bird, & Heyes, 2014; Cook, Bird, Catmur, Press, & Heyes, 2014; Heyes, 2010); it suggests that the mirrorness of MNs is produced in the course of individual development by sensorimotor associative learning. We will also argue that the associative model has major methodological implications for research investigating the functions of MNs.

The first section outlines key background information regarding MNs in macaques and humans. Next, we present the adaptation and associative accounts. In the following section, we introduce four kinds of evidence that have the potential to favor one of these hypotheses over the other, and discuss each of these types of evidence in turn. Finally, we examine the implications of the associative account for future research investigating the functions of MNs.

MN Background Information

Where are they found, and what qualifies as an MN?

In the macaque, "classical" MN areas include ventral PMC and IPL (see Figure 20.1). However, MNs have also been found in "nonclassical" areas, including primary motor cortex and dorsal PMC (Dushanova & Donoghue, 2010; Tkach, Reimer, & Hatsopoulos, 2007). In humans, there is evidence at both the single-cell and population level of neurons with sensorimotor matching properties. These have been found both in "classical" MN areas, including inferior frontal gyrus (IFG; considered the human homolog of macaque F5) (Kilner, Neal, Weiskopf, Friston, & Frith, 2009) and inferior parietal cortex (Chong, Cunnington, Williams, Kanwisher, & Mattingley, 2008), and in nonclassical areas, including dorsal PMC, superior parietal lobule, and cerebellum (Molenberghs *et al.*, 2012), occipitotemporal cortex (Oosterhof, Tipper, & Downing, 2012), supplementary motor area, and medial temporal lobe (Mukamel, Ekstrom, Kaplan, Iacoboni, & Fried, 2010).

Although some researchers only refer to neurons found in classical areas as MNs (e.g., Molenberghs *et al.*, 2012), many others, like us, use the term "MN" to refer to neurons in both classical and nonclassical areas (Gallese & Sinigaglia, 2011; Keysers & Gazzola, 2010). Functional definitions of what constitutes a MN also vary. In some cases, the term "MN" is used to refer to any neuron that fires during both the execution and observation of action, regardless of whether the executed and observed actions are similar to one another (Gallese, Fadiga, Fogassi, & Rizzolatti, 1996; Rizzolatti & Craighero, 2004). In contrast, and following the majority of researchers in the field, we consider that MNs' "mirrorness" is defined by the fact that they respond to observation and execution of similar actions. However, following common usage, we also refer to "logically related" MNs (see following subsection), which fire during observation and execution of dissimilar actions that have some functional relation, as "MNs."

MN response properties in the macaque

Macaque MNs have been broadly divided into three types (Figure 20.2), based on their field properties, the sensory and motoric conditions in which they fire: "Strictly congruent" MNs discharge during observation and execution of the same action, for example, a "precision" grip made with thumb and index finger. "Broadly congruent" MNs fire during the execution of one action (e.g., precision grip) and during the

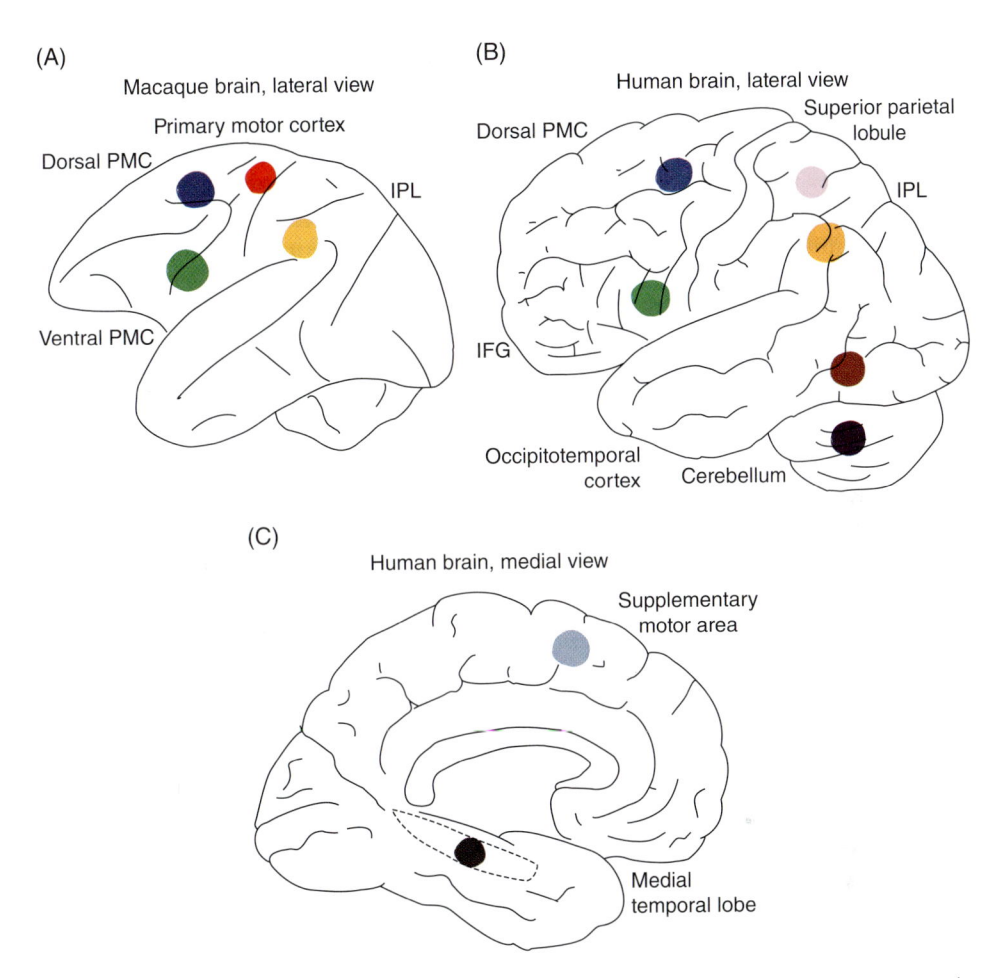

Figure 20.1 MN areas in (A) the macaque and (B, C) the human brain. These are areas in which there is evidence at the single-cell or population level of neurons with sensorimotor matching properties. IFG = inferior frontal gyrus; IPL = inferior parietal lobule; PMC = premotor cortex.

observation of one or more similar, but not identical, actions (e.g., only power grip; or multiple actions e.g. precision grip, power grip, *and* grasping with the mouth). So-called "logically related" MNs (di Pellegrino *et al.*, 1992) respond to different actions in observe and execute conditions. For example, they fire during the observation of an experimenter placing food in front of the monkey, and when the monkey executes a grasp on the food in order to eat it (it is likely that cells with these properties were dubbed "logically related," not because there is a formal relationship between their eliciting conditions, but to acknowledge that, unlike other MNs, they do not match or "mirror" observed and executed actions). MNs do not respond to the presentation of objects alone (di Pellegrino *et al.*, 1992). However, "canonical neurons," which are active during object observation and also during execution of an action that is commonly performed on that object, are located alongside MNs in both

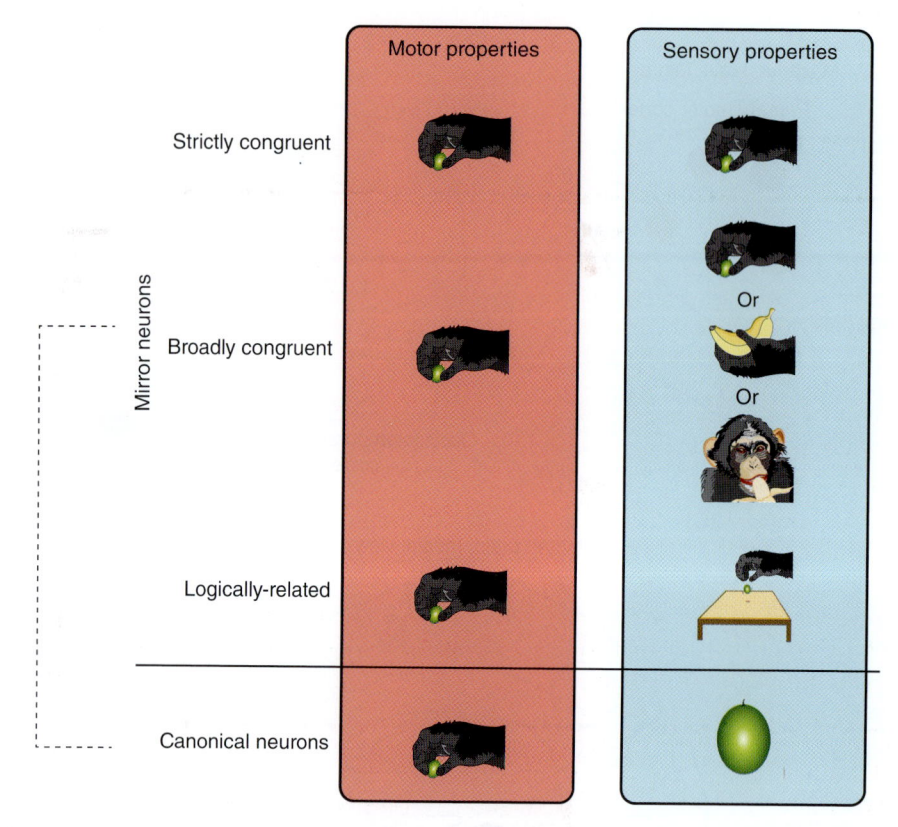

Figure 20.2 Types of MN in the macaque. Typical sensory properties of four different types of sensorimotor neuron are shown; for simplicity, the same motor property (a precision grip) is shown for each MN type.

premotor and parietal areas (Murata *et al.*, 1997; Murata, Gallese, Luppino, Kaseda, & Sakata, 2000).

Macaque MNs fire during execution and observation of a broad range of hand and mouth actions. The hand actions include grasping, placing, manipulating with the fingers, and holding (di Pellegrino *et al.*, 1992). The mouth actions include ingestive behaviors, such as breaking food items, chewing, and sucking; and communicative gestures, such as lip-smacking, lip protrusion, and tongue protrusion (Ferrari, Gallese, Rizzolatti, & Fogassi, 2003).

MNs in humans

Only one study offers single-cell recording evidence of MNs in the human brain (Mukamel *et al.*, 2010). However, a considerable body of evidence from neuroimaging, TMS, and behavioral studies, summarized in the following subsections, suggests that human brains contain Mirror Neurons or comparable "mirror mechanisms" (Glenberg, 2011; referred to throughout this chapter as "MNs").

Functional magnetic resonance imaging (fMRI) has identified regions of PMC and inferior parietal areas that respond during both action observation and execution (Gazzola & Keysers, 2009; Iacoboni et al., 1999; Vogt et al., 2007). More recently, "repetition suppression" effects, whereby the neural response is reduced when events activating the same neuronal population are repeated (Grill-Spector, Henson, & Martin, 2006), provide further evidence for the presence of "mirror" neuronal populations. Action observation followed by execution of the same action, or vice versa, elicits a suppressed response in inferior parietal regions (Chong et al., 2008; Lingnau, Gesierich, & Caramazza, 2009) and in PMC (Kilner et al., 2009; Lingnau et al., 2009), indicating that the same neuronal population is active when observing and executing the same action. Multivariate pattern analysis has also revealed cross-modal action-specific representations consistent with the presence of "mirror" neuronal populations (Oosterhof et al., 2012): A "classifier" program trained to discriminate neural responses to the execution of different actions can subsequently, when tested with neural responses to the observation of those actions, detect which action was observed, suggesting that the same neural representations encode action observation and execution.

"Mirror" patterns of MEPs further suggest a human mirror mechanism (Fadiga, Fogassi, Pavesi, & Rizzolatti, 1995). When TMS is applied to M1 during passive action observation, the amplitude of MEPs recorded from the muscles required to execute that action increases. For example, observing index and little finger movements selectively facilitates the amplitude of MEPs recorded from the muscles responsible for index and little finger movements (Catmur, Mars, Rushworth, & Heyes, 2011). That action observation selectively increases corticospinal excitability to action relevant muscles is suggestive of "mirror" sensorimotor connectivity.

Behaviorally, automatic imitation occurs when observation of an action involuntarily facilitates performance of a topographically similar action and/or interferes with performance of a topographically dissimilar action (Brass, Bekkering, & Prinz, 2001; Stürmer, Aschersleben, & Prinz, 2000). Humans show robust automatic imitation when they observe hand, arm, foot, and mouth movements (Heyes, 2011). This is regarded by many researchers as evidence of a human mirror mechanism (Ferrari, Bonini, & Fogassi, 2009; Iacoboni, 2009; Kilner, Paulignan, & Blakemore, 2003).

MNs' "mirrorness": Adaptation or association?

Here, we outline the standard, adaptation account of the origin of MNs, and the alternative associative account. Both accounts assume that genetic information and experience contribute to the development of MNs. They differ in the roles they assign to genetic evolution and to learning in producing MNs' characteristic matching properties.

The adaptation account suggests that the matching properties of MNs are an adaptation for action understanding and/or related social cognitive abilities (the term "adaptation" is used here to describe a phenotypic characteristic that is genetically inherited, and that was favored by natural selection to fulfill a particular function or "purpose"; Williams, 1966). Specifically, the adaptation account assumes that among common ancestors of macaques and humans, some individuals had a stronger genetic predisposition to develop MNs with matching properties, and that these individuals were more reproductively successful than those with a weaker genetic predisposition because the development of MNs enhanced their capacity to understand others' actions. Consequently, a genetic predisposition to develop MNs became universal, or nearly universal, in macaques and humans. The adaptation account further suggests that motor experience (executing actions) and/or visual experience (observing actions) plays a facilitative or "triggering" (Gottlieb, 1976; Ariew, 2006) role in the development of MNs, but their "mirror," sensory-to-motor matching properties are due to this genetic predisposition.

The adaptation account has largely been set out in discussions of the "evolution" of MNs (Gallese & Goldman, 1998; Rizzolatti & Arbib, 1998; Rizzolatti & Craighero, 2004; Rochat et al., 2010). For example, it was suggested that "the mirror neuron mechanism is a mechanism of great evolutionary importance through which primates understand actions done by their conspecifics" (Rizzolatti & Craighero, 2004, p. 172). A number of discussions have also suggested that MNs are present at birth (Ferrari et al., 2009; Gallese et al., 2009; Lepage & Theoret, 2007; Rizzolatti & Fadiga, 1998), a feature commonly associated with adaptations (Mameli & Bateson, 2006).

In contrast, the associative account suggests that the matching properties of MNs are not a product of a specific genetic predisposition, but instead result from domain-general processes of associative learning (Catmur et al., 2014; Cook et al., 2014; Heyes, 2010). Associative learning is found in a wide range of vertebrate and invertebrate species, indicating that it is an evolutionarily ancient and highly conserved adaptation for tracking predictive relationships between events (Heyes, 2012; Schultz & Dickinson, 2000).

Figure 20.3 represents a theory (Heyes, 2010; Heyes & Ray, 2000) of how MNs might acquire their matching properties through sensorimotor associative learning. Before associative learning, sensory neurons responsive to different high-level visual properties of observed action (Oram & Perrett, 1994, 1996) are weakly connected, directly or indirectly, to motor neurons in parietal cortex (Gallese et al., 2002) and PMC (Rizzolatti et al., 1988). Although some of these connections may be stronger than others, the links between sensory and motor neurons coding similar actions are not consistently stronger than other, nonmatching links. Correlated (i.e., contiguous and contingent) excitation of sensory and motor neurons that code similar actions produces MNs. For example, when an adult imitates an infant's facial movements, there might be correlated excitation of neurons that are responsive to the observation and execution of lip protrusion. Correlated excitation of the sensory and motor neurons increases the strength of the connection between them, so that subsequent excitation of the sensory neuron propagates to the motor neuron. Thereafter, the motor neuron fires, not only during execution of lip protrusion, but also during observation of lip protrusion, via its connection with the sensory neuron; what was originally a motor neuron has become a lip protrusion MN. In humans, there are many possible sources of correlated excitation of sensory and motor neurons encoding the same action. It occurs not only when we are imitated, but also when we observe our own actions – directly or using an optical mirror; when we observe others during synchronous activities – for example, in sports and dance training; and via "acquired equivalence" experience, for example, when the same sound (a word, or a sound produced by an action, e.g. lip-smacking) is paired sometimes with observation of an action and sometimes with its execution (Ray & Heyes, 2011). In all of

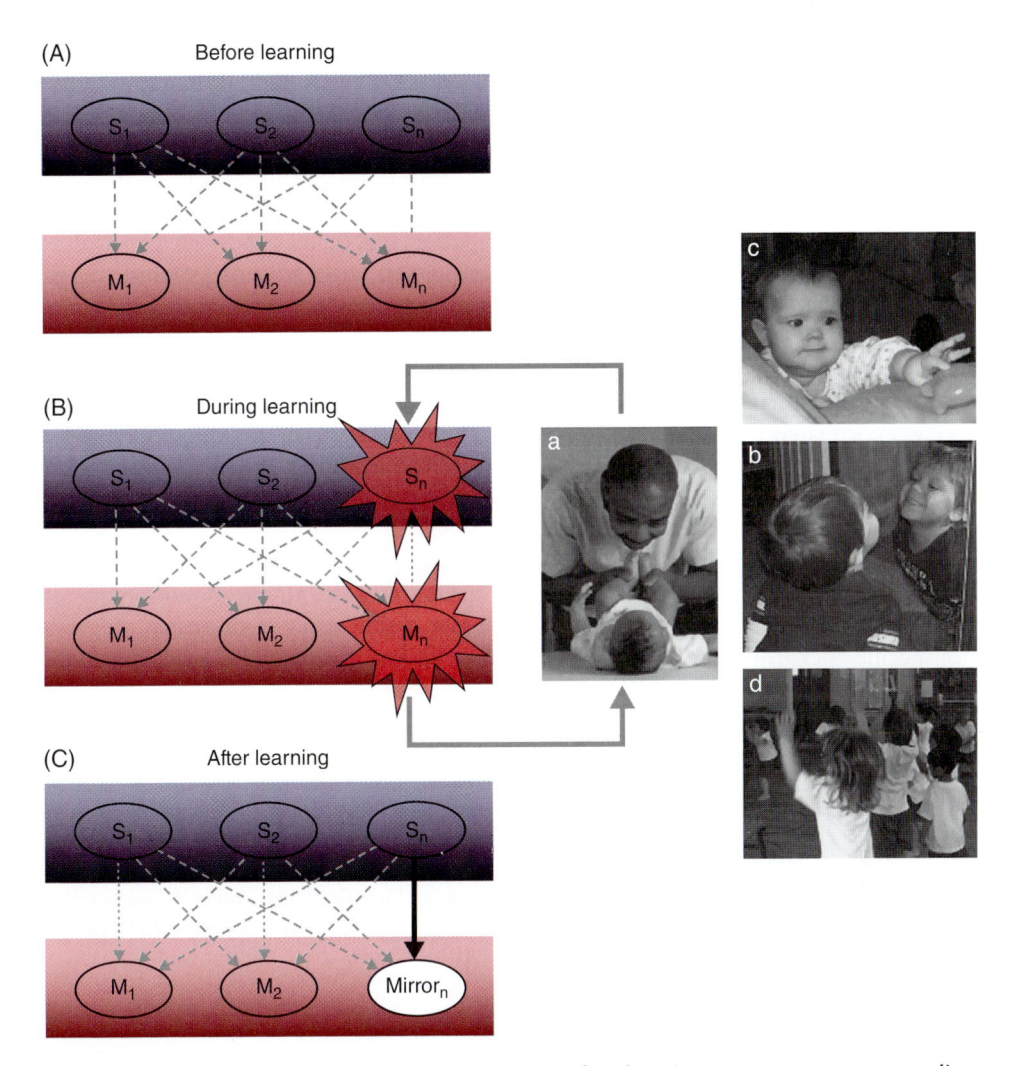

Figure 20.3 MNs from associative learning. (A) Before learning, sensory neurons encoding visual descriptions of observed action are not systematically connected to motor neurons in parietal and premotor areas involved in the production of similar actions. (B, a–d) Through social interaction and self-observation in the course of typical development, agents receive correlated sensorimotor experience; they see and do the same action at about the same time (contiguity), with one event predicting the other (contingency). This experience produces correlated activation of sensory and motor neurons coding similar actions, and, through associative learning, (C) strengthens connections between these neurons. Owing to these connections, neurons that were once involved only in the execution of action will also discharge during observation of a similar action; motor neurons become MNs. Figure reproduced with permission from Heyes (2010).

these situations, motor activity is not initiated by, but it is correlated with, observation of matching actions.

Thus, the associative account identifies sources in everyday life of the kind of correlated sensorimotor experience necessary for MN development, and many of these sources are sociocultural; to a large extent, MNs are built through social interaction.

Another important point to note about the associative account is its emphasis on contingency. Following contemporary associative learning theory, it anticipates that the mature properties of MNs will covary, not only with the number of occasions on which observation of an action has been paired with its execution (contiguity), but also, as a result of context blocking, with the relative predictiveness of observation for execution, or vice versa (contingency; Cook, Press, Dickinson, & Heyes, 2010). Experiments testing the associative account are discussed below.

In summary: The associative account implies that the characteristic, matching properties of MNs result from a genetically evolved process, associative learning, but that this process was not "designed" by genetic evolution specifically to produce matching MNs. It just happens to produce matching MNs when the developing system receives correlated experience of observing and executing similar actions. When the system receives correlated experience of observing objects and executing actions, the same associative process produces canonical neurons. When the system receives correlated experience of observing one action and executing a different action, the same associative process produces logically related MNs.

Thus, the adaptation account says that genetic evolution has played a specific and decisive role, and learning plays a merely facilitative role, in the development of matching MNs. In contrast, the associative account says that evolution has played a nonspecific background role, and that the characteristic matching properties of MNs are forged or "induced" (Gottlieb, 1976) by sensorimotor learning.

Distinguishing the Adaptation and Associative Accounts

Here, we present the four evidence-based arguments that aid in distinguishing between the adaptation and associative accounts. The first argument provides the foundation for the adaptation account. It suggests that examination of the field properties of MNs – and, in particular, their "goal" coding – forces the conclusion that MNs are "designed" (Williams, 1966) for action understanding. In the following subsection, we examine the field properties of MNs and suggest that this argument is not compelling.

The second argument suggests that research using conditioning procedures shows associative learning to be the right kind of learning to produce MNs. Specifically, the ways in which associative learning tracks contingent relationships, and enables contextual modulation of these connections, make it apt to produce MNs (and nonmatching visuomotor neurons) in typical developmental environments.

We then draw on research examining the development of MNs and their modification through sensorimotor experience. First, we discuss research with infants and adults that has been used to support a "poverty of the stimulus" argument (Chomsky, 1975); to suggest that MNs emerge too early in development, after too little sensorimotor experience, to have been forged by associative learning. In contrast, we offer a "wealth of the stimulus" argument.

Finally, we focus on evidence that, even in adulthood, the properties of MNs can be changed in radical ways by relatively brief periods of sensorimotor experience. This evidence supports the associative account in two ways: It confirms novel predictions of the associative account and indicates that the development of MNs is not buffered or protected from perturbation in the way one would expect if MNs were an adaptation for action understanding.

Do MNs encode the "goal" of an action?

Supporters of the adaptation account (e.g., Rizzolatti & Sinigaglia, 2010) argue that examination of the field properties of MNs indicates that they encode "goals." They further argue that this property suggests that MNs evolved to mediate action understanding. We first, therefore, consider how well the neurophysiological data accord with this view. The term "goal" has numerous interpretations (Hickok, 2009). We will consider two commonly adopted definitions, assuming that MNs encode "goals" if they encode (1) object-directed actions or (2) high-level action intentions.

Early descriptions of MN field properties reported that intransitive, that is nonobject-directed, actions (e.g., tongue protrusion) and pantomimed actions (e.g., miming a precision grip without an object) did not elicit MN responses (di Pellegrino et al., 1992; Gallese et al., 1996). In contrast, robust responses were reported when monkeys observed object-directed actions. This pattern raises the possibility that MNs encode "goals" in the sense that they are responsive only to object-directed actions. However, a close reading of the single-cell data suggests that only a small subset of MNs appear to encode action goals in these terms. A subset of the MNs described in the early reports continued to respond, albeit less strongly, to pantomimed or intransitive actions (di Pellegrino et al., 1992; Gallese et al., 1996, figure 5b). Subsequent studies confirmed that sizable proportions, perhaps the majority, of MNs exhibit robust responses to the observation of object-free body movements, such as lip-smacking, lip protrusion, and tongue protrusion (Ferrari et al., 2003). Also, as reported by Kraskov, Dancause, Quallo, Shepherd, and Lemon (2009), 73% of MN responses modulated by observation of object-directed grasping showed similar modulation during observation of pantomimed grasping.

As well as referring to the object of an action, the term "goal" has also been used to refer to what the actor intends to achieve – for example, "grasp in order to eat" (Fogassi et al., 2005) or "taking possession of an object" (Rochat et al., 2010). Rizzolatti and Sinigaglia (2010, p. 269) stated: "only those [neurons] that can encode the goal of the motor behavior of another individual with the greatest degree of generality can be considered to be crucial for action understanding." The suggestion that MNs encode high-level action intentions is consistent with reports that some broadly congruent MNs respond to the observation of multiple actions; for example any "grasping" action executed with the hand or mouth (Gallese et al., 1996). It is also made plausible by reports that MN responses to grasping can be modulated by the final outcome of the motor sequence (Bonini et al., 2010; Fogassi et al., 2005).

However, the single-cell data again suggest that relatively few MNs have the field properties one would expect of a system designed to represent high-level action intentions. For example, Gallese et al. (1996) reported that during action observation, 37.5% of MNs responded differently depending on whether the action was executed with the left or right hand, and 64% showed direction sensitivity, preferring either left-to-right or right-to-left grasping actions. Similarly, many MNs (53%) respond selectively to the observation of actions executed within ("peripersonal" MNs) or beyond ("extrapersonal" MNs), not the actor's, but the observing monkey's reach (Caggiano, Fogassi, Rizzolatti, Thier, & Casile, 2009). The majority (74%) of MNs also exhibit view-dependent responses; some MNs are tuned to egocentric (first-person) presentation, while others respond maximally to allocentric (third-person) perspectives (Caggiano et al., 2011). Each of these classes of MN is sensitive to features of action that fall well below the "greatest degree of generality," and of intentions such as "grasping in order to eat" or "taking possession of an object."

Associative learning: the right kind of learning to generate MN field properties?

The previous subsection suggested that many MNs have field properties incompatible with the hypothesis that they were designed by evolution to mediate action understanding via goal coding. Here, in complementary fashion, we argue that research on the roles of contingency and contextual modulation in associative learning enables the associative account to provide a unified explanation of all MN field properties reported to date.

Associative learning depends not only on contiguity – events occurring close together in space and time – but also on contingency: the degree to which one event reliably predicts the other (Elsner & Hommel, 2004; Rescorla, 1968; Schultz & Dickinson, 2000). The associative account therefore anticipates that MNs will acquire sensorimotor matching properties only when an individual experiences systematic contingencies between sensory events and performed actions (Cooper, Cook, Dickinson, & Heyes, 2013). This feature of associative learning ensures that the matching properties of MNs reflect sensorimotor relationships that occur reliably in the individual's environment, rather than chance co-occurrences. Cook, Press, Dickinson, and Heyes (2010) described evidence that the human mirror mechanism is modified by contingent, but not by noncontingent, sensorimotor experience.

Sensitivity to contingency explains the mix of strictly congruent MNs, sensitive to the low-level features of observed actions (type of grip, effector used, direction of movement, viewpoint, proximity to the observer), and broadly congruent MNs, responsive to multiple related actions irrespective of the manner of their execution. Both visual and motor systems are known to be organized hierarchically (Jeannerod, 1994; Perrett et al., 1989), comprising different populations encoding relatively low-level (e.g., descriptions of particular "precision" or "power" grips) and more abstract representations (e.g., descriptions of "grasping"). Crucially, contingencies can be experienced between both low- and high-level sensory and motor representations. When a monkey observes itself performing a precision grip, the excitations of sensory and motor populations encoding a specific grip (low-level) are correlated. However, during group feeding, a monkey might observe and perform a range of grasping actions, thereby causing correlated excitation of higher-level visual and motoric descriptions of grasping. Contingency sensitivity therefore explains the existence of both strictly congruent MNs, tuned to a particular sensory representation (e.g., a right-to-left precision grip executed with the right hand viewed allocentrically in extrapersonal space), and broadly congruent MNs, responsive to the observation of a number of related actions (see Figure 20.4).

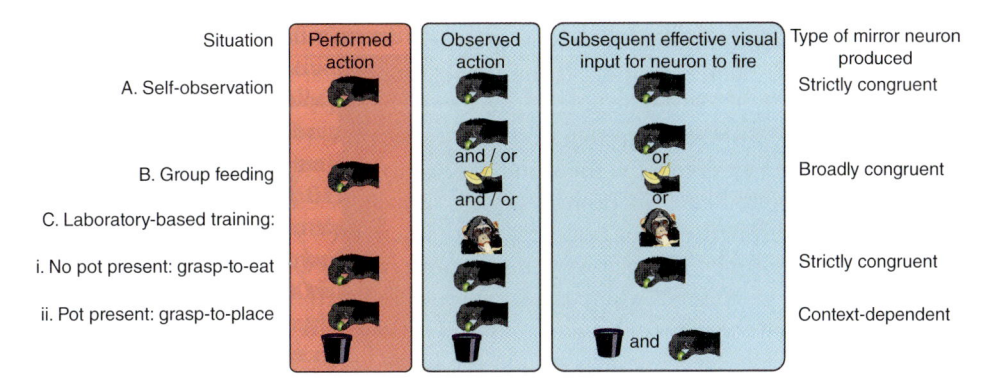

Situation	Performed action	Observed action	Subsequent effective visual input for neuron to fire	Type of mirror neuron produced
A. Self-observation				Strictly congruent
B. Group feeding		and / or	or	Broadly congruent
C. Laboratory-based training:		and / or	or	
i. No pot present: grasp-to-eat				Strictly congruent
ii. Pot present: grasp-to-place			and	Context-dependent

Figure 20.4 Examples of contingencies that would produce (A) strictly congruent, (B) broadly congruent, and (C) context-dependent ("grasp-to-place") MNs. (A) When a monkey watches its own actions while feeding, alone or in a group, the probability of seeing a particular grip (e.g., a precision grip) while performing exactly the same grip is high. (B) When a monkey watches the actions of others during group feeding, the probability of seeing a range of grasping actions while performing a particular (e.g., precision) grip is also high (and, crucially, it is higher than the probability of seeing an unrelated action, e.g. a kick). (C) Before testing for the presence of "grasp-to-place" MNs, monkeys are trained: (i) when a pot is not present, food items should be eaten, but (ii) when a pot is present, food items should be placed in the pot (in return for a higher-value food reward). Self-observation during this training ensures that, in the presence of a pot, the probability of seeing a grasp-to-place action while performing a grasp-to-place action is high. Subsequently, in the presence of a pot, the sight of a grasping action activates grasp-to-place (rather than grasp-to-eat) motor commands.

Contingency sensitivity also explains other MN properties. According to the associative account, MNs acquire sensorimotor properties whenever individuals experience a contingency between "seeing" and "doing." Crucially, there is no requirement that contingencies be between action execution and observation of the same action. Both monkeys and humans frequently experience nonmatching sensorimotor contingencies, where the observation of one action predicts the execution of another; for example, you release, and I grasp (Newman-Norlund, van Schie, van Zuijlen, & Bekkering, 2007). The associative account therefore explains the existence of logically related MNs that respond to different actions in observe and execute conditions. Equally, there is no requirement that contingencies be between action execution and the perception of "natural" action-related stimuli, such as the sight of animate motion or sounds that could have been heard by ancestors of contemporary monkeys. Thus, the associative account explains why "tool-use" MNs (Ferrari, Rozzi, & Fogassi, 2005) develop when action execution (e.g., grasping a food item) is reliably predicted by the sight of actions performed with tools (e.g., seeing food items being gripped with pliers) and why "audiovisual" MNs (Keysers *et al.*, 2003; Kohler *et al.*, 2002) develop when action performance predicts characteristic action sounds (e.g., paper tearing or plastic crumpling; Cook, 2012): There is a high contingency between the sight of the experimenter gripping food with pliers and the subsequent execution of a grasp by the macaque; and between the sound of paper tearing and the execution of the ripping action that produces that sound.

Studies of conditioning that have supported the role of contingency indicate that learned responses acquired under contingency control are often also subject to contextual control; if a stimulus is associated with two responses, each in a different context, then the context determines which association, representing a response–outcome contingency, is cued by the stimulus (Bouton, 1993, 1994; Peck & Bouton, 1990). For example, Peck and Bouton (1990) initially placed rats in a conditioning chamber with a distinctive scent (e.g., coconut) where they learned to expect electric shock following a tone. The rats were then transferred to a second chamber with a different scent (e.g., aniseed) where the same tone predicted the delivery of food. The rats quickly learned the new contingency, and conditioned foraging responses replaced conditioned freezing. However, learning in the second phase was context dependent. When returned to the first chamber, or transferred to a third chamber with a novel scent, the tone once again elicited freezing. The associative account of MN properties draws on the components of associative learning theory that explain this kind of effect.

Using associative learning theory in this way, several findings from the MN literature can be interpreted in terms of contextual modulation of MN firing (Cook, Dickinson, & Heyes, 2012). For example, some MNs show stronger visual responses to object-directed grasping than to pantomimed grasping in object-absent contexts (Gallese et al., 1996), and in some cases, the modulating influence of the object context can be seen even when the target object is occluded prior to contact with the hand (Umilta et al., 2001). Similarly, MN responses during the observation of grasping may be modulated by the type of object being grasped (Caggiano et al., 2012), with some MNs responding strongly in the presence of high-value objects (food, non-food objects predictive of reward), and some in the presence of low-value objects (nonfood objects not associated with reward). In the clearest example, the same motor act, grasping with a precision grip, elicits different MN responses dependent on whether the action is observed in the presence ("grasp to place") or absence ("grasp to eat") of a plastic cup (Bonini et al., 2010; Fogassi et al., 2005). Rather than the plastic cup providing a cue to the actor's intention, it may act as a cue modulating the operation of two associations. In the same way that the sound of the tone elicited different behaviors when presented in the coconut and aniseed contexts (Peck & Bouton, 1990), observing a precision grip may excite different MNs in the cup-present and cup-absent contexts (see Figure 20.4). Thus, while many of the field properties described above are frequently cited as evidence of goal (intention) coding by MNs, they are equally consistent with contextual modulation within an associative framework.

Sufficient opportunity for learning before MNs emerge?

MNs have not been measured directly in neonates. However, other research involving infants has been used to support a "poverty of the stimulus" (Chomsky, 1975) argument suggesting that MNs emerge too early in development, after too little sensorimotor experience, to have been forged by associative learning. Specifically, it has been claimed that imitation is mediated by MNs, and that both human and macaque infants are able to imitate when they have had minimal opportunity for sensorimotor learning. However, the evidence supporting the second claim is not compelling. Building on previous analyses (e.g., Anisfeld, 1996), a recent review found evidence that human neonates "copy" only one action – tongue protrusion – and that, since tongue protrusion occurs in response to a range of arousing stimuli, this "copying" does not show the specificity that is characteristic of imitation or of MNs (Ray & Heyes, 2011).

Turning to macaque infants, Ferrari et al. (2006) reported immediate imitation of tongue protrusion and lip-smacking in 3-day-old macaques. However, the effects were not present on days 1, 7, and 14 postpartum, and it is not clear whether they were replicated in a subsequent study (Paukner, Ferrari, & Suomi, 2011). The later study did report imitation of lip-smacking in macaques less than 1 week old, but this effect seems to have been due to a low frequency of lip-smacking in the control condition, rather than to an elevated frequency of lip-smacking when the infants were observing lip-smacking. Therefore, in common with the data from human infants, studies of imitation in newborn macaques do not currently support the conclusion that infants can imitate before they have had the opportunity for relevant sensorimotor learning.

A related argument has suggested that the associative account must be wrong because suppression of electroencephalographic (EEG) activity in the alpha frequency range (~6–13 Hz) during action observation (and execution) reflects the operation of MNs; and that both human and macaque infants show alpha suppression when they have had minimal opportunity for sensorimotor learning. In this case, both of the claims are weak. Alpha suppression is found over central cortical regions when observing and executing actions, but it may not reflect the activity of MNs. First, the functional significance of lower band EEG activity is poorly understood, even in adults, and is yet more difficult to interpret in infants where, for example, less information is available about the source (Marshall & Meltzoff, 2011). Alpha suppression in other locations is interpreted differently (e.g., as evidence of increased visual processing), and the only neonatal action observation study (Ferrari et al., 2012) has insufficient spatial resolution to provide source information. Second, adult studies have traced the likely source of alpha suppression during action execution to the somatosensory cortex (Hari & Salmelin, 1997), suggesting that alpha suppression during action observation may not index motor processing (and thus MNs) at all (Coll, Bird, Catmur, & Press, 2015). Third, even if alpha suppression does index motor processing, it does not show that the motor activation matches or mirrors the observed actions (Marshall & Meltzoff, 2011). Thus, alpha suppression during observation of lip-smacking, which has been reported in neonatal monkeys (Ferrari et al., 2012), may reflect a generalized readiness to act, or motor activation of tongue protrusion or hand movement, rather than motor activation of lip-smacking. Furthermore, it has not been shown that alpha suppression occurs when infants have had insufficient correlated sensorimotor experience to build MNs through associative learning. Indeed, studies of human infants suggest an age-related trend consistent with the associative account: For example, Nyström (2008) found no evidence of alpha suppression when 6-month-old infants observed actions, but effects have been obtained at 9 and 14 months (Marshall, Young, & Meltzoff, 2011; Southgate, Johnson, El Karoui, & Csibra, 2010).

It is important to note that although MN activity in newborns would be inconsistent with the associative model, the associative account is predicated on a "wealth of the stimulus" argument, and therefore anticipates MN activity in young infants following sufficient correlated sensorimotor experience (Ray & Heyes, 2011). This "wealth argument" points out that typical human developmental environments contain multiple sources of the kind of correlated sensorimotor experience necessary to build MNs; that each of these sources is rich; and that the mechanisms of associative learning can make swift and efficient use of these sources. The range of sources available to young human infants includes self-observation, being imitated by adults, being rewarded by adults for imitation, and acquired equivalence experience in which, for example, the infant hears the same tapping sound when she hits an object herself and when she sees the object hit by another person. A common misconception about associative learning is that it always occurs slowly. On the contrary, when contingency is high, infants can learn action–effect associations in just a few trials (Paulus, Hunnius, van Elk, & Bekkering, 2012; Verschoor, Weidema, Biro, & Hommel, 2010) and human adults demonstrate rapid learning even with complex contingencies (e.g., Baker, Vallée-Tourangeau, & Murphy, 2000).

Influence of sensorimotor learning

The associative account has been explicitly tested in experiments examining the effects of laboratory-based sensorimotor training on MNs in human adults. Building on the results of more naturalistic studies (Calvo-Merino, Glaser, Grezes, Passingham, & Haggard, 2005; Calvo-Merino, Grezes, Glaser, Passingham, & Haggard, 2006; Ferrari *et al.*, 2005; Vogt *et al.*, 2007), these experiments have isolated the effects of sensorimotor experience from those of purely visual and purely motor experience. Using all the measures of MN activity commonly applied to humans (imitation, motor evoked potentials, and fMRI measures including repetition suppression), they have shown that relatively brief periods of sensorimotor experience can enhance (Press, Gillmeister, & Heyes, 2007), abolish (Cook *et al.*, 2010, 2012; Gillmeister, Catmur, Liepelt, Brass, & Heyes, 2008; Heyes, Bird, Johnson, & Haggard, 2005; Wiggett, Hudson, Tipper, & Downing, 2011), reverse (Catmur *et al.*, 2008, 2011; Catmur, Walsh, & Heyes, 2007; Cavallo, Heyes, Becchio, Bird, & Catmur, 2014), and induce (Landmann, Landi, Grafton, & Della-Maggiore, 2011; Petroni, Baguear, & Della-Maggiore, 2010; Press *et al.*, 2012) MN activity (details below). These findings reveal the kind of flexibility one would expect if MNs are forged by sensorimotor associative learning. In contrast, this kind of flexibility is hard to reconcile with the adaptation account. If MNs were a genetic adaptation, one would expect their development to be protected or "buffered" against environmental perturbations that were occurring when MNs evolved and that could interfere with their adaptive function (Cosmides & Tooby, 1994; Pinker, 1997). Thus, if MNs are indeed an adaptation for "action understanding," their development should be buffered to prevent them from coding stimulus–response and response–outcome relationships that could interfere with that function. For example, MNs should be prevented from coding inanimate, rather than action, stimuli; and from coding dissimilar, rather than similar, observed and executed actions.

Evidence that MNs are not resistant to coding inanimate stimuli comes from studies showing that arbitrary sound, color and shape stimuli can induce mirror motor evoked potentials (D'Ausilio, Altenmüller, Olivetti Belardinelli, & Lotze, 2006; Petroni *et al.*, 2010), fMRI responses (Landmann *et al.*, 2011; Press *et al.*, 2012), and behavioral effects (Press *et al.*, 2007) following sensorimotor training. For example, Press and colleagues (2007) gave participants approximately 50 min of sensorimotor training in which they repeatedly opened their hand when seeing a robotic pincer open, and closed their hand when seeing the robotic pincer close. Prior to this training, the pincer movement elicited less automatic imitation than human hand movement, but 24 hr after training, the automatic imitation effect was as strong for the pincer movement as for the human hand.

Evidence that MNs are not resistant to coding dissimilar actions comes from studies showing that nonmatching (or "counter-mirror") sensorimotor training abolishes automatic imitation (Cook *et al.*, 2010, 2012; Gillmeister *et al.*, 2008; Heyes *et al.*, 2005; Wiggett *et al.*, 2011) and reverses both fMRI (Catmur *et al.*, 2008) and MEP mirror responses (Catmur *et al.*, 2007). For example, Catmur and colleagues (2007) gave participants approximately 90 min of nonmatching sensorimotor training in which they repeatedly made an index-finger movement while observing a little-finger movement, and vice versa. Before this training, they showed mirror MEP responses. That is, observation of index-finger movement elicited more activity in an index-finger muscle than observation of little-finger movement, and vice versa for the little-finger muscle. After training, this pattern was reversed. For example, observation of index-finger movement elicited more activity in the little-finger muscle than observation of little-finger movement. Similarly, following sensorimotor training in which observation of hand actions was paired with execution of foot actions and vice versa, fMRI responses to action observation were reversed: Premotor and parietal areas normally more responsive to the sight of hand actions now showed stronger responses to observation of foot actions (Catmur *et al.*, 2008).

Thus, a substantial body of evidence from studies of training and expertise has confirmed the predictions of the associative account, showing that mirror responses can be changed in radical ways by sensorimotor learning. In particular, these studies suggest that MNs are not buffered or protected against sensorimotor experience of a kind that makes them code inanimate stimuli and dissimilar actions.

Investigating the contribution of MNs to social behavior

The associative account suggests that MNs do not have a specific biological purpose or "adaptive function," distinct from that of other neurons with visuomotor properties. However, the associative account leaves open the possibility that MNs are recruited in the course of development to contribute to one or more "psychological functions." They could be useful – possibly they could contribute to a variety of social functions – without having been designed by evolution for a particular use. Thus, the associative account is functionally permissive; however, it implies that a radically new approach is required to find out what, if anything, MNs contribute to social behavior.

Theories relating to MN function have mainly been inspired by "reflection" on the field properties of MNs found in a sample of laboratory monkeys with unreported (and usually unknown) developmental histories. This method asks what neurons with these field properties might enable the animal to do. For example, early reports that MNs discharged when monkeys saw and produced object-directed actions inspired the theory that MNs mediate action understanding via "motor resonance." Even now, opposition to the idea that MNs mediate action understanding tends to be answered by focusing on the conditions in which they fire (Gallese *et al.*, 2011). The associative account suggests that the "reflection" method needs to be changed and extended by embedding MN research in system-level theories of social behavior, by considering individuals' developmental history, and by carrying out experimental investigation of MN function.

If MNs were an adaptation, one could argue that new categories of psychological functioning – such as "action understanding" and "motor resonance" – are necessary to characterize what they do. In contrast, by showing that established psychological theory – associative learning theory – can cast light on the origin of MNs, the associative account underlines the value of embedding research on MN function within system-level psychological and computational theories of how the brain produces behavior. This implies that hypotheses about MN function should specify a part in a process – a process that goes all the way from peripheral sensory input to overt motor output – that MNs are thought to fulfill. The name assigned to this part is not important in itself. What is important is that the hypothetical function of MNs is distinguished clearly from other components of the same overall process. For example, in this kind of system-level, theory-guided approach, "action understanding" would be distinguished from components that are more purely perceptual (which might be called "action perception" or "action recognition") or more purely motoric (e.g., "action execution"), or constitute a higher level of "understanding" (e.g., mentalizing). This approach would also make it clear whether the hypothetical function is thought to be optional or obligatory; whether it can be, or must be, done by MNs. The kind of system-level theoretical approach required in research on the functions of MNs is exemplified by studies of their role in speech perception (Lotto, Hickok, & Holt, 2009; Scott, McGettigan, & Eisner, 2009).

Regarding MN development, if MNs were an adaptation, it is likely that their properties would be relatively invariant across developmental environments. Therefore, it would be possible to make valid inferences about species-typical properties of MNs based on a relatively small and developmentally atypical sample of individuals. If MNs are instead a product of associative learning, this kind of inference is not valid. Whether or not an individual has MNs, which actions are encoded by their MNs, and at what level of abstraction, will all depend on the types of sensorimotor experience received by the individual in the course of their development. Therefore, the associative account implies that it is crucial for studies of laboratory monkeys to report, and ideally to control, the animals' developmental history; the kinds of sensorimotor experience to which they have been exposed. A corollary of this is that we cannot assume that the mirror mechanisms found in the members of one human culture are representative of the whole human species. With its emphasis on the role of social practices in driving the development of MNs, the associative account provides specific, theory-driven motivation for cross-cultural studies of mirroring.

In terms of function, a system-level theoretical approach would overcome a problem that has haunted discussions of the action understanding hypothesis since MNs were discovered: Is this hypothesis claiming that MN activity causes or constitutes action understanding? The former is an empirically testable hypothesis suggesting that there is a distinctive behavioral competence, called action understanding, to which the activity of MNs contributes. The latter implies that the firing of MNs during action observation is, in itself, a form of action understanding; it does not need to have further consequences in order to qualify as action understanding. This claim is not subject to empirical evaluation; it is true, or otherwise, by virtue of the meanings of words.

Empirical (rather than constitutive) claims about the function of MNs need to be tested by experiments looking for, at a minimum, covariation between MN activity and behavioral competence, and, ideally, testing for effects on behavioral competence of interventions that change MN activity. At present, this research faces two major challenges. First, because the hypothetical functions of MNs typically are not defined in the context of a system-level theory, it is difficult to design appropriate control tasks. For example, if an experiment is testing the hypothesis that MNs play a causal role in action understanding, should it control for the possibility that they instead play some role in action perception? If so, what kind of behavioral competence is indicative of action perception rather than action understanding? To date, only a small number of studies (e.g., Pobric & Hamilton, 2006) have made a serious attempt to tackle this problem. The second challenge is that, with rare exceptions (Mukamel et al., 2010), MN activity cannot be localized precisely within the human brain. Consequently, many studies assume that activity in the ventral PMC and IPL – areas homologous to those in which MNs have been found in macaques – is MN activity, and that behavioral changes brought about through interference with the functioning of these areas are due to interference with MNs. This is unsatisfactory because, in macaques, it is likely that fewer than 20% of the neurons in these classical mirror areas are actually MNs, and because there is evidence of MNs in nonclassical areas in both macaques and humans (see first section). Techniques such as fMRI repetition suppression, multivariate pattern analysis, and TMS adaptation (Cattaneo et al., 2011; Silvanto, Muggleton, Cowey, & Walsh, 2007) hold some promise as means of overcoming the localization problem with human participants, by isolating behavioral effects to specific populations of neurons. Guided by system-level theory, future studies could use these techniques with a range of tasks to isolate the processes in which MNs are involved.

Alongside such future studies with human participants, animal studies could be conducted, not only to document the field properties of MNs, but to examine how those properties relate to behavioral competence. For example, are animals with MNs for actions X and Y better than other animals of the same species at behavioral discrimination of X and Y, or at imitating X and Y? Studies of this kind have been dismissed as impractical on the assumption that they would have to involve monkeys, and that between-group variation in MN activity would have to be induced via lesions or disruptive TMS. However, the associative account suggests that between-group variation in the number and type of MNs could be induced using sensorimotor training, either in monkeys or by establishing a rodent model. If the associative account is correct, rodents, birds, and other animals are likely to have the potential to develop MNs because they are capable of associative learning. Whether or not they receive in the course of typical development the sensorimotor experience necessary to realize this potential, relevant sensorimotor training could be provided in the laboratory.

Conclusion

The associative account of the origin of MN properties paves the way for an alternative approach to MN research. It acknowledges that MNs were a fascinating discovery and is open to the possibility that they play one or more important roles in social interaction. It differs from the adaptation account in suggesting that sensorimotor learning plays a crucial, inductive role in the development of MNs, and, because of this, we will obtain reliable information about the function of MNs only by applying an approach based on system-level theory, developmental history, and experimentation. These methodological implications underline the fact that, relative to the adaptation account, the associative account shifts the balance of explanatory power from MNs themselves to the environments in which they develop. In some ways, this is inconvenient because developmental environments are much harder to study in the laboratory, but there are significant potential payoffs. As a rich source of testable predictions about when, where, and how MNs develop, associative learning theory can provide clear guidance for future research on the taxonomic distribution, typical properties, and functional roles of MNs.

Acknowledgments

CC is supported by the ESRC (ES/K00140X/1). We are also very grateful to Richard Cook and Geoff Bird with whom we developed the associative account of MNs.

References

Anisfeld, M. (1996). Only tongue protrusion modeling is matched by neonates. *Developmental Review*, *16*, 149–161.
Ariew, A. (2006). Innateness. In M. Matthen & C. Stevens (Eds.), *Handbook of the philosophy of science* (Vol. 3, pp. 567–584). Oxford, UK: Elsevier.
Baker, A. G., Vallée-Tourangeau, F., & Murphy, R. A. (2000). Asymptotic judgment of cause in a relative validity paradigm. *Memory & Cognition*, *28*, 466–479.
Blakesee, S. (2006). Cells that read minds. *The New York Times, January 10*.
Bonini, L., Rozzi, S., Serventi, F. U., Simone, L., Ferrari, P. F., & Fogassi, L. (2010). Ventral premotor and inferior parietal cortices make distinct contribution to action organization and intention understanding. *Cerebral Cortex*, *20*, 1372–1385.
Bouton, M. E. (1993). Context, time, and memory retrieval in the interference paradigms of Pavlovian learning. *Psychological Bulletin*, *114*, 80–99.
Bouton, M. E. (1994). Context, ambiguity, and classical-conditioning. *Current Directions in Psychological Science*, *3*, 49–53.
Brass, M., Bekkering, H., & Prinz, W. (2001). Movement observation affects movement execution in a simple response task. *Acta Psychologica*, *106*, 3–22.
Caggiano, V., Fogassi, L., Rizzolatti, G., Casile, A., Giese, M. A., & Thier, P. (2012). Mirror neurons encode the subjective value of an observed action. *Proceedings of the National Academy of Sciences of the United States of America*, *109*, 11848–11853.
Caggiano, V., Fogassi, L., Rizzolatti, G., Pomper, J. K., Thier, P., Giese, M. A., & Casile, A. (2011). View-based encoding of actions in mirror neurons of area f5 in macaque premotor cortex. *Current Biology*, *21*, 144–148.
Caggiano, V., Fogassi, L., Rizzolatti, G., Thier, P., & Casile, A. (2009). Mirror neurons differentially encode the peripersonal and extrapersonal space of monkeys. *Science*, *324*, 403–406.

Calvo-Merino, B., Glaser, D. E., Grezes, J., Passingham, R. E., & Haggard, P. (2005). Action observation and acquired motor skills: An fMRI study with expert dancers. *Cerebral Cortex, 15*, 1243–1249.

Calvo-Merino, B., Grezes, J., Glaser, D. E., Passingham, R. E., & Haggard, P. (2006). Seeing or doing? Influence of visual and motor familiarity in action observation. *Current Biology, 16*, 1905–1910.

Catmur, C., Gillmeister, H., Bird, G., Liepelt, R., Brass, M., & Heyes, C. (2008). Through the looking glass: counter-mirror activation following incompatible sensorimotor learning. *European Journal of Neuroscience, 28*, 1208–1215.

Catmur, C., Mars, R. B., Rushworth, M. F., & Heyes, C. (2011). Making mirrors: Premotor cortex stimulation enhances mirror and counter-mirror motor facilitation. *Journal of Cognitive Neuroscience, 23*, 2352–2362.

Catmur, C., Press, C., Cook, R., Bird, G., & Heyes, C. M. (2014) Mirror neurons: tests and testability. *Behavioral and Brain Sciences, 37*, 221–241.

Catmur, C., Walsh, V., & Heyes, C. (2007). Sensorimotor learning configures the human mirror system. *Current Biology, 17*, 1527–1531.

Cattaneo, L., Barchiesi, G., Tabarelli, D., Arfeller, C., Sato, M., & Glenberg, A. M. (2011). One's motor performance predictably modulates the understanding of others' actions through adaptation of premotor visuo-motor neurons. *Social Cognitive and Affective Neuroscience, 6*, 301–310.

Cavallo, A., Heyes, C., Becchio, C., Bird, G., & Catmur, C. (2014). Timecourse of mirror and counter-mirror effects measured with transcranial magnetic stimulation. *Social Cognitive and Affective Neuroscience, 9*, 1082–1088.

Chomsky, N. (1975). *Reflections on language.* New York, NY: Pantheon Books.

Chong, T. T. J., Cunnington, R., Williams, M. A., Kanwisher, N., & Mattingley, J. B. (2008). fMRI adaptation reveals mirror neurons in human inferior parietal cortex. *Current Biology, 18*, 1576–1580.

Coll, M.-P., Bird, G., Catmur, C., & Press, C. (2015). Cross-modal repetition effects in the mu rhythm indicate tactile mirroring during action observation. *Cortex, 63*, 121–131.

Cook, R. (2012). The ontogenetic origins of mirror neurons: evidence from "tool-use" and "audiovisual" mirror neurons. *Biology Letters, 8*, 856–859.

Cook, R., Bird, G., Catmur, C., Press, C., & Heyes, C. M. (2014). Mirror neurons: from origin to function. *Behavioral and Brain Sciences, 37*, 177–192.

Cook, R., Dickinson, A., & Heyes, C. (2012). Contextual modulation of mirror and countermirror sensorimotor associations. *Journal of Experimental Psychology: General, 141*, 774–87.

Cook, R., Press, C., Dickinson, A., & Heyes, C. (2010). Acquisition of automatic imitation is sensitive to sensorimotor contingency. *Journal of Experimental Psychology: Human Perception and Performance, 36*, 840–852.

Cooper, R., Cook, R., Dickinson, A., & Heyes, C. (2013). Associative (not Hebbian) learning and the mirror neuron system. *Neuroscience Letters, 540*, 28–36.

Cosmides, L., & Tooby, J. (1994). Beyond intuition and instinct blindness: toward an evolutionary rigorous cognitive science. *Cognition, 50*, 41–77.

D'Ausilio, A., Altenmüller, E., Olivetti Belardinelli, M., & Lotze, M. (2006). Cross-modal plasticity of the motor cortex while listening to a rehearsed musical piece. *European Journal of Neuroscience, 24*, 955–958.

di Pellegrino, G., Fadiga, L., Fogassi, L., Gallese, V., & Rizzolatti, G. (1992). Understanding motor events: a neurophysiological study. *Experimental Brain Research, 91*, 176–180.

Dushanova, J., & Donoghue, J. (2010). Neurons in primary motor cortex engaged during action observation. *European Journal of Neuroscience, 31*, 386–398.

Elsner, B., & Hommel, B. (2004). Contiguity and contingency in action–effect learning. *Psychological Research, 68,* 138–154.

Fadiga, L., Fogassi, L., Pavesi, G., & Rizzolatti, G. (1995). Motor facilitation during action observation: a magnetic stimulation study. *Journal of Neurophysiology, 73,* 2608–2611.

Ferrari, P. F., Bonini, L., & Fogassi, L. (2009). From monkey mirror neurons to primate behaviours: possible "direct" and "indirect" pathways. *Philosophical Transactions of the Royal Society B: Biological Sciences, 364,* 2311–2323.

Ferrari, P. F., Gallese, V., Rizzolatti, G., & Fogassi, L. (2003). Mirror neurons responding to the observation of ingestive and communicative mouth actions in the monkey ventral premotor cortex. *European Journal of Neuroscience, 17,* 1703–1714.

Ferrari, P. F., Rozzi, S., & Fogassi, L. (2005). Mirror neurons responding to observation of actions made with tools in monkey ventral premotor cortex. *Journal of Cognitive Neuroscience, 17,* 212–226.

Ferrari, P. F., Vanderwert, R. E., Paukner, A., Bower, S., Suomi, S. J., & Fox, N. A. (2012). Distinct EEG amplitude suppression to facial gestures as evidence for a mirror mechanism in newborn monkeys. *Journal of Cognitive Neuroscience, 24,* 1165–1172.

Ferrari, P. F., Visalberghi, E., Paukner, A., Fogassi, L., Ruggiero, A., & Suomi, S. J. (2006). Neonatal imitation in rhesus macaques. *PLoS Biology, 4*(e302).

Fogassi, L., Ferrari, P. F., Gesierich, B., Rozzi, S., Chersi, F., & Rizzolatti, G. (2005). Parietal lobe: from action organization to intention understanding. *Science, 308,* 662–667.

Gallese, V., Fadiga, L., Fogassi, L., & Rizzolatti, G. (1996). Action recognition in the premotor cortex. *Brain, 119,* 593–609.

Gallese, V., Fadiga, L., Fogassi, L., & Rizzolatti, G. (2002). Action representation and the inferior parietal lobule. In W. Prinz & B. Hommel (Eds.), *Common mechanisms in perception and action: attention and performance XIX.* Oxford, UK: Oxford University Press.

Gallese, V., Gernsbacher, M., Hickok, G., Heyes, C., & Iacoboni, M. (2011). Mirror neuron forum. *Perspectives on Psychological Science, 6,* 369–407.

Gallese, V., & Goldman, A. (1998). Mirror neurons and the simulation theory of mind-reading. *Trends in Cognitive Sciences, 2,* 493–501.

Gallese, V., Rochat, M., Cossu, G., & Sinigaglia, C. (2009). Motor cognition and its role in the phylogeny and ontogeny of action understanding. *Developmental Psychology, 45,* 103–113.

Gallese, V., & Sinigaglia, C. (2011). What is so special about embodied simulation? *Trends in Cognitive Sciences, 15,* 512–519.

Gazzola, V., & Keysers, C. (2009). The observation and execution of actions share motor and somatosensory voxels in all tested subjects: single-subject analyses of unsmoothed fMRI data. *Cerebral Cortex, 19,* 1239–1255.

Gillmeister, H., Catmur, C., Liepelt, R., Brass, M., & Heyes, C. (2008). Experience-based priming of body parts: A study of action imitation. *Brain Research, 1217,* 157–170.

Glenberg, A. (2011). Introduction to the Mirror Neuron Forum. *Perspectives on Psychological Science, 8,* 363–368.

Gottlieb, G. (1976). The roles of experience in the development of behavior and the nervous system. In G. Gottlieb (Ed.), *Neural and behavioral plasticity* (pp. 24–54). New York, NY: Academic Press.

Grill-Spector, K., Henson, R., & Martin, A. (2006). Repetition and the brain: neural models of stimulus-specific effects. *Trends in Cognitive Sciences, 10,* 14–23.

Hari, R., & Salmelin, R. (1997). Human cortical oscillations: A view through the skull. *Trends in Neuroscience, 20,* 44–49.

Heyes, C. (2010). Where do mirror neurons come from? *Neuroscience and Biobehavioral Reviews, 34,* 575–583.

Heyes, C. (2011). Automatic imitation. *Psychological Bulletin, 137*, 463–483.

Heyes, C. (2012). Simple minds: A qualified defence of associative learning. *Philosophical Transactions of the Royal Society B: Biological Sciences, 367*, 2695–703.

Heyes, C., Bird, G., Johnson, H., & Haggard, P. (2005). Experience modulates automatic imitation. *Cognitive Brain Research, 22*, 233–240.

Heyes, C. M., & Ray, E. (2000). What is the significance of imitation in animals? *Advances in the Study of Behavior, 29*, 215–245.

Hickok, G. (2009). Eight problems for the mirror neuron theory of action understanding in monkeys and humans. *Journal of Cognitive Neuroscience, 21*, 1229–1243.

Iacoboni, M. (2008). The mirror neuron revolution: Explaining what makes humans social. *Scientific American*, July 1.

Iacoboni, M. (2009). Imitation, empathy, and mirror neurons. *Annual Review of Psychology, 60*, 653–670.

Iacoboni, M., Woods, R. P., Brass, M., Bekkering, H., Mazziotta, J. C., & Rizzolatti, G. (1999). Cortical mechanisms of human imitation. *Science, 286*, 2526–2528.

Jeannerod, M. (1994). The representing brain. Neural correlates of motor intention and imagery. *Behavioral and Brain Sciences, 17*, 187–245.

Keysers, C., & Gazzola, V. (2010). Social neuroscience: mirror neurons recorded in humans. *Current Biology, 20*, R353–R354.

Keysers, C., Kohler, E., Umilta, M. A., Nanetti, L., Fogassi, L., & Gallese, V. (2003). Audiovisual mirror neurons and action recognition. *Experimental Brain Research, 153*, 628–636.

Kilner, J. M., Neal, A., Weiskopf, N., Friston, K. J., & Frith, C. D. (2009). Evidence of mirror neurons in human inferior frontal gyrus. *Journal of Neuroscience, 29*, 10153–10159.

Kilner, J. M., Paulignan, Y., & Blakemore, S. J. (2003). An interference effect of observed biological movement on action. *Current Biology, 13*, 522–525.

Kohler, E., Keysers, C., Umilta, M. A., Fogassi, L., Gallese, V., & Rizzolatti, G. (2002). Hearing sounds, understanding actions: action representation in mirror neurons. *Science, 297*, 846–848.

Kraskov, A., Dancause, N., Quallo, M. M., Shepherd, S., & Lemon, R. N. (2009). Corticospinal neurons in macaque ventral premotor cortex with mirror properties: a potential mechanism for action suppression? *Neuron, 64*, 922–930.

Landmann, C., Landi, S. M., Grafton, S. T., & Della-Maggiore, V. (2011). fMRI supports the sensorimotor theory of motor resonance. *PLoS One, 6*, 1–8.

Lepage, J. F., & Theoret, H. (2007). The mirror neuron system: grasping others' actions from birth? *Developmental Science, 10*, 513–523.

Lingnau, A., Gesierich, B., & Caramazza, A. (2009). Asymmetric fMRI adaptation reveals no evidence for mirror neurons in humans. *Proceedings of the National Academy of Sciences of the United States of America, 106*, 9925–9930.

Lotto, A. J., Hickok, G. S., & Holt, L. L. (2009). Reflections on mirror neurons and speech perception. *Trends in Cognitive Sciences, 13*, 110–114.

Mameli, M., & Bateson, P. (2006). Innateness and the sciences. *Biology and Philosophy, 21*, 155–188.

Marshall, P. J., & Meltzoff, A. N. (2011). Neural mirroring systems: Exploring the EEG mu rhythm in human infancy. *Developmental Cognitive Neuroscience, 1*, 110–123.

Marshall, P. J., Young, T., & Meltzoff, A. N. (2011). Neural correlates of action observation and execution in 14-month-old infants: An event-related EEG desynchronization study. *Developmental Science, 14*, 474–480.

Molenberghs, P., Cunnington, R., & Mattingley, J. B. (2012). Brain regions with mirror properties: a meta-analysis of 125 human fMRI studies. *Neuroscience and Biobehavioral Reviews, 36*, 341–349.

Mukamel, R., Ekstrom, A. D., Kaplan, J., Iacoboni, M., & Fried, I. (2010). Single-neuron responses in humans during execution and observation of actions. *Current Biology, 20,* 750–756.

Murata, A., Fadiga, L., Fogassi, L., Gallese, V., Raos, V., & Rizzolatti, G. (1997). Object representation in the ventral premotor cortex (area F5) of the monkey. *Journal of Neurophysiology, 78,* 2226–2230.

Murata, A., Gallese, V., Luppino, G., Kaseda, M., & Sakata, H. (2000). Selectivity for the shape, size, and orientation of objects for grasping in neurons of monkey parietal area AIP. *Journal of Neurophysiology, 83,* 2580–2601.

Newman-Norlund, R. D., van Schie, H. T., van Zuijlen, A. M. J., & Bekkering, H. (2007). The mirror neuron system is more active during complementary compared with imitative action. *Nature Neuroscience, 10,* 817–818.

Nyström, P. (2008). The infant mirror neuron system studied with high density EEG. *Social Neuroscience, 3,* 334–347.

Oosterhof, N. N., Tipper, S. P., & Downing, P. E. (2012). Viewpoint (in)dependence of action representations: an MVPA study. *Journal of Cognitive Neuroscience, 24,* 975–989.

Oram, M. W., & Perrett, D. I. (1994). Responses of anterior superior temporal polysensory (STPa) neurons to biological motion stimuli. *Journal of Cognitive Neuroscience, 6,* 99–116.

Oram, M. W., & Perrett, D. I. (1996). Integration of form and motion in the anterior superior temporal polysensory area (STPa) of the macaque monkey. *Journal of Neurophysiology, 76,* 109–129.

Paukner, A., Ferrari, P. F., & Suomi, S. J. (2011). Delayed imitation of lipsmacking gestures by infant rhesus macaques (*Macaca mulatta*). *PLoS ONE, 6,* e28848.

Paulus, M., Hunnius, S., van Elk, M., & Bekkering, H. (2012). How learning to shake a rattle affects 8-month-old infants' perception of the rattle's sound: Electrophysiological evidence for action–effect binding in infancy. *Developmental Cognitive Neuroscience, 2,* 90–96.

Peck, C. A., & Bouton, M. E. (1990). Context and performance in aversive-to-appetitive and appetitive-to-aversive transfer. *Learning and Motivation, 21,* 1–31.

Perrett, D. I., Harries, M. H., Bevan, R., Thomas, S., Benson, P. J., Mistlin, A. J., ... Ortega, J. E. (1989). Frameworks of analysis for the neural representation of animate objects and actions. *Journal of Experimental Biology, 146,* 87–113.

Petroni, A., Baguear, F., & Della-Maggiore, V. (2010). Motor resonance may originate from sensorimotor experience. *Journal of Neurophysiology, 104,* 1867–1871.

Pinker, S. (1997). *How the mind works.* London, UK: The Penguin Press.

Pobric, G., & Hamilton, A. F. (2006). Action understanding requires the left inferior frontal cortex. *Current Biology, 16,* 524–529.

Press, C., Catmur, C., Cook, R., Widmann, H., Heyes, C., & Bird, G. (2012). fMRI evidence of "mirror" responses to geometric shapes. *PLoS One, 7,* e51934.

Press, C., Gillmeister, H., & Heyes, C. (2007). Sensorimotor experience enhances automatic imitation of robotic action. *Proceedings of the Royal Society B: Biological Sciences, 274,* 2509–2514.

Ramachandran, V. S. (2009). The neurons that shaped civilization. *TED,* from http://www.ted.com/talks/vs_ramachandran_the_neurons_that_shaped_civilization.html

Ray, E., & Heyes, C. (2011). Imitation in infancy: the wealth of the stimulus. *Developmental Science, 14,* 92–105.

Rescorla, R. A. (1968). Probability of shock in the presence and absence of CS in fear conditioning. *Journal of Comparative and Physiological Psychology, 66,* 1–5.

Rizzolatti, G., & Arbib, M. A. (1998). Language within our grasp. *Trends in Neurosciences, 21,* 188–194.

Rizzolatti, G., Camarda, R., Fogassi, L., Gentilucci, M., Luppino, G., & Matelli, M. (1988). Functional organization of inferior area 6 in the macaque monkey. II. Area F5 and the control of distal movements. *Experimental Brain Research, 71,* 491–507.

Rizzolatti, G., & Craighero, L. (2004). The mirror-neuron system. *Annual Review of Neuroscience, 27,* 169–192.

Rizzolatti, G., & Fadiga, L. (1998). Grasping objects and grasping action meanings: the dual role of monkey rostroventral premotor cortex (area F5). *Novartis Foundation Symposium, 218,* 81–95; discussion 95–103.

Rizzolatti, G., Fadiga, L., Gallese, V., & Fogassi, L. (1996). Premotor cortex and the recognition of motor actions. *Cognitive Brain Research, 3,* 131–141.

Rizzolatti, G., & Sinigaglia, C. (2010). The functional role of the parieto-frontal mirror circuit: interpretations and misinterpretations. *Nature Reviews Neuroscience, 11,* 264–274.

Rochat, M. J., Caruana, F., Jezzini, A., Escola, L., Intskirveli, I., Grammont, F., ... Umiltà, M. A. (2010). Responses of mirror neurons in area F5 to hand and tool grasping observation. *Experimental Brain Research, 204,* 605–616.

Schultz, W., & Dickinson, A. (2000). Neuronal coding of prediction errors. *Annual Review of Neuroscience, 23,* 473–500.

Scott, S. K., McGettigan, C., & Eisner, F. (2009). A little more conversation, a little less action-candidate roles for the motor cortex in speech perception. *Nature Reviews Neuroscience, 10,* 295–302.

Silvanto, J., Muggleton, N. G., Cowey, A., & Walsh, V. (2007). Neural activation state determines behavioral susceptibility to modified theta burst transcranial magnetic stimulation. *European Journal of Neuroscience, 26,* 523–528.

Southgate, V., Johnson, M. H., El Karoui, I., & Csibra, G. (2010). Motor system activation reveals infants' online prediction of others' goals. *Psychological Science, 21,* 355–359.

Stürmer, B., Aschersleben, G., & Prinz, W. (2000). Correspondence effects with manual gestures and postures: a study of imitation. *Journal of Experimental Psychology: Human Perception and Performance, 26,* 1746–1759.

Tkach, D., Reimer, J., & Hatsopoulos, N. G. (2007). Congruent activity during action and action observation in motor cortex. *Journal of Neuroscience, 27,* 13241–13250.

Umilta, M. A., Kohler, E., Gallese, V., Fogassi, L., Fadiga, L., Keysers, C., & Rizzolatti G. (2001). I know what you are doing: A neurophysiological study. *Neuron, 31,* 155–165.

Verschoor, S. A., Weidema, M., Biro, S., & Hommel, B. (2010). Where do action goals come from? Evidence for spontaneous action–effect binding in infants. *Frontiers in Psychology, 1,* 1:6.

Vogt, S., Buccino, G., Wohlschlager, A. M., Canessa, N., Shah, N. J., Zilles, K., ... Fink G. R. (2007). Prefrontal involvement in imitation learning of hand actions: effects of practice and expertise. *Neuroimage, 37,* 1371–1383.

Wiggett, A. J., Hudson, M., Tipper, S. P., & Downing, P. E. (2011). Learning associations between action and perception: effects of incompatible training on body part and spatial priming. *Brain and Cognition, 76,* 87–96.

Williams, G. C. (1966). *Adaptation and natural selection.* Princeton, NJ: Princeton University Press.

21

Associative Approaches to Lexical Development

Kim Plunkett

Associative or What?

An associative approach to lexical acquisition assumes that the principles of associative learning are adequate to account for the representations and processes underlying the mature use of words. Theoretical constructs available to contemporary associative learning theory are powerful and varied. They include processes such as classical and instrumental conditioning, discrimination learning, blocking, extinction, and so forth, and do not shy away from using constructs such as attention, representation, categorization and memory, which will be familiar to modern-day cognitivists (see Dickinson, 1980; Pearce, 2008, for overviews). Nevertheless, it is still commonly assumed by many developmental psycholinguists that associative approaches to language acquisition became obsolete with Chomsky's (1959) critique of Skinner's (1957) *Verbal Behavior*. For example, a common interpretation of associative learning among many developmentalists is that associations can only be formed between stimuli that are present in the organism's immediate environment. Yet associative learning theory can readily account for the formation of associations between a stimulus and a memory representation of another stimulus not present in the current environment (see Holland, 1990; Chapter 4).

Cognitivists might object that admission of theoretical constructs, such as attention and representation, transform associative theory into a cognitive one. Similar arguments have been put forward in criticisms of connectionist modeling of cognitive processes, where some of the elementary processing units might themselves have a symbolic character (Fodor & Pylyshyn, 1988; Lachter & Bever, 1988). The validity of this critique depends much upon the manner in which the constituent theoretical constructs are used. If, for example, standard cognitive machinery is needed to get the associative explanation to work, then clearly the associative account fails. In this chapter, I consider whether cognitive machinery is needed to explain early lexical development by entertaining the possibility that associative mechanisms are sufficient to account for some of the important findings in the field. My strategy is to apply constructs taken from associative learning theory, including those implemented in contemporary connectionist learning models, to erstwhile cognitive explanations of

---

The Wiley Handbook on the Cognitive Neuroscience of Learning, First Edition.
Edited by Robin A. Murphy and Robert C. Honey.
© 2016 John Wiley & Sons, Ltd. Published 2016 by John Wiley & Sons, Ltd.

lexical development. I should acknowledge at the outset that this strategy may fall foul of the criticism of being "merely implementational" (Pinker & Prince, 1988). However, it is offered in the spirit of the connectionist insight that some cognitive explanations may merely be "descriptive conveniences" (Rumelhart & McClelland, 1986), and that the associative approach provides a closer view of the mechanisms at work.

The Problem

A central question in early lexical development is how infants learn to understand the meaning of words. In a typical labeling situation, the caregiver points at an object (*Fido* the dog) and says "Look, this is a dog!" The infant has then to rule out a huge number of possible meanings in order to decipher the intended meaning: Do the words refer to the size, to the shape, to the color, to the individual *Fido* or to the intended meaning: "Dog" is a label that can be used for this dog *and* for all dogs. An influential solution to this conundrum was introduced over 50 years ago: Language learners make use of linguistic constraints in order to narrow the hypothesis space in order to assign meaning to words (Quine, 1960). Three such constraints have proved particularly influential in informing cognitive approaches to lexical development (Markman, 1990, p. 57):

Whole object constraint: toddlers interpret novel terms as labels for objects – not parts, substances, or other properties of objects;
Taxonomic constraint: toddlers consider labels as referring to objects of like kind, rather than to objects that are thematically related;
Mutual exclusivity: toddlers expect each object to have only one label.

These constraints "guide children's initial hypotheses and eliminate numerous hypotheses from consideration and thereby help them solve the inductive problem posed by word-learning" (Markman, 1990, p. 75). A common interpretation of these claims is that infants are already in possession of knowledge underlying the use of these word-learning constraints at the outset of lexical development. This raises the question as to whether such knowledge is learnable and/or whether lexical learning contributes to the establishment of such constraints. Phrased more bluntly, are Markman's word-learning constraints an emergent property of linguistic and cognitive development, or are they innate? I will consider each constraint in turn and attempt to demonstrate that each can emerge from associative learning processes.

Whole Object Constraint

The whole object constraint (WOC) strikes at the heart of the Quinean conundrum, solving it at a stroke by stipulating that toddlers interpret novel labels as names for whole objects. The constraint takes it as given that toddlers can readily identify novel labels in the speech stream and segment objects in the visual scene. These are not trivial capacities and have been the focus of intensive programs of research for decades.

However, I will assume along with Markman (1990) that the infant's perceptual system delivers words and objects as feature packages for further processing. I will also assume that there are situational characteristics, such as joint attention, that facilitate the operation of the constraint. Of course, all of these assumptions require additional explanation to be rendered amenable to an associative account. For the moment, the problem is to account for the WOC whereby a package of linguistic features constituting a novel label is preferentially associated with a package of visual features defining the whole object rather than some subset (or superset) of these features. For the present purposes, I will assume that a whole object is represented as a bundle of features defining shape, coloring, texture, and spatio-temporal location. Likewise, I will assume that novel words are represented as bundles of phonetic or phonological features.[1]

A simple associative implementation of the WOC might exploit an *auto-associator*. An auto-associator (Figure 21.1) consists of a set of units (represented by circles) with incoming and outgoing connections (represented by arrows). Each unit possesses a set of connections to every other unit in the network (represented by small black circles). Activity entering the network along the input lines initiates a buildup of activity in the units that is passed forward along the output lines and to the other units in the network. A reverberating cycle of activation is thereby launched in the network. If the strength of the connections in the network is suitably chosen, the auto-associator will eventually stabilize to a state of equilibrium in the activity of the units. Usually, the pattern of activation achieved by the auto-associator is just the same pattern of activity that was used to initiate the cycle, hence the term auto-association. It may seem strange to build a network that just replicates the pattern of activity to which it is exposed. However, there are a several desirable properties associated with networks of this type:

1. The network can act as a store for many input patterns simultaneously, thereby functioning as a memory system.
2. The network can be trained to reproduce new patterns by adapting the connections using a simple Hebbian learning algorithm.
3. If the auto-associator is presented with a noisy version of one of the patterns in its memory, the final stable state of the network will look more like the original pattern than the noisy input. The auto-associator performs pattern completion (sometimes described as *clean-up*).

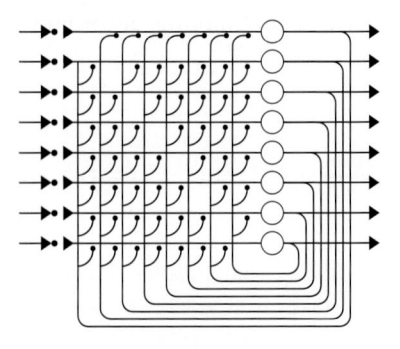

Figure 21.1 An auto-associator.

There is a substantial body of evidence indicating that neural networks in the hippocampus store episodic memories and that their computational/architectural structure resembles that of an auto-associator (e.g., Treves & Rolls, 1994). Of particular relevance to a discussion of the WOC is the auto-associator's capacity to compute correlations (positive or negative) in the activity of different components of the input signal, and adjust the connections appropriately (excitatory or inhibitory). Assume for the moment that input to the auto-associator is a compound audio-visual stimulus such as a visual scene depicting a dog and somebody pointing and saying *dog*. Since each component unit is connected to every other unit, the pattern of correlations encoded in the device can be complex (many-to-one and one-to-many). The WOC can then be construed as encoding a pattern of correlations between a package of linguistic features and a package of visual features in a compound audio-visual stimulus. Spurious correlations (such as whether a dog is moving or standing still, or indeed the breed of the dog, when the word *dog* is uttered) between the activities of the units of auto-associator will eventually be weeded out by the Hebbian learning algorithm with subsequent occurrences of similar events, leaving the essential ingredients of the word–object association in place: If the trained auto-associator is then presented with just auditory input (even noisy auditory input), it will reactivate just that pattern of visual activity with which it correlates, namely the bundle of visual features that were consistently presented with the auditory stimulus. For example, hearing *dog* will activate a visual representation of dogs, and vice versa.

This implementation of the WOC comes at a price: Multiple exposures to a particular object–word pairing are required for identification of the appropriate set of visual features for a given package of linguistic features. The learner cannot know at the outset which visual features (or, for that matter, which linguistic features) are relevant – the original Quinean conundrum. Consequently, initial solutions to the conundrum will have a global or holistic character whereby a broader range of visual features will be associated with the auditory label than is necessary. Furthermore, frequent exposures to identical (or highly similar) auditory-visual pairings will bias the learner to highlight certain features over others, even though they may not be central to the correct association. In fact, there is empirical evidence that early word meanings capture a broader context compared with adult meanings (e.g., Barrett, Harris, & Chasin, 1991; Kuczaj & Barrett, 1986; Meints, Plunkett, Harris, & Dimmock, 2004) and that these meanings are gradually de-contextualized to their core conceptual components. Similarly, highly frequent objectword pairings can be mastered surprisingly early by infants, as early as 6–9 months according to Bergelson and Swingley (2012) and Tincoff and Jusczyk (1999), suggesting that the WOC emerges incrementally rather than all at once.

It might be objected that this solution loses the force of the WOC. After all, on this associative account, the learner may include background context, in addition to the whole object, as part of the meaning of the word until subsequent experience teaches otherwise. A one-shot application of the WOC is not guaranteed in infants or adults. Several exposures, at least, are required to learn the meaning of words from an associative perspective. As much has been shown for toddlers: Horst and Samuelson (2008) have demonstrated the time-dependent and incremental nature of word learning in 24-month-olds. Of course, previous learning may fine-tune the learner's attention to specific features, such as the shape of an object, when a labeling event occurs (Landau, Smith, & Jones, 1988). When processing novel word–object associations, the connections in the auto-associator associated with these specific features may already be strong enough to highlight their role in the association, or equivalently, the learning algorithm may adapt to strengthen such connections more quickly than others (Kruschke, 1992).

Taxonomic Constraint

The taxonomic constraint (TC) assumes that "labels refer to objects of like kind rather than objects that are thematically related" (Markman, 1992, p. 57). An equivalent formulation is that labels refer to objects that belong to the same taxonomic category, where a category can be defined in terms of visual features (visible or hidden) or functional relations (dynamic or abstract). Importantly, labels do not refer to groups of objects that merely co-occur, either by virtue of their presence in the same event (e.g., dog–bone) or because they are mentioned in the same utterance. This does not exclude the possibility that taxonomically related objects occur in the same event or are mentioned in the same utterance, but that such co-occurrence is insufficient.

Markman and Hutchinson (1984) initially introduced a "weak" form of the TC as infants' relative preference for taxonomic over thematic extension of labels. They presented one group of young children (2–3-year-olds) with an object (say, a toy dog) that was labeled with a novel word (e.g., "dax"). The children were subsequently asked to find "another dax" from a pair of stimuli consisting of a taxonomic alternative (e.g., a cat) and a thematic alternative (e.g., a bone). For other children, the object was not labeled. Instead, they were asked to find "another one" from the same pair of stimuli (the taxonomic and the thematic alternatives). Children were more likely to pick the taxonomic alternative (the cat) when asked to find "another dax" than when asked for "another one," suggesting that children take novel words to refer to taxonomic categories and not to groups of objects defined by thematic relations.

In its strong form, the TC assumes that: "when infants embark upon the process of lexical acquisition, they are initially biased to interpret a word applied to an object as referring to that object and to other members of its kind" (Waxman & Markow, 1995, p. 257). In other words, from a single labeling event, the infant infers that every object that belongs to the same category is called by the same name. In this form, the TC equips the infant with a powerful communication tool, since she can now refer to objects she has never seen before, provided they belong to known categories.

At first glance, the TC might seem difficult to implement in an associative mechanism, since it involves one-to-many associations: The label *dog* is used to refer to many different types of dogs. If the target referent is sufficiently different from the initial referent, then *stimulus generalization*[2] (Moore, 1972) will fail. For example, if *dog* is used initially to refer to a German Shepherd, then *dog* may fail to be used appropriately to identify a Chihuahua. A simple way to fix this problem from an associative perspective is to ensure that all objects belonging to the category Dog are labeled *dog*. Of course, this is not a realistic solution, as the child will often encounter dogs she has never seen before and still name them correctly. However, if she is exposed to Dog labeling events across a representative sample of the species, then stimulus generalization can fill in the gaps allowing appropriate usage in the presence of novel exemplars, provided they fit in the space of possible dogs as defined by the child's experience.

Solution 1

An example of an associative vocabulary learner of this kind was proposed by Plunkett, Sinha, Møller, and Strandsby (1992). The learner is an auto-encoder network that has computational properties similar to that of the auto-associator shown in Figure 21.1, in that its task is to reproduce its input at the output. Unlike the auto-associator, which is fully recurrent, the auto-encoder is a structured network with intermediate layers of hidden units between the input and output. The hidden units function as information bottlenecks, forcing the network to encode the input patterns into a more compact, abstract representation that can then be decoded to reproduce the original input at the output.

The auto-encoder network architecture consists of two partially merging subnetworks: a visual subnetwork and a linguistic subnetwork (see Figure 21.2). The visual pathway is presented with random dot images (Posner & Keele, 1968) that are preprocessed by input receptors with Gaussian receptive fields. The second input pathway processes linguistic input corresponding to the names of the random dot patterns. Thirty two categories, each containing eight objects derived from a different random dot prototype, and 32 labels are presented to the auto-encoder network in a three-phase training cycle involving the object alone, the label alone, and the object-label pair, aimed at capturing the attention switching process to the label, the object, and finally the object–label pair. The performance of the network is evaluated by analyzing the network's ability to produce the correct label when only an image is presented (analogous to production) and to produce the correct image when only a label is presented (analogous to comprehension). The model successfully captures the well-known vocabulary spurt, patterns of over- and underextension errors, prototype effects, and the comprehension production asymmetry observed during infant vocabulary development. In particular, this associative learner behaves taxonomically: After

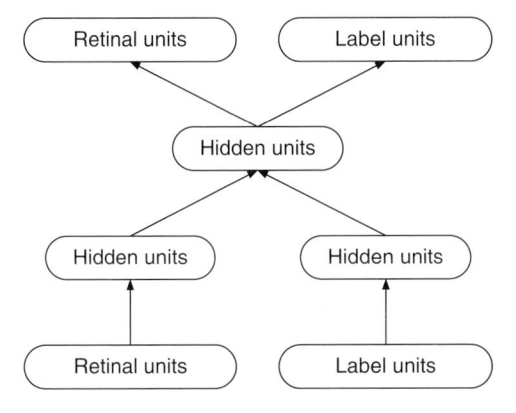

Figure 21.2 Auto-encoder used by Plunkett *et al.* (1992). Reproduced with permission from Taylor & Francis.

training, the network is able to assign the correct label to images that it has never seen before, just so long as those images are taken from the space of random dot patterns that span the category associated with the label. Prototypes of each category are responded to more robustly than peripheral members of the category, though this discrepancy decreases with training. The prototype effect is evident, even though the network has never been trained on the original pattern.

Again, this implementation of TC comes at a price: During the early stages of training, the network only responds appropriately to the range of examples presented in the training set. If the sampling of this space is not representative of the category, the network will underextend the assignment of the label. In fact, there is empirical evidence that infants respond in this way, too. Meints, Plunkett, and Harris (1999) showed that 12-month-old infants only correctly identify typical members of a category (GERMAN SHEPHERDS for *dog*) in a preferential looking task. Atypical members of categories (such as CHIHUAHUAS) are not identified as appropriate referents until around 18 months. Similar findings have been reported for action words (Meints, Plunkett, & Harris, 2008) and location terms (Meints, Plunkett, & Harris, 2002).

On this account, the TC is an emergent property of the associative learner's exposure to a representative sample of object–label pairings. If these pairings sample the full space of the target category, then the learner will be able to interpolate to novel object tokens and hence respond taxonomically. However, this explanation of taxonomic responding falls short of the stronger version of the TC described earlier: From a single labeling event, the infant infers that every object that belongs to the same category is called by the same name. The associative learner described by Plunkett *et al.* (1992) requires exposure to multiple object–label tokens. In order for this kind of one-shot learning and generalization to occur, the learner must have prior knowledge of the category boundaries.

Solution 2

Mayor and Plunkett (2010) addressed this problem by separating the visual and auditory pathways in the network and by using self-organizing maps (SOMs; Kohonen, 1984) to extract category representations from the auditory and object tokens presented in the training set (Figure 21.3). SOMs are associative learners that offer an efficient computational method for forming categories in a complex input space. They extract statistical regularities from the input and form categories of similar objects without explicit supervision. They achieve this result through dimensionality reduction and self-organization around topological maps. SOMs are thereby able to capture the *natural clustering* of objects that share properties with each other. At the end of the process of self-organization, similar objects activate neighboring neurones in the map.

The model consists of two separate SOMs, visual and auditory, that receive visual input and input from acoustic tokens, respectively. Again, it is assumed that infants have already developed the ability to segment objects out of complex visual scenes (e.g., Kellman, Spelke, & Short, 1986) and labels from continuous speech (e.g., Jusczyk & Aslin, 1995) by the time they start forming categories of objects and word types. Through the separate presentation of multiple object and label tokens, both SOMs form categories based on the similarity of the complex set of input patterns.

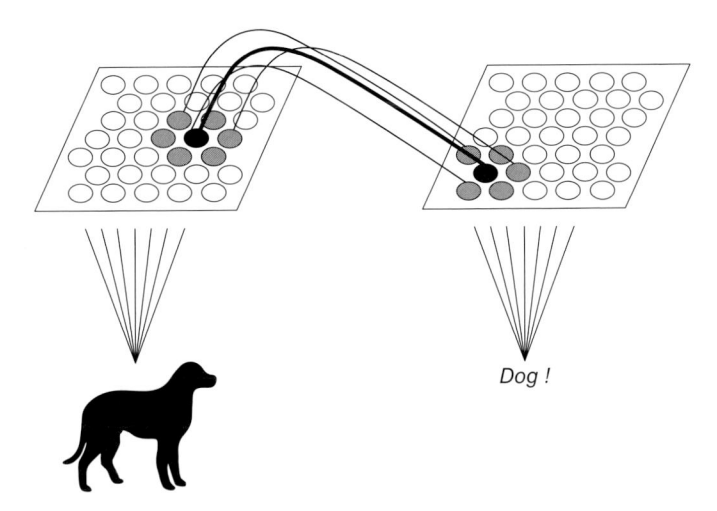

Figure 21.3 Sketch of the network in a joint attentional event. When a dog is presented to the visual map, a coherent activity pattern emerges. Similarly, when an acoustic token of the label *dog* is presented to the auditory map, a selection of neurones will be activated. Synapses connecting the two maps are modulated according to the Hebb rule. The reinforcement of synapses originating from neurones neighboring the maximally active neurone is a key element in generalizing single associations and therefore taxonomic responding.

The organization of the stimuli on the maps mimics the infant's perceptual refinement of her sensory cortices, based on the unsupervised experience of seeing different objects and hearing different speech fragments. By the time infants are able to engage in joint attentional activities with their caregivers (usually toward the end of the first year), their perceptual systems are already well organized. Both the visual and auditory maps have undergone self-organization, so that when a joint attentional event occurs, effective associations between the preestablished categories can be formed.

Joint attentional events, such as the caregiver looking at a dog and saying *dog* at the same time as the infant is paying attention to the dog, are mimicked through the simultaneous presentation of objects and their labels, and constitute the supervised component of word learning that is essential for learning the arbitrary mappings between labels and objects. Synapses connecting active neurones on both maps are reinforced through Hebbian learning (Hebb, 1949) as shown in Figure 21.3 (see also Chapter 3). Owing to the topographical organization of the maps that takes place in early development, many neighboring neurones on each map will be activated by the presentation of an object and its corresponding sound pattern. Crossmodal Hebbian learning will then take place for neighboring neurones on each map. Therefore, the association between the paired object and its corresponding sound pattern will be generalized, automatically building associations between all objects in its category to all sound patterns of the appropriate type. A single labeling event is thereby able to induce a taxonomic response with the label extended to all objects of like type: The novel word is learned.

Within this framework, the TC emerges from architectural constraints built into the network: The topographic organization of the SOM ensures that similar objects (auditory and visual) activate neighboring regions of the map, and Hebbian learning ensures that these regions form homogeneous crossmodal connections. This explanation can thus be regarded as a form of architectural/computational innateness (Elman *et al.*, 1996). The TC is the result of associative learning within specified microcircuitry of the brain (probably somewhere in the infero-temporal cortex) and suggests that no *cognitive* preprogramming is needed to explain this word-learning constraint.

Mutual Exclusivity

New words from old

An efficient strategy available to young word learners is to use their existing vocabulary to help them decipher the meaning of new words. An infant might see two objects, say, a shoe and a key, while knowing only the name for the shoe. Upon hearing the word "key," she might decide that it refers to the key, ruling out the shoe as a potential referent, because she already knows what the shoe is called. This strategy is commonly known as *mutual exclusivity* (ME).[3] Although the inference is not foolproof – objects always have at least two names whether you are monolingual (*Fido/dog/mammal/animal*) or multilingual (*Fido/dog/chien/hund*) – researchers generally agree that young children exploit ME to acquire new words (Halberda, 2003; Markman, 1989; Merriman & Bowman, 1989). Yet, the age when ME is first used, and the nature of the underlying mechanism that drives ME, remains a matter of dispute (cf. Mather & Plunkett, 2010, 2012).

Markman, Wasow, and Hansen (2003) have shown that 15- to 17-month-old infants, upon hearing a novel word, will search for an alternative object if the only object they can see is name-known. On the basis of these findings, they argue that ME is operative at 15 months and may contribute to the spurt in productive vocabulary often observed during the second half of the second year of life (e.g., Benedict, 1979; Goldfield & Reznick, 1992; Mervis & Bertrand, 1994). Similarly, Halberda (2003) has shown that 17-month-olds will look significantly longer at a name-unknown object image than a name-known one upon hearing a novel word. In contrast, Mervis and Bertrand (1994) have argued that the ability to select a name-unknown object in response to a novel word in 16- to 20-month-olds only appears at the onset or after the vocabulary spurt has begun. And Merriman and Bowman (1989) argued that ME is not available to word learners until they are over 2 years, as illustrated by a series of object selection experiments. A review by Merriman, Marazita, and Jarvis (1995) suggested that only toddlers aged over 2.5 years will reliably demonstrate ME.

Differing task demands may be responsible for these reported age differences in the use of ME. The failure of Mervis and Bertrand (1994) to find ME in prevocabulary spurt infants may be due to the processing demands of the task, as infants were presented with several name-known objects. In Markman *et al.* (2003), infants were presented with only a single name-known object. Halberda (2003) used looking time, argued to be a more sensitive measure of processing than the object selection measures used in Merriman and Bowman (1989) and Mervis and Bertrand (1994).

In considering this earlier research, it is important to keep in mind that an ME response to a novel word, that is, preferential attention to the novel object, is not itself evidence that an association has been formed with the name-unknown object. The mechanism underlying ME might guide attention toward the name-unknown object, but only subsequently might this lead to learning. Studies such as Halberda (2003), Markman *et al.* (2003), and Merriman and Bowman (1989) demonstrate the ME response, but do not test for formation or retention of any association. Other studies, for example, Liitschwager and Markman (1994) and Mervis and Bertrand (1994) test comprehension, but their testing procedures are problematic. For example, the test objects might differ in familiarity, or the test might compare a trained word with a novel control word. In either case, confounds created by differences in stimulus novelty could influence responding. To determine whether ME makes a direct contribution to vocabulary development, both a test of ME and a carefully controlled test of comprehension are required. Mather and Plunkett (2011) provided such a test by exposing 16-month-olds to two novel objects, first independently in two ME scenarios, each involving a familiar object, one of the novel objects, and a novel label (Figure 21.4A), and subsequently in a test with only the two novel objects and either of the novel labels (Figure 21.4B). Infants looked systematically longer at the appropriate novel object upon hearing one of the novel labels, indicating that an association had been formed between that object and the novel label during the initial ME scenario. Interestingly, if the novel label sounded similar to an existing word (e.g., "pok' – similar to "clock"), infants failed to demonstrate a systematic looking preference for the appropriate novel object. These results indicate that prevocabulary spurt infants can acquire new word-referent associations through ME and that label novelty is not all or nothing but graded.

In addition to disagreement about the timing of the onset of ME, a second point of dispute is the nature and ontogenesis of the mechanism underlying ME. ME is commonly argued to involve some form of reasoning. Some theorists (Golinkoff, Mervis, & Hirsh-Pasek, 1994; Mervis & Bertrand, 1994) argued that infants use a Novel-Name-Nameless-Category principle that operates specifically on linguistic input and states that "novel terms map to previously unnamed objects." Alternatively, ME could be the outcome of a more general cognitive process not specific to language. Markman's (1989, 1992) ME principle leads infants to reject second names for already-name-known objects, as part of a general preference for one-to-one mapping regularities. More recently, Halberda (2003) proposed that ME is driven by syllogistic reasoning of the form "A or B, not A, therefore B," where A is the name-known object, and B is the name-unknown object.

What all these explanations have in common, aside from supposing an inferential process, is the assumption that the mechanism underlying ME operates on the basis of the lexical status of objects, that is, that they have a name. However, in most experiments on ME, the lexical status of the objects is confounded with their novelty. That is, the name-known object is familiar, whereas the name-unknown object is typically novel (e.g., Halberda, 2003; Mervis & Bertrand, 1994). This leaves open the possibility that infants displaying ME could be responding on the basis of object novelty, rather than lexical status.

In order to evaluate these alternatives, Mather and Plunkett (2012) presented 22-month-olds with a choice of one name-known object and two name-unknown objects,

(A) Training: Look *meb*

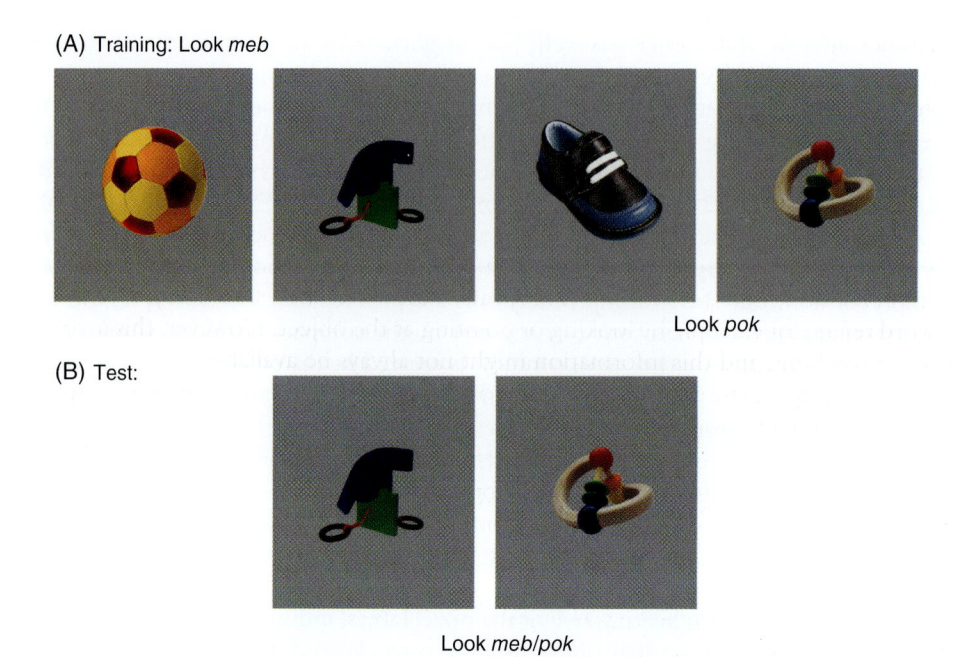

Look *pok*

(B) Test:

Look *meb/pok*

Figure 21.4 Training and test used by Mather and Plunkett (2011) for 16-month-old infants. During training (A), the 16-month-old infants were presented with two ME scenarios, and the novel labels *meb* and *pok* were introduced. At test (B), infants were shown both novel objects and either of the novel labels. Reproduced with permission from Cambridge University Press.

of which one was novel at test, whereas the other was previously familiarized to the infants. Upon hearing a novel label, the infants increased their attention to the novel object, but not the preexposed object, despite the fact that both the novel and preexposed objects were unfamiliar kinds for which the infants did not have names. This finding is compelling evidence that the ME response is sensitive to object novelty, and that nameability alone cannot account for infants' behavior. However, it was not clear that the novel label directly guided attention to the novel object. The novel label may have only prompted infants to reject the nameable object as a referent, with the novel object subsequently favored as an outcome of habituation to the preexposed object. In a follow-up experiment identical to the first, apart from the omission of the nameable object, infants looked longer at the novel object than the preexposed object upon hearing the novel label. This provided confirmation that a novel label can directly guide attention toward a novel object even when the competing object is name-unknown. Mather and Plunkett (2012) concluded that object novelty was both necessary and sufficient for the ME response.

A novelty-based mechanism

Given the contribution of novelty to ME, it is not unreasonable to conjecture that "attention to novelty" might play a role in the development of the response. Attention to the novelty of words and objects could lead to the acquisition of ME: As an infant becomes familiar with the words of her language, an appreciation of the correlation between the familiarity of words and the familiarity of the objects to which they refer might emerge. If a word is familiar, then it probably refers to a familiar object, but if a word is novel to an infant, it will probably refer to a novel object. If infants can detect this correlation, they could learn ME. This learning process would require infants to abstract a general correlation between a property of words and a property of objects, namely their novelty. This is potentially a difficult task, as any given word will be heard in the presence of many objects, so the infant will need to attend to the correct referent. One possibility is that speakers draw attention to the object to which a word refers, for example by looking or pointing at the object. However, this involves explicit teaching, and this information might not always be available.

Alternatively, infants might be able to detect the correlation without explicit teaching. If infants already have some vocabulary, they will attend to familiar objects when hearing familiar words, because they know the referents of the words. Conversely, infants might attend to novel objects in the presence of novel words because they have a general tendency to attend to novelty; thus, in the absence of a comprehended word that directs attention elsewhere, the infant may persist in attending to a novel object. If the infant associates the novel word with the novel object based on their temporal contiguity,[4] this information could be used eventually to abstract an ME principle.

Evidence of behavior similar to the ME response at the earliest stages of vocabulary development provides additional support for a novelty-based mechanism. Mather and Plunkett (2010) presented 10-month-olds with pairs of familiar and novel objects and different labeling phrases. Prior to naming, the infants preferred to look at the novel objects; yet their looking behavior diverged upon hearing different phrases. When the infants heard novel labels, their interest in the novel object was maintained and enhanced; yet when they heard familiar labels or a control phrase (e.g., "look"), they lost interest in the novel object. The authors concluded that as young as 10 months of age, novel labels have a specific role in supporting attention to novel objects. Importantly, a further experiment suggested that the 10-month-olds did not comprehend the names of the familiar objects. Hence, their responses appeared to be guided by novelty, rather than object nameability.

Associative learning is readily applied to ME through the process known as *blocking* (Kamin, 1969). Blocking involves "the disruption in conditioning with one element of a compound when it is accompanied by another element that has already been paired with the unconditioned stimulus" (Pearce, 2008, p.53). Note that infants implicitly name the objects with which they are familiar (Mani & Plunkett, 2010). Hence, the implicit name can block the formation of an associative link between the familiar object and a novel label, whereas no such blocking occurs for novel objects. Blocking itself is readily explained by the Rescorla and Wagner (1972) theory of learning which is itself a theory for measuring an animal's degree of surprise on encountering a stimulus in a given context. Alternatively, *latent inhibition* (Lubow, 1973) could account for the ME response: Latent inhibition is the "reduction in effectiveness of pairing a conditioned stimulus with an unconditioned stimulus, as a result of prior exposure to the conditioned stimulus" (Pearce, 2008, p. 76). In the context of ME, the familiarity of the name-known object reduces the associability of the object as a result of latent inhibition. A basic learning mechanism of this kind could guide the infant toward selectively associating a novel label with a novel object even without the need to retrieve the names of familiar objects to exclude them as potential referents.

There are several implications of these associative accounts of ME. First, familiar words should be better blockers than recently learned words. This prediction follows directly from Rescorla and Wagner's (1972) theory in which the strength of association between a familiar label and familiar object (an index of surprise) attenuates any change in strength of association formed between the novel label and familiar object. Second, any implicit label generated in the ME situation ought to be available, together with the novel label, to form associations with the novel object. There is no direct evidence, for or against, in the infant literature to evaluate these predictions. However, Mather and Plunkett's (2012) finding that the relative familiarity of objects influences the strength of an ME response points to the role of surprise – a well-established associative construct.

Conclusions

A compelling strategy in evaluating associative approaches to language development is to compare the human potential for language acquisition with that of other great apes, in particular bonobos and chimpanzees. It is commonly agreed that our closest relatives are not well prepared for language acquisition. The obvious and probably inescapable conclusion is that humans have some special genetic endowment that supports the construction of specialized microcircuitry in the brain without which language acquisition is difficult, if not impossible. From an associative perspective, this raises a perplexing paradox: Given the powerful associative processes at work in the brains of the great apes (or corvids, or any number of species, for that matter), why should they be inept at language if this capacity is based on associative learning processes? Only two solutions seem valid:

1. Language must rely on processes of acquisition that are nonassociative and lacking in other species.
2. There are associative processes at work in humans that we do not find in other species.

Since virtually the whole of contemporary associative learning theory is based on work with animals, the likelihood of finding an answer based on associative learning skills that are uniquely human seems remote.[5]

The demonstration in this chapter of word-learning constraints entirely reliant on learning processes that are exploited in nonhuman brains leaves us with the perplexing problem as to why nonhuman brains cannot acquire a human-like lexical system. One solution to this problem is that "the ability of associative processes to implement cognition… could arise from the constraints imposed by a particular processing architecture" (Dickinson, 2012, p. 2739). General associative learning processes can then operate within the confines of a dedicated architecture to produce a specialized processing mechanism. A similar solution is offered by Elman *et al.* (1996) in which architectural/computational considerations, rather than innate representations, underlie the acquisition of knowledge. On this account, general associative learning processes implemented in connectionist networks with prespecified architectures construct mental representations for language processing. The uniquely human capacity to construct a lexical system so rapidly in early childhood need appeal not to built-in cognitive constraints but rather the unique configuration of initially innocent neural systems guided in their growth by general learning processes in a highly structured environment. As I suggested at the start of this chapter, cognitivists might object that this type of account of word-learning constraints is merely implementational. If this objection turns out to be correct, then at least we have seen how an associative approach can provide a closer view of the mechanisms at work, rather than just giving them a name.

Notes

1 At the risk of overlaboring the point, these featural representations of objects and words are theoretical entities in search of a mechanism: Further machinery will be needed in order to account for their emergence.
2 "Stimulus generalization: Responding to a test stimulus as a result of training with another stimulus" (Pearce, 2008, p. 37).
3 There is some confusion in the literature in the use of the terms *mutual exclusivity* and *fast mapping*. In this chapter, I use the term *fast mapping* in a neutral manner to indicate that older infants can quickly form an association between a label and an object (or category of objects).
4 This mechanism might also constitute the basis of recent reports of word learning via cross-situational statistics, for example, Smith and Yu (2008).
5 Of course, one might also contemplate the possibility that animal minds are nonassociative, as do many contemporary scholars of comparative cognition (see Heyes, 2012, for further discussion).

References

Barrett, M., Harris, M., & Chasin, J. (1991). Early lexical development and maternal speech: A comparison of children's initial and subsequent uses of words. *Journal of Child Language, 18*, 21–40.
Benedict, H. (1979). Early lexical development: Comprehension and production. *Journal of Child Language, 6*, 183–200.
Bergelson, E., & Swingley, D. (2012). At 6–9 months, human infants know the meanings of many common nouns. *Proceedings of the National Academy of Sciences of the United States of America, 109*, 3253–3258.
Chomsky, N. (1959). Review of Skinner's Verbal Behaviour. *Language, 35*, 26–58.
Dickinson, A. (1980). *Contemporary animal learning theory*. Cambridge, UK: Cambridge University Press.
Dickinson, A. (2012). Associative learning and animal cognition. *Philosophical Transactions of the Royal Society of London B Biological Sciences, 367*, 2733–2742.
Elman, J. L., Bates, E. A., Johnson, M. H., Karmiloff-Smith, A., Parisi, D., & Plunkett, K. (1996). *Rethinking innateness: A connectionist perspective on development*. Cambridge, MA: MIT Press.

Fodor, J., & Pylyshyn, Z. (1988). Connectionism and cognitive architecture: A critical analysis. *Cognition, 28*, 3–71.

Goldfield, B., & Reznick, J. S. (1992). Rapid change in lexical development in comprehension and production. *Developmental Psychology, 28*, 406–413.

Golinkoff, R. M., Mervis, C. B., & Hirsh-Pasek, K. (1994). Early object labels: The case for a developmental lexical principles framework. *Journal of Child Language, 21*, 125–155.

Halberda, J. (2003). The development of a word-learning strategy. *Cognition, 87*, B23–B24.

Hebb, D. (1949). *The organization of behavior: A neuropsychological theory.* New York, NY: John Wiley & Sons.

Heyes, C. (2012). Simple minds: a qualified defence of associative learning. *Philosophical Transactions of the Royal Society B: Biological Sciences, 367*, 2695–2703.

Holland, P. C. (1990). Event representation in Pavlovian conditioning: image and action. *Cognition, 37*, 105–131.

Horst, J. S., & Samuelson, L. K. (2008). Fast mapping but poor retention by 24-month-old infants. *Infancy, 13*, 128–157.

Jusczyk, P., & Aslin, R. N. (1995). Infant's detection of sound patterns of words in fluent speech. *Cognitive Psychology, 29*, 1–23.

Kamin, L. J. (1969). Selective association and conditioning. In N. J. Mackintosh & W. K. Honig (Eds.), *Fundamental issues in associative learning* (pp. 42–64). Halifax, Canada: Dalhousie University Press.

Kellman, P., Spelke, E., & Short, K. (1986). Infant perception of object unity from translatory motion in depth and vertical translation. *Child Development, 57*, 72–86.

Kohonen, T. (1984). *Self-organization and associative memory.* Berlin: Springer.

Kruschke, J. K. (1992). Alcove: An exemplar-based connectionist model of category learning. *Psychological Review, 99*, 22–44.

Kuczaj, S. I., & Barrett, M. (1986). *The development of word meaning: Progress in cognitive development research.* New York, NY: Springer.

Lachter, J., & Bever, T. G. (1988). The relation between linguistic structure and associative theories of language learning–a constructive critique of some connectionist learning models. *Cognition, 28*, 195–247.

Landau, B., Smith, L. B., & Jones, S. (1988). The importance of shape in early lexical learning. *Cognitive Development, 3*, 299–321.

Liitschwager, J. C., & Markman, E. M. (1994). Sixteen- and 24 month-olds' use of mutual exclusivity as a default assumption in second-label learning. *Developmental Psychology, 30*, 955–968.

Lubow, R. E. (1973). Latent inhibition. *Psychological Bulletin, 79*, 398–407.

Mani, N., & Plunkett, K. (2010). In the infant's mind's ear: Evidence for implicit naming in 18-month-olds. *Psychological Science, 21*, 908–913.

Markman, E. M. (1989). *Categorization and naming in children: Problems of induction.* Cambridge, MA: MIT Press.

Markman, E. M. (1990). Constraints children place on word meanings. *Cognitive Science, 14*, 57–77.

Markman, E. M. (1992). Constraints on word learning: speculations about their nature, origins and domain specificity. In M. R. Gunnar & M. P. Maratsos (Eds.), *Modularity and constraints in language and cognition: The Minnesota symposium on child psychology* (pp. 59–101). Hillsdale, NJ: Erlbaum.

Markman, E. M., & Hutchinson, J. (1984). Children's sensitivity to constraints on word meaning: Taxonomic versus thematic relations. *Cognitive Psychology, 16*, 1–27.

Markman, E. M., Wasow, J. L., & Hansen, M. B. (2003). Use of the mutual exclusivity assumption by young word learners. *Cognitive Psychology, 47*, 241–275.

Mather, E., & Plunkett, K. (2010). Novel labels support 10 month-olds' attention to novel objects. *Journal of Experimental Child Psychology, 105*, 232–242.

Mather, E., & Plunkett, K. (2011). Mutual exclusivity and phonological novelty constrain word learning at 16 months. *Journal of Child Language, 38*, 933–950.

Mather, E., & Plunkett, K. (2012). The role of novelty in early word learning. *Cognitive Science, 36*, 1157–1177.

Mayor, J., & Plunkett, K. (2010). A neuro-computational model of taxonomic responding and fast mapping in early word learning. *Psychological Review, 117*, 1–31.

Meints, K., Plunkett, K., & Harris, P. L. (1999). When does an ostrich become a bird: The role of prototypes in early word comprehension. *Developmental Psychology, 35*, 1072–1078.

Meints, K., Plunkett, K., & Harris, P. L. (2002). What is "on" and "under" for 15-, 18- and 24-month-olds? Typicality effects in early comprehension of spatial prepositions. *British Journal of Developmental Psychology, 20*, 113–130.

Meints, K., Plunkett, K., & Harris, P. L. (2008). Eating apples and houseplants: Typicality constraints on thematic roles in early verb learning. *Language and Cognitive Processes, 23*, 434–463.

Meints, K., Plunkett, K., Harris, P. L., & Dimmock, D. (2004). The cow on the high: Effects of background context on early naming. *Cognitive Development, 19*, 275–290.

Merriman, W. E., & Bowman, L. L. (1989). The mutual exclusivity bias in children's word learning. *Monographs of the Society for Research in Child Development, 54*, 1–132.

Merriman, W. E., Marazita, J., & Jarvis, L. (1995). Children's disposition to map new words onto new referents. In M. Tomasello & W. E. Merriman (Eds.), *Beyond names for things: Young children's acquisition of verbs* (pp. 147–183). Hillsdale, NJ: Erlbaum.

Mervis, C. B., & Bertrand, J. (1994). Acquisition of the novel name nameless category (N3C) principle. *Child Development, 65*, 1646–1662.

Moore, J. W. (1972). Stimulus control: studies of auditory generalization in the rabbit. In A. H. Black & W. F. Prokasy (Eds.), *Classical conditioning II: Current research and theory* (pp. 206–320). New York, NY: Appleton-Century-Crofts.

Pearce, J. M. (2008). *Animal learning & cognition* (3rd ed.). Hove, UK: Psychology Press.

Pinker, S., & Prince, A. (1988). On language and connectionism: Analysis of a parallel distributed processing model of language acquisition. *Cognition, 29*, 73–193.

Plunkett, K., Sinha, C., Møller, M. F., & Strandsby, O. (1992). Symbol grounding or the emergence of symbols? Vocabulary growth in children and a connectionist net. *Connection Science, 4*, 293–312.

Posner, M., & Keele, S. (1968). On the genesis of abstract ideas. *Journal of Experimental Psychology, 77*, 353–363.

Quine, W. V. O. (1960). *Word and object*. Cambridge, MA: MIT Press.

Rescorla, R. A., & Wagner, A. R. (1972). A theory of Pavlovian conditioning: Variations in the effectiveness of reinforcement and non-reinforcement. In A. H. Black & W. F. Prokasy (Eds.), *Classical conditioning* (Vol. II, pp. 64–99). New York, NY: Appleton-Century-Crofts.

Rumelhart, D. E., & McClelland, J. L. (1986). On learning the past tense of English verbs. In J. L. McClelland & D. E. Rumelhart (Eds.), *Parallel distributed processing: explorations in the microstructure of cognition*. Cambridge, MA: MIT Press.

Skinner, B. F. (1957). *Verbal behavior*. New York, NY: AppletonCentury-Crofts.

Smith, L., & Yu, C. (2008). Infants rapidly learn word-referent mappings via cross-situational statistics. *Cognition, 106*, 1558–1568.

Tincoff, R., & Jusczyk, P. (1999). Some beginnings of word comprehension in 6-month-olds. *Psychological Science, 10*, 172.

Treves, A., & Rolls, E. (1994). Computational analysis of the role of the hippocampus in memory. *Hippocampus, 4*, 374–391.

Waxman, S., & Markow, D. B. (1995). Words as invitations to form categories: Evidence from 12 to 13-month-old infants. *Cognitive Psychology, 29*, 257–302.

22

Neuroscience of Value-Guided Choice

Gerhard Jocham, Erie Boorman, and Tim Behrens

Introduction

When studying the neural mechanisms of choice, one of the first obvious questions that comes to mind is *why* one should make a decision at all. Decisions can be quite effortful, so there needs to be some value in making a choice. In other words, different courses of action ought to have different values; otherwise choosing one over the other would have no obvious advantage. Accordingly, frameworks of decision-making often start off by assuming that we need to have some representation of the available set of options, assign value to them, and then choose between them on the basis of these values. Finally, after observing the outcome of our choice, we can use this result to update our estimate of this option's value: We can learn from the outcome (Rangel, Camerer, & Montague, 2008). In the following chapter, we will first describe some of the various representations of value that have been found in the brain. It will become evident that value correlates are very widespread in the brain; however, as we discuss, not all of them bear a direct relationship to choice. Next, we will discuss which value representations might constitute signatures of a decision process, and what such a decision mechanism might look like. We will then highlight that different brain regions come to the fore depending on a number of factors. Particular attention will be given to different frames of reference, such as deciding between stimuli as opposed to deciding between motor actions. Finally, in a second section, we will consider behavioral adaptation from a currently preferred default position and strategic decision-making.

Ubiquity of Value Representations

From functional magnetic resonance imaging (fMRI) and single-unit recording studies in animals, we know today that representations of value can be found in many regions throughout the brain. They have been found in frontal and parietal association cortices, the basal ganglia, but even in early sensory and motor cortical areas. However, finding a value correlate in one brain region does not necessarily imply that this area is also involved in choice. It is important to consider exactly what kind of value representation is found. A correlation with the *overall value* of available options is not of much use for deciding between options, but can rather serve motivational and/or attentional purposes. *Action value* representations, a correlation with the value of specific motor actions, are more likely an input to a decision process, or alternatively may reflect motor preparation. By contrast, a correlation with the value of the chosen option, a *chosen value* signal, is more intimately linked to choice. If neural activity correlates with the value of a selected option, independent of whether the subject chose left or right, and independent of the trial's overall value, this provides a hint that neural activity in this area relates to a choice between options, rather than between preparing a particular motor command. We will come back to these issues in the next section.

Of the areas studied so far, the frontal lobe, in particular the orbitofrontal cortex (OFC), arguably is the part of the brain that first attracted scientific interest. It has been known for decades that primates with lesions to the OFC are severely compromised at adjusting their behavior when the value of options is suddenly changed. Behavioral flexibility is often probed using reversal learning, reinforcer devaluation, or extinction (Chapter 16). In reversal learning, stimulus–outcome contingencies are suddenly changed, such that a rewarded option becomes incorrect, and a previously nonrewarded option becomes the correct option. Reinforcer devaluation tests degrade the value of a reward (usually food or liquid) either by feeding to satiety or by pairing the reward with malaise. Extinction measures the reduction in instrumental responding when a previously rewarded response is no longer reinforced. Primates with lesions to the OFC are impaired at all of these tests: Extinction of instrumental responding is slowed (Butter, Mishkin, & Rosvold, 1963), animals keep responding for a devalued food (Baxter, Parker, Lindner, Izquierdo, & Murray, 2000; Pickens, Saddoris, Gallagher, & Holland, 2005; Pickens *et al.*, 2003), and they take longer to relearn stimulus–outcome contingencies following reversals (Dias, Robbins, & Roberts, 1996; Iversen & Mishkin, 1970; Izquierdo, Suda, & Murray, 2004; Jones & Mishkin, 1972; Mishkin, 1964). Similar deficits in reversal learning, have been found in humans with lesions to the OFC and adjacent ventromedial prefrontal cortex. When stimulus–outcome contingencies are reversed, those patients make more errors (selecting the previously correct option) than controls or patients with dorsolateral prefrontal lesions (Fellows & Farah, 2003; Hornak *et al.*, 2004). Patients with OFC lesions seem to have general difficulty in using option values to make beneficial choices, despite otherwise entirely intact cognitive abilities (Bechara, Damasio, Damasio, & Anderson, 1994; Bechara, Tranel, & Damasio, 2000; Tsuchida, Doll, & Fellows, 2010).

These effects of lesions to OFC correspond well with what is known about its responses to reward and reward-predicting stimuli. Neural activity in the OFC appears to reflect the reward value of stimuli across diverse modalities. Human neuroimaging studies have found OFC activity to correlate with the pleasantness of music (Blood, Zatorre, Bermudez, & Evans, 1999) or odors (Anderson *et al.*, 2003), monetary or erotic rewards (Sescousse, Redoute, & Dreher, 2010), and the subjective desirability of food (Plassmann, O'Doherty, & Rangel, 2007). When a food reward is no longer valued (by feeding to satiety), OFC responses to this food, or stimuli that predict it, are diminished (Kringelbach, O'Doherty, Rolls, & Andrews, 2003; O'Doherty *et al.*,

2000; Rolls, Sienkiewicz, & Yaxley, 1989; Figure 22.1A). Furthermore, OFC neurons respond not only to reward itself, but also to stimuli that predict it, and their responses rapidly adjust when cue–outcome associations are changed (Roesch & Olson, 2004; Schoenbaum, Chiba, & Gallagher, 1999; Thorpe, Rolls, & Maddison, 1983; Tremblay & Schultz, 1999). Two features about the reward-predictive properties of OFC neurons are particularly important. First, they encode the expected value of stimuli, irrespective of their physical or spatial properties, or motor responses to the stimuli (Padoa-Schioppa & Assad, 2006; Tremblay & Schultz, 1999). In other words, an OFC neuron might respond similarly to two visual stimuli that look very different and are presented in opposite spatial positions, but predict the same outcome. Second, and perhaps more importantly, their reward-predictive responses are relative, or context-dependent. Imagine a monkey that prefers raisins over banana, but banana over apples. An OFC neuron might only display little responding to a cue predicting banana, when the monkey is in a situation where the rewards are the best-liked raisins and bananas. The same neuron might display a pronounced response to the same banana-predicting cue when the alternative reward is the least-preferred apple. Thus, the neuron reflects the primate's relative reward preferences (Tremblay & Schultz, 1999). It has to be noted, however, that whether OFC value representations follow an absolute or relative code may depend on the specific features of the task at hand, in particular whether trials of a given type are presented in blocks or in an interleaved fashion (Padoa-Schioppa & Assad, 2006). Second, OFC neurons adjust the range of their firing to the range of available rewards. An OFC neuron will respond with a strong increase in firing rate to a stimulus that predicts two units of reward when this is the highest reward currently available, but show only a modest increase to the same reward when the highest reward amount is 10 units of reward (Padoa-Schioppa, 2009; Figure 22.1B). Such flexible, context-dependent representations are extremely important for everyday life situations. A price difference of 5 euros makes no difference

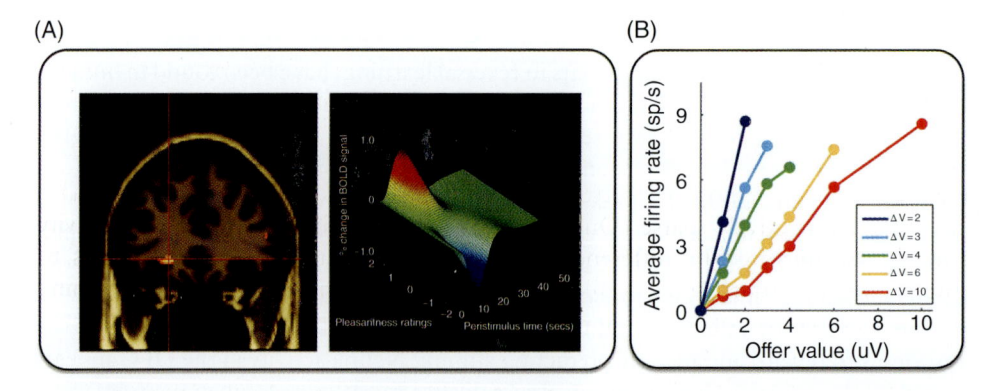

Figure 22.1 (A) Activity in OFC correlates with the subjective pleasantness of a liquid food (left). The BOLD response (right) is diminished with decreasing pleasantness ratings that ocurred when the food was devalued by feeding to satiety. (B) Orbitofrontal neuronal responses to reward cues adapt to the range of available rewards. The figure shows neuronal responses (spikes/s) for a range of offer values (in ascending order on the the x-axis) for different value ranges (ΔV). Reproduced with permission from Kringelbach *et al.* (2003), *Cerebral Cortex* (A) and Padoa-Schioppa (2009).

when choosing betweeen two cars that may cost tens of thousands of euros. However, the same 5 euros may be a crucial determinant when deciding between two dishes in a restaurant. Firing rates of cortical neurons typically do not exceed 60 Hz, so there is only a limited dynamic range. If neurons could not adjust to the current context, they would have to represent the entire range of possible values from zero to, say one million Euro within 1–60 Hz. Making a food choice in a restaurant would become impossible! A further interesting feature about OFC neurons is that they appear to code subjective, rather than objective, values. In a now famous experiment, Padoa-Schioppa and Assad (2006) offered monkeys choices between different types of juice rewards. They determined the subjective value of each juice by making the animals select between two juices of varying quantities and determining an indifference point. For example, an animal might display a strong preference for apple juice over water, when offered one drop of each. However, it might be equally likely to select either of the two when offered a choice between four drops of water and one drop of apple juice. The authors found that OFC neurons coded the subjective value of the options, rather than the reward quantity. In other words, an OFC neuron would show the same response to one drop of apple juice as to four drops of water. It has to be noted that the value-coding properties of these cells reflected diverse features; in particular, the authors found subsets of neurons that represented "offer value" (the sum of the subjective value of available options), "chosen value" (the subjective value of the option the monkey would end up choosing), or simply the identity of the chosen taste. The latter finding also highlights the fact that not only does OFC represent abstract values independent of stimulus properties, but it is a highly polymodal association cortex that receives inputs from all five senses (Carmichael & Price, 1995). Accordingly, OFC neurons signal sensory properties of both rewards but also of stimuli independent of their association with reward (Critchley Rolls, 1996; Rolls & Baylis, 1994). Taken together, OFC value representations display a number of properties that make them ideally suited for guiding choices based on *specific* expected outcomes, and lesions in this region have a profound impact on these kinds of value-guided choices.

An important distinction that needs to be highlighted is that between medial and lateral sectors of OFC. Anatomical studies provide evidence for two distinct networks, a lateral orbitofrontal network (LOFC) and a medial orbital/ventromedial prefrontal cortex (mOFC/vmPFC) network. Regions within both the LOFC and the mOFC/vmPFC network are heavily interconnected, but connections between the two networks are relatively sparse (Öngür & Price, 2000). These different connectivity patterns are mirrored by differences in functional specialization. While lesions to mOFC/vmPFC impair reward-guided choice, LOFC seems to be critical for learning from the outcomes of these choices (Noonan *et al.*, 2010; Rushworth, Noonan, Boorman, Walton, & Behrens, 2011). LOFC is particularly important for a certain kind of learning called contingent learning, in which an outcome is associated with the precise choice that caused it. Primates with LOFC lesions still do learn, but they are no longer able to assign credit for a reward to the causative choice and instead distribute credit to the average recent choice history (Walton, Behrens, Buckley, Rudebeck, & Rushworth, 2010). It is important to note that most human fMRI studies have reported value correlates in vmPFC, whereas primate neurophysiological studies have typically recorded from more lateral OFC areas, likely because (among other reasons) the vmPFC is difficult to access for recording. Given these functional differences, it would be highly interesting to explore what the behavior of single neurons in primate vmPFC looks like. Motivated by the surge of evidence from human functional imaging, researchers have only begun recording from primate vmPFC during value-guided choice (Bouret & Richmond, 2010; Monosov & Hikosaka, 2012; Rich & Wallis, 2014; Strait, Blanchard, & Hayden, 2014).

Value representations have been found in other frontal cortical areas, in particular in the lateral prefrontal cortex (LPFC) and anterior cingulate cortex (ACC). ACC and LPFC value correlates share many properties with those found in OFC, but there are also some clear distinctions. OFC neurons show barely any coding of motor responses (Wallis & Miller, 2003) and, as we have noted above, they code the value of stimuli independent of movement parameters or stimulus characteristics (Kennerley, Dahmubed, Lara, & Wallis, 2009a; Padoa-Schioppa & Assad, 2006, 2008). In contrast, neuronal activity in ACC seem to reflect more the value of actions, rather than stimuli. In a task that required monkeys to make either a go- or nogo-response to one of two cues, only a few cells coded for the visual cue. In contrast, many ACC neurons represented the upcoming motor response, the expected reward, or the interaction of action and reward (Matsumoto, Suzuki, & Tanaka, 2003). Likewise, firing rates of ACC neurons are correlated with the probability that an action will be rewarded (Amiez, Joseph, & Procyk, 2006). Studies examining both ACC and OFC have, however, reported that cells representing the value of stimuli and actions exist in both areas (Luk & Wallis, 2013), which might also explain why medial OFC and the adjacent ventromedial prefrontal cortex (vmPFC) have been found to correlate with the value of both stimuli and actions in human fMRI studies (Glascher, Hampton, & O'Doherty, 2009). Nevertheless, the relative abundance differs, such that cells representing stimulus values are more prevalent in OFC than in ACC, and vice versa for cells correlating with the value of actions (Luk & Wallis, 2013). These differences between ACC and OFC in representing stimulus versus action values reflect the connectional anatomy of those two regions. While the ACC has very direct access to the motor systems, with the cingulate motor area directly targeting the premotor and primary motor cortex and even motor neurons in the ventral horn of the spinal cord, the OFC is several synapses away from the motor system. In contrast, OFC receives direct input from all five senses, in particular highly processed visual input about object identity, information to which the ACC has far less direct access (Carmichael & Price, 1995; Cavada, Company, Tejedor, Cruz-Rizzolo and Reinoso-Suarez, 2000; Dum & Strick, 1991; He, Dum, & Strick, 1995). Accordingly, lesions to the OFC impair stimulus–reward learning without affecting action–reward learning, while ACC lesions interfere with action–reward learning, but not with stimulus reward learning in both macaques (Kennerley, Walton, Behrens, Buckley, & Rushworth, 2006; Rudebeck *et al.*, 2008) and humans (Camille, Tsuchida, & Fellows, 2011). ACC has strong connections with LPFC, which, like ACC, also is strongly connected with the motor system (Petrides & Pandya, 1999), and the two areas are often found coactive in various cognitive tasks in human functional imaging (Duncan & Owen, 2000).

Very much like ACC neurons, the firing of LPFC cells reflects motor response, outcome, and the interaction of the two (Matsumoto *et al.*, 2003; Watanabe, 1996). It has been shown that LPFC neuron firing is modulated by actions, outcomes, and action–outcome combinations not only of the current trial, but also of previous trials (Barraclough, Conroy, & Lee, 2004; Seo, Barraclough, & Lee, 2007). Such coding of previous choices and outcomes might be a potential mechanism for linking actions with delayed outcomes. While these characteristics of LPFC neurons are remarkably similar to those of ACC neurons, it has also been shown that responses reflecting action–outcome associations emerge only late in the trial in LPFC, whereas they were evident almost immediately after cue onset in ACC (Matsumoto *et al.*, 2003). A notable feature of ACC neurons is that they are able to "multiplex" several decision variables. Kennerley and colleagues (2009a) simultaneously recorded from macaque OFC, LPFC, and ACC while the animals chose between two options that varied on each trial along the expected reward magnitude, reward probability, or cost (lever presses required to obtain reward). Neurons that encoded one of the three value parameters were found in all three areas in roughly equal proportions. However, neurons whose activity was modulated by two or even three value parameters were far more abundant in ACC than in OFC, or even LPFC, where only a few neurons showed such multiplexing. Another striking feature of value representations by individual neurons and the BOLD signal in the ACC is that they encode not only the reward associated with the action actually selected, but also the counterfactual reward that would have resulted from an alternative course of action (Boorman, Behrens, & Rushworth, 2011; Hayden, Pearson, & Platt, 2009). Together with the monitoring of extended action–outcome histories that has been described in both primate and human ACC (Behrens, Woolrich, Walton, & Rushworth, 2007; Jocham, Neumann, Klein, Danielmeier, & Ullsperger, 2009; Kennerley *et al.*, 2006; Seo & Lee, 2007), these "counterfactual" value signals may play an important role when deciding to switch away from a current behavior, which we will discuss below.

The dorsal striatum receives dense projections from the ACC (Kunishio & Haber, 1994), and movement-related activity of cells in the primate striatum is modulated by expected reward (Cromwell & Schultz, 2003; Kawagoe, Takikawa, & Hikosaka, 1998; Shidara, Aigner, & Richmond, 1998). There is some heterogeneity in the exact value parameter that is found to be represented by striatal neurons. Some neurons in the caudate and putamen code action values, for example, the value of a left- or rightward movement (Samejima, Ueda, Doya, & Kimura, 2005), but a large fraction of cells in both dorsal and ventral striatum represent the overall value of options (Cai, Kim, & Lee, 2011; Wang, Miura, & Uchida, 2013). Representations of overall value are important for the response-invigorating effects of high-value options: An organism should be motivated to expend more effort when much reward is at stake, regardless of what option it ends up choosing. Thus, signaling of overall value in the striatum is consistent with its role in response invigoration (McGinty, Lardeux, Taha, Kim, & Nicola, 2013; Salamone, Correa, Farrar, & Mingote, 2007), rather than choice (Wang *et al.*, 2013). In contrast, correlations with chosen value, which is, by definition, more tightly linked to the outcome of a decision process, have only seldom been reported in the striatum (Lau & Glimcher, 2008).

In addition to these prefrontal and subcortical regions, value correlates have been found in a number of further areas. Largely separate from the research that focused on frontal cortical areas and the basal ganglia, another research community investigated an area in the primate parietal cortex, the lateral intraparietal area (LIP). This area contains neurons that are involved in the generation of eye movements, and they usually show selectivity for gazes toward a particular direction in space, that is, they have a preferred direction. LIP had been intensively studied in the domain of perceptual choice (Gold & Shadlen, 2007; Shadlen & Newsome, 1996). While a discussion of this extremely influential research is outside the scope of this chapter, it was these studies that laid the foundation for investigations on decision variables related to value rather than perceptual evidence. In a pivotal study, Platt and Glimcher (1999) were able to demonstrate that LIP neurons were sensitive to the reward value associated with a saccade to a particular direction. Importantly, value-related activity in these neurons was independent of movement-related parameters and also emerged early in the trial, prior to movement onset. Later, it was shown that LIP neurons track the local relative reward rate in a dynamically changing environment (Sugrue, Corrado, & Newsome, 2004). Further studies corroborated these findings, but also showed that LIP neurons carry diverse value representations. For instance, they were shown to display modulation by the value difference of two options, the value sum, but also the animal's upcoming and previous choices (Seo, Barraclough, & Lee, 2009). Some of these characteristics bear some resemblance to what has been described above for LPFC, with which LIP has strong connections (Blatt, Andersen, & Stoner, 1990). However, a debate has recently arisen as to whether LIP responses do indeed reflect value, rather than motivational salience (Leathers & Olson, 2012). In addition to these parietal cortices, value correlates have even been found as early as in visual cortex (Serences, 2008; Shuler & Bear, 2006) and throughout premotor and supplementary motor areas (Pastor-Bernier & Cisek, 2011; Roesch & Olson, 2003). Again, value-related activity in the motor system appears to pertain more to action values, rather than chosen values. Finally, value signals have also been observed in primate posterior cingulate (PCC; McCoy, Crowley, Haghighian, Dean, & Platt, 2003; McCoy & Platt, 2005), but the role of PCC in cognition is still fairly mysterious (Pearson, Heilbronner, Barack, Hayden, & Platt, 2011).

From Value to Choice

We have stated that signals related to economic value are widespread across the brain and are even observed in sensory and motor cortical areas. Two obvious questions arise: First, are all of these value representations used in the service of decision-making? Second, if a neural signal related to value is indeed used for a decision, then exactly how is this value representation transformed into a choice? Correlates of value could serve a number of functions, choice only being one of them. In fact, what appears to be a value correlate may in many cases reflect other aspects, such as motivational factors, motor preparation, attention, or modulation of sensory processing, as has been discussed in detail recently (O'Doherty, 2014). Sometimes, the exact nature of the value representation can already give some clues. For instance, one of the studies described above found cells in the ventral striatum whose firing rate correlated with the value sum of the two available options (Cai *et al.*, 2011). Such a representation is unlikely to be used for a choice, since the value sum can be high either whenever there is a high value of one option and a low value of the other option (regardless of which option is the high-value one) or when both options have intermediate value. Therefore, it does not inform about what option to choose. Instead, it is useful for motivational purposes, such as invigoration of responding. If an organism is in a situation in which a large amount of reward is at stake, it should be willing to exert more effort to obtain that goal. By contrast, value representations indicating a difference between two options' values are more informative, as they directly reflect how good one option is relative to an alternative. Nevertheless, in action-based tasks, some of the authors have interpreted this relative value signal as an indication of motor preparation, rather than of a decision (Pastor-Bernier & Cisek, 2011). In human fMRI studies, subjects are often asked to make choices between two options that are not prelearned, but instead vary from trial to trial, for instance by drawing randomly from a distribution and explicitly presenting reward magnitudes and probabilities on the screen. In a number of these studies, a correlate of the chosen option's value was found in the vmPFC (Boorman, Behrens, Woolrich, & Rushworth, 2009; Jocham, Hunt, Near, & Behrens, 2012a; Wunderlich, Rangel, & O'Doherty, 2009). In some of these studies, the fMRI signal in vmPFC correlated not only positively with the value of the chosen option, but also negatively with the value of the unchosen option (Boorman et al., 2009; Jocham et al., 2012a; Kolling, Behrens, Mars, & Rushworth, 2012). Such a representation of value difference between chosen and unchosen option would appear to reflect the outcome of a decision process, rather than motor preparation. Because, in these studies, values for the left and right options were generated afresh on each trial, the chosen and unchosen values are not tied to a particular response side.

Wunderlich and colleagues further dissected this in two very elegant studies. In the first, they made subjects decide on each trial whether to perform a saccade to a particular location or to press a button. Each of these two motor responses was associated with a probability of being rewarded that drifted slowly over time. By coupling the choice to two effectors that are represented in separable regions of the brain, they were able to test whether there were any separable correlates of the value of the particular motor actions, and where in the brain activity would correlate with the value of the option chosen, regardless of the effector required to execute the choice. It was found indeed that the value of the exact motor action ("action value") was correlated with activity in the brain areas responsible for that movement. Thus, the value of the hand movement correlated with activity in the supplementary motor area, while the value of making a saccade correlated with activity in the presupplementary eye field on each trial, regardless of which movement was ultimately performed. In contrast, activity in vmPFC was related neither to the value of the eye nor to hand movement, but instead correlated with the value of the movement chosen by the participant (Wunderlich et al., 2009). In the next study, the authors went on to show that representations of chosen value in the vmPFC were even evident without subjects knowing the exact motor output required to obtain an option. Subjects were first shown two options on each trial that were again associated with time-varying reward probabilities. However, only several seconds later, it was revealed to participants which motor response (again, saccade or button press) was required for which of the two options. It was found that the correlation of vmPFC activity with the value of the chosen option emerged before the stimulus–action pairing was revealed (Wunderlich, Rangel, & O'Doherty, 2010). Thus, representations of choice in the vmPFC could be found in an abstract "goods space," independent of the action needed to obtain that good. Intriguingly, a value correlated in vmPFC is observed even when people are not actively making choices. When subjects were asked to perform a cover task during fMRI, and only later were asked about their preferences between options, activity in vmPFC nevertheless covaried with the subjective value of the options (Lebreton, Jorge, Michel, Thirion, & Pessiglione, 2009). It therefore appears as if the brain automatically makes choices, even when they are not expressed behaviorally. Taken together, value representations in the vmPFC appear to fulfill the required criteria for a neural signal reflecting choice. This does not imply that vmPFC alone is important for making decisions. After all, patients and primates with vmPFC lesions still are able to make reward-guided choices, albeit showing suboptimal decisions and altered behavioral strategies (Camille, Griffiths, Vo, Fellows, & Kable, 2011; Fellows, 2006; Noonan et al., 2010). In fact, it appears likely that several brain areas may be capable of transforming value representations into choice, depending on the kind of decision to be made or on contextual factors, as we will discuss below.

Mechanisms of Choice

Because a correlate of chosen value, or value difference between chosen and unchosen options, reflects the outcome of a decision process (by definition, those signals are related to choice), brain areas carrying such representations are likely candidate regions for transforming value into choice. However, this also implies that we only observe the end-point of a decision process, or the neural representation we can measure after a neural network has made a choice. It therefore does not inform us how a population of neurons could have made this decision. A crucial impetus for research on the neural mechanisms of value-guided choice again came from the field of perceptual decision-making. The drift diffusion model is a very successful mathematical formulation of continuous evidence accumulation that has been able to capture behavior and neural dynamics during continuous evidence accumulation such as during the random dot motion task (Bogacz, 2007; Smith & Ratcliff, 2004). In this kind of task, a subject is observing a noisy sensory stimulus, in this particular case a cloud of dots moving around randomly on the screen. A certain fraction of these dots is moving toward either the left or right side, and the subject is asked to perform a saccade to the direction of net motion. Decision difficulty is manipulated by varying the percentage of dots moving coherently into one direction (motion coherence). This class of models assumes that a decision for a left or right motion is made whenever a decision variable reaches a predetermined threshold. This decision variable evolves according to a differential equation by sampling at each timepoint the momentary evidence in favor of a left or right decision. The drift rate, the steepness at which the decision variable ramps up to the threshold, is determined by the strength of evidence, that is, by the motion coherence. These models successfully capture both the longer reaction times (slower drift rates) and decreased accuracy (stronger influence of noise on the decision variable more often leads to passing the incorrect decision threshold) on trials with low motion coherence. They are purely mathematical descriptions in the sense that they do not care about how this process would be realized neurally, and in fact, some of their features are not realistic from a biophysical perspective.

Some researchers have therefore devised biophysically realistic neural network models capable of performing evidence accumulation similar to that in drift diffusion models (Lo & Wang, 2006; Wang, 2002; Wong & Wang, 2006). In this class of models, a decision circuit in area LIP is simulated. The model contains two pools of neurons, L and R, that are sensitive to left and right motion direction, respectively. The receive inputs from motion-sensitive cells in area MT in the temporal lobe that are known to increase firing in their preferred direction with increasing motion coherence. Therefore, the inputs to both L and R are proportional to the evidence in favor of left or right, respectively. The connections of these two pools display two key features. First, each pool of neurons has recurrent excitatory connections endowed with NMDA and AMPA receptors. Second, both pools of neurons excite a pool of GABAergic interneurons that provides feedback inhibition to both pools (Figure 22.2A). This architecture leads to so-called attractor dynamics: While, initially, both pools of neurons fire in proportion to their inputs, at the end of the dynamics, only one pool of neurons ends up in a persistent, high-firing state (Figure 22.2B). The recurrent excitation at NMDA receptors is crucial for these dynamics, as it allows slow evidence integration over a time span of several hundred milliseconds, comparable with behavioral reaction times. When recurrent excitation is governed only by AMPA receptors, their short time constant (about 5 ms compared with ~100 ms for NDMA receptors) causes the network almost immediately to latch onto one of the two attractor states. This results in very fast but also inaccurate decisions. The second key feature is GABAergic inhibition. With more GABA, the attractor dynamics are slowed down (corresponding to lower drift rates in the diffusion models), allowing more time for evidence integration and making the decision less susceptible to noise. The noise in these models arises from two sources, the sensory stimulus, but also from within the nervous system. These attractor models governed by recurrent excitation and mutual inhibition have not only captured behavioral data but also very accurately reproduced LIP firing rates during the random dot motion task.

Recently, these models have been adapted to value-guided decision-making. Now, the two pools of neurons represent two options, rather than left or right motion, and they receive input proportional to the options' values. Furthermore, the noise arises exclusively from within the neural circuit, not from the sensory stimulus, but everything else about the model is the same. In a recent study, this adapted model was used to simulate synaptic currents (rather than spikes) in order to predict MEG data during decision-making (Hunt *et al.*, 2012). The motivation was to generate a bottom-up prediction of what neural activity would look like if a brain area used a mechanism like that in the model for transforming value into choice. The model simulation revealed that overall network activity first represented overall value and then transitioned to represent the value difference between the chosen and unchosen option. This occurred in a frequency range of 2–10 Hz (Figure 22.2C,D). That is, within the same brain area, two different representations would be observed in rapid temporal succession. Such rapid dynamics would be invisible to fMRI, so the investigators used MEG to test these predictions. It was found that activity in two brain areas, vmPFC and posterior parietal cortex, exhibited the very dynamics predicted by the model (Figure 22.2E). Therefore, it appears likely that activity in these regions reflects the

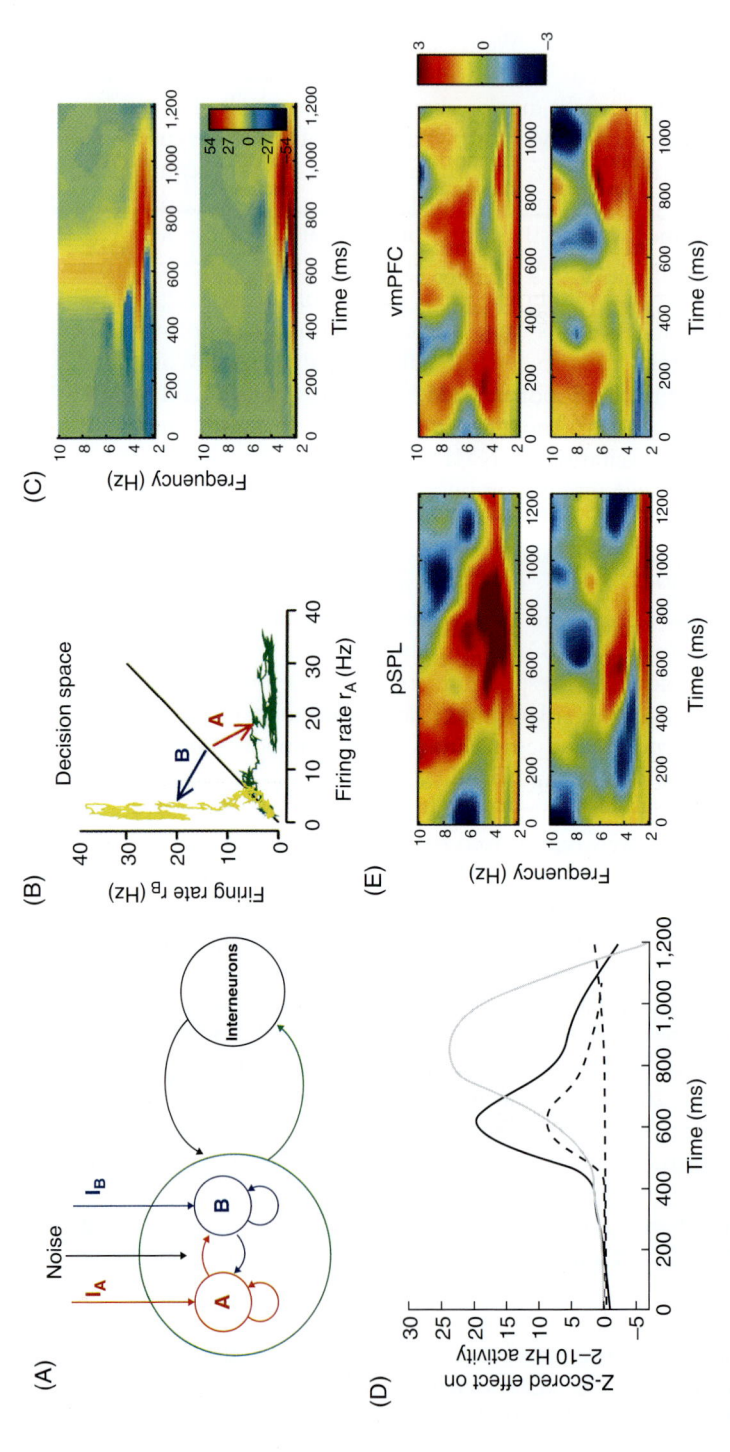

Figure 22.2 (A) Recurrent network model for decision-making. Pools 1 and 2 corresponds to pools representing leftward or rightward choice and receive inputs I1 and I2 from motion-sensitive cells in area MT. In the model variant adapted for value-guided choice, the two pools correspond to pools representing the left and right option, and they receive input proportional to the value of that option. Recurrent excitation is dominated by NMDA receptors (indicated by the coupling parameter w+). Both pools indirectly inhibit each other indirectly by exciting a pool of GABA interneurons that provides feedback inhibition. (B) Attractor dynamics. Initially, firing is high in both pools A and B, but as the competition is resolved (a decision is made), only one pool ends up in a high-firing attractor state while activity in the other pool is suppressed. (C) Biophysical model predictions of MEG data. Network activity in the range of 2–10 Hz represents the overall value (top panel) and value difference between the chosen and unchosen option (bottom). (C) Z-scored effect of the overall value and value difference. Solid lines are correct trials; dashed lines are incorrect trials. This reveals that the effect of the value sum occurs first before the network activity transitions to represent value difference. Furthermore, value difference representations are only observed on correct trials. (E) MEG data from two key brain areas for decision-making, the posterior superior parietal lobule (pSPL), and the ventromedial prefrontal cortex (vmPFC) matched with model predictions. The top panels show the effect of the value sum, and the bottom panels the effect of the value difference. Colors indicate the z-scores. Reproduced with permission from Wong and Wang (2006) (A), Wang (2002) (B), and Hunt et al. (2012) (C–E).

(A)

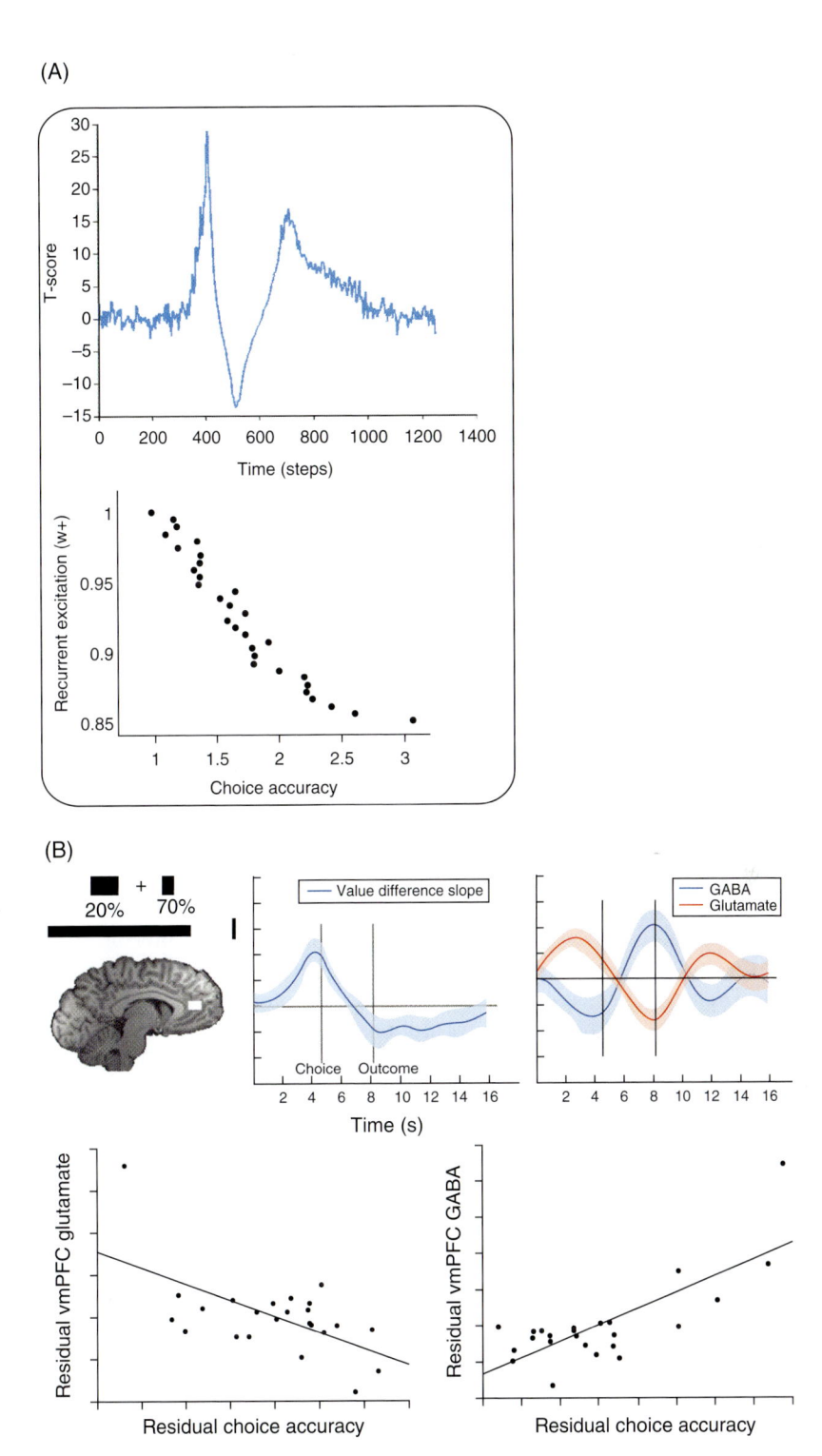

(B)

Figure 22.3 (A) Biophysical model predictions on the effect of increasing the degree of recurrent excitation (w+) in the network. The model predicts that the value difference correlate (top), a neural signature of a decision process, ramps up steeper followed by a faster decline

fact that they are involved in making a decision by using a mechanism as specified in the model. The model makes further testable predictions. Because the key components in the network are recurrent glutamatergic excitation and GABAergic inhibition, the network will vary predictably, depending on the level of excitation and inhibition. We simulated how interindividual differences in the concentrations of GABA and glutamate would translate into differences in neural dynamics and choice behavior. The simulations predicted that choices would become more accurate with higher levels of GABA, and less accurate with higher levels of glutamate. Neurally, the evolution of the value difference representation would be slower with high levels of GABA, and faster with high levels of glutamate (Figure 22.3A). We found that interindividual differences in vmPFC GABA and glutamate concentrations (measured by MR spectroscopy) were related to choice performance and neural dynamics consistent with model predictions. Subjects with high levels of GABA and low levels of glutamate in vmPFC were most accurate at choices on difficult trials. Furthermore, ramping up of the value difference signal (as measured with fMRI) was positively related to glutamate, and negatively to GABA (Jocham *et al.*, 2012a; Figure 22.3B). In other words, with high levels of GABA relative to glutamate, the decision was implemented slower in vmPFC, which led to more accurate choices. Together, these findings strongly suggest that the representations of the chosen value and value difference found in vmPFC reflect the outcome of a choice mechanism on the basis of competition via mutual inhibition. A recent single unit recording study provides direct neuronal evidence for mutual inhibition in vmPFC. When monkeys were presented with two options successively, neural activity reflected the value of the first and second option, respectively, at the time they were presented. Importantly, at the time of the second option presentation, cells were tuned to the value of both option 1 and option 2, but they were tuned in the opposite direction. In other words, if a cell was positively modulated by the value of option 1 during presentation of the second option, this same cell was negatively modulated by the value of option 2 during the same interval, despite the values of the two options being uncorrelated. Furthermore, even after the authors regressed all value-related activity out of firing rates, neural activity was still predictive of the upcoming choice the monkey would make (Strait *et al.*, 2014). Together with studies showing that lesions to primate vmPFC impair value-guide choice (Noonan

---

with increased levels of recurrent excitation. Behaviorally, the model's choice accuracy on difficult trials (as measured by the softmax inverse temperature) is reduced with a higher w+. (B) Experimental results. Subjects performed a simple binary choice paradigm. Participants tried to maximize their payoffs by making repeated selections between two options that differed in terms of reward magnitude and probability. GABA and glutamate concentrations were measured with MR spectroscopy in the vmPFC (white rectangle indicating the voxel position) and a control region in the parietal cortex (not shown). The slope of the value difference correlate (middle panel in the top row) depended on both GABA and glutamate (right). With high basal vmPFC concentrations of glutamate and low concentrations of GABA, the value difference correlate emerged very quickly but also decayed very rapidly. Behaviorally, performance (softmax inverse temperature) was best in subjects with high levels of GABA and low levels of glutamate. Reproduced with permission from Jocham *et al.* (2012a).

et al., 2010; Rushworth et al., 2011), these findings strongly suggest vmPFC as a brain region that implements a choice, and it appears to do so through a mechanism of competition via mutual inhibition.

Multiple Brain Mechanisms for Choice?

The evidence outlined above supports a role for vmPFC in value-guided choice, yet a good deal of evidence suggests decisions can be made in different frames of reference using (at least partly) different neural circuitry: Sometimes, a choice is made between two stimuli, whereas in other cases, choices are made between motor actions. In some situations, choices are made between options that are presented simultaneously; in other situations, the options are presented sequentially. How much the role of particular brain regions depends on these different frames of reference is probably best illustrated by the finding that lesions to ACC impair performance when choices are made between actions rather than stimuli, whereas OFC lesions produce the exact opposite deficit (Rudebeck et al., 2008). Another study using MEG found that value representations were found in vmPFC when options were displayed side by side, but were found in the motor cortex and not in vmPFC when options were presented sequentially, separated by a brief delay. In these sequential trials, the first option was shown on the left, the second option always on the right. At the time of the first option presentation, a correlate of this option's value was found in beta-band power in contralateral motor cortex. At the time the second option was presented, beta power represented the value difference between the contra- and ipsilateral option (Hunt, Woolrich, Rushworth, & Behrens, 2013). These findings suggest that when choices can be made in the space of motor actions, rather than abstract goods, valuation, choice, and motor preparation may proceed in parallel, rather than serially. This is further supported by a study using transcranial magnetic stimulation to study the relationship between value and corticospinal excitability as measured by motor-evoked potentials at the effector muscle. The authors found that corticospinal excitability was greater on trials with a high value difference, and this effect of value gradually evolved over the course of a trial, suggesting that motor preparation is facilitated by a high value difference (Klein-Flugge & Bestmann, 2012). It is important to note that our discussion does not argue against serial models of decision-making, as suggested by Kable and Glimcher (2009). They propose a two-stage progression, in which valuation occurs in circuits involving vmPFC and striatum, and circuitry spanning lateral prefrontal and parietal cortex using these value signals for choice. Above, we have presented mechanistic evidence on how the progression from value to choice over time can be implemented within a single brain area. However, we do not think that those two proposals are mutually exclusive. Rather, we suggest that choice mechanisms are deployed bespoke to the particular demands of the task at hand.

In addition to these different frames of reference, even more subtle details of the particular choice context can matter. In the study by Hunt and colleagues (2012), a value difference correlate was only found in the vmPFC when participants had to compute an abstract value estimate by integrating a reward magnitude and probability, but not when both stimulus dimensions mandated the same choice. In addition, the value difference correlate was only evident in vmPFC in the first half of the experiment, while in the second half it became more pronounced in posterior parietal cortex. Because reaction times declined steeply during the course of the experiment, it was suggested that choices gradually became more automated and less deliberative; hence, parietal cortex was interpreted as guiding behavior when choices are made fast, nearly automated, without long deliberation. In agreement with this, we have recently shown that when forcing subjects to make choices very rapidly, a pronounced value difference correlate is found in parietal cortex, but not in vmPFC. The situation exactly reversed when allowing subjects much time to decide – the value difference came to be represented in vmPFC but was absent from parietal cortex (Jocham et al., 2014).

Finally, it is important to point out the intricate relationship between valuation and choice with attention. A recent fMRI study provided evidence that vmPFC value signals are anchored to attention, not choice. The authors manipulated subjects' visual fixation orthogonally to option values in order to decorrelate attention from choice. Using this procedure, they found that the vmPFC fMRI signal correlated positively with the value of the attended, and negatively with the value of the unattended option. However, even though attention was deliberately decoupled from choice, they also found that guiding subjects' attention to one option also made them more likely to select that option (Lim, O'Doherty & Rangel, 2011). Indeed, moment-to-moment fluctuations of a decision variable were closely tracked by a drift-diffusion model under the control of visual attention (Krajbich, Armel, & Rangel, 2010). However, from that study, the direction of effect is unclear: Did people value an item more because they fixated on it, or did they fixate longer on it because they already assigned a higher value to it? Indeed, recent evidence has shown that visually salient options are more likely to be chosen than less salient alternatives during consumer choice (Milosavljevic, Navalpakkam, Koch, & Rangel, 2012). Furthermore, a descriptive accumulator model that integrates measures of salience and value in guiding fixations and ultimately value-based choice has recently been shown to outperform similar models without a salience component (Towal, Mormann, & Koch, 2013).

Most of our everyday decisions involve choices between items with multiple attributes, such as when deciding between two pairs of trousers that may vary in price, quality of the material, color, and so forth. In our laboratory experiments, we often mimic these situations by giving subjects two options that each have an amount of reward, and a probability with which that reward can be obtained. Economic theory posits that we compute an integrated value estimate, which, in our laboratory example, would be the Pascalian value (probability × magnitude), and in the trousers example a somewhat more abstract estimate of "how good" the item is. However, there is evidence to suggest that we do not always compute an integrated value. A notable study investigated the choice behavior of patients with vmPFC lesions and controls. Rather than looking at which option the subject ended up choosing, the study examined how information about options was gathered. Patients were asked to choose between three apartments that varied along three attributes (noisiness, neighborhood, and size). There were thus three pieces of information for each flat. Each of the resulting nine fields was covered with a card, and participants were allowed to turn over one card at a time. It was found that patients with vmPFC lesions gathered information *across attributes*, that is, they first uncovered all information for one flat, before proceeding to the next. In contrast, healthy individuals and patients with LPFC lesions sampled *within attributes*, that is, they first uncovered information, for example, for the prize for all of the flats, before proceeding to the next attribute (Fellows, 2006). These data suggest that healthy individuals make choices by comparing items with respect to specific attributes, and then either compare across attributes or select the one that compares best in the attribute(s) most relevant to the individual. By contrast, the vmPFC patient's behavior appears more consistent with the computation of an integrated value. Taken together, it seems that healthy individuals choices' are guided not only by how good an items is overall but also by attending to particular features most important to the individual. In sum, it does not appear implausible that similar or overlapping neural computations subserve attention, valuation, and choice.

Behavioral Adaptation

A useful distinction in value-guided choice can be drawn between comparative evaluative choices and sequential choices (Boorman, Rushworth, & Behrens, 2013; Freidin, Aw, & Kacelnik, 2009; Kolling *et al.*, 2012; Vasconcelos, Monteiro, Aw, & Kacelnik, 2010). Comparative evaluative choices are made between simultaneously presented, well-defined choice options, whose attributes, including any uncertainty (also called risk in this context), are known. An example of a comparative evaluative choice is a decision between a Snickers bar and a Mars bar at the canteen. Much of the evidence and modeling discussed in this chapter so far has stemmed from experiments implementing comparative evaluative choices, in part because they simplify the decision problem, facilitating a tractable examination of the decision-making mechanism. Sequential choices, on the other hand, are made in series or repeatedly, often under unknown uncertainty (also called ambiguity), which may or may not be resolvable with further experience. Examples of sequential choices abound in the real world, ranging from a foraging animal deciding whether to hunt a gazelle or search for prey further afield to a homeowner deciding whether to hold onto or sell their house.

In sequential choices, the animal frequently faces a decision about whether to continue selecting an option or to adapt its choice, to a known or unknown set of alternatives. This means it is adaptive to *track* several decision variables: rewards, costs, and uncertainties associated with choice options. Tracking options' rewards and costs is clearly advantageous, since these variables should guide behavior on the basis of current expectations about their future values – the expected reward relative to the cost that pursuing the options would likely entail. Yet in an ever-changing world, different courses of action are pervaded by uncertainty. Consequently, exploring less-known options with lower expected values enables the animal to gain potentially valuable information it could exploit in the future to obtain even better rewards. Both value-guided and information-guided behavioral adaptation can be described as either undirected or directed – in other words as a decision concerning whether to switch away from a known alternative to *any* alternative or to a *specific* alternative or portion of the sampling space guided by expected outcomes based on previous experience.

Default choices

In everyday life, animals face a daunting problem: How do they make good choices given the multitude of potential options to select between at any given moment? Reinforcement learning models often assume that agents perfectly track decision variables associated with each possible choice option and select the one that maximizes the agent's expected future reward (Sutton & Barto, 1998). Yet finding the optimal solution to this problem in the real world is not only difficult; it is impossible. The brain requires some means of constraining the decision space to reduce the computational demand of such continual effortful comparisons. One appealing heuristic to this problem is to form a default position, or long-term preferred option or limited set of options, based on their history of predicting favorable outcomes such as reward (Boorman et al., 2013); for a similar problem concerning identification of relevant stimulus dimensions, see Wilson and Niv (2011). This strategy dramatically simplifies the computational demand of the decision problem, rendering it tractable.

A default option can be readily identified in many everyday decisions: shopping for breakfast at the supermarket, choosing an airline for travel to an upcoming conference, or surfing the Internet. These sequential choices can often be reduced to a decision about whether to stick with the default position or switch to something else. Cross-species lesion and recording evidence from rodents, monkeys, and humans supports a central role for dorsal ACC (dACC) and adjacent pre-SMA in making such decisions. Both the BOLD response and single unit activity in dorsal ACC increase markedly at response time when subjects switch behavioral responses, especially when these are made volitionally based on the history of reinforcement, as opposed to an external cue (Procyk, Tanaka, & Joseph, 2000; Shima & Tanji, 1998; Walton, Devlin, & Rushworth, 2004). In the same vein, lesions to dorsal ACC produce deficits selecting options based on reinforcement history (Chudasama et al., 2013; Hadland, Rushworth, Gaffan, & Passingham, 2003; Rudebeck et al., 2008), particularly following a change in contingencies (Kennerley et al., 2006).

More recently, it has been proposed that decision-related dACC/pre-SMA activity reflects a decision variable amounting to the accumulated evidence favoring behavioral adaptation from a long-term or default option during sequential decisions (Boorman et al., 2011, 2013; Hayden, Pearson, & Platt, 2011; Hunt et al., 2012; Kolling, Wittmann, & Rushworth, 2014; Figure 22.4). Rather than merely increasing activity during switches, in each of these studies the dACC signal at choice scales monotonically with the value-based evidence for adapting behavior – that is, the difference or ratio between subjective values associated with adapting away from the default option and continuing to select it. Importantly, the signal is present independently of whether or not the subject does in fact switch, but is notably absent if the default option is transiently removed from the menu of available options (Boorman et al., 2013). In each of several tasks, dACC is sensitive to the task-relevant variable that is relevant on the longer term, whether it is reward probability (Boorman et al., 2013), average environmental reward size (Kolling et al., 2012), travel time between reward "patches" (Hayden et al., 2011), time pressure (Kolling et al., 2014), or a predictable spatial location (O'Reilly et al., 2013). Moreover, it integrates this long-term variable with other short-term variables in the form of subjective value comparisons relevant for the decision at hand (Boorman et al., 2009, 2013; Kolling et al., 2012).

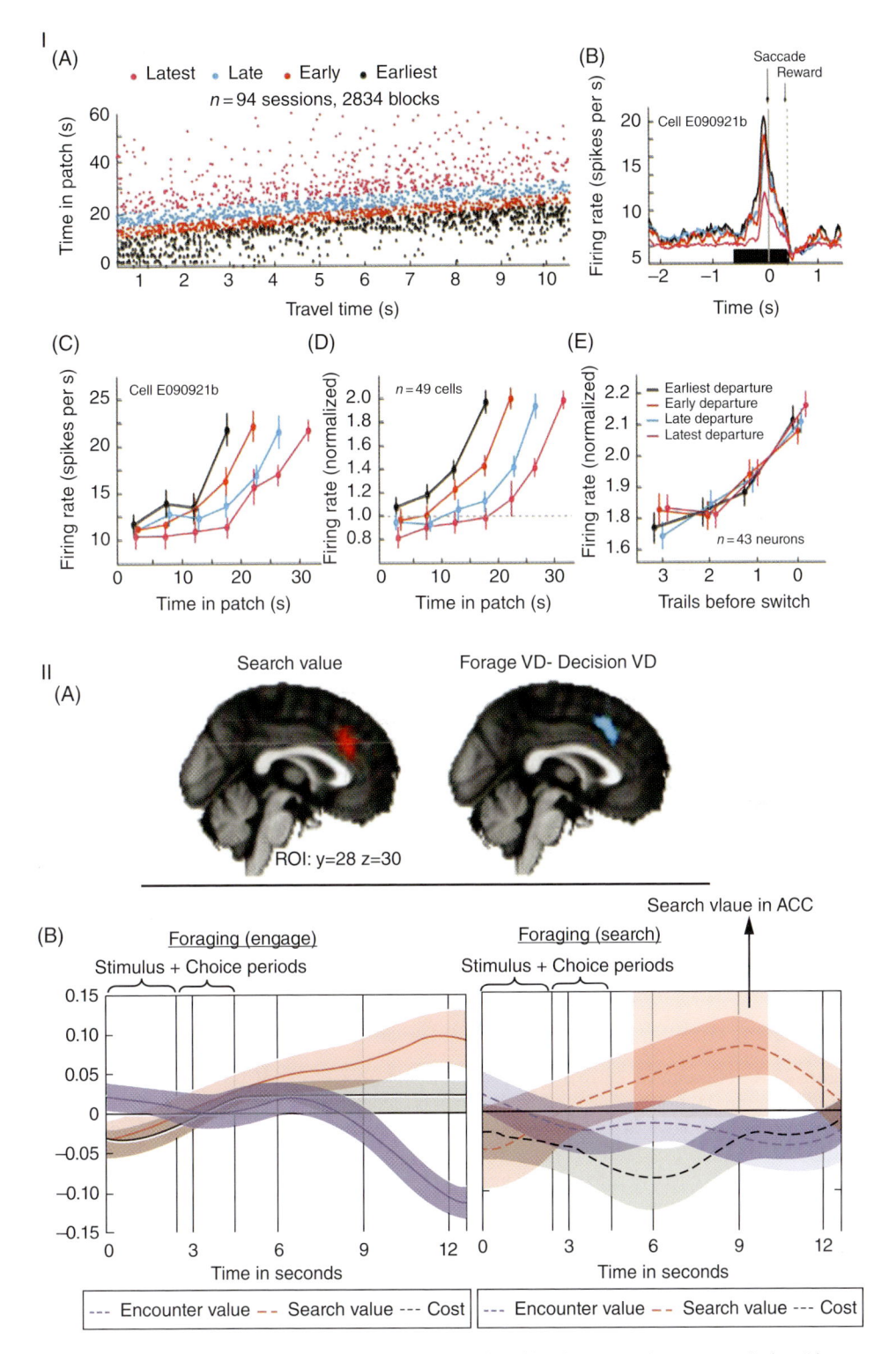

Figure 22.4 dACC and default adaptation. I. Monkey dACC neurons integrate switch evidence across trials. (A) Departure times of monkey choices are plotted as a function of travel time between patches and residence time within a patch, color-coded from the earliest to the latest departure times. (B) Saccade-locked phasic responses of a single dACC neuron, color-coded as in (A). (C) Same single neuron's firing rate plotted as a function of both travel time between patches and residence time in a patch. The gain of the response is inversely proportional to travel time.

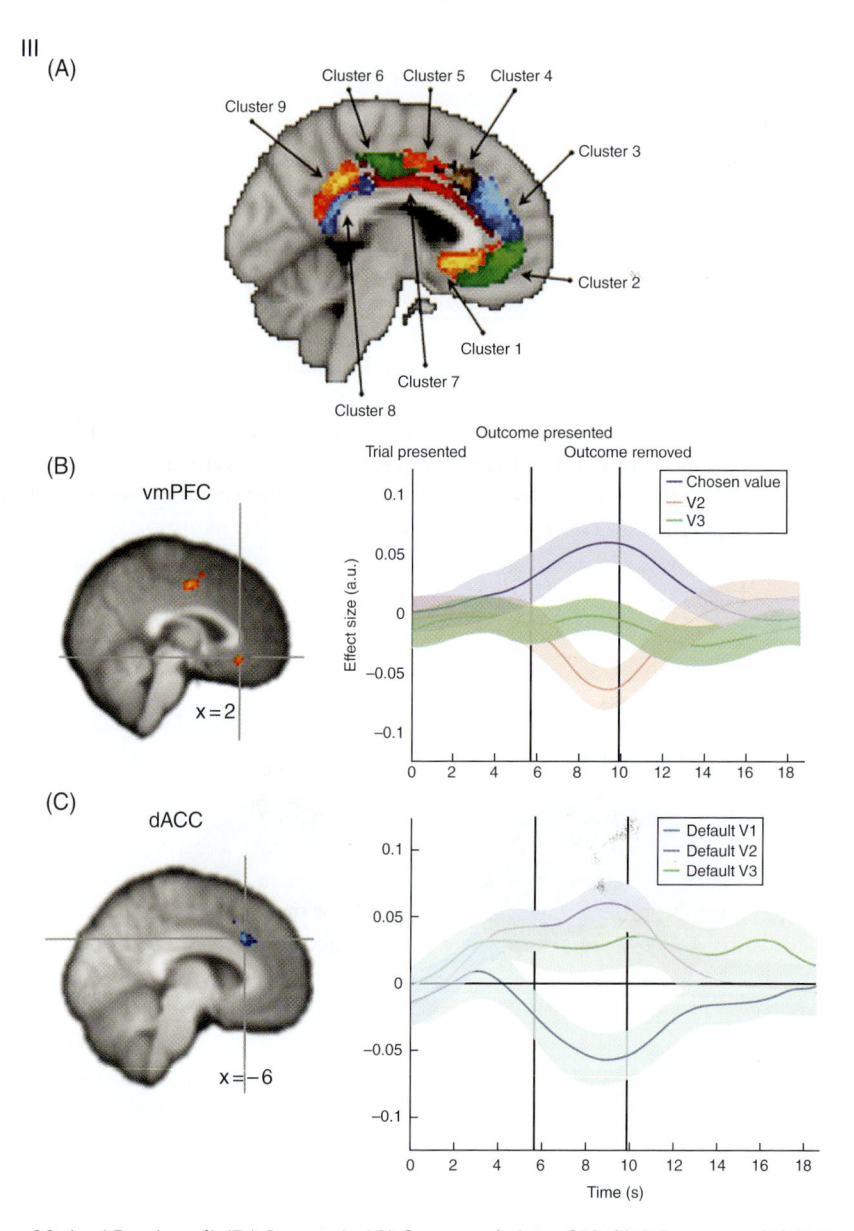

Figure 22.4 (Continued) (D) Same as in (C) for a population of 49 dACC neurons. (E) Firing rate for different travel times overlaid for the three trials preceding a switch and on switches, illustrating a rise to similar putative decision thresholds. Reproduced with permission from Hayden *et al.* (2011). II. dACC activity and average search value in foraging-style decisions. (A) dACC activity reflected the main effect of search value during foraging decisions (left) and was better related to VD during foraging-style decisions than decision VD during comparative evaluative decisions (right). (B) dACC time courses during "engage" decisions (left) and "search" decisions (right). Adapted from Kolling *et al.* (2012) with permission from the American Association for the Advancement of Science. III. Choice and default value coding during multialternative choice. (A) Reference image for comparison with (B) and (C) showing diffusion-weighted imaging-based parcellation of the cingulate cortex based on clustering of probabilistic connectivity profiles. (B, C) Left: sagittal slices through z-statistic maps relating to subjective expected value of the chosen option (chosen EV) during decisions. Positive effects are shown in red–yellow (B) and negative effects in blue–light blue (C). Right, top: time course of the effect size of the chosen EV, short-term next-best (V2), and short-term worst (V3) option EV plotted across the decision vmPFC. Right, bottom: the same for the long-term best (default V1), long-term next-best (default V2), and long-term worst (default V3) option EV in dACC. Thick lines: mean; shadows: SEM. Adapted with permission from Boorman *et al.* (2013).

Although there has been some debate surrounding whether decision-related dACC activity informs the current choice or instead predicts choice outcomes or monitors decision quality for learning (Alexander & Brown, 2011; Blanchard & Hayden, 2014), there are several properties of the dACC signal that are reminiscent of a mechanism that integrates evidence for behavioral change (Figure 22.4). In one particularly compelling study (Hayden et al., 2011), Hayden and colleagues trained monkeys to perform a "patch foraging" task, which required them either to choose to stay in a "patch," whose reward depleted with patch residence time, or to leave the "patch" and "travel" to a new one with some variable delay between patches. This is in essence a stay/switch decision, where staying can be seen as the default option because it is chosen again and again until the monkey has accumulated sufficient evidence to motivate a switch. Monkeys' decisions to leave a patch depended on both travel time between patches and handling time within a patch, and were predicted quantitatively by marginal value theorem (MVT), an optimal solution to foraging in a "patchy habitat" under certain assumptions (Charnov, 1976). Response-locked phasic responses in both single dACC neurons and the population integrated patch residence time and travel time over multiple stay decisions (Figure 22.4). Perhaps most convincingly, the gain of dACC firing rate with respect to patch residence time was inversely proportional to the travel time between patches but terminated at a similar threshold across departure times (Figure 22.4). These properties of integration across multiple sequential decisions, adaptive response gain with switch evidence, and rise to a threshold are consistent with an evidence accumulation-to-bound process, here guiding behavioral change.

This putative mechanism for behavioral change can be contrasted with the neural signatures of decision mechanisms for comparative evaluative decisions discussed earlier in the chapter. Notably the vmPFC and posterior parietal cortex value comparison signals measured during comparative evaluative choices initially reflect the sum of values and then transition to the difference between chosen and unchosen (or attended and unattended) subjective values (Boorman et al., 2009, 2013; Hunt et al., 2012; Jocham, Hunt, Near, & Behrens, 2012b; Lim et al., 2011). In many paradigms, the sign of this comparison signal is the inverse of the value comparison signals recorded in dACC described here. We propose that the dACC signal is inversely proportional to vmPFC and portions of posterior parietal cortex in many paradigms because it adopts a different reference frame: one of staying versus changing behavior, rather than a decision between well-defined options or goals (Boorman et al., 2013; Kolling et al., 2012). This distinction supports the view that decisions are governed by multiple controllers, whose recruitment depends on the type of decision required by current environmental demands (Rushworth, Kolling, Sallet, & Mars, 2012).

Undirected behavioral adaptation

MVT has proven powerful in capturing the sequential foraging behavior of many species, including bees, birds, monkeys, and human hunters in their respective ecological contexts (Hayden et al., 2011; Smith & Winterhalder, 1992; Stephens & Krebs, 1986). At the core of the stay/leave decision rule implied by MVT is a comparison between two terms: the marginal energy intake rate in a patch and the average energy intake rate for the habitat. When the latter exceeds the former, animals should leave the patch and search elsewhere. Notably, the intake rate is a function of rewards and energetic costs, including delay and effort. As mentioned earlier in this chapter, there is evidence that dACC activity reflects the abstract value of choices and the environment on average. A large proportion of dACC neurons multiplex over several decision variables, including reward probability, reward size, effort, and time, and this coding is significantly more prevalent than in LPFC or lOFC (Hosokawa, Kennerley, Sloan, & Wallis, 2013; Kennerley, Behrens, & Wallis, 2011; Kennerley, Dahmubed, Lara, & Wallis, 2009b). Furthermore, dACC neurons encode pure reward-prediction errors in these multiplexed values (Kennerley et al., 2011), which may be important for tracking these values. In humans, dACC BOLD activity was shown to reflect the average reward value of the environment in a foraging-style task when this information guided behavioral change from a long-term preferred or default option (Figure 22.4; Hunt et al., 2012). Finally, lesions to the ACC in rats impair decisions that require reward size to be weighed against effort costs (Floresco & Ghods-Sharifi, 2007; Rudebeck, Walton, Smyth, Bannerman, & Rushworth, 2006; Walton, Bannerman, Alterescu, & Rushworth, 2003; Walton, Bannerman, & Rushworth, 2002), and BOLD activity in human dACC, but not vmPFC, reflects a comparison between options' values that increase with reward size and decrease with effort cost (Lim, Colas, O'Doherty, & Rangel, 2013; Prevost, Pessiglione, Metereau, Clery-Melin, & Dreher, 2010). Collectively, these findings suggest that dACC decision-related activity is ideally suited to comparing marginal and average energy intake rates for sequential decisions.

Behavioral adaptation can be described as directed or undirected. The decision rule implemented by MVT is essentially undirected. Animals need only maintain a representation of the marginal value of the current option and the environment's average value, without any required representation of the value of specific alternatives they may choose when they do adapt their behavior (or transitions to subsequent states they may visit). Conversely, directed behavioral adaptation requires a representation of the reinforcement or information potential of specific alternatives in the environment. The role of dorsomedial frontal cortex in directed and undirected behavioral adaptation may depend on the structures with which it interacts, contingent upon contextual demands.

One candidate neuromodulator known to heavily innervate dACC that is well positioned to inform undirected behavioral adaptation is dopamine (DA; Berger, 1992; Lindvall, Bjorklund, & Divac, 1978). A noteworthy theory proposed that reward-prediction errors are integrated into an average reward rate encoded by tonic DA levels (Niv, Daw, Joel, & Dayan, 2007). Although there has been limited empirical support for this hypothesis to date, there is nevertheless evidence to suggest that DA may perform computations important for guiding undirected sequential decisions. In one tour-de-force study (Hamid et al., 2016), optogenetics was combined with fast cyclic voltammetry to measure changes in DA in NAc both with and without physiologically titrated ventral tegmental area stimulation in a decision-making task between two options with independently varying reward probabilities. The authors isolated two temporally dissociable DA signals that causally impacted behavior in distinct ways: a phasic burst in response to a tone marking the onset of a trial and a graded reward-prediction error at the time of a tone indicating a reward would be delivered for the animal's preceding choice. Optically stimulating DA neurons at the first tone led to vigorous approach behavior but did not impact learning, whereas stimulating at the second tone led to increased preference for the selected arm. Crucially, the DA reward-prediction error signal recorded in NAc took the form of the reward obtained minus the expected reward based on the state value of the environment, rather than the chosen or left/right action value. This reward-prediction error, comprising the obtained reward minus the expected reward on average, is precisely the form of prediction error useful for learning about the average energy-intake rate.

In a second study, Constantino and Daw (2015) developed a foraging task for humans and showed that an adaptation of MVT to incorporate a learning rule captured human choices dramatically better than a canonical temporal difference-learning algorithm in this setting. Comparing Parkinson's patients on and off DA medication with matched controls, they found that patients harvested longer in a patch before switching when on relative to off medication and also relative to matched controls. This finding is consistent with a reduced estimate of the average reward rate of the environment when off DA medication, suggesting that DA is critical for tracking average reward rate. Although untested to our knowledge, these DA signals may modulate dACC activity, facilitating decisions about when to continue or adapt behavior based on the local average reward, thereby guiding undirected behavioral adaptation.

Although MVT can capture much of the sequential behavior of diverse species, animals' behavior is also governed by the drive to gather information, which is not explicitly modeled by MVT. As with value, information-guided behavioral adaptation can be described as directed or undirected (Johnson, Varberg, Benhardus, Maahs, & Schrater, 2012). Setting aside the important interplay between value and uncertainty for now (discussed in a subsequent section), one formalization of undirected information foraging posits that animals continue sampling surprising locations they encounter, given prior experience at that location (Johnson et al., 2012). Similar to MVT, undirected information-guided behavioral adaptation can also be conceptualized as guided by a comparison between the information available from a currently observed sample relative to the expected information in the habitat on average, based on previous experience. In other words if the animal encounters a sufficiently surprising sample, an information-seeking animal should continue sampling that location to resolve the high uncertainty, relative to the animal's experiences in the environment on average (assuming equated expected values). Conversely, if the sample is relatively unsurprising, and the environment is sufficiently information rich, it should sample elsewhere. This simple information-based comparison can also inform undirected sequential decisions concerning whether to continue sampling an option or adapt behavior to sample elsewhere.

While it is challenging to disentangle the contributions of uncertainty and value on behavior, two productive approaches have been to remove reward from the experimental setting or to match expected rewards across options. In these circumstances, rats, monkeys, and humans all exhibit a preference for novel stimuli (Baillargeon, Spelke, & Wasserman, 1985; Berlyne, Koenig, & Hirota, 1966; Bromberg-Martin & Hikosaka, 2009, 2011), which can be shown to emerge naturally from formal treatments of information foraging and active Bayesian inference (Johnson et al., 2012; Schwartenbeck, Fitzgerald, Dolan, & Friston, 2013). Intriguingly, the very same DA and lateral habenula neurons that encode reward-prediction errors also encode information prediction errors, even when the options are carefully matched for expected reward value (Bromberg-Martin & Hikosaka, 2009, 2011). This surprising finding suggests that information may be inherently rewarding and points to a potential role for DA in undirected information-guided, as well as value-guided, behavioral adaptation.

Another candidate neuromodulator likely to be important for undirected information adaptation is norepinephrine (NE). An influential theoretical framework has proposed that NE tracks unknown uncertainty, or ambiguity (Yu & Dayan, 2005), which can be used both to modulate learning and to motivate exploration. There is indirect evidence to suggest that NE plays a role in tracking uncertainty, which theoretically should and empirically does control the rate of learning in rats (Gallistel, Mark, King, & Latham, 2001), monkeys (Rushworth & Behrens, 2008), and humans (Behrens et al., 2007). Release of NE from the locus coeruleus (LC) nucleus correlates with dilation of the pupils (Joshi, Kalwani, & Gold, 2013). This observation enables an indirect but noninvasive putative measure of LC activity. Matthew Nassar and colleagues have measured pupil diameter while subjects performed a change-detection task (Nassar et al., 2012). In this task, there are two computational factors that should make subjects amenable to changes of belief: the long-term probability that the world might change, and a term known as the relative uncertainty, which captures mathematically the subject's doubt that his previous belief was correct. As these factors are varied throughout the experiment, they both exhibit strong and separable influences on pupil diameter. Perhaps most impressively, if the experimenter introduces a surprising stimulus (a loud noise) at an unexpected time in the experiment, this not only causes an increase in pupil diameter but also results in a rapid period of revising beliefs about the subject's completely unrelated task. Another recent study showed that during decision-making, baseline pupil diameter is increased directly preceding exploratory compared with exploitative choices, a difference that predicted an individual's tendency to explore (Jepma & Nieuwenhuis, 2011). Notably, LC and dACC have strong reciprocal connections (Chandler, Lamperski, & Waterhouse, 2013; Jones & Moore, 1977). These observations suggest that interactions between NE and dACC may regulate both the rate at which new information replaces old during learning (Behrens et al., 2007; Jocham et al., 2009; O'Reilly et al., 2013) and also the extent to which overall uncertainty drives changes in exploratory behavior.

Directed behavioral adaptation

When animals do adapt from a default position or status quo, how do they know what to choose? So far, we have discussed behavioral and neural evidence pertaining to decisions to stay or switch to any option. According to such accounts, when the status quo becomes unrewarding or uninformative, animals switch randomly, akin to injecting noise into the choice process (Cohen, McClure, & Yu, 2007). However, in many scenarios, animals change behavior in a directed manner (Johnson et al., 2012). Both the computations and neural structures underpinning such directed adaptation differ in some noteworthy respects from those underpinning undirected adaptation.

Computationally, directed behavioral adaptation requires some representation of the expected values and/or uncertainties of specific alternatives that serve to guide behavioral change toward those options, as opposed to, for example, only the average value. Formally, this can be defined by the Bayesian belief (or probability distribution over rewards) describing how much reward is likely to be available from selecting each possible alternative outcome or location (Johnson et al., 2012), or only a subset of sufficiently valuable/informative alternatives in the environment (Koechlin & Hyafil, 2007), where the mean and variance of the distribution can be taken to represent the value and the uncertainty in that belief. Recent evidence suggests that interactions between dACC and hippocampus (HIPP) contribute to such directed behavioral change in sequential decision-making. Although it is not often highlighted, rat dACC projects throughout parahippocampal cortex, including presubiculum, parasubiculum, entorhinal cortex, and postrhinal cortex, and also sparsely to subiculum (Jones & Witter, 2007), and cingulate activity has been shown to be phase-locked to the well-described hippocampal theta rhythm (Colom, Christie, & Bland, 1988), supporting the plausibility of coordination between HIPP and dACC neural ensembles during behavior.

Evidence for the involvement of these structures in directed adaptation comes from studies with both rats and humans. Using a sequential choice task, Remondes and Wilson (2013) trained rats to learn to perform sequences of four trajectories in a "wagon-wheel maze" to ultimately obtain a chocolate reward while they recorded multiunit activity in HIPP and ACC. In this task, rats start at the center of the wagon-wheel maze, enter an outer circle via an exit arm, navigate around the outer circle, and choose whether to enter each of several entry arms (or trajectories) that return to the maze center. They then leave the exit arm again and return to the outer circle from where they will select the next arm in the sequence. This task is comparable with a choice adaptation paradigm in that continuing along the outer circle can be conceptualized as a default option; at each choice point (or entry arm), the rat has to select whether to continue along the outer circle or adapt behavior and select to enter the encountered entry arm. Both HIPP and ACC neural populations decoded choice trajectories in the intervals directly preceding these choice points, with HIPP trajectory content arising earlier than ACC. The authors then tested whether these changes in information content were reflected in distinct patterns of HIPP–ACC coherence of the local field potential. This revealed a progression in HIPP–ACC coherence initially dominated at high-frequency theta to wide-band theta as the animals progressed toward choice points. Moreover, they found that this change in coherence was accompanied by increases in the amount of trajectory information encoded by HIPP and ACC, again with HIPP preceding ACC. Finally, they investigated the relative timing and Granger causality, a test for inferring whether one time series is useful in predicting another, between HIPP and ACC spikes and local field potential, and found that HIPP spikes were Granger causal for ACC neural activity. Taken together, these findings suggest that lower-frequency HIPP–ACC theta coherence coordinates the integration of contextual information from hippocampus to ACC to adapt from current choices to specific trajectories in a directed manner.

Complementary evidence has arisen from an active visual exploration experiment in humans (Voss, Gonsalves, Federmeier, Tranel, & Cohen, 2011; Voss, Warren, et al., 2011). In this paradigm, subjects explore a visual grid to learn about the location of different occluded objects one at a time in an active condition, where they control which item is revealed and for how long, and a passive condition, where they observe the objects as seen by the previous subject, thus enabling precise control of viewing sequence, duration, and information content between pairs of subjects. The sole difference between conditions is whether the joystick movements are volitional or passive, and hence, the authors contend, whether information acquisition is active or passive. In the active condition, subjects spontaneously revisited recently viewed object locations, which they termed spontaneous revisitation. Spontaneous revisitation led to striking memory enhancements in both object identification and spatial memory in the active, but not passive, conditions. Superficially, such spontaneous revisitation behavior may seem to have little in common with the sequential decision-making paradigms discussed so far, but they do in fact share some key features. Subjects have to volitionally change their behavior from continuing to the next sample and instead direct it toward specific previously viewed objects to gain information and resolve uncertainty. Interestingly, the degree of memory enhancement afforded by such spontaneous revisitation was associated with coactivation of dACC and HIPP but only in the volitional condition (Voss, Gonsalves, et al., 2011). Moreover, spontaneous revisitation, and its benefits on subsequent memory performance, was only rarely observed in amnesic patients with severe damage to the hippocampus.

Another brain region that plays a key role in directed behavioral adaptation in humans is the lateral frontopolar cortex (lFPC). In one line of research, subjects were asked to make sequential choices on the basis of two separate pieces of information that an ideal observer should integrate: reward probabilities that drifted slowly but independently and could be tracked; and independent reward magnitudes that were generated randomly at the onset of a trial and hence could not be tracked (Boorman et al., 2009, 2011). This manipulation meant that future choices should only be dependent upon the options' reward probabilities, whereas current choices should be dependent upon both the options' reward probabilities and reward magnitudes, thus enabling variables important for long-term strategies and short-term behavior to be dissociated. In two studies, changes to future behavior could be shown to depend upon the relative unchosen reward probability: the difference (or ratio) between the reward probability associated with the best alternative in the environment and the reward probability associated with the selected option, with no impact of a third inferior option. Because subject switching behavior was driven by a comparison between the best two alternatives' reward probabilities, but not by the third inferior option, it can be described as directed. Neurally, lFPC BOLD activity uniquely encoded the reward probability of the best alternative option relative to the reward probability of the selected option but was not sensitive to the randomly generated magnitudes only relevant for current decisions (Figure 22.5). These findings suggest that lFPC compares the future reward potential of specific valuable counterfactual options with a selected or default option for upcoming choices. Consistent with this interpretation, subjects in whom this evidence was better represented in lFPC switched to the previous next-best alternative more frequently when advantageous. Notably, this pattern of coding contrasted with other brain regions such as vmPFC, dACC, posterior parietal cortex, and ventral striatum whose signals reflected the integration of reward probabilities and magnitudes into expected values relevant for current choices. The evidence for directed future behavioral change, reflected in lFPC activity, may also help coordinate decisions about whether to adapt behavior with interconnected dACC (Neubert, Mars, Thomas, Sallet, & Rushworth, 2014), where long-term variables were integrated with short-term variables relevant for current choices.

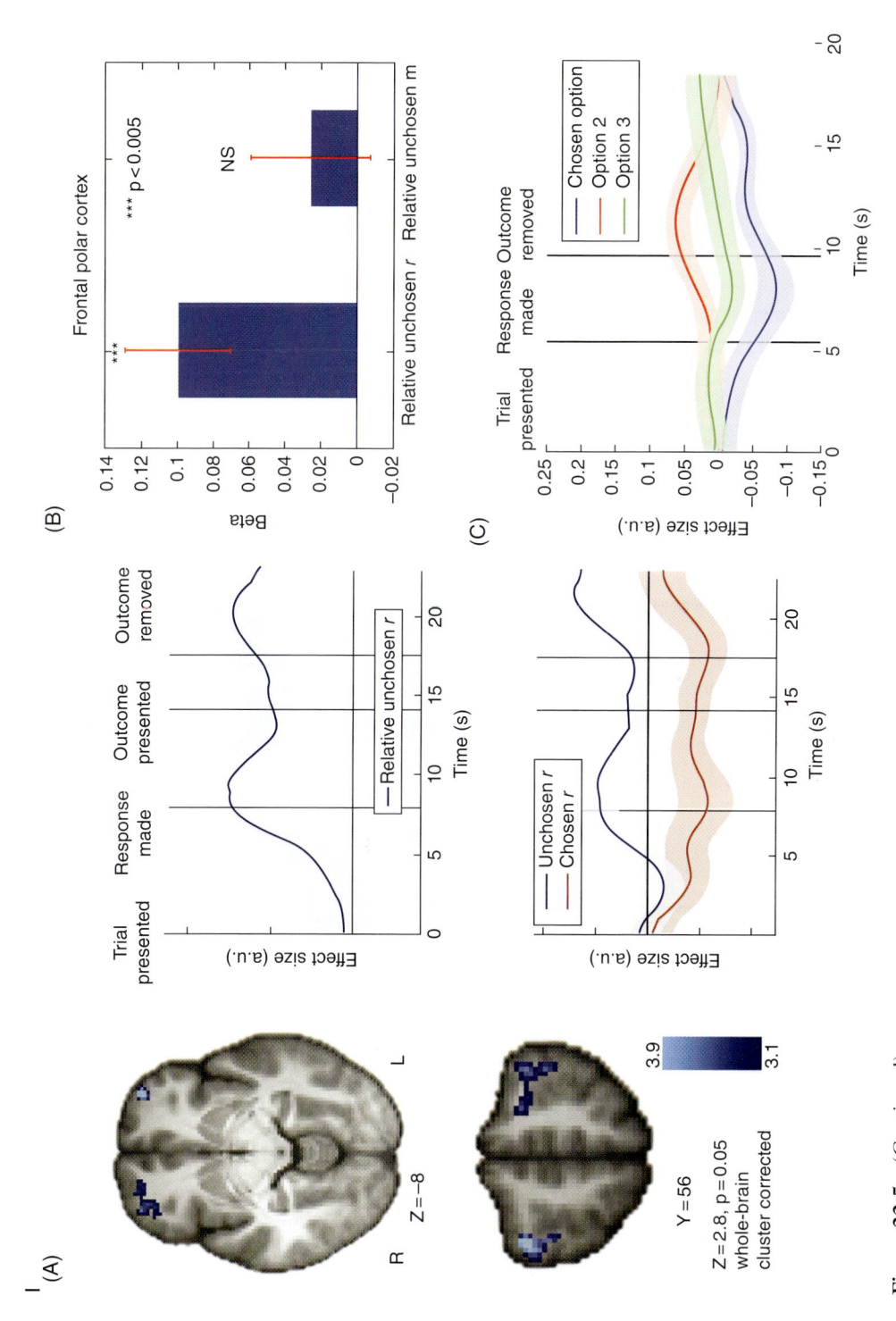

Figure 22.5 (Continued)

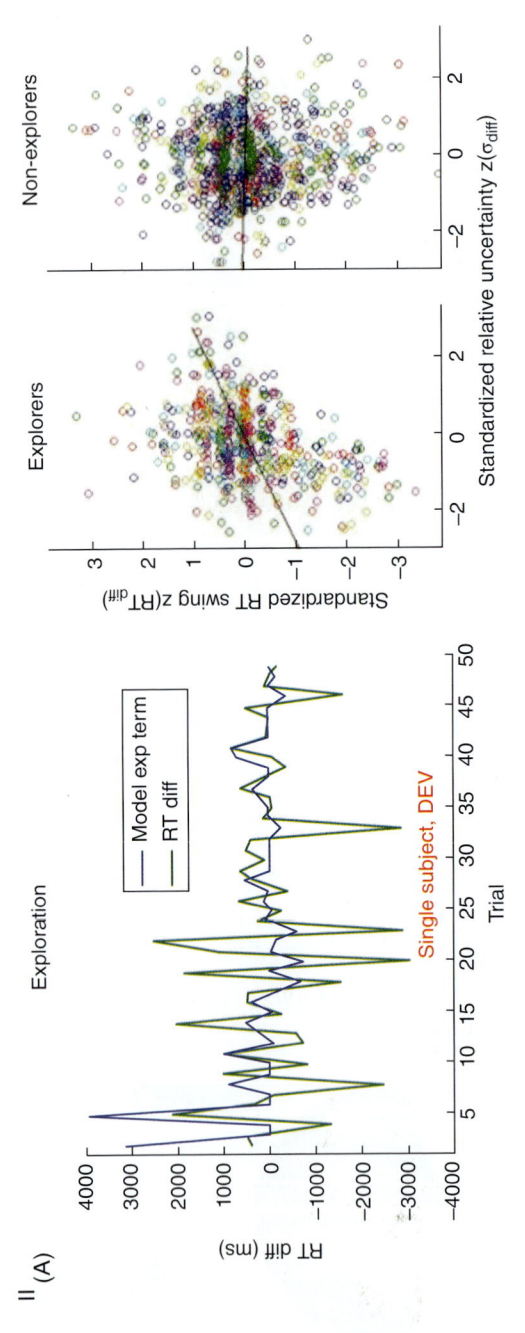

Figure 22.5 IFPC and strategic adaptation to counterfactuals. I. IFPC and adaptation to next best alternatives based on *relative value*. (A) Axial and coronal slices through z-statistic maps relating to the relative unchosen probability, log(unchosen action probability / chosen action probability). Maps are corrected for multiple comparisons across the whole-brain by means of cluster-based correction at $p < 0.05$. (B) Top panel: time course for the effect size of the relative unchosen probability in the IFPC shown throughout the duration of the trial. Bottom panel: same time course shown with the signal decomposed into log unchosen and log chosen option probabilities. Thick lines: mean effect sizes. Shadows: standard error of the mean (±SEM). Adapted with permission from Boorman et al. (2009). (B) IFPC signal reflecting reward probabilities, which are relevant for both current and future choices, but not reward magnitudes, which are only relevant for current choices. (C) Second study involving trinary choices (Boorman et al., 2011), time course of IFPC effect of the reward probability associated with the chosen option, best unchosen option (option 2), and worst unchosen (option 3). The signal reflects a directed comparison between option 2 and the chosen option. II. IFPC and strategic exploration based on *relative uncertainty*. (A) Left: plot from a representative participant illustrating that changes in the Explore term (blue) partially capture trial-to-trial swings in RT (green). Right: correlation between RT swings and relative uncertainty among explorers (left, [mean $r = 0.36$, $p < 0.0001$]) and nonexplorers (mean $r = -0.02$, $p > 0.5$). All trials in all participants are plotted in aggregate with color distinguishing individuals.

(B)

Explore participants only

Explore minus non-explore participants

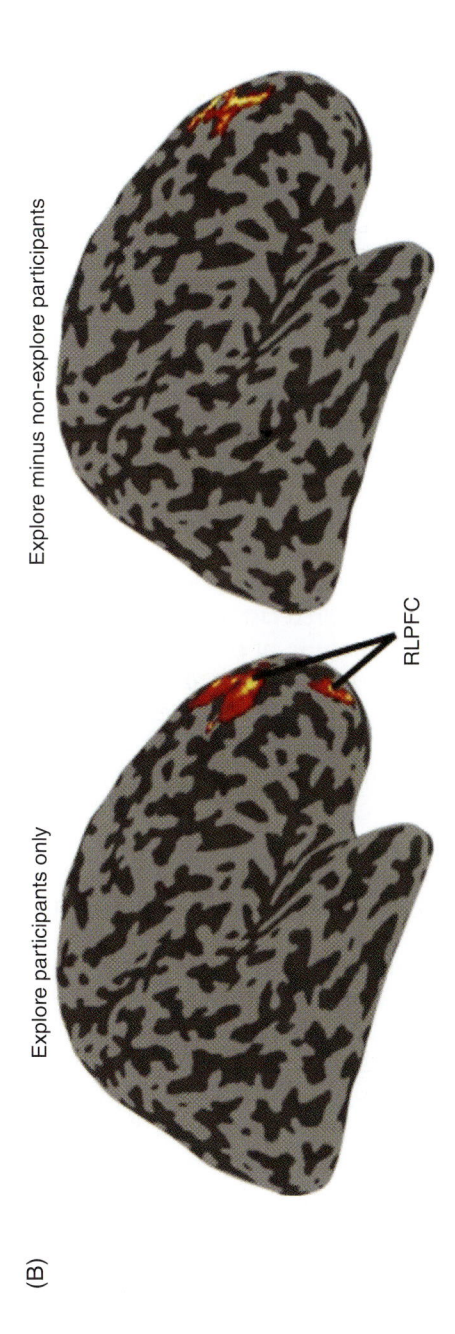

RLPFC

Figure 22.5 (Continued) (B) Left: effect of relative uncertainty, controlling for mean uncertainty and restricted to explore participants, revealing activation in dorsal and ventral lFPC regions, rendered at $p < 0.05$ FWE corrected (cluster level). Right: contrast of relative uncertainty effect, controlling for mean uncertainty, in explore versus nonexplore participants revealing a group difference in lFPC, rendered at $p < .05$ FWE corrected (cluster level). Adapted with permission from Badre *et al.* (2012).

In the real world, value and uncertainty both impact animal choices. Animals must trade off maximizing reward by exploiting well-known options with changing strategy and exploring less well-known options to gain information that may reveal even better rewards, a classic problem known as the exploration–exploitation dilemma (Sutton & Barto, 1998). Theoretical work has proposed that adaptive exploration can be directed toward options in proportion to the difference in uncertainty between them (Kakade & Dayan, 2002). In practice, however, isolating the influence of uncertainty on exploration has proven challenging (e.g., Daw, O'Doherty, Dayan, Seymour, & Dolan, 2006), partly because it requires very precise modeling of exploitation. In one elegant study, Michael Frank and colleagues (Frank, Doll, Oas-Terpstra & Moreno, 2009) accomplished this using a clock-stopping task. In this task, subjects have to decide when to stop a clock hand moving clockwise one full rotation over an interval of 5 s in different contexts with different reward structures: an increasing expected value (iEV), decreasing expected value (dEV), and constant expected value (cEV) condition. After accounting for the influence of incrementally learned Go and No-Go action values, among other factors, the authors found that the model failed to capture large swings in subjects' reaction times (RTs; Figure 22.5). These RT swings were accounted for by introducing an explore term that could influence both RTs and choices in proportion to the relative Bayesian uncertainty between "fast" and "slow" responses (those faster or slower than the local average). Inclusion of this term significantly improved model performance by capturing these large swings from fast to slow responses or vice versa. This indicated that subjects explored fast and slow responses at key points in the experiment to learn about the structure of the reward environment, critically doing so in proportion to the relative uncertainty about obtaining positive reward-prediction errors from categorical fast and slow choices. These directed behavioral changes from an exploitative to exploratory strategy, driven by relative uncertainty, were associated with variation in the expression of catechol-*O*-methyltransferase, a gene preferentially controlling prefrontal DA expression, but not with genes preferentially controlling striatal DA function. These results add to evidence indicating that the impact of DA on behavior depends upon its afferent targets and further suggest that its modulatory effects in prefrontal cortex, but not striatum, contribute to directed behavioral change.

In a second study, Badre, Doll, Long, and Frank (2012) investigated the neural correlates of such directed exploration in the same task using fMRI. They found that some subjects could be described as "explorers," while others could not, based on whether they used the relative uncertainty to drive strategic exploratory RT swings as described above. Only explorers showed an effect of the relative uncertainty in a region of lFPC that neighbored those reported by Boorman *et al.* (2009, 2011; Figure 22.5). By contrast, overall uncertainty, rather than relative uncertainty, was reflected in the activity of more posterior lateral regions of PFC, among other regions, but not in lFPC. Collectively, these studies suggest that lFPC compares variables, which may themselves be represented individually elsewhere, to guide directed or strategic changes to upcoming behavior toward counterfactual options, whether those variables are values or uncertainties. Whether and how lFPC, hippocampus, DA, NE, and other structures and neuromodulators, together orchestrate such directed behavioral change, or are selectively recruited depending on current environmental demands, remains an open question likely to be addressed in the coming years.

In this chapter, we have described how widespread value representations in the brain can result from distinct mechanisms, and how one might go about generating more mechanistic predictions about signatures of a decision-making system. Although it may be tempting to think about a single common decision-making system, evidence reviewed in this chapter suggests that contextual demands might determine the extent to which decisions are in fact implemented by distinct or at least partly distinct neural systems specialized for distinct kinds of decisions. According to this view, parallel neural circuits mediate decisions depending on the type of decision at hand, whether they are made between stimuli or actions, between well-defined options presented simultaneously or potentially changing options presented sequentially and under uncertainty, or finally, directed or undirected changes to behavior. Despite this apparent diversity in anatomical implementation, it is likely that these different kinds of decisions deploy a conserved computational architecture.

References

Alexander, W. H., & Brown, J. W. (2011). Medial prefrontal cortex as an action–outcome predictor. *Nature Neuroscience, 14*, 1338–1344.

Amiez, C., Joseph, J. P., & Procyk, E. (2006). Reward encoding in the monkey anterior cingulate cortex. *Cerebral Cortex, 16*, 1040–1055.

Anderson, A. K., Christoff, K., Stappen, I., Panitz, D., Ghahremani, D. G., Glover, G., ... Sobel, N. (2003). Dissociated neural representations of intensity and valence in human olfaction. *Nature Neuroscience, 6*, 196–202.

Badre, D., Doll, B. B., Long, N. M., & Frank, M. J. (2012). Rostrolateral prefrontal cortex and individual differences in uncertainty-driven exploration. *Neuron, 73*, 595–607.

Baillargeon, R., Spelke, E. S., & Wasserman, S. (1985). Object permanence in five-month-old infants. *Cognition, 20*, 191–208.

Barraclough, D. J., Conroy, M. L., & Lee, D. (2004). Prefrontal cortex and decision making in a mixed-strategy game. *Nature Neuroscience, 7*, 404–410.

Baxter, M. G., Parker, A., Lindner, C. C., Izquierdo, A. D., & Murray, E. A. (2000). Control of response selection by reinforcer value requires interaction of amygdala and orbital prefrontal cortex. *The Journal of Neuroscience, 20*, 4311–4319.

Bechara, A., Damasio, A. R., Damasio, H., & Anderson, S. W. (1994). Insensitivity to future consequences following damage to human prefrontal cortex. *Cognition, 50*, 7–15.

Bechara, A., Tranel, D., & Damasio, H. (2000). Characterization of the decision-making deficit of patients with ventromedial prefrontal cortex lesions. *Brain: A Journal of Neurology, 123*, 2189–2202.

Behrens, T. E., Woolrich, M. W., Walton, M. E., & Rushworth, M. F. (2007). Learning the value of information in an uncertain world. *Nature Neuroscience, 10*, 1214–1221.

Berger, B. (1992). Dopaminergic innervation of the frontal cerebral cortex. Evolutionary trends and functional implications. *Advances in Neurology, 57*, 525–544.

Berlyne, D. E., Koenig, I. D., & Hirota, T. (1966). Novelty, arousal, and the reinforcement of diversive exploration in the rat. *Journal of Comparative and Physiological Psychology, 62*, 222–226.

Blanchard, T. C., & Hayden, B. Y. (2014). Neurons in dorsal anterior cingulate cortex signal postdecisional variables in a foraging task. *The Journal of Neuroscience, 34*, 646–655.

Blatt, G. J., Andersen, R. A., & Stoner, G. R. (1990). Visual receptive field organization and cortico-cortical connections of the lateral intraparietal area (area LIP) in the macaque. *The Journal of Comparative Neurology, 299*, 421–445.

Blood, A. J., Zatorre, R. J., Bermudez, P., & Evans, A. C. (1999). Emotional responses to pleasant and unpleasant music correlate with activity in paralimbic brain regions. *Nature Neuroscience, 2*, 382–387.

Bogacz, R. (2007). Optimal decision-making theories: linking neurobiology with behaviour. *Trends in Cognitive Sciences, 11*, 118–125.

Boorman, E. D., Behrens, T. E., & Rushworth, M. F. (2011). Counterfactual choice and learning in a neural network centered on human lateral frontopolar cortex. *PLoS Biology, 9*, e1001093.

Boorman, E. D., Behrens, T. E., Woolrich, M. W., & Rushworth, M. F. (2009). How green is the grass on the other side? Frontopolar cortex and the evidence in favor of alternative courses of action. *Neuron, 62*, 733–743.

Boorman, E. D., Rushworth, M. F., & Behrens, T. E. (2013). Ventromedial prefrontal and anterior cingulate cortex adopt choice and default reference frames during sequential multi-alternative choice. *The Journal of Neuroscience, 33*, 2242–2253.

Bouret, S., & Richmond, B. J. (2010). Ventromedial and orbital prefrontal neurons differentially encode internally and externally driven motivational values in monkeys. *The Journal of Neuroscience, 30*, 8591–8601.

Bromberg-Martin, E. S., & Hikosaka, O. (2009). Midbrain dopamine neurons signal preference for advance information about upcoming rewards. *Neuron, 63*, 119–126.

Bromberg-Martin, E. S., & Hikosaka, O. (2011). Lateral habenula neurons signal errors in the prediction of reward information. *Nature Neuroscience, 14*, 1209–1216.

Butter, C. M., Mishkin, M., & Rosvold, H. E. (1963). Conditioning and extinction of a food-rewarded response after selective ablations of frontal cortex in rhesus monkeys. *Experimental Neurology, 7*, 65–75.

Cai, X., Kim, S., & Lee, D. (2011). Heterogeneous coding of temporally discounted values in the dorsal and ventral striatum during intertemporal choice. *Neuron, 69*, 170–182.

Camille, N., Griffiths, C. A., Vo, K., Fellows, L. K., & Kable, J. W. (2011). Ventromedial frontal lobe damage disrupts value maximization in humans. *The Journal of Neuroscience, 31*, 7527–7532.

Camille, N., Tsuchida, A., & Fellows, L. K. (2011). Double dissociation of stimulus-value and action-value learning in humans with orbitofrontal or anterior cingulate cortex damage. *The Journal of Neuroscience, 31*, 15048–15052.

Carmichael, S. T., & Price, J. L. (1995). Sensory and premotor connections of the orbital and medial prefrontal cortex of macaque monkeys. *The Journal of Comparative Neurology, 363*, 642–664.

Cavada, C., Company, T., Tejedor, J., Cruz-Rizzolo, R. J., & Reinoso-Suarez, F. (2000). The anatomical connections of the macaque monkey orbitofrontal cortex. A review. *Cerebral Cortex, 10*, 220–242.

Chandler, D. J., Lamperski, C. S., & Waterhouse, B. D. (2013). Identification and distribution of projections from monoaminergic and cholinergic nuclei to functionally differentiated subregions of prefrontal cortex. *Brain Research, 1522*, 38–58.

Charnov, E. L. (1976). Optimal foraging, the marginal value theorem. *Theoretical Population Biology, 9*, 129–136.

Chudasama, Y., Daniels, T. E., Gorrin, D. P., Rhodes, S. E., Rudebeck, P. H., & Murray, E. A. (2013). The role of the anterior cingulate cortex in choices based on reward value and reward contingency. *Cerebral Cortex, 23*, 2884–2898.

Cohen, J. D., McClure, S. M., & Yu, A. J. (2007). Should I stay or should I go? How the human brain manages the trade-off between exploitation and exploration. *Philosophical Transactions of the Royal Society of London B Biological Sciences, 362*, 933–942.

Colom, L. V., Christie, B. R., & Bland, B. H. (1988). Cingulate cell discharge patterns related to hippocampal EEG and their modulation by muscarinic and nicotinic agents. *Brain Research, 460*, 329–338.

Constantino, S., & Daw, N. D. (2015). Learning the opportunity cost of time in a patch-foraging task. *Cognitive, Affective, & Behavioral Neuroscience, 1–17.*

Critchley, H. D., & Rolls, E. T. (1996). Olfactory neuronal responses in the primate orbitofrontal cortex: analysis in an olfactory discrimination task. *Journal of Neurophysiology, 75,* 1659–1672.

Cromwell, H. C., & Schultz, W. (2003). Effects of expectations for different reward magnitudes on neuronal activity in primate striatum. *Journal of Neurophysiology, 89,* 2823–2838.

Daw, N. D., O'Doherty, J. P., Dayan, P., Seymour, B., & Dolan, R. J. (2006). Cortical substrates for exploratory decisions in humans. *Nature, 441,* 876–879.

Dias, R., Robbins, T. W., & Roberts, A. C. (1996). Dissociation in prefrontal cortex of affective and attentional shifts. *Nature, 380,* 69–72.

Dum, R. P., & Strick, P. L. (1991). The origin of corticospinal projections from the premotor areas in the frontal lobe. *The Journal of Neuroscience, 11,* 667–689.

Duncan, J., & Owen, A. M. (2000). Common regions of the human frontal lobe recruited by diverse cognitive demands. *Trends in Neurosciences, 23,* 475–483.

Fellows, L. K. (2006). Deciding how to decide: ventromedial frontal lobe damage affects information acquisition in multi-attribute decision making. *Brain: A Journal of Neurology, 129,* 944–952.

Fellows, L. K., & Farah, M. J. (2003). Ventromedial frontal cortex mediates affective shifting in humans: evidence from a reversal learning paradigm. *Brain, 126,* 1830–1837.

Floresco, S. B., & Ghods-Sharifi, S. (2007). Amygdala–prefrontal cortical circuitry regulates effort-based decision making. *Cerebral Cortex, 17,* 251–260.

Frank, M. J., Doll, B. B., Oas-Terpstra, J., & Moreno, F. (2009). Prefrontal and striatal dopaminergic genes predict individual differences in exploration and exploitation. *Nature Neuroscience, 12,* 1062–1068.

Freidin, E., Aw, J., & Kacelnik, A. (2009). Sequential and simultaneous choices: testing the diet selection and sequential choice models. *Behavioural Processes, 80,* 218–223.

Gallistel, C. R., Mark, T. A., King, A. P., & Latham, P. E. (2001). The rat approximates an ideal detector of changes in rates of reward:implications for the law of effect. *Journal of Experimental Psychology Animal Behavior Processes, 27,* 354–372.

Glascher, J., Hampton, A. N., & O'Doherty, J. P. (2009). Determining a role for ventromedial prefrontal cortex in encoding action-based value signals during reward-related decision making. *Cerebral Cortex, 19,* 483–495.

Gold, J. I., & Shadlen, M. N. (2007). The neural basis of decision making. *Annual Review of Neuroscience, 30,* 535–574.

Hadland, K. A., Rushworth, M. F., Gaffan, D., & Passingham, R. E. (2003). The anterior cingulate and reward-guided selection of actions. *Journal of Neurophysiology, 89,* 1161–1164.

Hamid, A. A., Pettibone, J. R., Mabrouk, O. S., Hetrick, V. L., Schmidt, R., Vander Weele, C. M., ... & Berke, J. D. (2016). Mesolimbic dopamine signals the value of work. *Nature Neuroscience, 19,* 117–126.

Hayden, B. Y., Pearson, J. M., & Platt, M. L. (2009). Fictive reward signals in the anterior cingulate cortex. *Science, 324,* 948–950.

Hayden, B. Y., Pearson, J. M., & Platt, M. L. (2011). Neuronal basis of sequential foraging decisions in a patchy environment. *Nature Neuroscience, 14,* 933–939.

He, S. Q., Dum, R. P., & Strick, P. L. (1995). Topographic organization of corticospinal projections from the frontal lobe: motor areas on the medial surface of the hemisphere. *The Journal of Neuroscience, 15,* 3284–3306.

Hornak, J., O'Doherty, J., Bramham, J., Rolls, E. T., Morris, R. G., Bullock, P. R., & Polkey, C. E. (2004). Reward-related reversal learning after surgical excisions in orbito-frontal or dorsolateral prefrontal cortex in humans. *Journal of Cognitive Neuroscience, 16,* 463–478.

Hosokawa, T., Kennerley, S. W., Sloan, J., & Wallis, J. D. (2013). Single-neuron mechanisms underlying cost–benefit analysis in frontal cortex. *The Journal of Neuroscience, 33*, 17385–17397.

Hunt, L. T., Kolling, N., Soltani, A., Woolrich, M. W., Rushworth, M. F., & Behrens, T. E. (2012). Mechanisms underlying cortical activity during value-guided choice. *Nature Neuroscience, 15*, 470–476, S1–3.

Hunt, L. T., Woolrich, M. W., Rushworth, M. F., & Behrens, T. E. (2013). Trial-type dependent frames of reference for value comparison. *PLoS Computational Biology, 9*, e1003225.

Iversen, S. D., & Mishkin, M. (1970). Perseverative interference in monkeys following selective lesions of the inferior prefrontal convexity. *Experimental Brain Research, 11*, 376–386.

Izquierdo, A., Suda, R. K., & Murray, E. A. (2004). Bilateral orbital prefrontal cortex lesions in rhesus monkeys disrupt choices guided by both reward value and reward contingency. *The Journal of Neuroscience, 24*, 7540–7548.

Jepma, M., & Nieuwenhuis, S. (2011). Pupil diameter predicts changes in the exploration–exploitation trade-off: evidence for the adaptive gain theory. *Journal of Cognitive Neuroscience, 23*, 1587–1596.

Jocham, G., Furlong, P. M., Kröger, I. L., Kahn, M. C., Hunt, L. T., & Behrens, T. E. (2014). Dissociable contributions of ventromedial prefrontal and posterior parietal cortex to value-guided choice. *NeuroImage, 100*, 498–506.

Jocham, G., Hunt, L. T., Near, J., & Behrens, T. E. (2012a). A mechanism for value-guided choice based on the excitation–inhibition balance in prefrontal cortex. *Nature Neuroscience, 15*, 960–961.

Jocham, G., Hunt, L. T., Near, J., & Behrens, T. E. (2012b). A mechanism for value-guided choice based on the excitation–inhibition balance in prefrontal cortex. *Nature Neuroscience, 15*, 960–961.

Jocham, G., Neumann, J., Klein, T. A., Danielmeier, C., & Ullsperger, M. (2009). Adaptive coding of action values in the human rostral cingulate zone. *The Journal of Neuroscience, 29*, 7489–7496.

Johnson, A., Varberg, Z., Benhardus, J., Maahs, A., & Schrater, P. (2012). The hippocampus and exploration: dynamically evolving behavior and neural representations. *Frontiers in Human Neuroscience, 6*, 216.

Jones, B., & Mishkin, M. (1972). Limbic lesions and the problem of stimulus – reinforcement associations. *Experimental Neurology, 36*, 362–377.

Jones, B. E., & Moore, R. Y. (1977). Ascending projections of the locus coeruleus in the rat. II. Autoradiographic study. *Brain Research, 127*, 25–53.

Jones, B. F., & Witter, M. P. (2007). Cingulate cortex projections to the parahippocampal region and hippocampal formation in the rat. *Hippocampus, 17*, 957–976.

Joshi, S., Kalwani, R. M., & Gold, J. I. (2013). The relationship between locus coeruleus neuronal activity and pupil diameter. *SFN Abstracts*.

Kable, J. W., & Glimcher, P. W. (2009). The neurobiology of decision: consensus and controversy. *Neuron, 63*, 733–745.

Kakade, S., & Dayan, P. (2002). Dopamine: generalization and bonuses. *Neural Networks, 15*, 549–559.

Kawagoe, R., Takikawa, Y., & Hikosaka, O. (1998). Expectation of reward modulates cognitive signals in the basal ganglia. *Nature Neuroscience, 1*, 411–416.

Kennerley, S. W., Behrens, T. E., & Wallis, J. D. (2011). Double dissociation of value computations in orbitofrontal and anterior cingulate neurons. *Nature Neuroscience*.

Kennerley, S. W., Dahmubed, A. F., Lara, A. H., & Wallis, J. D. (2009a). Neurons in the frontal lobe encode the value of multiple decision variables. *Journal of cognitive neuroscience, 21*, 1162–1178.

Kennerley, S. W., Dahmubed, A. F., Lara, A. H., & Wallis, J. D. (2009b). Neurons in the frontal lobe encode the value of multiple decision variables. *Journal of Cognitive Neuroscience, 21*, 1162–1178.

Kennerley, S. W., Walton, M. E., Behrens, T. E., Buckley, M. J., & Rushworth, M. F. (2006). Optimal decision making and the anterior cingulate cortex. *Nature Neuroscience, 9*, 940–947.

Klein-Flugge, M. C., & Bestmann, S. (2012). Time-dependent changes in human corticospinal excitability reveal value-based competition for action during decision processing. *The Journal of Neuroscience, 32*, 8373–8382.

Koechlin, E., & Hyafil, A. (2007). Anterior prefrontal function and the limits of human decision-making. *Science, 318*, 594–598.

Kolling, N., Behrens, T. E., Mars, R. B., & Rushworth, M. F. (2012). Neural mechanisms of foraging. *Science, 336*, 95–98.

Kolling, N., Wittmann, M., & Rushworth, M. F. (2014). Multiple neural mechanisms of decision making and their competition under changing risk pressure. *Neuron, 81*, 1190–1202.

Krajbich, I., Armel, C., & Rangel, A. (2010). Visual fixations and the computation and comparison of value in simple choice. *Nature Neuroscience, 13*, 1292–1298.

Kringelbach, M. L., O'Doherty, J., Rolls, E. T., & Andrews, C. (2003). Activation of the human orbitofrontal cortex to a liquid food stimulus is correlated with its subjective pleasantness. *Cerebral Cortex, 13*, 1064–1071.

Kunishio, K., & Haber, S. N. (1994). Primate cingulostriatal projection: limbic striatal versus sensorimotor striatal input. *The Journal of Comparative Neurology, 350*, 337–356.

Lau, B., & Glimcher, P. W. (2008). Value representations in the primate striatum during matching behavior. *Neuron, 58*, 451–463.

Leathers, M. L., & Olson, C. R. (2012). In monkeys making value-based decisions, LIP neurons encode cue salience and not action value. *Science, 338*, 132–135.

Lebreton, M., Jorge, S., Michel, V., Thirion, B., & Pessiglione, M. (2009). An automatic valuation system in the human brain: evidence from functional neuroimaging. *Neuron, 64*, 431–439.

Lim, S. L., Colas, J. T., O'Doherty, J. O., & Rangel, A. (2013). Primary motor cortex encodes relative action value signals that integrate stimulus value and effort cost at the time of cost. *SFN Abstracts*.

Lim, S. L., O'Doherty, J. P., & Rangel, A. (2011). The decision value computations in the vmPFC and striatum use a relative value code that is guided by visual attention. *The Journal of Neuroscience, 31*, 13214–13223.

Lindvall, O., Bjorklund, A., & Divac, I. (1978). Organization of catecholamine neurons projecting to the frontal cortex in the rat. *Brain Research, 142*, 1–24.

Lo, C. C., & Wang, X. J. (2006). Cortico-basal ganglia circuit mechanism for a decision threshold in reaction time tasks. *Nature Neuroscience, 9*, 956–963.

Luk, C. H., & Wallis, J. D. (2013). Choice coding in frontal cortex during stimulus-guided or action-guided decision-making. *The Journal of Neuroscience, 33*, 1864–1871.

Matsumoto, K., Suzuki, W., & Tanaka, K. (2003). Neuronal correlates of goal-based motor selection in the prefrontal cortex. *Science, 301*, 229–232.

McCoy, A. N., Crowley, J. C., Haghighian, G., Dean, H. L., & Platt, M. L. (2003). Saccade reward signals in posterior cingulate cortex. *Neuron, 40*, 1031–1040.

McCoy, A. N., & Platt, M. L. (2005). Risk-sensitive neurons in macaque posterior cingulate cortex. *Nature Neuroscience, 8*, 1220–1227.

McGinty, V. B., Lardeux, S., Taha, S. A., Kim, J. J., & Nicola, S. M. (2013). Invigoration of reward seeking by cue and proximity encoding in the nucleus accumbens. *Neuron, 78*, 910–922.

Milosavljevic, M., Navalpakkam, V., Koch, C., & Rangel, A. (2012). Relative visual saliency differences induce sizable bias in consumer choice. *Journal of Consumer Psychology, 22*, 67–74.

Mishkin, M. (1964). Perseveration of central sets after frontal lesions in monkeys. In J. M. Warren & K. Akert (Eds.), *The frontal granular cortex and behavior* (pp. 219–241). New York, NY: McGraw-Hill.

Monosov, I. E., & Hikosaka, O. (2012). Regionally distinct processing of rewards and punishments by the primate ventromedial prefrontal cortex. *The Journal of Neuroscience, 32*, 10318–10330.

Nassar, M. R., Rumsey, K. M., Wilson, R. C., Parikh, K., Heasly, B., & Gold, J. I. (2012). Rational regulation of learning dynamics by pupil-linked arousal systems. *Nature Neuroscience, 15*, 1040–1046.

Neubert, F. X., Mars, R. B., Thomas, A. G., Sallet, J., & Rushworth, M. F. (2014). Comparison of human ventral frontal cortex areas for cognitive control and language with areas in monkey frontal cortex. *Neuron, 81*, 700–713.

Niv, Y., Daw, N. D., Joel, D., & Dayan, P. (2007). Tonic dopamine: opportunity costs and the control of response vigor. *Psychopharmacology (Berlin), 191*, 507–520.

Noonan, M. P., Walton, M. E., Behrens, T. E., Sallet, J., Buckley, M. J., & Rushworth, M. F. (2010). Separate value comparison and learning mechanisms in macaque medial and lateral orbitofrontal cortex. *Proceedings of the National Academy of Sciences of the United States of America, 107*, 20547–20552.

O'Doherty, J. P. (2014). The problem with value. *Neuroscience and Biobehavioral Reviews, 43*, 259–268

O'Doherty, J., Rolls, E. T., Francis, S., Bowtell, R., McGlone, F., Kobal, G., ... Ahne, G. (2000). Sensory-specific satiety-related olfactory activation of the human orbitofrontal cortex. *Neuroreport, 11*, 893–897.

O'Reilly, J. X., Schuffelgen, U., Cuell, S. F., Behrens, T. E., Mars, R. B., & Rushworth, M. F. (2013). Dissociable effects of surprise and model update in parietal and anterior cingulate cortex. *Proceedings of the National Academy of Sciences of the United States of America, 110*, E3660–E3669.

Öngür, D., & Price, J. L. (2000). The organization of networks within the orbital and medial prefrontal cortex of rats, monkeys and humans. *Cerebral Cortex, 10*, 206–219.

Padoa-Schioppa, C. (2009). Range-adapting representation of economic value in the orbitofrontal cortex. *The Journal of Neuroscience, 29*, 14004–14014.

Padoa-Schioppa, C., & Assad, J. A. (2006). Neurons in the orbitofrontal cortex encode economic value. *Nature, 441*, 223–226.

Padoa-Schioppa, C., & Assad, J. A. (2008). The representation of economic value in the orbitofrontal cortex is invariant for changes of menu. *Nature Neuroscience, 11*, 95–102.

Pastor-Bernier, A., & Cisek, P. (2011). Neural correlates of biased competition in premotor cortex. *The Journal of Neuroscience, 31*, 7083–7088.

Pearson, J. M., Heilbronner, S. R., Barack, D. L., Hayden, B. Y., & Platt, M. L. (2011). Posterior cingulate cortex: adapting behavior to a changing world. *Trends Cogn Sci, 15*, 143–151.

Petrides, M., & Pandya, D. N. (1999). Dorsolateral prefrontal cortex: comparative cytoarchitectonic analysis in the human and the macaque brain and corticocortical connection patterns. *The European Journal of Neuroscience, 11*, 1011–1036.

Pickens, C. L., Saddoris, M. P., Gallagher, M., & Holland, P. C. (2005). Orbitofrontal lesions impair use of cue–outcome associations in a devaluation task. *Behavioral Neuroscience, 119*, 317–322.

Pickens, C. L., Saddoris, M. P., Setlow, B., Gallagher, M., Holland, P. C., & Schoenbaum, G. (2003). Different roles for orbitofrontal cortex and basolateral amygdala in a reinforcer devaluation task. *The Journal of Neuroscience, 23*, 11078–11084.

Plassmann, H., O'Doherty, J., & Rangel, A. (2007). Orbitofrontal cortex encodes willingness to pay in everyday economic transactions. *The Journal of Neuroscience, 27*, 9984–9988.

Platt, M. L., & Glimcher, P. W. (1999). Neural correlates of decision variables in parietal cortex. *Nature, 400*, 233–238.

Prevost, C., Pessiglione, M., Metereau, E., Clery-Melin, M. L., & Dreher, J. C. (2010). Separate valuation subsystems for delay and effort decision costs. *The Journal of Neuroscience, 30*, 14080–14090.

Procyk, E., Tanaka, Y. L., & Joseph, J. P. (2000). Anterior cingulate activity during routine and non-routine sequential behaviors in macaques. *Nature Neuroscience, 3*, 502–508.

Rangel, A., Camerer, C., & Montague, P. R. (2008). A framework for studying the neurobiology of value-based decision making. *Nature Reviews Neuroscience, 9*, 545–556.

Remondes, M., & Wilson, M. A. (2013). Cingulate-hippocampus coherence and trajectory coding in a sequential choice task. *Neuron, 80*, 1277–1289.

Rich, E. L., & Wallis, J. D. (2014). Medial-lateral organization of the orbitofrontal cortex. *Journal of cognitive neuroscience, 26*, 1347–1362.

Roesch, M. R., & Olson, C. R. (2003). Impact of expected reward on neuronal activity in prefrontal cortex, frontal and supplementary eye fields and premotor cortex. *Journal of Neurophysiology, 90*, 1766–1789.

Roesch, M. R., & Olson, C. R. (2004). Neuronal activity related to reward value and motivation in primate frontal cortex. *Science, 304*, 307–310.

Rolls, E. T., & Baylis, L. L. (1994). Gustatory, olfactory, and visual convergence within the primate orbitofrontal cortex. *The Journal of Neuroscience, 14*, 5437–5452.

Rolls, E. T., Sienkiewicz, Z. J., & Yaxley, S. (1989). Hunger modulates the responses to gustatory stimuli of single neurons in the caudolateral orbitofrontal cortex of the macaque monkey. *The European Journal of Neuroscience, 1*, 53–60.

Rudebeck, P. H., Behrens, T. E., Kennerley, S. W., Baxter, M. G., Buckley, M. J., Walton, M. E., & Rushworth, M. F. (2008). Frontal cortex subregions play distinct roles in choices between actions and stimuli. *The Journal of Neuroscience, 28*, 13775–13785.

Rudebeck, P. H., Walton, M. E., Smyth, A. N., Bannerman, D. M., & Rushworth, M. F. (2006). Separate neural pathways process different decision costs. *Nature Neuroscience, 9*, 1161–1168.

Rushworth, M. F., & Behrens, T. E. (2008). Choice, uncertainty and value in prefrontal and cingulate cortex. *Nature Neuroscience, 11*, 389–397.

Rushworth, M. F., Kolling, N., Sallet, J., & Mars, R. B. (2012). Valuation and decision-making in frontal cortex: one or many serial or parallel systems? *Current Opinion in Neurobiology, 22*, 946–955.

Rushworth, M. F., Noonan, M. P., Boorman, E. D., Walton, M. E., & Behrens, T. E. (2011). Frontal cortex and reward-guided learning and decision-making. *Neuron, 70*, 1054–1069.

Salamone, J. D., Correa, M., Farrar, A., & Mingote, S. M. (2007). Effort-related functions of nucleus accumbens dopamine and associated forebrain circuits. *Psychopharmacology (Berlin), 191*, 461–482.

Samejima, K., Ueda, Y., Doya, K., & Kimura, M. (2005). Representation of action-specific reward values in the striatum. *Science, 310*, 1337–1340.

Schoenbaum, G., Chiba, A. A., & Gallagher, M. (1999). Neural encoding in orbitofrontal cortex and basolateral amygdala during olfactory discrimination learning. *The Journal of Neuroscience, 19*, 1876–1884.

Schwartenbeck, P., Fitzgerald, T., Dolan, R. J., & Friston, K. (2013). Exploration, novelty, surprise, and free energy minimization. *Frontiers in Psychology, 4*, 710.

Seo, H., Barraclough, D. J., & Lee, D. (2007). Dynamic signals related to choices and outcomes in the dorsolateral prefrontal cortex. *Cerebral Cortex, 17*, i110–i117.

Seo, H., Barraclough, D. J., & Lee, D. (2009). Lateral intraparietal cortex and reinforcement learning during a mixed-strategy game. *The Journal of Neuroscience, 29*, 7278–7289.

Seo, H., & Lee, D. (2007). Temporal filtering of reward signals in the dorsal anterior cingulate cortex during a mixed-strategy game. *The Journal of Neuroscience, 27*, 8366–8377.

Serences, J. T. (2008). Value-based modulations in human visual cortex. *Neuron, 60*, 1169–1181.

Sescousse, G., Redoute, J., & Dreher, J. C. (2010). The architecture of reward value coding in the human orbitofrontal cortex. *The Journal of Neuroscience, 30*, 13095–13104.

Shadlen, M. N., & Newsome, W. T. (1996). Motion perception: seeing and deciding. *Proceedings of the National Academy of Sciences of the United States of America, 93*, 628–633.

Shidara, M., Aigner, T. G., & Richmond, B. J. (1998). Neuronal signals in the monkey ventral striatum related to progress through a predictable series of trials. *The Journal of Neuroscience, 18*, 2613–2625.

Shima, K., & Tanji, J. (1998). Role for cingulate motor area cells in voluntary movement selection based on reward. *Science, 282*, 1335–1338.

Shuler, M. G., & Bear, M. F. (2006). Reward timing in the primary visual cortex. *Science, 311*, 1606–1609.

Smith, E. A., & Winterhalder, B. (1992). *Evolutionary ecology and human behavior*. New York, NY: de Gruyer.

Smith, P. L., & Ratcliff, R. (2004). Psychology and neurobiology of simple decisions. *Trends in Neurosciences, 27*, 161–168.

Stephens, D. W., & Krebs, J. R. (1986). *Foraging theory*. Princeton, NJ: Princeton University Press.

Strait, C. E., Blanchard, T. C., & Hayden, B. Y. (2014). Reward value comparison via mutual inhibition in ventromedial prefrontal cortex. *Neuron*.

Sugrue, L. P., Corrado, G. S., & Newsome, W. T. (2004). Matching behavior and the representation of value in the parietal cortex. *Science, 304*, 1782–1787.

Sutton, R. S., & Barto, A. G. (1998). *Reinforcement learning: an introduction*. Cambridge, MA: MIT Press.

Thorpe, S. J., Rolls, E. T., & Maddison, S. (1983). The orbitofrontal cortex: neuronal activity in the behaving monkey. *Experimental Brain Research, 49*, 93–115.

Towal, R. B., Mormann, M., & Koch, C. (2013). Simultaneous modeling of visual saliency and value computation improves predictions of economic choice. *Proceedings of the National Academy of Sciences of the United States of America, 110*, E3858–E3867.

Tremblay, L., & Schultz, W. (1999). Relative reward preference in primate orbitofrontal cortex. *Nature, 398*, 704–708.

Tsuchida, A., Doll, B. B., & Fellows, L. K. (2010). Beyond reversal: a critical role for human orbitofrontal cortex in flexible learning from probabilistic feedback. *The Journal of Neuroscience, 30*, 16868–16875.

Vasconcelos, M., Monteiro, T., Aw, J., & Kacelnik, A. (2010). Choice in multi-alternative environments: a trial-by-trial implementation of the sequential choice model. *Behav Processes, 84*, 435–439.

Voss, J. L., Gonsalves, B. D., Federmeier, K. D., Tranel, D., & Cohen, N. J. (2011). Hippocampal brain-network coordination during volitional exploratory behavior enhances learning. *Nature Neuroscience, 14*, 115–120.

Voss, J. L., Warren, D. E., Gonsalves, B. D., Federmeier, K. D., Tranel, D., & Cohen, N. J. (2011). Spontaneous revisitation during visual exploration as a link among strategic behavior, learning, and the hippocampus. *Proceedings of the National Academy of Sciences of the United States of America, 108*, E402–E409.

Wallis, J. D., & Miller, E. K. (2003). Neuronal activity in primate dorsolateral and orbital prefrontal cortex during performance of a reward preference task. *The European Journal of Neuroscience, 18*, 2069–2081.

Walton, M. E., Bannerman, D. M., Alterescu, K., & Rushworth, M. F. (2003). Functional specialization within medial frontal cortex of the anterior cingulate for evaluating effort-related decisions. *The Journal of Neuroscience, 23*, 6475–6479.

Walton, M. E., Bannerman, D. M., & Rushworth, M. F. (2002). The role of rat medial frontal cortex in effort-based decision making. *The Journal of Neuroscience, 22*, 10996–11003.

Walton, M. E., Behrens, T. E., Buckley, M. J., Rudebeck, P. H., & Rushworth, M. F. (2010). Separable learning systems in the macaque brain and the role of orbitofrontal cortex in contingent learning. *Neuron, 65*, 927–939.

Walton, M. E., Devlin, J. T., & Rushworth, M. F. (2004). Interactions between decision making and performance monitoring within prefrontal cortex. *Nature Neuroscience, 7*, 1259–1265.

Wang, A. Y., Miura, K., & Uchida, N. (2013). The dorsomedial striatum encodes net expected return, critical for energizing performance vigor. *Nature Neuroscience, 16*, 639–647.

Wang, X. J. (2002). Probabilistic decision making by slow reverberation in cortical circuits. *Neuron, 36*, 955–968.

Watanabe, M. (1996). Reward expectancy in primate prefrontal neurons. *Nature, 382*, 629–632.

Wilson, R. C., & Niv, Y. (2011). Inferring relevance in a changing world. *Frontiers in Human Neuroscience, 5*, 189.

Wong, K. F., & Wang, X. J. (2006). A recurrent network mechanism of time integration in perceptual decisions. *The Journal of Neuroscience, 26*, 1314–1328.

Wunderlich, K., Rangel, A., & O'Doherty, J. P. (2009). Neural computations underlying action-based decision making in the human brain. *Proceedings of the National Academy of Sciences of the United States of America, 106*, 17199–17204.

Wunderlich, K., Rangel, A., & O'Doherty, J. P. (2010). Economic choices can be made using only stimulus values. *Proceedings of the National Academy of Sciences of the United States of America, 107*, 15005–15010.

Yu, A. J., & Dayan, P. (2005). Uncertainty, neuromodulation, and attention. *Neuron, 46*, 681–692.

Index

acquisition processes 10, 11, 12, 15, 16, 69, 76
action(s) 411–28, 489
   choice between 417–18
   definition and distinction from response 435
   goal-directed *see* goal-directed processes
   habits as sequences of 422–3
   habitual *see* habit
   object-directed, mirror neurons and 523, 529
   selection and execution 504–5
   value of 555
action–outcome (A–O) 412–18
   habit formation and 412–18
   value-guided choice and 559
action understanding 529, 530, 531
active avoidance 442, 443, 458, 460, 460
adaptation
   behavioral 569–83
   in mirror neuron origin 519–22, 532
      distinction from associative accounts 522–31
   in perceptual learning 206–7, 209, 212
addiction, drug 129–30, 287
adolescents, anxiety 468–88
adults
   mirror neurons 520, 522–3, 527, 528
   perceptual learning 226, 228, 229, 232, 233, 234, 239

allergy, food (experiment) 116–17, 119, 394
alpha suppression 527
Alzheimer's disease (AD) 271
   mouse model 155, 275
ambiguity 104–5
   cue 292, 293
   feature 255, 257, 267–9, 270
amnesia, medial temporal lobe 272, 274
AMPA receptors
   recognition memory and subunit GluA1 of 189–92
   value-guided choice and 563
amygdala 98–9, 459–61
   basolateral
      child and adolescent anxiety and 473, 477
      habit formation and 431, 432
      prediction error and 104
      reduction in attention and 101
      reward and 100–1
   central/central nucleus (CeA) 98–9
      avoidance and 459, 460
      habit formation and 427–8
      prediction error and 104
      reward and 98, 99, 100, 101
   contextual conditioning and 295, 305
   fear conditioning 32–3, 291–2, 295
   fear learning/conditioning and 473, 474, 475, 477, 478

The Wiley Handbook on the Cognitive Neuroscience of Learning, First Edition.
Edited by Robin A. Murphy and Robert C. Honey.
© 2016 John Wiley & Sons, Ltd. Published 2016 by John Wiley & Sons, Ltd.

contextual conditioning and 32–3, 291–2, 295
lateral 27, 32, 33
animal learning
  contemporary 70–2
  historical studies 69–70
anxiety, child and adolescent 468–88
  see also fear
Aplysia
  epigenetics 144, 147, 160, 164, 165
  Hebbian hypothesis 27
appetitive conditioning (incl. appetitive instrumental conditioning) 5–7, 77, 287, 427, 442, 443, 447, 455, 457, 460
  inhibitory processes and 495, 496, 497, 500, 505, 506
  timing 360–1, 362, 363, 364, 365, 371
arenas and navigations 317–18, 321–2, 323, 324, 328, 332, 333, 334, 337
arousal, general enhancement of 288
associative learning 1–176
  central problem of standard models 78–9
  conditions for 49–57
  theoretical elaboration 78–80
associative representations 177–407
associative stream in perceptual learning 201, 202
attention 86–135
  brain regions involved *see* brain
  derived, humans 114–35
  joint, and lexical development 545
  perception and 131, 225–9
  reductions in 100–1
  reward learning *see* reward
  set *see* set
  spatial learning and changes in 330–1
  value-guided choice and 568
  weighting 225–9
auditory stimuli and their processing
  lexical development 541, 544, 545
  perceptual learning 226, 230
auto-associator
  causal learning and 383, 387, 390, 393
  lexical development and 540–1, 543
autocatalytic loops 142
auto-encoder and lexical development 543
automatic imitation 519, 529
automatization 502, 503, 505, 506
autoshaping, pigeon 16–17, 20, 23, 25
aversion
avoiding the experience of *see* avoidance
  flavor/taste 14–15, 71, 72–3, 74, 77, 80, 229, 315, 413–14, 417, 419, 427, 455–6, 492
  inhibition and 492, 495, 496–7, 499–500, 502, 504, 505, 506, 507
  timing and aversive unconditioned stimulus 357, 359, 362
avoidance 442–67
  acquisition 450–1
  active 442, 443, 458, 460, 460
  associative theories 444–50
  conditions necessary for 450–3
  maintenance 451–2
  mechanisms 458–61
  passive 442, 443

Babbage, Charles 57
backward conditioned inhibition 493
basal ganglia and response inhibition 501
beacons in mazes 320, 325, 327, 330–1, 332
behavioral adaptation 569–83
behavioral inhibition 497
  top-down 500–1
belongingness (stimulus–reinforcer relevance) 21, 23
blocked exposure in perceptual learning 205, 209, 213–17
blocking effect 19, 24, 31, 32, 33, 35, 94–6
  causation and 381–2
  lexical development and 549
  spatial learning 331, 332, 333, 337
BNDF (brain-derived neurotrophic factor) gene 145, 148, 157, 159, 161, 162, 163, 165, 166
brain (incl. neural mechanisms/correlates)
  attentional processes 212
    attentional set 90–6
    reduction in attention 101–2
    reward 98–101
  avoidance behavior and 458–61
  epigenetics and areas involved in 157–65
  fear learning and 473–4
  habitual behavior and 423–8
  imaging *see* neuroimaging
  inhibition and 498–9
  learning and conditioning (in general) 26–33
  mediated learning and 74–7

brain (incl. neural mechanisms/correlates) (*cont'd*)
  mirror neuron populations 519, 531
  outcome expectations and 393–5
  plasticity *see* plasticity
  prediction error and 33, 57–65, 102–3, 393–5
  timing mechanisms and 356–62
  value-guided choice and 554, 557, 558, 561, 562, 563, 566, 568, 582, 591
  see also specific parts
brain-derived neurotrophic factor (BDNF) gene 145, 148, 157, 159, 161, 162, 163, 165, 166

CA1 of hippocampus and temporal cognition 358, 359, 360, 361
CA3 of hippocampus and temporal cognition 358, 361, 362
Caenorhabditis elegans 160, 164, 165, 168
calcineurin 145, 162
calcium/calmodulin-dependent protein kinase II 142
Cambridge Neuropsychological Test Automated Battery (CANTAB) ID–ED task 90, 91
cAMP response element-binding(CREB) 1 and CREB2 143, 147
cannabinoid (CB) receptors 425, 426
canonical neurons 517, 522
capture, value-driven 122–3, 124
catechol-*O*-methyltransferase enzyme gene 399–400
categorical perception 236–9
categorization (category learning) 223–35, 236, 237
causation 380–407
  inferring larger causal structures from individual causal links 340–3
cell
  epigenetic mechanisms and formation of cellular associations 150–1
  heredity 139
  memory 136, 137, 139, 143
cerebellum and eyeblink conditioning 29–30, 31–2
Chasmagnathus granulatus 159
checkerboards 202, 205, 213, 230, 233
children
  anxiety 468–88
  development *see* development

perceptual learning 226, 228
  see also infancy; neonates
choice and decision-making 554–91
  between two actions 417–18
  information processing and 351–2
  mechanisms 562–7
  risky 104–6
  value-guided 554–91
cholinergic systems
  reduction in attention and 101
  temporal learning and 367
chromatin markings 139–41
  storage of memory and 152
cingulate cortex, anterior (ACC), value-guided choice and 558, 559, 567, 570, 573–4, 575, 576, 577, 578
cognitive expectancy 448–90
cognitive expectancy *see* expectations
cognitive impairment, mild (MCI) 276, 277
cognitive inhibition 489, 497
cognitive maps 318–25, 326, 327, 329, 330, 331, 332, 336, 337, 338
color (walls of arena) and spatial learning 318, 333
comparison/comparator processes 25–6, 34
  in perceptual learning 205–7
competition (between)
  cues *see* cues
  recognition memory 187–9
    short-term and long-term habituation 180–1
    short-term and long-term memory 184, 189
    short-term and long-term spontaneous novelty preference behaviour 181–2
complete serial compound temporal difference simulator 355
compound discrimination 90, 91
computation(s) 65
  associative 48–9
computational models of memory 249–82
computer simulations *see* simulation
conceptual knowledge and low-level perception 239–40
concurrent processing of CS–US 22–3, 25, 26, 33, 34
condition(s) (for learning/Pavlovian learning) 35–6
  associative learning 49–57
  avoidance learning 450–3

fear learning 468–74, 476, 477
spatial learning 327–36
conditioned excitation *see* excitatory conditioning
conditioned inhibition *see* inhibitory conditioning; inhibitory control
conditioned response (CR) 349, 353, 357, 360, 362, 363
  acquisition 351, 353
  timing 351
conditioned stimuli (CS) 8–35
  contextual learning and 286
  intensity 10
  novelty 10
  prediction and 52–4
  timing 348–71
conditioned stimuli–unconditioned stimuli (CS–US)
  avoidance learning and 450–2
  concurrent processing of representations of 22–3, 25, 26, 33, 34
  contingency degradation effects 35
  convergence 27, 31
  pairings 11–13, 22, 24, 27, 28
    number 10–12
    order 12–13
    similarity 18–21
  training trials 11–12
conditioning
  appetitive *see* appetitive conditioning
  context-specific/dependent *see* contextual processes
  fear *see* fear
  instrumental *see* instrumental learning
  neural principles 26–33
  Pavlovian *see* Pavlovian learning
  serial 97–8
  timing and *see* temporal characteristics
  trace *see* trace conditioning
conflict (competition between response options) 499–500
congruency tasks 497, 499
connectivity (neural network) 138
  habit formation and 424, 425
  lexical development and 541
  memory and 138, 151–2, 541
contents of learning 35–6
  avoidance and 454
context chamber and context testing room conditioning 289–90

contextual (context-specific/dependent) processes/conditioning 285–312
  definition of context 286
  excitatory 294, 295–6, 298, 300–1, 301–2
  inhibitory 294–306, 307
  long-term habituation 184
  mirror neurons and 526
  US associations 286, 287–94, 306–7
contiguity
  mirror neurons and 522
  spatial 17–18
  temporal 13–15, 20, 24, 26–30, 348–50
contingency (learning) 19–20
  action–outcome, manipulating 412–13
  degradation 35, 418
  instrumental 412, 422, 432, 445, 452–3
  mirror neurons and 522, 522–6, 528
  overt attention during 116
  Pavlovian 340–2
correlation
  in lexical development 541, 549
  response rate–reward rate 414–16
cortico-striatal and cortico-striato-thalamic circuitry
  attentional set and 92–4
  habit formation and 424, 426, 433
  value-guided choice and 559
CpG (cytosine–guanine) dinucleotides (CpG) 139, 140, 161, 162
CREB1 and CREB2 (cAMP response element-binding 1 and 2) 143, 147
cue(s)
  ambiguity 292, 293
  blocking 19, 24, 31, 32, 33, 35, 94–6, 381, 382
  competition between 19
    spatial learning and 331–6
    temporal difference and 354
  contextual 286, 292–3, 298–302
  priority 52–3
  relative cue validity 20, 23, 24, 25, 33
  unblocking 32, 33, 62, 99, 100–1
cue–outcome (A–O) associations and causal learning 381–90
"cycle" to "trial" (C/T) ratio 16–17, 20, 23, 24, 25, 28
cytosine–guanine (CpG) dinucleotides 139, 140, 161, 162

dead reckoning 313, 321
decision-making *see* choice and decision-making
declarative memory 251, 252, 253, 258
default choices 570–3
defensive reactions 444
delay-dependent memory deficits/forgetting 254, 264–6
dementia 271
dendritic spines 145–6, 148, 151
    medium spiny neurons (MSNs) in dorsal striatum and 368, 369
depolarization, postsynaptic 27, 28
derived attention in humans 114–35
devaluation (outcome) 413–18, 419, 432, 433–5
    reinforcer 455–8
    unconditioned stimuli 11
development (incl. childhood)
    fear learning 471, 472–7, 478, 479
    lexical 538–53
    mirror neuron 519, 520, 521, 522, 523, 526, 528, 529, 530
diagonal band, vertical limb of 101
Dicer 145, 147, 149, 163
differential reinforcement of low rates (DRL) of behavior 358
differentiation in perceptual learning 229–33, 235
direct learning vs. mediated learning 79
directed behavioral adaptation 576–83
directional information in spatial learning 319, 325–6, 336
discrimination (learning) 87, 89, 90–1, 93, 294, 423, 424
    contextual 294, 295
        fear conditioning 289–93, 294, 307
        visual discrimination 296–8
    perceptual learning and 203–5, 209
    spatial learning 330
    temporal learning and 359
    visual *see* visual discrimination
dispositions, specific inherited 153
dissociations
    double 250, 258, 262
    neuroanatomical 179
    triple, within a triple dissociation 296–7
distinctiveness, acquired 87, 88, 90, 226
DNA methylation 137, 139–41, 143, 144, 152, 154, 161–3, 166, 167
    fear conditioning 145, 146, 147, 148, 149

dopamine (DA) system 47–68, 363–5, 366–7, 395–400
    avoidance and 458
    blocking and latent inhibition and 95
    habit formation and 424, 425, 426
    midbrain 30–1, 34, 61, 99, 459
    phasic firing of dopaminergic neurons 363–4, 394
    prediction error and 31, 57–65, 102, 103, 104, 395–9
    reward and 58–64, 98, 99
    temporal learning and 363–5
    transporter gene 398–9
    value-guided choice and 574–6, 582
dopamine D2 receptor 49
    gene, and polymorphisms 395–8
    habit formation and 424, 425
dot probe procedure 117–19, 130
double dissociations 250, 258, 262
drift diffusion model of choice 562
"drive" conditioning 35
Drosophila
    conditioned stimuli–unconditioned stimuli 13
    epigenetics 148, 159, 160, 164, 165, 168
drug addiction 129–30, 287
dual processes and systems
    avoidance behavior 454–7
    recognition memory 179, 188, 192–3, 195
    short and long-term memory 253, 256
duration
    of cues, fixed vs. from trial to trial 353
    of salience, perceived 131

EEG *see* electroencephalography
effective salience 119, 120, 126, 129, 130
eight-arm radial maze *see* radial maze
electroencephalography (EEG) perceptual learning 211, 212, 231
    mirror neurons and 527
elements in perceptual learning 202–3, 206–9
    common 202, 203, 205, 206, 207, 208
    unique 202, 203, 206, 207, 208, 209
eligibility trace 355
emotional learning and memory 294
encoding (memory) 137
    of context-specific inhibitory association 298
    epigenetics 138, 150, 152
endocannabinoids 425, 426

English language 236
　children and 226
engrams 136–7, 138
environment
　contextual 286
　in spatial learning
　　exploration 328–30
　　familiar 321, 327, 331
　　geometry 324, 332–6, 337
　　shape 321, 324, 333
epigenetics 136–76
　mechanisms 139–42
　　cellular associations and 150–1
equivalence 224
　acquired 224, 226, 520, 528
Eriksen flanker task 497, 499
Espinet effect 492–3, 493, 496
event-related potentials and evoked potentials
　motor *see* motor evoked potentials
　N2pc component 122, 125
evolution
　associative learning 154
　mirror neurons 515, 519, 520, 522, 524, 529
excitatory conditioning/learning 12, 13, 16, 21, 22, 25, 33, 34–5, 389, 482, 489
　causation and 387, 388–90, 393
　contextual 294, 295–6, 298, 300–1, 301–2
executive control 489, 497, 506
exosomes 151–2
expectations/expectancy (outcome)
　avoidance and 448–50
　brain and 393–5
experiential transmission 152
exploration (visual/of environment) 328–30
　directed behavioral adaptation and an experiment in 577–8
　recognition memory and 187, 190, 194
exposure schedule in perceptual learning 203–6
　brain imaging and 212–17
extinction 304–5, 492
　contextual control 286, 304–5
　fear *see* fear
eye movements 116, 122, 123, 124, 125
　eye gaze 62, 122, 123, 560
　eye tracking 116, 117, 119, 122, 125
　saccades 121, 122, 560, 561, 562
eyeblink conditioning 13, 17, 20, 29, 31–2, 33, 34

face (and its perception) 232–3, 271
　adults imitating infants facial movements 520
　categorization 226
　processing 234
familiarity 179, 188, 203, 205, 265, 266, 549, 550
　environmental, spatial learning and 321, 327, 331
fear 145–50, 468–88
　conditioning/learning 32–3, 72, 75–6, 453, 459, 470, 471, 473, 476
　　anxious and non-anxious youths 469–70
　　children and adolescents 468–88
　　in contextual paradigms 288–94
　　deficits 471
　　discriminative 289–93, 294, 307
　　epigenetics 145–50, 153, 155–7, 160, 161, 162, 163, 164, 167
　　individual differences (in humans) 469–70
　　nondiscriminative 288, 289, 290, 291, 292
　　temporal cognition and 357
　extinction 145, 398, 469, 474–5, 477–8
　　anxious and non-anxious youths 469
　　epigenetics 145–50
　　retention 474–5
　generalized (enhancement of) 288, 289
　multiple measures of 291
　reactivation/reinstatement 474, 476
　reduction 445, 446, 447, 449
　return/spontaneous recovery (after extinction) 476–7
　spontaneous forgetting 474
　see also anxiety
feature ambiguity 255, 257, 267–9, 270
flavor (taste) aversion 14–15, 71, 72–3, 74, 77, 80, 229, 315, 413–14, 417, 419, 427, 455–6, 492
flexibility of avoidance behavior 454–5
flooding 453
food
　allergy (experiment) 116–17, 119, 394
　flavor/taste aversion 14–15, 71, 72–3, 74, 77, 80, 229, 315, 413–14, 417, 419, 427, 455–6, 492
foot shock 19, 20, 80, 144, 145, 288, 289, 290, 294
　avoidance and 453
　temporal cognition 357

forebrain
  basal, and reductions in attention 101
  fear conditioning and 291–2
  memory systems 291–2
forebrain bundle, medial 60
forgetting
  of fear, spontaneous 474
  over a delay (delay-dependent memory deficits/forgetting) 254, 264–6
forward conditioned inhibition 493
frames of reference and value-guided choice 554, 567
free-operant procedures 366, 445, 447, 451, 459
freezing behavior 75, 144, 288, 289, 357
frontal brain areas
  attentional set and 90–2
  response inhibition and 501
  value-guided choice and 555
frontopolar cortex, lateral (lFPC), 578, 582
functional imaging *see* neuroimaging
functional specialization of memory 249–82

GABAergic system 32
  interneurons 31, 563
  value-guided choice and 563, 566
Gallus gallus 168
gametes, direct transmission of epigenetic information via 152–3
gaze 62, 122, 123, 560
gene
  RNA-mediated targeted deletions 141
  silencing 141–2, 149
generative causes (learning about) 380–6
  asymmetries between preventive learning and 388–90
genetic manipulation experiments, dopamine and reward 62–3
genetic markers 394–400
geometry learning in navigation 324, 332–6, 337
germline transmission of epigenetic information 152–3
globus pallidus (GP) and conditioned inhibitory control 498
GluA1 AMPA receptor subunit 189–92
go pathways and responses 397, 498, 500–7, 558
goal-directed processes/behaviours/actions 127–8, 315, 316, 412–14, 421, 423, 454, 455, 456, 457, 458
  avoidance and 454
  habitual actions and 416
    comparing 414
    differentiating between 412–14, 432
    interaction between 423, 428–35
  mirror neurons and 523–4
Gryllus pennsylvanicus 168

habenula, lateral 103, 575
habit (habitual actions) 412–41
  definition 411–12
  formation 412–41
    perspectives on 414–23
  goal-directed processes and *see* goal-directed processes
  as model-free reinforcement learning 419–22
  neural correlates 423–8
habituation 180–1
  long-term 181–2, 183, 184, 185, 191
  short-term 180–1, 182, 183, 184, 191
Hall and Pearce model 86, 94, 95, 96–8, 98–9, 100–1, 102, 105, 106, 107, 495
hand actions and mirror neurons 518, 523, 524, 529
head direction cells 319, 336
heat avoidance 456
Hebb, Donald 26, 50, 349
Hebbian learning 26–30
  lexical development and 540, 541, 545, 546
  timing and 349
Helix lucorum 159
heredity *see* inheritance and heredity
hexagonal maze 320
hierarchies
  in habitual action–goal-directed action interactions 423, 428–35
  in perceptual learning, reverse (RHT) 217, 239, 240
  representational–hierarchical framework for object memory 254–77
hippocampus
  attention and its reduction 101
  contextual conditioning and 301–6
    fear conditioning 32–3, 291–2
    inhibitory 294, 295, 296, 301–6
  fear conditioning 357
    contextual conditioning and 32–3, 291–2
  latent inhibition and 101, 305

lexical development and 541
mnemonic processes 75
recognition memory and 192–6
simultaneous visual discrimination and 270–2
spatial learning
  cognitive maps 318, 319
  conditions of learning 327
  performance 336
  place cells 318, 319, 327, 336, 337
temporal cognition and 193–5, 357–62
value-guided choice and 577–8
histone
  modification (acetylation/methylation etc.) 141, 143, 152, 155, 157–60, 161, 162, 166, 167
  deacetylation and deacetylases (HDACs) 141, 145, 146, 148, 155, 156, 157, 158, 159, 160, 162
  fear conditioning and 144, 145
  variants 141
Homer1a 144, 156
humans
  derived attention 114–35
  fear learning 470–1, 477–8
  inhibition in 493–4
  mirror neurons and 518–19, 520, 524, 525, 526–8, 529, 530, 531
  perceptual learning *see* perception
  see also adolescents; adults; children; infancy
5-hydroxytryptaminergic (serotonergic) system and temporal learning 366–7

imaging of brain *see* neuroimaging
imitation 526, 527, 528
  automatic 519, 529
incidental learning and associations 296–8
  spatial 327, 328, 330
independent race model 500–1, 501
individual differences fear learning in humans 469–70
infancy
  fear conditioning 472, 478, 484
  lexical development 541–50
  mirror neurons 522, 526–7
  see also neonates
information processing theory 351–2, 366
infralimbic cortex 427
  attentional set and 93, 94
  avoidance and 460

fear learning and 473, 475
habit formation and 427, 431
value-guided choice and 563, 564
inheritance and heredity
  cell 139
  epigenetic 139, 166–8
    transgenerational 137, 142, 152–3, 154, 155–8
inhibitory conditioning/learning (and conditioned inhibition) 13, 19, 34–5, 307, 387–93, 489–514
  backward 493
  causation and 387, 387–93
  context-specific 294–306, 307
  defining 489
  dopamine and reward and 63
  forward 493
  humans 493–4
  integration of association and 505–7
  latent *see* latent inhibition
  learning and what is learned during 494–7
  mediated 492–3
  tests for inhibition 491
inhibitory control 489
  acquisition 491–2
  conditioned 497–505, 506, 507
instrumental learning/conditioning 7, 432, 505, 506–7
  appetitive *see* appetitive conditioning
  contingency 412, 422, 432, 445, 452–3
  dopamine and 61
  habits and 411–12
  serial model of instrumental behavior 432
  visual 296
intercellular neuronal connections and their formation, memory and 151–2
interference control 497, 497–8
intermixed exposure in perceptual learning 205, 206, 213–16
interneurons, GABAergic 31, 563
interpositus nucleus, cerebellar (IPN) 29, 30, 31–2
intertrial interval (ITI) and I/T ratio 11, 16, 23, 350–1, 356, 359–60, 364, 445
interval vs. ratio schedules of reinforcement 416–17
intracranial stimulation 59–60
intradimensional–extradimensional (ID–ED) shift effect 89, 90, 91, 331
intraparietal area (LIP), lateral, and value-guided choice 559–60, 563

Japanese language 230
joint attentional events and lexical development 545

landmarks in spatial learning 325–34
language, categorization in 226, 230, 236
latent inhibition 10, 94–6, 305, 306, 330
  cholinergic systems and 101
  context-specific 305, 306
    fear conditioning and extinction and 144
  hippocampus and 101, 305
  mutual exclusivity and 549
latent spatial learning 328–30, 330, 336
learning curves and epigenetics 150–1
lexical development 538–53
light (experiments using)
  attentive processes 94–5, 97–8, 100
  sensory preconditioning 70–1, 79
  short-term effects of stimulus exposure on orienting to a 191–2
lip movements and mirror neurons 518, 520, 523, 527
lithium chloride (LiCl) and taste aversion 11, 15, 21, 72, 229, 315, 413–14, 418, 432, 455, 492
localization claims in functional MRI 3
location *see* place
long-term depression (LTD) 151, 424, 425
long-term habituation 181–2, 183, 184, 185, 191
long-term memory (LTM) 145, 147, 191, 251, 253, 254, 266, 352, 359, 367
  short-term memory and
    competition between 184, 189
    dual system of 253, 256
    interactions between 190
long-term potentiation (LTP) 27–30, 151, 424, 426
long-term spontaneous novelty preference 185

macaques
  mirror neurons and 515, 516, 516–18, 519–20, 525, 526, 527, 531
  temporal order learning tasks 362
Mackintosh's model attention and associative learning 86, 88, 94–7, 102, 103, 105, 106–7, 126

magnetic resonance imaging, functional *see* neuroimaging
magnetoencephalography (MEG) and value-guided choice 563, 567
map(s)
  cognitive 318–25, 326, 327, 329, 330, 331, 332, 336, 337, 338
  self-organizing, and lexical development 544–5
MAPK (mitogen-activated protein kinase) 474, 475
marginal value theorem (MVT) 573, 574, 575
marmoset monkey 90, 106, 163
mathematics, associative learning 57
mazes
  beacons 320, 325, 327, 330–1, 332
  radial *see* radial mazes
  sunburst 319, 320
  T 87, 91, 92, 314, 427
  water 316, 318, 321, 323, 325, 326, 330, 331, 332
  Y *see* Y-maze
Mecp2 146, 161
medial forebrain bundle 60
medial nucleus and thalamus and attentional set 92–3
medial prefrontal cortex *see* prefrontal cortex
medial septum and reductions in attention 101
medial temporal lobe *see* temporal lobe
mediated inhibition 492–3
mediated learning 69, 71, 72–7
  brain mechanisms 74–7
  direct learning vs. 79
  sensory preconditioning and 72–4
  trace conditioning as 77–8
medium spiny neurons (MSNs; spiny projection neurons)
  habit formation and 424, 425
  temporal learning and 368, 369
memory 136–76, 249–82
  cellular 136, 137, 139, 143
  computational and functional specialization 249–82
  declarative 251, 252, 253, 258
  delay-dependent deficits in (delay-dependent forgetting) 254–6
  dissociations between perception and 258–62
  emotional 294

epigenetics 136–76
fear conditioning and 291–2
forebrain and 291–2
general characterization 138–9
long-term *see* long-term memory
multiple memory systems 251, 252, 262, 294
recognition *see* recognition memory
retinal snapshot in (in spatial learning) 336
retrieval *see* retrieval
short-term *see* short-term memory
working 400
see also forgetting
mental representations *see* representations
mesencephalon *see* midbrain
methylation
DNA *see* DNA methylation
histone 144, 146, 160
mice *see* mouse
microRNAs 141–2, 151, 152, 154
fear conditioning and extinction 145–6, 147, 149
microstimuli 355
midbrain (mesencephalon)
dopamine system 30–1, 34, 58, 59, 61, 62, 99, 459
structures in 58, 59
mild cognitive impairment (MCI) 276, 277
mirror neurons 515–37
localization 515, 516
mitogen-activated protein kinase 474, 475
mnemonic processes/tasks 250, 260
hippocampus 75
model-free and model-based reinforcement learning 419–22
modules
of learning 35
of visual memory and perception in brain 249–53, 258, 262
motor evoked potentials (MEPs)
mirror patterns of 519, 529
testing of response inhibition 498
motor inhibition 490, 497
motor resonance 530, 531
mouse
Alzheimer's disease model 155, 275
epigenetics 157–8, 161–2, 163–4, 166–7
mouth actions and mirror neurons 518, 519, 523
multiple attribute items, choices with 568–9

multiple memory and learning systems 251, 252, 262, 294
mutual exclusivity 546–50
mutual inhibition between habitual and goal-directed systems 428

N2pc component of event-related potential 122, 125
navigation 313–36
negative priming 499, 502
neonates (newborns) and mirror neurons 526, 527
networks
in lexical development 540, 543, 544, 545
neural *see* connectivity
neuroimaging/brain imaging (incl. functional imaging/MRI)
habit formation 424
inhibitory control 497
localization claims 3
perceptual learning 207–17
exposure schedule and 212–17
visual memory and perception and their modular organization in 249
neurons
dendritic spines *see* dendritic spines
epigenetics 139–52
memory systems 143–4
memory and formation of connections between 151–2
see also specific types
neurotransmitters and neuromodulators
prediction errors 64, 65
timing behavior and 365–7
value-guided choice and 574, 576
see also specific neurotransmitters
newborns (neonates) and mirror neurons 526, 527
nigrostriatal dopaminergic projection and habit formation 426
NMDA receptors 75, 82
fear learning and 473, 475
value-guided choice 563
nogo pathways and responses 498, 500, 558
nonassociative processes
fear 288
language 550
recognition memory 184, 188, 189, 192–6
noncoding RNA *see* RNA
noncontingent outcomes 418–19

nonhistone proteins 141
nonspatial and spatial learning, relation between 313, 338
norepinephrine (NE) and value-guided choice 576, 582
no-US representation 495, 496, 499
novelty 548–50
  objects *see* object recognition
  preference 180–2, 189–90
    spatial 181, 182, 183, 189, 190
    spontaneous 179, 180, 183–7, 189
  words 540, 542, 545, 546, 547, 549
nucleus accumbens (NAc)
  attentional set and 92, 93, 95
  avoidance and 458–9
  value-guided choice and 574, 575

object constraint, whole 539, 539–42
object-directed actions and mirror neurons 523, 529
object recognition
  memory (ORM) 251, 253, 254, 262–7, 272–7
  novel 179, 180, 182, 185, 192, 193, 234, 266, 273–6
    epigenetics 156, 157, 158, 163, 174
  lexical development and 547–50
  temporal order of presentation and 193–5
object representation 237, 249, 321, 361
  representational–hierarchical framework for object memory 254–77
obsessive–compulsive disorder (OCD) 453, 456–7, 462
oculomotor inhibition 497
oddity tasks/tests 269, 271–2
olive, inferior (IO) 31, 32
omission trials (of reward) 63, 100, 102, 104, 123–4
optional shift task 93, 94
orbitofrontal cortex (OFC) and value-guided choice 555–9, 567, 574
outcome *see* action–outcome; cue–outcome; devaluation; expectations; noncontingent outcomes; value
overshadowing 52, 350
  spatial learning and 331, 332, 333, 334, 337
overt attention 116, 117, 119, 120, 124, 125
overtraining in habit formation 415, 417–18, 422, 424, 426, 427, 432

parallel models of decision-making 567, 583
Paramecia 138, 143
parietal brain areas and response inhibition 501
parietal cortex, posterior (PPC) 100, 125
  value-guided choice and 563, 568, 573
parietal lobule, inferior, mirror neurons and 515, 516, 531
passive avoidance 442, 443
path integration (dead reckoning) 313, 321
Pavlov, Ivan 48
Pavlovian contingency 340–2
Pavlovian learning and conditioning 1–2, 7–46, 48
  conditions for 35–6
  contents of *see* contents
  dopamine and 61
  fear and 32–3, 453, 459
  major variables supporting 9–21
  neural principles 26–33
  psychological principles 21–3
Pavlovian-to-instrumental task 12
Pearce–Hall model 86, 94, 95, 96–8, 98–9, 100–1, 102, 105, 106, 107, 495
perception (perceptual learning) 201–48
  animals 201–22
  attention and 131, 225–9
  categorical 236–9
  of causality
    redundancy and its role in 381–2
    temporal information in 382–6
  definition 201, 223
  dissociations between memory and perception and 258–62
  of duration of stimulation 131
  humans 223–48
    mechanisms of change 225–37
  quality vs. quantity 207–8
  terminology 202–3
performance, spatial learning 336–7
periaqueductal gray -3(PAG) 32
perirhinal cortex (PRC) 251–8, 259, 260–6, 267, 269, 271–4, 275, 276
phasic firing of dopaminergic neurons 363–4, 394
physically-defined contextual cues 286
pigeon autoshaping 16–17, 20, 23, 25
Piwi-interacting RNAs (piRNAs) 142, 146, 147, 149
place (location) 314–37
  place cells 318, 319, 327, 336, 337
  see also space

Index

place preference task, conditioned (CPP) 287
plasticity (neural incl. brain) 1
  epigenetics 136, 137, 139, 142, 143, 145, 146, 151, 152, 155–65
  fear conditioning and 32
  Hebbian 26, 27
  perception and 239
  synaptic *see* synaptic plasticity
point of subjective equality (PSE) 366
polymorphisms 395–8, 399
pontine nuclei (PN) 31
pop-out in visual search tasks 234
postsynaptic depolarization 27, 28
posttranscriptional silencing 141
PP1 145
PPP1R1B (protein phosphatase 1 regulatory subunit 1B) 395–8
prediction (and predictiveness) 52–3, 57–65, 87–96, 115–19
  effects of predictiveness 87–96
  error 23–6, 31, 32, 48–9, 102–4, 126–7, 385–400
    brain and 33, 57–65, 102–3, 393–5
    causal learning and 382, 385–400
    dopamine and 31, 57–65, 102, 103, 104, 395–9
    signed 102–3, 103
    temporal learning and 354, 364
    unsigned 103–4
prefrontal cortex (PFC)
  active avoidance and 460–1
  attentional set and 90–2, 93
  dopaminergic genes and 396
  dorsolateral, perceptual learning and 211–12, 215
  extinction and extinction retention and 475
  fear learning and 473
  medial/ventromedial 92, 93, 94, 473
    avoidance and 460–1
    infralimbic cortex of *see* infralimbic cortex
    lateral, value-guided choice and 558–9, 560, 569, 574
    prelimbic cortex of *see* prelimbic cortex
    value-guided choice and 557–9, 561–2, 564, 566–7, 568–9, 573, 574, 578
    visual discrimination learning and 302
  prediction errors and 33
prelimbic (PL) cortex/region
  attentional set shifting and 94
  fear learning and 473–4, 475
  habit formation and 428–31

premotor complex (PMC) 432–3, 535
  habit formation and 432–3
  mirror neurons and 515, 516, 519, 531
presupplementary motor area (PMA; pre-SMA) 433, 499, 561, 570
presynaptic stimulation 27, 28
preventive causes (learning about) 387–8
  asymmetries between generative and 388–90
  redundancy and its role 387–8
priming
  negative 499, 502
  repetition 502
prion(s) 151–2
prion-like proteins 147, 150, 165
priority (of occurrence or predictiveness) 52–3
protein phosphatase 1 regulatory subunit 1B 395–8
psychological principles of Pavlovian learning 21–3
psychophysical tradition of perceptual learning research 201, 210–12
psychosis 129–30
Purkinje cells (PCs) 31, 32
putamen 424, 559

quality vs. quantity in perceptual learning 207–8
Quinean conundrum 539, 541

radial mazes and alleys (incl. eight-arm) 293, 295, 296, 296–7, 297, 299, 306, 315, 331
  dark arm 296, 298, 298–300, 300, 301
  spatial learning and 321–2, 331, 332
rate expectancy theory (RET) 10, 12, 351, 352, 353, 356
ratio vs. interval schedules of reinforcement 416–17
reactivation and reinstatement (of forgotten original experience) 294
  fear 474, 476
real-time models, temporal information implemented in 383–6
receiver operating characteristic (ROC) curves 187–8
receiver operating characteristic (ROC) curves and recognition memory 187–8

recognition memory 179–200
　hippocampus and 192–6
　nonassociative processes 184, 188, 189, 190, 192–6
　objects see object recognition
recollection 179, 188, 192, 195
redundancy
　implemented in an error-correction rule 382
　in perception of causality, role of 381–2
　in preventive learning 387–8
regulatory RNA see RNA
reinforcers (and reinforcement) 49–50, 51
　devaluation in avoidance 455–8
　interval vs. ratio schedules of reinforcement 416–17
　model-free and model-based reinforcement learning 419–22
　secondary reinforcers 50, 51, 60
　stimulus–reinforcer relevance 21, 23
　see also differential reinforcement of low rates
reinstatement see reactivation
relative cue validity 20, 23, 24, 25, 33
renewal tests 298
repetition priming effects 502
representations (associative) 201–22
　content of 454
　contextual 286
　CS–US 22–3, 25, 26, 33, 34
　No-US 495, 496, 499
　object see object representation
　US 490, 493, 494, 495, 497, 499
　of value 554–60, 560, 561, 562, 567, 583
Rescorla–Wagner model 23, 24, 25, 34, 54, 55, 57, 60, 63, 64, 65, 100–1, 102, 156, 183, 262, 337, 354, 364, 370, 381, 452, 494, 550
response
　conditioned, see also conditioned response; conflict; stimulus–organism–response task; stimulus–response associations
　correlation between reward rate and rate of 414–16
　definition and distinction from action 435
　inhibition of 497–503, 506, 507
response–no US contingency 452–3
retardation tests 298–9, 491, 492, 495, 503
retinal snapshot (in spatial learning) 336

retrieval (memory) 71, 75, 77, 79, 81, 137, 185, 186, 193, 194, 305
　epigenetics 138, 145
　inhibition and 493, 499, 502, 504, 505
　spontaneous novelty preference and 185–7
retrieval see memory
reversal learning 298, 300–1, 301, 302, 306, 555
reverse hierarchy theory (RHT) 217, 239, 240
reward 58–64, 98–101, 555–62
　correlation between response rate and rate of 414–16
　dopamine and 58–64, 98, 99
　omission trials 63, 100, 102, 104, 123–4
　sensitivity to downshifts in 98–100
　sensitivity to upshifts in 100–1
　unexpected 103, 104
　　temporally 265, 363–4
　value and 119–25, 126, 555–62
risky decision-making 104–6
RNA (regulatory/non-coding) 141–2, 163–5
　fear conditioning and extinction and 145, 147
Russian language 236

saccades 121, 122, 560, 561, 562
salience 115–16, 130, 206, 333, 334, 568
　aberrant 129
　conditioned stimuli (CS) 10
　effective 119, 120, 126, 129, 130
　perceived duration of 131
scalar expectancy theory (SET) 352, 359–60, 363, 367, 370
schizophrenia 129, 130
selective associations 21, 56, 64
self-organizing maps and lexical development 544–5
self-sustaining autocatalytic loops 142
semantic dementia 271
Semon, Richard 136–7
sensorimotor learning and mirror neurons and 526, 527, 528–9, 532
sensory preconditioning 70–80, 82, 329, 492
　mediated learning during 72–4
septum, medial, and reductions in attention 101

serial conditioning 97–8
  WBP (Wilson, Boumphrey and Pearce) task 98, 99, 100, 101
serial models
  of decision-making 567
  of instrumental behavior 432
serotonergic system and temporal learning 366–7
set (attentional)
  neural correlates 90–4
  shifting 87–9, 91, 92, 93, 94, 95, 106
shape
  of environment in spatial learning, shape 321, 324, 333
  perception 224, 225, 239–40
short-term habituation 180–1, 182, 183, 184, 191
short-term memory (STM) 251, 252, 253, 254
  long-term memory and
    competition between 184, 189
    dual system of 253, 256
    interactions 190
signed prediction error 102–3, 103
simulations (and simulation data)
  attentional theory 128
  causation learning 293, 383, 390
  computational and functional specialization of memory 254, 262, 266
simultaneous conditioning/training 14–15
simultaneous visual discrimination 269–72
single unit recording
  attentional processes 125
  choice and 566
  perceptual learning 234
  prediction error 102
  temporal cognition 359–62
small noncoding RNA molecules (small ncRNAs) 141, 142, 143, 152
  fear conditioning and extinction and 147
social behavior and mirror neurons 529–31
soma-soma transmission 152
sometimes opponent process (SOP; Standard Operating Procedures) theory 22, 24, 80, 96, 183–4, 186, 188, 189, 190, 192, 193, 195, 196, 354, 356
space (and spatial learning) 203–407
  conditions of learning 327–36
  contiguity 17–18

novelty preference 181, 182, 183, 189, 190
spatial relations 325–7
translation of learning to performance 336–7
true spatial learning 327, 328, 330, 332, 338
see also place
species-specific defensive reactions 444
spiny projection neurons *see* medium spiny neurons
spontaneous novelty preference 179, 180, 183–7, 189
S–R associations *see* stimulus–response associations
S–S (stimulus–stimulus) associations in spatial learning 314–18, 328, 329, 337
standard operating procedures (SOP; sometimes opponent process) theory 22, 24, 80, 96, 183–4, 186, 188, 189, 190, 192, 193, 195, 196, 354, 356
stimulus (and stimuli in Pavlovian learning)
  associative strength 24, 54, 55–7, 88, 96, 126, 127, 189, 355
  attention to *see* attention
  avoidance response and the degree of change in (after avoidance response) 447
  conditioned *see* conditioned stimuli
  derived attention and the processing of 126–9
  generalization, lexical development and 542–3
  intensity 9–10
  present vs. not present 69–85
  selection 19, 20, 23, 33, 151
  substitution 50–2
  unconditioned *see* unconditioned stimuli
stimulus-driven process 126, 127, 128, 207, 216, 217, 218
stimulus-onset asynchrony (SOA) 117–19
stimulus–organism–response (SOR) task 273, 274–5
stimulus–reinforcer relevance 21, 23
stimulus–response (S–R) associations
  habit formation 412, 414, 416, 418, 419, 422, 426, 428
  spatial learning 313–14, 324, 336

stimulus–stimulus (S–S) associations in spatial learning 314–18, 328, 329, 337
stop pathways/processors 500–7
storage (memory) 137
  epigenetics 138, 150, 152
stream
  associative, in perceptual learning 201, 202
  ventral visual (VVS) 249, 250, 255, 258, 259, 260, 262, 263
striatum
  conditioned inhibitory control and 498, 499
  dopaminergic genes and 396
  dorsal/dorso-lateral (DLS) 367–70, 424–6
    beat frequency 368–70
    contextual conditioning and 294, 295, 296, 301
    habit formation and 424–6, 427, 428, 429, 432
    timing behavior and 367–70
  dorsomedial (DMS), habit formation and 431, 432
  outcome expectations and prediction errors and 394
  see also cortico-striatal and cortico-striato-thalamic circuitry; nigrostriatal dopaminergic projection
structural templating 142
substance (drug) addiction 129–30, 287
substantia innominata
  reductions in attention and 100
  reward and 99–100
substantia nigra 58, 62, 459
  pars compacta (SNc)
    habit formation and 424, 427, 428
    reward and 99
    projections to 428, 430
summation tests 298–300, 489, 491, 492, 503
sunburst maze 319, 320
supplementary motor area (SMA) 433, 499, 560, 561
swimming and navigation 316, 322, 324, 329
  see also water maze
synaptic plasticity 27, 30, 137, 146, 151, 473
  fear learning and 473
  see also postsynaptic depolarization; presynaptic stimulation

T-maze 87, 91, 92, 314, 427
task relevance 122–3, 124, 125, 498
taste (flavor) aversion 14–15, 71, 72–3, 74, 77, 80, 229, 315, 413–14, 417, 419, 427, 455–6, 492
taxonomic constraint 539, 542–6
tegmental area, ventral (VTA) 21, 64, 99, 102, 103, 104, 363
temporal characteristics and information (time and timing) 25–6, 348–79
  hippocampus and 357–62
  neural substrates 356–62
  perception of causality and 382–6
  temporal contiguity 13–15, 20, 24, 26–30, 348–50
  see also duration
temporal cortex, inferior 232
temporal difference (TD) model 354–6, 359, 363, 364, 365
temporal lobe
  dopamine and reward and 59
  medial (MTL) 249, 250, 251, 262
    amnesia 272, 274
    damage or degeneration 252, 253, 269, 271, 276, 277
    object-recognition memory (ORM) and 262
  value-guided choice and 563
thalamus
  attentional set and the medial nucleus of 92–3
  conditioned inhibitory control and 498–9
  prediction errors and 33
time-accumulation models 352, 353, 356, 359, 363, 367, 370
  see also duration; temporal characteristics
tool-use mirror neurons 525
top-down response inhibition 497–501, 506
  aftereffects 499–500
  of behavior 500–1
total intertrial interval (TII) 10–11
trace conditioning 80, 349, 350, 355, 356, 357
  as mediated learning 77–8
tracking of several decision variables 569
training (and training trials) 11–12, 120, 289, 292, 295
  CS–US 11–12
transcriptional silencing 141, 149

transgenerational inheritance/transmission 137, 142, 152–3, 154, 155–8
trial-based associative theories 348, 350, 351, 367, 369, 370
   challenges to 252–62
triple dissociation within a triple dissociation 296–7
two-factor theory of avoidance 445–8

unblocking effect 32, 33, 62, 99, 100–1
uncertainty 96–102, 106
   value and 569, 575, 576, 577, 578, 582
unconditioned stimuli (US) 8–35
   contextual learning and 286, 287–94, 306–7
   fear learning and 468, 469, 470, 471, 472, 473, 474
   intensity 9–10
   novelty 10
   representations (US-representations) 490, 493, 494, 495, 497, 499
   surprise and prediction error 23–6, 32–3, 34, 35
      neural evidence for importance 30
   timing and 348–71
   see also conditioned stimuli–unconditioned stimuli; response–no US contingency
unconditioned stimuli–conditioned stimuli (US–CS) intervals/pairings, backward 13, 22
undirected behavioral adaptation 573–6
unitization 233–5
unsigned prediction error 103–4

value (outcome) 119–25
   choice guided by 554–91
   manipulating 413–14
   reward and 119–25, 126, 555–62
   see also devaluation
vector learning 325, 326, 336
ventral tegmental area (VTA) 21, 64, 99, 102, 103, 104, 363

ventral visual stream (VVS) 249, 250, 255, 258, 259, 260, 262, 263
vertical limb of diagonal band 101
visual cortex and perceptual learning 210–12, 214, 215–16
   human 225–6, 231, 239
visual discrimination 250, 252, 254–62, 263, 267–72, 295, 296–300, 301–2, 305–6, 307
   simultaneous 269–72
   spatial learning 330
visual exploration *see* exploration
visual features and lexical development 541, 542
visual memory, modular organization in brain 249–53, 258, 262
visual perception and processing (of stimuli)
   humans 223–4, 228, 229, 230–1, 234, 236–7, 239
   lexical development and 543, 544, 545
   modular organization in brain 249–53, 258, 262
visual stream, ventral (VVS) 249, 250, 255, 258, 259, 260, 262, 263
vocabulary and lexical development 538–53

Wagner's Standard Operating Procedures (SOP; sometimes opponent process) theory 22, 24, 80, 96, 183–4, 186, 188, 189, 190, 192, 193, 195, 196, 354, 356
water maze 316, 318, 321, 323, 325, 326, 330, 331, 332
   see also swimming
whole object constraint 539, 539–42
Wisconsin Card Sorting Task (WCST) 90
word-learning and lexical development 538–53
working memory 400

Y-maze 181, 189, 190, 315, 330, 472
   modified 273